Applied Choic Analysis

A Primer

David A. Hensher
The University of Sydney

John M. Rose
The University of Sydney

William H. Greene
New York University

CAMBRIDGE UNIVERSITY PRESS
Cambridge, New York, Melbourne, Madrid, Cape Town, Singapore, São Paulo

Cambridge University Press
The Edinburgh Building, Cambridge CB2 2RU, UK

Published in the United States of America by Cambridge University Press, New York

www.cambridge.org
Information on this title: www.cambridge.org/9780521605779

First published 2005

Printed in the United Kingdom at the University Press, Cambridge

A catalogue record for this book is available from the British Library

ISBN-13 978-0-521-84426-0 hardback
ISBN-10 0-521-84426-6 hardback
ISBN-13 978-0-521-60577-9 paperback
ISBN-10 0-521-60577-6 paperback

Contents

Figures

Tables

Preface

> I'm all in favor of keeping dangerous weapons out of the hands of fools. Let's start with typewriters. (Frank Lloyd Wright, 1868–1959)

Almost without exception, everything human beings undertake involves a *choice* (consciously or sub-consciously), including the choice not to choose. Some choices are the result of habit while others are fresh decisions made with great care, based on whatever information is available at the time from past experiences and/or current inquiry.

Since the 1970s, there has been a steadily growing interest in the development and application of quantitative statistical methods to study choices made by individuals (and, to a lesser extent, groups of individuals). With an emphasis on both understanding how choices are made and forecasting future choice responses, a healthy literature has evolved. Reference works by Louviere, Hensher, and Swait (2000), and Train (2003) synthesize the contributions. However while these two sources represent the state of the art (and practice), they are technically advanced and often a challenge for the beginner and practitioners.

Discussions with colleagues over the last few years have revealed a gap in the literature of choice analysis – a book that assumes very little background and offers an entry point for individuals interested in the study of choice regardless of their background. Writing such a book increasingly became a challenge for us. It is often more difficult to explain complex ideas in very simple language than to protect one's knowledge-base with complicated deliberations.

There are many discussion topics in this primer that are ignored in most books on the subject, yet are issues which students have pointed out in class as important in giving them a better understanding of what is happening in choice modeling. The lament that too many books on discrete choice analysis are written for the well informed is common and is sufficient incentive to write this book.

This primer for beginners is our attempt to meet the challenge. We agreed to try and write the first draft without referring to any of the existing material as a means (hopefully) of encouraging a flow of explanation. Pausing to consult can often lead to terseness in the code (as writers of novels can attest). Further draft versions leading to the final product did, however, cross-reference to the literature to ensure we had acknowledged appropriate material. This primer, however, is not about ensuring that all contributors to the literature on choice are acknowledged, but rather to ensure that the novice choice analyst is given a fair go in their first journey through this intriguing topic.

We dedicate this book to the beginners but we also acknowledge our research colleagues who have influenced our thinking as well as co-authored papers over many years. We especially recognize Dan McFadden (2000 Nobel Laureate in Economics), Ken Train, Chandra Bhat, Jordan Louviere, Andrew Daly, Moshe Ben-Akiva, and David Brownstone. Colleagues and doctoral students at the University of Sydney read earlier versions. In particular, we thank Sean Puckett, Kwang Kim and Louise Knowles and the January 2004 graduate class in Choice Analysis at The University of Sydney, who were guinea pigs for the first full use of the book in a teaching environment. Sean Puckett also contributed to the development of the glossary.

Part I

Basic topics

If knowledge can create problems, it is not through ignorance that we can solve them. (Isaac Asimov, 1920–1992)

1 In the beginning

Education is a progressive discovery of our own ignorance. (Will Durant, 1885–1991)

Why did we *choose* to write this primer? Can it be explained by some inherent desire to seek personal gain, or was it some other less self-centered interest? In determining the reason, we are revealing an underlying objective. It might be one of maximizing our personal satisfaction level or that of satisfying some community-based objective (or social obligation). Whatever the objective, it is likely that there are a number of reasons why we made such a *choice* (between writing and not writing this primer) accompanied by a set of constraints that had to be taken into account. An example of a reason might be to "promote the field of research and practice of choice analysis"; examples of constraints might be the time commitment and the financial outlay.

Readers should be able to think of choices that they have made in the last seven days. Some of these might be repetitive and even habitual (such as taking the bus to work instead of the train or car), buying the same daily newspaper (instead of other ones on sale); other choices might be a one-off decision (such as going to the movies to watch a latest release or purchasing this book). Many choice situations involve *more than one choice*, such as choosing a destination and means of transport to get there, or choosing where to live and the type of dwelling.

The storyline above is rich in information about what we need to include in a study of the choice behavior of individuals. To arrive at a choice, an individual must have considered a set of *alternatives*. These alternatives are usually called the *choice set*. Logically one must evaluate at least two alternatives to be able to make a choice (one of these alternatives may be "not to make a choice" or "not participate at all"). At least one actual choice setting must exist (e.g. choosing where to live), but there may be more than one choice (e.g. what type of dwelling to live in, whether to buy or rent, and how much to pay per week if rented). The idea that an individual may have to consider a number of choices leads to a set of *inter-related choices*.

Determining the set of alternatives to be evaluated in a choice set is a crucial task in choice analysis. Getting this wrong will mean that subsequent tasks in the development of a choice model will be missing relevant information. We often advise analysts to devote considerable time to the identification of the choices that are applicable in the study of a specific problem. This is known as *choice set generation*. In identifying the relevant choices, one must also consider the range of alternatives and start thinking about what influences the decision to choose one alternative over another. These influences are called *attributes* if they relate to the description of an alternative (e.g. travel time of the bus alternative), but an individual's prejudices (or tastes) will also be relevant and are often linked to socio-economic *characteristics* such as personal income, age, gender, and occupation.

To take a concrete example, a common problem for transportation planners is to study the transport-related choices made by a sample of individuals living in an urban area. Individuals make many decisions related to their transportation needs. Some of these decisions are taken occasionally (e.g. where to live and work) while others are taken more often (e.g. departure time for a specific trip). These examples highlight a very important feature of choice analysis – the *temporal perspective*. Over what time period are we interested in studying choices? As the period becomes longer, the number of possible choices that can be made (i.e. are not fixed or predetermined) are likely to increase. Thus if we are interested in studying travel behavior over a five-year period then it is reasonable to assume that an individual can make choices related to the locations of both living and working, as well as the means of transport and departure time. That is, a specific choice of means of transport may indeed be changed as a consequence of the person changing where they reside or work. In a shorter period such as one year, choosing among modes of transport may be conditional on where one lives or works, but the latter is not able to be changed given the time that it takes to relocate one's employment.

The message in the previous paragraphs is that careful thought is required to define the choice setting so as to ensure that all possible behavioral responses (as expressed by a set of choice situations) can be accommodated when a change in the decision environment occurs. For example, if we increase fuel prices, then the cost of driving a car increases. If one has studied only the choice of mode of transport then the decision maker will be "forced" to modify the choice among a given set of modal alternatives (e.g. bus, car, train). However it may be that the individual would prefer to stay with the car but to change the time of day they travel so as to avoid traffic congestion and conserve fuel. If the departure time choice model is not included in the analysis, then experience shows that the modal choice model tends to force a substitution between modes which in reality is a substitution between travel at different times of day by car.

Armed with a specific problem or a series of associated questions the analyst now recognizes that to study choices we need a set of choice situations (or outcomes), a set of alternatives, and a set of attributes that belong to each alternative. But how do we take this information and convert it to a useful framework within which we can study the choice behavior of individuals? To do this, we need to set up a number of *behavioral rules* under which we believe it is reasonable to represent the process by which an individual considers a set of alternatives and makes a choice. This framework needs to be sufficiently realistic to explain past choices and to give confidence in likely behavioral responses in the future that result in staying with an existing choice or making a new choice. The framework should also be capable of assessing the likely support for alternatives that are not currently available, be they new alternatives in the market or existing ones that are physically unavailable to some market segments.

The following sections of this primer will introduce the main rules that are needed to start understanding the richness of methods available to study. We will start right from the beginning and learn to "walk before we run." We will be pedantic in the interest of clarity, since what is taken for granted by the long-established choice analyst is often gobbledy-gook to the beginner. Intolerance on the part of such "experts" has no place in this primer.

We have found in our courses that the best way to understand the underlying constructs that are the armory of choice analysis is to select one specific choice problem and follow it through from the beginning to the end. We will do this here. Selecting such a single case study is always fraught with problems since, no matter what we select, it will not be ideal for every reader. To try and offer a smorgasbord of case studies would (in our view) defeat the purpose of this primer. While readers will come from different disciplinary backgrounds such as economics, geography, environmental science, marketing, health science, statistics, engineering, transportation, logistics, and so forth and will be practicing in these and other fields, the tools introduced through one case study are universally relevant.

A reader who insists that this is not so is at a disadvantage; she is committing the sin of assuming uniqueness in behavioral decision making and choice response. Indeed the great virtue of the methods developed under the rubric of choice analysis is their universal relevance. Their portability is amazing. Disciplinary boundaries and biases are a threat to this strength. While it is true that specific disciplines have a lot to offer to the literature on choice analysis, we see these offerings as contributions to the bigger multi-disciplinary effort.

The case study focuses on a transport choice – the choice between a number of public and private modes of transport for travel within an urban area. The data were collected in 1994 as part of a larger study that resulted in the development of an environmental impact simulator to assess the impact of policy instruments on the demand for travel. We have selected this specific context because we have a real data set (provided on the primer website) that has all of the properties we need to be able to illustrate the following features of choice analysis:

1. There are *more than two alternatives* (in particular, car drive alone, car ride share, train, and bus). This is important because a choice situation involving more than two alternatives introduces a number of important behavioral conditions that do not exist when studying a binary choice.
2. It is possible to view the set of alternatives as *more than one choice* (e.g. choosing between public and private modes, choosing among the private modes, and choosing among the public modes). This will be important later to show how to set up a choice problem with more than one (inter-related) choice decision.
3. Two types of choice data have emerged as the primary sources of choice response. These are known as *revealed preference* (RP) and *stated preference* (SP) data. RP data refer to situations where the choice is actually made in real market situations; in contrast, SP data refer to situations where a choice is made by considering hypothetical

situations (which are typically the same alternatives in the RP data set, but are described by different levels of the same attributes to those observed in actual markets as well as additional attributes not in the data collected from actual markets). SP data are especially useful when considering the choice among existing and new alternatives since the latter are not observed in RP data. The case study data have both RP and SP choice data with the SP choice set comprising the exact same four alternatives in the RP data set plus two "new" alternatives – light rail and a dedicated busway system.

4. Often in choice modeling we *over- and under-sample* individuals observed to choose specific alternatives. This is common where particular alternatives are dominant or popular (in this data it is use of the car compared to public transport). The case study data have over-sampled existing choosers of bus and train and under-sampled car users. In establishing the relative importance of the attributes influencing the choice among the alternatives we would want to correct for this over- and under-sampling strategy by *weighting the data* to ensure reproduction of the population choice shares. These weighted choice shares are more useful than the sample choice shares.
5. The data have a large number of *attributes* describing each alternative and *characteristics* describing the socio-economic profile of each sampled trip maker (e.g. personal income, age, car ownership status, occupation). This gives the analyst plenty of scope to explore the contributions of attributes of alternatives and characteristics of individuals to explaining choice behavior.
6. The alternatives are *well-defined modes of transport* that are described by labels such as bus, train, car drive alone, and car ride share. A data set with labeled alternatives is preferred over one where the alternatives are not well defined in terms of a label such as abstract alternatives that are only defined by combinations of attributes. Labeled alternatives enable us to study the important role of alternative-specific constants.
7. Finally, most analysts have had *personal experience* in choosing a mode of transport for the journey to work. Thus the application should be very familiar.

The following chapters set out the process of choice analysis in a logical sequence consistent with what researchers and practitioners tend to do as they design their study and collect all the necessary inputs to undertake data collection, analysis, and reporting. We begin with a discussion on what we are seeking to understand in a study of choice; namely the role of an individual's preferences and the constraints that limit the ability to choose alternatives that are the most preferred in an unconstrained setting. Having established the central role of preferences and constraints, we are ready to formalize a framework within which a set of behavioral rules can be introduced to assist the analyst in accommodating these individual preferences, recognizing that the analyst does not have as much information about these individual preferences as the individual decision maker being studied. The behavioral rules are used to develop a formal *model of choice* in which we introduce the sources of individual preferences (i.e. attributes), constraints on such preferences (i.e. characteristics of individuals, peer influences, and other contextual influences), and the available set of alternatives to choose from. This is where we introduce choice models such as multinomial logit and nested logit.

With a choice-modeling framework set out, we are ready to design the data stage. Important issues discussed are survey design and administration, data paradigms, data collection strategies, and data preparation for model estimation. Many analysts have difficulties in preparing their data in a format suitable for model estimation. Although there are a number of software options available for model estimation, we have selected NLOGIT for two reasons – it is the most popular software package for choice model estimation and it is the package that the authors have greatest expertise in using (William Greene and David Hensher are the developers of NLOGIT). We set out, step by step, what the analyst must do to run a simple choice model and then introduce more advanced features. The results are interpreted in a way that ensures that the main outputs are all considered and reported as appropriate. Estimating models is only one critical element of the choice-modeling process. The findings must be used in various ways such as forecasting, scenario analysis, valuation (willingness to pay or WTP), and understanding of the role of particular attributes and characteristics. We discuss the most common ways of applying the results of choice models such as simulating the impact of changes in levels of attributes, deriving marginal rates of substitution (or values) of one attribute relative to another (especially if one attribute is measured in monetary units), and in constructing empirical distributions of specific attributes and ratios of attributes. Throughout the book we add numerous hints under the heading of "**As an aside**". This format was chosen as a way of preserving the flow of the argument but placing useful tips where they would best be appreciated. Before we can delve into the foundations of choice analysis we need to set out the essential statistical concepts and language that readers new to statistics (or very rusty) will need to make the rest of the book easier to read.

2 Basic notions of statistics

> If scientific reasoning were limited to the logical processes of arithmetic, we should not get very far in our understanding of the physical world. One might as well attempt to grasp the game of poker entirely by the use of the mathematics of probability. (Vannevar Bush 1890–1974)

2.1 Introduction

This chapter is intended to act as a review of the basic statistical concepts, knowledge of which is required for the reader to fully appreciate the chapters that follow. It is not designed to act as a substitute for a good grounding in basic statistics but rather as a summary of knowledge that the reader should already possess. For the less confident statistician, we recommend that in reading this and subsequent chapters, that they obtain and read other books on the subject. In particular, we recommend for the completely statistically challenged *Statistics without Tears: A Primer for Non-Mathematicians* (Rowntree 1991). More confident readers may find books such as those by Howell (1999) and Gujarati (1999, chapters 2–5) to be of particular use.

2.2 Data

Data are fundamental to the analysis and modeling of real world phenomena such as consumer and organizational behavior. Understanding data are therefore critical to any study application and nowhere more than to studies involving discrete choice analysis. The data sets which we use, whether collected by ourselves or by others, will invariably be made up of numerous observations on multiple variables (an object that can take on many different values). Only through understanding the qualities possessed by each variable will the analyst be capable of deriving the most benefit from their data.

We may define variables on a number of different dimensions. Firstly, variables may be *qualitative* or *quantitative*. A qualitative variable is one in which the "true" or naturally occurring levels or categories taken by that variable are not described as numbers but rather by verbal groupings (e.g. the levels or categories that hair color may take might include red, blond, brown, black). For such variables, comparisons are based solely on the *qualities* possessed by that particular variable. Quantitative variables on the other hand are those in which the natural levels take on certain quantities (e.g. price, travel time). That is, quantitative variables are measurable in some *numerical* unit (e.g. dollars, minutes, inches, etc.).

A second dimension is whether the variable is *continuous* or *non-continuous* in nature. A continuous variable is one in which it can theoretically assume any value between the lowest and highest points on the scale on which it is being measured (e.g. speed, price, time, height). For continuous variables, it is common to use a scale of measure such as minutes to quantify the object under study; however, invariably, such scale measures are potentially infinitely divisible (e.g. one could measure time in seconds, or thousandths of seconds, and so on). As such, continuous-level data will only be an approximation of the true value taken of the object under study, with the precision of the estimate dependent upon the instrument of measure. Non-continuous variables, sometimes referred to as *discrete variables*, differ from continuous variables in that they may take on a relatively few possible distinct values (e.g. male and female for gender).

A third dimension used in describing data are that of *scales of measurement*. Scales of measurement describe the relationships between the characteristics of the numbers or levels assigned to objects under study. Four classificatory scales of measurement were developed by Stevens (1951) and are still in use today. These are nominal, ordinal, interval, and ratio.

Nominal scaled data

A nominal scaled variable is a variable in which the levels observed for that variable are assigned unique values – values which provide classification but which do not provide any indication of order. For example, we may assign the values zero to represent males and one to represent females; however, in doing so, we are not saying that females are better than males or males are better than females. The numbers used are only to *categorize objects*. As such, it is common to refer to such variables as categorical variables (note that nominal data must be discrete). For nominal scaled data, all mathematical operations are meaningless (i.e. addition, subtraction, division and multiplication).

Ordinal scaled data

Ordinal scaled data are data in which the values assigned to levels observed for an object are (1) unique and (2) provide an indication of order. An example of this is ranking of products in order of preference. The highest-ranked product is more preferred than the second-highest-ranked product, which in turn is more preferred than the third-ranked product, etc. While we may now place the objects of measure in some order, we cannot determine *distances between the objects*. For example, we might know that product *A* is preferred to product *B*; however, we do not know by how much product *A* preferred to product *B*. Thus, addition, subtraction, division and multiplication are meaningless in terms of ordinal scales.

Interval scaled data

Interval scaled data are data in which the levels of an object under study are assigned values which are (1) unique, (2) provide an indication of order, and (3) have an equal distance between scale points. The usual example is temperature (Centigrade or Fahrenheit). In either scale, 41 degrees is higher than 40 degrees, and the increase in heat required to go from 40 degrees to 41 degrees is the same as the amount of heat to go from 20 degrees to 21 degrees. However, zero degrees is an arbitrary figure – it does not represent an absolute absence of heat (it does represent the temperature at which water freezes however when using the Centigrade scale). Because of this, you may add and subtract interval scale variables meaningfully but ratios are not meaningful (that is 40, degrees is not strictly twice as hot as 20 degrees).

Ratio scaled data

Ratio scaled data are data in which the values assigned to levels of an object are (1) unique, (2) provide an indication of order, (3) have an equal distance between scale points, and (4) the zero point on the scale of measure used represents an absence of the object being observed. An example would be asking respondents how much money was spent on fast food last week. This variable has order ($1 is less than $2), has equal distances among scale points (the difference between $2 and $1 is the same as the difference between $1000 and $999), and has an absolute zero point ($0 spent represents a lack of spending on fast food items). Thus, we can add, subtract and divide such variables meaningfully ($1 is exactly half of $2).

2.2.1 The importance of understanding data

Information such as that given in the previous section can be found in any of a number of statistics books. This fact alone suggests that understanding the types of data one has is an important (perhaps the most important) element in conducting any study. It is sometimes lost on the practitioner that the type of data she has (whether she collected it herself or not) dictates the type of analysis that can be undertaken. All statistical analysis makes assumptions with regard to the data used. For example, if one has collected data on income to use as the dependent variable in a linear regression analysis, the income variable must be collected in a format that meets the data requirements of the analytical technique for which it was collected to be used. Thus, in collecting data (i.e. in writing surveys), one must always be cognizant of the *types of analysis* one intends to conduct, even if the analysis is not to be conducted for another six months. Statistics, like a game of chess, requires the players to always be thinking several moves ahead.

2.3 A note on mathematical notation

In this section we outline the mathematical notion that is used throughout the book.

2.3.1 Summation

The Greek capital letter sigma, Σ, indicates summation or addition. For example:

$$\sum_{i=1}^{n} X_i = X_1 + X_2 + \cdots + X_n$$

where i is an index of summation indicating that for some variable X, we take the first value of X ($i = 1$) and add to each subsequent value taken by X up to the nth appearance of X. The subscript i is important in mathematical notation as it is used to denote a *variable* as opposed to a constant term. A variable, as the name suggests, is a quantity that is able to assume any set of values (i.e. has no fixed quantitative value). A constant is a quantity which is fixed at some level and as such does not vary. Constant terms are generally denoted without a subscript i (e.g. k).

In practice, one can abbreviate the summation as follows:

$$\sum_{i=1}^{n} X_i \text{ or simply } \sum X_i$$

The summation operator has several useful properties:

1. The *summation of a constant term* (note we drop the subscript i for constant terms):

$$\sum_{i=1}^{n} k = k + k + \cdots + k = nk$$

   For example, where $n = 3$ and $k = 4$, $\sum_{i=1}^{3} 4 = 4 + 4 + 4 = 3 \times 4 = 12$

2. The *summation of a constant term multiplied by a variable*:

$$\sum_{i=1}^{n} kX_i = kX_1 + kX_2 + \cdots + kX_n = k(X_1 + X_2 + \cdots + X_n)$$
$$= k\left(\sum_{i=1}^{n} X_i\right)$$

   For example, where $k = 3$ and $X_1 = 2$, $X_2 = 3$, and $X_3 = 4$

$$\sum_{i=1}^{n} 3X_i = (3 \times 2) + (3 \times 3) + (3 \times 4) = 3(2 + 3 + 4) = 3\left(\sum_{i=1}^{n} X_i\right) = 27$$

3. *Summing two variables*:

$$\sum_{i=1}^{n} (X_i + Y_i) = \sum_{i=1}^{n} X_i + \sum_{i=1}^{n} Y_i$$

   For example, assume $X_1 = 2$, $X_2 = 3$, and $X_3 = 4$ and $Y_1 = 4$, $Y_2 = 3$, and $Y_3 = 2$

$$\sum_{i=1}^{n} (X_i + Y_i) = \sum_{i=1}^{n} X_i + \sum_{i=1}^{n} Y_i = (2 + 3 + 4) + (4 + 3 + 2) = 18$$

4. *Adding and multiplying constants*:

$$\sum_{i=1}^{n}(z + kX)_i = nz + k\sum_{i=1}^{n} X_i$$

For example assume $z = 5$, $k = 3$, and $X_1 = 2$, $X_2 = 3$, and $X_3 = 4$

$$\sum_{i=1}^{n}(5 + 3X)_i = 3 \times 5 + 3\sum_{i=1}^{n} X_i = 3 \times 5 + 3(2 + 3 + 4) = 15 + 27 = 42$$

Occasionally, you may observe a double summation sign. An example of the double summation is shown below:

$$\sum_{i=1}^{n_1}\sum_{j=1}^{n_2} X_1 X_2$$

The summation operator is used extensively throughout the chapters that follow. Slightly less common is the product operator, which we discuss next.

2.3.2 Product

Represented by the Greek capital pi, $\prod$, the product symbol is used to denote that the analyst is to take the product of (multiply) the terms indicated:

$$\prod_{i=1}^{n} X_i$$

As with the summation operand, the product operand is usually abbreviated. Common abbreviations include:

$$\prod X_i$$

To demonstrate the product operand, consider a situation where $X_1 = 2$, $X_2 = 3$, and $X_3 = 4$

$$\prod_{i=1}^{n} X_i = 2 \times 3 \times 4 = 24$$

In the next section we discuss the topic of probability, which is central to understanding discrete choice modeling.

2.4 Probability

Consider the possible set of outcomes of an experiment in which each potential outcome is *mutually exclusive* (i.e. only one outcome can be observed at any one time) and equally likely to occur. Given n possible outcomes and m sets of circumstance that are likely to result in outcome A, the probability that outcome A will occur is given as:

$$P(A) = \frac{m}{n} \tag{2.1}$$

For example, assume that our experiment consisted of the rolling of a single die (note that "die" is the singular, "dice" the plural). From a single role of our die, the possible set of outcomes (known collectively as the *population* or *sample space*) consists of six possibilities. We will observe a one, a two, a three, a four, a five, or a six. The outcomes are mutually exclusive in that we cannot observe a one and a two at the same time, and each potential outcome, assuming the die has not been tampered with, is equally likely to occur. Assuming that our desired outcome, A, was to observe a roll of three. Only one possible circumstance, m, out of six possible outcomes (i.e. $n = 6$) will result in our desired outcome. Hence, from (2.1), the probability that we will observe a three in a single roll of our dice is given as

$$P(A) = \frac{1}{6}$$

In the above example, the nature of the experiment was such that the probability of any outcome may be known *a priori* (i.e. in advance). But what if the universal set of outcomes is not finite or the possibility of any two outcomes occurring is not equal? In order to understand the probabilities associated with such problems, one must consider *relative frequencies*.

2.4.1 Relative frequencies

Consider table 2.1. In table 2.1 we show the observed frequency counts for various travel times to work. These observed frequency counts, sometimes referred to as absolute frequency counts, are given in the second column of the table. The relative frequencies, given

Table 2.1. *Calculating the relative frequencies for travel to work*

Travel time to work (minutes)	Absolute frequency observed	Relative frequency	
$0 \le X \le 5$	8	0.07	$8 \div 115$
$5 < X \le 10$	15	0.13	$15 \div 115$
$10 < X \le 15$	17	0.15	$17 \div 115$
$15 < X \le 20$	24	0.21	$24 \div 115$
$20 < X \le 25$	19	0.17	$19 \div 115$
$25 < X \le 30$	15	0.13	$15 \div 115$
$30 < X \le 35$	10	0.09	$10 \div 115$
$35 < X \le 40$	7	0.06	$7 \div 115$
Total	115	1	

in the third column of the table, are calculated as the ratio of the absolute frequency counts over the sum of the absolute frequency counts. For example, the relative frequency for those traveling to work taking between 20 and 25 minutes is 0.17 (i.e. 19 ÷ 115). Given that we do not know *a priori* the probability of a given outcome occurring (i.e. that we will observe an individual with a travel time to work of 21–25 minutes), we must rely on the relative frequencies to establish the probabilities for us. That is, we will use the *relative frequencies as the probabilities themselves*. Note that this requires knowledge of the absolute frequency counts, which we cannot know in advance with certainty (we can guess or estimate them in advance, however). Thus, from table 2.1, we can state that the probability that we will observe a randomly chosen individual with a travel time to work of between 20 and 25 minutes is 0.17.

We may use the relative frequencies of outcomes of an event as probabilities provided the sample size of absolute frequencies is sufficiently large. The law of large numbers suggests that a sample size of 30 may be sufficiently large; however, for some types of problems, much larger samples may be required.

In the next sections, we discuss distribution functions. Before we do so however, we need to formally define random variables.

2.4.2 Defining random variables

The concept of random variables is central to the understanding of probability. A *random variable*, sometimes referred to as a *stochastic variable*, is a variable in which the value the variable is observed to take is determined as part of an experiment. That is to say, we do not know the exact value the variable will be observed to take with any certainty *a priori*. The two preceding illustrations provide examples of random variables. In the case of rolling a single die, the exact outcome of each roll cannot be known before the roll takes place (though the probabilities for each outcome can be calculated with certainty). In the second example, while the probability that we will observe an individual with a specific travel-to-work time may be calculated, we cannot say for certain that the next randomly observed individual will have a specific travel time to work value.

When dealing with random variables, it is necessary to study the *distributions of outcomes* that may be observed. In the next two sections we discuss two very important concepts related to the distribution functions of random variables; the probability distribution function and the cumulative distribution function.

2.4.3 Probability distribution functions

Consider the roll of a single die. The probability that the value observed will be a one is the same as the probability that the value observed will be a three or a six. In each case, the probability that any particular value will be observed is exactly 1/6. Now consider the rolling of two dice. The sum of the values of the two dice must lie between two and twelve; however, the probability that a particular value will be observed is not necessarily equal to the probability of any of the other values being observed. Why?

Table 2.2. *The PDF of a discrete random variable*

Number observed (X)	Value (die1, die2)	Value (die1, die2)	Value (die1, die2)	Value (die1, die2)	Value (die1, die2)	Value (die1, die2)	Number of possible outcomes	$f(X)$
2	1, 1						1	1/36
3	1, 2	2, 1					2	1/18
4	1, 3	3, 1	2, 2				3	1/12
5	1, 4	2, 3	3, 2	4, 1			4	1/9
6	1, 5	2, 4	3, 3	4, 2	5, 1		5	5/36
7	1, 6	2, 5	3, 4	4, 3	5, 2	6, 1	6	1/6
8	2, 6	3, 5	4, 4	5, 3	6, 2		5	5/36
9	3, 6	4, 5	5, 4	6, 3			4	1/9
10	4, 6	5, 5	6, 4				3	1/12
11	5, 6	6, 5					2	1/18
12	6, 6						1	1/36
						Sum:	36	1

In table 2.2, we show all possible outcomes that may be observed in the rolling of our two dice. Only one combination of circumstance will result in the sum of our two dice equalling two. That is, we will only ever observe the sum of our two dice equalling two if the face values of both of our dice happen to equal one. Two possible outcomes will result in the sum of our dice equalling three however; if the first die equals one and the second equals two, or if the first die equals two and the second die equals one. Similarly, there are six possible outcomes that will result in the sum of our dice equalling seven. Given that six different independent outcomes will result in the sum of our two dice equalling seven, but only one independent outcome will result in an observed value of two, it stands to reason that the probability of observing the sum of our two dice equalling seven is greater than the probability of observing our two dice equalling two.

From table 2.2, it can be seen that there are 36 independent possible outcomes that we might witness. The probability that any one outcome will be observed is therefore 1/36; however, the probability that we will observe a particular outcome in terms of summing the face values of our two dice will generally be much larger. We can calculate the probability of observing a particular value for our two dice by dividing the number of outcomes that will result in that value being observed (given in the second last column) by the total number of possible outcomes (which in this case is 36). The resulting values, given in the last column of table 2.2, represent the probability that for any one roll of our two dice, the sum of the values observed will equal a particular value.

The last column, labeled $f(X)$ is known as the *probability density function* (PDF). The PDF of a (discrete random) variable (in this case the roll of two dice) represents the probability distribution over the various values that the (discrete random) variable might take. As the 36 possible outcomes shown in table 2.2 represent the exhaustive set of possible outcomes, the probabilities will sum to one.

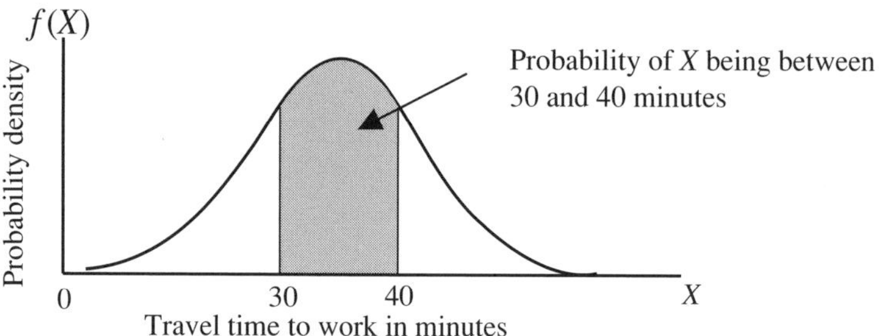

Figure 2.1 The PDF of a continuous random variable

Mathematically, we may represent the PDF of a discrete random variable as (2.2).

$$\begin{aligned} f(X) &= P(X = x_i) \qquad && \text{for } i = 1, 2, \ldots, n \\ &= 0 && \text{for } X \neq x_i \end{aligned} \tag{2.2}$$

In words, (2.2) states that the probability of a discrete random variable takes the value x_i is equal to zero for X not equal to x_i and that the probability for X equal to x_i is given as the PDF.

The PDF of a continuous random variable, though similar to that of a discrete random variable, cannot be treated the same. Consider a continuous random variable such as travel time to work, represented as X. Travel time to work is a continuous random variable which, when measured in (say) minutes, may take on any value within a range. The probability that we will observe an exact event for a continuous random variable is said to be zero. For example, the probability that it will take exactly 34.00000 minutes to get to work tomorrow is zero. Rather than establish the probability that a specific event will be observed to occur, when dealing with a continuous random variable, it is necessary to establish the probability within a range of events rather than for a specific event. Hence, when dealing with continuous random variables such as travel time to work, we say things such as "the probability that it will take between 30 and 40 minutes may be non-zero." Note that the probability may still be zero (you may work at home), but there may also be a non-zero probability attached to observing an outcome within the specified range. Figure 2.1 shows the probability for observing a travel time to work between 30 and 40 minutes.

2.4.4 Cumulative distribution functions

Related to the PDF of a random variable is the *cumulative distribution function* (CDF). The CDF, denoted as $F(X)$ may be mathematically defined as in (2.3).

$$F(X) = P(X \leq x) \tag{2.3}$$

In words, (2.3) states that the CDF is equal to the probability that a random variable, X, is observed to take on a value less than or equal to some known value, x. To demonstrate the CDF of a random variable, reconsider our earlier example of rolling two dice. The PDF of

Table 2.3. *PDF and CDF for a discrete random variable*

	PDF		CDF	
Number observed (X)	Value observed for X	$f(X)$	Value observed for X	$F(X)$
2	$2 \leq X < 3$	1/36	$X = 2$	1/36
3	$3 \leq X < 4$	1/18	$X \leq 3$	1/12
4	$4 \leq X < 5$	1/12	$X \leq 4$	1/6
5	$5 \leq X < 6$	1/9	$X \leq 5$	5/18
6	$6 \leq X < 7$	5/36	$X \leq 6$	5/12
7	$7 \leq X < 8$	1/6	$X \leq 7$	7/12
8	$8 \leq X < 9$	5/36	$X \leq 8$	13/18
9	$9 \leq X < 10$	1/9	$X \leq 9$	5/6
10	$10 \leq X < 11$	1/12	$X \leq 10$	11/12
11	$11 \leq X < 12$	1/18	$X \leq 11$	35/36
12	$12 \leq X$	1/36	$X \leq 12$	1

observing any outcome is as before. The CDF is calculated as the sum of the PDF values of X less than or equal to a given value of x. Mathematically,

$$F(X) = \sum_{i=1}^{x} f(X) \tag{2.4}$$

where $\sum_{i=1}^{x} f(X)$ suggests the sum of the PDF values of X less than or equal to the some specified value, x. We show this relationship between the PDF and the CDF in table 2.3. For example, in table 2.3, the probability that X takes a value less than four (i.e. $x = 4$) is $1/12$ (i.e. $1/36 + 1/18$). Similarly, the probability that X takes a value less than nine (i.e. $x = 9$) is $13/18$ (i.e. $1/36 + 1/18 + 1/12 + 1/9 + 5/36 + 1/6 + 5/36$).

The information in table 2.3 pertains to a discrete random variable. As X, the sum of the values obtained from the role of two dice, is discrete, the CDF is discontinuous in form and the CDF is drawn as a *step function*, as shown in figure 2.2. This is because X can only take on a discrete indivisible value (i.e. we cannot observe $X = 4.2$). For continuous random variables, however, one may observe fractions of events, for example, we may observe a travel time to work of 34.23697 minutes. The CDF of a continuous random variable is therefore continuous, as shown in figure 2.3.

2.4.5 Multivariate probability density functions

All the examples we have considered above have related to a single random variable. The PDF of table 2.2 and the CDF of table 2.3 are known as *univariate* distribution functions. In this section we consider the case of experiments where the observed outcomes are dependent on two or more random variables. The probability distributions of such experiments are known as *multivariate* probability functions. In the examples that follow, we discuss the case of bivariate (or two variable) problems.

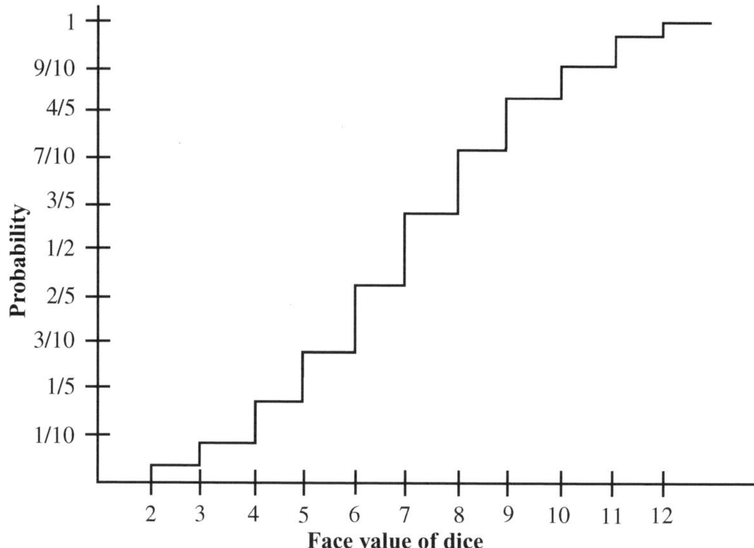

Figure 2.2 The CDF of a discrete random variable

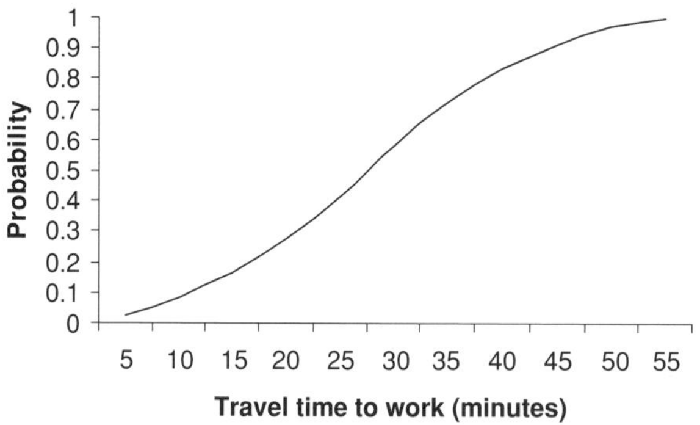

Figure 2.3 The CDF of a continuous random variable

2.4.6 The multivariate probability function

Consider the example of travel times to and from work. Given different traffic densities over a day, the amount of time spent traveling to work may not necessarily be the same as the amount of time spent traveling home from work. The total time spent traveling to and from work will be a function of the two separate journeys. Table 2.4 shows the frequency counts for home–work and work–home travel times observed for 115 individuals.

As with the previous travel time to work example, the probability of observing a specific set of events (e.g. a work–home trip of 11–15 minutes and a home–work trip of 6–10 minutes) is given as the relative frequency for that event. Table 2.5 shows the relative frequencies for each cell of table 2.4. Each relative frequency is calculated as the ratio of the cell's absolute value over the total population of events (i.e. 115). Table 2.5 represents the

Table 2.4. *Frequency counts for home–work and work–home trips*

Travel time to work (minutes) / Travel time from work (minutes)	$0 \leq X \leq 5$	$5 < X \leq 10$	$10 < X \leq 15$	$15 < X \leq 20$	$20 < X \leq 25$	$25 < X \leq 30$	$30 < X \leq 35$	$35 < X \leq 40$	Total
$0 \leq X \leq 5$	3	5	2	0	0	0	0	0	10
$5 < X \leq 10$	4	7	2	2	0	0	0	0	15
$10 < X \leq 15$	1	2	8	6	1	0	0	0	18
$15 < X \leq 20$	0	1	5	11	3	2	0	0	22
$20 < X \leq 25$	0	0	0	4	11	2	1	0	18
$25 < X \leq 30$	0	0	0	1	3	7	2	1	14
$30 < X \leq 35$	0	0	0	0	1	3	6	2	12
$35 < X \leq 40$	0	0	0	0	0	1	1	4	6
Total	8	15	17	24	19	15	10	7	115

Table 2.5. *The bivariate distribution for home–work and work–home trips*

Travel time from work (minutes) \ Travel time to work (minutes)	$0 \le X \le 5$	$5 < X \le 10$	$10 < X \le 15$	$15 < X \le 20$	$20 < X \le 25$	$25 < X \le 30$	$30 < X \le 35$	$35 < X \le 40$	Total
$0 \le X \le 5$	0.026	0.043	0.017	0.000	0.000	0.000	0.000	0.000	0.087
$5 < X \le 10$	0.035	0.061	0.017	0.017	0.000	0.000	0.000	0.000	0.130
$10 < X \le 15$	0.009	0.017	0.070	0.052	0.009	0.000	0.000	0.000	0.157
$15 < X \le 20$	0.000	0.009	0.043	0.096	0.026	0.017	0.000	0.000	0.191
$20 < X \le 25$	0.000	0.000	0.000	0.035	0.096	0.017	0.009	0.000	0.157
$25 < X \le 30$	0.000	0.000	0.000	0.009	0.026	0.061	0.017	0.009	0.122
$30 < X \le 35$	0.000	0.000	0.000	0.000	0.009	0.026	0.052	0.017	0.104
$35 < X \le 40$	0.000	0.000	0.000	0.000	0.000	0.009	0.009	0.035	0.052
Total	0.070	0.130	0.148	0.209	0.165	0.130	0.087	0.061	1

bivariate probability distribution for our example. Tables such as table 2.5 are commonly referred to as *joint probability density functions*, or simply JPDF.

The values calculated for each cell of a JPDF indicate the joint probability associated with two or more (two in this case) random variables being observed to take on specific values. For example, from table 2.5, the probability that we will observe an individual with a home–work trip time of 15–20 minutes and a travel time of 20–25 minutes for a work–home trip is equal to 0.035. Similarly, the probability that we will observe an individual with a home–work travel time of 5–10 minutes and a work–home trip travel time of 15–25 minutes is zero.

Formally, let X_1 be the travel time to work random variable and X_2 be the time from work random variable. Mathematically, the JPDF is given in (2.5):

$$f(X_1, X_2) = P(X_1 = x_1 \text{ and } X_2 = x_2) \tag{2.5}$$

In words, (2.5) states that the JPDF is equal to the probability that X_1 takes the value x_1 and X_2 takes the value x_2.

2.4.7 Marginal probability density functions

The column and row totals of table 2.5 give what are known as the marginal PDF (MPDF) of the random variables used in constructing the table. The column totals may be used to calculate the probabilities of observing a particular travel time to work independent of what value is observed for time spent traveling from work. Similarly, the row totals provide the probabilities of observing particular travel times from work, apart from the value observed for traveling to work. For example, the probability of observing an individual whose travel time to work is 10–15 minutes, irrespective of how long it took them to travel from work, is 0.148. Note that this is the same value we observe from table 2.1. Thus, by ignoring the other random variables, the MPDFs are calculated as if the problem we are examining is univariate.

2.4.8 Conditional probability density functions

The MPDFs we discussed in the previous section are sometimes referred to as "unconditional PDFs." The reference to "unconditional" is derived from the fact that the MPDF for one random variable is not conditional on a specific value being observed for any other random variable being considered. In effect, the MPDF is calculated irrespective of what values are observed for all other random variables. It is often useful to consider the *conditional probability density function* (CPDF). Consider two random variables, X_1 and X_2. Mathematically, the CPDF of X_2 is:

$$f(X_2 \mid X_1) = P(X_2 = x_2 \mid X_1 = x_1) \tag{2.6}$$

In words, (2.6) states that the probability that we will observe a particular value of X_2, x_2, is conditional on X_1 being observed to take the value of x_1. For example, assuming X_1 and X_2 are our travel to work and travel from work random variables, respectively, what is the

Table 2.6. *Marginal probability distributions*

Travel time to work (minutes)	$f(X_1)$	Travel time from work (minutes)	$f(X_2)$
$0 \leq X \leq 5$	0.07	$0 \leq X \leq 5$	0.09
$5 < X \leq 10$	0.13	$5 < X \leq 10$	0.13
$10 < X \leq 15$	0.15	$10 < X \leq 15$	0.16
$15 < X \leq 20$	0.21	$15 < X \leq 20$	0.19
$20 < X \leq 25$	0.17	$20 < X \leq 25$	0.16
$25 < X \leq 30$	0.13	$25 < X \leq 30$	0.12
$30 < X \leq 35$	0.09	$30 < X \leq 35$	0.10
$35 < X \leq 40$	0.06	$35 < X \leq 40$	0.05
Total	1.00	*Total*	1.00

probability that X_2 will take on the value 10–15 minutes given that X_1 is 15–20 minutes. The CPDF may be calculated using (2.7):

$$f(X_2 \mid X_1) = \frac{f(X_2, X_1)}{f(X_1)} \tag{2.7}$$

To demonstrate (2.7), the probability given as the CPDF of observing an individual whose travel time to work is 10–15 minutes given that there time from work is known to be 15–20 minutes is shown below:

$$f(10\text{–}15 \text{ minutes} \mid 15\text{–}20 \text{ minutes}) = \frac{f(X_2, X_1)}{f(X_1)} = \frac{0.03}{0.19} = 0.16$$

where $f(X_1, X_2)$ is the JPDF as defined in (2.5) and $f(X_1)$ is the PDF of the X_1 random variable as defined in (2.2). Note that the examples we are using are for discrete random variables (hence $f(X_1)$ is defined as per (2.2) and not (2.3)). The JPDF and MPDF for continuous variables are similarly calculated for continuous variables although the mathematical computations are far more involved. We therefore leave it to other sources to demonstrate the JPDF, MPDF, and CPDF case for continuous random variables.

In calculating the CPDF (the numerator of (2.7)) for the above example, the JPDF for an individual whose travel time to work is 10–15 minutes and travel time from of 15–20 minutes is obtained from table 2.5. The PDF for the travel time to work random variable designated X_1 (the denominator), is obtained from table 2.6.

Note that the probability that we would observe an individual whose travel time from work is 10–15 minutes when considered independent of the travel time to work for that same individual would be 0.15, less than the probability when we have additional information with regard to the time spent traveling to from home to work. The lesson to be learned from this is that the addition of information changes our assessment of the probabilities associated with observing certain outcomes of events. That is, when we know X_1, our assessment of the probability will change for X_2.

Table 2.7. *Demonstrating statistical independence of two random variables*

Die two \ Die one	1	2	3	4	5	6	Total
1	1/36	1/36	1/36	1/36	1/36	1/36	1/6
2	1/36	1/36	1/36	1/36	1/36	1/36	1/6
3	1/36	1/36	1/36	1/36	1/36	1/36	1/6
4	1/36	1/36	1/36	1/36	1/36	1/36	1/6
5	1/36	1/36	1/36	1/36	1/36	1/36	1/6
6	1/36	1/36	1/36	1/36	1/36	1/36	1/6
Total	1/6	1/6	1/6	1/6	1/6	1/6	1

2.4.9 Defining statistical independence

To demonstrate the concept of *statistical independence*, consider table 2.7. In table 2.7, the joint probability for any outcome is equal to the product of the related marginal probabilities. This property is both necessary and sufficient for the two random variables to be considered statistically independent.

For example, the marginal probability for observing a one from a single roll of die one is 1/6. The marginal probability for observing a one from a single roll of die two is also 1/6. Multiplying these two marginal probabilities together produces 1/36, the same value as the joint probability.

Table 2.8 shows the products of the MPDFs for table 2.5. The marginal probability of observing a travel time from home to work between 10 and 15 minutes is 0.15 and the marginal probability of observing a work to home journey between 15 and 20 minutes is 0.19. Multiplying these to values together yields a value of 0.0285 which is different to the joint probability value of 0.04. Clearly the home–work and work–home travel times are not statistically independent when compared to the actual JPDF calculated in table 2.5.

2.5 Properties of random variables

Rather than work with the PDF or CDF of a distribution, both of which require consideration of the entire set of possible outcomes and the probabilities associated with each possible outcome, it is more common to work with single statistical measures used to describe the distribution. The two most common statistical measures, referred to as "population moments," used to describe distributional forms are the expected value or the mean (referred to as the first population *moment*) and the *variance* (commonly referred to as the second population moment). In the following sections, we outline in detail the characteristics of both population moments.

Table 2.8. *Demonstrating that the home–work and work–home travel times are not statistically independent*

Travel time from work (minutes) \ Travel time to work (minutes)	$0 \le X \le 5$	$5 < X \le 10$	$10 < X \le 15$	$15 < X \le 20$	$20 < X \le 25$	$25 < X \le 30$	$30 < X \le 35$	$35 < X \le 40$	Total
$0 \le X \le 5$	0.03	0.04	0.02	0.00	0.00	0.00	0.00	0.00	0.09
$5 < X \le 10$	0.03	0.06	0.02	0.02	0.00	0.00	0.00	0.00	0.13
$10 < X \le 15$	0.01	0.02	0.07	0.05	0.01	0.00	0.00	0.00	0.16
$15 < X \le 20$	0.00	0.01	0.04	0.10	0.03	0.02	0.00	0.00	0.19
$20 < X \le 25$	0.00	0.00	0.00	0.03	0.10	0.02	0.01	0.00	0.16
$25 < X \le 30$	0.00	0.00	0.00	0.01	0.03	0.06	0.02	0.01	0.12
$30 < X \le 35$	0.00	0.00	0.00	0.00	0.01	0.03	0.05	0.02	0.10
$35 < X \le 40$	0.00	0.00	0.00	0.00	0.00	0.01	0.01	0.03	0.05
Total	0.07	0.13	0.15	0.21	0.17	0.13	0.09	0.06	1

Table 2.9. *The expected value of rolling two dice*

Number observed (X)	$f(X)$	$Xf(X)$
2	1/36	1/18
3	1/18	1/6
4	1/12	1/3
5	1/9	5/9
6	5/36	5/6
7	1/6	1 1/6
8	5/36	1 1/9
9	1/9	1
10	1/12	5/6
11	1/18	11/18
12	1/36	1/3
	E(X) =	7

2.5.1 Expected value

The *expected value* (also known as the mean or average) of a random variable, X, is defined as a number that purports to typify or describe X in a single value. More generally, we define the expected value as the average of the set of values that a random variable can assume. Mathematically, the expected value is often denoted as E(X), read as "E of X" while the mean of X is often denoted as $\bar{x}$, read as "x bar," if we are dealing with a sample or μ_x, read as "mu" of x, if we are dealing with a population. The relationship between the PDF of a random variable and mean or expected value of that PDF is given in (2.8):

$$\mathrm{E}(X) = \sum_{X=1}^{n} Xf(X) \tag{2.8}$$

where $f(X)$ is, as defined previously, the PDF of X.

Equation (2.8) suggests that the expected value of a random variable X is the sum over all values of X multiplied by the PDF of each potential outcome occurring. For example, reconsider our earlier example of rolling two dice and summing the observed values obtained. The set of possible outcomes make up the set of X. The PDF, given as $f(X)$ is obtained from table 2.2. From (2.8), the expected value of X is obtained by multiplying the PDF of each outcome with the associated outcomes value of X and summing the resulting values. We do this in table 2.9.

The expected value of summing the observed values of two dice in a single roll is calculated as being seven. This figure is arrived at by summing the last column of table 2.9. We can similarly calculate the expected travel times to and from work, however, in doing so we will have to take the mid-point of the travel time ranges. We do so in table 2.10, showing that the average travel time for home–work trips is 19.28 minutes and for work–home trips is 18.55.

Table 2.10. *Calculating the average home–work and work–home travel times*

Travel time to work (minutes) X_1	$f(X_1)$	$Xf(X_1)$	Travel time from work (minutes) X_2	$f(X_2)$	$Xf(X_2)$
2.5	0.07	0.18	2.5	0.09	0.23
7.5	0.13	0.98	7.5	0.13	0.98
12.5	0.15	1.88	12.5	0.16	2.00
17.5	0.21	3.68	17.5	0.19	3.33
22.5	0.17	3.83	22.5	0.16	3.60
27.5	0.13	3.58	27.5	0.12	3.30
32.5	0.09	2.93	32.5	0.10	3.25
37.5	0.06	2.25	37.5	0.05	1.88
	$E(X_1) =$	19.28		$E(X_2) =$	18.55

Table 2.11. *The expected values of two separate rolls of a die*

X_1	$f(X_1)$	$Xf(X_1)$	X_2	$f(X_2)$	$Xf(X_2)$
1	1/6	1/6	1	1/6	1/6
2	1/6	1/3	2	1/6	1/3
3	1/6	1/2	3	1/6	1/2
4	1/6	2/3	4	1/6	2/3
5	1/6	5/6	5	1/6	5/6
6	1/6	1	6	1/6	1
	$E(X_1)$	3.5		$E(X_2)$	3.5

2.5.1.1 Properties of expected values

The expected values of random variables display certain important properties. These are:

(1) The expected value of a constant is the same constant. That is:

$$E(k) = k \tag{2.9a}$$

For example, if $k = 6$, then $E(6) = 6$.

(2) The expected value of the sum of two random variables, X_1 and X_2, is equal to the sum of the expected values of X_1 and X_2:

$$E(X_1 + X_2) = E(X_1) + E(X_2) \tag{2.9b}$$

For example, from table 2.9, the expected value for rolling two dice was estimated as being equal to seven. In table 2.11, we consider each roll of the die as distinct random variable. The expected values for each roll of the die represented as random variables

Table 2.12. *The expected value of a random variable multiplied by a constant*

X	$f(X)$	$Xf(X)$	k	$kXf(X)$
1	1/6	1/6	2	1/3
2	1/6	1/3	2	2/3
3	1/6	1/2	2	1
4	1/6	2/3	2	1 1/3
5	1/6	5/6	2	1 2/3
6	1/6	1	2	2
			E(kX)	7

X_1 and X_2 are both equal to 3.5. Summing the expected value over both random variables suggests an expected value of seven; the exact same value we obtained earlier when treating the two outcomes as a single event.

(3) The ratio of two random variables, X_1 and X_2 is not equal to the sum of the ratios of the expected values of those same two random variables. Mathematically, this is given as (2.9c):

$$\mathrm{E}(X_1 \div X_2) \neq \frac{\mathrm{E}(X_1)}{\mathrm{E}(X_2)} \tag{2.9c}$$

(4) When two random variables are not statistically independent, the expected value of the product of two random variables is not equal to the product of two expected values. This is given in (2.9d):

$$\mathrm{E}(X_1 \times X_2) \neq \mathrm{E}(X_1) \times \mathrm{E}(X_2) \tag{2.9d}$$

If the two random variables are statistically independent, the expected value of the product of two random variables is equal to the product of two expected values, as shown in (2.9e):

$$\mathrm{E}(X_1 \times X_2) = \mathrm{E}(X_1) \times \mathrm{E}(X_2) \tag{2.9e}$$

(5) The fifth property associated with expected values of random variables is that the expected value of a random variable multiplied by a constant is equal to the constant times the expected value of the random variable. This is shown in (2.9f):

$$\mathrm{E}(kX) = k \times \mathrm{E}(X) \tag{2.9f}$$

To demonstrate, consider table 2.12. In table 2.12 we multiply $Xf(X)$ by a constant of two over each value of X, a roll of a single die. The expected value given as the sum of the last column is equal to 7. From table 2.11 we know that the expected value from rolling a single die is equal to 3.5. If we multiply this value by two, we arrive at the same value we calculate in table 2.12, as expected from (2.9f).

Note that the roll of two dice is not the same as two times the roll of one die.

(6) The last property is a composite of properties (1) and (5). Mathematically, if k and j are constants:

$$E(kX + j) = k \times E(X) + j \tag{2.9g}$$

For example, if $k = 6$ and $j = 2$, $E(6X + 2) = 6 \times E(X) + 2$.

The expected value or mean represents the first population moment of a distribution. In the next section we discuss the characteristics and outline the properties related to the second population moment – the *variance*. We then go on to discuss the important concept of *covariance*.

2.5.2 Variance

The second population moment of a distribution, known as the variance, provides the analyst with an understanding of how *dispersed or spread observations are around the mean*. Mathematically, the variance is given by (2.10):

$$\text{var}(X) = \sigma_x^2 = E(X - \mu_x)^2 \tag{2.10}$$

where X is a random variable, σ_x^2, read "sigma squared of x," is the notation used to represent variance and the remaining terms are as previously defined. Examination of the right-hand side of (2.10) shows that the variance of a random variable is the expected value of the squared difference between each observed outcome of X and the mean of X. While (2.10) defines the variance of a random variable, it is necessary to use (2.11) in order to calculate the correct value:

$$\text{var}(X) = \sigma_x^2 = \sum_{X \neq 1}^{n} (X - \mu_x)^2 f(X) \tag{2.11}$$

In table 2.13 we demonstrate the use of (2.11) to calculate the variance for our sum of the observed values from the roll of two dice example. Using (2.11) the variance for our example is calculated as 5.833.

Related to the variance is the *standard deviation*. The standard deviation, denoted σ_x, is calculated simply as the square root of the variance. For the above example, the standard deviation is equal to 2.415.

2.5.2.1 Properties of variance

As with the expected value, the variance measure has several useful properties. These include.

(1) The variance of a constant, k, is equal to zero:

$$\text{var}(k) = 0 \tag{2.12a}$$

Table 2.13. *Calculating the variance of rolling two dice*

X	$f(x)$	$(X-\mu_x)^2$	$(X-\mu_x)^2 f(X)$
2	1/36	25	0.694
3	1/18	16	0.889
4	1/12	9	0.750
5	1/9	4	0.444
6	5/36	1	0.139
7	1/6	0	0.000
8	5/36	1	0.139
9	1/9	4	0.444
10	1/12	9	0.750
11	1/18	16	0.889
12	1/36	25	0.694
		Sum	5.833

Table 2.14. *The variance of two independent throws of a die*

Die one				Die two			
X_1	$f(X_1)$	$(X_1-\mu_{x1})^2$	$(X_1-\mu_{x1})^2 f(X_1)$	X_2	$f(X_2)$	$(X_2-\mu_{x2})^2$	$(X_2-\mu_{x2})^2 f(X_2)$
1	1/6	6.25	1.042	1	1/6	6.25	1.042
2	1/6	2.25	0.375	2	1/6	2.25	0.375
3	1/6	0.25	0.042	3	1/6	0.25	0.042
4	1/6	0.25	0.042	4	1/6	0.25	0.042
5	1/6	2.25	0.375	5	1/6	2.25	0.375
6	1/6	6.25	1.042	6	1/6	6.25	1.042
		Sum	2.917			*Sum*	2.917

(2) If k is a constant term and X is a random variable, then

$$\text{var}(X+k) = \text{var}(X) \tag{2.12b}$$

(3) If X_1 and X_2 are two statistically independent random variables then the variance of the sum of X_1 and X_2 is equal to the sum of the variances of X_1 and X_2. Mathematically:

$$\text{var}(X_1+X_2) = \text{var}(X_1) + \text{var}(X_2) \tag{2.12c}$$

For example, returning to our earlier example of throwing two dice, the variance of the sum of the two random variables representing the outcome of the throw of the two dice was calculated in table 2.13 as 5.833. In table 2.14, for the same problem we calculate the sum of the variances of each throw separately.

From table 2.14, it can clearly be seen that the variance of each random variable is 2.917. Adding these two values together produces a variance of 5.833, which is precisely the value we obtained from table 12.13.

(4) Similar to property (3):

$$\text{var}(X_1 - X_2) = \text{var}(X_1) + \text{var}(X_2) \tag{2.12d}$$

(5) If k is a constant, then

$$\text{var}(kX) = k^2 \,\text{var}(X) \tag{2.12e}$$

(6) If k and j are both constants, then

$$\text{var}(kX + j) = k^2 \,\text{var}(X) \tag{2.12f}$$

For example, assuming $k = 6$ and $j = 2$, $\text{var}(6X + 2) = 36\,\text{var}(X)$

(7) From properties (3) and (5), it follows that

$$\text{var}(kX_1 + jX_2) = k^2 \,\text{var}(X_1) + j^2 \,\text{var}(X_2) \tag{2.12g}$$

For example, if $k = 6$ and $j = 2$, $\text{var}(6X_1 + 2X_2) = 36\,\text{var}(X_1) + 4\,\text{var}(X_2)$

The expected value and variance represent the two most commonly used statistics to describe a univariate distribution. When we move to the multivariate case, however, it is common to use other statistical descriptors of the data. Two of the more common multivariate statistics reported are the covariance and correlation. We discuss both of these now.

2.5.3 Covariance

The *covariance* is a statistical measure representative of the degree to which two random variables vary together. Mathematically, the covariance between two random variables X_1 and X_2 is given as (2.13).

$$\text{cov}(X_1, X_2) = \text{E}[(X_1 - \mu_{x1})(X_2 - \mu_{x2})] \tag{2.13}$$

where $\text{cov}(X_1, X_2)$, read as "the covariance between X_1 and X_2," E[ ], is as previously defined, and μ_{x1} and μ_{x2} are the means of X_1 and X_2 respectively (i.e. $\text{E}(X_1) = \mu_{x1}$ and $\text{E}(X_2) = \mu_{x2}$).

Rather than use (2.13) to compute the covariance between two random variables, we use (2.14) instead:

$$\text{cov}(X_1, X_2) = \sum_{X_1=1}^{n_1} \sum_{X_2=1}^{n_2} X_1 X_2 f(X_1, X_2) - \mu_{x1}\mu_{x2} \tag{2.14}$$

To demonstrate the use of (2.14), consider the home–work and work–home example used earlier. Ignoring the double summation sign for the present, let us first calculate values of $X_1 X_2 f(X_1, X_2)$ for each potential outcome. Taking X_1 and X_2 at their mid-points, we calculate $X_1 X_2 f(X_1, X_2)$ for each cell of tables 2.4 and 2.5. For the first cell, X_1 and X_2 both equal 2.5, hence $X_1 X_2$ equals 6.25. From table 2.5, we obtain a value for $f(X_1, X_2)$

Table 2.15. *Calculating $X_1X_2f(X_1, X_2)$ for home–work and work–home trips*

X_2 \ X_1	2.5	7.5	12.5	17.5	22.5	27.5	32.5	37.5
2.5	0.163	0.815	0.543	0.000	0.000	0.000	0.000	0.000
7.5	0.652	3.424	1.630	2.283	0.000	0.000	0.000	0.000
12.5	0.272	1.630	10.870	11.413	2.446	0.000	0.000	0.000
17.5	0.000	1.141	9.511	29.293	10.272	8.370	0.000	0.000
22.5	0.000	0.000	0.000	13.696	48.424	10.761	6.359	0.000
27.5	0.000	0.000	0.000	4.185	16.141	46.033	15.543	8.967
32.5	0.000	0.000	0.000	0.000	6.359	23.315	55.109	21.196
37.5	0.000	0.000	0.000	0.000	0.000	8.967	10.598	48.913

of 0.026. Multiplying 6.25 by 0.026 gives a value of 0.1625, as reported in cell one of table 2.15. The remaining cells of table 2.15 are obtained similarly.

Once each cell has been calculated, the double summation sign suggests that we sum every cell over every column and row. Summing all cells in table 2.15, gives a value of 439.293. Thus, $X_1X_2f(X_1, X_2)$ of (2.14) is equal to 439.293. μ_{x1} and μ_{x2} were estimated as part of table 2.10 and are equal to 19.28 and 18.55, respectively. Multiplying these two values together to obtain an estimate of $\mu_{x1} \times \mu_{x2}$ yields 357.551. With all the elements of (2.14), we are now able to calculate the covariance for the home–work, work–home example:

$$\text{cov}(X_1, X_2) = 439.293 - 357.551 = 81.742$$

The interpretation of the covariance statistic is generally limited to the observed sign of the statistic as the magnitude of the statistic will depend on the magnitude of the units of X_1 and X_2. A positive covariance indicates that as the observed values of one random variable increase, so to do the values of the other random variable: a positive relationship. A negative covariance indicates that as one random variable increases, the values observed for the other random variable tend to decrease: a negative relationship. A zero covariance indicates that no relationship exists between the two random variables. For the above example, a covariance of 81.742 indicates that those with longer home–work travel times tend towards longer work–home travel times; a not altogether surprising result.

2.5.3.1 Properties of covariance

Six properties of covariances are important:

(1) The covariance between two independent random variables will be zero.

To demonstrate, consider the covariance between the roll of two dice. Intuitively, the value observed from one die will not impact upon the value observed for the second. This intuitive independence translates to statistical independence as shown

Table 2.16. *Calculating $X_1 X_2 f(X_1, X_2)$ for the roll of two dice*

Die two \ Die one	1	2	3	4	5	6
1	0.03	0.06	0.08	0.11	0.14	0.17
2	0.06	0.11	0.17	0.22	0.28	0.33
3	0.08	0.17	0.25	0.33	0.42	0.50
4	0.11	0.22	0.33	0.44	0.56	0.67
5	0.14	0.28	0.42	0.56	0.69	0.83
6	0.17	0.33	0.50	0.67	0.83	1.00

in table 2.7. From (2.14) and table 2.7, each $X_1 X_2 f(X_1, X_2)$ is calculated as shown in table 2.16. Summing each of the non-marginal cells of table 2.16 produces a value of 12.25.

From table 2.11, we know that the average for each independent roll of a die is 3.5. Multiplying the expected value of 3.5 for each roll of the two dice, we obtain an estimate of 12.25 representing the $\mu_{x1} \times \mu_{x2}$ component of (2.14). Taking each constituent part of (2.14), we observe a zero covariance:

$$\text{cov}(X_1, X_2) = 12.25 - 12.25 = 0$$

(2) Where k and j are constants

$$\text{cov}(kX_1, jX_2) = kj\,\text{cov}(X_1, X_2)$$

For example, if $k = 6$ and $j = 2$, $\text{cov}(6X_1, 2X_2) = 12\,\text{cov}(X_1, X_2)$

(3) Where k, j, are constants

$$\text{cov}(k + X_1, j + X_2) = \text{cov}(X_1, X_2)$$

(4) From properties (2) and (3), if k, j, h and g are all constants

$$\text{cov}(h + kX_1, g + jX_2) = kj\,\text{cov}(X_1, X_2)$$

(5) Where X_1 and X_2 are two random variables

$$\text{cov}(X_1, X_2) = \text{cov}(X_2, X_1)$$

(6) The covariance between a random variable and itself is equal to the variance of that random variable. That is:

$$\text{cov}(X_1, X_1) = \text{var}(X_1)$$

2.5.4 The variance–covariance matrix

Consider an example of traveling to work in which there are two possible modes from which to choose: car or bus. Further, assume that there are only two attributes considered by each decision maker for each mode: travel time (TT) and cost. In the estimation of our model, we cannot know with certainty the weight each decision maker will place on each of these attributes. In practical terms, this uncertainty translates into the concept of an *error component* of the model. As we cannot observe the error component of each decision process, we are forced to make assumptions as to how it might look in order to estimate our models (see chapters 3, 13 and 15).

For each parameter we estimate within our model, there will be an associated *error term*. Each error term is treated within the model estimation process as a random component or random variable over decision makers. In treating the error components of our model as random variables, it is common practice to examine the distribution of the error terms, particularly in terms of their variances and covariances. These are most often shown in the form of a variance–covariance matrix.

For the above example, there will exist four variance terms, each linked to an error component of our four attributes. Each variance is shown as the diagonal element of the variance–covariance matrix. The off-diagonal elements of the variance–covariance matrix represent each of the covariances between the error terms of the model variables. The total number of covariances reported within a variance–covariance matrix may be calculated using (2.15).

$$n(n-1) \tag{2.15}$$

For the above example, n, the number of attributes in our model, is equal to four. Thus, from (2.15), the total number of covariances may be calculated as:

$$4 \times (4-1) = 12$$

For $j = j$, let σ_{ij}^2 represent the variance and for $i \neq j$, let σ_{ij} represent the covariance between the error term for attributes i and j. For the above example, the variance–covariance matrix may be written as (2.16):

$$\begin{array}{c} \\ \text{TT}_{\text{car}} \\ \text{Cost}_{\text{car}} \\ \text{TT}_{\text{bus}} \\ \text{Cost}_{\text{car}} \end{array} \begin{array}{c} \begin{array}{cccc} \text{TT}_{\text{car}} & \text{Cost}_{\text{car}} & \text{TT}_{\text{bus}} & \text{Cost}_{\text{bus}} \end{array} \\ \begin{bmatrix} \sigma_{11}^2 & \sigma_{12} & \sigma_{13} & \sigma_{14} \\ \sigma_{21} & \sigma_{22}^2 & \sigma_{23} & \sigma_{24} \\ \sigma_{31} & \sigma_{32} & \sigma_{33}^2 & \sigma_{34} \\ \sigma_{41} & \sigma_{42} & \sigma_{43} & \sigma_{44}^2 \end{bmatrix} \end{array} \tag{2.16}$$

From (2.16), it can be seen that there are four variance terms and 12 covariance terms. Given property (5), however, we know that $\sigma_{ij} = \sigma_{ji}$, hence although the variance–covariance matrix shown as (2.16) has 12 covariances, exactly half of these will be allowed to differ. This is often referred to as the *lower off-diagonal matrix*.

2.5.5 Correlation

Within the choice modeling literature, much discussion relates to the covariances that exist between random variables of the fitted models. As described previously, the sign of a covariance statistic may be used to indicate the direction of relationship between two random variables, however, the magnitude of the statistic is not generally informative as to the strength of relationship that may exist between the two random variables. An associated statistic to the covariance statistic is the *correlation statistic*. Unlike the covariance statistic, the correlation coefficient is used to determine not only the direction of a relationship, but also the strength of magnitude of the relationship that may exist between two random variables.

The correlation coefficient, ρ (read "rho") is calculated using (2.17):

$$\rho = \frac{\text{cov}(X_1, X_2)}{\sigma_{x1}\sigma_{x2}} \tag{2.17}$$

where σ_{x1} is the standard deviation of random variable X_1 and σ_{x2} is the standard deviation of random variable X_2.

2.5.5.1 Properties of the correlation coefficient

The correlation coefficient defined as (2.17) displays several properties of note:

(1) The sign of the correlation coefficient may be either negative or positive and will always be the same as that of the covariance statistic. To explain why, consider (2.17). The standard deviation of a random parameter must always be positive as one cannot have a negative variance (the expected value of a distribution may be negative, but the variance must always be equal to or greater than zero). Given that the standard deviation of a random variable must always be positive, the denominator of (2.17) must be positive. From our earlier discussion, the covariance between two random variables may be either positive or negative. As such, it is the sign of the covariance statistic, represented as the numerator of (2.17), which determines the sign of the correlation coefficient.

(2) The correlation coefficient will always lie between -1 and 1. Mathematically:

$$-1 \leq \rho \leq 1 \tag{2.18}$$

The closer a correlation coefficient is to one or minus one, the stronger the relationship is said to be between the two random variables. A correlation coefficient of zero suggests that there is no relationship between the two random variables.

As an aside, note that mathematically it is only ever possible to observe a zero correlation coefficient if the covariance between the two random variables is equal to zero. If the standard deviation of either random variable is equal to zero, the denominator of (2.17) will be equal to zero and hence the correlation coefficient will be inestimable. Thus, the statistics assumes that the standard deviations of both random variables are non-zero (and positive). If, on the other hand, the covariance is equal to zero, the correlation coefficient will also equal zero. As noted earlier, the covariance between two random variables will equal zero only if the two are statistically independent. Hence, the correlation between two statistically independent variables must equal zero.

Table 2.17. *Estimating the variances for home–work and work–home trips*

Home–work				Work–home			
X_1	$f(X_1)$	$(X_1 - \mu_{x1})^2$	$(X_1 - \mu_{x1})^2 f(X_1)$	X_2	$f(X_2)$	$(X_2 - \mu_{x2})^2$	$(X_2 - \mu_{x2})^2 f(X_2)$
2.5	0.07	281.57	19.71	2.5	0.09	257.86	23.21
7.5	0.13	138.77	18.04	7.5	0.13	122.28	15.90
12.5	0.15	45.97	6.90	12.5	0.16	36.70	5.87
17.5	0.21	3.17	0.67	17.5	0.19	1.12	0.21
22.5	0.17	10.37	1.76	22.5	0.16	15.54	2.49
27.5	0.13	67.57	8.78	27.5	0.12	79.96	9.60
32.5	0.09	174.77	15.73	32.5	0.10	194.38	19.44
37.5	0.06	331.97	19.92	37.5	0.05	358.80	17.94
		Sum	91.50			*Sum*	94.65

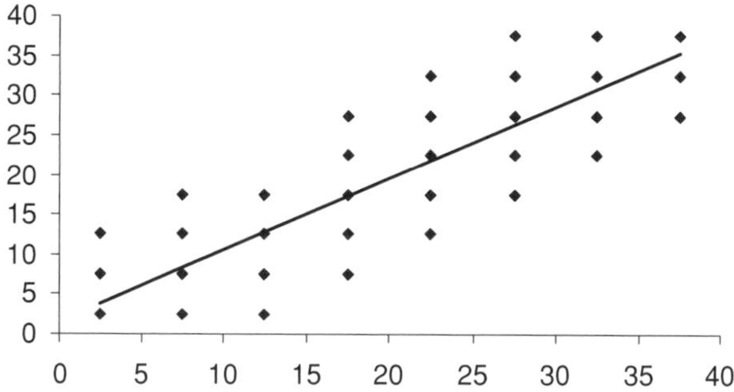

Figure 2.4 Plotting the home–work, work–home trip times

To demonstrate the correlation coefficient, let us return to our home–work, work–home example. Previously we estimated the covariance for this example as 81.742. The variances for the home–work and work–home trips are calculated in table 2.17 (estimated at the mid-points and with μ_1 and μ_2 equal 19.28 and 18.55 respectively).

Using equation (2.17), the correlation coefficient for the home–work and work–home example is calculated thus (noting that equation (2.17) calls for the use of the standard deviations and not variances):

$$\rho = \frac{81.742}{\sqrt{91.5} \times \sqrt{94.65}} = \frac{81.742}{93.06} = 0.878$$

A correlation coefficient of 0.878 suggest that there exists a strong positive relationship in terms of the times taken for home–work and work–home trips, such that those with a longer work–home trip, generally have a longer home–work trip. This relationship can clearly be seen by plotting the trip times, as shown in figure 2.4. Note that we have added a trendline to the figure to better demonstrate the relationship.

As an aside, (2.17) is the Pearson product moment correlation coefficient. The Pearson product moment correlation coefficient is the appropriate measure of similarity only when the two random variables being tested are ratio scaled. Other correlation measures are appropriate for non-ratio scaled data (see Hensher and Smith 1984). We describe these measures in appendix 2A (pp. 60–1).

2.5.6 Correlation and variances

Properties (3) and (4) of variance relate to the variances of two independent random variables. What if the two random variables are not independent? From our discussion just now, we know that two non-independent random variables will have a non-zero covariance and a non-zero correlation. In such cases, (2.12c) and (2.12d) are no longer valid and we are required to use (2.19a) and (2.19b) instead:

$$\text{var}(X_1 + X_2) = \text{var}(X_1) + \text{var}(X_2) + 2\text{cov}(X_1, X_2) \tag{2.19a}$$

$$\text{var}(X_1 - X_2) = \text{var}(X_1) + \text{var}(X_2) - 2\text{cov}(X_1, X_2) \tag{2.19b}$$

From (2.19a) and (2.19b), it can clearly be seen that if the two random variables X_1 and X_2 are statistically independent, then the covariances are zero and (2.19a) and (2.19b) are equivalent to (2.12c) and (2.12d), respectively.

For the home–work, work–home travel example, we calculated the variances as 91.5 and 94.65 for both trip types, respectively, and the covariance between the two as 81.742. From (2.19a) and (2.19b).

$$\text{var}(X_1 + X_2) = 91.5 + 94.65 + (2 \times 84.442) = 351.394$$

$$\text{var}(X_1 - X_2) = 91.5 + 94.65 - (2 \times 84.442) = 21.626$$

2.6 Sample population statistics

The above presentation of statistics may be unfamiliar to many. The equations we used and our explanations are likely to be familiar only to those with a background in classical statistics obtained from an econometric perspective. This is because the discussion is centered on population-level statistics, while most students are taught statistics performed on samples of populations. As it is more likely that we will have data on samples rather than populations, it is worthwhile discussing the types of statistics that are often applied at this level of analysis. We do so here, starting with the concept of the sample mean.

2.6.1 The sample mean

In the previous sections, we discussed the concept of expected value and stated that the expected value of a random variable is the same as the mean of that random variable. In

Table 2.18. *Respondent ratings of two soft drinks*

Respondent	Drink 1	Drink 2
1	8	6
2	10	4
3	8	6
4	4	4
5	6	8
6	6	2

discussing the expected value, we framed our discussion in terms of population-level data. In this section we discuss the concept of sample mean. Before we discuss the sample mean, however, let us first clarify some notation. The mean of a random variable obtained from a population is generally denoted as μ_x (read "mu of x") which is, as expressed previously, known as the expected value. The mean of a sample however is generally represented as $\bar{X}$ read "X bar," and is generally referred to as the sample mean.

The formula to calculate the sample mean is given as (2.20):

$$\bar{X} = \sum_{i=1}^{n} \frac{X_i}{n} \tag{2.20}$$

where $\sum_{i=1}^{n}$ is as previously defined, X_i is a random variable and n is the number of observations taken of the random variable X_i.

To demonstrate, consider an example. Suppose that the management of a soft drink manufacturer had six respondents rate their product and a competitor's product in a blind taste test on a ten-point scale. The results of this task are shown in table 2.18.

Using (2.20), the means for drinks 1 and 2 are

$$\bar{X}_1 = \frac{8 + 10 + 8 + 4 + 6 + 6}{6} = 7$$

$$\bar{X}_2 = \frac{6 + 4 + 6 + 4 + 8 + 2}{6} = 5$$

The mean ratings for drinks 1 and 2 are seven and five, respectively. These mean ratings are derived from the sample drawn. Again, we stress that these values are calculated as sample means and not population expected values which would require the collection of data on each population element. While it is possible that $\bar{X}$ might equal E(X), this does not necessarily have to be the case. Without explicit knowledge of the population expected value, however, we will use these values as *estimates* of the true population values.

2.6.2 The sample variance

Clearly, the observations for each soft drink shown in table 2.18 differ from the mean rating for each product (e.g. the first observation for soft drink 1 is 8 while the average for this soft drink is 7). Indeed, in both cases, not a single observation is the same as the sample means calculated. It is therefore worthwhile calculating a *measure of dispersion* around the sample mean to determine how spread the data are. As with the population variance statistic, the most common measure of spread at the sample level is also the variance, although the formula used in its calculation is not the same. The sample variance is given by (2.21):

$$s_x^2 = \frac{\sum_{i=1}^{n} (X_i - \bar{X})^2}{n - 1} \tag{2.21}$$

where all notation is as previously defined and $n - 1$ represents the *degrees of freedom* of the statistic.

For the above example, the sample variance is calculated as follows:

$$s_1^2 = \frac{(8-7)^2 + (10-7)^2 + (8-7)^2 + (4-7)^2 + (6-7)^2 + (6-7)^2}{6-1} = 4.4$$

$$s_2^2 = \frac{(6-5)^2 + (4-5)^2 + (6-5)^2 + (4-5)^2 + (8-5)^2 + (2-5)^2}{6-1} = 4.4$$

Another common statistic related to the sample variance is the *sample standard deviation*. As with the population standard deviation discussed previously, the sample standard deviation is calculated as the square root of the sample variance. In the above example, the sample standard deviation for both soft drinks is equal to $\sqrt{4.4}$ or 2.1.

2.6.3 The sample covariance

As with the variance, the population covariance also has a sample-level equivalent statistic. The sample covariance between X_1 and X_2 is calculated not as (2.14) but rather as (2.22):

$$\text{Sample cov}(X_1, X_2) = \frac{\sum (X_1 - \bar{X}_1)(X_2 - \bar{X}_2)}{n - 1} \tag{2.22}$$

with $n - 1$ degrees of freedom.

For our soft drink example, the numerator of the sample covariance between the ratings of soft drink one and soft drink two may be calculated as in table 2.19.

The numerator of (2.22) is equal to 2. The denominator, $n - 1$, is equal to 5 (i.e. $6 - 1$). Hence the sample covariance is:

$$\text{cov}(X_1, X_2) = \frac{2}{5} = 0.4$$

A covariance of 0.4 is positive, suggesting that respondents who gave a high rating for one soft drink were more likely to give a high rating on the other soft drink. To determine the

Table 2.19. *Calculating the sample covariance between the ratings of two soft drinks*

	Drink 1		Drink 2		
Respondent	X_1	$X_1 - \bar{X}_1$	X_2	$X_2 - \bar{X}_2$	$(X_1 - \bar{X}_1)(X_2 - \bar{X}_2)$
1	8	$8 - 7 = 1$	6	$6 - 5 = 1$	1
2	10	$10 - 7 = 3$	4	$4 - 5 = -1$	−3
3	8	$8 - 7 = 1$	6	$6 - 5 = 1$	1
4	4	$4 - 7 = -3$	4	$4 - 5 = -1$	3
5	6	$6 - 7 = -1$	8	$8 - 5 = 3$	−3
6	6	$6 - 7 = -1$	2	$2 - 5 = -3$	3
				Sum	2

strength of the relationship, however, it will be necesary to look at the sample correlation statistic.

2.6.4 The sample correlation coefficient

Equation (2.17) defined the population correlation coefficient. Analogous to this is the sample correlation coefficient, the formula for which we show as (2.23):

$$r = \frac{\text{cov}(X_1, X_2)}{S_{x1} S_{x2}} \tag{2.23}$$

where r is the sample correlation coefficient.

For the above example, the $\text{cov}(X_1, X_2) = 0.4$ and S_{x1} and S_{x2} both equalled 2.1. Hence the sample correlation coefficient is equal to:

$$r = \frac{0.4}{2.1 \times 2.1} = 0.09$$

where r defines the sample correlation coefficient.

A sample correlation coefficient of 0.09 is close to zero, suggesting that any relationship between the two ratings tasks is marginal.

2.7 Sampling error and sampling distributions

Assume that we sampled a number of individuals from some population and asked each individual their age. From our sample, it would be easy to calculate a number of statistics that describe the distribution of our sample – we described several such statistics in earlier sections of this chapter. Assume that we were interested only in the *mean age* of our sample. An interesting question arises as to how representative our mean age would be in terms of the true population mean value. Before we answer this question, however, let us ponder what would happen if we drew a different sample. Would the mean age be the same as that from the first sample drawn? What if we drew 100 samples? Would the mean ages of all 100 samples be the same? Of course, the means of the samples drawn would depend on the ages of the people in the samples which will, in all likelihood, differ from sample to sample.

The phenomenon that if we drew different samples we would likely observe different means (and variances, correlations and covariances as well) is known as *sampling variation*. The concept of sampling variation suggests that a sample statistic will likely deviate from the population statistic it is supposed to be measuring as a result of the particular observations that belong to the sample drawn. Thus, we may think of sampling variation in terms of *random variability* resulting from the particular sample that we draw, and not an error made by the analyst in terms of how the sample was drawn (though the analyst may also be in error here).

All of the above suggests that over repeated samples we would expect to observe a number of different values for whatever statistical measure we are using to describe the sample population from which the statistics are calculated. This leads us to the concept of *sampling distributions*. A sampling distribution is defined as the distribution of a sample statistic over repeated sampling from a fixed population. A sampling distribution may therefore be thought of as a measure of sample-to-sample variability.

Assuming the analyst were to take repeated samples, a profile of the sampling distribution could be built such that a determination of the sample distribution mean and standard deviation could be made. In such a case, the *sampling distribution mean* would represent the distribution of the means over repeated samples from the (fixed) population from which the samples were drawn. The standard deviation of the sample distribution of sample means, called the *standard error*, represents the standard deviation of the sampling distribution. For example, assume that an analyst drew 1000 samples from some fixed population ("fixed" suggests that the underlying population is unchanged for each draw). The distribution of the 1000 draws is shown in figure 2.5. For this example, the data for the 1000 sample draws was derived by randomly sampling 1000 observations from a normal distribution with a mean of 50 and a standard deviation of 16.6667. The sampling distribution from the 1000 random draws shows a sampling distribution mean of 49.5 and a standard error of the distribution of 16.29.

The sampling distribution shown in figure 2.5 suggests that a high number of sample draws generated had a sample mean between the values of 30 and 70. Were we to pick one of the sample draws at random, the distribution shown in figure 2.5 suggests that we would have a higher probability of selecting a sample with a sample mean between 30 and 70 than we would of selecting a sample with a mean lower than 30 or higher than 70: there are simply more of them to pick. That does not suggest that there is a zero probability of randomly selecting a sample with a mean that is not between 30 and 70, however. As we rarely draw more than one sample for a study, knowledge of sampling distributions becomes critically important.

Given that sample statistics are dependent on the sample drawn from a population, such statistics are known as estimates of the population parameters which they represent (e.g.

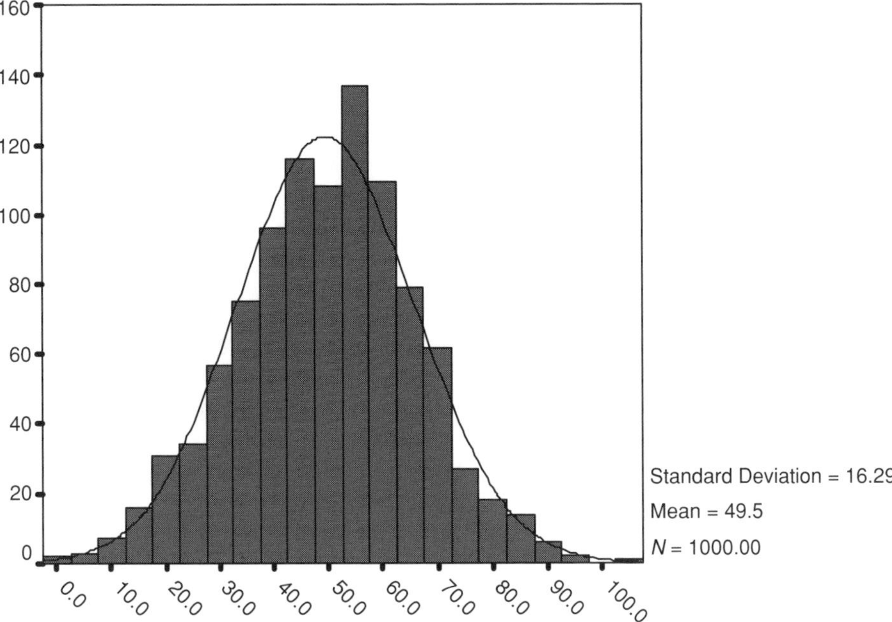

Figure 2.5 Sampling distribution for 1000 draws

the sample mean, $\bar{X}$, is an estimate of the population parameter E(X)). Once an estimate of a population parameter has been obtained, the question arises as to how good an estimate of that population parameter the estimate is. The method by which we answer this question is known as hypothesis testing.

2.8 Hypothesis testing

The process by which we determine how good an estimate of a population parameter a sample parameter is is known as *hypothesis testing*. Hypothesis testing is heavily reliant upon the assumptions analysts are willing to make with regard to the underlying distributional form of the random variables used in the test. Indeed, the majority of the statistical tests available to the analyst assume that the random variables used in the tests follow some (parametric) distributional form (e.g. a normal distribution). More often than not, it is only through the assumptions made about the distributional forms of the random variables that we are able to perform the statistical tests. For example, an analyst may wish to test whether that the population means underlying two samples drawn are equal. To test such an hypothesis, an assumption must first be made with regards to the *underlying distributional forms* of the populations from which the samples were drawn. For example, if the analyst is willing to assume that the two populations are distributed normally, then such a test can be performed using a simple t-test. If the assumption is not correct or the analyst is not willing to make the assumption in the first place, then the analyst will have to use one of a series of tests that do not assume anything about the distributions of the underlying data. Such distribution free tests are known as non-parametric tests (non-parametric tests are beyond the scope of this text; those interested in such tests are referred to Siegal and Castellan 1988).

Nevertheless, whether we are using parametric or non-parametric tests, the basic premise of most statistical tests is the testing of the pattern of the observed data against a hypothesized or assumed pattern of data. It is on this basis that *hypothesis testing* is designed. In the sections that follow, we outline the steps necessary to undertake hypothesis testing but note that hypothesis testing works by comparing the sample statistics obtained from one or more random samples and comparing these to the known properties of the assumed population distributions from which the random variables were drawn (i.e. such known properties are represented within the statistical tables at the back of most statistics texts and which may be calculated as shown in sub-section 2.8.3).

We begin our discussion on the steps usually undertaken in performing hypothesis testing by discussing the concepts of *null* and *alternative hypotheses*.

2.8.1 Defining the null and alternative hypotheses

In undertaking any hypothesis test, it is only ever possible to observe one of two outcomes. Either we will *reject* the hypothesis based on some evidence at hand or we will *not reject* the hypothesis based on that same evidence. Related to these two possible outcomes are the concepts of the null and alternative hypotheses. In statistical terms, the *null hypothesis* is often a statement that outlines the possible outcome of the hypothesis test that we do not want to observe (e.g. we may hypothesize the existence of a relationship between two random variables, the null hypothesis would therefore be that no such relationship exists between the two random variables). The *alternative hypothesis* would represent the outcome of the hypothesis test that we wish to find supporting evidence for.

In the preceding paragraph, we were extremely careful in our wording. In scientific terms, we can never *accept* a hypothesis. It is sufficient for us as scientists not to reject a hypothesis based on the sample data collected; however, at no stage would we claim that had a different sample been collected, we would have definitely rejected that same hypothesis. Thus, as scientists we are always searching for evidence to reject a hypothesis, not to accept one. A hypothesis is always assumed true until evidence is found to reject it. While this is but a subtle distinction, it is one that is often lost upon the student of statistics. It is for this reason that the null hypothesis is the dominant proposition in classical statistics. Nearly all of classical statistics is about trying to find evidence that disproves what we hope is true.

The null hypothesis (commonly denoted as H_0) also represents the starting point of hypothesis testing. To demonstrate, consider an example in which company *X* will introduce a new product to market if the individuals in the intended target population are likely to spend, on average, more than at least \$10 per week on the product. From the company's perspective, it would be hoped that those acting in the market will spend more than the \$10 per week necessary for product launch. As such, the null hypothesis representing the

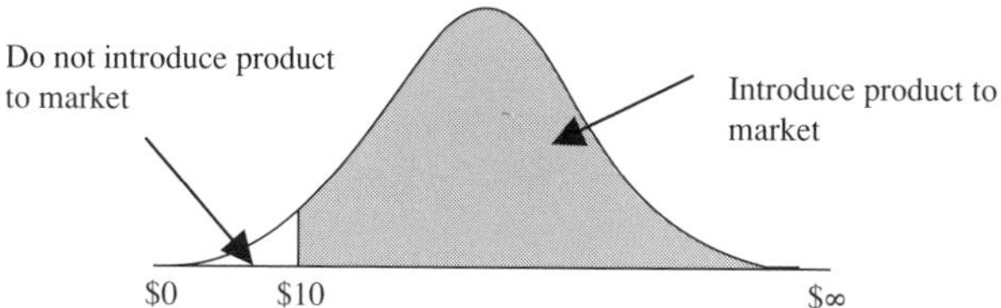

Figure 2.6 One-tailed test distribution

contrary position is that those in the market will not spend the necessary amount required for product launch to take place. Our discussion has not made reference yet to any sample. At present, we have confined ourselves to discussion of a population (a population mean, to be specific). In establishing the null hypothesis of a test, we discuss population parameters and not the sample parameters. For the above example, that means that the null (and alternative) hypothesis is framed in terms of the population mean, μ, not the sample mean, $\bar{X}$. In this instance, the null hypothesis may be framed as:

$$H_0: \mu \leq \$10$$

The alternative hypothesis is therefore given as:

$$H_1: \mu > \$10$$

In establishing our example, we have framed the problem in terms of what is known as a "one-tailed test." If we drew a single sample of respondents from the intended population target market and asked them how much they would be willing to spend on the product per week (provided it was introduced to market), a response on average less than \$10 would provide evidence supporting the null hypothesis. Any value less than \$10 will do. Alternatively, a response on average of greater than or equal to \$10 would provide evidence rejecting the null hypothesis, thus supporting the introduction to market of the new product. We show this in figure 2.6. Such tests are known as one-tailed tests because the range of values resulting in the support of the null hypothesis are confined to *one tail* of the population distribution from which the sample is drawn.

Hypothesis tests may also be created such that evidence supporting the null hypothesis may come from values observed in both tails of the distribution. The most common test in statistics is testing whether a parameter is statistically different from zero. Such a test is not direction specific. The parameter may deemed to be different from zero if the estimate of it is either less than or greater than zero (unlike the one-tailed test in which the direction of the test is predefined). Using the example of testing whether a parameter is statistically different to zero, the null and alternative hypothesis would be:

$$H_0: \mu = 0$$
$$H_1: \mu \neq 0$$

We show such a test graphically in figure 2.7.

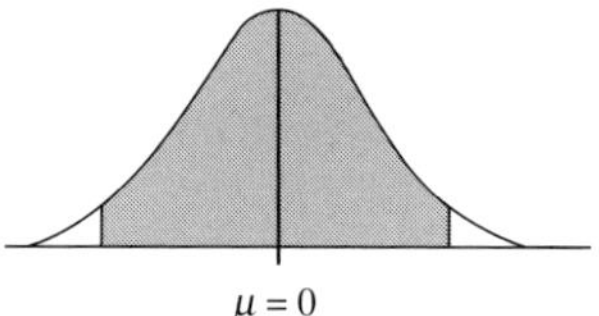

Figure 2.7 Two-tailed test distribution

Figure 2.7 suggests that if we observe a sample mean value that is very different from zero, then we will reject the null hypothesis that the population mean is equal to zero. How much different the sample statistic has to be from zero before we reject the null hypothesis is determined by hypothesis testing.

2.8.2 Selecting the test-statistic

Once the null and alternative hypotheses have been decided, the next stage in hypothesis testing is to determine the appropriate test-statistic to use. Previously, we defined the concepts of population and sample statistics. These, respectively, define some aspect of the population and sample distributions. A *test-statistic* is defined as the results of a statistical test that relates some sample statistic to that of a population statistic. Once calculated, the test-statistic acts as a basis of comparison between what we observe in the sample data and what we would expect to observe in the population given certain properties of the assumed population distribution. Hypothesis testing, as we have discussed, is about testing the probability of whether a sample observation is likely to have come from (or represent) the true population level statistic. Unless we know the true population level statistic, we will never know, with mathematical certainty, whether the sample statistic really is equal to exactly, close to but not exactly equal to, or not even close to the true population statistic. There is therefore some level of probability that any statistical test we perform will provide an erroneous result. One benefit of classical statistics is that while the analyst will never know for certain whether the hypothesis test conducted has given the wrong result or not, the probability that an erroneous result will occur can be calculated. The test-statistic allows us to test relationships within the sample, and infer, up to a probability, that any relationship that is found (or not found) to exist within the population. The specific statistical test assumed is dependent upon the underlying distribution assumed for the population. For the present, we will assume that the underlying distribution for a population random variable is normal.

Two statistical tests are commonly associated with hypothesis tests involving normally distributed random variables. These are the *Z*- and *t*-tests. The *Z*-test relates the population statistic to the sample statistic through the following equation. Under the hypothesis

$$H_0\colon \mu = \mu_x$$
$$H_1\colon \mu \neq \mu_x$$

where μ_x is the assumed population mean, the Z-test-statistic is:

$$Z = \frac{(\bar{X} - \mu_x)}{\sigma/\sqrt{n}} \sim N(0, 1) \tag{2.24}$$

where Z is the test-statistic, $\bar{X}$ is the sample mean, μ_x is the population mean defined in the hypothesis, σ is the population standard deviation, n is the sample size drawn for the test, $\sim$ (read "tilde") means "is distributed as," and $N(0,1)$ is normally distributed with a mean of zero and a standard deviation of one.

The Z-test-statistic assumes knowledge of the population standard deviation, σ, which means that unless this value is known, the test cannot be performed. It is therefore more common to use the t-test which makes no such presumption of knowledge. The t-test test-statistic is given as:

$$t = \frac{(\bar{X} - \mu_x)}{S/\sqrt{n}} \tag{2.25}$$

where t is the test-statistic, $\bar{X}$, μ_x and n are as previously defined and S is the sample standard deviation calculated as (2.26). Note that this is the same as (2.21):

$$S\sqrt{\frac{(X_i - \bar{X})^2}{n - 1}} \tag{2.26}$$

The t-statistic requires no prior knowledge of the population standard deviation as the test uses the sample standard deviation as an estimate of the population statistic instead. This is because the population standard deviation is unlikely to be known in advance. Thus, the analyst is required to use the sample standard deviation as a proxy.

Other test statistics are available depending upon the underlying population distribution assumed by the analyst. Two common distributions assumed are the Chi-square distribution (χ^2) and the F-distribution.

The Z- and t-tests (associated with the normal distribution) relate the mean of the sample statistic to the mean of the population statistic while the Chi-square- and F-tests relate the sample standard deviation of the sample to the standard deviation of the population in the case of the Chi-square and the sample standard deviation of one random variable to that of another in the case of the F-test. As such, the choice of test-statistic is reliant not only on the belief of the underlying population distribution but also on the purpose of the test.

2.8.3 Significance of the test and alpha

The *statistical significance* of a test is an estimated measure of the degree to which the test result obtained from the sample reflects the truth as to what is occurring within the population (i.e. how reliable the conclusion drawn from the sample is in inferring what is occurring within the population). Given that we can never be certain as to how representative a conclusion obtained from a sample is of the population (unless we take a census), statistical significance is represented in the form of a probability known as a p-value. The higher the p-value obtained for a test, the less able the analyst is to conclude that the finding obtained from the sample may be inferred to the population. Specifically, the p-value for a test represents the probability of an erroneous finding in terms of accepting the conclusion drawn from a test conducted on a sample as being valid, or representative of the population. In interpreting a p-value, the p-value represents the probability that the conclusion drawn from a statistical test conducted on a sample is erroneous simply due to bad luck. For example, a p-value of 0.2 indicates that there is a 20 percent probability that we would find a relationship within the sample that does not exist within the population – or, alternatively, find no relationship within the sample when one does exist within the population.

The upper level of acceptable error, called alpha (represented as α), must be determined by the analyst. In most research, a p-value of 0.05 is generally accepted as the upper level of acceptable error, although other values are equally valid. The α level of the test is critical as it is this value which we use to determine what is known as the *critical value* of the test. Over time, we have come to understand quite well the properties of various population distributions. The accumulated knowledge of this understanding is often reflected in the statistical tables provided at the back of most statistical texts (rather than reproduce such tables, we prefer to calculate the values using Excel, we show how to do this on p. 50). For given numbers of degrees of freedom (d.f.), statisticians have established for different distributions, the critical values at which we may reject or not reject null hypotheses. These critical values depend both on the degrees of freedom and on α.

Hypothesis testing works by comparing the critical value of the test as determined by the value of α selected by the analyst (and the number of observations over the sample) to that of the test-statistic calculated for the test conducted on the sample. Needless to say, the lower the significance level selected by the analyst, the more stringent the test. That is, the smaller we define α, the lower the probability of rejecting the hypothesis when it is true.

To understand this concept, it is necessary first to define *Type I* and *Type II errors*. Let us begin by offering a formal definition of these errors and then explain why they are important to us as researchers. We define a *Type I error* as occurring when we reject the null hypothesis when it is true. A *Type II error* is said to occur when we fail to reject the null hypothesis when it is false. Thus, when we talk about Type I and Type II errors, we are talking about making a mistake in terms of the inferences drawn from our statistical tests. With Type I and Type II errors formally defined we may now formally define the level of significance, alpha (α). We formally define α as the probability of making a Type I error. We define beta (β) as the probability of making a Type II error. One minus β is known as the *power of the test*.

In establishing the level of significance for the test, α, the analyst effectively determines some critical value for the hypothesis test which is compared to the test-statistic. That is, you the analyst are setting the probability that you may make an erroneous conclusion. As stated previously, usually we set α to equal 5 percent and in doing so, we are resigning ourselves to the fact that there is a 5 percent chance that we will draw the wrong conclusion from the test as a result of bad luck. The temptation is therefore to use ever-smaller values of α so as to ensure that we will not make a Type I error. While it is typical in academic

Table 2.20. *The relationships between H_0, H_1, Type I errors, and Type II errors*

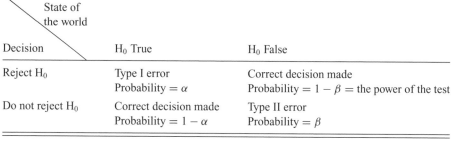

Decision \ State of the world	H_0 True	H_0 False
Reject H_0	Type I error Probability $= \alpha$	Correct decision made Probability $= 1 - \beta =$ the power of the test
Do not reject H_0	Correct decision made Probability $= 1 - \alpha$	Type II error Probability $= \beta$

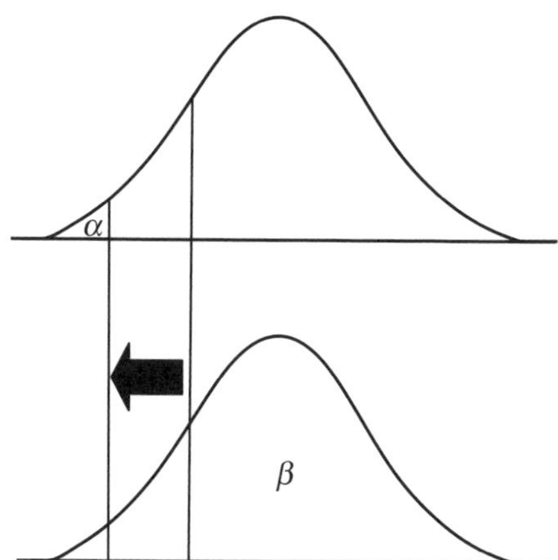

Figure 2.8 The relationship between α and β

settings to set α to equal 0.05 (i.e. a 5 percent level of confidence), why not use $\alpha = 0.01$ instead and therefore have a 1 percent chance of making such a Type I error rather than a 5 percent chance? Or why not set α to 0.001 for an even more stringent test? While this is a perfectly legitimate response, we need to realize that if we do this we increase the probability of making a Type II error. That is, the more stringent the criteria you set to reduce the possibility of making a Type I error, the more likely we will make a Type II error. This is shown in figure 2.8.

Figure 2.8 shows that as we decrease the level of α, β increases. Given that the probability of an outcome is given as the area under the curve, decreasing the probability of a Type I error occurring must, for any specific alternative hypothesis, necessarily increase the probability of a Type II error. Table 2.20 shows the relationships between the null and alternative hypotheses and α and β.

As an aside, the concept of Type I and Type II errors suggest that from a statistical standpoint, we are better off performing as few tests as possible. This is called parsimony. Let us consider the possibility where we can use two relatively simple tests or one relatively difficult test to test some hypothesis. Assuming a significance level of $\alpha = 0.05$, the probability of making a Type I error using the single test is 5 percent. The probability of making a Type I error using the two tests is 9.75 percent. We will demonstrate how we got this figure below, but you can see clearly that we are better performing one test instead of two. And the more tests you perform the higher the probability of making a Type I error.

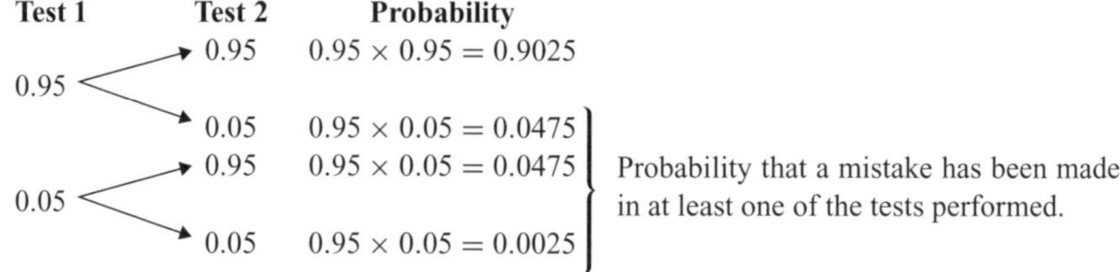

We can see that for the first test there is a 95 percent chance of not making a Type I error and a 5 percent chance of making a Type I error. Assuming that the tests are independent of one another, there is also a 95 percent chance of not making a Type I error and a 5 percent chance that we will make a Type I error when performing the second test. As the tests are assumed to be independent of each other, we can multiply the probabilities together to arrive at the probability of the two events occurring together. Thus there is a 0.95×0.95 or 90.25 percent probability of no Type I error occurring during either test. However as each test has a probability of a Type I error being made (and remember we will not know if it has been made), we can also multiply the probabilities together where we (suspect that we) have made a mistake during at least one of the tests. There are three branches in the tree diagram above where we have made a Type I error during at least one test. The sum of the probabilities associated with these outcomes provides us with the probability that a Type I error was made during at least one test. Thus, from the example, there is a $0.0475 + 0.0475 + 0.0025$ or 0.0975 probability of a Type I error occurring during the performance of our two tests.

Once the significance level has been determined by the analyst, the *critical value* for the test may be determined using Microsoft Excel. We now show the Excel formulas to calculate the critical values for normal, student *t*-, Chi-square- and *F*-distributions:

=NORMINV(<probability>, <mean>, <standard deviation>)
=TINV(<probability>, <degrees of freedom>)
=CHIINV(<probability>, <degrees of freedom>)
=FINV(<probability>, <degrees of freedom numerator>, <degrees of freedom denominator>)

For example:

=NORMINV(0.975,0,1) = 1.96
=TINV(0.05,1) = 12.706
=CHIINV(0.95,1) = 3.84
=FINV(0.05,2,3) = 9.55

The critical value of the test thus obtained is then used to create what is known as the *rejection region(s)* for the test. Two-tailed tests will have two rejection regions, one in

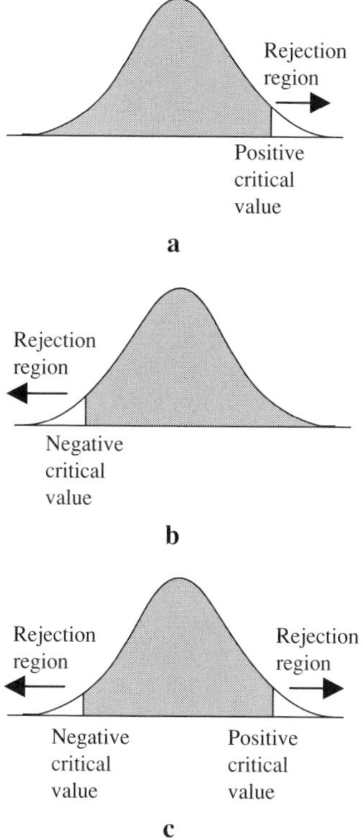

Figure 2.9 The rejection region for one- or two-tailed tests

each tail; one-tailed tests will have a single rejection region located in only one tail of the distribution. Test statistics that fall into the rejection, or critical region(s) of the test support the rejection of the null hypothesis. Figure 2.9a–c shows the rejection regions relative to the critical values for a normal distribution. For one-tailed tests, the rejection region of the test is dependent upon the sign of the test-statistic and the null hypothesis stated. Generally, the rejection regions for positive critical values encompass values greater than the critical value (see figure 2.9a). Negative critical values generally are associated with rejection regions less than the critical value (i.e. more negative in value; see figure 2.9b). Two-tailed tests relate to both tails of the distribution, hence values in the rejection region encompass the area of the distribution greater than the critical value and less than the negative of the critical value; this is shown in figure 2.9c.

The statistical hypothesis-testing method outlined in the previous example requires that the analyst choose the significance level, α, independent of the collection of any data and the computing of the test-statistic. The selection of α, in effect, fixes the rejection region of the test. As such, no matter how large or small the value of the test-statistic, the decision rule is fixed: reject the null hypothesis if the test-statistic falls into the region of the distribution known as the rejection region, as dictated by the critical value for the test.

Table 2.21. *Comparing alpha to the probability value*

Test	Action taken by analyst
Alpha greater than the p-value	*Reject* the null hypothesis of the test
Alpha less than the p-value	*Do not reject* the null hypothesis of the test

The fixed nature of the rejection region means that a hypothesis is rejected if the value of the test-statistic relative to that of the critical value places the test-statistic in the rejection region of the distribution for the test. Such decision rules allow for no margin for interpretation as to how significant a test-statistic is. For example, assume that for a particular test, an analyst observes a critical value of 2.262. The null hypothesis for the test would be rejected if the test-statistic was observed to be 2.263, just the same as if the test-statistic was observed to be 100. Given the proximity of a test-statistic of 2.263 to the cut-off point dictated by the critical value of the test, the analyst would be more certain that the null hypothesis should be rejected should a test-statistic of 100 be observed than a test-statistic of 2.263. The use of critical values to determine statistical significance does not therefore reflect the degree of certainty in the mind of the analyst as to reliability of the inference being made from the test.

For this reason, a growing number of researchers prefer to examine the probabilities (i.e. the p-values) of the outcome of tests rather than use the cut-and-dried results dictated by the use of critical values (nevertheless, as the analyst arbitrarily selects the level of α which in part determines the critical value, the use of critical values is not as cut and dried as some would have you think). The use of p-values allows the analyst to determine the relative significance of the test. If the p-value is less than the level of α, then the analyst rejects the null hypothesis of the test. If on the other hand the p-value exceeds the level of alpha, then the analyst cannot reject the null hypothesis. To clarify the action taken, given the relative magnitude of α to the p-value shown in the output, look at table 2.21.

For example, a p-value of 0.01 is said to be more significant than a p-value of 0.1. As with critical values, however, an arbitrary decision is required concerning at what p-value the test-statistic is deemed to be statistically insignificant. Is the test statistically significant if the p-value is less than 0.1 or 0.05?

p-values for the more common distributions may be calculated in Microsoft Excel. We now show the Microsoft Excel formulas to calculate the p-values for the normal, t-, Chi-square- and F-distributions:

=NORMDIST(<test-statistic>, <mean>, <standard deviation>, 1)
=TDIST(<test-statistic>, <degrees of freedom>, <number of tails in the test>)
=CHIDIST(<test-statistic>, <degrees of freedom>)
=FDIST(<test-statistic>, <degrees of freedom numerator>, <degrees of freedom denominator>)

For example:

=NORMDIST(-1.64,0,1,1) = 0.050503
=TDIST(1.99,265,2) = 0.047618
=CHIDIST(3.98,1) = 0.046044
=FDIST(9.91,9,9) = 0.001078

In explaining the above examples, we will use a value of α equal to 0.05. The first example shows the p-value from a normal distribution test (Z-test) in which the test-statistic is -1.64. The test is calculated for a standard normal (mean $= 0$, standard deviation $= 1$). The p-value calculated is 0.050503, which strictly speaking would not result in the rejection of the null hypothesis if the level of α was 0.05. The next example shows a two-tailed student-t-distribution test with a test-statistic of 1.99 and 265 degrees of freedom. The p-value of 0.047618 is less than an α of 0.05 (we do not need to divide α by two; Excel automatically adjusts the p-value for this) suggesting that the test-statistic is statistically significant. The third example is that of a Chi-square-test with a test-statistic of 3.98 and one degree of freedom. The resulting p-value for the test is 0.046044, less than α of 0.05. At α equal to 0.05, we would reject the null hypothesis of the test. The last example shown above is that of an F-test in which the test-statistic is 9.91 and the degrees of freedom for the numerator and denominator are both equal to 9. The resulting p-value is equal to 0.001078, much less than α equal to 0.05. Once more, we would reject the null hypothesis of the test. The above shows the arbitrary nature in selecting a value for α. At α equal to 0.05, all but the first example would result in the rejection of the null hypothesis; however, had we selected α equal to 0.06, all of the above examples would result in the rejection of the null hypothesis.

Once the significance level has been determined by the analyst, the critical value for the test may be determined using Microsoft Excel. In the next section, we show an example of hypothesis testing.

2.8.4 Performing the test

Now that the stages of hypothesis testing have been outlined, all that remains is to perform the test and draw the appropriate conclusions. To demonstrate our discussion of hypothesis testing, we now provide a detailed example. We do so in the context of a statistical test known as the once sample t-test.

2.8.5 Example hypothesis test: the one sample t-test

The one sample t-test is calculated using equations (2.25) and (2.26), reproduced below.

$$t = \frac{(\bar{X} - \mu_x)}{S/\sqrt{n}}$$

where S is

$$S = \sqrt{\frac{\sum (X_i - \bar{X})^2}{n - 1}}.$$

Consider an example, in which a new product will be introduced to the market if it receives a mean of at least six on a ten-point scale. A sample of 40 respondents was asked to rate a prototype of the product. The results indicated a mean rating of 6.9 with a standard deviation of 1.4. The researcher chose an alpha level of 0.05. Should the new product be introduced? The analysis would proceed thus:

$$H_0 : \mu \leq 6$$
$$H_1 : \mu > 6$$

$$t = \frac{\bar{x} - \mu}{s_{\bar{x}}} = t = \frac{6.9 - 6}{\frac{1.4}{\sqrt{40}}} = 4.065786$$

The critical value at which we reject the null hypothesis is calculated using Excel as shown below. Note that we use an α value of 0.05 and 39 d.f. (why?).

= tinv(0.1,39)

We use 0.1 instead of 0.05 as Excel calculates the test as a two-tailed test. As this is a one-tailed test, using 0.1 instead of 0.05 forces Excel to calculate the critical value at the correct probability for the one-tailed test.

The critical value for this test is 1.6848, and hence t observed is greater than t critical, suggesting that the null hypothesis should be rejected and that the new product should be introduced to the market. To confirm this finding, we can also calculate the p-value for the test using Excel. We show this below.

=tdist(4.065786,39,1)

Excel calculates the p-value for the test as 0.00011242. This is much smaller than our α value of 0.05, and hence, using the p-value for the test, we also would reject the null hypothesis for the test.

2.9 Matrix algebra

In this section, we discuss the concept of matrix algebra and relate some of the mathematical operations associated with matrices. Our discussion is limited, in that we do not give full coverage to the mathematical operations of matrices. That is, we relate only those operations which have importance to the estimation of models of discrete choice. A wider coverage of matrix algebra is given in Greene (2003).

A *matrix* is a rectangular array of numeric or algebraic quantities, the elements of which are arranged into columns or rows. For example, consider the following matrix denoted A:

$$A = \begin{bmatrix} 2 & 1 & 3 & 4 \\ 4 & 2 & 3 & 7 \end{bmatrix}$$

A is said to be of the order 2×4 matrix where the first number is the number of rows of the matrix and the second number the number of columns. Matrices with only one row (i.e. $1 \times n$) are termed *row vectors* while matrices with only one column (i.e. $m \times 1$) are termed *column vectors*. For example:

$$a = \begin{bmatrix} 2 & 1 & 3 & 4 \end{bmatrix}$$

$$b = \begin{bmatrix} 2 \\ 4 \end{bmatrix}$$

a is a 1×4 row vector and b a 2×1 column vector. Note that vectors are represented by lower case letters (e.g. a) while matrices are represented by capital letters (e.g. A).

A *scalar* is defined as a single constant. For example, a scalar might be equal to 2. Note that a scalar is a 1×1 matrix.

There are a number of important properties and operations that are associated with matrices. We detail the more important of these now.

2.9.1 Transposition

The transpose of a matrix involves the interchanging of the columns of the matrix with the rows. Mathematically we write the transpose of matrix A as A′ (read "A transpose"). We show this for matrix A given above. Note that A′ is now a 4×2 matrix:

$$A = \begin{bmatrix} 2 & 4 \\ 1 & 2 \\ 3 & 3 \\ 4 & 7 \end{bmatrix}$$

2.9.2 Matrix addition and subtraction

It is possible to add or subtract two matrices if they are of the same order (i.e. have the same number of rows and columns). The addition or subtraction of two matrices requires the addition or subtraction of the corresponding elements of the two matrices. Consider the two matrices, B and C:

$$B = \begin{bmatrix} 2 & 1 & 3 \\ 4 & 2 & 3 \end{bmatrix} \text{ and } C = \begin{bmatrix} 4 & 7 & 8 \\ 2 & 3 & 1 \end{bmatrix}$$

$$B + C = \begin{bmatrix} 6 & 8 & 11 \\ 6 & 5 & 4 \end{bmatrix} \text{ and } B - C = \begin{bmatrix} -2 & -6 & -5 \\ 2 & -1 & 2 \end{bmatrix}$$

The resulting matrices will be of the same order as the original two matrices. B − C won't equal C − B unless B = C:

$$\mathrm{C}+\mathrm{B}=\begin{bmatrix} 6 & 8 & 11 \\ 6 & 5 & 4 \end{bmatrix} \text{ and } \mathrm{C}-\mathrm{B}=\begin{bmatrix} 2 & 6 & 5 \\ -2 & 1 & -2 \end{bmatrix}$$

2.9.3 Matrix multiplication by a scalar

As with addition and subtraction, matrix multiplication of a scalar involves each element of the matrix being multiplied by the scalar. For example:

$$2 \times \mathrm{B}=\begin{bmatrix} 4 & 2 & 6 \\ 8 & 4 & 6 \end{bmatrix}$$

2.9.4 Matrix multiplication

Two matrices may be multiplied if the number of columns of the first matrix is equal to the number of rows of the second matrix. Thus if A is of the order 4 × 2 and B of the order 2 × 4, then the two matrices may be multiplied together. If, on the other hand, A is of the order 4 × 2 and B is of the order 4 × 2, the matrices may not be multiplied together. Assuming that two matrices may be multiplied together, the order of the resulting matrix is given as the number of rows of the first matrix and the number of columns of the second matrix. For example, if A is of the order 4 × 3 and B is of the order 3 × 5, the resulting matrix is of the order 4 × 5.

The multiplication process of two matrices is that the rows of the first matrix be treated as a series of row vectors and the second matrix be treated as a series of column vectors.

Assuming that D is a $n \times k$ matrix and E a $k \times m$ matrix, we may write out D as a set of n row vectors and E as m column vectors:

$$\mathrm{D}=[\mathrm{d}_1\ \mathrm{d}_2 \ldots \mathrm{d}_n] \text{ and } \mathrm{E}=\begin{bmatrix} \mathrm{e}_1 \\ \mathrm{e}_2 \\ \cdot \\ \cdot \\ \cdot \\ \mathrm{e}_m \end{bmatrix}$$

DE is then defined as:

$$\mathrm{DE}=\begin{bmatrix} \mathrm{d}_1\mathrm{e}_1 & \mathrm{d}_1\mathrm{e}_2 & \ldots & \mathrm{d}_1\mathrm{e}_m \\ \mathrm{d}_2\mathrm{e}_1 & \mathrm{d}_2\mathrm{e}_2 & \ldots & \mathrm{d}_2\mathrm{e}_m \\ \cdot & \cdot & & \cdot \\ \cdot & \cdot & & \cdot \\ \cdot & \cdot & & \cdot \\ \mathrm{d}_n\mathrm{e}_1 & \mathrm{d}_n\mathrm{e}_2 & \ldots & \mathrm{d}_n\mathrm{e}_m \end{bmatrix}$$

which is of the order $n \times m$.

Assuming that B and C are as described previously, B × C is not defined; however B × C′ is:

$$B \times C' = \begin{bmatrix} 2 & 1 & 3 \\ 4 & 2 & 3 \end{bmatrix} \begin{bmatrix} 4 & 2 \\ 7 & 3 \\ 8 & 1 \end{bmatrix}$$

$$= \begin{bmatrix} (2 \times 4) + (1 \times 7) + (3 \times 8) & (2 \times 2) + (1 \times 3) + (3 \times 1) \\ (4 \times 4) + (2 \times 7) + (3 \times 8) & (4 \times 2) + (2 \times 3) + (3 \times 1) \end{bmatrix} = \begin{bmatrix} 39 & 10 \\ 54 & 17 \end{bmatrix}$$

C × B is not defined; however C′ × B is:

$$C' \times B = \begin{bmatrix} 4 & 2 \\ 7 & 3 \\ 8 & 1 \end{bmatrix} \begin{bmatrix} 2 & 1 & 3 \\ 4 & 2 & 3 \end{bmatrix}$$

$$= \begin{bmatrix} (4 \times 2) + (2 \times 4) & (4 \times 1) + (2 \times 2) & (4 \times 3) + (2 \times 3) \\ (7 \times 2) + (3 \times 4) & (7 \times 1) + (3 \times 2) & (7 \times 3) + (3 \times 3) \\ (8 \times 2) + (1 \times 4) & (8 \times 1) + (1 \times 2) & (8 \times 3) + (1 \times 3) \end{bmatrix} = \begin{bmatrix} 16 & 8 & 18 \\ 26 & 13 & 30 \\ 12 & 10 & 27 \end{bmatrix}$$

Clearly, B × C′ does not give the same result as C′ × B. Assuming two matrices, A and B may be multiplied, A × B does not necessarily have to have the same order as B × A, nor should the resulting matrices be equal.

2.9.5 Determinants of matrices

For each square matrix (i.e. a matrix where the number of rows equals the number of columns), there exists a scalar value known as the *determinant*. In matrix algebra, determinants are useful in the analysis and solution of systems of linear equations. Many texts such as Greene (2003) and Maddala (1992) show how to calculate the determinant of a square matrix. As it is highly unlikely, however, that one will ever have to calculate the determinant of a matrix of order greater than 3 × 3 by hand, we refer the reader to these texts for further details. In general, the determinant of a 2 × 2 matrix is given as:

$$\begin{vmatrix} a_{11} & a_{12} \\ a_{21} & a_{22} \end{vmatrix} a_{11} \times a_{22} - a_{12} \times a_{21}$$

The determinant of a 3 × 3 matrix is given as

$$\begin{vmatrix} a_{11} & a_{12} & a_{13} \\ a_{21} & a_{22} & a_{23} \\ a_{31} & a_{32} & a_{33} \end{vmatrix} = a_{11}a_{22}a_{33} + a_{12}a_{23}a_{31} + a_{13}a_{32}a_{21} - a_{31}a_{22}a_{13} + a_{21}a_{22}a_{13} + a_{11}a_{23}a_{32}$$

For matrices greater than 3 × 3, it is far simpler to calculate the determinant using a fx =MDETERM(C1:F4)

C	D	E	F
4	2	0	0
0	1	0	2
1	3	1	1
2	3	5	0
64			

Figure 2.10 Calculating the determinant of a matrix in Excel

fx =MDETERM(C1:F4)

C	D	E	F
1	1	0	0
1	1	0	0
1	1	2	0
1	0	0	1
0			

Figure 2.11 A singular matrix

computer. Microsoft Excel allows the calculation of the determinant using the formula:

=mdeterm(<cells of matrix>)

$$\text{Let A} = \begin{bmatrix} 4 & 2 & 0 & 0 \\ 0 & 1 & 0 & 2 \\ 1 & 3 & 1 & 1 \\ 2 & 3 & 5 & 0 \end{bmatrix}$$

The determinant of A, $|A|$, is calculated in Excel as shown in figure 2.10.

If the determinant of a matrix is zero, the matrix is said to be singular. An example of a singular matrix is given in figure 2.11.

Note that for the matrix shown in figure 2.11, column C equals column D plus column F. That is, the columns in the matrix are not independent. We will discuss the concept of singularities further when we discuss matrix inversion.

2.9.6 The identity matrix

A square matrix (i.e. an $n \times n$ matrix) in which the diagonal elements are all equal to one and the off-diagonal elements are all equal to zero is called an *identity matrix*, denoted I_n.

For example:

$$I_4 = \begin{bmatrix} 1 & 0 & 0 & 0 \\ 0 & 1 & 0 & 0 \\ 0 & 0 & 1 & 0 \\ 0 & 0 & 0 & 1 \end{bmatrix}$$

2.9.7 The inverse of a matrix

The inverse of a square matrix, A, denoted A^{-1} is a matrix such that the multiplication of A by its inverse equals an identity matrix (i.e. $AA^{-1} = I$):

$$\text{Let } A = \begin{vmatrix} a_{11} & a_{12} & a_{13} \\ a_{21} & a_{22} & a_{23} \\ a_{31} & a_{32} & a_{33} \end{vmatrix}$$

The inverse of A is given as

$$A^{-1} = \frac{1}{|A|} \begin{vmatrix} a_{11} & a_{12} & a_{13} \\ a_{21} & a_{22} & a_{23} \\ a_{31} & a_{32} & a_{33} \end{vmatrix}'$$

where A^{-1} will be of the same order as A (i.e. a 3×3 matrix).

Again, texts such as Greene (2003) explain in great detail the complexities of calculating the inverse of matrices such as A without the aid of a computer. Given the prevalence of computers in society today, however, rarely, if ever, will one have to calculate the inverse of a matrix by hand (the reader interested in doing so is referred to Greene 2003). Microsoft Excel will calculate the inverse of a matrix using the following formula:

=minverse(<cells of the matrix>)

Figure 2.12 shows the use of this formula for the matrix shown in figure 2.10.

As an aside, in order for Excel to calculate the inverse of a matrix, the analyst must first select the correct number of destination cells (i.e. the cells where the inverse of the matrix will be displayed) and type the formula into the first cell of the selected cells only (see figure 2.13). After the formula has been entered into the first cell, Excel will calculate the elements of the inverse of the selected matrix in the destination cells after the **Ctrl + Alt + Enter** keys are pressed simultaneously.

If the determinant of a matrix, A, is equal to zero then a square matrix is said to be singular and non-invertible, i.e. A^{-1} is not defined (i.e. A^{-1} does not exist). If $|A|$ is not equal to zero then a square matrix is said to be non-singular and invertible (i.e. $|A|^{-1}$ is defined). Thus the matrix shown in figure 2.13 is non-invertible.

As an aside, a not uncommon error reported in the estimation of choice models is that the variance–covariance (VC) matrix is singular (e.g. see Appendix 7A, error 1026, p. 211). This is usually due to the fact that the elements in at least one column of the VC matrix are

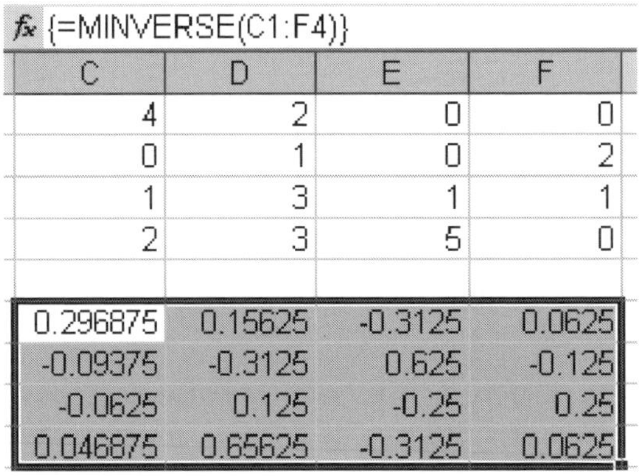

{=MINVERSE(C1:F4)}

C	D	E	F
4	2	0	0
0	1	0	2
1	3	1	1
2	3	5	0
0.296875	0.15625	-0.3125	0.0625
-0.09375	-0.3125	0.625	-0.125
-0.0625	0.125	-0.25	0.25
0.046875	0.65625	-0.3125	0.0625

Figure 2.12 The inverse of a matrix in Microsoft Excel

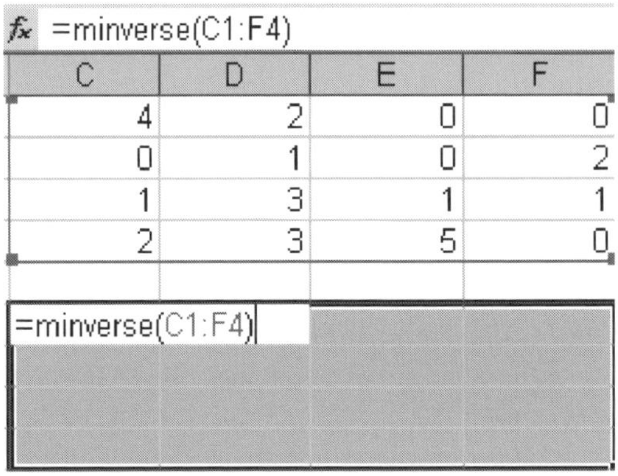

=minverse(C1:F4)

C	D	E	F
4	2	0	0
0	1	0	2
1	3	1	1
2	3	5	0
=minverse(C1:F4)			

Figure 2.13 Calculating the inverse of a matrix in Microsoft Excel

made up entirely of zeros which will automatically result in a singular or non-invertible matrix. As such, when NLOGIT attempts to invert the matrix as part of the estimation process, it is unable to do so and an error is reported.

2.9.8 Linear and quadratic forms

Let a and x be two column vectors and A a matrix of dimensions $k \times k$:

$$\mathrm{a} = \begin{bmatrix} a_1 \\ a_2 \\ a_3 \end{bmatrix} \qquad \mathrm{x} = \begin{bmatrix} x_1 \\ x_2 \\ x_3 \end{bmatrix} \qquad \mathrm{A} = \begin{bmatrix} \mathrm{a}_{11} & \mathrm{a}_{12} & \mathrm{a}_{13} \\ \mathrm{a}_{21} & \mathrm{a}_{22} & \mathrm{a}_{23} \\ \mathrm{a}_{31} & \mathrm{a}_{32} & \mathrm{a}_{33} \end{bmatrix}$$

$\mathrm{B} = \mathrm{a}'\mathrm{x} = \mathrm{a}_1\mathrm{x}_1 + \mathrm{a}_2\mathrm{x}_2 + \mathrm{a}_3\mathrm{x}_3$ is said to be a *linear form of xs* and $\mathrm{C} = \mathrm{x}'\mathrm{A}\mathrm{x} = a_{11}x_1^2 + a_{12}x_1x_2 + a_{13}x_1x_3 + a_{22}x_2^2 + a_{23}x_2x_3 + a_{31}x_1x_3 + a_{32}x_2x_3 + a_{33}x_3^2$ is a *quadratic form in the xs*.

2.9.9 Positive definite and negative definite matrices

A positive definite matrix is a symmetric matrix, A, for which the quadratic form x Ax is positive for all non-zero vectors of x (i.e. x Ax > 0). Positive definite matrices are of both theoretical and computational importance given that they are often used in the optimization algorithms used to estimate various regression-based models. Occasionally, the analyst will note an error reported in NLOGIT such as:

```
Hessian is not positive definite at start values.
  Error   803: Hessian is not positive definite at start
values.
B0 is too far from solution for Newton method.
Switching to BFGS as a better solution method.
Line search does not improve fn. Exit iterations. Status=3
  Error   806: Line search does not improve fn. Exit
iterations. Status=3
Function=  .34146087789D+04, at entry,  .32150403881D+04 at
exit
```

This error suggests that the Hessian matrix (the second-order partial derivatives used in optimizing the search over the log likelihood function; see chapter 10) is not positive definite. Such errors are usually associated with problems within the data set, usually but not always associated with the attempt to estimate a parameter for which the data are invariant within the data set (e.g. the variable always takes the value zero).

2.10 Conclusion

This chapter has introduced the most basic statistical concepts that a choice modeler should be aware of to be able to make sensible interpretations of their data and their model outputs. In doing so, we left our discussion fairly broad. Further details can be sourced from the many statistical and econometric books (particularly, Gujarati 1999; Greene 2003).

In chapter 3 we establish the theory of demand and outline the basis of the most basic model we use to model choice: the multinomial logit model (MNL).

Appendix 2A Measures of correlation or similarity

The most commonly used measure of correlation is the Pearson product moment (PPM) correlation coefficient, ρ. While popular, the PPM correlation coefficient is strictly valid only when the two random variables for which correlation is being measured are ratio scaled. When one or the both random variables are not ratio scaled, other correlation measures are appropriate and PPM is at best an aproximation. Table 2A.1, adapted from Hensher and Smith (1984), shows the appropriate formulae to use for different scaled data. We refer you to this article for a more in-depth discussion on these measures.

Table 2A.1. *Appropriate correlation formula*

Random variable scale definitions: R: ratio; I: interval, O: Ordinal; D: dichotomous; N: nominal

Scale pair (X_1, X_2)	Formula 1, 2, ..., N observations 1, 2, ..., m levels X_1, X_2 = random variables	Test name
R, R or R, I	$r\rho(X_1, X_2) = \dfrac{\sum_{i=1}^{N}(X_{1i} - \bar{X}_1)(X_{2i} - \bar{X}_2)}{\sqrt{\sum_{i=1}^{N}(X_{1i} - \bar{X}_1)^2} \times \sqrt{\sum_{j=1}^{N}(X_{2i} - \bar{X}_2)^2}}$	Pearson product moment correlation coefficient [ρ]
D, D	$rG(X_1, X_2) = \dfrac{A - B - C + D}{A + B + C + D}$ where A = sum of positive agreeing responses ($X_1 = +ve$, $X_2 = +ve$) B = sum of negative agreeing responses ($X_1 = -ve$, $X_2 = -ve$) C = sum of non-agreeing responses ($X_1 = -ve$, $X_2 = +ve$) D = sum of non-agreeing responses ($X_1 = +ve$, $X_2 = -ve$) When the dichotomous variable (0, 1) is coded (−1, +1)	G index [G]
N, N or N, D	$r\rho(X_1, X_2) = \dfrac{\sum_{i=1}^{N}\sum_{s=1}^{N} X_{1i}^{(S)} X_{2i}^{(S)}}{\sqrt{\sum_{i=1}^{N}\sum_{s=1}^{N} X_{1i}^{(S)2}} \times \sqrt{\sum_{i=1}^{N}\sum_{s=1}^{N} X_{2i}^{(S)2}}}$ where $d_i^2 = \begin{cases} d_x = -1 \text{ if } X_i = X_s \\ \quad -1 \text{ otherwise} \end{cases}$ and d_x = number of categories for X	J index [J]
O, O	$rSR(X_1, X_2) = \dfrac{\sum_{i=1}^{m}(X_{1i} - \bar{X}_1)^2 + \sum_{i=1}^{m}(X_{2i} - \bar{X}_2) - \sum_{i=1}^{m} d_i^2}{2\left[\sqrt{\sum_{i=1}^{m}(X_{1i} - \bar{X}_1)^2} \times \sqrt{\sum_{j=1}^{m}(X_{2i} - \bar{X}_2)^2}\right]}$ where $d_i^2 = \sum_{i=1}^{m}(X_{1i} - \bar{X})^2 - 2\sum_{i=1}^{m}(X_{1i} - \bar{X})(X_{2i} - \bar{X}) + \sum_{i=1}^{m}(X_{2i} - \bar{X})$	Spearman rank correlation [SR]

Table 2A.1. (*Cont.*)

Scale pair (X_1, X_2)	Formula 1, 2, ..., N observations 1, 2, ..., m levels X_1, X_2 = random variables	Test name
D, R	$r_{PB}(X_1^D, X_2^R) = \frac{\mu_{21} - \mu_{2o}}{\sigma_{X_2}} \sqrt{P(1-p)}$ where σ_{X_2} is the standard deviation of the ratio scaled random variable X_2, μ_{21} and μ_{20} are the means of the values of X_2, corresponding to the dichotomous X_1 variables values 1 and 0.	Point biserial correlation [*PB*]
N, I	$r_{CP}(X_1^I, X_2^N) = \frac{d \overbrace{\sum_{i=1}^{N}\sum_{j=1}^{N}}^{X_{2i} = X_{2j}} (X_{1i} - \bar{X}_1)(X_{1j} - \bar{X}_1)}{\sqrt{N^2 + d(d-2)\sum N_r^2 \times \sum_{i=1}^{N}(X_i - \bar{X})^2}}$ where n_r is the number of individuals with $Y = r$; d is the number of categories of the nominal attribute	*CP* coefficient [*CP*]
I, I	$r_H(X_1, X_2) = \frac{\sum_{i=1}^{N} X_{1i}X_{2i}}{\sqrt{\sum_{i=1}^{N}(X_{1i}^2)} \times \sqrt{\sum_{i=1}^{N}(X_{2i}^2)}}$	H-INDEX [*H*]

The popularity of the PPM correlation coefficient is such that very few computer software packages offer any other correlation measures. Both Microsoft Excel and NLOGIT estimate the Pearson product moment correlation coefficient only. SPSS offers the Spearman rank correlation and Kendall's tau-b (refered to as the *G* index in table 2A.1) as well as the PPM correlation coefficient. NLOGIT also computes the rank correlation. If variables **x1** and **x2** are a set of ranks, **Calc;sprman=RKC(x1,x2)** computes the rank correlation.

3 Choosing

> As soon as questions of will or decision or reason or choice of action arise, human science is at a loss. (Noam Chomsky 1928–30)

3.1 Introduction

Individuals are born traders. They consciously or sub-consciously make decisions by comparing alternatives and selecting an action which we call a *choice outcome*. As simple as the observed outcome may be to the decision maker (i.e. the chooser), the analyst who is trying to explain this choice outcome through some captured data will never have available all the information required to be able to explain the choice outcome fully. This challenge becomes even more demanding as we study the population of individuals, since differences between individuals abound.

If the world of individuals could be represented by one person, then life for the analyst would be greatly simplified because whatever choice response we elicit from that one person could be expanded to the population as a whole to get the overall number of individuals choosing a specific alternative. Unfortunately there is a huge amount of variability in the reasoning underlying decisions made by a population of individuals. This variability, often referred to as *heterogeneity*, is in the main not observed by the analyst. The challenge is to find ways of observing and hence measuring this variability, maximizing the amount of measured variability (or *observed* heterogeneity) and minimizing the amount of unmeasured variability (or *unobserved* heterogeneity). The main task of the choice analyst is to capture such information through data collection and to recognize that any information not captured in the data (be it known but not measured or simply unknown) is still relevant to an individual's choice and must somehow be included in the effort to explain choice behavior.

3.2 Individuals have preferences, and they count

What we need is a conceptual framework that focuses on identifying the underlying influences on an individual's choice behavior. A useful way of revealing the necessary information is to start with a search for what these influences are. We will draw on ideas (in the main) from economics and (to a lesser extent) psychology, starting with the notion that it is an individual's *preferences* for specific alternatives (be they goods or services) that best determine what alternative is chosen. The word "preference" is used in common parlance – we often state that "we prefer to drive a car to work than catch public transport." If we delve deeper and try and understand this statement a little better, we would find that the reasons for preferring the car over public transport are related to travel time, comfort, convenience, security, and even status (depending on what type of car is driven). We might also be told however that not all reasoning is grounded in positive issues – parking is a problem at the destination (in terms of availability and price), and one might even include "good-citizen" considerations such as air pollution, global warming, and car crashes leading to huge costs to society in terms of lost productivity, not to mention trauma.

Even taking into account these underlying reasons that drive preferences, there will always be a number of *constraints* that deny the full achievement of the most preferred alternative. For example, an individual may not be able to afford to purchase a car (an income constraint). Assuming that the income constraint is not binding (for the time being), it makes very good sense to try and find out more about the preferences so that, regardless of the current budget constraint, if in the future this constraint is modified (i.e. tightened or relaxed) we can usefully establish what set of alternatives would be most preferred. To progress along this line of reasoning we need to take a closer look at how preferences are formed.

Where to start? Let us assume that we are discussing whether an individual will choose the car as a driver or the train for the journey to work. We will keep it simple, limiting the discussion to two alternatives, although we can easily generalize to many alternatives once we have a basic understanding on how preferences are revealed. Let us also assume that we have had extensive discussions with a sample of travelers and have identified the many reasons for choosing car or train. This list is likely to be quite long but we will take the top two attributes – travel time and out-of-pocket cost. Later you will see that the selection of these two attributes is a gross simplification of what are the underlying influences on preferences for car or train travel; in our serious data collection we have to measure a greater number of the potentially relevant attributes. Indeed even travel time itself is a complex attribute because it includes all types of travel time – walking to a train station, waiting for a train, time in the train, time in the car, time parking a car, time walking to the workplace after parking the car or alighting from the train.

To be able to progress we have to decide on how we might measure the underlying influences that define an individual's preferences for car over train or vice versa. Putting aside a concern about the image of a particular form of transport (which may ultimately be an important influence on preference formation, especially for new means of transport), we have assumed that the choice between car and train is determined by a comparison of the travel times and costs of the trip. But how relevant or important is time compared to cost and does it differ within each alternative? Throughout the development of choice analysis, we have sought to find a way of measuring an individual's preferences through what we call the "sources of preferences." Once the sources are identified they have to be measured in units that enable us to compare various combinations of the attributes across the alternatives and hopefully be confident that the alternative with the highest (positive) value or index is the most preferred. Whether we can say that an alternative is preferred by an exact number (i.e. a cardinal measure) or simply state it is more preferred (i.e. an ordinal measure) is a more challenging question, but for this primer we can safely put that issue aside.

The best way of progressing the measurement of preferences is to recognize that if the only influencing attribute were travel time, then it would be a simple exercise to compare the travel times and conclude that the alternative that has the shorter travel time to the given destination would be preferred. However, here we have two attributes (and usually many more). So how do we measure an individual's preferences in a multi-attribute environment?

We will begin by looking at each mode of transport separately. Take the car with its travel time and cost. To reveal an individual's preferences we will invite them to evaluate different combinations of travel time and cost associated with a particular trip (whose distance traveled is known). We need to ensure that all combinations are realistic although at the same time noting that some combinations may be outside of the individual's existing experiences (in the sense that there is no current technology available that can deliver a particular combination – e.g. an automatic pilot operating the vehicle using global positioning system (GPS) technology to steer; or institutional constraints such as 90 mph that limit a particular travel time over the fixed distance). To be able to convert the combinations of time and cost into a unit (or metric) that enables a comparison it is common practice to define a *response space* in either satisfaction or utility space. We need to explain this since it is crucial that the reader understands the meaning.

The build-up of knowledge of an individual's preferences begins by taking one commodity or good (which we call an *alternative*). Let us begin with the bus alternative and seek out an individual's preference for different combinations of travel time and cost (i.e. bus fare). We might start by selecting a range over which we will select a number of travel times and fares. Let this be 10–60 minutes and $0.20–$5.00. Preferences are revealed by asking an individual to evaluate combinations of travel time and cost and to provide either a numerical score or a ranking. A numerical score implies an ability to quantify with some precision a preference order and is referred to as *cardinal measurement*. A ranking score implies relativity (including equivalence) but admits that precision by cardinal measurement is not possible. Such a ranking is known as *ordinal measurement*. Despite the ongoing debate about the relative merits of cardinal and ordinal measurement, we will be adventurous and assume a capability to assign a numerical measure to each combination of travel time and cost. But what might this numerical measure be? In psychology it is referred to as "level of satisfaction"; in economics it is called "level of utility." These are essentially the same (although economists typically reserve the nomenclature "utility" for ordinal measurement).

Using the notion of satisfaction we need to give it some numerical dimension (i.e. a scale) that is easy to understand and is capable of being used to compare combinations of travel time and cost. We will use a scale over the range 0 to 100, where 100 is the highest

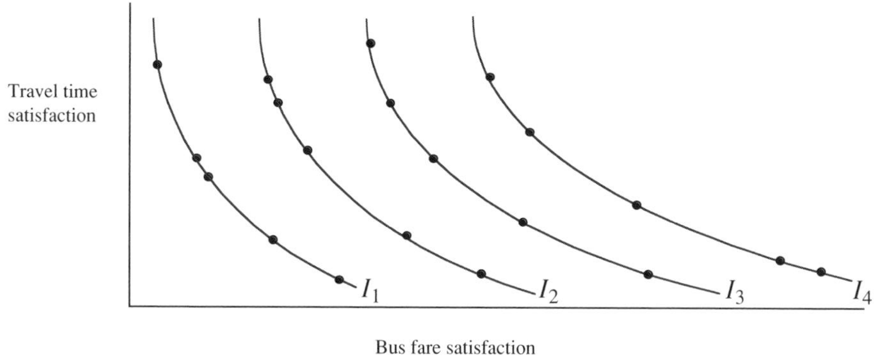

Figure 3.1 The identification of an individual's preferences for bus use

level of satisfaction. We will further assume that the scale has a meaningful zero and hence we can compare pairs of levels on the scale. A pair is a ratio and hence it is known as a *ratio scale*. If we were to assume that zero was not meaningful then we could not infer that a fixed difference between two combinations (e.g. 20 versus 30 on the satisfaction scale with 30 versus 40) was exactly the same on satisfaction. Another way of saying this is that over a fixed interval the preference is not linear.

Continuing with a ratio scale satisfaction response, we would elicit a response from an individual for each offered combination of travel time and cost. Although in theory one can offer an infinite number of combinations subject to the range of travel time and cost, in practice we tend to select a sufficient number to be able to trace out the levels of satisfaction that are likely to arise from the "consumption" of any one of the total (but finite) set of possible combinations. What we are doing here is plotting the combinations of travel time and cost in satisfaction space as a way of revealing preferences.

To illustrate what such a plot might look like, for one alternative (the bus mode) we define in figure 3.1 the vertical axis as levels of satisfaction associated with travel time, and the horizontal axis as levels of satisfaction associated with bus fares. Assume that we invited an individual to evaluate the 20 combinations by indicating on a satisfaction rating scale what rating they would assign to each combination of time and fare, and then we plotted the responses in satisfaction space. A closer look at each of these 20 points will show that some of them have identical levels of satisfaction. We have specifically plotted a number of combinations with the same levels of satisfaction to be able to introduce another way of representing preferences. If we join together all points with the same level of satisfaction we can conclude that an individual is *indifferent* as to which of these combinations is chosen. This indifference in level of satisfaction has led to the definition of a set of *indifference curves* as a way of depicting individual preferences.

In the satisfaction space in figure 3.1 there are literally thousands of possible points of difference and equality in satisfaction. The indifference curves enable us to make some meaningful sense out of all the potentially useful information on what we might call the *shape of the preferences of individuals*. This exercise can be repeated for each alternative since it is likely that the same combinations of levels of attributes might produce different levels of satisfaction across the alternative modes of transport. For example, holding cost fixed, 20 minutes in a bus might be associated with a different level of satisfaction than 20 minutes in a car as a driver. What we are starting to recognize is that the preferences (as revealed through levels of satisfaction) of an individual across alternatives will vary, and indeed this is likely to be the case even across individuals.

This heterogeneity in preferences is what choice analysis is all about – to try and explain these preferences across a sample of individuals given the choice set. In taking stock of what information we now have about preferences, it should be recognized that we have made a number of (implicit) assumptions to assist in measuring the levels of satisfaction (which we might also start to refer to as levels of utility):

(1) We have assumed that any other influences on preference formation except levels of travel time and cost of a specific alternative are held fixed at whatever levels they might be at the time of the evaluation.
(2) These other influences include the state of technology, an individual's ability to pay (i.e. their personal income), the levels of attributes associated with that alternative that are additional to travel time and cost, the levels of all attributes associated with other (competing and/or complementary) alternatives, and preferences for other alternatives.

The *state of technology* refers to the levels of attributes offered in the market by existing modes of transport. By referring to these other potential influences on choice behavior as fixed influences, we commonly use the nomenclature that an individual chooses levels of the two attributes (travel time and cost) and assigns a level of satisfaction, holding "all other influences constant." This statement hints at a preference for the combination of travel time and cost that provides the highest level of satisfaction (or utility). To be able to say that an individual prefers this combination implies that an individual acts as if they are maximizing the level of satisfaction. This is commonly referred to as a behavioral rule expressed as "utility maximizing behavior."

As desirable as the selection of the combination of attributes is, all other things equal, that gives the highest level of utility, this solution may not be achievable. This is because a person's income (or budget) cannot afford the cost, and/or the state of technology does not permit that combination. The next task is to recognize these constraints and establish the utility maximizing combination within the financial budget.

We need to make a modification to the presentation now. Instead of working with two attributes of a single alternative (i.e. time and cost for bus), we will instead introduce an additional alternative (i.e. car) and look at the preferences for bus versus car travel (either in terms of a single attributes such as cost or in terms of combinations of attributes such as time and cost). Note that if we evaluate more than one attribute associated with each alternative then to be able to stay with a simple two-dimensional diagram we will need to add up each attribute. In the current context, we would have to convert travel time to dollars and add it to fares for bus and operating costs for car to get what is referred to as the *generalized cost* or price of a trip. We discuss issues of converting attributes into dollar units in chapter 10 on willingness to pay (WTP) but for the time being we will

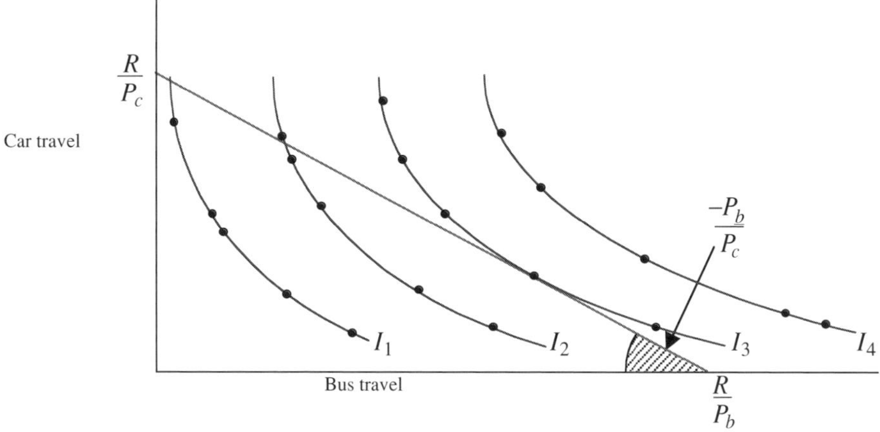

Figure 3.2 The budget or resource constraint

assume that we have a single attribute associated with bus and car called "cost." Within this revised setting of two modes, we will define the budget constraint as an individual's personal income. In figure 3.2 we overlay this budget constraint on a set of preference (or indifference) curves to identify the domain within which preferences can be realized. How do we present the budget constraint? There are three main elements in the definition of the budget constraint:

(1) The total resources (R) available (e.g. personal income) over a relevant time period (which we refer to as resources available per unit of time)
(2) The unit price associated with car (P_c) and bus (P_b) travel
(3) Whether these unit prices are influenced by the individual (as a price maker) or the individual has no influence and simply takes prices as given (i.e. a price taker).

Let us define the price of a unit of car travel as P_c and the price of a bus trip as P_b. We will also assume that the individual is a price taker and so has no influence over these unit prices. The slope of the budget constraint is the ratio of the prices of the two modal trips. To explain why this is so, if we assume that all of the budget is spent on car travel then the maximum amount of car travel that one can "consume" is the total resources (R) divided by P_c. Likewise the total amount of bus travel that can be undertaken is R/P_b. As a price taker, the unit price is constant at all levels of car and bus travel cost, and so is a straight line. To illustrate what happens to the budget line when we vary price and resources, in figure 3.3, starting with the original budget constraint (denoted as line A) we present line B for a reduction in the price of car travel, line D for an increase in the price of car travel, and line C for an increase in total resources (holding prices fixed at P_c and P_b).

In figure 3.4, when we overlay the budget constraint with the preference curves we can see what are the possible combinations of the two modal trips that an individual can choose to maximize utility subject to the resource constraint. This will be at point E where an indifference curve is tangential to the budget constraint for the prices P_c and P_b and

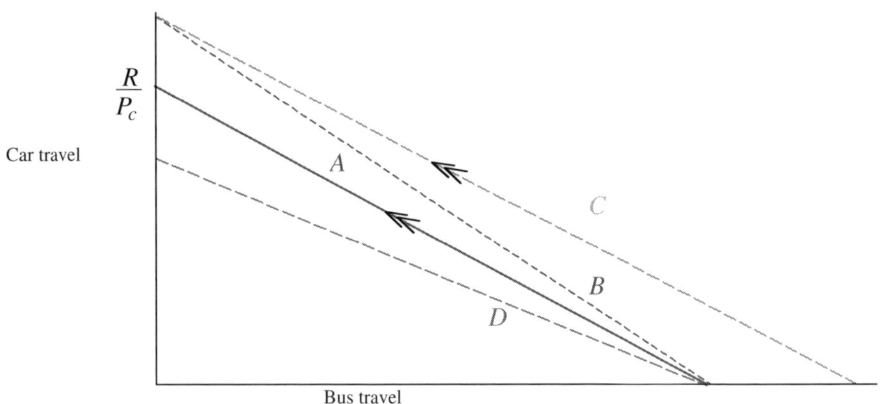

Figure 3.3 Changes to the budget or resource constraint

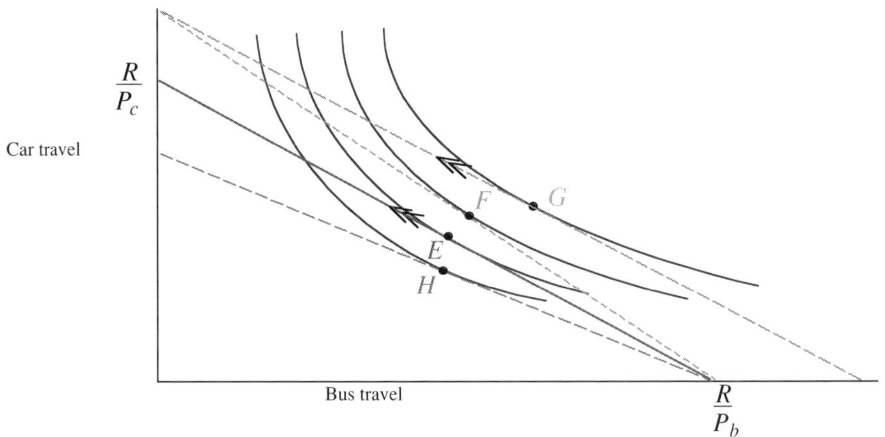

Figure 3.4 Individual preferences subject to a budget constraint

resources R. The individual cannot improve their level of utility without varying the total amount of resources and/or the unit prices of the two modal trips. In figure 3.4 we show other utility maximizing solutions under a reduction in the unit price of car travel (point F), an increase in total personal income (point G), and an increase in the unit price of bus travel (point H).

In the discussion above we have used a car trip being traded against a bus trip. It is common, however, in developing an understanding of the role of preferences and constraints to select one attribute of an alternative (or good or service) and evaluate its role *vis-à-vis* not spending money on that alternative, given the total available resources. This single attribute is typically the unit price of the alternative (e.g. the bus fare). However we can see from figure 3.1 that alternatives have many attributes as descriptors of sources of satisfaction (or utility) and hence we would want to preserve this detail in a real application.

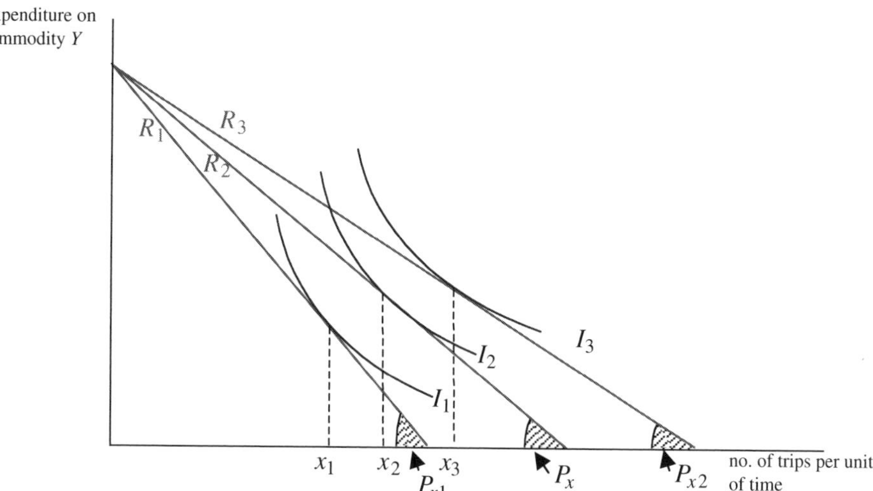

Figure 3.5 Indifference curves with budget constraint

This would be achieved by converting each attribute's level into a dollar value and adding them up to produce what is called a generalized price. In presenting the material in a two-dimensional diagram, the best way to continue the discussion is to treat the horizontal axis as the amount of the travel mode (i.e. bus) consumed as defined by the number of trips per unit of time (say, over a month), and the vertical axis as another use of resources that are available after allocating funds to bus use (call it savings or expenditure on commodity Y).

Figure 3.5 has three budget constraints and three indifference curves that serve to illustrate how utility maximizing levels of bus travel and expenditure on other activities are determined. You will see that the amount of bus travel varies as we vary the price of bus travel, increasing as bus fares decrease and decreasing as bus fares increase. Figure 3.5 is especially useful in establishing a relationship between the frequency of choice and an attribute influencing such a choice, all other things being equal (or constant). We can now make a very important statement: "Given an individual's preferences (as represented by the shapes of the indifference curves), available budget and unit prices of alternatives (in this example, bus travel and all other activities), and holding all other considerations constant, under the rule of utility maximization we can trace out the relationship between the unit price of bus travel and the amount of bus travel." What we have here is the *individual's demand function*.

We have avoided using the word "demand" up to now since our focus is on "choice." These two constructs are related and need to be clarified. When we observe an individual doing something such as undertaking a bus trip, we have observed the outcome of a choice and also information that represents the demand for the activity (i.e. bus travel). The observed choice outcome observed over a period of time enables us to measure the number of times a specific choice is made (whether it is made under habitual choice or a

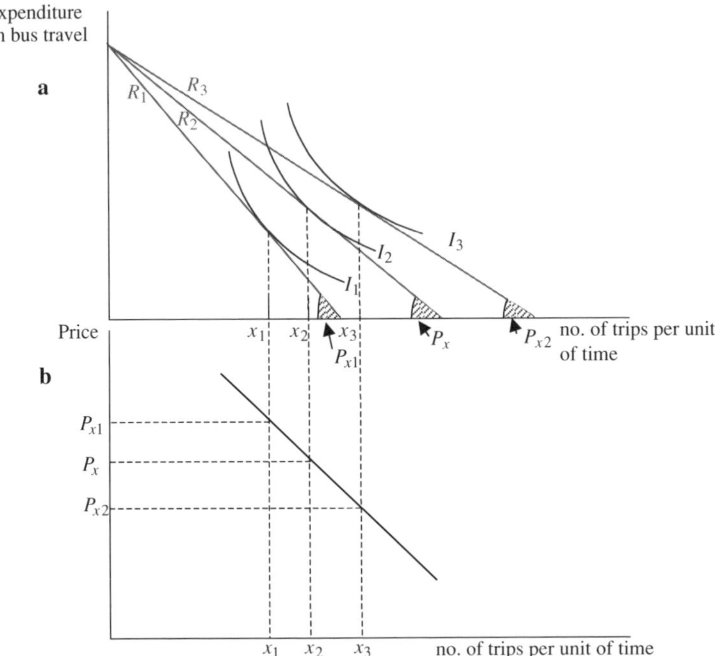

Figure 3.6 Demand curve construction

fresh re-evaluation each time). Importantly, to be able to interpret the sum of all choice outcomes as a measure of an individual's demand for a specific activity (be it a purchase of a durable good (e.g. a car), a consumption of a good (e.g. a chocolate bar), or use of an alternative such as bus) we must record situations where such an activity is not undertaken at all. This has led to a useful distinction between *conditional and unconditional choice.* The former tells us that a specific choice is conditional on something else. For example, the choice of mode of transport for the journey to work is conditional on a prior choice to work or not to work. It may also be conditional on the prior choice to work away from home versus work at home (conditional on the decision to work). An unconditional choice is one that is not conditioned on any prior choice. It is only when we have taken into account all of these prior (or in some cases joint) conditions that we can refer to individual (unconditional) demand. An important point to recognize for later is that the alternative "not to choose any of the alternatives offered" is a very important alternative if we are to convert an individual choice outcome into a measure of individual demand.

With this distinction clarified, we can now use the information in figure 3.5 to derive the individual's demand function for a specific alternative. We do this by simply reading off from figure 3.4 the combinations of unit price and number of bus trips and plotting them in figure 3.6 against a vertical axis for price and a horizontal axis for the quantity demanded.

Figure 3.6 has provided the necessary information to derive one demand curve for an individual. Movements along this demand curve are attributed to changes in the price of

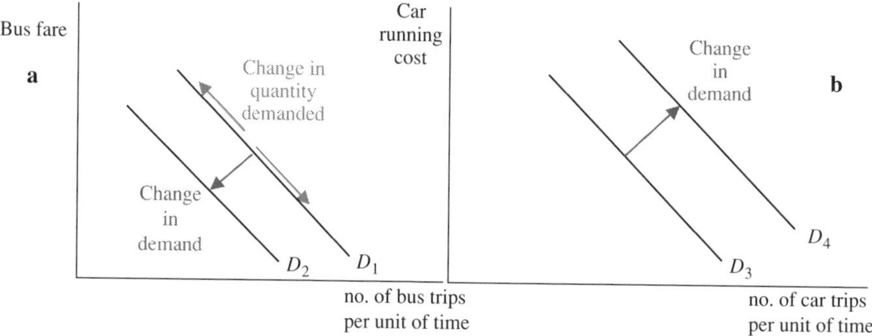

Figure 3.7 Changes in demand and changes in quantity demanded

bus travel, all other considerations held constant. However other influences may change from time to time for many reasons and then we have a problem in interpreting movements along a given demand curve. Simply put, we cannot observe movements along a given demand curve (called change in the *quantity* demanded) when something other than what is on the vertical axis changes. If an individual's personal income increases, we might expect a change in the quantity of bus travel because the additional income might enable the individual to buy a car and switch from bus to car travel for some of the trips per unit of time. What we now have is more than a change in the quantity of bus travel but also a change in the *level of* demand.

That is, the *demand curve itself* will change, resulting in an additional demand curve that accounts for both the reduction in bus travel and the increase in car travel. Since figure 3.6 is focused on bus travel we will be able to observe only the change in bus travel in this diagram. We will also need an additional diagram (figure 3.7) to show the amount of travel that has substituted car for bus. A movement between demand curves is referred to as *a change in demand* (in contrast to a change in the quantity demanded when an individual moves along a given demand curve). We now have a substitution effect and an income effect; the latter due to a change in income and the former due to a change in the unit price. These concepts are developed in more detail in Hensher and Brewer (2001, 197–201).

3.3 Using knowledge of preferences and constraints in choice analysis

We are now able to focus back on choice analysis, armed with some very important constructs. The most important is an awareness of how we identify an individual's preferences for specific alternatives and the types of constraints that might limit the alternatives that can be chosen. The shapes of the preference curves will vary from individual to individual, alternative to alternative, and even at different points in time. Identifying the influences molding a specific set of preferences is central to choice analysis. Together with the constraints that limit the region within which preferences can be honored and the behavioral decision rule used to process all inputs, we establish a *choice outcome*.

The challenge for the analyst is to find a way of identifying, capturing and using as much as possible of the information that an individual takes on board when they process a situation leading to a choice. There is a lot of information, much of which the analyst is unlikely to observe. Although knowledge of an individual's choice and factors influencing it is central to choice analysis, the real game is in being able to explain choices made by a population of individuals. When we go beyond an individual to a group of individuals (as a sample or a full population census) we reveal an even greater challenge for the analyst – how best to take into account the huge amount of variation in reasoning underlying the same choice outcome and indeed the rejection of the non-chosen alternatives.

Choice analysis is about explaining variability in behavioral response in a sampled population of individuals (or other units of choice making such as households, firms, community groups, etc.). An early reminder of the importance of this is in order, and there are some relatively simple ways of attacking this matter. One might limit the compilation of data to a few easy-to-measure attributes of alternatives and descriptors of individuals. Furthermore one might use relatively aggregate measures of these. For example, it is not uncommon in transport studies to use the average income of individuals living in a specific suburb instead of an individual's actual income. It is also not uncommon to use the average travel time between specific locations based on a sample of individuals traveling between those locations, instead of an individual's actual (or most likely perceived) travel time. It is also not uncommon to then take the proportion of travelers choosing an alternative as the dependent variable, effectively moving away from a study on individual choice to a study of spatially aggregated individuals. What we will observe is that much of the variability in sources of potential influence on choice behavior associated with individuals is eliminated by *aggregation* (or averaging). When this occurs, we have indeed less variability to explain and indeed statistical methods will handle this in a way that produces a higher explanation of behavioral response. This is a fallacy – when there is less variability to explain, it is easier to explain and you tend to get a better fitting statistical model (e.g. a very high overall goodness of fit measure such as R-squared in a linear model). You feel good, but you should not. There is a very high chance that you have explained a high amount of only a small amount of the true behavioral variance in the data on individuals. What we still have left is a huge amount of *unobserved variability* that is central to explaining the choice made. Its relevance increases when the analyst adopts so-called simple ways of trying to explain choice behavior. One is not eliminating the problem, simply ignoring (or avoiding) it.

The next step is to set out a framework within which we can capture the sources of behavioral variability at the individual decision-making level. We must recognize that the sources of variability are initially unobserved by the analyst (but known with certainty by the decision maker); and that the analyst's challenge is to try and capture as much as possible of the variability through a set of observed influences while finding ways of accommodating the remaining unobserved (to the analyst) influences. We cannot ignore the latter because they are very much relevant sources of variability. How we account for these unobserved influences is at the center of choice analysis.

To begin, let us assume the existence of a well-defined (closed) population of individuals. We will select a random sample of individuals to represent this closed population. We will also limit our inquiry initially to the study of the choice of mode of transport for a specific travel purpose – the journey to work – and assume that this activity is undertaken on a regular basis, five times per week (essentially ignoring the frequency of such travel). We will also fix the set of alternatives to four and assume that they are all available. These alternatives are car as driver only, car ride share, bus, and train. In defining the choice set we are assuming that the alternatives are *mutually exclusive*. That is, the individual chooses one of them. (If it is more realistic to use a bus to connect to a train and not as alternative to the train, then we might redefine our choice set to be three alternatives, replacing bus and train with combined access mode (*bus*) and line-haul mode (*train*). This example illustrates the importance of careful definition of alternatives since, once defined, they are deemed to be mutually exclusive.)

For a sampled individual, we assume that they have full knowledge of the factors that influence their choice decision. This does not mean that all attributes of alternatives as observed in reality are indeed taken into account and even measured (consciously or subconsciously) the way we assume they are depicted in the marketplace. How an individual perceives the level of an attribute is what clearly influences their choice. We as analysts may follow someone in a car and record a 35-minute trip, but if the chooser perceives it as 25 minutes then that is what matters to them. This creates challenges for the analyst because in real world applications we typically evaluate changes in attribute levels based on actual attribute levels and not the equivalent perceived level.

What attributes do matter to an individual? This is a crucial issue and must involve extensive inquiry on the part of the analyst. Establishing through focus groups, literature reviews, talking to experts, etc. what are generally accepted as the main attributes is often fraught with many challenges. Measurement is one in particular. In studies of travel mode choice it is common to be told that in addition to travel time, cost and frequency (the latter for public transport), comfort, convenience, safety, and image matter. Ask anyone to define these last four attributes and we guarantee you will get as many different answers as there are respondents. "Safety" can refer to personal safety from assault, the vehicle having a crash or trains being derailed. "Comfort" can refer to the temperature in the vehicle, quality of seating – material, shape and amount of space. "Convenience" can mean simply the time its takes to get to work, but also time waiting for a train or bus, traffic congestion on the road, and even uncertainty of timetable for public transport. Some individuals dislike using buses and trains simply because they are public transport; however other individuals prefer public transport because it is more attuned to their beliefs on sustainable transport than the car. What these examples highlight is the ambiguity inherent in establishing the meaning of what attributes influence an individual's choice of mode of transport for the journey to work.

Analysts must recognize this and commit substantial amounts of effort to working through this sea of ambiguity to try and recover as much clarity of attribute content (in meaning and measurement) as is possible. Any information that is excluded (for whatever reason, including ignorance of the phenomenon) still remains as unobserved sources of influence on choice behavior. For example, with respect to measurement, if instead of asking an individual how long a trip took we calculate it based on distance and average speed, then the difference between the measured and perceived travel time is actually information that is "forced" into the unobserved influences (after all, where else can it go?). If comfort (however defined) is really relevant and we ignore it then it also ends up with the growing list of relevant but unobserved influences. If we measure comfort in terms of seating shape (on some scale) but ignore the material of the seating and it is relevant, then again important information is assigned to the unobserved influences. If the unobserved influences start to dominate the observed influences then we are already signaling a major concern about the analyst's ability to explain choice behavior. Without jumping too far ahead, we may be able to find a way of accommodating the dominating unobserved influences by clever specification of how they are distributed among the sampled population, but one needs more than one observation to be able to do this, which means either lots of observation on one person or a sample of individuals.

Clearly the ideal situation is to be able to measure all relevant attributes (i.e. sources of utility) through observed attributes, essentially limiting the unobserved sources of utility to "pure noise." Sometimes we feel confident in including an attribute but have difficulty with its measurement. Analysts have been heard to comment that they excluded an important attribute because they did not know how to forecast its future levels for applications. While there is some sense in the comment, it is a risky strategy because it limits the behavioral capability of the choice exercise. A preferred strategy (in our view) is to leave such relevant attributes in the model as part of the observed set, but to either use a scenario-based ("what-if") application method or simply fix the attribute at its base levels over time. The scenario approach enables the analysts to at least get some sense as to whether the attribute might actually impact noticeably on choice responses when changed.

3.4 Setting up a behavioral choice rule

Section 3.3 has promoted the idea of a set of observed and a set of unobserved influences on choice behavior. When we talk about "sources of influence" we really refer to *attributes that are sources of utility*. We are now ready to introduce some simple notation to summarize the way that we introduce attributes in order to establish their role in the identification of the level of utility (or satisfaction) contributed by that attribute to the overall level of (relative) utility associated with each alternative in a choice set. In some literature, the contribution of a specific attribute to overall utility of an alternative is called a "part-worth."

Let us represent overall utility of an alternative as U_i, where i refers to a specific alternative. For example, i could be a bus or a train. From now on, the utility level we refer to is a relative measure and all that matters is the level of utility associated with an alternative relative to that of another alternative *in the same choice set*. This is a very important issue, because it implies that there is some base reference against which we can compare the utility of each alternative. This base reference is called the "scale of utility" (or the scale parameter, for short) and is a warning that one must not look at the absolute utility calculated for an alternative in one study (or choice set) and compare it with another study or choice set. You will see later what we mean when we introduce two data sets derived from the same individual to study the same choice (in particular, the use of revealed and stated preference data to study the choice of mode for the journey to work). A comparison of data sets or choices requires revealing this scale parameter as a mechanism for making the results comparable.

The overall utility associated with the ith alternative can be divided into the contributions that are observed by the analyst and those that are not observed by the analyst. Let us denote these sources of (relative) utility respectively by V_i and ε_i. Epsilon (ε) is common notation which dates back to a literature that used to refer to the unobserved influences as error. This is a most unfortunate labeling since it potentially denies recognition of the behavioral content of this part of the utility expression.

In choice analysis we treat both V_i and ε_i as of great relevance, and set ourselves as analysts the task of unraveling the sources of variability in behavioral response resident in both parts of the utility expression. We need to assume a relationship between V_i and ε_i. Studies generally assume that these two components are independent and additive. We can now write out the first expression:

$$U_i = V_i + \varepsilon_i \tag{3.1}$$

There are as many equations as there are alternatives in the choice set. We have four such expressions for the mode-choice case study and we have assumed that all alternatives are available from which an individual chooses one. We define this as a choice of $j = 1, \ldots, i, \ldots, J$ alternatives, where J is the number of available alternatives in the choice set faced by an individual. It is often the situation that not all alternatives in the universal (but finite) choice set are available to every individual, for whatever reason (be it physically not available or some perceptual threshold of lack of interest in respect of one of more attributes).

As an aside, we sometimes have a very large number of alternatives and have to find ways of including all of them in the analysis without resorting to a very large (and often not affordable) sample size. For example, in Australia there are over 4,000 makes and models (by vintage) of cars in the market. It is impossible to treat each as an alternative available to each individual and to develop a model to explain the choice between 4,000 alternatives. One would need at least 240,000 observations where each had a minimum of 60 individuals observed to choose each alternative (to ensure efficient parameter estimates). One strategy to get around this that is commonly used is to define each individual's choice set as their chosen alternative plus a randomly selected set from the remaining 3,999, typically about 20 non-chosen alternatives. Randomization is fine under certain conditions (see the IID property below). Some analysts ask respondents to indicate what alternatives would be chosen if they had not made their current choice. The downside of this is that we have no idea of knowing why the alternatives that are excluded were not chosen. That is, we have not explained the choice of an alternative being in or out of a choice set. Looking ahead, the true probability of an individual choosing an alternative from the total set of available alternatives in the market is the probability of choosing an alternative given that it is in the choice set and the probability of it being in or out of the choice set.

The next task is to decide on how V_i and ε_i are to be represented. V_i is often referred to as the "representative component of utility," because it is where the set of attributes that are observed and measured (for a representative individual q) reside. Their residency is accompanied by a set of weights that establish the relative contribution of each attribute to the observed sources of relative utility. In its simplest form, we can define the representative component of utility as a linear expression in which each attribute is weighted by a unique weight (called a parameter or coefficient) to account for that attribute's marginal utility input. Formally, we can write this out as (3.2), using f as a generalized notation for functional form, but recognizing that the functional form can be different for each attribute:

$$V_i = \beta_{0i} + \beta_{1i} f(X_{1i}) + \beta_{2i} f(X_{2i}) + \beta_{3i} f(X_{3i}) + \cdots + \beta_{Ki} f(X_{Ki}) \qquad (3.2)$$

where

β_{1i} is the weight (or parameter) associated with attribute X_1 and alternative i
β_{0i} is a parameter not associated with any of the observed and measured attributes, called the *alternative-specific constant*, which represents on average the role of all the unobserved sources of utility.

There are $k = 1, \ldots, K$ attributes in (3.2). This expression has included subscripts on every element to recognize that the weights, the attribute levels, and the constant are specific to the ith alternative. The inclusion of $f(\ldots)$ is our notation for indicating that the ways that the attributes enter the utility expression are many and varied. If we were to treat each attribute as linear then we would simply define $f(X) = X$. However, each attribute can be specified in a logarithmic form (e.g. the natural log of X), or as a quadratic (i.e. X^2), or even as a linear and a quadratic term (e.g. $\beta_{2i} X_{2i} + \beta_{2i} X_{2i}^2$). Interactions between attributes are also interesting (e.g. $\beta_{5i} X_{2i} X_{3i}$).

As an aside, when a linear and a quadratic term are included, one must ensure that they are lowly correlated otherwise you will get confoundment and be unable to establish the role of each term. The same applies to interacting attributes. The inclusion of the quadratic enables the analyst to establish if a change in the level of an attribute causes the marginal utility to increase at an increasing or decreasing rate or decrease at an increasing or decreasing rate.

Initially we will assume that the V_i component is linear additive in the attributes and the parameters. This means that each parameter is a single fixed estimate (called a fixed parameter in contrast to a random parameter, where the latter has a mean and a standard deviation that delivers a distribution of estimated values).

The unobserved component, ε_i, now needs careful definition. As an index of the unobserved influences, we know virtually nothing behaviorally about it. The task is to reconstruct as well as we can what we might reasonably assume. The best place to start is to recognize that each individual will have some utility associated with an alternative that is captured by the unobserved component. Across the sample of individuals, each person will have such data. That is, there will exist a distribution of such unobserved sources of utility across the sampled population. What might this distribution look like, and how can we quantify each point on an unknown distribution, in utility units? To progress this argument we have to introduce some assumptions that we refer to as *maintained assumptions*.

As an aside, there are two broad classes of assumptions – testable and maintained. As the names imply, a *testable assumption* is one that can be introduced and varied to establish its behavioral implications. A maintained assumption is one that cannot be tested. An example of the latter is the additivity of V_i and ε_i.

The first (maintained) assumption we will introduce is that the unobserved utility associated with each individual is located on some (unknown) distribution and randomly allocated to each sampled individual. The density of utility along the real line is dependent on the distribution of such information in the population, which is an unknown. We have to choose a particular distribution and then work out how each individual might be assigned appropriate amounts of utility as a measure of the role of the unobserved influences in the establishment of overall utility associated with a particular alternative.

The next (testable) assumption is that each alternative has its own unobserved component represented by some unknown distribution with individuals assigned locations randomly within the distribution that defines the range of utility values. We have indexed ε_i in recognition that the index is different across the alternatives. Indeed, they may be correlated between pairs of alternatives and have different-shaped distributions. However, the simplest starting assumption is that the set of unobserved components, while each having their own unique mean value (to reveal different alternative-specific constants as in (3.2) above), are independent (i.e. with no cross-correlated terms) with the exact same distributions (i.e. identically distributed). This set of assumptions is referred to as the IID condition (IID is "independently and identically distributed").

To appreciate exactly what IID implies, we will illustrate it with four alternatives and define the full potential correlation structure between the alternatives in terms of a variance–covariance matrix (often called the covariance matrix). For the case study with four alternatives, it will be a 4×4 (or 16-cell) matrix as shown in (3.3). This specification has the maximal amount of information that is theoretically (at least) in the covariance matrix. When we impose the IID assumption we get a simplified matrix as in (3.4). Under IID, all subscripts have been removed since each unobserved component is *identically distributed*, and all covariances (or cross-correlated terms) are set to zero since the alternatives are *independent*. The variances (on the diagonal) remain, but are identical. To enable us to identify each variance relative to the others (remember the scaling issue above), it is common practice to arbitrarily normalize one of the variances to equal 1.0. In the simplest specification with all variances equal, all diagonal elements are equal to 1.0. This is known as the *constant variance assumption* and is equivalent to IID:

$$\begin{bmatrix} \sigma_{11}^2 & \sigma_{12} & \sigma_{13} & \sigma_{14} \\ \sigma_{21} & \sigma_{22}^2 & \sigma_{23} & \sigma_{24} \\ \sigma_{31} & \sigma_{32} & \sigma_{33}^2 & \sigma_{34} \\ \sigma_{41} & \sigma_{42} & \sigma_{43} & \sigma_{44}^2 \end{bmatrix} \tag{3.3}$$

$$\begin{bmatrix} \sigma^2 & 0 & 0 & 0 \\ 0 & \sigma^2 & 0 & 0 \\ 0 & 0 & \sigma^2 & 0 \\ 0 & 0 & 0 & \sigma^2 \end{bmatrix} = \begin{bmatrix} 1 & 0 & 0 & 0 \\ 0 & 1 & 0 & 0 \\ 0 & 0 & 1 & 0 \\ 0 & 0 & 0 & 1 \end{bmatrix} \tag{3.4}$$

To provide an intuitive explanation of how (3.3) operates in an outcome setting, think of the task as being one of representing sources of variance that contribute to explaining a specific outcome. For a specific individual, (3.1) has variance potential associated with the parameter attached to each observed characteristic (i.e. β), to each observed characteristic itself (i.e. X), and to the unobserved effects term (ε). We could expand this equation out to reflect these sources of variance for three characteristics, defining "*OB*" as observed and "*U*" as unobserved, as (dropping the q and to subscripts):

$$\begin{aligned} U_i = &(\beta_{OB1} X_{OB1} + \beta_{u1} X_{u1}) + (\beta_{OB2} X_{OB2} + \beta_{u2} X_{u2}) \\ &+ (\beta_{OB3} X_{OB3} + \beta_{u3} X_{u3}) + \varepsilon_i \end{aligned} \tag{3.5a}$$

Each characteristic is now represented by a set of observed and unobserved influences. In addition, each parameter and characteristic can itself be expressed as some function of other influences, giving more depth in the explanation of sources of variance. As we expand the function out we reveal deeper parameters to identify. In the most restrictive (or simplest) versions of the utility expression, we would gather all the unobserved sources together and replace (3.5a) with (3.5b):

$$U_i = \beta_{OB1} X_{OB1} + \beta_{OB2} X_{OB2} + \beta_{OB3} X_{OB3} + (\beta_{u1} X_{u1} + \beta_{u2} X_{u2} + \beta_{u3} X_{u3} + \varepsilon_i) \tag{3.5b}$$

and would collapse the unobserved influences into a single unknown by assuming that all unobserved effects cannot be related in any systematic way with the observed effects:

$$U_i = \beta_{OB1} X_{OB1} + \beta_{OB2} X_{OB2} + \beta_{OB3} X_{OB3} + \varepsilon_i \tag{3.5c}$$

Furthermore by defining a utility expression of the form in (3.5c) for each alternative, and imposing a further assumption that the unobserved influences have the same distribution and are independent across alternatives, we can remove the i subscript attached to e. What we have is the functional form for the utility expressions of a multinomial logit (MNL) model. This intuitive discussion has highlighted the way in which an MNL model restricts through assumption the opportunity to reveal the fuller range of potential sources of influence on utility as resident throughout the full dimensionality of (3.5a). Explaining these fuller sources is equivalent to explaining the broader set of sources of observed and unobserved heterogeneity on a choice outcome.

Although (3.3) is very general, it has been shown to be impossible to impose such a general set of relationships on a choice model in order to get a behaviorally richer choice model than the model associated with the IID condition. A number of authors have shown that one full row of (3.3) has to be normalized (by setting the terms to zero) to ensure that the choice model can be estimated.

There are a number of useful insights we can obtain from this set of strong assumptions in (3.3):

(1) The attributes that are not included in the observed part of the utility expression are by definition represented by the unobserved component and of identical impact for

each alternative. Thus if trip comfort is missing in all alternatives, it is seen as having the exact same influence on the choice of each alternative. This may be unrealistic when comparing public transport with the car.

(2) An attribute that is common to two or more alternatives suggests the presence of correlation across alternatives. If it is excluded from the observed part of the utility expression, then its inclusion in the unobserved component must introduce correlation between alternatives. This information should reside in the off-diagonal elements. Since they are all set to zero in (3.4), we have a potential violation of the IID condition.

(3) Where there is concern about possible violation of constant variance and/or correlated alternatives because of an inability to accommodate the sources of this in the observed part of the utility expression, one should consider a choice model that allows less restrictive assumptions. For this primer, we limit this ability to relax simplifying assumptions on the structure of the covariance matrix to those that can be handled within a nested logit, a heteroskedastic extreme value, and a mixed logit setting (see chapters 13–16). Essentially the nested logit structure allows us to partition the choice set in such a way that the constant variance assumption holds among alternatives in the same partition while allowing differential variance between partitions and correlation among alternatives within a partition. For example, the four alternatives in our case study might be partitioned in such a way that bus and train are separated from car driver and car ride share to reflect the presence of unobserved attributes that have more in common in respect of their utility influence *within* public transport modes and *within* car modes than *between* public transport and car modes. Whatever partition is chosen, it is important to recognize that it is a way of taking into account the influence of unobserved attributes and has nothing to say about how individuals make choices. For example, intuitively an individual may choose between public transport or car and given their choice (say, car), they then choose to drive. What we have here is a conditional choice (i.e. car drive conditional on choosing car) and a marginal choice (i.e. car versus public transport). Mixed logit (chapters 15 and 16) permits a more general specification of the components of the covariance matrix.

We now have information to understand the meaning of the utility expression for each alternative. With such an expression associated with each alternative, we are ready to talk about how an individual evaluates the alternatives to arrive at a most preferred alternative which is the chosen alternative. For the first time, we have to talk about an underlying behavioral rule that an individual might use to arrive at a choice outcome. In contemplating this important matter, we introduce the maintained assumption that all individuals act rationally. While this might seem a rather innocuous statement, it has nevertheless been associated with a lot of controversy. We take the position that all individuals act rationally in the sense that they take into account all matters they deem relevant regardless of the amount of information they have at their disposal to assist their deliberations. The resulting choice is what the analyst must try to explain as well as they can, and the exclusion of an attribute that an analyst deems important is no basis for saying that someone acts irrationally. Indeed once we recognize the presence of both $V_i + \varepsilon_i$ then we can no longer say anything about rationality in respect of the contents of V_i across the alternatives since there is information in ε_i that matters.

Given the maintained assumption that an individual acts rationally in choosing an alternative, we are able to introduce a formal mechanism for placing this assumption within utility space. The assumption we now introduce is that an individual acting rationally is assumed to *compare alternatives* and to choose that one which gives the *greatest level of satisfaction or utility*. Formally we state that "*an individual acts as if they are maximizing utility.*" This says nothing about the choice set, the alternatives, and the attributes, and thus is seen as a global assumption that does not permit the exclusion of any relevant information (from the individual's perspective). If the analyst excludes information it can be for many reasons including an inability to afford an alternative, non-availability of an alternative in the geographical setting of the individual, the effort and transaction cost involved in evaluating a large number of alternatives, and many other possible influences. Thus we often talk of "an individual acting as if they maximize global utility subject to constraints." If as a consequence of such constraints we observe individuals ignoring certain alternatives, we cannot say that they are not maximizing utility in a global sense; rather that they have chosen, for whatever reason, to exclude some alternatives entirely. Constructs such as *bounded rationality* and *satisficing* have been used to describe these "local" minimum effort choices.

This issue has engendered a debate on what should be in the choice set, with market researchers distinguishing *consideration sets* (i.e. the sub-set of alternatives from a universal choice set that are considered by an individual as candidates to be chosen) from choice sets. We find the distinction interesting but not very useful. Rather, the critical issue is how the analyst defines the framework within which they establish an individual's choice set. Broadly, there are two main methods. We can simply ask an individual what alternatives are in the choice set from which a particular alternative was observed to be chosen; or we can list the universal but finite set of alternatives and establish which one was chosen. If we adopt the former approach, then we are running the risk of violating the global utility maximizing assumption. Specifically, by asking an individual what is the chosen alternative and what other alternatives were considered (usually limited to one or two), we have introduced a *threshold constraint* on the utility maximizing outcome. Another way of stating this is that we have set up a choice problem in which an individual is assumed to choose among a set of alternatives within bounded utility space.

Some analysts refer to this as the *bounded rationality* paradigm. While appealing, it has failed to provide some crucial information – namely, why were the other alternatives excluded? Is there enough information in the bounded set to be confident that one can extrapolate to any subsequent setting and establish the correct choice shares in the presence of an alternative that was excluded through asking an individual for the composition of the choice set? The way to ensure such potentially important information is included in the analysis is to seek out information on why an alternative was excluded. This suggests a model structure wherein we have the choice of an alternative given a choice set and a choice of choice sets. In reality, this is very difficult to accommodate because of the large number of choice sets, which proliferate very fast as the number of alternatives increases. A practical compromise is to sample alternatives; however, this is strictly valid only if alternatives are truly independent (which requires the underlying covariance matrix as discussed above to have no non-zero off-diagonal elements). Clearly we have a very complex issue and while we admit that it has not been solved (and is beyond the confines of this primer), it is nevertheless of sufficient importance and interest to recognize.

The alternative whereby we do not ask an individual to define their choice set but to admit the universal but finite choice set as the permissible set under which an individual chooses an alternative, aligns with the global utility maximizing rule. It is the challenge of the analyst to ensure that the observed set of attributes are able to establish the relevance of each alternative and we would hope that a useful choice model would predict that many alternatives will not be chosen by a specific individual for many reasons. Often, however, the size of the choice set is so large that one is "forced" to sample alternatives.

As an aside, sampling of alternatives is not necessarily desirable. Doing so imposes restrictions. Two in particular should be noted. Suppose one has 2,000 alternatives and decides to sample 20 for each individual (plus one for the chosen alternative) giving a choice set of 21 alternatives. Each individual will have a different set of 21 alternatives. It is certain that you will not have enough individuals with a specific alternative in their choice set to be able to treat all 2,000 alternatives as unique alternatives (what we refer to as "labeled" or "ranked" alternatives). Thus alternatives must be *grouped*. This can be done by either (i) defining 21 unlabeled utility expressions and randomly assigning an alternative to one of the 21 alternative utility expressions or (ii) grouping alternatives and replacing them with classes of alternatives. The problem with classes is that one has to establish criteria for classification: this is a form of *aggregation bias*. Although we can preserve the actual levels of attributes of alternatives in the classification system, we cannot allow different parameter estimates (i.e. marginal utilities) for alternatives in the same class. However if we adopt the former unlabeled strategy we also cannot allow any differences in marginal utilities across the entire choice set – it simply makes no sense when a specific alternative can be randomly spread throughout all 21 alternatives. At least one can establish class-specific marginal utilities in the latter structure.

A concrete example may help in making these points clearer if there is still some doubt. Some years ago a student undertook research into a household's choice of type of car. The student chose to seek information on the alternatives in the choice set by asking the household. Taking one household who owned one vehicle, their chosen vehicle was a Mazda 323. When asked for up to three alternatives that would have been purchased had they not bought the Mazda 323, the stated vehicles were Honda Civic, Toyota Corolla, and Ford Escort. After collecting the data and undertaking the model estimation it was found that the vehicle price attribute had a positive sign (and was marginally significant). After much thought it became clear what the problem was. By limiting the choice set to vehicles listed by the respondent, we were limiting the analysis to the choice among similarly priced vehicles. Consequently more expensive vehicles (and much less expensive ones) were not being assessed in the data although some process of rejection had clearly taken place by the household. The price attribute was at best a proxy for quality differences among the vehicles (subject to whatever other vehicle attributes were included in the observed part of the utility expression). Price would be better placed in explaining what alternatives were in or out of the choice set. If the student had simply listed all vehicles on the market (by make, model, vintage) and considered all eligible, then regardless of which grouping strategy was used (as discussed above) one would expect price to have a negative parameter; and indeed the model if well specified should have assigned a very low likelihood of the particular household purchasing a vehicle in a higher and a lower price range. An important lesson was learned.

3.5 Deriving a basic choice model

We are now ready to start translating the behavioral choice rule and associated maintained and testable assumptions into a model that can be used to estimate the parameters that represent the contribution of attributes and socio-demographic characteristic(s) (SDC(s)) of alternatives to the overall choice outcome.

Formally, each alternative is compared, and the one that yields the highest level of utility is chosen by an individual. The analyst is less confident in picking the most preferred alternative because he has less information to play with than the decision maker. This inability to "look into the head" of the individual decision maker and capture all the information used by the individual means that the analyst can use only the sub-set of information they have managed to compile. This is equivalent to saying that the analyst can explain an individual's choice only up to a probability of an alternative being chosen. Let us see how we write this out in terms of the utility expression notation we have used in (3.1) above.

An individual will evaluate each alternative as represented by U_j; $j = 1, \ldots, J$ alternatives. The individual decision maker's rule is that they will compare $U_1, U_2, \ldots, U_j, \ldots, U_J$ and choose the one with maximum utility, i.e. max (U_j).

However the analyst has a specific representation of U_j in terms of two additive components. The individual's behavioral choice rule available to the analyst is as follows.

In words, the probability of an individual choosing alternative i is equal to the probability that the utility of alternative i is greater than (or equal to) the utility associated with alternative j after evaluating each and every alternative in the choice set of $j = 1, \ldots i, \ldots J$ alternatives.

In notation:

$$\text{Prob}_i = \text{Prob}\,(U_i \geq U_j)\ \forall\ j \in j = 1, \ldots, J; i \neq j) \tag{3.6}$$

For the analyst this is equivalent to:

$$\text{Prob}_i = \text{Prob}\,[(V_i + \varepsilon_i) \geq (V_j + \varepsilon_j)\ \forall\ j \in j = 1, \ldots, J; i \neq j] \tag{3.7}$$

Equation (3.7) contains information that is measurable by the analyst (i.e. V_j) through a set of observed attributes and information that is not directly measurable (i.e. ε_j). This equation is recognition that the analyst's lack of full information limits the analysis to a modified behavioral choice rule which states that "the information available to the analyst conditions the individual decision maker's utility maximization rule to be a *random utility maximization* rule."

It is useful to rearrange (3.7) to reflect this:

$$\text{Prob}_i = \text{Prob}\,[(\varepsilon_j - \varepsilon_i) \leq (V_i - V_j)\ \forall\ j \in j = 1, \ldots, J; i \neq j] \qquad (3.8)$$

In words, the probability of an individual choosing alternative i is equal to the probability that the difference in the unobserved sources of utility of alternative j *compared to* i is less than (or equal to) the difference in the observed sources of utility associated with alternative i compared to alternative j after evaluating each and every alternative in the choice set of $j = 1, \ldots i, \ldots J$ alternatives.

Randomness in the utility maximization rule comes about because we have to establish a way of handling the information in ε_j associated with each individual. These steps involve consideration of how we might account for the unobserved elements of the utility expressions associated with each alternative. After considerable reflection, we have decided to limit the derivation of the basic choice model to a few broad comments and to refer the curious beginner to chapter 3 of Louviere, Hensher, and Swait (2000, 37–47), where the step-by-step derivation is set out. What is important here is a recognition that the component of a utility expression associated with an individual and an alternative that is unobserved is treated as a random piece of information in the sense that we really have no idea what numerical value to assign to it. However to move forward we must impose some structure on it (what we might think of as a containment strategy), which we do by introducing a number of *assumptions*, some maintained and some testable. The maintained assumption is that each individual in a sampled population resides along a real (bounded) line and since we do not know where they are located, they are randomly assigned a location. The first testable assumption is that this real line has an allocation rule that is driven by a specific statistical distribution (e.g. a normal distribution). As a consequence the location of each individual, although randomly assigned, will ensure that the mapping takes a specific shape in utility space, typically with more individuals assigned to the central area of the distribution in contrast to the tails. The analyst can choose any distribution they wish although practice has tended to limit the set considered.

The distributions that have "survived" in choice analysis are those that have plausible behavioral properties and which lead to parsimonious forms of a practical choice model. In the beginning, this was a critical concern because of the problems of implementing such models and the ability of software developers to write code that would work. We have come a long way since these days (up to the late 1980s) and new methods have enabled the development of choice models with more complex "open forms" that have been successfully programmed. The 2002 release of NLOGIT 3.0 by Econometric Software, Inc., for example, delivers the opportunity for practitioners (including beginners) to estimate a large number of simple and complex choice models. We say more on this later.

Once a particular distribution of the random component has been selected, the analyst is well on their way to having all the necessary data to derive a choice model. A popular distribution in discrete choice analysis is the extreme value type 1 (EV1) distribution. The name is intriguing but before explaining it we should write out the form of this distribution in (3.9):

$$\text{Prob}\,(\varepsilon_j \leq \varepsilon) = \exp\,(-\exp - \varepsilon) \tag{3.9}$$

noting that Prob $[\varepsilon_j \leq (\varepsilon_i + V_i - V_j)]$ is equivalent to (3.9) except that in (3.9) we are attributing all information as unobserved, and "exp" is shorthand for the exponential function. Distributions are analytical constructs that we hope bear a good relationship to the role of such information in explaining actual choices. While we can never be totally sure we have got the "best" behavioral representation through a specific distribution, we do have statistical tests to provide some broad based clues (discussed later).

As an aside, the phrase "extreme value" arises relative to the normal distribution. The essential difference between the EV1 and normal distributions is in the tails of the distribution where the extreme values reside. With a small choice set such as two alternatives this may make little difference because the resulting differences in the choice probabilities between the normal and EV1 is usually negligible. When one has numerous alternatives, however, one gets many very small choice probabilities and it is here that differences between the distributions can be quite noticeable. For example a choice probability of 0.02 compared to 0.04 is significant, and when aggregated across a population can amount to sizeable differences in overall choice shares.

Returning to (3.9), the focus is on the unobserved component of a utility expression for a specific alternative (j). It is contrasted with the generically defined ε. As stated, (3.9) treats all information as unobserved and randomly distributed across an unknown distribution according to this specific distribution. But we know that some information is measured and hence observed in our language. Thus if we take this on board we can replace ε with the other information revealed in (3.8) that is additional to ε_j. This is $(\varepsilon_i + V_i - V_j)$. There will be an equivalent expression for each and every alternative in the choice set. In a formal derivation of a choice model (given in Louviere, Hensher, and Swait 2000, chapter 3) we recognize that utility expressions are relative constructs and so any derivation contrasts the utility expression of one alternative with another. Actually, the contrast is a little more restrictive than this due to the fact that we know only what alternative was chosen and by implication that all other alternatives were not chosen. Consequently, the most information typically available suggests a specification of the choice model that contrasts the utility expression of the chosen alternative with that of each of the non-chosen alternatives.

As an aside, we could establish additional information on the relative preferences for the non-chosen alternatives by asking for a ranking (or even rating) of each alternative. Choice analysis allows for choice responses that are more than simply choosing the most preferred. We limit this primer to the first preference choice since it is the most "popular" approach. It has some strong appeal in reflecting reality where we only ever observe an individual making a choice of one alternative and rejecting the others. Nevertheless there is useful information in a full or partial rank (or rate), and this should be recognized.

We are now ready to take the information available and integrate it into a setting where we recognize the distributional assumption associated with each ε_j. Before doing so, we have to decide what relationship will exist between the full set of ε_js. In an earlier section we had suggested that the IID assumption was an appropriate starting position for the derivation of the choice model because of its simplicity. While behaviorally restrictive it is nevertheless a convenient assumption to work with initially, opening up the opportunity to test less restrictive assumptions once you have got sufficient confidence in estimating and interpreting the outputs of a model based on the IID assumption.

Acceptance of this assumption enables us to treat each ε_j as independent (i.e. uncorrelated, so no off-diagonal terms) as well as identically distributed (i.e. the *j*th subscript can be removed). One more important task remains. We have given some structure to the unobserved influences through the EV1 distribution, and we have recognized the assignment of each sampled individual to this distribution associated with a specific alternative (given it is in their choice set). Importantly you will see that there are two unknowns when we contrast two alternatives, and in order to establish the relative values of the unknowns through some solution mechanism we have to impose a further restriction. This is referred to as *identification*. We achieve this here (assuming the IID condition) so there are only two elements to worry about – namely two variances – by fixing the value of one of the unknowns and solving for the other one that is unconstrained. A typical restriction to satisfy identification is to set the value to 1.0. Under IID, this is the same as setting the variance estimate of one of the unobserved indices (e.g. ε_1) to 1.0.

When we relax the IID condition to allow correlated alternatives, we will introduce additional elements of the unobserved effects through the covariance terms. Further challenges will exist in securing identification. We will not discuss this here but simply note that one cannot include all of the off-diagonal elements but must set at least one row of them to zero (namely impose a zero correlation condition). Which covariance terms to select is the choice of the analyst, reflecting which ones are thought to be close to zero in reality. This is testable.

Armed with all this information, we are ready to put the finishing touches to the derivation of a basic choice model. The ultimate aim is to establish a relationship between the observed attributes, the unobserved attributes, and the observed (or stated) choice outcome. The unknowns are the weights attached to the attributes (as presented in (3.2)) and the information in the random components now established in functional form through the EV1 and IID conditions. The next step in a formal derivation (left to Louviere, Hensher, and Swait, 2000, chapter 3) is to find a way of using the information contained in the ε_j set to establish the choice probabilities associated with each alternative. Since the EV1 distribution has an area (called its *density*) it seems appropriate to use integration methods in calculus to account for this information. What integration does is essentially to use the unknown information present across the entire space in which it is bounded (typically from $-\infty$ to ∞) and replace it with something that contributes to the measurement of the choice probability. The full derivation set out in Louviere, Hensher, and Swait (2000, chapter 3), results in the most important choice model known as the multinomial logit (MNL) model. It has become known as the "workhorse" of discrete choice analysis. The form of the model is given in (3.10). It is referred to as a closed-form model because applications do not require any further estimation:

$$\text{Prob}_i = \frac{\exp V_i}{\sum_{j=1}^{J} \exp V_j}; \quad j = 1, \ldots, i, \ldots, J \quad i \neq j \tag{3.10}$$

In words, (3.10) states that the probability of an individual choosing alternative i out of the set of J alternatives is equal to the ratio of the (exponential of the) observed utility index for alternative i to the sum of the exponentials of the observed utility indices for all J alternatives, including the ith alternative. V_i is defined in (3.2).

The MNL model form is the result of imposing the IID condition on the random components of the set of utility expressions. We are now ready to take this model and learn all about its capabilities, and in the process of implementing this model to understand its great empirical value as well as areas where it might benefit from some less restrictive assumptions. We always believe that this learning experience should be done in the setting of a case study. We are almost ready to introduce the case study (chapter 9) and then show you how the data are used in estimating a series of MNL models. At this juncture, it is important to state that all data preparation and model estimation is focused on the Limdep computer package (renamed as NLOGIT 3.0 for those using the discrete choice modeling features). All applications here use NLOGIT 3.0 (released in September 2003).

3.6 Concluding overview

This chapter has developed the main economic concepts that underpin the behavioral appeal of the discrete choice modeling paradigm. The major link between the microeconomic ideas and choice analysis is in the definition and representation of preferences and associated constraints on choice behavior. Constraints such as personal income impact on both the definition of an individual's choice set and on the role of specific attributes of alternatives in influencing the relative utility, and hence probability, of choosing an alternative. As such, the constraints should be interacted with attributes of alternatives if one believes that they impact on the influence of such attributes on choice outcomes. Including such constraints as independent influences (through the characteristics of individuals and other influences) recognizes that they are proxies for attributes of alternatives that are not observed and which would reside in the unobserved component of utility if not proxied by such explicitly modeled influences. This last point is important since it recognizes that all sources of utility are associated with attributes of alternatives and not characteristics of individuals.

In this chapter, we have spent a great deal of time in formally deriving the choice function and its demand equivalent. We have then taken such knowledge and used it in constructing a choice model, with the centerpiece being the utility (or preference) expression associated with each alternative. It is important to appreciate that what we have done in deriving a demand function is applicable to each alternative. Thus a choice model with four alternatives is essentially a set of four demand equations, complicated by the fact that not all sources of demand are observed. The relationships between the demand for each product (i.e. alternative) are specified through assumptions underlying the structure of the variance–covariance matrix. The IID condition provides the most restrictive assumption of interdependencies between alternatives.

We are now ready to look at the range of other tasks that need to be undertaken as part of the larger task of developing an empirical choice model, including relaxing the IID condition and estimating more complex, and hopefully more behaviorally realistic, discrete choice models.

4 Paradigms of choice data

Statistics: The only science that enables different experts using the same figures to draw different conclusions. (Evan Esar, 1899–1995)

4.1 Introduction

We noted in chapter 3 the existence of two sources of influences on choice behavior. We termed these influences *attributes* if they relate to the description of an alternative, and *characteristics* if they are related to an individual's prejudices (or tastes) represented by socio-economic variables and context influences such as the data collection strategy. These sources of influence are all essential to both the development and estimation of the basic choice model as they represent the constituent ingredients of the representative component of the utility function. It is these influences that we hope to attach weights to through some estimation process so as to develop an understanding of their relative importance on the decision-making process.

In order to estimate a model and derive the relative weights for the attributes, socio-demographic characteristics (SDC), and contextual influences, we require data. We write this chapter with the aim of introducing the issues surrounding choice data. Given the differences between attributes and SDC characteristics, you will see below that different data are required for each.

In chapter 1 we briefly introduced the concepts of stated preference (SP) and revealed preference (RP) data, the former often referred to as "stated choice data." In the choice literature, these two data paradigms are associated with the *attributes* of the alternatives. The collection of SDC data and data on contextual influences is not associated with any particular data paradigm within the literature, being collected via traditional survey means.

Given that SP and RP data paradigms are more likely to be new to the reader, while traditional survey methods are not, the major focus of this chapter is the discussion of SP and RP data. While not ignoring the issue of SDC and contextual influences, we advise the reader not familiar with the writing of questionnaires and other forms of survey instruments to consult other reference material that provides more coverage of the topic (for example see, among others, Aakar, Kumar, and Day 1998; Lehman, Gupta, and Steckel 1998; or Churchill 1999).

4.2 Data consistent with choice

The behavioral rules established in chapter 3 used to derive the basic choice model primarily relate to the concept of *utility*. Recall (3.1). Equation (3.1) suggests that for any given individual, there will exist an amount of utility for each alternative within the universal (but finite) set of alternatives, the amount of which is formed from the (preference) weights the individual decision maker places upon the attribute levels inherent for that alternative (observed or unobserved). Assuming the existence of four alternative modes of travel to choose from, we may rewrite (3.1) as

$$U_{car} = V_{car} + \varepsilon_{car} \tag{4.1a}$$

$$U_{bus} = V_{bus} + \varepsilon_{bus} \tag{4.1b}$$

$$U_{train} = V_{train} + \varepsilon_{train} \tag{4.1c}$$

$$U_{plane} = V_{plane} + \varepsilon_{plane} \tag{4.1d}$$

Each decision maker will derive an amount of utility for each of the alternatives within the universal (but finite) set of alternatives. This utility is likely to exist for every alternative even if the individual has not had occasion to sample one or more of the alternatives. In doing so, decision makers are likely to impose *perceptual beliefs* in revealing the attribute levels of non-experienced (or even rarely used) alternatives. This perceptual correspondence may transfer to the attribute levels of the experienced alternatives as well. For example, an individual who has never used a bus may hold the belief that the travel time for a given journey using a bus will be 40 minutes when in reality it is only 30 minutes. The same individual may also believe that the same journey will take 30 minutes when using a train when in fact the train trip will take 35 minutes. This belief about the travel time for the train alternative may prevail despite the decision maker having frequently used this mode of transport in the past.

Equations (4.1a)–(4.1d) suggest that the element of interest is utility. An implied assumption in choice analysis is that a decision maker will choose the alternative that provides her with the highest level of utility, provided there are no constraints to choice (e.g. income, availability, etc.). As such, what we desire is a *direct measure of utility*.

Given the abstract nature of utility to a decision maker, it makes no sense to ask them what their utility is for a particular alternative. We premise this statement by noting that currently no theory exists to guide us in establishing the best metric for representing utility. Indeed, economists refer to the unit of measure of utility as "*utils*". Consider asking decision makers how many utils they derived from driving to work!

Some have attempted to overcome this by using various response mechanisms that purport to map directly to utility space. The most common method is to use some form of ranking or rating of the alternatives. We discourage these approaches, for a number of reasons. First and foremost is that decision makers are not asked to make a choice (as they are in real settings), but rather to rank or rate the alternatives. At best, this provides the analyst with information on *preference*, not choice. We say "at best," as debate currently exists as to the appropriateness of the response mechanism employed. Take the case of rating. First, the scale mechanism must be arbitrarily chosen by the analyst (e.g. why a 10-point scale, why not a 100-point scale?). Secondly, individual decision makers are assumed to use the response scale in a cognitively similar fashion. To explain, assume that decision maker one has rated alternative i a 6 on a 10-point scale and decision maker two has rated the same alternative a 5. Does decision maker one prefer alternative i more than decision maker two? To answer this question requires that the analyst know what a 6 means to decision maker one and what a 5 means to decision maker two. It is not unforeseeable that, were we to map both decision makers' preferences for alternative i into utility space, that even though they provided different ratings, by attaching different cognitive meanings to the scales they would reside at the same location in utility space.

Data collected using ratings or ranking data also pose problems at the time of estimation. The most common form of estimation technique used to model this type of data are *regression analysis* where the rating or ranking is the dependent variable within the model. While this appears innocuous, a quick review of the properties of scale types will reveal that ratings may at best be assumed to be interval scaled but are more likely to be measured on an ordinal scale. Rankings are, by definition, ordinal scale measures. Using such data as the dependent variable in a regression violates the requirement that the dependent variable be continuous.

Estimation problems aside, even if one assumes a direct mapping from rating or rankings to utility space, preference does not necessarily translate to choice. As we have stated several times, constraints on the decision maker often prevent preference from becoming choice (perhaps this is why one author still drives a Volvo instead of a Porsche!). What is required is not preference data, but *choice data*.

Choice data are data collected on *choices made*. As such, the choices as observed are made within the constraints imposed upon individual decision makers. Further, the response mechanism for choice data are binary (i.e. 0 or 1). Either an alternative was chosen (1) or it was not chosen (0). We note this because such a response mechanism cannot by criticized as to the possibility of cognitively perceptual differences in response between decision makers. The choice of the car alternative is the same choice for decision maker one as it is for decision maker two.

As an aside, under the umbrella of choice response we can permit frequency data to indicate the number of times an alternative is chosen either at a single point in time or over a given period. Although we focus on a single 0, 1 choice response, frequency response represented by the absolute number of times each alternative is chosen or the proportion of all choices associated with each alternative are both permissible and can be accommodated in NLOGIT.

With choice data, we do not directly observe the utilities derived for every alternative for each decision maker. Rather we estimate them having witnessed the choices that were made. To do so, we introduce the assumption that within the constraints faced by a decision maker, the selected alternative will be the alternative that produces the highest level of utility (or the least amount of negative utility or disutility). At the level of the individual decision maker, the analyst obtains understanding as to what the most preferred alternative is. Among the non-chosen alternatives, the analyst knows only that they are less preferred to the chosen alternative. No information about the order of preference among the non-chosen alternatives is gained. However in the aggregate (i.e. over a number of decision makers and/or repeated observations for one decision maker) the analyst is able to collect enough information on preference formation to be able to proceed.

While the above is of interest, let us return to (4.1a)–(4.1d). These equations suggest that the analyst is required to obtain data on a number of different elements. Examination of the right-hand side of (4.1a)–(4.1d) suggests the necessity to collect information on the attribute levels of the alternatives as well as on the SDC of the decision makers (and perhaps even on the context in which the decision was made). The analyst may collect this information in a number of different ways. Ignoring SDC and contextual influences for the present, the analyst may elect to venture to the point of physical distribution (e.g. surveying on a bus or at a supermarket) and observe the *actual* attribute levels of each of the alternatives. Alternatively, the analyst may elect to obtain information on the attribute levels of the alternatives by asking decision makers operating within the market what they believe the levels to be. Thus on the one hand we have what might usefully be termed *authentic* real world data and on the other hand we have *perceptual* data.

Which type of data are best to use is a matter of debate. Authentic real world data on real attribute levels often produces "cleaner" data which is preferable for modeling purposes. Perceptual data, on the other hand, often produces data that has outliers which pose problems for the analyst at the time of estimation. That said, however, it is more likely that preference – and hence choice – will be the result of perceptual beliefs of attribute levels rather than the real levels as they appear. For example, if a decision maker believes that the travel time associated with a bus trip to work is 40 minutes then the choice of alternative will be premised on this belief, even if in reality the actual trip takes only 30 minutes.

Returning to (4.1a)–(4.1d), we note that we do not capture direct information on the utility amounts associated with each alternative (other than by obtaining information on which is the most preferred alternative). Indeed we estimate these utility levels from our model. Following our earlier logic, the response mechanism in a choice model is not utility but rather choice. Thus the analyst is required to obtain information as to which of the alternatives was observed to be chosen. Two approaches exist as to how the analyst may collect this data on choice (the right-hand side of our equations). These are the two data paradigms of RP and SP data collection.

As an aside, we relate the collection of RP and SP data to the collection of data on choice. While both paradigms suggest strategies of collecting information on the elements on the right-hand side of our utility equations, SP and RP data strictly relate to the collection of data on choice.

We are now ready to discuss the paradigms of RP and SP data collection. We begin with the RP data paradigm.

4.3 Revealed preference data

Revealed preference data (RP data) represents data collected on choices that are made in an actual market. As such, RP data represent events that have been observed to have *actually occurred*. Several possibilities exist as to how such data may be collected. First, the analyst may elect to observe a market and note the alternatives as chosen and non-chosen. Alternatively, some other (probably electronic) means may be available to record choices within a market (e.g. shopping center scanner panels or television meters). No matter how data are collected, the analyst must consider how data are to be collected on the attribute levels and SDC of the decision makers operating within the market. With regard to attribute levels, we noted two methods earlier, collecting actual data on the real attributes levels or asking decision makers what they perceive the attribute levels to be. With regard to SDC, if the analyst chooses to *observe* decision makers, then only simple information on SDC may be obtainable (e.g. gender and possibly an age range), which may or may not be significant to preference formation. Alternatively, a questionnaire survey of decision makers may yield more useful information.

Despite problems in how RP data are collected, the use of RP data provides the analyst with a number of possible advantages and disadvantages that should be considered before such data are collected. We present these below.

Real world representation (market equilibrium)

The collection of RP data represents the collection of data on *real life choices*. Given that the total realized demand for any good or service is the sum of the amount of times that a good or service was actually chosen in the marketplace, it follows that if RP data are collected on a representative sample of the population, we can in theory replicate the actual market shares for all the goods and services within that market. This "replication" is in effect a replication of the market "equilibrium."

Embodiment of constraints

Through the examination of real market data, the choices as made by individual decision makers are bound by the real constraints confronted by those same decision makers. That is, constraints that limit choices are necessarily a part of RP data. In contrast, such constraints are not necessarily limiting when one asks a decision maker what choice they would make given a hypothetical situation (as with SP data). Consider one such constraint, the income constraint. The old adage of someone having a "champaign taste on a beer income" has the very real world (read RP) consequence of potentially leading to a declaration of bankruptcy. However in the world of hypothetical situations (read "SP") one can afford to indulge a little without fear of such a consequence. We are, however, by no means limited to the single issue of budget constraints. Other issues such as accessibility to the good or service are also contained within RP data.

Moving away from the individual decision maker, we also must note that constraints exist on the market itself. Environmental and technological constraints impact on the choices we make within a market. While personal constraints affect individuals and thus impact unevenly across a market (e.g. a low income level may preclude the purchase of a Ferrari, a constraint not imposed upon the wealthy), market constraints impact upon all acting in that market more or less evenly (e.g. the removal from service of the Concorde means that no person may now travel from the United States to Europe in four hours, not even the wealthy). Once more, market-wide constraints are pre-existent in RP data.

Reliability and validity

Those familiar with surveys will immediately recognize that such data also provide the analyst with the properties of reliability and face validity. "Reliability" refers to the idea that with repeated measures of a choice – we will obtain similar results up to a sampling error (provided that representative samples are drawn in each of the repeated measures); "face validity" refers to the relationship between what was observed to be chosen and what actually was chosen.

Limitations on alternatives, attributes, and attribute levels

As RP data are by definition data collected on choices made in real markets, we are limited to collecting data only on currently existing alternatives within those markets. This will not be a problem if the market being studied has a stable market equilibrium without the possibility of *new entrants* coupled with no possibility of *innovative behavior*. *New entrants*, whether defined as new firms or new products/brands, equate to new alternatives within a market with possible impacts on choice behavior through competition. *Innovation*, whether from existing competitors or new entrants, suggests new attribute levels and possibly even new attributes being introduced to the market that may potentially impact upon choice behavior.

Thus if new market entrants appear or new innovations are introduced to the market, we will be required to collect further data so as to produce new models. As such, RP data provide little if any benefit to those who wish to predict market changes *a priori* to the introduction of new alternatives or innovations. Given research and development (R&D) costs and the probability of failure among new products, having an understanding of market equilibrium after a product's launch is likely to be of little benefit to the analyst.

As an aside, the definition of a new alternative is itself an interesting issue. Given that alternatives are essentially packages of attributes and associated levels (complicated often by attributes such as image) we might reasonably suggest that an alternative is new when its attribute profile differs significantly from that of an existing alternative. Determining what "differs significantly" means is the challenge. In general, we suggest that if attribute levels vary from levels observed for existing alternatives in ways that stretch outside the range observed in real markets for the existing alternative then there are good grounds for promoting a new alternative in the choice set. For example, high-speed rail is often unlike a conventional train or air mode since it is typically much faster than conventional train but slower than air, but much more expensive than conventional train and much less expensive than air.

Attribute-level invariance

Experience has shown that many markets provide limited variability in the levels of attributes we wish to use for modeling purposes. Before we divulge why this represents a problem for the analyst, let us discuss the reasons why this may be so. Possible reasons for attribute level invariance include (1) market structure, (2) lack of patent or copyright, (3) costs in changing the marketing mix, and (4) marketing strategies.

First, the market structure itself may be the cause. Basic economic theory suggests that in markets with perfect competition, the attributes of the goods and services offered are homogeneous. Secondly, in many markets, patents or copyrights are not often sought or granted, and hence given R&D costs, imitation is often a better strategy than innovation. Thirdly, examination of the "four Ps" of marketing – *price*, *product*, *place*, and *promotion* – suggest that for firms it is often easier and less costly to change prices than to change other aspects of the marketing mix (i.e. changing the product requires time and money in R&D, changing the place (the distribution channel) is also costly in terms of both time and money, as are changes to the promotional mix). Depending on the market, changes in price will often be met with similar changes in the price of goods or services offered by the competition, with the possible result being a price war. In such markets, the status quo is likely to prevail.

The first three possible reasons for attribute-level invariance described above suggest the existence of "real" attribute-level invariance within the market. Yet even if attribute-level invariance does not exist, consumers may behave as if it does. As marketers will tell you, "*reality often counts for little, perceptions count for everything.*" Accepting this view, marketers have adopted a psychological theory known as Just Noticeable Difference (JND) or alternatively as Weber's Law. In application, this theory suggests the existence of a *psychological threshold*, below which marketing mix changes will not be noticed. Identifying this threshold, marketers make subtle changes that are not perceptually identified by consumers. Data collected on perceptual data may not pick up changes in the marketing mix (the attributes) that have occurred.

Attribute-level invariance has implications for how RP data are collected. One possibility is for the analyst to collect RP data from the marketplace itself. The collection of such data does not provide for the decision maker perceptual inferences from which choice behavior is really made. Alternatively, RP data may be collected on information provided by decision makers operating within the market. In this case, what is really being collected is not the "*actual*" market data but rather the decision maker's "*perceptions*" of the actual market data.

Independent of the cause, attribute invariance also poses modeling problems for the analyst. The reason for this is that over a population there will exist a distribution of utility for each and every alternative. The purpose of undertaking a choice study is to explain why some individuals reside at one point on the distribution while others reside at other points along the same distribution. An attribute that takes on the same value for all alternatives cannot help explain why individuals reside at the point of the distribution that they do. The point to take away from this dialog is that we require variation in order to explain variation.

Non-chosen alternatives

Whether one collects information directly from the market (e.g. from scanner panel data) or from respondents operating within the market, we often fail to obtain information on the alternatives *not chosen*. Taking the example of asking decision makers operating within the market, we are required to ask about the attributes and attribute levels of the alternatives as observed within the market. If decision makers have had no experience of non-chosen alternatives, they may not be in a position to relate information on the attribute levels associated with those alternatives. We therefore are confined to collecting data solely on chosen alternatives.

As an aside, contemplate a further related problem. Consider the case of collecting data directly from the market. For example, where scanner panel data are collected, not only are data collected solely on the alternative purchased, but also no information is obtained on the SDC of the purchaser (unless collected as part of a separate study). Further, while we may know that a "*Reach*" toothbrush was purchased, we collect no information on the attributes of the toothbrush itself (again information must be obtained at a separate time). What is therefore required is that the analyst should conduct research at each of the physical distribution centers.

Correlation

Experience has shown that a considerable proportion of markets tend to exhibit significant levels of attribute correlations which in turn poses problems for model estimation. For example, consider so called *price–quality trade-offs* which suggest that "higher"-quality goods and services are higher priced (a positive correlation). A further example exists in the automobile market whereby higher-priced vehicles come standard with airbags, an item not associated with lower-priced vehicles. In such instances, certain attributes and attribute levels may become associated with certain types of goods or service, often categorized using price as a heuristic.

Cost

We will finish our discussion on RP data with one further point of consideration. Collection of RP data can be costly, in terms of both time and money – perhaps prohibitively so depending upon how the analyst chooses to collect the data. Given the time and cost in collecting such data, the analyst may be tempted to cut corners. Such temptation should be avoided at all costs as at the end of the day the models we produce are only as good as the data we collect.

4.3.1 Choice-based sampling

At this point, we deviate from our discussion and consider the concept of choice-based sampling (CBS) since it is a popular way of capturing attribute variability and sufficient observations on each alternative within RP settings. CBS involves the analyst specifically selecting decision makers such that across all those sampled, all alternatives were observed to have been chosen by a significant proportion of sampled decision makers. CBS usually involves the analyst disproportionately over-sampling, relative to the market share, decision makers whose choices were for less popular alternatives and under-sampling, relative to the market share, from alternatives that are more popularly selected across the sampled population. As a way of clarification, assume that less than 1 percent of the population ride pushbikes to work, while 60 percent drive. Taking a representative sample of 400 commuters, we would expect to sample less than 4 pushbike riders but 240 drivers. Clearly we capture more information on car drivers than we do on pushbike riders. To overcome this we over-sample pushbike riders and under-sample car drivers.

As an aside, CBS applies to RP data only and has nothing to do with SP data. SP data, as we will see, requires that decision makers are presented with a number of hypothetical scenarios and asked, for each scenario, which alternative they would choose given the alternatives as they are described. The scenarios are assigned in a pre-arranged manner suggesting that the analyst has no means to force a decision maker to select a specific alternative. As such, one cannot perform CBS on SP data.

For the example above, the true mode shares are likely to be such that the numbers observed to travel by car greatly outnumber those who travel by other means. Using CBS, we may have elected to sample 50 decision makers observed to have selected each of the alternative modes of travel (i.e. 50 car drivers, 50 bus passengers, etc.). As such, CBS is not representative sampling and hence we can no longer aggregate RP data to estimate market shares accurately. For example, assuming we sample as suggested above, the sample market shares for each alternative will be 25 percent each. Clearly, this outcome is unrealistic. We therefore require some method to regain the ability to estimate accurately market shares.

Fortunately, a solution exists. This solution requires the choice model outcomes be weighted to correspond to the actual market shares. The analyst is required to have *a priori* knowledge as to what the actual (i.e. population) market shares are. Independent of where the information on actual market shares are sourced, the analyst is able to weight the choice outcomes using NLOGIT. We show how to weight choice data in chapter 11.

4.4 Stated preference (or stated choice) data

We have seen that RP data offer a number of advantages to the analyst as well as a number of disadvantages. If life were kind, then the alternative paradigm, that of SP data, would offer only advantages, thus making the choice of data paradigm to employ easy. Unfortunately, life is not so kind. In this section, we detail the major strengths and weaknesses of SP data.

Hypothetical scenarios

Let us begin by restating that SP data represents choices "made" or stated given hypothetical situations. We noted earlier that this may lead to situations in which personal constraints are not considered as constraints at the time of choice. This will particularly be the case if the SP task is not taken seriously by subjects ("Sure, I'll take two Ferraris"). The task of the analyst is therefore to make the hypothetical scenarios as realistic as possible.

The hypothetical nature of SP data also offers the analyst a significant benefit over RP data. We noted in section 4.3 that RP data are constrained in terms of being able to collect information solely on currently existing alternatives. As such, the alternatives, the attributes, and the attribute levels are fixed in terms of what is currently on offer. Since predicting outside of the ranges of data provides notoriously unreliable estimates from most statistical models, what we require is an approach that will either allow for accurate model predictions outside of the existing data range or alternatively an approach that allows for the

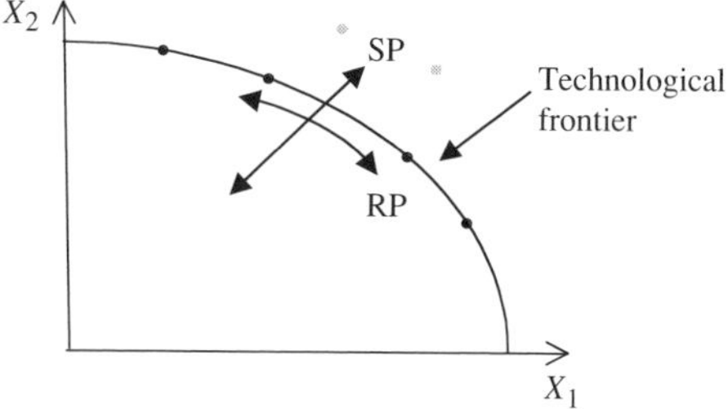

Figure 4.1 The technological frontier and the roles of RP and SP data

collection of data outside of these ranges which may be used with conventional modeling techniques for predictive purposes.

Figure 4.1 is a reproduction of figure 2.1 from Louviere, Hensher, and Swait (2000, 23). This figure illustrates clearly our discussion above. RP data represent information up to the extent of the technological frontier as it currently exists. SP data allow us to explore issues outside of the technological frontier.

We can extend the above discourse to products that are not traded in real markets. Consider the example of environmental pollutants such as aerosol pollutants from a factory. How much are people willing to pay for clean air? Unless there exists a government tax on air pollutants, there will be no data on how much individuals are willing to pay. In such instances, RP data may not be available. The hypothetical nature of SP data provides one approach to gather the missing data required.

Mapping to utility

With SP experiments, the analyst must specify the attributes and attribute levels in advance. This allows the analyst to manipulate the relationship between attributes and investigate specific hypotheses about the functional form that utility should take (e.g. linear additive ($X_1 + X_2$) or interactive (X_1X_2)). Continuing from section 4.3, there now exists the ability to map utility functions from previously non-existing alternatives and test the functional form of these.

4.5 Further comparisons

From a practical standpoint, two further differences become apparent between the two data paradigms. First, as noted, with SP experiments the attribute levels are pre-specified by the analyst and given to the decision maker by the researcher as determined by some statistical design (discussed in detail in chapter 5). The onus is therefore on the analyst to identify the salient attributes and attribute levels which determine choice behavior within the population.

With RP data, the levels of the attributes are provided by either the decision makers themselves or directly from the market, such as in the case of scanner panel data. Unless open-ended questions are used when collecting data from decision makers, the attributes must also be known *a priori*. Nevertheless, the attribute levels need not be known in advance as this is the information that the analyst is seeking to gather.

The second difference lies in the number of observations obtained from the two methods. With SP data, respondents are usually shown multiple choice sets, each of which has different attribute levels (and possibly even different alternatives present, depending on the design). Thus for each respondent, we gain multiple observations over the number of choice sets completed. RP data, however, usually provide the analyst with information about the single choice that was made. We say "usually," as this depends on the data collection methodology employed by the analyst. This will be the case if RP data are collected using a cross-sectional survey. If panel data are collected then information on multiple choices will be gathered from the same individuals, however at considerable cost.

4.6 Why not use both RP and SP data?

A quick scan of the preceding paragraphs will show that the advantages of RP data appear, in the main, to mirror the disadvantages of SP data and vice versa. The logical question from this observation is whether the analyst can in some way combine the two data sources so as to promote the strengths of both and minimize the disadvantages of each. The answer to this question is, fortunately, "yes." Indeed, we are able to combine any number of data sources including RP and SP data sources, or combinations thereof. We discuss this further in chapter 14.

4.7 Socio-demographic characteristic data

What we have not yet mentioned is how to include the SDC of the decision maker. Assuming that SDC are important sources of explanation, (3.2) then becomes

$$\begin{aligned} V_i = \beta_{0iq} + \beta_{1iq} f(X_{1iq}) + \beta_{2iq} f(X_{2iq}) + \cdots + \beta_{Kiq} f(X_{Kiq}) + \beta_{1qi} f(S_{1q}) \\ + \beta_{2qi} f(S_{2q}) + \cdots + \beta_{nqi} f(S_{nq}) \qquad (4.2) \end{aligned}$$

Where β_{nqi} is the weight for the nth SDC for alternative i for person q and S_{nq} is some measurement of the associated nth SDC for person q. Since a person's SDC are invariant across alternatives, the subscript i drops from this part of the equation.

What (4.2) shows is that while SDC are invariant across alternatives, their impact (weight) may be a significant predictor for some alternatives but not for others. The observant reader will notice another subtle change to (4.2). We have added a subscript q to the attributes and attribute weights. This simple addition suggests that the weights for attributes may vary from individual to individual. This gives rise to the interesting notion of modeling segments within the population, either through their SDC or through their reactions to changes in the attribute levels. We will discuss this in more detail later.

As an aside, even if SDC are not thought to be important in utility/preference formation, collecting such information is often a worthwhile exercise. While this may place an additional burden on respondents through an increase in survey length, such data can often be useful in checking whether the sample collected matches known characteristics of the population of interest. As an example, assume that we have prior knowledge that the age group of the population of interest is 25–40-year-olds. Collecting information on respondent age, in this example, will allow us to confirm that we have indeed sampled from the correct population.

The reader interested in learning more on the collection of such data are referred to any number of social science texts that provide coverage on this topic. Indeed, there exists a plethora of such texts in the area of marketing research, a number of which we mentioned in the introduction to this chapter.

5 Processes in setting up stated choice experiments

As far as the laws of mathematics refer to reality, they are not certain, and as far as they are certain, they do not refer to reality. (Albert Einstein, 1879–1955)

5.1 Introduction

We focus in this chapter on explaining the processes used in generating an experimental design, although we warn that the reader will not become an expert after having completed this chapter. Like choice modeling, experimental design is very much owned by the specialist. We have decided to concentrate on the practical aspect of experimental design, as conversations with both colleagues and students over many years have confirmed that it is perhaps this topic which is the least understood subject matter related to choice modeling. We refer those readers interested in the theoretical aspects of experimental design to other texts such as Louviere, Hensher, and Swait (2000) which provide a more detailed treatment of the topic.

If at the end of this chapter the reader can understand the jargon used in the experimental design literature and generate simple experimental designs then we will be satisfied that we have achieved our aim.

5.2 What is an experimental design?

The foundation for any SP experiment is an *experimental design*. An *experiment* defined in scientific terms involves the observation of the effect upon one variable, a *response variable*, given the manipulation of the levels of one or more other variables. The manipulation of the levels of the variables does not occur in a haphazard manner. Rather we turn to a specialized form of statistics to determine what manipulations to make and when to make them. Thus we can say that the manipulations occur by design. Hence the name "experimental design"!

Many different fields have developed a rich literature related to the concept of experimental design. Unfortunately, they have done so with little broad consultation. The result has been a diverse use of terminology that has contributed only to the mystique of this topic. For example, the manipulated variables mentioned in the previous paragraph have alternatively been termed *factors*, independent variables, explanatory variables, and attributes (when they are related to the characteristics of a good or service), depending upon which literature one reads. The levels have been called *factor levels*, attribute levels, or simply just levels. Given our earlier distinction between attributes and socio-demographic characteristics (SDC), we have chosen to continue with the terms *attribute* and *attribute levels*. We do so noting that the experimental designs we discuss throughout this book involve the manipulation of the levels of goods and services only.

We also note that much of the literature refers to each individual attribute level as a *treatment*. Combinations of attributes, each with unique levels is called a *treatment combination*. Treatment combinations thus describe the profile of the alternatives within the choice set. Again, different literatures have developed their own terminology – for example, marketing, which refers to treatment combinations as *profiles*. We will use the terms "treatment" and "treatment combination" throughout. The language associated with the field of experimental design can become quite complicated, quickly. For this reason, we have included a glossary at the end of the book (p. 696) that you may refer to at any stage of your reading.

Figure 5.1 summarizes the process used to generate stated preference experiments. This process begins with a refinement of the problem, to ensure that the analyst has an acute understanding of what the research project hopes to achieve by the time of completion.

Once the problem is well understood, the analyst is required to *identify and refine the stimuli* to be used within the experiment. It is at this stage of the research that the analyst decides upon the list of alternatives, attributes and attribute levels to be used. This refinement may result in further scrutiny of the problem definition, and as a result a return to the problem refinement stage of the process. Moving from stimuli refinement, the analyst must now make several decisions as to the statistical properties that will be allied with the final design.

As an aside, the first two stages of the process consist of refining the analyst's understanding of behavioral aspects of the problem as they relate to decision makers. It is hoped that this understanding of behavioral impacts will regulate the decision process of the analyst at the time of considering the statistical properties of the design. Often, however, statistical considerations must take precedence. Statistically inefficient designs, designs which are unwieldy in size, or possibly even the non-availability of a design that fits the behavioral requirements established in the earlier stages, may trigger a return to the first two stages of the design process.

Provided that the analyst is sufficiently happy to continue at this point, the experimental design may be generated. While it is preferable to generate such designs from first principles, such a derivation requires expert knowledge. For the beginner, we note that several statistical packages are capable of generating simple experimental designs that may be of use (e.g. SPSS, Minitab and SAS). Following the generation of the experimental design, the analyst must allocate the attributes selected in stage 2 to specific columns of the design. Again, a return to previous stages of the design process may be

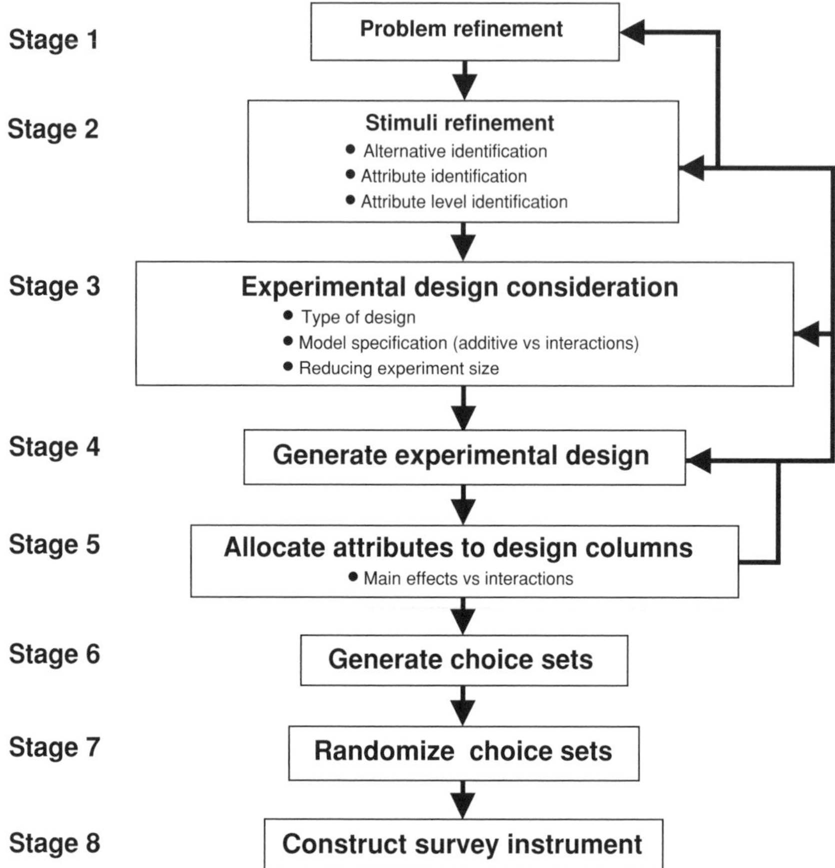

Figure 5.1 The experimental design process

necessary if the design properties do not meet the criteria established at earlier stages of the process.

Once the attributes have been allocated to columns within the design, the analyst manipulates the design to produce the response stimuli. While several forms of response stimuli are available to the analyst, we concentrate in this primer on only one type, that of *choice*. Thus, stage 6 of the design process sees the analyst construct choice sets that will be used in the survey instrument (e.g. a questionnaire). To overcome possible biases from order effects, the order of appearance of these choice sets are randomized across questionnaires. As such, several questionnaire versions are created for each single choice experiment undertaken. The final stage of the experimental design process is to construct the survey, by inserting the choice sets as appropriate into the different versions and inserting any other questions that the analyst may deem necessary to answer the original research problem (such as questions on RP data or SDC).

The remainder of this chapter provides a more in-depth examination of stages 1–5 as described above. The following chapter deals specifically with issues related to stages 6–8 of this process, which specifically relate to questionnaire construction.

5.2.1 Stage 1: problem definition refinement

Let us continue our discussion on experimental design through the use of an example. Rather than use the case study mentioned previously, the design for which is extremely complicated (as will be shown in chapter 9) let us introduce a simple hypothetical example that will demonstrate how the specialist (or at least the authors) go about deriving experimental designs for choice experiments. Consider an example whereby an analyst has been approached by an organization to study inter-city transport demand between two interior cities. The first stage in an analyst's journey towards deriving an SP choice experiment is to refine their understanding of the problem being studied. The analyst begins by asking the question: "Why is this research being undertaken?" By defining the problem clearly from the outset, the questions that "need" to be asked may be determined, as well as irrelevant questions that can be avoided.

Let us assume that the organization that approached our analyst wishes to estimate mode share changes given the introduction of a new alternative means of travel between the two cities. With such a brief, the analyst may ask several questions:

- What are the existing modal alternatives available?
- What are their attributes?
- What determinants drive demand for travel between the two cities?
- Who are travelers?
- Are travel patterns consistent over time or are they seasonal?

Many more *research questions* exist that the analyst may wish to ask. Through asking questions such as those mentioned above, the analyst has begun to refine their understanding of the problem.

As an aside, we note that at this stage of research, the analyst should not be wed to any particular methodological approach to answer the research questions. Rather the questions the analyst arrives at from the problem refinement process should decide the approach to be taken. Hence the approach does not decide which questions should be asked.

As a further aside, we note that, given the possibility of deriving several possible research questions from a single research problem, the analyst may be required to employ several research approaches to satisfactorily resolve the research problem.

One benefit of establishing research questions is that they aid in *hypothesis generation*. The generation of hypotheses hones even further the questions that the analyst may be required to ask of the population under study. For example, the analyst may hypothesize that one of the determining factors affecting modal choice in traveling between the two cities of interest is the conditions of the roads between the two cities. For example, poorly maintained roads may result in higher patronage of modes that do not rely on the road system (i.e. trains or aircraft). In setting up such hypotheses, the analyst begins to build up the types of questions that need to be asked of the population of travellers. For the above example, without asking questions related to the road conditions experienced and without attempting to obtain information as to the impacts of such conditions upon mode choice, this hypothesis will remain just that, a hypothesis.

Only once the research problem has been properly refined should the analyst proceed. We will assume that the analyst has garnered a sufficient understanding of the problem to meaningfully proceed. We will further assume that given the necessity to estimate modal market shares in the presence of a new modal alternative, the analyst has decided upon the use of a stated preference (SP) experiment. Proceeding, the next stage of the design process is the refinement of the stimuli to be used in the experimental design.

5.2.2 Stage 2: stimuli refinement

5.2.2.1 Refining the list of alternatives

The next stage of the experimental design process is *stimuli refinement*. Beginning with alternative identification and refinement, we now have a two-stage process. The first stage involves defining the universal but finite list of alternatives available to decision makers within the context being studied. In defining such a list, one must identify each and every possible alternative (even if a number of alternatives are available to only a small sub-set of the total number of decision makers) in order to meet the global utility maximizing rule first introduced in chapter 3. We recall that this rule states that failure to identify all alternatives produces a constraint, a threshold on the utility maximizing outcome.

In deriving the universal but finite list of alternatives it is suggested that the analyst expend a considerable level of effort. Secondary data searches, in-depth interviews, and focus groups may aid in alternative identification. Often attending the location at which the decision is to take place can also prove insightful.

Stage 2 involves the culling of alternatives from the list. While this breaks with the global utility maximizing rule, for studies that have identified large numbers of alternatives the analyst may be left with little choice but to cull alternatives in order to reach a manageable number to study. We note several ways to reduce the number of alternatives to be used within a study. First, the analyst may assign a randomly sampled number of alternatives taken from the universal but finite list of alternatives to each decision maker (plus the chosen). Hence, each decision maker is presented with a different sub-set of alternatives. Thus, while in the aggregate (provided enough decision makers are surveyed) the entire population of alternatives may be studied, each individual decision maker views a reduced set of alternatives within their given choice set. While such an approach appears more appealing than simply removing alternatives from all decision makers' choice sets, the experimental designs for such studies tend to be quite large and extremely complex. This process, however, under the strict condition of IID (see chapter 3), does not violate the global utility maximisation assumption. When we deviate from IID, the global utility maximisation assumption is violated.

The second approach to reducing the alternatives is to exclude "insignificant" alternatives. The problem here is that the analyst is required to make the somewhat subjective decision as to what alternatives are to be considered "insignificant" and therefore removed from the study. However in making such a decision, the analyst is placing more weight on practical, as opposed to theoretical, considerations. A third approach (one that we will explore in more detail later) is to use experiments that do not name the alternatives (i.e. the analyst defines *generic* or *unlabeled* alternatives).

If the universal, but finite, list of alternatives is relatively small (typically up to 10 alternatives although we have often studied the choice amongst 20 alternatives), the analyst may decide not to reject alternatives from the choice analysis at all. We end this discussion by stating that the analyst should be guided in their decision by the research problem in determining how best to proceed.

5.2.2.2 Refining the list of attributes and attribute levels

Having identified the list of alternatives to be studied, the analyst must now determine the attributes and *attribute levels* for those alternatives. This is not an easy task. First, we note that each alternative may incorporate a mix of common as well as different attributes and even if two alternatives have similar attributes, the levels of those attributes may differ from alternative to alternative. For example, in selecting between two modes of transport for a trip to work, consider the attributes which result in preference formation if those two transport modes are train and automobile. In looking at the train alternative, decision makers are likely to examine such attributes as frequency of service, waiting times (which may incorporate time spent waiting at the station and time taken walking to the station), and fares. None of these attributes is associated with driving a car to work. Instead, decision makers are likely to consider such car-related attributes as fuel, toll, and parking costs. Both modes do share some attributes that decision makers are likely to consider. For example, departure time from home, arrival time at work, and comfort. Yet despite these attributes being shared by both alternatives, the levels decision makers cognitively associate with each alternative are likely to be different. There is no need for the decision maker to travel to the station if they choose to travel by car, and hence they are likely to be able to leave home later if this mode of transport is selected (assuming favorable traffic conditions). The levels one attaches to comfort may differ across the alternatives. Indeed we invite the reader to consider what the attribute "comfort" means in the context of traveling to work either by train or by car. A discussion of the meaning of comfort is an excellent group discussion theme. It reveals the ambiguities in meaning and measurement of many attributes one may wish to use as part of a choice study.

Continuing with the example of "comfort," interesting questions are raised as to how the analyst is to communicate attributes and attribute levels to decision makers (recalling that in SP tasks the analyst relates the attributes and attribute levels to respondents). What does the word "comfort" really mean and does it mean the same thing to all decision makers? In the context of a train trip, does "comfort" refer to the softness of the seats aboard the train? Or could "comfort" relate to the number of other patrons aboard which affects the personal space available for all on board. Alternatively, could "comfort" refer to the temperature or ambience aboard the train? Or is it possible that decision makers perceive "comfort" to be some combination of all of the above, or perhaps even none of the above, but rather some other aspect that we have missed such as getting a seat? And what does "comfort" refer to in the context of a car trip?

As an aside, the consequences of attribute ambiguity may not be apparent at first. We note that what the analyst has done by inclusion of an ambiguous attribute is more than likely add to the unobserved variance in choice between the alternatives without adding to their ability to explain any of the new increase in variation observed. Further, looking ahead, consider how the analyst may use such attributes after model estimation. Assuming that the attribute is statistically significant for the train alternative, what recommendations can the analyst make? The analyst may recommend improving comfort aboard trains; however, questions remain as to how the organization responsible for the running of the trains may proceed. What aspects of comfort should be improved? Will the specific improvements result in persuading all decision makers to switch modes, or just those who perceive comfort as relating to those areas in which improvements were made? Failure to correctly express attribute descriptors results in lost time and money for all parties.

Earlier, we hinted at the solution to attribute ambiguity, although we did not mention it at the time. Returning to waiting time, we noted different components of travel time that may be important to how preferences are formed. Decision makers may attach a different importance weight (or marginal utility) to time spent walking to a station than they do to time spent waiting at the station itself. Walking to the station, it is unlikely that they will be able to drink a coffee and read the newspaper (unless they walk slowly). Waiting at the station, these actions become relatively easy, although waiting may be monotonous compared to walking. Or consider how decision makers perceive time spent while in (1) heavily congested (but still moving) traffic, versus (2) heavily congested traffic that frequently requires stopping, versus (3) free-flowing traffic conditions. Can the analyst attach a single meaning to "travel time" that captures the importance of "travel time" under all three conditions, or are separate weights required? If one believes the answer is that separate weights are required, then the analyst is required to break the attribute into unambiguous components that are well understood by decision makers.

When identifying attributes to be used in an experiment, the analyst must consider the concept of *inter-attribute correlation*. Despite the use of the word "correlation," inter-attribute correlation is not a statistical concept. Rather, inter-attribute correlation refers to the cognitive perceptions decision makers bind to the attribute descriptions provided. As we will show later, an experimental design may be statistically uncorrelated (i.e. orthogonal) in terms of the design used but correlated perceptually in terms of the attributes employed. For example, consider the frequently noted price–quality heuristic often employed by decision makers. This heuristic suggests that decision makers act as if higher-priced alternatives display higher levels of quality (however "quality" is defined). That is, *price acts as a proxy for quality*. Thus, while we may generate an experimental design that allows for the independent estimation of importance weights for price and quality, decision makers may not necessarily treat these attributes as being independent. While we may test for this at the time of estimation, dependent upon the characteristics of the design used, the problem remains that inter-attribute correlation may result in cognitively unacceptable combinations of attributes within the design. Assuming a price–quality heuristic, how will decision makers react to a high-price, low-quality alternative? One possible result of such combinations is that they will stop taking the experiment seriously, thus biasing the results. Design strategies exist to overcome the problem of inter-attribute correlations, such as nested designs; however, implementing such designs may prove beyond the beginner (nevertheless we discuss the nesting of attributes in appendix 5A, p. 154). In such cases, we suggest that the beginner identify attributes that may act as proxies for other attributes and select and use the most appropriate attribute for the study.

Having identified the attributes to be used in the experiment, the analyst must now derive *attribute levels* and *attribute-level labels*. We define "attribute levels" as the levels assigned to an attribute as part of the experimental design process. These are represented by numbers which will have meaning to the analyst but not to the decision maker being surveyed. "Attribute-level labels" on the other hand are assigned by the analyst and are related to the experimental design only insofar as the number of attribute-level labels must equal the number of attribute levels for a given attribute. Attribute-level labels are the narrative assigned to each attribute level that will (if the experiment is designed correctly) provide meaning to the decision maker. Attribute-level labels may be represented as numbers (i.e. quantitative attributes such as travel time may have attribute-level labels of "10 minutes," "20 minutes," etc.) or as words (i.e. qualitative attributes such as color may have attribute-level labels of "green" and "black").

The identification and refinement of the attribute levels and attribute-level labels to be used in an experiment is not an easy task, requiring several important decisions to be made by the analyst. The first decision is how many attribute levels to assign to each attribute, noting that the number of levels does not have to be the same for each attribute. Let us consider the attribute "travel time" for a single alternative. For any given decision maker, there will exist for this attribute different quantities of utility associated with the various levels that may be taken. That is, the utility for 5 minutes of travel time is likely to be different to the utility attached to 10 minutes of travel time. Is the utility attached to 5 minutes of travel time likely to be different to the utility attached to 5 minutes and 10 seconds of travel time? Each "possible" attribute level may be mapped to a point in utility space. The more levels we measure of an attribute, the more information (and hopefully accuracy) we capture in utility space.

Figure 5.2 illustrates this point. Figure 5.2 shows, in utility space, the level of utility derived from a single attribute at varying levels. The utility brought about by the levels of a single attribute has been referred to as *part-worth* utility in some literatures such

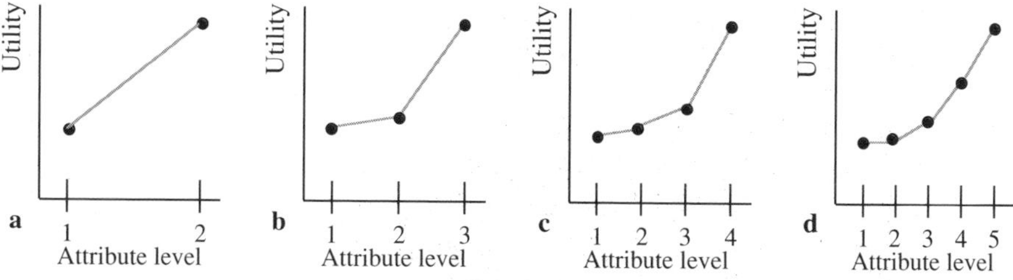

Figure 5.2 Mapping part-worth utility

as marketing or *marginal utility* in others. As we move from figure 5.2a to 5.2d we note the analyst's ability to detect more complex utility relationships as more levels (and hence more observations) are added. Indeed, starting with figure 5.2a, the analyst would be forced to conclude that the utility relationship for the attribute is linear given an change in the attribute level from level 1 to level 2. Examination of figure 5.2b in which a third attribute level is added suggests a non-linear relationship in terms of utility over the range of the attributes levels. This relationship would go undetected if only two attribute levels been used. Figures 5.2c and 5.2d suggest that had only three levels been used, the analyst still would not have a true understanding of the real relationship that exists (although, three attribute levels would suffice to provide knowledge of a good approximation of the true underlying utility function).

Ultimately we would like to observe the level of satisfaction at each point in utility space by taking observations for each level of an attribute. As we will see later, this is not always possible. The analyst may thus be forced to compromise in terms of the number of attribute levels to use. Deciding on the number of attribute levels to assign is a complex issue relating to the number of observations in utility space one wishes to obtain. A separate, but no less important, issue is how to identify the *extreme ranges* (sometimes referred to as the *end-points*) of the attribute levels to use.

The analyst is best able to identify the attribute-level label extremes by examining the experiences related to that attribute of the decision makers being studied. Returning to the example of travel time for a single alternative, a process consisting of a secondary data search combined with focus groups may have identified that decision makers experience travel times varying from 11 hours to 15 hours for travel between two cities. The analyst may use these experiences to derive the extremes of the attribute-level labels to be used in their experiment. However, rather than use these (observed) levels, the analyst should consider using values outside of the identified range. We suggest this for modeling purposes. It is well known that statistical models generally predict poorly outside of the range of data used for model estimation. Assume that 11 hours and 15 hours represent the extremes of the travel times used to estimate a model. If conditions change such that journeys now take much less than 11 hours or longer than 15 hours, any predictions from the model for the new conditions should be treated with caution.

Selecting attribute-level labels outside of conditions experienced, however, must be done with care. This is because the selected levels must be such that decision makers may reasonably believe them to be feasible and the analyst has confidence in the shape of the utility expression outside of the empirically identified domain. Taking the car alternative, for example, if trip lengths are currently on average around 11–15 hours, presenting decision makers with a hypothetical car trip of 8 hours is likely to have a detrimental effect on how seriously the decision maker takes the SP task.

As an aside, while we have concentrated on a quantitative example (see appendix 5B for further discussion on the assignment of attribute-level labels to quantitative attributes) we note that the above holds for qualitative attributes as well. We make a distinction between nominal and ordinal scale qualitative attributes. A *nominal* qualitative attribute may be one such as the color used for the bus alternative, where no natural order exists between the levels assumed. Selecting attribute levels to use for such attributes involves in-depth study as to what levels are likely to result in changes to preference (e.g. should the analyst use as levels the colors blue, or red, or green?). Ordinal qualitative attributes assume that some natural order exists amongst the levels. Taking the bus alternative as an example once more, the demeanor of the bus driver may be a significant attribute in preference formation for this alternative. Demeanor may be measured on some non-quantitative continuum ranging from "grumpy" to "gregarious," where "gregarious" is naturally rated higher than "grumpy." Assigning attribute-level labels to points between these extremes is a tedious task requiring much work for the number of descriptive labels which may exist between them.

To conclude, we note the existence of the axiom "garbage in, garbage out." The meaning of this axiom is quite simple. If a computer programmer enters invalid data into a system, the resulting output produced will also be invalid. Although originating in computer programming, the axiom applies equally well to other systems, including systems dealing with decision making. The point to take away from this is that the analyst is well advised to spend as much time as possible identifying and refining the lists of *alternatives*, *attributes*, *attribute levels*, and *attribute-level labels* to be used before proceeding to the formal design of the experiment.

5.2.3 Stage 3: experimental design considerations

Having identified the alternatives, attributes, the number of attribute levels, and the attribute-level labels, the analyst must now make decisions as to the *design* to be used. Let us reiterate from the outset that it is best if the analyst's understanding of the behavioral impacts regulate the decision process at the time of considering the statistical characteristics of the design. While this represents the best outcome, you will find that the designs available will often constrain the behavior(s) that the analyst is able to explore.

That said, a number of different classes of designs are available to the analyst. To explore each class of design here is impossible. We therefore choose to discuss the most common designs that the reader may wish to make use of in the future. We begin with the most general class of design available, the full factorial design.

We define a *full factorial design* as a design in which all possible treatment combinations are enumerated. To demonstrate, we return to our earlier example. Assume that through a process of secondary data search and focus groups our analyst identifies two salient attributes, comfort and travel time. For the time being we will assume the existence of only one alternative. During the preliminary research phase, relevant ranges of the attributes are also obtained. Those interviewed suggest three relevant levels for the "comfort" attribute. For convenience we designate these, low, medium, and high. Typical ranges for the "travel time" attribute lead our analyst to propose the use of three levels, 10 hours, 12 hours, and 14 hours. A full factorial design is a design in which all possible combinations of the attribute alternatives are used. We show these combinations in table 5.1.

Rather than write out the combinations as in table 5.1, the experimental design literature has created a coding format that may be used to represent the possible combinations. This coding format assigns a unique number to each attribute level, beginning with 0, then 1 and proceeding to L–1, where L is the number of levels for that attribute. Thus given 3 levels

Table 5.1. *Full factorial design*

Treatment combination	*Comfort*	*Travel time* h(hours)
1	Low	10
2	Low	12
3	Low	14
4	Medium	10
5	Medium	12
6	Medium	14
7	High	10
8	High	12
9	High	14

Table 5.2. *Full factorial design coding*

Treatment combination	*Comfort*	*Travel time*
1	0	0
2	0	1
3	0	2
4	1	0
5	1	1
6	1	2
7	2	0
8	2	1
9	2	2

the coding would be 0, 1, and 2. For attributes with 4 levels the coding used would be 0, 1, 2, and 3. Using this coding scheme, table 5.1 becomes table 5.2.

We could use any coding that allows for a unique mapping between the level and the assigned value. A useful alternative to the coding structure demonstrated in table 5.2 is known as *orthogonal coding*. Orthogonal coding uses values for codes which, when summed over any given *column* (not row), equals 0. To achieve this effect we code an attribute such that when we assign one level a positive value, we assign a second level the same value, only negative. This works in the case where we have an even number of levels. In the case of odd numbers of levels, the median level is assigned the value 0. For example, in the case of a two-level attribute, we assign the values of 1 and −1 for the two levels. For a three-level attribute we assign the values −1, 0, and 1.

As an aside, convention suggests that we use only odd numbers in such coding (i.e. −3, −1, 0, 1, 3, etc.). Table 5.3 shows the orthogonal codes for the equivalent design codes used in table 5.2 for attributes up to six levels. Note that by convention, −5 and 5 are not used in orthogonal coding.

Table 5.3. *Comparison of design codes and orthogonal codes*

Number of levels	Design Code	Orthogonal Code
2	0	−1
	1	1
3	0	−1
	1	0
	2	1
4	0	−3
	1	−1
	2	1
	3	3
5	0	−3
	1	−1
	2	0
	3	1
	4	3
6	0	−7
	1	−3
	2	−1
	3	1
	4	3
	5	7

The analyst may choose to stop at this point of the design process and use the design as it is. By having decision makers rate or rank each of the treatment combinations, the analyst has elected to perform *conjoint analysis*. We focus on choice analysis and not conjoint analysis and as such require some mechanism that requires decision makers to make some type of choice. To proceed, we note that the treatment combinations above represent possible product forms that our single alternative may take. For a choice to take place we require treatment combinations that describe some other alternative (recalling that choice requires at least two alternatives).

Assuming that the second alternative also has two attributes that are deemed important to preference formation, we now have a total of four attributes: two attributes for each alternative. As discussed earlier, these attributes do not have to be the same across alternatives and, even if they are, the attribute levels each assumed do not have to be the same. For ease, we will assume the attributes for the two alternatives are the same. Let us assume the attribute levels for the "comfort" attribute are the same for both alternatives but for the second alternative we observe attribute levels of 1 hour, 1.5 hours, and 2 hours for the travel time attribute (as opposed to 10, 12, and 14 hours for alternative 1). Taking the full factorial design for two alternatives, each with two attributes with three levels, 81 different treatment combinations exist. How did we arrive at this number?

The full enumeration of possible choice sets is equal to L^{MA} for labeled choice experiments (defined in the next section) and L^{A} for unlabeled experiments, where L is the number of levels, M the number of alternatives, and A the number of attributes. The above example thus yields 81 (i.e. $3^{(2\times2)} = 3^4$) possible treatment combinations (assuming a labeled choice experiment; for an unlabeled choice experiment, we could reduce this to nine treatment combinations (i.e. 3^2)).

5.2.3.1 Labeled versus unlabeled experiments

Rather than have decision makers rate or rank a treatment combination, we may now have them choose which of the alternatives they would select given the levels each alternative assumes. Table 5.4 shows the first treatment combination for the example described above. As we will show later, the treatment combinations for designs such as that represented in table 5.4 become the choice sets we use in the experiment. In table 5.4, the analyst elected to use generic titles for each of the alternatives. The title *Alternative 1* does not convey any information to the decision maker other than that this is the first of the alternatives. Experiments that use generic titles for the alternatives are called *unlabeled experiments*. Instead, the analyst may have elected to label each of the alternatives in the experiment (e.g. *car*). We have done this in table 5.5. We term such experiments *labeled experiments*.

The decision as to whether to use labeled or unlabeled experiments is an important one. One of the main benefits of using unlabeled experiments is that they do not require the identification and use of all alternatives within the universal set of alternatives. Indeed, alternative 1 above may be used to describe alternatives as diverse as cars, buses, and trains. That is, the attribute levels are sufficiently broad to relate to various modes of travel.

Table 5.4. *Choice treatment combination*

Treatment	Alternative 1		Alternative 2	
combination	*Comfort*	*Travel time*	*Comfort*	*Travel time*
1	Low	10 hours	Low	1 hour

Table 5.5. *Labeled choice experiment*

Treatment	*Car*		*Plane*	
combination	*Comfort*	*Travel time*	*Comfort*	*Travel time*
1	Low	10 hours	Low	1 hour

We acknowledge a further benefit in the use of unlabeled experiments. Recall the IID assumption introduced in chapter 3 which imposed the restriction that the alternatives used in the modeling process be uncorrelated. This assumption is less likely to be met under labeled experiments than under unlabeled experiments. To explain, we note that a label attached to an alternative acts somewhat like an attribute for that alternative (albeit an attribute whose level is constant across treatment combinations). This has several consequences. First, if we acknowledge that an alternative's name becomes an attribute in labeled experiments (the different alternatives being the attribute levels), the perceptions decision makers hold with regard to the alternatives may be correlated with the attributes used within the experiment. That is, the alternative *plane*, may be correlated with both the *comfort* and *travel time* attributes. This represents a failure in terms of meeting the IID model assumption.

As an aside, a further problem arising from the use of labeled experiments develops from the perceptual assumptions decision makers hold for each labeled alternative. To date, we have kept our example simple for pedagogical purposes. Clearly, however, in reality, mode choice depends on more than the two attributes we have identified. Decision makers may use assumptions surrounding the labels attached to alternatives as proxies for these omitted attributes. We invite the reader to return to our earlier discussion on the IID assumption in chapter 3 to see how omitted attributes are treated. The message here is that one should spend as much time as is feasible in identifying which attributes, attribute levels, and attribute-level labels to use in an experiment.

In using labeled experiments, if the analyst identifies the relevant attributes for the experiment then problems brought about by decision makers making inferences about the levels of omitted attributes from the labels will also be minimized. Further, violations of the IID assumption are testable, and if observed may be dealt with through the use of more advanced modeling techniques such as nested logit modeling (chapters 13 and 14).

The above does not suggest that one should avoid labeled experiments. Indeed, the decision to use a labeled as opposed to an unlabeled experiment should be made in the context of the research problem. Indeed, if one wishes to estimate alternative-specific parameter estimates, it is best to use labeled experiments (we discuss this in more detail later). Also, one may elect to use labeled experiments for the purpose of realism. When decision makers venture to a point of physical distribution (e.g. a supermarket), they do not select amongst generic alternatives, but rather from a number of branded goods and services. Having decision makers select from breakfast cereal A or B may not represent a realistic task. Further, the branded name for a good or service may be an important contributor to choice amongst segments of decision makers. For example, some decision makers may elect to fly with Qantas, without consideration of the attribute levels associated with Qantas or their competitors, simply because of the brand name Qantas. The brand name connotes an *historical accumulation of utility* associated with attribute levels experienced in the past, and as such is a very powerful influence on choice, often downgrading the role of currently observed (actual or perceived) attribute levels.

As an aside, in general, where the focus is on prediction and forecasting in contrast to establishing willingness to pay (WTP) for specific attributes, a labeled experiment is preferred. However, one can take a set of parameters estimated from an unlabeled experiment

Table 5.6. *Attribute levels for expanded number of alternatives*

Attribute \ Alternative	*Car*	*Bus*	*Train*	*Plane*
Comfort	Low Medium High	Low Medium High	Low Medium High	Low Medium High
Travel time	10 hours 12 hours 14 hours	10 hours 12 hours 14 hours	10 hours 12 hours 14 hours	1hour 1.5 hours 2 hours

and, provided one is happy to stay with generic parameters for all attributes, then introduce alternative-specific constants as *calibration constants* to fit the model to a set of actual labeled alternatives to reproduce actual market shares. These calibrated constants are not part of the SP estimation process but are introduced in the application stage.

Whether the analyst decides upon a labeled or unlabeled experiment, several more considerations are required to be made in selecting a design. We note in our example that the analyst requires decision makers to make 81 choices, one for each treatment combination. The analyst may believe that presenting decision makers with 81 choice sets may place a significant level of cognitive burden on respondents, with the likely result of a decrease in response rates and/or a decrease in response reliability. There are a number of different strategies that may be adopted to reduce the number of choice sets given to decision makers. These are (1) reducing the number of levels used within the design, (2) using fractional factorial designs, (3) blocking the design, and (4) using a fractional factorial design combined with a blocking strategy.

Before we discuss each of these strategies, let us expand upon the example. Rather than two alternatives, let us now assume the existence of four alternative modes of transport – *car*, *bus*, *train*, and *plane*. Retaining the initial two attributes, the attribute levels associated with each alternative are shown in table 5.6. Using this as the basis for a design, there are now 6,561 possible treatment combinations (recall L^{MA}).

5.2.3.2 Reducing the number of levels

Reducing the number of levels within the design will dramatically reduce the design size; however, such a reduction comes at a cost in terms of the amount of information the design obtains in terms of observations gained. One such strategy often employed is to utilize the attribute levels at the extremes only. That is, each attribute will have only two attribute levels, both at the two extremes of the attribute level range. Such designs are known as *end-point* designs (as promoted in Louviere, Hensher, and Swait 2000, chapter 5). For the example above, using an *end-point* design reduces the number of treatment combinations to 256. End-point designs are particularly useful if the analyst believes that linear relationships exist amongst the part-worth utilities or if the analyst is using the experiment as an exploratory tool.

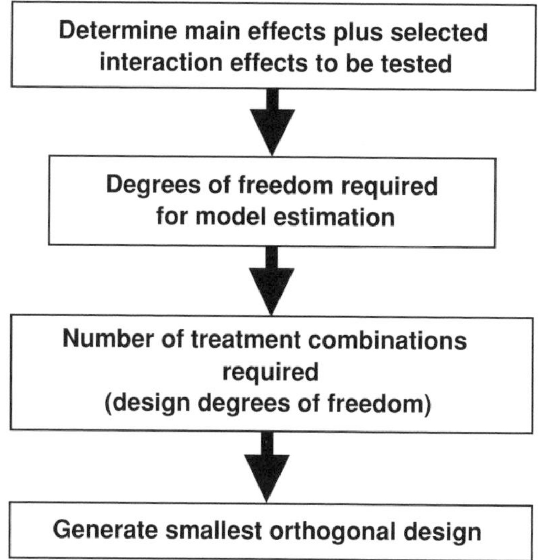

Figure 5.3 Stages in deriving fractional factorial designs

5.2.3.3 Reducing the size of experimental designs

Rather than use all 6561 possible treatment combinations, it is possible for the analyst to use only a fraction of the treatment combinations. Designs in which we use only a fraction of the total number of treatment combinations are called *fractional factorial* designs. To choose which treatment combinations to use, the analyst may randomly select a number of treatment combinations from the total number of treatment combinations without replacement. However, random selection is likely to produce statistically inefficient or sub-optimal designs. What is required is a scientific method that may be used to select the optimal treatment combinations to use. Figure 5.3 shows the steps used to derive a statically efficient fractional factorial design.

In order to proceed, the analyst must have an understanding of a number of statistical concepts. We begin with the concept of *orthogonality*. Orthogonality is a mathematical constraint requiring that all attributes be statistically independent of one another. As such, orthogonality implies zero correlations between attributes. An orthogonal design is therefore a design in which the columns of the design display zero correlations (note that the attributes themselves may be perceptually correlated but statistically independent).

As an aside, the number of rows which represent the number of alternative combinations of attribute levels are critical to the determination of column orthogonality; but once the orthogonality is established for a given number of rows, we can easily remove columns without affecting the orthogonality. Removing rows, however, will affect the orthogonality. In studies, we often give individuals sub-sets of rows, which is fine assuming that when we pool the data for analysis we retain an equal number of responses for each row. The importance of *sampling* becomes paramount in preserving the orthogonality.

As with multicollinearity in linear multiple regression, non-orthogonal designs render determination of the contribution of each independent attribute difficult, as the attributes are confounded with one another. Statistically, non-orthogonality tends to produce higher amounts of shared variation with lower unique variation from which individual attribute estimates are derived. Parameters estimated from non-orthogonal designs are likely to be incorrectly estimated and, in some instances, have the incorrect sign. As an aside, full factorial designs mathematically display orthogonality, which is why we have ignored this important concept to date.

A second concept which requires exploration is that of *main and interaction effects*. We define an effect as the impact a particular treatment has upon some response variable. In choice analysis, the response variable is choice. Thus, an effect is the impact a particular attribute level has on choice. For experimental designs, we define an effect as the difference in treatment means. A main effect is defined as the direct independent effect of each attribute upon the response variable, choice. The main effect, therefore, is the difference in the means of each level of an attribute and the overall or grand mean. An interaction effect is an effect upon a response variable, choice, obtained by combining two or more attributes which would not have been observed had each of the attributes been estimated separately.

The following illustrates the differences. Equation (5.1) is the linear representative component of utility first presented in chapter 3:

$$V_i = \beta_{0i} + \beta_{1i} f(X_{1i}) + \beta_{2i} f(X_{2i}) + \beta_{3i} f(X_{3i}) + \cdots + \beta_{Ki} f(X_{Ki}) \tag{5.1}$$

where

β_{1i} is the weight (or parameter) associated with attribute X_1 and alternative i
β_{0i} is a parameter not associated with any of the observed and measured attributes, called the alternative-specific constant, which represents on average the role of all the unobserved sources of utility.

Using (5.1), a *main effect* (ME) is the effect each attribute has on the response variable (V_i in (5.1)) independent of all other attribute effects. Examination of (5.1) suggests that the impact of any attribute, for example X_{1i}, upon V_i is equivalent to its associated parameter weight, in this instance β_{1i}. Thus the β_{Ki}s represent our estimates of MEs. For any given design, the total number of MEs that we can estimate is equivalent to the number of attributes present in the design (see sub-section 5.3.2.4 to see how MEs may be estimated for attribute levels).

What we have not shown in (5.1) are the *interaction terms*. An interaction occurs when the preference for the level of one attribute is dependent upon the level of a second attribute. A good example of this is nitro-glycerine. Kept separately, nitric acid and glycerine are relatively inert; however, when combined an explosive compound is created. This is not a chemistry text, however, and a useful example for students of choice is warranted. The part-worth utility functions might thus look like (5.2):

$$\begin{aligned} V_i = {} & \beta_{0i} + \beta_{1i} f(X_{1i}) + \beta_{2i} f(X_{2i}) + \beta_{3i} f(X_{3i}) + \cdots + \beta_{Ki} f(X_{Ki}) \\ & + \beta_{Li} f(X_{1i} X_{2i}) + \beta_{Mi} f(X_{1i} X_{3i}) + \cdots + \beta_{Oi} f(X_{1i} X_{Ki}) \\ & + \beta_{Pi} f(X_{2i} X_{3i}) + \cdots + \beta_{Zi} f(X_{1i} X_{2i} X_{3i \ldots} X_{Ki}) \end{aligned} \tag{5.2}$$

where

$f(X_{1i}X_{2i})$ is the two-way interaction between the attributes X_{1i} and X_{2i} and β_{Ki} is the interaction effect.

$f(X_{1i}X_{2i}X_{3i\ldots}X_{Ki})$ is the kth-way interaction and β_{Zi} is the related interaction effect.

Returning to our example, assume the that analyst identified color as being an important attribute for the bus alternative. Research showed that for trips of 10 hours or less, decision makers had no preference for the color of the bus. However, for trips over 10 hours, bus patrons prefer light-colored buses to dark-colored buses (the analyst suspects that dark-colored buses become hotter and therefore more uncomfortable over longer distances). As such, the preference decision makers have for the bus alternative is not formed by the effect of color independent of the effect of travel time but rather is formed due to some combination of both.

Because the level of one attribute when acting in concert with a second attribute's level affects utility for that alternative, the analyst should not examine the two variables separately, but rather in combination with one another. That is, the bus company should not look at the decision of which color bus to use as separate to the decision of what route to take (affecting travel times). Rather, the two decisions should be considered together in order to arrive at an optimal solution. In terms of our model, if an interaction effect is found to be significant, then we need to consider the variables collectively (though the model itself does not tell us what the optimal combination is). If the interaction effect is found not to be significant, then we examine the main effects by themselves in order to arrive at the optimal solution.

As an aside, one might confuse the concept of interaction with the concept of *correlation*. Correlation between variables is said to occur when we see movement in one variable similar to the movement in a second variable. For example, a positive correlation may be said to exist if, as price increases, we also observe quality increasing. While this looks remarkably like the concept of interactions discussed above, it is not. The concept of an interaction between two attributes is about the *impact* two attributes are having when acting in concert. Thus, in the example described earlier, we are not interested in whether, as the level of color changes from light to dark, travel time increases. Rather we are interested in the impact certain combinations of color and travel time may have on bus patronage (i.e. increasing utility for the bus alternative relative to the other alternatives). That is, which combinations of color and travel time will sell more bus tickets? Put simply, a correlation is said to be a relationship between two variables, whereas an interaction may be thought of as the impact two (or more) variables have on a third (response) variable.

Interaction and main effects are important concepts and must be fully understood by the analyst. One benefit of using full factorial designs is that all the main effects and all the interaction effects may be estimated independent of one another. That is, the analyst may estimate parameters for all main effects and interaction effects such that there is no confoundment present. Unfortunately, in reducing the number of treatment combinations, fractional factorial designs force confoundment upon these effects. Strategies exist to minimize these confoundments such that those effects of interest may be estimated independent of all other effects. We address these strategies later.

Finally, we define *degrees of freedom*. The degrees of freedom for an experiment are the number of observations in a sample minus the number of independent (linear) constraints placed upon it during the modeling process. The independent (linear) constraints are the β-parameters we estimate. In non-expert terms, a degree of freedom represents a single piece of information available to the analyst. As the analyst requires a certain amount of information (degrees of freedom) in order to estimate a model, the analyst requires knowledge of how much information is present within a design and how much information is required to estimate a model.

To determine the minimum number of treatment combinations necessary for a fractional factorial, the analyst is obligated to establish how many degrees of freedom are required for estimation purposes. This determination is dependent upon the number of parameters to be estimated at the time of modeling, which in turn is dependent on how the analyst is likely to specify the model. To demonstrate, recall that the representative component of utility (ignoring interactions) for any alternative may be written as a linear function such that:

$$V_i = \beta_{0i} + \beta_{1i} f(X_{1i}) + \beta_{2i} f(X_{2i}) + \beta_{3i} f(X_{3i}) + \cdots + \beta_{Ki} f(X_{Ki}) \tag{5.3}$$

If, for argument's sake, the attribute *comfort* for the car alternative is the first attribute associated with alternative i then using our notation, this attribute enters the utility function of (5.3) through X_{1i}. At the time of modeling, we will derive a weight, β_{1i} associated with this attribute.

Using the coding suggested in table 5.6, the imposition of a linear effect on utility can easily be shown. Our estimate of the level of utility associated with a low level of comfort is obtained by substituting 0 (the non-orthogonal code used in the design for a low level of comfort; this value would be -1 if using the orthogonal coding method) into $f(X_{1i})$ to obtain:

$$V_i = \beta_{0i} + (\beta_{1i} \times 0) = \alpha_i + 0 \tag{5.4}$$

ceteris paribus (all other things being equal). The utility we estimate for the medium level of comfort, *ceteris paribus*, is given as:

$$V_i = \beta_{0i} + (\beta_{1i} \times 1) = \alpha_i + \beta_{1i} \tag{5.5}$$

and for a high level of comfort:

$$V_i = \beta_{0i} + (\beta_{1i} \times 2) = \alpha_i + 2\beta_{1i} \tag{5.6}$$

Note that every time we increase the amount of comfort by one unit, *ceteris paribus*, our utility level increases by the amount β_{1i}. That is, the utility for the difference between a low level of comfort and a medium level of comfort is the same as the utility for the difference between a medium level of comfort and a high level of comfort. This is unlikely to be true. Consider the case of air travel. The three levels of comfort may translate to comfort levels experienced in coach, business, and first class. Those who are lucky enough to have traveled first class will acknowledge a significant difference between first class and business class, much more so than between business and coach. The answer to this problem lies in two alternative coding approaches.

Table 5.7. *Dummy coding*

Attribute level \ Variable	*comfort1*	*comfort2*
High	1	0
Medium	0	1
Low	0	0

5.2.3.4 Dummy and effects coding

Dummy coding allows for non-linear effects in the levels of attributes. This is accomplished through the creation of a number of variables for each attribute being coded. The number of new variables created is equivalent to the number of levels of the attribute being coded, minus one. Thus in the example above where we have three comfort levels, we need to create two variables. For simplicity's sake, let us call these new variables *comfort1* and *comfort2*. We associate *comfort1* with the high level of comfort such that every time the attribute *comfort* is at the high level, we will place a 1 in the column *comfort1* of a our data set. If the attribute was other than high then we will place a 0 in the *comfort1* column. Similarly *comfort2* will equal 1 if a medium level of comfort was experienced and 0 otherwise. As we have only two variables but three levels, the third level, a low comfort level, is represented as a 0 in both *comfort1* and *comfort2*. This coding is shown in table 5.7.

Such coding allows for non-linear effects to be tested in the levels of the attributes. Returning to (5.3), *comfort1* would now be associated with $f(X_{1i})$ and *comfort2* with $f(X_{2i})$. Consequently we now have two β-parameters associated with our single comfort attribute, β_{1i} and β_{2i}. The utility associated with a high level of comfort, *ceteris paribus*, now becomes:

$$V_i = \beta_{0i} + \beta_{1i} \times 1 + \beta_{2i} \times 0 = \beta_{0i} + \beta_{1i} \tag{5.7}$$

and for medium comfort:

$$V_i = \beta_{0i} + \beta_{1i} \times 0 + \beta_{2i} \times 1 = \beta_{0i} + \beta_{2i} \tag{5.8}$$

The utility associated with a low comfort level becomes:

$$V_i = \beta_{0i} + \beta_{1i} \times 0 + \beta_{2i} \times 0 = \beta_{0i} \tag{5.9}$$

What we now have is a different value of utility associated with each level of the attribute coded. We have therefore overcome the problem noted with the more traditional coding method of linear changes in the response variable given one unit changes in the explanatory variable.

We have left β_{0i} in (5.4)–(5.9) quite deliberately. Examination of (5.9) shows that the utility associated with the base level will always, by default, equal β_{0i}. That is, we are not measuring the utility associated with low comfort at all, but rather the average overall utility

Table 5.8. *Effects coding structure*

Attribute level \ Variable	*comfort1*	*comfort2*
High	1	0
Medium	0	1
Low	−1	−1

level when we look at the utility for the base level. The above suggests that by dummy coding the data we have perfectly confounded the base level of an attribute with the overall or *grand mean*. Each attribute we dummy code will also be perfectly confounded with the grand mean. The question is then, what have we measured? Have we measured the utility for the base level or the overall or grand mean?

It is for the above reason that we prefer effects coding as opposed to dummy coding. Effects coding has the same advantage of dummy coding in that non-linear effects in the attribute levels may be measured, but dispenses with the disadvantage of perfectly confounding the base attribute level with the grand mean of the utility function.

To effects code, we follow the procedure set out above for dummy coding; however, instead of coding the base level 0 across our newly created variables, we now code the base level as −1 across each of these new variables. Thus for our example we have the situation in table 5.8.

As we have not changed the coding for the high and medium comfort levels, (5.7) and (5.8) still hold. However the estimate of utility associated with the change of the coding for the low level of comfort, now becomes:

$$V_i = \beta_{0i} + \beta_{1i} \times (-1) + \beta_{2i} \times (-1) = \beta_{0i} - (\beta_{1i} + \beta_{2i}) \tag{5.10}$$

We note that the utility for the base level is now no longer perfectly confounded with the alternative i's grand mean, but rather may be estimated as $\beta_{0i} - \beta_{1i} - \beta_{2i}$. As such, the effect of the base level is therefore equivalent to $-\beta_{1i} - \beta_{2i}$ around β_{0i}.

In table 5.9 we show the coding structure for attributes up to five levels. For attributes with more than five levels, the analyst is simply required to add more variables.

To demonstrate the importance of the coding choice (i.e. the use of a single (linear) attribute or several dummy or effects coded variables representing a single attribute), consider figure 5.4.

Figure 5.4 assumes the existence of some complex part-worth (marginal) utility function (taken from figure 5.2d). Assuming the estimation of a single parameter (i.e. slope coefficient) for this attribute, we arrive at the case represented by 5.4a. In such a case, the analyst will not be able to establish the true utility function to any degree of accuracy. As we estimate more parameters (i.e. more slope coefficients) for the attribute through the use of dummy or effects codes, the analyst may obtain a better understanding of the true utility function as shown in figures 5.4b–5.4d.

Table 5.9. *Effects coding formats*

	Variable 1	Variable 2	Variable 3	Variable 4
Level 1	1			
Level 2	−1			
Level 1	1	0		
Level 2	0	1		
Level 3	−1	−1		
Level 1	1	0	0	
Level 2	0	1	0	
Level 3	0	0	1	
Level 4	−1	−1	−1	
Level 1	1	0	0	0
Level 2	0	1	0	0
Level 3	0	0	1	0
Level 4	0	0	0	1
Level 5	−1	−1	−1	−1

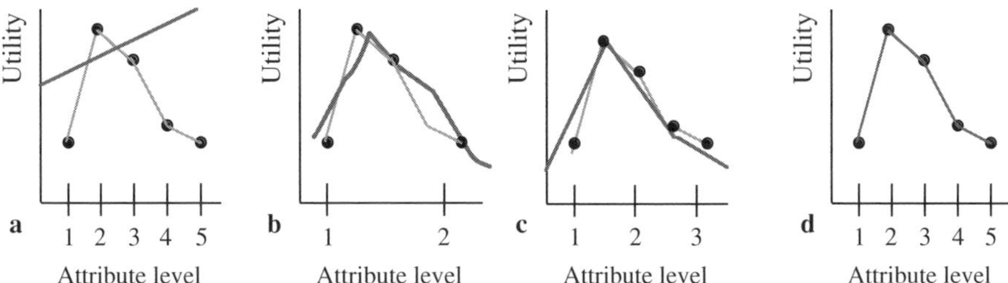

Figure 5.4 Estimation of linear vs quadratic effects

As an aside, because the estimation of a single parameter for an attribute will produce a linear estimate (i.e. slope), we refer to such estimates as linear estimates. An attribute estimated with two dummy (or effects) parameters is known as a quadratic estimate and subsequent dummy (or effects) parameters are known as polynomials of degree L−1 (where L is the number of dummy or effects parameters) estimates.

What the above discussion suggests is that the more complex the part-worth utility function, the better off one is to move to a more complex coding structure capable of estimating more complex non-linear relationships. Of course, prior to model estimation, beyond experience and information gleaned from other studies, the analyst will have no information as to the complexity of a part-worth utility function. This would suggest that the analyst is best to assume the worst and produce models capable of estimating extremely complex non-linear relationships. However as we shall see, this comes at a considerable cost, and may be far from the best strategy to employ.

5.2.3.5 Calculating the degrees of freedom required

Recall the earlier definition provided for degrees of freedom.

> The degrees of freedom for an experiment are the number of observations in a sample minus the number of independent (linear) constraints placed upon it during the modeling process. The independent (linear) constraints are the β-parameters we estimate.

The above definition suggests that the more parameters an analyst desires to estimate, the greater the number of degrees of freedom required for estimation purposes. That is, the more complex non-linear relationships we wish to detect, the more parameters we are required to estimate and in turn the more degrees of freedom we require for model estimation. As we shall show, *more degrees of freedom mean larger designs.*

Assuming the estimation of a main effects only model (ignoring interactions between attributes), the degrees of freedom required of a design depend upon the types of effects to be estimated and whether the design is labeled or unlabeled. For our example, each (labeled) alternative (i.e. car, bus, train, and plane) has two attributes defined on three levels. Assuming estimation of linear effects only, the degrees of freedom required for the design is equal to nine (i.e. $4 \times 2 + 1$). As noted above, the degrees of freedom required of a design corresponds to the number of parameters to be estimated over all alternatives. Consider the utility functions for each of the four alternatives given that the marginal utilities (or part-worths) are assumed to be linear. The utility functions will be estimated as shown below (ignoring constant terms):

$$
\begin{aligned}
V_{car} &= \beta_{1car} \times comfort + \beta_{2car} \times TT \\
V_{bus} &= \beta_{1bus} \times comfort + \beta_{2bus} \times TT \\
V_{train} &= \beta_{1train} \times comfort + \beta_{2train} \times TT \\
V_{plane} &= \beta_{1plane} \times comfort + \beta_{2plane} \times TT
\end{aligned}
$$

Over the four alternatives, the number of parameters to be estimated is 8, however in order to estimate the model, one additional degree of freedom is required. Thus, a minimum of 9 degrees of freedom would be required for the design used to estimate all of the parameters within the above system of utility functions.

Assuming the estimation of non-linear effects, the degrees of freedom required increases to 17 (i.e. $((3 - 1) \times 4 \times 2 + 1)$. Under the assumption that the marginal utilities for each attribute are non-linear, the utility functions become:

$$
\begin{aligned}
V_{car} &= \beta_{1car} \times comfort\,(low) + \beta_{2car} \times comfort\,(medium) \\
&\quad + \beta_{3car} \times TT(10\ hours) + \beta_{4car} \times TT(12\ hours) \\
V_{bus} &= \beta_{1bus} \times comfort\,(low) + \beta_{2bus} \times comfort\,(medium) \\
&\quad + \beta_{3bus} \times TT(10\ hours) + \beta_{4bus} \times TT(12\ hours) \\
V_{train} &= \beta_{1train} \times comfort\,(low) + \beta_{2train} \times comfort\,(medium) \\
&\quad + \beta_{3train} \times TT(10\ hours) + \beta_{4train} \times TT(12\ hours)
\end{aligned}
$$

$$V_{plane} = \beta_{1plane} \times comfort\,(low) + \beta_{2plane} \times comfort\,(medium) + \beta_{3plane} \times TT(1\ hour) + \beta_{4plane} \times TT(1^1/_2\ hours)$$

A total of 16 parameters are required to be estimated (ignoring constant terms). Given the requirement of an additional degree of freedom, the above model specification would require a minimum of 17 degrees of freedom.

For unlabeled choice experiments, the degrees of freedom required are somewhat reduced (see section 5.3, "A note on unlabeled experimental designs"). The minimum degrees of freedom required of a design may be calculated using the formulas given in table 5.10.

As with main effects, the degrees of freedom required for an interaction effect depends on how the interaction effect is to be specified in the model. To demonstrate, consider the three utility specifications below:

$$V_i = \beta_{0i} + \beta_{1i} \times comfort + \beta_{2i} \times TT + \beta_{3i} \times comfort \times TT$$

$$V_i = \beta_{0i} + \beta_{1i} \times comfort(low) + \beta_{2i} \times comfort\,(medium) + \beta_{3i} \times TT(10\ hours) + \beta_{4i} \times TT(12\ hours) + \beta_{5i} \times comfort\,(low) \times TT(10\ hours) + \beta_{6i} \times comfort\,(low) \times TT(12\ hours) + \beta_{7i} \times comfort\,(medium) \times TT(10\ hours) + \beta_{8i} \times comfort\,(medium) \times TT(12\ hours)$$

$$V_i = \beta_{0i} + \beta_{1i} \times comfort\,(low) + \beta_{2i} \times comfort\,(medium) + \beta_{3i} \times TT(10\ hours) + \beta_{4i} \times TT(12\ hours) + \beta_{5i} \times comfort \times TT$$

In the first utility specification, the main effects are estimated as linear effects and the interaction effect as the multiplication of the two linear main effects. The interaction effect thus requires the estimation of only a single parameter and hence necessitates only a single degree of freedom. In the second utility specification, the main effects have been estimated as non-linear effects (i.e. they have been either dummy or effects coded). Interaction effects may thus be estimated for each combination of the non-linear main effects. Under this specification, four interactions are generated, requiring four parameter estimates and an additional four degrees of freedom. The last utility specification shows an example whereby the main effects are estimated as non-linear effects; however, the interaction effect is estimated as if the main effects were linear in effect. As such, only a single parameter

Table 5.10. *Minimum treatment combination requirements for main effects only fractional factorial designs*

Effects \ Experiment	Unlabeled	Labeled
Linear	A + 1	MA + 1
Non-linear (dummy or effects coded variables)	(L − 1) × A + 1	(L−1) × MA + 1

will be estimated for the interaction effect requiring only a single degree of freedom for estimation. The total number of degrees of freedom required for this specification is six.

The degrees of freedom required for the estimation of interaction terms therefore depend on how the utility functions are likely to be estimated. The degrees of freedom from an interaction term estimated from linear main effects (two or more) will be one. Two-way interaction terms estimated from non-linear main effects will be equal to $(L_1 - 1) \times (L_2 - 1)$ where L_1 is the number of levels associated with attribute one and L_2 is the number of levels associated with attribute two. The degrees of freedom associated with the addition of attributes to an interaction (e.g. three-way interactions) requires the addition of multiplication terms (e.g. $(L_1 - 1) \times (L_2 - 1) \times (L_3 - 1)$).

Given knowledge of all of the above, we are now ready to proceed with the design of an experiment. First, the analyst is required to determine which effects of interest are to be modeled. It is usual to model all main effects (either treated as linear or non-linear) and ignore any possible interaction effects; hence, the smallest number of effects to be estimated is equivalent to the number of main effects (i.e. parameters). This will produce a model equivalent to (5.1). Such designs are called *orthogonal main effects only designs*. We noted earlier that reducing the number of treatment combinations through the use of fractional factorial designs results in confoundment of effects. Main effects only designs are designs in which the main effects are independently estimable of all other effects but the interaction effects will be confounded with one another.

For our example, we have eight attributes each with three levels (two attributes for each of the four alternatives). Assuming non-linear estimates are required, each attribute requires 2 degrees of freedom for main effects to be estimated, suggesting that the design generated requires at minimum 16 degrees of freedom (each attribute requires 2 degrees of freedom (i.e. 3 − 1) to estimate each of the dummy or effects coded parameters. Estimating all eight attributes therefore requires a total of 16 degrees of freedom (i.e. 8 × 2)). This is not strictly true as the analyst requires an additional degree of freedom for the random error component of the model (when it is treated as one component if we are using an IID model such as multinomial logit or MNL), hence, the minimum degrees of freedom required is actually 17. Thus the minimum number of treatment combinations (rows) needed is 17. Unfortunately, if the analyst wishes to maintain orthogonality, the search for an orthogonal array with eight columns, each with three levels, will reveal that a greater number of treatment combinations is required. That is, while we can generate a 17-row design, such a design will not be orthogonal. Indeed, the minimum number of rows for eight attributes each with three levels and maintaining orthogonality is 18. Eighteen treatment combinations may be far more manageable for a decision maker to handle than the full 6,561 treatment combinations generated by the full factorial design. The point to note is that orthogonality is often found by selecting designs that satisfy the number of degrees of freedom but often have more rows than the number of degrees of freedom.

The use of a main effects only design significantly reduces the number of treatment combinations required. However, this reduction comes at a cost. Recall that each treatment combination represents a separate piece of information. By using only a fraction of the

Table 5.11. *Enumeration of all two-way interactions*

A	B	C	D	E	F	G	H
AB	BC	CD	DE	EF	FG	GH	
AC	BD	CE	DF	EG	FH		
AD	BE	CF	DG	EH			
AE	BF	CG	DH				
AF	BG	CH					
AG	BH						
AH							

total number of possible treatment combinations, the analyst has in effect thrown away a significant proportion of information. The effect of this lost information will never be known. To emphasize the point, consider what information has been lost through the use of a main effects only design. The analyst is capable of estimating only the main effects. No interaction terms are estimable (a degree of freedom problem) and even if they were, they are likely to be confounded with one another. The analyst has thus assumed that all interaction effects are not significant, an assumption that cannot be tested. For our example, there exist 28 two-way interaction terms. Assuming eight attributes (we will call them attributes A, B, C, D, E, F, G, and H) the 28 treatment combinations are shown in table 5.11.

There also exist a number of three-, four-, five-, six-, seven- and eight-way interactions as well. All these *are assumed* to be statistically insignificant (i.e. their parameters in (5.2) are equal to 0). Recalling our earlier discussion on interaction terms, if any one of these interaction terms is in reality not statistically insignificant, then ignoring the non-significant interactions will produce sub-optimal results in terms of our model estimated and predictions derived from that model.

Fortunately the analyst is able to generate designs that allow for the estimation of selected interaction effects. Such designs require advance knowledge as to which interactions are likely to be statistically significant. The ability to estimate interaction effects comes at the cost of design size, however. The more interaction effects the analyst wishes to estimate, the more treatment combinations are required. Let us assume that our analyst believes that the interaction between comfort and travel time will be significant for the car alternative and similarly for the bus alternative. Therefore, the analyst wishes to estimate two two-way interaction effects. Taking the two-way interaction effect for the car alternative and assuming non-linear effects, the degrees of freedom for the interaction effect is 4 (i.e. $(3 - 1) \times (3 - 1)$) (1 if linear effects are used). Similarly, the two-way interaction for the bus alternative is also 4. The analyst thus now requires a design with 25 degrees of freedom (16 main effects degrees of freedom plus 8 two-way interaction degrees of freedom plus 1 degree of freedom for the model error). Again, a search for an orthogonal array shows that the smallest number of treatment combinations is 27 and not 25. Thus the analyst must generate a design with 27 treatment combinations. So how do we determine which 27 treatment combinations to select (recall that there exist 6,561 such combinations)?

5.2.3.6 Blocking the design

Before answering the above question, let us finish this section by discussing another method used to reduce the number of treatment combinations shown to any particular respondent. This technique is known as blocking. *Blocking* involves the analyst introducing another orthogonal column to the design, the attribute levels of which are used to segment the design. That is, if this new attribute has three levels, then the design will be broken down into three different segments (blocks). Each block is then given to a different respondent, the result of which is that three different decision makers are required to complete the full design. Assuming the analyst has done as described above, then for the design with 27 treatment combinations, each decision maker would receive 9 of the 27 treatment combinations. If a nine-level column was used, then 9 respondents would each receive 3 treatment combinations. Note that we could have blocked the full factorial design (although the block would not be orthogonal; full factorial designs allocate all possible orthogonal columns to the attributes); however, as you can see from the above, the sample size required for a blocked design increases exponentially as the number of treatment combinations within a block decreases for a fixed number of treatment combinations.

As an aside, a design is orthogonal only if the complete (fractional factorial or full factorial) design is used. Thus, if blocks of block size 9 are used and only two of the three decision makers complete the experiment, the (pooled) design used at the time of estimation will not be orthogonal. Acknowledgement of this fact has largely been ignored by both academics and practitioners alike. One wonders how many carefully crafted orthogonal designs have in reality maintained their statistical properties after data are collected and used in model estimation!

As a further aside, note that we suggested a blocking strategy that involves the use of an extra column that is orthogonal to the other design columns. By using an orthogonal column for the block, the attribute parameter estimates will be independent of the assigned blocks. This is important statistically; however, it may not always be possible to add an extra design column for the purpose of blocking without increasing the number of treatment combinations as, for every design, there exists a finite number of orthogonal columns available that the analyst may choose from. It is therefore not uncommon to move to a larger design in order to locate an additional design column that may be allocated as a blocking variable. Note, however, that unless it is the desire of the analyst to test the effect of a blocking variable, assuming that there exists an additional design column that may be allocated as the blocking variable, we do not have to increase the number of treatment combinations as a result of an increase in the degrees of freedom required.

Increasing the number of treatment combinations within a design is but one alternative in accommodating an additional blocking column. Nevertheless, more complex designs may make this strategy unworkable. In such cases, the analyst may elect to randomly allocate treatment combinations to different decision makers. While this strategy may result in a confoundment between the treatment combinations given to decision makers and the parameter estimates, this approach may be the only strategy available to the analyst.

5.2.4 Stage 4: generating experimental designs

Generating the actual experimental design is not a straightforward task. Indeed, conversations with colleagues and students have led us to believe that this is the least understood concept related to the choice modeling process. In this section, we will lay bare how the reader may generate simple experimental designs using computer software. Using software to generate experimental designs is not the preferred method; however, to describe exactly how the expert generates experimental designs would require an entire book. We have therefore chosen to demonstrate, using SPSS as an example, how to obtain workable designs. The reader who wishes to become a serious choice analyst is advised to research beyond this book to learn exactly how experts generate designs (for example, see Cochran and Cox 1957; Cox 1958; Kuehl 2000). We have developed a stated choice design generator to handle the majority of popular designs for our own research although, like many of these tools, it is not widely available.

To proceed from this point, the analyst must consider whether a main effects only design is to be generated or whether a main effects plus selected interactions design is required. Given a main effects only design, the analyst may name the attributes such that each design column that will be generated will be assigned to a specific attribute (e.g. SPSS will generate a column in the design called *comfort*). Examination of the design process outlined in figure 5.1 suggests that for main-effects only designs, the generation of the design (stage 4) and the allocation of attributes to design columns (stage 5) occur simultaneously. If the analyst wishes to test for specific interaction effects (e.g. the two-way interaction between the *comfort* and *travel time* attributes for the car alternative) then stages 4 and 5 of the design process occur sequentially such that the analyst provides SPSS with generic attribute names and assigns the generated design columns at a later stage of the design process. We see why this is so as our discussion progresses.

Returning to our earlier example we note that the analyst requires a main effects plus selected (two-way) interaction design (i.e. the two-way interaction between the attributes "comfort" and "travel time" for the car alternative, and the two-way interaction between "comfort" and "travel time" for the bus alternative). Note that the analyst must pre-specify which interactions are to be tested before a design can be generated, as well as whether linear or non-linear effects (or some combination of the two) are to be estimated.

To generate an experimental design in SPSS, the following actions are required. Go to the *Data* option in the toolbar menu. In the pop down menu select *Orthogonal Design* and then *Generate*... This will open the *Generate Orthogonal Design* dialog box. We show these dialog boxes in figure 5.5.

To progress, the analyst uses the *Generate Orthogonal Design* dialog box to name the attributes to be generated. We do this by typing the names of the attributes (factors) into the Factor Name box and pressing the *Add* button after each entry. Once the *Add* button has been pressed, the attribute name will appear in the box next to the add button. Note that SPSS allows for designs with up to 10 attributes (we discuss later how one may generate larger designs). Continuing with our example, the analyst provides each of the attributes with generic titles. For this example, we will use the names, A, B, C, D, E, F, G, H, and I.

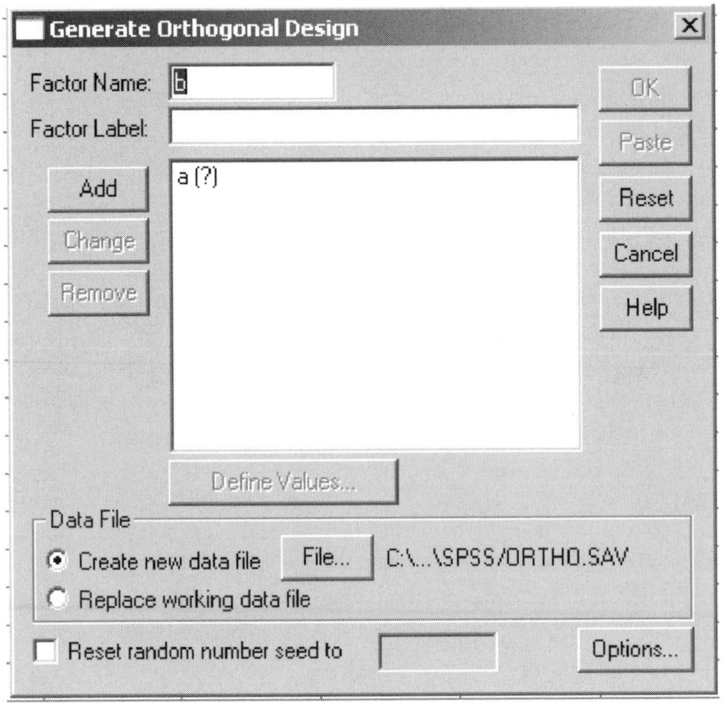

Figure 5.5 Generating designs using SPSS

Note that we have provided nine attribute names, and not eight. We will use one of these attributes (we do not know which yet) as a *blocking attribute*.

Next, the analyst must specify the number of *attribute levels*. For main-effects only designs, the analyst provides attribute names that are specific to the attribute. As such, the number of attribute levels to be related to a specific attribute must specifically be applied to that attribute (e.g. we must assign three levels to the "comfort" attribute for the car alternative). If for the case of main effects plus selected interactions designs, generic titles have been used, the analyst must be careful to assign the correct number of attribute levels as required in the experiment (e.g. if two attributes are at two levels and four are at three levels, then attributes A and B will be assigned two levels and attributes C, D, E, and F will be assigned three levels each). To assign the attribute levels, we note that there appears a [?] next to each attribute name. This symbol signifies that there are no attribute levels assigned to this attribute. To assign levels, select the attribute and press the *Define Values*... pushbutton. This will open the *Generate Design: Define Values* dialog box (see figure 5.6). Note that you may select more than one attribute at a time to assign attribute levels if the numbers of levels for the attributes are the same.

SPSS allows for up to nine attribute levels for each attribute. For our example, we wish to assign each attribute three attribute levels. We will title these 0, 1, and 2 in line with our

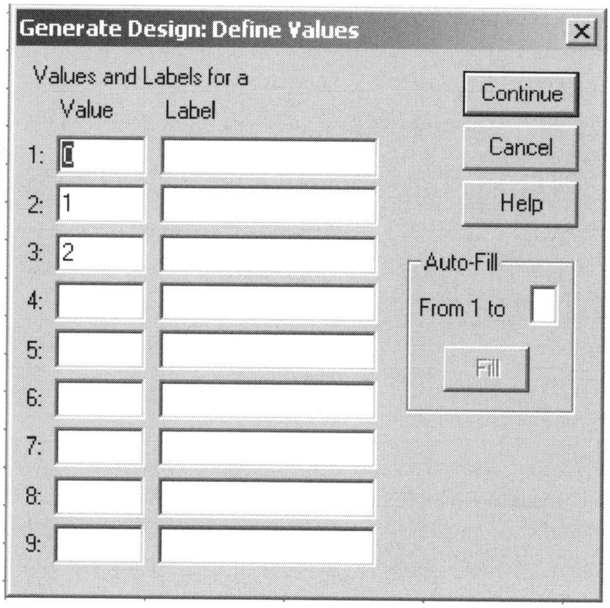

Figure 5.6 Specifying the number of attribute levels per attribute

coding format established earlier. We enter these values as shown in figure 5.6. Once the attribute levels have been correctly specified we press *Continue*.

Upon returning to the *Generate Orthogonal Design* dialog box, the analyst will notice that the attribute levels are now specified next to the attribute names. Before we can continue, the analyst must be aware of the number of treatment combinations required due to the degrees of freedom necessary for estimation purposes. In generating a design for any number of attributes and attribute levels, SPSS will generate the smallest design available (although this is not strictly true, as we will see) capable of estimating non-linear effects. As we have seen, the smallest experimental design possible (that we would consider using) is a main effects only design. Thus, if a larger design as a result of a greater number of degrees of freedom is required for estimation purposes (e.g. due to the necessity to estimate interaction effects), we are required to inform SPSS of this. We do this by selecting the options button in the *Generate Orthogonal Design* dialog box. This will open the *Generate Orthogonal Design: Options* dialog box. Following on from our earlier example, we note that the minimum number of treatment combinations required for a design with main effects plus two two-way interactions, where each attribute within the design has three levels, is 25. We therefore place 25 in the *Minimum number of cases to generate:* box and press *Continue* (figure 5.7).

The analyst is now ready to generate an experimental design. Before doing so, however, the analyst may elect to generate the design in a file saved somewhere on their computer, or to have the design replace the active worksheet in SPSS. This decision is made in the

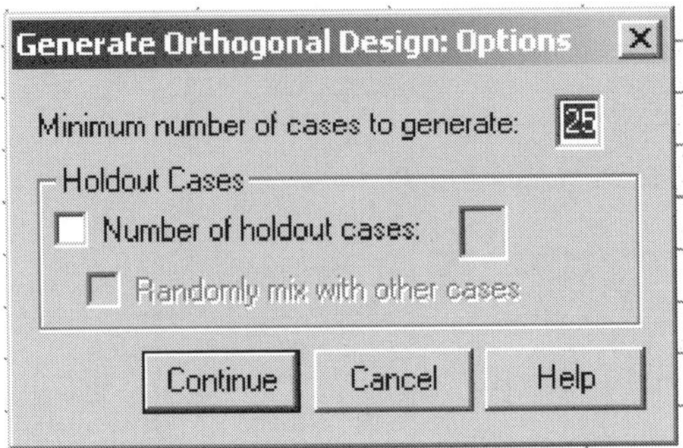

Figure 5.7 Specifying the minimum number of treatment combinations to generate

Generate Orthogonal Design dialog box in the section titled *Data File*. Having selected where the design is outputted to generate the design, press the *OK* button.

As an aside, note that the reader should generate statistical designs from first principles rather than use statistical packages such as SPSS. To prove why, we invite the reader to generate a design with eight attributes each with three levels without specifying the minimum number of treatment combinations to generate. In doing so, the reader should note that the design generated will have 27 treatment combinations. This is certainly not the smallest design possible. As we noted earlier, we are able to generate a workable design capable of estimating non-linear effects for each attribute from first principles that has only 18 treatment combinations for the attributes and attribute levels as specified. While the 27-treatment combination is useful, this highlights one problem in using computer programs to generate designs.

As a further aside, note that SPSS will generate a different design each time the process described is followed. Thus, if the reader uses SPSS to generate two designs without changing any inputs to the program, two completely different designs will be generated. As such, the reader is advised that should they follow our example and attempt to replicate the design we display in the next section, it is probable that they will obtain a different-looking design. No matter what the design generated, SPSS ensures that the design generated will be orthogonal.

5.2.4.1 Assigning an attribute as a blocking variable

We noted earlier that the analyst may chose to create a blocking variable in order to reduce the number of choice sets each decision maker will be given. Optimally, this blocking variable will be orthogonal to the other design attributes. As such, we generate the blocking variable at the time of design generation. For main-effects only designs, the analyst should name the specific variable in some fashion that will specifically identify the design column generated as being related to the blocking variable. For main effects plus selected interaction designs, the analyst does not pre-specify which design column will be used as the blocking variable, although there exists an exception to this rule.

Consider our example in which 27 treatment combinations are generated using SPSS. If we allocate to each attribute of the design three levels (as we have in the example), then the blocking variable (whichever design column it may be) will have to assume three levels also. As such, each block will have nine treatment combinations (i.e. have a block size of nine, worked out by dividing 27 by three). If however we wish to show each decision maker three choice sets and not nine, then we would have to allocate at least one attribute with nine levels and use this attribute as our blocking variable (i.e. we would have nine blocks of block size three).

5.2.5 Stage 5: allocating attributes to design columns

We noted in the previous section that if a main effects only design is required, stages 4 and 5 of the design process are conducted simultaneously. As such, the analyst may proceed directly to stage 6 of the design process. If, however, main effects plus selected interactions are of interest, then the generation of the design is separated from the allocation of the attributes to the design columns generated.

To allocate the attributes to design columns, the analyst is required to code the attribute levels using *orthogonal codes*, as opposed to the design codes used up until this point. Table 5.12 shows a design generated using SPSS in which we have coded the attribute levels using orthogonal codes.

We prefer to use orthogonal coding due to some desirable properties we observe from such coding. Primarily, orthogonal codes allow the analyst to observe the design columns for the interaction effects. To generate the interaction columns of a design, the analyst simply multiplies the appropriate main effects columns together. For example, columns A and B represent the main effects columns for two attributes (although we are unsure which two attributes at this stage). To obtain the interaction column for the A and B columns (i.e. the AB interaction) the analyst multiplies each of the terms of the A and B columns. Taking the first treatment combination of table 5.12, the AB interaction term is equal to 1 (i.e. -1×-1). This process is followed for higher-order interactions. For example, the ADEF interaction column is obtained by multiplying the A, D, E, and F columns together. For the first treatment, the ADEF interaction is observed to take the level, 0 (i.e. $-1 \times 0 \times 0 \times -1$). For our example, the analyst may generate columns for the two-way interactions, three-way interactions, four-way interactions, up to the nine-way interaction (e.g. ABCDEFGHI).

As an aside, it is good practice to test the effect of blocks on the experiment. This may include testing the interaction of the blocking variable with the attribute columns of the design. If we use up to the nine-way interaction, then we have included the blocking variable in the interaction effect. Doing so, however, will require that the blocking variable be included in the model, which in turn requires that the degrees of freedom for that variable be included in the determination of how many treatment combinations are required.

The analyst is not required to generate all of the interaction columns in order to determine which attributes to allocate to which design columns. As a rule of thumb, the analyst should generate all interactions up to the order of the highest-order interaction the analyst

Table 5.12. *Orthogonal coding of fractional factorial design*

Treatment combination	A	B	C	D	E	F	G	H	I
1	−1	−1	1	0	0	−1	0	−1	1
2	1	0	1	−1	−1	0	0	−1	−1
3	0	0	1	0	−1	−1	1	0	0
4	0	0	0	1	0	−1	−1	0	−1
5	1	−1	0	−1	1	1	−1	0	1
6	0	1	0	−1	−1	1	1	−1	−1
7	−1	1	0	0	−1	0	−1	0	0
8	0	−1	0	0	1	0	0	1	−1
9	1	0	0	0	0	0	1	−1	1
10	1	1	1	0	1	−1	−1	1	−1
11	0	−1	−1	1	−1	0	1	1	1
12	−1	0	−1	0	1	1	1	1	−1
13	−1	1	−1	1	0	0	0	0	−1
14	1	1	−1	−1	0	−1	1	1	0
15	−1	−1	0	1	1	−1	1	−1	0
16	0	−1	1	−1	0	0	−1	1	0
17	−1	0	1	1	−1	1	−1	1	1
18	−1	−1	−1	−1	−1	−1	−1	−1	−1
19	1	−1	−1	0	−1	1	0	0	0
20	−1	1	1	−1	1	0	1	0	1
21	1	0	−1	1	1	0	−1	−1	0
22	0	1	−1	0	0	1	−1	−1	1
23	−1	0	0	−1	0	1	0	1	0
24	1	1	0	1	−1	−1	0	1	1
25	0	1	1	1	1	1	0	−1	0
26	1	−1	1	1	0	1	1	0	−1
27	0	0	−1	−1	1	−1	0	0	1

wishes to estimate. For our example, the highest-order interaction the analyst desires to test is a two-way interaction. Thus, all two-way interaction columns should be produced. Had it been the desire of the analyst to test a four-way interaction (e.g. the interaction between the travel time attributes for each of the alternatives) then all two-way, three-way, and four-way design columns should be examined. Table 5.13 shows the design columns for all main effects and all two-way interactions columns for the design shown in table 5.12.

As an aside, table 5.13 was derived using Microsoft Excel, as shown in figure 5.8. In Figure 5.8 cells K2 through Q2 show the calculations of the two-way interaction effects while cells K3 through Q28 show the results of similar calculations for each remaining row of the design.

The next stage of the process is to generate the complete correlation matrix for all main effects and interaction terms. This is shown in table 5.14. Examining the correlation matrix

	A	B	C	D	E	F	G	H	I	J	K	L	M	N	O	P	Q
1	**Treatment Combination**	**A**	**B**	**C**	**D**	**E**	**F**	**G**	**H**	**I**	**AB**	**AC**	**AD**	**AE**	**AF**	**AG**	**AH**
2	1	-1	-1	1	0	0	-1	0	-1	1	=$B2*C2	=$B2*D2	=$B2*E2	=$B2*F2	=$B2*G2	=$B2*H2	=$B2*I2
3	2	1	0	1	-1	-1	0	0	-1	-1	0	1	-1	-1	0	0	-1
4	3	0	0	1	0	-1	-1	1	0	0	0	0	0	0	0	0	0
5	4	0	0	0	1	0	-1	-1	0	-1	0	0	0	0	0	0	0
6	5	1	-1	0	-1	1	1	-1	0	1	-1	0	-1	1	1	-1	0
7	6	0	1	0	-1	-1	1	1	-1	-1	0	0	0	0	0	0	0
8	7	-1	1	0	0	-1	0	-1	0	0	-1	0	0	1	0	1	0
9	8	0	-1	0	0	1	0	0	1	-1	0	0	0	0	0	0	0
10	9	1	0	0	0	0	0	1	-1	1	0	0	0	0	0	1	-1
11	10	1	1	1	0	1	-1	-1	1	-1	1	1	0	1	-1	-1	1
12	11	0	-1	-1	1	-1	0	1	1	1	0	0	0	0	0	0	0
13	12	-1	0	-1	0	1	1	1	1	-1	0	1	0	-1	-1	-1	-1
14	13	-1	1	-1	1	0	0	0	0	-1	-1	1	-1	0	0	0	0
15	14	1	1	-1	-1	0	-1	1	1	0	1	-1	-1	0	-1	1	1
16	15	-1	-1	0	1	1	-1	1	-1	0	1	0	-1	-1	1	-1	1
17	16	0	-1	1	-1	0	0	-1	1	0	0	0	0	0	0	0	0
18	17	-1	0	1	1	-1	1	-1	1	1	0	-1	-1	1	-1	1	-1
19	18	-1	-1	-1	-1	-1	-1	-1	-1	-1	1	1	1	1	1	1	1
20	19	1	-1	-1	0	-1	1	0	0	0	-1	-1	0	-1	1	0	0
21	20	-1	1	1	-1	1	0	1	0	1	-1	-1	1	-1	0	-1	0
22	21	1	0	-1	1	1	0	-1	-1	0	0	-1	1	1	0	-1	-1
23	22	0	1	-1	0	0	1	-1	-1	1	0	0	0	0	0	0	0
24	23	-1	0	0	-1	0	1	0	1	0	0	0	1	0	-1	0	-1
25	24	1	1	0	1	-1	-1	0	1	1	1	0	1	-1	-1	0	1
26	25	0	1	1	1	1	1	0	-1	0	0	0	0	0	0	0	0
27	26	1	-1	1	1	0	1	1	0	-1	-1	1	1	0	1	1	0
28	27	0	0	-1	-1	1	-1	0	0	1	0	0	0	0	0	0	0

Figure 5.8 Calculating interaction design codes using Microsoft Excel

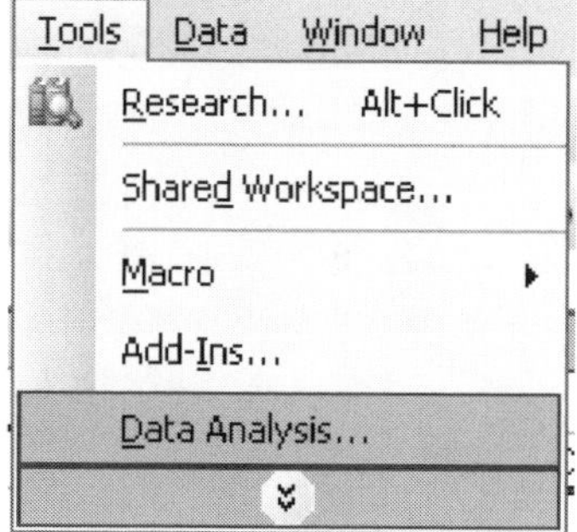

Figure 5.9 Microsoft Excel commands to generate correlations

in table 5.14 reveals that all of the main effects are uncorrelated with all other main effects. Using the terminology of the experimental design literature, we say that the main effects are *un-confounded with each other*.

As an aside, the correlation matrix shown as table 5.14 was also derived using Microsoft Excel. This can be done by first selecting the *Tools* toolbar option followed by the *Data Analysis... option* as shown in figure 5.9. Note that the *Data Analysis...* option is not automatically installed with Microsoft Excel. If the option is not present in the Tools Toolbar drop down menu, the reader will need to add the option via the *Add-Ins...* option, also shown in figure 5.9.

Table 5.13. *Orthogonal codes for main effects plus all two-way interaction columns*

Treatment combination	1	2	3	4	5	6	7	8	9	10	11	12	13
A	−1	1	0	0	1	0	−1	0	1	1	0	−1	−1
B	−1	0	0	0	−1	1	1	−1	0	1	−1	0	1
C	1	1	1	0	0	0	0	0	0	1	−1	−1	−1
D	0	−1	0	1	−1	−1	0	0	0	0	1	0	1
E	0	−1	−1	0	1	−1	−1	1	0	1	−1	1	0
F	−1	0	−1	−1	1	1	0	0	0	−1	0	1	0
G	0	0	1	−1	−1	1	−1	0	1	−1	1	1	0
H	−1	−1	0	0	0	−1	0	1	−1	1	1	1	0
I	1	−1	0	−1	1	−1	0	−1	1	−1	1	−1	−1
AB	1	0	0	0	−1	0	−1	0	0	1	0	0	−1
AC	−1	1	0	0	0	0	0	0	0	1	0	1	1
AD	0	−1	0	0	−1	0	0	0	0	0	0	0	−1
AE	0	−1	0	0	1	0	1	0	0	1	0	−1	0
AF	1	0	0	0	1	0	0	0	0	−1	0	−1	0
AG	0	0	0	0	−1	0	1	0	1	−1	0	−1	0
AH	1	−1	0	0	0	0	0	0	−1	1	0	−1	0
AI	−1	−1	0	0	1	0	0	0	1	−1	0	1	1
BC	−1	0	0	0	0	0	0	0	0	1	1	0	−1
BD	0	0	0	0	1	−1	0	0	0	0	−1	0	1
BE	0	0	0	0	−1	−1	−1	−1	0	1	1	0	0
BF	1	0	0	0	−1	1	0	0	0	−1	0	0	0
BG	0	0	0	0	1	1	−1	0	0	−1	−1	0	0
BH	1	0	0	0	0	−1	0	−1	0	1	−1	0	0
BI	−1	0	0	0	−1	−1	0	1	0	−1	−1	0	−1
CD	0	−1	0	0	0	0	0	0	0	0	−1	0	−1
CE	0	−1	−1	0	0	0	0	0	0	1	1	−1	0
CF	−1	0	−1	0	0	0	0	0	0	−1	0	−1	0
CG	0	0	1	0	0	0	0	0	0	−1	−1	−1	0
CH	−1	−1	0	0	0	0	0	0	0	1	−1	−1	0
CI	1	−1	0	0	0	0	0	0	0	−1	−1	1	1
DE	0	1	0	0	−1	1	0	0	0	0	−1	0	0
DF	0	0	0	−1	−1	−1	0	0	0	0	0	0	0
DG	0	0	0	−1	1	−1	0	0	0	0	1	0	0
DH	0	1	0	0	0	1	0	0	0	0	1	0	0
DI	0	1	0	−1	−1	1	0	0	0	0	1	0	−1
EF	0	0	1	0	1	−1	0	0	0	−1	0	1	0
EG	0	0	−1	0	−1	−1	1	0	0	−1	−1	1	0
EH	0	1	0	0	0	1	0	1	0	1	−1	1	0
EI	0	1	0	0	1	1	0	−1	0	−1	−1	−1	0
FG	0	0	−1	1	−1	1	0	0	0	1	0	1	0
FH	1	0	0	0	0	−1	0	0	0	−1	0	1	0
FI	−1	0	0	1	1	−1	0	0	0	1	0	−1	0
GH	0	0	0	0	0	−1	0	0	−1	−1	1	1	0
GI	0	0	0	1	−1	−1	0	0	1	1	1	−1	0
HI	−1	1	0	0	0	1	0	−1	−1	−1	1	−1	0

14	15	16	17	18	19	20	21	22	23	24	25	26	27
1	−1	0	−1	−1	1	−1	1	0	−1	1	0	1	0
1	−1	−1	0	−1	−1	1	0	1	0	1	1	−1	0
−1	0	1	1	−1	−1	1	−1	−1	0	0	1	1	−1
−1	1	−1	1	−1	0	−1	1	0	−1	1	1	1	−1
0	1	0	−1	−1	−1	1	1	0	0	−1	1	0	1
−1	−1	0	1	−1	1	0	0	1	1	−1	1	1	−1
1	1	−1	−1	−1	0	1	−1	−1	0	0	0	1	0
1	−1	1	1	−1	0	0	−1	−1	1	1	−1	0	0
0	0	0	1	−1	0	1	0	1	0	1	0	−1	1
1	1	0	0	1	−1	−1	0	0	0	1	0	−1	0
−1	0	0	−1	1	−1	−1	−1	0	0	0	0	1	0
−1	−1	0	−1	1	0	1	1	0	1	1	0	1	0
0	−1	0	1	1	−1	−1	1	0	0	−1	0	0	0
−1	1	0	−1	1	1	0	0	0	−1	−1	0	1	0
1	−1	0	1	1	0	−1	−1	0	0	0	0	1	0
1	1	0	−1	1	0	0	−1	0	−1	1	0	0	0
0	0	0	−1	1	0	−1	0	0	0	1	0	−1	0
−1	0	−1	0	1	1	1	0	−1	0	0	1	−1	0
−1	−1	1	0	1	0	−1	0	0	0	1	1	−1	0
0	−1	0	0	1	1	1	0	0	0	−1	1	0	0
−1	1	0	0	1	−1	0	0	1	0	−1	1	−1	0
1	−1	1	0	1	0	1	0	−1	0	0	0	−1	0
1	1	−1	0	1	0	0	0	−1	0	1	−1	0	0
0	0	0	0	1	0	1	0	1	0	1	0	1	0
1	0	−1	1	1	0	−1	−1	0	0	0	1	1	1
0	0	0	−1	1	1	1	−1	0	0	0	1	0	−1
1	0	0	1	1	−1	0	0	−1	0	0	1	1	1
−1	0	−1	−1	1	0	1	1	1	0	0	0	1	0
−1	0	1	1	1	0	0	1	1	0	0	−1	0	0
0	0	0	1	1	0	1	0	−1	0	0	0	−1	−1
0	1	0	−1	1	0	−1	1	0	0	−1	1	0	−1
1	−1	0	1	1	0	0	0	0	−1	−1	1	1	1
−1	1	1	−1	1	0	−1	−1	0	0	0	0	1	0
−1	−1	−1	1	1	0	0	−1	0	−1	1	−1	0	0
0	0	0	1	1	0	−1	0	0	0	1	0	−1	−1
0	−1	0	−1	1	−1	0	0	0	0	1	1	0	−1
0	1	0	1	1	0	1	−1	0	0	0	0	0	0
0	−1	0	−1	1	0	0	−1	0	0	−1	−1	0	0
0	0	0	−1	1	0	1	0	0	0	−1	0	0	1
−1	−1	0	−1	1	0	0	0	−1	0	0	0	1	0
−1	1	0	1	1	0	0	0	−1	1	−1	−1	0	0
0	0	0	1	1	0	0	0	1	0	−1	0	−1	−1
1	−1	−1	−1	1	0	0	1	1	0	0	0	0	0
0	0	0	−1	1	0	1	0	−1	0	0	0	−1	0
0	0	0	1	1	0	0	0	−1	0	1	0	0	0

Table 5.14. *Design correlation*

	A	B	C	D	E	F	G	H	I	AB	AC	AD
A	1	0	0	0	0	0	0	0	0	0	0	0
B	0	1	0	0	0	0	0	0	0	0	0	0
C	0	0	1	0	0	0	0	0	0	0	0	0
D	0	0	0	1	0	0	0	0	0	0	0	0
E	0	0	0	0	1	0	0	0	0	0	0	0
F	0	0	0	0	0	1	0	0	0	−0.6	0	0
G	0	0	0	0	0	0	1	0	0	0	0	0
H	0	0	0	0	0	0	0	1	0	0	0	0
I	0	0	0	0	0	0	0	0	1	0	−0.6	0
AB	0	0	0	0	0	−0.6	0	0	0	1	0	0
AC	0	0	0	0	0	0	0	0	−0.6	0	1	0
AD	0	0	0	0	0	0	0	0	0	0	0	1
AE	0	0	0	0	0	0	−0.6	0	0	0	0	0
AF	0	−0.6	0	0	0	0	0	−0.6	0	−0.3	0	0
AG	0	0	0	0	−0.6	0	0	0	0	0	0	0
AH	0	0	0	0	0	−0.6	0	0	0	0.5	0	0
AI	0	0	−0.6	0	0	0	0	0	0	0	0.25	0
BC	0	0	0	0	0	0	0	0	0	0	0	0.25
BD	0	0	0	0	0	0	−0.6	0	0	0	0.25	0
BE	0	0	0	0	0	0	0	0	0	0	0	0.25
BF	−0.6	0	0	0	0	0	0	−0.6	0	0.25	0	0
BG	0	0	0	−0.6	0	0	0	0	0	0	−0.3	0
BH	0	0	0	0	0	−0.6	0	0	0	0.5	0	0
BI	0	0	0	0	0	0	0	0	0	0	0	0.5
CD	0	0	0	0	0	0	0	0	0	0.3	0	0
CE	0	0	0	0	0	0	0	0	0	0	0	0.3
CF	0	0	0	0	0	0	0	0	0	0	0	0
CG	0	0	0	0	0	0	0	−0.6	0	−0.3	0	0.5
CH	0	0	0	0	0	0	−0.6	0	0	0	0	0.25
CI	−0.6	0	0	0	0	0	0	0	0	0	−0.3	0
DE	0	0	0	0	0	0	0	−0.6	−0.6	0.25	0.25	0
DF	0	0	0	0	0	0	0	0	0	0	0	0
DG	0	−0.6	0	0	0	0	0	0	0	0	0.5	0
DH	0	0	0	0	−0.6	0	0	0	0	0	0.25	0
DI	0	0	0	0	−0.6	0	0	0	0	0.5	0	0
EF	0	0	0	0	0	0	0	0	0	0	0.25	0.25
EG	−0.6	0	0	0	0	0	0	0	0	0	0	0
EH	0	0	0	−0.6	0	0	0	0	−0.6	0	0.5	0
EI	0	0	0	−0.6	0	0	0	−0.6	0	−0.3	0	0
FG	0	0	0	0	0	0	0	0	−0.6	0	0.5	0.5
FH	−0.6	−0.6	0	0	0	0	0	0	0	0	0	0
FI	0	0	0	0	0	0	−0.6	0	0	0	0	−0.3
GH	0	0	−0.6	0	0	0	0	0	0	0	0	0.25
GI	0	0	0	0	0	−0.6	0	0	0	0.25	0	0.25
HI	0	0	0	0	−0.6	0	0	0	0	0	0	0

AE	AF	AG	AH	AI	BC	BD	BE	BF	BG	BH	BI
0	0	0	0	0	0	0	0	−0.6	0	0	0
0	−0.6	0	0	0	0	0	0	0	0	0	0
0	0	0	0	−0.6	0	0	0	0	0	0	0
0	0	0	0	0	0	0	0	0	−0.6	0	0
0	0	−0.6	0	0	0	0	0	0	0	0	0
0	0	0	−0.6	0	0	0	0	0	0	−0.6	0
−0.6	0	0	0	0	0	−0.6	0	0	0	0	0
0	−0.6	0	0	0	0	0	0	−0.6	0	0	0
0	0	0	0	0	0	0	0	0	0	0	0
0	−0.3	0	0.5	0	0	0	0	0.25	0	0.5	0
0	0	0	0	0.25	0	0.25	0	0	−0.3	0	0
0	0	0	0	0	0.3	0	0.3	0	0	0	0.5
1	0	0.25	0	0	0	0.25	0	0	0	0	−0.3
0	1	0	0.25	0	0	0	0	0.25	0	0	0
0.25	0	1	0	0	−0.3	0	0	0	0	0.5	0.25
0	0.25	0	1	0	0	0	0	0	0	0	0
0	0	0	0	1	0	0.5	−0.3	0	0.25	0	0
0	0	−0.3	0	0	1	0	0.5	0	0	0	0
0.25	0	0	0	0.5	0	1	0	0	0.25	0	0
0	0	0	0	−0.3	0.5	0	1	0	0	0	0
0	0.25	0	0	0	0	0	0	1	0	−0.3	0
0	0	0	0	0.25	0	0.25	0	0	1	0	0
0	0	0	0.5	0	0	0	0	−0.3	0	1	0
−0.3	0	0.25	0	0	0	0	0	0	0	0	1
0.3	0	0.5	0.3	0	0	0	0	0	0	0.3	0.3
0	0.3	0	0.5	0	0.5	0	0.5	0	0	0	0
0.3	0	0.5	0	0	0	0	0	0	0.3	0	0.3
0	0.5	0	0	0	0	0	0	0.25	0	0	0.5
0.5	0	0	0	0	0	0.25	0	0	0	0	0.25
0	0	0	0	0.25	0	0.25	0	0.25	0.5	0.25	0
0	0.25	0	0	0	0	0	0	0.5	0	0	0
0.25	0	0.5	0	−0.3	0	0	0.5	0	0	0	0.25
0	0.5	0	0.25	0.25	0	0.25	0	0	−0.3	0	0
0	0	0.25	0	0	0.25	0	0	0	0	0	0
0	−0.3	0.25	0	0	0.25	0	0	0.25	0	0	0
0	0	0	0	0.5	0	0.5	0	0	0.25	0	0.25
−0.3	0	0.25	0	0	0	0	0	0.25	0	0.25	0.5
0	0	0	0	0	0	0	0	0	0.25	0	0
0	0.5	0	0	0	0	0	0	0.25	0.5	0	0
0	0	0	0	0	0.25	0	0.25	0	0	0	0
0	0.25	0	−0.3	0	0	0	0	0.25	0	0.25	0
0.5	0	0	0	0	0.25	0.25	0.25	0	0	0	0
0	0	0	0	0.25	0	0	0.25	0	0	0	0.25
0	0	0	0.25	0	0.5	0	0.5	0	0	0.25	0
0	0	0.25	0	0	0.25	0	0	0	0.25	0	0

(*cont.*)

Table 5.14. (*Cont.*)

	CD	CE	CF	CG	CH	CI	DE	DF	DG	DH	DI
A	0	0	0	0	0	−0.6	0	0	0	0	0
B	0	0	0	0	0	0	0	0	−0.6	0	0
C	0	0	0	0	0	0	0	0	0	0	0
D	0	0	0	0	0	0	0	0	0	0	0
E	0	0	0	0	0	0	0	0	0	−0.6	−0.6
F	0	0	0	0	0	0	0	0	0	0	0
G	0	0	0	0	−0.6	0	0	0	0	0	0
H	0	0	0	−0.6	0	0	−0.6	0	0	0	0
I	0	0	0	0	0	0	−0.6	0	0	0	0
AB	0.25	0	0	−0.3	0	0	0.25	0	0	0	0.5
AC	0	0	0	0	0	−0.3	0.25	0	0.5	0.25	0
AD	0	0.3	0	0.5	0.3	0	0	0	0	0	0
AE	0.25	0	0.25	0	0.5	0	0	0.25	0	0	0
AF	0	0.25	0	0.5	0	0	0.25	0	0.5	0	−0.3
AG	0.5	0	0.5	0	0	0	0	0.5	0	0.25	0.25
AH	0.25	0.5	0	0	0	0	0	0	0.25	0	0
AI	0	0	0	0	0	0.25	0	−0.3	0.25	0	0
BC	0	0.5	0	0	0	0	0	0	0	0.25	0.25
BD	0	0	0	0	0.25	0.25	0	0	0.25	0	0
BE	0	0.5	0	0	0	0	0	0.5	0	0	0
BF	0	0	0	0.25	0	0.25	0.5	0	0	0	0.25
BG	0	0	0.25	0	0	0.5	0	0	−0.3	0	0
BH	0.25	0	0	0	0	0.25	0	0	0	0	0
BI	0.25	0	0.25	0.5	0.25	0	0	0.25	0	0	0
CD	1	0	0.5	0	0	0	0	0.5	0	0	0
CE	0	1	0	0	0	0	0	0	0.3	0	0
CF	0.5	0	1	0	0	0	0	0.5	0	0	0
CG	0	0	0	1	0.25	0	0.25	0	0	0	−0.3
CH	0	0	0	0.25	1	0	0	0	0	0	0
CI	0	0	0	0	0	1	0	0	−0.3	0	0
DE	0	0	0	0.25	0	0	1	0	0	−0.3	0.25
DF	0.5	0	0.5	0	0	0	0	1	0	0	0
DG	0	0.25	0	0	0	−0.3	0	0	1	0	0
DH	0	0	0	0	0	0	−0.3	0	0	1	0.5
DI	0	0	0	−0.3	0	0	0.25	0	0	0.5	1
EF	0	0	0	0.25	−0.3	0.25	0	0	0.25	0	0
EG	0.25	0	0.25	0	0	0.5	0	0.25	0	0	0
EH	0	0	−0.3	0	0	0	0.25	0	0	0.25	0
EI	0	0	0.25	0.5	0	0	0.25	0	0	0	−0.3
FG	0	0.25	0	0	0	0	0.25	0	0	0.25	0
FH	0	−0.3	0	0	0	0.5	0	0	0.25	0	0
FI	0	0.25	0	0	0.5	0	0	0	0	0	0
GH	0	0	0	0.25	−0.3	0	0	0.25	0	0	0
GI	−0.3	0.5	0	0	0	0	0	0	0	0	0
HI	0	0	0.5	0	0	0	0	0	0	0.5	0.5

EF	EG	EH	EI	FG	FH	FI	GH	GI	HI
0	−0.6	0	0	0	−0.6	0	0	0	0
0	0	0	0	0	−0.6	0	0	0	0
0	0	0	0	0	0	0	−0.6	0	0
0	0	−0.6	−0.6	0	0	0	0	0	0
0	0	0	0	0	0	0	0	0	−0.6
0	0	0	0	0	0	0	0	−0.6	0
0	0	0	0	0	0	−0.6	0	0	0
0	0	0	−0.6	0	0	0	0	0	0
0	0	−0.6	0	−0.6	0	0	0	0	0
0	0	0	−0.3	0	0	0	0	0.25	0
0.25	0	0.5	0	0.5	0	0	0	0	0
0.3	0	0	0	0.5	0	−0.3	0.3	0.3	0
0	−0.3	0	0	0	0	0.5	0	0	0
0	0	0	0.5	0	0.25	0	0	0	0
0	0.25	0	0	0	0	0	0	0	0.25
0	0	0	0	0	−0.3	0	0	0.25	0
0.5	0	0	0	0	0	0	0.25	0	0
0	0	0	0	0.25	0	0.25	0	0.5	0.25
0.5	0	0	0	0	0	0.25	0	0	0
0	0	0	0	0.25	0	0.25	0.25	0.5	0
0	0.25	0	0.25	0	0.25	0	0	0	0
0.25	0	0.25	0.5	0	0	0	0	0	0.25
0	0.25	0	0	0	0.25	0	0	0.25	0
0.25	0.5	0	0	0	0	0	0.25	0	0
0	0.3	0	0	0	0	0	0	−0.3	0
0	0	0	0	0.3	−0.3	0.3	0	0.5	0
0	0.3	−0.3	0.3	0	0	0	0	0	0.5
0.25	0	0	0.5	0	0	0	0.25	0	0
−0.3	0	0	0	0	0	0.5	−0.3	0	0
0.25	0.5	0	0	0	0.5	0	0	0	0
0	0	0.25	0.25	0.25	0	0	0	0	0
0	0.25	0	0	0	0	0	0.25	0	0
0.25	0	0	0	0	0.25	0	0	0	0
0	0	0.25	0	0.25	0	0	0	0	0.5
0	0	0	−0.3	0	0	0	0	0	0.5
1	0	0	0	0	0	0	0.5	0	0
0	1	0	0	0	0.5	0	0	0	0
0	0	1	0.25	0.5	0	0	0	0	−0.3
0	0	0.25	1	0	0	0	0	0	0.25
0	0	0.5	0	1	0	−0.3	0	0.25	0
0	0.5	0	0	0	1	0	0	0	0
0	0	0	0	−0.3	0	1	0	0.25	0
0.5	0	0	0	0	0	0	1	0	0
0	0	0	0	0.25	0	0.25	0	1	0
0	0	−0.3	0.25	0	0	0	0	0	1

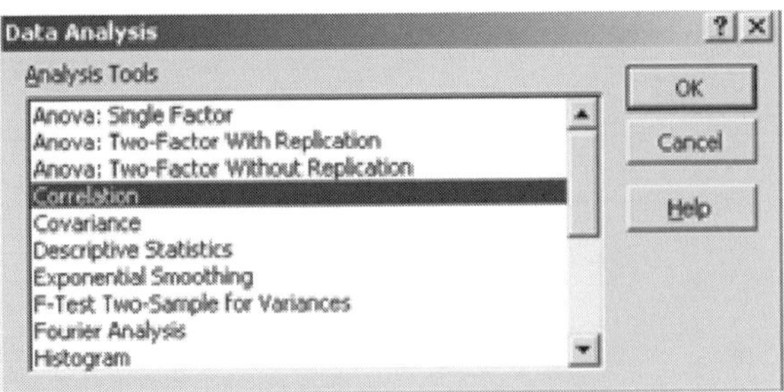

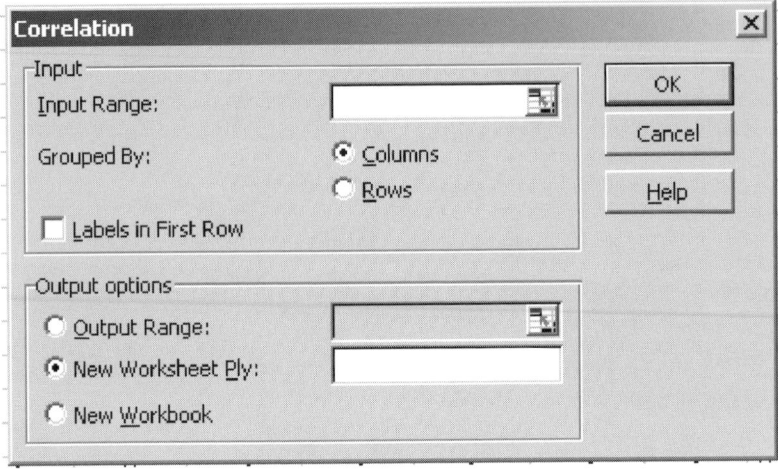

Figure 5.10 Microsoft Excel Data Analysis and Correlation dialog boxes

Selecting *Data Analysis*... from the *Tools* drop down menu will open the *Data Analysis* dialog box (see figure 5.10). From the *Data Analysis* dialog box the analyst next selects the heading *Correlation* before pressing *OK*. This will open the *Correlation* dialog box, also shown in figure 5.10.

As an aside, the correlation coefficient used by Microsoft Excel is the Pearson product moment (PPM) correlation coefficient. As noted in chapter 2, this statistic is strictly appropriate only when the variables used in the test are ratio scaled. This is clearly not the case here. The full design with interaction columns (table 5.13) could be exported into SPSS and either the Spearman rho or Kendall's tau-b correlations be calculated; however, neither of these is strictly appropriate for the data either (see table 2A.1 in appendix 2A, p. 60). The appropriate measure to use for the design would be the J-index (see table 2A.1), however, unless the analyst has access to specialized software, this correlation coefficient will need to be calculated manually. This calculation is beyond the scope of this book and, as such, we rely on the PPM correlation coefficient, assumed to be an approximation for all similarity indices.

In the *Correlation* dialog box, all cells shown in figure 5.10 are selected in the *Input Range*: cell. By selecting the first row which includes the column headings, the analyst is also required to check the *Labels in First Row box*. This will show the column headings as part of the Excel correlation output otherwise Excel will assign generic column headings to the resulting correlation matrix output.

Note, however, the existence of correlations with the main effects columns and several of the interaction effects columns (e.g. design column A is correlated with the BF interaction column) as shown in table 5.14. This is an unfortunate consequence of using fractional factorial designs. By using only a fraction of the available treatment combinations, fractional factorial designs must confound some of the effects. Unless designs are generated from first principles, the analyst has no control over which effects are confounded (another reason why the serious choice analyst is best to learn how to generate statistical designs from first principles and not rely on computer packages).

As an aside, experience suggests that it is more likely that two-way interactions are statistically significant than three-way or higher interactions. Thus, designs in which all main effects are un-confounded with all two-way interactions are preferable. To demonstrate why this is so, return to our earlier discussion of the effects of confoundment. Confoundment produces model effects similar to the effects of multicollinearity in linear regression models. That is, the parameter estimates we obtain at the time of estimation are likely to be incorrect, as are their standard errors, and as such so are any tests we perform on attribute significance. Taking this example, unless the analyst tests specifically the statistical significance of the attributes assigned to the B and F design columns (we have not yet allocated attributes to columns), the analyst can never be sure that the parameter estimate for the main effect for the attribute assigned to column A are correct. We note that design column A is also confounded with the CI, EG, FH interaction columns. As with the BF interaction, significance of any of these interactions also poses problems for model estimation. We draw the reader's attention to the fact that the other main effects columns are also correlated with other interaction effects. Does the analyst test for these effects also? To do so will require larger designs due to the requirement for degrees of freedom. The only way to proceed is thus to assume that these interaction effects are insignificant in practice. While this assumption may seem unwise, the analyst can cut the odds in assuming interaction effects to be insignificant through selecting specific interaction effects to test. The selection of which effects to test for occurs prior to design generation. For example, the analyst in our example believed that the interaction between the comfort attribute and travel time attribute for the car and bus alternatives are likely to be significant. This determination was made in advance of the design generation.

To continue, the analyst first assigns the attributes for which interaction effects are to be tested. The analyst revisits the correlation matrix and identifies the two-way interaction columns for correlations with the main effects columns. Examination of table 5.14 reveals that the AD, BC, BE, BI, CD, CE, CF, DF, and EF two-way interaction columns are all un-confounded with all main effects design columns (but not with other two-way interaction columns). The analyst requires four design columns (two for the car interaction and two for the bus interaction). What is required is to determine which of the columns to use given the correlations amongst the main effects and two-way interaction columns. The analyst may assign any of the columns as suggested by the interaction combinations suggested above. That is, for the interaction between the *comfort* and *travel time* attributes the analyst may assign the *comfort* attribute to column A and the *travel time* attribute to column D (or *comfort* to D and *travel time* to A). Alternatively, the B and C, B and E, B and I, C and D, C and E, C and F, D and F, or E and F columns could be used. The analyst must also assign the attributes for the bus alternative to one of these combinations.

But which combinations should be used? Again the correlation matrix provides the answer. Once the analyst has identified which interaction design columns are un-confounded with the main effects design columns, the next step is to examine the correlations amongst the two-way interactions. Doing so, we note that the AD interaction column is confounded with the BC, BE, BI, CE, and EF design interaction columns. Hence, if the analyst were to assign the attributes of the car alternative to the A and D columns and the bus alternative attributes to any of the combinations of the interaction columns mentioned above, then the estimated interaction effects will be confounded. Thus, should the analyst decide to use the A and D columns for one interaction effect, the other interaction attributes should be assigned to the C and D, C and F, or the D and F columns. Note that we cannot assign two attributes to the D column; therefore, the second two attributes for which an interaction effect is to be tested must be assigned to the C and F columns. Had the B and C columns been utilized for the car attributes, the reader is invited to check that either D and F or E and F columns may be used for the second two attributes that the analyst wishes to obtain interactions for.

As an aside, assuming the A and D columns and C and F columns were the ones used, the two-way interactions may be treated as being independent of all main effects, but not of all other two-way interaction effects. Indeed, as with the main effects, the analyst must assume that the two-way interactions for the BC, BE, BI, CE, and EF interaction terms are insignificant in order to proceed (and that is only for the AD interaction). If, however, it turns out in practice any other interactions are significant, then the problem of estimating models with correlated data arises once more. That these interactions are insignificant statistically is an assumption for which there exists no way of testing. We have said nothing of confoundment that exists with higher-order interaction terms.

Assuming that the analyst elected to assign the car alternative attributes to the A and D columns and the bus alternative attributes to the C and F design columns, the remainder of the attributes may be distributed to the remaining design columns. No interaction terms are required for these and hence confoundment of the interaction terms for these remaining attributes is not an issue. Note that for our example, all attributes have three levels each, hence it matters not to which design columns we assign the remaining attributes. Had the design required one attribute to have four levels, then that attribute would be assigned to the design column with four attribute levels (or a pair of design columns each of two levels). Table 5.15 shows the attributes as they might be allocated to the design columns for the experimental design introduced in table 5.11. Note that we have allocated column I to be the block variable.

As an aside, the reader should be aware of the issue of *balanced versus unbalanced designs*. A balanced design is a design in which the levels of any given attribute appear the same number of times as all other levels for that particular attribute. For example, for the design described in table 5.15, for each attribute, the level coded -1 occurs nine times, 0 nine times, and 1 nine times. An unbalanced design is a design in which the attribute levels do not appear the same number of times within each attribute for the design. The use

Table 5.15. *Attributes assigned to design columns*

	comf1 (*car*)	*ttime1* (*car*)	*comf2* (*bus*)	*ttime2* (*bus*)	*comf3* (train)	*ttime3* (*train*)	*comf4* (*plane*)	*ttime4* (*plane*)	*block*
Design column / Treatment combination	A	D	C	F	E	B	G	H	I
1	−1	0	1	−1	0	−1	0	−1	1
2	1	−1	1	0	−1	0	0	−1	−1
3	0	0	1	−1	−1	0	1	0	0
4	0	1	0	−1	0	0	−1	0	−1
5	1	−1	0	1	1	−1	−1	0	1
6	0	−1	0	1	−1	1	1	−1	−1
7	−1	0	0	0	−1	1	−1	0	0
8	0	0	0	0	1	−1	0	1	−1
9	1	0	0	0	0	0	1	−1	1
10	1	0	1	−1	1	1	−1	1	−1
11	0	1	−1	0	−1	−1	1	1	1
12	−1	0	−1	1	1	0	1	1	−1
13	−1	1	−1	0	0	1	0	0	−1
14	1	−1	−1	−1	0	1	1	1	0
15	−1	1	0	−1	1	−1	1	−1	0
16	0	−1	1	0	0	−1	−1	1	0
17	−1	1	1	1	−1	0	−1	1	1
18	−1	−1	−1	−1	−1	−1	−1	−1	−1
19	1	0	−1	1	−1	−1	0	0	0
20	−1	−1	1	0	1	1	1	0	1
21	1	1	−1	0	1	0	−1	−1	0
22	0	0	−1	1	0	1	−1	−1	1
23	−1	−1	0	1	0	0	0	1	0
24	1	1	0	−1	−1	1	0	1	1
25	0	1	1	1	1	1	0	−1	0
26	1	1	1	1	0	−1	1	0	−1
27	0	−1	−1	−1	1	0	0	0	1

of balanced versus unbalanced designs is of interest as early research conducted suggests that the unbalanced attributes of an unbalanced design are often found to be statistically significant, not so much because the attribute itself is statistically significant, but because attention is drawn to that attribute at the time of the survey (Wittink and Nutter 1982; Wittink, Krishnamurti, and Reibstein 1990).

As an aside, the formulas shown in table 5.10 are used to calculate the minimum degrees of freedom necessary for estimating the desired number of parameters. The numbers derived may, however, not represent the true minimum number of treatment combinations necessary to achieve an orthogonal design, due to the necessity to maintain attribute-level balance within each attribute. For example, let M = 2, A = 3, and L = 2. The minimum number of treatment combinations assuming the estimation of non-linear effects in the marginal utilities in a labeled choice experiment is equal to $(2 - 1) \times 2 \times 3 + 1$ or seven. However, such a design will not be balanced as each attribute has two levels which must appear an equal number of times over seven choice sets. This represents an additional constraint, such that the smallest possible design will have a number of treatment combinations equal to or greater than that calculated using the relevant formula shown in table 5.10, but also be a number that produces an integer when divided by all L.

Before proceeding to stage 6 of the design process, the analyst may wish to sort the experimental design by the blocking variable. Doing so informs the analyst which mixture of treatment combinations will be shown to various decision makers. Looking at table 5.16, we see that one out of every three decision makers will be given treatment combinations 2, 4, 6, 8, 10, 12, 13, 18, and 26. Other decision makers will be presented with treatment combinations 3, 7, 14, 15, 16, 19, 21, 23, and 25. Yet other decision makers will be given treatment combinations 1, 5, 9, 11, 17, 20, 22, 24, and 27.

We have, in generating a fractional factorial design for the example described, managed to reduce the number of treatment combinations from 6561 (the full factorial design) to 27. Further, we have managed to reduce the 27 treatment combinations to nine in terms of how many treatment combinations each decision maker will be presented with (in the guise of choice sets). We have done so by confounding higher-order interaction effects which we are required to assume will be statistically insignificant.

The experimental design shown in table 5.16 represents a workable design capable of estimating all main effects and two two-way interactions. However returning to the method of how the design was derived, we note that the degrees of freedom used to determine the number of treatment combinations for the design was such that non-linear effects could be estimated for each attribute. That is, the analyst may elect to dummy or effects code each attribute and estimate a parameter for each dummy or effect variable thus created. It is therefore worthwhile examining how the design will look should the analyst elect to use effects codes (for dummy codes one simply has to replace all -1s with 0s). Using the orthogonal code of -1 in table 5.15 to represent the base level (i.e. the level that will take the value -1 in our effects code), the design will look as in table 5.17.

Note that we did not effects code column I of table 5.16. This is because this column represents the blocking column of the design for which we will not be estimating a parameter when we estimate our choice model (although we could in order to determine whether the block assigned was a significant contributor to the choice outcome). Table 5.18 shows the correlation matrix for the design shown in table 5.17.

Examination of table 5.18 shows that there now exist correlations within the design. Design orthogonality has been lost. Indeed, design orthogonality will exist for linear main effects designs only. Once one moves towards designs capable of estimating non-linear effects using such methods as effects or dummy coding, one automatically introduces correlations (we leave it to the reader to show the correlation structure formed when dummy codes are used instead of effects codes for the above example).

There therefore exists a trade-off in being able to detect non-linear effects and the introduction of correlations. Unfortunately, programs such as SPSS are able to generate

Table 5.16. *Using blocking variables to determine allocation of treatment combinations*

	comf1 (car)	*ttime1 (car)*	*comf2 (bus)*	*ttime2 (bus)*	*comf3 (train)*	*ttime3 (train)*	comf4 (*plane*)	*ttime4 (plane)*	*block*
Design column / Treatment combination	A	D	C	F	E	B	G	H	I
2	1	−1	1	0	−1	0	0	−1	−1
4	0	1	0	−1	0	0	−1	0	−1
6	0	−1	0	1	−1	1	1	−1	−1
8	0	0	0	0	1	−1	0	1	−1
10	1	0	1	−1	1	1	−1	1	−1
12	−1	0	−1	1	1	0	1	1	−1
13	−1	1	−1	0	0	1	0	0	−1
18	−1	−1	−1	−1	−1	−1	−1	−1	−1
26	1	1	1	1	0	−1	1	0	−1
3	0	0	1	−1	−1	0	1	0	0
7	−1	0	0	0	−1	1	−1	0	0
14	1	−1	−1	−1	0	1	1	1	0
15	−1	1	0	−1	1	−1	1	−1	0
16	0	−1	1	0	0	−1	−1	1	0
19	1	0	−1	1	−1	−1	0	0	0
21	1	1	−1	0	1	0	−1	−1	0
23	−1	−1	0	1	0	0	0	1	0
25	0	1	1	1	1	1	0	−1	0
1	−1	0	1	−1	0	−1	0	−1	1
5	1	−1	0	1	1	−1	−1	0	1
9	1	0	0	0	0	0	1	−1	1
11	0	1	−1	0	−1	−1	1	1	1
17	−1	1	1	1	−1	0	−1	1	1
20	−1	−1	1	0	1	1	1	0	1
22	0	0	−1	1	0	1	−1	−1	1
24	1	1	0	−1	−1	1	0	1	1
27	0	−1	−1	−1	1	0	0	0	1

only designs based on the number of degrees of freedom necessary to estimate non-linear effects. As such, should one be interested in non-linear effects, one will have to use a much larger design than is necessary if the design one wishes to produce is constructed by programs such as SPSS, another reason why one should learn how to generate designs from first principles.

Independent of whether we wish to detect linear effects or non-linear effects, we have left ourselves open to one major criticism. This criticism does not relate to the processes in generating the design. Rather, we may be criticized for failing to heed our own advice. The astute reader will note that our original research problem was framed such that the

Table 5.17. *Effects coding design of table 5.15*

Treatment combination \ Design column	A1	A2	D1	D2	C1	C2	F1	F2	E1	E2	B1	B2	G1	G2	H1	H2	I
2	1	0	−1	−1	1	0	0	1	−1	−1	0	1	0	1	−1	−1	−1
4	0	1	1	0	0	1	−1	−1	0	1	0	1	−1	−1	0	1	−1
6	0	1	−1	−1	0	1	1	0	−1	−1	1	0	1	0	−1	−1	−1
8	0	1	0	1	0	1	0	1	1	0	−1	−1	0	1	1	0	−1
10	1	0	0	1	1	0	−1	−1	1	0	1	0	−1	−1	1	0	−1
12	−1	−1	0	1	−1	−1	1	0	1	0	0	1	1	0	1	0	−1
13	−1	−1	1	0	−1	−1	0	1	0	1	1	0	0	1	0	1	−1
18	−1	−1	−1	−1	−1	−1	−1	−1	−1	−1	−1	−1	−1	−1	−1	−1	−1
26	1	0	1	0	1	0	1	0	0	1	−1	−1	1	0	0	1	−1
3	0	1	0	1	1	0	−1	−1	−1	−1	0	1	1	0	0	1	0
7	−1	−1	0	1	0	1	0	1	−1	−1	1	0	−1	−1	0	1	0
14	1	0	−1	−1	−1	−1	−1	−1	0	1	1	0	1	0	1	0	0
15	−1	−1	1	0	0	1	−1	−1	1	0	−1	−1	1	0	−1	−1	0
16	0	1	−1	−1	1	0	0	1	0	1	−1	−1	−1	−1	1	0	0
19	1	0	0	1	−1	−1	1	0	−1	−1	−1	−1	0	1	0	1	0
21	1	0	1	0	−1	−1	0	1	1	0	0	1	−1	−1	−1	−1	0
23	−1	−1	−1	−1	0	1	1	0	0	1	0	1	0	1	1	0	0
25	0	1	1	0	1	0	1	0	1	0	1	0	0	1	−1	−1	0
1	−1	−1	0	1	1	0	−1	−1	0	1	−1	−1	0	1	−1	−1	1
5	1	0	−1	−1	0	1	1	0	1	0	−1	−1	−1	−1	0	1	1
9	1	0	0	1	0	1	0	1	0	1	0	1	1	0	−1	−1	1
11	0	1	1	0	−1	−1	0	1	−1	−1	−1	−1	1	0	1	0	1
17	−1	−1	1	0	1	0	1	0	−1	−1	0	1	−1	−1	1	0	1
20	−1	−1	−1	−1	1	0	0	1	1	0	1	0	1	0	0	1	1
22	0	1	0	1	−1	−1	1	0	0	1	1	0	−1	−1	−1	−1	1
24	1	0	1	0	0	1	−1	−1	−1	−1	1	0	0	1	1	0	1
27	0	1	−1	−1	−1	−1	−1	−1	1	0	0	1	0	1	0	1	1

analyst wished to estimate mode share changes given the introduction of a new alternative means of travel between the two cities. The design we have generated is for currently existing alternatives only. We require additional design columns for the attributes of the new alternative. Taking this into account we are required to generate another (probably larger) design.

Let us assume that this new alternative has two attributes that the analyst believes will be significant in determining whether the alternative will be chosen or not (perhaps focus groups were conducted to determine these). Each attribute will have three attribute levels. The full factorial design will have 59,049 possible treatment combinations (i.e. $3^{(5\times2)}$). Given this, it is likely the analyst will wish to generate a fractional factorial design to reduce the number of treatment combinations. Unfortunately this is not possible using

Table 5.18. *Correlation matrix for effects coded design*

	A1	A2	D1	D2	C1	C2	F1	F2	E1	E2	B1	B2	G1	G2	H1	H2	I
A1	1																
A2	0.5	1															
D1	0	0	1														
D2	0	0	0.5	1													
C1	0	0	0	0	1												
C2	0	0	0	0	0.5	1											
F1	0	0	0	0	0	0	1										
F2	0	0	0	0	0	0	0.5	1									
E1	0	0	0	0	0	0	0	0	1								
E2	0	0	0	0	0	0	0	0	0.5	1							
B1	0	0	0	0	0	0	0	0	0	0	1						
B2	0	0	0	0	0	0	0	0	0	0	0.5	1					
G1	0	0	0	0	0	0	0	0	0	0	0	0	1				
G2	0	0	0	0	0	0	0	0	0	0	0	0	0.5	1			
H1	0	0	0	0	0	0	0	0	0	0	0	0	0	0	1		
H2	0	0	0	0	0	0	0	0	0	0	0	0	0	0	0.5	1	
I	0	0	0	0	0	0	0	0	0	0	0	0	0	0	0	0	1

SPSS as the total number of attributes that may be handled are 10. The analyst requires 11 (10 attributes and one blocking variable). Fortunately the analyst may proceed by using SPSS to generate a base design and then use this base design to generate the other attribute columns as required. Let us use a simpler (smaller) design example to demonstrate how. Table 5.19 shows a design generated by SPSS for four attributes each with four levels. Note that we have used orthogonal coding.

The analyst may generate the additional design columns required using a number of different approaches. First, the analyst may use the existing treatment combinations and use these as the additional design columns. To do so, the analyst might randomize the treatment combinations and assign these randomized treatment combinations to the new design columns while retaining the existing design for the original columns. We do this in table 5.20.

In assigning the randomized treatment combinations, it is important that the analyst check that a randomized treatment combination is not assigned next to its replicate treatment combination (i.e. randomized treatment combination one is not assigned next to the original treatment combination one).

Table 5.21 shows the correlation matrix for the above design. The design produced, as is the case here, is not likely to be orthogonal. As such, the problems associated with modeling with correlated data are likely to be experienced.

An alternative approach is to take the *foldover* of the design and to use the foldover as the new design columns. Taking the foldover involves the reproduction of the design such that the factor levels of the design are reversed (e.g. replace 0 with 1 and 1 with 0). If orthogonal codes have been used we may achieve this effect by multiplying each column

Table 5.19. 3^4 *Fractional factorial design*

Treatment combination	A	B	C	D
1	−3	−3	−3	−3
2	1	1	−3	1
3	3	3	−3	3
4	−1	−1	−3	−1
5	−1	3	1	−3
6	3	1	−1	−3
7	1	−1	3	−3
8	−3	3	3	1
9	3	−3	3	−1
10	−3	1	1	−1
11	−1	1	3	3
12	−1	−3	−1	1
13	1	−3	1	3
14	1	3	−1	−1
15	3	−1	1	1
16	−3	−1	−1	3

Table 5.20. *Randomizing treatment combinations to use for additional design columns*

Treatment combination	A	B	C	D	Random treatment combination	E	F	G	H
1	−3	−3	−3	−3	2	1	1	−3	1
2	1	1	−3	1	16	−3	−1	−1	3
3	3	3	−3	3	15	3	−1	1	1
4	−1	−1	−3	−1	6	3	1	−1	−3
5	−1	3	1	−3	4	−1	−1	−3	−1
6	3	1	−1	−3	10	−3	1	1	−1
7	1	−1	3	−3	9	3	−3	3	−1
8	−3	3	3	1	14	1	3	−1	−1
9	3	−3	3	−1	8	−3	3	3	1
10	−3	1	1	−1	1	−3	−3	−3	−3
11	−1	1	3	3	12	−1	−3	−1	1
12	−1	−3	−1	1	5	−1	3	1	−3
13	1	−3	1	3	3	3	3	−3	3
14	1	3	−1	−1	7	1	−1	3	−3
15	3	−1	1	1	11	−1	1	3	3
16	−3	−1	−1	3	13	1	−3	1	3

Table 5.21. *Correlation matrix for randomizing treatment combinations*

	A	B	C	D	E	F	G	H
A	1							
B	0	1						
C	0	0	1					
D	0	0	0	1				
E	−0.1	−0.05	−0.15	0.2	1			
F	0.2	−0.4	0	0	0	1		
G	0.6	−0.05	0.15	0	0	0	1	
H	0.25	−0.25	0	0.5	0	0	0	1

Table 5.22. *Using the foldover to generate extra design columns*

Treatment combination	A	B	C	D	E	F	G	H
1	−3	−3	−3	−3	3	3	3	3
2	1	1	−3	1	−1	−1	3	−1
3	3	3	−3	3	−3	−3	3	−3
4	−1	−1	−3	−1	1	1	3	1
5	−1	3	1	−3	1	−3	−1	3
6	3	1	−1	−3	−3	−1	1	3
7	1	−1	3	−3	−1	1	−3	3
8	−3	3	3	1	3	−3	−3	−1
9	3	−3	3	−1	−3	3	−3	1
10	−3	1	1	−1	3	−1	−1	1
11	−1	1	3	3	1	−1	−3	−3
12	−1	−3	−1	1	1	3	1	−1
13	1	−3	1	3	−1	3	−1	−3
14	1	3	−1	−1	−1	−3	1	1
15	3	−1	1	1	−3	1	−1	−1
16	−3	−1	−1	3	3	1	1	−3

by −1. Table 5.22 shows how the foldover for our simplified example. Columns E–H of table 5.22 represent the foldover columns.

Unfortunately, the way SPSS generates designs means that using the foldover to generate extra design columns is not a desirable approach to the problem. Examination of the correlation matrix for the design presented in table 5.22 shows that the additional attribute columns are perfectly (negatively) correlated with the existing design columns. As such, using the foldover to generate additional design columns is not an option for those using SPSS to generate designs.

As an aside, assuming the analyst wishes to estimate non-linear effects, even had no correlations been observed, the above designs would be unusable as a result of insufficient

Table 5.23. *Correlation matrix for designs using foldovers to generate additional columns*

	A	B	C	D	E	F	G	H
A	1							
B	0	1						
C	0	0	1					
D	0	0	0	1				
E	−1	0	0	0	1			
F	0	−1	0	0	0	1		
G	0	0	−1	0	0	0	1	
H	0	0	0	−1	0	0	0	1

degrees of freedom. That is, for four attributes each with four levels, 16 treatment combinations provide a sufficient amount of degrees of freedom for estimation purposes (i.e. we require $3 \times 4 = 12$ degrees of freedom for main effects only). For eight attributes each with four levels we require 24 degrees of freedom (i.e. 3×8) for a main effects only design (table 5.23). As such, 16 treatment combinations will provide an insufficient amount of degrees of freedom. In our defense, the above is used only as an example of procedure. The reader should note that had we done the above correctly, we would specify the minimum number of treatment combinations to be generated as 25 before proceeding to generate the additional columns.

We conclude that the analyst is best to use the first method to generate additional design columns (at least if SPSS is used to generate the design). Unless all decision makers respond to the questionnaire, then the design as entered into the computer will not be orthogonal anyway (i.e. for orthogonality, it is the *rows* of the design which are important and not the columns). We can remove columns and not lose orthogonality. If we lose rows (treatment combinations) then the design will no longer be orthogonal. Thus if a block of a design is not returned by one decision maker, orthogonality will be lost. In practice, this fact is largely ignored. We continue our discussion on the experimental design process in chapter 6.

5.3 A note on unlabeled experimental designs

The example used throughout this chapter is a *labeled experiment*. While it is possible to construct unlabeled experiments in the same manner as we would construct a labeled experiment, doing so may prove grossly inefficient. To explain why, consider exactly what an unlabeled experiment is.

An unlabeled experiment is by definition, an experiment in which the heading or title of each alternative is *generic or uninformative* to the decision maker. If this is the case and no other information is available to the decision maker, then the only way of differentiating between each alternative is via the attributes and attribute-level labels as assigned by the experimental design. But as the attribute-level labels are varied as part of the experimental design, each alternative within an unlabeled experiment must, over the entire experiment, be undefinable. Unless the attributes and attribute-level labels are such that Alternative A may be viewed as a proxy for a known alternative when compared to the attribute level labels of other alternatives (consider table 5.4), over the entire experiment, Alternative A may indeed represent a car, a bus and even a horse-drawn carriage. So, too, may Alternative B.

The above concept has implications with regard to how one is likely to model data from an unlabeled experiment, which in turn has implications as to how one may go about constructing the experiment in the first place. Consider (5.1). The subscript i in (5.1) suggests that it is possible to estimate a utility function for all j alternatives. Thus, one can define a utility function for a car alternative that is different to the utility function for a bus alternative. In an unlabeled experiment, one may also estimate a utility function for each alternative within the choice set. Thus one can estimate a utility function for (the undefinable) Alternative A just as one can estimate a second utility function for (the undefinable) Alternative B. If, however, each alternative is undefinable, the estimation of a unique utility function for each makes no sense.

Some information is known, however, about each alternative other than that given by the attributes and attribute-level labels displayed. As part of the experiment, it is necessary that the decision maker know that each alternative belongs to a general class of good or service. For example both Alternative A and Alternative B may be modes of transport. Note, however, that this information applies equally to all alternatives within the experiment and cannot be used to differentiate between the alternatives.

Given the above, it hopefully makes more sense to the reader to estimate a utility function *generic to the general class of good or service* rather than estimate a utility function specific to each alternative within the experiment when dealing with unlabeled experiments. Thus, for example, one will estimate a parameter for a price that applies equally to all alternatives within the experiment.

Knowing in advance that one is going to estimate a generic parameter has a significant impact upon how to construct an experimental design. Note that we did not specify that the experiment be unlabeled. It is not uncommon to estimate generic parameters for labeled designs although the estimation of generic parameters is mandatory with unlabeled experiments. That said, the construction of an experimental design, whether labeled or unlabeled, when constructed in the knowledge that generic parameter estimates will be produced, requires a different manner of thinking as to how to proceed.

First, the analyst must reconsider the degrees of freedom required to estimate the model. By definition, the degrees of freedom are given as the number of parameters to be estimated plus one. Unlike the case of alternative-specific parameter estimates where a parameter may be estimated for each attribute of each alternative, in the case where a generic parameter is to be estimated, *only a single parameter will be estimated independent of how many alternatives there are*. For example, there will not be a two price parameters, one for a car alternative and one for a bus alternative, but rather a single price parameter. As smaller degrees of freedom suggest smaller designs, all other things being equal, unlabeled experiments will tend to require smaller experimental designs. It is still possible to estimate both linear and non-linear effects when estimating generic parameters.

The estimation of generic parameter estimates also requires a rethink of the concept of orthogonality. Consider, for example, the treatment of the *comfort* attribute in the experimental design shown in table 5.15. Here, the *comfort* attribute for the car alternative was constructed such that it is orthogonal to the *comfort* attribute of all other alternatives. Such construction allows for the independent estimation of a *comfort* parameter specific to the car alternative. If as in the case with unlabeled experiments, a generic parameter is to be estimated, the question is "does an attribute that appears in more than one alternative have to be orthogonal to attributes of a similar nature?" That is, does the price attribute of Alternative A have to be orthogonal to the price attribute of Alternative B?

The answer is "no." What is of importance to unlabeled experiments (or labeled experiments with generic parameter estimates) is *within-alternative orthogonality*. As long as within-alternative orthogonality is maintained, the experimental design is useful. Across-alternative orthogonality is of little concern to the analyst.

Given this new evidence, let us reconsider the design shown in table 5.19. Examination of the design's related correlation matrix reveals correlations which previously suggested that the design should be discarded. We may now reconsider this when the experiment be unlabeled. Thus, should the analyst assign Alternative A to design columns A–D and Alternative B to design columns E–H, within-alternative orthogonality will be maintained.

5.4 Optimal designs

The designs that SPSS produce are known as *orthogonal fractional factorial designs*. Recently, researchers have suggested that from a statistical perspective, experimental designs underlying SP tasks should impart the maximum amount of information about the parameters of the attributes relevant to each specific choice task (Sandor and Wedel 2001), something that cannot be guaranteed with an orthogonal fractional factorial design. This has resulted in the introduction of a class of designs known as *optimal or statistically efficient designs*. The generation of statistically efficient designs has been addressed by several authors (Kuhfeld, Toblas, and Garratt 1994; Lazari and Anderson 1994; Huber and Zwerina 1996; Bunch, Louviere, and Anderson 1996; Sandor and Wedel 2001; Kanninen 2002), each of whom offers differing construction strategies to generate such designs.

While we do not demonstrate how to construct such designs here (the interested reader is referred to any of the above articles, or alternatively to Rose and Bliemer 2004), it is worth noting the differences between the two. Orthogonal fractional factorial designs are generated so that the attributes of the design are *statistically independent* (i.e. uncorrelated). Orthogonality between the design attributes represents the foremost criterion in the generation process; the statistical efficiency of the design is rarely considered. Thus, while optimal designs optimize the amount of information obtained from a design, the construction process for orthogonal fractional factorial designs minimizes to zero the correlations evidenced within a design. Optimal designs will be statistically efficient but will likely have correlations; orthogonal fractional factorial designs will have no correlations but may not be the most statistically efficient design available. Hence, the type of design generated reflects the belief of analysts as to what is the most important property of the constructed design.

In determining what constitutes the most statistically efficient design, the literature has tended towards designs which maximize the determinant of the variance–covariance matrix, otherwise known as the Fisher information matrix, of the model to be estimated. Such designs are known as *D-optimal designs*. In determining the D-optimal design, it is usual to use the inversely related measure to calculate the level of D-efficiency – that is, minimize the determinant of the inverse of the variance–covariance matrix. The determinant of the inverse of the variance–covariance matrix is known as *D-error* and will yield the same results maximizing the determinant of the variance–covariance matrix.

The log likelihood function of the MNL model is shown as (5.11)

$$L = \sum_{n=1}^{N} \sum_{s=1}^{S} \sum_{j=1}^{J} y_{njs} \ln(P_{njs}) + c \tag{5.11}$$

where y_{njs} is a column matrix where 1 indicates that an alternative j was chosen by respondent n in choice situation $s$and 0 otherwise, P_{njs} represents the choice probability from the choice model, and c is a constant. Maximizing (5.11) yields the maximum likelihood estimator, $\hat{\beta}$, of the specified choice model given a particular set of choice data. McFadden (1974) showed that the distribution of $\hat{\beta}$ is asymptotically normal with a mean, β, and covariance matrix:

$$\Omega = \left(X'PX\right) = \left[\sum_{m=1}^{M} \sum_{j=1}^{J} x'_{njs} P_{njs} x_{njs}\right] \tag{5.12}$$

and inverse:

$$\Omega^{-1} = \left(X'PX\right)^{-1} = \left[\sum_{m=1}^{M} \sum_{j=1}^{J} x'_{njs} P_{njs} x_{njs}\right]^{-1} \tag{5.13}$$

where P is a $JS \times JS$ diagonal matrix with elements equal to the choice probabilities of the alternatives, j over choice sets, s and $M = NS$.

For Ω, several established summary measures of error have been shown to be useful comparing between designs. The most often used summary measure is known as D-error which is inversely related to D-efficiency:

$$\text{D-error} = \left(\det \Omega^{-1}\right)^{\frac{1}{K}} \tag{5.14}$$

where K is the total number of *generic* parameters to be estimated from the design.

Minimization of (5.14) will produce the design with the smallest possible errors around the estimated parameters.

Appendix 5A Designing nested attributes

In certain circumstances, particular combinations of attribute-level labels may appear as part of an experimental design that contradicts expectations. Consider, for example, the attributes price and quality. Decision makers will expect low prices to appear with low quality levels and high prices to appear with higher levels of quality. One may not expect, however, low prices with high quality levels or high prices with low quality levels. For example, one would not expect to pay $20,000 for a new BMW sports car nor $80,000 for a new Mini Minor (we are not suggesting that Mini Minors are of low quality). In such cases, the appearance of an attribute-level label of one attribute is tied to the appearance (or perhaps non-appearance) of another attribute-level label for a second attribute. Such attributes are said to be *nested*.

Consider an experiment in which a *price* attribute takes the attribute levels low, medium, and high and a *quality* attribute which takes the attribute levels of low and high. In this experiment, the analyst believes that low quality is feasible only with a low or medium price and high quality with a medium or high price. A low price may not appear with high quality and a high price with a low quality. There thus exist four possible combinations, which we show in table 5A.1.

Rather than create two attributes, one for *price* and one for *quality*, the analyst may create a single attribute, the attribute levels of which are based upon each possible combination. For the example above, this attribute will be the *price–quality* column of table 5A.1.

Assuming that the experiment requires two other attributes, each with three levels, a possible experimental design is shown as table 5A.2. Note that for convenience we have called the two new attributes A and B. The last two columns of table 5A.2 separate the *price* and *quality* attributes, as per table 5A.1.

Nesting attributes in the manner described above produces the results required by the analyst. Low price never appears with high quality and high price never appears with low quality. However, this has come at a cost. First, the medium attribute level of price appears eight times while the low and high levels appear a total of four times each. While in the *price–quality* attribute, each price–quality combination appears an equal number of times, when price is separated the number of levels becomes unbalanced. Examination of table 5A.1 shows why this is the case. It is therefore suggested that, where possible, each attribute level appear an equal number of times within the combinations formed. But there exists a second potential problem with what we have done.

Table 5A.1. *Price–quality combinations*

price–quality	*price*	*quality*
0	Low	Low
1	Medium	Low
2	Medium	High
3	High	High

Table 5A.2. *Fractional factorial of a $6^1 \times 3^2$ design with price–quality nested attribute*

price–quality	A	B	*price*	*quality*
0	0	2	0	0
0	2	1	0	0
2	1	0	1	1
3	0	1	2	1
1	0	0	1	0
0	0	0	0	0
3	1	2	2	1
2	0	0	1	1
2	2	2	1	1
0	1	0	0	0
2	0	1	1	1
1	2	0	1	0
3	2	0	2	1
1	1	1	1	0
1	0	2	1	0
3	0	0	2	1

Table 5A.3. *Correlation matrix of a fractional factorial of a $6^1 \times 3^2$ design with price–quality nested attribute*

	price–quality	A	B	*price*	*quality*
Price-quality	1				
A	0	1			
B	0	0	1		
Price	0.948683	0	0	1	
Quality	0.894427	0	0	0.707107	1

Table 5A.3 shows the correlation matrix for the design including the separated price and quality attributes.

Examining the correlation matrix for the design shown in table 5A.2 reveals several potentially significant correlations. The first two correlations are between the *price–quality* nested attribute and the separated *price* and *quality* attributes. As it is unlikely that the analyst will include both the nested attribute and the two separated attributes within a single model this correlation is unlikely to be of any concern. The correlation between the two separated attributes, however, may be of particular concern. Until such time as the data are collected and tests of multicollinearity have been performed, the analyst will not know the full extent of the problem.

Constructing nested attributes in the manner described provides for cognitively sensible designs at the possible cost of a potentially significant loss of design orthogonality. Yet while alternative methods of construction may retain design orthogonality, the additional effort required on behalf of the analyst may far exceed the benefits of using such construction methods.

The above discussion assumes that the analyst intends to use the separated attributes as opposed to the nested attribute for modeling purposes. While doing so (ignoring correlations that are prevalent) will allow for the independent estimation of the desired attributes (e.g. for the above example the *price* and *quality* attributes), it is possible that the analyst use the single nested attribute (e.g. *price–quality*) at the time of model estimation. While this approach may have a number of downsides, such as not being able to separate the attributes, the analyst will nevertheless be able to estimate *price–quality* effects. Indeed, if the analyst were to either effect or dummy code a nested attribute, the result would be somewhat similar to testing for interaction effects of the two (or more) attributes concerned.

Let us conclude by reconsidering the above example again. The design required by our analyst requires three attributes with three levels each (i.e. A, B, and *price*) and one attribute with two levels. That is, the full factorial design is a $3^3 \times 2^1$ with a total of 54 treatment combinations. Of this 54, there might be a sufficient number of treatment combinations in which the non-desired *price–quality* attribute-level combinations do not exist. Finding these and retaining orthogonality may prove impossible (in the interests of orthogonality, one cannot simply pick which treatment combinations are retained). As such, unless the analyst is sufficiently familiar with the design of experiments, the only way to proceed is to have programs such as SPSS iteratively generate more and more designs until a design is found in which the offending combinations are not present. This assumes that such a design exists in the first place.

Appendix 5B Assignment of quantitative attribute-level labels

Consider the coding formats available to an analyst when entering data obtained from a choice experiment. First, if the intention of the analyst is to estimate linear effects only, the analyst may use either design or orthogonal codes (or possibly some other unique coding format) when entering data. Secondly, for attributes where the attribute-level labels are described numerically (e.g. travel time), the analyst may replace the design or orthogonal codes with the actual numerical attribute-level labels shown to each decision maker as part of the experiment. Thirdly, if it is the intention of the analyst to estimate non-linear effects then the data will be entered either as dummy or effects codes. Finally, the analyst may use a combination of coding formats to test various effects (e.g. use both design and dummy codes). For a travel time attribute with three attribute levels, we show these various coding formats in table 5B.1.

Ignoring the non-linear coding formats which we have shown induce a loss of orthogonality by the method in which they are constructed, the three remaining (linear) coding formats are design coding, orthogonal coding, and the direct use of numerical

Table 5B.1. *Comparison of coding formats*

Travel time (hours)	Design codes	Orthogonal codes	Attribute-level labels	Effect level 1	Effect level 2	Dummy level 1	Dummy level 2
10	0	−1	10	1	0	1	0
12	1	0	12	0	1	0	1
14	2	1	14	−1	−1	0	0

attribute-level labels. For qualitative attributes such as *comfort* the attribute-level labels will be non-numerical (e.g. low comfort) which precludes entering the attribute-level labels directly into a statistical package (one cannot analyse words). As such, qualitative attributes must be formatted using either design coding or orthogonal coding (ignoring the possibility of effects or dummy coding).

One appealing feature of using the attribute-level labels directly when dealing with quantitative attributes is that one can meaningfully predict over the entire range of the attribute-level labels from models estimated specified with such attributes. That is, for the above example, one could predict from a model, utility estimates not only for 10, 12, or 14 hours but also for 11 and 13 hours, or even 10 ½, 11 ½ hours, etc. Note that for both non-linear coding formats, one is constrained to examining utility estimates at the discrete points used for the attribute-level labels only.

The assignment of numerical values as attribute-level labels must be carefully considered if the data are to be entered using the attribute-level labels directly. If orthogonality is to be maintained, it is important that the attribute-level labels assigned must be such that they are equally spaced along the continuum on which the attribute is measured. Consider the mode choice experiment used throughout chapter 5. In this example we used the attribute level labels 10, 12, and 14 hours for the car, bus, and train alternatives and 1, 1.5, and 2 hours for the plane alternative. Examining the attribute labels assigned to the travel time attribute for the car, bus, and train alternatives, the values increase in increments of 2 hours, such that difference between the 10-hour and 12-hour attribute-level labels is the same as the difference between the 12-hours and 14-hour attribute-level labels. Similarly, for the plane alternative, the attribute-level labels used are equidistant by 30 minutes. That is, the difference between one and 1.5 hours is 30 minutes, the same difference as between 1.5 and 2 hours. It does not matter that different attribute-level labels were assigned for the same attribute associated with different alternatives. What matters is that within each attribute, the attribute-level labels for quantitative attributes are *equally spaced*. Substituting the values suggested above, the design shown in table 5.16 now becomes table 5B.2.

In table 5B.3 we show the correlation matrix for the design shown in table 5B.2. Examining this correlation matrix reveals that using the attribute-level labels directly as opposed to the orthogonal codes used in chapter 5 does not impact upon the overall orthogonality of the design.

Consider the case where the travel times for the *car*, *bus*, and *train* alternatives no longer assume the values of 10, 12, and 14 hours. Rather, let the travel times for the *car* alternative

Table 5B.2. *Estimating linear effects using quantitative attributes*

	comf1 (*car*)	*ttime1* (*car*)	*comf2* (*bus*)	*ttime2* (*bus*)	*comf3* (*train*)	*ttime3* (*train*)	*comf4* (*plane*)	*ttime4* (*plane*)	*block*
Treatment combination \ Design column	A	D	C	F	E	B	G	H	I
2	1	10	1	12	−1	12	0	1	−1
4	0	14	0	10	0	12	−1	1.5	−1
6	0	10	0	14	−1	14	1	1	−1
8	0	12	0	12	1	10	0	2	−1
10	1	12	1	10	1	14	−1	2	−1
12	−1	12	−1	14	1	12	1	2	−1
13	−1	14	−1	12	0	14	0	1.5	−1
18	−1	10	−1	10	−1	10	−1	1	−1
26	1	14	1	14	0	10	1	1.5	−1
3	0	12	1	10	−1	12	1	1.5	0
7	−1	12	0	12	−1	14	−1	1.5	0
14	1	10	−1	10	0	14	1	2	0
15	−1	14	0	10	1	10	1	1	0
16	0	10	1	12	0	10	−1	2	0
19	1	12	−1	14	−1	10	0	1.5	0
21	1	14	−1	12	1	12	−1	1	0
23	−1	10	0	14	0	12	0	2	0
25	0	14	1	14	1	14	0	1	0
1	−1	12	1	10	0	10	0	1	1
5	1	10	0	14	1	10	−1	1.5	1
9	1	12	0	12	0	12	1	1	1
11	0	14	−1	12	−1	10	1	2	1
17	−1	14	1	14	−1	12	−1	2	1
20	−1	10	1	12	1	14	1	1.5	1
22	0	12	−1	14	0	14	−1	1	1
24	1	14	0	10	−1	14	0	2	1
27	0	10	−1	10	1	12	0	1.5	1

now be 10, 12, and 18 hours, for the *bus* alternative 11, 12, and 20 hours, and for the *train* alternative 3, 12, and 18 hours. For the *plane* alternative, let us assume that the travel-time attribute may now take the values 1, 1.5 and 3 hours. Ignoring the implausibility of some of the values used, substituting these values, table 5.16 now becomes table 5B.4.

The correlation matrix for table 5B.4 is shown in table 5B.5.

The use of attribute-level labels which are not equally spaced along the travel–time continuum induces correlations within the experimental design, although the underlying experimental design specified using either design or orthogonal codes retains orthogonality (i.e. table 5.15 from which table 5B.4 was derived remains orthogonal). Note that we need

Table 5B.3. *Correlation matrix for design shown in table 5B.2*

	comf1 (*car*)	*ttime1* (*car*)	*comf2* (*bus*)	*ttime2* (*bus*)	*comf3* (*train*)	*ttime3* (*train*)	*comf4* (*plane*)	*ttime4* (*plane*)	*block*
comf1 (*car*)	1								
ttime1 (*car*)	0	1							
comf2 (*bus*)	0	0	1						
ttime2 (*bus*)	0	0	0	1					
comf3 (*train*)	0	0	0	0	1				
ttime3 (*train*)	0	0	0	0	0	1			
comf4 (*plane*)	0	0	0	0	0	0	1		
ttime4 (*plane*)	0	0	0	0	0	0	0	1	
block	0	0	0	0	0	0	0	0	1

Table 5B.4. *Estimating linear effects using different quantitative attribute-level labels*

	comf1 (*car*)	*ttime1* (*car*)	*comf2* (*bus*)	*ttime2* (*bus*)	*comf3* (*train*)	*ttime3* (*train*)	*comf4* (*plane*)	*ttime4* (*plane*)	*block*
Treatment combination \ Design column	A	D	C	F	E	B	G	H	I
2	1	10	1	12	−1	12	0	1	−1
4	0	18	0	11	0	12	−1	1.5	−1
6	0	10	0	20	−1	18	1	1	−1
8	0	12	0	12	1	3	0	3	−1
10	1	12	1	11	1	18	−1	3	−1
12	−1	12	−1	20	1	12	1	3	−1
13	−1	18	−1	12	0	18	0	1.5	−1
18	−1	10	−1	11	−1	3	−1	1	−1
26	1	18	1	20	0	3	1	1.5	−1
3	0	12	1	11	−1	12	1	1.5	0
7	−1	12	0	12	−1	18	−1	1.5	0
14	1	10	−1	11	0	18	1	3	0
15	−1	18	0	11	1	3	1	1	0
16	0	10	1	12	0	3	−1	3	0
19	1	12	−1	20	−1	3	0	1.5	0
21	1	18	−1	12	1	12	−1	1	0
23	−1	10	0	20	0	12	0	3	0
25	0	18	1	20	1	18	0	1	0
1	−1	12	1	11	0	3	0	1	1
5	1	10	0	20	1	3	−1	1.5	1
9	1	12	0	12	0	12	1	1	1
11	0	18	−1	12	−1	3	1	3	1
17	−1	18	1	20	−1	12	−1	3	1
20	−1	10	1	12	1	18	1	1.5	1
22	0	12	−1	20	0	18	−1	1	1
24	1	18	0	11	−1	18	0	3	1
27	0	10	−1	11	1	12	0	1.5	1

Table 5B.5. *Correlation matrix for the design shown in table 5B.3*

	comf1 (car)	*ttime1 (car)*	*comf2 (bus)*	*ttime2 (bus)*	*comf3 (train)*	*ttime3 (train)*	*comf4 (plane)*	*ttime4 (plane)*	*block*
comf1 (car)	1								
ttime1 (car)	−0.11	1							
comf2 (bus)	0	−0.11	1						
ttime2 (bus)	0	0.05	0	1					
comf3 (train)	0	0.11	0	0	1				
ttime3 (train)	0	−0.01	0	1.3E-17	0	1			
comf4 (plane)	0	0	0	0	0	0	1		
ttime4 (plane)	−1.2E-17	0.09	0	0	0	−1.6E-18	0	1	
block	0	0.11	0	0	0	0	0	0	1

not worry about this, however, if the analyst intends to use non-linear effects or use either design or orthogonal code formats. Nevertheless, as is likely to be the case, if the analyst is unsure as to the final model specification, the use of non-equidistant attribute-level labels for quantitative attributes will preclude the use of linear effects without inducing some loss of design orthogonality.

6 Choices in data collection

USA Today has come out with a new survey – apparently, three out of every four people make up 75 percent of the population. (David Letterman, 1947–)

6.1 Introduction

To estimate a statistical model one requires data. To estimate a statistical model of choice, one requires choice data. Chapters 4 and 5 provided the reader with an understanding of the data requirements for modeling choice. But having an understanding of the theoretical requirements is one thing. How do we gather choice data in practice?

While this chapter is devoted to questionnaire construction, we remind the reader that the overall purpose of this book is to educate on matters related to choice modeling. We therefore offer only limited discussion on general questionnaire construction and reiterate that, should the reader seek a greater understanding of questionnaire construction beyond the bounds of choice, they seek information elsewhere (some specific texts on questionnaire construction include Foddy 1994; Dillman 2000, a book the authors recommend be on any self-respecting researcher's bookshelf; Frazer and Lawley 2000).

6.2 General survey instrument construction

The writing of questionnaires for the collection of choice data are an in-depth process that adds to the already existing complexities of more traditional questionnaire construction. While the analyst must adhere to the well-documented conventions of questionnaire construction, added burdens (as we will show) associated with the collection of choice data also require consideration. Yet, as with any survey, the more time spent in preparation, the less problems are likely to occur, problems which the analyst may not be able to rectify at a later stage of the research project. We thus advise that the analyst spend as much time as is possible in testing and pre-testing their survey instrument before commencing any field work.

In chapter 5, we introduced the concept of problem refinement and exploratory research. Though we did so in the context of SP data collection, problem refinement and exploratory research should not be confined to studies involving the use of SP data collection. Studies calling for the collection of RP data also require problem refinement, for one does not know what questions to ask unless the problem is first understood, irrespective of the data that is to be collected. We therefore offer the refinement of the problem as the starting point for questionnaire construction, without regard to the data requirements of the study at hand. Once we have defined the problem sufficiently, we can then proceed to the research design. In arriving at a research design, the analyst decides how the research project will proceed in terms of how the information will be gathered to answer the problem formulated in the first stage of the process. Two questions that need to be answered are what *type* of data are to be collected and how best to *collect* that data. The most important aspect of this stage of the survey design process is that the research design be consistent with the problem definition. That is, the *research process should conform to the problem definition* and not vice versa. Of course, one can always return to the problem definition stage and reformulate the task.

It is during the research design phase that the questionnaire itself is written. But before the questionnaire can be written, the analyst must decide how the survey is to be implemented. The types of questions that can be answered by decision makers are largely dependent upon the delivery mechanism of the survey. Consider the following question:

> *Thinking about the last time you traveled by bus, rank in order of importance (1 being most important, 6 being least important) the following attributes in influencing your decision to choose a bus trip.*
>
> 1. *Seat availability*
> 2. *Fare*
> 3. *Travel time*
> 4. *Waiting time for bus*
> 5. *Driver friendliness*
> 6. *Bus cleanliness*

Despite having only six attributes in the above example, consider the difficulty in asking such a question over the phone:

> *Interviewer "Thinking about the last time you traveled by bus, rank in order of importance (1 being most important, 6 being least important) the following attributes in influencing your decision to choose a bus trip.*
>
> 1. *Seat availability*
> 2. *Fare*
> 3. *Travel time*
> 4. *Waiting time for bus*
> 5. *Driver friendliness*
> 6. *Bus cleanliness."*

Respondent: "Sorry, what was that first one . . . ?"
Interviewer: "Seat availability."
Respondent: "And the second . . . "

Similar problems exist for phone surveys if we wish to ask the respondent a question about some visual stimuli. This is not to suggest that phone interviews are bad. The point we wish to make is that the *survey delivery method* must be *appropriate to the questions being asked*.

Similarly, the questions being asked must correspond to the type of data necessary for the analysis to be conducted. On more than one occasion, the authors have witnessed students who have completed a semester going through the research process of some project only to find that they were unable to perform the appropriate analysis due to a failure to fully appreciate the underlying data assumptions of the analysis they had planned to undertake. If, for example, you plan to undertake a regression analysis with the dependent variable being income, collecting data on income in a questionnaire as a categorical variable will only result in embarrassment later on (an assumption of regression analysis is that the dependent variable is continuous in nature; this suggests that the related question in the survey should be open-ended as opposed to close-ended[1]). This suggests that in writing the questionnaire, the analyst must consider not only the preceding stages of questionnaire design (problem definition), but also the stages yet to come (data collection, sampling, data analysis, etc.).

The research design phase is an *iterative process*. One must weigh considerations such as costs and time available to the study versus each delivery mechanism's ability to ask questions in a manner appropriate to answering the research problem. One may thus be required to review the problem definition in the light of budgetary or other constraints.

Once we are satisfied that we have an appropriate research design in place, we must draft the questionnaire. Writing the questions for the questionnaire is not an easy task. Consider an example where a wife is suspected in the death of her husband. Listed below are just some of the ways a detective might ask the question as to the wife's responsibility in her husband's death:

Did you kill your husband?
Did you murder your husband?
Did your husband die due to your actions?
Are you responsible for your husband's death?
What part did you have in your husband's death?

In answering each of the above questions, the response the detective will get will be different. What if the wife was involved in the accidental death of her husband? How will her response differ for each of the above questions? While in a police interview, the detective may correct herself and ask the question in a different form, with a questionnaire,

[1] A trade-off exists here in terms of the likelihood of decision makers answering such questions. With sensitive questions such as these related to income and age, decision makers may feel more comfortable answering closed-ended questions as opposed to open-ended questions. To somewhat offset this problem, one may increase the number of categories or use the mean or median of the category range in the analysis.

unless we are willing to conduct a second survey to correct our mistakes, the questions we ask – and hence the data we collect – cannot be changed once the survey is complete.

We must therefore consider very carefully how we word our questions. There are several pitfalls that one should consider when writing a question for a questionnaire. We will briefly discuss several of the more common of these in turn.

Firstly, is the question *appropriate* for the study? "Appropriateness" here relates to whether the question is necessary or not. In our bus questionnaire example, is it appropriate to ask the respondent questions on their household level of income or their marital status? The measure of appropriateness lies in the hypotheses established during the problem definition phase. If income or marital status relate to a specific hypothesis then their inclusion in the survey is warranted. If, however, you plan to ask such questions only because everyone else does, then they are "nice to know" questions and not "need to know" questions. Nice to know questions are nice to know but make only for longer surveys.

The caveat here is that sometimes we wish to ask questions that are not directly related to our research problem. If we have some prior knowledge about the population of interest, then it is often useful to ask questions that will confirm that the final sample is from the intended population. Screening questions perform a similar function.

Another important issue is whether the respondent will *understand* the question. Respondent confusion may arise for several reasons. We all like to appear intelligent; however, it is suggested that you *eschew pretentious obfuscation* (or avoid using large words). Confusion may also arise as a result of question *ambiguity*. Earlier we innocently used the word "convenience" when deriving our research hypothesis. But what is "convenience" in terms of traveling to and from work? Does "convenience" mean the ability to travel from door to door or to choose from any of the available routes? Or does "convenience" mean having the flexibility of choosing when to travel and not having to rely on the timetabled travel times of public transport? Are these two definitions the same, or does each result in different implications for our research study? Further, do you define the word "convenience" the same way as your neighbor? Worse yet, does "convenience" mean the same thing to you all the time, or is it context-specific? As you can see, if we do not explain what we mean by the word convenience, then how do we know what exactly the respondent was responding to?

Understanding may also be lost if the respondent uses a different *vernacular* to that used by the analyst. What was (in Western society) once "cool" to teenagers is now (at least at the time of writing) "sick." Different cultural segments have their own language that may be foreign to those not included within that segment. Using the language of the sub-culture will substantially reduce respondent confusion.

Understanding may be further reduced if the respondent does not have the *technical expertise* in the area under investigation. If the pool of decision makers is from 6–12-year-old children (ethical considerations aside), then asking questions as to their opinions on the macroeconomic impacts of supply-side economic policies will probably result in few productive answers.

Another pitfall to avoid is asking *biased or leading questions*. Such questions, often associated with political push polling (where political parties survey respondents on policies in such a manner as to get the results they want to obtain), provide the analyst with the results before the question is even asked. One such example might be the question, "Do you support strict federal gun control laws, or do you support the wholesale murder of our children?" By asking such questions, decision makers are compelled to answer in a manner that they might not necessarily support simply for fear of ostracism should they answer in the manner that best represents their true position.

The above question also displays another pitfall to avoid, *double-barreled questions*. However improbable, one might support strict gun control measures while also supporting the wholesale murder of children. In answering "no" to the above question, how do we know what the respondent answered "no" to?

Several other pitfalls exist in writing questions such as the use of *non-mutually exclusive categories*. Nevertheless, we must remember that the purpose of this book is not solely on survey writing. Indeed, there is enough material on survey writing to write just such a book. However, as several books have already been written, we ask that any reader interested in this topic obtain one of these (Foddy 1994; Dillman 2000; Frazer and Lawley 2000).

Once the analyst feels that the draft questionnaire is ready, a *code book* should be developed. A code book can take many forms, but no matter what the form taken, the purpose remains the same. A code book describes how the data will look when entered into a computer for analysis. The drafting of a code book will help explain the type of data that will be collected. Consider the example above, where sampled individuals were asked to rate the importance of six different attributes. What if we had asked the individuals to select which of the attributes was important to them, as opposed to having them rank them? If the respondent was free to select more than one attribute, then how do we enter the data? If they selected both *seat availability* and *fare*, do we code the answer as 12? But what if they ticked all six attributes? To handle this type of data we must create a separate variable for each attribute and code each variable as either being important or not being important. How does this type of data affect any proposed analysis? Assuming we left the question as is, how do we enter data for ranked questions? A useful exercise is for the reader to write a code book for the question as it is described above and decide what type of data analysis is possible with such a coding.

The final stage before actual data collection is to *pilot the questionnaire*. As the drafter of the survey instrument, we sometimes become so close to the document that we fail to see the obvious flaws that may exist. How many times have we stared at something, unable to find the mistake, only to have someone with fresh eyes come along and pick up the mistake straight away? To pilot the survey, the analyst should sample from the population of interest and conduct the survey exactly as they plan to for the main survey. In our experience, pilot studies should include 30–40 respondents. Sampling more than 40 individuals tends to result in diminishing returns in terms of the information gained to evaluate the survey instrument (as distinct to using data in preliminary statistical analysis). The conducting of a pilot study should identify any potential problems that may occur at the data collection stage, in terms of both survey administration as well as identifying problems with the instrument itself. At this stage, it may be worthwhile spending extra time asking decision makers not only to complete the survey but also ask them to indicate what improvements to the instrument might be made. This may result in a revision of the instrument; however it is best to spend time revising now than to find out later that you cannot answer your research problem after you have collected all of your data. It is strongly recommended that the same interview team is used in the pilot as in the main survey so that you can test the quality of the interview team as well.

6.3 Questionnaires for choice data

The above discussion provides a brief exposition on how to write questionnaires in general. While the issues raised also relate to survey instruments designed for choice data collection, the specific and pedantic nature of choice data requires further in-depth examination. We begin by returning to the example introduced in chapter 5. Although expressly related to SP choice data, following sections discuss issues specifically related to the collection of RP choice data.

Returning to the example in chapter 5, we concluded our discussion at stage 5 of the experimental design process. We are yet to complete stages 6–8 (reproduced in figure 6.1). We begin with the *generation of choice sets*.

6.3.1 Stage 6: generation of choice sets

A *choice set* represents the basic mechanism of conveying information to decision makers about the alternatives, attributes and attribute levels that exist within the hypothetical scenarios of a study. More than that, a choice set represents the machinery by which we gather information on the choices made by sampled decision makers given the alternatives, attributes and attribute levels as determined through some experimental design such as that generated in chapter 5.

When we began our discussion on experimental design, the first design we generated (table 5.1) enumerated all possible combinations of the attribute levels (i.e. a full factorial design), the levels of which were expressed in words which convey (we hope) some level of cognitively meaningful information (ignoring any ambiguity associated with the attribute *comfort* and the attribute levels of high, medium, low) to potentially sampled decision makers. To progress our discussion, we were forced to abandon descriptive attribute-level labels and use a coding structure. In doing so, by stage 5 of the experimental design process we were able to arrive at a useable experimental design (table 5.15) expressed in the coding structure adopted earlier. While the design reported in table 5.1 is useful, some transformation is required in order to make the design ready for field distribution. We begin

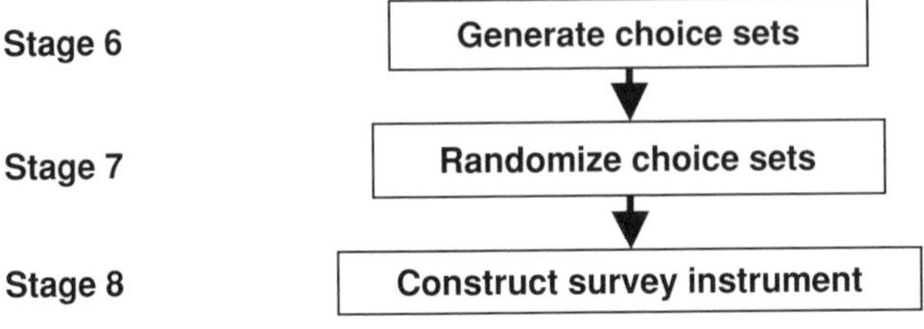

Figure 6.1 Stages 6–8 of the experimental design process

Table 6.1. *Attaching cognitively meaningful attribute labels to attribute levels*

Attribute \ Alternative	*car*	*bus*	*train*	*plane*
Comfort	−1: Low 0: Medium 1: High	−1: Low 0: Medium 1: High	−1: Low 0: Medium 1: High	−1: Low 0: Medium 1: High
Travel time	−1: 10 hours 0: 12 hours 1: 14 hours	−1: 10 hours 0: 12 hours 1: 14 hours	−1: 10 hours 0: 12 hours 1: 14 hours	−1: 1 hours 0: 1.5 hours 1: 2 hours

this process by attaching the relevant attribute labels to the design. Taking the attribute-level labels reported in table 5.6, the analyst may, either in Microsoft Word or Excel, use the replace command (**Ctrl + H** on the keyboard) to replace the numerical coding with the relevant descriptive labels already decided upon. For our example, for each alternative, the attribute-level labels of the experiment are exactly the same for the *comfort* attribute. Thus, for all alternatives, every time the analyst observes a −1 in any design column related to the attribute *comfort*, the −1 should be replaced with the word *Low*. Similarly, a 0 should be replaced with the word *Medium* and a 1 with the word *High*. For the *car*, *bus*, and *train* alternatives, for the *travel time* attribute −1, are replaced with 10 hours, 0s are replaced with 12 hours, and 1s are replaced with 14 hours. We show the attribute labels and corresponding attribute levels in table 6.1.

As an aside, the actual transformation need not correspond to the manner related above. As each attribute level is unique within the experimental design, there is no reason that −1 represents the low level and 1 represents the high level. Indeed, the analyst may wish to change the code such that −1 represents the medium level while 0 represents the high level and 1 represents the low level. Any mapping from attribute level to attribute-level label is possible. The only caveat to this exists for unbalanced experimental designs in which each attribute has levels that occur a varying number of times. In such cases, the analyst may prefer that a given attribute-level label be observed more than other attribute-level labels; in this situation, a haphazard allocation of the attribute-level labels to the attribute-level codes cannot occur.

Taking the attribute-level labels and allocating them as discussed above to the experimental design related in table 5.15, we arrive at table 6.2. It is from table 6.2 that the analyst generates the choice sets to be shown to the sampled individuals. Recall that each row of the design is called a *treatment combination* and consists of attribute levels that are related directly to a set of attributes, which are in turn related specifically to a set of alternatives. By changing the attribute levels observed between the rows, the underlying experimental design forces each treatment combination to act as a separate and independent hypothetical scenario – or choice set. As such, each treatment combination is a separate choice set.

What remains is for the analyst to rearrange each treatment combination into a workable choice set that not only provides information on the attribute levels of the various

Table 6.2. *A reproduction of the first two treatment combinations for the table 5.11 design*

Treatment combination \ Design column	*comf1* (*car*) A	*ttime1* (*car*) D	*comf2* (*bus*) C	*ttime2* (*bus*) F	*comf3* (*train*) E	*ttime3* (*train*) B	*comf4* (*plane*) G	*ttime4* (*plane*) H	block I
2	High	14	High	12	Low	12	Medium	2	1
4	Medium	10	Medium	14	Medium	12	Low	$1\frac{1}{2}$	1
6	Medium	14	Medium	10	Low	10	High	2	1
8	Medium	2	Medium	12	High	14	Medium	1	1
10	High	12	High	14	High	10	Low	1	1
12	Low	12	Low	10	High	12	High	1	1
13	Low	10	Low	12	Medium	10	Medium	$1\frac{1}{2}$	1
18	Low	14	Low	14	Low	14	Low	2	1
26	High	10	High	10	Medium	14	High	$1\frac{1}{2}$	1
3	Medium	12	High	14	Low	12	High	$1\frac{1}{2}$	2
7	Low	12	Medium	12	Low	10	Low	$1\frac{1}{2}$	2
14	High	14	Low	14	Medium	10	High	1	2
15	Low	10	Medium	14	High	14	High	2	2
16	Medium	14	High	12	Medium	14	Low	1	2
19	High	12	Low	10	Low	14	Medium	$1\frac{1}{2}$	2
21	High	10	Low	12	High	12	Low	2	2
23	Low	14	Medium	10	Medium	12	Medium	1	2
25	Medium	10	High	10	High	10	Medium	2	2
1	Low	12	High	14	Medium	14	Medium	2	3
5	High	14	Medium	10	High	14	Low	$1\frac{1}{2}$	3
9	High	12	Medium	12	Medium	12	High	2	3
11	Medium	10	Low	12	Low	14	High	1	3
17	Low	10	High	10	Low	12	Low	1	3
20	Low	14	High	12	High	10	High	$1\frac{1}{2}$	3
22	Medium	12	Low	10	Medium	10	Low	2	3
24	High	10	Medium	14	Low	10	Medium	1	3
27	Medium	14	Low	14	High	12	Medium	$1\frac{1}{2}$	3

alternatives, but also allows the decision maker some mechanism for selecting one of the alternatives available. Taking the first two treatment combinations from table 6.2, we present two possible choice sets in figure 6.2. We note that the formatting of choice sets is not limited to the format presented in figure 6.2. Indeed, the reader may elect to choose any format for the presentation of choice sets so long as the choice sets relay the relevant information and provide a means for decision makers to make a choice.

A picture is worth a thousand words (the picture tells a story)

A requirement of stated preference experiments is that the attribute levels be well defined. That is, the attribute level must have the same meaning to all decision makers surveyed.

Scenario 1

Trip Description	Car	Bus	Train	Plane
Comfort	High	High	Low	Medium
Travel Time (hours)	14	12	12	2
If I had to take the trip I would choose	☐	☐	☐	☐

Scenario 2

Trip Description	Car	Bus	Train	Plane
Comfort	Medium	Medium	Low	Medium
Travel Time (hours)	10	14	12	2
If I had to take the trip I would choose	☐	☐	☐	☐

Figure 6.2 Example choice sets

Blue A	Blue B	Blue C	Blue D	Blue E

Figure 6.3 The meaning of grey

Abstract or ill-defined attribute levels that may be ambiguously interpreted by decision makers add to the variability in choice without adding to the explanatory ability of the analyst. This is particularly the case for qualitatively defined attributes. We have already discussed the attribute *comfort* and the disparate meanings that decision makers may attach to it. Yet consider even a simple attribute, say color. The analyst may consider that color is a well-defined attribute; however, consider the effect of color on the choice of automobile. Figure 6.3 illustrates several different shades of the color grey, each of which are likely to result in different levels of preference for an automobile should that color scheme be adopted by the manufacturer. Should the analyst believe that color is a significant determinate of automobile choice and that grey is one of the attribute levels to be used in the experiment, the analyst must decide how this attribute is to be described to the sampled decision makers. Should the analyst elect to describe the attribute level grey simply as "grey," how might decision makers interpret this description?

Yet given the fact that the analyst believes color to be a significant determinant of automobile choice, what is required is some mechanism of describing unambiguously what is meant by each attribute level (i.e. each color, grey being but one level). Rather than attempt to describe the color "grey," the analyst may make use of the specific color that the manufacturer intends to use as part of their choice set.

Consider another example where the good under study is jogging shoes. In figure 6.4 we present a choice set in which two different jogging shoes are shown. We offer as an interesting exercise for the reader to generate their own choice set to replace the one shown in figure 6.4, using only words to describe the attributes of the pair of jogging shoes shown. We then challenge the reader to show their choice set to a third party and to compare their description to that shown in figure 6.4 in order to determine whether the derived description indeed does describe the pair of shoes displayed below.

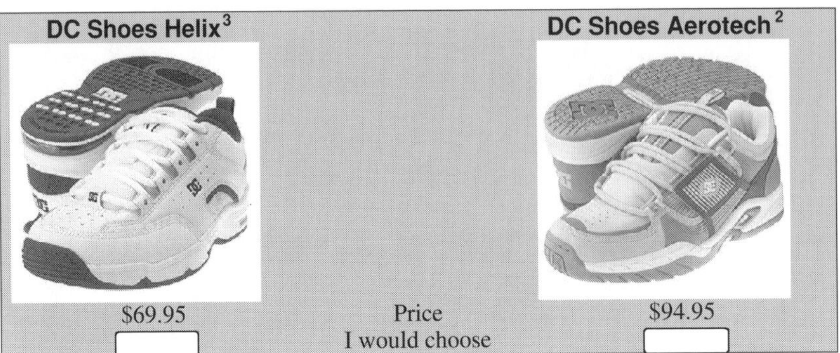

Figure 6.4 Example shoe choice set
Source: http://shop.zappos.com/, 13 December 2002.

6.3.2 Stage 7: randomizing choice sets

The last column in table 6.2 is the blocking column. Recall from chapter 5 that we use the blocking variable to assign the treatment combinations (choice sets) that are to be observed by individual decision makers. For the above example, each decision maker will observe nine choice sets and three different decision makers will be required to complete the full experimental design of 27 choice sets (this raises interesting questions as to sampling which we will discuss later in this chapter). The analyst may generate 27 choice sets similar to those in figure 6.2 (or however many is applicable to their particular study) and present them in the order suggested in table 6.2 to the sampled decision makers. In doing so, however, the analyst would be ignoring possible biasing from the order in which the choice sets appear. Perhaps there exists some learning in which the first few choice sets are used by the respondent to gain an understanding of the process required by the analyst. If this is the case, then the choices made in later choice sets are likely not to be the same in terms of the utility or preferences revealed than in the first one or two choice sets.

Alternatively, decision makers may get bored towards the end of the survey, particularly if each decision maker is presented with a large number of choice sets (however, it is an open debate as to how many choice sets is a large number) which may affect the responses of choice sets displayed later in the survey. In the past, analysts generated extra choice sets from which decision makers could "practice" and "learn" from. These practice choice sets were then discarded by the analyst from the analysis. However this only added to the amount of time required to complete the survey and little evidence in terms of the effects of reducing bias was found. As such, the use of practice choice sets has fallen somewhat out of favor. The recent trend for choice modelers is to randomize the choice sets shown to individual decision makers such that two decision makers presented with the same block will ultimately observe the same choice sets, but in different orders to one another (i.e. randomized choice sets within blocks). This then allows the analyst to test for order effect bias at the time of model estimation.

The randomization of choice sets raises interesting questions for the choice analyst in terms of the data collection mechanism adopted. Should the analyst elect to use traditional paper and pencil surveys, the ramification of randomization needs to be thought through carefully. Returning to our mode example with 27 choice sets and assuming a sample of 100 decision makers, does the analyst present each of the 100 decision makers with a different randomized survey or does the analyst generate, say, 10 different randomized surveys and randomly assign the 100 decision makers to each of the 10 randomized surveys? In the first instance, the analyst has to construct each of the 100 surveys separately and therefore loses any benefit that may be gained from being able to reproduce a survey multiple times through photocopying. In the second instance, has the analyst strictly accounted for order biases? Is 10 different survey versions enough? Should the analyst produce 20 randomized versions and assign five decision makers to each instead of 10 decision makers to 10 different survey versions?

To our knowledge, the problem of how to handle the randomization of choice sets is yet to be formally studied. As such, we can only offer advice as to what we understand is current practice. While theoretically the complete randomization of the choice set presentation to each decision maker would be ideal, in practice the problem of logistics means that different survey versions representing different randomizations of the choice sets are created which are then presented to more than one decision maker. Unfortunately, no clear guideline exists as to how many randomized versions are optimal and to how many decision makers those versions should be physically distributed.

As an aside, the authors have on occasion generated additional blocking variables within an experimental design which are then used to generate the randomized survey versions after the additional blocking variables have been sorted. For example, consider a simple experiment involving two alternatives, each with two attributes with two levels (i.e. a 2^4 design). The smallest main effects only orthogonal design possible has eight treatment combinations (ignoring the extra degree of freedom required for model estimation). Assuming that we wish to present each decision maker with four of the eight treatment combinations, we would generate a blocking variable with two levels (eight treatment combinations divided by two equals four). We might then generate a second blocking variable also with two levels. Table 6.3 shows just such a design. Note that we have sorted the two blocking variables, first by block one and then again by block two.

Table 6.3. *A 2^4 orthogonal design with two blocking variables*

Treatment combination	A1	A2	B1	B2	block1	block2	
1	1	1	0	1	0	0	A
2	0	0	1	1	0	0	
3	1	0	0	0	0	1	B
4	0	1	1	0	0	1	
5	0	1	0	0	1	0	C
6	1	0	1	0	1	0	
7	0	0	0	1	1	1	D
8	1	1	1	1	1	1	

Table 6.4. *Randomization of choice sets across surveys*

ABCD	ABDC	CDAB	CDBA
BACD	BADC	DCAB	DCBA

By sorting the two blocking variables of the design as shown, we can combine the two together as suggested in table 6.3 to produce four combinations (A, B, C, and D). Using block one as the true blocking variable, decision makers will always observe treatment combinations 1, 2, 3, and 4 (combinations A and B) or 5, 6, 7, and 8 (combinations C and D). Thus, combinations A and B will always be presented together as will combinations C and D. The randomization occurs by randomizing the order in which decision makers observe the combinations. For example, a decision maker assigned to block one may either observe the combination in the order A and B (treatment combinations 1, 2, 3, and 4) or in the order of B and A (treatment combinations 3, 4, 1, and 2), not both. Similarly, decision makers assigned to block two may observe combinations C and D either in the order of C and D (treatment combinations 5, 6, 7, and 8) or D and C (treatment combinations 7, 8, 6, and 5). In taking this approach, we reduce the number of possible randomized survey versions from 576[2] to eight (see table 6.4).

The advantage of using this strategy is that the order of presentation is orthogonal to the design attributes. Nevertheless, this strategy is sub-optimal to a strategy allowing the complete randomization of choice set presentation to individual decision makers. As suggested, however, the use of paper and pencil surveys may pose insurmountable logistical problems preventing the use of a complete randomization of the choice sets to individuals. Computer surveys have been used to overcome this logistical problem by allowing the computer program to randomize the choice sets observed by individual decision makers. These are called Computer Aided Personal Interviews (CAPI). Even more recently, choice surveys have made their debut on the web. In either case, the choice sets can be easily randomized and the data automatically entered into a database ready for analysis (data entry being another problem associated with the randomization of choice sets).

6.3.3 Stage 8: survey construction

Once the analyst has generated the choice sets, it is then time to construct the survey. Considerations for the construction of the choice survey are similar to the considerations for more conventional surveys in terms of when and how to ask the questions. For example, we suggest that demographic questions be asked in the last section of the survey. Given that much has been already written about questionnaire construction, we advise the reader

[2] Within each block there exist 24 possible permutations, thus over two blocks there exist 576 possible permutations (24 × 24).

unfamiliar with questionnaire design to seek out other sources on the subject. However, much can still be said with regard to questionnaires designed for the collection of choice data.

6.3.3.1 Choice context

Every choice we make as human beings is made within a *decision context*. Returning to our mode choice example, consider two individual decision makers making the same journey. The first individual decision maker is a business person making the journey for business purposes. The second individual decision maker has decided to make the journey with his family for a sightseeing holiday. The context of the two decision makers is therefore very different – business or holiday. Are the decision processes likely to be the same for both parties? If the analyst thinks not, then several decisions need to be made.

Can the two be included in the same sample? If so, what impact will any differences between the two (a form of heterogeneity) have at the time of model estimation? If not, should the analyst sample only those making holiday trips or those making business trips, or should both be sampled and the samples treated separately for model estimation purposes?

Assuming that the context in which a decision is made is likely to impact upon choice (as will be the case in most if not all situations), the analyst must not only decide upon whom to sample but, in the case of SP data, also clearly define the context in which decision makers are to assess each choice set in order to make a meaningful decision. Usually this takes the form of a *descriptive story* which explains to the decision maker the context in which to consider their choice of alternative within each choice set. In the case of RP data, the context under which choice data are collected also needs to be clearly defined at the time of the survey.

Returning to our example and assuming that the analyst wishes to sample holiday makers only, the analyst may present the following decision context in which decision makers are to consider each of the choice sets:

> *Imagine a situation where you are taking a holiday to <Insert City name here> with your immediate family. After some research you have identified five different modes of transport that you may use to get to <Insert City name here>. Each mode is described by the level of comfort likely to be experienced and the estimated travel time given in hours. Please consider the following scenarios and choose the mode that you would take for your holiday.*

If the analyst was interested in business trips, the choice context detailed above could easily be changed to reflect the change in decision emphasis. If both business and holiday makers are to be sampled, the choice context may have to be completely rewritten to account for both types of travelers. Alternatively, the different choice contexts could be presented in different survey versions to the relevant traveler. Again, the latter case suggests sampling and sample size considerations that need to be made. We discuss sampling issues later in this chapter.

Imagine a situation where you are taking a business trip to <Insert City name here>. After some research you have identified four different modes of transport that you may use to get to <Insert City name here>. Each mode is described by the level of comfort likely to be experienced and the estimated travel time given in hours. Please consider the following scenarios and choose the mode that you would take for your trip.

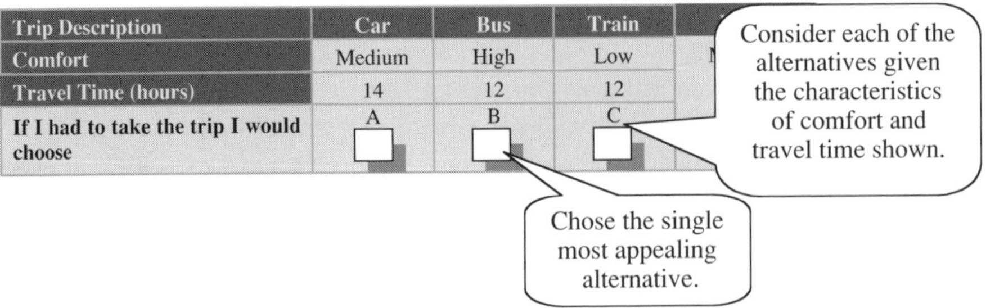

Trip Description	Car	Bus	Train
Comfort	Medium	High	Low
Travel Time (hours)	14	12	12
If I had to take the trip I would choose	A ☐	B ☐	C ☐

Consider each of the alternatives given the characteristics of comfort and travel time shown.
Chose the single most appealing alternative.

Figure 6.5 Mode-choice example

6.3.3.2 Use an example

Earlier, we said that decision makers may require several choice sets before they fully understand the task that they are being asked to undertake. At the time, we mentioned that in the past choice modelers provided extra choice sets which the decision maker could use to practice and learn the task required and which the choice analyst discarded from analysis. We also mentioned that this practice has fallen out of favor. By way of compensation, the current trend is for the analyst to provide an example of the choice task, explaining exactly what it is the analyst requires the decision maker to do. Figure 6.5 shows an example choice task for our mode-choice example.

6.3.3.3 Independence of choice sets

One problem that has been largely ignored by both academics and practitioners alike is the necessity of decision makers to treat the decision made in each choice set as an *independent decision* to the decisions made in all other choice sets. That is, the hypothetical scenario presented in each choice set is not to be compared to the hypothetical scenario presented in any other choice set observed. Consider the situation of a survey in which the respondent is able to observe all or some of the choice sets simultaneously. This is likely to be the case for paper and pencil surveys although computer and internet surveys may also display such characteristics. Given such a situation it is not unforeseeable that the decision maker may observe both prior and subsequent choice sets and make their choices with those choice sets in mind. In the worst case, decision makers may even return to already completed choice sets and change their choices in light of subsequent choice sets.

In order to overcome this, the analyst may adopt several strategies. Firstly, the analyst may express to the decision maker that each scenario is to be treated as a *separate hypothetical situation* and should not be considered in conjunction with other choice sets. However, such

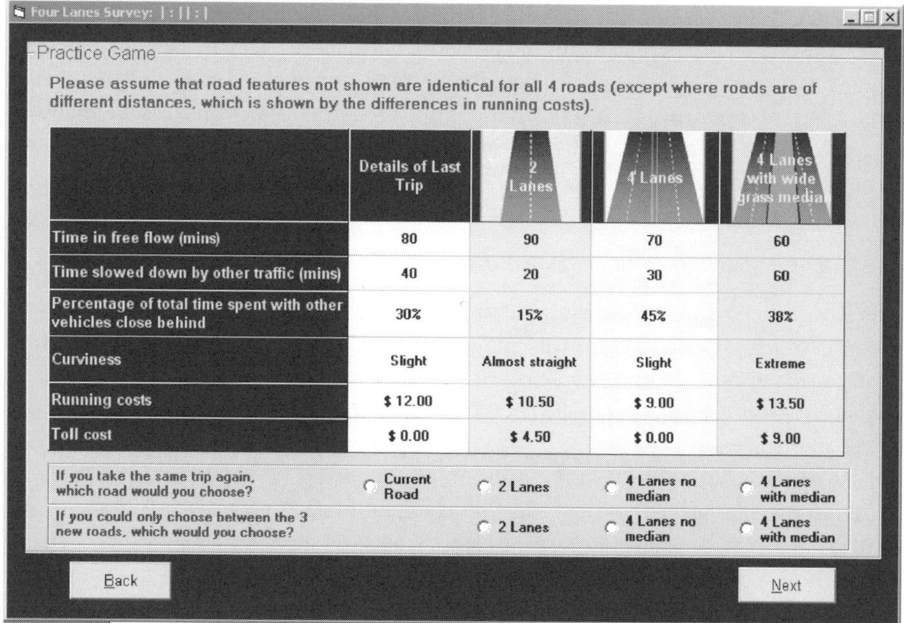

Four Lanes Survey: | : | | : |

Practice Game

Please assume that road features not shown are identical for all 4 roads (except where roads are of different distances, which is shown by the differences in running costs).

	Details of Last Trip	2 Lanes	4 Lanes	4 Lanes with wide grass median
Time in free flow (mins)	80	90	70	60
Time slowed down by other traffic (mins)	40	20	30	60
Percentage of total time spent with other vehicles close behind	30%	15%	45%	38%
Curviness	Slight	Almost straight	Slight	Extreme
Running costs	$ 12.00	$ 10.50	$ 9.00	$ 13.50
Toll cost	$ 0.00	$ 4.50	$ 0.00	$ 9.00

If you take the same trip again, which road would you choose?	Current Road	2 Lanes	4 Lanes no median	4 Lanes with median
If you could only choose between the 3 new roads, which would you choose?		2 Lanes	4 Lanes no median	4 Lanes with median

Back Next

Figure 6.6 Example of choice set with more than two choices

a statement may not be enough to prevent decision makers from failing to treat each choice set independently. The analyst may thus have to consider using personal interviews so that the way a decision maker completes the survey can be monitored and strictly controlled. Alternatively, computer and internet surveys may be utilized, the programming of which may allow for the viewing of only one choice set at a time and prevention of the return to previous choice sets.

6.3.3.4 More than one choice

Figure 6.6 shows a screenshot from a study using a computer choice survey undertaken by one of the authors (Hensher and Sullivan, 2003). A close examination of figure 6.6 reveals that decision makers were asked to make two decisions. The first decision requires the analyst to consider four alternatives, the last trip and trips involving 2 lanes, 4 lanes, or 4 lanes with a wide grass median (the grass that separates the lanes moving in two opposite directions) (we discuss the last trip alternative in some detail later). Once that choice has been made, decision makers are required to consider the same hypothetical scenario, however this time with only three alternatives: 2 lanes, 4 lanes, or 4 lanes with a wide grass median. As such, the second choice in the example shown in figure 6.6 represents a constraint in the available set of alternatives. While not strictly the case, the analyst may view such experiments as an availability problem (see Louviere, Hensher, and Swait 2000, chapter 5 for an example of a true availability experiment).

Asking decision makers to make two choices per choice set is not uncommon. In establishing the experiment in this manner, the analyst is able to model decisions under the two choice scenarios – the full choice set and a constrained choice set. Indeed, the analyst obtains two choice experiments for the price of one. This has become a popular strategy where the attribute levels associated with the alternatives in a stated choice set are pivoted from a current experience (as in figure 6.6). The dual-choice response enables the analyst to undertake statistical analysis with and without the pivot-base alternative. This is discussed in more detail below.

6.3.3.5 The no-choice or delay-choice alternative

The most common example of having decision makers make two choices involves experiments in which one of the alternatives available is a *non-choice* (the choice not to select one of the available alternatives) or a *delay-choice* alternative. In nearly all decision contexts decision makers are faced with, the decision maker will have the option not to select one of the alternatives or to delay their choice for the present. Consider a trip to the supermarket. At no stage during the visit is a decision maker compelled to purchase their favorite breakfast cereal. They may elect to either purchase the breakfast cereal, delay the purchase until another visit, or not to purchase the cereal at all. Nor, despite what some may believe, can a salesperson force an unwilling consumer to purchase some unwanted good or service (and even if they could, the act would be illegal).

We said above that *nearly all decisions* allow for the choice alternatives "not to choose any alternative" or to "delay the choice." Some choices, however, must require a choice of one of the available alternatives. If the decision has already been made to go to work today and assuming no telecommuting, a decision (or a continuation of habit based on an earlier decision) must be made on what mode to use for the commute. Similarly, a person traveling inter-state and planning on returning the next day must decide where to stay overnight.

Including the *no-choice* or *delay-choice* alternative is a decision that must be made in light of the objective of the study. If the objective is to estimate the demand for various alternatives within a market then the inclusion of a non-choice alternative is warranted. Unrealistically forcing decision makers to select among the available alternatives is likely to over inflate any estimates obtained.[3] If, however, the objective is to study the impact of the relationships different attribute levels have upon choice, then any non-choice alternative is likely to be a hindrance to the analyst. We say this as the only information obtained from a non-choice alternative is that the decision maker would prefer not to choose any of the available alternatives. We obtain no information as to why this may be the case, however. By forcing decision makers to make a choice, we oblige decision makers to trade off the attribute levels of the available alternatives and thus obtain information on the relationships that exist between the varying attribute levels and choice. Of course, the analyst may set up experiments collecting both decisions with and without a non-choice alternative to reap the benefits that both experimental formats have to offer.

[3] We caution readers from using SP experiments to estimate market demand. The best practice is to use both SP and RP data (see chapter 14).

6.4 Revealed preferences in questionnaires

The collection of RP data are not unlike the collection of any other data collected using a questionnaire (with the exception of SP data). With SP data, the analyst provides the decision maker with the attribute levels and gathers information on choice. With both traditional and RP data the analyst simply asks questions as to what was observed to have occurred (i.e. the level taken by some attribute – or, in the case of more traditional data types, perhaps some socio-demographic characteristic).

However, as discussed in chapter 4, with RP data the decision maker is often able to report accurately their observations with regard to the chosen alternative only. In such cases, the analyst must make the important decision as to whether or not to collect data from each decision maker with regard to non-chosen alternatives. If such information is not collected then further decisions regarding how to obtain data on non-chosen alternatives (required for model estimation) need to be made (discussed in chapter 8). If the analyst elects to ask each decision maker about the attribute levels of the non-chosen alternatives, further questions about the accuracy of their answers must be raised given that the decision maker may never have experienced the attribute levels of several of the available alternatives. Given that decision makers' preferences are formed based upon perceptions, however, theoretically this should not represent a problem. Nevertheless, perceptual data of this nature are more likely to produce outliers and reported levels out of line with actual levels if the individual has experienced that alternative, which are likely to cause problems for model estimation.

The decision to collect data on the non-chosen alternatives is likely to impact upon questionnaire construction. The analyst will be required to prepare additional questions and decision makers will be faced with longer questionnaires, requiring more time to complete. Given the necessity to handle data on non-chosen alternatives, however, the analyst should not automatically discard this option (again we discuss this in more detail in chapter 8). If the analyst decides not to collect data on the non-chosen alternatives then further decisions regarding survey construction also arise. How does the analyst handle the collection of data on the attribute levels if the alternatives under study do not share common attributes? The analyst may either use screening questions to move decision makers towards the survey questions relevant to their chosen alternative or prepare separate questionnaires specific to each alternative. The latter strategy may be worthwhile if the data are to be collected at the point at which the decision is being made (e.g. on the bus or at the supermarket), otherwise the former strategy is likely to prevail.

6.5 Studies involving both RP and SP data

As we noted in chapter 4, it is often worthwhile to collect and study both RP and SP data combined within a single study. We discuss this further in chapter 14. For the present, however, the challenge for the analyst in such cases is to ask questions that are consistent across both data sources. That is, if the analyst has established an SP experiment in which the attributes observed by each decision maker have been pre-defined for each alternative, information as to the levels observed by the decision maker to have occurred naturally must be collected on those same attributes. If, for example, price was used in the SP experiment then information about price should be collected as part of the RP data collection process also. Although we can handle cases in which the attributes differ between the two data sources quite easily, questions remain as to how best to combine such data and the effect upon the final model results, and therefore the analyst is best to remain consistent between the two in terms of the information collected.

6.6 Using RP data in SP experiments: the "current alternative"

An interesting approach to data collection is to include the current RP experience as part of an SP experiment. We show one such experiment in figure 6.6, in which the last trip alternative represents data collected on an actual trip previously undertaken by the decision maker. Figure 6.7 shows the screenshot for the questions asked to gather the information for the last trip attribute levels shown within the experiment for the same study. Although the attribute levels relate to the current chosen alternative, we cannot develop an RP choice model *per se* since we would need at least two RP alternatives. The situation below is often described as a *switching model* in which the choice response is strictly SP.

Across each choice set of the SP experiment, the alternative formed from each decision maker's previous experience remains constant (i.e. that attribute levels are invariant across choice sets). It is the attribute levels of the remaining alternatives which change from choice

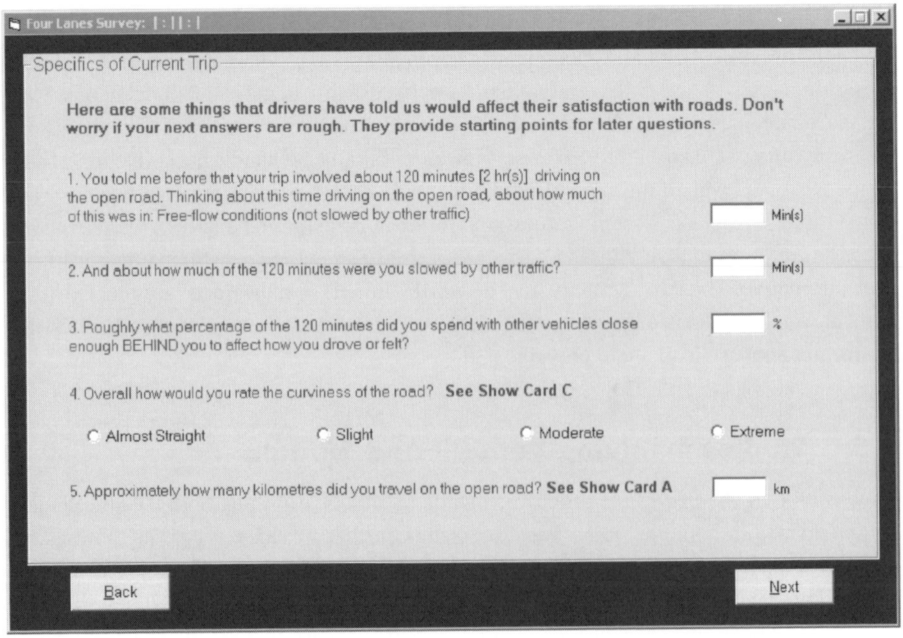

Figure 6.7 Collecting RP data for inclusion in an SP experiment

Table 6.5. *Reported attribute levels and SP attribute-level labels, different approaches*

Table	Reported experience		Fixed-attribute levels (car)		Fixed-attribute levels (bus)	
Attribute	Person A	Person B	0	1	0	1
Price ($)	5	8	3	10	2	6
Travel time (minutes)	20	30	15	35	25	35

Table 6.6. *Attribute-level labels for a* 2^4 *orthogonal design*

Treatment combination	Car price ($)	Car travel time (minutes)	Bus price ($)	Bus travel time (minutes)
1	10	35	2	35
2	3	15	6	35
3	10	15	2	25
4	3	35	6	25
5	3	35	2	25
6	10	15	6	25
7	3	15	2	35
8	10	35	6	35

set to choice set. Nevertheless, given that different decision makers may report different experiences, each decision maker will view different attribute levels for the alternative relating to their prior experiences.

To show how the analyst might proceed, consider an experiment with only two decision makers, A and B. Each decision maker is asked about the current attribute levels experienced for commutes to work for two attributes, price and travel time, when using their current mode of transport. The reported values are shown in table 6.5. Clearly decision maker A experiences travel times less than decision maker B as well as experiencing lower travel costs.

Using the experimental design shown in table 6.3, each decision maker will view a total of 8 treatment combinations if we ignore the blocking variables. If the analyst were to proceed as suggested in chapter 5, attribute-level labels cognitively sensible to each decision maker would have to be pre-defined as part of the experiment. Let us assume that the analyst elects to use the attribute-level labels shown in table 6.5 as reported under the columns titled *fixed attribute levels*, which have been derived to correspond to the attribute levels 0 and 1 in table 6.3. Using these attribute-level labels, table 6.3 may be rewritten as table 6.6.

Combing the reported attribute levels with those of the SP experiment as shown in table 6.6 and assuming that the choice sets have not been randomized, figures 6.8a and 6.8b show the first two choice sets as they might be shown to decision makers A and B, respectively.

Scenario 1

Trip Description	Current Means of transport	New car trip	New bus trip
Price	$5	$10	$2
Travel Time (minutes)	20	35	40
I would choose	☐	☐	☐
If I could no longer use my current means I would choose		☐	☐

Scenario 2

Trip Description	Current Means of transport	New car trip	New bus trip
Price	$5	$4	$6
Travel Time (minutes)	20	15	40
I would choose	☐	☐	☐
If I could no longer use my current means I would choose		☐	☐

a

Scenario 1

Trip Description	Current Means of transport	New car trip	New bus trip
Price	$8	$10	$2
Travel Time (minutes)	30	35	40
I would choose	☐	☐	☐
If I could no longer use my current means I would choose		☐	☐

Scenario 2

Trip Description	Current Means of transport	New car trip	New bus trip
Price	$8	$4	$6
Travel Time (minutes)	30	15	40
I would choose	☐	☐	☐
If I could no longer use my current means I would choose		☐	☐

b

Figure 6.8 Choice sets using fixed attribute-level labels
a Decision maker A
b Decision maker B

Notice that the larger the range of the experiences reported the harder it will be for the analyst to derive cognitively sensible attribute-level labels for each decision maker sampled as part of the experiment (this will be true whether the analyst wishes to use the decision maker's prior experiences as part of the SP experiment or not). In such cases, the analyst

Table 6.7. *Pivoting SP attribute levels from reported attribute levels using percentages*

		Percentages (car)		Percentages (bus)	
		0	1	0	1
	Reported levels (%)	−10	+10	0	+20
Person A					
	$5	$4.50	$5.50	$5.00	$6.00
	20	18	22	20	24
Person B					
	$8	$7.20	$8.80	$8.00	$9.60
	30	27	33	30	36

may be required to treat different decision makers as belonging to separate but identifiable segments, each of which could be presented with different attribute-level labels within the range of experiences for that particular segment. In such cases, the same experimental design may be used for each segment (alternatively, different experimental designs may be generated for each segment); however, the attribute-level labels assigned to each attribute level of the design may differ from segment to segment (as we will show, this approach is used in the main case study discussed in chapter 9).

As an alternative to the analyst separating the sample into segments, a process which is likely to be arbitrary in any case, the analyst may instead assign values to the attribute levels that are not fixed in an absolute sense across the entire sample (or segment), but rather which are some percentage change from the attribute levels reported by each decision maker. As such, the attribute levels of the SP design alternatives will be pivoted from the reported values of each decision maker. As an example consider table 6.7. In table 6.7 the analyst has defined attribute levels for the car alternative as −10 percent and 10 percent of the decision maker's reported attribute levels for both price and travel time. The attribute levels attached to the design for the bus alternative are 0 percent and 20 percent, respectively.

Taking the attribute-level labels assigned in table 6.7, table 6.3 now becomes table 6.8.

Note that the analyst does not show decision makers the percentages as given in table 6.8 but rather uses these percentages to calculate the attribute levels to be shown. Returning to table 6.7, we note that for decision maker A for the car attribute price, −10 percent is replaced by $4.50 while +10 percent is replaced by $5.50. For decision maker B, −10 percent will be replaced by $7.20 while +10 percent will be replaced by $8.80. Each decision maker observes different attribute levels dependent upon the attribute levels they reported, although the attribute levels shown are the same in terms of the percentage change from the reported levels. Assuming that the choice sets are not randomized, figures 6.9a and 6.9b show possible choice sets for the first two treatment combinations for decision makers A and B, respectively.

Table 6.8. *Attribute-level labels as percentage changes for a 2^4 orthogonal design*

Treatment combination	Car price (%)	Car travel time (%)	Bus price (%)	Bus travel time (%)
1	10	10	0	20
2	−10	−10	20	20
3	10	−10	0	0
4	−10	10	20	0
5	−10	10	0	0
6	10	−10	20	0
7	−10	−10	0	20
8	10	10	20	20

Table 6.9. *Pivoting SP attribute levels from reported attribute levels using wider percentages*

		Percentages (car)		Percentages (bus)	
		0	1	0	1
	Reported levels (%)	−20	+20	−10	+30
Person A					
	$5	$4.00	$6.00	$4.50	$6.50
	20	16	24	18	26
Person B					
	$8	$6.40	$9.60	$7.20	$10.40
	30	24	36	27	39

A comparison of the choice sets shown in figures 6.9a and 6.9b to those shown in figures 6.8a and 6.8b suggests that the attribute levels shown to the decision makers for the SP alternatives are more likely to be akin to the expectations of decision makers when the attributes are pivoted from the reported alternative than when fixed attribute levels are used. For example, in figure 6.8a, in the first scenario for the car alternative the price level is twice that which is currently experienced while the price of the bus alternative is under half of that currently experienced. For the same scenario, the travel time is almost twice that of the currently experienced travel time. Given these significant differences it is possible that the alternatives presented in this scenario represent an unrealistic proposition to decision maker A.

The percentages assigned to the attribute levels by the analyst will have a dramatic impact upon such a comparison. In table 6.9 we increase the range of the percentages and show the new attribute levels that each decision maker would be shown. As such, the analyst must be careful in selecting the percentages to assign to the attribute levels, considering

Scenario 1

Trip Description	Current Means of transport	New car trip	New bus trip
Price	$5	$5.50	$5
Travel Time (minutes)	20	22	24
I would choose	☐	☐	☐
If I could no longer use my current means I would choose		☐	☐

Scenario 2

Trip Description	Current Means of transport	New car trip	New bus trip
Price	$5	$4.50	$6
Travel Time (minutes)	20	18	24
I would choose	☐	☐	☐
If I could no longer use my current means I would choose		☐	☐

a

Scenario 1

Trip Description	Current Means of transport	New car trip	New bus trip
Price	$8	$8.80	$9.60
Travel Time (minutes)	30	33	36
I would choose	☐	☐	☐
If I could no longer use my current means I would choose		☐	☐

Scenario 2

Trip Description	Current Means of transport	New car trip	New bus trip
Price	$8	$7.20	$9.60
Travel Time (minutes)	30	27	36
I would choose	☐	☐	☐
If I could no longer use my current means I would choose		☐	☐

b

Figure 6.9 Choice sets using percentage attribute-level labels
a Decision maker A
b Decision maker B

the likely impacts the assigned percentages will have upon the attribute levels observed by each decision maker within the experiment.

As an aside, should an analyst approach an SP experiment as shown above, the model estimate results will be in the form of percentage changes from some current experienced level. While fixed attribute levels will allow the analyst to estimate the impact upon preference formation if prices are raised from, say, \$10 to \$15 (an absolute change), by taking the percentage of the attribute levels, the estimation of impacts of absolute changes in the attribute levels is no longer possible. Rather the results will suggest the impact upon preference formation given a percentage change in some given attribute level: for example, changing prices by 5 percent of the current experienced price, whatever that may be. Again, the analyst should not attempt to predict outside of the ranges used within the experiment. Thus, if the percentages used are those reported in table 6.7, then the analyst is restricted to examining percentage changes within the bounds of ± 10 percent from the currently experienced prices and travel times for the car alternative, and increases of between zero and 20 percent of the prices and travel times of the currently experienced bus alternative.

As a further aside, careful consideration is required in selecting the data collection mechanism used if the analyst elects to pivot the SP design attribute levels off of the reported levels obtained in advance from decision makers. If the analyst is using a paper and pencil survey then a two-stage process is required, in which the attribute levels currently experienced must first be obtained from decision makers before a second survey with the new attribute levels can be generated, overall a cumbersome process. It is thus suggested that the analyst use either computer aided or internet aided questionnaires in which the underlying computer program automatically calculates the percentage changes in the attribute levels and displays these within the same survey.

6.7 Sampling for choice data: the theory

Sampling, alongside experimental design, remains one of the least understood areas of choice analysis. While the choice of sample population is usually easy to determine, being a function of the objective of the study, *who* to sample and *what strategy* to use to sample from the chosen population is often much less clear.

To clarify the sample population, the analyst is best to start by defining the *sampling frame* for the study. The sampling frame represents the universal but finite set of decision makers to whom the analyst may administer the data collection instrument. Far from being a simple task, the sampling frame must remain consistent with the spirit of the objectives of the study, yet remain operationally viable. Consider the sampling frame for our inter-city travel example in which the population of interest is easily defined – inter-city travelers – yet the operational translation in terms of how we identify decision makers belonging to this population remains unclear. How do we identify travelers or potential travelers out of the total city population from whom we can sample? While bus, rail, and air travelers may be easily found, what about car travelers? For the sampling frame to be of use, the *location* of those identified within the sampling frame must also be known.

Assuming that the analyst is able to obtain lists of decision makers consistent with the defined population, the *sampling strategy* must then be determined. Possible sampling strategies include simple random samples (SRS), stratified random samples, and a choice-based sample (CBS). Non-random samples are also possible; however, the results of the analysis may not be readily transferable to the larger population of interest. As such, non-random samples as used in many academic studies may be used to identify the relationships between attributes but will often produce highly dubious market share or market demand estimates.

We have already discussed CBS in chapter 4 and so omit further detailed discussion on the topic here. With regard to SRS, if the sampling procedure is conducted properly, the proportions of those sampled should equal the proportions of those observed who actually have selected or are likely to select each of the available alternatives. That is, if we aggregate an SRS to the population, the true market shares should be reproduced.

6.7.1 Simple random samples

For SRS, the minimum acceptable sample size, n, is determined by the desired level of accuracy of the estimated probabilities, $\hat{p}$. Let p be the true choice proportion of the relevant population, a be the level of allowable deviation as a percentage between $\hat{p}$ and p, and β be the confidence level of the estimations such that $\Pr(|\hat{p} - p| \leq ap) \geq \beta$ for a given n, where $\beta = 1 - \alpha$. The minimum sample size is defined as[4]:

$$n \geq \frac{q}{pa^2}\left[\Phi^{-1}\left(1 - \frac{\alpha}{2}\right)\right]^2 \tag{6.1}$$

where q is defined as $1 - p$ and $\Phi^{-1}(1 - \frac{\alpha}{2})$ is the inverse cumulative distribution function of a standard normal (i.e. $N \sim (0,1)$) taken at $(1 - \frac{\alpha}{2})$.

As noted earlier, p represents the true choice proportion of the population. The observant reader will have noted that both here and earlier we used the singular *proportion* as opposed to the plural *proportions*. By taking the singular case, the analyst is confined to examples in which decision makers are limited to one of two alternatives; each individual decision maker is observed to either choose the alternative or not (e.g. the proportion of bus users is 0.2 (i.e. $p = 0.2$) compared to 0.8 (i.e. $q = 0.8$) for the proportion of non-bus users). But what if there exist *multiple alternatives* from which decision makers may choose (e.g. bus, car, train, and plane)? There now exist a number of proportions equal to the number of alternatives available.

To demonstrate how we handle such cases, let us return to our inter-city mode choice example. Assuming that the true proportions for each mode are known *a priori* (i.e. the market shares) the analyst must first decide on the level of accuracy, α, specified as a percentage that the sample proportions drawn are allowed to deviate from the true population proportions. Let us assume that the analyst can tolerate the sampled proportion of decision makers, $\hat{p}$ being within ± 5 percent of the true population proportions, p, and that the market shares for car, bus, train, and plane are 0.5, 0.03, 0.07, and 0.4, respectively.

[4] **As an aside**, those familiar with Louviere, Hensher, and Swait (2000) should note that (6.1) is different to (9.4) in that text. This is because (9.4) in Louviere, Hensher, and Swait (2000) has been misreported as a result of a typing error which was not discovered until after publication (as was (9.5)). We use this opportunity now to correct this error.

	A	B	C	D
1	**Alpha**	**1-Alpha/2**	**Z**	**Z^2**
2	0.1	=1-A2/2	=NORMINV(B2,0,1)	=D2^2
3	0.05	=1-A2/2	=NORMINV(B3,0,1)	=D2^2
4	0.01	=1-A2/2	=NORMINV(B4,0,1)	=D2^2
5				
6	**Alpha**	**1-Alpha/2**	**Z**	**Z^2**
7	0.1	0.95	1.64	2.71
8	0.05	0.975	1.96	3.84
9	0.01	0.995	2.58	6.63

Figure 6.10 Calculating Z^2 using Microsoft Excel

The next step is to obtain an estimate of the inverse cumulative normal distribution function, $\Phi^{-1}(1 - \frac{\alpha}{2})$. Elementary statistics tells us that the cumulative distribution function (CDF) of a normal distribution is the probability that a standard normal variable will take a value less than or equal to z (i.e. $P(Z \leq z)$ where z is some established numerical value of Z. However, we are not interested in the inverse normal distribution function but rather its square. Statistical theory shows that the square of a standard normal variable is distributed as a Chi-square with one degree of freedom. That is, Z^2.

The analyst is therefore required to find values of Z^2 in order to complete (6.1) and obtain estimates of the minimum sample size required. Using Excel, it is possible to calculate Z^2. We show this below (see also sub-section 2.8.3).

Figure 6.10 shows a screenshot for the formula as they would appear in Microsoft Excel to first calculate the probability of Z taken at $\left(1 - \frac{\alpha}{2}\right)$ for varying levels of α. The first step is to divide whatever value of α the analyst wishes to use by 2 and minus this value from 1. This will produce the required value for a single tail of the distribution. Next, using the *NORMINV* formula, the Z statistic can be calculated. The *NORMINV* formula is used in Excel to calculate the inverse normal distribution function for different normal distribution functions with varying means, standard deviations, and at varying levels of α. The first input into this formula as shown in figure 6.10 is the value of alpha we worked out as belonging to a single tail of the distribution in the C column of the spreadsheet. This level of α precedes the mean and standard deviation of the normal distribution. Note that we have entered a mean of zero and a standard deviation of 1 into the *NORMINV* formula. This suggests that we are using a standard normal distribution such that

$$Z \sim N(0, 1) \tag{6.2}$$

In words: Z is normally distributed with a mean of zero and standard deviation of one.

The *NORMINV* formula in Microsoft Excel will provide the analyst with the same Z-value they would obtain if they had used standard statistical tables. What remains is to square the Z, as shown in figure 6.10.

Table 6.10. *Differences between relative and absolute treatment of sample proportions*

	Proportion	Absolute difference	Upper and lower bound	Range	Relative difference	Upper and lower bound	Range
car	0.5	±0.05	(0.45, 0.55)	0.1	±0.025	(0.475, 0.525)	0.05
bus	0.03	±0.05	(0, 0.08)	0.1	±0.0015	(0.0285, 0.0315)	0.003
train	0.07	±0.05	(0.02, 0.12)	0.1	±0.0035	(0.0665, 0.0735)	0.007
plane	0.4	±0.05	(0.35, 0.45)	0.1	±0.02	(0.38, 0.42)	0.04

	A	B	C	D	E	F	G	H
1	**Alt**	**P**	**A**	**Q**	**R**	**Z^2**	**A**	**N/R**
2	Car	0.5	0.05	=1-B2	9	3.84	=D2/(B2*C2^2)*F2	=G2/E2
3	Bus	0.03	0.05	=1-B3	9	3.84	=D3/(B3*C3^2)*F3	=G3/E3
4	Train	0.07	0.05	=1-B4	9	3.84	=D4/(B4*C4^2)*F4	=G4/E4
5	Plane	0.4	0.05	=1-B5	9	3.84	=D5/(B5*C5^2)*F5	=G5/E5
6								
7	**Alt**	**P**	**A**	**Q**	**R**	**Z^2**	**A**	**N/R**
8	Car	0.5	0.05	0.5	9	3.84	1536	171
9	Bus	0.03	0.05	0.97	9	3.84	49664	5518
10	Train	0.07	0.05	0.93	9	3.84	20407	2267
11	Plane	0.4	0.05	0.6	9	3.84	2304	256

Figure 6.11 Calculating sample sizes using Microsoft Excel

Returning to our example, figure 6.11 shows the remainder of the calculation. Notice that we have calculated the sample sizes for each of the alternatives. This is because the calculation used is based upon the *allowable error* relative to each of the true population proportions and not upon the absolute value of the allowable error around each of the population proportions. Had we treated the error as an absolute, then the range in which we would expect to observe our sample proportions would have been ±5 percent around the true population proportion for each alternative. In treating the error as a relative value, there will exist a differential impact in terms of the range of proportions from which we might observe the sample proportions for each of the alternatives. We show this in figure 6.11.

To explain, we invite the reader to calculate the value of 0.05 of 0.5 and compare this to 0.05 of 0.03 (we have actually done this for you in table 6.10). Intuitively, we would expect 5 percent of 0.5 to be a larger value than 5 percent of 0.03, which is what we observe in table 6.10. Indeed from table 6.10, 5 percent of 0.5 is 0.025 while 5 percent of 0.03 is 0.0015.

It is at this point that the analyst must make a decision as to which population proportion to use to calculate the sample size to be used for the study. If the analyst were to use 0.5 as the proportion (the proportion associated with the *car* alternative) in (6.1) then, as shown in figure 6.11, the minimum sample size of the study would be 1,536 decision makers (this is not strictly true, as we will show later). If, on the other hand, the analyst chose to use the population proportion for the *bus* alternative (0.03) then the minimum sample size suggested would be 49,664 decision makers, a significant increase over the sample size suggested when using the proportion for the car alternative.

Why would the analyst sample 49,664 decision makers when they could sample only 1,536? To answer this question we must rearrange (6.1) to show the impact of altering sample sizes on the tolerable error, α. Rearranging (6.1) we get:

$$a \leq \sqrt{\frac{q}{pn}\left[\Phi^{-1}\left(1-\frac{\alpha}{2}\right)\right]^2} \tag{6.3}$$

Assuming that the sample size for the *car* alternative is used, calculating the allowable error for the *bus* alternative we get:

$$a \leq \sqrt{\frac{0.97}{0.03 \times 1536}[1.96]^2}$$

$$a \leq 0.28$$

While the tolerable error for the *car* alternative remains 0.05, for the *bus* alternative the allowable error is 0.28. That is, the sample proportion obtained will be within the range of 0 and 0.31 (i.e. 0.03 ± 0.28; as a proportion cannot be negative we censor the lower bound to be 0). Should the analyst use the population proportion for the *bus* alternative to determine the sample size then the allowable error would remain at 0.05 for the bus alternative but would become 0.01 for the *car* alternative. Again these calculations are easily performed in Microsoft Excel, as shown in figure 6.12.

From the above, it is clear that the analyst is best to calculate the sample size based upon the alternative with the smallest population proportion as this will ensure that the allowable error for the remaining alternatives will be smaller than that specified for the alternative used to calculate the sample size.[5] However, this strategy is likely to result in very large minimum sample sizes. The more common approach is therefore to calculate the sample size based upon what the analyst believes to be the more important of the alternatives in the study. Thus, if the analyst was more interested in the car alternative, then the true population proportion for the car alternative would be used to calculate the sample size. Alternatively, if the train alternative was deemed to be more important or of more interest in the study, then the true population proportion for the train alternative would be used to calculate the sample size. In taking this approach, the analyst must be aware that the acceptable error will be exact only for the alternative in which the analyst used the population proportion and that the acceptable error will be higher for alternatives with smaller true population proportions, and lower for alternatives with larger true population proportions relative to the proportion used in the calculation.

[5] If there exists a rarely chosen alternative, then the analyst should consider the use of CBS.

	A	B	C	D	E	F	G
1	**Alt**	**P**	**N**	**Q**	**R**	**Z^2**	**A**
2	Car	0.5	1536	=1-B2	9	3.84	=SQRT((D2/(B2*C2))*F2)
3	Bus	0.03	1536	=1-B3	9	3.84	=SQRT((D2/(B2*C2))*F2)
4	Train	0.07	1536	=1-B4	9	3.84	=SQRT((D2/(B2*C2))*F2)
5	Plane	0.4	1536	=1-B5	9	3.84	=SQRT((D2/(B2*C2))*F2)
6							
7							
8	**Alt**	**P**	**N**	**Q**	**R**	**Z^2**	**A**
9	Car	0.5	1536	0.5	9	3.84	0.05
10	Bus	0.03	1536	0.97	9	3.84	0.28
11	Train	0.07	1536	0.93	9	3.84	0.18
12	Plane	0.4	1536	0.6	9	3.84	0.06
13							
14	**Alt**	**P**	**N**	**Q**	**R**	**Z^2**	**A**
15	Car	0.5	49664	0.5	9	3.84	0.01
16	Bus	0.03	49664	0.97	9	3.84	0.05
17	Train	0.07	49664	0.93	9	3.84	0.03
18	Plane	0.4	49664	0.6	9	3.84	0.01

Figure 6.12 Calculating the allowable error using Microsoft Excel

As an aside, it is not always possible to obtain the true population proportions in advance of the study. In such instances, the analyst may have to best guess what the true population proportions are. While this represents a weak point in any choice study, we note that calculations similar to those shown above are also required for studies not associated with choice analysis and therefore represent a weakness in nearly all scientific research requiring the calculation of sample size, and not just for choice analysis.

To conclude the discussion on SRS, recall earlier that the minimum sample sizes calculated do not strictly represent the minimum sample sizes required. The calculation determines the sample size required if each decision maker is shown a single choice set. As such, the sample size is not strictly the minimum sample size necessary for the study, but rather the minimum number of choices that are required to replicate the *true population proportions* within the acceptable error. Thus for SP studies where decision makers may be shown more than one choice set, the minimum number of decision makers required for any given study is equal to the minimum number of choices divided by the number of choices each decision maker is to be shown as part of the survey (the number of choice sets). In figures 6.11 and 6.12, we define the number of choice sets to be shown to each decision maker as r, and use this to calculate the minimum number of decision makers required for the sample. As shown in figure 6.11, using the car alternative to calculate the minimum number of choices required and setting r to equal 9, the total number of decision makers required is 171 and not 1,536 (i.e. $1536 \div 9 = 171$).

As an aside, the above holds only if decision makers treat each choice set as being an *independent decision task* (see sub-section, 6.3.3.3, *Independence of choice sets*). If this does not hold, then one cannot increase the number of choice sets shown to each decision maker in order to decrease the number of decision makers required to be sampled. Further, the analyst should be aware that by reducing the number of decision makers sampled, there exists a corresponding decrease in the variability of socio-demographic characteristics and contextual effects observed within the sample, which in turn is likely to pose problems at the time of model estimation if these socio-demographic characteristics are to be included within the model.

6.7.2 Stratified random sampling

With stratified random sampling, the population is first divided into G mutually exclusive groups each representing a proportion of the total population, W_g. As discussed in Louviere, Hensher, and Swait (2000), the basis for creating the groups can be any characteristic common to the population (e.g. age, income, location, gender etc.) with the exception of choice. That is, the analyst cannot form groups based upon the observed choice of alternative as would occur with CBS. To maintain randomness within the sample (a desirable property if one wishes to generalize to the population), a *random sample* is drawn within each stratum. The sample sizes drawn within each stratum need not be equal across stratums.

To calculate the sample size for a stratified random sample, the analyst may either (1) apply (6.1) to establish the minimum total sample size and subsequently partition the total sample size into the G groups, or (2) apply (6.1) to each stratum and sum the sample sizes calculated for each stratum to establish the total sample size. Strategy (1) produce smaller minimum sample sizes than strategy (2); however, the analyst must recognize the effect on the acceptable error in using strategy (1), as the accuracy of the results when using strategy (1) will be related to the overall proportion while the accuracy of the results for strategy (2) will be relative to the within-group proportions.

For example, assume that the analyst has divided the inter-city mode choice population into two strata; those traveling for business purposes and those traveling for other reasons. Assuming a total population of travelers of 1 million, 40 percent of whom are traveling for business purposes, table 6.11 summarizes the population proportions broken down by purpose of travel. As table 6.11 shows, the population proportions are significantly

Table 6.11. *Breakdown of inter-city travelers, by purpose of trip*

Mode	Overall proportions	Total travelers	Business traveler proportions	Total business travelers	Other traveler proportions	Total other travelers
car	0.5	500,000	0.4	160,000	0.566	340,000
bus	0.03	30,000	0.01	4000	0.043	26,000
train	0.07	70,000	0.04	16,000	0.09	54,000
plane	0.4	400,000	0.55	220,000	0.3	180,000

Table 6.12. *Strata sample sizes calculated using the overall population proportions*

Mode	Minimum number of decision makers	Bus	Other
Car	171	68	102
Bus	5518	2207	3311
Train	2267	907	1360
Plane	256	102	154

Table 6.13. *Strata sample sizes calculated using the strata population proportions*

	Business			Other			
Mode	Proportion	Choices	Decision makers	Proportion	Choices	Decision makers	Total
Car	0.40	2304	256	0.57	1159	129	385
Bus	0.01	152064	16896	0.04	36864	4096	20992
Train	0.04	36864	4096	0.09	15531	1726	5822
Plane	0.55	1257	140	0.30	3584	398	538

different for mode choice suggesting that a stratified random sample is warranted in this instance.

Strategy (1) suggests the use of the overall population proportions to first derive the minimum sample size. We have already computed these sample sizes; however, in using a stratified random sample the analyst is next required to determine the sample sizes of each of the G groups. While the analyst may elect to divide the total sample size into the G groups equally, let us assume here that the analyst has decided to apportion the total sample size in accordance with the observed division of strata (i.e. 40 percent of the total sample size will be business travelers while 60 percent will be those traveling for other reasons). Using such a division, the minimum acceptable sample sizes for each strata are shown in table 6.12 (assuming $r = 9$). The analyst is once more left to decide which population proportion to use in order to calculate the minimum sample size requirements.

Strategy (2) suggests calculating the minimum sample size requirements for each of the strata, G, and summing the derived minimum samples sizes for each strata to calculate the overall minimum sample size required. Using the proportions reported in table 6.11, we report the sample sizes in table 6.13 (once more assuming $r = 9$).

Tables 6.12 and 6.13 report the minimum number of decision makers and not the minimum number of *choices* required. To calculate the effect upon the acceptable error, we require the minimum number of choices and thus multiply the number of decision makers by the number of choice set replications they will be shown; nine in this example.

	A	B	C	D	E	F	G	H	I	J	K	L	M
1	**Overall**												
2	**Business**							**Other**					
3	Car							Car					
4	**P**	**N**	**Q**	**R**	**Z^2**	**A**		**P**	**N**	**Q**	**R**	**Z^2**	**A**
5	0.5	68	0.5	9	3.84	0.24		0.5	102	0.5	9	3.84	0.19
6	0.03	68	0.97	9	3.84	1.35		0.03	102	0.97	9	3.84	1.10
7	0.07	68	0.93	9	3.84	0.86		0.07	102	0.93	9	3.84	0.71
8	0.4	68	0.6	9	3.84	0.29		0.4	102	0.6	9	3.84	0.24
9	Bus							Bus					
10	**P**	**N**	**Q**	**R**	**Z^2**	**A**		**P**	**N**	**Q**	**R**	**Z^2**	**A**
11	0.5	2207	0.5	9	3.84	0.04		0.5	3311	0.5	9	3.84	0.03
12	0.03	2207	0.97	9	3.84	0.24		0.03	3311	0.97	9	3.84	0.19
13	0.07	2207	0.93	9	3.84	0.15		0.07	3311	0.93	9	3.84	0.12
14	0.4	2207	0.6	9	3.84	0.05		0.4	3311	0.6	9	3.84	0.04
15	Train							Train					
16	**P**	**N**	**Q**	**R**	**Z^2**	**A**		**P**	**N**	**Q**	**R**	**Z^2**	**A**
17	0.5	907	0.5	9	3.84	0.07		0.5	1360	0.5	9	3.84	0.05
18	0.03	907	0.97	9	3.84	0.37		0.03	1360	0.97	9	3.84	0.30
19	0.07	907	0.93	9	3.84	0.24		0.07	1360	0.93	9	3.84	0.19
20	0.4	907	0.6	9	3.84	0.08		0.4	1360	0.6	9	3.84	0.07
21	Plane							Plane					
22	**P**	**N**	**Q**	**R**	**Z^2**	**A**		**P**	**N**	**Q**	**R**	**Z^2**	**A**
23	0.5	102	0.5	9	3.84	0.19		0.5	154	0.5	9	3.84	0.16
24	0.03	102	0.97	9	3.84	1.10		0.03	154	0.97	9	3.84	0.90
25	0.07	102	0.93	9	3.84	0.71		0.07	154	0.93	9	3.84	0.58
26	0.4	102	0.6	9	3.84	0.24		0.4	154	0.6	9	3.84	0.19

Figure 6.13 Within-stratum acceptable error using overall population proportions

Using (6.4), we show the impact upon the acceptable level of error as calculated in Microsoft Excel for sample sizes calculated using the overall population proportions (strategy (1)) in figure 6.13. Thus while the overall acceptable error will be 0.05, within each stratum, the acceptable error can be anywhere up to 1.35 or 135 percent for an individual alternative.

Figure 6.14 shows the calculated acceptable errors for sample sizes calculated using within-strata population proportions (strategy (2)). Dependent upon the proportion used to calculate the minimum sample size, there are dramatic improvements in terms of the acceptable error generated from the sample size drawn.

6.7.3 Conclusion to the theory of calculating sample sizes

These improvements come at the substantial cost of dramatic increases in sample size which, in many instances, is dependent upon the available budget of the study.

To conclude the discussion on calculating the minimum sample size necessary for choice studies a few remarks are necessary. First, in calculating the minimum sample sizes in the manner suggested, we have largely ignored the impact of *task complexity* on model

29	**Within Group**											
30	**Business**						**Other**					
31	Car						Car					
32	**P**	**N**	**Q**	**R**	**Z^2**	**A**	**P**	**N**	**Q**	**R**	**Z^2**	**A**
33	0.5	2304	0.5	9	3.84	0.04	0.5	1159	0.5	9	3.84	0.06
34	0.03	2304	0.97	9	3.84	0.23	0.03	1159	0.97	9	3.84	0.33
35	0.07	2304	0.93	9	3.84	0.15	0.07	1159	0.93	9	3.84	0.21
36	0.4	2304	0.6	9	3.84	0.05	0.4	1159	0.6	9	3.84	0.07
37	Bus						Bus					
38	**P**	**N**	**Q**	**R**	**Z^2**	**A**	**P**	**N**	**Q**	**R**	**Z^2**	**A**
39	0.5	152064	0.5	9	3.84	0.01	0.5	36864	0.5	9	3.84	0.01
40	0.03	152064	0.97	9	3.84	0.03	0.03	36864	0.97	9	3.84	0.06
41	0.07	152064	0.93	9	3.84	0.02	0.07	36864	0.93	9	3.84	0.04
42	0.4	152064	0.6	9	3.84	0.01	0.4	36864	0.6	9	3.84	0.01
43	Train						Train					
44	**P**	**N**	**Q**	**R**	**Z^2**	**A**	**P**	**N**	**Q**	**R**	**Z^2**	**A**
45	0.5	36864	0.5	9	3.84	0.01	0.5	15531	0.5	9	3.84	0.02
46	0.03	36864	0.97	9	3.84	0.06	0.03	15531	0.97	9	3.84	0.09
47	0.07	36864	0.93	9	3.84	0.04	0.07	15531	0.93	9	3.84	0.06
48	0.4	36864	0.6	9	3.84	0.01	0.4	15531	0.6	9	3.84	0.02
49	Plane						Plane					
50	**P**	**N**	**Q**	**R**	**Z^2**	**A**	**P**	**N**	**Q**	**R**	**Z^2**	**A**
51	0.5	1257	0.5	9	3.84	0.06	0.5	3584	0.5	9	3.84	0.03
52	0.03	1257	0.97	9	3.84	0.31	0.03	3584	0.97	9	3.84	0.19
53	0.07	1257	0.93	9	3.84	0.20	0.07	3584	0.93	9	3.84	0.12
54	0.4	1257	0.6	9	3.84	0.07	0.4	3584	0.6	9	3.84	0.04

Figure 6.14 Within-stratum acceptable error using strata population proportions

estimation. The estimation of any statistical model requires a certain amount of degrees of freedom. Insufficient sample sizes are likely to result in an inability by the analyst to estimate statistical models capable of detecting statistically significant results, and in some instances from estimating any models at all.

Second, we wish to reiterate the important point made earlier regarding socio-demographic characteristics and sample sizes. While the analyst may decrease the number of physical decision makers necessary for a study by increasing the number of choice set replications shown to each, this will lower the variability observed within the socio-demographic characteristics, which in turn decreases the likelihood of detecting significant socio-demographic characteristics at the time of modeling. We leave you to ponder the question: are 100 decision makers making 10 decisions the same as 10 decision makers making 100 decisions?

6.8 Sampling for choice data: the reality

Section 6.7 outlined theories related to sampling as they apply to studies of choice. Unfortunately, while such theories are well advanced, experience suggests that they are more often than not ignored for more practical considerations. With specific regard to studies of choice, this has resulted in the development of a series of *rules of thumb*, the origins of which exist not in the minimization of the acceptable error allowed by an analyst, but rather in attempts to identify the minimal sample size required to estimate models of choice. Budgetary considerations often take precedence over theoretical considerations. In this section, we discuss not how sampling should occur, but rather how sampling (in our experience) tends to occur for studies of choice.

With the collection of RP choice data, the guiding rule of thumb is simple. Experience suggests that the *best strategy* for sampling is CBS with minimum sample sizes of 50 decision makers choosing each alternative. For example, two alternatives suggest a minimum sample size of 100 decision makers; three alternatives a minimum of 150 decision makers, and so forth. Sampling on the chosen alternative to conform to a minimum quota of 50 decision makers per alternative involves a non-random sampling process, which in turn means that the sample is unlikely to represent the true population market shares. If one takes such an approach to sampling with the intention of prediction, some form of data (re-)weighting is required. We explore this in detail in chapters 8 (Data implications) and 11 (Modeling).

If one elects to use a form of random sampling, the question of minimum sample size is no longer so straightforward. In the case of a study consisting of two alternatives, randomly sampling 100 decision makers is unlikely to produce 50 decision makers per each alternative. Indeed, in cases where selection of one of the alternatives is relatively rare in the population being sampled, it is highly probable that the majority of decision makers sampled will have chosen the more popular of the two alternatives. Such disparity in numbers, while perhaps replicating the true market shares, will likely result in little variability in the variables of interest (both attributes and SDC) for the least-chosen alternative(s).

Since statistical modeling is about explaining variability, one requires variability in order that it can be explained. No variation means no statistical model, while little variation often translates to poor model results. It is for this reason that the somewhat arbitrary number of 50 decision makers per alternative has been suggested as an experiential lower limit which provides adequate variation in the variables of interest for which *robust* models may be fitted.

Taking the above into account, one of two approaches is available to the analyst, although we are not aware that either approach is commonly used in practice (the authors use CBS). The first approach assumes knowledge of the *true market proportions*. Knowing the true market proportions in advance, the analyst may set the sample size for the alternative with the smallest proportion to 50 and calculate the sample sizes for the remaining alternatives in recognition of the known population proportions. For example, if one alternative is chosen five times more than a second alternative, setting the sample size for the second alternative to 50 would suggest a sample size for the first alternative of 250. In randomly sampling 300 decision makers, we would expect to obtain the minimum number of 50 decision makers for the least-popular alternative while at the same time maintaining the true market proportions.

We might wish to reject this strategy, as it will produce unnecessarily high sample sizes. In knowing the true market proportions, the analyst may use CBS and sample 50 decision makers for each alternative, later weighting the data to obtain the true market proportions. For the above example, this would require a minimum sample size of 100 in contrast to 300 decision makers.

Assuming that the population proportions are unknown, the second strategy involves the use of a *flexible sample size*. The suggestion here is to randomly sample until at least 50 decision makers have been sampled who have selected each alternative. Again, this may result in excessively large sample sizes in cases where selection of one of the alternatives is relatively rare. In such instances, one is best to use non-random sampling techniques such as *snowballing*[6] to obtain decision makers for the rarely chosen alternative. However without knowing the true population proportions, one may then have to guess as to which weights to apply at the time of model estimation in order to replicate the true population choice or market shares.

Variability is less of an issue in collecting SP choice data if any analysis is to be confined to the attributes used as part of the experimental design. This is because variability is induced within these attributes as part of the experimental design employed. The moment the analyst wishes to include any covariates (i.e. SDC or other non-design attribute) into the analysis, variability becomes as much an issue as when one collects RP choice data. The issue of establishing a minimum sample size for SP choice data therefore relates to whether the analyst intends to estimate models using the design attributes only, or the design attributes combined with covariates.

For SP choice data, experience suggests that the most commonly used criteria for establishing a minimum sample size is the number of observations required to estimate robust models. "Observations" here refers to the choice sets and not rows of data (as we show chapter 10, the two are not necessarily the same). There appear to be no practical well-defined rules to guide the analyst. Given that the chosen alternatives are not known in advance (as with RP data), a *quota strategy* appears to be the best approach, in which a frequent check is made of the number of times an alternative is chosen in each choice set. Given that an individual may be faced with 16 choice sets it may not take too many observations to satisfy this condition. However, given that some alternatives will be less popular (especially if they are labeled such as *car vs train vs bus* in contrast to unlabeled alternatives (*Alternative A vs B vs C*), the minimum sample size will again be dictated by the 50 observation cut-off for the least-popular alternative. Where the alternatives are unlabeled, and hence all parameters will be generic across all alternatives, the minimum can be relaxed since the variability required is far less. There is no magic number, but one suspects a total sample of 50 individuals each with 16 choice sets and fully generic parameter specification for design attributes and no contextual or covariate effects might just be acceptable.

[6] "Snowballing" is a non-random sampling technique in which the analyst identifies potential respondents by asking those already surveyed for details of other potential respondents that they may know. These new potential respondents are then contacted and surveyed, after which the process repeats itself.

As an aside, practitioners utilizing RP and/or SP data often start with alternative-specific parameters and find that one is statistically insignificant on an alternative, or even of the wrong sign. They then impose a constraint across alternatives through a generic parameter to produce statistical significance and the correct sign. Is this wise if indeed one is covering up a deficiency rather than truly establishing common behavioral response (i.e. marginal utility) for an attribute across more than one alternative?

7 NLOGIT for applied choice analysis: a primer

Programming today is a race between software engineers striving to build bigger and better idiot-proof programs, and the Universe trying to produce bigger and better idiots. So far, the Universe is winning. (Rich Cook)

7.1 Introduction

This book includes a companion computer program, NLOGIT/ACA, which will enable you to replicate, extend and explore the models that are discussed in the book using your own computer and the data set on which the examples are based. NLOGIT/ACA is a special version of NLOGIT, a major commercial package published by Econometric Software, Inc., which is used world-wide by discrete choice modellers in transport, economics, marketing, statistics, and all the social sciences (you might want to visit the company's website, www.NLOGIT.com). This chapter will describe how to install and use this program on your computer. There are relatively few steps involved, and getting started should take only a few minutes.

7.2 About the software

7.2.1 About NLOGIT

NLOGIT is an extension of another very large, integrated econometrics package, LIMDEP, that is used world-wide by analysts of models for regression, discrete choice, sample selection, censored data, count data, models for panel data, etc. NLOGIT includes all of the capabilities of LIMDEP plus the package of estimators for models of multinomial choice, such as the multinomial logit (MNL), multinomial probit (MNP), nested logit, mixed logit and several others and, in addition, some tools for analyzing discrete choice models such as the model simulator described in chapters 11 and 12 in this book.

7.2.2 About NLOGIT/ACA

This version of NLOGIT is restricted to use with the data set that is provided on the website with the program and analyzed in the text. You will be free to compute new variables based on those in the data set, and transformations of the data as well. However, the program is not able to accept any other data set. NLOGIT is a very large model estimation and analysis package that contains roughly 200 built-in estimators for a variety of models for regression, discrete choice, counts, survival, sample selection and a wide variety of others. NLOGIT/ACA is limited to a small sub-set of these: descriptive statistics, linear regression, and the binomial and multinomial discrete choice models described in this book. Aside from these two restrictions, all features of the program are available, including, for example, specifying sub-samples of the data, transformations of the data set, the scientific calculator and the matrix algebra package. NLOGIT/ACA includes all of the capabilities that are special to NLOGIT but, once again, these are limited to the data set provided with the text.

7.2.3 Installing NLOGIT/ACA

NLOGIT/ACA is a Windows-based program (there is no Macintosh version). It will self-install on most machines. Just download the file from the website for the book to your computer and double click the installation program in any Windows explorer. Windows will find the program and invoke the installation package. This in turn will install the program and place startup icons in your *Start* menu, in the programs menu, and on your desktop. You can start NLOGIT/ACA from any of these icons just by double clicking it.

7.3 Starting NLOGIT/ACA and exiting after a session

7.3.1 Starting the program

You can start NLOGIT/ACA from any of the program icons or menu entries. The main desktop will appear as shown in figure 7.1.

7.3.2 Inputting the data

In order to do any analysis, you must now input the data to the program. Data for your analysis are placed in an NLOGIT data file named <*AppliedChoice.lpj*> (the *lpj* suffix is a Windows recognized file type which stands for "*limdep projectfile*"). This file is provided at the website for this book. You can (and should) make a copy of this file and place it in some familiar place on your computer. To read the data into NLOGIT, use *File*, *Open Project*..., then make your way to this file, either on the book's website or to wherever you have copied it. Select it by double clicking the file name, and you are ready to begin. The process is shown in figure 7.2. Figure 7.3 shows how your desktop will appear after you load your

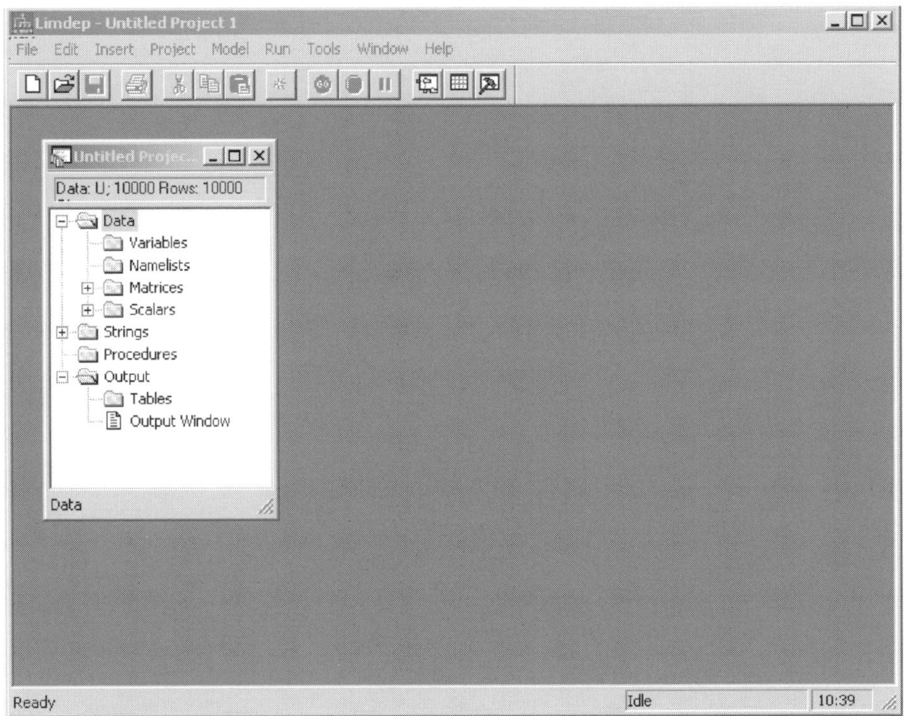

Figure 7.1 Initial NLOGIT desktop

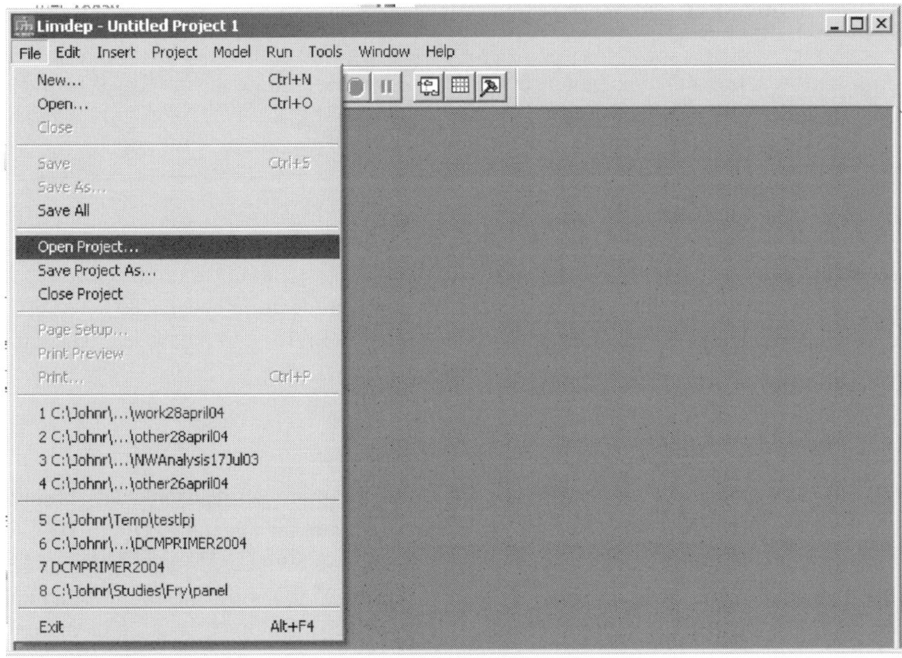

Figure 7.2 File Menu on Main Desktop and Open Project . . . Explorer

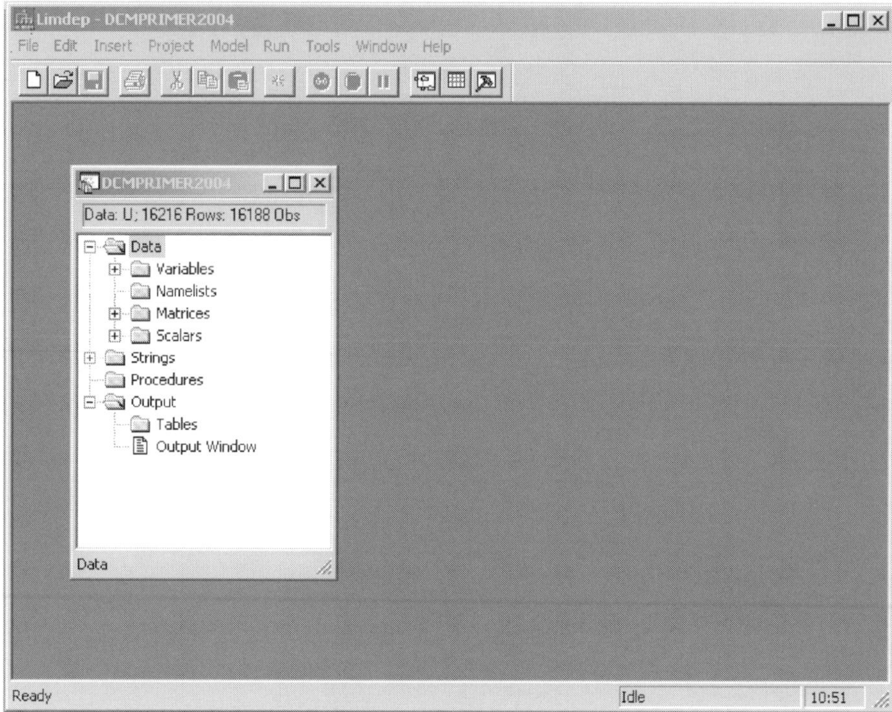

Figure 7.3 NLOGIT desktop after Project File Input

project into the program (you will have more than 840 observations in your data set – there are 840 in our small test data set).

7.3.3 Reading data

NLOGIT can read many kinds of data files, including rectangular ASCII files and spreadsheet files from programs such as Microsoft Excel. The program operation to do so is a **READ** command. The **READ** command is discussed in detail in chapter 8 (note, once again, this version of the program will be able only to **READ** its own data set). The data set specific to this text is discussed in chapter 9.

7.3.4 The project file

All your data are stored in your project file. Your program can read only *this* project file named <*AppliedChoice.lpj*> (this file contains an internal signature, NLOGIT/ACA cannot read a different file with this name – for this reason, we strongly urge you to make and save at least one, possibly several, copies of this file). You will be able to create new variables and add them to your project file. When you leave NLOGIT, you will be offered a chance to save the project file. You should do this. Later, when you restart the program, you will find *AppliedChoice.lpj* in the bottom part of the file menu in the recent files, and you can load the data into the program by selecting this file from the *File* menu.

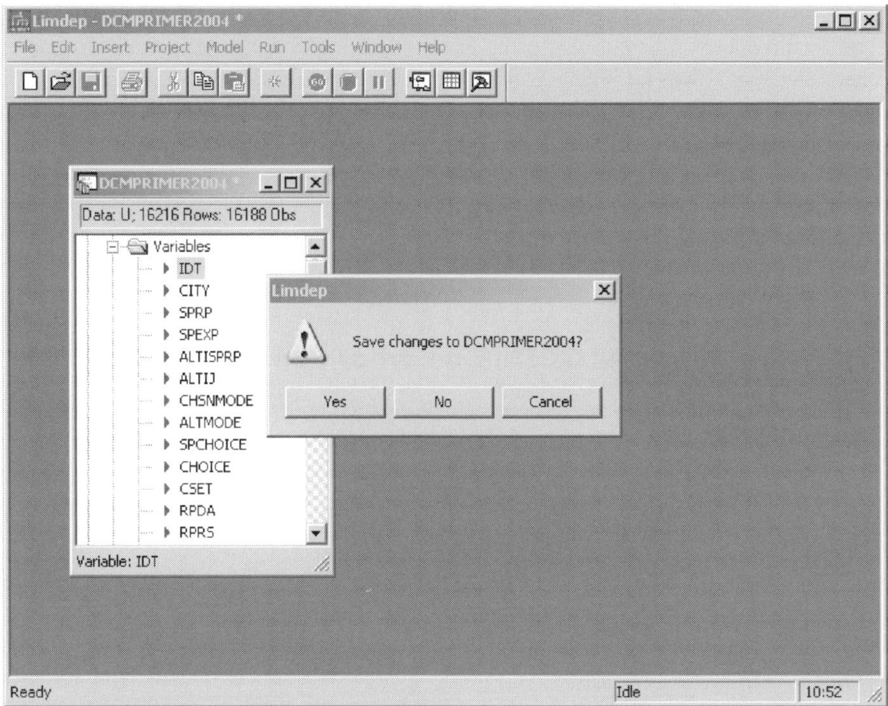

Figure 7.4 Dialog for Exiting NLOGIT and Saving the Project File

7.3.5 Leaving your session

When you are ready to leave your session, you should use *File*, *Exit* to close the program (double clicking the NLOGIT icon at the extreme upper left of the desktop, or single clicking the red × button at the extreme upper right will also close the program). When you leave NLOGIT, you are given an opportunity to save your work, as shown in figure 7.4. You should save your project file if you have made any changes that you wish to keep.

7.4 Using NLOGIT

Once you have started the program and input your data, you are ready to analyze them. The functions you will perform with NLOGIT/ACA will include the following:

(a) Compute new variables or transform existing variables
(b) Set the sample to use particular sets of observations in your analyses
(c) Use program tools such as the scientific calculator to compute statistics
(d) Use the descriptive statistics package to learn about your data set
(e) Compute linear regressions
(f) Use the NLOGIT features to estimate and analyze discrete choice models.

We note the following with respect to this version of the larger program. You have the full functionality of NLOGIT for functions (a)–(c). Function (d) is also unrestricted but, again, only for analysis of the data provided with the text. Your program can compute any linear regression model you would like, using least squares, and will produce a wide range of related statistics. However, many features of the linear regression package, such as panel data estimators, two stage least squares, etc. are not supported. Likewise, roughly 200 other model estimation packages for many single and multiple equation models (you can find a listing of these at Econometric Software Inc.'s website) are also disabled. All of the model estimation and analysis tools of the NLOGIT suite of discrete choice estimators, as well as the LOGIT command in LIMDEP are contained in NLOGIT/ACA.

7.5 How to get NLOGIT to do what you want

There are two methods of giving "commands" or instructions to NLOGIT. Both will produce identical results. The row of desktop commands at the top of your screen – *File*, *Edit*, *Insert*, *Project*, etc. – all invoke dialog boxes that will query you for the information needed to carry out your instructions. There are also dialog boxes for specifying models invoked by the *Model* command. These are standard, Windows-style dialogs that generally require minimal information from you, sometimes nothing more than clicking boxes or buttons to indicate a decision. The alternative method is for you to type "commands" to NLOGIT and to submit these commands to a processor which carries them out for you. The two methods have their advantages and disadvantages. The dialog boxes are convenient, but have three shortcomings:

(1) It is usually necessary to redo all steps completely if you want to repeat an operation. Dialog boxes do not remember anything.
(2) The dialog boxes do not always provide all the different variations for an instruction you want carried out.
(3) Ultimately, command entry by the dialog boxes will become tedious and slow.

The command entry is *self-documenting* – once you enter a command by the method discussed below, the command itself is retained and you can re-use it. Also, commands look like what they are trying to do. For example, the command **CREATE; LOGX = Log(X) $** carries out a function similar to what it looks like (i.e. creates a variable called logx which is the log of a variable called **X**). The discussion below will describe how to use the text editor to enter instructions. You may want to experiment with the menus and dialogs as well.

7.5.1 Using the Text Editor

In order to submit commands to NLOGIT's command processor, you will first type them in the Text Editor. The command (Text) Editor is a basic, standard text processor in which you enter lines of text that are commands to NLOGIT. The editor also uses standard features such as Cut/Copy/Paste, highlight, drag and drop, etc. Use *File*, *New* then *OK* (assuming Text/Command Document is highlighted, as in figure 7.5) to open the text editing screen. This will appear as in figure 7.6. You are now ready to type your instructions. Figure 7.7 shows some examples (the format of the instructions is discussed below and later in the

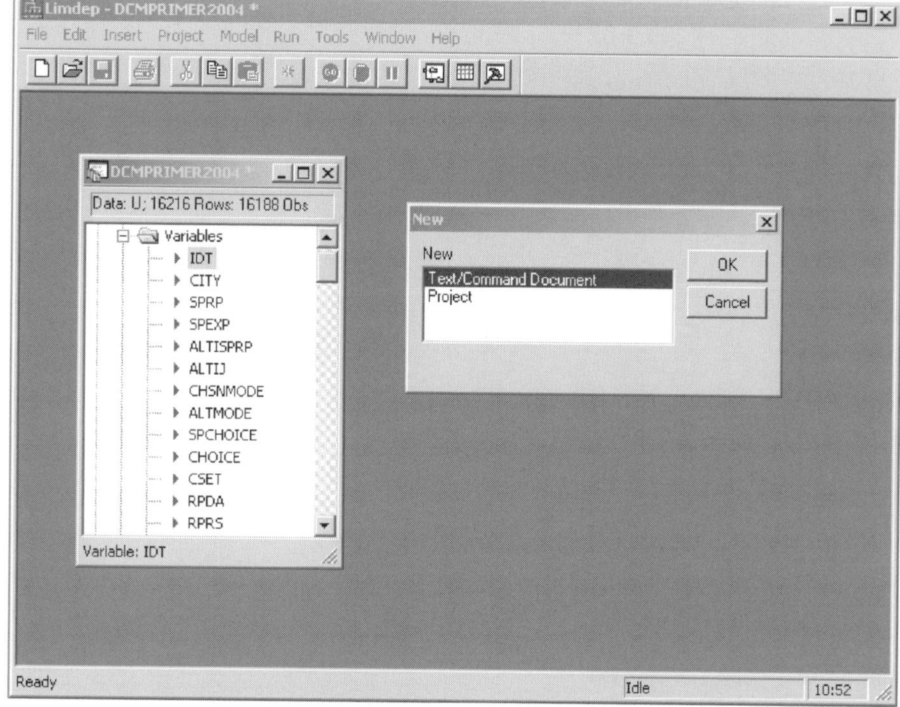

Figure 7.5 Dialog for Opening the Text Editor

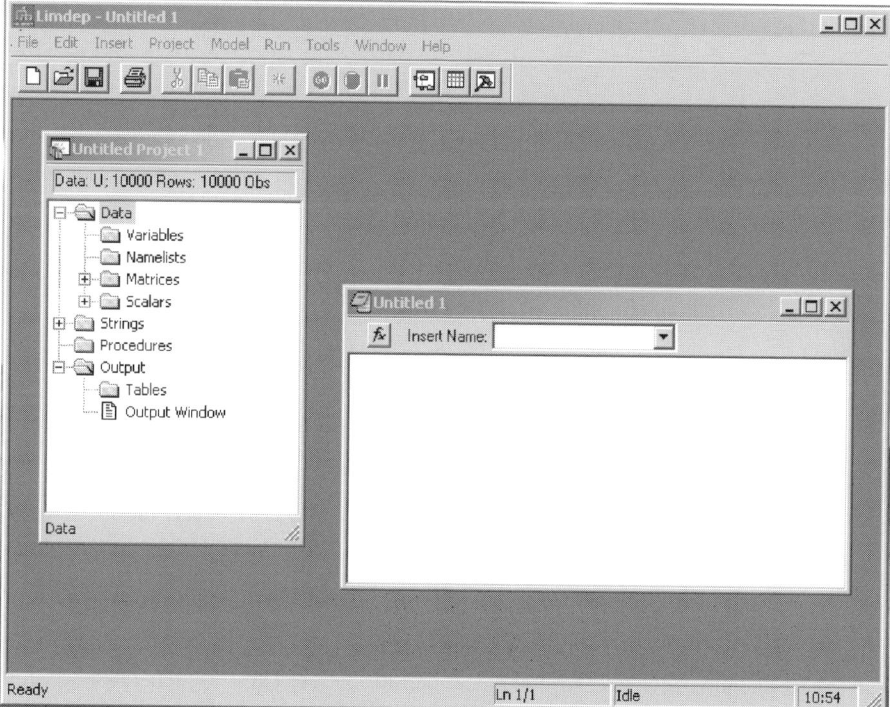

Figure 7.6 Text Editor Ready for Command Entry

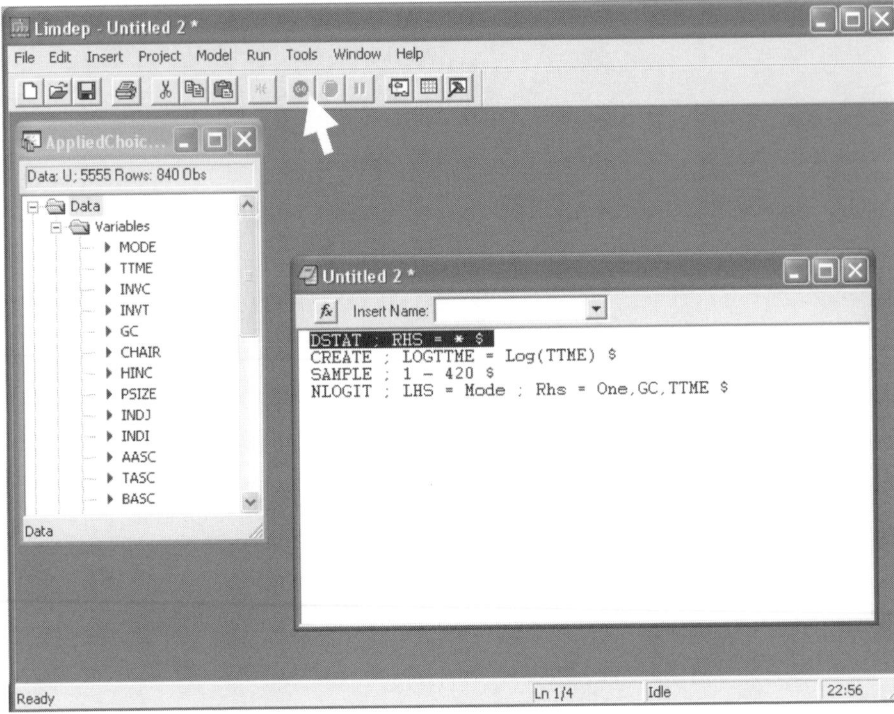

Figure 7.7 Commands in the Text Editor

book). Typing an instruction in the Editor is the first step in getting your command carried out. You must then "submit" the instruction to the program. This is done in two ways, both using the "*Go*" button that is marked in figure 7.7. To submit a single line of text to the program for execution, put the blinking text cursor on that line, then with your mouse, press the *Go* button. The instruction will then be executed (assuming it has no errors in it). To submit more than one line at the same time (or one line), highlight the lines as you would in any word processor, then, again, press "*Go*."

7.5.2 Command format

NLOGIT instructions all have the same format. Each new instruction must begin on a new line (see figure 7.7). Within an instruction, you may use lower case or capital letters, and you may place spaces anywhere you wish. An instruction may use as many lines as desired. The general format of a command is:

VERB; other information . . . $

The command always begins with a verb followed by a semi-colon and ends with a dollar sign (**$**). Commands often give several pieces of information. These are separated by semi-colons. For example, when you wish to compute a regression, you must tell NLOGIT what the dependent (LHS) and independent (RHS) variables are. You might do this as follows:

REGRESS ; LHS = y ; Rhs = One,X $

The order of command parts generally doesn't matter either – the RHS variables could appear first. The other element of commands that you need at this point is the *naming convention*. NLOGIT operates on variables in your data set. Variables all have names, of course. In NLOGIT, variable names must have one to eight characters, must begin with a letter, and may use only letters, digits, and the underscore character.

7.5.3 Commands

NLOGIT recognizes hundreds of different commands, but for your purposes, you will need only a small number of them – they are differentiated by the verbs. The functions of the program that you will use (once your data are read in and ready to analyze) are:

(1) Data analysis

DSTATS; RHS = the list of variables $? For descriptive statistics.

REGRESS; Lhs = dependent variable; Rhs = independent variable $

Note: ONE is the term used for the constant term in a regression. NLOGIT does not put one in automatically: you must request that a constant be estimated.

LOGIT; Lhs = variable; Rhs = variables $? For a binomial logit model.

PROBIT; Lhs = variable; Rhs = variables $? For a binomial probit model.

NLOGIT; various different forms $? The NLOGIT command is the command most used throughout this text. The various forms are discussed at length in chapters 10, 11, 14, and 16.

CROSSTAB; Lhs = variable; RHS = Variable $

HISTOGRAM; Rhs = a variable $

(2) Sample setting

SAMPLE; first observation – last observation $

SAMPLE; ALL $? To use the entire data set.

REJECT; decision rule $? For removing observations from the sample. They are not "deleted". They are just marked and bypassed until you restore them in the sample.

(3) New variables

CREATE; name = expression; name = expression . . . $

(4) Scientific calculations

CALCULATE; expression $? Examples appear below.

MATRIX; expression $? Examples appear below.

As an aside, any text after a question mark (**?**) is *not read* by NLOGIT. This allows the analyst to make comments in command editor that may be useful in future sessions. Also note that spacing of characters in the commands typed is not essential (i.e. the words may run into each other); however the use of spacing often makes it easier to follow what the command is, and will help in locating errors.

7.5.4 Using the Project File Box

The variables in the data set, once loaded, may be accessed using the Project File Box. The Project File Box is the box shown to the left-hand side of the NLOGIT desktop. Before loading the data set, the Project File Box is titled "**Untitled Project 1**" (see figure 7.1). Once a project file (i.e. a *lpj* file) has been read into NLOGIT, the name of the Project File Box will take on the name of the file read (see figure 7.3). If data are read into NLOGIT using a file extension other than *lpj* (e.g. *.TXT*, *.XLS*, *.SAV*) then the Project File Box will retain the "**Untitled Project 1**" title.

As an aside, the *.SAV* file extension is the file extension name used by SPSS but also was historically used by NLOGIT. The two are not compatible, hence those attempting to read data from SPSS must first save the data into another format (such as *.TXT*, *.XLS*, etc.) before reading it into NLOGIT.

The Project File Box contains several folders that will allow the analyst to access various useful screens. Double clicking on the Data folder, for example, will open up several other sub-folders, one of which is a Folder titled Variables (figure 7.7). Double clicking on the Variables folder will allow the analyst to view the names of all the variables in the data set (including any the analyst has created since reading in the data). By double clicking on any one of the variable names, the Data Editor will be opened displaying the data for each of the variables. The Data Editor in NLOGIT (and NLOGIT/ACA) will display only the first 120 variables in a data set and the first 1900 rows of data. Variables greater than the 120th variable in the data set and rows greater than the 1900th row cannot be viewed by the analyst in NLOGIT (NLOGIT makes no claims to be a spreadsheet program. If spreadsheet capabilities are required, the authors tend to use other programs such as Microsoft Excel or SPSS and import the data into NLOGIT). Other useful NLOGIT functions may be accessed via the Project File Box, such as the scientific calculator (see section 10.7, "The **Calc** command").

7.6 Useful hints and tips

NLOGIT is an extremely powerful program allowing the analyst to perform many statistical functions and estimate a wide variety of models (NLOGIT/ACA allows for only a sub-set of these, however). Yet despite its wide range of capabilities, those new to NLOGIT often have difficulties with the program. While in the chapters that follow we use the Text/command Editor to write out the full set of commands for the models we estimate, the slightest error in spelling or omission of a necessary character will result in the program being unable to carry out the desired function. This is not the fault of the program, but of the analyst. Thus, extreme care must be made in writing out the commands correctly. As mentioned above, the analyst may use the command toolbars rather than the Text/command Editor; however, this usually comes at the cost of flexibility. While the authors prefer to use the Text/command editor to write out the commands, it is sometimes useful to use the command toolbars if the source of an error cannot be located. Even when using the command toolbars NLOGIT will provide the command syntax for the initiated command in the output file, thus allowing the analyst to see what the command should look like and perhaps help in locating the original error. Nevertheless, as noted earlier, the command toolbars do not always offer the full range of outputs that may be generated using the Text/command editor and as such, this error locating strategy may not always be possible.

As an aside, the most common errors in the output that are associated with the estimation of discrete choice models are given in appendix 7A.

7.6.1 Limitations in NLOGIT (and NLOGIT/ACA)

There are a number of limitations on the commands used and models that may be estimated in NLOGIT. The two most specific limitations worth noting are:

1. A 2500 character limit to commands (including spaces; but not including comments made after question marks)
2. A 100 parameter limit in estimation.

Only in extreme cases will these limitations be a barrier for the analyst. Indeed, it is highly unlikely that the beginner will need a command that has greater than 2500 characters or estimate a model that has more than 100 parameters. Even if the 2500 character limit is reached, often creative renaming of variables and parameters may overcome the problem. The issue of estimating 100 parameters is less easily solved; however, very few studies will ever require the estimation of a choice model with this number of parameters.

7.7 NLOGIT software

The full NLOGIT package includes many features not listed above. These include nearly 100 varieties of regression models, models for count data, discrete choice models such as probit and logit, ordered discrete data models, limited dependent variable models, panel data models and so on. There are also a large variety of other features for describing and manipulating data. You can learn more about these on the website for the program, www.NLOGIT.com.

7.7.1 Support

Please note, NLOGIT/NCA is free software. It has been tested to reproduce the results in your book and for normal operation with your data set. As it is free, the program comes with no warranty and no technical support. Please understand that ESI is not able to support this program, nor can they answer modeling questions or questions about operation. You can learn more about NLOGIT at Econometric Software Inc.'s website. You may, of course, also purchase the full package, which operates exactly the same as this one. However, your purchase of *Applied Choice Analysis: A Primer* and, with it, this demonstration version of NLOGIT, does not imply other than normal purchase arrangements for the full package, as an initial purchase.

7.7.2 The program installed on your computer

As noted earlier, NLOGIT is an expanded version of LIMDEP. *The program that is installed on your computer is actually called LIMDEP* – it is NLOGIT, however. There are a number of signatures in the program that will indicate this to you, if you have any doubt. You will be able to see the name NLOGIT on the program icons, and you may find some additional data in the Help About box after you start the program.

7.7.3 Using NLOGIT/ACA in the remainder of the book

We have provided NLOGIT/NCA as part of the book. As noted, this program is limited in the applications you are allowed to perform and in the data you will be able to use. The remainder of the text is written as if you are using the full version of NLOGIT and not NLOGIT/ACA. Where a capability in NLOGIT/ACA is not available (e.g. reading single line data, see chapter 8) we make a note of this. NLOGIT/NCA will allow access only to the *AppliedChoice.lpj*. This data may be read into NLOGIT/NCA as described in this chapter. For those with access to the full version of NLOGIT, we not only provide the *AppliedChoice.lpj* but also the data in the *.TXT* format and each of the commands used in each chapter as *.LIM* files. In chapter 9, we describe how to read in data using these other formats, noting now that these files will be accessible only to those using the full version of NLOGIT (project files (i.e. *lpj* files)) can become quite large, hence using alternative file extensions is often quite useful. It is for this reason that we offer these files as an alternative to the *AppliedChoice.lpj* for those with the full NLOGIT program. Those with access to the full program will still be able to use the *AppliedChoice.lpj* file if this is preferred.

Appendix 7A Diagnostic and error messages

Introduction

The following is a complete list of diagnostics that will be issued only by *NLOGIT*. Altogether, there are over 1000 specific conditions that are picked up by the command translation and computation programs in *LIMDEP* and *NLOGIT*. Those listed here are specific to *NLOGIT*. A complete list of the full set of diagnostics is given in chapter R17 of the

LIMDEP Reference Guide. Nearly all the error messages listed below identify problems in commands that you have provided for the command translator to parse and then to pass on to the computation programs.

Most diagnostics are self-explanatory and will be obvious. For example:

```
82 ;Lhs - variable in list is not in the variable names table.
```

states that your Lhs variable in a model command does not exist. No doubt this is due to a typographical error – the name must be misspelled. Other diagnostics are more complicated, and in many cases, it is not quite possible to be precise about the error. Thus, in many cases, a diagnostic will say something like "the following string contains an unidentified name" and a part of your command will be listed – the implication is that the error is somewhere in the listed string. Finally, some diagnostics are based on information that is specific to a variable or an observation at the point at which it occurs. In that case, the diagnostic may identify a particular observation or value. In the listing below, we use the conventions:

<AAAAAAAA> indicates a variable name that will appear in the diagnostic
<nnnnnnnnnnn> indicates an integer value, often an observation number, that is given
<xxxxxxxxxxxx> indicates a specific value that may be invalid, such as a "time" that is negative

The listing below contains the diagnostics and, in some cases, additional points that may help you to find and/or fix the problem. The actual diagnostic you will see in your output window is shown in the `Courier` font, such as appears in diagnostic 82 above.

We note it should be extremely rare, but occasionally, an error message will occur for reasons that are not really related to the computation in progress (we can't give an example – if we knew where it was, we'd remove the source before it occurred). This is on the same level as the ubiquitous "page fault" that Windows often throws up when something entirely different has occurred. You will always know exactly what command produces a diagnostic – an echo of that command will appear directly above the error message in the output window. So, if an absolutely unfathomable error message shows up, try simplifying the command that precedes it to its bare essentials and, by building it up, reveal the source of the problem.

Finally, there are the "program crashes." Obviously, we hope that these never occur, but they do. The usual ones are division by zero and "page fault." Once again, we cannot give specific warning about these, since if we could, we'd fix the problem. If you do get one of these and you cannot get around it, let us know at Econometric Software, if at all possible, with sufficient resources attached so that we can reproduce the error.

Discrete choice (CLOGIT) and NLOGIT errors

1000 `FIML/NLOGIT is not enabled in this program.`

1001 `Syntax problem in tree spec or expected ; or $ not found.`

1002 `Model defines too many alternatives (more than 100).`

1003 `A choice label appears more than once in the tree specification.`

1004 `Number of observations not a multiple of # of alternatives.`

This occurs when you have a fixed choice set with J alternatives. In this case, the number of observations in the sample must be $J \times N$, where N is the number of individuals in your sample.

1005 `Problem reading labels, or weights for choice based sample.`

1006 `Number of weights given does not match number of alternatives.`

1007 `A choice-based sampling weight given is not between zero and one.`

1008 `The choice-based sampling weights given do not sum to one.`

1009 `An expected [ in limb specification was not found.`

1010 `An expected ( in branch specification was not found.`

1011 `A branch label appears more than once in the tree.`

1012 `A choice label in a branch spec. is not in the ;CHOICES list.`

1013 `The branch specifications are not separated by commas.`

1014 `One or more ;CHOICE labels does not appear in the tree.`

1015 `One or more ;CHOICE labels appears more than once in the tree.`

1016 `The model must have either 1 or 3 LHS variables. Check specification.`

1017 `Nested logit model must include ;MODEL:...or ;RHS spec.`

`Found neither Model: nor RhS/Rh2. Model is incomplete.`

1018 `There is an unidentified variable name in the equation.`

This occurs in your **;Model** specification for the utility functions.

1019 `Model specification exceeds an internal limit. See documentation.`

NLOGIT has a few internal limits, such as 100 choices and 25 branches. When you exceed a limit on the model size, estimation must halt at that point: your model is too large.

1020 `Not used specifically.`

This diagnostic may show up with a self-explanatory message. Error 1020 is an internal template that is used at many points where a problem with a data set, observation or command shows up. The actual diagnostic given will show the error.

1021 `You are using the Box-Cox function on a variable that equals 0.`

1022 `There are insufficient valid observations to fit a model.`

The actual requirement is only 2, so if you have less than this, your sample must be badly constructed.

1023 `Mismatch between current and last models.`

This occurs when you are using the **;Simulation= ...** part of the NLOGIT package. The model used for the simulation must match exactly the one that was estimated by the previous command. If the specification appears to be different based on the saved command, then the simulation must be halted.

1024 `Failure estimating DISCRETE CHOICE model.`

Since this is the starting value for other models, if estimation fails here, it won't succeed in the more complicated model.

1025 `Failed to fit model. See earlier diagnostic.`

1026 `Singular VC may mean model is unidentified. Check tree.`

What looks like convergence of a nested logit model may actually be an unidentified model. In this case, the covariance matrix will show up with at least one column of zeros.

1027 `Models - estimated variance matrix of estimates is singular.`
`Non P.D. 2nd derivatives. Trying BHHH estimator instead.`

This is just a notice. In almost all cases, the Hessian for a model that is not the simple MNL model will fail to be positive definite at the starting values. This does not indicate any kind of problem. Estimation will continue. Look for the exit code at the end of the iterations. If it is zero, the diagnostic should be ignored.

1028 In ;SIMULATION=list of alternatives, a name is unknown.

1029 Did not find closing] in labels[list].

1030 Error in specification of list in ;Choices=...labels[list].

1031 List in ;Choices=...labels[list] must be 1 or NALT values.

The following three errors, all numbered 1032, will occur when you are merging revealed and stated preference data: Error 1033 also occurs with this merging procedure.

1032 Merging SP and RP data. Not possible with 1 line data setup.
Merging SP and RP data requires LHS=choice,NALTi, ALTij form.
Check :MERGERPSP(id=variable, type=variable) for an error.

1033 Indiv. <nnnnnn> with ID= <nnnnn> has the same ID as another individual.

This makes it impossible to merge the data sets.

Errors 1034–1048 will be produced by incorrect specifications of the **;Simulation** feature of NLOGIT.

1034 Specification error. Scenario must begin with a colon.

1035 Expected to find Scenario: specification = value.

1036 Unbalanced parentheses in scenario specified.

1037 Choice given in scenario: attr(choice...) is not in the model.

1038 Cannot identify attribute specified in scenario.

1039 Value after = in scenario spec is > 20 characters.

1040 Cannot identify RHS value in scenario spec.

1041 Transformation asks for divide by zero.

1042 Can only analyze 5 scenarios at a time.

1043 Did not find any valid observations for simulation.

1044 Expected to find ; LIST : name_x (choices). Not found.

1045 Did not find matching (or [in <scenario specification is given>.

1046 Cannot recognize the name <AAAAAAAA> in <scenario specification is given>.

1047 Same as 1046.

1048 None of the attributes requested appear in the model.

1049 Model has no free parameters among slopes!

This occurs during an attempt to fit the MNL model to obtain starting values for a nested logit or some other model.

1050 DISC with RANKS. Obs= <nnnnnn>. Alt= <nn>. Bad rank given = <nnnn>.

1050 DISC w/RANKS. Incomplete set of ranks given for obs. <nnnnnn>.

These two errors are data problems with the coding of the Lhs variable. With ranks data, your dependent variable must take values $1, \ldots, R$ (where R may be the tied last place ranking of more than one observation).

1051 Singular VC matrix trying to fit MNL model.

When the MNL breaks down, it will be impossible to fit a more elaborate model such as a nested logit model.

1052 You did not provide ;FCN=label(distn),...for RPL model.

1053 Scaling option is not available with HEV, RPL, or MNP model.
Ranks data may not be used with HEV, RPL, or MNP model.
Nested models are not available with HEV, RPL, or MNP model.
Cannot keep cond. probs. or IVs with HEV, RPL, or MNP model.
Choice-based sampling not useable in HEV, RPL, or MNP model.

These diagnostics are produced by problems setting up the scaling option for mixed data sets. Errors numbered 1053 are all related to the **;Scale** option. All the diagnostics listed in the group will use the same number. Only one of them will be given.

1054 Scaling option is not available with one line data setup.
Ranks data may not be used with one line data setup.

Choice set may not be variable with one line data setup.
One line data setup requires ;RHS and/or ;RH2 spec.
Nested models are not available with one line data setup.
Cannot keep probabilities or IVs with one line data setup.

Errors numbered 1054 are all related to the option that allows you to provide data for the discrete choice model on a single line instead of on one line per alternative. All the diagnostics listed in the group will use the same number. Only one of them will be given.

1055 Did not find closing paren in ;SCALE(list) spec.
The list of variables to be scaled has an error.
Only 40 or fewer variables may be scaled.
You are attempting to scale the LHS variable.
The list of values given for SCALE grid is bad.
Grid must = Lo,Hi,N or Lo,Hi,N,N2. Check spec.
Grid must have Low > 0 and High > low. Check #s.
Number of grid points must be 2,3,...up to 20.

Errors numbered 1055 are all related to the **;Scale** option. All the diagnostics listed in the group will use the same number. Only one of them will be given.

1056 Unidentified name in IIA list. Procedure omitted.

1057 More than 5 names in IIA list. Limit is 5.

1058 Size variables only available with (Nested) MNL

1059 Cannot locate size variable specified.

1060 Model is too large: Number of betas up to 90.

Model is too large: Number of alphas up to 30.

Model is too large: Number of gammas up to 15.

Model is too large: Number of thetas up to 10.

1061 Number of RHS variables is not a multiple of # of choices.

This occurs when you are using a one line setup for your data. See 1054 above, as well.

1062 Expected ;FIX=name[...]. Did not find [or].

1063 In ;FIX=name[...], name does not exist: <name is given>.

1064 Error in fixed parameter given for <name is given>.

1065 Wrong number of start values given.

This occurs with nested logit and other models, not the random parameters logit model.

1066 Command has both ;RHS and Model: U(alts). This is inconsistent.

1067 Syntax problem in ;USET:(names list)= list of values.

1068 ;USET: list of parms contains an unrecognized name.

1069 Warning, ;IUSET: # values not equal to # names.

1070 Warning, ;IUSET: # values not equal to # names.

1071 Spec for RPL model is label(type) or [type]. Type=N,C,or L.

1072 Expected ,; $ in COR/SDV/HFN/REM/AR1=list not found.

1073 Invalid value given for correl. or std.dev. in list.

1074 ;COR/SDV=list did not give enough values for matrix.

1075 Error. Expected [in ;EQC=list[value] not found.
Error:Value in EQC=list[value] is not a correlation.
Error. Unrecognized alt name in ;EQC=list[value].
Error:List needs more than 1 name in EQC=list[value].
Error. A name is repeated in ;EQC=list[value].

1076 Your model forces a free parameter equal to a fixed one.

1077 Covariance heterogeneity model needs nonconstant variables.

1078 Covariance heterogeneity model not available with HEV model.
Covariance heterogeneity model is only for 2 level models.
Covariance heterogeneity model needs 2 or more branches.

1079 At least one variance in the HEV model must be fixed.

1080 Multiple observation RPL/MNP data must be individual.

1081 Mismatch of # indivs. and number implied by groups.
WARNING Halton method is limited to 25 random parameters.

1082 Not used.

1083 MODEL followed by a colon was expected, not found.

1084 Expected equation specs. of form U(...) after MODEL.

1085 Unidentified name found in <string is given>.

This occurs during translation of **;MODEL:U(...)** specifications.

1086 U(list) must define only choices, branches, or limbs.

1087 An equals sign was not found where expected in utility function definition.

1088 Mismatched [or (in parameter value specification.

1089 Could not interpret string; expected to find number.

1090 Expected to find ;IVSET:=defn. at this point. ??

1091 Expected to find a list of names in parens in IVSET.

1092 IVSET:(list)...Unidentified name appears in (list).

1093 You have given a spec for an IV parm that is fixed at 1.

1094 You have specified an IV parameter more than once.

1095 Count variable <nnnnnn> at row <nnnnnn> equals <nnnn>.

A peculiar value for the count variable has thrown off the counter that keeps track of where the estimator is in the data set.

1096 Choice variable <AAAAAAAA> at row <nnnnn>: Choice= <nnnnn>.

This looks like a coding error or some other kind of bad data.

1097 Obs. <nnnnnn>: Choice set contains <nnnn> <nnnn> times.

The choice variable for this individual's data have more than one 1.0 in it. NLOGIT cannot tell which alternative they actually chose.

1098 Obs. <nnnnnn> alt. <nnn> is not an integer nor a proportion.

1099 Obs. <nnnnnn> responses should sum to 1.0. Sum is <xxxxxx>.

1100 Cannot classify obs. <nnnnnn> as IND, PROPs, or FREQs. (???)

Your data appear to be a mix of individual and frequency data. This occurs when an individual's lhs variable data include zeros. It then becomes difficult to figure out what kind of data you have. You can settle the question by including **;FREQUENCIES** in your command if that is appropriate.

1101 `# of parms in < list > greater than # choices in U(list).`

1102 `RANK data can only be used for 1 level (nonnested) models`

8 Handling choice data

It is a capital mistake to theorize before one has data. Insensibly one begins to twist facts to suit theories, instead of theories to suit facts. (Sir Arthur Conan Doyle, 1859–1930)

8.1 Introduction

In teaching courses on discrete choice modeling, we have increasingly observed that many participants struggle with *the look of choice data*. Courses and texts on econometrics often provide the reader with an already formatted data set (as does this book) yet fail to mention how (and why) the data were formatted in the manner they were. This leaves the user to work out the whys and the hows of data formatting by themselves (albeit with the help of lists such as the Limdep List: see http://limdep.its.usyd.edu.au). The alternative is for the non-expert to turn to user manuals; however, such manuals are often written by experts for experts. We have found that even specialists in experimental design or econometrics have problems in setting up their data for choice modeling.

We now focus on how to format choice data for estimation purposes. We concentrate on data formatting for the program NLOGIT from Econometric Software. While other programs capable of modeling choice data exist in the market, we choose to concentrate on NLOGIT because this is the program that the authors are most familiar with (indeed, Greene and Hensher are the developers of NLOGIT). NLOGIT also offers all of the discrete choice models that are used by practitioners and researchers. The release of NLOGIT 3.0 in August 2002 comes with a comprehensive set of (four) manuals. The discussion herein complements the 2002 manuals (Greene 2002). All the features of NLOGIT that are used herein are available in version 3.0 (dated September 2003).

NLOGIT is specific in terms of how data must be formatted. The second listed author will readily admit to spending many a frustrated hour cursing the many and varied errors that NLOGIT is capable of generating only to learn that the difficulty arose solely due to incorrect data formatting (always as a result of his own doing). Our objective in writing this chapter is to help the novice avoid these many frustrating hours.

8.2 The basic data setup

The data setup for choice analysis using NLOGIT is somewhat unique. While those familiar with panel data formats may acknowledge some similarity, those accustomed to more general statistical modeling techniques using other statistical packages are likely to be unfamiliar with the data requirements of NLOGIT. Unlike other statistical packages where each row of data represents an independent observation (usually that of a separate subject), in the main NLOGIT requires the assignment of several rows of data to represent a single subject (although NLOGIT is equipped to handle the more traditional data format, as we will later see). As such, when using NLOGIT data formats, each row of data are strictly not independent of each other and cannot be treated as such.

To illustrate the most general data format setup, let us use an example. Let us assume that choice data were collected on three individuals (a rather small sample but sufficient to illustrate the data formatting required). Let us assume that each individual was shown a total of two choice sets, each with four alternatives – say, *bus*, *train*, *plane*, and *car*. Keeping our example simple, we assume that each alternative has only two attributes, say *comfort* (clearly defined in some manner) and *travel time*. We divide the data format into a number of blocks, each block representing an individual choice set as given to each subject. Each row within a block corresponds to an alternative within that choice set. Taking the example as described above, each individual subject will be represented by two blocks (the two choice sets), and within each separate block there will exist four rows of data (the four alternatives). As such, each individual will be represented by eight rows of data (number of blocks multiplied by the number of alternatives within each block). The data as described will look as shown in table 8.1 (as a quick aside, the reader does not have to use the attribute names we have used below; in NLOGIT names are limited to eight characters and must begin with an alpha code, but are otherwise unrestricted).

Each decision maker in this example will be represented by eight rows of data. The *alti* variable is an accounting index that informs NLOGIT which alternative is assigned to a line of data. In the example above, we have assumed a fixed choice set size with each alternative appearing in each and every choice set. As you will see with the main case study detailed in chapter 9, some designs allow for alternatives to appear in one choice set but not in others. For example, let us add a fifth alternative to our example, Very Fast Train (*VFT*). If we retain the fixed choice set size of four alternatives then within each choice set, one alternative will have to fall out. In table 8.2 the first decision maker was presented with a choice set which consisted of a choice between travel using a *car*, a *bus*, a *plane*, or a *VFT*. The second choice set for this decision maker consisted of the alternatives, *car*, *bus*, *train*, and *plane*.

The choice set size does not have to be a fixed size. The variable *cset* is designed to inform NLOGIT of the number of alternatives within a particular choice set. In both tables 8.1 and 8.2 the choice set sizes were fixed at four alternatives. With RP data some alternatives may not be present at a particular physical distribution point at the time of purchase (choice). The SP equivalent is to use availability designs (see Louviere, Hensher, and Swait 2000, chapter 5). In either case, the number of alternatives present varies across choice sets. In

Table 8.1. *Most general choice data format in NLOGIT*

	id	*alti*	*cset*	*choice*	*comfort1*	*comfort2*	*ttime*
Car	01	1	4	1	1	0	14
Bus	01	2	4	0	1	0	12
Train	01	3	4	0	−1	−1	12
Plane	01	4	4	0	0	1	2
Car	01	1	4	0	0	1	10
Bus	01	2	4	1	0	1	14
Train	01	3	4	0	0	1	12
Plane	01	4	4	0	−1	−1	1.5
Car	02	1	4	0	0	1	12
Bus	02	2	4	0	1	0	14
Train	02	3	4	0	−1	−1	12
Plane	02	4	4	1	1	0	1.5
Car	02	1	4	0	−1	−1	12
Bus	02	2	4	0	0	1	12
Train	02	3	4	1	−1	−1	10
Plane	02	4	4	0	−1	−1	1.5
Car	03	1	4	0	−1	−1	12
Bus	03	2	4	1	1	0	14
Train	03	3	4	0	0	1	14
Plane	03	4	4	0	0	1	2
Car	03	1	4	1	1	0	14
Bus	03	2	4	0	0	1	10
Train	03	3	4	0	1	0	14
Plane	03	4	4	0	−1	−1	1.5

Table 8.2. *Varying alternatives within choice sets*

	id	*alti*	*cset*	*choice*	*comfort1*	*comfort2*	*ttime*
Car	01	1	4	1	1	0	14
Bus	01	2	4	0	1	0	12
Plane	01	4	4	0	0	1	2
VFT	01	5	4	0	1	0	8
Car	01	1	4	0	0	1	10
Bus	01	2	4	1	0	1	14
Train	01	3	4	0	0	1	12
Plane	01	4	4	0	−1	−1	1.5

table 8.3 the first choice set has only three of the five alternatives present while the second choice set has all five alternatives present.

The *choice* variable indicates which alternative within a choice set was chosen. A “1” indicates that an alternative was selected, while a 0 indicates that it was not. As such, the

Table 8.3. *Varying the number of alternatives within choice sets: (1)*

	id	*alti*	*cset*	*choice*	*comfort1*	*comfort2*	*ttime*
Car	01	1	3	1	1	0	14
Bus	01	2	3	0	1	0	12
VFT	01	5	3	0	1	0	8
Car	01	1	5	0	0	1	10
Bus	01	2	5	1	0	1	14
Train	01	3	5	0	0	1	12
Plane	01	4	5	0	−1	−1	1.5
VFT	01	5	5	0	−1	−1	6

sum of the choice variable should equal 1 within each choice set and within an individual sum to the number of choice sets given to that individual. Across individuals, this variable should sum to the total number of choice sets. Returning to table 8.1, decision maker one chooses alternative one, *car*, in the first choice set and alternative two, *bus*, in the second. Decision maker two chooses *plane* and *train*, respectively.

As an aside, for situations where every observation has the exact same alternatives (and listed in the same order) it is not necessary to define *alti* and *cset*. NLOGIT will count the number of alternatives based on the names assigned to the choice alternatives in the NLOGIT input command syntax (see chapter 10) and assume that each observation has these alternatives – and, most importantly, that the alternatives are in the same order in each decision maker's choice sets.

The last three variables in our mock data set require some explanation. Taking the case of *comfort*, we began with only one *comfort* attribute, but in our data set we have two *comfort* variables. Comfort, being a qualitative attribute, requires that words rather than numbers be attached as descriptors at the time of survey. For analytical purposes we are required to numerically code these word descriptors. One possible way of coding qualitative data are to attach a unique numeric value for each level of the attribute within one variable. Thus, assuming three levels of comfort (low, medium, and high), we could create a single variable (call it comfort) such that low = 0, medium = 1, and high = 2 (note that any unique values could have been used). Taking this coding structure, for decision maker one, table 8.1 becomes table 8.4.

The reason we do not code qualitative (or any classification) data in the manner suggested by table 8.4 is simple. The use of such a coding structure unnecessarily ascribes a *linear relationship* to the effects of the levels of the attribute. That is, at the time of modeling, we will derive a single parameter associated with the attribute *comfort*. Note that each alternative will have its own β-parameter if we allow for an alternative-specific model specification (we will discuss this in chapter 10). This is the problem that led us to effects and dummy coding in chapter 5.

As an aside, we have included in appendix 8A the effects coding for the design generated in chapter 5.

We did not effects code the *travel time* attribute. This is not to suggest that we could not have effects or dummy coded the variable (by partitioning it into a series of ranges).

Table 8.4. *Varying the number of alternatives within choice sets: (2)*

	id	*Alti*	*cset*	*choice*	*comfort*	*ttime*
Car	01	1	4	1	0	14
Bus	01	2	4	0	0	12
Train	01	3	4	0	2	12
Plane	01	4	4	0	1	2
Car	01	1	4	0	1	10
Bus	01	2	4	0	1	14
Train	01	3	4	0	1	12
Plane	01	4	4	1	2	1.5

Indeed, to test for non-linear effects over the range of the attribute, it is necessary to do so. Nevertheless doing so at this stage will not add to our general discussion, and hence we will assume linearity over the ranges of the *travel time* attributes.

Thus far we have said little about *socio-demographic characteristics* (SDCs). The SDCs of a decision maker are invariant across decisions provided that there is not a significant time lapse involved in the decision making process. As such, when we enter socio-demographic data, the levels the data take are constant for an individual (but vary across individuals). For our example, let us assume that we have collected data on the age of each decision maker. We show how this age variable is entered into NLOGIT in table 8.5. Other socio-demographic characteristics would be entered in a similar fashion.

8.2.1 Entering multiple data sets: stacking and melding

The analyst may have occasion to combine multiple choice data sets, the most common amalgamation being a combination of SP and RP data. When combining different data sources, whether the data are SP and RP or some other combination, the data sources will be stacked, one upon the other. If, however, the two data sources are collected from the same decision makers, we may meld the two data sets such that the data for each decision maker are kept intact independent of which data source it originated from.

8.2.2 Handling data on the non-chosen alternative in RP data

RP data pose significant challenges for the analyst in terms of how they should be handled. As noted in previous chapters, the analyst often is able to capture information only on the chosen alternative. Further, we often collect RP data only for a single decision context. As such, if we enter RP data as suggested above, for each individual we would have only one line of data. The *choice* variable would therefore take on the constant value of one given that the single line of data represents the chosen alternative for each individual. Given that there is no information on the non-chosen alternatives, it would appear that at no stage was

Table 8.5. *Entering socio-demographic characteristics*

	id	*alti*	*cset*	*choice*	*comfort1*	*comfort2*	*ttime*	*age*
Car	01	1	4	1	1	0	14	40
Bus	01	2	4	0	1	0	12	40
Train	01	3	4	0	−1	−1	12	40
Plane	01	4	4	0	0	1	2	40
Car	01	1	4	0	0	1	10	40
Bus	01	2	4	1	0	1	14	40
Train	01	3	4	0	0	1	12	40
Plane	01	4	4	0	−1	−1	1.5	40
Car	02	1	4	0	0	1	12	32
Bus	02	2	4	0	1	0	14	32
Train	02	3	4	0	−1	−1	12	32
Plane	02	4	4	1	1	0	1.5	32
Car	02	1	4	0	−1	−1	12	32
Bus	02	2	4	0	0	1	12	32
Train	02	3	4	1	−1	−1	10	32
Plane	02	4	4	0	−1	−1	1.5	32
Car	03	1	4	0	−1	−1	12	35
Bus	03	2	4	1	1	0	14	35
Train	03	3	4	0	0	1	14	35
Plane	03	4	4	0	0	1	2	35
Car	03	1	4	1	1	0	14	35
Bus	03	2	4	0	0	1	10	35
Train	03	3	4	0	1	0	14	35
Plane	03	4	4	0	−1	−1	1.5	35

a choice made (recalling that we need at least two alternatives for a choice). This represents a modeling problem.

What is required is information on (at least one) non-chosen alternative(s). The best solution is to gather the information from those making the decision; however, as we have already discussed in chapters 3 and 5, this is not always possible. In practice, four solutions have been employed. We will assume that, in the aggregate, information on the attribute levels for all alternatives within the choice set are available, although at an individual observation level they are available only for the chosen alternative.

The first approach involves taking the averages of the attribute levels (or medians for qualitative attributes) for each alternative for those who chose each of them. For any given individual, the chosen alternatives' attribute levels as observed are retained. The calculated averages (or median) attribute levels are then substituted as the attribute levels for the non-chosen alternatives. This first method involves taking the average for the attribute levels of each observed alternative and substituting these averages (or medians) as the values for the attribute levels of the non-chosen alternatives for those who did not choose them. Thus for each individual, while we retain the information on the individual's chosen alternative, we generate data on the non-chosen alternatives by using the averages of the non-chosen alternative's attribute levels as chosen by the other decision makers. It is worth noting that there is a risk that these averages promote a better set of attribute levels than what would be the levels if we knew the actual levels available to the person who has the alternative as the non-chosen. Indeed, we note that such a strategy certainly reduces the variance of the attribute-level distribution in the sampled population.

The second method employs a similar approach. We sample across a distribution of decision makers such that we have a proportion of decision makers observed to have chosen each of the alternatives. Rather than taking the average of the observed attribute levels for each alternative and substituting these as the attribute levels for the non-chosen alternatives, as in method one, we take the observed levels unamended and distribute these as the attribute levels for those who did not choose those alternatives. This distribution can be done randomly, or alternatively we may attempt to match the non-chosen alternatives attribute levels to specific decision makers through a matching of SDCs. For transport studies, a matching of trip origin and destination is also very useful. The benefit of this approach is the preservation of *variability* in the attribute-level distribution.

As an aside, both methods are far from desirable. We would prefer to capture information on the attribute levels of non-chosen alternatives as they actually exist for the decision maker. While the above represent strategies to estimate what these levels might actually be, it is likely that the actual attribute levels for the non-chosen alternatives are somewhat different. A better strategy may be to gain information from the decision maker based on his perception of the attribute levels for the non-chosen alternative. As discussed in chapter 3, this approach is likely to produce data which will require much data cleansing; however as also noted in chapter 3 it is more likely that decision makers base their choices on their perceptions of what attribute levels an alternative takes rather than the actual levels (or some view from others) that alternative takes. It may thus be argued that the capturing of perceptual data will produce more realistic behavioral models. This is the third "solution" to the problem of capturing information on the non-chosen alternative.

The fourth solution, similar to the first two, is to synthesize the data. This requires expert knowledge as to how the data are to be synthesized. The norm is to use known information such as travel distances or other socio-demographic characteristics and to condition the synthesized data on these. But like the first two approaches, synthesising the data leaves one open to the criticism that the created data may not represent the alternatives actually faced by decision makers and as such the estimation process will be tainted. If such synthesized data can be developed from perceptual maps associated with non-chosen alternatives, this may be an appealing solution.

8.2.3 Combining sources of data

Returning to our example, we no longer have enough decision makers to obtain information on the non-chosen alternatives. We will therefore increase our sample size to 200 (i.e. four alternatives each with 50 respondents), and assume that among those 200 decision makers each alternative was observed to have been chosen at least once. We may now use the observed attribute levels for those who choose car as the attribute levels

Table 8.6. *Combining SP and RP data*

	id	*alti*	*cset*	*choice*	*sprp*	*comfort1*	*comfort2*	*ttime*	*age*
Car	01	1	4	1	1	0	1	10.5	40
Bus	01	2	4	0	1	−1	−1	11.5	40
Train	01	3	4	0	1	−1	−1	12	40
Plane	01	4	4	0	1	1	0	1.3	40
Car	01	5	4	1	0	1	0	14	40
Bus	01	6	4	0	0	1	0	12	40
Train	01	7	4	0	0	−1	−1	12	40
Plane	01	8	4	0	0	0	1	2	40
Car	01	5	4	0	0	0	1	10	40
Bus	01	6	4	1	0	0	1	14	40
Train	01	7	4	0	0	0	1	12	40
Plane	01	8	4	0	0	−1	−1	1.5	40
Car	02	1	4	0	1	0	1	10	32
Bus	02	2	4	0	1	−1	−1	11.5	32
Train	02	3	4	0	1	−1	−1	12	32
Plane	02	4	4	1	1	1	0	1.25	32
Car	02	5	4	0	0	0	1	12	32
Bus	02	6	4	0	0	1	0	14	32
Train	02	7	4	0	0	−1	−1	12	32
Plane	02	8	4	1	0	1	0	1.5	32
Car	02	5	4	0	0	−1	−1	12	32
Bus	02	6	4	0	0	0	1	12	32
Train	02	7	4	1	0	−1	−1	10	32
Plane	02	8	4	0	0	−1	−1	1.5	32

for the car alternative associated with individuals who choose the bus, train, and plane alternatives.

In combining data sources into a single data set, such as SP and RP data, we need to create a dummy variable that specifies which data set the data originated from. In table 8.6, we call this variable SPRP. This variable takes the value 1 if the observation is RP or 0 if SP. The SPRP variable will allow the analyst to estimate SP and RP models separately but will not be used in models combing both data sources. For combined models, this is done through the *alti* variable. The *alti* variable is adjusted to reflect the fact that some alternatives belong to one data source (e.g. RP) while others belong to a second data source (e.g. SP). In table 8.6, we use values of 1 through 4 for the *alti* variable to denote the alternatives belong to the RP sub-data set and 5 through 8 to represent alternatives from the SP sub-data set. Thus, the car alternative is represented as 1 in the *alti* variable when dealing with the RP data and 5 when dealing with the SP data set (we discuss the combining of data sources further in chapter 14).

Table 8.6 presents the data set for the first two of our 200 decision makers. We observe that individual one in reality selected to travel by car, a trip which took $10\frac{1}{2}$ hours and which they described as being of medium comfort. As this person did not take a bus, train, or plane, we have inserted the average (medium for qualitative attributes) attribute levels from those who did select those modes. Thus the average travel time from those decision makers observed to have chosen the bus mode was $11^1/_2$ hours. Similarly, the average travel time for those selecting the train was 12 hours and 1 hour and 20 minutes for those choosing the plane. Individual two was observed to have chosen to travel by plane.

The observant reader will note that if we combine the data sources as suggested above, we have only one RP data choice set but multiple SP data choice sets per individual traveler. Some researchers have suggested that, when combined, RP data should be weighted so as to have equal representation as the SP data set. Weighting each observation is really something that should be decided by the analyst according to what behavioural strengths each data source has. We call this "Bayesian determination." If we believe that the RP data are equally as useful as the SP data then we may wish to equally weight it. With, say, one RP observation and eight SP observations, one would either weight the RP data by 8.0 or the SP data by 0.125. We are of the opinion that such weighting should not take place. We reason that RP data are by its very nature ill-conditioned (i.e. it may be invariant and is likely to suffer from multicollinearity, see chapter 4) while SP data arguably provides better-quality inputs to estimation, especially on the attributes of alternatives. As such, while we use the RP data to provide information on market shares and to capture information on real choices, we believe that we are best to obtain our parameters or taste weights associated with each attribute from SP data sources (except for the alternative-specific constant in labeled choice sets) and (as shown in chapter 14) export the SP attribute parameters to the RP environment where the model is calibrated to reproduce the actual market shares of observed alternatives.

As an aside, calibration cannot and should not be undertaken on new alternatives, for obvious reasons. What does the analyst calibrate against? In addition, CBS is valid only for RP alternatives.

We thus remain unconcerned that SP data may *swamp* RP data at the time of estimation. We do remind the analyst, however, that if the interest is in prediction and deriving elasticities, that the RP model should be used but with the transferred attribute parameters from the SP model. We discuss this in chapter 14. SP models as stand-alone models are useful only for measuring the WTP for attributes (i.e. in valuation) and not for prediction and behavioural response (i.e. in deriving elasticities) unless the SP model is calibrated through alternative-specific constants in order to reproduce the base RP shares for the sub-set of alternatives observed in real markets.

8.2.4 Weighting on an exogenous variable

The choice variable in an RP data set represents an endogenous variable within our system of equations. When we wish to correct for over-sampling and under-sampling on the choice response we refer to choice-based weights (which were discussed in chapter 4). However it is often the situation that the sample is drawn using some non-choice (or exogenous) criteria such as income and gender, drawing observations in a way that over-samples in cells (e.g. income by gender) with a small population incidence and under-sampling in cells with a high population incidence. To correct for such sampling, we can re-weight the

Table 8.7. *Exogenous weights entered*

	id	*alti*	*cset*	*choice*	*weight*	*sprp*	*comfort1*	*comfort2*	*ttime*	*age*
Car	01	1	4	1	0.6	1	0	1	10.5	40
Bus	01	2	4	0	0.6	1	−1	−1	11.5	40
Train	01	3	4	0	0.6	1	−1	−1	12	40
Plane	01	4	4	0	0.6	1	1	0	1.3	40
Car	01	5	4	1	0.6	0	1	0	14	40
Bus	01	6	4	0	0.6	0	1	0	12	40
Train	01	7	4	0	0.6	0	−1	−1	12	40
Plane	01	8	4	0	0.6	0	0	1	2	40
Car	01	5	4	0	0.6	0	0	1	10	40
Bus	01	6	4	1	0.6	0	0	1	14	40
Train	01	7	4	0	0.6	0	0	1	12	40
Plane	01	8	4	0	0.6	0	−1	−1	1.5	40
Car	02	1	4	0	0.3	1	0	1	10	32
Bus	02	2	4	0	0.3	1	−1	−1	11.5	32
Train	02	3	4	0	0.3	1	−1	−1	12	32
Plane	02	4	4	1	0.3	1	1	0	1.25	32
Car	02	5	4	0	0.3	0	0	1	12	32
Bus	02	6	4	0	0.3	0	1	0	14	32
Train	02	7	4	0	0.3	0	−1	−1	12	32
Plane	02	8	4	1	0.3	0	1	0	1.5	32
Car	02	5	4	0	0.3	0	−1	−1	12	32
Bus	02	6	4	0	0.3	0	0	1	12	32
Train	02	7	4	1	0.3	0	−1	−1	10	32
Plane	02	8	4	0	0.3	0	−1	−1	1.5	32

data using exogenous weights based on the criteria used to design the sample. The analyst may establish an exogenous weighting variable within the data set to be used to weight the data during estimation. For example, we may wish to weight the data differently for the different sexes. For our example, we do not have a gender variable, so let us assume that the analyst wishes to weight the data on the age variable. For example, assume that the analyst wishes to weight the data such that data for those 40 years and older are weighted by 0.6 and those under the age of 40, by 0.3. The weight variable is shown in table 8.7 (we discuss in chapter 11 how to exogenously weight data for a choice model).

8.2.5 Handling rejection: the "no option"

As discussed in chapter 6, a significant number of choice contexts allow the chooser *not to choose* (although not choosing is technically a choice) or to delay their choice. In our example we have ignored the *no choice* alternative and constrained the decision maker into making a choice from the listed alternatives. We call this a *conditional* choice. However, what if the decision maker may elect not to travel? Figure 8.1 presents an example of a choice set for our travel example with the *elect not to travel* alternative.

Mode Description	Car	Bus	Train	Plane	I would not travel
Comfort Level	Medium	High	Low	Low	
Travel Time	12 hours	12 hours	10 hours	1.5 hours	
Given these options I would choose	☐	☐	☐	☐	☐

Figure 8.1 Choice set with the "no-travel" alternative

As an aside, it is useful to think of any choice analysis in which the *no choice* alternative is excluded as a conditional choice. Given the definition of demand in chapter 3, another way of expressing this is that any choice analysis that ignores no choice is effectively a conditional demand model. That is, conditional on choosing an alternative, we can identify a probability of choosing it. The only circumstance in which the conditional demand is equivalent to unconditional demand is where the probability of making no choice is zero.

If one elects not to travel then we have no observable attribute levels for this alternative. We see this in the choice set shown in figure 8.1. Given that the attribute levels are not observed we treat them as *missing values*. As each row of data represents an alternative we are required to insert a row of data for the not-travel alternative in which the attribute levels are coded as missing. The (default) missing value code for NLOGIT is −999.

As an aside, when collecting data for use in NLOGIT, we recommend that any missing data be either imputted in the data set or assigned a −999 code (the default in NLOGIT for missing data). This is especially important with data formats such as a comma delimited text file or a free format file, since data items are well defined and cannot be left blank. While it is worthwhile converting spreadsheets to a text format to compress the size of a data file (spreadsheets, especially Excel, have lots of redundant code embedded in them that is not required by NLOGIT but makes the file very large), importing data from the resulting file format will move the data one variable to the left for each blank. Therefore, while NLOGIT will read blanks as −999 when importing data directly from Excel, the analyst must be careful as the same is not true of non-spreadsheet formats.

In adding the "no-choice" or "delay-choice" alternative we add to the number of existing alternatives within our data set. As such we need to adjust our *alti* and *cset* variables. In the example, we now have five alternatives (ignoring *VFT* as a possible alternative) and hence the *cset* variable will take on the value 5. The *alti* variable will now take on the values 1–5, 5 equating to the choice not to travel alternative. We show this in table 8.8. In table 8.8, the attribute levels for the *choose not to travel* alternative are set to the missing value code of −999: SDCs remain unchanged over the new alternative, hence we are not required to treat such data as missing. Again, the reader can see this in table 8.8. In table 8.8, individual one elected not to travel in the second choice set.

As an aside, in NLOGIT the *alti* indexing must begin at 1 and include all values up to the maximum number of alternatives. This does permit each individual to have a different number of alternatives in their choice set. For example, individual one may have alternatives 1, 2, 4, 5 and individual two may have alternatives 1, 2, 3, 4, 5. The only situation in which we do not need to have an *alti* variable (and a *cset* variable) is where all individuals have

Table 8.8. *Adding the "no-choice" or "delay-choice" alternative*

	id	*alti*	*cset*	*choice*	*comfort1*	*comfort2*	*ttime*	*age*
Car	01	1	5	1	1	0	14	40
Bus	01	2	5	0	1	0	12	40
Train	01	3	5	0	−1	−1	12	40
Plane	01	4	5	0	0	1	2	40
None	01	5	5	0	−999	−999	−999	40
Car	01	1	5	0	0	1	10	40
Bus	01	2	5	0	0	1	14	40
Train	01	3	5	0	0	1	12	40
Plane	01	4	5	0	−1	−1	1.5	40
None	01	5	5	1	−999	−999	−999	40
Car	02	1	5	0	0	1	12	32
Bus	02	2	5	0	1	0	14	32
Train	02	3	5	0	−1	−1	12	32
Plane	02	4	5	1	1	0	1.5	32
None	02	5	5	0	−999	−999	−999	32
Car	02	1	5	0	−1	−1	12	32
Bus	02	2	5	0	0	1	12	32
Train	02	3	5	1	−1	−1	10	32
Plane	02	4	5	0	−1	−1	1.5	32
None	02	5	5	0	−999	−999	−999	32
Car	03	1	5	0	−1	−1	12	35
Bus	03	2	5	1	1	0	14	35
Train	03	3	5	0	0	1	14	35
Plane	03	4	5	0	0	1	2	35
None	03	5	5	0	−999	−999	−999	35
Car	03	1	5	1	1	0	14	35
Bus	03	2	5	0	0	1	10	35
Train	03	3	5	0	1	0	14	35
Plane	03	4	5	0	−1	−1	1.5	35
None	03	5	5	0	−999	−999	−999	35

choice sets with identical alternatives which are presented in the data in the same order for each individual. We call the latter a *fixed-choice set* and the case of varying *alti* and *cset* a *variable-choice set*. Analysts who use RP and SP data in a combined data set must take this into account when using the sub-data set (e.g. SP) as the *alti* values for the second data set will begin at the value immediately following the last value of the first data set (e.g. in table 8.6, it will need to be transformed back to 1, 2, etc.). This is very easy. One simply creates a new *alti* index (say *altz*) equal to *alti-z* where *z* is the highest RP *alti* value. The variable *altz* then replaces *alti* in the SP stand-alone analysis after you have rejected the RP data lines.

As a further aside, it is interesting to consider the *no choice* or *delay choice* alternatives in terms of RP data studies. Although we have placed the *no choice* alternative in the context of an SP experiment in table 8.8, the analyst should be prepared to collect RP data on individuals who have elected not to choose or to delay choice. In doing so, one not only captures information on market shares (the aggregates of those who choose among the alternatives) but also on potential demand (those who choose plus those who operate within the market but have elected not to purchase in the current period). Gathering data on non-choosers also allows the analyst to test hypotheses as to differences between decision makers who elected to choose and those that did not.

8.3 Entering data into NLOGIT

There are two possible methods of entering data into NLOGIT. First, the analyst may choose to enter the data directly into the program. Alternatively, the analyst may elect to import the data from another source. We explore both these options now.

8.3.1 Entering data directly into NLOGIT

To enter data directly into NLOGIT, the analyst must first create the new variables before proceeding to enter the data values into the cells for each variable. To do so, it is necessary for the analyst to select the following commands. In the *Project* command in the program's toolbars, select *New*. After New has been selected, select the *Variable*... command. We show this in figure 8.2.

This procedure opens the *New Variable* dialog box which is used to name each new variable. Figure 8.3 shows the naming of a new variable titled ID. After naming each variable, the analyst is required to select the *OK* button in order to proceed.

Once all the variables have been named, the analyst next enters the data into the Data Editor in a manner similar to most other statistics and spreadsheet programs. To gain access to the Data Editor, the analyst double clicks on the variable name in the *Project* dialog box shown in figure 8.4. This will open up the Data Editor in which the data may be entered.

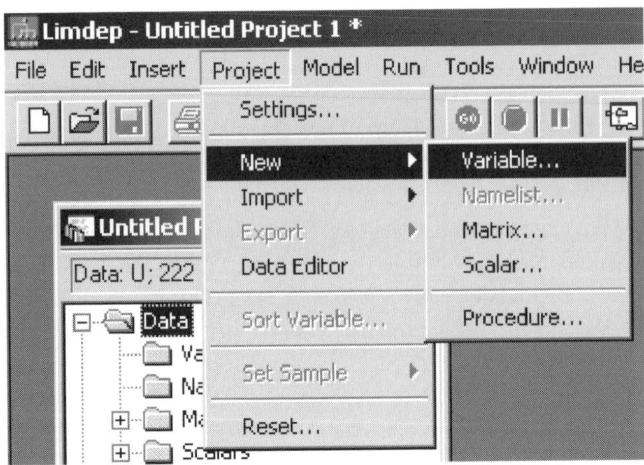

Figure 8.2 Creating new variables using the toolbar commands

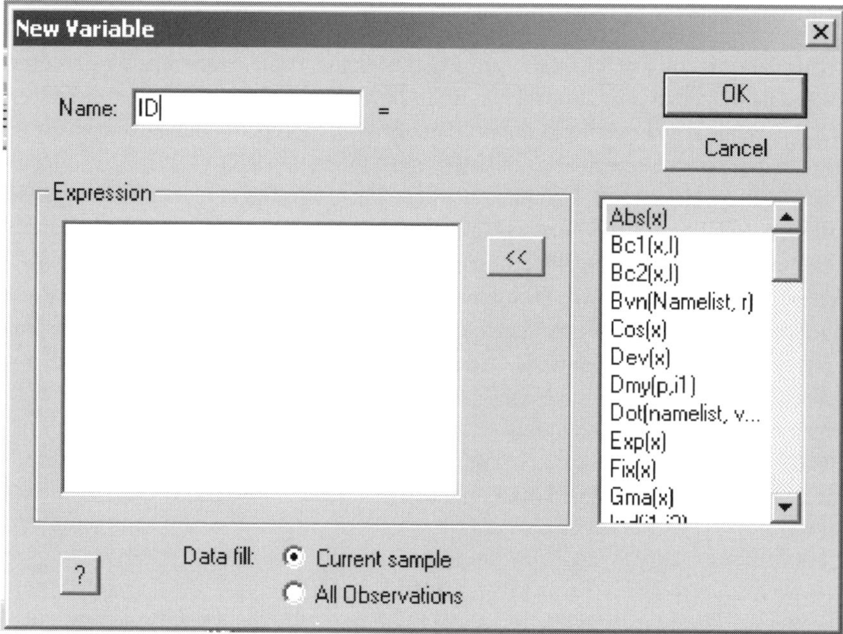

Figure 8.3 Naming new variables using the *New Variable* dialog box

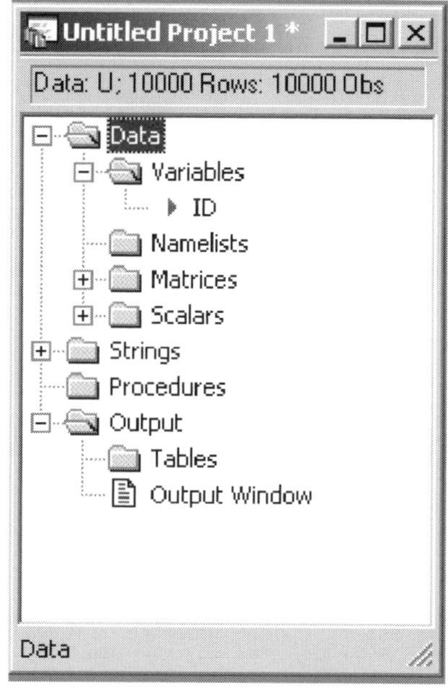

Figure 8.4 *Project* dialog box

8.3.2 Importing data into NLOGIT

Entering data directly into NLOGIT can be cumbersome. For this reason, the authors prefer to enter data into other programs such as SPSS or Microsoft Excel and import the data into NLOGIT. While it is possible to import data using the toolbar command menus, we opt instead to discuss an alternative method. For most functions in NLOGIT, two mechanisms are available to the analyst to initiate actions. These are the command menus and the Text/Document Editor. The commands as described in this and the following chapters are commands that are to be entered into the Text/Document Editor. While perhaps less awkward for the beginner, we have elected not to discuss the command menus in any further detail unless certain commands contained in the command menus are absolutely necessary to access some other NLOGIT function. We made this decision not so much for space limitation reasons but because the authors tend not use the command menus and feel that those considering becoming serious choice modellers are best to learn how to use NLOGIT using the *Text/Document Editor* from an early stage. We therefore leave it to the interested individual to explore NLOGIT's command menus on their own.

8.3.2.1 The Text/Document editor

To access the *Text/Document Editor* select the *File* toolbar button followed by the *New* command. This opens the *New Dialog* box. . . . In the *New Dialog* box, select *Text/Command Document*. Alternatively, select the *New* pushbutton from the toolbar menu (shown in figure 8.5).

The *Text/Document Editor* functions much like Microsoft's *Notepad*, in which the commands are typed as they appear here in the primer. To initiate the action dictated by a particular command, the analyst selects the relevant command syntax before pushing the *Go* button located in the command menu (see figure 8.6).

One benefit of using the *Text/Document Editor* over the toolbar command menus is that the analyst may save the *Text/Document Editor* for use at later sessions (we discuss this in chapter 9). In using the command menus, the analyst is required to input the commands into the relevant dialog boxes each time some analysis is required.

8.3.3 Reading data into NLOGIT

The following section does not apply to those using NLOGIT/ACA (see chapter 7). Imported data may be either **READ, WRITTEN** or **LOADED** into NLOGIT. The **READ**

Figure 8.5 The New Text/Document Editor pushbutton

Figure 8.6 The Go pushbutton

command in NLOGIT is used to import data saved in an ASCII format, although with a few minor alterations to the command syntax the **READ** command can be used to import data saved in either binary or spreadsheet formats. For files saved in the ASCII format, the **READ** command will be written in the *Text/Document Editor* in the following arrangement:

> **READ; file= <File location and name><.File format type>; Nobs = N; Nvar = K; Names = <variable name 1, variable name 2, . . . , variable name K> $**

We use the notation < > to indicate that a set of NLOGIT statements are required to replace the descriptor. For example, the above command may appear as:

> **READ; file=c:\choice_models_are_fun\choicedata. DAT; Nobs = 30; Nvar = 8; Names = id, alti, cset, choice, comfort1, comfort2, ttime, age $**

As can be seen above, in using the **READ** command to import ASCII formatted files the analyst must specify the file location and name. In this instance, the file location is in a folder named "**choice_models_are_fun**" located on the analyst's C drive of their computer. The file name is called "*choicedata*". Note that while later versions of Microsoft Windows allow file and folder names to be named with spaces, NLOGIT works best if the file and folder names have no spaces. Hence above we use the underscore character (_) in the folder name as opposed to spaces. The file format used in this example is .DAT, but NLOGIT will accept many formats.

The **Nobs** specification requires the analyst to specify the number of observations or rows of data in the data set to be imported. If this value is unknown, the analyst may specify a number greater than the number of rows in the imported file. Provided that the number given is actually greater than the total number of rows in the file, NLOGIT will continue reading the data until the last value in the data set is located and then stop. For the example, command syntax shown above, the total number of rows of data to be imported is 30.

The **Nvar** specification specifies the number of variables in the data set to be imported. It is important that the analyst provides the correct information here, otherwise **NLOGIT** will assign data to the wrong rows. The number provided must match the number of names given in the **Names** = < > command, otherwise NLOGIT will produce an error. For the example above, the imported file has eight variables. The names of these eight variables are *id*, *alti*, *cset*, *choice*, *comfort1*, *comfort2*, *ttime*, and *age*.

As an aside, NLOGIT uses the value −999 as the default missing value. For ASCII formatted files, blank values which may indicate missing values in the ASCII format are not treated as such by NLOGIT. This may potentially result in problems with imported data sets where NLOGIT will insert the number of variables specified by the **Nvar** command into a row before moving on to the next row. Further, alphanumeric or non-numeric data will be treated as missing values by NLOGIT which is unable to handle such data.

The **Names** specification shown above suggests that the analyst must specify each variable name in the order they appear in the data set. This need not be the case if the variable names are provided within the data set itself. The base command for non-spreadsheet data sets shown above assumes that the first row(s) of data does not contain the variable names. Assuming the data set has variable names included, NLOGIT will read the names provided one includes **;names=1** for one line of names or **;names=2** for two lines of names, etc. If this is not the case and the names specification is not given, NLOGIT will assign generic names to the variables such as X1. In such cases we may change the variable names using the *Project* dialog box.

Syntax commands in NLOGIT are concluded with a dollar sign ($). The dollar sign instructs NLOGIT that a command has been concluded and unless a known command heading such as **READ** follows on a separate line after the dollar sign, everything following will be ignored by NLOGIT.

It is not uncommon for the analyst to be working with data which is formatted in the data file in accordance with some uniform structure. This will particularly be the case if the data set is large. In such cases, the analyst may append the **Format** specification to the read command. Note that in doing so, the format specification must be situated before the dollar sign of the **READ** command syntax. The format specification appears as follows:

;Format =(<Fortran format>)

For example, the format might appear as:

;Format = (8(F5.3,1X)) $

In the above format specification the first number, 8, represents the total number of variables (columns) that will be created in the new data set. The remaining **(F5.3,1X)** format component requires some explanation. The number immediately following the **F**, i.e. 5.3, informs NLOGIT that the maximum number of digits any value will take will be five, with up to three decimal places. For example, the number 51854 will be read as 51.854. The **,1X** component of the format specification instructs NLOGIT to leave a single space between each of the read values, making it easy to read the data via a spreadsheet or a free format specification at a later stage. The example, we have provided is rather simple. For reasons of brevity we refer the reader to NLOGIT's extensive reference manuals for a more detailed understanding of this aspect of data entry.

For data first entered into a spreadsheet program (e.g. Lotus 123 (.WKS, WK1) or Microsoft Excel (.XLS) as opposed to being formatted as an ASCII type file, e.g. as a .TXT or .DAT file), the analyst may dispense with the **Nobs** and **Nvar** specifications in the **READ** command. Instead, the **READ** command is re-written such that the Format specification replaces both the **Nobs** and **Nvar** specifications. However, when importing data from a spreadsheet, the **Format** specification is used differently than described above (note that for ASCII formatted data sets, when using the **Format** specification, NLOGIT requires the **Nobs** and **Nvar** specifications). In such cases, the Format specification is written in the following arrangement:

;Format = <File type>

For example, if the data were first entered into Microsoft Excel, the Format specification would be:

;Format = XLS

As an aside, NLOGIT is unable to read data saved in the .XLS file format if the data are saved as a workbook (i.e. has more than one worksheet). As such, when using the .XLS file format, the analyst is best to save the file as a worksheet. Also note that NLOGIT will not be able to read Excel formulas (this is one of the most common problems in reading in data).

Using the format specification above, the entire **READ** command therefore might appear as:

> **READ; file=c:\choice_models_are_fun\choicedata ;Nobs = 30; Nvar = 8; Names = id, alti, cset, choice, comfort1, comfort2, ttime, age ;Format = XLS $**

8.3.4 Writing data into NLOGIT

The **WRITE** command allows the NLOGIT user to create a new data set from an existing data set. As we show later, this capability is particularly useful when converting single-line data to the multiple, panel-style data format we use for choice modeling as described earlier. The **WRITE** command syntax in NLOGIT takes the following form:

> **WRITE ; <variable name 1, variable name 2, . . . , variable name k > ;File = <wherever the analyst specifies > $**

The default format for the **WRITE** command is (**6G15.7**). The 15.7 format code provides a 15-column field with 7 significant digits in the number. Should the analyst desire another format, a different **Format** specification may be appended to the **WRITE** command. We demonstrate the **WRITE** command and the use of a different **Format** specification with an example when we discuss the conversion of single-line data formats to multiple-line data formats later this chapter.

8.3.5 Saving data sets

The following section does not apply to those using NLOGIT/ACA (see chapter 7). Once data have been read into NLOGIT, the user may save the data set using the following command syntax:

> **SAVE; file= <File location and name>.SAV $**

The analyst must specify the file location and file name in the appropriate area indicated in the command syntax above. Using the .SAV file format allows the user to load the data as a binary format into NLOGIT's Data Editor in future sessions rather than having to draw upon the **READ** command function. As we discuss in sub-section 8.3.5, loading data provides substantial time savings over reading data into NLOGIT, particularly if the data set being imported is of substantial size.

As an aside, the .SAV file format is not the same as the .SAV file format used by SPSS. If the data set being imported is a .SAV file of SPSS origin, the analyst must save the data using SPSS under another file format (e.g. .WK1). Similarly, .SAV files saved using

NLOGIT are not compatible with SPSS and cannot be opened using that program (or any other program except Stat Transfer or DBMS Copy).

Alternatively, data may be saved via the command menus. To save data using the command menus, use the *Save Project As* command under the *File* menu. Using the *Save Project As* command will save the data in a *lpj* format (short for Limdep project file). The *lpj* file is a file format unique to NLOGIT and hence does not have the problem associated with the .SAV file format.

8.3.6 Loading data into NLOGIT

NLOGIT/ACA is restricted to reading the *AppliedChoice.lpj* file only. As such, the discussion below relates to the full version of NLOGIT only.

The **LOAD** command in NLOGIT is designed to open data sets which have already been written or read into NLOGIT and saved during previous work sessions. This command provides substantial time savings in opening data sets in NLOGIT, as the command assumes that the data are in a format that has embedded information including variable names as well as information regarding the spacing of data within cells. Unlike the **READ** command, the **LOAD** command does not involve NLOGIT having to determine what data belongs to what cell. The location of data are already assumed to be known. Further, the analyst does not have to spend time typing the names of the all variables as with the **READ** command in the *Text/Document Editor*.

Assuming that the analyst has saved the data set in a previous NLOGIT session using the .SAV file format, the **LOAD** command will take the following appearance.

LOAD; file= <File location and name> <.SAV > $

Once more, the analyst is required to provide a specific file location and name. The **LOAD** command does not require that the number of observations or number of variables be given. Nor, as suggested earlier, are the variable names required. All this information is embedded into the data set already. As with all other NLOGIT commands, the command is concluded with a dollar sign.

As with the **SAVE** command, the analyst may load data via the NLOGIT command menus. .LPJ and .SAV files may be opened via the *Open Project* command under the file menu.

8.3.6.1 Changing the maximum default size of the Data Editor

Independent of how data are entered into the NLOGIT, the analyst needs to be wary of the size of the data set. NLOGIT has set as a default the ability to accept data sets with up to 200 columns and up to 1000 rows (i.e. a total of 900,000 cells). The program will adjust automatically.

To make permanent changes to the default setting, select the *Tools* command in the toolbar followed by *Options* (see figure 8.7). This will open up the *Options* dialog box. In

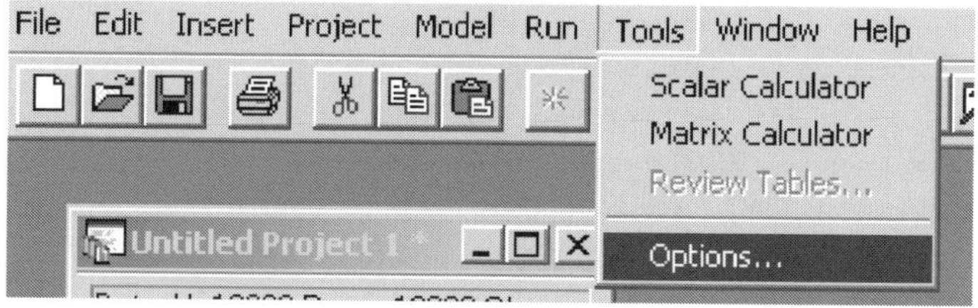

Figure 8.7 Changing the default workspace available in NLOGIT

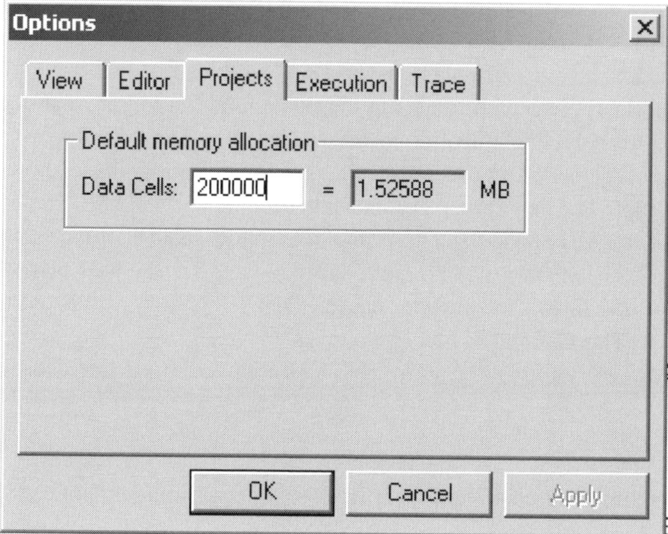

Figure 8.8 The *Options* dialog box

the *Options* dialog box select the *Projects* tab and change the default setting to the number of cells required for the new project (see figure 8.8). By changing the default workspace in the manner described, the newly specified workspace will become the new default setting for any future projects.

8.4 Data entered into a single line

This section is not applicable to those using NLOGIT/ACA. The data format described previously is the most commonly used format for choice analysis using NLOGIT. An alternative formatting approach is to enter each choice set into a single line of data as opposed to allocating each alternative within a choice set to a separate row of data. Using the single row per choice set data format, the total number of rows related to any given individual is the total number of choice sets associated with that individual.

Table 8.9 shows how data are entered such that each choice set is represented by a single row of data (for space reasons, table 8.9 shows only the first three alternatives). In this data context, the choice variable no longer consists of a vector of 0s and 1s but rather assumes a unique number corresponding to the alternative chosen. In our example, the first alternative is *car*. Hence if this was the alternative chosen the choice variable is coded 1. Similarly the choice variable is coded 2 for *bus*, 3 for *train*, or 4 for *plane*. We have created an index variable, *ind* which specifies to which individual the choice set belongs. (This is the format that is used by some other programs.)

Although NLOGIT can estimate models using data in the above format, we prefer the data format as set out earlier in the chapter. In the interests of brevity we do not discuss the modeling procedures associated with single-line data analysis. Rather we refer those interested in modeling with such data to the NLOGIT user manual.

Assuming the analyst enters the data into the single-line data format as shown in table 8.9, it is possible to use NLOGIT to reformat the data into the preferred multiple-line format described earlier. The commands to convert the single-line data example shown in table 8.9 into the multiple-line data format are shown in detail in appendix 8B. To demonstrate the commands here, we provide a smaller, simpler example. Table 8.10 shows the RP data for the first two decision makers as first introduced in table 8.6. We have placed this data into a single-line data format and included data on the first three alternatives only, although the commands we show are for all four alternatives.

The commands to convert the data in table 8.10 into a multiple-line data format are shown below:

```
CREATE
;car=(choice=1);bus=(choice=2);train=(choice=3);plane=(choice=4)
;cset=4
;alt1=1;alt2=2;alt3=3;alt4=4 $

WRITE
;id, alt1, cset, car, comfort1, comfort2, ttime1, age,
id, alt2, cset, bus, comfort3, comfort4, ttime2, age,
id, alt3, cset, train, comfort5, comfort6, ttime3, age,
id, alt4, cset, plane, comfort7, comfort8, ttime4, age
;File= <wherever the analyst specifies>
;Format=((8(F5.3,1X))) $
```

This may look overly complicated but is, under examination, quite simple. The first command **CREATE** allows the analyst to construct new variables. The lines following the **CREATE** command are the new variables that will be constructed. The first line after the **CREATE** command constructs four new variables, each associated with one of the alternatives. **car=(choice=1)** tells NLOGIT to create a new variable called *car*. This variable will take the value 1 if the existing choice variable equals 1 or 0 otherwise. Similarly **bus=(choice=2)** constructs a new variable called *bus* that will take the value 1 if choice equals 2 or 0 otherwise. In NLOGIT, if we write a command such that some variable equals another variable which in turn equals a specific value (the other variable and value being

Table 8.9. *Data entered into a single line*

id	*choice*	*ind*	*comfort1* (*car*)	*comfort2* (*car*)	*ttime1* (*car*)	*comfort3* (*bus*)	*comfort4* (*bus*)	*ttime2* (*bus*)	*comfort5* (*train*)	*comfort6* (*train*)	*ttime3* (*train*)	*age*
01	1	1	1	0	14	1	0	12	−1	−1	12	40
01	2	1	0	1	10	0	1	14	0	1	12	40
02	4	2	0	1	12	1	0	14	−1	−1	12	32
02	3	2	−1	−1	12	0	1	12	−1	−1	10	32
03	2	3	−1	−1	12	1	0	14	0	1	14	35
03	1	3	1	0	14	0	1	10	1	0	14	35

Table 8.10. *RP data in a single-line data format*

id	*choice*	*comfort1*	*comfort2*	*ttime1*	*comfort3*	*comfort4*	*ttime2*	*comfort5*	*comfort6*	*ttime3*	*age*
1	1	0	1	10.5	−1	−1	11.5	−1	−1	12	40
2	4	0	1	10	−1	−1	11.5	−1	−1	12	32

placed in brackets), the newly created variable will equal 1 if what is in the brackets is true, or 0 otherwise.

The second line after the **CREATE** command, **cset=4,** creates a new variable called *cset* which will always take the value 4. Similarly, **alt1=1** creates a new variable which will take the constant value 1. We complete any command with a **$**. The **$** instructs NLOGIT to perform the specified function, in this case the **CREATE** command up to the **$** sign. We note that within commands, we are often able to have multiple sub-commands, as in the case above, with several new variables being created through the single **CREATE** command. Sub-commands are separated by a semi-colon (i.e. ;). Once more, we end the command with **$**.

The next command is the **WRITE** command. The **Format** command we have specified is the same as that which we explained earlier:

;Format=((8(F5.3,1X))) $

In the **Format** command, the first number, 8, represents the total number of variables (columns) that will be created in the new data set. For our example, there will be eight columns, one for each of the *id*, *alt*, *cset*, *choice*, *comfort1*, *comfort2*, *ttime*, *age* variables. The (F5.3,1X) format component requires some explanation. The number immediately following the F, i.e. 5.3, informs NLOGIT that the maximum number of digits any value will take will be five, rounded up to three decimal places.

As an aside, we have been conservative here, as the greatest number of digits any value takes in our mock data set is three with one decimal place. It is better to be conservative than to understate the number of digits and decimal places, which will avoid the data being incorrectly formatted (typically being shown in the data set as *****). As before, the **,1X** component of the format command instructs NLOGIT to leave a single space between each of the written values, making it easy to read the data via a spreadsheet.

As a further aside, data formatted by the **WRITE** command are not automatically converted into a format consistent with the way the command is written. We have written the commands immediately following the write statement as we wish them to appear in the new data set (i.e. in a four-line data format). We have done this for ease of checking mistakes. Command lines presented in separate rows do not correspond to rows of data containing the variables as they appear in the data. As such, the following is equivalent to the commands written above:

WRITE
;id, alt1, cset, car, comfort1, comfort2, ttime1, age, id, alt2, cset, bus, comfort3, comfort4, ttime2, age, id, alt3,
cset, train, comfort5, comfort6, ttime3, age, id, alt4, cset, plane, comfort7, comfort8, ttime4, age
;File= <wherever the analyst specifies>
;Format=((8(F5.3,1X))) $

It is through the **Format** command that the data are appropriately formatted. We have 32 variables listed under the **WRITE** command. The commands immediately following the

WRITE command instruct NLOGIT on the order the variables will feed into the new data set. Given that the **Format** command instructs NLOGIT that the new data set will have a total of eight variables, the first eight variables are assigned to the first row of data. The next eight variables are placed in the second row of data, and so forth.

This process begins with the first row of data within the active data set. Hence, in the above example, the first four rows of data will all relate to the variables in the first row of data in the original data set (36 variables into eight columns). The **WRITE** command initiates an iterative process so that once the command locates a semi-colon (in this instance, this occurs at the line beginning **;File**), it will immediately proceed to the next row of data in the active data set and restart from the beginning. This process will continue until the last row of data in the original data set has been properly formatted.

As an aside, the **WRITE** command does not effect changes in the active data set. Rather, the write command creates a new data set in a location specified by the analyst in the line of code:

;File= <wherever the analyst specifies>

For example:

;File=c:\choice_models_are_fun\NLOGIT_data.SAV or
;File=c:\ choice_models_are_fun\NLOGIT_data.LPJ

As suggested previously, we prefer either the .SAV or the .LPJ file formats (although .DAT and .TXT are fine for relatively small data sets). As suggested earlier, the **WRITE** command has as a default format (G15.7 per attribute) for the data or you may specify a format. We recommend a data-specific format for a large number of attributes to try and limit the size of the file. Imagine 100 attributes each at G15.7. The data set that is currently open, the active data set, remains untouched by the **WRITE** command. Therefore it may be worthwhile for the analyst to save any changes made through the **CREATE** command before continuing with the **WRITE** command. Indeed a user-provided format is essential to allocate variables to specific rows in creating a new NLOGIT data set of one alternative per row.

8.5 Data cleaning

The final task for the analyst in entering data should, as always, be the cleaning of the data. There is no conceivable circumstance in which the analyst should not check their data for inaccuracies before analysis. The simplest and quickest check of data are to perform an analysis of descriptive statistics. The command to generate descriptive statistics is:

Dstats;rhs=*$

The * signifies in NLOGIT, all variables. Thus the above command will generate descriptive statistics for all variables within the data set. Inserting specific names (separated by commas) instead of * will generate descriptive statistics only for those variables named. The descriptive statistics for the *all variable* case is shown below. What the analyst should look for is unusual-looking data. Examination of the output reveals that all variables are within their expected ranges (for example, we would expect the *alti* variable to have a minimum value of 1 and a maximum value of 4). A quick examination of such output can save the analyst a significant amount of time and avoid problems at the time of model estimation:

```
Descriptive Statistics
All results based on nonmissing observations.
======================================================================
Variable            Mean        Std.Dev.        Minimum        Maximum Cases
======================================================================
----------------------------------------------------------------------
All observations in current sample
----------------------------------------------------------------------
ID             1.50000000    .534522484    1.00000000    2.00000000    8
ALTI           2.50000000    1.19522861    1.00000000    4.00000000    8
CSET           4.00000000    .000000000    4.00000000    4.00000000    8
CHOICE         .250000000    .462910050    .000000000    1.00000000    8
COMFORT1      -.250000000    .886405260   -1.00000000    1.00000000    8
COMFORT2      -.250000000    .886405260   -1.00000000    1.00000000    8
TTIME          8.75625000    4.66946292    1.25000000    12.0000000    8
AGE            36.0000000    4.27617987    32.0000000    40.0000000    8
```

Examination of the descriptive statistics table is useful for locating possible data entry errors as well as possibly suspect data observations. The analyst, however, needs to be aware that the output table generated above is inclusive of observations for *all* alternatives. Examining the descriptive statistics for alternatives independently may yield further interesting information. The command we would use for the example above is:

Dstats ;rhs=*; str=alti $

The addition of the **;str=alti** to the **Dstats** command has NLOGIT produce descriptive statistics specific to each value present within the *alti* variable.

The output generated using the **REJECT** command as described above is shown below. Note the average travel time for each of the alternatives. We see that the average travel time for the *car* is 10.25 hours, for *bus* 11.5 hours, for *train* 12 hours, and for *plane* 1.3 hours. Compare this to the average travel time shown in the previous output which is the overall average for this variable (8.76 hours rounding). Using the overall average in this instance as an indicator of the averages for the alternatives is likely to be misleading. The SDC, *age*, is the same for each alternative. This will be true of all SDCs:

```
Descriptive Statistics
All results based on nonmissing observations.
==============================================================================
Variable          Mean      Std.Dev.       Minimum        Maximum Cases
==============================================================================
------------------------------------------------------------------------------
All observations in current sample
------------------------------------------------------------------------------
ID           1.50000000   .707106781    1.00000000     2.00000000     2
ALTI         1.00000000   .000000000    1.00000000     1.00000000     2
CSET         4.00000000   .000000000    4.00000000     4.00000000     2
CHOICE       .500000000   .707106781    .000000000     1.00000000     2
COMFORT1     .000000000   .000000000    .000000000     .000000000     2
COMFORT2     1.00000000   .000000000    1.00000000     1.00000000     2
TTIME        10.2500000   .353553391    10.0000000     10.5000000     2
AGE          36.0000000   5.65685425    32.0000000     40.0000000     2

Descriptive Statistics
All results based on nonmissing observations.
==============================================================================
Variable          Mean      Std.Dev.       Minimum        Maximum Cases
==============================================================================
------------------------------------------------------------------------------
All observations in current sample
------------------------------------------------------------------------------
ID           1.50000000   .707106781    1.00000000     2.00000000     2
ALTI         2.00000000   .000000000    2.00000000     2.00000000     2
CSET         4.00000000   .000000000    4.00000000     4.00000000     2
CHOICE       .000000000   .000000000    .000000000     .000000000     2
COMFORT1    -1.00000000   .000000000   -1.00000000    -1.00000000     2
COMFORT2    -1.00000000   .000000000   -1.00000000    -1.00000000     2
TTIME        11.5000000   .000000000    11.5000000     11.5000000     2
AGE          36.0000000   5.65685425    32.0000000     40.0000000     2

Descriptive Statistics
All results based on nonmissing observations.
==============================================================================
Variable          Mean      Std.Dev.       Minimum        Maximum Cases
==============================================================================
------------------------------------------------------------------------------
All observations in current sample
------------------------------------------------------------------------------
ID           1.50000000   .707106781    1.00000000     2.00000000     2
ALTI         3.00000000   .000000000    3.00000000     3.00000000     2
```

```
CSET         4.00000000    .000000000    4.00000000    4.00000000     2
CHOICE        .000000000   .000000000     .000000000    .000000000    2
COMFORT1    -1.00000000    .000000000   -1.00000000   -1.00000000     2
COMFORT2    -1.00000000    .000000000   -1.00000000   -1.00000000     2
TTIME        12.0000000    .000000000    12.0000000    12.0000000     2
AGE          36.0000000   5.65685425     32.0000000    40.0000000     2

Descriptive Statistics
All results based on nonmissing observations.
==================================================================
Variable          Mean        Std.Dev.       Minimum       Maximum    Cases
==================================================================
------------------------------------------------------------------
All observations in current sample
------------------------------------------------------------------
ID           1.50000000    .707106781    1.00000000    2.00000000     2
ALTI         4.00000000    .000000000    4.00000000    4.00000000     2
CSET         4.00000000    .000000000    4.00000000    4.00000000     2
CHOICE        .500000000   .707106781     .000000000   1.00000000     2
COMFORT1     1.00000000    .000000000    1.00000000    1.00000000     2
COMFORT2      .000000000   .000000000     .000000000    .000000000    2
TTIME        1.30000000    .000000000    1.30000000    1.30000000     2
AGE          36.0000000   5.65685425     32.0000000    40.0000000     2
```

As well as examining the descriptive statistics, the analyst may find it worthwhile to examine the correlation structure of the data. The command to do so is:

Dstats ;rhs=*; output=2 $

As an aside, the analyst may wish to examine the covariance matrix. The command for this is **output=1$**. Using the command **output=3$** will generate both the covariance and correlation matrices. The correlation matrix for our example is shown below. As with descriptive statistics, it may be worthwhile examining the correlation matrix for each alternative independently. In NLOGIT, the correlation matrix is based on a Pearson product moment (PPM) specification between two variables. Strictly, this is valid when contrasting ratio scaled variables (and is usually acceptable for interval scaled variables); however, for classificatory variables (e.g. ordinal scaled) other indicators of similarity are preferred. The Prelis pre-processor in LISREL is useful in this task:

```
Correlation Matrix for Listed Variables
                ID     ALTI    CSET   CHOICE COMFORT1 COMFORT2  TTIME     AGE
ID          1.00000  .00000  .00000   .00000  .00000   .00000 -.01434 -1.00000
ALTI         .00000 1.00000  .00000   .00000  .40452  -.40452 -.67613   .00000
CSET         .00000  .00000  .00000   .00000  .00000   .00000  .00000   .00000
CHOICE       .00000  .00000  .00000  1.00000  .52223   .52223 -.37930   .00000
```

COMFORT1	.00000	.40452	.00000	.52223	1.00000	.63636	-.92986	.00000
COMFORT2	.00000	-.40452	.00000	.52223	.63636	1.00000	-.31053	.00000
TTIME	-.01434	-.67613	.00000	-.37930	-.92986	-.31053	1.00000	.01434
AGE	-1.00000	.00000	.00000	.00000	.00000	.00000	.01434	1.00000

Examining the correlations within the data set is important but often a neglected aspect of getting to know and cleaning the data. Significant correlations may result in *multicollinearity* at the time of modeling, which has implications for both model estimation and prediction. It is suggested that the analyst spend time examining the data for the possibility of multicollinearity.

To premise the importance of this, consider an SP choice experiment with three blocks. As previously mentioned, one can remove columns (i.e. attributes) from the design without loss of orthogonality; however, the same is not true for the removal of rows (i.e. treatment combinations or choice sets). As such, design orthogonality requires the return of all data for all blocks of the design: there can be no missing data. For small sample sizes (e.g. the total sample size is three respondents, each assigned to one of three blocks of a design) maintaining orthogonality is relatively straightforward. For larger sample sizes (e.g. when the sample size is in the hundreds), maintaining orthogonality is a non-trivial task.

For example, consider a design blocked into three. If 100 decision makers complete the first block and 100 complete the second but only 99 complete the third block, design orthogonality will be lost over the entire sample. The degree of the loss of orthogonality is a question of correlation and hence multicollinearity.

As an aside, for an experimental design to remain orthogonal, either the entire design must be given to each decision maker (and any missing data result in the entire data related to that individual being removed from the data set) or some *sampling strategy* put in place to ensure that complete designs are returned across all decision makers. Unfortunately, any such strategy is likely to result in questions being raised regarding sampling bias. Computer Aided Personal Interviews (CAPI) or Internet Aided Surveys (IASs) may help alleviate this problem somewhat by detecting portions of a design (blocks) that have been under-utilized in sampling and assign new individuals to these. Alternatively, the randomization process might involve randomly assigning the first decision maker to a block and subsequent decision makers to other unused blocks without replacement. Once the entire design is complete, the process repeats itself, starting with the next decision maker sampled. In either case, the analyst must consider whether such strategies are strictly random. At the end of the day, it is likely that the analyst will have to live with some design non-orthogonality.

As a further aside, the authors have observed a recent but undocumented trend among some analysts to do away with the formal generation of experimental designs. Instead such "researchers" generate the treatment combinations of the experimental design by some random process. While this is likely to result in non-orthogonal designs, unless handled with extreme care the survey and sampling process is likely to destroy any orthogonality that might have once existed in an orthogonal experimental design anyway. Further, the random generation of treatment combinations is a far less convoluted process than that required for the formal generation of an experimental design. While not *yet* ready to condone this practice, the authors welcome more research to establish the extent of bias in randomization in contrast to the practice of orthogonal design.

8.5.1 Testing for multicollinearity using NLOGIT

A loss of design orthogonality represents the introduction of correlations among the design attributes which, if significant enough, may result in multicollinearity (see p. 116 for a discussion of the effects of multicollinearity). Fortunately, the analyst is able to test for the presence of multicollinearity; however, if detected, there is little that the analyst can do to rectify the problem short of ignoring all but one of the affected attributes. Thus the analyst is best to avoid multicollinearity in the first place. The use of paper and pencil surveys makes this difficult; however the advent of CAPI and IASs means that this is likely to be less of a problem in the future.

Several methods exist to test for multicollinearity. The most commonly used involves the generation of some bivariate or pairwise correlation coefficient, usually Pearson's r. The correlation coefficients are then used in conjunction with some arbitrary rule of thumb to determine whether correlation exists among the explanatory variables of the model to an extent which may produce multicollinearity. For example, a cut-off of 0.8 may be used to determine whether the correlation between two variables is sufficient to cause problems for model estimation.

A more scientifically rigorous test is to use the method of auxiliary regressions (Gujarati 1995). The three steps of this test are:

(1) *Regress each attribute on the remaining attributes of the design*. An experimental design with six attributes will thus require six separate regressions, with five explanatory variables. Each individual regression should also include the constant term.

(2) *Compute the R^2 of each (auxiliary) regression* and *calculate R_i* for each regression using the following formula:

$$R_i = \frac{R^2_{x1.x2x3...xk} / (k-2)}{\left(1 - R^2_{x1.x2x3...xk}\right) / (n-k+1)} \tag{8.1}$$

where

$R^2_{x1.x2x3...xk}$ is the coefficient of determination (i.e. the R^2) of the regression of attribute x_i on the remaining attributes, k is the number of explanatory variables in the model, and n is the sample size.

(3) Compare each R_i to a critical F-statistic with degrees of freedom $k-2$ and $n-k+1$. If an R_i for an auxiliary regression exceeds the critical F-statistic, then the attribute x_i is collinear or correlated with the remaining attributes, raising issues of multicollinearity in model estimation.

a

Alt 1		Alt 2	
Attribute 1	Attribute 2	Attribute 3	Attribute 4

b

Alt 1	Attribute 1	Attribute 2	Attribute 3	Attribute 4
Alt 2	Attribute 1	Attribute 2	Attribute 3	Attribute 4

Figure 8.9 Differences between the data and experimental design setups
a Experimental design data setup
b Data set setup

An additional test using the auxiliary R^2 values is to use Klein's rule (Klein 1962). For this test, the coefficients of determination of the auxiliary regressions are compared to the R^2 of a regression of the dependent variable (i.e. choice) on the attributes of the model as used in the auxiliary regression models. If the R^2 of any auxiliary regression model exceeds the R^2 of the regression on choice of the design attributes, then multicollinearity is thought to be of significant concern to the analyst.

As an aside, the analyst must consider differences in how the attributes and alternatives are set up in the data to how they appear in the experimental design. In the experimental design, the attributes and alternatives are in the columns. In the data, the attributes are in the columns but the alternatives are in the rows. We show this in figures 8.9a and 8.9b.

Because of the way the data are set up, the analyst cannot blindly test for multicollinearity over all of the attributes. Rather, the analyst will have to select each alternative one at a time and conduct the tests described above selectively. Thus, assuming two attributes for each of two alternatives the analyst will now have to perform eight auxiliary regressions and not four (i.e. four for each alternative). We demonstrate how this is done in chapter 9; however, it is worth noting now that although we have couched this discussion in terms of the experimental design attributes, multicollinearity is not just a problem for design attributes but may also be present within SDC. As such, these tests should be conducted for all variables included within a model specification, an arduous and time-consuming task.

Because of the way the data are set up, it will only ever be possible to conduct tests for multicollinearity within an alternative. Between-alternative correlations cannot be tested. While this may not pose a problem for unlabeled experiments where between-alternative correlations are of no concern, multicollinearity may remain an undetected problem for labeled experiments. The keen analyst may either re-arrange the data so that each line of data are that of an individual choice set as opposed to each row corresponding to an alternative, thus allowing for tests of multicollinearity to be performed on both within- and between-alternative attributes, or use lag commands to place each alternative on a single line of data while at the same time retaining the multiple-row data format for the remainder of the data set. Unfortunately, in practice, keen analysts are few and far between.

Once the analyst is comfortable with the data and is certain that the data are clean, it is time to start modeling. We demonstrate the commands necessary and detail the output generated in chapters 10 and 11. In chapter 9 we provide a detailed description of a transportation case study. The data for this case study which we will use to demonstrate NLOGIT's modeling capabilities may be found on the website provided with this book.

Appendix 8A Design effects coding

Table 8A.1 shows the coding for the design introduced in chapter 5 (from table 5.12). The left-hand side shows the design. The right-hand side shows the effects coding as would be entered into NLOGIT at the time of analysis.

Table 8A.1. *Design effects coding*

mode	*choice set*	*comfort*	*ttime*	*block*	*comfort1*	*comfort2*	*ttime*
Car	2	1	14	−1	1	0	14
Bus	2	1	12	−1	1	0	12
Train	2	−1	12	−1	−1	−1	12
Plane	2	0	2	−1	0	1	2
Car	4	0	10	−1	0	1	10
Bus	4	0	14	−1	0	1	14
Train	4	0	12	−1	0	1	12
Plane	4	−1	1.5	−1	−1	−1	1.5
Car	6	0	14	−1	0	1	14
Bus	6	0	10	−1	0	1	10
Train	6	−1	10	−1	−1	−1	10
Plane	6	1	2	−1	1	0	2
Car	8	0	12	−1	0	1	12
Bus	8	0	12	−1	0	1	12
Train	8	1	14	−1	1	0	14
Plane	8	0	1	−1	0	1	1
Car	10	1	12	−1	1	0	12
Bus	10	1	14	−1	1	0	14
Train	10	1	10	−1	1	0	10
Plane	10	−1	1	−1	−1	−1	1
Car	12	−1	12	−1	−1	−1	12
Bus	12	−1	10	−1	−1	−1	10
Train	12	1	12	−1	1	0	12
Plane	12	1	1	−1	1	0	1
Car	13	−1	10	−1	−1	−1	10
Bus	13	−1	12	−1	−1	−1	12
Train	13	0	10	−1	0	1	10
Plane	13	0	1.5	−1	0	1	1.5
Car	18	−1	14	−1	−1	−1	14
Bus	18	−1	14	−1	−1	−1	14

Table 8A.1. (*Cont.*)

mode	*choice set*	*comfort*	*ttime*	*block*	*comfort1*	*comfort2*	*ttime*
Train	18	−1	14	−1	−1	−1	14
Plane	18	−1	2	−1	−1	−1	2
Car	26	1	10	−1	1	0	10
Bus	26	1	10	−1	1	0	10
Train	26	0	14	−1	0	1	14
Plane	26	1	1.5	−1	1	0	1.5
Car	3	0	12	0	0	1	12
Bus	3	1	14	0	1	0	14
Train	3	−1	12	0	−1	−1	12
Plane	3	1	1.5	0	1	0	1.5
Car	7	−1	12	0	−1	−1	12
Bus	7	0	12	0	0	1	12
Train	7	−1	10	0	−1	−1	10
Plane	7	−1	1.5	0	−1	−1	1.5
Car	14	1	14	0	1	0	14
Bus	14	−1	14	0	−1	−1	14
Train	14	0	10	0	0	1	10
Plane	14	1	1	0	1	0	1
Car	15	−1	10	0	−1	−1	10
Bus	15	0	14	0	0	1	14
Train	15	1	14	0	1	0	14
Plane	15	1	2	0	1	0	2
Car	16	0	14	0	0	1	14
Bus	16	1	12	0	1	0	12
train	16	0	14	0	0	1	14
Plane	16	−1	1	0	−1	−1	1
Car	19	1	12	0	1	0	12
Bus	19	−1	10	0	−1	−1	10
Train	19	−1	14	0	−1	−1	14
Plane	19	0	1.5	0	0	1	1.5
Car	21	1	10	0	1	0	10
Bus	21	−1	12	0	−1	−1	12
Train	21	1	12	0	1	0	12
Plane	21	−1	2	0	−1	−1	2
Car	23	−1	14	0	−1	−1	14
Bus	23	0	10	0	0	1	10
Train	23	0	12	0	0	1	12
Plane	23	0	1	0	0	1	1
Car	25	0	10	0	0	1	10
Bus	25	1	10	0	1	0	10
Train	25	1	10	0	1	0	10
Plane	25	0	2	0	0	1	2
Car	1	−1	12	1	−1	−1	12
Bus	1	1	14	1	1	0	14
Train	1	0	14	1	0	1	14

(*cont.*)

Table 8A.1. (*Cont.*)

mode	*choice set*	*comfort*	*ttime*	*block*	*comfort1*	*comfort2*	*ttime*
Plane	1	0	2	1	0	1	2
Car	5	1	14	1	1	0	14
Bus	5	0	10	1	0	1	10
Train	5	1	14	1	1	0	14
Plane	5	−1	1.5	1	−1	−1	1.5
Car	9	1	12	1	1	0	12
Bus	9	0	12	1	0	1	12
Train	9	0	12	1	0	1	12
Plane	9	1	2	1	1	0	2
Car	11	0	10	1	0	1	10
Bus	11	−1	12	1	−1	−1	12
Train	11	−1	14	1	−1	−1	14
Plane	11	1	1	1	1	0	1
Car	17	−1	10	1	−1	−1	10
Bus	17	1	10	1	1	0	10
Train	17	−1	12	1	−1	−1	12
Plane	17	−1	1	1	−1	−1	1
Car	20	−1	14	1	−1	−1	14
Bus	20	1	12	1	1	0	12
Train	20	1	10	1	1	0	10
Plane	20	1	1.5	1	1	0	1.5
Car	22	0	12	1	0	1	12
Bus	22	−1	10	1	−1	−1	10
Train	22	0	10	1	0	1	10
Plane	22	−1	2	1	−1	−1	2
Car	24	1	10	1	1	0	10
Train	22	0	10	1	0	1	10
Plane	22	−1	2	1	−1	−1	2
Car	24	1	10	1	1	0	10
Bus	24	0	14	1	0	1	14
Train	24	−1	10	1	−1	−1	10
Plane	24	0	1	1	0	1	1
Car	27	0	14	1	0	1	14
Bus	27	−1	14	1	−1	−1	14
Train	27	1	12	1	1	0	12
Plane	27	0	1.5	1	0	1	1.5

Appendix 8B Converting single-line data commands

The commands to convert the data in table 8.9 into multiple-line choice data are recreated below. We have also included the commands to generate the additional descriptive tables for each alternative as well as the correlation matrix, as described in the main text.

```
CREATE
;car=(choice=1);bus=(choice=2);train=(choice=3);plane=(choice=4)
;cset=4
;alt1=1
;alt2=2
;alt3=3
;alt4=4 $

WRITE
;id, alt1, cset, car, comfort1, comfort2, ttime1, age,
id, alt2, cset, bus, comfort3, comfort4, ttime2, age,
id, alt3, cset, train, comfort5, comfort6, ttime3, age,
id, alt4, cset, plane, comfort7, comfort8, ttime4, age
;File= <wherever the analyst specifies.DAT>
;Format=((8(F5.2,1X))) $

RESET
READ; file = <specified file location .dat>; nvar = 8 ;nobs = 24
;Names = id, alt, cset, choice, comfort1, comfort2, ttime, age $
Dstats;rhs=*$

Dstats ;rhs=*; str=alti $
Dstats;rhs=*  ;output=two $
```

The descriptive statistics output generated from this example is now shown:

```
Descriptive Statistics
All results based on nonmissing observations.
==============================================================================
Variable              Mean       Std.Dev.       Minimum        Maximum  Cases
==============================================================================
------------------------------------------------------------------------------
All observations in current sample
------------------------------------------------------------------------------
ID             2.00000000    .834057656    1.00000000    3.00000000      24
ALT            2.50000000    1.14208048    1.00000000    4.00000000      24
CSET           4.00000000    .000000000    4.00000000    4.00000000      24
CHOICE         .250000000    .442325868    .000000000    1.00000000      24
COMFORT1       .083333333    .829702234    1.00000000    1.00000000      24
COMFORT2      .0416666667    .858672720    1.00000000    1.00000000      24
TTIME          9.16666667    4.70352936    1.00000000    14.0000000      24
AGE            35.6666667    3.37080389    32.0000000    40.0000000      24
```

The descriptive statistics for each alternative are shown below:

```
Descriptive Statistics
All results based on nonmissing observations.
==================================================================
Variable          Mean       Std.Dev.       Minimum       Maximum    Cases
==================================================================
------------------------------------------------------------------
All observations in current sample
------------------------------------------------------------------
ID          2.00000000   .894427191   1.00000000   3.00000000        6
ALTI        1.00000000   .000000000   1.00000000   1.00000000        6
CSET        4.00000000   .000000000   4.00000000   4.00000000        6
CHOICE      .333333333   .516397779   .000000000   1.00000000        6
COMFORT1    .000000000   .894427191  -1.00000000   1.00000000        6
COMFORT2    .000000000   .894427191  -1.00000000   1.00000000        6
TTIME       11.0000000   1.67332005   10.0000000   14.0000000        6
AGE         35.6666667   3.61478446   32.0000000   40.0000000        6

Descriptive Statistics
All results based on nonmissing observations.
==================================================================
Variable            Mean       Std.Dev.         Minimum       Maximum Cases
==================================================================
------------------------------------------------------------------
All observations in current sample
------------------------------------------------------------------
ID            2.00000000   .894427191    1.00000000   3.00000000    6
ALTI          2.00000000   .000000000    2.00000000   2.00000000    6
CSET          4.00000000   .000000000    4.00000000   4.00000000    6
CHOICE        .333333333   .516397779    .000000000   1.00000000    6
COMFORT1     -.166666667   .983192080   -1.00000000   1.00000000    6
COMFORT2     -.333333333   .816496581   -1.00000000   1.00000000    6
TTIME         12.3333333   1.96638416    10.0000000   14.0000000    6
AGE           35.6666667   3.61478446    32.0000000   40.0000000    6

Descriptive Statistics
All results based on nonmissing observations.
==================================================================
Variable           Mean       Std.Dev.         Minimum       Maximum Cases
==================================================================
------------------------------------------------------------------
All observations in current sample
------------------------------------------------------------------
ID           2.00000000   .894427191    1.00000000   3.00000000     6
ALTI         3.00000000   .000000000    3.00000000   3.00000000     6
```

```
CSET          4.00000000   .000000000    4.00000000  4.00000000      6
CHOICE         .166666667  .408248290     .000000000  1.00000000      6
COMFORT1     -.333333333   .816496581   -1.00000000  1.00000000      6
COMFORT2     -.166666667   .983192080   -1.00000000  1.00000000      6
TTIME         11.6666667  1.96638416    10.0000000  14.0000000      6
AGE           35.6666667  3.61478446    32.0000000  40.0000000      6


Descriptive Statistics
All results based on nonmissing observations.
====================================================================
Variable          Mean      Std.Dev.       Minimum      Maximum  Cases
====================================================================
--------------------------------------------------------------------
All observations in current sample
--------------------------------------------------------------------
ID          2.00000000   .894427191    1.00000000  3.00000000      6
ALTI        4.00000000   .000000000    4.00000000  4.00000000      6
CSET        4.00000000   .000000000    4.00000000  4.00000000      6
CHOICE       .166666667  .408248290     .000000000  1.00000000      6
COMFORT1     .166666667  .752772653   -1.00000000  1.00000000      6
COMFORT2     .333333333  .816496581   -1.00000000  1.00000000      6
TTIME       1.66666667   .408248290    1.00000000  2.00000000      6
AGE         35.6666667  3.61478446    32.0000000  40.0000000      6
```

The correlation matrix for this example is now shown:

```
Correlation Matrix for Listed Variables
              ID       ALT     CSET   CHOICE COMFORT1 COMFORT2 TTIME    AGE
ID        1.00000   .00000  .00000   .00000   .18848   .00000   .06650 -.61859
ALTI       .00000  1.00000  .00000  -.17213   .04588   .15517  -.69607  .00000
CSET       .00000   .00000  .00000   .00000   .00000   .00000   .00000  .00000
CHOICE     .00000  -.17213  .00000  1.00000   .53311   .25756   .06269  .00000
COMFORT1   .18848   .04588  .00000   .53311  1.00000   .54416  -.13555 -.08809
COMFORT2   .00000   .15517  .00000   .25756   .54416  1.00000  -.24042  .22031
TTIME      .06650  -.69607  .00000   .06269  -.13555  -.24042  1.00000  .03931
AGE       -.61859   .00000  .00000   .00000  -.08809   .22031   .03931 1.00000
```

9 Case study: mode-choice data

Few things are harder to put up with than the annoyance of a good example. (Mark Twain, 1835–1910, *Pudd'nhead Wilson*, 1884)

9.1 Introduction

In this chapter, we provide a detailed description of the case study alluded to throughout the book. You should already be familiar with aspects of the case study from your reading to date. The question for us was whether we detailed the case study early in the book, later in the book (as we have here) or discussed aspects of it throughout the book without ever providing the reader with a detailed overview of how the actual study proceeded.

Detailing the case study earlier in the book risked alienating the reader through the use of the expert language necessary to relate the hows and whys of the study. By leaving the detailed description to now, we feel that the reader should be equipped with a level of expertise in the language of choice to understand what actually occurred. We will, for this chapter, use the language of the expert (or, at least, the more informed). If you have absorbed the material in previous chapters, then what we write here should be easily understood.

9.2 Study objectives

The case study, the data for which we use in later chapters to demonstrate the more practical aspects of choice modeling, was part of a 1994 study into Greenhouse Gas Emissions (GGE) commissioned by the Australian Federal Government. An important feature of the GGE study was to develop a data base to describe the characteristics of the population of households and passenger vehicles in a base year. Households comprise individuals who participate in travel activities; they have available in varying degrees automobiles of many types, as well as public transport. Although a major data component of the GGE study is a household travel survey, administered to over 1400 households in the six capital cities in mainland Australia (excluding Darwin), placing the sampled households in the context of the population requires additional data.

The primary data related to the socio-economic and demographic data of individuals and households, the characteristics of the population of passenger vehicles, and descriptors of traffic levels and urban locations for residential and work activity in the year 1994. This information was used to develop classes of passenger vehicles (defined by size and vintage), scrappage rates of vehicles, and classes of "synthetic" households (defined on core classifiers such as life cycle stage and household income, and non-core classifiers such as number of workers). These outputs enabled the study to define population weighted synthetic households, the population of vehicles available for "allocation" to each synthetic household, and the consequent patterns of travel behavior which provided measures of GGE and other useful outputs such as modal accessibility, vehicle kilometers, consumer surplus, and energy consumption.

An important objective of the GGE study was to put in place a set of procedures for both developing and maintaining an ongoing data base for use in future studies of urban passenger transport. It is for this reason that a lot of effort was devoted to careful sourcing and documentation of secondary data. The Institute of Transport Studies at the University of Sydney (hereafter referred to as ITS) set up a specialized Data Sourcing and Maintenance Unit (DSMU) with the initial task of delivering useful data for passenger transport analyses.

The GGE study involved, *inter alia*, consideration of the effects of a variety of possible policies that might be used to reduce enhanced GGE in urban areas in Australia. An SP approach was justified by the fact that (a) some of the proposed strategies (i.e. combinations of instruments) had not been tried and, hence, their potential effects had not been observed; and (b) some of the levels or ranges of variables representing strategies had not been observed and, hence, it was not possible or at least risky to assume that one could extrapolate from known data to these unobserved values. As well, in many cases individuals or households might have reacted to the strategies in a variety of ways and the SP approach used allowed the researchers to examine the types of decisions that might be made and how they inter-related.

Two SP surveys were developed. The first addressed the commuter's choice of mode and departure time when faced with congestion pricing, higher fuel prices, and "new" forms of public transport such as a bus priority system and light rail. The second addressed the choice of vehicle and fuel types when faced with higher fuel prices for conventional fuels but lower fuel prices for other fuels, the limitations of range and boot space of electric and alternative fueled vehicles (e.g. LPG and CNG), greater variability in registration fees, and a new regime of vehicle purchase prices. We refer to the first experiment as the "mode-choice experiment" and the second as the "vehicle-choice experiment."

The process leading to the testable set of instruments in the pilot survey and then the main survey involved a large number of iterations. By the time the full pilot questionnaire was ready, a number of skirmish and pre-pilot tests had already been completed on a small number of respondents, which had resolved most of the items of concern that the main empirical study was likely to face.

To the extent possible, joint estimation of RP and SP models was planned. This meant that it was necessary to design the experiments with a response metric which was common to that of the RP model and that there were some common attributes across both data sets. Some choices such as mode choice were easily transferable between the two data methodologies and, hence, amenable to joint estimation. Other choices, however, such as departure time choice on a congestion priced tollway, could not be observed.

The focus in this chapter and book is on the *mode-choice experiment for commuters*. The vehicle-choice experiment is discussed in detail together with estimation of choice models in Hensher and Greene (2001). Readers interested in seeing how the entire data set was utilized to estimate and apply models for household choice of residential location, vehicle type and fleet size, as well as employed individual household member choice of commuter departure time and mode choice and choice of workplace location, can refer to Hensher (2002).

9.3 The pilot study

The primary objective of the pilot study was to test the contents and logistics of the survey process. More specifically, the research set out to test the following:

(1) *Readability* of the questionnaires in general
(2) Ability to complete the *entire questionnaire* – home interview, household, and commuter questionnaires
(3) Ability to complete the *choice modeling* sections of the home interview questionnaire;
(4) *Correct skips or logic* in the questionnaires
(5) Interviewers' understanding of the study and how it is to be *administered*
(6) Interview *length*
(7) *Additional questions* needed
(8) *Omission* of questions
(9) *Interviewing process* can be carried out smoothly.

The pilot study enabled the testing of the following elements of the interviewing process:

(1) Interviewer briefing
(2) 40–45 minute interview with respondent
(3) Drop-off and pick-up of household and commuter questionnaires
(4) Interviewer de-briefing.

The initial mode-choice experiment included a choice set of six alternatives: a *non-toll auto trip*, a *tolled auto trip*, *bus*, *busway*, *heavy rail*, and *light rail*. The public transport options were rotated in the SP design such that for each replication a respondent would have to consider only two public transport modes together with the two automobile options. Six attributes defined a commuter trip by car: *travel time*, *fuel cost*, *parking cost*,

Table 9.1. *Attributes and levels used for the initial mode choice showcards*

travel by car/van/light truck	*free (non-toll) route*	*tollway with congestion toll*
Travel time	15, 25, 35 minutes	4, 8, 12 minutes less
Fuel cost ($)	0.70, 1.00, 1.30, 1.60, 1.90, 2.20	(Same as Free route)
Parking cost ($ per day)	Free, 5, 10	(Same as Free route)
Fee to avoid congestion ($)	Free route no fee	0.50, 1.00, 1.50
Time you have to depart	When you do now	30, 20, 10 minutes earlier, current time, 10, 20, 30 minutes later
What the tolls are used for	Not applicable	Roads/public transport, non-transport needs
travel by public transport	*train or bus*	*busway or light rail (tram)*
Total time spent in vehicle	10, 15, 20 minutes	10, 15, 20 minutes
Frequency of service	Every 10, 15, 20 minutes	Every 10, 15, 20 minutes
Closest stop to your home	10, 15, 20 minutes walk	10, 15, 20 minutes walk
Closest stop to your destination	10, 15, 20 minutes walk	10, 15, 20 minutes walk
Fare ($)	1, 2, 3 (one-way)	1, 2, 3 (one-way)

a fee to avoid congestion, *departure time*, and a *toll fee*. Five attributes defined a public transport trip to work: *travel time in the vehicle*, *frequency of service*, *travel time walking to the closest public transport stop*, *travel time walking from the public transport mode to the destination*, and the *one-way fare*. The rotation of the public modes added another attribute to the design. We show the alternatives, attributes and attribute levels in table 9.1.

From the experimental design the researchers designed showcards to be shown to each respondent. Rather than produce several surveys corresponding to each of the blocks of the experimental design, the researchers produced a survey that provided space for the respondent to select the most attractive alternative but did not show the choice sets themselves. The choice sets were placed on showcards that the interviewer could show to each respondent. The instructions and an example of the survey response mechanism are shown in figure 9.1.

Each respondent was given nine choice sets from the full set of 81 choice sets and asked to indicate the actions they might take in the short term and in the longer term. To ensure a meaningful interpretation of the travel times, the researchers identified the current trip length for the commute and segmented the showcard sets into three trip lengths. Three sets of 81 showcards were required. The trip lengths were (a) up to 30 minutes, (b) 30–45 minutes, and (c) over 45 minutes. These trip lengths are the same for each urban area, even though the number of commuters in each category was expected to differ. Table 9.2 and 9.3 shows the full experimental design used for the pilot study.

This section of the survey should be interesting and fun. We're going to show you nine possible future scenarios involving transport conditions and options in your area. To our knowledge, no one has suggested that any of the scenarios you'll see are likely to happen. We're using these scenarios to understand how individuals and households choose to cope with future changes that might make transport more expensive and less convenient than at present.

For example, you're probably aware that pollution levels in many cities have become major health and environmental concerns in many countries. Likewise, as city populations rise and new workplaces spring up in suburbs or edges of cities, road congestion increases, travel becomes less convenient in some areas and more demands are placed on public funds to solve transport problems and meet future needs. Thus, we need your help to try to understand how transport facilities can best serve your needs under a variety of possible future conditions.

What we want you to do is relatively simple. We will show you 9 scenarios that describe possible future transport conditions in your area that might apply to your typical trips to get to/from work or tertiary education. We want you to evaluate each scenario with reference to your most recent trip and other future trips like it.

Specifically, we want to know: If the transport conditions described in each scenario were to occur and last for some months or years, what would you be most likely to do to deal with the situation?

To answer this question, we give you with a number of possible options from which to choose. Or, if you would choose to do something not included in our list, we give you space to tell us about that choice. So, your job is fairly simple: examine each scenario and think about what it would be like to travel to work or tertiary education in this situation for months or years. Then tell us which actions you would be most likely to take to deal with the situation.

Figure 9.1 Instructions and format of the initial mode-choice survey

Actions available to respondents in the short-term include: (i) which mode they would most likely choose for their usual commute; (ii) how many trips they would likely make by each mode in a typical week; (iii) if they chose (used) drive alone or rideshare, how many times per week would they use the congestion priced tollway. Longer-term actions include: (i) changing workplace location to make commuting less expensive, faster and/or more convenient; (ii) changing residence location to make commuting less expensive, faster and/or more convenient; (iii) trying to change how or when they work (more flexible schedule, working at home more, new shift time(s), or making no work changes); (iv) changing their vehicle mix or use strategy, such as making fewer trips in vehicle(s), selling or giving up at least one vehicle, trading one or more vehicles on a more fuel efficient or alternative fuel vehicle, converting one or more vehicles to alternative fuels, or making no changes to what they own or use. Both long-term and short-term actions were tested as part of the pilot study.

An advantage of posing the survey questions in this way is the ability to model these decisions in a variety of ways to reflect possible issues of interest to policy analysis. For example, it is possible to estimate mode-choice models, and forecast the likely effect of changes in fuel costs and congestion pricing on such choices to determine changes in

Table 9.2. *Instructions and format of the initial mode-choice survey*

travel by car/van/light truck	*free (non-toll) route*	*tollway with congestion toll*
Travel time	25 minutes	12 minutes less
Fuel cost	$1.60	(Same as Free route)
Parking cost	$5.00 per day	(Same as Free route)
Fee to avoid congestion	Free route no fee	$1.00
Time you have to depart	When you do now	10 minutes early
What the tolls are used for	Not applicable	Non-transport needs
travel by public transport	*train or bus*	*light rail (tram)*
Total time spent in vehicle	15 minutes	20 minutes
Frequency of service	Every 15 minutes	Every 20 minutes
Closest stop to your home	10 minutes walk	10 minutes walk
Closest stop to your destination	20 minutes walk	15 minutes walk
Weekly fare	$2.00 (one-way)	$3.00 (one-way)

If the above conditions applied to your most recent or typical work or tertiary education trip, what would you be most likely to do to cope with that? Answer each question below as realistically as possible.

Things You Could Do In The Short Term

1. In a typical week, I would probably try to use each mode the following number of times per week (Write number of times in boxes below. Note: there are at most 10 round trips per week.)

Drive alone	Share a ride	Bus	Commuter train	Light rail (tram)	Busway
❐	❐	❐	❐	❐	❐

2. If you used Drive alone or Rideshare above, how many times per week would you use the Tollway (write numbers in box. Note: there are at most 10 round trips per week)? ❐ Drive alone ❐ Rideshare

Things You Could Do In The Longer Term

3. Try to change where you work to make trip less expensive, faster and/or more convenient (TICK ONLY 1 BOX AT RIGHT): ❐ Yes ❐ No

4. Try to change where you live to make trip less expensive, faster and/or more convenient (TICK ONLY 1 BOX AT RIGHT): ❐ Yes ❐ No

5. Try to do one of the following with how or when you work (TICK ONLY 1 BOX AT RIGHT): ❐ Get a more flexible schedule ❐ Work at home more ❐ Get new shift time(s) ❐ Make no work changes

6. Try to do the following with the vehicles you own or operate (TICK ONLY 1 BOX AT RIGHT): ❐ Make fewer trips in my vehicle(s) ❐ Sell or give up at least one vehicle ❐ Trade one or more vehicles on a more fuel efficient or alternative fuel vehicle ❐ Convert one or more vehicles to an alternative fuel ❐ Make no changes to what I own or how I use them

7. Any other things you might try to do in this situation? Please tell us about them in the space provided:

Table 9.3. *Orthogonal fractional factorial mode-choice pilot experimental design*

car (with toll)				*car (no toll)*			*train or bus*						*busway or light railway*					
time	*depart*	*toll*	*fuel*	*time*	*parking*	*fuel*	*time*	*freq*	*acct*	*egt*	*fare*	*switch*	*time*	*freq*	*egt*	*fare*	*fare*	*block*
1	3	1	1	2	1	2	1	1	0	2	1	1	2	2	0	1	2	0
0	3	1	0	0	2	5	0	2	2	1	0	0	0	2	1	2	2	0
2	1	0	1	2	2	0	0	0	1	1	0	0	0	1	2	1	0	0
1	4	0	0	0	1	6	1	2	2	2	1	1	1	0	1	0	0	0
0	1	0	1	0	0	4	2	1	2	0	0	1	1	2	0	0	0	0
0	5	2	0	1	1	1	1	0	0	0	2	1	0	0	2	0	1	0
1	0	2	1	2	0	3	0	1	1	2	1	1	1	1	2	2	1	0
2	2	1	1	1	2	3	2	2	0	1	2	0	2	0	0	2	1	0
2	5	2	0	1	0	3	2	0	1	0	2	0	2	1	1	1	2	0
2	3	1	1	2	0	5	0	0	0	0	2	1	1	0	1	1	0	1
2	4	2	1	1	2	2	1	0	2	0	1	0	0	2	2	2	1	1
1	3	2	0	1	0	6	2	1	1	1	2	1	2	2	0	2	0	1
0	1	1	0	0	1	1	0	1	0	1	1	0	0	1	0	1	1	1
0	5	2	1	2	2	3	1	2	2	1	6	1	1	1	0	0	0	1
1	5	0	1	2	1	0	2	0	1	2	0	0	1	2	1	2	2	1
2	2	0	0	0	0	3	1	1	2	2	2	0	2	1	2	0	2	1
1	1	1	1	0	2	4	2	2	1	0	1	1	0	0	1	0	1	1
0	0	0	0	1	1	3	0	2	0	2	0	1	2	0	1	1	2	1
0	1	2	1	0	2	6	0	0	0	2	1	0	2	1	2	2	0	2
1	2	2	0	2	2	4	2	0	0	0	1	1	0	2	0	1	2	2
0	1	0	0	2	1	6	1	0	2	2	2	0	1	1	0	2	1	2
2	0	2	1	0	0	1	2	2	1	1	0	1	1	0	1	2	1	2
1	3	0	1	2	0	3	1	1	0	1	0	0	0	0	0	0	2	2
1	4	1	1	1	0	3	0	2	1	2	2	1	0	1	2	0	2	2
0	3	1	0	1	2	3	1	2	1	0	0	1	1	2	2	1	0	2

2	5	1	0	1	1	0	0	1	2	0	1	0	2	2	1	0	1	2
2	5	0	1	0	1	2	2	1	2	1	2	1	2	0	1	1	0	2
2	1	1	1	2	1	3	1	2	1	1	2	1	0	2	2	0	0	3
2	1	2	1	0	1	3	0	2	0	0	0	0	2	2	0	0	2	3
0	5	1	0	0	0	2	0	0	1	2	2	1	0	0	0	2	0	3
1	0	1	0	2	2	6	1	0	0	1	2	0	1	2	1	1	1	3
1	5	2	0	0	2	3	1	1	2	0	0	0	1	0	2	1	2	3
1	2	0	1	1	1	5	2	1	1	0	1	1	0	1	2	2	0	3
0	4	0	0	2	0	0	2	2	2	1	1	1	2	1	0	1	1	3
2	3	0	1	1	2	1	2	0	0	2	1	1	1	1	1	0	2	3
0	3	2	1	1	0	4	0	1	2	2	0	0	2	0	1	2	1	3
0	1	2	0	1	2	3	2	1	1	2	1	0	1	0	0	1	0	4
2	2	2	1	2	1	6	0	1	2	1	0	1	0	0	2	1	1	4
0	5	0	1	1	0	3	0	0	0	1	1	1	0	2	1	0	0	4
2	0	1	0	0	2	2	2	0	2	2	0	1	0	1	0	0	2	4
1	3	0	1	2	2	1	0	2	2	0	2	1	2	1	0	2	2	4
1	5	2	1	0	1	5	2	2	0	2	2	0	1	2	2	0	1	4
1	3	1	0	0	0	0	1	3	0	0	1	0	2	0	2	2	0	4
0	4	1	1	1	1	4	1	1	1	1	2	0	1	1	1	1	0	4
2	1	0	0	2	0	3	1	0	1	0	0	1	2	2	1	2	1	4
2	1	1	0	1	0	1	1	1	2	1	1	1	1	2	2	2	2	5
0	0	1	1	2	1	3	2	1	0	0	1	0	2	1	1	0	0	5
0	4	2	1	0	0	5	2	0	0	1	0	1	2	2	2	1	2	5
1	5	0	1	0	2	3	1	0	1	1	1	1	2	0	0	1	1	5
0	3	0	1	2	2	2	0	1	1	0	2	0	1	0	2	0	1	5
1	2	1	0	0	1	3	0	0	2	0	0	1	1	1	1	2	0	5
2	5	2	0	2	0	4	1	2	0	2	2	0	0	1	0	2	0	5
1	1	2	1	1	2	0	0	2	2	2	2	1	0	0	1	1	2	5
2	3	0	0	1	1	6	2	2	1	2	0	0	0	2	0	0	1	5
1	5	1	0	1	2	5	0	1	1	1	0	1	2	1	0	0	1	6
1	3	2	1	0	0	3	1	0	2	1	1	0	0	1	1	0	1	6

(cont.)

Table 9.3. (*Cont.*)

car (with toll)				car (no toll)			train or bus						busway or light railway					
time	*depart*	*toll*	*fuel*	*time*	*parking*	*fuel*	*time*	*freq*	*acct*	*egt*	*fare*	*switch*	*time*	*freq*	*egt*	*fare*	*fare*	*block*
1	1	0	0	1	0	2	2	2	0	0	0	0	1	1	2	1	1	6
2	4	1	0	2	2	3	2	1	0	2	0	0	0	0	1	2	0	6
2	5	0	0	2	1	4	0	2	0	1	1	1	1	0	2	2	2	6
0	1	1	1	2	0	6	2	0	2	0	2	1	2	0	2	0	2	6
2	3	2	1	1	1	3	0	0	2	2	1	1	1	2	0	1	0	6
0	0	2	1	0	1	0	1	1	1	0	2	1	0	2	0	2	2	6
0	2	0	1	0	2	1	1	2	1	2	2	0	2	2	1	1	6	6
0	2	1	1	1	0	0	1	0	0	2	0	1	1	0	0	0	1	7
2	4	0	1	0	2	3	0	1	0	0	2	1	1	2	0	2	1	7
0	3	2	0	2	1	3	2	2	2	0	2	1	0	1	1	1	1	7
1	0	0	0	1	2	4	0	0	2	1	2	0	2	2	2	0	0	7
0	3	0	0	0	1	3	2	0	1	1	1	0	0	0	2	2	2	7
1	1	2	1	1	1	2	1	2	0	1	0	1	2	1	1	2	0	7
2	5	1	1	0	0	6	0	2	1	0	1	0	1	1	0	1	2	7
2	1	2	0	2	2	5	1	1	1	2	1	1	2	0	1	0	2	7
1	5	1	1	2	0	1	2	1	2	2	0	0	0	2	2	1	0	7
0	5	0	1	1	2	6	1	1	0	0	0	1	0	1	1	2	2	8
1	4	2	0	2	1	1	0	0	1	0	0	0	2	0	0	0	0	8
2	3	1	1	0	1	4	1	0	1	2	0	1	2	1	2	1	1	8
1	1	0	0	0	0	3	0	1	0	2	2	1	0	2	1	1	1	8
2	0	0	1	1	0	5	1	2	2	0	1	0	0	0	0	1	0	8
0	5	1	1	2	2	3	2	2	2	2	1	1	2	2	2	2	1	8
2	3	2	0	0	2	0	2	1	0	1	2	1	1	1	2	0	0	8
1	1	1	1	1	1	3	2	0	2	1	2	0	1	0	0	2	2	8
0	2	2	0	2	0	2	0	2	1	1	1	0	1	2	1	0	2	8

mode-choice mixes and numbers of weekly trips. Alternatively, it is possible to recognize that the mode-choice decision might be accompanied by a locational- or vehicle-choice decision and model the joint choices implied in such decisions. An important feature of the surveys was that the researchers deliberately designed them to allow the testing of violations of the IID error assumptions of simple choice models such as Multinomial Logit (MNL). Thus, if individuals use nested or hierarchical choice processes, we will be able to estimate these models from the data (discussed in chapters 13 and 14).

This starting experimental design was pre-tested in Australia and in California. The design proved problematic for a number of reasons. The most important concerns identified were associated with (1) the number of replications initially suggested, namely nine per respondent, drawn from 81 showcards, (2) the ability of a respondent to meaningfully identify their long-run actions, (3) the suitability of an essentially attitudinal question on support for how the revenue raised from a congestion toll might influence one's travel choice, and (4) the wording used in the contextual introduction and on each showcard. Concern was expressed about the length of the contextual statement and the reference to "future" scenarios without a clear statement as to when in the future and what assumptions does the respondent make about household conditions at this unknown future date. A number of the attributes were vague in respect of whether their levels referred to a one-way or a round trip. The access and egress trip times for public transport, expressed as walk times, were problematic for respondents who would use a motorized access/egress mode. Most importantly, with an interest in departure time-choice this design was unable to establish the influence that time-of-day road pricing (i.e. congestion pricing) might have on departure time-choice and hence peak spreading. Having a toll imposed without a time context is rather limiting.

Together with a number of more minor concerns the "first pass" experimental design was revised substantially for the pilot study.

9.3.1 Pilot sample collection

The sample census collection districts (CCDs) for metro Sydney were selected from a cumulative count of dwellings, by CCD, taken from the 1986 Census. From this cumulative list, the total number of dwellings for each particular region (e.g. Statistical Division) was divided by the number of CCDs (start points) required. This provided an interval between dwelling numbers. To determine the first start point or dwelling number, a random number between one and the interval size was selected. This random number represents a dwelling number. This gives an interval between dwelling numbers. The next dwelling and consequential CCD was selected by incrementing the dwelling number by the interval.

This process was then repeated for the number of start points (CCDs) required. Interviewing commenced at each start point and was continued until five interviews had been achieved.

9.3.1.1 Interviewer briefing

On April 15, 1994 an interviewer briefing for the pilot survey was held in Sydney. The field supervisor, field co-ordinator, project director, ITS, and the interviewers who were conducting the pilot interviews were all present. A full set of briefing notes was provided by ITS. The interview briefing was held to ensure that the interviewers knew exactly what the study was about, how they were to conduct the interview, and how the respondents were supposed to complete the additional questionnaires which were left with them.

Each of the questions in the home interview was reviewed thoroughly and all questions from the interviewers were answered. The choice modeling and choice sets were reviewed carefully and questions were answered by the representative from ITS.

Once the questionnaires were reviewed a practice interview was conducted with all the interviewers.

9.3.1.2 Interviewing

Interviewing was carried out face-to-face using a home interview questionnaire. This was completed by a member of the household who was responsible for making decisions on where the household lived and what vehicle they purchased. The home interview took approximately 45 minutes to be completed. The household and commuter questionnaires were left for the respondent to complete and then were picked up approximately three days later by the same interviewer who left them.

For the pilot study, all respondent households had to have a member who commuted to a regular place of work, although in the final study 10 percent could be a non-commuting household.

Interviews began on Saturday April 16 and were completed by Thursday April 21, 1994.

9.3.1.3 Analysis of contacts

The 13 interviewers each completed five interviews in the pilot study except for one interviewer who completed only three interviews. A total of 58 interviews were conducted. In order to obtain these 58 interviews there were a total of 809 door knocks; 404 of those were unusable for reasons such as not being home or there was no access to the dwelling. There were 391 people not home at the time of the interviewing and 13 where there was no access to the dwelling, such as a locked gate.

There were 405 total contacts which includes those interviews which were terminated for the following reasons: the eligible person was away at the time of the interview (a child was home), there was contact but the qualified person (commuter) was not there, refusal to participate, too busy to complete the interview, or the household did not speak English; 118 were made where the household was not qualified to complete the interview, such as an elderly couple who do not commute. There were four questionnaires deemed to be unreliable due to the responses to questions such as having an income of Au $1 million and living in a lower-income location. The contact, but no access, occurred five times, which meant there was contact made but the interviewer was not able to gain access, due to a security intercom system, for example.

Of those 405 contacts there were 158 households who refused to complete the home interview which is a refusal rate of 39 percent. The response rate was therefore 14 percent – that is, 58 completed questionnaires out of 405 total contacts.

9.3.1.4 Interviewer debriefing

On April 21, 1994, the interviewers, field supervisor, field co-ordinator, coding and data processing managers, project director and the ITS representative reconvened for a debrief of the pilot survey.

The interviewers were each given the chance to discuss issues regarding the interview process, the questionnaires, wording of the questionnaires etc. within the meeting. Problems were discussed and suggestions made on the most effective manner in which the problems could be resolved. The skips and logic of the questionnaire were also discussed and changes made where appropriate.

There was no coding or data entry undertaken on the returned data. The data were not being used in the full study, therefore it was unnecessary to follow through to the coding, editing and data entry stages. However, the coding and editing co-ordinators had a great deal of input into the pilot study. They confirmed that all the questions were coded with the right numbers, "other specifics" were completed correctly and questionnaire logic was correct.

Very few changes were made to the survey instruments as a result of the pilot survey. Minor changes were made to the wording of the introduction of the home interview questionnaire and some revision was made to the multiple-option responses to some questions as a result of pilot responses. The only problem which emerged from the pilot was concern over securing completed self-completion questionnaires. So as to ensure that key data items were obtained, the question on the number of kilometers traveled by each household vehicle was added to the home interview questionnaire (as well as being left in the household questionnaire for cross-reference purposes). The question on the commuter's travel patterns to work over the past seven days, a rich source of data for the commuter's departure-timechoice model, was also moved from the commuter questionnaire to the home interview questionnaire as it was found that in a self-completion mode respondents had difficulty following through this question. The experience of the main survey proved that this was a correct decision, as the question worked very well in the interview situation.

The consistency of the responses to the stated choice questions was also carefully checked. The researchers were satisfied that they had been administered correctly by the interviewers and answered validly. The only change made to either the questions or the showcards was a modification of the registration fee for alternative fueled vehicles, which was considered to be too high.

9.4 The main survey

Data for the main survey was collected by means of three survey instruments: an interviewer-administered home interview and two self-completion questionnaires which were left with the respondent and collected a few days later. The two self-completion questionnaires were a general questionnaire called the household questionnaire and a questionnaire specifically for a household commuter called a commuter questionnaire.

There was a considerable amount of detailed data relating to the household's vehicle fleet and the commuting patterns of one member of the household which had to be collected in this survey. There were also two stated choice experiments, one on the modal- and departure time-choices of a household commuter (i.e. the mode-choice experiment) and one on the vehicle purchasing preferences of the household (i.e. the vehicle-choice experiment). This was too much data to be collected by any one survey instrument. There was certainly too much information to be collected in a telephone interview and the complex stated-choice experiments could not be administered in that manner. There was also too much data to be collected in one face-to-face interview as interviews in excess of 45–60 minutes are difficult to secure.

Given these difficulties, the above strategy was employed for a number of reasons. The initial proposal of contacting respondents first with a telephone interview and then inviting them to take part in a home interview and accept some self-completion questionnaires was abandoned on the advice of the survey firm. They believed that, based on experience, it would be more efficient to secure the required response rate by randomly seeking the home interview as the first contact with respondents. It was felt that there was too much opportunity for respondents to later refuse the home interview and the self-completion questionnaires, even if they had previously agreed to this, and would ensure that the most important data were collected at the initial point of contact. Supplementary information which was either too detailed to be collected at the home interview or which had to be left out of that questionnaire in order to keep it within a manageable time frame, was asked for in the two self-completion questionnaires which were left with the respondent.

The complete questionnaire covered a number of topics and was divided into six sections:

Section 1:	Your vehicles	The number and type of vehicles in the household
Section 2:	Vehicles and the environment issue	Opinions and awareness of greenhouse gases
Section 3:	Where you live	Reasons why the household lives at this location
Section 4:	Your trip to work	Some choices on options of traveling to work
Section 5:	Buying a vehicle	Some choices of purchasing vehicles
Section 6:	About you	Socio-economic questions

The aim of the questionnaire was to collect sufficient data on the household's *vehicle fleet* to determine the number and type of vehicles in the household. More detailed information on those vehicles was collected in the household self-administered questionnaire. Essential data to map the household vehicles into the population of vehicle data bases was sought in the first section.

This section was followed by some general questions about the respondent's knowledge and perceptions of *environmental problems*, including the GGE. This information was used to provide an understanding of the overall level of community awareness of the GGE problem, which assisted in identifying needs for a community education program.

The third section asked questions about the household's *residential location*. Specifically, how long had respondents lived in the area, what were the main reasons they chose to live in that area, and were they considering moving; and, if so, why? This data were needed for a residential location model to explain what factors influenced the choice made by households as to where to live.

The fourth section turned to the collecting of data on the *journey to work* for regular commuters. The respondent who answered this section was required to make regular commutes to a place of work for either full-time or part-time employment. Of note, the respondent of this section may not necessarily have been the same respondent for the other sections of the questionnaire if that person was not a regular commuter at the time of the survey. Thus the potential existed for two respondents completing the questionnaire, a primary respondent who answered sections 1, 2, 3, 5, and 6 and a commuting respondent who answered section 4.

The fourth section of the survey began by asking the commuter questions about their work and travel pattern over the previous seven days. This provided information on the regularity and variations around the regular pattern of respondents commuting activity which comprised an important input for the departure time-choice model.

9.4.1 The mode-choice experiment

The fourth section of the survey also included the refined stated preference mode-choice experiment. As with the pilot experiment, to initiate this experiment the trip length in terms of travel time relevant for each respondent's current commuting trip was first established so that the travel choices could be given in a context which had some reality for the respondent. The travel choice sets were divided into trip lengths of:

Less than 30 minutes	Short trip
30–45 minutes	Medium trip
Over 45 minutes	Long trip

In participating in the choice experiments, each respondent was asked to consider a context in which the offered set of attributes and levels represented the only available means of undertaking a commuter trip from the current residential location to the current workplace location. It was made clear that the purpose was to establish each respondent's *coping strategies* under these circumstances.

Four alternatives appear in each mode choice scenario; *car no toll*, *car toll road*, *bus or busway*, and *train or light rail* (hereafter referred to as *LR*). The five attributes for the public transport alternatives are in-vehicle time, frequency of service, closest stop to home, closest stop to destination, and fare. The attributes for the *car* alternatives are *travel time*, *fuel cost*, *parking cost*, *travel time variability*, and, for the toll road, *departure time* and *toll charge*. Three levels were selected for each attribute. The design allows for six alternative specific main effect models for *car no toll*, *car toll road*, *bus*, *busway*, *train*, and *light rail*.

SA101	1. *car, toll road*		2. *car, non-toll road*	
Travel time to work	10 min.		15 min.	
Time variability	None		None	
Toll (one way)	$1.00		Free	
Pay toll if you leave at this time (otherwise free)	6–10 am		–	
Fuel cost (per day)	$1.00		$3.00	
Parking cost (per day)	Free		Free	
	3. *bus*		4. *train*	
Total time in the vehicle (one way)	10 min.		10 min.	
Time from home to your closest stop	Walk	Car/Bus	Walk	Car/Bus
	5 min.	4 min.	5 min.	4 min.
Time to your destination from the closest stop	Walk	Bus	Walk	Bus
	5 min.	4 min.	5 min.	4 min.
Frequency of service	Every 5 min.		Every 5 min.	
Return fare	$1.00		$1.00	

Figure 9.2 Example of the format of the mode-choice experiment showcard

Linear by linear interactions are estimable for both *car* models, and generically for the *bus/busway* and *train/light rail* models. While cross-effects have been assumed negligible, the four-alternative design is perfectly balanced across all attributes.

Four alternatives appeared in each travel choice scenario: (a) *car (no toll)*, (b) *car (toll)*, (c) *bus or busway*, and (d) *train or light rail*. Twelve types of showcards described scenarios involving combinations of trip length (3) and public transport pairs (4): *bus* vs *light rail*, *bus* vs *train* (*heavy rail*), *busway* vs *light rail*, and *busway* vs *train*. Appearance of public transport pairs in each card shown to respondents was based on an experimental design. Attribute levels are summarized in table 9.4 and an illustrative showcard is displayed in figure 9.2. The contextual statement for the mode choice experiment is given in appendix 9A.

The master design for the travel choice task was a $27 \times 3^{20} \times 2^{2}$ orthogonal fractional factorial, which produced 81 scenarios or choice sets. The 27-level factor was used to block the design into 27 versions, each with three choice sets containing the four alternatives. Versions were balanced such that each respondent saw every level of each attribute exactly once. The 3^{20} portion of the master design is an orthogonal main effects design, which permits independent estimation of all effects of interest. The two two-level attributes were used to describe *bus/busway* and *train/light rail* modes, such that *bus/train* options appear in 36 scenarios and *busway/light rail* in 45. Given the method used to determine which public transport methods were present within a choice set, the *bus and LR* and *train and busway* alternatives never appeared within the same choice set. Table 9.5 shows the 81 treatment combinations of the experimental design. Table 9.6 shows the correlation matrix for this design (the correlation matrix is for linear effects only). Note that there exist small

Table 9.4. *The set of attributes and attribute levels in the mode-choice experiment*

All cost items are in Australian $, all time items are in minutes

short (<30 mins.)	*car no toll*	*car toll rd*	*public transport*	*bus*	*train*	*busway*	*light rail*
Travel time to work	15, 20, 25	10, 12, 15	Total time in the vehicle (one-way)	10, 15, 20	10, 15, 20	10, 15, 20	10, 15, 20
Pay toll if you leave at this time (otherwise free)	None	6–10, 6:30–8:30, 6:30–9	Frequency of service	Every 5, 15, 25	Every 5, 15, 25	Every 5, 15, 25	Every 5, 15, 25
Toll (one-way)	None	1, 1.5, 2	Time from home to closest stop	Walk 5, 15, 25	Walk 5, 15, 25	Walk 5, 15, 25	Walk 5, 15, 25
Fuel cost (per day)	3, 4, 5	1, 2, 3	Time to destination from closest stop	Walk 5, 15, 25	Walk 5, 15, 25	Walk 5, 15, 25	Walk 5, 15, 25
Parking cost (per day)	Free, $10, 20	Free, $10, 20	Return fare	1, 3, 5	1, 3, 5	1, 3, 5	1, 3, 5
Time variability	0, ±4, ±6	0,±1,±2					
medium (30–45 mins.)	*car no toll*	*car toll rd*	*public transport*	*bus*	*train*	*busway*	*light rail*
Travel time to work	30, 37, 45	20, 25, 30	Total time in the vehicle (one-way)	20, 25, 30	20, 25, 30	20, 25, 30	20, 25, 30
Pay toll if you leave at this time (otherwise free)	None	6–10, 6:30–8:30, 6:30–9	Frequency of service	Walk 5, 15, 25	Walk 5, 15, 25	Walk 5, 15, 25	Walk 5, 15, 25
Toll (one-way)	None	2, 3, 4	Time from home to closest stop	Walk 5, 15, 25	Walk 5, 15, 25	Walk 5, 15, 25	Walk 5, 15, 25
Fuel cost (per day)	6, 8, 10	2, 4, 6	Time to destination from closest stop	Walk 5, 15, 25	Walk 5, 15, 25	Walk 5, 15, 25	Walk 5, 15, 25
				Bus 4, 6, 8	Bus 4, 6, 8	Bus 4, 6, 8	Bus 4, 6, 8
Parking cost (per day)	Free, $10, 20	Free, $10, 20	Return fare	2, 4, 6	2, 4, 6	2, 4, 6	2, 4, 6
Time variability	0, ±7, ±11	0, ±2, ±4					
long (>45 mins.)	*car no toll*	*car toll rd*	*public transport*	*bus*	*train*	*busway*	*light rail*
Travel time to work	45, 55, 70	30, 37, 45	Total time in the vehicle (one-way)	30, 35, 40	30, 35, 40	30, 35, 40	30, 35, 40
Pay toll if you leave at this time (otherwise free)	None	6–10, 6:30–8:30, 6:30–9	Frequency of service	Walk 5, 15, 25	Walk 5, 15, 25	Walk 5, 15, 25	Walk 5, 15, 25
Toll (one-way)	None	3, 4.5, 6	Time from home to closest stop	Walk 5, 15, 25	Walk 5, 15, 25	Walk 5, 15, 25	Walk 5, 15, 25
Fuel cost (per day)	9, 12, 15	3, 6, 9	Time to destination from closest stop	Walk 5, 15, 25	Walk 5, 15, 25	Walk 5, 15, 25	Walk 5, 15, 25
				Bus 4, 6, 8	Bus 4, 6, 8	Bus 4, 6, 8	Bus 4, 6, 8
Parking cost (per day)	Free, $10, 20	Free, $10, 20	Return fare	3, 5, 7	3, 5, 7	3, 5, 7	3, 5, 7
Time variability	0, ±11, ±17	0, ±7, ±11					

Table 9.5. *Mode-choice experimental design*

car (no toll)				*car (toll)*						*bus/busway*					*train/light rail*							
time	*fuel*	*parking*	*timevar*	*time*	*tollpred*	*toll*	*fuel*	*parking*	*timevar*	*time*	*freq*	*acctime*	*egtime*	*fare*	*time*	*freq*	*acctime*	*egtime*	*fare*	*Switch1*	*Switch2*	*block*
0	0	0	0	0	0	0	0	0	0	0	0	0	0	0	0	0	0	0	0	0	0	0
2	2	2	2	2	2	2	2	2	2	1	1	1	1	1	1	1	1	1	1	1	1	0
1	1	1	1	1	1	1	1	1	1	2	2	2	2	2	2	2	2	2	2	1	0	0
2	1	1	2	2	2	2	1	2	2	0	2	2	2	0	0	0	0	0	0	1	0	1
0	2	2	0	0	0	0	2	0	0	2	1	1	1	2	2	2	2	2	2	1	1	1
1	0	0	1	1	1	1	0	1	1	1	0	0	0	1	1	1	1	1	1	0	0	1
2	0	0	2	2	2	2	0	2	2	2	0	0	0	2	2	2	2	2	2	0	1	2
1	2	2	1	1	1	1	2	1	1	0	1	1	1	0	0	0	0	0	0	1	1	2
0	1	1	0	0	0	0	1	0	0	1	2	2	2	1	1	1	1	1	1	0	1	2
0	1	0	1	1	2	0	1	1	2	1	1	0	1	0	1	0	0	2	2	0	1	3
2	0	2	0	0	1	2	0	0	1	2	2	1	2	1	2	1	1	0	0	0	1	3
1	2	1	2	2	0	1	2	2	0	0	0	2	0	2	0	2	2	1	1	1	1	3
0	0	2	1	1	2	0	0	1	2	0	2	1	2	2	0	2	2	1	1	0	0	4
2	2	1	0	0	1	2	2	0	1	1	0	2	0	0	1	0	0	2	2	1	1	4
1	1	0	2	2	0	1	1	2	0	2	1	0	1	1	2	1	1	0	0	1	0	4
2	1	0	0	0	1	2	1	0	1	0	1	0	1	2	0	2	2	1	1	1	0	5
1	0	2	2	2	0	1	0	2	0	1	2	1	2	0	1	0	0	2	2	0	0	5
0	2	1	1	1	2	0	2	1	2	2	0	2	0	1	2	1	1	0	0	1	1	5
1	0	1	0	0	2	1	0	0	2	1	1	2	1	2	1	2	2	0	0	0	0	6
0	2	0	2	2	1	0	2	2	1	2	2	0	2	0	2	0	0	1	1	1	1	6
2	1	2	1	1	0	2	1	1	0	0	0	1	0	1	0	1	1	2	2	1	0	6
2	0	1	1	1	0	2	0	1	0	2	1	2	1	0	2	0	0	1	1	0	1	7
1	2	0	0	0	2	1	2	0	2	0	2	0	2	1	0	1	1	2	2	1	1	7
0	1	2	2	2	1	0	1	2	1	1	0	1	0	2	1	2	2	0	0	0	1	7
0	0	1	2	2	1	0	0	2	1	0	1	2	1	1	0	1	1	2	2	0	0	8
1	1	2	0	0	2	1	1	0	2	2	0	1	0	0	2	0	0	1	1	1	0	8
2	2	0	1	1	0	2	2	1	0	1	2	0	2	2	1	2	2	0	0	1	1	8

2	2	0	0	2	2	0	0	1	0	0	0	2	1	1	1	2	0	2	0	1	0	9
0	0	1	1	0	0	1	1	2	1	2	2	1	0	0	0	1	2	1	2	1	1	9
1	1	2	2	1	1	2	2	0	2	1	1	0	2	2	2	0	1	0	1	0	0	9
0	2	0	1	0	0	1	0	2	1	1	0	2	1	2	2	0	1	0	1	1	0	10
1	0	1	2	1	1	2	1	0	2	0	2	1	0	1	1	2	0	2	0	1	1	10
2	1	2	0	2	2	0	2	1	0	2	1	0	2	0	0	1	2	1	2	0	0	10
0	1	2	1	0	0	1	2	2	1	0	1	0	2	1	1	2	0	2	0	0	1	11
2	0	1	0	2	2	0	1	1	0	1	2	1	0	2	2	0	1	0	1	1	1	11
1	2	0	2	1	1	2	0	0	2	2	0	2	1	0	0	1	2	1	2	0	1	11
2	0	0	1	0	1	0	1	2	2	1	1	2	2	1	2	2	0	1	2	1	1	12
0	1	1	2	1	2	1	2	0	0	0	0	1	1	0	1	1	2	0	1	0	1	12
1	2	2	0	2	0	2	0	1	1	2	2	0	0	2	0	0	1	2	0	0	1	12
2	2	2	1	0	1	0	0	2	2	0	2	0	0	0	1	1	2	0	1	1	0	13
1	1	1	0	2	0	2	2	1	1	1	0	1	1	1	2	2	0	1	2	0	0	13
0	0	0	2	1	2	1	1	0	0	2	1	2	2	2	0	0	1	2	0	1	1	13
1	0	0	0	2	0	2	1	1	1	0	1	2	2	0	1	1	2	0	1	1	1	14
0	2	2	2	1	2	1	0	0	0	1	2	0	0	1	2	2	0	1	2	1	0	14
2	1	1	1	0	1	0	2	2	2	2	0	1	1	2	0	0	1	2	0	0	0	14
0	2	1	0	2	1	1	0	1	2	1	1	1	2	0	2	1	2	2	0	1	0	15
2	1	0	2	1	0	0	2	0	1	2	2	2	0	1	0	2	0	0	1	0	0	15
1	0	2	1	0	2	2	1	2	0	0	0	0	1	2	1	0	1	1	2	1	1	15
1	2	1	1	0	2	2	0	2	0	2	1	1	2	1	0	2	0	0	1	0	1	16
0	1	0	0	2	1	1	2	1	2	0	2	2	0	2	1	0	1	1	2	0	1	16
2	0	2	2	1	0	0	1	0	1	1	0	0	1	0	2	1	2	2	0	1	1	16
0	0	2	0	2	1	1	1	1	2	2	0	0	1	1	0	2	0	0	1	1	1	17
1	1	0	1	0	2	2	2	2	0	1	2	2	0	0	2	1	2	2	0	0	0	17
2	2	1	2	1	0	0	0	0	1	0	1	1	2	2	1	0	1	1	2	1	0	17
1	1	0	0	1	1	0	0	2	0	0	0	1	2	2	2	1	0	1	0	1	1	18
0	0	2	2	0	0	2	2	1	2	1	1	2	0	0	0	2	1	2	1	1	0	18
2	2	1	1	2	2	1	1	0	1	2	2	0	1	1	1	0	2	0	2	0	0	18
2	1	0	1	2	2	1	0	0	1	1	0	1	2	0	0	2	1	2	1	1	1	19
1	0	2	0	1	1	0	2	2	0	2	1	2	0	1	1	0	2	0	2	1	0	19

(*cont.*)

Table 9.5. (*Cont.*)

car (no toll)				*car (toll)*						*bus/busway*					*train/light rail*							
time	*fuel*	*parking*	*timevar*	*time*	*tollpred*	*toll*	*fuel*	*parking*	*timevar*	*time*	*freq*	*acctime*	*egtime*	*fare*	*time*	*freq*	*acctime*	*egtime*	*fare*	*Switch1*	*Switch2*	*block*
0	2	1	2	0	0	2	1	1	2	0	2	0	1	2	2	1	0	1	0	0	0	19
1	2	1	0	1	1	0	1	2	0	1	2	0	1	0	0	2	1	2	1	0	1	20
0	1	0	2	0	0	2	0	1	2	2	0	1	2	1	1	0	2	0	2	1	1	20
2	0	2	1	2	2	1	2	0	1	0	1	2	0	2	2	1	0	1	0	0	1	20
0	1	2	0	1	2	2	0	2	1	2	2	2	1	0	1	2	1	1	0	1	1	21
1	2	0	1	2	0	0	1	0	2	1	1	1	0	2	0	1	0	0	2	0	1	21
2	0	1	2	0	1	1	2	1	0	0	0	0	2	1	2	0	2	2	1	0	1	21
0	0	1	0	1	2	2	2	2	1	1	0	0	2	2	0	1	0	0	2	1	0	22
2	2	0	2	0	1	1	1	1	0	2	1	1	0	0	1	2	1	1	0	0	0	22
1	1	2	1	2	0	0	0	0	2	0	2	2	1	1	2	0	2	2	1	1	1	22
2	1	2	2	0	1	1	0	1	0	1	2	2	1	2	0	1	0	0	2	1	1	23
1	0	1	1	2	0	0	2	0	2	2	0	0	2	0	1	2	1	1	0	1	0	23
0	2	0	0	1	2	2	1	2	1	0	1	1	0	1	2	0	2	2	1	0	0	23
2	1	1	0	1	0	1	0	2	2	1	1	0	0	1	0	0	2	1	0	1	1	24
1	0	0	2	0	2	0	2	1	1	2	2	1	1	2	1	1	0	2	1	1	0	24
0	2	2	1	2	1	2	1	0	0	0	0	2	2	0	2	2	1	0	2	0	0	24
0	1	1	1	2	1	2	0	0	0	2	1	0	0	2	1	1	0	2	1	1	1	25
2	0	0	0	1	0	1	2	2	2	0	2	1	1	0	2	2	1	0	2	0	1	25
1	2	2	2	0	2	0	1	1	1	1	0	2	2	1	0	0	2	1	0	0	1	25
2	2	2	0	1	0	1	1	2	2	2	0	2	2	2	1	1	0	2	1	0	0	26
0	0	0	1	2	1	2	2	0	0	1	2	1	1	1	0	0	2	1	0	1	0	26
1	1	1	2	0	2	0	0	1	1	0	1	0	0	0	2	2	1	0	2	1	1	26

Note: To determine whether the choice set has *bus/busway* or *train/light rail* present, the switch factors must be considered concurrently.
Switch1 = 0, Switch2 = 0: bus and train present; Switch1 = 0, Switch2 = 1: bus and busway present;
Switch1 = 1, Switch2 = 0: train and light rail present; Switch1 = 1, Switch2 = 1: busway and light rail present.

Table 9.6. *Correlation matrix for mode-choice experimental design*

	car (no toll)				car (toll)						bus/busway					train/light railway							
	time	*fuel*	*parking*	*timevar*	*time*	*tollpred*	*toll*	*fuel*	*parking*	*timevar*	*time*	*freq*	*acctime*	*egtime*	*fare*	*time*	*freq*	*acctime*	*egtime*	*fare*	*PTmode1*	*PTmode2*	*block*
time	1																						
fuel	0	1																					
parking	0	0	1																				
timevar	0	0	0	1																			
time	0	0	0	0	1																		
tollpred	0	0	0	0	0	1																	
toll	0	0	0	0	0	0	1																
fuel	0	0	0	0	0	0	0	1															
parking	0	0	0	0	0	0	0	0	1														
timevar	0	0	0	0	0	0	0	0	0	1													
time	0	0	0	0	0	0	0	0	0	0	1												
freq	0	0	0	0	0	0	0	0	0	0	0	1											
acctime	0	0	0	0	0	0	0	0	0	0	0	0	1										
egtime	0	0	0	0	0	0	0	0	0	0	0	0	0	1									
fare	0	0	0	0	0	0	0	0	0	0	0	0	0	0	1								
time	0	0	0	0	0	0	0	0	0	0	0	0	0	0	0	1							
freq	0	0	0	0	0	0	0	0	0	0	0	0	0	0	0	0	1						
acctime	0	0	0	0	0	0	0	0	0	0	0	0	0	0	0	0	0	1					
egtime	0	0	0	0	0	0	0	0	0	0	0	0	0	0	0	0	0	0	1				
fare	0	0	0	0	0	0	0	0	0	0	0	0	0	0	0	0	0	0	0	1			
PTmode1	−6.7E-18	−6.7E-18	0	0	0	0	−6.7E-18	−6.7E-18	0	0	−6.7E-18	−6.7E-18	−6.7E-18	−6.7E-18	0	−6.7E-18	0	0	0	0	1		
PTmode2	−6.7E-18	−6.7E-18	0	0	0	0	−6.7E-18	−6.7E-18	0	0	−6.7E-18	0	0	0	0	−6.7E-18	0	0	0	0	0	1	
block	0	0	0	0	0	0	0	0	0	0	0	0	0	0	0	0	0	0	0	0	5.6E-18	8.4E-18	1

correlations among some of the attributes, however, these are so small as to be considered equal to zero.

9.4.1.1 Detailed description of attributes

In the experiment, respondents are asked to consider their daily commute trip. The aim of the experiment is to test a range of instruments for altering mode and departure time choice. There were 12 types of showcards, with three trip lengths and four combinations of public transport. The public transport combinations are: *bus* vs *light rail*, *bus* vs *train* (*heavy rail*), *busway* vs *light rail*, and *busway* vs *train*. The trip length showcards were printed in different colors for ease of use by interviewers when matching respondents' current trip lengths with those on the showcards. The four public transport combinations appeared in each showcard with incidence determined by the statistical design.

travel time to work

There were three different sets of showcards representing short (under 30 minutes), medium (30–45 minutes), and long (45 minutes and over) commutes. These were matched to the commute times currently experienced by respondents. Within each set of showcards, there were three levels of travel times. All public transport options had the same levels as each other, allowing for different combinations across the public transport pairs in each replication. Having the levels the same enables the analyst to investigate the influence that image (through the mode-specific constants) plays in determining preferences within the public transport modes after allowing for the influence of the balanced set of attributes and levels in the design. Travel times on the tolled road were selected so that it is never worse than the time on the non-tolled route.

pay toll if you leave at this time (otherwise free)

The tolled route option had a toll only at peak congestion times. The peak over which the toll applied was varied to determine what impact a short, medium, and long toll period would have on mode and departure time decisions.

toll (one-way)

The toll alternative applied only to the tolled routes when the respondent's commute trip commenced within the times specified by the previous variable. There were three levels of toll for each travel time set, with toll levels increasing for the longer travel time sets. Tolls in excess of current tolls in the Sydney metropolitan area were included to assess the impact of increases beyond the then-current levels in one city. The toll on the M4 (M standing for Motorway) in Sydney was at the time $1.50 for a car and $2 on the then-completed section of the M5. At the time it was anticipated that the toll for the M5 would increase to $4 when the second section was completed. Tolls in the experiment vary from $1 to $6.

fuel cost (per day)

Fuel cost was varied from the current levels to a tripling of the current levels to assess possible changes commuters would make as a response to large increases in fuel prices.

The daily fuel cost for the commute trip on the tolled road was assumed to be equal to or lower than that experienced on the non-tolled route. Fuel costs were allowed up to $15 per day for trips in excess of 45 minutes on a free route, representing a tripling of fuel prices.

parking cost (per day)

Another method for reducing the attractiveness of private vehicle use, particularly in central city areas, is to increase parking charges. Three levels of parking charge were used in the experiment to see how sensitive respondents were to parking costs. A fixed set of charges ranging from free to $20 were evaluated.

travel time variability

This attribute was calculated for private vehicle modes only, with levels based on 0, ±20 percent, and ±30 percent of the average trip time on "no-toll" roads, and 0, ±5 percent, and ±10 percent of the average trip time for "tolled routes." Toll roads were always equal to or better than non-tolled roads on trip reliability.

total time in the vehicle (one-way)

For public transport only, this attribute referred to the time spent traveling on a train, bus, light rail, or busway. There were three travel time sets to match those of private vehicles. Only two public transport systems were compared or traded off at once to make the experiment more realistic for the respondent. Thus, there were four sets of public transport combinations, listed above, any other combinations being not meaningful. All public transport options shared the same experimental levels, enabling the investigation of the role of image in respondent's preferences.

frequency of service

This variable gave the number of minutes between each service, and had three levels. The frequency for all modes had a range from a low of 5 minutes to a high of 25 minutes.

time from home to your closest stop

The distance from the respondent's home to the public transport stop, in minutes, is measured in both walk time and time traveling by a motorized form of transport. The respondent was asked to indicate which means of access they would us if they were to use public transport. There are three levels: 5, 15, and 25 minutes walk time, and 4, 6, and 8 minutes by a motorized mode. This same logic is applied to the *time to your destination from the closest stop*, except that the only motorized mode available is bus. It is very rare that a commuter will use a car to complete a trip after alighting from public transport. The taxi option is excluded.

return fare

This variable gives the return fare in dollars. This has three levels, with the same fare sets being used for all public transport modes for each trip length.

9.4.1.2 Using the showcards

The experimental design shown in table 9.5 was used for each of the three trip lengths such that the attribute levels of the design were assigned different attribute-level labels dependent upon the trip length reported by the respondent. These were color coded as Short trip – pink cards, Medium trip – green cards, and Long trip – yellow cards, for easy identification by the interviewers in the field. The 81 choices for each trip length were grouped into 27 sets of three. These were numbered for example S01A, S01B, and S01C to S27A, S27B, and S27C. The prefix S, M, or L was given to identify the trip length. So that the interviewers did not have to carry 81 $\times$ 3 cards in the field to all interviews, each interviewer was given a field kit containing three sets of each trip length from which they were instructed to randomly select one relevant set, according to trip length, for each respondent. This procedure also increased the probability of each set being used, thus increasing the variation of choices offered across the sample.

The interviewer was instructed to first establish the trip length of the respondent, and then to select at random one set of choice cards from the three that were given for that trip length. For example, if it was a long trip the set selected might be L17A, L17B, and L17C. The respondent was then shown these choices one at a time and asked to consider the attributes and select their most preferred option for their trip to work. Respondents were not given the option of not making a choice, as it was explained that these were to be considered as long-run situations and that given that they had to continue to go to work, they had to choose one of these packages of traveling. Interviewers were briefed to rotate the administering of the order of the cards so as to reduce *order bias* which might have been introduced if they had always been administered in the A, B, and C order.

The respondent was also asked some additional questions about the travel choices to clarify the reasoning behind their decision. They were asked to indicate how they considered they would get from their home to the public transport choices, either walk or drive/catch a car/bus, and from the public transport to their workplace, either walk or catch a bus. They were also asked that if they had chosen to go by car they would have traveled alone or shared the ride. There were also some questions to determine the impact of the choice made by the respondent on their workplace location and residential location, and on their departure time for work.

9.4.2 RP data

As part of the study protocol, each respondent was asked about their current commute experience to work. So as to remain consistent across respondents, the "current commute" was defined as the last commute to work undertaken. As well as gathering information on the attribute levels of their last mode used, defined as the primary mode, the questionnaire also asked respondents to intimate the attribute levels of a single alternative means of traveling to work as perceived by that respondent. This second mode was deemed the alternative mode.

The above survey strategy was employed to capture RP data such that information on at least one non-chosen alternative per respondent was captured. While it would have been better to capture information on all non-chosen alternatives, to do so, it was felt, would place an increased burden upon respondents in terms of time and cognitive effort required to complete the questionnaire. As such, the above represented a compromize solution that allowed in the aggregate for information to be gathered on all non-chosen alternatives while reducing respondent burden in completing the questionnaire.

The alternatives present for the RP task were somewhat different to those of the SP choice experiment. Given that the *busway* and *light rail* alternatives did not exist at the time, these alternatives were not present within the set of alternatives for the RP data. Further, the *toll* and *no-toll privately owned vehicle* alternatives were classified as *drive alone* (*DA*) or *ride share* (*RS*). Also present in the RP task but not in the SP task were the alternatives of *walk* and "*other*" mode.

9.4.3 The household questionnaire

The household questionnaire could be completed by any adult member of the household. There were three sections in this questionnaire. Section 1 asked for information on the household's use of taxis and other public transport. Section 2 expanded the information collected on the vehicles in the household to add to the basic details which were obtained in the home interview. Section 3 contained questions on each member in the household to give a profile of the household life cycle stage.

Section 2 asked for detailed information on all the vehicles in the household, information which required the respondent to check their financial records and perhaps consult with other members of the household and was thus considered to be inappropriate to ask in the home interview. In that interview, we had ordered the vehicles in the household as Vehicle 1, Vehicle 2, etc., starting with the vehicle which had been in the household the longest. So that we were sure that the order was consistent in the household questionnaire with that assigned in the home interview we asked the interviewers to record the first four data items for each vehicle – i.e. make, model, year came into the household, and year of manufacture – for each vehicle in the household questionnaire, leaving the respondent to complete the remainder of the details.

9.4.4 The commuter questionnaire

The commuter questionnaire had to be completed by a member of the household who was a regular commuter to a set workbase location for either full- or part-time employment. It could not be someone who traveled around to different workplaces (for example, a self-employed tradesperson). This commuter also had to be the same person that answered section 4 in the home interview questionnaire which contained the travel choice questions.

The commuting respondent was identified by their person number, as assigned in the household questionnaire. There were five sections to this questionnaire. Section 1 contained some general opinion questions relating to environmental issues and possible policy actions as well as some questions on possible lifestyle changes considered by the respondent.

Section 2 was a short section, with a few questions about the respondent's work situation. Section 3 was an important section, collecting details of the respondent's trip to work and the most likely alternative means by which they would make that trip. Section 4 explored the issues of flexible working arrangements, such as compressed work weeks and telecommuting, and the degree of flexibility available to the commuter in terms of their start and finish times. Section 5 was also a short section, with a couple of questions relating to the availability of parking at the commuter's workplace. The questionnaire concluded with the commuter's personal income.

9.4.5 The sample

The targeted sample size is given in table 9.7, by capital city.

A national survey firm was contracted to supply 1400 completed interviews with the sample distribution by capital city as set out in table 9.7. A completed interview required the three questionnaires of the survey being complete for each household – that is, the home interview questionnaire, the household questionnaire, and the commuter questionnaire. ITS decided which were the key data items to be completed for the interview to be counted as acceptable.

The sample was a stratified random sample of households according to the vehicle fleet size. The survey firm was supplied with ABS data on household fleet size in the categories "zero vehicles, 1 vehicle, 2 vehicles and 3 or more vehicles" for households at a statistical sub-division level for each of the metropolitan areas to be surveyed. Except that for Brisbane it was not appropriate to use the statistical sub-divisions sub-area classification because one statistical sub-division (Brisbane City) includes most of the metropolitan area of Brisbane. The sub-area classification to be used for Brisbane was statistical regions. From this tabulation, the number of target interviews to be conducted in each sub-area was calculated. Table 9.8 summarizes the target interviews in each urban area; table 9.9 summarizes the profile of households, by fleet size. From the Australian Standard Geographical Classification the relevant tables to show the mapping between local government areas and the selected sub-areas have been reproduced.

Table 9.7. *Number of interviews for each city*

City	Number of interviews
Sydney	300
Melbourne	300
Brisbane	250
Adelaide	200
Perth	200
Canberra	150
Total	1400

Table 9.8. *Targeted number of interviews, by location*

	Target interviews by vehicles in household (rounded values)				
	Number of vehicles				
	0	1	2	3+	Total
SYDNEY					
Inner Sydney	4	9	7	5	25
Eastern Suburbs	3	8	7	4	22
St George–Sutherland	5	11	10	7	33
Canterbury–Bankstown	3	8	7	5	23
Fairfield–Liverpool	3	7	6	4	20
Outer South Western Sydney	2	5	4	3	14
Inner Western Sydney	2	5	4	3	14
Central Western Sydney	3	8	6	4	21
Outer Western Sydney	3	7	6	4	20
Blacktown–Baulkham Hills	4	8	7	5	24
Lower Northern Sydney	4	9	8	5	26
Hornsby–Ku-ring-gai	3	6	5	4	18
Manly–Warringah	3	7	6	4	20
Gosford–Wyong	3	7	6	4	20
Total	45	105	89	61	300
MELBOURNE					
Central Melbourne	3	9	9	5	26
Western Inner Melbourne	1	5	5	3	14
Western Outer Melbourne	2	7	7	4	20
Western Fringe Melbourne	1	3	3	2	9
Northern Inner Melbourne	1	3	3	2	9
Northern Middle Melbourne	2	6	6	4	18
Northern Fringe Melbourne	1	4	4	2	11
Northern Outer Melbourne	2	6	6	3	17
Eastern Inner Melbourne	1	5	5	3	14
Eastern Middle Melbourne	2	8	8	5	23
Eastern Outer Melbourne	3	10	9	5	27
Eastern Fringe Melbourne	1	4	5	2	12
Southern Inner Melbourne	2	7	7	4	20
Southern Outer Melbourne	2	6	6	4	18
South Eastern Inner Melbourne	1	5	5	3	14
South Eastern Outer Melbourne	1	5	5	3	14
Mornington Peninsula Inner	1	4	4	2	11
Mornington Peninsula Outer	1	3	3	2	9
Geelong	1	5	5	3	14
Total	29	105	105	61	300

Table 9.8. (*Cont.*)

	Target interviews by vehicles in household (rounded values)				
	Number of vehicles				
	0	1	2	3+	Total
ADELAIDE					
Northern	6	16	15	9	46
Western	6	16	15	9	46
Eastern	8	22	20	12	62
Southern	6	16	15	9	46
Total	26	70	65	39	200
PERTH					
Central Metropolitan	2	8	8	5	23
East Metropolitan	3	11	11	6	31
North Metropolitan	6	21	21	12	60
South West Metropolitan	4	14	14	8	40
South East Metropolitan	5	16	16	9	46
Total	20	70	70	40	200
CANBERRA					
Central Canberra	3	11	12	6	32
Belconnen	4	14	14	8	40
Woden Valley	2	7	6	4	19
Weston Creek	2	4	4	3	13
Tuggeranong	3	11	12	6	32
Queanbeyan	1	5	5	3	14
Total	15	52	53	30	150
BRISBANE					
Brisbane City Inner Ring	8	27	27	15	77
Brisbane City Outer Ring	7	25	25	14	71
South and East BSD Balance	5	16	17	9	47
North and West BSD balance	6	19	19	11	55
Total	26	87	88	49	250

It was not stipulated that interviews had to meet the strict quotas of vehicle fleet size for each statistical sub-division but that the quotas had to be met, within a margin of error of ±10 percent, for the metropolitan area as a whole. The fleet size profile for all statistical sub-divisions was supplied as a guide to the survey firm in determining their sampling clusters, an accepted means of securing an effective sample in the field. Table 9.9 is limited to the metropolitan areas of the capital cities where all surveys were undertaken.

Table 9.9. *Summary at urban area-wide level of profile of households, by fleet size*

		COUNTS OF HOUSEHOLDS					
		Number of motor vehicles					
Area	Code	0	1	2	3+	Not stated	Total
Sydney	105	204,838	513,154	339,552	114,256	48,250	1,220,050
Canberra	805	8098	38,634	32,897	11,253	1848	92,730
Melbourne	205	129,147	389,430	361,795	133,879	34,385	1,048,636
Brisbane	305	56,640	185,679	148,212	53,477	12,687	456,695
Adelaide	405	51,018	159,814	121,821	39,542	7638	379,833
Perth	505	41,478	156,678	142,280	54,598	8379	403,413
Hunter	110	24,654	80,944	53,989	18,084	4062	181,733
Illawarra	115	15,172	54,774	34,951	10,511	3160	118,568

		PERCENTAGE (INCLUDING NOT STATED)					
		Number of motor vehicles					
Area	Code	0 (%)	1 (%)	2 (%)	3+ (%)	Not stated (%)	Total (%)
Sydney	105	17	42	28	9	4	100
Canberra	805	9	42	35	12	2	100
Melbourne	205	12	37	35	13	3	100
Brisbane	305	12	41	32	12	3	100
Adelaide	405	13	42	32	10	2	100
Perth	505	10	39	35	14	2	100
Hunter	110	14	45	30	10	2	100
Illawarra	115	13	46	29	9	3	100

		% OF HOUSEHOLDS (BASED ON A STATED RESPONSE)					
		Number of motor vehicles					
Area	Code	0 (%)	1 (%)	2 (%)	3+ (%)	Not stated	Total (%)
Sydney	105	17	44	29	10		104
Canberra	805	9	43	36	12		102
Melbourne	205	13	38	36	13		103
Brisbane	305	13	42	33	12		103
Adelaide	405	14	43	33	11		102
Perth	505	10	40	36	14		102
Hunter	110	14	46	30	10		102
Illawarra	115	13	47	30	9		103

Table 9.9. (*Cont.*)

		ESTIMATED COUNTS OF VEHICLES					
		Number of motor vehicles					
Area	Code	0	1	2	3+	Not stated	Total
Values Used		*0*	*1*	*2*	*3.2*		
Sydney	105	0	513,154	679,104	365,619		1,557,877
Canberra	805	0	38,634	65,794	36,010		140,438
Melbourne	205	0	389,430	723,590	428,413		1,541,433
Brisbane	305	0	185,679	296,424	171,126		653,229
Adelaide	405	0	159,814	243,642	126,534		529,990
Perth	505	0	156,678	284,560	174,714		615,952
Hunter	110	0	80,944	107,978	57,869		246,791
Illawarra	115	0	54,774	69,902	33,635		158,311

		% OF VEHICLES (BASED ON A STATED RESPONSE)					
		Number of motor vehicles					
Area	Code	0 (%)	1 (%)	2 (%)	3+ (%)	Not stated	Total (%)
Sydney	105	0	33	44	23		100
Canberra	805	0	28	47	26		100
Melbourne	205	0	25	47	28		100
Brisbane	305	0	28	45	26		100
Adelaide	405	0	30	46	24		100
Perth	505	0	25	46	28		100
Hunter	110	0	33	44	23		100
Illawarra	115	0	35	44	21		100

9.4.5.1 Screening respondents

Interviewers were instructed to interview adults over 18 years of age who were involved in the household's decisions as to where to live and buying motor vehicles. It was also important to ensure that a respondent was at home at the time of the interview who fulfilled the commuter criteria to answer Section 4 of the home interview questionnaire. This could be the primary respondent who first agreed to the interview but, in the event that this person was not a regular commuter, another commuter in the household could become the commuting respondent. Interviewers were instructed that a maximum of 10 percent of their interviews could be conducted in households which did not have a commuter.

9.4.5.2 Interviewer briefing

Each metropolitan city had two interviewer briefings held between May 9 and May 13, 1994. The briefings were undertaken by the field supervisor in each state. In addition to the field supervisor, an ITS representative was present. A full set of briefing notes was provided by ITS. The interviewers were given the briefing notes as well as the set of questionnaires, showcards, and choice sets.

The briefing was held to ensure that the interviewers knew exactly what the study was about, how they were to conduct the interview and how the respondents were supposed to complete the additional questionnaires which were left with them. The briefing took the interviewers through each question of the home interview and then all questions from the interviewers were answered thereafter. The choice modeling and choice sets were reviewed carefully and questions were answered by the representative from ITS.

After the questionnaires were reviewed, a practice interview was conducted with all interviewers.

9.4.5.3 Interviewing

As in the pilot survey, interviewing was carried out face-to-face using a home interview questionnaire. This was completed by a member of the household who was responsible for making decisions on where the household lives and what vehicle(s) they purchase. The home interview took approximately 45 minutes to be completed.

The commuter mode-choice and vehicle-choice questions were completed in the face-to-face home interview where the interviewer could answer any questions the respondent had.

The household and commuter questionnaires were left for the respondent to complete and then were picked up approximately three days later by the same interviewer who left them. This procedure differed slightly from state to state; however, only in respect to the number of days which the questionnaire was left for the respondent to complete. For example, the interviewers in Sydney left the questionnaire for three days while in Brisbane the questionnaires were picked up the same day as the interview.

Interviews began Saturday May 14 and it took longer than anticipated to conduct the required number of interviews within each state. The interviewing was in field for approximately five weeks instead of the scheduled three weeks. The problems were primarily in the zero car households, which remained an issue throughout the interviewing process. In the end, each state targeted specific areas, in order to fulfil the quota requirements for household fleet size.

9.4.5.4 Analysis of total contacts

There were a total of 1571 interviews conducted throughout the metropolitan cities of Australia of which 1529 were entered after the editing process. Although the contracted sample size was 1400 interviews it was necessary to over-sample, given the likelihood that a proportion of these interviews would found to be unsuitable for further analysis.

There were a total of 19,752 door knocks. Of these, there were 9492 interviews which were unusable for reasons such as not home or no access to the home. There were 8970 people not home at the time of the interviewing or where there was no access to the dwelling, such as a locked gate.

There were 10,257 total contacts which includes those interviews which were terminated for the following reasons: the eligible person was away at the time of the interview (a child was home), there was contact but the qualified person (commuter) was not there, the refusals, too busy to complete the interview, or the household did not speak English; 4168 contacts were made where the household was not qualified to complete the interview, such as an elderly couple who did not commute. There were only 15 questionnaires deemed to be unreliable due to the responses to questions such as the household reported having 15 cars and not having a driver's license.

Contact, but no access, occurred 172 times, which meant there was contact made but the interviewer was not able to gain access – due to a security intercom system, for example. Of those 10,257 contacts there were 2268 households who refused to complete the home interview, which is a refusal rate of 22 percent. The response rate was 15 percent – that is, 1571 completed questionnaires out of 10,257 total contacts.

There were only a few variations between the states in regard to the proportion of people who terminated, were away at the time of the interview, were temporarily busy, etc. A few noted variations include the high proportion of respondents in Victoria which did not qualify for the study – 1219 out of 400 required compared to the other states such as 726 in the state of New South Wales (NSW).

There was a slight difference between NSW and the other states in terms of their refusal rate. NSW had 721 out of 400 required (1.8 percent), Western Australia (WA) had 343 out of 200 required (1.7 percent) while South Australia (SA) only had 211 refusals out of 200 required (1.0 percent). Western Australia had the highest number of people who were not home while the interview was to be conducted, while the Australian Capital Territory (ACT) had the lowest number of people who were not home at that time.

9.4.5.5 Questionnaire check edit

ITS was responsible for the first stage of the check edit process. Once the interviews were completed and the household and commuter questionnaires were collected, the complete sets of the three questionnaires were sent to ITS. Each questionnaire was examined to ascertain the completeness and validity of the responses. The questionnaires were then sent back to the survey firm for second check editing and the coding process.

9.4.5.6 Coding and check edit

The survey firm received the questionnaires in stages as ITS completed the check editing. It was agreed ITS would do the majority of the check editing as the survey firm usually takes self-completes as they come rather than cross-checking the information

Table 9.10. *Final questionnaire totals, by state (after ITS editing)*

	Incompletes	Non-commuter	Commuter	Other incomplete	Total
NSW	16	28	246	31	321
ACT	8	14	123	13	158
VIC	25	47	239	17	328
SA	21	22	162	19	224
QLD	5	25	244	4	278
WA	8	18	190	4	220
Final total	83	154	1204	88	1529

Table 9.11. *Breakdown, by city, for the SP and RP data sets*

	RP	SP	30 minutes or less	30–45 minutes	Greater than 45 minutes
Sydney	167	246	123 (0.5)	60 (0.24)	63 (0.26)
Canberra	96	123	104 (0.84)	13 (0.10)	6 (0.04)
Melbourne	173	239	148 (0.61)	51 (0.21)	40 (0.16)
Adelaide	119	162	122 (0.75)	28 (0.17)	12 (0.07)
Brisbane	167	244	155 (0.63)	56 (0.22)	33 (0.13)
Perth	144	190	138 (0.72)	31 (0.16)	21 (0.11)
Total	866	1204	790 (0.65)	239 (0.19)	175 (0.14)

from other parts of the questionnaire. Therefore, the check edit process completed by the survey firm was more of a procedure of logic checks within the home interview questionnaire.

The "other" and "other specify" were coded by the survey firm. That is, 350 questionnaires were used to determine the code frames for each question where there was an "other" or "other specify". In order for a code to be established it had to have been stated at least 11 times. The "other" and "other specify" questions and their code frames were documented in a separate report by the survey firm.

Table 9.10 documents the total number of questionnaires which were keypunched after the coding and editing process. ITS requested there be four different categories in which to put the questionnaires: (1) incompletes, (2) non-commuter, (3) commuter, and (4) other incompletes, as shown in table 9.11. The incompletes included questionnaires which had only the home interview completed ($N = 83$). The commuters were those who completed all three sections of the questionnaire ($N = 1204$). Non-commuters were the respondents who did not commute and therefore completed only the home interview and the household questionnaire ($N = 154$). The other incompletes was a category which ITS devised to represent those which were quite badly incomplete and had other problems such as the personal information was not completed ($N = 88$). The survey firm agreed to attempt to obtain the missing data; however after encountering many aggravated and despondent respondents, this effort was ceased.

9.4.5.7 Data entry

The data entry of the questionnaires was conducted by the survey firm. The questionnaires were all finalized in terms of their responses before any keypunching was completed. That is, nothing was revised on the questionnaires once the keypunching had begun. This process took approximately a week to complete.

9.4.5.8 SPSS setup

Each question of the questionnaire was set up in SPSS by the survey firm. This process involved keypunching several questionnaires to establish the variable names and lengths within SPSS. Once the variables were created within SPSS, a check was run to validate that the information was in the right variable. The completed data files were handed over to ITS for analysis. ITS undertook extensive pre-analysis of the base survey data to ensure that the data were "clean" and ready for analysis.

9.5 The case study data

The data accompanying this primer is the actual data collected for the GGE mode choice experiment. This data may be downloaded from http://cambridge.org/0521605776. With the exception of the exclusion of the non-commuting sample data, the data remains undoctored. It exists as it did in 1994 when first collected and as such exhibits all of the nuisances of real life data (which it is). It is this data set that we will use in the remaining chapters to demonstrate the more practical exercises in choice modeling.

Table 9.11 shows the breakdown for the data, by city, of the sample sizes for both the SP and RP components of the study (from this point on, we refer to capital cities of each state instead of the states themselves as the data were collected in these urban centers and not across the remainder of the states). Note that there exist 338 fewer respondents for the RP data than the SP data. This is despite the fact that the same respondent completed both the SP and RP component of the survey. Thus these 338 missing respondents for the RP data represent missing data that were either missing at the time of data collection or have been lost for reasons unknown since.

Table 9.11 also breaks down the SP sample data, by city, into the trip lengths as sampled in 1994; 790 commuters were sampled with trips to work of less than 30 minutes, 239 with trips to work of between 30 to 45 minutes, and 175 commuters with trips to work of greater than 45 minutes. The proportions belonging to each trip length segment for each city are given in brackets.

Share profiles of RP choices for each of the six cities and the overall totals for all six cities are summarized in tables 9.12 and 9.13; *walk* and "*other*" were eliminated in the RP models because insufficient individuals chose *walk*. "*other*" is uninformative.

Table 9.12. *Profile of RP modal share (%), chosen main mode*

	CAN	SYD	MEL	BRS	ADL	PER	TOTAL
Drive alone	52.0	51.0	62.4	50.0	54.3	61.4	55.3
Ride share	22.0	16.0	14.8	26.3	21.3	17.4	19.4
Bus	19.5	7.4	1.3	7.2	11.6	9.2	8.3
Train	0.0	19.8	13.5	11.0	3.0	7.1	10.4
Walk	1.6	3.3	3.0	1.7	1.2	0.5	2.0
Other[a]	4.9	2.5	5.1	3.8	8.5	4.3	4.6
Total number	123	243	237	236	164	184	1187

Note: [a] "Other" is taxi, ferry (in SYD, BRS), motorbike, and bicycle.

Table 9.13. *Profile of RP modal share (%), alternative mode*

	CAN	SYD	MEL	BRS	ADL	PER	TOTAL
Drive alone	10.6	15.6	15.6	13.1	9.8	7.6	12.6
Ride share	22.8	21.8	21.5	24.6	25.0	24.5	23.3
Bus	41.5	23.0	15.6	24.6	28.0	28.8	25.4
Train	0.0	18.1	22.8	18.6	9.8	17.9	16.1
Walk	4.9	6.6	6.3	5.1	9.1	8.2	6.7
Other[a]	20.3	14.8	18.1	14.0	18.3	13.0	16.1
Total number	123	243	237	236	164	184	1187

Note: [a] "Other" is taxi, ferry (in SYD, BRS), motorbike, and bicycle.

The data set used for the case study is a combined RP–SP data set consisting of 109 columns and 16,188 rows of data. We provide a detailed description of these variables in appendix 9B and appendix 9C. The data set is presented in two different formats: (1) in a project file format (*AppliedChoice.lpj*) or (2) as a text file (.TXT) format. Chapter 7 described how to load the project file format. This section describes how to load the text file format of the data. Those using NLOGIT/ACA must use the project file data. Those using the full version of NLOGIT may use either the project file format or the text file format.

To load the text file format, you will need to go to http://cambridge.org/0521605776 and save the data to your PC. NLOGIT/ACA, which accompanies this book, will automatically be opened if you use the .LPJ file; however the .TXT file is appropriate only if you have access to the full version of the program and cannot be accessed using NLOGIT/ACA (they are exactly the same data; however, NLOGIT/ACA has restricted functionality, see chapter 7). If you are using the .TXT format, you will need to use the following command (note that we have assumed that the data have been saved to the C drive of your PC; if this is not the case you will need to change the drive letter in the command line **;File=c:\Appliedchoiceanalysis \SPRP.TXT** to whatever drive letter is appropriate):

```
RESET
READ
;File=c:\Appliedchoiceanalysis\SPRP.TXT
;Nobs=16188
;Nvar=109
;Names =ID, CITY, SPRP, SPEXP, ALTISPRP, ALTIJ, CHSNMODE, ALTMODE,
SPCHOICE, CHOICE, CSET, RPDA, RPRS, RPBUS, RPTN, RPWALK, RPBIKE, SPCART,
SPCARNT, SPBUS, SPTN, SPBW, SPLR, CN, SPMISS, RPMISS, SPRPMISS, RPSPWKBK,
RPCAR, BEFORPTR, AFTERPTR, MPTRFARE, OPTRFARE, HOMTOPTR, PTRTOWK,
HHLDVEH, WKKMVEH, WALKTIME, MPTRTIME, WAITTIME, OPTRTIME, AUTOPASS,
MAXPASS, HLDAUTO, AUTONA, AUTOMAKE, AUTOYEAR, AUTOWKKM, AUTOTIME,
AUTOWKTM, AUTWKWLK, AUTWKBUS, AUTWKTRN, AUTWKOTH, VEHPPARK,
VEHPRKCT,
VEHPTOLL,VEHTOLCT, VEHPOTHE, VEHOTHCT, VEHPNOTH, DRPPTRAN,
DRPCCARE,
DRPSCHOL,DRPTEDUC, DROPWORK, DROPOTHE, DROPDWEL, NODROPOF,
DROPTIME,
TRIPTIME, DEPTIME, DISDWCBD, VEHSTATU, CHAWKTR, CHADWTR, SPLENGTH,
TIME,TIMEVAR, TOLL, TOLLPRED, FUEL, PARKING, FREQ, FARE, START24,
ACCTIME, EGTIME, HWEIGHT, NUMBVEHS, HLDINCOM, NHLDBCAR, NCOMPCAR,
NDRIVLIC, HLDSIZE, NWORKERS, WKREMPLY, WKROCCUP, PERAGE, DRIVLIC,
PINCOME, PERSEX, PEREDUC, ACCEGGT, CAN, SYD, MEL, BRS, ADL$
Dstats ;rhs=* $
```

The commands as written are entered into a new Text/Command Document and the program initiated by selecting the relevant text before pressing the *Go* button, as described in chapter 6. Rather than have to retype commands such as those above every time an analyst wishes to re-explore a previously conducted analysis, NLOGIT allows Text/Command Documents to be saved and re-opened at a later time. To save a Text/Command Document the analyst may either press the *Save to disk* pushbutton in the toolbar or select the *File* command followed by either *Save* or *Save As* and specify the location and file name for the Text/Command Document. Text/Command Documents are saved as a .LIM format by NLOGIT.

As an aside, so that the reader does not have to enter the above commands themselves we have saved the Text/Command Document along with the commands shown in the remainder of the chapter which may be downladed from the web site mentioned above. The relevant .LIM file is titled *Chap9.lim*. This may be opened either by selecting the *File* command followed by the *Open* command or by selecting the *Open file* pushbutton on the NLOGIT toolbar and locating the file on your C drive. While we have provided this file with the relevant commands, we suggest that the reader attempt to write the commands to a new Text/Command Document themselves, as the best method of learning in our experience is "by doing." NLOGIT can be unforgiving in terms of mistakes made in the writing of commands to Text/Command Documents, with tiny mistakes resulting in frustration as the analyst is forced to examine each line of the command looking for the mistake much like a programmer looking through programming code in order to debug an errant program. Learning the nuances of NLOGIT's "programming code" now rather than later may represent a good investment in the long term.

The reader will find it quicker if the data are saved to the hard drive of their computer not as a .TXT format but rather as a .SAV format using NLOGIT. Thus, the reader will be required to read the data into NLOGIT using the command syntax above, but can save the data as a .LPJ or .SAV file using the following command structure.

SAVE;file=c:\<File name>.LPJ $ or
SAVE;file=c:\<File name>.SAV $

The reader will be required to specify the drive letter (we have assumed C above) and the location of the drive (not **<File name>**, as we have shown) to where the file will be saved. The .LPJ or .SAV file format is similar to a spreadsheet file, meaning that the names of the variables are saved as the first row of data and do not have to be read into NLOGIT separately. As such, the reader will find that using the .LPJ or .SAV file formats will save a significant amount of time in placing the data into the NLOGIT program.

Once saved, the analyst may load (not read) the data into NLOGIT during future sessions using the command syntax shown below. Note that as with the **READ** command, the file location must be specified; however, the names of the variables are no longer required as these are now included as part of the file. The **RESET** command is necessary only if an existing data set is open, as NLOGIT will attempt to add any new data to the end of an open data set. While it is not necessary to use the **RESET** command for the first session, both authors have found it is a good habit to use it anyway.

9.5.1 Formatting data in NLOGIT

We have already discussed the **RESET**, **READ**, and **CREATE** commands in chapter 8 and it is not necessary to reiterate our earlier comments here. We do, however, draw the reader's attention to the different way in which we now use the **CREATE** commands. Previously we used the **CREATE** command to construct new variables within the data set, the values of which were not contingent upon the values of already existing variables. By including the **;if** statement as below, the values taken by the newly created variables are conditional upon the level taken by a second variable. For example, the command

```
CREATE
;if(wkremply=1)ftime=1
;if(wkremply=2)ptime=1
;if(wkremply=3)ftime=-1
;if(wkremply=3)ptime=-1 $
```

creates two new variables, *ftime* and *ptime* such that *ftime* takes the value one if the existing variable *wkremply* equals one, minus one if *wkremply* equals three, and zero otherwise, and *ptime* takes the value one if the existing variable *wkremply* equals two, minus one if *wkremply* equals three, and zero otherwise. So why have we done this?

Examining the levels taken by the variable *wkremply* reveals that one equates to the surveyed decision maker being employed full-time, two to the decision maker being employed

Table 9.14. *Effects coding for the* wkremply *variable*

Attribute level \ Variable	*ftime*	*ptime*
Full time	1	0
Part time	0	1
Self-employed	−1	−1

part-time, and three to the decision maker being self-employed (note that the study examined commutes to work and therefore there exists no need to provide a value for unemployed decision makers). While the analyst could employ (no pun intended) the variable as is within a choice model, the model produced would have a single parameter associated with the *wkremply* variable. Given a single parameter, the above suggests a change in utility as we move from a full-time to a part-time employed decision maker, being exactly the same change observed as we move from a part-time to self-employed decision maker. For classificatory variables, this is meaningless. This is the precise problem discussed in chapter 5 that led us to effects coding (or dummy coding).

A close examination of the **CREATE** command above suggests that the *wkremply* variable has been recoded as shown in table 9.14. The observant reader will note that we have used the **CREATE** command in NLOGIT to effects code the variable as described earlier in chapter 8. In this instance, the self-employed category will be the base level.

Had the analyst wished to dummy code the *wkremply* variable instead, the last two lines of the command would be redundant as it is these two lines which code the base level of the variable as minus one. That is, the analyst could dummy code the same variable using the command:

```
CREATE
;if(wkremply=1)ftime=1
;if(wkremply=2)ptime=1 $
```

This works because the **CREATE** command generates the desired value for the new variable if the **if** command is true or zero otherwise. As such, when *wkremply* equals three, both *ftime* and *ptime* will equal zero.

Note that we have also effects coded the variables *wkroccup* and *tollpred*, but have not made coding changes to any of the remaining variables. As way of explanation, first note that we have already effects coded several of the variables within the data set (examine the minimum and maximum values for each of the variables using the **Dstats=* $** command). Those variables that we have dummy coded are, with the exception of the *choice* variable, not to be used as part of any choice models. We will use these variables to select certain segments of data to be used in our modeling. We therefore will not use them directly in the models we employ. Even so, one needs to be careful in examining data using the **Dstats** command in this manner, as it is possible to observe variables bounded within a 0–1 range which are continuous and not categorical in nature. Such variables do not need to be effects coded as we will show – this highlights the necessity for the analyst to have more than a thorough understanding of the data set before attempting any analysis.

Variables such as number of vehicles (*numbvehs*) and household size (*hldsize*) are continuous in nature and are thus difficult (but not impossible) to effects code. This is because the largest observed value for such variables can often be considerable (suggesting a large number of possible levels), and as the analyst is required to create L – 1 new variables (where L is the number of levels) for each variable to be effects coded, the number of variables required to be created becomes substantial. For example, if it were observed that the maximum household size was 12, then the analyst would have to create 11 household size variables for effects coding (assuming that household sizes cannot be zero or fewer). One could, however, group household sizes but we would not recommend this. At the extreme, variables such as income or age may require far too many new variables to warrant such a coding practice.

But what of the SP design attributes? While the experimental design employed suggests categorical levels, the attribute-level labels used for all but one of the design attributes (i.e. *tollpred*) were continuous. For example, the design codes as shown in table 9.3 are 0, 1, and 2 for each alternative mode of transport but the attribute-level labels for the *bus* alternative for commutes of less than 30 minutes duration, were 10, 15, and 20 minutes. The analyst could easily recode the travel time attribute for each mode so that the attributes are effects coded. Doing so would have the benefit of allowing for the testing of non-linear impacts upon utility for each mode between changes in travel time from the low level (i.e. 10 minutes for the *bus* alternative) and the medium level (i.e. 15 minutes) and between the medium level and the high level (i.e. 20 minutes) or between the low and high level. However, one problem with effects coding (or any other form of categorical coding) is that the analyst may capture information only about the models' dependent variable (i.e. utility) at the discrete points at which the data are collected (i.e. at 10, 15, and 20 minutes).

But what level of utility do decision makers derive from 12 minutes of travel time? By retaining the variables as continuous in format, the analyst may investigate the level of utility derived for any value of an attribute between the lower and upper value of which data on that variable were collected. As such, the decision to effects code (or dummy code) a continuous variable represents a trade-off between the ability to test for non-linear effects upon the dependent variable (i.e. utility) and the ability to predict values for the dependent variable beyond, but not outside the range of, the values observed within the data set for that variable. The important point to make here is that, while not often done (even by the authors), it is theoretically advisable that the analyst investigate models with both continuous and categorically recoded (preferably effects coded) variables to test for non-linear effects and to allow for predictions for values not observed within the data. For this primer, we do not recode continuous formatted variables and as such complete only half the story. We ask that the diligent reader recode these variables (at the very least the SP attributes) themselves and test how this recoding impacts upon the models employed within this book. We would welcome knowing the outcome.

As an aside, the **CREATE** command with the **;if** statement can be used to recode new variables contingent upon the values taken by more than one variable. For example, assume that the analyst decides to create a new variable dependent on the values taken by the *wkremply* and *wkroccup* variables. A single **;if** statement is used in which the two variables *wkremply* and *wkroccup* are separated by an ampersand character (**&**). Thus

```
CREATE
;if(wkremply=1 & wkroccup=1)manft=1$ or,
CREATE
;manft = (wkremply=1)*(wkroccup=1) $
```

will create a new variable titled *manft* such that this new variable equals one if *wkremply* and *wkroccup* both simultaneously equal one or equal zero otherwise. This new variable, *manft*, represents the "interaction" between the two currently existing variables.

9.5.2 Getting to know and cleaning the data

Before proceeding to chapter 10, we invite the reader to get to know the data set using the techniques mentioned in the section titled Data cleaning in (section 8.5). We leave it to the reader to generate the descriptive statistics and correlation matrices using the command syntax shown in that section. Nevertheless, in that section we detailed the test for multicollinearity using auxiliary regressions and noted at the time that we would provide an example later as to how to undertake this test using NLOGIT. We provide such an example now. Before we do so, however, we note that for chapter 10 we utilize only the data for the commute segment with trips to work of less than 30 minutes. Thus to remain consistent with this chapter, we demonstrate the auxiliary regression test on this segment of data only.

To obtain the desired segment of decision makers, it is necessary to use the **REJECT** command in order to ignore the data for decision makers from other segments. Two **REJECT** commands are required, the first to reject the RP data (we will be using only the SP data chapter 10; we use the RP data in later chapters) and the second to reject decision makers with commutes of greater than 30 minutes. From appendix 9A and 9B, the *sprp* variable indicates whether the data belong to the SP or RP component of the GGE study and the variable *splength* is used to indicate the trip length segment to which the decision maker belongs. As such, the command syntax will be shown below:

```
Sample;all $
Reject;sprp=1 $
Reject;splength#1 $
Dstats;rhs=* $
```

Once the correct commuter segment is selected, the analyst may undertake the auxiliary regression test for multicollinearity. The first step of this test requires the analyst to regress each variable on the remaining explanatory variables. As the data requirements for choice modeling require each alternative to be in a separate row of data, the analyst will be required to select each alternative one at a time and undertake this test. For the mode case study, this will constitute a total of 30 auxiliary regressions for the design attributes alone (see the *Chapter 9.lim* file which you may download from the text website).

The analyst will begin by using the **REJECT** command to select the first alternative:

```
REJECT;altij#1 $
```

Once the first alternative is selected, the analyst will need to generate the required number of auxiliary regressions. For the mode-choice case study, this will involve seven such regressions, considering the SP design attributes only. In NLOGIT, the command **REGRESS** is used to perform a regression analysis. Following the command **REGRESS** the analyst specifies the dependent or left-hand side variable using the command **;lhs = <variable name>**. The explanatory or right-hand side variable(s) are specified by the command **;rhs = <variable name(s)>**. If the analyst uses as a variable name, the name **one** (one is a reserved name in NLOGIT – you cannot call a variable "one"), NLOGIT will estimate the constant parameter. Omitting the command **one** in the **;rhs = <variable name(s)>** command syntax will mean that no constant parameter will be estimated. As a concrete example, the auxiliary regression for the time attribute on the remaining SP design attributes (including a constant term) will be accomplished with the following NLOGIT command syntax:

```
REGRESS
;lhs = time
;rhs = one, timevar, toll, tollpred, fuel, parking $
```

Assuming the trip length up to 30 minutes is selected, the above NLOGIT command will generate the following output:

```
+-----------------------------------------------------------------------+
| Ordinary    least squares regression    Weighting variable = none     |
| Dep. var. = TIME         Mean= 12.33685099      , S.D.= 2.050378272     |
| Model size: Observations =     2369, Parameters =    6,  Deg.Fr.= 2363 |
| Residuals: Sum of squares = 9929.121204       ,  Std.Dev.=    2.04986 |
| Fit:        R-squared =      .002619, Adjusted R-squared =      .00051 |
| Model test: F[  5,    2363] =    1.24,        Prob value =      .28719 |
| Diagnostic: Log-L = -5058.8587, Restricted(b=0) Log-L =   -5061.9649 |
|             LogAmemiyaPrCrt.= 1.438, Akaike Info. Crt.=         4.276 |
| Autocorrel: Durbin-Watson Statistic = 2.67465, Rho =          -.33733 |
+-----------------------------------------------------------------------+
+----------+------------+---------------+---------+----------+-----------+
| Variable | Coefficient | Standard Error | b/St.Er. | P[|Z|>z] | Mean of x |
+----------+------------+---------------+---------+----------+-----------+
Constant       12.39429298        .15610769      79.396     .0000
TIMEVAR   -.3017156040E-01  .51641645E-01      -.584     .5591      1.0008442
TOLL        .4201788985E-01  .55409620E-01       .758     .4483      1.0666948
TOLLPRED -.7709942223E-01  .51729312E-01     -1.490     .1361      .99746729
FUEL        .4226010685E-01  .51489017E-01       .821     .4118      1.9949346
PARKING   -.7916645654E-02  .51586049E-02     -1.535     .1249      10.037991
(Note: E+nn or E-nn means multiply by 10 to + or -nn power.)
```

The regression output of NLOGIT is analogous to the regression output from most other statistical packages. Included in the output are the ANOVA or F-test, R^2 and adjusted R^2, parameter estimates, standard errors, t-statistics and probability values along with other useful statistics. For the auxiliary regression test for multicollinearity, it is the R^2 value that is of interest to the analyst. For the above regression, the reported R^2value is 0.002619.

The next step of the test is to use the R^2 value to calculate the R_i statistic. Using (8.1), where k (i.e. the number of explanatory variables in the model) equals 6 (including the constant term) and n (the sample size) is 2369 (given as the number of observations in the output), R_i equals

$$R_i = \frac{R^2_{x1.x2x3...xk} \big/ (k-2)}{(1 - R^2_{x1.x2x3...xk}) \big/ (n-k+1)} = \frac{0.002619 \big/ (6-2)}{(1 - 0.002619) \big/ (2369 - 6 + 1)} = 1.55189$$

Comparing the R_{time} statistic of 1.55 for the auxiliary regression of the time attribute on the remaining design attributes for the first alternative to the F-critical value with four (6–2) and 2364 (2369 – 6 + 1) degrees of freedom (i.e. 2.38) we note that R_{time} does not exceed F-critical. This suggests that the time attribute is not collinear or correlated with the remaining attributes. Although there exists some correlation, the correlation is not likely to be of significance.

The remaining auxiliary regressions can be estimated using the following commands (these apply only to alternative one; we will still need to test the remaining alternatives by resetting the sample and rejecting the other alternatives one at a time):

```
REGRESS
;lhs = timevar
;rhs = one, time, toll, tollpred, fuel, parking $
REGRESS
;lhs = toll
;rhs = one, time, timevar, tollpred, fuel, parking $
REGRESS
;lhs = tollpred
;rhs = one, time, timevar, toll, fuel, parking $
REGRESS
;lhs = fuel
;rhs = one, time, timevar, toll, tollpred, parking $
REGRESS
;lhs = parking
;rhs = one, time, timevar, toll, tollpred, fuel $
```

We omit the NLOGIT output for each auxiliary regression, however, showing the calculated

R_i statistic for each below:

$$R_{timevar} = 1.73434; \quad R_{toll} = 4.83520; \quad R_{tollpred} = 5.72317;$$
$$R_{fuel} = 0.53416; \quad R_{parking} = 2.07457$$

The F-critical statistic remains equal to 2.38 for each test, as the degrees of freedom for each auxiliary regression does not change. As such, it can be seen that multicollinearity is not a problem for the *timevar*, *fuel*, and *parking* attributes, but the *toll* and *tollpred* R_i statistics exceed the F-critical value for the test, suggesting problems involving multicollinearity. Therefore for both the *toll* and *tollpred* attributes, the attribute is collinear or correlated with the remaining attributes. Design orthogonality has been lost!

The above represents a most important learning point for the reader. While significant time and effort was spent in designing an orthogonal experimental design, any resemblance of orthogonality has been lost through missing data and a poor procedure in allocating choice sets to decision makers. One can always say this in hindsight and, to be fair to the original researchers, the procedures used in the choice case study represent, even today, the standard of practice.

The second point to take away from the above discourse is that once the survey has been conducted, the data entered into the computer and cleaned, and the analyst made ready to conduct the analysis (this involves lots of coffee), any problem detected at this stage cannot be satisfactorily rectified unless there exists sufficient time and budget to return to the field. Assuming that there is neither sufficient time nor budget, and knowing now that there exists multicollinearity in the data, what can the analyst do about it? The answer unfortunately is "very little."

Firstly, the analyst may simply pretend that the problem does not exist (the authors are economists and hence can do this!). The second alternative consists of manipulating the data to remove any offending multicollinearity (this will require both advanced knowledge of statistics as well as luck). The third alternative, particularly relevant to experimental designs, is to remove observations till one obtains zero correlations (but what biases this may introduce is not known). All three alternatives are not preferable and hence it is in the analyst's best interests to implement strategies before the survey to minimize correlations before reaching the analysis phase of the project.

As an aside, we have created a number of dummy variables within the data set that will allow the reader to remove certain observations from analysis. One such variable, titled *spmiss*, is a dummy variable that will remove any decision maker with missing SP data (i.e. with fewer than three choice sets). Hence, the command **Reject ;spmiss = 1** will remove any such decision maker from any future analysis. Nevertheless, doing so is a necessary but not sufficient strategy for the removal of multicollinearity from the experimental design attributes, as multicollinearity arises not solely as a result of missing SP observations, but also as a result of different numbers of decision makers being exposed to different blocks of the design. We leave it to the reader to test this.

We have conducted the multicollinearity test for the first alternative only. We leave it to the reader to complete the remaining tests for the remaining alternatives. Also, the thorough reader will conduct these tests, not just with the SP design attributes, but with SDCs.

Appendix 9A The contextual statement associated with the travel choice experiment

We would now like to ask some questions about your trip TO work. We need to speak to the person in the household who completed the Commuter Questionnaire.

IF THERE IS NO COMMUTER IN THE HOUSEHOLD GO TO QUESTION 14

How long does it take you to travel to work, door to door, on a normal day (i.e. without any abnormal traffic or public transport delays) READ OPTIONS

Less than 30 minutes 1
30 to 45 minutes 2
Over 45 minutes 3

SELECT THE RELEVANT SET OF CHOICE CARDS FOR THE RESPONDENT'S TRAVEL TIME

We are going to show you 3 possible choices of transport options in your area. We are not suggesting that these changes will happen in your area, we are just using these options to understand how individuals and households choose to cope with possible changes to transport. We need your help to try to understand how transport facilities can best service your needs under a variety of possible conditions.

We would like you to consider each choice with reference to your current trip TO work.

TRAVEL CHOICE 1.

CHOOSE A SET OF THREE CARDS AT RANDOM FROM THE TRAVEL TIME SET WHICH IS RELEVANT FOR THE RESPONDENT. TAKE ONE OF THOSE CARDS. WHAT IS THE NUMBER OF THE CARD __________

This is the first choice. (SHOW THE RESPONDENT THE CARD AND EXPLAIN THE FEATURES OF THE OPTIONS)
If these were the options available for your trip to work, which one would you choose?

Car toll route 1
Car no toll route 2
Bus 3
Train 4
Light rail (Tram) 5
Busway 6
(A busway is a dedicated lane for buses which extends for most of your trip)

Which set of times did you consider when you were thinking about getting to/from the public transport options (regardless of whether you chose public transport)?

From home:		To your destination:	
Walk	1	Walk	1
Car/bus	2	Bus	2

If you were to travel by private vehicle on either a toll or a no toll route (regardless of whether you chose these options), would you

Drive alone 1
Carpool or share a ride as driver 2
Carpool or share a ride as passenger 3

If these were the set of travel choices that were available for your trip to work, do you find them so unattractive that you would seriously consider

	Yes	No
Changing your work place	1	2
Changing where you live	1	2

IF THE RESPONDENT CHOSE EITHER OF THE CAR OPTIONS CONTINUE WITH THE FOLLOWING QUESTION, IF NOT GO TO CHOICE 2.

Given the choice that you have made to travel by private vehicle on a (TOLL/NO TOLL ROUTE) how would this affect the time that you leave home compared with now. Would you leave

Earlier, if so by how many minutes .... 1 ____mins
Later, if so by how many minutes .... 2 ____mins
At the same time 3

Appendix 9B Mode-choice case study data dictionary

Variable name	Units	Data set	Variable description	Mean	Std.Dev.	Minimum	Maximum	NumbCases
ID	number	SP,RP	Id	3678.97	1584.12	1000	6503	16186
CITY	1 to 6	SP,RP	City	3.54	1.58	1	6	16186
SPRP	1,2	SP,RP	1 = RP 2 = SP	1.89	0.31	1	2	16186
SPEXP	0,1,2,3	SP	Experiment number	1.79	0.99	0	3	16186
ALTISPRP	1 to 12	SP,RP	Combined SPRP modes 1–12	8.37	2.65	1	12	16186
ALTIJ	1 to 6	SP,RP	SP Mode 1–6; RP Mode 1–6	3.01	1.76	1	6	16186
CHSNMODE	0 to 16	RP	Mode chosen in RP choice set	1.00	3.18	0	16	16186
ALTMODE	0 to 16	RP	Alternative mode present in RP choice set	0.73	2.81	0	16	16186
SPCHOICE	0 to 6	SP	Travel options to work	2.86	1.95	0	6	16186
CHOICE	0,1	SP,RP	Chosen mode	0.28	0.45	0	1	16186
CSET	2,4	SP,RP	Choice set size	3.79	0.62	2	4	16186
RPDA	0,1	RP	Mode chosen dummy – drive alone	0.58	0.49	0	1	1730
RPRS	0,1	RP	Mode chosen dummy – ride share	0.16	0.36	0	1	1730
RPBUS	0,1	RP	Mode chosen dummy – bus	0.09	0.29	0	1	1730
RPTN	0,1	RP	Mode chosen dummy – train	0.11	0.31	0	1	1730
RPWALK	0,1	RP	Mode chosen dummy – walk	0.02	0.15	0	1	1730
RPBIKE	0,1	RP	Mode chosen dummy – bicycle	0.03	0.17	0	1	1730
SPCART	0,1	SP	Mode chosen dummy – car with toll	0.22	0.42	0	1	14456
SPCARNT	0,1	SP	Mode chosen dummy – car with no toll	0.23	0.42	0	1	14456
SPBUS	0,1	SP	Mode chosen dummy – bus	0.12	0.32	0	1	14456
SPTN	0,1	SP	Mode chosen dummy – train	0.12	0.33	0	1	14456
SPBW	0,1	SP	Mode chosen dummy – busway	0.16	0.36	0	1	14456
SPLR	0,1	SP	Mode chosen dummy – light rail	0.15	0.35	0	1	14456
CN	0 to 4	SP	Alternatives present within choice set	2.38	1.37	0	4	16186
SPMISS	0,1	SP	Decision maker has missing choice sets	0.01	0.09	0	1	16186
RPMISS	0,1	RP	Decision maker has missing RP data	0.26	0.44	0	1	16186
SPRPMISS	0,1	SP,RP	Analyst created variable	0.26	0.44	0	2	16186

RPSPWKBK	0,1	RP	Walk and/or Bike alternative present in RP choice set	0.15	0.36	0	1	16186
RPCAR	0,1	RP	Car alternative present in RP choice set	0.02	0.13	0	1	16186
BEFORPTR	1 to 5	RP	Point before main point	0.03	0.26	0	5	16186
AFTERPTR	1 to 5	RP	Point after main point	0.02	0.28	0	5	16186
MPTRFARE	dollars	RP	Cost main form public transport	0.12	0.67	0	15	16186
OPTRFARE	dollars	RP	Cost other form public transport	0.06	0.57	0	17.5	16186
HOMTOPTR	1 to 6	RP	Mode of travel from home to first point	0.14	0.72	0	6	16186
PTRTOWK	1 to 6	RP	Last point to work	0.15	0.76	0	6	16186
HHLDVEH	number	RP	Household vehicle used to point	0.01	0.15	0	4	16186
WKKMVEH	km	RP	Vehicle km to/from point	0.06	1.09	0	60	16186
WALKTIME	minutes	RP	Time walking: last trip to work	0.46	2.88	0	90	16186
MPTRTIME	minutes	RP	Time on main public transport	1.18	6.95	0	95	16186
WAITTIME	minutes	RP	Time waiting for public transport	0.39	2.45	0	60	16186
OPTRTIME	minutes	RP	Time on other public transport	0.23	2.24	0	80	16186
AUTOPASS	number	RP	Number & type passengers in car to work	0.13	0.69	0	6	16186
MAXPASS	number	RP	Maximum number of passengers	0.08	0.39	0	6	16186
HLDAUTO	number	RP	Household vehicle driven to work	0.07	0.35	0	6	16186
AUTONA	−1,1	RP	Car not applicable	−0.99	0.17	−1	1	16186
AUTOMAKE	number	RP	Make/model of vehicle driven to work	193.03	973.75	0	9620	16186
AUTOYEAR	year	RP	Year manufacture of car driven to work	4.17	18.36	0	94	16186
AUTOWKKM	km	RP	Distance traveled by car to work	0.90	5.01	0	120	16186
AUTOTIME	minutes	RP	Time spent traveling by car to work	1.31	6.57	0	120	16186
AUTOWKTM	minutes	RP	Time in car to work	0.05	0.71	0	51	16186
AUTWKWLK	number	RP	Walk – from car to work	−0.89	0.46	−1	1	16186
AUTWKBUS	number	RP	Bus – from car to work	0.00	0.04	0	2	16186
AUTWKTRN	number	RP	Train – from car to work	0.00	0.00	0	0	16186
AUTWKOTH	number	RP	Other mode – from car to work	0.00	0.08	0	4	16186
VEHPPARK	number	RP	Paid parking on last trip to work	−0.99	0.14	−1	1	16186
VEHPRKCT	dollars	RP	Cost of parking on last trip to work	0.01	0.29	0	14	16186

(cont.)

Appendix 9B (*Cont.*)

Variable name	Units	Data set	Variable description	Mean	Std.Dev.	Minimum	Maximum	NumbCases
VEHPTOLL	number	RP	Paid toll on last trip to work	0.00	0.05	0	2	16186
VEHTOLCT	dollars	RP	Toll costs on last trip to work	0.00	0.07	0	6	16186
VEHPOTHE	number	RP	Paid other on last trip to work	0.01	0.12	0	3	16186
VEHOTHCT	dollars	RP	Other costs on last car trip to work	0.01	0.22	0	20	16186
VEHPNOTH	number	RP	Paid nothing on last car trip to work	0.19	0.85	0	4	16186
DRPPTRAN	number	RP	Drop passengers in car at public transport	0.00	0.03	0	1	16186
DRPCCARE	number	RP	Drop passengers in car at childcare	0.00	0.07	0	2	16186
DRPSCHOL	number	RP	Drop passengers in car at school	0.01	0.17	0	3	16186
DRPTEDUC	number		Drop passengers in car at tertiary edu	0.00	0.07	0	4	16186
DROPWORK	number	RP	Drop passengers in car at work	0.01	0.27	0	5	16186
DROPOTHE	number	RP	Drop passengers in car at other places	0.00	0.12	0	6	16186
DROPDWEL	number	RP	Drop passengers in car at dwelling	0.05	0.61	0	7	16186
NODROPOF	number	RP	Don't drop any passengers in car off	0.21	1.20	0	7	16186
DROPTIME	minutes	RP	Time taken to drop passengers from car	0.05	0.96	0	73	16186
TRIPTIME	minutes	RP	Trip time walk and bike	0.38	4.61	0	145	16186
DEPTIME	24hrtime	RP	Departure time	86.76	272.79	0	2400	16186
DISDWCBD	km	RP	Distance from dwelling to CBD	2.03	9.68	0	500	16186
VEHSTATU	0,1,2,3	RP	Vehicle status	0.06	0.29	0	3	16186
CHAWKTR	1,2	SP	Move work closer to home	1.71	0.65	0	2	16186
CHADWTR	1,2	SP	Move home closer to work	1.71	0.65	0	2	16186
SPLENGTH	0,3	SP	SP experiment segment	1.33	0.83	0	3	16186
TIME	minutes	SP	Travel time to work	19.00	12.66	0	70	16186
TIMEVAR	minutes	SP	Time variability	0.95	1.86	0	7	16186
TOLL	dollars	SP	Toll cost	0.38	1.01	0	6	16186
TOLLPRED	times	SP	Times applied to tolls	0.22	0.57	0	2	16186
FUEL	dollars	SP	Fuel cost	2.00	3.03	0	15	16186
PARKING	dollars	SP	Parking cost	4.47	7.38	0	20	16186
FREQ	number	SP	Frequency of service	6.69	9.23	0	25	16186

FARE	dollars	SP	Return fare	1.56	2.11	0	7	16186
START24	24hrtime	SP	Normal depart time	825.06	309.60	200	2400	15724
ACCTIME	minutes	SP	Public transport access time	5.10	7.59	0	25	16186
EGTIME	minutes	SP	Public transport egress time	5.18	7.67	0	25	16186
HWEIGHT	number	SP,RP	Household weight	1.00	0.42	0.118	3.35	16186
NUMBVEHS	number	SP,RP	Number vehicles in household	1.75	1.03	0	6	16186
HLDINCOM	1 to 12	SP,RP	Household's income	6.15	2.41	1	12	15338
NHLDBCAR	number	SP,RP	Number household business cars	0.11	0.43	0	6	16186
NCOMPCAR	number	SP,RP	Number company cars	0.10	0.31	0	2	16186
NDRIVLIC	number	SP,RP	Number licenses in household	1.99	0.96	0	7	16186
HLDSIZE	number	SP,RP	Household size	2.87	1.36	1	8	16186
NWORKERS	number	SP,RP	Number workers in household	1.76	0.78	1	5	16186
WKREMPLY	1,2,3	SP,RP	Employment type	1.32	0.59	0	3	16186
WKROCCUP	1 to 9	SP,RP	Occupation category	3.91	2.38	0	9	16186
PERAGE	years	SP,RP	Person age	38.65	11.17	16	79	15352
DRIVLIC	1,2,3	SP,RP	Person driver's license	1.07	0.27	0	3	16186
PINCOME	dollars,000's	SP,RP	Personal income	32.62	16.91	0	80	16155
PERSEX	1,2	RP	Person sex	0.81	1.16	−1	2	16186
PEREDUC	1 to 5	RP	Person highest education	3.88	0.89	2	5	11828
ACCEGGT	number	SP,RP	Access time plus egress time	10.28	13.75	0	50	16186
CAN	1,0,−1	SP,RP	Canberra	−0.05	0.51	−1	1	16186
SYD	1,0,−1	SP,RP	Sydney	0.04	0.60	−1	1	16186
MEL	1,0,−1	SP,RP	Melbourne	0.04	0.60	−1	1	16186
BRIS	1,0,−1	SP,RP	Brisbane	0.04	0.60	−1	1	16186
ADEL	1,0,−1	SP,RP	Adelaide	−0.02	0.54	−1	1	16186

Appendix 9C Mode-choice case study variable labels

Variable name	Labels
ID	Respondent ID
CITY	1 = Canberra 2 = Sydney 3 = Melbourne 4 = Brisbane 5 = Adelaide 6 = Perth
SPRP	1 = RP 2 = SP
SPEXP	0 = RP 1 = CHOICE SET 1 (SP) 2 = CHOICE SET 2 (SP) 3 = CHOICE SET 3 (SP)
ALTISPRP	1 = DRIVE ALONE (RP) 2 = RIDE SHARE (RP) 3 = BUS (RP) 4 = TRAIN (RP) 5 = WALK (RP) 6 = BICYCLE (RP) 7 = CAR (TOLL) (SP) 8 = CAR (NOT TOLL) (SP) 9 = BUS (SP) 10 = TRAIN (SP) 11 = LIGHT RAIL (SP) 12 = BUSWAY (SP)
ALTIJ	1 = DRIVE ALONE (RP) 2 = RIDE SHARE (RP) 3 = BUS (RP) 4 = TRAIN (RP) 5 = WALK (RP) 6 = BICYCLE (RP) 1 = CAR (TOLL) (SP) 2 = CAR (NOT TOLL) (SP) 3 = BUS (SP) 4 = TRAIN (SP) 5 = LIGHT RAIL (SP) 6 = BUSWAY (SP)
	0 = SP 1 = Train (RP) 2 = Bus (RP) 3 = Tram (RP) 4 = Ferry (RP) 5 = Taxi (RP) 8 = Walk (RP)

Appendix 9C (*Cont.*)

Variable name	Labels
CHSNMODE	9 = Motorbike (RP)
	10 = Bicycle (RP)
	11 = Drive alone (RP)
	12 = Drive & household passenger (RP)
	13 = Drive + other passenger (RP)
	14 = Drive + household passenger & other passenger (RP)
	15 = Passenger household vehicle (RP)
	16 = Passenger other vehicle (RP)
	0 = SP
	1 = Train (RP)
	2 = Bus (RP)
	3 = Tram (RP)
	4 = Ferry (RP)
	5 = Taxi (RP)
	8 = Walk (RP)
ALTMODE	9 = Motorbike (RP)
	10 = Bicycle (RP)
	11 = Drive alone (RP)
	12 = Drive & household passenger (RP)
	13 = Drive + other passenger (RP)
	14 = Drive + household passenger & other passenger (RP)
	15 = Passenger household vehicle (RP)
	16 = Passenger other vehicle (RP)
	0 = RP
	1 = car with toll (SP)
	2 = car without toll (SP)
SPCHOICE	3 = bus (SP)
	4 = train (SP)
	5 = busway (SP)
	6 = light rail (SP)
CHOICE	0 = not chosen
	1 = chosen
CSET	2 = RP
	4 = SP
RPDA	1 = DRIVE ALONE CHOSEN (RP)
	0 = DRIVE ALONE NOT CHOSEN (RP)
RPRS	1 = RIDE SHARE CHOSEN (RP)
	0 = RIDE SHARE NOT CHOSEN (RP)
RPBUS	1 = BUS CHOSEN (RP)
	0 = BUS NOT CHOSEN (RP)
RPTN	1 = TRAIN CHOSEN (RP)
	0 = TRAIN NOT CHOSEN (RP)
RPWALK	1 = WALK CHOSEN (RP)
	0 = WALK NOT CHOSEN (RP)

(*cont.*)

Appendix 9C (*Cont.*)

Variable name	Labels
RPBIKE	1 = BICYCLE CHOSEN (RP) 0 = BICYCLE NOT CHOSEN (RP)
SPCART	1 = CAR WITH TOLL CHOSEN (SP) 0 = CAR WITH TOLL NOT CHOSEN (SP)
SPCARNT	1 = CAR WITH NO TOLL CHOSEN (SP) 0 = CAR WITH NO TOLL NOT CHOSEN (SP)
SPBUS	1 = BUS CHOSEN (SP) 0 = BUS NOT CHOSEN (SP)
SPTN	1 = TRAIN CHOSEN (SP) 0 = TRAIN NOT CHOSEN (SP)
SPBW	1 = BUSWAY CHOSEN (SP) 0 = BUSWAY NOT CHOSEN (SP)
SPLR	1 = LIGHT RAIL CHOSEN (SP) 0 = LIGHT RAIL NOT CHOSEN (SP)
CN	0 = Walk and other alternative included (RP) 1 = Bus – Train (SP) 2 = Bus – Busway (SP) 3 = Train – Light Rail (SP) 4 = Busway – Light Rail (SP)
SPMISS	0 = All choice sets present 1 = One or more choice sets missing
RPMISS	0 = Respondent's RP data present 1 = Respondent's RP data missing
SPRPMISS	0 = Use 1 = Reject
RPSPWKBK	0 = Walk and/or bike alternatives not present in RP choice set 1 = Walk and/or bike alternatives are present in RP choice set
RPCAR	0 = Ride share and/or drive alone alternatives not present in RP choice set 1 = Ride share and/or drive alone alternatives are present in RP choice set
BEFORPTR	1 = TRAIN 2 = BUS 3 = TRAM 4 = FERRY 5 = TAXI
AFTERPTR	1 = TRAIN 2 = BUS 3 = TRAM 4 = FERRY 5 = TAXI
MPTRFARE	As specified by respondent
OPTRFARE	As specified by respondent
	1 = CAR THEN PARK

Appendix 9C (*Cont.*)

Variable name	Labels
HOMTOPTR	2 = CAR THEN DROPPED OFF 3 = MOTORBIKE 4 = WALKED 5 = TAXI 6 = BICYCLE
PTRTOWK	1 = CAR THEN PARK 2 = CAR THEN DROPPED OFF 3 = MOTORBIKE 4 = WALKED 5 = TAXI 6 = BICYCLE
HHLDVEH	As specified by respondent
WKKMVEH	As specified by respondent
WALKTIME	As specified by respondent
MPTRTIME	As specified by respondent
WAITTIME	As specified by respondent
OPTRTIME	As specified by respondent
AUTOPASS	As specified by respondent
MAXPASS	As specified by respondent
HLDAUTO	As specified by respondent
AUTONA	As specified by respondent
AUTOMAKE	As specified by respondent
AUTOYEAR	As specified by respondent
AUTOWKKM	As specified by respondent
AUTOTIME	As specified by respondent
AUTOWKTM	As specified by respondent
AUTWKWLK	As specified by respondent
AUTWKBUS	As specified by respondent
AUTWKTRN	As specified by respondent
AUTWKOTH	As specified by respondent
VEHPPARK	As specified by respondent
VEHPRKCT	As specified by respondent
VEHPTOLL	As specified by respondent
VEHTOLCT	As specified by respondent
VEHPOTHE	As specified by respondent
VEHOTHCT	As specified by respondent
VEHPNOTH	As specified by respondent
DRPPTRAN	As specified by respondent
DRPCCARE	As specified by respondent
DRPSCHOL	As specified by respondent
DRPTEDUC	As specified by respondent
DROPWORK	As specified by respondent
DROPOTHE	As specified by respondent
DROPDWEL	As specified by respondent
NODROPOF	As specified by respondent

(*cont.*)

Appendix 9C (*Cont.*)

Variable name	Labels
DROPTIME	As specified by respondent
TRIPTIME	As specified by respondent
DEPTIME	As specified by respondent
DISDWCBD	As specified by respondent
VEHSTATU	1 = PRIVATE VEHICLE 2 = HOUSEHOLD BUSINESS VEHICLE 3 = COMPANY VEHICLE
CHAWKTR	As specified by respondent
CHADWTR	As specified by respondent
SPLENGTH	0 = RP 1 = Less than 30 minutes 2 = 30 to 45 minutes 3 = over 45 minutes
TIME	As per table 9.4
TIMVAR	As per table 9.4
TOLL	As per table 9.4
TOLLPRED	As per table 9.4
FUEL	As per table 9.4
PARKING	As per table 9.4
FREQ	As per table 9.4
FARE	As per table 9.4
START24	As specified by respondent
ACCTIME	As per table 9.4
EGTIME	As per table 9.4
HWEIGHT	Household weight variable
NUMBVEHS	As specified by respondent
HLDINCOM	1 = Less than 5000 2 = 5000–12000 3 = 12001–20000 4 = 20001–30000 5 = 30001–40000 6 = 40001–50000 7 = 50001–60000 8 = 60001–70000 9 = 70001–80000 10 = 80001–90000 11 = 90001–120000 12 = Greater than 120000
NHLDBCAR	As specified by respondent
NCOMPCAR	As specified by respondent
NDRIVLIC	As specified by respondent
HLDSIZE	As specified by respondent
NWORKERS	As specified by respondent
WKREMPLY	1 = Full Time 2 = Part Time 3 = Self Employed

Appendix 9C (*Cont.*)

Variable name	Labels
	1 = Managers and Admin
	2 = Professionals
	3 = Para-professional
	4 = Tradespersons
WKROCCUP	5 = Clerks
	6 = Sales
	7 = Plant operators
	8 = Laborers
	9 = Other
PERAGE	As specified by respondent
	1 = YES
DRIVLIC	2 = NO
	3 = NOT APPLICABLE
PINCOME	As specified by respondent
PERSEX	1 = Male
	−1 = Female
	1 = PRE-PRIMARYSCHOOL
	2 = PRIMARYSCHOOL
PEREDUC	3 = SECONDARYSCHOOL
	4 = TECH/COLLEGE
	5 = UNIVERSITY
ACCEGGT	As specified by respondent
	1 = CANBERRA
CAN	−1 = PERTH
	0 = OTHER
	1 = SYDNEY
SYD	−1 = PERTH
	0 = OTHER
	1 = MELBOURNE
MEL	−1 = PERTH
	0 = OTHER
	1 = BRISBANE
BRS	−1 = PERTH
	0 = OTHER
	1 = ADELAIDE
ADL	−1 = PERTH
	0 = OTHER

10 Getting started modeling: the basic MNL model

An economist is an expert who will know tomorrow why the things he predicted yesterday didn't happen today. (Laurance J. Peter, 1919–88)

10.1 Introduction

It is now time to get your hands dirty. In chapter 9, we provided you with a detailed description of a real life project undertaken in 1994, along with information on the data collected in that project. This data set may be downloaded from the web site associated with this text (see chapters 7 and 9).

In this chapter, we demonstrate through the use of the mode-choice data set how to model choice data by means of NLOGIT. In writing this chapter we have been very specific. We demonstrate line by line the commands necessary to estimate a model in NLOGIT. We do likewise with the output, describing in detail what each line of output means in practical terms. Knowing that "one must learn to walk before one runs," we begin with estimation of the most basic of choice models, the multinomial logit (MNL). We devote chapter 11 to additional output that may be obtained for the basic MNL model and later chapters to more advanced models.

10.2 Modeling choice in NLOGIT: the MNL command

The basic commands necessary for the estimation of choice models in NLOGIT are as follows:

```
NLOGIT
;lhs = choice, cset, altij
;choices =<names of alternatives>
;Model:
```

U(alternative 1 name) = <utility function 1> /

U(alternative 2 name) = <utility function 2> /

...

U(alternative i name) = <utility function i> $

While other command structures are possible (e.g. using RHS and RH2 instead of specifying the utility functions – we do not describe these here and refer the interested reader to NLOGIT's vast help references), the above format provides the analyst with the greatest flexibility in specifying choice models. It is for this reason that we use this command format over the other formats available.

The first line of the above command, as with all commands in NLOGIT, informs the program as to the specific function being undertaken by the analyst. This is similar to the **CREATE** and **Dstats** commands discussed previously. The command **NLOGIT** informs the program that the analyst intends to perform a discrete choice model. Alternatively, the analyst might use the command **Discretechoice** in place of **NLOGIT**, used in earlier versions of LIMDEP.

The next command line specifies the components of the left-hand side of the choice model (**lhs**). *The semi-colon is obligatory*. The order of the command is always the choice variable (*choice*, in this instance) followed by the variable representing the number of alternatives within each choice set (i.e. *cset*) followed by the variable indicating the alternative represented within each row of data (i.e. *altij*). If these commands are placed in an order other than that shown, NLOGIT is likely to produce an error message such as

```
Error:  1099: Obs.   1 responses should sum to 1.0. Sum is 2.0000.
Error:  1099: Obs.   1 responses should sum to 1.0. Sum is 2.0000.
```

indicating that there exists more than one choice per choice set somewhere within the data set. Such an error is likely if (1) the data has been incorrectly inputted or (2) the order of the command line has been incorrectly entered as suggested above.

The next command

;choices = <names of alternatives>

requires the analyst to name each of the alternatives. It is important that the names appear in the exact order as the coding of the *altij* variable, otherwise the analyst is likely to misinterpret the resulting output. This is the only place in the command syntax where order matters. For example, in the *altij* variable for the case study, the car alternative with toll is coded one while the car alternative without toll is coded two. As such, whatever names the analyst gives these two alternatives should appear in the order of the car with toll followed by the car without toll. The remaining alternatives should also appear in the same order indicated by the *altij* variable.

The remaining commands specify the utility functions (in any order) for each of the alternatives:

```
;Model:
U(<alternative 1 name>) = <utility function 1> /
U(<alternative 2 name>) = <utility function 2> /
...
U(<alternative i name>) = <utility function i> $
```

The utility specification begins with the command **;Model:** and each new utility function is separated by a slash (/). The last utility function ends with a dollar sign (**$**), informing NLOGIT that the entire command sequence is complete. Note the use of a colon (**:**) after the word **Model** rather than a semi-colon (**;**).

The utility function for an alternative represents a linear equation corresponding to the functional relationship between the attributes and SDCs and the utility associated with that alternative. Each utility function is equivalent to the utility function shown in (3.2) and reproduced as (10.1):

$$V_i = \beta_{0i} + \beta_{1i} f(X_{1i}) + \beta_{2i} f(X_{2i}) + \beta_{3i} f(X_{3i}) + \cdots + \beta_{Ki} f(X_{Ki}) \qquad (10.1)$$

where

β_{1i} is the weight (or parameter) associated with attribute X_1 and alternative i

β_{0i} is a parameter not associated with any of the observed and measured attributes, called the alternative-specific constant, which represents on average the role of all the unobserved sources of utility.

As an aside, the constant β_{0i} need not be made specific to each alternative (i.e. an alternative-specific constant in the literature); however, it is debatable as to why an analyst would ever wish to constrain a constant to be equal across two or more alternatives (known as a generic parameter) when the alternatives are labeled (we discuss the case of unlabeled experiments in appendix 10A). Given that the constant term is representative of the average role of all the unobserved sources of utility, constraining the constant terms of two or more labeled alternatives to be equal forces the average role of all the unobserved sources of utility for those alternatives to be equal. In most cases, this is a questionable proposition for labeled alternatives.

The utility functions specified by the analyst need not be the same for each alternative. Different attributes and SDCs may enter into one or more utility functions or may enter into all or several utility functions but be constrained in different ways or transformed differently across the utility functions (e.g. with log transformations). Indeed, some utility functions may have no attributes or SDCs enter into them at all.

In specifying a utility function, the analyst must define both the parameters and the variables of the linear utility equation. This is done in a systematic manner with the parameter specified first and the variable specified second. Both are separated with an asterisk (*):

```
;Model:
U(<alternative 1 name>) = <parameter>*<variable> /
```

The variable name must be consistent with a variable present within the data set. A parameter may be given any name, so long as the name is no more than eight characters long and begins with an alpha code. In naming the parameter, the analyst is best to choose names that represent some meaning to the variable related to that parameter although, as mentioned, any name will suffice.

If the same parameter name is used more than once across (and within) alternatives, the parameter estimated will be the same for however many utility functions that name was used. That is to say that the parameter will be generic across those alternatives. For example:

;Model:
U(<alternative 1 name>) = <parameter 1>*<variable 1> /
U(<alternative 2 name>) = <parameter 1>*<variable 1> /....

will produce a single-parameter estimate which is generic to both utility functions for variable one. If different parameter names are used for similar variables, then parameter estimates specific to each alternative will be generated. Thus:

;Model:
U(<alternative 1 name>) = <parameter 1>*<variable 1> /
U(<alternative 2 name>) = <parameter 2>*<variable 1> /....

will estimate a specific parameter for alternative one which may be different to the parameter estimated for alternative two.

To specify that the analyst wishes to estimate a constant term for an alternative, a parameter name for that constant term must also be specified (although no variable name is required). For example:

;Model:
U(<alternative 1 name>) = <constant> + <parameter>*<variable> /

will produce an estimate of the constant term for alternative one. Note that only one constant can be specified per utility function. Thus:

;Model:
U(<alternative 1 name>) = <constant > + <mistake> + <parameter>*<variable> /

will produce an error in the output stating that NLOGIT was unable to estimate standard errors or reliable parameter estimates for the model specified:

```
+---------+-------------+--------------+--------+---------+
|Variable | Coefficient | Standard Error |b/St.Er.|P[|Z|>z] |
+---------+-------------+--------------+--------+---------+
CONSTANT        .09448145      .70978218        .133   .8941
MISTAKE         .09448145    ......(Fixed Parameter).......
PARAMETE       -.08663454    ......(Fixed Parameter).......
```

As an aside, for this book, we are using a version of NLOGIT 3.0 released after August 2003. For versions released before this date, NLOGIT uses scientific notation in reported values, such that the above would appear as follows. We will point out further differences between this and earlier versions of NLOGIT as necessary:

```
+---------+-------------+---------------+--------+---------+
|Variable | Coefficient  | Standard Error  |b/St.Er.|P[|Z|>z] |
+---------+-------------+---------------+--------+---------+
CONSTANT    .9448144526E-01      .70978218     .133    .8941
MISTAKE     .9448144526E-01........(Fixed Parameter)........
PARAMETE   -.8663454472E-01........(Fixed Parameter)........
(Note: E+nn or E-nn means multiply by 10 to + or -nn power.)
```

Using a specific example, the utility function for an alternative named *cart* (i.e. *car with toll*) might look thus:

;Model:
U(cart) = asccart + cst*fuel /

If a second utility function were specified as shown below, the model output will have a single generic parameter associated with the *fuel* variable for both alternatives but will estimate constant terms specific to each alternative (these are known as alternative specific constants or ASCs):

U(carnt) = asccarnt + cst*fuel /

We show this in the following NLOGIT output table. For this example, a single generic parameter named *cst* is estimated for both alternatives while separate ASC terms are estimated:

```
+---------+-------------+---------------+--------+---------+
|Variable | Coefficient  | Standard Error |b/St.Er.|P[|Z|>z] |
+---------+-------------+---------------+--------+---------+
ASCCART          .24813894        .09376555      2.646    .0081
CST             -.08639310        .04013500     -2.153    .0314
ASCCARNT         .51347752        .16677288      3.079    .0021
```

As an aside, the name used for the parameter may be whatever the analyst so desires so long as the number of characters used in naming the parameter does not exceed eight (although there are one or two reserved names, **one** being just such a name). While we might name the parameter **cst** for the fuel design attribute we could have used **fuel** instead (i.e. **fuel*fuel**). While the parameter can take any name, the variable name must be that of a variable located within the data set. Thus should the analyst mistakenly type the command:

;Model:
U(cart) = cst*fual /

the following error message would appear as no such variable exists (i.e. fual) within the data set:

```
Error:  1085: Unidentified name found in FUAL
```

It is very important to check the spelling within each of the command lines to avoid unwanted errors. Returning to (10.1), the utility functions may be written as (10.2a) and (10.2b)

$$V_{cart} = 0.2481 - 0.0864 \times \text{Fuel} \quad (10.2a)$$
$$V_{carnt} = 0.5134 - 0.0864 \times \text{Fuel} \quad (10.2b)$$

We have highlighted where these parameter estimates are obtained in the output and discuss their exact meaning in following sections. For the present, we note that the parameter estimates for the fuel attribute are equal for both alternatives (i.e. −0.0864) but the constant terms of each of the alternatives differ (i.e. 0.2481 for *cart* and 0.5134 for *carnt*).

If the fuel parameter in the second utility function were given a different name than that in the first utility function (e.g. *carntcst*), separate alternative specific parameters would be estimated. For example:

;Model:
U(cart) = asccart + cst*fuel /
U(carnt) = asccarnt + carntcst*fuel /

might produce the following parameter estimates:

Variable	Coefficient	Standard Error	b/St.Er.	P[|Z|>z]
ASCCART	.24687557	.12447977	1.983	.0473
CST	-.08575065	.05782493	-1.483	.1381
ASCCARNT	.51589556	.22882210	2.255	.0242
CARNTCST	-.08700203	.05628216	-1.546	.1221

The utility functions from (10.1) thus become

$$V_{cart} = 0.2469 - 0.0858 \times \text{Fuel} \quad (10.3a)$$
$$V_{carnt} = 0.5159 - 0.0870 \times \text{Fuel} \quad (10.3b)$$

The parameter estimates for the fuel attribute are allowed to vary across the alternatives (i.e. we now have two parameter estimates, −0.0858 for *cart* and −0.0870 for *carnt*, one for each alternative). This demonstrates the difference between generic and alternative-specific parameters.

As an aside, if a parameter is given a name with nine or more characters (e.g. a parameter is given the name parameter), NLOGIT will make use of the first eight characters only. A not uncommon mistake when specifying alternative specific parameters is to provide two

Table 10.1. *Reproduction of table 8.8*

	id	*alti*	*cset*	*choice*	*comfort1*	*comfort2*	*ttime*	*age*
Car	01	1	4	1	1	0	14	40
Bus	01	2	4	0	1	0	12	40
Train	01	3	4	0	−1	−1	12	40
Plane	01	4	4	0	0	1	2	40
Car	01	1	4	0	0	1	10	40
Bus	01	2	4	1	0	1	14	40
Train	01	3	4	0	0	1	12	40
Plane	01	4	4	0	−1	−1	1.5	40

or more parameters with names which are differentiated only after the eighth character (e.g. parameter1 and parameter2). As NLOGIT makes use only of the first eight characters the estimated model will produce a single generic parameter titled *paramete* rather than the two or more alternative specific parameters desired by the analyst (e.g. *parameter1* and *parameter2*).

One final note is necessary before the reader can begin estimating models. The logit model, from which the basic choice model is derived, is homogeneous of degree zero in the attributes. In layman's terms, this suggests that attributes and SDCs which are invariant across alternatives, such as age, number of vehicles, etc., will fall out of the probabilities and the model will not be estimable. This is true also of the constant term.

To explain, return to the example given in chapter 8. Table 10.1 replicates table 8.8 for the first decision maker only. If we examine the data in table 10.1, we note that within and across each choice set, the attribute levels of both *comfort* and *ttime* vary. However the SDC *age* variable is invariant both within and across choice sets for this decision maker (i.e. it is always 40). This invariance means that the analyst cannot estimate a parameter for this variable for each and every utility function within the model. To establish some variance, the analyst can estimate only an age parameter for a maximum of $J - 1$ alternatives (where J is the number of alternatives).

With this in mind, the NLOGIT command for the six alternatives in the case study

```
NLOGIT
;lhs = choice, cset, altij
;Choices = cart, carnt, bus, train, busway, lr
;Model:
U(cart)     = asccart + cartcst*fuel + age*perage /
U(carnt)    = asccarnt + carntcst*fuel + age*perage /
U(bus)      = ascbus + buscst*fare + age*perage /
U(train)    = asctn + tncst*fare + age*perage /
U(busway)   = ascbusw + buswcst*fare + age*perage /
U(LR)       = lrcst*fare $
```

would work as there is no constant or *age* parameter estimated for the final utility function (i.e. for the light rail (*LR*) alternative).

As an aside, in the command above, we have specified alternative specific parameter estimates for the *fuel* and *fare* attributes but a generic parameter estimate for the *age* SDC. NLOGIT allows for both parameter estimate types to coexist within the same model. It is possible to specify a parameter such that it is generic for two or more alternatives but alternative specific for others.

Moving on, the command

```
NLOGIT
;lhs = choice, cset, altij
;Choices = cart, carnt, bus, train, busway, lr
;Model:
U(cart)    = asccart + cartcst*fuel + age*perage /
U(carnt)   = asccarnt + carntcst*fuel + age*perage /
U(bus)     = ascbus + buscst*fare + age*perage /
U(train)   = asctn + tncst*fare + age*perage /
U(busway)  = ascbusw + buswcst*fare + age*perage /
U(LR)      = asclr + lrcst*fare + age*perage $
```

will not work as the analyst has specified a constant for each alternative as well as an age parameter. The following errors will appear in the output:

```
Hessian is not positive definite at start values.
  Error 803: Hessian is not positive definite at start values.
B0 is too far from solution for Newton method.
Switching to BFGS as a better solution method.
Normal exit from iterations. Exit status=0.

+---------+-------------+---------------+--------+---------+
|Variable | Coefficient  | Standard Error |b/St.Er.|P[|Z|>z] |
+---------+-------------+---------------+--------+---------+
ASCCART        -.29803117        .42542188      -.701    .4836
CARTCST        -.09908627        .05819220     -1.703    .0886
AGE           -.137549D-11       .40551099       .000   1.0000
ASCCARNT        .00157358     ......(Fixed Parameter).......
CARNTCST       -.10292040        .00696498    -14.777    .0000
ASCBUS         -.10367187        .04727961     -2.193    .0283
BUSCST         -.15858230     ......(Fixed Parameter).......
ASCTN          -.02171056     ......(Fixed Parameter).......
TNCST          -.21310941     ......(Fixed Parameter).......
ASCBUSW         .25189778     ......(Fixed Parameter).......
BUSWCST        -.25838977     ......(Fixed Parameter).......
ASCLR           .16994223     ......(Fixed Parameter).......
LRCST          -.26770154     ......(Fixed Parameter).......
```

There is no such restriction on variables which are not fixed within the data range representative of each decision maker. The analyst is thus able to estimate parameters for each utility function of an SP attribute, because such attributes are allowed to vary within the data representative of each decision maker by design.

10.3 Interpreting the MNL model output

In this section, we interpret the output from an MNL model fitted using the data accompanying this primer. For the present, we will concentrate on interpreting the output from this basic model and not concern ourselves with how to improve the model's overall performance. Subsequent sections will add to the output generated as well as to our understanding of choice analysis. We leave it to the reader to explore the data in their own time and produce improved choice models than those shown here.

For this and other sections, the command that generates the output that we use for demonstrative purposes is shown below. This command will generate a generic cost parameter for the *fuel* and *fare* attributes and alternative-specific constants for five of the six alternatives:

```
NLOGIT
;lhs = choice, cset, altij
;Choices = cart, carnt, bus, train, busway, LR
;Model:
U(cart)     = asccart + cst*fuel /
U(carnt)    = asccarnt + cst*fuel /
U(bus)      = ascbus + cst*fare /
U(train)    = asctn + cst*fare /
U(busway)   = ascbusw + cst*fare /
U(LR)       = cst*fare $
```

Using the above command structure, NLOGIT will generate the following output:

```
+-----------------------------------------------+
| Discrete choice (multinomial logit) model      |
| Maximum Likelihood Estimates                   |
| Model estimated: Feb 30, 2003 at 06:00:00AM.   |
| Dependent variable                 Choice      |
| Weighting variable                   None      |
| Number of observations               2369      |
| Iterations completed                    5      |
| Log likelihood function         -3220.150      |
| R2=1-LogL/LogL*  Log-L fncn  R-sqrd  RsqAdj    |
| No coefficients  -4244.6782  .24137  .24073    |
| Constants only.  Must be computed directly.    |
|                 Use NLOGIT ;...; RHS=ONE   $   |
| Chi-squared[ 1]               = 1639.08085     |
| Prob [ chi squared > value ]  =     .00000     |
| Response data are given as ind. choice.        |
| Number of obs.=  2369, skipped    0 bad obs.   |
+-----------------------------------------------+
```

Variable	Coefficient	Standard Error	b/St.Er.	P[|Z|>z]
ASCCART	-.08252881	.07552527	-1.093	.2745
CST	-.20180890	.01916932	-10.528	.0000
ASCCARNT	.41384399	.07640648	5.416	.0000
ASCBUS	.01966141	.09923321	.198	.8429
ASCTN	-.04174518	.09373128	-.445	.6561
ASCBUSW	.09250653	.08587656	1.077	.2814

Breaking this output into two sections, the first section provides the analyst with useful information regarding the data used to estimate the model as well as the model fit. The heading informs the analyst that a discrete choice model was estimated using the method of maximum likelihood estimation (MLE).

10.3.1 Maximum likelihood estimation

To explain the concept of MLE, we provide a simple example. Consider the probability of observing a head given the toss of an unbiased coin. The probability of observing such an outcome is clearly 0.5. The probability of observing two heads given two tosses of the same coin (or two unbiased coins) is 0.25. If we toss the same coin (or a number of coins) a number of times the probability distribution will be that of a binomial probability distribution ("binomial" meaning two possible outcomes: in this case, heads or tails). In mathematical terms, the likelihood function of the binomial distribution may be written as (10.4):

$$\mathrm{LL} = \frac{n!}{h!(n-h)!} p^h (1-p)^{n-h} \tag{10.4}$$

where LL is the likelihood, n is the total number of coin tosses, h is the total number of heads observed to have occurred, and p is the probability of observing a head on any one coin toss. ! is the mathematical symbol for factorial, such that $3! = 3 \times 2 \times 1 = 6$.

Over 1000 coin tosses, we would expect that the overall probability of observing a head is 0.5 for any given coin toss, and that in the aggregate 500 tosses would result in a head. If we were to produce a model predicting the number of heads observed over a number of coin tosses, the "*heads*" parameter, which is equivalent to the probability of observing a head, p, would be 0.5. That is:

$$\text{Predicted number of heads} = 0.5 \times n \tag{10.5}$$

This intuitive result, however, is ignorant of any data collected on the phenomenon. Over 1000 tosses, would we expect to observe exactly 500 heads?

MLE works not by intuition but by examining sample data and estimating parameters such as our "*heads*" parameter based on that data. The use of the word "*likelihood*" is intentional. Without wishing to get overly technical, we describe an MLE as an estimator that calculates parameters for which the observed sample is most *likely* to have occurred.

Continuing the example, consider that we toss a coin 1000 times and observe 580 heads (i.e. $n = 1000$ and $h = 580$). MLE will search for values of p (i.e. the heads parameter) for which the observed sample data are *most likely to have occurred*. This search procedure is iterative, searching for a single value of p that will maximize the likelihood function, L^* (i.e. given the information we have that can be applied to the problem, what set of parameters can be assumed making it more likely that we can reproduce the true parameters of the sample? As we have more information, we would expect to get closer to the true solution).

Assuming $p = 0.5$, substitution into (10.4) suggests

$$\text{LL} = \frac{1000!}{580!(1000-580)!} 0.5^{580}(1-0.5)^{(1000-580)} = 6.6761 \times 10^{-08}$$

But what if $p = 0.51$? Using the same substitution procedure, the value of L^* becomes

$$\text{LL} = \frac{1000!}{580!(1000-580)!} 0.51^{580}(1-0.51)^{(1000-580)} = 1.3415 \times 10^{-06}$$

which is a larger value of L^* than when $p = 0.5$. Thus the value of p is more likely to be equal to 0.51 than 0.5. But does a value of p equal to 0.51 maximize L^*? Searching over a range of values for p, we note that L^* is maximized when p equals 0.58, as shown in table 10.2 and plotted in figure 10.1.

We have used a simple example to demonstrate MLE which, in this instance, produced a rather intuitive result. If 580 heads are observed out of 1000 coin tosses, then from the data, the probability of observing a head in any one coin toss must be 0.58 (and not 0.5). We need not have used MLE to estimate this. So why use MLE?

Generally, we will use MLE to solve more complex problems involving the simultaneous estimation of a number of parameters. Indeed, MLE has become a popular method

Table 10.2. *Searching over a range of values to maximize L^**

P	LL
0.54	0.00100275
0.55	0.00411279
0.56	0.0113162
0.57	0.02082996
0.58	0.02555401
0.59	0.02079253
0.60	0.0111543
0.61	0.00391706
0.62	0.00089292

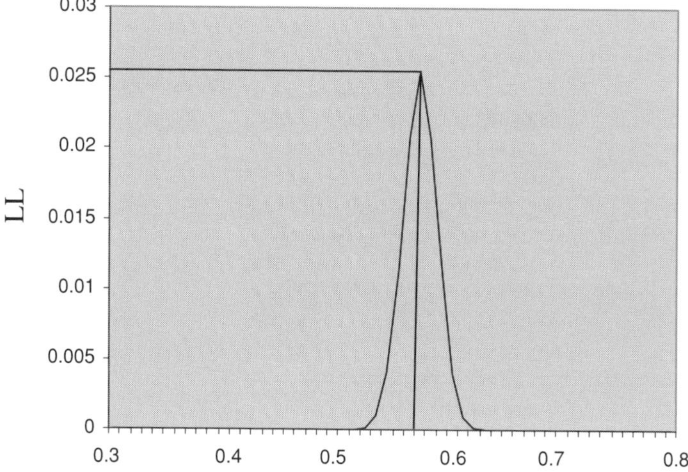

Figure 10.1 Likelihood surface

of model estimation because of its robustness and ability to deal with complex data. Taking the example of the MNL model, the maximum likelihood function may be written as:

$$L(\theta|s_1, s_2, \ldots, s_T) = \prod_{t=1}^{T} P_s(s_t|\theta) \tag{10.6}$$

where θ is the parameter to be estimated (i.e. p in the previous coin toss example or β in the choice models we wish to estimate), and s_t is one of the many possible samples the analyst may take from the total population of decision makers.

In mathematical terms, the search for the maximum value of a likelihood function, LL, may be thought of as a search along the likelihood function surface (e.g. figure 10.1) for a point at which the slope or gradient of that surface equals zero. At this point, the first derivative of the function will equal zero (i.e. at this point we cannot improve the statistical fit of the model). While easy to locate for less complicated likelihood functions, more complex functions present certain difficulties in locating this point (see below). For this reason, it is more common to use the log of the likelihood function rather than the likelihood function itself. To explain why this is so, consider (10.6). In (10.6), we use the mathematical symbol $\prod$ to denote that what follows should be multiplied (i.e. the product of a set of terms). If, as is common, the values taken by what follows this symbol are extremely small (e.g. 0.00000001), the resulting value of the multiplication can be so small as to escape detection by most computer packages due to a limitation in the number of decimal places used.

Noting the mathematical principle

$$\ln(\text{AB}) = \ln(\text{A}) + \ln(\text{B}) \tag{10.7}$$

Table 10.3. *Calculating log likelihood values*

P	LL	ln(LL)
0.54	0.00100275	−6.90501
0.55	0.00411279	−5.49365
0.56	0.0113162	−4.48152
0.57	0.02082996	−3.87136
0.58	0.02555401	−3.66696
0.59	0.02079253	−3.87316
0.60	0.0111543	−4.49593
0.61	0.00391706	−5.54241
0.62	0.00089292	−7.02102

and taking the log of (10.6) we obtain

$$\ln(L(\theta)) = L^*(\theta) = \ln\left(\prod_{t=1}^{T} P_{s_t}(s_t|\theta)\right)$$

$$= \sum_{t=1}^{T} \ln\left(P_{s_t}(s_t|\theta)\right) \quad (10.8)$$

In (10.8), we no longer have to deal with multiplication but rather summation.[1]

Considering that the values being summed are likely to be small in magnitude, taking the log of such small values will produce negative log likelihood values (this is true for any value smaller than one). Returning to our coin toss example, we show the logs of the likelihood functions calculated at different parameter values in table 10.3.

Once more, maximizing the likelihood or minimizing the absolute value of the log likelihood (LL) function, suggests a parameter estimate of 0.58 consistent, with our earlier finding. Indeed, the optimal solution for the LL function will be that closest to zero.

As an aside, in our coin toss example, we have searched for values that maximize the likelihood and minimize the LL function in steps of 0.01 (e.g. we searched at the value of 0.54 then 0.55, etc.). The value at which this step takes place (e.g. 0.01) is known as the *tolerance level*. In NLOGIT, the default tolerance level is 0.000001; however, this may be changed by the analyst to whatever level desired. To do so, the command for this would be

;tlg = <desired tolerance level>

[1] For example consider $1/2 \times 1/2 = 1/4$ compared with $1/2 + 1/2 = 1$. Multiplying fractions or decimals produces smaller values while summing fractions or decimals results in larger values. However, strictly, we must use $\ln(1/2) + \ln(1/2)$ and not $1/2 + 1/2$.

As an aside, the smaller the tolerance set, the more demanding the test employed to search for the model solution. For example:

```
NLOGIT
;lhs = choice, cset, altij
;Choices = cart, carnt, bus, train, busway, lr
;tlg = 0.02
;Model:
U(cart)    = asccart + cartcst*fuel + age*perage /
U(carnt)   = asccarnt + carntcst*fuel + age*perage /
U(bus)     = ascbus + buscst*fare + age*perage /
U(train)   = asctn + tncst + age*perage /
U(busway)  = ascbusw + buswcst*fare + age*perage /
U(LR)      = lrcst*fare $
```

would change the tolerance level from 0.000001 to 0.02 (a less exacting test). We advise that the beginner refrain from changing the tolerance level from its default setting. A word of warning: different tolerances will affect the comparison of model results.

To conclude the discussion on MLE for the present, we draw the reader's attention to one potential problem in using such an estimation strategy. Except for the MNL (which guarantees a global solution) the possibility of locating local but sub-optimal solutions is very real for more advanced choice models. Before we discuss this, however, it is worth mentioning that most search algorithms (i.e. optimisation programs) search for minima and not maxima. Thus, while NLOGIT reports the LL function, the solution search undertaken within the program involves locating the minimum of the negative LL function and not the maximum of the LL function itself. We mention this now as it pertains to the following likelihood surface shown in figure 10.2 which relates to the negative of some complex but undefined LL function.

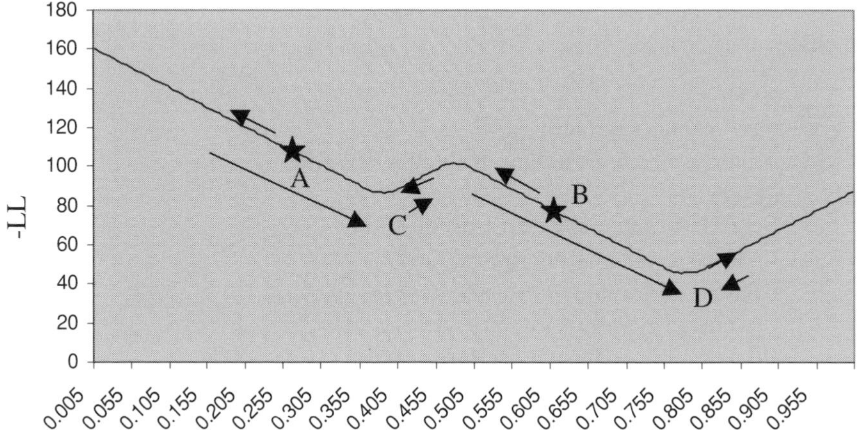

Figure 10.2 A complex negative LL surface with local sub-optimal solutions

Assuming that figure 10.2 represents the negative of some LL function surface, if the optimization algorithm begins its search at point A, movement to the left of the surface will produce increasing values of the negative LL. Movement to the right will produce smaller minimizing values of the negative LL until point C is reached. Given further searches to the right of point C, the algorithm will produce ever-increasing values and will settle back towards point C. The program will conclude that this is the optimal (minimum) negative LL value. But clearly point D represents the minimum of this negative LL function surface and not point C. If the search algorithm begins at point B, following the same logic as starting with point A, the algorithm will locate point D as the minimum point along the surface. As such, the solutions of MLE are reliant upon the point at which the search commences on the (negative) LL function surface. Fortunately, this is not a problem for the simple MNL model which is just as happy starting with no prior information on parameter estimates.

Point C is called a *local minimum*. Unless one is prepared to search over the entire negative LL surface, there will always exist the possibility that the search algorithm will produce a model solution from some local *minima* (this is not a problem for the logit model, as the log likelihood is globally concave). However, searching over the entire surface would require complex computations with ever-increasing computer requirements. NLOGIT allows the analyst to specify the starting point for a search although we strongly recommend that the beginner refrain from changing NLOGIT from its default start value. Assuming the analyst wishes to change the default starting point, this must be done for each variable in the model specification for which the starting point is to be changed. That is, there is no global way in NLOGIT to change the starting point for all parameters to be estimated. The command to change the starting value for a parameter involves placing to the right of the parameter the starting value that the analyst wishes the search algorithm to begin with, in brackets (( )). This can also be done for constant terms. That is:

```
;Model:
U(<alternative 1 name>) = <constant(value_i)> + <parameter(value_j)>*<variable> /
```

will commence the search for the constant coefficient at $value_i$ and the search for the variable parameter at $value_j$ (note that i can equal j). For example:

```
NLOGIT
;lhs = choice, cset, altij
;Choices = cart, carnt, bus, train, busway, LR
;Model:
U(cart)     = asccart(-0.5) + ptcst(-1)*fuel /
U(carnt)    = asccarnt + pntcst*fuel /
U(bus)      = ascbus + cst(-0.8)*fare /
U(train)    = asctn + cst*fare /
U(busway)   = ascbusw + cst*fare /
U(LR)       = cst*fare $
```

Note that the starting point for the search for the *cart* alternative ASC will be −0.5 and −1 for the *cart* fuel attribute. The above also specifies that the search start point for the fare attribute of the *bus* alternative will be −0.8. The astute reader will note that in the above command, the fare attribute has been specified as generic across all of the public transport alternatives. In the case of generic parameter estimates, it is necessary only to specify the start point for one alternative. Thus, the start point for the fare attributes of the *train*, *busway*, and *light rail* alternatives will also be −0.8. The start values for the fuel parameter of the *carnt* alternative will be zero, as will the constant terms (save for the *cart* alternative) as no starting point was given for these. We omit the results from this exercise for this example, as the results generated are no different to the results if no start point is given.

As an aside, NLOGIT has a command called **;Start=logit**. This is a useful command for advanced choice models, using the parameter estimates from a multinomial logit model as starting values. We recommend the use of this command (see Hensher 1986) for such models. However, as should be obvious, it is not relevant for the simpler multinomial logit choice model being discussed in the current chapter.

As a further aside, it will often be necessary to constrain certain parameters of choice models so that they equal some value. One form of constraint, already discussed, occurs when the analyst specifies generic parameter estimates across the utility functions of two or more alternatives. The estimated value will not be known in advance by the analyst. Often, however, the analyst will be required to fix one or more parameters so that they equal some known fixed value.

To constrain a parameter (or a constant) to some predetermined fixed value we place to the right of the parameter to be fixed, square brackets (**[ ]**) and write in the specific parameter value. We do not use round brackets, which indicate a starting value for a parameter to be estimated – see above. The command syntax is:

;Model:
U(<alternative 1 name>) = <constant[value$_i$]> + <parameter[value$_j$]>*<variable>

An example of this procedure is provided in chapter 11.

10.3.2 Determining the sample size and weighting criteria used

Returning to the NLOGIT output, the analyst is next informed of the time when the analysis was conducted, after which the dependent or left-hand side variable is named as well as any weighting variable used:

```
Model estimated: Feb 30, 2003 at 06:00:00AM.
Dependent variable                 Choice
Weighting variable                   None
```

The choice variable used was *choice* which is consistent with the commands used for the analysis. We have not used any variable to weight the data. The number of observations refers to the number of *choice sets* used within the analysis, and not the number of individual respondents:

```
Number of observations 2369
```

To identify the number of sampled individuals in the estimation data set, the analyst must divide the number of observations by the number of choice sets shown to each individual. This is a relatively straightforward task for studies involving fixed-choice set sizes. Here, each individual was presented with three choice sets each; thus dividing 2,369 (i.e. the number of observations) by three should yield the total number of sampled individuals (or, in this instance, the number of individuals within the commute trip length segment of less than 30 minutes). However, dividing 2,369 by three suggests that 786.67 respondents were sampled from the parent population. Clearly we cannot sample 0.67 of an individual, which indicates that a potential problem exists for the analyst. What happened to the other 0.33 of the individual respondent?

Indeed, the total number of individuals sampled from this segment was 790 and not 786.67. What has occurred here is that not all the individuals completed all three choice sets (or they did and the data was not entered correctly), and hence there exists missing data. This is important in that missing choice data corresponds to data missing on treatment combinations of the experimental design. Missing treatment combinations in turn translates to missing rows of the experimental design and, as we explained previously, missing rows of an experimental design means that, in the aggregate, the design is no longer orthogonal. To add to this, the choice sets as shown to individual respondents were randomly selected and not assigned systematically. As such, in the aggregate, each treatment combination of the experimental design was shown a different number of times, the probable result of which is likely to be further erosion in design orthogonality (see sub-section 8.5.1, Testing for multicollinearity using NLOGIT).

10.3.3 Interpreting the number of iterations to model convergence

Continuing with our interpretation of the NLOGIT output, the next line of output informs the analyst how many iterations were taken to locate the solution reported (i.e. to fit the model):

```
Iterations completed                           5
```

We have already mentioned that MLE is an *iterative process*. A large number of iterations before model convergence is an indication to the analyst that something is amiss. With a few exceptions, the number of iterations taken for simple choice models will rarely exceed 25. If, for MNL models, more than 25 iterations are observed to have occurred, the analyst should be suspicious of the final model produced. However more complex models may require up to 100 iterations before convergence.

As an aside, the analyst may specify the maximum number of iterations allowable by NLOGIT in estimating any given model. This is achieved by adding the command **;Maxit = n** (where **n** = the maximum number of iterations). That is:

```
NLOGIT
;lhs = choice, cset, altij
;Choices = <names of alternatives>
; Maxit = n
;Model:
```

U(<alternative 1 name>) = <utility function 1> /
U(<alternative 2 name>) = <utility function 2> /
...
U(<alternative i name>) = <utility function i> $

By specifying the maximum number of iterations, the analyst must be aware that the model produced may be sub-optimal if convergence was not achieved prior to this number of iterations being reached. For example, adding the command **;Maxit = 1** to the commands for the generic parameters model of p. 316 produces the following output.

```
+----------------------------------------------+
| Discrete choice (multinomial logit) model     |
| Maximum Likelihood Estimates                  |
| Model estimated:  Feb 30, 2003 at 06:15:00AM. |
| Dependent variable                 Choice     |
| Weighting variable                   None     |
| Number of observations               2369     |
| Iterations completed                    2     |
| Log likelihood function         -3226.778     |
| R2=1-LogL/LogL*  Log-L fncn  R-sqrd  RsqAdj   |
| No coefficients  -4244.6782  .23981  .23916   |
| Constants only.  Must be computed directly.   |
|                 Use NLOGIT ;...; RHS=ONE  $   |
| Chi-squared[ 1]              = 1625.82376     |
| Prob [ chi squared > value ] =     .00000     |
| Response data are given as ind. choice.       |
| Number of obs.= 2369, skipped    0 bad obs.   |
+----------------------------------------------+
+---------+-------------+---------------+--------+---------+
|Variable | Coefficient  | Standard Error |b/St.Er.|P[|Z|>z] |
+---------+-------------+---------------+--------+---------+
ASCCART        -.17536878       .07577349    -2.314    .0206
CST            -.24320777       .01915907   -12.694    .0000
ASCCARNT        .40371942       .07687471     5.252    .0000
ASCBUS          .13542754       .09758776     1.388    .1652
ASCTN           .03525459       .09229401      .382    .7025
ASCBUSW         .11012079       .08530599     1.291    .1967
```

Comparing this output to that of p. 316, the parameter estimates are different to when we allowed NLOGIT to converge without a maximum iteration constraint. The output suggests that two iterations occurred and not one. That is, the iterations allowed are strictly **n** + **1** and not **n** as suggested previously.

The final point to note about iterations is that for more complex models in which more iterations may be required, the amount of time required to estimate a model can be significant.

It is not uncommon for the analyst to use the **;Maxit** command to limit the maximum number of iterations to a reasonable number (say, 150), in order to save time on a model that is not likely to be desirable. Indeed, some analysts have reported upwards of over 1000 iterations before model convergence (Greene 2002). It is likely that if a model has not converged by 150 iterations, it will never converge, or that the model produced will be so poor as to be worthless.

10.3.4 Determining overall model significance

The next line of output provide the log likelihood (LL) function estimate and the LL function estimate for the choice model.

```
Log likelihood function          -3220.150
```

Because we have used MLE and not ordinary least squares (OLS) as the estimation procedure, we cannot rely upon the use of statistical tests of model fit commonly associated with OLS regression. We cannot use the F-statistic to determine whether the overall model is statistically significant or not.

As an aside, pre-August 2003 versions of NLOGIT, NLOGIT will provide two LL functions:

```
Log likelihood function    -3220.150
Log–L for Choice model = -3220.14968
```

For simple MNL models, these two should be equal, although the LL function estimate for the choice model will be reported to a larger number of decimal places.

To determine whether the overall model is statistically significant, the analyst must compare the LL function of the choice model at convergence to the LL function of some other "base model." To explain why this is so, recall that values of LL functions closer to zero represent better model fits. For this example, the LL function at convergence is -3220.15 but we invite the reader to consider just how close -3220.15 is to zero if there exists no upper bound on the value that a LL function can take. Unless we have some point of comparison, there is no way to answer this question.

Traditionally, two points of comparison have been used. The first point of comparison involves comparing the LL function of the fitted model with the LL function of a model fitted independent of any information contained within the data. The second point of comparison involves comparing the LL function of the fitted model against the LL function of a model fitted using only information of the market shares as they exist within the data set. To explain the origin of these two base comparison models (note that different literature has alternatively referred to these models as base models, constants only models and null models) an understanding of two important properties of discrete choice models is necessary.

The first property relates the dependent variable of a discrete choice model to the output of the model estimation process. The dependent variable of a discrete choice model, assuming the data format coincides with that described in chapter 8, is binary (i.e. 0, 1), yet the outcome of the model estimation process is choice probabilities, not choices *per se* (see

(3.10)). As we show later, summing the choice probabilities for an alternative estimated from a choice model over all observations will reproduce the choice or market share for that alternative.

The second property pertains to the role constant terms play within the model. The simplest explanation is that a constant term represents the average influence of unobserved factors influencing choice decisions. If a constant is estimated such that it is specific to an alternative (i.e. an alternative-specific constant, ASC) then the constant represents the unobserved factors influencing choice decisions as they pertain to the particular alternative for which it was estimated. An interesting question then becomes: if a constant term is representative of "unobserved" influences, how is it estimated?

Consider (3.10), the basic equation of a discrete choice model. Assume a binary choice model (i.e. the model has only two alternatives) in which the only parameters estimated for that model are the constant terms. Further, assume that the utilities (i.e. V_is of (3.10)) for the two alternatives are equal to one and zero. Why zero?

Recall that logit models are homogeneous of degree zero in the attributes. As such, the analyst is only ever able to estimate the utility for *J*–1 ASCs. In estimating a model with *J*–1 ASCs with no other attributes or SDC, at least one utility function is estimated with an average utility of zero (i.e. the utility function for the *J*th–1 alternative). As the exponential of zero equals one, the utility for this alternative will be represented within the denominator of (3.10) as one.

Assuming utility values of one and zero for the two alternatives respectively, the probability of the first alternative being chosen, all else being equal, is calculated using (3.10) as shown below:

$$p = \frac{e^1}{e^1 + e^0} = \frac{2.72}{2.72 + 1} = 0.73$$

An increase of one unit in the utility level associated with the first alternative produces an increase in probability of selecting that alternative to 0.88. We show this calculation below:

$$p = \frac{e^2}{e^2 + e^0} = \frac{2}{2 + 1} = 0.88$$

Increasing the utility of the first alternative from one to two produced an increase in the probability of selecting that alternative of a magnitude of 0.15. Now consider a further one unit increase in the utility associated with the first alternative (i.e. the utility increases from two to three), the probability of selecting the first alternative now becomes

$$p = \frac{e^3}{e^3 + 1} = 0.95$$

representing an increase in the probability of choosing the first alternative of 0.07 from when the utility of the first alternative was observed to be two. An equal change in magnitude in the utility level (e.g. a one-unit increase) produced a differential change in the magnitude of the change in the choice probabilities. A discrete choice model is non-linear in the probabilities (note that plotting the probabilities over changes in a utility function, holding everything else equal, will produce the familiar S-shaped or sigmoid curve, see figure 10.3).

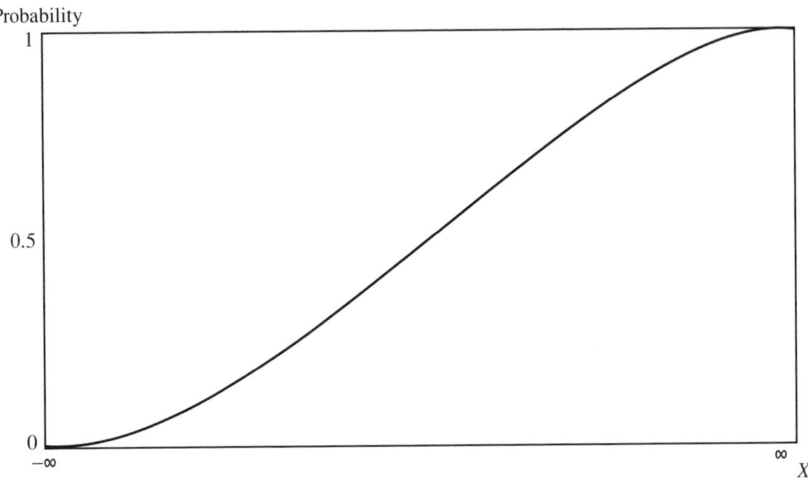

Figure 10.3 The sigmoid curve

While the probabilities outputted from a choice model will be non-linear when plotted, the utility functions (i.e. the V_is) are estimated as per the functional form suggested in (3.2). That is, the utility functions themselves are linear. Noting this point and following the same logical argument used to show that the base level of a dummy coded variable is perfectly confounded with the average utility of a given alternative (see chapter 5, p. 119), it can be shown that if the utility function for an alternative is estimated with only an ASC (i.e. no other parameters are estimated associated with any design attributes or SDC), the ASC will be equal to the average utility for that alternative (we demonstrate this formally later).

Returning to our initial binary choice example, and assuming that the two utilities discussed are utilities estimated from a model employing ASC only, the two utilities represent the average utilities for the two alternatives. Assuming that the original utilities are the true utilities for each alternative, the average utilities for alternatives one and two are one and zero, respectively (as we discuss later, these are relative utilities hence the average utility for the second alternative is not strictly zero) and the probabilities of choice as calculated from (3.10) for these two alternatives are 0.73 and 0.27, respectively, *ceteris paribus*.

But what of the first base comparison model? This model is estimated ignorant of any information contained within the data (hence it is sometimes referred to as the "no information" model). For this model, the true choice proportions are ignored and instead the model is estimated as if the choice or market shares are equal across the alternatives. This is equivalent to estimating a model with only a generic constant term for each of the $J-1$ alternatives (assuming fixed-choice sets).

Independent of whether one uses the first or second model as a basis of comparison, if the fitted model does not statistically improve the LL function (i.e. the LL of the model is statistically closer to zero than the comparison or base model's LL function value) then the additional attributes and/or SDCs do not improve the overall model fit beyond the comparison or base model. That suggests that the best estimate available to the analyst is the market share assumed (i.e. either the actual market shares or equal market shares, dependent upon the comparison model employed).

The first comparison model assuming equal market shares among the alternatives has fallen out of favor. This is because an assumption of equal market shares is likely to be unrealistic, and given information in the data on choices the analyst has available information on the actual sample market shares. So why not use the information available? For this reason, it is now more common to use the actual sample market shares available in the data as the comparison or base model to test for improvements in model fits.

A base model using the market shares within the data are equivalent to a model estimated with alternative specific constants only. The commands necessary in NLOGIT to generate this base model involves providing unique names for the constant terms for each alternative. The NLOGIT command for this model might therefore look like:

```
NLOGIT
;lhs= choice, cset, altij
;Choices= cart, carnt, bus, train, busway, LR
;Model:
U(cart)     = asccart /
U(carnt)    = asccarnt /
U(bus)      = ascbus /
U(train)    = asctrain /
U(busway)   = ascbusw $
```

We show the output for this below:

```
+-----------------------------------------------+
| Discrete choice (multinomial logit) model      |
| Maximum Likelihood Estimates                   |
| Model estimated: Feb 30, 2003 at 06:30:00AM.   |
| Dependent variable                 Choice      |
| Weighting variable                   None      |
| Number of observations               2369      |
| Iterations completed                    5      |
| Log likelihood function         -3277.012      |
| R2=1-LogL/LogL*  Log-L fncn  R-sqrd RsqAdj     |
| No coefficients  -4244.6782  .22797 .22743     |
| Constants only. Must be computed directly.     |
|                  Use NLOGIT ;...; RHS=ONE  $   |
| Response data are given as ind. choice.        |
| Number of obs.= 2369, skipped 0 bad  obs.      |
+-----------------------------------------------+
```

```
+---------+--------------+----------------+--------+---------+
|Variable | Coefficient  | Standard Error |b/St.Er.|P[|Z|>z] |
+---------+--------------+----------------+--------+---------+
ASCCART          .10014136       .07332614      1.366   .1720
ASCCARNT         .19241663       .07231745      2.661   .0078
ASCBUS           .02563012       .09810350       .261   .7939
ASCTRAIN        -.04432724       .09285080      -.477   .6331
ASCBUSW          .09941552       .08479863      1.172   .2410
```

To continue, recall that the constant term of a linear model estimated with no other parameters will equal the average of the dependent or left-hand side component of the equation. Discrete choice models are non-linear; however, as we discussed earlier, the derived utility functions are estimated as linear functions. As such, the parameter estimates provided in the above output represent the average estimated utility for each of the alternatives, given the data. We show this in (10.10a)–(10.10e):

$$V_{cart} = \beta_{0cart} = 0.1001413574 = \bar{V}_{cart} \tag{10.10a}$$

$$V_{carnt} = \beta_{0carnt} = 0.1924166335 = \bar{V}_{carnt} \tag{10.10b}$$

$$V_{bus} = \beta_{0bus} = 0.02563011826 = \bar{V}_{bus} \tag{10.10c}$$

$$V_{train} = \beta_{0train} = -0.04432723711 = \bar{V}_{train} \tag{10.10d}$$

$$V_{busway} = \beta_{0busway} = -0.09941552072 = \bar{V}_{busway} \tag{10.10e}$$

To determine whether a model is statistically significant, the analyst compares the LL function of the estimated model to that of the base comparison model. If the LL function of an estimated model can be shown to be a statistical improvement over the LL function of the base model (i.e. statistically closer to zero), then the model may be thought of as being statistically significant overall. Put another way, the base model represents the average utility for each of the alternatives and through (3.10) represents the market shares present within the data set. If an estimated model does not improve the LL function in comparison to the base model, then the additional parameters estimated do not add to the predictive capability of the base model. The analyst is best to use the average utility (and hence the market shares observed within the data set) as the estimate of the utility derived for each alternative for each decision maker.

The test to compare the LL function of an estimated model against the LL of its related base model is called the LL *ratio-test*. The formula for the test is:

$$-2(LL_{base\ model} - LL_{estimated\ model}) \sim \chi^2_{(\text{number of new parameters estimated in the estimated model})} \tag{10.11}$$

As an aside, we call this test the LL ratio-test because the difference between the logs of two values is mathematically equivalent to the log of the ratio of the two values. That is

$$\ln(A) - \ln(B) = \ln\left(\frac{A}{B}\right) \tag{10.12}$$

	A	B	C	D	E	F
1	**Model**	**LL**	**DF**	**DF diff**	**-2LL Function**	**Chi Critrical**
2	Base Model	-3277.01154	5			
3	Estimated Model	-3220.14968	6	=C3-C$2	=-2*(B$2-B3)	**3.841**
4						
5	**Model**	**LL**	**DF**	**DF diff**	**-2LL Function**	**Chi Critrical**
6	Base Model	-3277.01154	5			
7	Estimated Model	-3220.14968	6	1	113.72372	**3.841**

Figure 10.4 Using Excel to perform the −2LL test

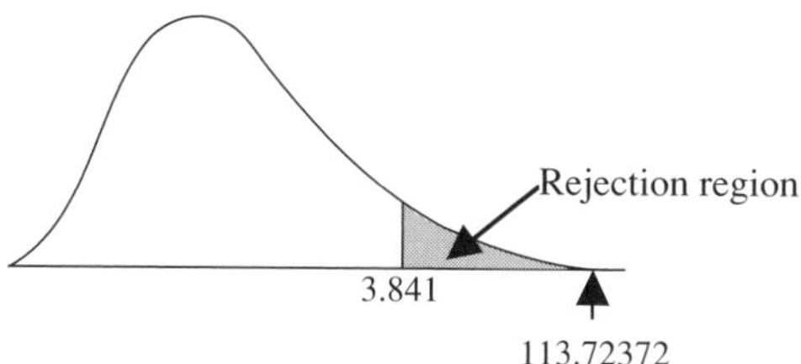

Figure 10.5 The −2LL Chi-square test

We demonstrate in figure 10.4 how to conduct this test using Microsoft Excel. Taking the difference of the LL reported for the base model in the output (i.e. −3277.01154) and the LL of the estimated model (i.e. −3220.14968) obtained from the output on p. 316) and multiplying this value by −2, the −2 log likelihood (−2LL) statistic equals 113.72372. To determine whether an estimated model is superior to its related base model, the −2LL value obtained is compared to a Chi-square statistic with degrees of freedom equal to the difference in the number of parameters estimated for the two models (assuming that the sample size remains constant). For this example, the base model requires five parameters be estimated (i.e. five ASC) while the estimated model estimates a total of six parameters (i.e. five ASC and one cost parameter). This suggests that the estimated model requires the estimation of one parameter more than the base comparison model. As such, the analyst is required to compare the calculated −2LL value to a χ^2 statistic with one degree of freedom. From Excel (see chapter 2), we note that $\chi^2_{(1)\text{d.f.}} = 3.841$ at $\alpha = 0.05$.

If the −2LL value exceeds the critical Chi-square value, then the analyst rejects the null hypothesis that the specified model is no better than the base comparison model. If on the other hand, the −2LL is less than the Chi-square value, then the analyst cannot conclude that the specified model is better than the base model – and, hence, the best estimate of utility is the average utility estimated from the base comparison model. We show this test in figure 10.5. Clearly, here, the generic parameters model outperforms the base model.

In the case of all constant terms being specified within the model as alternative-specific constants, NLOGIT will automatically perform the LL ratio-test (however, this test is performed using the equal choice shares for the base comparison model). This is represented by the lines of output:

```
Chi-squared[ 1]               = 1639.08085
Prob [ chi squared > value ] = .00000
```

To interpret the above output, the analyst compares the value shown in the line *Prob [chi squared > value]* (i.e. 0.00000 here) known as the *significance* or *p-value* (short for probability value) to some level of acceptance, commonly referred to as alpha, α, for that test. Usually the level of acceptance is taken as 0.05. If the p-value is less than the level of alpha, then the analyst *rejects* the null hypothesis that the estimated model is no better than the base comparison model. If on the other hand the p-value exceeds the level of alpha, then the analyst *cannot reject* the hypothesis and must conclude that the estimated model is no better than the base comparison model.

As an aside, those purchasing NLOGIT post-February 2004 may use the additional command, **;asc**, to have NLOGIT automatically estimate the ASC-only base model. Using the **;asc** command not only has NLOGIT estimate the ASC model automatically but also compute the Chi-square test using the LL function for this model as well. We demonstrate this below:

```
NLOGIT
;lhs = choice, cset, altij
;Choices = cart, carnt, bus, train, busway, LR
;asc
;Model:
U(cart)     = asccart + cst*fuel /
U(carnt)    = asccarnt + cst*fuel /
U(bus)      = ascbus + cst*fare /
U(train)    = asctn + cst*fare /
U(busway)   = ascbusw + cst*fare /
U(LR)       = cst*fare $
```

Adding the command **asc** to the command syntax produces the following model results:

```
+----------------------------------------------+
| Discrete choice (multinomial logit) model    |
| Maximum Likelihood Estimates                 |
| Model estimated: Feb 30, 2003 at 06:35:00AM. |
| Dependent variable               Choice      |
| Weighting variable                 None      |
| Number of observations             2369      |
| Iterations completed                  5      |
| Log likelihood function       -3277.012      |
| R2=1-LogL/LogL*  Log-L fncn  R-sqrd RsqAdj   |
| No coefficients  -4244.6782  .22797 .22743   |
| Constants only   -4039.6901  .18880 .18823   |
```

```
| Response data are given as ind. choice.          |
| Number of obs.= 2369, skipped   0 bad obs.       |
+--------------------------------------------------+

+-----------------------------------------------+
| Notes No coefficients=> P(i,j)=1/J(i).        |
|      Constants only => P(i,j) uses ASCs       |
|        only. N(j)/N if fixed choice set.      |
|        N(j) = total sample frequency for j    |
|        N    = total sample frequency.         |
|      These 2 models are simple MNL models.    |
|      R-sqrd = 1 - LogL(model)/logL(other)     |
|      RsqAdj=1-[nJ/(nJ-nparm)]*(1-R-sqrd)      |
|        nJ   = sum over i, choice set sizes    |
+-----------------------------------------------+

+---------+-------------+---------------+--------+---------+
|Variable | Coefficient | Standard Error |b/St.Er.|P[|Z|>z] |
+---------+-------------+---------------+--------+---------+
 A_CART        .10014136      .07332614     1.366    .1720
 A_CARNT       .19241663      .07231745     2.661    .0078
 A_BUS         .02563012      .09810350      .261    .7939
 A_TRAIN      -.04432724      .09285080     -.477    .6331
 A_BUSWAY      .09941552      .08479863     1.172    .2410


Normal exit from iterations. Exit status=0.
+----------------------------------------------+
| Discrete choice (multinomial logit) model    |
| Maximum Likelihood Estimates                 |
| Model estimated: Feb 30, 2003 at 06:35:01AM. |
| Dependent variable               Choice      |
| Weighting variable                 None      |
| Number of observations             2369      |
| Iterations completed                  5      |
| Log likelihood function       -3220.150      |
| R2=1-LogL/LogL*  Log-L fncn  R-sqrd  RsqAdj  |
| No coefficients  -4244.6782  .24137  .24073  |
| Constants only   -3277.0115  .01735  .01652  |
| Chi-squared[ 1]          =     113.72373     |
| Prob [ chi squared > value ] =    .00000     |
| Response data are given as ind. choice.      |
| Number of obs.= 2369, skipped     0 bad obs. |
+----------------------------------------------+
```

```
+----------------------------------------------+
| Notes No coefficients=> P(i,j)=1/J(i).        |
|  Constants only => P(i,j) uses ASCs           |
|    only. N(j)/N if fixed choice set.          |
|    N(j) = total sample frequency for j        |
|    N    = total sample frequency.             |
|  These 2 models are simple MNL models.        |
|  R-sqrd = 1 - LogL(model)/logL(other)         |
|  RsqAdj=1-[nJ/(nJ-nparm)]*(1-R-sqrd)          |
|    nJ   = sum over i, choice set sizes        |
| (Constants only model was fit separately.     |
| Test statistics are meaningless if this       |
| model does not contain a set of constants. )|
+----------------------------------------------+
```

```
+---------+--------------+----------------+--------+---------+
|Variable | Coefficient  | Standard Error |b/St.Er.|P[|Z|>z] |
+---------+--------------+----------------+--------+---------+
 ASCCART       -.08252881        .07552527     -1.093   .2745
 CST           -.20180890        .01916932    -10.528   .0000
 ASCCARNT       .41384399        .07640648      5.416   .0000
 ASCBUS         .01966141        .09923321       .198   .8429
 ASCTN         -.04174518        .09373128      -.445   .6561
 ASCBUSW        .09250653        .08587656      1.077   .2814
```

NLOGIT will first estimate the ASC-only base model and provide the output for this model. The model, with additional parameters, will be given next in the output. Unlike pre-February 2004 versions, NLOGIT will undertake the LL ratio-test using the ASC-only model automatically rather than using the "no-information" model to perform the test (as noted previously, this is the preferred test of model significance). We reproduce the relevant output below:

```
| Constants only   -3277.0115  .01735  .01652 |
| Chi-squared[ 1]           =   113.72373     |
| Prob [ chi squared > value ] =   .00000     |
```

The ASC-only model LL function is exactly the same as when we estimated the ASC-only model ourselves. The Chi-square statistic of 113.72 is also no different to that when calculated manually. The p-value reported is for this test and not the no-information model comparison also. The results shown above conform with those of the test when performed manually.

The **;asc** command is applicable only for the MNL model. The command will not work for more advanced models such as the nested logit model (chapter 14) and the mixed logit model (chapter 16).

As a further aside, note that if a generic constant is specified anywhere within the model (even if only two constants are generic and the rest are alternative-specific), the analyst will need to perform the LL ratio-test themselves, using the procedure shown in figure 10.3. The reason for this is because when generic constants are present within the model, the predicted and actual shares no longer match. When the Chi-squared statistic is computed by NLOGIT using the actual shares, a negative value is observed, which statistically should not be possible. Indeed, for labeled choice experiments and choice models based upon RP data we do not recommend generic constants. Nevertheless, we note that for unlabeled choice experiments, ASCs make no sense.

10.3.5 Comparing two models

Assuming that the same choice variable is used, the analyst may compare two different choice model specifications using the log ratio-test described in section 10.3.4. To demonstrate, consider the following model in which the cost attribute is allowed to vary across alternatives (i.e. the cost attribute is now alternative-specific):

```
NLOGIT
;lhs = choice, cset, altij
;Choices = cart, carnt, bus, train, busway, lr
;Model:
U(cart)    = asccart + cartcst*fuel /
U(carnt)   = asccarnt + carntcst*fuel /
U(bus)     = ascbus + buscst*fare /
U(train)   = asctn + tncst*fare /
U(busway)  = ascbusw + buswcst*fare /
U(LR)      = lrcst*fare $
```

Using the above command, NLOGIT produces the following output:

```
+-----------------------------------------------+
| Discrete choice (multinomial logit) model      |
| Maximum Likelihood Estimates                   |
| Model estimated: Feb 30, 2003 at 06:45:00AM.   |
| Dependent variable                 Choice      |
| Weighting variable                   None      |
| Number of observations               2369      |
| Iterations completed                    5      |
| Log likelihood function         -3214.241      |
| R2=1-LogL/LogL*  Log-L fncn  R-sqrd  RsqAdj    |
| No coefficients  -4244.6782  .24276  .24159    |
| Constants only.  Must be computed directly.    |
|                  Use NLOGIT ;...; RHS=ONE $    |
| Chi-squared[ 6]              = 1650.89911      |
| Prob [ chi squared > value ] =     .00000      |
```

```
| Response data are given as ind. choice.                |
| Number of obs.= 2369, skipped     0 bad obs.    |
+----------------------------------------------+
```

Variable	Coefficient	Standard Error	b/St.Er.	P[|Z|>z]
ASCCART	-.43353076	.17456286	-2.484	.0130
CARTCST	-.09766455	.05795105	-1.685	.0919
ASCCARNT	-.16668466	.26069361	-.639	.5226
CARNTCST	-.09243679	.05646700	-1.637	.1016
ASCBUS	-.18885515	.19430843	-.972	.3311
BUSCST	-.17877650	.04576476	-3.906	.0001
ASCTN	-.15244648	.18561589	-.821	.4115
TNCST	-.21490349	.04577121	-4.695	.0000
ASCBUSW	.11529699	.17866515	.645	.5187
BUSWCST	-.26642705	.04168628	-6.391	.0000
LRCST	-.25775069	.04182220	-6.163	.0000

Before commencing the LL ratio-test as described in section 10.3.4, we note that the p-value for the Chi-square statistic for our new model is 0.0000, which is less than our α level of 0.05. As such, we reject the hypothesis that this new model is no better than the base comparison model (i.e. the same base comparison model used previously) and conclude that this model is statistically significant overall.

Using the LL ratio-test we compute the -2LL ratio using the same procedure as before, only this time the LL of the base comparison model is replaced by the largest LL of the two models under comparison. If we naively use the first-estimated model's LL function value first and the second-estimated model's LL second, the possibility exists that the LL function for the first model will be smaller than that of the second model. In such cases, the computed Chi-square test-statistic will be negative (i.e. the same problem when generic constants are specified). Thus the test becomes:

$$-2(LL_{largest} - LL_{smallest}) \sim \chi^2_{(\text{difference in the number of paramaters estimated between the two models})} \tag{10.13}$$

The LL of the previous model was -3220.14968 while the LL of the new model is -3214.24055, hence we replace the LL for the base model with the LL of the second model. Substituting the LL values for the old and new model into (10.13) we obtain

$$-2 \times (-3214.24055 - (-3220.14968)) \sim \chi^2_{(11-6)\text{d.f.}} 11.81826 \sim \chi^2_{(5)\text{d.f.}}$$

The degrees of freedom for the critical Chi-square statistic is equal to the difference between the number of parameters estimated between the two models. As the first model estimated 6 parameters (i.e. five ASC and one cost parameter) and the new model 11 parameters (i.e. 5 ASC and 6 cost parameters), the degrees of freedom for the test is 5. The Chi-square critical value with 5 degrees of freedom taken at a 95 percent confidence level is 11.07 (see sub-section 2.8.3).

Comparing the test-statistic of 11.82 to the Chi-square critical value of 11.07, we note that the test-statistic is greater than the critical value (only just). Given this, the analyst is able to reject the hypothesis that the new model does not statistically improve the LL over the previous model and conclude that the LL of the new model is statistically closer to zero than that of the previous model.

10.3.6 Determining model fit: the pseudo-R^2

The next section of output informs the analyst as to the model pseudo-R^2, pseudo-R^2 adjusted, and the LL function, assuming no coefficients are estimated:

```
R2=1-LogL/LogL* Log-L fncn R-sqrd RsqAdj
No coefficients -4244.6782 .24137 .24073
```

The generation of such output is unfortunate in some ways as the R^2 statistic associated with choice models is not exactly analogous to the R^2 statistic of the linear regression model. This is because the linear regression model is, as the name suggests, linear, while the MNL model underlying choice analysis is non-linear. As such, an R^2 of 0.24 for a regression model is not equal to a pseudo-R^2 of 0.24 for a choice model. We show this later.

As shown in the above output, it is possible to calculate a pseudo-R^2 for a choice model. To do so we use the following equation:

$$R^2 = 1 - \frac{LL_{Estimated\ model}}{LL_{Base\ model}} \tag{10.14}$$

Note that some analysts reportedly use the algebraically equivalent (10.15) instead of (10.14) to calculate the pseudo-R^2. In either case, the same R^2 value will be calculated:

$$R^2 = \frac{LL_{Base\ model} - LL_{Estimated\ model}}{LL_{Base\ model}} \tag{10.15}$$

Substituting the values from estimated model output and base model output into (10.14) we obtain

$$R^2 = 1 - \frac{-3220.14968}{-3277.01154} = 0.01735$$

Figure 10.6 shows the calculation of the pseudo-R^2 for the choice model by means of both (10.14) and (10.15) using Microsoft Excel.

As an aside, the R^2 we calculate is different to that calculated by NLOGIT. This is because NLOGIT calculates the R^2 using the LL function for the model estimated with no coefficients (the equal market share model discussed earlier) instead of the LL function for the model estimated with ASC only (i.e. from the market shares from data) which we

	A	B	C
1	**Model**	**LL**	**Pseudo R Square (1)**
2	Base Model	−3276.833	=1-(B3/B2)
3	Estimated Model	−3219.011	
4			
5	**Model**	**LL**	**Pseudo R Square (1)**
6	Base Model	−3276.833	0.017645696
7	Estimated Model	−3219.011	

Figure 10.6 Using Excel to calculate a pseudo-R^2

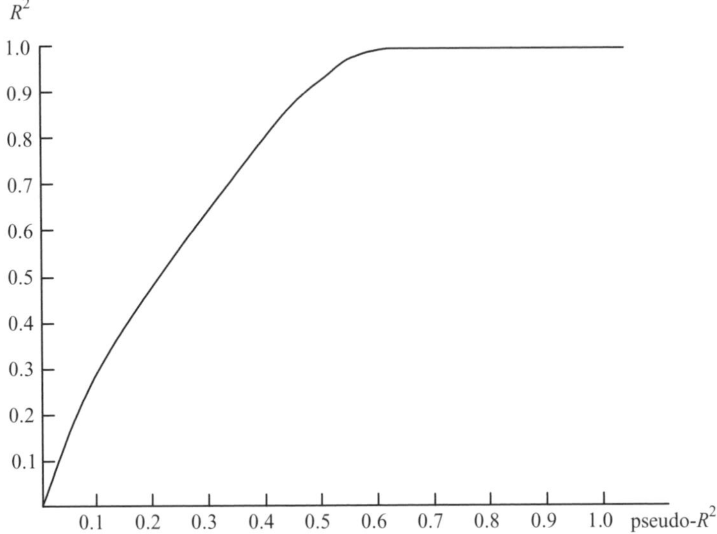

Figure 10.7 Mapping the pseudo-R^2 to the linear R^2

have used in our calculation. The LL function for the no-coefficients estimated model is given in the output as −4224.6782. Substitution of this value into (10.15) instead of that used yields the same R^2 as reported by NLOGIT.

For this example, we use the pseudo-R^2 value of 0.017. As noted previously, the pseudo-R^2 of a choice model is not exactly the same as the R^2 of a linear regression model. Fortunately, there exists a direct empirical relationship between the two (Domencich and McFadden 1975). Figure 10.7 shows the mapping of the relationship between the two indices.

Figure 10.7 suggests that a pseudo-R^2 value of 0.017 still represents a bad model fit. This is not a surprising result, given that the model fitted included a single attribute parameter.

As an aside, in our experience, a pseudo-R^2 of 0.3 represents a decent model fit for a discrete choice model. Indeed from figure 10.7 it can be seen that a pseudo-R^2 of 0.3

represents an R^2 of approximately 0.6 for the equivalent R^2 of a linear regression model. In fact pseudo-R^2 values between the range of 0.3 and 0.4 can be translated as an R^2 of between 0.6 and 0.8 for the linear model equivalent.

10.3.7 Type of response and bad data

The last remaining output of the first section of output reports the type of response data used and the number of observations used for modeling:

```
Response data are given as ind. choice.
Number of obs.= 2369, skipped 0 bad obs.
```

NLOGIT allows modeling of a number of different types of choice data. For this primer, we concentrate solely on individual-level data; however, it is also possible to model choices based on proportions data, frequency data, and ranked data. It is more likely that the beginner will be exposed to individual-level choice data. For those wishing to explore these other data formats, the NLOGIT reference manuals accompanying the software provide an excellent discussion on how to use them.

The number of observations used for modeling is reported a second time in the output; however, this time it is accompanied with a record of how many *bad* observations were skipped in model estimation. For simple MNL models, this record of bad observations becomes relevant when conducting the test of the Independence of Irrelevant Alternatives (IIA) (discussed in chapter 14).

10.3.8 Obtaining estimates of the indirect utility functions

The second section of output for the simple MNL discrete choice model is that of the parameter estimates of the choice model. Those familiar with regression output from most other statistical packages will note a parallel with the output provided by NLOGIT for discrete choice models and those of regression analysis. Any similarity is deceptive:

Variable	Coefficient	Standard Error	b/St.Er.	P[|Z|>z]
ASCCART	-.08252881	.07552527	-1.093	.2745
CST	-.20180890	.01916932	-10.528	.0000
ASCCARNT	.41384399	.07640648	5.416	.0000
ASCBUS	.01966141	.09923321	.198	.8429
ASCTN	-.04174518	.09373128	-.445	.6561
ASCBUSW	.09250653	.08587656	1.077	.2814

The first column of output provides the variable names supplied by the analyst. The second column provides the parameter estimates for the variables mentioned in the first column of output. Ignoring the statistical significance of each of the parameters (or the lack thereof) for the present, we can use the information gleaned from the above output to write out the utility functions for each of the alternatives. Doing so requires knowledge of how the utility functions were specified earlier. For the above example, writing out the utility functions to conform to the earlier model specification yields (10.16a)–(10.16f).

$$V_{cart} = -0.08252881153 - 0.2018089032 \times \text{Fuel} \tag{10.16a}$$

$$V_{carnt} = 0.4138439919 - 0.2018089032 \times \text{Fuel} \tag{10.16b}$$

$$V_{bus} = -0.01966140957 - 0.2018089032 \times \text{Fare} \tag{10.16c}$$

$$V_{train} = -0.04174517962 - 0.2018089032 \times \text{Fare} \tag{10.16d}$$

$$V_{busway} = -0.09250652924 - 0.2018089032 \times \text{Fare} \tag{10.16e}$$

$$V_{LR} = -0.2018089032 \times \text{Fare} \tag{10.16f}$$

To demonstrate, consider the utility an individual derives when faced with a fuel price of \$1 (per trip). Holding everything else constant and considering only the impact upon the utility of traveling by car on toll roads, (10.16a) becomes

$$\begin{aligned} V_{cart} &= -0.08252881153 - 0.2018089032 \times 1 \\ &= -0.284337715 \end{aligned}$$

The utility derived from a choice model as shown above is meaningful only when considered relative to that of the utility for a second alternative. Thus, a utility of −0.284 is meaningful only when compared with the utility calculated for that of a second alternative. Assuming the utility for the *carnt* alternative was estimated as being 0.212, the utility of the *cart* alternative relative to that of the *carnt* alternative is given as the difference of the two. That is

$$\begin{aligned} V_{cart} - V_{carnt} &= -0.284 - 0.212 \\ &= -0.496 \end{aligned}$$

Clearly, the non-toll car alternative is preferred to that of the car traveling on a toll road, *ceteris paribus*.

Each of the utility functions shown in (10.16a)–(10.16f) represent the constituent components of (3.10) reproduced as (10.17) below:

$$\text{Prob}(i \mid j) = \frac{\exp V_i}{\sum\limits_{j=1}^{J} \exp V_j}; j = 1, \ldots, i, \ldots, J \quad i \neq j \tag{10.17}$$

To calculate the probability that an alternative will be selected over all other available alternatives, the utility function for that alternative is treated as the numerator in (10.17) (i.e. V_i). As such, to calculate the selection probabilities of each of the alternatives will require as many equations as there exist alternatives.[2]

[2] This is not strictly true, as the probabilities must sum to one and hence one can calculate the probability of the last alternative given knowledge of the probabilities of all other alternatives.

Using a specific example, assuming the analyst wishes to determine the probability of selection of the *cart* alternative, expanding (10.17) for the mode case study we obtain:

$$\text{Prob}(CART\,|\,j) = \frac{e^{V_{CART}}}{e^{V_{CART}} + e^{V_{CANT}} + e^{V_{BUS}} + e^{V_{TRAIN}} + e^{V_{BUSWAY}} + e^{V_{LR}}} \qquad (10.18)$$

and substituting (10.16a)–(10.16f) we arrive at:

$$\text{Prob}(CART\,|\,j) = \frac{e^{(-0.08252881153-0.2018089032\times \text{Fuel})}}{\begin{array}{l}\left(e^{(-0.08252881153-0.2018089032\times \text{Fuel})} + e^{(0.4138439919-0.2018089032\times \text{Fuel})}\right.\\ + e^{(-0.01966140957-0.2018089032\times \text{Fare})} + e^{(-0.04174517962-0.2018089032\times \text{Fare})}\\ \left. + e^{(-0.09250652924-0.2018089032\times \text{Fare})} + e^{(-0.2018089032\times \text{Fare})}\right)\end{array}} \qquad (10.19)$$

Similarly, the probability of selecting the bus alternative could be calculated by substituting the utility function for bus as the numerator in (10.18) as shown in (10.20):

$$\text{Prob}(BUS\,|\,j) = \frac{e^{(-0.019661\ 40957\ -0.2018089032\times \text{Fare})}}{\begin{array}{l}\left(e^{(-0.082528\ 81153\ -0.2018089032\times \text{Fuel})} + e^{(0.4138439\ 919\ -0.2018089032\times \text{Fuel})}\right.\\ + e^{(-0.019661\ 40957\ -0.2018089032\times \text{Fare})} + e^{(-0.04175\ 17962\ -0.20180890\ 32\times \text{Fare})}\\ \left. + e^{(-0.092506\ 52924\ -0.2018089032\times \text{Fare})} + e^{(-0.2018089032\times \text{Fare})}\right)\end{array}} \qquad (10.20)$$

As noted previously, while the utility functions derived from a discrete choice model are linear, the probability estimates are not. It is possible to provide a direct behavioral interpretation of the parameter estimates when discussing utilities (although only in a relative sense) but not when discussing probabilities. This is a result of the use of exponentials in (10.17). In chapter 11, we discuss the concepts of marginal effects and elasticities which provide a direct and meaningful behavioral interpretation of the parameter estimates when dealing with probabilities. The next column of output lists the standard errors for the parameter estimates:

Variable	Coefficient	Standard Error	b/St.Er.	P[|Z|>z]
ASCCART	-.08252881	.07552527	-1.093	.2745
CST	-.20180890	.01916932	-10.528	.0000
ASCCARNT	.41384399	.07640648	5.416	.0000
ASCBUS	.01966141	.09923321	.198	.8429
ASCTN	-.04174518	.09373128	-.445	.6561
ASCBUSW	.09250653	.08587656	1.077	.2814

The parameter estimates obtained are subject to error. The amount of error is given by the standard error of the coefficient. A common question asked by analysts is whether a variable contributes to explaining the choice response. What we are attempting to accomplish through modeling is an explanation of the variation in the dependent variable (i.e. choice) observed within the population of sampled individuals. Why do some individuals choose alternative A over alternative B while others ignore these alternatives completely and choose alternative C? By adding variables to a model, the analyst is attempting to explain this variation in choice of alternative.

If an explanatory variable does not add to the analyst's understanding of choice, statistically the weight attached to that variable will equal zero. That is

$$\beta_i = 0 \tag{10.21}$$

In linear regression analysis, this test is usually performed via a t- or F-test. For choice analysis based upon MNL models, neither the t- nor F-statistic is available. Fortunately, the asymptotic equivalent test is available. Known as the Wald-statistic, the test-statistic is both calculated and interpreted in the same manner as the t-test associated with linear regression models. The Wald-statistic is given as:

$$Wald = \frac{\beta_i}{\text{standard error}_i} \tag{10.22}$$

The Wald-statistic for each parameter is given in the fourth column of the output:

Variable	Coefficient	Standard Error	b/St.Er.	P[|Z|>z]
ASCCART	-.08252881	.07552527	-1.093	.2745
CST	-.20180890	.01916932	-10.528	.0000
ASCCARNT	.41384399	.07640648	5.416	.0000
ASCBUS	.01966141	.09923321	.198	.8429
ASCTN	-.04174518	.09373128	-.445	.6561
ASCBUSW	.09250653	.08587656	1.077	.2814

To determine whether an explanatory variable is statistically significant (i.e. $\beta_i \neq 0$) or not (i.e. $\beta_i = 0$), the analyst compares the Wald-statistic given in the output to a critical Wald-value. In the limit, this critical Wald-value is equivalent to the t-statistic and hence the value used for comparison is that of the t-statistic taken at various levels of confidence (see sub-section 2.8.3 on how to calculate this value). Assuming a 95 percent confidence level (i.e. alpha = 0.05) the critical Wald-value is 1.96 (many round this to 2.0). If the absolute value of the Wald-test statistic given in the output is greater than the critical Wald-value, the analyst may reject the hypothesis that the parameter equals zero and conclude that the explanatory variable is statistically significant. If, on the other hand, the absolute value of the Wald-test statistic given in the output is less than the critical Wald-value, the analyst cannot reject the hypothesis that the parameter equals zero and therefore must conclude that the explanatory variable is not statistically significant.

The final column of output provides the probability value (known as a p-value) for the Wald-test of the previous column:

```
+---------+-------------+---------------+--------+---------+
|Variable | Coefficient | Standard Error |b/St.Er.|P[|Z|>z] |
+---------+-------------+---------------+--------+---------+
ASCCART       -.08252881       .07552527   -1.093    .2745
CST           -.20180890       .01916932  -10.528    .0000
ASCCARNT       .41384399       .07640648    5.416    .0000
ASCBUS         .01966141       .09923321     .198    .8429
ASCTN         -.04174518       .09373128    -.445    .6561
ASCBUSW        .09250653       .08587656    1.077    .2814
```

As with the log-ratio Chi-square test, the analyst compares the p-value to some predetermined confidence level as given by alpha. Assuming a 95 percent confidence level, alpha equals 0.05. p-values less than the determined level of alpha suggest that that parameter is not statistically equal to zero (i.e. the explanatory variable is statistically significant) while p-values that exceed the level of alpha as assigned by the analyst indicate that a parameter is statistically equal to zero (and hence the explanatory variable is not statistically significant). At the same level of confidence, both the Wald-test and the p-value will draw the same conclusion for the analyst.

10.3.8.1 Matrix: LastDsta/LastOutput

At the end of each NLOGIT output, you will notice a box similar to that shown in figure 10.8.

By double clicking on this button, NLOGIT will open the output preceding the button in a pop-up box that appears in a similar format to Microsoft Excel. This may prove extremely useful if one wishes to transfer the output into a second program such as Excel (keep this in mind when reading the next two sections). Figure 10.9 shows one such pop-up screen for the choice model output for our mode choice example.

It is far easier to select the cells in these pop-up matrices and copy these into a second program than to copy and paste the output from NLOGIT's output editor. For some (but not all) output, these pop-up matrices provide additional output not shown in the output editor. For example, the output matrix for the descriptive statistics output provides the analyst with information on both skewness and kurtosis, information not available in the general output editor.

As an aside, the output produced by NLOGIT is best saved to a word file in courier font with point size 8. When you copy and paste the output as is, it will look very messy in other default fonts and sizes (e.g. 12 point Times Roman).

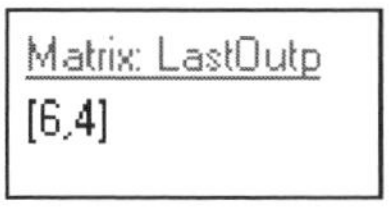

Matrix: LastOutp
[6,4]

Figure 10.8 *Matrix: LastDsta* button

Matrix - LastOutp

[6, 4] Cell:

	Coeff.	Std.Err.	t-ratio	P-value
ASCCART	-0.0825288	0.0755253	-1.09273	0.274512
CST	-0.201809	0.0191693	-10.5277	2.88658e-015
ASCCARNT	0.413844	0.0764065	5.41635	6.08291e-008
ASCBUS	0.0196614	0.0992332	0.198133	0.842941
ASCTN	-0.0417452	0.0937313	-0.445371	0.656052
ASCBUSW	0.0925065	0.0858766	1.0772	0.281389

Figure 10.9 *Matrix: LastOutp* example

10.4 Interpreting parameters for effects and dummy coded variables

Throughout this chapter, we have explored models with variables specified as linear effects only. An interesting question is: how do we handle models that incorporate non-linear effects derived either by the effects or dummy coding of variables to be used within models of discrete choice?

Let us consider the case of dummy coding (effects codes will be handled in exactly the same manner). The following command syntax may be used to dummy code the fare attribute for the public transport modes for the commutes segment of 30 minutes or less. This syntax will divide the fare attribute into two new variables (recall that the fare attribute may take the values \$1, \$3, or \$5) such that the newly created *fare1d* variable will equal one if the fare attribute equals one or zero otherwise and the newly created *fare3d* variable will equal one if the fare attribute equals three or zero otherwise. When the fare attribute takes the value five, both *fare1d* and *fare3d* will simultaneously take the value zero, hence representing the base level for the recoded fare attribute.

```
CREATE
;if(fare=1)fare1d=1
;if(fare=3)fare3d=1 $
```

It is possible within a model specification that an attribute that relates to two or more alternatives be linear for one alternative yet enter the utility functions of other alternatives as non-linear terms. We show this in the following model specification, in which the analyst assigns the non-linear dummy coded fare attribute to the busway alternative but retains the linear effects format for the remaining alternatives:

```
NLOGIT
;lhs = choice, cset, altij
;Choices=cart, carnt, bus, train, busway, LR
;Model:
```

U(cart) = asccart + cst*fuel /
U(carnt) = asccarnt + cst*fuel /
U(bus) = ascbus + cst*fare /
U(train) = asctn + cst*fare /
U(busway) = ascbusw + fare1d*fare1d + fare3d*fare3d /
U(LR) = cst*fare $

The above syntax produces the following model results:

```
+-----------------------------------------------+
| Discrete choice (multinomial logit) model     |
| Maximum Likelihood Estimates                  |
| Model estimated: Feb 30, 2003 at 07:00:00AM.  |
| Dependent variable              Choice        |
| Weighting variable                None        |
| Number of observations            2369        |
| Iterations completed                 5        |
| Log likelihood function      -3217.960        |
| R2=1-LogL/LogL*  Log-L fncn  R-sqrd  RsqAdj   |
| No coefficients  -4244.6782  .24188  .24103   |
| Constants only.  Must be computed directly.   |
|                 Use NLOGIT ;...; RHS=ONE  $   |
| Chi-squared[ 3]             = 1643.45932      |
| Prob [ chi squared > value ] =    .00000      |
| Response data are given as ind. choice.       |
| Number of obs.= 2369, skipped   0 bad obs.    |
+-----------------------------------------------+
+----------+-------------+----------------+--------+---------+
| Variable | Coefficient | Standard Error |b/St.Er.|P[|Z|>z] |
+----------+-------------+----------------+--------+---------+
 ASCCART     -.06486119     .07603214       -.853     .3936
 CST         -.18202714     .02173768      -8.374     .0000
 ASCCARNT     .39187088     .07707979       5.084     .0000
 ASCBUS       .02057009     .09912476        .208     .8356
 ASCTN       -.04100211     .09358635       -.438     .6613
 ASCBUSW     -.95673266     .15650056      -6.113     .0000
 FARE1D      1.05038514     .16650421       6.308     .0000
 FARE3D       .38559604     .17653647       2.184     .0289
```

Ignoring the overall model fit, the parameter estimates for the *fare1d* and *fare3d* variables are 1.05 and 0.386, respectively. Noting our earlier discussion on interpreting parameter estimates with regard to the probabilities produced by the model, extrapolating behavioral meaningful interpretations from either parameter beyond the sign, relative magnitude, and statistical significance is not possible without first undertaking some form of logit transformation. Nevertheless, we are able to examine the utility function derived from our model without the requirement of such a transformation. We do so below, showing the utility function for the busway alternative only:

$$V_{busway} = -0.9567326611 + 1.050385138 \times \text{Fare1d} + 0.3855960448 \times \text{Fare3d}$$

Before examining the utility function and estimating the relative utilities for the different fare attribute levels, we note that the fare parameters for the busway alternative are of the correct sign and are both statistically significant. That is, the parameter estimate for the *fare1d* variable is of greater magnitude than the parameter estimate for the *fare3d* variable, and hence the model will predict a higher probability of selecting the busway alternative for a busway fare of \$1 than for a busway fare of \$3. Similarly, the utility estimated by the above model for a busway fare of \$1 will be higher than the utility associated with a busway fare of \$3. We show this by a process of substitution. The relative (dis)utilities for the various fare levels are calculated as 0.09 for a busway fare of \$1 (i.e. $fare1d = 1$ and $fare3d = 0$), -0.57 for a busway fare of \$3 (i.e. $fare1d = 0$ and $fare3d = 1$), and -0.96 for a busway fare of \$5 (i.e. $fare1d = 0$ and $fare3d = 0$), *all else being equal*. We plot these (dis)utilities in figure 10.10.

The utility values estimated from the model are shown in figure 10.10 in grey. The light grey columns show the relative utilities at each discrete point of measure (i.e. attribute level; effects or dummy codes measure utilities at discrete points in preference space, hence one should not use linear lines to represent relationships between the points). Comparing the columns representing the utility estimates for the non-linear in effects dummy coded fare attribute (dark grey) to that of the linear in effects fare attribute suggests that the utility estimates of the non-linear in effects impact could sufficiently be explained using a less complicated linear specification. Specifically, this is a question as to whether the slopes for the utility estimates over the range of the non-linear coded variables are equal, and as such would best be represented as a single linear function. Formally this may be tested statistically using the Wald-test for linear restrictions.

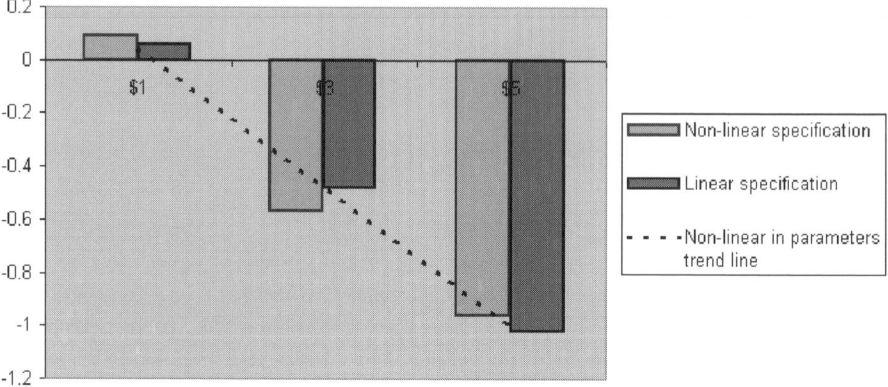

Figure 10.10 Linear and non-linear in parameters marginal utilities

We show the general command format for the Wald-test of linear restrictions below. Note the use of a colon (**:**) after the command **Wald** and not a semi-colon (**;**):

;Wald: <linear restriction>

In providing the specific linear restriction required for the test, the analyst specifies the test in terms of the restriction(s) to be placed upon the parameters required for the relevant test. The linear restriction specification for the above problem is entered into NLOGIT in the following format:

;Wald: b(<j>) - b(<k>) = 0

We use j and k to specify which parameters in the NLOGIT output the test is to be applied to. Examining the NLOGIT output, the two parameters of interest appear seventh and eighth in the model output and hence we substitute the value 7 for j and 8 for k in the above specification. Explicitly, the command as entered into NLOGIT for the above problem would appear as shown below:

;Wald: b(7) - b(8) = 0

We show the entire NLOGIT command syntax below:

```
NLOGIT
;lhs = choice, cset, altij
;Choices=cart, carnt, bus, train, busway, LR
;Wald:b(7) - b(8) = 0
;Model:
U(cart) = asccart+ cst*fuel /
U(carnt) = asccarnt + cst*fuel /
U(bus) = ascbus + cst*fare /
U(train) = asctn + cst*fare /
U(busway) = ascbusw + fare1d*fare1d + fare3d*fare3d /
U(LR) = cst*fare $
```

The first section of NLOGIT output generated from the above NLOGIT command syntax is shown below. We omit the output showing the parameter estimates for the above command syntax as there are no changes in these estimates from the previous output shown.

Highlighted in the output is the section pertaining to this test produced by NLOGIT:

```
+----------------------------------------------+
| Discrete choice (multinomial logit) model    |
| Maximum Likelihood Estimates                 |
| Model estimated: Feb 30,  2003 at 07:15:00AM. |
| Dependent variable                 Choice    |
| Weighting variable                   None    |
| Number of observations               2369    |
| Iterations completed                    5    |
| Log likelihood function         -3217.960    |
```

```
| R2=1-LogL/LogL*    Log-L fncn  R-sqrd  RsqAdj    |
| No coefficients    -4244.6782  .24188  .24103    |
| Constants only.    Must be computed directly.    |
|                    Use NLOGIT ;...; RHS=ONE $    |
| Chi-squared[ 3]             = 1643.45932         |
| Prob [ chi squared > value ]  =   .00000         |
| Response data are given as ind. choice.          |
| Number of obs.= 2369,  skipped    0 bad obs.     |
| Wald-test of 1 linear restrictions               |
| Chi-squared =   18.73,   Sig. level =   .00002   |
+--------------------------------------------------+
```

In this particular case, we requested a test involving only a single linear restriction. For dummy or effects coded variables with more than two associated parameter estimates, more linear restrictions will be required to test the slopes over the entire range of the variable of interest (discussed below). The test-statistic for this test is a Chi-square statistic with degrees of freedom equal to the number of linear restriction imposed upon the model (i.e. one for this example). We use the probability value provided to determine whether the hypothesis (shown below) for the test is rejected or not. The hypothesis for this test is:

$$\mathrm{H}_0 : \beta_7 - \beta_8 \neq 0; \text{or } \beta_7 \neq \beta_8$$
$$\mathrm{H}_1 : \beta_7 - \beta_8 = 0; \text{or } \beta_7 = \beta_8$$

Examining the probability value shown in the output, the value of 0.0002 is less than our alpha of 0.05. Hence we reject the null hypothesis and conclude that, at the 95 percent level of confidence, the slopes of the dummy variable parameter estimates are equal. This finding suggests that a single linear effect would sufficiently capture the information observed using the non-linear effect specification used.

We show the command syntax for the model with the fare attribute for the busway specified as a linear effect below:

```
NLOGIT
;lhs = choice, cset, altij
;Choices=cart, carnt, bus, train, busway, LR
;Model:
U(cart) = asccart+ cst*fuel /
U(carnt) = asccarnt + cst*fuel /
U(bus) = ascbus + cst*fare /
U(train) = asctn + cst*fare /
U(busway) = ascbusw + buswfare*fare /
U(LR) = cst*fare $
```

For the 30 minutes or less commuter segment, the above NLOGIT command produces the following result:

```
+--------------------------------------------------+
| Discrete choice (multinomial logit) model         |
| Maximum Likelihood Estimates                      |
| Model estimated: Feb 30,  2003 at 07:30:00AM.     |
| Dependent variable                Choice          |
| Weighting variable                  None          |
| Number of observations              2369          |
| Iterations completed                   5          |
| Log likelihood function        -3218.441          |
| R2=1-LogL/LogL*  Log-L fncn  R-sqrd  RsqAdj       |
| No coefficients  -4244.6782  .24177  .24102       |
| Constants only.  Must be computed directly.       |
|                  Use NLOGIT ;...; RHS=ONE $       |
| Chi-squared[ 2]              = 1642.49914         |
| Prob [ chi squared > value ]     = .00000         |
| Response data are given as ind.  choice.          |
| Number of obs.= 2369, skipped 0 bad obs.          |
+--------------------------------------------------+
+----------+-------------+----------------+--------+---------+
| Variable | Coefficient | Standard Error |b/St.Er.|P[|Z|>z] |
+----------+-------------+----------------+--------+---------+
 ASCCART    -.06565401      .07603514       -.863    .3879
 CST        -.18276235      .02172310      -8.413    .0000
 ASCCARNT    .39256214      .07707012       5.094    .0000
 ASCBUS      .02150109      .09910716        .217    .8282
 ASCTN      -.04096956      .09358895       -.438    .6616
 ASCBUSW     .32598510      .15223518       2.141    .0322
 BUSWFARE   -.26940378      .04163606      -6.470    .0000
```

Ignoring the model fit for the present, the linear effect fare attribute is statistically significant and of the correct sign (i.e. higher busway fares will result in lower utility levels for the busway alternative as well as a lower probability of that alternative being selected, *all else being equal*). The utility function for the busway alternative specified with a linear effect busway fare attribute is given below:

$$V_{busway} = 0.3259850999 - 0.269403771 \times \text{Fare}$$

Substituting busway fare values of \$1, \$3, and \$5 into the above equation suggests utility levels of 0.06, −0.48, and −1.02, respectively, *ceteris paribus*. We plot these values in figure 10.10 along with those derived from the non-linear specification.

From figure 10.10, the estimated utilities derived from the linear specification of the busway fare almost perfectly match those shown from the linear trend line fitted from the utility estimates derived from the non-linear estimates. While this need not necessarily be the case, it does provide substantive weight to the argument of using a linear effect rather than non-linear effects for the busway fare attribute in the above example.

Above, we have relied on an example which has required only two parameter estimates for a single non-linear coded variable. What if a non-linear coded variable requires more than two associated parameter estimates? In such cases, the analyst is required to perform multiple Wald-tests for linear restrictions simultaneously. That is, the analyst is required to test whether each slope associated with the non-linear coded variable is equal to every other slope. In general, the command syntax used in NLOGIT is of the following form:

;Wald: <linear restriction 1>, <linear restriction 2>, . . . , <linear restriction n>

By separating each linear restriction with a comma (,), the analyst is able to conduct several Wald-tests simultaneously. For example, assume an attribute has four attribute levels which are effects coded into three separate variables. A model estimated using these effects coded variables will produce three parameter estimates (assuming that they are not specified as generic parameters). Assuming that these parameters are the seventh, eighth, and ninth parameters estimated within the model, the NLOGIT command syntax for the Wald-test of linear restriction would look as shown below:

;Wald: b(7) - b(8) = 0, b(7)-b(9)=0, b(8)-b(9)=0

The total number of linear restrictions required for the test may be calculated using (10.23):

$$\text{Number of linear combinations} = \frac{n(n-1)}{2} \tag{10.23}$$

where n is the number of parameters estimated as part of the non-linear coding system.

For the preceding example, using (10.23) we obtain the following number of combinations:

$$\text{Number of linear combinations} = \frac{3(3-1)}{2} = 3$$

Thus, for the above hypothetical variable specified as a non-linear effect using effects (or dummy) coding will require three linear restrictions to be tested simultaneously.

The use of the Wald-test for linear restrictions to test whether the slopes of non-linear coded variables are equal is but the first step in determining whether a variable should be specified as being either linear or non-linear. The analyst is also required to consider the impact upon the overall model fit. We advise that not only should the analyst conduct the Wald-test for linear restrictions but also the log likelihood ratio-test described earlier. This test will determine whether the overall model fit is improved when a variable is treated either as a linear or non-linear effect by examining the LL function of models estimated specifying a variable as linear and non-linear effects.

For the above example, we leave it to the reader to show that the specification of the busway fare attribute as a non-linear effect does not statistically improve the model beyond the model fit derived when the busway fare attribute is specified as a linear effect. Nevertheless, it is foreseeable that a situation may arise whereby the Wald-test of linear restrictions suggests that a variable is best represented as a linear effect yet the overall model is improved statistically if the variable is specified as a non-linear effect (or vice versa). In such a case, the analyst must make a choice between overall model performance (and perhaps parsimony) and the estimates derived for that single variable.

To conclude the discussion on non-linear coded variables, consider the commonly asked question of what one should do if one or more parameter components of a variable that has been dummy or effects coded are found to be statistically insignificant. To demonstrate, consider the following NLOGIT output derived when the dummy coded fare attribute is related to the train alternative and not the busway alternative:

```
+---------+-------------+---------------+--------+---------+
|Variable | Coefficient  | Standard Error |b/St.Er.|P[|Z|>z] |
+---------+-------------+---------------+--------+---------+
ASCCART       -.08183882       .07579985     -1.080    .2803
CST           -.20090871       .02090049     -9.613    .0000
ASCCARNT       .41295828       .07713362      5.354    .0000
ASCBUS         .02315993       .09921531       .233    .8154
ASCTN         -.89160160       .15865305     -5.620    .0000
FARE1D         .78442543       .17629246      4.450    .0000
FARE3D        -.07905742       .19509511      -.405    .6853
ASCBUSW        .09300017       .08587716      1.083    .2788
```

In the above example output, the *fare1d* parameter is statistically significant while *fare3d* is statistically insignificant (i.e. $\beta_{fare\,1d} \neq 0$; $\beta_{fare\,3d} = 0$). This suggests that, *ceteris paribus*, a fare of \$1 is statistically different to the base fare of \$5 (really, the average unobserved effect for the train alternative given that we have used dummy codes and not effects codes). The positive sign suggests that a \$1 train fare is preferred to a \$5 train fare. The negative but insignificant *fare3d* parameter suggests that a fare of \$3 is statistically the same as the \$5 fare (where $\beta_{fare\,5d} = 0$). The question is: "should the analyst include the *fare3d* in the model specification or should the variable be removed and the model re-estimated (as is common practice when a variable is found to be insignificant)?"

Traditionally, the answer to this question is that when multiple variables are derived from a single attribute or variable due to dummy or effects coding, unless the entire system of dummy coded or effects coded variables is found to be statistically insignificant, then all of the variables are included within the model specification. The reason for this is that when a variable in the system of linked variables is removed and the model re-estimated, the impact of that variable, albeit statistically insignificant, enters the model via the constant term of the utility function from which the variable was removed. As such, the removal of an insignificant component of a dummy- or effects-coded variable may be viewed as confoundment with the constant term of the associated utility functions.

Tradition aside, if the removal of one or more components of a dummy- or effects-coded variable due to statistical insignificance is observed to have little or no impact upon the constant term of the associated utility function, and given that the overall model fit is not adversely affected by their removal, the analyst should seriously consider their removal. This should particularly be the case for complex models where parsimony may be a factor in determining the final model specification.

10.5 Handling interactions in choice models

The examples we have used to this point have assumed that there are no significant interaction effects present within the data. This assumption is somewhat justifiable given the well-known findings of Dawes and Corrigan (1974), who found that the vast majority of variance within linear models (recall that choice models are linear in the utility functions) can be explained by main effects attributes only. Indeed, Dawes and Corrigan found that:

- 70–90 percent of variance may be explained by main effects
- 5–15 percent of variance may be explained by two-way interactions
- Higher-order interactions account for the remaining variation.

The Dawes and Corrigan findings suggest that models incorporating all main effects and all two-way interactions will account for between 75 and 100 percent of the variation!

It is possible that non-design variables also have significant interaction effects upon choice. Consider the case of the number of vehicles owned and the number of licensed drivers within that household. It is possible that the number of vehicles owned within a household will have a differential impact upon the choice of mode when considered in concert with the number of licensed drivers within that same household. As such, the analyst may consider estimating a model inclusive of the interaction effect between the number of vehicles owned within a household (*numbvehs* in the data set) and the number of licensed drivers within each household (*drivlic*). The following NLOGIT command syntax may be used to generate just such an interaction variable:

```
CREATE
;vehlic=numbvehs*drivlic $
```

For the *carnt* alternative, to estimate a model that includes the "number of vehicles–number of licensed drivers" interaction, the following command syntax may be employed. We have not included the number of vehicles and number of drivers with licenses as separate variables within the model specification. Unlike attributes from an experimental design which may be manufactured such that the interaction of two or more attributes may be treated orthogonally to the main effects of the interacted attributes, the interaction of non-design variables will likely be highly collinear with the variables that were used to produce the interaction. Thus the inclusion of the separate variables along with their associated interaction is likely to induce multicollinearity within the model:

```
NLOGIT
;lhs = choice, cset, altij
;Choices=cart, carnt, bus, train, busway, LR
;Model:
U(cart) = asccart + cst*fuel /
U(carnt) = asccarnt + cst*fuel + vehlic*vehlic /
U(bus) = ascbus + cst*fare /
U(train) = asctn + cst*fare /
U(busway) = ascbusw + cst*fare /
U(LR) = cst*fare $
```

The above command syntax produces the following NLOGIT output:

```
+-----------------------------------------------+
| Discrete choice (multinomial logit) model      |
| Maximum Likelihood Estimates                   |
| Model estimated: Feb 30, 2003 at 07:45:00AM.   |
| Dependent variable              Choice         |
| Weighting variable                None         |
| Number of observations            2369         |
| Iterations completed                 5         |
| Log likelihood function      -3214.791         |
| R2=1-LogL/LogL*  Log-L fncn  R-sqrd  RsqAdj    |
| No coefficients  -4244.6782  .24263  .24188    |
| Constants only. Must be computed directly.     |
|                 Use NLOGIT ;...; RHS=ONE   $   |
| Chi-squared[ 2]  =          1649.79774         |
| Prob [ chi squared > value ] =    .00000       |
| Response data are given as ind. choice.        |
| Number of obs.=  2369,  skipped  0 bad obs.    |
+-----------------------------------------------+

+----------+------------+----------------+----------+----------+
| Variable | Coefficient | Standard Error | b/St.Er. | P[|Z|>z] |
+----------+------------+----------------+----------+----------+
 ASCCART    -.08134599     .07552487       -1.077      .2814
 CST        -.20179932     .01917615      -10.523      .0000
 ASCCARNT    .14618264     .11271695        1.297      .1947
 VEHLIC      .14212966     .04326984        3.285      .0010
 ASCBUS      .02211412     .09926283         .223      .8237
 ASCTN      -.04219174     .09373865        -.450      .6526
 ASCBUSW     .09484292     .08589973        1.104      .2695
```

The "number of vehicles–number of drivers" interaction is a statistically significant contributor in explaining mode choice. From the output above, the utility function for the *carnt* alternative may be stated as follows:

$$V_{carnt} = 0.1461826366 + 0.1421296639 \times vehlic$$

Table 10.4 shows the part-worth utility estimates for various combinations of number of vehicles owned and number of licensed drivers within a household, *holding everything else constant*.

Figure 10.11 graphs the part-worth or marginal utilities shown in table 10.5. Given the different marginal utility levels representing the estimated part-worth utilities for each combination of number of vehicles owned and number of licensed drivers within a household,

Table 10.4. *Part-worth utility estimates for the "number of vehicles-number of drivers" interaction*

Number of licensed drivers	Number of vehicles 0	Number of vehicles 1	Number of vehicles 2	Number of vehicles 3
0	0	0	0	0
1	0	0.1421	0.2843	0.4264
2	0	0.2843	0.5685	0.8528
3	0	0.4264	0.8528	1.2792

Table 10.5. *Part-worth utility estimates for the fare–time interaction*

	Time		
Fare ($)	10 min	15 min	20 min
1	0.565991	0.321553	0
3	1.923311	1.632061	0
5	0	0	0

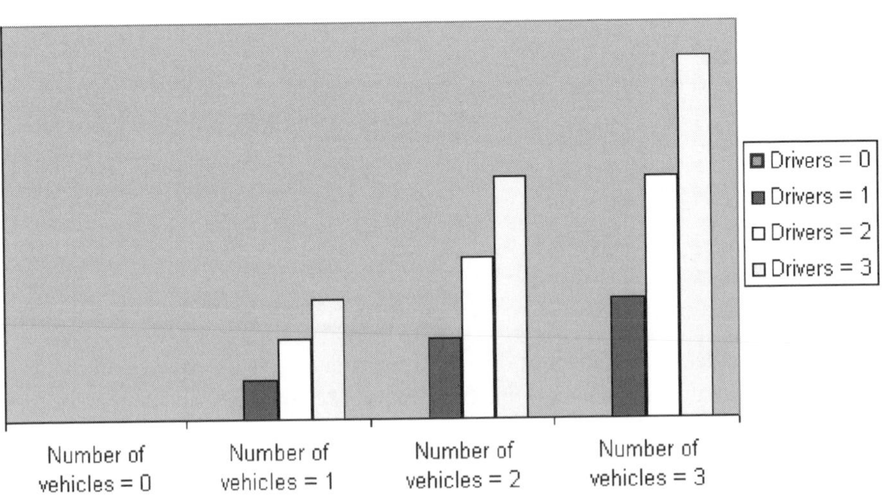

Figure 10.11 Marginal utility estimates for the "number of vehicles–number of drivers" interaction

the number of vehicles owned and number of licensed drivers resident within a household have a differential impact upon preference formation for the *carnt* alternative over different combinations of values of each variable. Had the model been specified with the variables treated as separate entities rather than as the interaction of the two, the model would likely have produced a sub-optimal solution in terms of the utilities and probabilities estimated.

The interaction of categorically coded variables poses problems in terms of the number of combinations that are created. Consider the interaction of the *fare* and *time* attributes. If both attributes are specified as linear in effects, then the interaction created by the multiplication of the two attributes will produce a single new interaction variable (i.e. *fare* × *time*). If on the other hand, one of the attributes is dummy or effects coded, the interaction created by the multiplication of each attribute requires that the linear in effects coded attribute be multiplied by each of the dummy coded variables associated with the second attribute (e.g. *fare1d* × *time*; *fare3d* × *time*). Finally, if multiple attributes are categorically coded (either dummy or effects coded), each combination of category codes must be multiplied in order to obtain the total interaction term over all the attributes (e.g. *fare1d* × *time10d*; *fare1d* × *time15d*; *fare3d* × *time10d*; *fare3d* × *time15d*). The above is of interest not only because the analyst may have to create a large number of new variables to estimate relatively simple interaction effects, but also because each new variable created will require an additional degree of freedom for estimation purposes.

The following command syntax will dummy code the design attributes *fare* and *time*. We have created these dummy codes for the 30 minutes or less travel segment only. As previous, the base level for the *fare* attribute will be \$5. The base attribute for the travel *time* attribute will be 20 minutes:

```
CREATE
;if(fare=1)fare1d=1
;if(fare=3)fare3d=1
;if(time=10)time10d=1
;if(time=15)time15d=1 $
```

From the above coding system, four interaction variables may be created, corresponding to the four non-zero combinations:

```
CREATE
;fr1tim10=fare1d*time10d
;fr1tim15=fare1d*time15d
;fr3tim10=fare3d*time10d
;fr3tim15=fare3d*time15d $
```

The following NLOGIT command syntax will specify the newly created fare–time interaction effects to the *bus* alternative. Unlike the previous example, below we have assigned the *fare* and *time* attributes as separate variables to the newly created interaction effects in the model specification. We leave it to the reader to show that the *fare* and *time* interaction is orthogonal to the main effects of the experimental design used (this can be done by estimating the interaction effect correlations from table 10.3):

```
NLOGIT
;lhs = choice, cset, altij
;Choices = cart, carnt, bus, train, busway, LR
;Model:
U(cart) = asccart + cst*fuel /
U(carnt) = asccarnt + cst*fuel /
```

```
U(bus) = ascbus + fare1d*fare1d + fare3d*fare3d + time10d*time10d + time15d*time15d
+ fr1tim10*fr1tim10 + fr1tim15*fr1tim15 + fr3tim10*fr3tim10 +fr3tim15*fr3tim15/
U(train) = asctn + cst*fare /
U(busway) = ascbusw + cst*fare /
U(LR) = cst*fare $
```

The above command syntax will produce the following NLOGIT output for the 30 minutes or less commuting segment:

```
+-----------------------------------------------+
| Discrete choice (multinomial logit) model      |
| Maximum Likelihood Estimates                   |
| Model estimated: Feb 30, 2003 at 08:00:00AM.   |
| Dependent variable                 Choice      |
| Weighting variable                   None      |
| Number of observations               2369      |
| Iterations completed                    5      |
| Log likelihood function         -3199.521      |
| R2=1-LogL/LogL*  Log-L fncn  R-sqrd  RsqAdj    |
| No coefficients  -4244.6782  .24623  .24474    |
| Constants only. Must be computed directly.     |
|                 Use NLOGIT ;...; RHS=ONE  $    |
| Chi-squared[ 9]         =      1680.33774      |
| Prob [ chi squared > value ] =     .00000      |
| Response data are given as ind. choice.        |
| Number of obs.= 2369, skipped   0 bad obs.     |
+-----------------------------------------------+
```

Variable	Coefficient	Standard Error	b/St.Er.	P[|Z|>z]
ASCCART	-.08707311	.07599997	-1.146	.2519
CST	-.20667650	.02151974	-9.604	.0000
ASCCARNT	.42027780	.07732727	5.435	.0000
ASCBUS	-.58526890	.23804503	-2.459	.0139
FARE1D	.18215774	.30647725	.594	.5523
FARE3D	-.78898243	.37082692	-2.128	.0334
TIME10D	-1.12908799	.38608573	-2.924	.0035
TIME15D	-.77819044	.37058594	-2.100	.0357
FR1TIM10	1.15126269	.48398644	2.379	.0174
FR1TIM15	.90682185	.47411641	1.913	.0558
FR3TIM10	2.50857566	.52587695	4.770	.0000
FR3TIM15	2.21733199	.51153916	4.335	.0000
ASCTN	-.03988432	.09384786	-.425	.6708
ASCBUSW	.09092551	.08591272	1.058	.2899

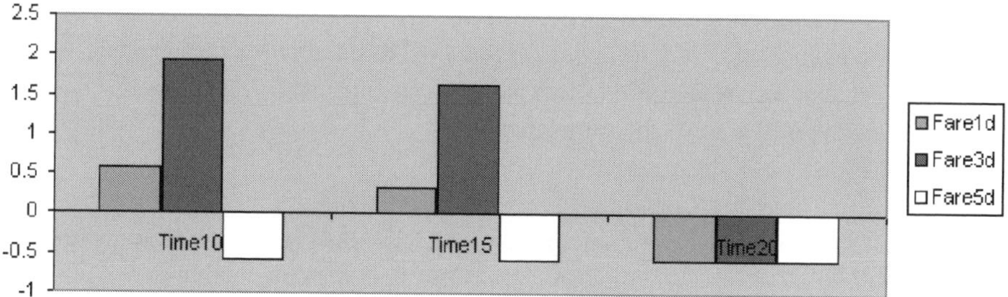

Figure 10.12 Marginal utility estimates for the "fare–time" interaction

At the 95 percent confidence level, three of the four interaction terms are statistically significant. The analyst may consider removing the non-significant interaction effect and re-estimating the model. We do not do this here.

From the above output, the utility function for the *bus* alternative may be expressed as follows:

$$
\begin{aligned}
V_{bus} = & -0.5852688990 + 0.1821577393 \times \text{fare1d} - 0.7889824297 \times \text{fare3d} \\
& -1.129087991 \times \text{time10d} \\
& - 0.7781904374 \times \text{time15d} + 1.151262686 \times \text{fr1}tim\text{10} \\
& + 0.9065218500 \times \text{fr1tim15} \\
& + 2.508575662 \times \text{fr3tim10} + 2.217331989 \times \text{fr3tim15}
\end{aligned}
$$

Examining the parameters for the *fare* attribute suggests that the highest utility will be derived for bus fares of \$1 and the lowest utilities from bus fares of \$3, *ceteris paribus*. Similarly, the negative parameter estimates associated with the *time* attribute suggests that shorter travel times will produce higher utilities for the *bus* alternative relative to the other alternatives, *all else being equal*. Ignoring the improbability of these findings, the significant "*fare–time*" interaction effects implies that one should not examine the *fare* and *time* parameters in isolation. That is to say that *fare* and *time* are in some manner acting in concert in the development of preference towards the *bus* alternative. As such, holding everything else constant, the part-worth utilities derived from the fare–time interaction are shown in table 10.5.

Figure 10.12 shows the part-worth (marginal) utility estimates as shown in table 10.5. As seen in table 10.5 and figure 10.12, the differing combinations of time and fare interact to create a differential impact upon the utility formation for the *bus* alternative, all else being equal. By dummy coding as opposed to effects coding, the utilities for combinations including either bus fares of \$5 and/or 20 minutes of travel time are confounded perfectly with the constant term.

10.6 Measures of willingness to pay

A common objective in the use of discrete choice models is the derivation of measures designed to determine the amount of money individuals are willing to forfeit in order to obtain some benefit from the undertaking of some specific action or task. Such measures are referred to as measures of *willingness to pay* (WTP). In simple linear models,[3] WTP measures are calculated as the ratio of two parameter estimates, *holding all else constant*. Provided at least one attribute is measured in monetary units, the ratio of the two parameters will provide a financial indicator of WTP.

One such important WTP measure in transportation studies is the *value of travel time savings* (VTTS), defined as the amount of money an individual is willing to outlay in order to save a unit of time spent traveling, *ceteris paribus*. Specifically, such measures are used in determining road and public transportation pricing. WTP measures are also important to environmental economic studies in which a not uncommon objective is the valuation of non-monetary attributes such as air or water quality.

The following NLOGIT command syntax may be used to estimate a model which will allow for the derivation of a VTTS measure for the *carnt* alternative:

```
;lhs = choice, cset, altij
;Choices=cart, carnt, bus, train, busway, LR
;Model:
U(cart) = asccart + cst*fuel /
U(carnt) = asccarnt + cst*fuel + time*time/
U(bus) = ascbus + cst*fare /
U(train) = asctn + cst*fare /
U(busway) = ascbusw + cst*fare /
U(LR) = cst*fare $
```

As an aside, if VTTS are to be estimated for two or more alternatives and all attributes to be used in the calculation of the WTP measure are specified generic, the resulting VTTS will be generic to all alternatives inclusive. For example:

```
U(cart) = asccart + cst*fuel + time*time /
U(carnt) = asccarnt + cst*fuel + time*time/
```

will allow for the estimation of the WTP for car travel, inclusive of travel on both toll and non-toll roads. Separate VTTS measures for each car alternative will not be possible. If at least one parameter is alternative-specific, alternative-specific WTP measures may be calculated. For example:

```
U(cart) = asccart + cstct*fuel + timect*time /
U(carnt) = asccarnt + cstcnt*fuel + timecnt*time /
```

will allow the estimation of VTTS specific to travel on toll and non-tolled roads when using a car. In the above example, as long as the time or cost parameter is alternative-specific, the use of a generic parameter for the second attribute would still allow for the estimation of alternative-specific measures of VTTS.

[3] As models of discrete choice are linear in the utility functions, the choice modeler is able to take advantage of this fact.

For the 30 minutes or less commuting segment, the following output was generated:

```
+----------------------------------------------+
| Discrete choice (multinomial logit) model    |
| Maximum Likelihood Estimates                 |
| Model estimated: Feb 30, 2003 at 08:15:00AM  |
| Dependent variable              Choice       |
| Weighting variable                None       |
| Number of observations            2369       |
| Iterations completed                 5       |
| Log likelihood function      -3214.722       |
| R2=1-LogL/LogL* Log-L fncn  R-sqrd  RsqAdj   |
| No coefficients  -4244.6782 .24265  .24190   |
| Constants only. Must be computed directly.   |
|               Use NLOGIT ;...; RHS=ONE  $    |
| Chi-squared[ 2]         =     1649.93536     |
| Prob [ chi squared > value ] =    .00000     |
| Response data are given as ind. choice.      |
| Number of obs.= 2369, skipped   0 bad obs.   |
+----------------------------------------------+
```

Variable	Coefficient	Standard Error	b/St.Er.	P[|Z|>z]
ASCCART	-.08020336	.07552448	-1.062	.2883
CST	-.20043709	.01917685	-10.452	.0000
ASCCARNT	1.15532467	.23689518	4.877	.0000
TIME	-.03739286	.01138050	-3.286	.0010
ASCBUS	.02092759	.09925844	.211	.8330
ASCTN	-.04028250	.09377288	-.430	.6675
ASCBUSW	.09261623	.08587024	1.079	.2808

In calculating a measure of WTP, it is important that both attributes to be used in the calculation are found to be statistically significant, otherwise no meaningful WTP measure can be established. For the above example, the VTTS are to be calculated from the cost and time parameters, which are both statistically significant. If, as is the case with VTTS, one attribute is measured in monetary terms, it is important that that attribute be treated as the denominator in the ratio of the two parameters to be used. As such, the VTTS from the above model may be calculated as follows:

$$\text{VTTS} = \left(\frac{\beta_{time}}{\beta_{cst}}\right) \times 60$$

$$= \left(\frac{-0.03739285660}{-0.2004370929}\right) \times 60 = 11.19\ \$/\text{per hour}$$

We have multiplied the VTTS measure by 60 to give a measure of WTP measured in dollars per hour rather dollars per minute.

As an aside, WTP measures are calculated as the ratios of two parameters, and as such are sensitive to the *attribute-level ranges* used in the estimation of both parameters. Some researchers have recently observed differences in WTP measures derived from SP and RP data sources, and have claimed that these differences may be the result of the hypothetical nature of SP data in which respondents are not bound by real life constraints in the choices made. As such, many prefer WTP measures derived from RP data where such constraints are binding. What is only now being acknowledged is that such differences may in part be the result of different attribute-level ranges being employed across different studies. Even for WTP measures derived from different data sets of similar type (e.g. SP and SP, or RP and RP), differences in the attribute-levels ranges may account for some if not all of any differences observed in WTP measures derived. It is important therefore that researchers report the attribute-level ranges used in deriving WTP measures if any objective comparison is to be made across studies.

More complex WTP measures can be obtained for non-linear models in which the valuation of an attribute is itself a function of the level of an attribute and other interacted influences. We discuss this in chapter 15 and 16 on mixed logit models.

10.7 Obtaining choice probabilities for the sample

NLOGIT has the capability to calculate the choice probabilities for each respondent within the sample. Rather than reproduce the probabilities as output, NLOGIT can save these probabilities as a *variable* in the data set (by resaving the .SAV file) which can then be used for further analysis. The command to produce these probabilities is:

```
;Prob = <name>
```

We append this command to the base choice model command below:

```
NLOGIT
;lhs = choice, cset, altij
;Choices = <names of alternatives>
;Model:
U(<alternative 1 name>) =<utility function 1> /
U(<alternative 2 name>) =<utility function 2> /
...
U(<alternative i name>) = <utility function i>
;Prob = <name> $
```

As an aside, we have placed the **;Prob = <name>** command at the end of the command syntax. Any additional command to the base MNL command, such as the **;Prob** or **;Maxit** commands may appear either before or after the utility function specifications.

In placing the **;Prob** command after the last utility function, the dollar sign (**$**) is no longer present after the last utility function. The dollar sign is not to be replaced with a slash (/) at the end of the last utility expression, but by a semi-colon.

Returning to our mode-choice example, we name the new probability variable *p1* although we could have used any name so long as it is no more than eight characters long. The command syntax thus becomes:

```
NLOGIT
;lhs = choice, cset, altij
;Choices = cart, carnt, bus, train, busway, LR
;Model:
U(cart)     = asccart + cst*fuel /
U(carnt)    = asccarnt + cst*fuel /
U(bus)      = ascbus + cst*fare /
U(train)    = asctn + cst*fare /
U(busway)   = ascbusw + cst*fare /
U(LR)       = cst*fare
;Prob       = p1 $
```

The output generated is unchanged, however, the analyst will note the existence of a new variable at the end of the Data Editor. We show this in figure 10.13.

Figure 10.13 shows the choice probabilities for the first decision maker as calculated by NLOGIT using (10.17). The first two probabilities are missing as these rows represent

TIME15D	FR1TIM10	FR1TIM15	FR3TIM10	FR3TIM15	P1
1	0	0	0	0	0.285731
0	0	0	0	0	0.209388
1	0	1	0	0	0.297625
0	0	0	1	0	0.207257
0	0	0	0	0	0.231392
1	0	0	0	0	0.310653
0	0	0	0	0	0.150463
0	0	0	0	0	0.307492
0	0	0	0	0	0.242487
0	0	0	0	0	0.325549
1	0	0	0	0	0.179383
0	0	0	0	0	0.252581
1	0	0	0	0	0.285731
0	0	0	0	0	0.209388
1	0	1	0	0	0.297625
0	0	0	1	0	0.207257
0	0	0	0	0	0.242487

Figure 10.13 Model probabilities saved within NLOGIT

	A	B	C	D	E	F	G	H
1	**alts**	**probs**	**alts**	**probs(all)**	**probs(rest)**			
2	Cart	0.285731	Cart	=(H11)/(SUM(H$11:H$16))	=H11/(H$11+H$12+H$14+H$16)			
3	Carnt	0.209388	Carnt	=(H12)/(SUM(H$11:H$16))	=H12/(H$11+H$12+H$14+H$16)			
4			Bus	=(H13)/(SUM(H$11:H$16))				
5	Train	0.297625	Train	=(H14)/(SUM(H$11:H$16))	=H14/(H$11+H$12+H$14+H$16)			
6			Busway	=(H15)/(SUM(H$11:H$16))				
7	LR	0.207257	LR	=(H16)/(SUM(H$11:H$16))	=H16/(H$11+H$12+H$14+H$16)			
8	Sum:	1.000001		=SUM(D2:D7)	=SUM(E2:E7)			
9								
10	**alts**					**Cost**		
11	Cart	ASCCart	-0.132949288	CST	-0.377367075	1	Cart	=EXP(C11+F11*E11)
12	Carnt	ASCPOVNT	0.33641144	CST	-0.377367075	5	Carnt	=EXP(C12+F12*E12)
13	Bus	ASCBUS	0.027860345	CST	-0.377367075		Bus	=EXP(C13+F13*E13)
14	Train	ASCTN	-0.036888768	CST	-0.377367075	1	Train	=EXP(C14+F14*E14)
15	Busway	ASCBUSW	0.094842646	CST	-0.377367075		Busway	=EXP(C15+F15*E15)
16	LR			CST	-0.377367075	3	LR	=EXP(E16*F16)
17								
18	**alts**	**probs**	**alts**	**probs(all)**	**probs(rest)**			
19	Cart	0.285731	Cart	0.158409702	0.285730667			
20	Carnt	0.209388	Carnt	0.116084866	0.209387467			
21			Bus	0.214687596				
22	Train	0.297625	Train	0.165003771	0.297624684			
23			Busway	0.230910232				
24	LR	0.207257	LR	0.114903831	0.207257181			
25	Sum:	1.000001		1	1			
26								
27	**alts**					**Cost**		
28	Cart	ASCCart	-0.0825288	CST	-0.201809	1	Cart	0.752512403
29	Carnt	ASCPOVNT	0.413844	CST	-0.201809	5	Carnt	0.551451713
30	Bus	ASCBUS	0.0196614	CST	-0.201809		Bus	1.019855958
31	Train	ASCTN	-0.0417452	CST	-0.201809	1	Train	0.783836991
32	Busway	ASCBUSW	0.0925065	CST	-0.201809		Busway	1.096920272
33	LR			CST	-0.201809	3	LR	0.545841303

Figure 10.14 Calculating choice probabilities using Excel

the RP data for that decision maker which has been excluded from the analysis. As each decision maker was given three choice sets, each with four alternatives, the first four probabilities represent the probabilities of selecting the alternatives present within that choice set. Each successive block of four probabilities thus represents a subsequent choice set.

To demonstrate how NLOGIT makes this calculation, we reproduce the probabilities for the first choice set of decision maker one using Microsoft Excel. We show this in figure 10.14. Using Excel, we have placed the choice probabilities as calculated by NLOGIT for decision maker one in cells B2 to B7 (note that the probabilities sum to one as is to be expected). For choice set one the four alternatives present are *cart*, *carnt*, *train*, and *LR*. Cells C11–C15 represent the parameter estimates for the ASCs while cells E11 through E16 correspond to the cost parameter for each of the alternatives as estimated by NLOGIT. In column F of figure 10.14 we have placed the values observed by this individual for the fuel and fare attributes of the alternatives present within the choice set (the reader is free to check the data to see that the first individual did indeed observe \$1 for the cost of the *cart* alternative, \$5 for the cost of the *carnt* alternative, a \$1 fare for the *train* alternative, and \$3 for the *LR* alternative). These correspond to the X_{ki}s in (10.1).

Cells H11–H16 estimate the exponential (i.e. **exp(...)** in Excel) of the utility functions. The choice probabilities, given by (10.17), are calculated in cells D2–D7. Cells D2–D7 calculate the choice probabilities for all six alternatives, two of which where not present within the choice set. We restrict the calculation of the choice probabilities for the alternatives present within the choice set in cells E2–E7.

The resulting probabilities from this exercise are shown in cells D19–D24 for the unrestricted probability set and E19–E24 for the restricted probability set. Comparing these to the probabilities as calculated by NLOGIT suggests that NLOGIT calculates the probabilities for the restricted set of alternatives and not the unrestricted set. This should act as a warning to the analyst using variable choice set sizes.

As an aside, the analyst may use spreadsheets such as Excel set up as per figure 10.14 to test "*what-if*" scenarios. This is somewhat redundant given NLOGIT's simulation capability (discussed in chapter 11); nevertheless, it is worthwhile for the reader to perform this task at least once to gain a better understanding on how choice models actually work. Figure 10.15 shows one such "*what-if*" scenario, illustrating the impact upon individual choice probabilities given a $1 dollar increase in the cost of fuel when traveling via a tollway (i.e. we change $1 to $2 in cell F28).

We conclude our discussion on choice probabilities by returning to our earlier discussion regarding the base comparison model. We noted earlier that the sum of the choice probabilities for a given alternative across the sample defines in aggregate the number of times that alternative was chosen across the entire data set. That is, the sum of the probabilities for a given alternative is equal to the sample data choice or market share for that alternative. Having obtained the choice probabilities, we are now in a position to demonstrate this property. Before we do so however, it is necessary to discuss the **Calc;** command.

The **Calc;** command

To sum the probabilities over an alternative using NLOGIT, the analyst must use the **Calc;** command. The **Calc;** command in NLOGIT allows the analyst to preform several mathematical functions, such as summing columns of data, obtaining means of columns of data, etc. In general, the command will be of the following format:

Calc;<scalar name> = function(<existing variable name>) $

Unlike the **;Prob** command, the **Calc;** command does not create a new variable in the data. Rather, the **Calc;** command is designed to calculate a single value, otherwise known as a *scalar*. The output of this command may be found in the *Project* dialog box as shown in figure 10.16. Unless the project has been saved as a project, the Project dialog box will be titled "**Untitled Project 1***."

Within the *Project* dialog box, by clicking on the *Scalars* folder, several different NLOGIT scalar outputs are shown. By clicking on the name of a scalar, NLOGIT will open the *New Scalar* dialog box, also shown in figure 10.16. The output of the **Calc;** command is given in this dialog box within the **Expression** text box.

Within the **calc;** command, the analyst provides the scalar with a name. After the command is run, the scalar will appear in the *Project* dialog box under that name. NLOGIT allows for several functions to be performed using the NLOGIT command. For the beginner,

18	alts	probs	alts	probs(all)	probs(rest)			
19	Cart	0.285731	Cart	0.133319998	0.246378837			
20	Carnt	0.209388	Carnt	0.119545618	0.220923423			
21			Bus	0.221087917				
22	Train	0.297625	Train	0.169922906	0.314021967			
23			Busway	0.237794187				
24	LR	0.207257	LR	0.118329374	0.218675772			
25	Sum:	1.000001		1	1			
26								
27	alts					Cost		
28	Cart	ASCCart	-0.0825288	CST	-0.201809	2	Cart	0.61499152
29	Carnt	ASCPOVNT	0.413844	CST	-0.201809	5	Carnt	0.551451713
30	Bus	ASCBUS	0.0196614	CST	-0.201809		Bus	1.019855958
31	Train	ASCTN	-0.0417452	CST	-0.201809	1	Train	0.783836991
32	Busway	ASCBUSW	0.0925065	CST	-0.201809		Busway	1.096920272
33	LR			CST	-0.201809	3	LR	0.545841303

Figure 10.15 Using Excel to perform "what-if" scenarios on the choice probabilities

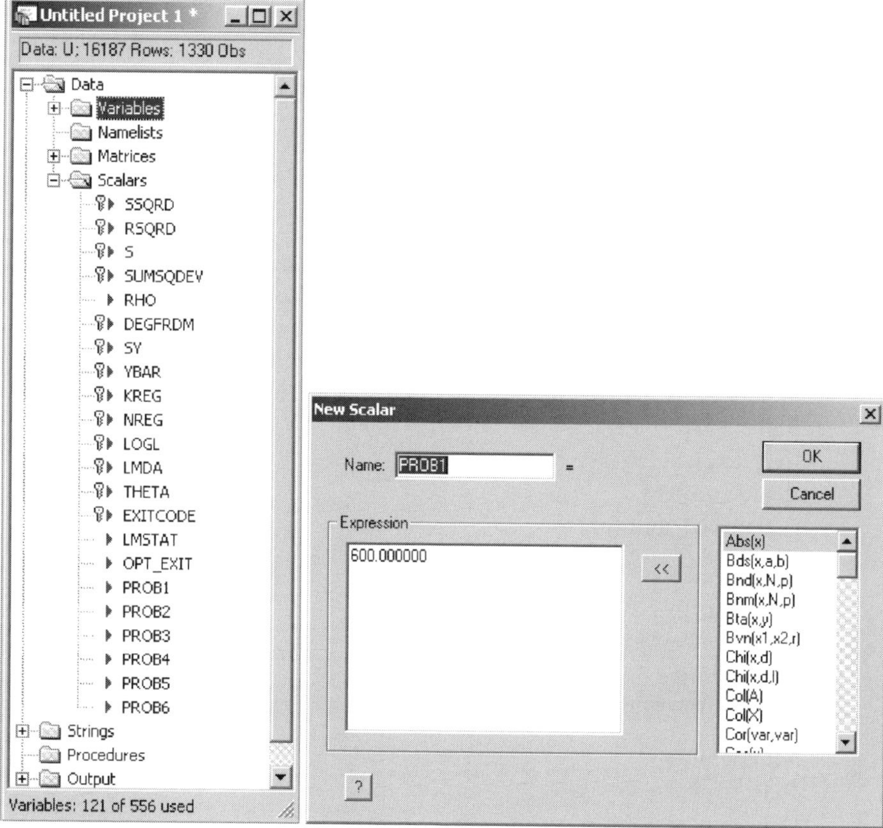

Figure 10.16 The *Project* dialog box and *New Scalar* dialog box

the most useful will consist of the following (this list is by no means definitive):

Calc; Sum(<existing variable name>)$? sum of sample values;
Calc; Xbr(<existing variable name>)$?mean of sample values;
Calc; Sdv(<existing variable name>)$?standard deviation of sample values;
Calc; Var(<existing variable name>)$?variance of sample values;
Calc; Min(<existing variable name>)$?sample minimum;
Calc; Max(<existing variable name>)$?sample maximum

The existing variable name is the name of a variable within the data set to which the calc; function is to be applied to. Thus, for example, to obtain the sum of the probabilities for alternative one, the command would look thus:

```
Calc;prob1=sum(p1) $
```

The above command will calculate the sum of a variable named *p1* and save the resulting value as a scalar called *prob1*. To obtain the sum of the probabilities for an alternative, the analyst will have to use the **Reject;** command so that NLOGIT will ignore the probabilities associated with other alternatives. Thus for the entire six alternatives of the mode choice case study, the analyst could use the following commands to obtain the sums of the probabilities for all six mode alternatives:

```
Reject;altij#1 $
Calc;prob1=sum(p1) $

Sample;all $
Reject;sprp=1 $
Reject;splength#1 $
Reject;altij#2 $
Calc;prob2=sum(p1) $

Sample;all $
Reject;sprp=1 $
Reject;splength#1 $
Reject;altij#3 $
Calc;prob3=sum(p1) $

Sample;all $
Reject;sprp=1 $
Reject;splength#1 $
Reject;altij#4 $
Calc;prob4=sum(p1) $

Sample;all $
Reject;sprp=1 $
Reject;splength#1 $
Reject;altij#5 $
Calc;prob5=sum(p1) $

Sample;all $
Reject;sprp=1 $
Reject;splength#1 $
Reject;altij#6 $
Calc;prob6=sum(p1) $
```

After the first **Reject;** command, the analyst is required to restore the entire sample before rejecting the other alternatives. The new scalar dialog box, shown in figure 10.16, shows the sum of the probabilities for the first alternative. The remaining sums of probabilities are 658, 244, 243, 319, and 305 for each of the alternatives, respectively. As we shall see in chapter 11, these choice sums exactly equal the choice or market shares observed within the data set.

10.8 Obtaining the utility estimates for the sample

NLOGIT allows the analyst to generate the utility estimates for the sampled individuals and to store them (by resaving the .SAV file) as a newly created variable at the end of the data set. The command to generate the utility estimates is:

```
;Utility =<name>
```

Similar to the command used to generate the choice probabilities, the command to generate the utility estimates may be placed either before or after the utility function specifications. For this example, we have decided to add the **Utility;** command to the end of the command syntax. We show this below.

As an aside, an analyst may wish to save a series of utility values from multiple runs of NLOGIT. This can be achieved by using a unique name for the saved set of utilities. Failure to do so will mean that the initial set of utilities are overwritten each time the NLOGIT is run. The same logic applies for saving the choice probabilities:

```
NLOGIT
;lhs = choice, cset, altij
;Choices = <names of alternatives>
;Model:
U<alternative 1 name>) =< utility function 1> /
U(<alternative 2 name>) = <utility function 2> /
...
U(<alternative i name>) = <utility function i>
;Utility = <name> $
```

The command syntax might be:

```
NLOGIT
;lhs = choice, cset, altij
;Choices = cart, carnt, bus, train, busway, LR
;Model:
U(CART)    = asccart + cst*fuel /
U(CARnot) = asccarnt + cst*fuel /
U(bus)      = ascbus + cst*fare /
U(train)   = asctn + cst*fare /
U(busway) = ascbusw + cst*fare /
U(LR)       = cst*fare
;Utility   = u1 $
```

This syntax will have NLOGIT create a new variable called *u1* in which the utilities for each alternative for each individual will be stored in memory. Figure 10.17 shows the utilities stored by NLOGIT in the variable *u1* for the first decision maker.

The first two rows of utilities are not present as these rows of data correspond to the not currently used RP data for the first individual. As each decision maker was given three choice sets, each with four alternatives, the first four utilities shown represent the utilities associated with the four alternatives present within the first choice set. Each successive block of four utilities thus represents subsequent choice sets.

We show in figure 10.18, using Excel, how NLOGIT calculates these utilities. The formulas shown in cells H10–H15 of figure 10.17 are equivalent to (10.16a)–(10.16f).

	FR3TIM10	FR3TIM15	P1	U1
0	0	0	0.285731	-0.284338
0	0	0	0.209388	-0.595201
1	0	0	0.297625	-0.243554
0	1	0	0.207257	-0.605427
0	0	0	0.231392	-0.486147
0	0	0	0.310653	-0.191583
0	0	0	0.150463	-0.916538
0	0	0	0.307492	-0.201809
0	0	0	0.242487	-0.687956
0	0	0	0.325549	-0.393392
0	0	0	0.179383	-0.989383
0	0	0	0.252581	-0.647172
0	0	0	0.285731	-0.284338
0	0	0	0.209388	-0.595201
1	0	0	0.297625	-0.243554
0	1	0	0.207257	-0.605427
0	0	0	0.242487	-0.687956

Figure 10.17 Estimated utilities saved within NLOGIT

Since not all alternatives were present in the choice set for this individual, we replicate the formulas in cells H10–H15 in cells C2–C7 for the restricted set of alternatives present within the choice set.

We show the results of this process in cells C18–C23, highlighting those cells which correspond to those alternatives present within the first choice set for individual one. Comparing these to the utilities estimated by NLOGIT as shown in cells B18–B23, this is exactly how NLOGIT calculated the choice probabilities. The analyst may use spreadsheets, set up as shown in figure 10.19, to test "*what-if*" scenarios by changing the values of the attributes and or SDC and observing how the utility estimates change. We do not show this here.

Returning to our earlier discussion of ASCs, it is now possible to demonstrate the direct relationship that exists between the ASCs and the average utility obtained when estimating a model, the functional form of which is specified with the estimation of ASCs only. To demonstrate, consider the following NLOGIT command syntax which will save the utilities for a model estimated with $J - 1$ ASCs only (note that this is the same model as the base model estimated using the choice or market share information available within the sample

	A	B	C	D	E	F	G	H
1	**alts**	**Utility**	**Working**					
2	Cart	-0.284338	=C10+E10*F10					
3	Carnt	-0.595201	=C11+E11*F11					
4								
5	Train	-0.243554	=C13+E13*F13					
6								
7	LR	-0.605427	=C15+E15*F15					
8								
9	**alts**					Cost		
10	Cart	ASCCart	-0.0825288	CST	-0.201809	1	Cart	=L10+N10*O10
11	Carnt	ASCPOVNT	0.413844	CST	-0.201809	5	Carnt	=L11+N11*O11
12	Bus	ASCBUS	0.0196614	CST	-0.201809		Bus	=L12+N12*O12
13	Train	ASCTN	-0.0417452	CST	-0.201809	1	Train	=L13+N13*O13
14	Busway	ASCBUSW	0.0925065	CST	-0.201809		Busway	=L14+N14*O14
15	LR			CST	-0.201809	3	LR	=L15+N15*O15
16								
17	**alts**	**Utility**	**Working**					
18	Cart	-0.284338	-0.2843378					
19	Carnt	-0.595201	-0.595201					
20								
21	Train	-0.243554	-0.2435542					
22								
23	LR	-0.605427	-0.605427					
24								
25	**alts**					Cost		
26	Cart	ASCCart	-0.0825288	CST	-0.201809	1	Cart	-0.2843378
27	Carnt	ASCPOVNT	0.413844	CST	-0.201809	5	Carnt	-0.595201
28	Bus	ASCBUS	0.0196614	CST	-0.201809		Bus	0.0196614
29	Train	ASCTN	-0.0417452	CST	-0.201809	1	Train	-0.2435542
30	Busway	ASCBUSW	0.0925065	CST	-0.201809		Busway	0.0925065
31	LR			CST	-0.201809	3	LR	-0.605427

Figure 10.18 Using Excel to test "what-if" scenarios on the utility estimates

data set):

```
NLOGIT
;lhs = choice,cset,altij
;Choices = cart, carnt, bus, train, busway, LR
;Show
;Model:
U(cart) = asccart /
U(carnt) = asccarnt /
U(bus) = ascbus /
U(train) = asctn /
U(busway) = ascbusw
;Utility=u1 $
```

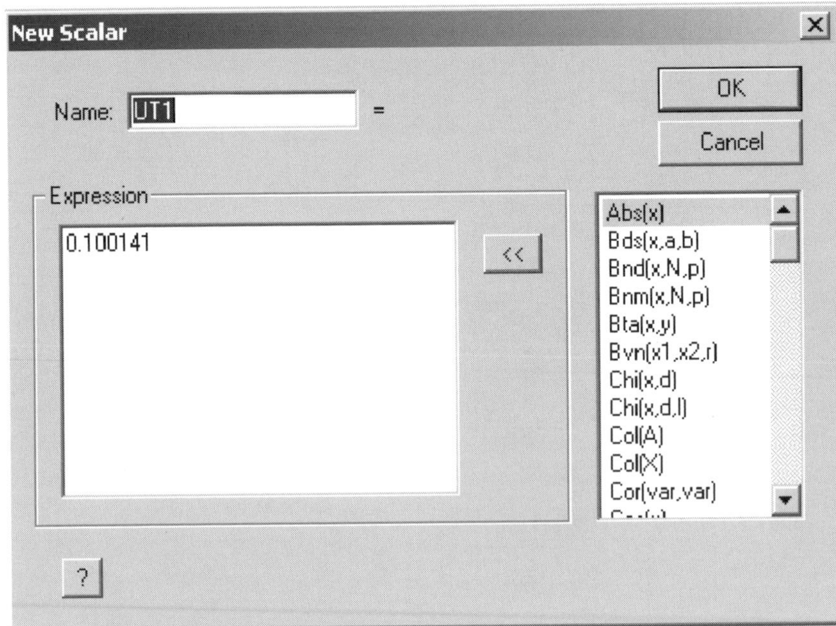

Figure 10.19 Obtaining the average utility using the **Calc;** command

To obtain the average utility for the first alternative, the analyst will first have to use the **reject** command to reject all other alternatives. Next, the analyst will have to use the **Calc;** command to find the average utility for that alternative. For the first alternative in the mode choice case study, the command would look thus:

```
Reject;altij#1 $
Calc;ut1=xbr(u1) $
```

For the 30 minute or less commute sample, the average utility as calculated via the above NLOGIT command syntax is shown in figure 10.19. Comparing this result to the parameter estimate for the above specified model (shown on p. 330), we note that the parameter for the first alternative (i.e. *cart*) is equal to the average utility for that alternative.

As with the calculation of the sum of the probabilities for differing alternatives, the analyst will be required to reset the sample before using the **Reject;** command to discard unwanted alternatives when using the **Calc;** command, to find the average utility level for a given alternative. We show this procedure below for the second alternative and 30 minutes or less travel segment:

```
Sample;all $
Reject;sprp=1 $
Reject;splength#1 $
Reject;altij#2 $
Calc;ut2=xbr(u1) $
```

Using the above procedure, the reader can confirm that the average utilities for the second through sixth alternative are 0.192417, 0.025630, −0.044327, 0.099416, and 0 respectively, which exactly match the parameter estimates for the model as shown on p. 330.

As an aside, the average utility for the last alternative is not strictly zero, as the utility outputs for an alternative derived from models of discrete choice are meaningful only when examined relative to the utility estimate obtained for a second alternative. As such, the sign and relative magnitude of the constant terms provide useful information to the analyst on the ranking of preferences for alternatives. The positive signs observed for *cart*, *carnt*, *bus*, and *busway* suggests that, on average, relative to the *LR* alternative, these alternatives have a higher utility, while the negative utility observed for the *train* alternative relative to that of the *LR* alternative, suggests that on average, the utility for the *train alternative* is smaller than that of the *LR alternative*. Indeed, the relative magnitudes and signs of the above reported average utilities suggest that, *holding all else constant*, the order of preference for the available modes over the sample is *carnt*, *cart*, *busway*, *bus*, *light rail*, and *train*. The above, however, is only ever meaningful for RP choice studies. As such, ranking the alternatives as has done here based on average utilities derived from an SP choice experiment is of limited value.

Appendix 10A Handling unlabeled experiments

The mode case study used throughout chapter 10 involves a labeled-choice experiment. Unlike labeled-choice experiments, the use of alternative-specific parameters makes no behavioral sense when the experiment is unlabeled (also referred to as "unranked" in some literature). To demonstrate why, consider an unlabeled experiment involving two alternatives, A and B. The experiment is unlabeled in the sense that the names, A and B, do not convey meaning to the respondent on what the alternatives represent in reality (e.g. a brand) and do not provide any useful information to suggest that there are unobserved influences that are systematically different for alternatives A and B. The first two choice sets from a hypothetical unlabeled choice experiment are shown in figure 10A.1.

From both choice set scenarios 1 and 2, we offer a set of attribute levels for alternatives A and B that have no association with any specific branded alternative (i.e. a car, a bus, a train, or any other mode of transport, real or imaginary). Unlabeled-choice experiments are often constructed to examine different (potential) configurations of a single alternative, although this need not be the only choice setting. A popular application in transportation is the choice between routes in terms of mixtures of levels of tolls and travel time. Labeled experiments are designed to explore different (potential) configurations of two or more branded alternatives. The single alternative being examined within the context of an unlabeled experiment should be expressly stated in establishing the scenario under which the choice is being made. For example, respondents for the above may be told that they are choosing between two cars (or buses, or trains, etc.) for the same journey.

For the above example, assuming alternative-specific parameter estimates including a constant assigned to alternative A, the utility functions for alternatives A and B might

Scenario 1

Trip Description	A	B
Comfort	High	High
Travel Time (hours)	14	12
If I had to take the trip I would choose	☐	☐

Scenario 2

Trip Description	A	B
Comfort	Medium	Medium
Travel Time (hours)	10	14
If I had to take the trip I would choose	☐	☐

Figure 10.A1 Two scenarios from an unlabeled choice experiment

appear as follows:

```
U(A) = ascA + comfA*Comfort + TTimeA*ttime /
U(B) =        comfB*Comfort + TTimeB*ttime $
```

This alternative-specific specification suggests that increases in travel time and comfort levels will have a differential impact upon the utilities, and hence the choice probabilities, for each alternative. Assuming travel time parameters for alternative A and B of −0.2 and −0.4, respectively, increasing travel time for alternative A by 1 minute will decrease the relative utility for alternative A by 0.2, while increasing the travel time for alternative B by 1 minute will decrease the utility for alternative B by 0.4. But what are alternatives A and B? Clearly this makes no sense since the trade-offs in the choice sets are between attribute levels that have no association with a brand or labels.

The parameters of unlabeled-choice experiments should be treated as generic parameter estimates). But how does one treat the constant terms of the alternatives within an unlabeled experiment? The analyst may only ever estimate J–1 constant terms (given J alternatives in a choice set). This suggests that the constant term for at least one alternative (the one for which a constant was not estimated) will be different (it will be zero) to all other estimated constant terms (which should be held generic across the remaining alternatives). Hence we have violated the meaning of "unlabeled" with the inclusion of alternative-specific (albeit generic across J–1) constants.

The correct way to proceed is to exclude constant terms for all (unlabeled) alternatives. That is, we constrain the average unobserved effect for all (unlabeled) alternatives to be zero. The preferred utility specification for the above example would be:

```
U(A) = comf*Comfort + TTime*ttime /
U(B) = comf*Comfort + TTime*ttime $
```

As an aside, the parameters from an unlabeled-choice model can be imported into a labeled-choice context in which there exist calibrated alternative-specific constants and alternative-specific variables. This is often a strategy when using a mix of stated choice (SC) data and RP data. The SC data provide the unlabeled (generic) parameters for a sub-set of attributes given the argument that certain parameters will be more robust and behaviorally useful when established from controlled experiments than from the real world reported data that have extensive measurement error.

The problem of alternative-specific parameter estimates with regard to unlabeled experiments is not limited to the attributes of the experimental design. As with the constant terms, it is possible to estimate parameters only for socio-demographic and/or contextual variables across J–1 utility functions. For unlabeled-choice experiments, this violates the necessity to maintain genericness in the parameter estimates across all alternatives. The inclusion of socio-demographic and contextual variables therefore requires the analyst to create interaction terms (or possibly ratios) for each socio-demographic and/or contextual variable with specific attributes in order for the model to be correctly specified. The creation of interaction terms (or ratios of variables to attributes) can be achieved through the use of **CREATE** commands; however, one should be careful as this may induce unacceptable levels of correlation.

To demonstrate, the following **CREATE** command will construct an interaction variable between the socio-demographic gender variable and the travel time variable:

```
CREATE
;ttgen=ttime*gender $
```

The utility specification for using the gender–travel time interaction would be as follows:

```
The utility fu
U(A) = comf*Comfort + TTgen*ttgen /
U(B) = comf*Comfort + TTgen*ttgen
```

Note that this works as the travel time attribute varies over the experimental design despite the gender (socio-demographic variable) being invariant over the same design.

11 Getting more from your model

Where facts are few, experts are many. (Donald R. Gannon)

11.1 Introduction

In chapter 10, we detailed the standard output generated by NLOGIT for the basic (multinomial logit) choice model. By the addition of supplementary commands to the basic command syntax, the analyst is able to generate further output which may aid in the understanding of choice. We outline these additional commands now. As before, we demonstrate how the command syntax should appear and detail line by line how to interpret the output.

Although we use many model specifications throughout to demonstrate our discussion, our primary discussion relates to the model estimated in chapter 10 (i.e. shown on p. 316), reproduced below:

```
+----------------------------------------------+
| Discrete choice (multinomial logit) model    |
| Maximum Likelihood Estimates                 |
| Model estimated: Feb 30, 2003 at 08:30:00AM  |
| Dependent variable              Choice       |
| Weighting variable                None       |
| Number of observations            2369       |
| Iterations completed                 5       |
| Log likelihood function      -3220.150       |
| R2=1-LogL/LogL* Log-L fncn R-sqrd   RsqAdj   |
| No coefficients -4244.6782 .24137   .24073   |
| Constants only. Must be computed directly.   |
|                 Use NLOGIT ;...; RHS=ONE $   |
| Chi-squared[ 1]           =   1639.08085     |
| Prob [ chi squared > value ] =   .00000      |
| Response data are given as ind. choice.      |
| Number of obs.= 2369, skipped   0 bad obs.   |
+----------------------------------------------+
```

```
+----------+------------+--------------+--------+----------+
|Variable  | Coefficient | Standard Error | b/St.Er. |P[|Z|>z] |
+----------+------------+--------------+--------+----------+
 ASCCART        -.08252881      .07552527     -1.093    .2745
 CST            -.20180890      .01916932    -10.528    .0000
 ASCCARNT        .41384399      .07640648      5.416    .0000
 ASCBUS          .01966141      .09923321       .198    .8429
 ASCTN          -.04174518      .09373128      -.445    .6561
 ASCBUSW         .09250653      .08587656      1.077    .2814
```

We begin our discussion on additional NLOGIT output with the **;Show** command.

11.2 Adding to our understanding of the data

11.2.1 Show

The **;Show** command in NLOGIT may be used to generate output informative of both the market shares and utility structures. As with the **;Maxit** command, the **;Show** command may either precede the utility function specifications or follow them. In the example below, we demonstrate the command as it would appear before the utility specifications:

```
NLOGIT
;lhs = choice, cset, altij
;Choices = <names of alternatives>
;Show
;Model:
U<alternative 1 name>) = < utility function 1> /
U(<alternative 2 name>) = <utility function 2> /
...
U(<alternative i name>) = <utility function i> $
```

Specifically, for the model shown in chapter 10, specified for the SP data restricted to commuting trips less than 30 minutes, the **;Show** command would look as follows:

```
NLOGIT
;lhs = choice, cset, altij
;Choices = cart, carnt, bus, train, busway, LR
;Show
;Model:
U(cart)     = asccart + cst*fuel /
U(carnt)    = asccarnt + cst*fuel /
U(bus)      = ascbus + cst*fare /
U(train)    = asctn + cst*fare /
U(busway)   = ascbusw + cst*fare /
U(LR)       = cst*fare $
```

The **;Show** command generates output in two sections. We show these below:

```
          Tree Structure Specified for the Nested Logit Model
          Sample proportions are marginal, not conditional.
          Choices marked with * are excluded for the IIA test.
----------------+----------------+----------------+----------------+------+---
Trunk     (prop.)|Limb      (prop.)|Branch    (prop.)|Choice (prop.)|Weight|IIA
----------------+----------------+----------------+----------------+------+---
Trunk{1} 1.00000|Lmb[1:1] 1.00000|B(1:1,1) 1.00000|CART     .25327| 1.000|
                |                |                |CARNT    .27775| 1.000|
                |                |                |BUS      .10300| 1.000|
                |                |                |TRAIN    .10257| 1.000|
                |                |                |BUSWAY   .13466| 1.000|
                |                |                |LR       .12875| 1.000|
----------------+----------------+----------------+----------------+------+--
Model Specification: Utility Functions for Alternatives
Table entry is the attribute that multiplies the indicated parameter.
      Parameter
      Row 1 ASCCART  CST      ASCCARNT  ASCBUS     ASCTN     ASCBUSW
Choice
CART        1 Constant FUEL
CARNT       1          FUEL  Constant
BUS         1          FARE            Constant
TRAIN       1          FARE                      Constant
BUSWAY      1          FARE                                Constant
LR          1          FARE
```

The first section of the **;Show** command output can be further divided into two segments. The first segment details information on the nested structure of the model. For the basic MNL model described in this chapter, we can ignore this output as no nesting structure exists (this is relevant to the nested logit model described in chapters 13 and 14):

```
----------------+----------------+----------------+
Trunk     (prop.)|Limb      (prop.)|Branch    (prop.)|
----------------+----------------+----------------+
Trunk{1} 1.00000|Lmb[1:1] 1.00000|B(1:1,1) 1.00000|
                |                |                |
                |                |                |
                |                |                |
                |                |                |
                |                |                |
----------------+----------------+----------------+
```

Part of the second segment of the **;Show** command output is relevant to the basic MNL choice model. In this section of the output NLOGIT details the choice proportions or market shares as they appear within the data:

```
+---------------+------+---
|Choice   (prop.)|Weight|IIA
+---------------+------+---
|CART      .25327| 1.000|
|CARNT     .27775| 1.000|
|BUS       .10300| 1.000|
|TRAIN     .10257| 1.000|
|BUSWAY    .13466| 1.000|
|LR        .12875| 1.000|
+---------------+------+---
```

From this output it can be seen that the *car* with toll represents 25.3 percent of the choices while the non-toll *car* alternative was chosen 27.7 percent of the time. The other choice proportions are also shown. While this information is important (indeed, the base comparison model used to determine overall model significance is in its essence a simple replication of these choice proportions), the analyst must be careful in interpreting these proportions when they are based on SP data as they are here. In the case of SP data, these choice proportions indicate the proportion of times an alternative was chosen across all choice sets. But what does it mean that in 25.3 percent of choice sets, the *cart* alternative was chosen? Given that the choice sets are not based upon what is occurring in the marketplace but rather upon some experimental design generated by the analyst, these choice proportions are largely meaningless with respect to predicting market shares and must not be treated as an estimate of the true market shares. However, for RP data the market shares should correspond to the actual market shares.

As an aside, one can always calibrate the constants in an SP choice set (limited to only those alternatives that exist in the real market) to establish a market-relevant prediction model. This is often done when an RP choice set is not available. This is an alternative to transferring the parameter estimates of the attributes (except the constants) from an SP choice set to an RP choice set and using the estimated RP mode-specific constants. We discuss this further in chapter 14.

The next two columns of output are not relevant to the basic MNL choice model as described to this point. The first of the two columns discloses any endogenous weighting that may have been utilized. We discuss this in a later section of the chapter. The last column discloses information with regard to a test of IID (behaviorally equivalent to the IIA assumption; see chapter 3). We discuss this test in chapter 14. The second section of the **;Show** command output reconstructs the shapes of the utility functions:

```
                 Parameter
     Row 1       ASCCART      CST      ASCCARNT ASCBUS   ASCTN    ASCBUSW
Choice
CART       1     Constant     FUEL
CARNT      1                  FUEL     Constant
BUS        1                  FARE              Constant
TRAIN      1                  FARE                       Constant
BUSWAY     1                  FARE                                Constant
LR         1                  FARE
```

The columns within this output detail the names given to the parameters estimated within the system of utility functions of the choice model. The rows of the output represent the alternatives. The cells within the matrix formed by the parameter names and alternatives available detail which alternative an estimated parameter is associated with and for which variable that parameter belongs. Thus, for the above, it can be seen that constants are estimated for all but the *LR* alternative while a parameter named *CST* is estimated for all of the alternatives, based upon the *fuel* attribute for the *cart* and *carnt* alternatives and the fare attributes of the remaining alternatives.

11.2.2 Descriptives

The next additional output we describe is generated by the command **;Descriptives**. As with all other commands such as **;Maxit** and **;Show** commands, the **;Descriptives** command may either precede the utility function specification within the command syntax or follow it as per our discussion on the **;Probs** and **;Utility** commands. We show the command as it would appear if it precedes the utility function specification below:

```
NLOGIT
;lhs = choice, cset, altij
;Choices = <names of alternatives>
;Descriptives
;Model:
U<alternative 1 name>) = < utility function 1> /
U(<alternative 2 name>) = <utility function 2> /
...
U(<alternative i name>) = <utility function i> $
```

Specifically for the mode-choice case study, the command syntax with the **;Descriptives** command for our example choice model would look thus:

```
NLOGIT
;lhs = choice, cset, altij
;Choices = cart, carnt, bus, train, busway, LR
?;Show
;Descriptives
;Model:
U(cart)    = asccart + cst*fuel /
U(carnt)   = asccarnt + cst*fuel /
U(bus)     = ascbus + cst*fare /
U(train)   = asctn + cst*fare /
U(busway)  = ascbusw + cst*fare /
U(LR)      = cst*fare $
```

As an aside, note that for the above syntax we have retained the **Show** command, however we have preceded it with a question mark (**?**). The question mark informs NLOGIT to ignore everything that follows within that line of the command. In this way, the analyst may use the question mark to make comments to the right of **?** that may aid in understanding what it is that the command is supposed to do – or, as we have done here, allow the analyst to return to a previous command without having to retype it, simply by deleting the question mark.

Using the above command syntax, NLOGIT generates the following output:

```
+---------------------------------------------------------------------+
|            Descriptive Statistics for Alternative CART             :
|      Utility Function               |                |      600.0 observs.|
|      Coefficient                   | All   2369.0 obs.| that chose CART    |
| Name            Value    Variable| Mean      Std. Dev.| Mean      Std. Dev. |
|---------------------------------------------------------------------|
| ASCCART        -.0825    ONE       |    1.000       .000|    1.000      .000 |
| CST            -.2018    FUEL      |    1.995       .818|    1.952      .825 |
+---------------------------------------------------------------------+
+---------------------------------------------------------------------+
|            Descriptive Statistics for Alternative CARNT            :
|      Utility Function               |                |     658.0 observs. |
|      Coefficient                   | All   2369.0 obs.| that chose CARNOT  |
| Name            Value    Variable| Mean      Std. Dev.| Mean    Std. Dev.  |
|----------------------------      | ----------------  | ------------------|
| CST            -.2018    FUEL      |    3.997       .816|    3.954      .813 |
| ASCCARNT        .4138    ONE       |    1.000       .000|    1.000      .000 |
+---------------------------------------------------------------------+
+---------------------------------------------------------------------+
|            Descriptive Statistics for Alternative BUS              :
|      Utility Function               |                |     244.0 observs. |
|      Coefficient                   | All   1039.0 obs.| that   chose   BUS |
| Name            Value    Variable| Mean      Std. Dev.| Mean     Std.   Dev. |
|----------------------------      | ----------------+-------------------|
| CST            -.2018    FARE      |    3.010     1.646|    2.607     1.510 |
| ASCBUS          .0197    ONE       |    1.000      .000|    1.000      .000 |
+---------------------------------------------------------------------+
+---------------------------------------------------------------------+
|            Descriptive Statistics for Alternative TRAIN            :
|      Utility Function               |                |     243.0 observs. |
|      Coefficient                   | All   1089.0 obs.| that chose TRAIN   |
| Name            Value    Variable| Mean      Std. Dev.| Mean       Std.   Dev.|
| ----------------------------     | ----------------+-------------------+
| CST            -.2018    FARE      |    3.017     1.639|    2.605     1.689 |
| ASCTN          -.0417    ONE       |    1.000      .000|    1.000      .000 |
+---------------------------------------------------------------------+
+---------------------------------------------------------------------+
|            Descriptive Statistics for Alternative BUSWAY           :
|      Utility Function               |                |     319.0 observs. |
|      Coefficient                   | All   1280.0 obs.| that chose BUSWAY  |
| Name            Value    Variable| Mean      Std. Dev.| Mean     Std.   Dev. |
| ----------------   ----------    | ----------------+-------------------+
| CST            -.2018    FARE      |    2.972     1.624|    2.448     1.585 |
| ASCBUSW         .0925    ONE       |    1.000      .000|    1.000      .000 |
+---------------------------------------------------------------------+
```

```
+-----------------------------------------------------------------------+
|              Descriptive Statistics for Alternative LR                 :
|      Utility Function              |                |     305.0 observs.  |
|      Coefficient                   | All    1330.0 obs.| that chose LR      |
| Name              Value   Variable| Mean     Std. Dev.| Mean    Std. Dev.  |
| -------------    -------------- | -----------------+-------------------+
| CST              -.2018   FARE   |    2.997     1.627|      2.508    1.583 |
+-----------------------------------------------------------------------+
```

To avoid repetition, we discuss this series of output for the *cart* alternative only. The remaining output generated is interpreted in exactly the same manner.

```
+-----------------------------------------------------------------+
|              Descriptive Statistics for Alternative CART           :
|    Utility Function          |                 |      600.0 observs.|
|    Coefficient               | All    2369.0 obs.|that chose CART    |
| Name      Value Variable | Mean      Std.  Dev.|Mean       Std.  Dev. |
| ------------  -------- | ----------------+--------------------|
| ASCCART -.0825 ONE       |        1.000      .000|      1.000     .000 |
| CST      -.2018 FUEL     |        1.995      .818|      1.952     .825 |
+-----------------------------------------------------------------+
```

The heading informs the analyst which alternative the output is associated with. After the heading, the **;Descriptives** command output is broken into three segments. The first segment of this output details the parameter estimates for the variables assigned to that alternative via the utility function specification:

```
|     Utility Function           |
|     Coefficient                |
| Name            Value  Variable |
| ----------------   --------  |
| ASCCART        -.0825  ONE      |
| CST            -.2018  FUEL     |
+------------------------------
```

As an aside, note that NLOGIT uses the name ONE to indicate the estimation of a constant term.

The second segment of the **;Descriptives** command output indicates the mean and standard deviation for each of the variables as specified within the utility function for that alternative for the entire sample used for the estimation of the model:

```
| All      2369.0 obs.|
| Mean       Std. Dev.|
| ------------------+
|    1.000        .000|
|    1.995        .818|
+---------------------
```

For the *cart* alternative, the mean and standard deviation for the entire sample of commuters with trips less than 30 minutes for the design attribute *fuel* was 1.995 and 0.818, respectively.

The last segment of this output is shown below:

```
|        600.0 observs.    |
|that     chose CART       |
|Mean             Std. Dev. |
+-----------------------|
|        1.000       .000 |
|        1.952       .825 |
------------------------+
```

This output details the mean and standard deviation for the variables assigned to that alternative for those who chose that alternative only. In this instance, there exist 2,369 choice sets across 790 decision makers. Within these 2,369 choice sets, the *cart* alternative was chosen 600 times (note that $600 \div 2369 = 0.25327$, the choice proportion revealed by the **;Show** command earlier). For the fuel design attribute, the mean and standard deviation for those choice sets in which the *cart* alternative was selected was 1.952 and 0.825, respectively.

As an aside, the data used for model estimation for this example is SP data. As such the means and standard deviations relate to choice sets and not to what has occurred within the marketplace. For RP data, the **;Descriptives** command will describe the actual means and standard deviations as observed over the sample data, which if representative of the population will prove more useful and easier to interpret.

11.2.3 Crosstab

The pseudo-R^2 we discussed in chapter 10 is but one method of determining how well a choice model is performing. An often more useful method of determining model performance is to examine a *contingency table* of the predicted choice outcomes for the sample as based upon the model produced versus the actual choice outcomes as they exist within the data. To generate such a contingency table, NLOGIT uses the command **;Crosstab**. We show how this command is used below:

```
NLOGIT
;lhs = choice, cset, altij
;Choices = < names of alternatives>
;Crosstab
;Model:
U<alternative 1 name>) = < utility function 1> /
U(<alternative 2 name>) = <utility function 2> /
...
U(<alternative i name>) = <utility function i> $
```

For our mode-choice case study, the **;Crosstab** command would look:

```
NLOGIT
;lhs = choice, cset, altij
;Choices = cart, carnt, bus, train, busway, LR
?;Show
?;Descriptives
;Crosstab
;model:
U(cart)     = asccart + cst*fuel /
U(carnt)    = asccarnt + cst*fuel /
U(bus)      = ascbus + cst*fare /
U(train)    = asctn + cst*fare /
U(busway)   = ascbusw + cst*fare /
U(LR)       = cst*fare $
```

For the case study example, NLOGIT will produce the following output. The contingency table generated by NLOGIT does not appear within the output file as with other output generated by NLOGIT. To access the contingency table, the analyst must use the *Matrix: Crosstab* button similar to the *LastOutp* button described in chapter 10. The authors and not NLOGIT have highlighted the diagonal elements of the resulting contingency table:

```
+-------------------------------------------------------+
| Cross tabulation of actual vs. predicted choices.     |
| Row indicator is actual, column is predicted.         |
| Predicted total is F(k,j,i)=Sum(i=1,...,N) P(k,j,i).  |
| Column totals may be subject to rounding error.       |
+-------------------------------------------------------+
```

	CART	CARNT	BUS	TRAIN	BUSWAY	LR	Total
CART	155	167	63	58	81	76	600
CARNT	166	185	69	72	84	83	658
BUS	61	68	61	27	27	0	244
TRAIN	60	70	25	59	0	28	243
BUSWAY	80	85	25	0	88	41	319
LR	70	84	0	27	40	77	305
Total	600	658	244	243	319	305	2369

Within the contingency table produced by NLOGIT the rows represent the number of choices made by those sampled for each alternative, while the columns represent the number of times an alternative was predicted to be selected as based on the choice model specified by the analyst. This prediction is based upon the choice probabilities with the predicted choice corresponding to the alternative to which the highest probability is observed.

The diagonal elements of the contingency table represent the number of times the choice model correctly predicted the choice of alternative as observed in the data. The off-diagonal elements represent in the aggregate, the number of times the choice model incorrectly

	CART	CARNT	BUS	TRAIN	BUSWAY	LR
CART	0.26	0.28	0.11	0.10	0.14	0.13
CARNT	0.25	0.28	0.10	0.11	0.13	0.13
BUS	0.25	0.28	0.25	0.11	0.11	0.00
TRAIN	0.25	0.29	0.10	0.24	0.00	0.12
BUSWAY	0.25	0.27	0.08	0.00	0.27	0.13
LR	0.25	0.27	0.00	0.09	0.13	0.25

Figure 11.1 Proportions of correct and incorrect predictions

predicted which alternative a decision maker would select given the levels of the attributes of the alternatives and SDC for that decision maker as they exist within the data set.

Figure 11.1 converts the raw observations for each of the cells in the contingency table to proportions. Examining the diagonal elements of figure 11.1 suggests that the choice model used for this example predicts, for the sampled decision makers, the *cart* alternative correctly 26 percent of the time, the *cartnt* alternative correctly 28 percent of the time, and the *bus*, *train*, *busway*, and *LR* alternatives correctly 25, 24, 27, and 25 percent of the time, respectively. For the *cart* alternative, the choice model incorrectly predicted 28 percent of the 600 choices in which the *cart* alternative was selected (i.e. this is based on an SP experiment; with RP data, this would translate to decision makers) as a choice for the *carnt* alternative. The model also incorrectly predicted 11, 10, 14, and 13 percent of the actual choices for the *cart* alternative as being choices for the *bus*, *train*, *busway*, and *LR* alternatives respectively. The remaining off-diagonal cells reveal where the choice model incorrectly predicted mode choice for the remaining alternatives.

Returning to the raw observations given in the contingency table by NLOGIT, it is possible to derive a measure of the aggregate proportion of correct predictions. This is done by summing across the number of correct predictions and dividing by the total number of choices made. Our mode choice model correctly predicted the mode chosen 625 (i.e.155 + 185 + 61 + 59 + 88 + 77) times out of the total of 2369 choices made. Thus the overall proportion of correct predictions equals

$$\frac{\text{Number of correct predictions}}{\text{Total number of observations}} = \frac{625}{2369} = 0.26 \tag{11.1}$$

Thus for the data, this particular choice model correctly predicted the actual choice outcome for only 26 percent of the total number of cases. The reader should not be surprised by this finding given that the model has but a single predictor, *cost*.

11.3 Adding to our understanding of the model parameters

A result of the logit transformation is that there exists no straightforward behavioral interpretation of a parameter estimate of a choice model beyond the sign of the parameter which indicates whether the associated variable of interest has either a positive or negative effect upon the choice probabilities. Indeed, for ordered logit models (in contrast to the unordered choices herein), even the sign has no behavioral meaning. To arrive at a behaviorally meaningful interpretation, it is possible for the analyst to calculate either the elasticities or marginal effects of the choice probabilities with respect to some particular attribute or SDC. We discuss both elasticities and marginal effects now.

11.3.1 **;Effects**: elasticities

Formally, *elasticity* may be defined as a unitless measure that describes the relationship between the percentage change for some variable (i.e. an attribute of an alternative or the SDC of a decision maker) and the percentage change in the quantity demanded, *ceteris paribus*. The percentage change in quantity demanded need not be confined to the alternative to which the attribute observed to change belongs, but may also be observed to occur in other competing alternatives. It is for this reason that economists have defined two types of elasticities; *direct elasticities* and *cross-elasticities*. From Louviere, Hensher, and Swait (2000, 58), direct and cross-elasticities may be defined as follows:

> A direct elasticity measures the percentage change in the probability of choosing a particular alternative in the choice set with respect to a given percentage change in an attribute of that same alternative. A cross elasticity measures the percentage change in the probability of choosing a particular alternative in the choice set with respect to a given percentage change in a competing alternative.

Not only is there a distinction between the form that elasticities may take, there exists also a distinction between how one may calculate the elasticity for an attribute or SDC. The two main methods of calculation are the *arc elasticity method* and the *point elasticity method*. We will ignore the differences between the two estimation methods for the present and note that NLOGIT outputs a point elasticity. We discuss arc elasticities in sub-section 11.3.2 and how they can be derived using NLOGIT's simulation capability.

The direct point elasticity for the MNL model is given as (11.2):

$$E^{P_{iq}}_{X_{ikq}} = \frac{\partial P_{iq}}{\partial X_{ikq}} \cdot \frac{X_{ikq}}{P_{iq}} \tag{11.2}$$

Equation (11.2) is interpreted as the elasticity of the probability of alternative i for decision maker q with respect to a marginal change in the kth attribute of the ith alternative (i.e. X_{ikq}), as observed by decision maker q.

Louviere, Hensher, and Swait (2000) show that through simplification, the direct *point* elasticity (11.2) for the MNL model for each observation becomes:

$$E^{P_{iq}}_{X_{ikq}} = -\beta_{ik} X_{ikq}(1 - P_{iq}) \tag{11.3}$$

and the cross-point elasticity

$$E^{P_{iq}}_{X_{jkq}} = -\beta_{jk} X_{jkq} P_{jq}. \tag{11.4}$$

As an aside, while it is possible to calculate point elasticities for categorically coded variables the results will be meaningless. Consider a gender variable where male is coded zero and female coded one. In such a case the elasticity would be interpreted as the percentage change in the probability of choice given a 1 percent change in gender (we will not offer a guess as to what this 1 percent change in gender is). Thus while NLOGIT will provide elasticity estimates for dummy and effects coded variables, the output generated cannot be meaningfully interpreted. Large changes in a variable such as a 100 percent change do, however, make sense when discussing categorically coded variables (e.g. from dummy code 1 to 0). Thus, such variables have to be handled using the arc elasticity formula discussed later if the analyst requires elasticities. We therefore calculate and interpret the point elasticities for continuous-level data only.

Examination of the subscripts used within (11.4) will reveal that the cross-point elasticity is calculated for alternative j independent of alternative i. As such, the cross-point elasticities with respect to a variable associated with alternative j will be the same for all $j, j \neq i$ and as a consequence, a choice model estimated using MNL will display uniform cross-elasticities across all $j, j \neq i$. This property relates to the MNL model because of the IID assumption of that model. More advanced models (such as those described in later chapters) which relax the IID assumption use a different formula to establish elasticities and as such allow for non-uniform cross-elasticities to be estimated. Equations (11.3) and (11.4) yield elasticities for each individual decision maker. To calculate sample elasticities (noting that the MNL choice model is estimated on sample data), the analyst may either (1) utilize the sample average X_{ik} and average estimated P_i for the direct point elasticity and X_{jk} and average estimated P_j for the direct cross-elasticities or (2) calculate the elasticity for each individual decision maker and weight each individual elasticity by the decision maker's associated choice probability (this last method is known as "probability weighted sample enumeration"). Aggregation method (3), known as "naive pooling," is to calculate the elasticity for each individual decision maker but not weight each individual elasticity by the decision maker's associated choice probability.

Louviere, Hensher, and Swait (2000) warn against using aggregation approaches (1) and (3). They reject (1) when using MNL models due to the non-linear nature of MNL models which means that the estimated logit function need not pass through the point defined by the sample averages. Indeed, they report that this method of obtaining aggregate elasticities may result in errors of up to 20 percent (usually overestimates) in elasticities. Approach (3) to aggregating elasticities is rejected on the grounds that it fails to recognize the contribution to the choice outcome of each alternative.

Heeding this warning and using the probability weighted sample enumeration (PWSE) technique, the aggregate elasticities are calculated using (11.5):

$$E_{X_{jkq}}^{\bar{P}_i} = \left(\sum_{q=1}^{Q} \hat{P}_{iq} E_{X_{jkq}}^{P_{iq}} \right) \Big/ \sum_{q=1}^{Q} \hat{P}_{iq} \tag{11.5}$$

where

$\bar{P}_i$ refers to the aggregate probability of choice of alternative i and $\hat{P}_{iq}$ is an estimated choice probability.

The use of PWSE has important ramifications for the direct cross-elasticities estimated. Because uniform cross-elasticities are observed as a result of the IID assumption when calculated for individual decision makers, the use of sample enumeration which weights each individual decision maker differently will produce non-uniform cross-elasticities. Naive pooling which does not weight each individual elasticity by the decision maker's associated choice probability will, however, display uniform cross-elasticities. Analysts should not be concerned that the sample cross-elasticities for an attribute differ between pairs of alternatives; the individual-level cross-elasticities are strictly identical for the IID model.

Independent of how the elasticities are calculated, the resulting values are interpreted in exactly the same manner. For direct elasticities we interpret the calculated elasticity as the percentage change of the choice probability for alternative i given a 1 percent change in X_{ik}. For cross-elasticities, we interpret the calculated elasticity as the percentage change of the choice probability for alternative j given a 1 percent change in X_{ik}. If the percentage change in the probability for either the direct or cross-elasticity is observed to be greater than 1, that elasticity is said to be *relatively elastic*. If the percentage change in the probability for either the direct or cross-elasticity is observed to be less than 1, that elasticity is said to be *relatively inelastic*. If a 1 percent change in a choice probability is observed given a 1 percent change in X_{ik} then the elasticity is described as being of *unit elasticity*. Table 11.1 summarizes each scenario, including the impact on revenue given that X_{ik} is the price of alternative i.

To calculate elasticities using NLOGIT, the analyst uses the command **;Effects**. For this command, the analyst must specify which variable the elasticity is to be calculated for (i.e. which X_{ik}) and for which alternative (i.e. which alternative is i). The command looks thus:

;Effects: <variable$_k$(alternative$_i$)>

For this command, the analyst types the variable name and not the parameter name for which the elasticity is to be calculated followed by the desired alternative which is placed in round (( )) brackets. It is possible using NLOGIT to calculate the elasticity for a single variable over several alternatives if that variable relates to more than one alternative. Thus one could calculate the point elasticities for the fuel variable for both the *cart* and *carnt* alternatives. This is done by typing the name of the alternatives within the round brackets separated by a comma, as shown below:

;Effects: <variable$_k$(alternative$_i$, alternative$_j$)>

It is also possible in NLOGIT to calculate the point elasticities for more than one variable at a time. For example, the analyst may calculate both the elasticity for the *fuel* variable for the *cart* alternative and the elasticity for the *fare* attribute for the *bus* alternative. In such cases, the commands indicating the point elasticities to be estimated are divided by a slash (/) thus:

;Effects: <variable$_k$(alternative$_i$) / variable$_h$(alternative$_i$)>

The default aggregation method employed by NLOGIT is that of naive pooling, a method that the authors advise against. To use the PWSE method, the command **;Pwt** must also be added to the command syntax. If this command is not added, the analyst will notice the tell-tale sign that the cross-point elasticities will all be equal. Note that the analyst may also have NLOGIT compute the point elasticities using the sample means of the data by replacing the **pwt** command with **;Means**. As stated previously, we advise against this approach as well.

Table 11.1. *Relationship between elasticity of demand, change in price, and revenue*

	Absolute value of elasticity observed	Direct elasticity	Cross-elasticity	Price increase	Price decrease
Perfectly inelastic	$E_{X_{ikq}}^{\bar{P}_i} = 0$	1 percent increase in X_i results in a $-\infty$ percent decrease in P_i	1 percent increase in X_i results in a $-\infty$ percent increase in P_j	Revenue increases	Revenue decreases
Relatively inelastic	$0 < E_{X_{ikq}}^{\bar{P}_i} < 1$	1 percent increase in X_i results in a less than 1 percent decrease in P_i	1 percent increase in X_i results in a less than 1 percent increase in P_j	Revenue increases	Revenue decreases
Unit elastic	$E_{X_{ikq}}^{\bar{P}_i} = 1$	1 percent increase in X_i results in no percent change in P_i	1 percent increase in X_i results in no percent change in P_j	Revenue unchanged	Revenue unchanged
Relatively elastic	$1 < E_{X_{ikq}}^{\bar{P}_i} < \infty$	1 percent increase in X_i results in a greater than 1 percent decrease in P_i	1 percent increase in X_i results in a greater than 1 percent increase in P_j	Revenue decreases	Revenue increases
Perfectly elastic	$E_{X_{ikq}}^{\bar{P}_i} = \infty$	1 percent increase in X_i results in an ∞ percent decrease in P_i	1 percent increase in X_i results in a ∞ percent increase in P_j	Revenue decreases	Revenue increases

In general form, the command syntax for point elasticities will be:

```
NLOGIT
;lhs = choice, cset, altij
;Choices = <names of alternatives>
;Effects: <variable_k(alternative_i)>
;Pwt
;Model:
U<alternative 1 name>) = < utility function 1> /
U(<alternative 2 name>) = <utility function 2> /
...
U(<alternative i name>) = <utility function i> $
```

Using a specific example, the mode-choice example becomes:

```
NLOGIT
;lhs = choice, cset, altij
;Choices = cart, carnt, bus, train, busway, LR
?;Show
?;Descriptives
?;Crosstabs
;Effects: fuel(*) / fare(*)
;Pwt
;Model:
U(cart)     = asccart + cst*fuel /
U(carnt)    = asccarnt + cst*fuel /
U(bus)      = ascbus + cst*fare /
U(train)    = asctn + cst*fare /
U(busway)   = ascbusw + cst*fare /
U(LR)       = cst*fare $
```

We have used the asterisk symbol (∗) to denote all alternatives. As such, the command syntax above will produce elasticities for all alternatives to which there belongs a fuel variable (*cart* and *carnt*) and all alternatives to which there belongs a fare variable (*bus*, *train*, *busway*, and *LR*). The output generated by NLOGIT from this exercise is shown below:

```
+----------------------------------------------------------+
| Partial effects = prob. weighted avg.                    |
|                                                          |
| dlnP[alt=k,br=j,lmb=i,tr=l]                              |
| ------------------------------ = D(m:K,J,I,L) = delta(m)*F |
| dx(m):alt=K,br=J,lmb=I,tr=L]                             |
|                                                          |
| delta(m) = coefficient on x(m) in U(K:J,I,L)             |
|  F = (l=L) (i=I) (j=J) [(k=K)-P(K:JIL)]                  |
| + (l=L) (i=I) [(j=J)-P(J:IL)] P(K:JIL)t(J:IL)            |
| + (l=L) [(i=I)-P(I:L)] P(J:IL) P(K:JIL)t(J:IL)s(I:L)     |
| + [(l=L)-P(L)] P(I:L) P(J:IL) P(K:JIL)t(J:IL)s(I:L)f(L)  |
|                                                          |
| P(K JIL)=Prob[choice=K  branch=J,limb=I,trunk=L]         |
| P(J IL), P(I^{3}L), P(L) defined likewise.               |
| (n=N) = 1 if n=N, 0 else, for n=k,j,i,l and N=K,J,I,L.   |
| Elasticity = x(l) * D(l:K,J,I)                           |
| Marginal effect = P(KJIL)*D = P(K:JIL)P(J:IL)P(I:L)P(L)D |
| F is decomposed into the 4 parts in the tables.          |
+----------------------------------------------------------+
+----------------------------------------------------------------+
| Elasticity          Averaged over observations.                |
| Attribute is FUEL   in choice CART                             |
| Effects on probabilities of all choices in the model:          |
```

```
| *indicates direct Elasticity effect of the attribute.                  |
|                        Decomposition of Effect                  Total  |
|                         Trunk      Limb      Branch    Choice    Effect|
| Trunk=Trunk{1}                                                        |
| Limb=Lmb[1:1]                                                         |
|    Branch=B(1:1,1)                                                    |
| *      Choice=CART     .000      .000      .000      -.288      -.288 |
|        Choice=CARNT    .000      .000      .000       .099       .099 |
|        Choice=BUS      .000      .000      .000       .098       .098 |
|        Choice=TRAIN    .000      .000      .000       .099       .099 |
|        Choice=BUSWAY   .000      .000      .000       .095       .095 |
|        Choice=LR       .000      .000      .000       .096       .096 |
+-----------------------------------------------------------------------+
+-----------------------------------------------------------------------+
| Elasticity            Averaged over observations.                     |
| Attribute is FUEL     in choice CARNT                                 |
| Effects on probabilities of all choices in the model:                 |
| * indicates direct Elasticity effect of the attribute.                |
|                        Decomposition of Effect                  Total  |
|                         Trunk      Limb      Branch    Choice    Effect|
| Trunk=Trunk{1}                                                        |
| Limb=Lmb[1:1]                                                         |
|   Branch=B(1:1,1)                                                     |
|        Choice=CART     .000      .000      .000       .221       .221 |
| *      Choice=CARNT    .000      .000      .000      -.568      -.568 |
|        Choice=BUS      .000      .000      .000       .218       .218 |
|        Choice=TRAIN    .000      .000      .000       .220       .220 |
|        Choice=BUSWAY   .000      .000      .000       .214       .214 |
|        Choice=LR       .000      .000      .000       .217       .217 |
+-----------------------------------------------------------------------+
+-----------------------------------------------------------------------+
| Elasticity            Averaged over observations.                     |
| Attribute is FARE     in choice BUS                                   |
| Effects on probabilities of all choices in the model:                 |
| * indicates direct Elasticity effect of the attribute.                |
|                        Decomposition of Effect                  Total  |
|                         Trunk      Limb      Branch    Choice    Effect|
| Trunk=Trunk{1}                                                        |
| Limb=Lmb[1:1]                                                         |
|   Branch=B(1:1,1)                                                     |
|        Choice=CART     .000      .000      .000       .054       .054 |
|        Choice=CARNT    .000      .000      .000       .054       .054 |
|  *     Choice=BUS      .000      .000      .000      -.406      -.406 |
|        Choice=TRAIN    .000      .000      .000       .065       .065 |
|        Choice=BUSWAY   .000      .000      .000       .047       .047 |
|        Choice=LR       .000      .000      .000       .000       .000 |
+-----------------------------------------------------------------------+
```

```
+------------------------------------------------------------------+
| Elasticity             Averaged over observations.               |
| Attribute is FARE      in choice TRAIN                           |
| Effects on probabilities of all choices in the model:            |
| * indicates direct Elasticity effect of the attribute.           |
|                        Decomposition of Effect            Total  |
|                        Trunk    Limb    Branch   Choice   Effect |
| Trunk=Trunk{1}                                                   |
| Limb=Lmb[1:1]                                                    |
|   Branch=B(1:1,1)                                                |
|       Choice=CART      .000     .000    .000     .057      .057  |
|       Choice=CARNT     .000     .000    .000     .057      .057  |
|       Choice=BUS       .000     .000    .000     .063      .063  |
|  *    Choice=TRAIN     .000     .000    .000    -.420     -.420  |
|       Choice=BUSWAY    .000     .000    .000     .000      .000  |
|       Choice=LR        .000     .000    .000     .048      .048  |
+------------------------------------------------------------------+
+------------------------------------------------------------------+
| Elasticity             Averaged over observations.               |
| Attribute is FARE      in choice BUSWAY                          |
| Effects on probabilities of all choices in the model:            |
| * indicates direct Elasticity effect of the attribute.           |
|                        Decomposition of Effect            Total  |
|                        Trunk    Limb    Branch   Choice   Effect |
| Trunk=Trunk{1}                                                   |
| Limb=Lmb[1:1]                                                    |
|   Branch=B(1:1,1)                                                |
|       Choice=CART      .000     .000    .000     .071      .071  |
|       Choice=CARNT     .000     .000    .000     .070      .070  |
|       Choice=BUS       .000     .000    .000     .062      .062  |
|       Choice=TRAIN     .000     .000    .000     .000      .000  |
|  *    Choice=BUSWAY    .000     .000    .000    -.400     -.400  |
|       Choice=LR        .000     .000    .000     .078      .078  |
+------------------------------------------------------------------+
+------------------------------------------------------------------+
| Elasticity             Averaged over observations.               |
| Attribute is FARE      in choice LR                              |
| Effects on probabilities of all choices in the model:            |
| * indicates direct Elasticity effect of the attribute.           |
|                        Decomposition of Effect            Total  |
|                        Trunk    Limb    Branch   Choice   Effect |
| Trunk=Trunk{1}                                                   |
| Limb=Lmb[1:1]                                                    |
|   Branch=B(1:1,1)                                                |
|       Choice=CART      .000     .000    .000     .071      .071  |
|       Choice=CARNT     .000     .000    .000     .071      .071  |
|       Choice=BUS       .000     .000    .000     .000      .000  |
```

```
|        Choice=TRAIN     .000      .000      .000        .058        .058 |
|        Choice=BUSWAY    .000      .000      .000        .074        .074 |
|   *    Choice=LR        .000      .000      .000       -.416       -.416 |
+--------------------------------------------------------------------------+
```

The first output box describes how NLOGIT calculated the point elasticities requested by the analyst. NLOGIT states that probability weighted averages have been used. The heading **prob. weighted avg.** indicates that sample enumeration was used in calculating the elasticities while the heading **Averaged over observations** indicates that naive pooling was used. The heading **Partial effects computed at data means** will indicate to the analyst that the sample data means were used to calculate the point elasticities.

The second section of output describes the direct and cross-point elasticities for each of the attributes and alternatives. For each section of output, the direct point elasticity effect is indicated with an asterisk (∗). For MNL models, the analyst can ignore the trunk and limb decomposition effects which pertain to the more advanced nested logit model (see chapter 13). The choice-effects column is what is of interest for the present.

Taking the example of the elasticity for the fare attribute on the *train* alternative, the direct effect is calculated as −0.42. This suggests that a 1 percent increase in train fare will decrease the probability of selecting the *train* alternative by 0.42 percent, all else being equal. As would be expected, raising one's own price is likely to decrease demand for one's own good or service. Comparing the absolute value of −0.42 to table 11.1, we note that the fare elasticity for the *train* alternative is relatively inelastic. For the train company, this suggests that the revenue gained by any increase in fare will more than make up for the loss of patronage the fare increase will bring.

The remaining point elasticities represent the cross-elasticity effects. Examining these effects, the specified model suggests that a 1 percent increase in the fare for the *train* alternative will result in a 0.057 percent increase in the choice probabilities for the *cart* and *carnt* alternatives and an increase of 0.063, 0 and 0.048 percent in the choice probabilities of the *bus*, *busway*, and *LR* alternatives, respectively, *ceteris paribus*. Once more, the findings conform to expectations. An increase in a price for our good or service is likely to increase the demand for competing goods or services, *ceteris paribus*. We caution the user against the cross-elasticity effects in using the basic MNL model. While they are still of some use they are constrained by the IID condition for MNL and as we have already indicated they only vary across the alternatives due to the aggregation condition.

As an aside, care needs to be taken in interpreting the cross-elasticity effect for the *busway* alternative. The design employed for the mode-choice case study was such that the *train* alternative never appeared in the same choice set as the *busway* alternative. Because the *train* alternative never appeared in the same choice set as the *busway* alternative, there is no way to determine the cross-elasticity effect of *train* attributes on the choice probabilities of the *busway* alternative. As such, NLOGIT must assign a zero to the cross-elasticity for the *busway* alternative. The opposite case is also true. Similarly, the *bus* alternative never appeared in the same choice set as the *LR* alternative hence producing a zero cross-elasticity for when those alternatives appear together.

11.3.2 Calculating arc elasticities

Consider the direct point elasticity for a decision maker given a unit increase in price from \$1 to \$2 and a decrease in the probability of choice from 0.6 to 0.55. Estimation using (11.2) yields the following elasticity:

$$E^{P_{iq}}_{X_{ikq}} = \frac{0.6 - 0.55}{1 - 2} \cdot \frac{2}{0.55} = -0.182$$

We interpret this result as being indicative of a 0.182 percent decrease in the probability of selecting the alternative to which the price change occurred given a 1 percent change in the price variable, *ceteris paribus*.

The above appears straightforward; however, note that we chose to use the after-change price and after-change probability to calculate the point elasticity. That is, X_{ikq} of (11.2) equals 2 and P_{iq} equals 0.55. What if we chose to use the before-change price and before-change probability to estimate the direct point elasticity for our decision maker? The elasticity then becomes:

$$E^{P_{iq}}_{X_{ikq}} = \frac{0.6 - 0.55}{1 - 2} \cdot \frac{1}{0.6} = -0.08$$

Using the before-change values for X_{ikq} and P_{iq} suggests that a 1 percent change in price will yield an 0.08 percent decrease in the probability of selecting the alternative for which the price change occurred, *ceteris paribus*. There thus exists a discrepancy of some 0.1 percent between using the before-change values and the after-change values to calculate the point elasticity for the above example.

Which is the correct elasticity to use? For multi-million dollar projects, the answer to this question may prove critical.

Rather than answer the above question, economists prefer to answer a different question. That is, is the magnitude of difference in an elasticity calculated using the before- and after-change values sufficiently large enough to warrant concern? If the difference is marginal, then it matters not whether the before- or after-change values are used. If the magnitude of difference is non-marginal, however, then the analyst may calculate the elasticity using another method, known as the *arc elasticity method*. What constitutes a marginal or non-marginal difference is up to the individual analyst.

The calculation of arc elasticity involves using an average of the before- or after-change values. Thus (11.2) becomes

$$E^{P_{iq}}_{X_{ikq}} = \frac{\partial P_{iq}}{\partial X_{ikq}} \cdot \frac{\bar{X}_{ikq}}{\bar{P}_{iq}} \tag{11.6}$$

For the previous example, using (11.6), the calculated elasticity now becomes:

$$E^{P_{iq}}_{X_{ikq}} = \frac{0.6 - 0.55}{1 - 2} \cdot \frac{1.5}{0.575} = -0.13$$

Note that the arc elasticity will lie somewhere, but not necessarily halfway, between the direct elasticities calculated using the before- and after-change values.

Early versions of NLOGIT[1] do not have the capability to calculate direct and cross-arc elasticities without having to resort to a series of syntax commands which are quite complex. While we describe the steps required here, due to the complexity of the commands required, we leave it to appendix 11A to demonstrate the workings of these steps with regard to the mode-choice case study.

The steps required to calculate both direct and cross-arc elasticities are:

(1) For choice studies involving non-fixed-choice sets, create an index variable from 1 to C where C is the number of alternatives present within each choice set
(2) Create a new variable representative of the change in X (see (11.6)) for which the elasticity is to be estimated
(3) Estimate a model using the pre-change variable of interest and save the choice probabilities
(4) Calculate the utilities for a model using the after change variable created in step (2)
(5) Using the utilities obtained in step (4), calculate the choice probabilities for a model estimated with the after-change variable
(6) Create variables consistent with the individual components of (11.6); this involves estimating the average choice probabilities and average change in the variable of interest
(7) Using the variables created in step (6), calculate the within-choice set or individual-level elasticities
(8) Aggregate the within-choice set or individual-level elasticities using probability weighted sample enumeration.

As indicated earlier, we show the command syntax required for steps (1)–(8) in appendix 11A. In this appendix, we also show how the commands will look for post-June 2003 versions of NLOGIT, using the simulation command to calculate arc elasticities.

11.3.3 **;Effects**: marginal effects

As with point elasticities, a *marginal effect* reflects the rate of change in one variable relative to the rate of change in a second variable. However, unlike elasticities, marginal effects are not expressed as percentage changes. Rather marginal effects are expressed as *unit changes*. More specifically, we interpret the marginal effect for a choice model as the change in probability given a unit change in a variable, *ceteris paribus*.

A further similarity exists between marginal effects and elasticities in that, as with elasticities, marginal effects may be represented as both direct and cross-effects. Direct marginal effects represent the change in the choice probability for an alternative given a

[1] Neither LIMDEP 7.0 nor the first release version of NLOGIT 3.0 has a command specific to the estimation of arc elasticities. Versions of NLOGIT 3.0 after June 2003 have the capacity through the simulation command to estimate arc elasticities without having to resort to the command syntax described in appendix 11A.

1-unit change in a variable of interest, that variable belonging to that same alternative, *ceteris paribus*. Cross-marginal effects represent the impact a 1-unit change in a variable has upon the choice probabilities of competing alternatives to which that attribute does not belong, *ceteris paribus*.

However unlike elasticities (unless treated as a 100 percent change), marginal effects assigned to categorically coded data do make sense. Returning to our earlier gender example, a 1-unit change in the gender variable represents the change in choice probabilities (i.e. both direct and cross) given a change from male to female (or vice versa). As we discuss later, however, the method of calculating marginal effects for categorical data are different to the calculation performed for continuous-level data.

A further difference concerns the notion that a marginal effect represents an absolute change in the choice probabilities while an elasticity represents a conditional change. To show why, consider a marginal effect of 0.1 and an elasticity of 0.1. For the marginal effect, we interpret this as a change in the choice probability for all decision makers of 0.1 given a 1-unit change in the variable for which the marginal effect was calculated, *ceteris paribus*. For the elasticity, we would say that a 1 percent change in the variable of interest will result in a 0.1 percent change in the choice probabilities, *ceteris paribus*. Assuming the observed choice probabilities for two alternatives are 0.5 and 0.4, a 0.1 percent change (i.e. an elasticity) represents changes of 0.005 and 0.004, respectively, not 0.1 (i.e. a marginal effect).

The direct marginal effect for the MNL model is given as (11.7). The astute reader will note the relationship between the marginal effect and elasticity formula of (11.2). It is the second component of (11.2) which translates a marginal effect to an elasticity. That is, it is the second component of (11.2) that converts equation (11.7) to a percentage rather than unit change in the dependent choice variable:

$$M_{X_{ikq}}^{P_{iq}} = \frac{\partial P_{iq}}{\partial X_{ikq}} \tag{11.7}$$

It can be shown that at the level of the individual decision maker, (11.7) is equivalent to (11.8) when calculating a direct marginal effect:

$$M_{X_{ikq}}^{P_{iq}} = \partial X_{ikq} = \frac{\partial P_{iq}}{\partial X_{ikq}} = [1 - P_{iq}]\beta_k \tag{11.8}$$

It can also be shown that for cross-marginal effects, (11.7) becomes (11.9) at the level of the individual decision maker:

$$M_{X_{jkq}}^{P_{iq}} = -\beta_{jk} P_{jq} \tag{11.9}$$

As with elasticities, since the MNL model is estimated on a sample of choice data and not choice data for a single individual, the marginal effect for a variable must be calculated for the aggregate sample and not at the level of the individual decision maker.

To calculate an aggregate marginal effect, the analyst may, as with the calculation of the aggregate elasticities, either (1) utilize the average estimated P_i for the direct marginal

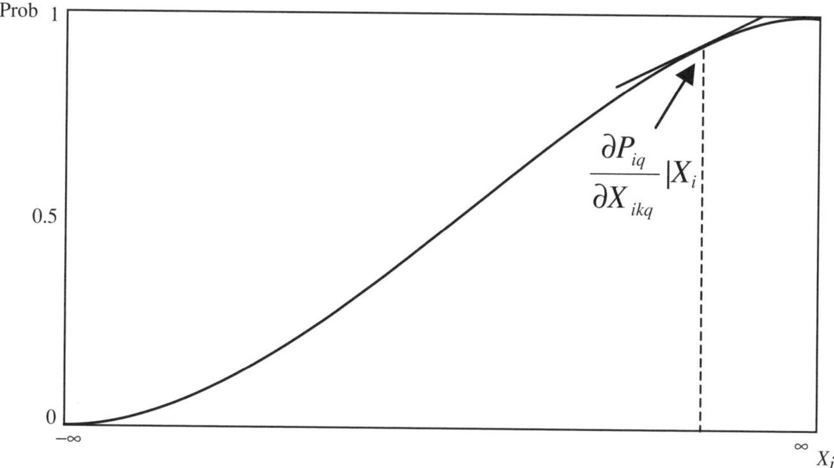

Figure 11.2 Marginal effects as the slopes of the tangent lines to the cumulative probability curve

effect and average estimated P_j for the cross-marginal effect (i.e. equivalent to using the sample means in estimated aggregate elasticities) or (2) calculate the marginal effect for each individual decision maker and weight each individual marginal effect by the decision maker's associated choice probability (i.e. probability weighted sample enumeration), or (3) calculate the marginal effect for each individual decision maker but not weight each individual marginal effect by the decision maker's associated choice probability (i.e. employ naive pooling). As with the calculation of aggregate elasticities, the authors advise against the use of the probability means and naive pooling and advocate the use of PWSE to calculate marginal effects for discrete choice models.

As an aside, to demonstrate why the marginal effect for a categorical variable is calculated differently to that of a continuous variable, note that marginal effects are mathematically equivalent to the slopes of lines tangential to the cumulative probability curve for the variable for which the marginal effect is being calculated, as taken at each distinct value of that variable (Powers and Xie 2001). We show this in figure 11.2 for an individual decision maker. Given that the tangent can be taken at any point along the cumulative distribution for the variable, X_i, our earlier discussion with regard to the use of the sample means, sample enumeration or naive pooling is of particular importance as it is these approaches which dictate where on the cumulative distribution curve that the tangent (i.e. the marginal effect) is calculated.

For categorical variables, a cumulative distribution function curve may be drawn for each level that the variable of concern may take. We show this for a dummy coded (0, 1) variable in figure 11.3, in which two curves are present. As with continuous-level data, the marginal effects as given by the tangents to the cumulative distribution functions are not constant over the range of the variable X_i. However as suggested by figure 11.3, the

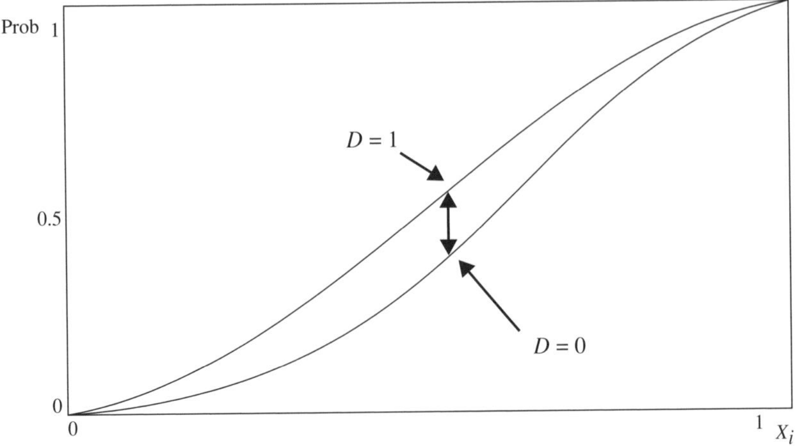

Figure 11.3 Marginal effects for a categorical (dummy coded) variable

maximum difference between the cumulative distribution function for the two levels occurs at Prob$(Y = 1) = 0.5$. It is at this point that many researchers calculate the marginal effects (i.e. the tangents to the curves).

NLOGIT treats the cumulative distribution function as a continuous variable when calculating a marginal effect, independent of whether the variable for which the marginal effect is sought is continuous or not. As such, the analyst is required to calculate the marginal effects manually (for categorically coded variables). We discuss this process after discussing the simulation capabilities of NLOGIT.

The command to generate marginal effects is similar to the command to generate point elasticities, the sole difference being that the round brackets used within the elasticity command (( )) are replaced with square brackets ([ ]). All else remains as for the elasticity command. Hence, in general the marginal effects command will look:

;Effects: <variable$_k$[alternative$_i$]>

As with elasticities, it is also possible to obtain marginal effects for a single variable on several alternatives through a single command. To do so, the command will take the following form:

;Effects: <variable$_k$[alternative$_i$, alternative$_j$]>

It is also possible to generate the marginal effects of several variables within a single command line by separating the individual marginal effects with a slash (/), as shown below:

;Effects: <variable$_k$[alternative$_i$] / variable$_h$[alternative$_i$]>

The command syntax in its entirety will therefore look as follows:

```
NLOGIT
;lhs = choice, cset, altij
;Choices = <names of alternatives>
;Effects: <variablek[alternativei]>
;Pwt
;Model:
U<alternative 1 name>)  =< utility function 1> /
U(<alternative 2 name>) = <utility function 2> /
...
U(<alternative i name>) = <utility function i> $
```

For the mode case study, the command to generate the marginal effects for *cart* fuel attribute will look as shown below. Note the use once more of the **;Pwt** command to indicate that probability weighted sample enumeration be used in the calculation. As with elasticities, if the **;Pwt** command is not included, NLOGIT will apply naive pooling to calculate the marginal effects. Similarly, the analyst may replace the **;Pwt** command with the command **means** to have NLOGIT calculate the marginal effects using the sample data means. Once more, the authors advise against the use of both naive pooling and the use of the probability means:

```
NLOGIT
;lhs = choice, cset, altij
;Choices = cart, carnt, bus, train, busway, LR
?;Show
?;Descriptives
?;Crosstabs
?Effects: fuel(*) / fare(*)
;Effects: fuel[cart]
;Pwt
;Model:
U(cart)     = asccart + cst*fuel /
U(carnt)    = asccarnt + cst*fuel /
U(bus)      = ascbus + cst*fare /
U(train)    = asctn + cst*fare /
U(busway)   = ascbusw + cst*fare /
U(LR)       = cst*fare $
```

Using the above command syntax for the mode case study for the segment with commutes of less than 30 minutes, NLOGIT will produce the following output:

```
+-----------------------------------------------------------+
| Partial effects = prob. weighted avg.                      |
|                                                            |
| dlnP[alt=k,br=j,lmb=i,tr=l]                                |
| ---------------------------- =  D(m:K,J,I,L) = delta(m)*F |
|                                                            |
```

```
| dx(m):alt=K,br=J,lmb=I,tr=L]                                  |
|                                                               |
| delta(m) = coefficient on x(m) in U(K:J,I,L)                  |
| F = (l=L) (i=I) (j=J) [(k=K)-P(K:JIL)]                        |
| + (l=L) (i=I) [(j=J)-P(J:IL)] P(K:JIL)t(J:IL)                 |
| + (l=L) [(i=I)-P(I:L)] P(J:IL) P(K:JIL)t(J:IL)s(I:L)          |
| + [(l=L)-P(L)] P(I:L) P(J:IL) P(K:JIL)t(J:IL)s(I:L)f(L)       |
|                                                               |
| P(K|JIL)=Prob[choice=K |branch=J,limb=I,trunk=L]              |
| P(J|IL), P(I3L), P(L) defined likewise.                       |
| (n=N) = 1 if n=N, 0 else, for n=k,j,i,l and N=K,J,I,L.        |
| Elasticity = x(l) * D(l:K,J,I)                                |
| Marginal effect = P(KJIL)*D = P(K:JIL)P(J:IL)P(I:L)P(L)D      |
| F is decomposed into the 4 parts in the tables.               |
+---------------------------------------------------------------+
+-----------------------------------------------------------------------+
| Derivative (times 100) Averaged over observations.                    |
| Attribute is FUEL  in choice CART                                     |
| Effects on probabilities of all choices in the model:                 |
| *indicates direct Derivative effect of the attribute.                 |
|                         Decomposition of Effect                Total  |
|                           Trunk     Limb    Branch   Choice   Effect |
| Trunk=Trunk{1}                                                        |
| Limb=Lmb[1:1]                                                         |
|     Branch=B(1:1,1)                                                   |
| *       Choice=CART      .000      .000     .000    -3.849    -3.849 |
|         Choice=CARNT     .000      .000     .000     1.460     1.460 |
|         Choice=BUS       .000      .000     .000     1.256     1.256 |
|         Choice=TRAIN     .000      .000     .000     1.999     1.199 |
|         Choice=BUSWAY    .000      .000     .000     1.307     1.307 |
|         Choice=LR        .000      .000     .000     1.217     1.217 |
+-----------------------------------------------------------------------+
```

As with the elasticity output, the first output given by NLOGIT for marginal effects provides advanced information as to how the marginal effects were calculated. For the beginner, only the heading of this output will be informative as the heading indicates to the analyst what form of aggregation was employed for the calculation of the marginal effects. The heading **prob. weighted avg.** indicates that PWSE was used while the heading **Averaged over observations** indicates that naive pooling was used instead. Observing the heading **Partial effects computed at data means** will indicate to the analyst that the sample data means were used to calculate the marginal effects.

It is the next NLOGIT output which is of more consequence to the analyst in determining the marginal effects for the variables specified. As with the output generated for elasticities, the analyst can, for the present, ignore the columns of output titled *Trunks, Limbs and Branches*. It is the *Choice* column which is of importance as it is this column which reports the marginal effects for the MNL model. Due to the small size often observed for marginal effects, the marginal effects as reported are the true marginal effects multiplied by 100. Thus, the analyst must divide the reported values by 100 to obtain the true marginal effects for the model.

As with the elasticities output, an asterisk (∗) is used to indicate the alternative for which the marginal effect was specified. For the above example, this is the *cart* alternative. The marginal effect for this alternative, alternative i, is interpreted as follows. An increase in the price of fuel attribute for the *cart* alternative of 1 unit will decrease the choice probability for the *cart* alternative by 0.03849, *ceteris paribus*. This is in the direction expected.

The remaining marginal effects represent the changes in the probabilities for competing alternatives. From the above output, a 1-unit increase in the *cart* fuel attribute will increase the probability of selecting the *carnt* alternative by 0.0146, *ceteris paribus*. Similarly, a 1-unit change in the *cart* fuel attribute will, according to the estimated model, increase the probabilities by 0.0146, 0.01256, 0.01199, 0.01307, and 0.01217 for the *carnt*, *bus*, *train*, *busway*, and *LR* alternatives respectively, *ceteris paribus*.

As an aside, as the choice probabilities must sum to one, the marginal effects which represent the change in the choice probabilities are mathematically constrained to sum to zero, thus representing a net zero change over all alternatives. This is not true of elasticities.

11.4 Simulation

Earlier, we described how to perform "what-if" scenarios using Microsoft Excel. In doing so, we used a simple example. Nevertheless, as the reader may appreciate, using spreadsheet programs such as Excel to establish "what-if" scenarios quickly becomes cumbersome the more complex the model specified. Rather than use spreadsheet programs, NLOGIT 3.0 (and LIMDEP 8.0) provides the analyst with a simulation capability which is not available in earlier versions.

The simulation capability of NLOGIT allows the analyst to use an existing model to test how changes in attributes and SDC impact upon the choice probabilities for each of the alternatives. This requires a two-step process:

(1) Estimate the model as previously described (automatically saving outputs in memory)
(2) Apply the simulation command (using the stored parameter estimates) to test how changes in the attribute and SDC levels impact upon the choice probabilities.

Step (1) involves the analyst specifying a choice model that will be used as a basis of comparison for subsequent simulations. Step (2) involves performing the simulation to test how changes in an attribute or SDC impact upon the choice probabilities for the model estimated in step (1).

We use the following model specification to demonstrate NLOGIT's simulation capability. Note that in the model specification below, we allow for ASCs and alternative-specific parameter estimates for the *fuel* and *fare* attributes:

```
NLOGIT
;lhs = choice, cset, altij
;Choices = cart, carnt, bus, train, busway, LR
;Model:
U(cart)     = asccart + cartcst*fuel /
U(carnt)    = asccarnt + carntcst*fuel /
U(bus)      = ascbus + buscst*fare /
U(train)    = asctn + tncst*fare /
U(busway)   = ascbusw + buswcst*fare /
U(LR)       = lrcst*fare $
```

For the 30 minutes or less commute segment, the above model specification will generate the following NLOGIT output:

```
+---------------------------------------------+
| Discrete choice (multinomial logit) model    |
| Maximum Likelihood Estimates                 |
| Model estimated: Feb 30, 2003 at 08:45:00AM. |
| Dependent variable               Choice      |
| Weighting variable                 None      |
| Number of observations             2369      |
| Iterations completed                  5      |
| Log likelihood function       -3214.241      |
| R2=1-LogL/LogL*  Log-L  fncn R-sqrd  RsqAdj  |
| No coefficients  -4244.6782  .24276  .24159  |
| Constants only.  Must be computed directly.  |
|                  Use NLOGIT ;...; RHS=ONE $  |
| Chi-squared[ 6]           =    1650.89911    |
| Prob [ chi squared > value ] =    .00000     |
| Response data are given as ind. choice.      |
| Number of obs.= 2369, skipped   0  bad  obs. |
+---------------------------------------------+
+---------+--------------+----------------+--------+---------+
|Variable | Coefficient  |Standard Error  |b/St.Er.|P[|Z|>z] |
+---------+--------------+----------------+--------+---------+
 ASCCART      -.43353076      .17456286     -2.484    .0130
 CARTCST      -.09766455      .05795105     -1.685    .0919
 ASCCARNT     -.16668466      .26069361      -.639    .5226
 CARNTCST     -.09243679      .05646700     -1.637    .1016
 ASCBUS       -.18885515      .19430843      -.972    .3311
 BUSCST       -.17877650      .04576476     -3.906    .0001
 ASCTN        -.15244648      .18561589      -.821    .4115
 TNCST        -.21490349      .04577121     -4.695    .0000
 ASCBUSW       .11529699      .17866515       .645    .5187
 BUSWCST      -.26642705      .04168628     -6.391    .0000
 LRCST        -.25775069      .04182220     -6.163    .0000
```

We leave it to the reader to interpret the output above, but note that we use this model as the basis for demonstrating the simulation capability that follows.

The **;Simulation** command in NLOGIT is as follows:

;Simulation = <list of alternatives>
;Scenario: <variable(alternative)> = <[action]magnitude of action> $

The command **;Simulation** may be used in one of two ways. First, the analyst may restrict the set of alternatives used in the simulation by specifying which alternatives are to be included. For example, the command

;Simulation = cart, carnt

will restrict the simulation to changes in the two privately owned vehicle alternatives. All public transport alternatives will be ignored.

The analyst may include all alternatives by not specifically specifying any alternatives. Thus:

;Simulation

will have NLOGIT perform the simulation on all alternatives specified within the **=<list of alternatives>** command.

The remainder of the command syntax instructs NLOGIT on what changes to simulate. A number of points are required to be made. First, the command begins with a semi-colon (**;**) but the command **;scenario** is followed with a colon (**:**). Next, the variable specified must be included within at least one of the utility functions and must belong to the alternative specified in the round brackets. It is possible to simulate a change in an attribute belonging to more than one alternative by specifying each alternative within the round brackets separated by a comma. Thus:

;Scenario: fuel(cart,carnt)

will simulate a change in the fuel attribute of both the *cart* and *carnt* alternatives.

The actions specifications are as follows:

= a specific value for which the variable indicated is to take for each decision maker (e.g. **fuel(Cart) = 2** will simulate a fuel price equal to $2 for the *cart* alternative for all individuals); or

= [+] will add the value following to the observed value within the data for each decision maker (e.g. **fuel(Cart) = [+]2** will add $2 to the observed value of the fuel attribute for the *cart* alternative for each individual); or

= [-] will subtract the value following to the observed value within the data for each decision maker (e.g. **fuel(Cart) = [-]2** will subtract $2 from the observed value of the fuel attribute for the *cart* alternative for each individual); or

= [*] will multiply the observed value within the data by the value following for each individual (e.g. **fuel(Cart) = [*]2** will double the observed value of the fuel attribute for the *cart* alternative for each decision maker); or

= [/] will divide the observed value within the data by the value following for each individual (e.g. **fuel(Cart) = [/]2** will halve the observed value of the fuel attribute for the *cart* alternative for each individual).

The **;Simulation** command may specify that more than one attribute is to change and that changes may be different across alternatives. To specify more than one change, the command syntax is as above; however, new scenarios are separated with a slash (/). We show this below:

;Simulation = <list of alternatives>
;Scenario: <variable$_1$(alternative$_i$)> = <[action]magnitude of action>
/<variable$_k$(alternative$_j$)> = <[action]magnitude of action> $

As a specific example:

;Scenario: fuel(cart,carnt) = [*]2 / fare(bus) = [/]2
/ fare(train) = [*]1.5 $

will double the fuel costs for the *privately owned vehicle* alternatives, halve the fare for the *bus* alternative, and multiply the fare for the *train* alternative by 1.5, all within the single simulation.

Within NLOGIT's command syntax, the **;Simulation** command is not treated separate to the remainder of the **NLOGIT** command syntax. Thus, even though the choice model has been estimated, the **;Simulation** and **;Scenario** commands are not used by themselves. Indeed, they are attached to the end of the model specification, as shown below:

NLOGIT
;lhs = choice, cset, altij
;Choices = <names of alternatives>
;Model:
U<alternative 1 name>) =< utility function 1> /
U(<alternative 2 name>) = <utility function 2> /
...
U(<alternative i name>) = <utility function i>
;Simulation = <list of alternatives>
;Scenario: <variable(alternative)> = <[action]magnitude of action> $

We show a specific example using the model estimated earlier as the base choice calibration model:

NLOGIT
;lhs = choice, cset, altij
;Choices = cart, carnt, bus, train, busway, LR

```
;Model:
U(cart)    = asccart + cartcst*fuel /
U(carnt)   = asccarnt + carntcst*fuel /
U(bus)     = ascbus + buscst*fare /
U(train)   = asctn + tncst*fare /
U(busway)  = ascbusw + buswcst*fare /
U(LR)      = lrcst*fare
;Simulation
;Scenario:fuel(cart)=[*]2 $
```

The output generated is as follows. Note that even though the model is specified as before, NLOGIT does not reproduce the standard results shown above. Only the simulation results shown below are produced:

```
+---------------------------------------------+
|Discrete Choice (One Level) Model            |
|Model Simulation Using Previous Estimates    |
|Number of observations            2369       |
+---------------------------------------------+
+-----------------------------------------------------+
|Simulations of Probability Model                     |
|Model: Discrete Choice (One Level) Model             |
|Simulated choice set may be a subset of the choices.|
|Number of individuals is the probability times the   |
|number of observations in the simulated sample.      |
|Column totals may be affected by rounding error.     |
|The model used was simulated with 2369 observations.|
+-----------------------------------------------------+
---------------------------------------------------------------------
Specification of scenario 1 is:
Attribute Alternatives affected        Change type              Value
--------- -------------------------- ------------------- ---------
FUEL      CART                         Scale base by value      2.000
---------------------------------------------------------------------
The simulator located 2369 observations for this scenario.
Simulated Probabilities (shares) for this scenario:
     +----------+--------------+-------------+------------------+
     |Choice    |     Base     |  Scenario   | Scenario - Base  |
     |          | %Share Number |%Share Number | ChgShare ChgNumber|
     +----------+--------------+-------------+------------------+
     |CART      | 25.327    600 | 21.927   519 |  -3.400%     -81 |
     |CARNT     | 27.775    658 | 29.074   689 |   1.298%      31 |
     |BUS       | 10.300    244 | 10.773   255 |    .473%      11 |
     |TRAIN     | 10.257    243 | 10.729   254 |    .471%      11 |
     |BUSWAY    | 13.466    319 | 14.051   333 |    .585%      14 |
     |LR        | 12.875    305 | 13.447   319 |    .572%      14 |
     |Total     |100.000   2369 |100.000  2369 |    .000%       0 |
     +----------+--------------+-------------+------------------+
```

The first output box indicates the total number of observations available for use for the simulation. This should equate to the number of observations used in the base choice model. The next output box informs the analyst that the simulation may be performed on a sub-set of the available alternatives as specified with the **;Simulation = <list of alternatives>** command. The remainder of information provided by this output box informs the reader as to how to interpret the remainder of the simulation output.

The third output box instructs the analyst what simulation change(s) were modeled and which attributes and which alternatives those changes apply to. We leave it to the reader to discover which heading applies to which action.

The last NLOGIT simulation output box indicates how the actions specified in the simulation impact upon the choice shares for each of the alternatives. The first section of this output provides the base shares for the base or constants-only model (not to be confused with the base choice calibration model estimated at step (1) of the simulation). The third column of the output demonstrates how the changes specified by the analyst impact upon these base-choice shares:

Choice	Base		Scenario		Scenario - Base	
	%Share	Number	%Share	Number	ChgShare	ChgNumber
CART	25.327	600	21.927	519	-3.400%	-81
CARNT	27.775	658	29.074	689	1.298%	31
BUS	10.300	244	10.773	255	.473%	11
TRAIN	10.257	243	10.729	254	.471%	11
BUSWAY	13.466	319	14.051	333	.585%	14
LR	12.875	305	13.447	319	.572%	14
Total	100.000	2369	100.000	2369	.000%	0

In the example, a doubling of the fuel cost for the *cart* alternative will produce an estimated market share for the *cart* alternative of 21.927, down from 25.327, *ceteris paribus*. The same change will produce market shares of 29.074, 10.773, 10.729, 14.051, and 13.447 for the *carnt*, *bus*, *train*, *busway*, and *LR* alternatives, respectively, *ceteris paribus*.

The final column provides the change in choice shares for each of the alternatives both as a percentage and in raw numbers for the sample. Thus, a doubling of the fuel attribute for the *cart* alternative, *ceteris paribus*, decreases the *cart* share as a percent by 3.4 which translates as 81 of the original 600 choices for that alternative now switching to another alternative. Of these 81, 31 of those choices are predicted to switch to the *carnt* alternative (i.e. an increase of 1.298 percent), the *bus* and *train* alternatives attract 11 each (i.e. increases of 0.473 and 0.471, percent respectively), and *busway* and *LR* attract 14 choices each (i.e. increases of 0.585 and 0.572 percent, respectively). We ignore any rounding errors.

Careful wording is used above, particularly the use of the word *choices*. The above simulation example was performed using SP data. As such, the changes in shares reported are representative of changes in *choice sets*, and not market shares. This is because with SP choice data, the choices are made within choice sets and not choices made in the real world.

Indeed, each individual reviewed three choice sets and thus made three choices when in the real world they may have made only one choice. Although the simulation may be of some use in determining how changes impact upon a model estimated using SP data, the resulting share outputs are of no real significance to the analyst. However, for RP data, the shares reported are of particular interest. Thus, unless the simulation is used for some other purpose such as estimating the marginal effects for categorically coded variables (see below), the simulation capability is generally confined to either RP data only or combined SP and RP data (see chapters 13 and 14).

As an aside, it is possible to conduct more than one simulation concurrently and compare the results of each simulation using NLOGIT. To do so, the analyst separates the simulations within the scenario command by use of the **&** character. We show this below for two simulations, although it is possible to perform more than two. The comparisons generated are pairwise comparisons, and as such NLOGIT will generate output comparing each possible combination of simulation scenario specified by the analyst:

```
;Simulation = <list of alternatives>
;Scenario: <variable(alternative)> = <[action]magnitude of action> & <vari-
able(alternative)> = <[action]magnitude of action > $
```

For the example, the following command syntax will compare the simulation of all individuals observing a fuel cost of $0.90 with a simulation in which all individuals incur a fuel cost of $0.80:

```
NLOGIT
;lhs = choice, cset, altij
;Choices = cart, carnt, bus, train, busway, LR
;Model:
U(cart) = asccart + cartcst*fuel /
U(carnt) = asccarnt + carntcst*fuel /
U(bus) = ascbus + buscst*fare /
U(train) = asctn + tncst*fare /
U(busway) = ascbusw + buswcst*fare /
U(LR) = lrcst*fare
;Simulation
;Scenario: fuel(cart,carnt) = 0.9 & fuel(cart,carnt) = 0.8 $
```

For the 30 minutes or less segment, the above syntax generates the following results:

```
+---------+---------------+---------------+------------------+
|Choice   |     Base      |   Scenario    | Scenario - Base  |
|         | %Share Number | %Share Number |ChgShare ChgNumber|
+---------+---------------+---------------+------------------+
|CART     | 25.327    600 | 25.096    595 |  -.231%       -5 |
|CARNT    | 27.775    658 | 32.926    780 |  5.151%      122 |
|BUS      | 10.300    244 |  9.196    218 | -1.104%      -26 |
|TRAIN    | 10.257    243 |  9.159    217 | -1.099%      -26 |
```

```
|BUSWAY   | 13.466     319 | 12.091     286 | -1.375%        -33 |
|LR       | 12.875     305 | 11.532     273 | -1.343%        -32 |
|Total    |100.000    2369 |100.000    2369 |   .000%          0 |
+---------+----------------+---------------+-------------------+
---------------------------------------------------------------------
                Specification of scenario 2 is:
Attribute  Alternatives affected          Change type          Value
---------  -------------------------      ---------------- --------
FUEL       CART    CARNT                  Fix at new value      .800
---------------------------------------------------------------------
  The simulator located 2369 observations for this scenario.
       Simulated Probabilities (shares) for this scenario:
+----------+---------------+---------------+------------------+
|Choice    |      Base     |    Scenario    | Scenario - Base   |
|          | %Share  Number |%Share   Number |ChgShare ChgNumber|
+----------+---------------+---------------+------------------+
|CART      | 25.327     600 | 25.202     597 |  -.126%        -3 |
|CARNT     | 27.775     658 | 33.047     783 |  5.272%       125 |
|BUS       | 10.300     244 |  9.146     217 | -1.154%       -27 |
|TRAIN     | 10.257     243 |  9.109     216 | -1.149%       -27 |
|BUSWAY    | 13.466     319 | 12.027     285 | -1.438%       -34 |
|LR        | 12.875     305 | 11.470     272 | -1.405%       -33 |
|Total     |100.000    2369 |100.000    2370 |   .000%         1 |
+----------+---------------+---------------+------------------+

  The simulator located 2369 observations for this scenario.
          Pairwise Comparisons of Specified Scenarios
          Base     for this comparison is scenario 1.
          Scenario for this comparison is scenario 2.
+----------+---------------+---------------+------------------+
|Choice    |      Base     |    Scenario    | Scenario - Base   |
|          | %Share  Number |%Share   Number |ChgShare ChgNumber|
+----------+---------------+---------------+------------------+
|CART      | 25.096     595 | 25.202     597 |  .105%          2 |
|CARNT     | 32.926     780 | 33.047     783 |  .121%          3 |
|BUS       |  9.196     218 |  9.146     217 | -.050%         -1 |
|TRAIN     |  9.159     217 |  9.109     216 | -.050%         -1 |
|BUSWAY    | 12.091     286 | 12.027     285 | -.064%         -1 |
|LR        | 11.532     273 | 11.470     272 | -.062%         -1 |
|Total     |100.000    2369 |100.000    2370 |  .000%          1 |
+----------+---------------+---------------+------------------+
```

The first two output boxes provide the simulated market shares under each a simulation scenario independent of the other simulation scenario specified. These are interpreted in the same manner described earlier. The last output box provides the analyst with a pairwise comparison of the different simulation scenarios. Examining the change in the market shares, the reader will note that, for the above example, a change from 0.9 units of fuel price to 0.8 units of fuel price increases the *cart* alternative market share by 0.105 percent and the *carnt* alternative market share by 0.121 percent, *ceteris paribus*. The same decrease in fuel costs decreases the market shares for the *bus*, *train*, *busway*, and *LR* alternatives by 0.050, 0.050, 0.064, and 0.062 percent, respectively, *ceteris paribus*.

11.4.1 Marginal effects for categorical coded variables

In the discussion of marginal effects, we noted that the marginal effects for categorically coded data are handled differently to those of continuous-level data. The marginal effects commands and output shown earlier relate to the calculation of marginal effects for continuous-level data and should not be applied to categorically coded data such as variables that have been effects or dummy coded.

We have developed a quick and simple technique to obtain the marginal effects for categorical data using NLOGIT's simulation capability. We demonstrate this technique here. Consider the following model specification in which the *fare* attribute is effects coded. We assign the effects coded *fare* attribute to the *busway* alternative only. To create the effects code for the *fare* attribute, the following command is required first:

```
CREATE
;if(fare=1)fare1d=1
;if(fare=3)fare3d=1
;if(fare=5)fare1d=-1
;if(fare=5)fare3d=-1 $
```

The model described above may be estimated using the following command syntax:

```
NLOGIT
;lhs= choice, cset, altij
;Choices = cart, carnt, bus, train, busway, LR
;Model:
U(cart)    = asccart /
U(carnt)   = asccarnt + cst*fuel /
U(bus)     = ascbus + cst*fare /
U(train)   = asctn + cst*fare /
U(busway)  = ascbusw + fare1d*fare1d + fare3d*fare3d /
U(LR)      = cst*fare $
```

Estimating of the above model for the 30 minutes or less commute segment, we obtain the following output:

```
+---------------------------------------------+
| Discrete choice (multinomial logit) model   |
| Maximum Likelihood Estimates                |
| Model estimated:  Feb 30,  2003 at 09:00:00AM.|
| Dependent variable                Choice    |
| Weighting variable                  None    |
```

```
| Number of observations                      2369     |
| Iterations completed                           5     |
| Log likelihood function               -3217.960     |
| R2=1-LogL/LogL*     Log-L fncn    R-sqrd   RsqAdj  |
| No coefficients     -4244.6782    .24188   .24103  |
| Constants only. Must be computed directly.          |
|                  Use NLOGIT ;...; RHS=ONE $         |
| Chi-squared[ 3]          =     1643.45932          |
| Prob [ chi squared > value ] =             .00000  |
| Response data are given as ind. choice.            |
| Number of obs.=    2369,   skipped    0 bad obs.  |
+----------------------------------------------------+
+---------+-------------+----------------+---------+---------+
|Variable | Coefficient  | Standard Error |b/St.Er.|P[|Z|>z] |
+---------+-------------+----------------+---------+---------+
ASCCART        -.06486119       .07603214      -.853    .3936
CST            -.18202714       .02173768     -8.374    .0000
ASCCARNT        .39187088       .07707979      5.084    .0000
ASCBUS          .02057009       .09912476       .208    .8356
ASCTN          -.04100211       .09358635      -.438    .6613
ASCBUSW        -.47807227       .10638508     -4.494    .0000
FARE1D          .57172474       .08911888      6.415    .0000
FARE3D         -.09306435       .09533799      -.976    .3290
```

The above model will act as the base-choice calibration model for the simulation. We omit further discussion of the above model, beyond noting that the *fare1d* parameter for the *busway* alternative is statistically significant while the *fare3d* parameter is not (at the alpha equals 0.05 level). We leave it to the reader to decide on the merits of this model specification.

Given the above model, the analyst may now use the base-choice calibration model to estimate the changes in the choice probabilities at each level of the effects or dummy coded variable. As suggested by figure 11.3, the analyst is required to calculate the marginal effects as movements from one level to another within a categorically coded variable. For this example, this represents three scenario simulations. We show the three scenarios below which correspond to the three bus fare levels:

(1) Estimating choice probability changes from a change in bus fare from \$1 to \$3:

```
;scenario:fare1d(busway)=1/fare3d(busway)=0 &
fare1d(bus)=0/fare3d(bus)=1 $
```

(2) Estimating choice probability changes from a change in bus fare from \$3 to \$5:

```
;scenario:fare1d(busway)=0/fare3d(busway)=1 &
fare1d(bus)=-1/fare3d(bus)=-1 $
```

(3) Estimating choice probability changes from a change in bus fare from \$1 to \$5:

```
;scenario:fare1d(busway)=1/fare3d(busway)=0 &
fare1d(bus)=-1/fare3d(bus)=-1 $
```

To simulate the marginal effect of a movement from a *busway* fare of \$1 to a *busway* fare of \$3, the following command syntax is used:

```
NLOGIT
;lhs = choice, cset, altij
;Choices = cart, carnt, bus, train, busway, LR
;Model:
U(cart) = asccart + cst*fuel /
U(carnt) = asccarnt + cst*fuel /
U(bus) = ascbus + fare1d*fare1d + fare3d*fare3d /
U(train) = asctn + cst*fare /
U(busway) = ascbusw + cst*fare /
U(LR) = cst*fare
;Simulation
;Scenario: fare1d(busway)=1 / fare3d(busway)=0 & fare1d(busway)=0 /
fare3d(busway)=1 $
```

For the 30 minutes or less commuter segment, the above model specification produces the following output. We have omitted all output save for the pairwise comparison of the two scenarios (i.e. *busway* fares at \$1 and \$3):

Choice	Base		Scenario		Scenario - Base	
	%Share	Number	%Share	Number	ChgShare	ChgNumber
CART	23.402	554	25.832	612	2.430%	58
CARNT	25.668	608	28.328	671	2.660%	63
BUS	9.597	227	10.444	247	.848%	20
TRAIN	10.257	243	10.257	243	.000%	0
BUSWAY	19.312	458	12.039	285	-7.273%	-173
LR	11.764	279	13.099	310	1.335%	31
Total	100.000	2369	100.000	2368	.000%	-1

Changing the *busway* fare from \$1 to \$3 increases the choice probabilities for the *cart* and *carnt* alternatives by 0.0243 and 0.0266, respectively, *ceteris paribus*. The same change in *busway* fares over the sample will increase the choice probabilities for the *bus*, *train*, and *LR* alternatives by 0.00848, 0, and 0.01335 respectively, *ceteris paribus*. This same change will reduce the choice probability over the sample for the *busway* alternative by 0.07273. Note that as the *train* alternative never appeared in the same choice set as the *busway* alternative, determining the cross-marginal effect for changes of the *busway* fare attribute upon the train alternative is not possible.

A second simulation is required to determine the marginal effects for a change in *busway* fare levels from \$3 to \$5. The command syntax will look thus:

```
NLOGIT
;lhs = choice, cset, altij
;Choices = cart, carnt, bus, train, busway, LR
;Model:
U(cart) = asccart + cst*fuel /
U(carnt) = asccarnt + cst*fuel /
U(bus) = ascbus + cst*fare /
U(train) = asctn + cst*fare /
U(busway) = ascbusw + fare1d*fare1d + fare3d*fare3d /
U(LR) = cst*fare
;Simulation
;Scenario: fare1d(busway)=0 / fare3d(busway)=1 & fare1d(busway)=-1 /
fare3d(busway)=-1 $
```

The mode-choice shares for a *busway* fare increase from \$3 to \$5 are provided below:

Choice	Base %Share	Base Number	Scenario %Share	Scenario Number	Scenario - Base ChgShare	Scenario - Base ChgNumber
CART	25.832	612	26.908	637	1.076%	25
CARNT	28.328	671	29.506	699	1.178%	28
BUS	10.444	247	10.818	256	.373%	9
TRAIN	10.257	243	10.257	243	.000%	0
BUSWAY	12.039	285	8.822	209	-3.217%	-76
LR	13.099	310	13.689	324	.590%	14
Total	100.000	2368	100.000	2368	.000%	0

The simulation estimates that increasing the *busway* fare from \$3 to \$5 will increase the choice shares for the *cart*, *carnt*, *bus*, *train*, and *LR* alternatives by 0.01076, 0.01178, 0.00373, 0, and 0.059 respectively, *ceteris paribus*. The same fare increase will have a direct marginal effect of a decrease in the choice probabilities for the *busway* alternative of 0.03217 for the sample, *ceteris paribus*.

The final simulation is designed to obtain the marginal effects for a *busway* fare increase from \$1 to \$5:

```
NLOGIT
;lhs = choice, cset, altij
;Choices = cart, carnt, bus, train, busway, LR
;Model:
U(cart) = asccart + cst*fuel /
U(carnt) = asccarnt + cst*fuel /
U(bus) = ascbus + cst*fare /
U(train) = asctn + cst*fare /
U(busway) = ascbusw + fare1d*fare1d + fare3d*fare3d /
```

U(LR) = cst*fare

;Simulation

;Scenario: fare1d(busway)=1 / fare3d(busway)=0 & fare1d(busway)=-1 / fare3d(busway)=-1 $

The above will produce the following choice share output:

Choice	Base %Share	Base Number	Scenario %Share	Scenario Number	Scenario - Base ChgShare	Scenario - Base ChgNumber
CART	23.402	554	26.908	637	3.507%	83
CARNT	25.668	608	29.506	699	3.838%	91
BUS	9.597	227	10.818	256	1.221%	29
TRAIN	10.257	243	10.257	243	.000%	0
BUSWAY	19.312	458	8.822	209	-10.490%	-249
LR	11.764	279	13.689	324	1.925%	45
Total	100.000	2369	100.000	2368	.000%	-1

Increasing the *busway* fare from \$1 to \$5 will increase the probabilities for the *cart* and *carnt* alternatives by 0.03507 and 0.03838, respectively, *ceteris paribus*. A similar change in *busway* fare will increase choice probabilities for the *bus*, *train*, and *LR* alternatives by 0.01221, 0, and 0.01925, respectively, *ceteris paribus*. Similarly, the indicated fare change will decrease the probability over the sample of selecting the *busway* alternative by 0.1049, *ceteris paribus*.

11.4.2 Reporting marginal effects

An often-asked question is how does one report marginal effects?[2] Several possibilities exist, although the authors prefer the method shown in table 11.2. In table 11.2, we show the marginal effects for the generic *fuel* attribute for the *cart* alternative as well as for the effects coded *busway* fare attribute as estimated in sub-section 11.4.1. The direct and cross-marginal effects for the *fuel* attribute associated with the *cart* alternative was estimated using the command:

Effects:fuel[cart]

We have therefore assumed that the *fuel* attribute is continuous in nature. This is perhaps somewhat of an optimistic assumption given that over the sample used for the estimation of the model the attribute took on only three discrete values (i.e. \$1, \$3, and \$5). In reporting the marginal effects, each marginal effect corresponds to an alternative, the order of which is provided in the header of the table. Given that we have assumed that the *fuel* attribute is

[2] This discussion may be extended to the reporting of elasticities.

Table11.2. *Reporting marginal effects*

Attribute	Alternative	Coefficient (Wald statistic)	Marginal effect [*cart*, *carnt*, *bus*, *train*, *busway*, *LR*]	
ASCCART	CART	–0.0648612 (–0.853076)		Δ from \$1 to \$3
ASCCARNT	CARNT	0.391871 (5.08396)		
ASCBUS	BUS	0.0205701 (0.207517)		
ASCTN	TRAIN	–0.0410021 (–0.438121)		
ASCBUSW	BUSWAY	–0.478072 (–4.49379)		
CST	CART, CARNT, BUS, TRAIN, LR	–0.182027 (–8.37381)	[–0.03412, 0.01284, 0.00468, 0.00475, 0.00593, 0.00592]	Δ from \$3 to \$5
FARE1D	BUSWAY	0.571725 (6.4153)	[0.0243, 0.0266, 0.00848, 0, –0.07273, 0.01335]	
FARE3D	BUSWAY	–0.0930644 (–0.976152)	[0.01076, 0.01178, 0.00373, 0, –0.03217, 0.0059]	
			[0.03507, 0.03838, 0.01221, 0, –0.1049, 0.01925]	Δ from \$1 to \$5

linear, the reported marginal effects relate to 1-unit changes in the *fuel* attribute for the *cart* alternative such that a change from $1 to $2 has the same impact upon the mode-choice probabilities as a change from $2 to $3.

The marginal effects for the effects coded *busway* fare attribute are similarly reported; each marginal effect corresponds to an alternative, the order of which is once more shown in the table header, only now there are now three sets of reported marginal effects (as opposed to one). Each set of marginal effects corresponds to one of the simulations used to estimate the marginal effects, as described in sub-section 11.4.1. The first set of marginal effects shows the marginal effects for a change from a *busway* fare of $1 to a *busway* fare of $3. The next relates the marginal effects for a change in *busway* fares of $3 to a *busway* fare of $5. The final set of marginal effects reported is for a change in the *busway* fare from $1 to $5.

The last set of marginal effects reported represents a change over the entire range of the attribute represented by the first two sets of marginal effects reported. Summing the marginal effects for the first two rows of marginal effects reported within each alternative will replicate, within rounding error, the last series of marginal effects reported.

11.5 Weighting

It is not an uncommon practice for an analyst to weight data so that the data conform to some prior view of the world. Consider an example where an analyst has sample data from a population for which Census data (i.e. data on the entire population) is also available. While the research objective studied by the analyst may mean that the sample data collected will contain data on variables not included in the Census data, any communality in terms of variables collected between the two data sets may be used to *re-weight* the sample data to correspond with the distributions of the total population as observed in the Census data.

The information held by the analyst may be used in one of two ways to weight the data. First, if the information pertains to the true market shares of the alternatives, the weighting criteria to be applied are said to be *endogenous*, "endogenous" meaning internal to the choice response. The market shares for the alternatives are represented by the choice variable within the data set. If the information held by the analyst relates to any variable other than the choice variable, the weighting criteria to be applied are said to be *exogenous*, "exogenous" meaning external to the system. The distinction between endogenous and exogenous weighting is important, as they are handled differently by NLOGIT. We discuss both forms of weighting now.

11.5.1 Endogenous weighting

In the case of discrete choice models, endogenous weighting of data occurs on the dependent choice variable and takes place when the analyst has information from other sources regarding the true market shares for each of the alternatives included within the model. This is of particular use when the analyst has employed choice-based weighting as the sampling technique.

The above should offer a clue as to the type of data in which the use of endogenous weighting should be employed. For SP data, the choice of alternative is made within the context of a choice set. Therefore, different decision makers may observe different choice sets with alternatives assigned different attribute levels dependent upon the experimental design, hence the concept of true market shares is meaningless. Thus both endogenous weighting and choice-based sampling is meaningful solely within the context of RP data collection.

To demonstrate endogenous weighting in an evocative manner, we are therefore required to do so using the RP data component of the mode-choice data set. We do so now mindful that everything said to this point also applies to the modeling of RP choice models.

To access the RP data, we must first resample all of the data and then reject the SP data source. The command to do so is given below:

```
Sample;all $
Reject;sprp=2 $ ? Includes RP only
```

The command syntax for handling RP choice models is identical to the syntax discussed above for SP choice models.

To apply endogenous weighting to a sample, supplementary command syntax indicating the true market shares is attached to the **;Choices = names of alternatives** command line. The additional command syntax is separated from the **;Choices = names of alternatives** command by a slash (/), and the population market shares as proportions (summing exactly to 1.00) are assigned in the order of the alternatives as given in the **;Choices = names of alternatives** syntax. The true shares are separated by a comma. We show this below:

```
NLOGIT
;lhs = choice, cset, altij
;Choices = <names of alternatives> / <weight assigned to alt1,> <weight assigned to alt2,>
..., <weight assigned to altj>
;Model:
U(<alternative 1 name>) = <utility function 1>
U(<alternative 2 name>) = <utility function 2>
...
U(<alternative i name>) = <utility function i $>
```

To demonstrate endogenous weighting, consider the following choice model. We have defined the alternatives for this model as *drive alone* (*DA*), *ride share* (*RS*), *bus*, *train*, *walk*, and *other* and assigned ASC to each of the alternatives. We have also specified alternative-specific parameters to time variables for each of the alternatives, time being *autotime* for the *car* alternatives, *mptrtime* for the *public transport* alternatives, and *triptime* for the *walk* and other alternatives:

```
NLOGIT
;lhs=choice,cset,altij
;Choices = da, rs, bus, train, walk, other
;Show
;Model:
```

U(da) = daasc + daautott*autotime /
U(rs) = rsasc + rsautott*autotime /
U(bus) = busasc + bustt*MPTRTIME /
U(train) = tnasc + tntt*MPTRTIME /
U(walk) = wkasc + wktt*triptime /
U(other) = othertt*triptime $

Without weighting, the above model specification produces the following NLOGIT output. We have also included the output generated from the **;Show** command:

```
          Tree Structure Specified for the Nested Logit Model
          Sample proportions are marginal, not conditional.
          Choices marked with * are excluded for the IIA test.
----------------+----------------+----------------+--------------+------+---
Trunk     (prop.)|Limb      (prop.)|Branch    (prop.)|Choice (prop.)|Weight|IIA
----------------+----------------+----------------+----------+------+---+---
Trunk{1} 1.00000|Lmb[1:1] 1.00000|B(1:1,1) 1.00000|DA       .58382| 1.000|
                |                |                |RS       .15723| 1.000|
                |                |                |BUS      .11098| 1.000|
                |                |                |TRAIN    .09364| 1.000|
                |                |                |WALK     .02312| 1.000|
                |                |                |OTHER    .03121| 1.000|
----------------+----------------+----------------+--------------+------+---

Model Specification: Utility Functions for Alternatives
Table entry is the attribute that multiplies the indicated parameter.
             Parameter
      Row  1 DAASC     DAAUTOTT RSASC     RSAUTOTT BUSASC    BUSTT     TNASC
      Row  2 TNTT      WKASC    WKTT      OTHERTT
Choice
DA         1 Constant AUTOTIME
           2
RS         1                    Constant AUTOTIME
           2
BUS        1                                       Constant MPTRTIME
           2
TRAIN      1                                                          Constant
           2 MPTRTIME
WALK       1
           2          Constant TRIPTIME
OTHER      1
           2                             TRIPTIME
+---------------------------------------------+
| Discrete choice (multinomial logit) model    |
| Maximum Likelihood Estimates                 |
| Model estimated: Feb 30, 2003 at 09:15:00AM. |
| Dependent variable                Choice     |
```

```
| Weighting variable                         None      |
| Number of observations                      865      |
| Iterations completed                          7      |
| Log likelihood function               -366.2101      |
| R2=1-LogL/LogL*    Log-L fncn  R-sqrd  RsqAdj        |
| No coefficients   -1549.8719  .76372   .76067        |
| Constants only.   Must be computed directly.         |
|                   Use NLOGIT ;...; RHS=ONE $          |
| Chi-squared[ 6]            =   1457.99565            |
| Prob [ chi squared > value ]   =   .00000            |
| Response data are given as ind. choice.              |
| Number of obs.=     865, skipped    0 bad obs.       |
+-----------------------------------------------+

+---------+-------------+---------------+--------+---------+
|Variable | Coefficient | Standard Error |b/St.Er.|P[|Z|>z] |
+---------+-------------+---------------+--------+---------+
 DAASC        1.01493034      .61151070      1.660    .0970
 DAAUTOTT     -.02915020      .00972699     -2.997    .0027
 RSASC       -1.41255607      .62606815     -2.256    .0241
 RSAUTOTT     -.00360506      .01061643      -.340    .7342
 BUSASC      -1.77418298      .67374525     -2.633    .0085
 BUSTT         .00417751      .00911158       .458    .6466
 TNASC       -1.37469500      .64740463     -2.123    .0337
 TNTT         -.02811428      .01007733     -2.790    .0053
 WKASC        1.00771756      .73342442      1.374    .1694
 WKTT         -.13895591      .03491549     -3.980    .0001
 OTHERTT      -.07059393      .02417283     -2.920    .0035
```

We ignore most of the above, and leave it to the reader to interpret the output generated. However, we draw the reader's attention to the choice proportions given in the **;Show** command output. Given that this model is estimated with RP data, assuming some form of random sampling, the choice proportions should equal the actual market shares for each of the alternatives.

Choice-based sampling (CBS) or the vagaries of random sampling may mean that the sample proportions do not match the true, known market shares, thus requiring endogenous weighting of the sample. Using the same model specification, we demonstrate the command syntax employed to endogenously weight the data below. Here we have assumed that the true market shares are 0.58, 0.16, 0.07, 0.08, 0.01, and 0.1 for the *DA*, *ride share RS*, *bus*, *train*, *walk*, and *other* alternatives, respectively:

NLOGIT
;lhs=choice,cset,altij
;Choices=da, rs, bus, train, walk, other / 0.58,0.16,0.07,0.08,0.01,0.1
;Show
;Model:

U(da) = daasc + daautott*autotime /
U(rs) = rsasc + rsautott*autotime /
U(bus) = busasc + bustt*MPTRTIME /
U(train) = tnasc + tntt*MPTRTIME /
U(walk) = wkasc + wktt*triptime /
U(other) = othertt*triptime $

The above choice model specification will produce the following NLOGIT output:

```
    Tree Structure Specified for the Nested Logit Model
    Sample proportions are marginal, not conditional.
    Choices marked with * are excluded for the IIA test.
----------------+----------------+----------------+--------------+------+---
Trunk    (prop.)|Limb     (prop.)|Branch   (prop.)|Choice (prop.)|Weight|IIA
----------------+----------------+----------------+------------+------+---
Trunk{1} 1.00000|Lmb[1:1] 1.00000|B(1:1,1) 1.00000|DA      .58382|  .993|
                |                |                |RS      .15723| 1.018|
                |                |                |BUS     .11098|  .631|
                |                |                |TRAIN   .09364|  .854|
                |                |                |WALK    .02312|  .432|
                |                |                |OTHER   .03121| 3.204|
----------------+----------------+----------------+--------------+------+---

+-------------------------------------------+
| Discrete choice (multinomial logit) model |
| Maximum Likelihood Estimates              |
| Model estimated: Feb 30, 2003 at 09:30:00AM.|
| Dependent variable              Choice    |
| Weighting variable                None    |
| Number of observations             865    |
| Iterations completed               101    |
| Log likelihood function      -338.3464    |
| R2=1-LogL/LogL*  Log-L fncn  R-sqrd RsqAdj |
| No coefficients  -1549.8719  .78169 .77888 |
| Constants only.  Must be computed directly. |
|                  Use NLOGIT ;...; RHS=ONE $ |
| Chi-squared[ 6]          =   1513.72306    |
| Prob [ chi squared > value ] =   .00000    |
| Vars. corrected for choice-based sampling  |
| Response data are given as ind. choice.    |
| Number of obs.=   865, skipped   0 bad obs. |
+-------------------------------------------+
+---------+-------------+---------------+--------+---------+
|Variable | Coefficient | Standard Error |b/St.Er.|P[|Z|>z] |
----------+-------------+---------------+--------+---------+
 DAASC        .17427849     .24459460      .713    .4761
 DAAUTOTT   -.02727235     .01055003    -2.585    .0097
```

```
RSASC          -2.19375497      .36032069    -6.088    .0000
RSAUTOTT        -.00261502      .01125596     -.232    .8163
BUSASC         -3.01372848      .48937209    -6.158    .0000
BUSTT            .00523917      .01047635      .500    .6170
TNASC          -2.46097967      .43843774    -5.613    .0000
TNTT            -.02385524      .01071998    -2.225    .0261
WKASC           -.62394958     1.20817499     -.516    .6055
WKTT            -.14553787      .09470653    -1.537    .1244
OTHERTT         -.05767990      .00728939    -7.913    .0000
```

The above output was generated using endogenous weighting of the choice variable. We have omitted the utility function specification given for the **;Show** command which is no different in form to that demonstrated previously. A close examination of the output will reveal that no weighting variable was used for model estimation (shown below). As we show in sub-section 11.5.2, the use of a weighting variable is associated with the exogenous weighting of a data set:

```
Weighting variable          None
```

The next point to note in the above output is that NLOGIT informs the analyst that CBS was applied. This is shown in the following line of output:

```
Vars. corrected for choice-based sampling
```

Next, the reader will note that the parameters estimated by NLOGIT differ from the model in which no weighting was applied. Indeed, for the parameter *RSAUTOTT* the sign has changed although, in either case, the time variable is not a significant predictor of choice for the ride share alternative. The *WKTT* parameter, which was originally statistically significant, is no longer significant after endogenous weighting takes place.

The output generated by the **;Show** command now displays the weights that were applied to obtain the choice shares specified by the analyst. Multiplying each of the choice proportions (which remain unchanged from the previous output) by the weights shown will reproduce the market shares specified by the analyst in the command syntax. For example, for the *walk* alternative, 0.2309 × 0.433 equals 0.01, the *walk* share expressed in the command syntax.

11.5.2 Weighting on an exogenous variable

The above discourse relates to the weighting of data for choice analysis based on the choice variable of that data. Weighting data on any variable other than the choice variable requires a different approach. In chapter 8, we described how to create a weighting variable in NLOGIT. It is this variable that we now use to weight the data.

The NLOGIT command for exogenous weighting is:

;wts = <name of weighting variable>

Returning to our original model estimated for the SP segment of commuting trips of less than 30 minutes, we show the exogenous weighting command, weighting on the variable *hweight* below:

NLOGIT
;lhs = choice, cset, altij
;Choices = cart, carnt, bus, train, busway, LR
;wts = hweight
;Model:
U(cart) = asccart + cst*fuel /
U(carnt) = asccarnt + cst*fuel /
U(bus) = ascbus + cst*fare /
U(train) = asctn + cst*fare /
U(busway) = ascbusw + cst*fare /
U(LR) = cst*fare $

The above command generates the following NLOGIT output:

```
+-----------------------------------------------+
| Discrete choice (multinomial logit) model     |
| Maximum Likelihood Estimates                  |
| Model estimated: Feb 30, 2003 at 09:45:00AM.  |
| Dependent variable              Choice        |
| Weighting variable             HWEIGHT        |
| Number of observations            2369        |
| Iterations completed                 5        |
| Log likelihood function      -3149.323        |
| R2=1-LogL/LogL*  Log-L fncn  R-sqrd  RsqAdj   |
| No coefficients  -4151.6930  .24144  .24080   |
| Constants only.  Must be computed directly.   |
|                  Use NLOGIT ;...; RHS=ONE $   |
| Chi-squared[ 1]          =   1643.90892       |
| Prob [ chi squared > value ] =   .00000       |
| Response data are given as ind. choice.       |
| Number of obs.=  2369, skipped  0 bad  obs.   |
+-----------------------------------------------+
+---------+--------------+----------------+--------+---------+
|Variable | Coefficient  | Standard Error |b/St.Er.|P[|Z|>z] |
+---------+--------------+----------------+--------+---------+
ASCCART        -.21287272      .07510346     -2.834   .0046
CST            -.20419221      .01924529    -10.610   .0000
ASCCARNT        .31694854      .07591828      4.175   .0000
ASCBUS          .03989567      .09769339       .408   .6830
ASCTN          -.14269852      .09358488     -1.525   .1273
ASCBUSW         .03321127      .08524396       .390   .6968
```

The only indication provided by NLOGIT to suggest that exogenous weighting has occurred is shown in the following line of output, in which NLOGIT names the variable used for weighting. No other indication is provided:

```
Weighting variable          HWEIGHT
```

Comparing the model weighted on an exogenous variable to that without such a weight, the reader will note a change in the LL function as well as changes in the parameters estimated. While not observed here, weighting the data by either an exogenous or endogenous variable has the potential to change the model fit through a change in the LL functions reported. Nevertheless, as shown, weighting on either criteria is likely to change the parameter estimates and, although not observed in this example, possibly the significance of the parameters as well.

11.6 Calibrating the alternative-specific constants of choice models estimated on SP data

When collected correctly, RP data will translate to accurate initial market share forecasts but will often (but not always) provide poor forecasts once the analyst predicts changes beyond the initial market conditions observed. This is because RP data collected on the attributes and attribute levels of goods and services *within* the market are likely to be ill conditioned (e.g. due to multicollinearity, little or no variation in the attribute levels, and the non-existence of new alternatives, attributes, and attribute levels within the data set etc.). Thus while the choices observed in RP data will reflect the market shares of the alternatives present, ill-conditioned data on the attributes and attribute levels will produce poor estimates in terms of the preference trade-offs decision makers make in real markets. SP data, on the other hand, often provide good estimates about the preference trade-offs decision makers make in markets but will not, unless by chance, reflect the true market shares observed in real markets. The above has implications for how the analyst handles the constant terms of discrete choice models.

The role played by the constant terms associated with each utility expression is extremely important. They not only represent the role, on average, of the unobserved effects associated with a particular alternative, they also represent (for an MNL model) the sample choice shares. When the sample data are RP data drawn from a random sample, the constant terms (when specified as ASCs) will reproduce the true market shares of the alternatives for the population from which the sample was drawn. If SP data are used, however, the ASCs reflect the choice shares across the choice sets of the data set, and not the market shares as observed in real markets. This is because the alternatives represented in each choice and set differ in terms of attributes and attribute levels from choice set to choice set and hence are not the same as real alternatives operating within real markets which are observed to have constant attribute levels.

A large amount of research has been conducted on how best to estimate models that capture initial market share conditions while at the same time accurately estimate the preference structures of those operating within the market in order to model shifts in demand given structural changes within the markets modeled. Much of this research has focused upon the combining of SP and RP data to take advantage of the strengths of both while negating the weaknesses of each data type. We discuss in detail, the combining of SP and RP data in chapter 14.

The combining of SP and RP data are possible only if both data sources are available. In this section, we discuss how the analyst might proceed if only SP data are available. By *calibrating* the constant terms of discrete choice models estimated from SP data only, the analyst may reproduce the initial market conditions while retaining the preference structures, the very reason that makes the use of SP data so appealing in the first place. The calibration of the constant terms of choice models requires that the population market shares for the alternatives modeled are either all known in advance or known for at least some alternatives.

As an aside, the calibration we discuss here relates only to the calibration of the constants of discrete choice models. It will often be the case, particularly for transport studies, that the estimated choice model will be used as part of a wider research effort and that the model will be embedded into some other, larger, model network. In such cases, a further calibration process may be required to be undertaken before correct market forecasts can be made. Other than noting this possibility, we refrain from further discussion on this point, as the calibration process will be specific to the network to which the choice model becomes wedded, too.

When the true market shares are known *a priori* for all alternatives, there are two stages required to calibrate the ASCs of discrete choice models estimated using SP choice data only:

(1) Estimate the SP model and obtain the parameter estimates
(2) Re-estimate the SP model while,
    (a) constraining the parameters for all attributes and SDC to be equal to those obtained in step (1) but allow the ASC free to vary, and
    (b) use exogenous weighting reflective of the known population shares.

When the true choice shares are not known *a priori* for all alternatives, stages (1) and (2) will prove insufficient to calibrate the ASC of choice models estimated from SP data only. This is because the analyst does not know in advance what exogenous weights to employ at stage (2(b)) of the process to alternatives for which the market shares are not known in advance. Given that SP choice experiments are often constructed to examine new alternatives not presently offered within real markets, such situations are likely to arise often.

When the real market shares are known for some but not all alternatives, the calibration of the ASCs of models estimated from SP data requires an additional step to those outlined above. The calibration process in its entirety becomes:

(1) Estimate the SP model and obtain the parameter estimates
(2) Re-estimate the SP model while,
    (a) constraining the parameters for all attributes and SDC to be equal to those obtained in step (1)

(b) constraining the ASC for those alternatives whose market shares are not known *a priori* to those obtained in step (1), at the same time allowing those with known market shares to vary, and
(c) use exogenous weighting to calibrate the ASC of alternatives with known population shares.

Below we use two examples to elucidate this process. Both examples relate to the following choice model estimated on the 30 minutes or less commuter segment of the mode choice case study. In the first example, we assume known market shares for all alternatives. In the second example, we assume that the market shares for the *busway* and *light rail* alternatives are unknown in advance by the analyst:

NLOGIT
;lhs = choice, cset, altij
;Choices = cart, carnt, bus, train, busway, LR
;Model:
U(cart) = asccart + cartcst*fuel /
U(carnt) = asccarnt + carntcst*fuel /
U(bus) = ascbus + buscst*fare /
U(train) = asctn + tncst*fare /
U(busway) = ascbusw + buswcst*fare /
U(LR) = lrcst*fare $

The above command produces the following NLOGIT output. In both examples that follow, we are interested in the parameter estimates of this model output and not in whether the model itself represents a good fit of the data. We therefore leave it to the reader to determine the merits of this model relative to others produced in this primer:

```
+-------------------------------------------+
| Discrete choice (multinomial logit) model  |
| Maximum Likelihood Estimates               |
| Model estimated: Feb 30, 2003 at 10:00:00AM.|
| Dependent variable               Choice    |
| Weighting variable                 None    |
| Number of observations             2369    |
| Iterations completed                  5    |
| Log likelihood function       -3214.241    |
| R2=1-LogL/LogL*  Log-L fncn  R-sqrd  RsqAdj |
| No coefficients  -4244.6782  .24276  .24159 |
| Constants only.  Must be computed directly. |
|                  Use NLOGIT ;...; RHS=ONE $ |
| Chi-squared[ 6]          =   1650.89911     |
| Prob [ chi squared > value ] =   .00000     |
| Response data are given as ind.  choice.    |
| Number of obs.=  2369, skipped   0 bad obs.|
+-------------------------------------------+
```

Variable	Coefficient	Standard Error	b/St.Er.	P[|Z|>z]
ASCCART	-.43353076	.17456286	-2.484	.0130
CARTCST	-.09766455	.05795105	-1.685	.0919
ASCCARNT	-.16668466	.26069361	-.639	.5226
CARNTCST	-.09243679	.05646700	-1.637	.1016
ASCBUS	-.18885515	.19430843	-.972	.3311
BUSCST	-.17877650	.04576476	-3.906	.0001
ASCTN	-.15244648	.18561589	-.821	.4115
TNCST	-.21490349	.04577121	-4.695	.0000
ASCBUSW	.11529699	.17866515	.645	.5187
BUSWCST	-.26642705	.04168628	-6.391	.0000
LRCST	-.25775069	.04182220	-6.163	.0000

11.6.1 Example (1) (the market shares of all alternatives are known *a priori*)

Consider an example where the true market population shares for our six alternatives are known in advance to be 0.25 for the *cart* alternative, 0.3 for the *carnt* alternative, and 0.18, 0.17, 0.04, and 0.06 for the *bus*, *train*, *busway*, and *LR* alternatives, respectively. Step one of the calibration process requires the estimation of the *choice model* for which the constants are to be calibrated. We have done this above. The second step, which we have broken into two parts, requires the analyst to estimate a second model, this time constraining the parameter estimates not estimated as constant terms to be equal to those observed in the first model estimated, while at the same time using *choice-based weighting* to calibrate the constant terms to reflect the known market shares.

Using the parameter estimates from the above model and constraining the parameters in the manner discussed earlier in this chapter, we show the NLOGIT command syntax for the second model, using the choice-based weights of our known market shares provided earlier:

```
NLOGIT
;lhs = choice, cset, altij
;Choices = cart, carnt, bus, train, busway, LR / 0.25, 0.3, 0.18, 0.17, 0.04, 0.06
;Model:
U(cart)     = asccart + cartcst[-0.0976645]*fuel /
U(carnt)    = asccarnt + carntcst[-0.0924368]*fuel /
U(bus)      = ascbus + buscst[-0.178777]*fare /
U(train)    = asctn + tncst[-0.214903]*fare /
U(busway)   = ascbusw + buswcst[-0.266427]*fare /
U(LR)       = lrcst[-0.257751]*fare $
```

Using the same sample as the model estimated at stage one of the process, the following model output is produced:

```
+---------------------------------------------+
| Discrete choice (multinomial logit) model    |
| Maximum Likelihood Estimates                 |
| Model estimated: Feb 30, 2003 at 10:15:00AM.|
| Dependent variable             Choice        |
| Weighting variable               None        |
| Number of observations           2369        |
| Iterations completed              101        |
| Log likelihood function     -3056.325        |
| R2=1-LogL/LogL*  Log-L fncn  R-sqrd  RsqAdj |
| No coefficients  -4244.6782  .27996  .27946 |
| Constants only.  Must be computed directly. |
|                  Use NLOGIT ;...; RHS=ONE $ |
|Chi-squared[ 6]          =   1966.73099      |
|Prob [ chi squared > value ] =    .00000      |
|Vars. corrected for choice-based sampling     |
|Response data are given as ind. choice.       |
|Number of obs.=  2369, skipped   0 bad obs.   |
+---------------------------------------------+
+---------+--------------+----------------+--------+---------+
|Variable | Coefficient  | Standard Error |b/St.Er.|P[|Z|>z] |
+---------+--------------+----------------+--------+---------+
ASCCART        .42004579       .16073071      2.613    .0090
CARTCST       -.09766450     ......(Fixed Parameter).......
ASCCARNT       .77440420       .15838075      4.890    .0000
CARNTCST      -.09243680     ......(Fixed Parameter).......
ASCBUS        1.24055134       .16427108      7.552    .0000
BUSCST        -.17877700     ......(Fixed Parameter).......
ASCTN         1.21028761       .15921110      7.602    .0000
TNCST         -.21490300     ......(Fixed Parameter).......
ASCBUSW        .33002421       .21919397      1.506    .1322
BUSWCST       -.26642700     ......(Fixed Parameter).......
LRCST         -.25775100     ......(Fixed Parameter).......
```

Once the model shown above has been estimated, the analyst may use the simulation capability of NLOGIT to model changes in the choice shares for the alternatives modeled.

11.6.2 Example (2) (the market shares for some alternatives are unknown)

When the market shares for some alternatives are not known in advance, the procedure used in example (1) will prove insufficient in calibrating the ASCs. Consider an example where there currently exist only four alternatives within the market. These are *cart*, *carnt*, *bus*, and *train*. The market shares for these four alternatives are currently 0.3, 0.35, 0.18, and 0.17, respectively. The analyst wishes to determine the impact two new alternatives may have upon the market shares of the existing alternatives should these two new alternatives be introduced to the market. For this example, an SP choice experiment was conducted including the four existing alternatives as well as the two new alternatives, *busway* and *light rail*. The market shares for these two new alternatives are not known in advance.

As with example (1), the first step required to calibrate the constant terms is first to estimate the model *free of any restrictions*. For this example, we will use the same model as in example (1). The second step first requires the constraining of the parameter estimates associated with the attributes and SDC associated with each of the utility functions. Simultaneously, the analyst constrains the constant terms to be equal to those estimated as part of the first model for those alternatives for which the market shares are not known in advance. Finally, the model is re-estimated using exogenous weighting to calibrate the ASC of alternatives with known market shares.

The use of exogenous weighting only on alternatives with known market shares suggests that the market shares in this weighting procedure for alternatives with unknown shares be set to zero. This does not represent a problem, however, as the constant terms for these alternatives were constrained as part of step (2(b)), and hence will not be estimated as zero for the model produced. To fix the market share for an alternative to zero, the analyst will use a choice-based weight for that alternative of 1.0 and not as one would expect, of zero. For example (2), we set the last two exogenous weights to 1.0 while retaining the weights indicative of the market shares for the remaining alternatives, as shown below:

```
NLOGIT
;lhs = choice, cset, altij
;Choices = cart, carnt, bus, train, busway, LR / 0.30, 0.35, 0.18, 0.17, 1.0, 1.0
;Model:
U(cart)     = cartcst[-0.0976645]*fuel /
U(carnt)    = asccarnt+ carntcst[-0.0924368]*fuel /
U(bus)      = ascbus + buscst[-0.178777]*fare /
U(train)    = asctn + tncst[-0.214903]*fare /
U(busway)   = ascbusw[0.5488277485] + buswcst[-0.266427]*fare /
U(LR)       = asclr[0.4335307566] +lrcst[-0.257751]*fare $
```

For the 30 minutes or less commuter segment, the above model produces the following results:

```
+-------------------------------------------+
| Discrete choice (multinomial logit) model |
| Maximum Likelihood Estimates              |
| Model estimated: Feb 30, 2003 at 10:30:00AM.|
| Dependent variable              Choice    |
| Weighting variable                None    |
| Number of observations            2369    |
| Iterations completed                 9    |
| Log likelihood function      -3208.917    |
| R2=1-LogL/LogL*  Log-L fncn  R-sqrd  RsqAdj |
| No coefficients  -4244.6782  .24401  .24369 |
| Constants only.  Must be computed directly. |
```

```
|                    Use NLOGIT ;...; RHS=ONE $ |
| Chi-squared[ 6]           =    1661.54640     |
| Prob [ chi squared > value ] =     .00000     |
| Vars. corrected for choice-based sampling     |
| Response data are given as ind. choice.       |
| Number of obs.=  2369, skipped   0 bad obs.   |
+-----------------------------------------------+
+---------+-------------+---------------+--------+---------+
|Variable | Coefficient  | Standard Error |b/St.Er.|P[|Z|>z] |
+---------+-------------+---------------+--------+---------+
CARTCST       -.09766450    ......(Fixed Parameter).......
ASCCARNT       .26195384       .05408472      4.843    .0000
CARNTCST      -.09243680    ......(Fixed Parameter).......
ASCBUS         .58485552       .06519271      8.971    .0000
BUSCST        -.17877700    ......(Fixed Parameter).......
ASCTN          .56311902       .06647278      8.471    .0000
TNCST         -.21490300    ......(Fixed Parameter).......
ASCBUSW        .54882775    ......(Fixed Parameter).......
BUSWCST       -.26642700    ......(Fixed Parameter).......
ASCLR          .43353076    ......(Fixed Parameter).......
LRCST         -.25775100    ......(Fixed Parameter).......
```

As with example (1), the model estimated here may be used to estimate changes to the market shares for all six alternatives given structural changes within the market, through changes to the attributes modeled.

Appendix 11A Calculating arc elasticities

For the mode-choice case study, the following NLOGIT syntax commands may be used to produce the direct and cross-arc elasticities for a change in the design attribute, *time*. Minimal changes may be made to the command syntax in order to calculate the direct and cross-elasticities for any other attribute or SDC within the data set.

For ease, we break these commands up into components, the workings of which we explain so that the reader may utilize similar syntax as required in their own choice studies.

Step 1

The first step necessary in the calculation of direct and cross-elasticities for the mode choice case study is the creation of an *index variable*. While this stage is not strictly necessary, in studies involving non-fixed-choice sets, the creation of an index variable will greatly aid in the estimation of the after-change choice probabilities.

To create an index from 1 to J where J is the number of alternatives within the choice set, the analyst may use the following command:

```
CREATE
;if(altij=1)index=1
;if(altij>1)index=index[-1]+1 $
```

The first part of the **CREATE** command shown above will create a new variable called *index* and assign to this new variable the value one when the variable *altij* equals one. The last line of the command has NLOGIT examine the *altij* variable for values greater than one and when such values are located, assign to the index variable one plus the value observed for the index variable in the row above. For example, if *altij* is observed to be equal 2, NLOGIT will assign the new index variable the value 1 plus the value the index variable took in the row before. As *altij* will have equalled 1 in the previous row, the index variable will have taken the value 1 in the previous row and hence the index variable will now equal 2. The index variable will continue increasing by a value of 1 until such time as the *altij* variable again takes the value 1, at which time the process will start anew. Using this procedure, the index variable will take the values 1–4 within each choice set for this example.

As an aside, in the case of fixed-choice-set sizes where the alternatives are also fixed, the *altij* (or equivalent) variable will ordinarily range from one to J, and hence the creation of an index variable in the manner described above will be redundant.

Step 2

The second step in the estimation of direct and cross-arc elasticities is the creation of a new variable representative of the changes the analyst requires to observe the cross- and direct arc elasticities for. For the example shown here, we create a new time variable called *time2*, which represents an increase in the time taken for the second alternative (car with no toll) of 2 minutes:

```
CREATE
;time2=time
;if(altij=2)time2=time+2 $
```

Step 3

The next step is to save the before-change choice probabilities using the **;Prob** command discussed in chapter 10. For this example, the command used would look as below. We have chosen to call the before-change probabilities *pbef*, although any unique name would have sufficed:

```
NLOGIT
;lhs = choice, cset, altij
;Choices= cart, carnt, bus, train, busway, LR
;Model:
U(cart) = asccart + time*time /
U(carnt) = asccarnt + time*time /
U(bus) = ascbus + time*time /
U(train) = asctn + time*time /
U(busway) = ascbusw + time*time /
U(LR) = time*time
;Prob = pbef $
```

Step 4

For models of discrete choice, an elasticity represents a percentage change in the choice probability for an alternative given a percentage change in some variable of interest. Whether the variable of interest belongs to the alternative to which the percentage change in the choice probability is observed determines if the elasticity estimated is direct or cross. Step 3 provides estimates of the before-change choice probabilities; however, in order to calculate any percentage change that may occur the analyst requires not only the before-change choice probabilities but also the after-change choice probabilities.

While it is tempting to re-estimate the model using the same model specification used in step 3, but replacing the *time* attribute with the *time2* variable created during step 2, such an approach will produce erroneous results. Any time the model specification is altered through the changing of a variable (i.e. a variable is added, removed, or replaced with a different variable), any subsequent re-estimation of the model will result in a change in the vector of parameters estimated, which in turn impacts upon the choice probabilities produced (i.e. all the parameters will differ, not only that for which we wish to observe the change). For the purposes of calculating changes in probabilities, as is required in the calculation of arc elasticities, the before- and after-probabilities are from two completely different models, and hence cannot be used. We have apples and oranges when what we really want is apples and apples.

The experienced NLOGIT user may be tempted to estimate the after-change choice model by constraining the time parameter for the after-change model to be equal to the time parameter estimated in the model at step 3. For the mode-choice study, fixing the time parameter to equal the parameter value observed in the model produced in step 3, the command syntax would look thus:

```
NLOGIT
;lhs = choice, cset, altij
;Choices = cart, carnt, bus, train, busway, LR
;Model:
U(cart) = asccart + time*time /
U(carnt) = asccarnt + time[-0.04084204415]*time2 /
U(bus) = ascbus + time*time /
U(train) = asctn + time*time /
U(busway) = ascbusw + time*time /
U(LR) = time*time
;Prob = paft $
```

Comparison of the output for the above model with that produced at step 3 will show that the parameters of the new model are the same as those produced earlier. This is misleading. The above statement is true only up to a number of decimal places and while the difference in the parameters due to differences in decimal places may be small, the difference is sufficiently large to produce probabilities incomparable for the purpose required. Once more we have apples and oranges instead of apples and apples.

The solution is to calculate the probabilities manually through a series of **CREATE** commands. In order to calculate the probabilities, the analyst requires estimates of the utilities (see (3.10)). As such, step 4 involves the estimation of the utilities for each alternative consistent with the model estimated in step 3 of the process. We show this below:

```
Reject;altij#1 $
CREATE
;uaft = -0.00606275-0.040842*time $
```

The estimation of the utility for each decision maker for the first alternative is shown above using the parameter estimates obtained in step 3. Note that we have elected to save the utilities as a variable called *uaft*. The utility estimates for the remaining alternatives are shown below. Note that for subsequent calculations the sample must be restored before proceeding:

```
Sample;all $
Reject;sprp=1 $
Reject;splength#1 $
Reject;altij#2 $
CREATE
;uaft = 0.395279-0.040842*time2 $

Sample;all $
Reject;sprp=1 $
Reject;splength#1 $
Reject;altij#3 $
CREATE
;uaft = 0.0204831-0.040842*time $

Sample;all $
Reject;sprp=1 $
Reject;splength#1 $
Reject;altij#4 $
CREATE
;uaft = -0.0432171-0.040842*time $

Sample;all $
Reject;sprp=1 $
Reject;splength#1 $
Reject;altij#5 $
CREATE
;uaft = 0.0924605-0.040842*time $

Sample;all $
Reject;sprp=1 $
Reject;splength#1 $
```

```
Reject;altij#6 $
CREATE
;uaft = -0.040842*time $
```

Only after the utilities have been calculated can the choice probabilities be formally estimated using (3.10). We do this in step 5.

Step 5

The last command of step 4 rejected all alternatives other than alternative 6. Thus before we can continue the analyst will be required to re-set the sample:

```
Sample;all $
Reject;sprp=1 $
Reject;splength#1 $
```

After the sample has been restored, the analyst will be able to calculate the choice probabilities through a complex **CREATE** command. It is only now that the importance of the index variable created in step 1 will become apparent in studies involving non-fixed-choice sets. In chapter 10 it was shown that the choice probabilities estimated by NLOGIT are calculated only for those alternatives present within each choice set. For studies involving non-fixed-choice sets, this has implications on what utility functions appear in the denominator of (3.10). Ordinarily, this would require different **CREATE** commands to accommodate whichever alternatives are present within each choice set. The use of the index variable removes this problem by allowing for a generic estimation of (3.10). We show this below:

```
CREATE
;if(index=1)paft=exp(uaft)/(exp(uaft) + exp(uaft[+1]) + exp(uaft[+2]) + exp(uaft[+3]))
;if(index=2)paft=exp(uaft)/(exp(uaft[-1]) + exp(uaft) + exp(uaft[+1]) + exp(uaft[+2]))
;if(index=3)paft=exp(uaft)/(exp(uaft[-2]) + exp(uaft[-1]) + exp(uaft) + exp(uaft[+1]))
;if(index=4)paft=exp(uaft)/(exp(uaft[-3]) + exp(uaft[-2]) + exp(uaft[-1]) + exp(uaft)) $
```

For index equal to one, NLOGIT will create a variable called *paft*, equal to the exponential (i.e. **exp**) of the variable *uaft* divided by the sum of the exponentials of the utilities for the alternatives within that choice set. The command **<variable>[+<n>]** has NLOGIT use the value for the specified variable **n** rows below specified for that command. Thus **exp(uaft[+1])** will take the exponential of the value observed for the variable *uaft* one row below any row in which the index variable takes the value one. Similarly **<variable>[-<n>]** will use the value observed **n** rows of data for the specified variable. Using the index variable in this way allows for the estimation of the choice probabilities within each choice set independent of which alternatives are present within a choice set. For fixed-choice sets, the analyst may use the *altij* (or equivalent) variable for the same purpose.

Step 6

Steps 3–5 are used to estimate the before- and after-change choice probabilities necessary in the calculation of elasticities, both point and arc. The next step is to re-arrange the data such that it is consistent with component parts of (11.6). The first component of equation (11.6) is the difference in the before- and after-change choice probabilities. Also required are the average of the before- and after-choice probabilities, the difference in the before and after change in times and the average of the before- and after-change in times. The command syntax required is shown below:

```
CREATE
;pdiff=paft-pbef
;pave=(pbef+paft)/2
;ttdiff=2
;ttave=(time+time2)/2 $
```

In calculating an elasticity, either direct or cross, the change in probability is not dependent upon whether the alternative is that to which the change in the variable of interest occurred. If, as is the case here, the change in the variable of interest occurred for the second alternative, the change in probability for the first alternative (i.e. a cross-elasticity) is equal to the difference in the before and after probabilities for the first alternative. The change in probability for the second alternative (i.e. a direct elasticity) is similarly the difference in the before- and after-choice probabilities for the second alternative. Both cases are catered for in the above command.

The same is not true for the change in the variable of interest. For the above example, the change in the variable of interest occurred for alternative two. For the cross-elasticity associated with alternative one, this suggests that we use the change in variable of interest as it occurred for alternative two. Indeed, no change occurred for alternative one (hence time minus *time2* will equal zero). Thus the difference in time for the mode-choice case study, as observed for alternative two, was the addition of 2 minutes to the time taken using that mode. Whether we are to estimate a direct or cross-elasticity, the difference in time will always be equal to 2 for the above example.

In the above command, **;ttdiff = 2** will produce the desired effect. With regard to alternatives for which the analyst desires cross-elasticities, the last line of the above command designed to estimate the average travel time will incorrectly calculate the average travel time, not for the alternative to which the change occurred, but for alternatives to which no change was observed to have occurred. To compensate for this, the following lag command may be used such that within each choice set, the average change in travel time used is that for the alternative to which the change actually occurred.

```
CREATE
;if(altij=1)ttave=ttave[+1]
;if(altij>2)ttave=ttave[-1] $
```

We show the results of the above data manipulation in figure 11A.1.

PBEF	PAFT	UAFT	PDIFF	PAVE	TTDIFF	TTAVE
0.238636	0.243155	-0.618693	0.00451922	0.240895	2	26
0.236952	0.222502	-0.707455	-0.0144503	0.229727	2	26
0.229932	0.234286	-0.655847	0.00435438	0.232109	2	26
0.29448	0.300057	-0.40842	0.00557672	0.297268	2	26
0.250615	0.256762	-0.414483	0.00614707	0.253688	2	16
0.305225	0.288183	-0.299035	-0.0170415	0.296704	2	16
0.276564	0.283347	-0.31596	0.00678353	0.279955	2	16
0.167597	0.171707	-0.81684	0.00411088	0.169652	2	16
0.271672	0.278056	-0.496167	0.00638403	0.274864	2	21
0.292716	0.276095	-0.503245	-0.0166206	0.284405	2	21
0.246809	0.252609	-0.592147	0.0057998	0.249709	2	21
0.188803	0.19324	-0.860057	0.00443675	0.191022	2	21
0.238636	0.243155	-0.618693	0.00451922	0.240895	2	26
0.236952	0.222502	-0.707455	-0.0144503	0.229727	2	26
0.229932	0.234286	-0.655847	0.00435438	0.232109	2	26
0.29448	0.300057	-0.40842	0.00557672	0.297268	2	26
0.271672	0.278056	-0.496167	0.00638403	0.274864	2	21

Figure 11A.1 Data Editor for calculating arc elasticities

Step 7

Once the data are correctly calculated, the analyst may now calculate the individual level (or within-choice set) elasticities, both direct and cross, as per (11.6). The command for this is shown below:

```
CREATE
;inde=(pdiff/ttdiff)*(ttave/pave) $
```

The above command will create the within-choice set elasticities. The results of this process for the first individual is shown in figure 11A.2. The elasticities are shown in the last column. The cross-elasticities are, as expected, all equal (given rounding error) within each choice set.

Step 8

The command shown in step 7 will produce the within-choice set elasticities. What is required by the analyst is an *aggregation* of these elasticities. While there exist three methods of aggregation, as discussed in chapter 11 the authors prefer the method of probability weighted sample enumeration (PWSE). This requires the estimation of (11.5) for the sample. For convenience we show (11.5) once more below:

$$E_{X_{jkq}}^{\bar{P}_i} = \left(\sum_{q=1}^{Q} \hat{P}_{iq} E_{X_{jkq}}^{P_{iq}} \right) \Big/ \sum_{q=1}^{Q} \hat{P}_{iq}$$

For ease of computation, we will break (11.5) into several constituent components. The

UAFT	PDIFF	PAVE	TTDIFF	TTAVE	INDE
-0.618693	0.00451922	0.240895	2	26	0.243881
-0.707455	-0.0144503	0.229727	2	26	-0.817727
-0.655847	0.00435438	0.232109	2	26	0.243881
-0.40842	0.00557672	0.297268	2	26	0.243878
-0.414483	0.00614707	0.253688	2	16	0.193846
-0.299035	-0.0170415	0.296704	2	16	-0.459487
-0.31596	0.00678353	0.279955	2	16	0.193846
-0.81684	0.00411088	0.169652	2	16	0.19385
-0.496167	0.00638403	0.274864	2	21	0.243874
-0.503245	-0.0166206	0.284405	2	21	-0.613618
-0.592147	0.0057998	0.249709	2	21	0.243875
-0.860057	0.00443675	0.191022	2	21	0.243877

Figure 11A.2 Within-choice-set elasticities

first component we estimate is $\hat{P}_{iq} E^{P_{iq}}_{X_{jkq}}$, which requires that the analyst multiply each individual elasticity by the estimated choice probability for the alternative to which the elasticity belongs. We do this through the following command. With this command, we create a new variable named *indep*. We have used the average of the before and after probabilities in this calculation:

```
CREATE
;indep=inde*pave $
```

To aggregate the elasticities over the sample, the analyst is next required to sum the *indep* variable over each alternative and divide the result by the sum of the probabilities for each relevant alternative. Given that this is required for each alternative, it is easier in NLOGIT to do this for each alternative one at a time. We show this for the first alternative below:

```
Reject;altij#1 $
Calc;sum1=sum(indep) $
Calc;sum2=sum(pave) $
Calc;arce1=sum1/sum2 $
```

The **reject** command ensures that what follows will be performed only for the first alternative. The second line of the above command uses the **Calc** command to sum the probability weighted individual-level elasticities (i.e. $\sum_{q=1}^{Q} \hat{P}_{iq} E^{P_{iq}}_{X_{jkq}}$). The second **Calc;** command sums the average probabilities required for estimation of (11.5) (i.e. $\sum_{q=1}^{Q} \hat{P}_{iq}$). The last **Calc;** command divides these two components to give the PWSE for the first alternative, as per (11.5).

The remaining elasticities are calculated in a similar manner. The sample must be re-set before the **Reject;** command can be used to select the relevant alternative. We show the necessary commands for the remaining five alternatives below:

```
Sample;all $
Reject;sprp=1 $
Reject;splength#1 $
Reject;altij#2 $
Calc;sum1=sum(indep) $
Calc;sum2=sum(pave) $
Calc;arce2=sum1/sum2 $

Sample;all $
Reject;sprp=1 $
Reject;splength#1 $
Reject;altij#3 $
Calc;sum1=sum(indep) $
Calc;sum2=sum(pave) $
Calc;arce3=sum1/sum2 $
```

```
Sample;all $
Reject;sprp=1 $
Reject;splength#1 $
Reject;altij#4 $
Calc;sum1=sum(indep) $
Calc;sum2=sum(pave) $
Calc;arce4=sum1/sum2 $

Sample;all $
Reject;sprp=1 $
Reject;splength#1 $
Reject;altij#5 $
Calc;sum1=sum(indep) $
Calc;sum2=sum(pave) $
Calc;arce5=sum1/sum2 $

Sample;all $
Reject;sprp=1 $
Reject;splength#1 $
Reject;altij#6 $
Calc;sum1=sum(indep) $
Calc;sum2=sum(pave) $
Calc;arce6=sum1/sum2 $
```

The above commands produce arc elasticities of 0.227222, −0.61291, 0.225157, 0.228219, 0.219773, and 0.224462 for the *cart*, *carnt*, *bus*, *train*, *busway*, and *LR* alternatives, respectively.

Releases of NLOGIT 3.0 after June 2003 have the capability to estimate arc elasticities without having to resort to the complicated commands above. The arc elasticities may be estimated through the **;Simulation** command with the addition of the command **;Arc**. For the above example, the command as it would appear in its entirety is shown below. As with any other simulation, the model must first be estimated without the simulation command to establish the base probability shares:

```
NLOGIT
;lhs=choice,cset,altij
;Choices=cart,carnt,bus,train,busway,LR
;Arc
;Model:
U(cart) = asccart + time*time /
U(carnt) = asccarnt + time*time /
U(bus) = ascbus + time*time /
U(train) = asctn + time*time /
U(busway) = ascbusw + time*time /
U(LR) = time*time
```

;Simulation

;Scenario: time(carnt) = [+]2 $

The above command using the 30 minutes or less commuting segment will produce the following results:

```
-----------------------------------------------------------------
Estimated Arc Elasticities Based on the Specified Scenario. Rows in
the table report 0.00 if the indicated attribute did not change in
the scenario or if the average probability or average attribute was
zero in the sample. Estimated values are averaged over all
individuals used in the simulation. Rows of the table in which no
changes took place are not shown.
-----------------------------------------------------------------
Attr Changed in | Change in Probability of Alternative
-----------------------------------------------------------------
Choice CARNT    | CART    CARNT    BUS      TRAIN    BUSWAY    LR
   x = TIME     |    .227   -.613   .225     .231     .222      .227
-----------------------------------------------------------------
```

The elasticities for the *cart*, *carnt*, *bus*, *train*, *busway*, and *LR* alternatives are, respectively, 0.227, −0.613, 0.225, 0.231, 0.222, and 0.2.27.

12 Practical issues in the application of choice models

The best way to predict the future is to invent it. (Alan Kay)

12.1 Introduction

The previous chapters have taken the reader, step by step, through all the essential tasks in problem definition, data specification, model preparation and estimation, and interpretation of the extensive number of outputs. Although we have introduced many application issues, it seems appropriate in the concluding chapter in part I to bring together what we regard as the range of issues that the analyst has to sort out when applying their empirically estimated choice models.

In giving some structure to applications, it is useful to recognize the main questions that will be asked by those wishing to apply the models (or wishing to have them applied by someone else). We make the distinction between applying the choice model today and in the future. Given the focus in this book on a cross-section approach (even if stated choice data are repeated observations on one individual – essentially an instantaneous "panel") any applications into the future (what we call "establishing market potential," but which is often referred to as "forecasting" or "prediction") take the form of a "*what-if*" scenario application or a forecast of levels of all explanatory variables based on externally provided information on a single best estimated future.

In this chapter, the following four issues cover necessary activities in applying a choice model to a population of interest:

(1) Calibration of the model for base and forecast year(s)
(2) Designing a population data base for applications – synthetic observations
(3) Updating the attributes of alternatives
(4) Designing a decisions support system

12.2 Calibration of a choice model for base and forecast years

A set of parameters estimated on a sample will apply to that sample at the point in time of data collection. They may also apply to the population from which the sample is drawn, especially if choice-based weights are used in model estimation to ensure reproduction of the population shares associated with the exact same unit of analysis and level of (dis)aggregation of data (see chapter 11).

However, when applying the choice model to a market setting in the future, we are not likely to have any additional information to use in model re-estimation. To make full use of the estimated choice model in the many possible settings in which it will be applied, we have to consider the range of tasks that the analyst has to undertake in preparing the parameter estimates and the data defining the attributes of alternatives and socio-economic characteristics of the observation unit of analysis (i.e. individual, household, business, etc.) that will apply in the application year.

Application options take a number of forms:

(1) *Applying a choice model exactly as is* (i.e. in terms of parameters associated with the sample data used in model estimation) without any calibration on the data representing the year of estimation or any future year.

(2) Calibrating the model (via adjustment of the alternative-specific constants) to reproduce the *known base-year choice shares* on the data that base-year "forecasts" will be developed. Importantly this may involve:
   (a) Calibration using the population shares and exactly the same data used in model estimation, or
   (b) Calibration with another data set that might be a hold-out sample of exactly the same data used in model estimation, or some re-specification of the original attributes and socio-economic characteristics used in model estimation:
      (i) In travel choice studies, it is common to apply the model at a level of aggregation that is greater than that used in model estimation. For example, model estimation may use a sample of individual trips associated with an individual traveler. The application might use data aggregated to some spatial unit (e.g. a traffic zone), in which the attribute levels (e.g. travel time, cost) are some aggregated level that is not the level actually experienced by an individual in the sample upon which the choice model was estimated. Such aggregated data are extracted from synthetic travel networks for highways and public transport modes.
      (ii) Likewise socio-economic data associated with the population might be re-defined as average levels for each census tract (e.g. average income in a particular Census tract or traffic zone) which is not the same as the specific income level associated with an individual used in model estimation. What we have here is some form of *aggregation bias*.

It is one challenge to re-calibrate a model to the data used in the base year application. It is another challenge when one wants to calibrate a model to obtain the forecast year baseline.

In the forecast year, one has very little idea of what the base-choice shares will be (i.e. through some projection over time without any change in the levels of attributes associated with a specific policy). The analyst needs to source information that will enable forecasts of the attribute levels and socio-economic characteristics to be made. Since the parameter estimates are unlikely to be changed in the absence of any additional information to guide the revision of preferences, we normally assume transferability of the exact parameter estimates developed in the estimation year, including calibration of the alternative-specific constants.

In section 12.3 we will detail methods that are available to calibrate the base-year choice shares on an application data set and show how one can adjust the socio-economic composition (and absolute number) of the population in a future year through the application of weights. The subsequent section will look at ways of updating attribute levels.

12.3 Designing a population data base: synthetic observations

There are two main methods of preparing the socio-economic profile of the application data set:

(1) Develop synthesized observations compatible with the decision making unit, and
(2) Impose averaging at various levels of aggregation.

To be more concrete, suppose we want to apply a model estimated and calibrated in 2004 to a situation in 2009, five years out. The first thing to do is to get the best information available on what levels each of the attributes of alternatives and characteristics of individuals will be in 2009. Ideally we would want to have a sample of data associated with individuals in 2009, but we are unlikely to get that unless one has access to a sophisticated forecasting model at the individual (or household) level. An alternative is to use the information already available from unit records of the sample used in model estimation (appropriately weighted to reflect the sampled population) or an external data source of unit records from the population. The latter may be from a Census.

In Australia, for example, we are able to obtain a 1 percent sample of unit records of the entire population of households. This 1 percent unit record sample can be used to create a set of synthetic households and individuals based on their socio-economic characteristics. The socio-economic characteristics define a multi-way cross-tabulation (e.g. personal income, by age, by gender). Each individual or synthetic household would be assigned a weight to reflect their representation in the population. Over time, we would adjust the weights to reflect their changing incidence in the population (in addition to a growth factor to allow for the increasing number of households). Given the usefulness of this method, we outline it in detail in the context of households; however, the method is sufficiently general to apply to any empirical setting. Software (Syn_HH) is provided on the Cambridge University Press website that produces a set of synthetic households for the Sydney metropolitan area for a base year 1998. By selecting a growth rate, the analyst can grow the number of households (while holding the mix constant) over time up to 2025.

As an aside, the current version of Syn_HH has some very specific interpretation. In particular, the program produces two files: (1) the 1998 synthetic household profile and (2) a file of weights for each application year. The 1998 synhhld file is expanded by rows to account for each worker in a household, so a household with three workers has three rows of data. The household data are common across workers but each worker has their own person data. The weights in the 1998 file are rather meaningless since they are duplicated for each worker associated within the same household. For each household in 1998 the weights in that file at a household level have been rescaled to ensure that they sum to total number of households in Sydney in 1998. This is what we see in the household weight file. The annual growth rate selected in the program front end is used to grow each household weight at same rate to give growth in total number of households. The current version of the program does not allow differential growth in types of households over time.

12.4 The concept of synthetic households

There have been a number of approaches to overcoming barriers to the practical use of discrete choice models in the context of forecasting choices. By far the simplest approach to forecasting with discrete choice models is to project population average values for the socio-economic variables (e.g. personal income of individuals living in a specific suburb or geographical location), calculate average choice probabilities, and factor these up by population size. This approach tends to lead to predictive error of perhaps quite substantial proportions due, among other reasons, to the non-linear nature of discrete choice models and the loss of information through averaging as a way of describing very heterogeneous populations.

An alternative approach is to segment the population of interest into a number of sub-categories, project average values for the socio-economic variables in each sub-population, use these to predict the average sub-population choice probabilities, weight the average choice probabilities by the number of households in the sub-population, and sum across sub-populations to obtain predictions for the population as a whole. Provided the sub-populations are relatively homogeneous in terms of the socio-economic variables, the predictive error from this method will be relatively small. To achieve homogeneous groupings with many socio-economic variables it is necessary to define very small sub-populations. In the limiting case, each segment will be populated by only one household. When this occurs the prediction method is labeled "sample enumeration" or the "Monte Carlo method."

Rather than predicting choice probabilities for every household in the population, a gargantuan task, when applying the sample enumeration method it is usual to predict *choice probabilities* for a synthetic or real sample drawn from the population, sum them up to obtain sample predictions, and then expand the predictions to the population level. Sample enumeration is regarded as superior to other forecasting methods (Daly 1982).

A "synthetic household" is defined as a household representing a known number of households in a classified structure of household types. Each synthetic household carries a weight to represent its contribution to the total population. Over time, the weights change to reflect the representation in the population. The application process is likened to "dropping" a sample of synthetic households into the spatial location of the sampled population, each such household being described by a bundle of socio-economic and demographic characteristics and a weight. For example, if a particular synthetic household carries a weight of 200 it indicates that this household represents 200 actual households in the total population. Through time, we can carry forward the base-year weights or, alternatively, modify the weights to represent the changing composition of households in the population.

The socio-economic descriptors of each synthetic household are explanatory variables in the utility expressions associated with one or more discrete choice models. These households move through the choice model(s) and get applied to the parameters associated with the socio-economic characteristics. Together with the attributes of the alternatives and their associated parameters, the predicted-choice probabilities are obtained for each alternative for each synthetic household. The weights are then applied to the probabilities associated with each alternative, and then summed across all observations to produce the number of times an alternative is chosen in the population.

The attractiveness of a synthetic sample stems from at least four sources (Hensher et al. 1992). First, provided the pertinent population information is available, the application can be commenced at any point in time. Second, births and deaths of households can be incorporated within a sampling scheme. Third, the synthetic sampling can be tailored to suit the application. For example, in an application looking at the impact of a downturn in the building and industrial sectors on motor vehicle sales it may make sense to adopt a stratified sampling strategy concentrating on households containing a worker from one of these sectors. Finally, similar methods can be used to obtain synthetic samples, as are applied in translating user-supplied scenarios into acceptable model inputs.

One crucial task in the generation of synthetic households is the establishment of a set of households that not only represent adequately the heterogeneity of the population but also are able to be implemented in a decision support system under acceptable computational running times.

12.4.1 Synthetic households' generation framework

A synthetic sample is developed through a cross-tabulation of existing population or survey data. For a choice-model system, suitable cross-tabulations designed to capture patterns of correlation between the socio-economic variables can be developed from existing household-level databases such as a population Census. With data from a single source, a way of automatically achieving this aim is to construct an n-way cross-tabulation where n is the number of socio-economic variables. However, when n becomes large, this approach will not be a practical option. It will require some assumptions on the pattern of correlation among socio-economic variables and hence a structure for the cross-tabulations. The approach described below is an interactive three-stage process using two different versions of the 1996 Australian Population Census, both illustrative of the types of available census-level data in many countries:

(1) Data source 1 is an aggregate 100 percent population census reported as 57 two-way tables for selected pairs of socio-economic characteristics
(2) Data source 2 is household-based 1 percent unit records from a population Census.

While smaller than data source 1, data source 2 enables the analyst to develop multi-way cross-tabulations and hence identify the 3-way and 4-way distributions that are not available

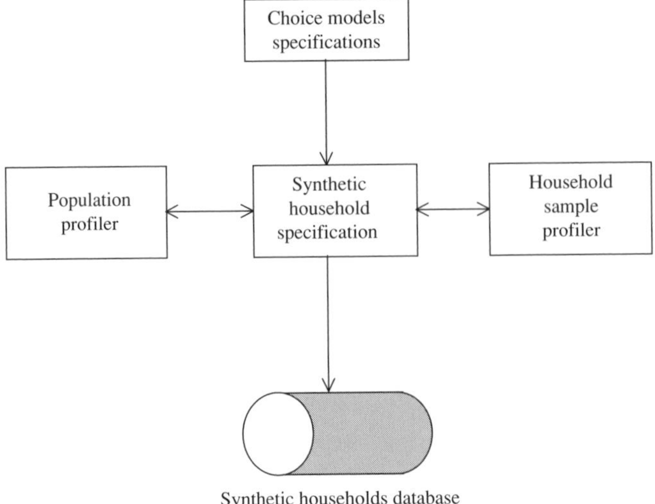

Figure 12.1 Synthetic household generation process

from the full Census tables. Data source 1 is limited by the cross-tabulations in each of the 57 tables, making it difficult (if not impossible) to establish new multi-way tables for combinations of socio-economic characteristics not provided in the 57 tables. Data source 1 is useful in checking aggregate totals derived from data source 2. The sequence in which each data source is used is presented below (and summarized in figure 12.1):

(1) First, the 100 percent population Census defining two-way tables of various combinations of socio-economic characteristics or data source 2 are used to produce a set of core household-level cells, selecting two socio-economic variables (in our example) that are key influences in the choice model. The output matrix provides a household distribution at the population level. This task is referred to as the *population profiler*.
(2) Second, the specification of a synthetic household sample size and a preferred distribution of within-core cell representation are determined as the basis of generating the final synthetic household distribution. The resulting matrix from the second phase will provide a guide to how many synthetic households in each category, specified by the two core socio-economic variables, are to be drawn. This task is called the *synthetic household specification*.
(3) In the third phase, a further cross-tabulation operation is performed on the remaining set of socio-economic variables that are significant influences in the choice model(s). The 1 percent population Census sample is used in this cross-tabulation. The output from this cross-tabulation provides a more detailed sampling rule for drawing specific records to represent the profile of households in each core cell, as described by the additional set of socio-economic variables. This task is the *household sample profiler*.
(4) Finally, after the synthetic sample is drawn, each synthetic household is assigned a weight to indicate their representation in the total population.

In our example, we have selected household type (*htype*: 5 categories) and household income (*hincome*: 5 categories) to define 25 core cells (but one can have as many core variables as required). The number of workers in a household (6 categories) is then used to sort households into the second-level cells within each core cell in the matrix of *htype* and *hincome*. Other socio-economic variables are selected for cross-tabulation to define the third-level cells where synthetic households are sampled.

12.5 The population profiler

The determining influences on the context within which synthetic households are derived are the set of statistically significant socio-economic variables in the choice model of interest for the appropriate unit of analysis (i.e. an individual or a household). In the mode-choice model estimated in previous chapters, the unit of analysis is the individual traveler; in a residential location-choice model, the unit of analysis is most likely to be a household.

Once the context is defined from the choice model, the generation process starts. We have assumed that household income and type are the two core variables to start the population profiler and the unit of analysis is the household:

htype: (household type)	*hincome:* (Household income category)
1. One parent family	1. Less than \$13,000
2. Two parent family	2. \$13,000–\$34,000
3. Couples without children	3. \$34,001–\$57,000
4. Single person households	4. \$57,001–\$91,000
5. Other household groups.	5. More than \$91,000

The 5 × 5 output matrix represents the household distribution at the population level based on the two selected variables. The 25 core cells in this matrix are indexed (table 12.1) so that they can be related to the next cross-tabulation for further selection of model attributes.

Table 12.1. *Household distribution at population level: indexing 25 core cells*

	hincome				
htype	< \$13,000: 1	\$13,000–\$34,000: 2	\$34,001–\$57,000: 3	\$57,001–\$91,000: 4	More than \$91,000: 5
One parent family: 1	C1	C2	C3	C4	C5
Two parent family: 2	C6	C7	C8	C9	C10
Couples without children: 3	C11	C12	C13	C14	C15
Single person households: 4	C16	C17	C18	C19	C20
Other household groups: 5	C21	C22	C23	C24	C25

Table 12.2. *Cross-tabulation of households at core-cell level*

a

htype	*hincome* 1	2	3	4	5	Sum
1	240	551	435	99	155	1480
2	196	850	1951	1192	719	4908
3	466	824	986	554	204	3034
4	1447	835	492	99	12	2885
5	1233	362	554	339	197	2685
Sum	3582	3422	4418	2283	1287	**14992**

b

htype	*hincome* 1	2	3	4	5	Sum
1	0.01601	0.03675	0.02902	0.00660	0.01034	
2	0.01307	0.05670	0.13014	0.07951	0.04796	
3	0.03108	0.05496	0.06577	0.03695	0.01361	
4	0.09652	0.05570	0.03282	0.00660	0.00080	
5	0.08224	0.02415	0.03695	0.02261	0.01314	
Sum	0.23893	0.22826	0.29469	0.15228	0.08585	1

As indicated above, either data source 1 or 2 can be cross-tabulated into the table. We have selected the 1 percent population Census that contains 14,992 sampled households with 39,898 records, representing 1,499,200 households with 3,989,800 residents in 1996 in the Sydney Metropolitan Area. Tables 12.2a and 12.2b show the number of cross-tabulated households in each cell and the proportion of households in each cell relative to all households. These matrices will be used as an input to the synthetic household specification block.

12.5.1 The synthetic household specification

Two decisions are required to develop the synthetic households (see figure 12.2, p. 445), the selection of a synthetic sample size and the selection of method for generating a synthetic household distribution. There are three methods for generating a synthetic household distribution (SHD):

(1) A one-to-one mapping of the population profile (i.e. where "*a priori*" knowledge of the household distribution at the population level is known). With this method the analyst might adopt the exact proportion of households at the population level (from the population profiler): SHD1.

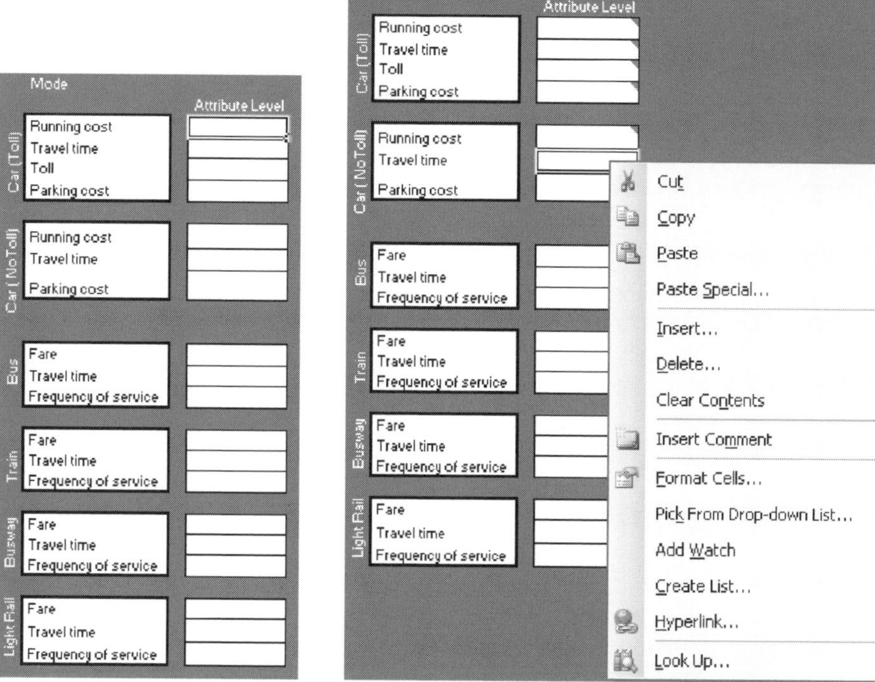

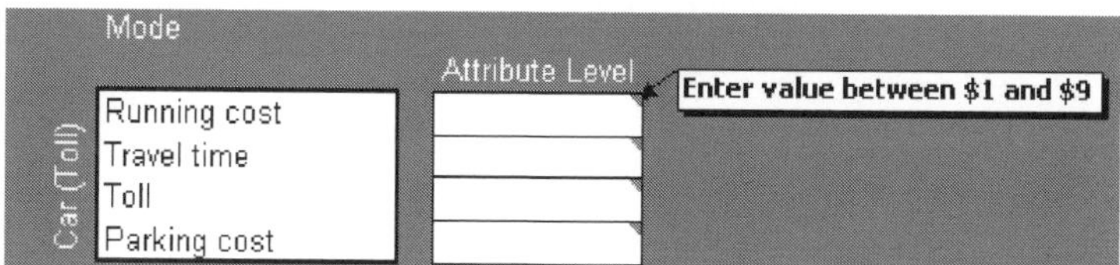

Figure 12.2 Constructing the front end of a DSS

(2) A uniform distribution of synthetic households (i.e. where there is missing information on the household distribution at the population level): SHD2.

(3) The adoption of any statistical distribution to replicate the household distribution at the population level (observed distribution) determined by the population profiler. For example, we can establish the mean and variance of the observed distribution and then employ a random number generator to generate a normal distribution: SHD3.

The following set of tables and associated formulae illustrate the three methods for generating a synthetic household distribution associated with a sample size of 401.

SHD1: Synthetic households are distributed into 25 core cells using the formula:

$$S_{ij} = \frac{N_{ij}}{N} * S$$

Table 12.3. *SHD1 method*

htype	*hincome* 1	2	3	4	5
1	S_{11}	S_{12}	S_{13}	S_{14}	S_{15}
2	S_{21}	S_{22}	S_{23}	S_{24}	S_{25}
3	S_{31}	S_{32}	S_{33}	S_{34}	S_{35}
4	S_{41}	S_{42}	S_{43}	S_{44}	S_{45}
5	S_{51}	S_{52}	S_{53}	S_{54}	S_{55}

a *Synthetic households allocated to each core cell*

htype	*hincome* 1	2	3	4	5	
1	6	15	12	3	4	
2	5	23	52	32	19	
3	12	22	26	15	5	
4	39	22	13	3	*0*	
5	33	10	15	9	5	
Sum	95	92	118	62	33	400

b *Adjusted synthetic households allocated to each core cell*

htype	*hincome* 1	2	3	4	5	
1	6	15	12	3	4	
2	5	23	52	32	19	
3	12	22	26	15	5	
4	39	22	13	3	*1*	
5	33	10	15	9	5	
Sum	95	92	118	62	34	401

where:

N_{ij} = the number of households in the household distribution at the population level in class (table 12.2a)
N = total number of households in the household distribution at the population level
S = total number of synthetic households (401)
S_{ij} = Number of synthetic households assigned to class

The calculated synthetic household distribution is given in table 12.3a. The Cell S_{45} is empty. To ensure that each cell is sampled, put a sample size of 1 into Cell S_{45}. This makes the total sample size 401, as shown in table 12.3b.

Table 12.4. *SHD2: uniform distribution method*

	hincome				
htype	1	2	3	4	5
1	S_{11^u}	S_{12^u}	S_{13^u}	S_{14^u}	S_{15^u}
2	S_{21^u}	S_{22^u}	S_{23^u}	S_{24^u}	S_{25^u}
3	S_{31^u}	S_{32^u}	S_{33^u}	S_{34^u}	S_{35^u}
4	S_{41^u}	S_{42^u}	S_{43^u}	S_{44^u}	S_{45^u}
5	S_{51^u}	S_{52^u}	S_{53^u}	S_{54^u}	S_{55^u}

Table 12.5. *Uniform distribution allocation*

	hincome				
htype	1	2	3	4	5
1	16	16	16	16	16
2	16	16	16	16	16
3	16	16	16	16	16
4	16	16	16	16	16
5	16	16	16	16	16

SHD2 – uniform distribution: the synthetic household distribution matrix can be established by multiplying *S* (total number of synthetic households) by every cell value in the matrix (table 12.4).

S^u_{ij} = total sample of synthetic households (e.g. 401) divided by the number of cells in the matrix and $S_{ij} = 401/25 = 16$. The uniform distribution allocates 16 synthetic households to each cell, as shown in table 12.5.

SHD3 – normal distribution: With the support of matrix and random sampling tools, the household distribution at the population level can be replicated. For example, the mean (μ_s) of the number of households per cell might be 2000 with a standard deviation (σ_s) of 800. A typical output from the application of a random number generator, given 401 synthetic households, is shown in table 12.6a, with absolute household numbers (rounded) in table 12.6b.

The cell values in the synthetic household distribution matrix represent the number of synthetic households to be drawn from the 1 percent unit record sample. For example in table 12.6b we need to draw 37 and 32 records of type (*htype* = 2 and *hincome* = 4) and (*htype* = 3 and *hincome* = 1), respectively. In what follows, we have selected the one–one mapping distribution method (table 12.3b).

The next question is how to draw these synthetic household records. One solution is a *random draw*. However, before the random sample can be drawn, it is advisable to further enhance the representation of the synthetic sample by developing additional multi-way

Table 12.6. *SHD3*

a *allocation by random assignment to obtain proportions*

	hincome					
htype	1	2	3	4	5	
1	0.053333	0.026667	0.013333	0.013333	0.026667	
2	0.066667	0.040000	0.026667	0.093333	0.106667	
3	0.080000	0.026667	0.053333	0.013333	0.026667	
4	0.026667	0.013333	0.066667	0.026667	0.013333	
5	0.026667	0.013333	0.080000	0.040000	0.026667	
Sum	0.253333	0.120000	0.240000	0.186667	0.200000	1.0

b *distribution of 401 synthetic households*

	hincome					
htype	1	2	3	4	5	
1	21	11	5	5	11	
2	27	16	11	37	43	
3	32	11	21	5	11	
4	11	5	27	11	5	
5	11	5	32	16	11	
Sum	102	48	96	74	81	401

tables for other socio-economic variables that are included in the choice model(s). This is undertaken within the sample profiler.

12.6 The sample profiler

The aim of the sample profiler, given the number of synthetic household records to be selected, is to specify the appropriate *sampling rule*. This guides the sampling procedure by providing additional information such as the frequency distribution of the given number of records to be drawn from the socio-economic variables in the choice model. The sample profiler involves three tasks:

(1) further cross-tabulating each core cell using additional socio-economic variables (as listed in table 12.7) to ensure the representative of each synthetic household
(2) drawing synthetic households as specified in the distribution matrix, and
(3) assigning a weight to each synthetic household, this is calculated as a ratio of the number of synthetic households to the number of households represented.

The resulting data are then multiplied by 100 to indicate that the source for drawing the synthetic sample is the 1 percent population census. To evaluate how well the 401

Table 12.7. *Household characteristics: a comparison of synthetic household projection to Census data*

Variables	Projected from synthetic household	Number of households in Census data	Scale factor
Total number of households	1499200	1499200	1.00
Household type			
One parent family	148000	148000	1.00
Two parent family	490800	490800	1.00
Couples without children	307207	303400	1.01
Single person households	288500	288500	1.00
Other household groups	264693	268500	0.99
Annual household income category			
Less than $13,000	354393	358200	0.99
$13,001– $34,000	346007	342200	1.01
$34,001–$57,000	441500	441500	1.00
$57,001–$91,000	228600	228600	1.00
More than $91,000	128700	128700	1.00
Number of workers in the household			
No worker in the household	516300	518800	1.00
One worker in the household	442200	438200	1.01
Two workers in the household	403200	405800	0.99
Three workers in the household	99000	97400	1.02
Four workers in the household	32700	31900	1.03
Five or more workers in the household	5800	7100	0.82
Age			
Average age of the head of the household	49.78	50.00	1.00
Number of members of the household			
One member	305429	365900	0.83
Two members	473252	463200	1.02
Three members	291054	250600	1.16
Four members	228323	240300	0.95
Five or more members	201142	179200	1.12
Average income of the household (in $000)	42.75	42.66	1.00
Number of children in the household			
No child	928973	964500	0.96
One child	256308	223400	1.15
Two children	218146	198800	1.10
Three or more children	95774	112500	0.85

Table 12.8. *Resident characteristics: a comparison of synthetic household projection to Census data*

Variables	Projected from synthetic household	Number of residents in Census data	Scale factor
Work status			
Full-time worker	1242761	1261900	0.98
Part-time worker	463239	444200	1.04
Self-employed worker	107953	73200	1.47
Gender			
Male	2043753	1934800	1.06
Age			
Average age of residents	37.02	36.00	1.03
Personal annual income			
Less than $3,000	445373	378000	1.18
$3,001–$7,000	462703	399700	1.16
$7,001–$10,000	216554	255900	0.85
$10,001–$18,000	584709	576400	1.01
$18,001–$28,000	656268	560200	1.17
$28,001–$57,000	289250	331700	0.87
$57,001 or more	398809	417400	0.96
Occupation			
Professional	367601	352900	1.04
Para-professional	110815	129100	0.86
Trade	197739	209800	0.94
Clerk	326159	315600	1.03
Sales	213335	218800	0.98
Plant	67908	71500	0.95
Labor	136604	128100	1.07
Management professional	643173	625800	1.03
Technical	265647	281300	0.94

synthetic households represent households in the Sydney Metropolitan Area, we compare projected household and person characteristics with those in Census data (tables 12.7 and 12.8).

The synthetic households can represent most household variables with reasonable accuracy. Whether this level of accuracy is acceptable is very much a decision that needs to be made by the analyst. Where errors are large (e.g. 18 percent for personal income less than $3000), the analyst might want to improve the accuracy by re-scaling variables in each synthetic household (using the inverse of scale factor in tables 12.7 and 12.8). While this strategy is theoretically reasonable, it is intuitively unacceptable. For example, it is not good practice to use 1.02 for full-time workers or 0.96 for the occupation class *clerical*, because these variables are originally treated as dummies. The best method for improving representativeness is to enlarge the number of synthetic households, subject to the constraint of computer capacity.

The weights that are derived from this process apply to the socio-economic distribution in the base year. In developing forecasts of choice outcomes, one has to decide on an updated set of weights that reflect the changing composition of the population over time. The data required to do this are usually obtained from government agencies that specialize in forecasting the population. Our experience suggests that many such organizations have a limited number of socio-economic variables in their forecasting set, typically the total population and selective occupation indicators including total jobs.

Subject to what externally available forecasted distributions are available, the analyst can make adjustments to the synthetic household weights based on this new information. Alternatively one uses the base-year weights but undertakes sensitivity assessment ("*what-if*") on the weights. For example, we know that many populations are aging and so it would be interesting to increase the relative weights for individuals in households that will be over 55 in, say, five years' time. This is an important point, highlighting that the analyst can undertake applications that involve changes beyond the attributes of the alternatives in a choice set. However the main use of choice models will be to assess the changes in choice shares associated with changing levels of one or more attributes describing the choice alternatives (be they existing or new alternatives). We now turn to this.

12.7 Establishing attribute levels associated with choice alternatives in the base year and in a forecast year

We have focused above on establishing a process to weight each application unit (in our example, of households) in a base year and at a future date to represent the population of interest. However, in choice models we have a number of attributes associated with each alternative, and these have to be defined in the base year and projected into the future.

There is a growing interest in *synthesized attributes*, but to date the majority of applications have adopted one or more of the following strategies:

For the *base year*:

(1) Adopt the data that was used to estimate the choice model, but calibrate the alternative-specific constants to ensure reproduction of *population choice shares*. If choice-based weights were used in model estimation this should guarantee the correct population shares, or

(2) Use another data set and re-calibrate the alternative-specific constants (ASCs) to account for the influence of the newly defined attribute levels. The exclusive use of the ASCs to "correct" for all sources of differences between the data set used in model estimation and that used in application also accommodates any differences in the data defining the observed attributes. For example, in estimation we may have

used an individual's actual travel time associated with a sample individual whereas in application we may be using an average travel time from a synthetic network associated with a synthetic individual. As long as the distribution of levels of an attribute used in estimation and in application overlay then the risk of significant error being attributed to the parameter estimate is minimal. Indeed, where the overlay is noticeably different we would not recommend using such data.

For the *application year*:

(1) Treat attribute levels as fixed into the future, based on the data in the estimation data set or a hold out sample, and/or
(2) Project the attribute levels into the future based on some broad assumptions (e.g. prices increase by the consumer price index), and/or
(3) Implement a "*what-if*" scenario approach in which a range of possible levels of each attribute represents the likely domain in which each attribute will reside and a distribution of forecasted choice shares are derived.

12.8 Bringing the components together in the application phase

Regardless of which strategy is adopted for the base and forecast years, the data representing the attributes have to be treated in a number of ways in developing choice probabilities and population choice shares, depending on how one selects the observation unit. The approaches that we recommend are summarized below:

(1) *Application approach 1:* Use synthetic observations to define the decision making unit and identify which observations in the estimation sample belong to the same socio-economic strata. For each identified member of the strata used in estimation, calculate the mean and standard deviation value for each attribute associated with each alternative. Then randomly generate a level for the attribute (assuming a particular distribution) and assign that value to the synthetic observation. Repeat for each attribute and each synthetic observation to produce the *attribute data base* for the application data set.
(2) *Application approach 2:* Use the estimation data set (socio-economic and attribute data), appropriately calibrated to base-year choice shares, and undertake a series of "*what-if*" scenario assessments by varying one or more of the attributes of alternatives and socio-economic characteristics of sampled individuals. The "*what-if*" scenarios can relate to the base year and/or a forecast year. For the forecast year, one would have to make assumptions about the representativeness of the calibrated base-year sample and re-weight the individual observations as appropriate. This can be done in NLOGIT (using **weights = <exogenous weighting variable>**) where the weight variable is included in the data set or developed using the **CREATE** command. For a forecast year, the analyst has to scale up the findings to account for the growth in the size of population that the observation unit belongs to.

(3) *Application approach 3:* Use exactly the same hold-out sample as the one used in model estimation and apply the calibrated model directly to that data set. This is typically used for a base year, in which another sample is drawn, but it can also be used in a forecast year if the hold out sample has been constructed to represent a year that has already passed and the analyst wishes to establish how reliable the base year model is.

(4) *Application approach 4:* Each sampled observation used in model estimation can be extrapolated into the future in terms of each of the socio-economic characteristics and the attribute levels associated with each alternative that apply to that observation unit. The analyst must recognize that samples do age and that each observation must be re-weighted to reflect any known changes in the composition of future populations. These weights should also account for the absolute growth in the population.

12.9 Developing a decision support system

It is popular practice to embed the utility expressions within a decision support system (DSS) so that analysts can predict the impact of changes in the levels of attributes on choice shares and absolute numbers choosing each alternative. A DSS can be written as the front end of a spreadsheet (for example using Microsoft Excel) or as a stand alone piece of software in virtually any programming language. In this section, we provide an example of how to create a DSS in Microsoft Excel using the utility expressions from the following MNL model. The creation of a stand alone .EXE proceeds in a similar fashion to that for a DSS created in Microsoft Excel. The model we use is on the entire commuting SP data:

```
Sample;all $
reject;sprp=1 $
dstats;rhs=* $

NLOGIT
;lhs = choice, cset, altij
;Choices  = cart, carnt, bus, train, busway, LR
;Model:
U(cart)    = asccart + cst1*fuel + tt1*time + toll*toll
+ park1*parking /
U(carnt)  = asccarnt + cst2*fuel + tt2*time + park2*parking /
U(bus)     = ascbus + pcst3*fare + ptt3*time + freq3*freq /
U(train)   =              pcst4*fare + ptt4*time + freq4*freq /
U(busway)= ascbusw + pcst3*fare + ptt3*time + freq3*freq /
U(LR) = asclr + pcst4*fare + ptt4*time + freq4*freq $
```

The above model estimated on all commuter segments produces the following results in NLOGIT:

```
+-----------------------------------------------+
| Discrete choice (multinomial logit) model      |
| Maximum Likelihood Estimates                   |
| Model estimated: Feb 28, 2003 at 10:45:00AM.   |
| Dependent variable                  Choice     |
| Weighting variable                    None     |
| Number of observations                3614     |
| Iterations completed                     5     |
| Log likelihood function          -4467.977     |
| R2=1-LogL/LogL*  Log-L fncn  R-sqrd  RsqAdj    |
| No coefficients  -6475.4187 .31001   .30886    |
| Constants only.  Must be computed directly.    |
|                  Use NLOGIT ;...; RHS=ONE $    |
| Chi-squared[13]              = 3751.62477      |
| Prob [ chi squared > value ]   = .00000        |
| Response data are given as ind. choice.        |
| Number of obs.= 3614, skipped    0 bad obs.    |
+-----------------------------------------------+
```

Variable	Coefficient	Standard Error	b/St.Er.	P[|Z|>z]
ASCCART	.41349306	.16612251	2.489	.0128
CST1	-.12866208	.03231945	-3.981	.0001
TT1	-.05434916	.00763454	-7.119	.0000
TOLL	-.06380674	.03613155	-1.766	.0774
PARK1	-.09918613	.00575726	-17.228	.0000
ASCCARNT	.74572566	.16723522	4.459	.0000
CST2	-.11970089	.02663205	-4.495	.0000
TT2	-.04255827	.00608713	-6.992	.0000
PARK2	-.08185763	.00546047	-14.991	.0000
ASCBUS	-.22434585	.18414475	-1.218	.2231
PCST3	-.17938212	.02261820	-7.931	.0000
PTT3	-.03132159	.00615091	-5.092	.0000
FREQ3	-.02092913	.00478812	-4.371	.0000
PCST4	-.26340390	.02470082	-10.664	.0000
PTT4	-.02878038	.00627536	-4.586	.0000
FREQ4	-.01696465	.00470297	-3.607	.0003
ASCBUSW	-.08239233	.18790491	-.438	.6610
ASCLR	-.09283715	.07399468	-1.255	.2096

In the paragraphs that follow, we demonstrate the steps required to create a DSS using the above model. The DSS we construct is provided on the book's website folder and is called *DSS.xls*. In creating the DSS, we demonstrate the two methods used to obtain the initial attribute levels as shown to the user of the program. The first method involves using, as the initial attribute levels shown to the program user, the average of the attribute levels within the sample data. Such an approach is quick to program and allows the user to define and explore explicit attribute-level values in exploring policy scenarios. The second method involves using the actual attribute levels contained within the sample data (or a sub-set of them) and have the user pivot the attribute levels around these levels (this is also what the simulation capability in NLOGIT does). The first method is by far the more popular of the two due to the simplicity and ease in which the DSS may be constructed. The second method requires far greater time to create and has the disadvantage of not being able to determine the choice-share changes for explicit attribute levels that may be of interest in policy exploration. Nevertheless, two disadvantages arise as a result of the use of the first method. First, it assumes that the attribute levels for the entire population are the same (i.e. at the sample average). Secondly, using the sample data averages to determine the attribute levels assumed for the population will not reproduce the initial choice shares. Despite being far more time-consuming, the second approach will reproduce the choice shares and does allow for different individuals within the population to experience different levels of attributes over the policy scenarios explored.

In detailing how we created the accompanying DSS, we first show the construction of the DSS using the data sample averages. In sub-section 12.9.2, we outline how to construct a DSS pivoting the scenario changes from the choice data used in model estimation.

12.9.1 Using the data sample averages in creating the DSS

The first step in creating a DSS is to create the *input screen* for the user. The input screen is the screen that will allow the user to interact with the program by changing the attribute levels of the underlying model in order to predict choice share changes. Figure 12.2 shows the construction steps that were used in designing the user interface accompanying DSS. Figure 12.2(a) shows the construction of the input cells in which users of the first DSS will be able to change the attribute level values of the underlying choice model. It is necessary to restrict the values that users may enter to avoid predicting outside of the data ranges used in model estimation. Figures 12.2(b) and 12.2(c) demonstrate how to insert comments to inform the user about the attribute-level ranges.

To restrict the attribute-level ranges that are entered, the analyst may use the Microsoft Excel *Data Validation* option. Figure 12.3 demonstrates this facility. To use the *Data Validation* option, first select the cell or cells to which the data validation is to be applied. Next select *Data* in the command menu, followed by *Validation*. This will open the *Data Validation* command box. The analyst may then select the inputs the user (or client) will be allowed to enter in each cell. The analyst may also select what messages will be displayed to the user upon entering a value or making an error in entering a value (i.e. entering a value outside the range of values allowed).

Before completing the front screens of the DSS, it is worthwhile organizing the back end of the program in which the model sits. NLOGIT output is easily copied and pasted into other programs such as excel (see figure 12.15, for example). In figure 12.4, we have copied the parameter values from the model shown on p. 454 into a separate worksheet

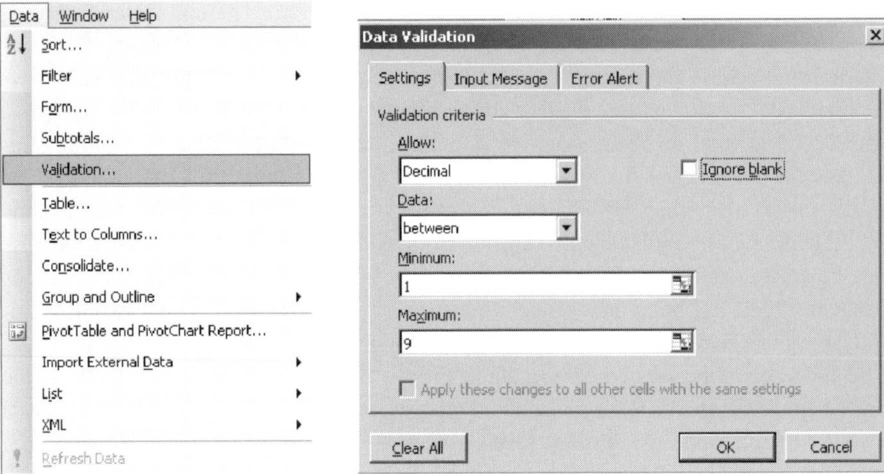

Figure 12.3 Using the Microsoft Excel Data Validation option

	A	B	C	D	E	F	G	H	I	J	K	L	M	N	O	P	Q	R
1	**Inputs**																	
2	**Cart**			**Carnt**			**Bus**			**Train**			**Busway**			**LR**		
3	ASCCART	0.413493		ASCCARNT	0.745726		ASCBUS	-0.224346					ASCBUSW	-0.0823923		ASCLR	-0.0928371	
4	CST	-0.128662	0	CST	-0.119701	0	PCST	-0.179382	0	PCST	-0.263404	0	PCST	-0.179382	0	PCST	-0.263404	0
5	TT	-0.0543492	0	TT	-0.0425583	0	PTT	-0.0313216	0	PTT	-0.0287804	0	PTT	-0.0313216	0	PTT	-0.0287804	0
6	TOLL	-0.0638067	0	PARK	-0.0818576	0	FREQ	-0.0209291	0	FREQ	-0.0169647	0	FREQ	-0.0209291	0	FREQ	-0.0169647	0
7	PARK	-0.0991861	0															
8																		
9																		
10		**Utility**		**Exp(U)**	**Prob**													
11	**Cart**	0.413493		1.5120903	0.20852527		208525											
12	**Carnt**	0.745726		2.1079713	0.29070042		290700											
13	**Bus**	-0.224346		0.7990386	0.11019166		110192											
14	**Train**	0		1	0.1379053		137905											
15	**Busway**	-0.0823923		0.9209106	0.12699846		126998											
16	**LR**	-0.0928371		0.9113419	0.12567889		125679											
17				**7.2513527**	**1**		1000000											

Figure 12.4 Creating the back end of a DSS

of Excel. In setting up the sheet, we have re-arranged the output so that the parameters for each alternative are in different columns. Next to each (non-constant) parameter we link the adjacent cell to the corresponding attribute in the front screens of the DSS. For example, cell C4 in figure 12.4 is linked to cell E4 in the front end worksheet of the DSS. This is done simply by making cell C4 of this worksheet equal cell E4 of the front end worksheet. Subsequent cells are related to the cells of the front end worksheet in a similar manner. In this way, the user inputs will be linked to the model in the back end of the DSS.

Once the user inputs from the front end of the DSS have been linked to the model in the back end of the DSS, the model outputs may be created. We have shown how this is done in chapter 11. In cells B11–B16, we have created the utilities for each of the alternatives based on the constants plus the sum of the products of the parameters and user input values for each alternative. Cells D11–D16 take the exponentials of the corresponding utilities defined in cells B11–B16. Cell D17 is the sum of cells D11–D16. The probability for any given alternative is given as (3.10). For the DSS, the probability that an alternative will be chosen is given as the division of the exponential of that alternative derived utility divided

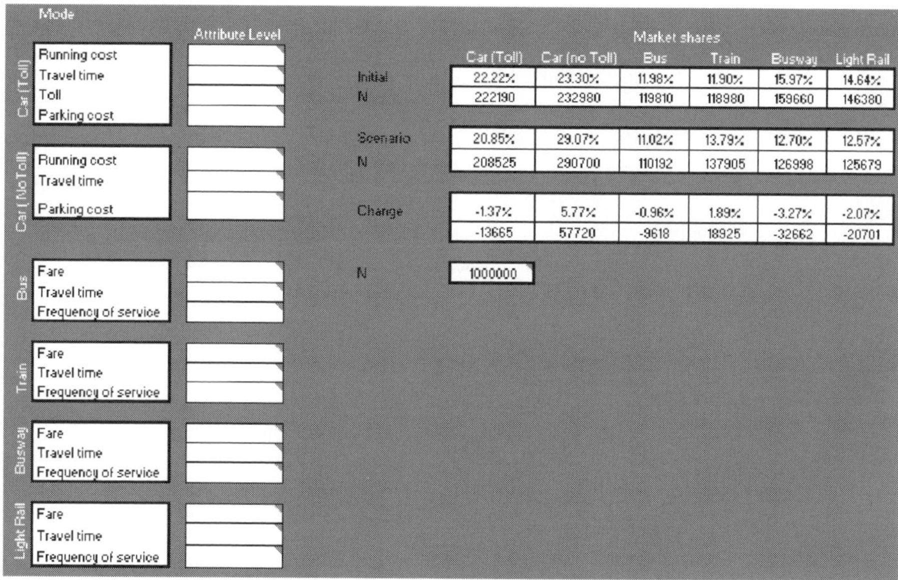

Figure 12.5 Setting up the output for the DSS

by the sum of the exponentials of the utilities for all alternatives. As such, the probabilities may be calculated by dividing each of the cells, D11–D16 by cell D17. These calculations are shown in cells E11–E16.

Returning to the front end of the DSS, we are now in a position to create the output cells that will be shown to the user. We show one such output configuration in figure 12.5. In this configuration, we have placed the initial choice shares at the top of the output (we have assumed that the choice shares are those from the model. These may be obtained using the **;Show** command when estimating the model). At the bottom of the output we have created a cell called N in which we allow the user to define the population size. Directly below the initial choice shares, the user-defined population value is multiplied by each choice share to generate the initial numbers selected for each alternative. The next cells below show the model choice shares as predicted under the scenario entered by the user. The choice shares shown are linked to cells E11–E16 in the back end of the DSS. The next row directly below these multiply each of these choice shares with the user-defined population size to estimate the predicted numbers choosing each alternative under the defined scenario. Finally, the differences between the initial and scenario choice and number shares are calculated and shown (figure 12.5 and 12.6).

Next, the analyst may use the initial and scenario choice shares to create a graph to show visually how the model predicts attribute-level changes will affect the market (see figure 12.7). This may be accomplished using the Microsoft Excel chart wizard.

The analyst is next required to insert the initial attribute levels that will be shown to the user upon opening the DSS. As is most common, the most common attribute levels are those taken at the attribute-level averages within the data set from which the model used

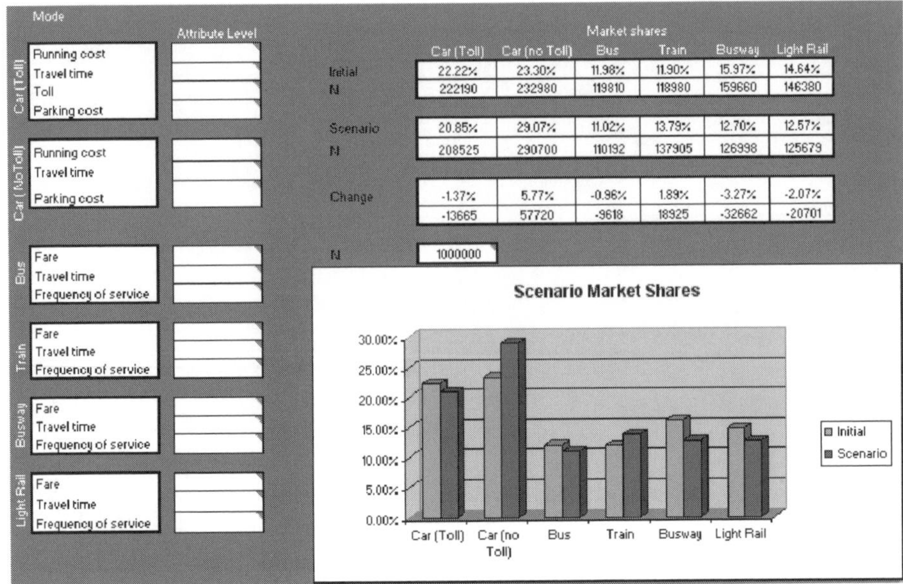

Figure 12.6 Creating a graph to visually represent predicted market adjustments due to policy changes

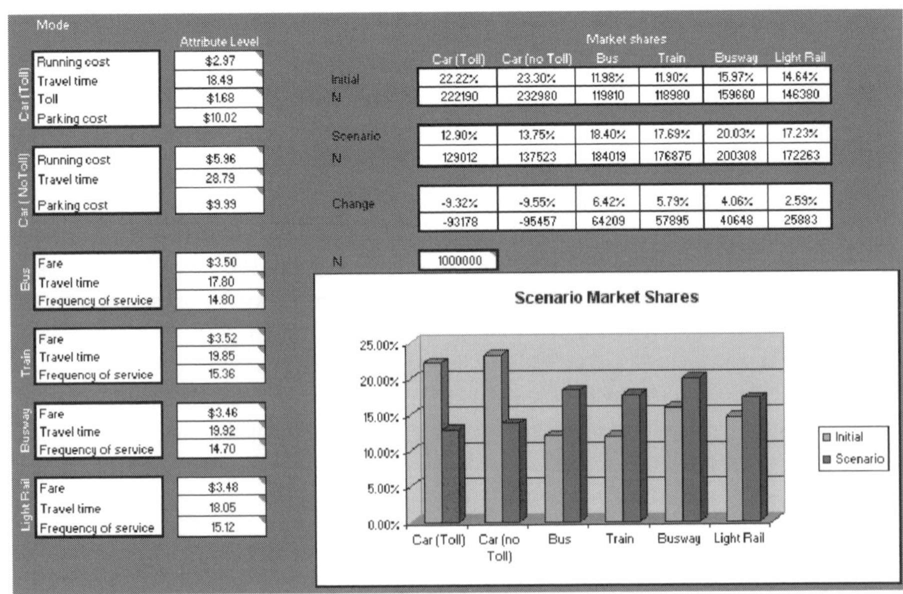

Figure 12.7 Using the attribute-level data averages as the initial DSS attribute levels

in the DSS was estimated. The NLOGIT command syntax below may be used to obtain these values:

```
Reject;altij#1 $
Dstats;rhs=fuel,time,toll,parking $

Sample;all $
Reject;sprp=1 $
Reject;altij#2 $
Dstats;rhs=fuel,time,parking $

Sample;all $
Reject;sprp=1 $
Reject;altij#3 $
Dstats;rhs=fare,time,freq $

Sample;all $
Reject;sprp=1 $
Reject;altij#4 $
Dstats;rhs=fare,time,freq $

Sample;all $
Reject;sprp=1 $
Reject;altij#5 $
Dstats;rhs=fare,time,freq $

Sample;all $
Reject;sprp=1 $
Reject;altij#6 $
Dstats;rhs=fare,time,freq $
```

The output generated from the above command syntax is shown below:

```
Descriptive Statistics
All results based on nonmissing observations.
====================================================================
Variable      Mean       Std.Dev.       Minimum       Maximum  Cases
====================================================================
--------------------------------------------------------------------
All observations in current sample
--------------------------------------------------------------------
FUEL     2.97648035   2.00338772   1.00000000   9.00000000  3614
TIME     18.4903154   9.82959095   10.0000000   45.0000000  3614
TOLL     1.68608190   1.52464848   .000000000   6.00000000  3614
PARKING  10.0221361   8.17397037   .000000000   20.0000000  3614
```

```
Descriptive Statistics
All results based on nonmissing observations.
==============================================================================
Variable       Mean         Std.Dev.        Minimum        Maximum    Cases
==============================================================================
------------------------------------------------------------------------------
All observations in current sample
------------------------------------------------------------------------------
FUEL     5.95877144    3.24695591     3.00000000      15.0000000  3614
TIME     28.7924737    14.5895249     15.0000000      70.0000000  3614
PARKING 9.99446597     8.16044291     .000000000      20.0000000  3614
```

```
Descriptive Statistics
All results based on nonmissing observations.
==============================================================================
Variable       Mean         Std.Dev.        Minimum        Maximum    Cases
==============================================================================
------------------------------------------------------------------------------
All observations in current sample
------------------------------------------------------------------------------
FARE     3.50188206     1.80716547     1.00000000      7.00000000  1594
TIME     17.7979925     8.12724269     10.0000000      40.0000000  1594
FREQ     14.7992472     8.13939137     5.00000000      25.0000000  1594
```

```
Descriptive Statistics
All results based on nonmissing observations.
==============================================================================
Variable       Mean         Std.Dev.        Minimum        Maximum    Cases
==============================================================================
------------------------------------------------------------------------------
All observations in current sample
------------------------------------------------------------------------------
FARE     3.51736746     1.80678852     1.00000000      7.00000000  1641
TIME     19.8507008     8.26351154     10.0000000      40.0000000  1641
FREQ     15.3595369     8.14082879     5.00000000      25.0000000  1641
```

```
Descriptive Statistics
All results based on nonmissing observations.
==============================================================================
Variable       Mean         Std.Dev.        Minimum        Maximum    Cases
==============================================================================
------------------------------------------------------------------------------
All observations in current sample
------------------------------------------------------------------------------
```

```
FARE    3.45970603    1.78227221    1.00000000    7.00000000   1973
TIME    19.9265079    8.54128334    10.0000000    40.0000000   1973
FREQ    14.6958946    8.17585425    5.00000000    25.0000000   1973

Descriptive Statistics
All results based on nonmissing observations.
==================================================================
Variable      Mean       Std.Dev.        Minimum        Maximum  Cases
==================================================================
------------------------------------------------------------------
All observations in current sample
------------------------------------------------------------------
FARE    3.47920792    1.77848664    1.00000000    7.00000000   2020
TIME    18.0470297    8.17771081    10.0000000    40.0000000   2020
FREQ    15.1188119    8.16410089    5.00000000    25.0000000   2020
```

For each alternative in the DSS, the means for each attribute may be used as the initial values shown to the user. We show this in figure 12.7. In using the average attribute levels to determine the initial attribute levels, the choice shares will not reflect (1) the market shares from the data or (2) the known market shares if the alternative specific constants have been calibrated to reflect these. Comparison of the initial market shares shown in figure 12.7 to those estimated from the attribute-level averages confirms this. In the example shown, the predicted-choice shares for the two car alternatives are much smaller than those estimated from the model. Use of, and changes about, the attribute-level averages in policy review therefore allow for analysis of changes in choice shares, not an analysis of the prediction of market share changes under differing scenarios tested.

In sub-section 12.9.2, we demonstrate how to create a DSS using the choice data as opposed to using the attribute averages obtained from the choice data in establishing the attribute levels shown to the DSS user.

12.9.2 Using the choice data in creating the DSS

The stages in creating a DSS when using the choice data (or a sub-set thereof) to determine the initial attribute levels shown are similar to the stages when using the sample data averages. As such, the first stage of the process involves the creation of the front end of the DSS. Figure 12.8 shows the front end of the accompanying DSS in which we make use of the actual choice data. In using the actual attribute levels contained within the choice data, the DSS will no longer have the user use explicit attribute values in determining the impacts of various policies upon the choice shares of the alternatives. Rather, in examining policy changes, the DSS will require the user to either pivot the attribute levels as a percentage around the attribute levels as they exist within the data for each sampled individual or pivot the attribute levels by some absolute amount. For the accompanying DSS, we have chosen to use percentage changes as opposed to absolute changes, though our discussion is easily extended to the use of absolute changes.

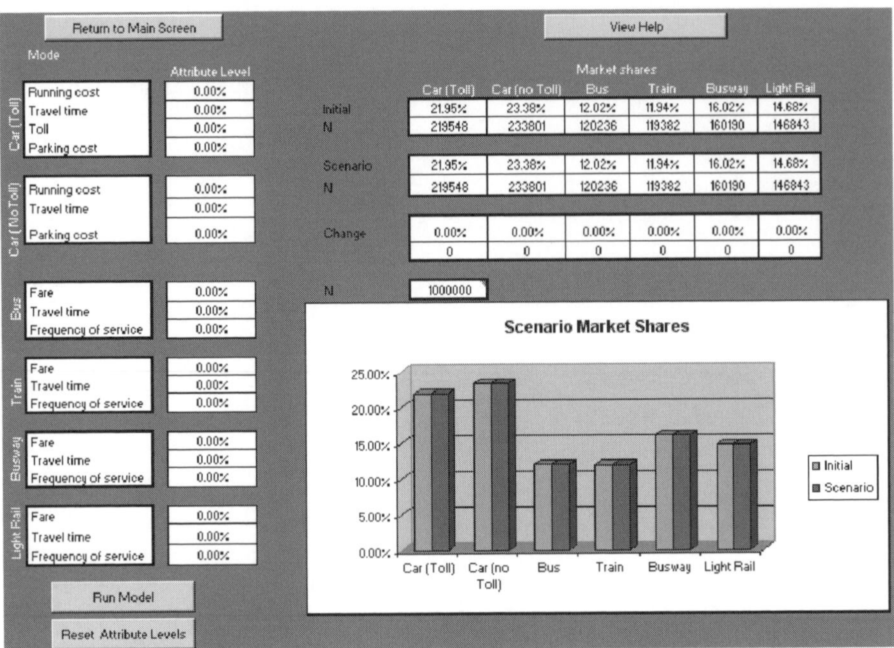

Figure 12.8 Creating a front end using percentage changes

The use of this strategy means that care is required in restricting the values users are allowed to adopt in the scenarios explored through the DSS. Unlike the previous method in which an explicit range of values could be determined and implemented, no such explicit range of values can now be used. To explain why, consider the values assumed in the data for two respondents for a car with toll travel times. Assuming travel times of 15 and 10 minutes, the analyst may desire to explore the impact of a decrease in travel times in the order of 10 percent. For the first respondent, such a scenario change would mean a travel time of 13.5 minutes. For the second respondent, the proposed scenario would suggest a travel time of 9 minutes. Given that the range of data collected for the car with toll travel time was between 10 and 45 minutes, for the second respondent we are now predicting outside of the data range. This is not a desirable result, and should be avoided where possible. Unfortunately, we cannot limit the range in which the analyst or user may change the values as any percentage change downwards for the second respondent will result in predictions being made out of range. For the first respondent, a negative over 33 percent will result in values being predicted out of range.

Given that different percentages (and absolute values) will result in different attribute levels being assigned to different respondents within the data, we are unable to limit the allowable changes in the front end of the DSS. As such, we do not use the data validation or comments options previously used in creating the front end of the DSS when using the choice data to establish the attribute levels.

	A	B	C	D	E	F	G	H
1		Raw Data						
2	ID	ALTIJ	TIME	TOLL	FUEL	PARKING	FREQ	FARE
3	1000	1	15	1	1	10	0	0
4	1000	2	25	0	5	0	0	0
5	1000	4	15	0	0	0	25	1
6	1000	6	10	0	0	0	5	3
7	1000	1	10	1.5	2	20	0	0
8	1000	2	15	0	3	10	0	0
9	1000	5	10	0	0	0	15	5

Figure 12.9 Copying the raw choice data into the DSS

Once the front end of the DSS has been created, the analyst may now turn their attention to the back end of the DSS. In using the choice data rather than the data point averages, the back end of the DSS becomes far more complex than shown in the previous example. The first step is to copy the relevant data into a new worksheet of the DSS. We show this in figure 12.9. For the example DSS, we have copied only those attributes used in the estimated model. We have also included the data from all respondents (SP data only) meaning that there are 14,466 rows of data. It is not uncommon in many applications that a random sample of the entire data set be used instead; however, in using a sub-set of the data (even if randomly selected), the choice shares derived by the DSS will not likely match those from when the entire data set is used.

After the raw data have been copied into the DSS, new columns of data must be created that reflect the policy changes inputted by the user in the front end of the DSS. This requires complex formulae. In the accompanying DSS, we have created a new worksheet (titled "Model2Values") in which we have placed all of the parameter estimates obtained from the model as well as a series of cells linked to the user inputted policy changes from the front end of the DSS. Cells A19–H25 of figure 12.10 show the cells linked to the front end of the DSS (at present, all cells show a value of zero as these are the values we have currently placed in cells E5–E29 in the front end of the DSS, see figure 12.8). Figure 12.10 omits some of the model parameters located in this screen for reasons of space.

Returning to the worksheet in which we have copied the raw choice data, we are now able to create the new columns of data that reflect the user derived policy changes. We show these new columns in figure 12.11. In figure 12.11, we have highlighted the formula used in cell I3. Cell I3 of figure 12.11 reflects the policy scenarios indicated by the DSS user. The formula we use in this cell is known as the *vlookup* command (*vlookup* stands for "vertical lookup"). The *vlookup* command requires three inputs as shown below:

=vlookup(Value to look up, Data source from which to look up the value, The column number from which to return the value in the source data)

In the example shown, the formula first looks up the value in cell B3. The dollar sign in front of B3 locks the column B so that copying the formula into another cell will always reference column B (but not row 3). Once Excel has identified the value given in cell B3 (i.e. 1), Excel will next look for that value in the first column of data located in cells

	A	B	C	D	E	F	G	H
1	Constants				Time			
2	ASCCART	1	0.413493		ASCCART	1	-0.0543492	
3	ASCCARNT	2	0.745726		ASCCARNT	2	-0.0425583	
4	ASCBUS	3	-0.224346		ASCBUS	3	-0.0313216	
5	ASCTRAIN	4	0		ASCTRAIN	4	-0.0287804	
6	ASCBUSW	5	-0.0823923		ASCBUSW	5	-0.0313216	
7	ASCLR	6	-0.0928371		ASCLR	6	-0.0287804	
8								
9								
10	Parking				Fare			
11	ASCCART	1	-0.0991861		ASCCART	1	0	
12	ASCCARNT	2	-0.0818576		ASCCARNT	2	0	
13	ASCBUS	3	0		ASCBUS	3	-0.179382	
14	ASCTRAIN	4	0		ASCTRAIN	4	-0.263404	
15	ASCBUSW	5	0		ASCBUSW	5	-0.179382	
16	ASCLR	6	0		ASCLR	6	-0.263404	
17								
18	1	2	3	4	5	6	7	8
19			**TIME**	**TOLL**	**FUEL**	**PARKING**	**FREQ**	**FARE**
20	1	CART	0	0	0	0		
21	2	CARNT	0		0	0		
22	3	BUS	0				0	0
23	4	TRAIN	0				0	0
24	5	BUSW	0				0	0
25	6	LR	0				0	0

Figure 12.10 Linking the back end to the front end of the DSS

I3 ▾ fx =VLOOKUP($B3,Model2values!$A$20:$H$25,3)*C3+C3

	A	B	C	D	E	F	G	H	I	J	K	L	M	N
1		Raw Data							Scenario					
2	**ID**	**ALTIJ**	**TIME**	**TOLL**	**FUEL**	**PARKING**	**FREQ**	**FARE**	**TIME**	**TOLL**	**FUEL**	**PARKING**	**FREQ**	**FARE**
3	1000	1	15	1	1	10	0	0	15.00	1.00	1.00	10.00	0.00	0.00
4	1000	2	25	0	5	0	0	0	25.00	0.00	5.00	0.00	0.00	0.00
5	1000	4	15	0	0	0	25	1	15.00	0.00	0.00	0.00	25.00	1.00
6	1000	6	10	0	0	0	5	3	10.00	0.00	0.00	0.00	5.00	3.00
7	1000	1	10	1.5	2	20	0	0	10.00	1.50	2.00	20.00	0.00	0.00
8	1000	2	15	0	3	10	0	0	15.00	0.00	3.00	10.00	0.00	0.00
9	1000	5	10	0	0	0	15	5	10.00	0.00	0.00	0.00	15.00	5.00
10	1000	6	20	0	0	0	25	1	20.00	0.00	0.00	0.00	25.00	1.00

Figure 12.11 Using the *vlookup* command in Microsoft Excel

A20–H25 in the worksheet "*Model2values*" (note that both the columns and rows of the cells in this command have been locked via the use of dollar signs in the formula). This is cell A20 in figure 12.10. Once the appropriate cell has been located in the "*Model2values*" worksheet, Excel will return the value located in the third column of the same row. Thus, for the example shown, Excel will first identify cell A20 and return the value in the third row starting from this cell. In this example, this corresponds to cell C20 (i.e. 0). The remainder of the formula shown in figure 12.11 firstly multiplies the value obtained in the *vlookup* command by the value in cell C3 (i.e. the corresponding raw data value), and then adds fx =IF(I3<10,10,IF(I3>45,45,I3))

I	J	K	L	M	N	O	P	Q	R	S	T
		Scenario						Scenario Data			
TIME	TOLL	FUEL	PARKING	FREQ	FARE	TIME	TOLL	FUEL	PARKING	FREQ	FARE
15.00	1.00	1.00	10.00	0.00	0.00	15.00	1.00	1.00	10.00	0.00	0.00
25.00	0.00	5.00	0.00	0.00	0.00	25.00	0.00	5.00	0.00	0.00	0.00
15.00	0.00	0.00	0.00	25.00	1.00	15.00	0.00	0.00	0.00	25.00	1.00
10.00	0.00	0.00	0.00	5.00	3.00	10.00	0.00	0.00	0.00	5.00	3.00
10.00	1.50	2.00	20.00	0.00	0.00	10.00	1.50	2.00	20.00	0.00	0.00
15.00	0.00	3.00	10.00	0.00	0.00	15.00	0.00	3.00	10.00	0.00	0.00
10.00	0.00	0.00	0.00	15.00	5.00	10.00	0.00	0.00	0.00	15.00	5.00
20.00	0.00	0.00	0.00	25.00	1.00	20.00	0.00	0.00	0.00	25.00	1.00

Figure 12.12 Using the *if statement* to restrict the possible attribute-level ranges in the data

this same value to the resulting number. This last part of the formula creates the percentage change around the value given in the raw data. Columns J–N use the *vlookup* formula in a similar manner to generate the percentage changes around the raw data for the remaining attributes used in the model.

As an aside, the *vlookup* command requires that the values in the lookup table (i.e. cells A20–H25 in the worksheet "*Model2values*") be in ascending order. If the lookup table is not in ascending order (it may skip values though), the *vlookup* command will not work. Thus, before using this command, make sure to sort the data by the first column of the lookup table data.

As noted earlier, the use of the raw data to create the attribute levels used in the DSS means that the attribute levels used in the scenarios created may extend beyond the range of the data used in model estimation. To avoid this possibility, we have created a number of new columns that use the *if statement* to restrict the possible values that an attribute may take. We show an example of one such *if statement* in figure 12.12. In figure 12.12, we show an *if statement* for the time attribute in which values less than 10 are made to equal 10 and values greater than 45 are made to equal 45. Values between 10 and 45 are left free. The restriction of the attribute range through this mechanism prevents attributes taking values outside of the range in which the model was estimated and prevents the possibility of having attributes take on values of an unexpected sign (e.g. a negative travel time). In making such restrictions, however, the analyst must be fully aware that it is possible that the policy changes examined by the user may not apply equally to all sampled respondents in the data set (e.g. those already with a travel time of 10 minutes, for example, will have no change in their travel times experienced in a policy examining a decrease in travel times experienced by the population while those with travel times greater than 10 minutes will have a downward shift in the travel times used in testing the policy impact). In making such restrictions, the impact upon the choice shares obtained from the DSS will be indeterminable. For this reason, some may elect not to place such restrictions on the attribute ranges allowed, even though this means estimating out of sample. Columns P–T use similar *if statements* to restrict the levels of the remaining attributes.

fx =VLOOKUP($B3,Model2values!$B$2:$C$7,2)

O	P	Q	R	S	T	U	V	W	X	Y	Z	AA
Scenario Data						Parameters						
TIME	TOLL	FUEL	PARKING	FREQ	FARE	constant	TIME	TOLL	FUEL	PARKING	FREQ	FARE
15.00	1.00	1.00	10.00	0.00	0.00	0.413493	-0.0543492	-0.0638067	-0.128662	-0.0991861	0	0
25.00	0.00	5.00	0.00	0.00	0.00	0.745726	-0.0425583	0	-0.119701	-0.0818576	0	0
15.00	0.00	0.00	0.00	25.00	1.00	0	-0.0287804	0	0	0	-0.0169647	-0.263404
10.00	0.00	0.00	0.00	5.00	3.00	-0.0928371	-0.0287804	0	0	0	-0.0169647	-0.263404
10.00	1.50	2.00	20.00	0.00	0.00	0.413493	-0.0543492	-0.0638067	-0.128662	-0.0991861	0	0
15.00	0.00	3.00	10.00	0.00	0.00	0.745726	-0.0425583	0	-0.119701	-0.0818576	0	0

Figure 12.13 Inserting the parameter estimates into the back end of the DSS

Next, the analyst is required to create new columns containing the parameter estimates obtained from the model. In the case of experiments involving fixed-choice sets, this is an easy process involving inserting the parameter estimates into the appropriate cells and copying them for each respondent or each choice set in the data. For studies involving non-fixed-choice sets (as in the mode-choice data set) a more complex approach is required. Figure 12.13 shows how we have inserted the appropriate parameters into the correct cells of the worksheet. Cell U3 in figure 12.13 demonstrates how we use the *vlookup* command to obtain the desired parameter estimates and insert them in the appropriate corresponding cells. The first row of data (Excel row 3) relates to alternative one (i.e. the car with toll alternative) hence the parameters inserted in this row of data must relate to this alternative. The second row (Excel row 4) relates to the second alternative; however, the third and forth rows of data relate to alternatives four and six respectively (see the *altij* variable in figure 12.11). For the next choice set (Excel rows 7–10 in figure 12.11), the choice set consists of alternatives one, two, five, and six (the different alternatives assigned to different choice sets is precisely why we cannot simply copy the parameters from one choice set to another).

The *vlookup* command shown in figure 12.13 works by looking for the value shown in cell B3 (the *altij* variable, in this case equal to one; see figure 12.11) in the first column of cells B2–C7 in the worksheet named "*Model2values*." Examining figure 12.10 suggests that it will locate the value 1 in cell B2 in the data range given of this worksheet. Once this cell is located, it will return the value in the second column of the same row of the data range indicated within the command. In this example, the second column in row 2 is that of the car with toll constant, precisely the parameter we wish to insert into cell U3. The remaining parameter estimates are inserted into the appropriate cells using the same mechanism.

The next step in setting up the back end of the DSS is shown in figure 12.14. In this step, the analyst calculates the utilities for each of the alternatives using (3.2). We show the calculation in Excel using (3.2) for the first alternative in figure 12.13. The formula shown in figure 12.13 multiplies each of the parameters by their related attribute levels and sums the total.

Once the utilities for each alternative have been calculated, the choice probabilities for each alternative may be derived. We show these calculations in figure 12.15. For the first alternative in figure 12.15, cell AC3 takes the exponential of the utility calculated in cell AB3. In column AD of figure 12.15, we sum all the exponentials of the utilities belonging

AB3 fx =U3+V3*O3+W3*P3+X3*Q3+Y3*R3

	A	U	V	W	X	Y	Z	AA	AB
1	F	Parameters							
2	ID	constant	TIME	TOLL	FUEL	PARKING	FREQ	FARE	Utilities
3	1000	0.413493	-0.0543492	-0.0638067	-0.128662	-0.0991861	0	0	-1.5860747
4	1000	0.745726	-0.0425583	0	-0.119701	-0.0818576	0	0	-0.9167365
5	1000	0	-0.0287804	0	0	0	-0.0169647	-0.263404	-1.1192275
6	1000	-0.0928371	-0.0287804	0	0	0	-0.0169647	-0.263404	-1.2556766
7	1000	0.413493	-0.0543492	-0.0638067	-0.128662	-0.0991861	0	0	-2.46675505
8	1000	0.745726	-0.0425583	0	-0.119701	-0.0818576	0	0	-1.0703275

Figure 12.14 Calculating the utilities for each alternative

AC3 fx =EXP(AB3)

	A	AB	AC	AD	AE	AF
1	F					
2	ID	Utilities	exp(U)	sum	alt	prob
3	1000	-1.5860747	0.204727654	0	1	0.168366492
4	1000	-0.9167365	0.399821732	0	2	0.328810404
5	1000	-1.1192275	0.326531943	0	4	0.268537429
6	1000	-1.2556766	0.284883031	1.215964361	6	0.234285675
7	1000	-2.46675505	0.084859778	0	1	0.095772956
8	1000	-1.0703275	0.342896201	0	2	0.3869935
9	1000	-1.6064548	0.200597513	0	5	0.22639485
10	1000	-1.3559666	0.257698083	0.886051575	6	0.290838694

Figure 12.15 Calculating the choice probabilities

to the same choice set. For ease of visual test, we have done so for the fourth alternative only. Column AE replicates the *altij* column, column B. Although this is unnecessary at the present, replicating this column now will help with future calculations. The final column in figure 12.15 calculates the probabilities for each alternative. From (3.9), the probability of an alternative being chosen is given as the exponential of the utility for that alternative divided by the sum of the utility exponentials for all alternatives. Thus, the probability for the first alternative is given as the division of cell AC3 by cell AD6. The remaining probabilities are calculated in a similar fashion.

As we demonstrated in chapter 10, the sum of the probabilities for an alternative will equal the choice or market shares for the data set. Thus, in order to calculate the market or choice-share changes resultant from scenario changes instigated by the DSS user, the DSS must sum the probabilities for each alternative in order to calculate the new choice or market shares for each new policy regime examined. There are several methods for doing this, however; the quickest method for large data sets is to use the *pivot table* function available in Microsoft Excel.

To create a pivot table, go to the *Data* option in the toolbar menu and select the *PivotTable and PivotChart Report* command (see figure 12.16). This will open the *PivotTable and PivotChart Wizard* box (see figure 12.17).

In the *PivotTable and PivotChart Wizard* box select the *Microsoft Excel list or Database* and *Pivot Table* radial buttons (these are the default alternatives: see figure 12.17). Once selected, press the *Next* button.

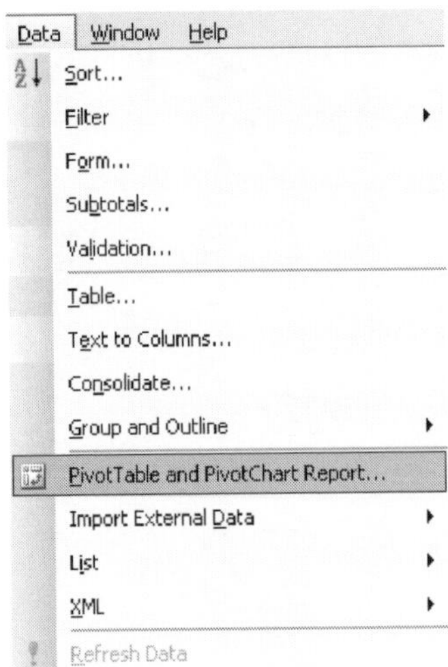

Figure 12.16 PivotTable and PivotChart Report command menu

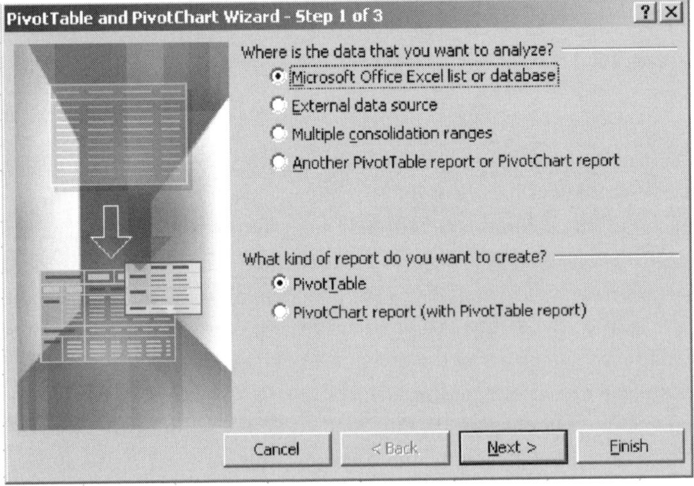

Figure 12.17 PivotTable and PivotChart Wizard box

Pressing *Next* will open step two of the Wizard. Step two allows the analyst to select the data that will be used to generate the pivot table. We show this in figure 12.18. For the pivot table we will generate, we select the data contained in columns AE and AF (i.e. the *altij* variable and probabilities).

Once the data have been selected, press the *Next* button.

This will open the step three box of the PivotTable Wizard (see figure 12.19). In this Wizard box, select the *Layout* button.

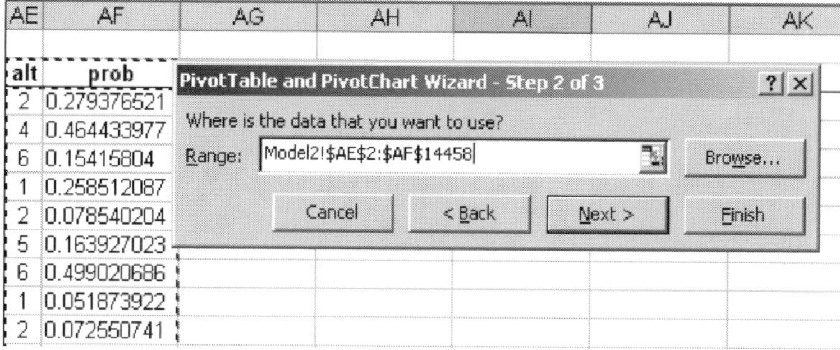

Figure 12.18 Selecting the pivot table data using the PivotTable Wizard

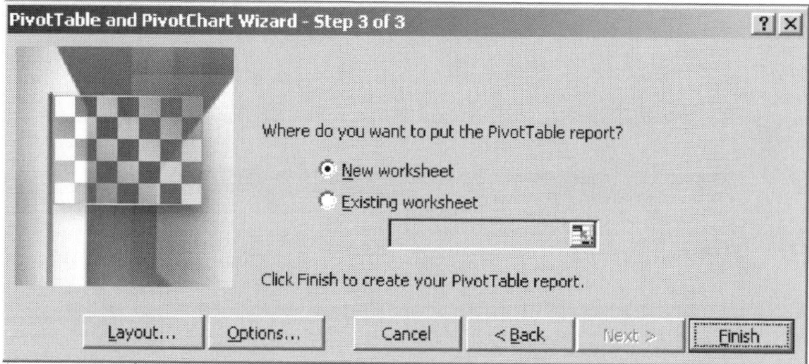

Figure 12.19 The third PivotTable and PivotChart Wizard

Pressing the *layout* button of the third PivotTable Wizard box will open the *PivotTable and PivotChart Wizard–Layout* box. Each variable in the data selected using the second Wizard box are shown as boxes in the right-hand side of the *PivotTable and PivotChart Wizard–Layout* box. In the center of the *PivotTable and PivotChart Wizard–Layout* box is a diagram showing the pivot table. The headings in the pivot table diagram are *Column*, *Row*, and *Data*. Dragging a variable (by using the cursor) onto one of the headings in the diagram will have Microsoft Excel place that variable in that position in the pivot table. Thus, if we want the alternatives to be the rows of the pivot table, we drag the *alt* variable box onto the *row* heading in the pivot table diagram. Any variable placed in the *Data* position of the pivot table diagram will be summed according to the variables placed in the *Row* and *Column* positions. Hence, if the *alt* variable is placed in the rows of the diagram and the probabilities in the *Data* position, the pivot tables will sum the probabilities for each of the alternatives within the data selected using the second Wizard (figure 12.18). Figure 12.20 shows how this looks for the example. Once the variables have been placed in their correct positions, press the *OK* button.

The analyst may next elect where the pivot table will appear. If the new pivot table is to appear on a new worksheet then simply select *Finish* (see figure 12.19). If the pivot table is to appear on an existing worksheet, the analyst will need to select the *existing worksheet*

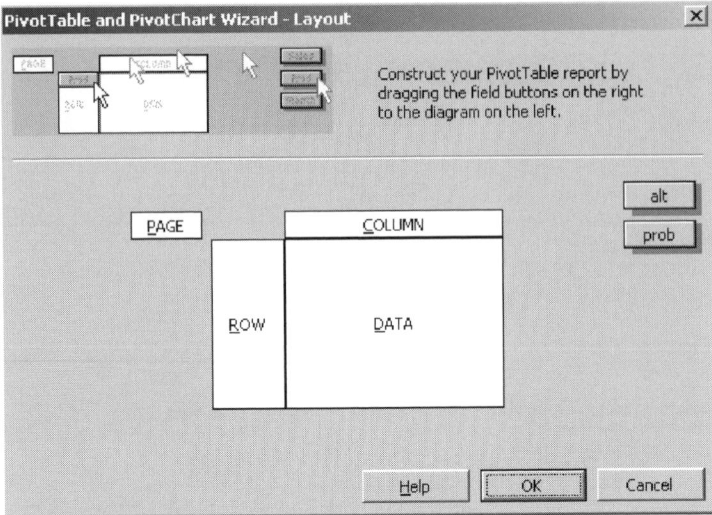

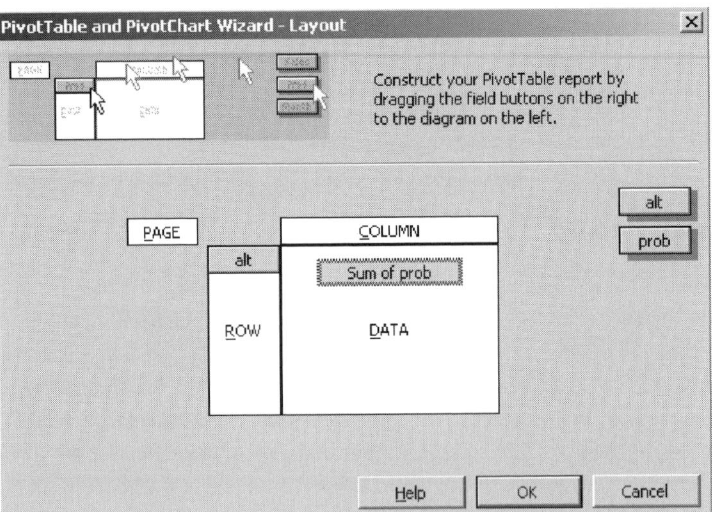

Figure 12.20 Creating the pivot table through the Layout Wizard

radial button and select the cells in which the pivot table is to appear. For the DSS, we have elected to have the pivot table appear in the AI3–AJ10 of the worksheet in which we have placed the data set used in calculating the probabilities. To generate the pivot table, select the *Finish* button.

Figure 12.21 shows the pivot table as generated for the DSS. The alternatives are numbered from 1 to 6 in the AI column and the corresponding sums of the probabilities are shown in column AK. In figure 12.21, we have placed the alternative names next to the numbers shown in column AI for ease of identification. The choice shares for each of the

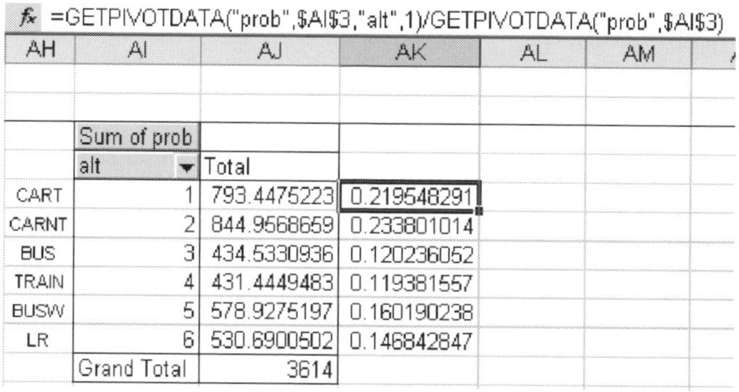

=GETPIVOTDATA("prob",$AI$3,"alt",1)/GETPIVOTDATA("prob",$AI$3)

AH	AI	AJ	AK	AL	AM
	Sum of prob				
	alt	Total			
CART	1	793.4475223	0.219548291		
CARNT	2	844.9568659	0.233801014		
BUS	3	434.5330936	0.120236052		
TRAIN	4	431.4449483	0.119381557		
BUSW	5	578.9275197	0.160190238		
LR	6	530.6900502	0.146842847		
	Grand Total	3614			

Figure 12.21 Calculating the choice shares using the Microsoft pivot table

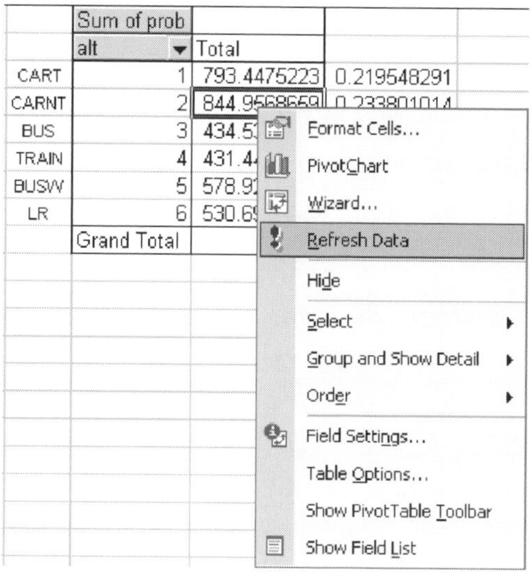

	Sum of prob		
	alt	Total	
CART	1	793.4475223	0.219548291
CARNT	2	844.9568659	0.233801014
BUS	3	434.5	
TRAIN	4	431.4	
BUSW	5	578.9	
LR	6	530.6	
	Grand Total		

Format Cells...
PivotChart
Wizard...
Refresh Data
Hide
Select
Group and Show Detail
Order
Field Settings...
Table Options...
Show PivotTable Toolbar
Show Field List

Figure 12.22 Refreshing the data of the pivot table

alternatives are calculated in column AK. The choice or market share for an alternative is calculated as the sum of the probabilities for that alternative divided by the sum of the probabilities for all alternatives. The calculation for this is shown in figure 12.21 where the predicted market share for alternative 1 is calculated as 0.2195. As we have used the entire choice data set in creating the DSS, this figure will match that predicted by the simulation command in NLOGIT as well as the initial choice shares derived from the model (using the **;Show** command).

The pivot table will not automatically update after a change has been made to the data. To update the table after a change has been made requires that the analyst to right-hand mouse click on any of the cells within the pivot table and select the *Refresh Data* option (see figure 12.22).

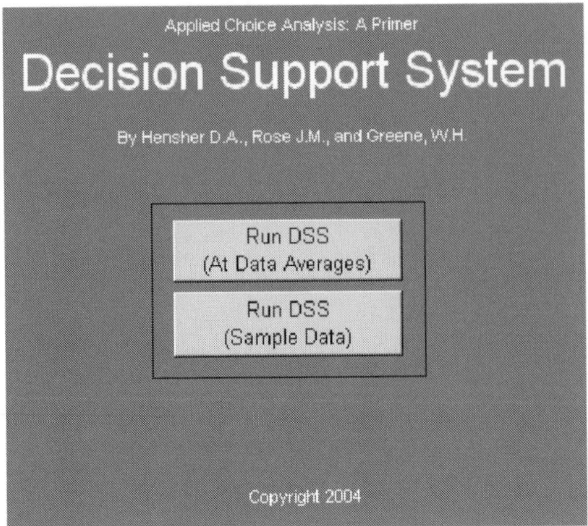

Figure 12.23 The Introduction screen buttons

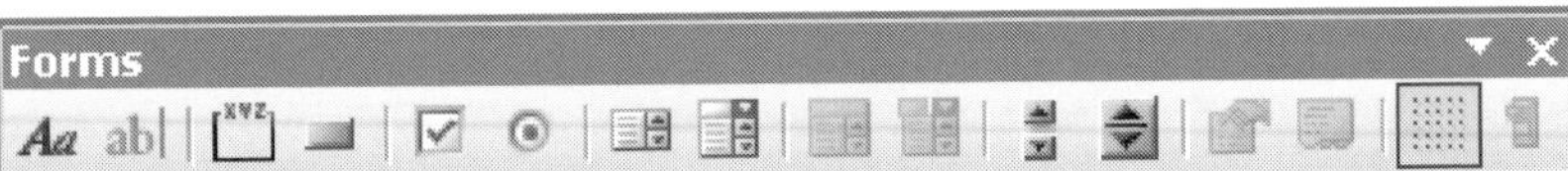

Figure 12.24 The Microsoft Excel Forms toolbar

Once the pivot table has been generated, the analyst must next link the probabilities derived from the pivot table to those in the front end of the DSS.

12.9.3 Improving the look of the DSS

All the major elements of DSS are now complete. All that remains is for the analyst to improve the presentation of the DSS. In the accompanying DSS, we have created a number of new worksheets; an introduction to the DSS and a *Help* screen for each of the two types of DSS created. In the *Introduction* screen, we have created two buttons (see figure 12.23) which when clicked on will lead to the front ends of the two DSS created earlier.

In order to create the buttons, go to *View* in the menu bar followed by *Toolbars*. Select the *Forms* toolbar. The Forms toolbar will now appear at the top of your screen (see figure 12.24).

To create a button, click on the button command in the *Forms* toolbar and place the button in the desired location on the worksheet. Once the button has been placed, the *Assign Macro* dialog box will automatically open (see figure 12.25). The analyst may use this box to define what exactly pushing the button will do to the DSS. This is done by creating *macros*. The analyst may give the macro any name; however, it is often useful to give each macro a name that is informative as to its function. If an existing macro name is used in naming the macro (the existing macro names are given in the large box located under the macro name box) then that existing macro will be assigned to that button. If a new name is given, the analyst should next select *Record*. Once the *Record* button in the

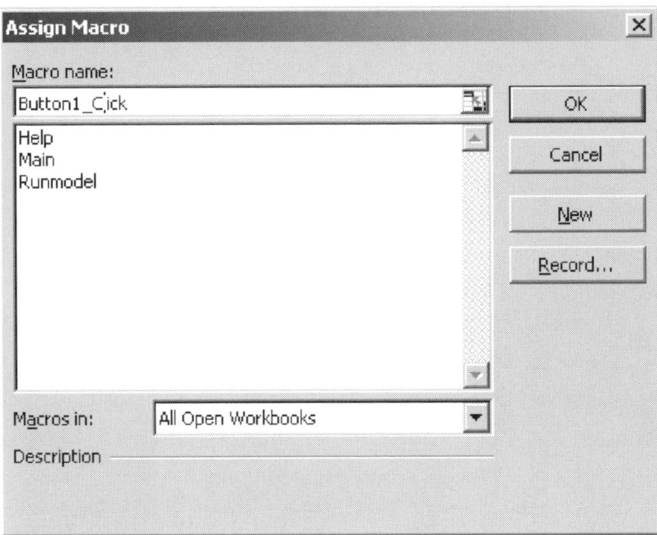

Figure 12.25 Recording macros

Assign Macro dialog box has been selected, anything that the analyst does in the workbook will be recorded into the macro (e.g. if the analyst opens another worksheet, then that will be written into the macro programming language). To stop recording, the analyst must select the *Tools* option in the menu bar, followed by *Macro* and *Stop Recording*. The two buttons created for a front page were created in this fashion (see figure 12.25).

The *Help* screens in the accompanying DSS is created using the print screen button when the front end screen is the active screen in the workbook. The resulting picture is then copied into the *Help* screen worksheet for the first DSS (see figure 12.26). Text and arrows were next added to aid the user with the various aspects of the front end of the DSS. Buttons are added with macros to navigate the user between all the DSS screens (except the back end screen which you do not want them to have access to).

For the second DSS menu, we have created two additional buttons; one that will automate the refreshing of the pivot table and one that will re-set all of the attribute level percentage changes to zero (see figure 12.27). These were both created using the *Record* macro option as described above. A button that resets the attribute-level values to the data averages was similarly created for the first DSS (see figure 12.26).

The last step in creating the DSS is to make it secure from *user interference*. In providing the DSS to a client or colleague, it is best that the client does not have access to the back end of the DSS where the model or data may inadvertently be changed. The simplest method to limit access to the back end where the DSS engine resides is to make the screen view full screen. This is done by going to *Screen* in the menu toolbar and selecting *Full screen*. Selecting *Full screen* will make the worksheet tabs disappear, meaning that the user may navigate about the DSS only using the buttons created, thus preventing access to areas of the DSS in which no button is linked. The DSS is now ready to deliver.

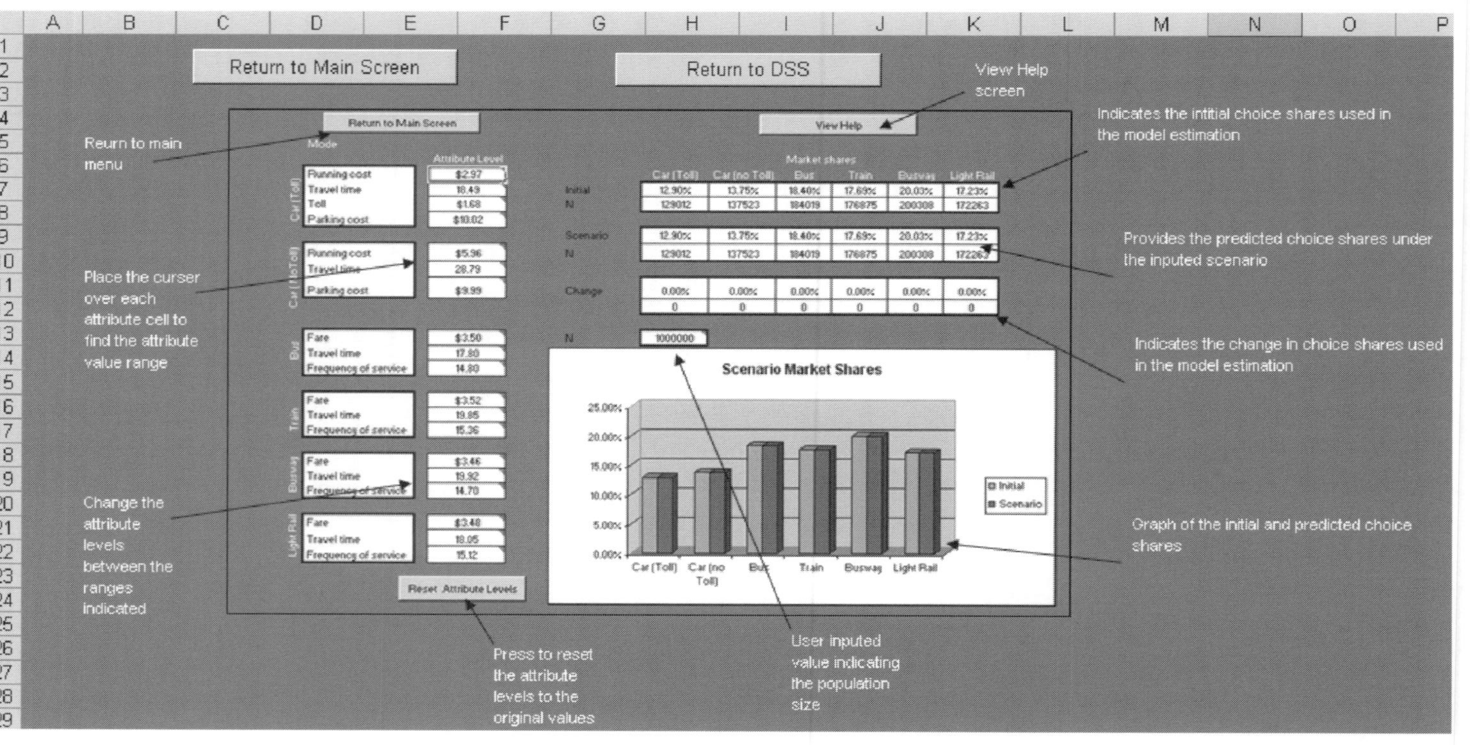

Figure 12.26 The DSS Help screen

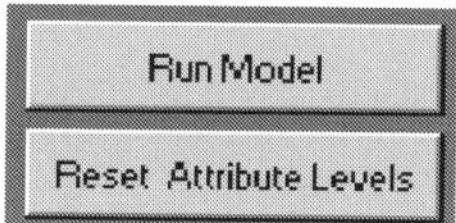

Figure 12.27 Run Model and Reset Attribute Levels for DSS2

12.9.4 Using the DSS

Once delivered, the DSS may be used to explore hypothetical policy scenarios on choice shares. By providing the DSS, we leave it to the reader to explore how the DSS works and the policy implications for various scenarios. Of particular interest is to investigate differences in how the two versions of the DSS perform.

12.10 Conclusion

The preceding twelve chapters have outlined the theory and practice of undertaking studies of discrete choice. Starting with the theory of the simple MNL model, we have proceeded to discuss the different types of data that one may use in estimating choice models, specific issues of SP data, data collection issues, sampling for choice studies and how to estimate models of discrete choice. Interspersed throughout these chapters, we have discussed very specific issues related to NLOGIT including getting started, data entry, the cleaning of data and the commands necessary to run choice models. This chapter concludes the basic introduction for the beginner. In it, we reveal (for the first time) much of what we do once we have our choice models. Nevertheless, we do not end here.

In part II, we move beyond the MNL model and discuss two more advanced discrete choice models: the nested logit and mixed logit models. Both models relax in different ways the important but restrictive IID assumption associated with the MNL model. We leave it up to the beginner to decide when they are ready to move to these more advanced topics. For many beginners, that might be a while, at least until they are comfortable with the previous twelve chapters. For others, they may feel ready now.

Part II

Advanced topics

Knowledge and timber shouldn't be much used till they are seasoned. (Oliver Wendell Holmes, 1809–94, *The Autocrat of the Breakfast-Table*, 1858)

13 Allowing for similarity of alternatives

For rarely are sons similar to their fathers: most are worse, and a few are better than their fathers. (Homer, c.800BC–c.700BC)

13.1 Introduction

The choice analysis undertaken in previous chapters has focused on the multinomial logit model (MNL). For many years this was the only easily estimated model in the sense of both available software and ease of interpretation and application. However, it was always recognized that the underlying IID condition was potentially limiting. IID had an equivalent behavioral association with a property known as the Independence of Irrelevant Alternatives (IIA).

In words, the IIA property states that the ratio of the choice probabilities of any pair of alternatives is independent of the presence or absence of any other alternative in a choice set. A particularly important behavioral implication of IIA is that *all pairs of alternatives are equally similar or dissimilar*. For the set of attributes that are not observed, this amounts to assuming that all the information in the random components is identical in quantity and relationship between pairs of alternatives and hence across all alternatives (hence the IID condition).

While on first appreciation this is a worrying assumption, it is on balance a very useful simplification that may not necessarily be too unreasonable. If the analyst can do a good job of maximizing the amount of information in the observed component of utility (i.e. V_j), resulting in a minimal amount of information in the unobserved component (i.e. ε_j), then any assumption imposed on ε_j, no matter how unrealistic, is likely to be of small consequence. Unfortunately the ability of the analyst to deliver such quality information cannot be assured.

Experience in choice analysis has shown us that there are some key issues that need to be given careful consideration as the analyst seeks to represent the influences on choice in a way that reduces the impact of violations in the strong conditions associated with IID and IIA. The key issues are set out below:

(1) *Selection of the relevant attributes that influence an individual's choice*. The more relevant attributes one can measure and include in V_j, the less likely that the ε_j term will influence the predicted choice outcome.

(2) *Measurement of the relevant attributes*. Including a relevant attribute requires careful consideration of how it is measured. As a simple rule of thumb, an attribute should be measured in a way that reflects how it is viewed and is processed by the individual decision maker. For example, a person's income is best measured as the actual income of the individual and not as a code for a range within which that income sits (e.g. 3 = \$30,000–\$40,000) or some average income for a segment of the population (e.g. all workers resident in a suburb or census collector's district (CCD)). Selecting a value in a range or using an average across individuals are both examples of *aggregation*, and as such involve the removal of information that is relevant to an individual. It is not uncommon in transport studies to use the average income of all workers living in the same traffic zone (the latter being the sum of a number of CCDs). As a result of averaging we are effectively creating a mean and a variation around a mean, and by including the mean income in the V_j expression we are assigning the variation around the mean to the ε_j. This is often called *naive aggregation*. As measurement error, it is confounded with other unobserved but relevant information resident in the distributions for ε_j.

(3) *Socio-economic characteristics as proxies for unobserved attributes*. The sources of utility are strictly linked to the *attributes of alternatives*. It is common, however, for analysts to include descriptors of an individual or their contextual setting as explanatory variables in the V_j expression. Although this is quite acceptable, it must be realized that they are included as proxies for unobserved attributes of an alternative. Socio-economic and contextual characteristics *per se* are not sources of utility of an alternative. However, such descriptors can condition the role of unobserved attributes and so can be considered as influences on the parameter estimates of observed attributes. This is another way of explicitly accounting for preference differences as explained by specific characteristics.

(4) *The functional form of the attributes*. The inclusion of an attribute in V_j does not mean that it is represented appropriately. Should it be a *linear* indicator (i.e. travel time)? Maybe it should be a *non-linear* indicator (e.g. (travel time)^2 or a natural logarithm). It might also be *interacted* with another attribute (e.g. (travel time/cost)) or with a socio-economic descriptor (e.g. cost/income).

(5) *The functional form of the parameters*. It is common to treat the parameters associated with each attribute as *fixed*. These fixed values are average (or point) estimates representing a distribution. However, other information in the distribution is not considered. When we consider the full distribution of a parameter estimate the fixed parameter becomes a random parameter. The phrase "random parameter" simply indicates that each individual has an associated parameter estimate on the distribution, but the location for each individual is not known. Hence each person is randomly assigned a location, given the particular shape of the distribution. In addition, the true distribution is not known and so we select an analytical distribution such as normal, lognormal, uniform or triangular.

These five types of issues are central to the analyst's consideration of the specification of the utility expression associated with each alternative and the relationship between the choice alternatives. Any element of this set that is relevant to the decision maker that is excluded in the definition of V_j ends up in ε_j. The more (relevant) information that ends up in ε_j, the greater the chance that the profile of this unobserved information is not consistent with the IID/IIA condition. Violation of IID/IIA then becomes a real concern.

There are (at least) two main ways of accommodating this potential outcome. One can work harder to ensure the richness of information in V_j while retaining the MNL model, or one can consider a choice model that is less restrictive and which can allow for violation of IID/IIA simply by removing the need for this set of conditions. The former is always encouraged initially because it provides the best way of getting to know your data. We have found that the statistically significant influences found in an MNL model are often the influences that are retained as we relax the strong conditions of IID/IIA, and so this effort is far from wasted.

As an aside, we often advise analysts to devote a considerable amount of time to exploratory data analysis using MNL, typically over 50 percent of the allocated model estimation time.

13.2 Moving away from IID between all alternatives

The choice model that was first introduced to try and accommodate violations of IID/IIA became known as the *nested logit model*. It has also been referred to as hierarchical logit and tree extreme logit. What exactly does the nested logit model offer? In simple terms, nested logit recognizes the possibility that each alternative may have information in the unobserved influences of each alternative that has a role to play in determining a choice outcome that is different across the alternatives. This difference means that the variances might be different (i.e. specific alternatives do not have the same distributions for ε_j). Differences might also mean that the information content could be similar among subsets of alternatives and hence some amount of correlation might exist among pairs of alternatives (i.e. non-zero and varying covariances for pairs of alternatives).

A concrete example may help. Using the mode-choice setting of our data, let us assume that "comfort" is an important attribute but that it has not been measured. Its exclusion may be due to the difficulty of measuring comfort (it means many things to different people). Furthermore, it is likely that when we investigate the meaning of comfort in a little more detail we find that comfort has a similar meaning for bus and train compared to car travel. Already we have made a statement that indicates that the information in the ε_j associated with bus and train is possibly more similar than the information in the ε_j associated with car. If "comfort" was deemed to be the only unobserved information influencing the choice outcome, then we can safely suggest that the ε_js for bus and train are likely to be correlated to some degree (due to the common element of comfort) and even have a similar variance (possibly identical) for bus and train which is different to the variance of car. Another way of thinking about this is to assume we can separate out two components of comfort for bus and train; one part that is unique to bus and unique to train and another part that is common to them because they are both forms of public transport. Indeed, it is this *common element* that engenders the correlation.

Nested logit is a choice method specifically designed to recognize the possibility of different variances across the alternatives and some correlation among sub-sets of alternatives. The presence of these possibilities is equivalent to relaxing IID and IIA *to some extent*. We would only totally relax these conditions if we allowed all variances to be different (i.e. free) and all covariances to be different.

With this background, we are now ready to modify the MNL model to see what the nested logit model looks like. One useful point to make is that a nested logit model is really a set of linked MNL models. You will see what we mean soon. To ensure that the reader grasps the great potential advantage of a nested choice model, we must state that *the entire purpose in creating a nested form is to try and accommodate violation of IID/IIA. It has nothing to do with any behavioral belief in the way that alternatives are assessed in the process of making a choice*. This distinction is very important because many analysts think that nested choice models are a way of defining the decision process that links behavioral choices. Using the case study data set where we have six modes of transport within the SP component of the data, a decision maker may well treat the alternatives in a number of ways. For example, an individual may first choose between car and public transport, and then given a choice (e.g. car) may choose among driving alone and ride sharing. Alternatively an individual may choose between all modes simultaneously. The former imposes a hierarchy which introduces a grouping of the modes – car and public transport. Nesting thus creates a set of conditional choices and a set of marginal choices. The marginal choices are the first choice made (although as you will see below they are the last choice modelled). In our example, we have two conditional choices: the choice between bus, train, busway, or light rail conditional on choosing public transport, and the choice between car driven along a toll road and car driven along a non-tolled road conditional on choosing car. The remaining choice is between car and public transport (and since it is not conditional on any other choice as described here, it is a marginal choice).

13.3 Setting out the key relationships for establishing a nested logit model

We can write the set of conditional and marginal choices out in terms of the probability of choosing an alternative from a choice set. For example, the probability of choosing car driven along a tolled road is equal to the joint probability of choosing car (i.e. Prob(*car*)) and choosing car along a tolled road (Prob(*cart*|*car*)). Formally this is shown in (13.1):

$$\text{Prob}(cart) = \text{Prob}(car) \times \text{Prob}(cart\,|car) \tag{13.1}$$

In this example, it is rather clear that the two decisions are related. However, there are situations where two choices may or may not be related (i.e. they are interdependent or correlated to some extent). For example, the choice of workplace destination and commuter mode may both be related in the sense that the mode chosen is influenced by the location of the *destination* (e.g. train use is more common if someone works in the central business district). In this case, we might make mode conditional on destination or possibly destination conditional on mode. It may go either way (or, indeed, vary according to some other criterion or segment of travellers). Alternatively, it may be that choice of mode and destination are independent. Where two (or more) choices are independent then the joint probability is simply the product of the two (or more) marginal choice probabilities. We can set these alternative specifications out in (13.2)–(13.4).

As an aside, these choices can be either different decisions (e.g. choice of mode of transport and choice of destination) or a single decision that is partitioned as in choice of train and choice of public transport (where the former is a member of the latter). We call the alternatives that are not composites, *elemental alternatives* (i.e. *cart*, *carnt*, *bus*, *train*, *busway*, *light rail*). The alternatives that summarize or represent one or more elemental alternatives are called *composite alternatives*. This distinction is very important because, as a general rule, we should always place the attributes that are unique in level for an elemental alternative with the elemental alternative and not with the composite alternative. For example, the travel time for a bus and for a train should enter the utility expressions for bus and train, respectively, and not for public transport. To enter the utility expression for public transport would require some assumption about what value to include (e.g. average of bus and train travel times or some weighted formula). The latter makes little sense. However, characteristics of individuals or context that are not attributes of alternatives (e.g. income, age, car ownership) can be included in both the elemental and composite alternative utility expressions. We find increasingly that they fit well in the composite alternatives utility expression. In the context of mode choice for example, a person's income often has a greater influence on choosing between car and public transport than between public transport modes or between the car alternatives.

The structure that is of especial interest here is where choices may be interdependent:

$$\text{Prob}(mode(m)\ \&\ destination(d)) = \text{Prob}(mode) \times \text{Prob}(destination|mode) \quad (13.2)$$

$$\text{Prob}(mode(m)\ \&\ destination(d)) = \text{Prob}(destination) \times \text{Prob}(mode|destination) \quad (13.3)$$

$$\text{Prob}(mode(m)\ \&\ destination(d)) = \text{Prob}(mode) \times \text{Prob}(destination) \quad (13.4)$$

Equations (13.2) and (13.3) recognize interdependencies between choices. When this occurs, we have to find a way of taking this into account. To see what we might do, if we look at (13.4), we can see that the right-hand side is the product of two independent choices – *mode* and *destination*. Since each choice decision can be viewed as a MNL model, then to calculate this joint probability of mode and destination we need two MNL models. There is nothing else to do but to estimate a model along the lines set out in previous chapters.

However, when two decisions are *not independent* we have to rethink this strategy. Fortunately, research undertaken in the later 1970s and early 1980s laid the foundations for a way of handling interdependent choices that is intuitive as well as recognizing the usefulness of the MNL model as the starting position. Most importantly, it results in a choice model that has built into it a capability of checking to ensure that the resulting structure is locally and globally consistent with utility maximization behavior. This latter point is very important, since any choice model that cannot be shown to satisfy the conditions of the behavioral choice rule of decision makers is not, in our view, worth pursuing.

What we are about to introduce is a neat idea that tells us that interdependency is nothing more than a recognition that specific alternatives associated with one choice are influenced by specific alternatives associated with another choice (such as the use of the train mode if working in the city destination). Furthermore, since alternatives are essentially a packaging of bundles of attributes, then the interdependencies of alternatives results from the *interdependencies of attributes*, some of which are unobserved.

If we return to the example in (13.1) that relates to the case study data, we have six elemental alternatives (*cart*, *carnt*, *bus*, *train*, *busway*, and *light rail*) and two composite alternatives (*car* and *public transport*). Focusing on one part of the choice setting, namely public transport, we now know that the utility associated with public transport must stem from the utility associated with the elemental alternatives that it is "representing." But how does it take the information that matters to individuals choosing or not choosing a train or a bus and ensure it is useful in representing the role of public transport? If we just concentrate on the attributes of bus and train for the time being (and ignore the characteristics of individuals and other contextual influences), we might suggest that the utility associated with public transport as an alternative (in a higher choice between car and public transport) is really some weighted average of the utility associated with each of bus and train. This makes good sense. But what might these weights be? The appropriate answer is that the analyst's best information is really the probability of an individual choosing each of the bus and the train. Hence a choice probability weighted utility expression for the composite alternative called "public transport" makes good sense.

Another way of looking at this is to introduce the idea of *expected maximum utility*. What this suggests is that the probability of an individual choosing a public transport alternative is really driven by the assessment of the utility associated with each public transport mode (bus and train), but that this utility does not all reside within the set of observed attributes defining the V_j component of the utility expressions for bus and train. Because we are seeking the maximum utility in a setting in which some of relevant information used by the individual decision maker resides in the random component (ε_j), then our search for the highest level of utility involves some *expectation* as to what we can extract from the ε_j terms for each elemental alternative associated with the composite alternative. It is the use of the word "expectation" that results in us talking about identifying the expected maximum utility associated with the set of elemental alternatives as relevant information in deriving the utility associated with the composite alternative.

We can now state that the utility associated with a composite alternative that is not independent of an elemental alternative is the sum of two parts – the utility associated with public transport *per se* and the expected maximum utility associated with the alternatives that deliver the elemental attributes of each elemental alternative. If the utility of public transport had nothing to do with the utility of bus and train then the expected maximum utility would not be relevant. This is unlikely to be the case in this example; however in (13.2) and (13.3), where we have two different decisions (mode and destination), it is quite possible that the two choices are not related and so the expected maximum utility might be of no consequence. Indeed, when this occurs we end up with (13.4). An example might be

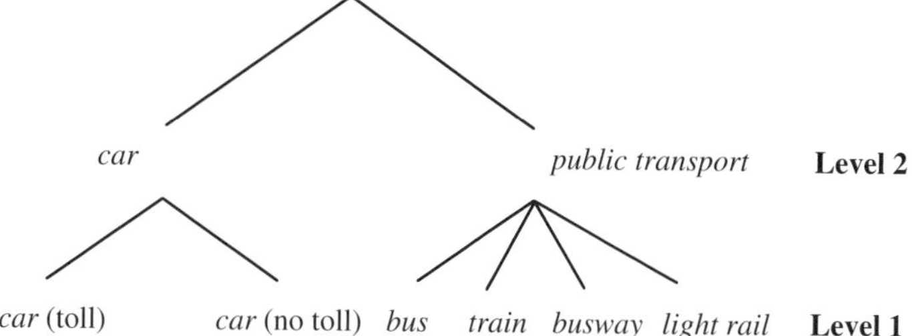

Figure 13.1 A tree diagram to recognize the (potential) linkages between choice sets

where the attributes of a destination determine which destination to visit and the attributes of the modes are irrelevant. Again, this example may fail the independence test. Maybe a more useful example is the choice of type of dwelling to live in and the mode used for the journey to work. Living in an apartment compared to a house may have little to do with whether you drive to work or use a train. But maybe there is a connection? For example, living in an apartment may mean that one has a lower income than someone living in a detached dwelling and hence one might use public transport for financial reasons. What we have here is not an attribute of the alternatives but an attribute of the *person* driving the link. If that is the case, then we should recognize this by including income in the utility expression for the elemental alternative. But, be warned, as indicated earlier, characteristics of people are really picking up unobserved attributes or they are acting as conditioning effects on the parameter estimates associated with observed attributes, accounting for difference sensitivities to an observed attribute in different socio-economic segments (such as in our example where high and low income might impact on the influence of travel cost).

We are now ready to use these ideas and write out a new form of the choice model, based on the MNL model. Using the formulation in (13.1), we can write out three choice models based on the following choice sets (CS):

CS1: car (with toll) vs car (not toll)
CS2: bus vs train vs busway vs light rail
CS3: car vs public transport

Think of these as three MNL models but recognize that the choice outcome associated with choice set 3 is influenced by the levels of utility associated with the elemental alternatives in CS1 and CS2. It is common to show this linkage with a tree diagram (figure 13.1).

The utility expressions for each elemental alternative can be written out as follows:

$$\begin{aligned} V_{cart} &= \beta_{0cart} + \beta_{1cart} f(X_{1cart}) + \beta_{2cart} f(X_{2cart}) \\ &\quad + \beta_{3cart} f(X_{3cart}) + \cdots + \beta_{Kcart} f(X_{Kcart}) \qquad (13.5) \\ V_{carnt} &= \beta_{0carnt} + \beta_{1carnt} f(X_{1carnt}) + \beta_{2carnt} f(X_{2carnt}) \\ &\quad + \beta_{3carnt} f(X_{3carnt}) + \cdots + \beta_{Kcarnt} f(X_{Kcarnt}) \qquad (13.6) \end{aligned}$$

$$\begin{aligned} V_{bs} &= \beta_{0bs} + \beta_{1bs} f(X_{1bs}) + \beta_{2bs} f(X_{2bs}) \\ &\quad + \beta_{3bs} f(X_{3bs}) + \cdots + \beta_{Kbs} f(X_{Kbs}) \end{aligned} \tag{13.7}$$

$$\begin{aligned} V_{tn} &= \beta_{0tn} + \beta_{1tn} f(X_{1tn}) + \beta_{2tn} f(X_{2tn}) \\ &\quad + \beta_{3tn} f(X_{3tn}) + \cdots + \beta_{Ktn} f(X_{Ktn}) \end{aligned} \tag{13.8}$$

$$\begin{aligned} V_{bsw} &= \beta_{0bsw} + \beta_{1bsw} f(X_{1bsw}) + \beta_{2bsw} f(X_{2bsw}) \\ &\quad + \beta_{3bsw} f(X_{3bsw}) + \cdots + \beta_{Kbsw} f(X_{Kbsw}) \end{aligned} \tag{13.9}$$

$$\begin{aligned} V_{lr} &= \beta_{1lr} f(X_{1lr}) + \beta_{2lr} f(X_{2lr}) + \beta_{3lr} f(X_{3lr}) \\ &\quad + \cdots + \beta_{Klr} f(X_{Klr}) \end{aligned} \tag{13.10}$$

where

cart = car (with toll), *carnt* = car (not toll), *bs* = bus, *tn* = train, *bsw* = busway, and *lr* = light rail

13.4 The importance of a behaviorally meaningful linkage mechanism between the branches on a nested structure

If we assume that the attributes of elemental alternatives that are linked to a composite alternative influence the choice between composite alternatives (a testable assumption), then we need to include this information in the utility expressions for each composite alternative. The linkage is achieved through an index of *expected maximum utility* (EMU). As discussed above, this information resides in the utility expressions associated with the elemental alternatives which are used to derive the MNL model by imposition of an IID condition for the unobserved influences.

Thus to establish the expected maximum utility we have to take the MNL form and search over the entire utility space in which the choice probabilities of each alternative is identified (i.e. for all values of V_j for all elemental alternatives associated with a composite alternative. This is equivalent to using integration within a 1, 0 bound with respect to changes in V_j. A formal derivation is given in Louviere, Hensher, and Swait 2000, 188). However, the final result of great importance for the beginner is that EMU is equal to the natural logarithm of the denominator of the MNL model associated with the elemental alternatives. The form is shown in (13.11) for the *bus* vs *train* vs *busway* vs *light rail* choice set:

$$\text{EMU (bus, train, busway, light rail)} = \log\{\exp V_{bs} + \exp V_{tn} + \exp V_{bsw} + \exp V_{lr}\} \tag{13.11}$$

A similar index exists for *car drive alone* and *car ride share*:

$$\text{EMU (cart, carnt)} = \log\{\exp V_{cart} + \exp V_{carnt}\} \tag{13.12}$$

These two indices are easily calculated once the MNL models are estimated for *train* vs *bus* and *car drive alone* vs *car ride share*. The next step is to recognize this as information relevant to the choice between public transport and car. This is achieved by including the EMU index in the utility expressions for the relevant composite alternative as just another explanatory variable, as shown in (13.13) and (13.14):

$$\begin{aligned} V_{car} &= \beta_{0car} + \beta_{1car} f(X_{1car}) + \beta_{2car} f(X_{2car}) \\ &\quad + \cdots + \beta_{Kcar} f(X_{Kcar}) + \beta_{K+1\ car} f(EMU_{K+1\ car}) \end{aligned} \tag{13.13}$$

$$\begin{aligned} V_{pt} &= \beta_{0pt} + \beta_{1pt} f(X_{1pt}) + \beta_{2pt} f(X_{2pt}) \\ &\quad + \cdots + \beta_{Kpt} f(X_{Kpt}) + \beta_{K+1\ pt} f(EMU_{K+1\ pt}) \end{aligned} \tag{13.14}$$

We now have an MNL model for the choice among composite alternatives which has one additional but crucial attribute in each of the utility expressions. When you read papers and books in choice modeling you will find that this EMU index is called by various names, most commonly as *inclusive value* (IV) and *logsum* but also *composite cost*. We will use IV from now on because it is the most common nomenclature and the one used in NLOGIT.

The parameter estimate of the IV index as the natural logarithm of the denominator of the MNL model at the elemental alternative level is the statistical test for the relevance of the interdependency.

As an aside, some nested models have more than two levels. When this occurs, the only level that has elemental alternatives is the bottom level (i.e. level 1). Thus we still refer to the IV as linking levels but the link between levels 2 and 3 involves an IV index based on a lower composite alternative (which itself is based on an even lower level where the elemental alternatives reside).

The numerical value of the parameter estimate for IV is the basis of establishing the extent of dependence or independence between the linked choices. To appreciate what we mean by this requires some careful explanation. Up to now we have suppressed a very important piece of information called the *scale parameter*. The reason why we have suppressed it thus far is because the MNL model has enabled us to essentially ignore it by the way we normalize the information in the variance–covariance matrix under IID, where the covariances are all zero and the variances are all the same (arbitrarily set to 1.0). However, when we want to relax the IID condition (to whatever degree) then we must make sure that we understand the information resident in the suppressed elements of the variance–covariance matrix. There are a number of underlying parameters (sometimes called "deep parameters" because they are largely hidden in simple models but become essential to identify in less restrictive models).

13.5 The scale parameter

To appreciate the importance of the scale parameter we have to formally define the variance of the unobserved effects. We will stay with the variance for the extreme value type 1 distribution which applies to the MNL model. A step-by-step derivation in Louviere,

Hensher, and Swait (2000, 142–3) shows that the variance is defined as (13.15):

$$\sigma^2 = \frac{\pi^2}{6\lambda^2} \tag{13.15}$$

where pi-squared (π^2) is a constant (equal to 3.14159^2), and lambda (λ) is an unknown, the latter referred to as the scale parameter. The scale parameter (squared) is what essentially describes the profile of the variance of the unobserved effects associated with an alternative. We often state that *the variance is an inverse function of the scale*. In the MNL model, where all variances are constant (identically distributed), we arbitrarily set all variances equal to 1.0 and hence we need not worry about the different scale parameters between alternatives. That is, the scale parameters for each alternative underlying the MNL model are set equal to 1.283.[1] When the scale parameters are allowed to vary due to the possibility of differential variances then we have to write out the choice model in a slightly different way. It is common to write out the MNL form as a starting point, in which we explicitly introduce the scale parameter (λ). When we relax to the constant variance assumption, λ subscripted to each alternative (i.e. λ_j) becomes an additional multiplicand of each attribute influencing choice, as shown in (13.16). Note that λ *is strictly inversely proportional to the standard deviation* rather than the variance:

$$V_j = \lambda_j \beta_{0j} + \lambda_j \beta_{1j} f(X_{1j}) + \cdots + \lambda_j \beta_{Kj} f(X_{Kj}) \tag{13.16}$$

Another way that (13.16) is often expressed is shown in (13.17), in which λ_j is moved to the left-hand side:

$$V_j / \lambda_j = \beta_{0j} + \beta_{1j} f(X_{1j}) + \cdots + \beta_{Kj} f(X_{Kj}) \tag{13.17}$$

Equations (13.16) and (13.17) do not include the IV index and its parameterization. Again, some messy manipulations are required to show the relationship between the parameter for IV and the scale parameter. Because we are dealing with more than one utility expression we have to be very careful indeed. First, we have to take into account the scale parameters associated with the elemental alternatives at level 1. Secondly, we have to take into account the scale parameter for the utility expression of the composite alternative at level 2. In our example, we have potentially five scale parameters for the IV of public transport (i.e. scale parameters for *bus*, *train*, *busway*, *light rail*, and *public transport*).

Fortunately, we can do some simplification. Given that the choice between *bus*, *train*, *busway*, and *light rail* is specified as MNL, we can impose the constant variance assumption for *bus*, *train*, *busway*, and *light rail* and so collapse four scale parameters into one scale parameter (i.e. the scale parameter as the inverse of the constant standard deviation). But we

[1] Rearranging (13.15), the scale parameter is equal to

$$\lambda = \sqrt{\frac{\pi^2}{6\sigma^2}}$$

Setting the variance to one (i.e. σ^2), $\lambda = 1.283$.

still have two scale parameters – one for level 1 and one for level 2. Showing the relationship between these two scale parameters is equivalent to showing the relationship between the two standard deviations and how this information impacts on the estimation parameter for the inclusive value index in level 2. The big breakthrough came when a number of researchers independently showed that the parameter of IV at level 2 is the ratio of the scale parameter at level 2 to the scale parameter at level 1. The literature often cites the Daly–Zachary–Williams proof after the major authors, although some credit this to Moshe Ben-Akiva and Steve Lerman. We will not venture into the debate as to who chronologically delivered the first proof but it has been contentious. With this breakthrough, we can write out the utility expression for a level 2 composite alternative as (13.18):

$$V_{pt} = \beta_{0pt} + \beta_{1pt} f(X_{1pt}) + \beta_{2pt} f(X_{2pt}) + \cdots + \beta_{Kpt} f(X_{Kpt}) + (\lambda_{pt}/\lambda_m) IV_{K+1pt} \tag{13.18}$$

where λ_m = the scale parameter associated with the *bus*, *train*, *busway*, and *light rail* modes (m). This is real progress, but unfortunately we cannot identify this model without imposing an additional restriction. This restriction is also very convenient. We can usefully assume that one of the λs can be normalized (i.e. fixed) at a specific value, typically 1.0.[2] Which one, however, is a really interesting question since it does influence the outcome (and especially the extent) to which we can ensure that our nested model satisfies the necessary and sufficient conditions for utility maximization. A number of researchers (notably, Koppelman, Wen, Hensher, Greene, and Hunt) have debated this issue in the period 1999–2001 (see Louviere, Hensher, and Swait 2000, 164–175) and have proposed two specifications – one in which the normalization is at level 1 or the lowest level of the tree (called RU1 in NLOGIT for Random Utility Model Specification 1) and the other in which the normalization is at level 2 or the top level of the tree (called RU2 in NLOGIT).[3] For the time being we will normalize level 1 leaving level 2 free to be estimated. This is shown in (13.19). The test for differences in scale between the levels is the extent to which the scale parameters of levels 1 and 2 are statistically different. Since we have already normalized the level 1 scale to 1.0, then the two scale parameters would be identical if the parameter estimate of IV equals 1.0:

$$V_{pt} = \beta_{0pt} + \beta_{1pt} f(X_{1pt}) + \beta_{2pt} f(X_{2pt}) + \cdots + \beta_{Kpt} f(X_{Kpt}) + \lambda_{pt} IV_{K+1pt} \tag{13.19}$$

Importantly, the behavioral implication of this is that if the parameter estimate of IV is equal to 1.0 then the level-2 variance equals the level-1 variance. Thus, what we have is recognition that the constant variance assumption is valid and so we can collapse the choice model into one level. There is no need for a nested model.

[2] In normalizing this scale parameter to 1.0, the associated variance becomes 1.645 and not 1.0 (see (13.15)).

[3] Normalization using RU2 is preferred to RU1 in the sense that RU2 guarantees that the model under any specification of all of the model's parameters (i.e. whether generic or alternative-specific) will be consistent with global utility maximization under random utility theory without having to introduce a dummy node level below level 1. See Hensher and Greene (2002) for more details.

As an aside, it is often unclear in software packages as to whether the resulting parameter estimate for an inclusive value is the standard deviation or the scale. Be careful, for obvious reasons. NLOGIT provides the scale parameter directly

$$\text{i.e.} \quad \lambda = \frac{\pi}{\sigma\sqrt{6}}$$

and hence the standard deviation would be (from (13.15))

$$\sigma = \frac{\pi}{\lambda\sqrt{6}}$$

We now have the essential concepts needed to understand the reasoning behind the use of a nested logit structure. What we have not yet discussed in sufficient detail is the process of inquiry leading up to the selection of a "preferred" tree structure. This is by no means a straightforward exercise. The most important rule that is used to establish the preferred tree structure only establishes the set of trees that are compliant with the underlying behavioral assumption of global utility maximization. There are many tree structures that satisfy the global utility maximization rule.

13.6 Bounded range for the IV parameter

To satisfy this rule, the parameter estimate associated with each and every IV variable must lie within the 0–1 range. Any value outside of this range has a particular behavioral implication that is not acceptable. We need to explain this in some detail because it is one of the most commonly asked questions: *why must it lie in the 0–1 band?* We will start with the ratio of the two parameters – λ_{pt}/λ_m from (13.18). Let us write out the full set of choice probabilities for a two-level nested logit model in the mode choice context:

$$\begin{aligned} \text{Prob}_{car} &= \text{Prob}\,\{[U_{car} + \max(U_{cart\,|car} + U_{carnt\,|car})] \\ &\quad > [U_{PT} + \max(U_{bs\,|PT} + U_{tn\,|PT} + U_{bsw\,|PT} + U_{lr\,|PT})]\} \end{aligned} \tag{13.20}$$

$$\text{Prob}_{cart} = \text{Prob}\,[U_{cart\,|car} > U_{carnt\,|car}] \tag{13.21}$$

$$\text{Prob}_{carnt} = \text{Prob}\,[U_{carnt\,|car} > U_{cart\,|car}] \tag{13.22}$$

$$\text{Prob}_{bs} = \text{Prob}\,[U_{bs\,|PT} > U_{\{pt1\}|PT}] \tag{13.23}$$

$$\text{Prob}_{tn} = \text{Prob}\,[U_{tn\,|PT} > U_{\{pt2\}|PT}] \tag{13.24}$$

$$\text{Prob}_{bsw} = \text{Prob}\,[U_{bsw\,|PT} > U_{\{pt3\}|PT}] \tag{13.25}$$

$$\text{Prob}_{lr} = \text{Prob}\,[U_{lr\,|PT} > U_{\{pt4\}|PT}] \tag{13.26}$$

where

$\{pt1\}$ is the set of all *PT* utilities not including U_{bs}; $\{pt2\}$ is the set of all *PT* utilities not including U_{tn},$\{pt3\}$ is the set of all *PT* utilities not including U_{bsw}; and $\{pt4\}$ is the set of all *PT* utilities not including U_{lr}.

And,

$$\max(U_{cart|car} + U_{carnt|car}) = \mathrm{E}\{\max(V_{cart|car} + V_{carnt|car})\} + [\varepsilon_{cart|car} + \varepsilon_{carnt|car}] \tag{13.27}$$

$$\max(U_{bs|PT} + U_{tn|PT} + U_{bsw|PT} + U_{lr|PT}) = \mathrm{E}\{\max(V_{bs|PT} + V_{tn|PT} + V_{bsw|PT} + V_{lr|PT})\} + [\varepsilon_{bs|PT} + \varepsilon_{tn|PT} + \varepsilon_{bsw|PT} + \varepsilon_{lr|PT}] \tag{13.28}$$

where

$\max(V_{cart\,|car} + V_{carnt\,|car})$ is the IV (IV_{car}) for the composite alternative "car" and $\max(U_{bs\,|PT} + U_{tn|\,|PT} + U_{bsw\,|PT} + U_{lr\,|PT})$ is the IV (IV_{PT}) for the composite alternative "public transport."

We can define also the assumptions associated with the random component of each of the six utility expressions:

$$\begin{aligned}
\mathrm{E}(\varepsilon_{car}) &= 0,\ \mathrm{var}(\varepsilon_{car}) = \sigma^2_{car},\ \mathrm{E}(\varepsilon_{PT}) = 0,\ \mathrm{var}(\varepsilon_{PT}) = \sigma^2_{PT}\\
\mathrm{E}[\varepsilon_{cart\,|car} + \varepsilon_{carnt\,|car}] &= 0,\ \mathrm{var}[\varepsilon_{cart|car} + \varepsilon_{carnt\,|car}] = \sigma^2_{cart\,|car} + \sigma^2_{carnt\,|car}\\
\mathrm{E}(\varepsilon_{cart\,|car}) &= 0,\ \mathrm{E}(\varepsilon_{carnt\,|car}) = 0,\ \mathrm{E}(\varepsilon_{bs\,|PT}) = 0,\\
\mathrm{E}(\varepsilon_{tn\,|PT}) &= 0,\ \mathrm{E}(\varepsilon_{bsw\,|PT}) = 0,\ \mathrm{E}(\varepsilon_{lr\,|PT}) = 0\\
\mathrm{var}(\varepsilon_{cart\,|car}) &= \sigma^2_{cart\,|car},\ \mathrm{var}(\varepsilon_{carnt\,|car}) = \sigma^2_{carnt\,|car},\\
\mathrm{var}(\varepsilon_{bs\,|PT}) &= \sigma^2_{bs\,|PT},\ \mathrm{var}(\varepsilon_{tn\,|PT}) = \sigma^2_{tn|PT},\ \mathrm{var}(\varepsilon_{bsw|PT})\\
&= \sigma^2_{bsw\,|PT},\ \mathrm{var}(\varepsilon_{lr\,|PT}) = \sigma^2_{lr\,|PT}
\end{aligned}$$

where

$\mathrm{E}(\varepsilon_{car})$ is the expected or mean error term for car and var (ε_{car}) is the variance for car.

We show this in (13.29), the variance–covariance matrix:

$$\begin{bmatrix}
\sigma^2_{cart|car} & 0 & 0 & 0 & 0 & 0 & 0 & 0\\
0 & \sigma^2_{carnt|car} & 0 & 0 & 0 & 0 & 0 & 0\\
0 & 0 & \sigma^2_{bs|PT} & 0 & 0 & 0 & 0 & 0\\
0 & 0 & 0 & \sigma^2_{tn|PT} & 0 & 0 & 0 & 0\\
0 & 0 & 0 & 0 & \sigma^2_{bsw|PT} & 0 & 0 & 0\\
0 & 0 & 0 & 0 & 0 & \sigma^2_{lr|PT} & 0 & 0\\
0 & 0 & 0 & 0 & 0 & 0 & \sigma^2_{car} & 0\\
0 & 0 & 0 & 0 & 0 & 0 & 0 & \sigma^2_{PT}
\end{bmatrix} \tag{13.29}$$

There are two branches in the nested structure for this example – the CAR branch and the PUBLIC TRANSPORT branch. Let us also define the total sources of variance associated with each branch of the nested structure as follows:

$$\sigma_{car}^{2*} = \sigma_{car}^2 + \left(\sigma_{cart\,|car}^2 + \sigma_{carnt|car}^2\right)$$

(we can add up variances because the elemental alternatives are independent).

$$\sigma_{PT}^{2*} = \sigma_{PT}^2 + \left(\sigma_{bs\,|PT}^2 + \sigma_{tn|PT}^2 + \sigma_{bsw\,|PT}^2 + \sigma_{lr\,|PT}^2\right)$$

Since we are interested in the variances (or standard deviations or scale parameters) at the upper level of the tree, we can re-arrange the variances as follows:

$$\sigma_{car}^2 = \sigma_{car}^{2*} - \left(\sigma_{cart\,|car}^2 + \sigma_{carnt\,|car}^2\right) \text{ and}$$
$$\sigma_{PT}^2 = \sigma_{PT}^{2*} - \left(\sigma_{bs\,|PT}^2 + \sigma_{tn\,|PT}^2 + \sigma_{bsw\,|PT}^2 + \sigma_{lr\,|PT}^2\right)$$

We can now replace the variance with the formula in (13.15):

$$\sigma_{car}^2 = \frac{\pi^2}{6\,\lambda_{car}^2} - \left(\frac{\pi^2}{6\,\lambda_{cart\,|car}^2} + \frac{\pi^2}{6\,\lambda_{carnt\,|car}^2}\right) \tag{13.30}$$

$$\sigma_{PT}^2 = \frac{\pi^2}{6\,\lambda_{PT}^2} - \left(\frac{\pi^2}{6\,\lambda_{bs\,|PT}^2} + \frac{\pi^2}{6\,\lambda_{tn|PT}^2} + \frac{\pi^2}{6\,\lambda_{bsw\,|PT}^2} + \frac{\pi^2}{6\,\lambda_{lr|PT}^2}\right) \tag{13.31}$$

By definition, a variance must be positive, hence all λs must also be greater than zero.[4] We should also note that the scale parameter associated with the elemental alternatives within a branch (e.g. $\sigma_{cart\,|car}^2 = \sigma_{carnt\,|car}^2 = \sigma_{**|car}^2$; $\sigma_{bs\,|PT}^2 = \sigma_{tn\,|PT}^2 = \sigma_{bsw\,|PT}^2 = \sigma_{lr\,|PT}^2 = \sigma_{..|PT}^2$) are identical and so we can from now on refer to a single lower-level scale parameter for each branch. This requires that $\lambda_{car}^2 \leq \lambda_{**|car}^2$ must hold otherwise σ_{car}^2 would be less than zero. Furthermore, for λ_{car}^2 and $\lambda_{**|car}^2$ to be defined values, each must be greater than zero.

Since $\lambda_{car}^2 \leq \lambda_{**|car}^2$, then

$$0 < \frac{\lambda_{car}^2}{\lambda_{**|car}^2} \leq 1 \tag{13.32}$$

We can express this in terms of the scale parameter (instead of the scale parameter squared):

$$0 < \frac{\lambda_{car}}{\lambda_{**|car}} \leq 1 \tag{13.33}$$

A useful way to think about this is to recognize that there is more variance in the upper level than in the lower level simply because the upper level(s) include the accumulated sources from lower levels. Since the scale parameters (λs) are inversely proportional to

[4] Statistical packages such as NLOGIT do not estimate the variances directly. Rather, such packages estimate a parameter that in theory has links to variance (the IV parameters are estimated as the coefficients that multiply the logsums in probability models such as the NL model). Numerically, these may have either a positive or negative sign and be of any magnitude. It is therefore theoretically possible for the analyst to observe a negative variance. Such cases are only likely to occur given an extremely bad model specification.

the variance then the scale parameter at the upper level must be lower than at a lower level. *That is, the scale parameter must decline in value as we move up a nested tree structure*. This is why the ratio of the λs in (13.33) has to be less than (or equal to) 1.0. However, if the two scale parameters had identical magnitude (the limiting case where all variances are the same either by assumption or by empirical evidence) then the ratio would equal 1.0. We now know that this is the assumption of a MNL model (i.e. constant variance) and so any nested logit model in which the ratio of the λs is equal to 1.0 (or not statistically significantly different from 1.0) collapses into a single level MNL model. Since we normalize on either the upper- or lower-level scale parameter (as discussed above) then any vale of the unconstrained λ would be judged against 1.0 for deviations from MNL.

As an aside, in normalizing an IV parameter, we are in fact treating that parameter as fixed. This suggests that the normalized parameter is not free to vary, and as such the variance for this parameter will be equal to zero. Thus, assuming that the *car* IV parameter is normalized to 1.0, the variance–covariance matrix of (13.29) becomes:

$$\begin{bmatrix} \begin{bmatrix} \sigma^2_{cart|car} & 0 \\ 0 & \sigma^2_{carnt|car} \end{bmatrix} & \begin{matrix} 0 & 0 & 0 & 0 \\ 0 & 0 & 0 & 0 \end{matrix} & \begin{matrix} 0 & 0 \\ 0 & 0 \end{matrix} \\ \begin{matrix} 0 & 0 \\ 0 & 0 \\ 0 & 0 \\ 0 & 0 \end{matrix} & \begin{bmatrix} \sigma^2_{bs|PT} & 0 & 0 & 0 \\ 0 & \sigma^2_{tn|PT} & 0 & 0 \\ 0 & 0 & \sigma^2_{bsw|PT} & 0 \\ 0 & 0 & 0 & \sigma^2_{lr|PT} \end{bmatrix} & \begin{matrix} 0 & 0 \\ 0 & 0 \\ 0 & 0 \\ 0 & 0 \end{matrix} \\ \begin{matrix} 0 & 0 \\ 0 & 0 \end{matrix} & \begin{matrix} 0 & 0 & 0 & 0 \\ 0 & 0 & 0 & 0 \end{matrix} & \begin{matrix} 0 & 0 \\ 0 & \sigma^2_{PT} \end{matrix} \end{bmatrix} \tag{13.34}$$

We have talked about the meaning of the upper limit 1.0, but what about the lower limit of zero, and what if we have a ratio that exceeds 1.0? What does this mean?

1. If the ratio is greater than 1.0, then we would find that an increase in the utility associated with a specific elemental alternative (e.g. car driven on a toll road) would lead to an increase in the probability of choosing the non-car composite alternative (e.g. public transport). This does not make sense under the global utility maximization assumption, and is equivalent to producing a cross-elasticity with the wrong sign.
2. When the ratio is equal to 0 we have two totally independent choice models for the upper and lower levels. Thus there is no need for a nested model. Sometimes this is called the "degenerate outcome."
3. When the ratio is equal to 1.0, we have equal cross-elasticities between an alternative and each of the other alternatives. Since this result is associated with the ratio that gives us the MNL form, we can now state that an MNL model always produces equal cross-elasticities between a specific alternative and each of the other alternatives. Nested logit models, however, allow for different cross-elasticities but only where one is using alternatives that are not in the same partition. The reason is hopefully obvious – four alternatives in the same partition (e.g. *bus*, *train*, *busway*, and *light rail*) are subject to the MNL assumption whereas two alternatives across partitions (e.g. *train* and *car driven along a non-tolled road*) are not subject to the MNL assumption.

In appendix 13A we provide the full technical details for a nested logit model with four levels, under the two normalizing strategies, RU1 and RU2. Appendix 13A is complex and may be left unread by the beginner without any loss of continuity with the remaining chapters.

13.7 Searching for the "best" tree structure

We now know that a nested structure that is consistent with the necessary conditions for global utility maximization must satisfy the 0–1 bound for the scale parameter and that the scale parameter should decline in value as we move up the tree (conversely the standard deviation of the random component associated with the alternatives should increase as we move up the tree). An analyst may estimate a number of tree structures and find that some of them satisfy these conditions. In deciding which of the evaluated set of tree structures is best in a statistical sense that has passed the behavioral test of compliance, we can use the overall goodness-of-fit measure (the log likelihood at convergence). This is the same exact test discussed in chapter 10 where the likelihood-ratio test is used to compare the log likelihood at convergence of two models (where the difference in degrees of freedom is the difference in the number of unique parameter estimates for each model). While this will guide the analyst in selecting the preferred model, it does not ensure that the "best" model has been identified. There may be a tree structure that is the best relative to all other trees that has been entirely ignored.

Establishing eligible trees that produce the "best" tree in terms of compliance with global utility maximization and lowest log likelihood involves investigating a large number of potential candidate trees. Although behavioral intuition can be invaluable, we now know that trees are selected in order to accommodate differences in variance or scale that exists in the unobserved components of the utility expressions. A way forward that we have found very useful as a search strategy is to use a specification of nested logit in which each branch has only one alternative. We call this degenerate nested logit (or NL-DG). In earlier publications we promoted the use of the Heteroskedastic Extreme Value (HEV) model as a search tool, but now prefer NL-DG because of the frequent difficulty of estimating HEV models that converge.[5] Each branch in the NL-DG has its own scale parameter (or equivalently standard deviation parameter) enabling the analyst to group alternatives into branches that appear most likely to have similar variances associated with the unobserved

[5] Hensher (1999) proposed HEV as a search strategy for the most likely preferred tree structure. This model is explained in detail in Louviere, Hensher, and Swait (2000, 189–194). It is a discrete choice model that adopts the EV1 assumption for each alternative but allows the variance to be totally free for each alternative (except for one alternative which is normalized to 1.0 for purposes of identification). It does not matter which alternative is normalized (although NLOGIT 3.0 normalize the last-named alternative in the list of choice alternatives). What the analyst does is to estimate an HEV model to reveal all of the variances (and scale parameters) and to use the findings to co-locate one or more alternatives to the same branch in a nested structure. Some amount of flexibility is required in the allocation since the scale parameter values may be spread quite a lot across the alternatives. For example, we may have the following scale parameters for *cart*, *carnt*, *bs*, *tn*, *bsw*, and *lr*: 1.5, 0.3, 1.2, 0.8, 0.6, and 1.6. Our view is that one might structure the tree by grouping *cart*, *carnt*, and *bs* and *lr* together, grouping *tn* and *bsw* together, and treating *carnt* as a separate branch with only one alternative.

influences. We illustrate this in chapter 14. We have found to our great delight (as have others we have advised) that using NL-DG as a search engine is very effective. It does, however, often reveal trees that would not normally be in an analyst's intuitive set. This again reminds one of the purpose of nesting.

As an aside, the HEV model reveals *differences in variance*, whereas the nested logit model also accounts for correlation among alternatives within a branch. This may appear to be legitimate grounds for rejecting the HEV model as a search engine for nested logit structures in preference for NL-DG. However, where the HEV model has converged, the empirical evidence suggests it still very useful despite the absence of correlation. It also may suggest that most of the richness delivered by nested logit is in the partitioning to reveal differential variances. We encourage the use of both NL-DG and HEV to search for appropriate nested structures.

We are now well positioned to estimate nested logit models in chapter 14 and to interpret the suite of new measures that enable us to determine if there are real behavioral gains in moving from MNL to NL.

Appendix 13: Technical details of the Nested Logit Model

For each trunk, limb, branch and elemental alternative of an NL model, there will exist a specific scale parameter. Using the notation recommended by Louviere et al., (2000), we represent these as follows.

Trunk: $\tau_{(l)}$
Limb: $\gamma_{(i,l)}$
Branch: $\lambda_{(j|i,l)}$
Elemental Alternative: $\mu_{(j|i,l,k)}$

Where

$\tau_{(l)}$ (pronounced tau) is the scale parameter for the lth trunk, $\gamma_{(i,l)}$ (pronounced gamma) is the scale parameter for the ith limb of trunk l, $\lambda_{(j|i,l)}$ (pronounced lambda) is the scale parameter for the jth branch of limb i of trunk l and $\mu_{(j|i,l,k)}$ (pronounced mu) is the scale parameter for the kth elemental alternative of branch j of limb i of trunk l.

Given that the variances of each elemental alternative present within branch j are equal, by implication the scale parameters must also be equal for each alternative present within any given branch. As such, the subscript notation k is redundant and hence we may represent the scale parameters for the elemental alternatives simply as:

Elemental Alternative: $\mu_{(j|i,l)}$

For all NL models there will also exist for each trunk, limb and branch specified as part of the tree structure, both an inclusive value variable (IV_V) and an inclusive value parameter (IV_P). Each IV_V is calculated as the natural logarithm of the sum of the exponentials of the utility expressions for the level directly below which the IV_V is calculated. Given that

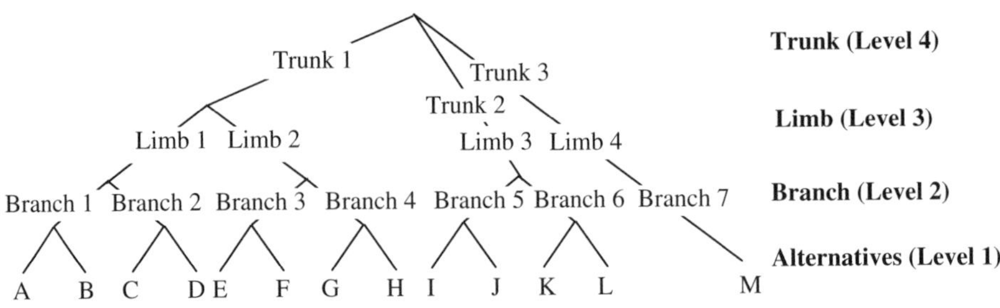

Figure 13A.1 A 4 Level NL tree structure

all utility expressions of an NL model are a function not only of the attributes and SDC as entered by the analyst, but also of the scale parameters, each IV_V will also be inclusive of the scale parameters of levels partitioned directly below the level for which the IV_V is estimated for. Indeed, the lower level scale parameters enter the IV_V via the IV_P which is the ratio of scale parameter associated with the level of for which the IV_V is being calculated for to the scale parameter of the levels directly below. For example, the IV_P for branch j is calculated as the ratio of the scale parameter for branch j to the scale parameter of the elemental alternatives partitioned within branch j, as shown in equation (13A.1).

$$\frac{\lambda_{(j|i,l)}}{\mu_{(j|i,l)}} \tag{13A.1}$$

Unfortunately, the NL model as described is overidentified (i.e., we are attempting to estimate too many variables with not enough information). For this reason, it is necessary to normalize at least one of the scale parameters to one in order to estimate the other. As we discuss in Chapter 13, the level at which we normalize the scale parameter has implications as to the system of equations that we employ in calculating the utility levels and probabilities at each level of the model as well as the necessary conditions required in order to remain consistent with the global utility maximization assumption.

To demonstrate, consider an NL with the following tree partitioning structure. We set out the probability choice system (PCS) for this tree under the situation whereby (1) we normalize on $\mu_{(j|i,l,k)}$, called random utility model 1 (RU1) and (2) we normalize on $\lambda_{(j|i,l)}$, called random utility model 2 (RU2).

Level 1 (Elemental alternative)

At the lowest level of the NL tree (i.e., at the level of the elemental alternatives), the utility functions for the above tree structure may be expressed as shown below.

$$V_A = \mu_1\beta_{1A}f(X_{1A}) + \mu_1\beta_{2A}f(X_{2A}) + \mu_1\beta_{3A}f(X_{3A}) + \ldots + \mu_1\beta_{KA}f(X_{KA})$$
$$V_B = \mu_2\beta_{0A} + \mu_2\beta_{1B}f(X_{1B}) + \mu_2\beta_{2B}f(X_{2B}) + \mu_2\beta_{3B}f(X_{3B}) + \ldots + \mu_2\beta_{KB}f(X_{KB})$$
$$V_C = \mu_3\beta_{0C} + \mu_3\beta_{1C}f(X_{1C}) + \mu_3\beta_{2C}f(X_{2C}) + \mu_3\beta_{3C}f(X_{3C}) + \ldots + \mu_3\beta_{KC}f(X_{KC})$$

$$\begin{aligned}
V_D &= \mu_4\beta_{0D} + \mu_4\beta_{1D}f(X_{1D}) + \mu_4\beta_{2D}f(X_{2D}) + \mu_4\beta_{3D}f(X_{3D}) \\
&\quad + \ldots. + \mu_4\beta_{KD}f(X_{KD}) \\
V_E &= \mu_5\beta_{0E} + \mu_5\beta_{1E}f(X_{1E}) + \mu_5\beta_{2E}f(X_{2E}) + \mu_5\beta_{3E}f(X_{3E}) + \ldots. + \mu_5\beta_{KE}f(X_{KE}) \\
V_F &= \mu_6\beta_{0F} + \mu_6\beta_{1F}f(X_{1F}) + \mu_6\beta_{2F}f(X_{2F}) + \mu_6\beta_{3F}f(X_{3F}) + \ldots. + \mu_6\beta_{KF}f(X_{KF}) \\
V_G &= \mu_7\beta_{0G} + \mu_7\beta_{1G}f(X_{1G}) + \mu_7\beta_{2G}f(X_{2G}) + \mu_7\beta_{3G}f(X_{3G}) + \ldots. + \mu_7\beta_{KG}f(X_{KG}) \\
V_H &= \mu_8\beta_{0H} + \mu_8\beta_{1H}f(X_{1H}) + \mu_8\beta_{2H}f(X_{2H}) + \mu_8\beta_{3H}f(X_{3H}) + \ldots. + \mu_8\beta_{KH}f(X_{KH}) \\
V_I &= \mu_9\beta_{0I} + \mu_9\beta_{1I}f(X_{1I}) + \mu_9\beta_{2I}f(X_{2I}) + \mu_9\beta_{3I}f(X_{3I}) + \ldots. + \mu_9\beta_{KI}f(X_{KI}) \\
V_J &= \mu_{10}\beta_{0J} + \mu_{10}\beta_{1J}f(X_{1J}) + \mu_{10}\beta_{2J}f(X_{2J}) + \mu_{10}\beta_{3J}f(X_{3J}) + \ldots. + \mu_{10}\beta_{KJ}f(X_{KJ}) \\
V_K &= \mu_{11}\beta_{0K} + \mu_{11}\beta_{1K}f(X_{1K}) + \mu_{11}\beta_{2K}f(X_{2K}) + \mu_{11}\beta_{3K}f(X_{3K}) \\
&\quad + \ldots. + \mu_{11}\beta_{KK}f(X_{KK}) \\
V_L &= \mu_{12}\beta_{0L} + \mu_{12}\beta_{1L}f(X_{1L}) + \mu_{12}\beta_{2L}f(X_{2L}) + \mu_{12}\beta_{3L}f(X_{3L}) + \ldots. + \mu_{12}\beta_{KL}f(X_{KL}) \\
V_M &= \mu_{13}\beta_{0M} + \mu_{13}\beta_{1M}f(X_{1M}) + \mu_{13}\beta_{2M}f(X_{2M}) + \mu_{13}\beta_{3M}f(X_{3M}) \\
&\quad + \ldots. + \mu_{13}\beta_{KM}f(X_{KM})
\end{aligned}$$

RU1 (normalize $\mu_{(j|i,l)} = 1$)

Normalizing on the scale parameters at the level of the elemental alternatives gives:

$$\mu_1 = \mu_2 = \mu_3 = \mu_4 = \mu_5 = \mu_6 = \mu_7 = \mu_8 = \mu_9 = \mu_{10} = \mu_{11} = \mu_{12} = \mu_{13} = 1$$

The utility functions under RU1 therefore become:

$$\begin{aligned}
V_A &= \beta_{1A}f(X_{1A}) + \beta_{2A}f(X_{2A}) + \beta_{3A}f(X_{3A}) + \ldots. + \beta_{KA}f(X_{KA}) \\
V_B &= \beta_{0B} + \beta_{1B}f(X_{1B}) + \beta_{2B}f(X_{2B}) + \beta_{3B}f(X_{3B}) + \ldots. + \beta_{KB}f(X_{KB}) \\
V_C &= \beta_{0C} + \beta_{1C}f(X_{1C}) + \beta_{2C}f(X_{2C}) + \beta_{3C}f(X_{3C}) + \ldots. + \beta_{KC}f(X_{KC}) \\
V_D &= \beta_{0D} + \beta_{1D}f(X_{1D}) + \beta_{2D}f(X_{2D}) + \beta_{3D}f(X_{3D}) + \ldots. + \beta_{KD}f(X_{KD}) \\
V_E &= \beta_{0E} + \beta_{1E}f(X_{1E}) + \beta_{2E}f(X_{2E}) + \beta_{3E}f(X_{3E}) + \ldots. + \beta_{KE}f(X_{KE}) \\
V_F &= \beta_{0F} + \beta_{1F}f(X_{1F}) + \beta_{2F}f(X_{2F}) + \beta_{3F}f(X_{3F}) + \ldots. + \beta_{KF}f(X_{KF}) \\
V_G &= \beta_{0G} + \beta_{1G}f(X_{1G}) + \beta_{2G}f(X_{2G}) + \beta_{3G}f(X_{3G}) + \ldots. + \beta_{KG}f(X_{KG}) \\
V_H &= \beta_{0H} + \beta_{1H}f(X_{1H}) + \beta_{2H}f(X_{2H}) + \beta_{3H}f(X_{3H}) + \ldots. + \beta_{KH}f(X_{KH}) \\
V_I &= \beta_{0I} + \beta_{1I}f(X_{1I}) + \beta_{2I}f(X_{2I}) + \beta_{3I}f(X_{3I}) + \ldots. + \beta_{KI}f(X_{KI}) \\
V_J &= \beta_{0J} + \beta_{1J}f(X_{1J}) + \beta_{2J}f(X_{2J}) + \beta_{3J}f(X_{3J}) + \ldots. + \beta_{KJ}f(X_{KJ}) \\
V_K &= \beta_{0K} + \beta_{1K}f(X_{1K}) + \beta_{2K}f(X_{2K}) + \beta_{3K}f(X_{3K}) + \ldots. + \beta_{KK}f(X_{KK}) \\
V_L &= \beta_{0L} + \beta_{1L}f(X_{1L}) + \beta_{2L}f(X_{2L}) + \beta_{3L}f(X_{3L}) + \ldots. + \beta_{KL}f(X_{KL}) \\
V_M &= \beta_{0M} + \beta_{1M}f(X_{1M}) + \beta_{2M}f(X_{2M}) + \beta_{3M}f(X_{3M}) + \ldots. + \beta_{KM}f(X_{KM})
\end{aligned}$$

The probability of selecting an elemental alternative is conditional on the branch to which that alternative belongs first being selected (which is conditional upon the limb to which the branch belongs being selected, which in turn is conditional upon the trunk to which the limb to which the branch belongs being selected). Ignoring these conditional probabilities for the present, at level 1 of the tree structure, the probability calculation for selecting an alternative is related only to those alternatives present within that branch. Hence, the probability for alternative A under RU1 may be calculated as

$$\mathrm{P}(A) = e^{V_A}/(e^{V_A} + e^{V_B})$$

This may be rewritten as:

$$\mathrm{P}(A) = \frac{e^{(\beta_{1A}\mathrm{f}(\mathrm{X}_{1A})+\beta_{2A}\mathrm{f}(\mathrm{X}_{2A})+\beta_{3A}\mathrm{f}(\mathrm{X}_{3A})+\ldots+\beta_{KA}\mathrm{f}(\mathrm{X}_{KA}))}}{e^{(\beta_{1A}\mathrm{f}(\mathrm{X}_{1A})+\beta_{2A}\mathrm{f}(\mathrm{X}_{2A})+\beta_{3A}\mathrm{f}(\mathrm{X}_{3A})+\ldots+\beta_{KA}\mathrm{f}(\mathrm{X}_{KA}))} + e^{(\beta_{0B}+\beta_{1B}\mathrm{f}(\mathrm{X}_{1B})+\beta_{2B}\mathrm{f}(\mathrm{X}_{2B})+\beta_{3B}\mathrm{f}(\mathrm{X}_{3B})+\ldots+\beta_{KB}\mathrm{f}(\mathrm{X}_{KB}))}}$$

The remaining probabilities may be written as:

$$\mathrm{P}(B) = e^{V_B}/(e^{V_A} + e^{V_B})$$
$$\mathrm{P}(C) = e^{V_C}/(e^{V_C} + e^{V_D})$$
$$\mathrm{P}(D) = e^{V_D}/(e^{V_C} + e^{V_D})$$
$$\mathrm{P}(E) = e^{V_E}/(e^{V_E} + e^{V_F})$$
$$\mathrm{P}(F) = e^{V_F}/(e^{V_E} + e^{V_F})$$
$$\mathrm{P}(G) = e^{V_G}/(e^{V_G} + e^{V_H})$$
$$\mathrm{P}(H) = e^{V_H}/(e^{V_G} + e^{V_H})$$
$$\mathrm{P}(I) = e^{V_I}/(e^{V_I} + e^{V_J})$$
$$\mathrm{P}(J) = e^{V_J}/(e^{V_I} + e^{V_J})$$
$$\mathrm{P}(K) = e^{V_K}/(e^{V_K} + e^{V_L})$$
$$\mathrm{P}(L) = e^{V_L}/(e^{V_K} + e^{V_L})$$

Nowhere within the entire tree structure, is alternative M partitioned within a branch, limb or trunk. Such alternatives are referred to as degenerative alternatives. Given that at level 1 of an NL tree, degenerate alternatives are the sole alternative that may be chosen within that branch, the probability of selection must be equal to one at this level of the tree. That is,

$$\mathrm{P}(M) = e^{V_M}/e^{V_M} = 1$$

The probability that a degenerate alternative will be chosen is therefore not usually calculated at this level, but rather at the highest level of the tree structure being explored. As such, we omit from further discussion, discourse on all levels related to alternative M, until it is time to discuss the highest level of the tree, that being the level 4.

RU2 (normalize$^{\tau(l)=1}$)

It is possible to normalize the scale parameters at any level of an NL model. Normalizing on the scale parameters at level 4 (RU2) leaves the scale parameters at levels 1 and 2 free to vary. Nevertheless, the NL model maintains the IID assumption within each partition of the NL tree structure. As such the variances, and hence, scale parameters of elemental alternatives within the same branch of a tree under RU2 are constrained so as to equal one another. Hence

$$\mu_1 = \mu_2 = \mu_{(1|1,1)}, \mu_3 = \mu_4 = \mu_{(2|1,1)}, \mu_5 = \mu_6 = \mu_{(3|2,1)}, \mu_7 = \mu_8 = \mu_{(4|2,1)},$$
$$\mu_9 = \mu_{10} = \mu_{(5|3,2)}, \mu_{11} = \mu_{12} = \mu_{(6|3,2)}, \text{ and } \mu_{13} = \mu_{(7|4,2)}$$

The utility functions under RU2 are therefore:

$$\begin{aligned}
V_A &= \mu_{(1|1,1)}\beta_{1A}f(X_{1A}) + \mu_{(1|1,1)}\beta_{2A}f(X_{2A}) + \mu_{(1|1,1)}\beta_{3A}f(X_{3A}) \\
&\quad + \ldots. + \mu_{(1|1,1)}\beta_{KA}f(X_{KA}) \\
V_B &= \mu_{(1|1,1)}\beta_{0B} + \mu_{(1|1,1)}\beta_{1B}f(X_{1B}) + \mu_{(1|1,1)}\beta_{2B}f(X_{2B}) + \mu_{(1|1,1)}\beta_{3B}f(X_{3B}) \\
&\quad + \ldots. + \mu_{(1|1,1)}\beta_{KB}f(X_{KB}) \\
V_C &= \mu_{(2|1,1)}\beta_{0C} + \mu_{(2|1,1)}\beta_{1C}f(X_{1C}) + \mu_{(2|1,1)}\beta_{2C}f(X_{2C}) + \mu_{(2|1,1)}\beta_{3C}f(X_{3C}) \\
&\quad + \ldots. + \mu_{(2|1,1)}\beta_{KC}f(X_{KC}) \\
V_D &= \mu_{(2|1,1)}\beta_{0D} + \mu_{(2|1,1)}\beta_{1D}f(X_{1D}) + \mu_{(2|1,1)}\beta_{2D}f(X_{2D}) + \mu_{(2|1,1)}\beta_{3D}f(X_{3D}) \\
&\quad + \ldots. + \mu_{(2|1,1)}\beta_{KD}f(X_{KD}) \\
V_E &= \mu_{(3|2,1)}\beta_{0E} + \mu_{(3|2,1)}\beta_{1E}f(X_{1E}) + \mu_{(3|2,1)}\beta_{2E}f(X_{2E}) + \mu_{(3|2,1)}\beta_{3E}f(X_{3E}) \\
&\quad + \ldots. + \mu_{(3|2,1)}\beta_{KE}f(X_{KE}) \\
V_F &= \mu_{(3|2,1)}\beta_{0F} + \mu_{(3|2,1)}\beta_{1F}f(X_{1F}) + \mu_{(3|2,1)}\beta_{2F}f(X_{2F}) + \mu_{(3|2,1)}\beta_{3F}f(X_{3F}) \\
&\quad + \ldots. + \mu_{(3|2,1)}\beta_{KF}f(X_{KF}) \\
V_G &= \mu_{(4|2,1)}\beta_{0G} + \mu_{(4|2,1)}\beta_{1G}f(X_{1G}) + \mu_{(4|2,1)}\beta_{2G}f(X_{2G}) + \mu_{(4|2,1)}\beta_{3G}f(X_{3G}) \\
&\quad + \ldots. + \mu_{(4|2,1)}\beta_{KG}f(X_{KG}) \\
V_H &= \mu_{(4|2,1)}\beta_{0H} + \mu_{(4|2,1)}\beta_{1H}f(X_{1H}) + \mu_{(4|2,1)}\beta_{2H}f(X_{2H}) + \mu_{(4|2,1)}\beta_{3H}f(X_{3H}) \\
&\quad + \ldots. + \mu_{(4|2,1)}\beta_{KH}f(X_{KH}) \\
V_I &= \mu_{(5|3,2)}\beta_{0I} + \mu_{(5|3,2)}\beta_{1I}f(X_{1I}) + \mu_{(5|3,2)}\beta_{2I}f(X_{2I}) + \mu_{(5|3,2)}\beta_{3I}f(X_{3I}) \\
&\quad + \ldots. + \mu_{(5|3,2)}\beta_{KI}f(X_{KI}) \\
V_J &= \mu_{(5|3,2)}\beta_{0J} + \mu_{(5|3,2)}\beta_{1J}f(X_{1J}) + \mu_{(5|3,2)}\beta_{2J}f(X_{2J}) + \mu_{(5|3,2)}\beta_{3J}f(X_{3J}) \\
&\quad + \ldots. + \mu_{(5|3,2)}\beta_{KJ}f(X_{KJ}) \\
V_K &= \mu_{(6|3,2)}\beta_{0K} + \mu_{(6|3,2)}\beta_{1K}f(X_{1K}) + \mu_{(6|3,2)}\beta_{2K}f(X_{2K}) + \mu_{(6|3,2)}\beta_{3K}f(X_{3K}) \\
&\quad + \ldots. + \mu_{(6|3,2)}\beta_{KK}f(X_{KK}) \\
V_L &= \mu_{(6|3,2)}\beta_{0L} + \mu_{(6|3,2)}\beta_{1L}f(X_{1L}) + \mu_{(6|3,2)}\beta_{2L}f(X_{2L}) + \mu_{(6|3,2)}\beta_{3L}f(X_{3L}) \\
&\quad + \ldots. + \mu_{(6|3,2)}\beta_{KL}f(X_{KL}) \\
V_M &= \mu_{13}\beta_{0M} + \mu_{13}\beta_{1M}f(X_{1M}) + \mu_{13}\beta_{2M}f(X_{2M}) + \mu_{13}\beta_{3M}f(X_{3M}) \\
&\quad + \ldots. + \mu_{13}\beta_{KM}f(X_{KM})
\end{aligned}$$

The probability for the first elemental alternative under RU2 may be calculated as:

$$P(A) = e^{V_A} / (e^{V_A} + e^{V_B})$$

Which we may rewrite as:

$$P(A) = \frac{e^{(\mu_{(1|1,1)}\beta_{1A}f(X_{1A}) + \mu_{(1|1,1)}\beta_{2A}f(X_{2A}) + \mu_{(1|1,1)}\beta_{3A}f(X_{3A}) + \ldots + \mu_{(1|1,1)}\beta_{KA}f(X_{KA}))}}{e^{(\mu_{(1|1,1)}\beta_{1A}f(X_{1A}) + \mu_{(1|1,1)}\beta_{2A}f(X_{2A}) + \mu_{(1|1,1)}\beta_{3A}f(X_{3A}) + \ldots + \mu_{(1|1,1)}\beta_{KA}f(X_{KA}))} + e^{(\mu_{(1|1,1)}\beta_{0B} + \mu_{(1|1,1)}\beta_{1B}f(X_{1B}) + \mu_{(1|1,1)}\beta_{2B}f(X_{2B}) + \mu_{(1|1,1)}\beta_{3B}f(X_{3B}) + \ldots + \mu_{(1|1,1)}\beta_{KB}f(X_{KB}))}}$$

The remaining probabilities may be written as:

$$P(B) = e^{V_B} / (e^{V_A} + e^{V_B})$$
$$P(C) = e^{V_C} / (e^{V_C} + e^{V_D})$$
$$P(D) = e^{V_D} / (e^{V_C} + e^{V_D})$$
$$P(E) = e^{V_E} / (e^{V_E} + e^{V_F})$$
$$P(F) = e^{V_F} / (e^{V_E} + e^{V_F})$$
$$P(G) = e^{V_G} / (e^{V_G} + e^{V_H})$$
$$P(H) = e^{V_H} / (e^{V_G} + e^{V_H})$$
$$P(I) = e^{V_I} / (e^{V_I} + e^{V_J})$$
$$P(J) = e^{V_J} / (e^{V_I} + e^{V_J})$$
$$P(K) = e^{V_K} / (e^{V_K} + e^{V_L})$$
$$P(L) = e^{V_L} / (e^{V_K} + e^{V_L})$$

As with RU1, the probability of the last alternative is not shown in the above system of equations, as the conditional probability collapses to one. We show the equation to calculate the probability for this alternative later.

Level 2 (Branch)

Figure 13A.2 shows the relationship between levels 1 and 2 of NL tree structures. We now discuss the calculation of the utilities and probabilities at the branch level under the RU1 and RU2 normalization profiles.

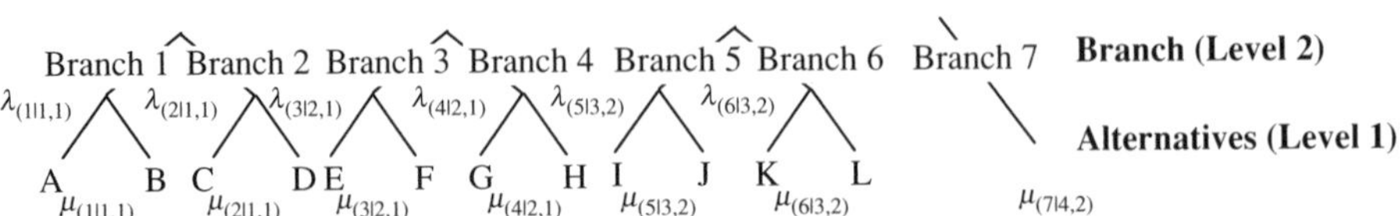

Figure 13A.2 Relationship between the scale parameters at levels 1 and 2 of an NL tree structure

For the first branch, (1|1,1), the utility may be expressed as:

$$V_{(1|1,1)} = \lambda_{(1|1,1)}\left[\beta_{0(1|1,1)} + \beta_{1(1|1,1)}f(X_{1(1|1,1)}) + \beta_{2(1|1,1)}f(X_{2(1|1,1)}) + \ldots + \beta_{K(1|1,1)}f(X_{K(1|1,1)}) + \frac{1}{\mu_{(1|1,1)}} \times IV_{(1|1,1)}\right]$$

Where

$$IV_{(1|1,1)} = \ln(e^{(\mu_{(1|1,1)}V_A)} + e^{(\mu_{(1|1,1)}V_B)}) \text{ and the IV parameter is } \frac{\lambda_{(1|1,1)}}{\mu_{(1|1,1)}}$$

RU1 (normalize $\mu_{(j|i,l)} = 1$)

Under RU1 $\mu_{(j|i,l)} = 1$, hence the IV parameter becomes $\lambda_{(j|i,l)}$.
We therefore obtain:

$$V_{(1|1,1)} = \lambda_{(1|1,1)}[\alpha_{(1|1,1)} + \beta_{1(1|1,1)}f(X_{1(1|1,1)}) + \beta_{2(1|1,1)}f(X_{2(1|1,1)}) + \ldots + \beta_{K(1|1,1)}f(X_{K(1|1,1)}) + IV_{(1|1,1)}]$$

Where the IV variable (not to be confused with the IV parameter) equals

$$IV_{(1|1,1)} = \ln(e^{(\mu_{(1|1,1)}V_A)} + e^{(\mu_{(1|1,1)}V_B)})$$

In full:

$$IV_{(1|1,1)} = \ln(e^{(\mu_{(1|1,1)}\times(\beta_{1A}f(X_{1A})+\beta_{2A}f(X_{2A})+\beta_{3A}f(X_{3A})+\ldots+\beta_{KA}f(X_{KA})))} + e^{(\mu_{(1|1,1)}\times(\beta_{0B}+\beta_{2B}f(X_{1B})+\beta_{2B}f(X_{2B})+\beta_{3B}f(X_{3B})+\ldots+\beta_{KB}f(X_{KB}))})$$

The remaining branches may be written as:

$$V_{(2|1,1)} = \lambda_{(2|1,1)}[\beta_{0(2|1,1)} + \beta_{1(2|1,1)}f(X_{2(1|1,1)}) + \beta_{2(2|1,1)}f(X_{2(2|1,1)}) + \ldots + \beta_{K(2|1,1)}f(X_{K(2|1,1)}) + IV_{(2|1,1)}]$$

where

$$IV_{(2|1,1)} = \ln(e^{(\mu_{(2|1,1)}V_C)} + e^{(\mu_{(2|1,1)}V_D)})$$

$$V_{(3|2,1)} = \lambda_{(3|2,1)}[\beta_{0(3|2,1)} + \beta_{1(3|2,1)}f(X_{2(3|2,1)}) + \beta_{2(3|2,1)}f(X_{2(3|2,1)}) + \ldots + \beta_{K(3|2,1)}f(X_{K(3|2,1)}) + IV_{(3|2,1)}]$$

where

$$IV_{(3|1,1)} = \ln(e^{(\mu_{(3|2,1)}V_E)} + e^{(\mu_{(3|2,1)}V_F)})$$

$$V_{(4|2,1)} = \lambda_{(4|2,1)}[\beta_{0(4|2,1)} + \beta_{1(4|2,1)}f(X_{2(4|2,1)}) + \beta_{2(4|2,1)}f(X_{2(4|2,1)}) + \ldots + \beta_{K(4|2,1)}f(X_{K(4|2,1)}) + IV_{(4|2,1)}]$$

where

$$\mathrm{IV}_{(4|1,1)} = \ln(e^{(\mu_{(4|2,1)}V_G)} + e^{(\mu_{(4|2,1)}V_H)})$$

$$\mathrm{V}_{(5|3,2)} = \lambda_{(5|3,2)}[\beta_{0(5|3,2)} + \beta_{1(5|3,2)}f(\mathrm{X}_{2(5|3,2)}) + \beta_{2(5|3,2)}f(\mathrm{X}_{2(5|3,2)}) + \ldots + \beta_{\mathrm{K}(5|3,2)}f(\mathrm{X}_{\mathrm{K}(5|3,2)}) + \mathrm{IV}_{(5|3,2)}]$$

where

$$\mathrm{IV}_{(5|3,2)} = \ln(e^{(\mu_{(5|3,2)}V_G)} + e^{(\mu_{(5|3,2)}V_H)})$$

$$\mathrm{V}_{(6|3,2)} = \lambda_{(6|3,2)}[\beta_{0(6|3,2)} + \beta_{1(6|3,2)}f(\mathrm{X}_{2(6|3,2)}) + \beta_{2(6|3,2)}f(\mathrm{X}_{2(6|3,2)}) + \ldots + \beta_{\mathrm{K}(6|3,2)}f(\mathrm{X}_{\mathrm{K}(6|3,2)}) + \mathrm{IV}_{(6|3,2)}]$$

where

$$\mathrm{IV}_{(6|3,2)} = \ln(e^{(\mu_{(6|3,2)}V_I)} + e^{(\mu_{(6|3,2)}V_J)})$$

The last alternative is degenerate, which requires special treatment. The utility function for a degenerative branch may be given as:

$$\mathrm{V}_{(7|3,3)} = \lambda_{(7|3,3)}\left[\beta_{0(7|3,3)} + \beta_{1(1|1,1)}f(\mathrm{X}_{1(7|3,3)}) + \beta_{2(7|3,3)}f(\mathrm{X}_{2(7|3,3)}) + \ldots + \beta_{\mathrm{K}(1|1,1)}f(\mathrm{X}_{\mathrm{K}(7|3,3)}) + \frac{1}{\mu_{(7|3,3)}} \times \mathrm{IV}_{(7|3,3)}\right]$$

The analyst may specify the utility for a degenerative alternative at any level of the model. For this example, we have assumed that the utility for the Mth alternative has been specified at level 1. As such, no attributes SDC are included in the utility function at this level of the model. Hence:

$$\mathrm{V}_{(7|3,3)} = \lambda_{(7|3,3)}\left[\frac{1}{\mu_{(7|3,3)}} \times \mathrm{IV}_{(7|3,3)}\right]$$

Under RU1, $\mu_{(j|i,l)} = 1$.

$$\mathrm{V}_{(7|3,3)} = \lambda_{(7|3,3)}\left[\frac{1}{1} \times \mathrm{IV}_{(7|3,3)}\right] = \lambda_{(7|3,3)} \times \mathrm{IV}_{(7|3,3)}$$

where

$$\mathrm{IV}_{(7|3,3)} = \ln(e^{(\mu_{(7|3,3)}V_M)}) = \mathrm{V_M}$$

Hence, the utility for the degenerative branch, M, at level 2 is:

$$\mathrm{V}_{(7|3,3)} = \lambda_{(7|3,3)} \times \mathrm{V_M}$$

As an aside, if the utility function for a degenerative alternative is located at the branch level, we have:

$$V_{(7|3,3)} = \lambda_{(7|3,3)}\left[\beta_{0(7|3,3)} + \beta_{1(1|1,1)} f(X_{1(7|3,3)}) + \beta_{2(7|3,3)} f(X_{2(7|3,3)}) + \ldots + \beta_{K(1|1,1)} f(X_{K(7|3,3)}) + \frac{1}{1} \times IV_{(7|3,3)}\right] \text{ and } V_M = 0$$

Hence:

$$IV_{(7|3,3)} = \ln(e^{(1\times0)}) = 0$$

Therefore,

$$V_{(7|3,3)} = \lambda_{(7|3,3)}\left[\beta_{0(7|3,3)} + \beta_{1(1|1,1)} f(X_{1(7|3,3)} + \beta_{2(7|3,3)} f(X_{2(7|3,3)}) + \ldots + \beta_{K(1|1,1)} f(X_{K(7|3,3)}) + \frac{1}{1} \times 0\right]$$

$$V_{(7|3,3)} = \lambda_{(7|3,3)}[\beta_{0(7|3,3)} + \beta_{1(1|1,1)} f(X_{1(7|3,3)}) + \beta_{2(7|3,3)} f(X_{2(7|3,3)}) + \ldots + \beta_{K(1|1,1)} f(X_{K(7|3,3)})]$$

This is equivalent to specifying the utility function at level 1 of the model.

As with the system of equations used to estimate the probabilities at level 1 of the NL tree structure, the probability of selecting a branch is conditional upon the limb and trunk to which that branch belongs, first being chosen. As such, the probably that a branch is chosen, is calculated only in relation to other branches partitioned within the same limb.

$$P(1|1,1) = e^{V_{(1|1,1)}} / (e^{V_{(1|1,1)}} + e^{V_{(2|1,1)}})$$

This may be rewritten in the following form:

$$P(1|1,1) = \frac{e^{\lambda_{(1|1,1)}[\beta_{0(1|1,1)}+\beta_{1(1|1,1)}f(X_{1(1|1,1)})+\beta_{2(1|1,1)}f(X_{2(1|1,1)})+\beta_{3(1|1,1)}f(X_{3(1|1,1)})+\ldots+\beta_{K(1|1,1)}f(X_{K(1|1,1)})+IV_{(1|1,1)}]}}{e^{\lambda_{(1|1,1)}[\beta_{0(1|1,1)}+\beta_{1(1|1,1)}f(X_{1(1|1,1)})+\beta_{2(1|1,1)}f(X_{2(1|1,1)})+\beta_{3(1|1,1)}f(X_{3(1|1,1)})+\ldots+\beta_{K(1|1,1)}f(X_{K(1|1,1)})+IV_{(1|1,1)}]} + e^{\lambda_{(2|1,1)}[\beta_{0(2|1,1)}+\beta_{1(2|1,1)}f(X_{1(2|1,1)})+\beta_{2(2|1,1)}f(X_{2(2|1,1)})+\beta_{3(2|1,1)}f(X_{3(2|1,1)})+\ldots+\beta_{K(2|1,1)}f(X_{K(2|1,1)})+IV_{(2|1,1)}]}}$$

The remaining probabilities may be written as:

$$P(2|1,1) = e^{V_{(2|1,1)}} / (e^{V_{(1|1,1)}} + e^{V_{(2|1,1)}})$$
$$P(3|2,1) = e^{V_{(3|2,1)}} / (e^{V_{(3|2,1)}} + e^{V_{(4|2,1)}})$$
$$P(4|2,1) = e^{V_{(4|2,1)}} / (e^{V_{(3|2,1)}} + e^{V_{(4|2,1)}})$$
$$P(5|3,1) = e^{V_{(5|3,1)}} / (e^{V_{(5|3,1)}} + e^{V_{(5|3,1)}})$$
$$P(6|3,1) = e^{V_{(6|3,1)}} / (e^{V_{(5|3,1)}} + e^{V_{(5|3,1)}})$$

RU2 (normalize $\tau_{(l)} = 1$)

Under RU2 $\tau_{(l)} = 1$, hence the IV parameter, $\frac{\lambda_{(1|1,1)}}{\mu_{(1|1,1)}}$, remains unaffected.

For the first branch we therefore obtain:

$$V_{(1|1,1)} = \lambda_{(1|1,1)}\left[\beta_{0(1|1,1)} + \beta_{1(1|1,1)}f(X_{1(1|1,1)}) + \beta_{2(1|1,1)}f(X_{2(1|1,1)}) + \ldots + \beta_{K(1|1,1)}f(X_{K(1|1,1)}) + \frac{IV_{(1|1,1)}}{\mu_{(1|1,1)}}\right]$$

Where

$$IV_{(1|1,1)} = \ln(e^{(\mu_{(1|1,1)}V_A)} + e^{(\mu_{(1|1,1)}V_B)})$$

The remaining equations for each branch may be written as:

$$V_{(2|1,1)} = \lambda_{(2|1,1)}\left[\beta_{0(2|1,1)} + \beta_{1(2|1,1)}f(X_{2(1|1,1)}) + \beta_{2(2|1,1)}f(X_{2(2|1,1)}) + \ldots + \beta_{K(2|1,1)}f(X_{K(2|1,1)}) + \frac{IV_{(2|1,1)}}{\mu_{(2|1,1)}}\right]$$

where

$$IV_{(2|1,1)} = \ln(e^{(\mu_{(2|1,1)}V_C)} + e^{(\mu_{(2|1,1)}V_D)})$$

$$V_{(3|2,1)} = \lambda_{(3|2,1)}\left[\beta_{0(3|2,1)} + \beta_{1(3|2,1)}f(X_{2(3|2,1)}) + \beta_{2(3|2,1)}f(X_{2(3|2,1)}) + \ldots + \beta_{K(3|2,1)}f(X_{K(3|2,1)}) + \frac{IV_{(3|2,1)}}{\mu_{(3|2,1)}}\right]$$

where

$$IV_{(3|1,1)} = \ln(e^{(\mu_{(3|2,1)}V_E)} + e^{(\mu_{(3|2,1)}V_F)})$$

$$V_{(4|2,1)} = \lambda_{(4|2,1)}\left[\beta_{0(4|2,1)} + \beta_{1(4|2,1)}f(X_{2(4|2,1)}) + \beta_{2(4|2,1)}f(X_{2(4|2,1)}) + \ldots + \beta_{K(4|2,1)}f(X_{K(4|2,1)}) + \frac{IV_{(4|2,1)}}{\mu_{(4|2,1)}}\right]$$

where

$$IV_{(4|1,1)} = \ln(e^{(\mu_{(4|2,1)}V_G)} + e^{(\mu_{(4|2,1)}V_H)})$$

$$V_{(5|3,2)} = \lambda_{(5|3,2)}\left[\beta_{0(5|3,2)} + \beta_{1(5|3,2)}f(X_{2(5|3,2)}) + \beta_{2(5|3,2)}f(X_{2(5|3,2)}) + \ldots + \beta_{K(5|3,2)}f(X_{K(5|3,2)}) + \frac{IV_{(5|3,2)}}{\mu_{(5|3,2)}}\right]$$

where

$$IV_{(5|3,2)} = \ln(e^{(\mu_{(5|3,2)}V_G)} + e^{(\mu_{(5|3,2)}V_H)})$$

$$V_{(6|3,2)} = \lambda_{(6|3,2)}\left[\beta_{0(6|3,2)} + \beta_{1(6|3,2)}f(X_{2(6|3,2)}) + \beta_{2(6|3,2)}f(X_{2(6|3,2)}) + \ldots + \beta_{K(6|3,2)}f(X_{K(6|3,2)}) + \frac{IV_{(6|3,2)}}{\mu_{(6|3,2)}}\right]$$

where

$$IV_{(6|3,2)} = \ln(e^{(\mu_{(6|3,2)}V_I)} + e^{(\mu_{(6|3,2)}V_J)})$$

Once more, no utility for alternative M may be expressed at the branch level.

$$V_{(7|3,3)} = \lambda_{(7|3,3)}\left[\beta_{0(7|3,3)} + \beta_{1(1|1,1)}f(X_{1(7|3,3)} + \beta_{2(7|3,3)}f(X_{2(7|3,3)}) + \ldots + \beta_{K(1|1,1)}f(X_{K(7|3,3)}) + \frac{1}{\mu_{(7|3,3)}} \times IV_{(7|3,3)}\right]$$

The analyst may specify the utility for a degenerative alternative at any level of the model. For this example, we have assumed that the utility for the Mth alternative has been specified at level 1. As such, no attributes SDC are included in the utility function at this level of the model.

Hence:

$$V_{(7|3,3)} = \lambda_{(7|3,3)}\left[\frac{1}{\mu_{(7|3,3)}} \times IV_{(7|3,3)}\right]$$

Under RU1, $\tau_{(l)} = 1$.

$$V_{(7|3,3)} = \left[\frac{\lambda_{(7|3,3)}}{\mu_{(7|3,3)}} \times IV_{(7|3,3)}\right]$$

where

$$IV_{(7|3,3)} = \ln(e^{(\mu_{(7|3,3)}V_M)}) = \mu_{(7|3,3)} \times V_M$$

Hence, the utility for the degenerative branch, M, at level 2 is:

$$V_{(7|3,3)} = \frac{\lambda_{(7|3,3)}}{\mu_{(7|3,3)}} \times \mu_{(7|3,3)} \times V_M = \lambda_{(7|3,3)} \times V_M$$

As an aside, if the utility function for a degenerative alternative is located at the branch level, we have:

$$V_{(7|3,3)} = \lambda_{(7|3,3)}\left[\beta_{0(7|3,3)} + \beta_{1(1|1,1)}f(X_{1(7|3,3)} + \beta_{2(7|3,3)}f(X_{2(7|3,3)}) + \ldots + \beta_{K(1|1,1)}f(X_{K(7|3,3)}) + \frac{1}{\mu_{(7|3,3)}} \times IV_{(7|3,3)}\right] \text{ and } V_M = 0$$

Hence:

$$\mathrm{IV}_{(7|3,3)} = \ln(e^{(1\times 0)}) = 0$$

Therefore,

$$\begin{aligned}
V_{(7|3,3)} &= \lambda_{(7|3,3)}\Big[\beta_{0(7|3,3)} + \beta_{1(1|1,1)} f(X_{1(7|3,3)} + \beta_{2(7|3,3)} f(X_{2(7|3,3)}) \\
&\quad + \ldots + \beta_{K(1|1,1)} f(X_{K(7|3,3)}) + \frac{1}{\mu_{(7|3,3)}} \times 0\Big] \\
V_{(7|3,3)} &= \lambda_{(7|3,3)}[\beta_{0(7|3,3)} + \beta_{1(1|1,1)} f(X_{1(7|3,3)} + \beta_{2(7|3,3)} f(X_{2(7|3,3)}) \\
&\quad + \ldots + \beta_{K(1|1,1)} f(X_{K(7|3,3)})]
\end{aligned}$$

This is equivalent to specifying the utility function at level 1 of the model.

The probability for the first branch under RU2 may be written as:

$$\mathrm{P}(1|1,1) = e^{V_{(1|1,1)}} / (e^{V_{(1|1,1)}} + e^{V_{(2|1,1)}})$$

Under RU2, this may be rewritten in the following form:

$$\mathrm{P}(1|1,1) = \frac{e^{\left(\lambda_{(1|1,1)}\left[\beta_{0(1|1,1)}+\beta_{1(1|1,1)}f(X_{1(1|1,1)})+\beta_{2(1|1,1)}f(X_{2(1|1,1)})+\beta_{3(1|1,1)}f(X_{3(1|1,1)})+\ldots+\beta_{K(1|1,1)}f(X_{K(1|1,1)})+\frac{IV_{(1|1,1)}}{\mu_{(1|1,1)}}\right]\right)}}{\left\{\begin{array}{l} e^{\left(\lambda_{(1|1,1)}\left[\beta_{0(1|1,1)}+\beta_{1(1|1,1)}f(X_{1(1|1,1)})+\beta_{2(1|1,1)}f(X_{2(1|1,1)})+\beta_{3(1|1,1)}f(X_{3(1|1,1)})+\ldots+\beta_{K(1|1,1)}f(X_{K(1|1,1)})+\frac{IV_{(1|1,1)}}{\mu_{(1|1,1)}}\right]\right)} \\ +e^{\left(\lambda_{(2|1,1)}\left[\beta_{0(2|1,1)}+\beta_{1(2|1,1)}f(X_{1(2|1,1)})+\beta_{2(2|1,1)}f(X_{2(2|1,1)})+\beta_{3(2|1,1)}f(X_{3(2|1,1)})+\ldots+\beta_{K(2|1,1)}f(X_{K(2|1,1)})+\frac{IV_{(2|1,1)}}{\mu_{(2|1,1)}}\right]\right)} \end{array}\right\}}$$

The remaining probabilities may be written as:

$$\begin{aligned}
\mathrm{P}(2|1,1) &= e^{V_{(2|1,1)}} / (e^{V_{(1|1,1)}} + e^{V_{(2|1,1)}}) \\
\mathrm{P}(3|2,1) &= e^{V_{(3|2,1)}} / (e^{V_{(3|2,1)}} + e^{V_{(4|2,1)}}) \\
\mathrm{P}(4|2,1) &= e^{V_{(4|2,1)}} / (e^{V_{(3|2,1)}} + e^{V_{(4|2,1)}}) \\
\mathrm{P}(5|3,1) &= e^{V_{(5|3,1)}} / (e^{V_{(5|3,1)}} + e^{V_{(5|3,1)}}) \\
\mathrm{P}(6|3,1) &= e^{V_{(6|3,1)}} / (e^{V_{(5|3,1)}} + e^{V_{(5|3,1)}})
\end{aligned}$$

Level 3 (Limb)

Figure 13A.3 reveals the relationship between levels 2 and 3 of NL tree structures. We now discuss these relationships by formally writing out the equations for calculating the utilities and probabilities for each limb under the RU1 and RU2 normalization profiles.

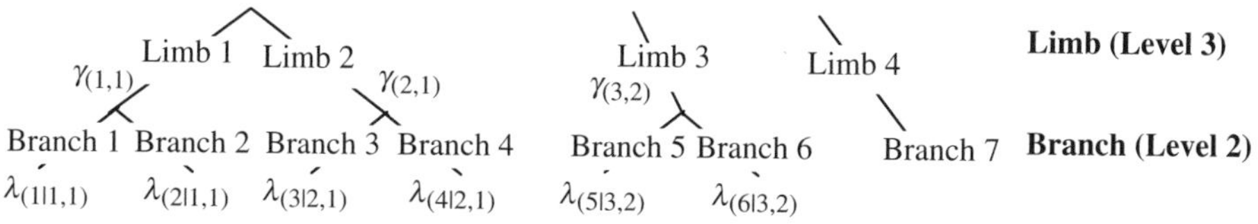

Figure 13A.3 Relationship between the scale parameters at levels 2 and 3 of an NL tree structure

For the first limb, (1,1), we may write the utility expression as follows.

$$V_{(1,1)} = \gamma_{(1,1)}\Big[\beta_{0(1,1)} + \beta_{1(1,1)}f(X_{1(1,1)}) + \beta_{2(1,1)}f(X_{2(1,1)}) + \ldots + \beta_{K(1,1)}f(X_{K(1,1)}) + \frac{1}{\lambda_{(1,1)}} \times IV_{(1,1)}\Big]$$

Where

$$IV_{(1,1)} = \ln(e^{(\lambda_{(1|1,1)}V_{(1|1,1)})} + e^{(\lambda_{(2|1,1)}V_{(2|1,1)})}) \text{ and the IV parameter is } \frac{\gamma_{(1,1)}}{\lambda_{(1,1)}}$$

RU1 (normalize $\mu_{(j|i,l)} = 1$)

Under RU1, the scale parameters at level 1 of the NL tree structure are normalized and the scale parameters for level 2 are free to vary. As the IID assumption is maintained within each partition of the tree, the scale parameters for each connected branch are constrained to equal. Hence, at level 3 of the NL model:

$$\lambda_{(1|1,1)} = \lambda_{(2|1,1)} = \lambda_{(1,1)},\ \lambda_{(3|2,1)} = \lambda_{(4|2,1)} = \lambda_{(2,1)},\ \lambda_{(5|3,2)} = \lambda_{(6|3,2)} = \lambda_{(3,2)} \text{ and } \lambda_{(7|3,3)} = \lambda_{(4,3)}$$

For the first limb, (1,1), we may therefore write the utility expression as follows.

$$V_{(1,1)} = \gamma_{(1,1)}\Big[\beta_{0(1,1)} + \beta_{1(1,1)}f(X_{1(1,1)}) + \beta_{2(1,1)}f(X_{2(1,1)}) + \ldots + \beta_{K(1,1)}f(X_{K(1,1)}) + \frac{1}{\lambda_{(1,1)}} \times IV_{(1,1)}\Big]$$

Where

$$IV_{(1,1)} = \ln(e^{(\lambda_{(1|1,1)}V_{(1|1,1)})} + e^{(\lambda_{(2|1,1)}V_{(2|1,1)})}) \text{ and the IV parameter is } \frac{\gamma_{(1,1)}}{\lambda_{(1,1)}}$$

The remaining equation for each limb may be written as:

$$V_{(2,1)} = \gamma_{(2,1)}\Big[\beta_{0(2,1)} + \beta_{1(2,1)}f(X_{1(2,1)}) + \beta_{2(2,1)}f(X_{2(2,1)}) + \ldots + \beta_{K(2,1)}f(X_{K(2,1)}) + \frac{1}{\lambda_{(2,1)}} \times IV_{(2,1)}\Big]$$

where

$$IV_{(2,1)} = \ln(e^{(\lambda_{(3|2,1)}V_{(3|2,1)})} + e^{(\lambda_{(4|2,1)}V_{(4|2,1)})}) \text{ and the IV parameter is } \frac{\gamma_{(2,1)}}{\lambda_{(2,1)}}$$

$$V_{(3,2)} = \gamma_{(3,2)}\Big[\beta_{0(3,2)} + \beta_{1(3,2)}f(X_{1(3,2)}) + \beta_{2(3,2)}f(X_{2(3,2)}) + \ldots + \beta_{K(3,2)}f(X_{K(3,2)}) + \frac{1}{\lambda_{(3,2)}} \times IV_{(3,2)}\Big]$$

where

$$IV_{(3,2)} = \ln(e^{(\lambda_{(5|3,2)}V_{(5|3,2)})} + e^{(\lambda_{(6|3,2)}V_{(6|3,2)})}) \text{ and the IV parameter is } \frac{\gamma_{(3,2)}}{\lambda_{(3,2)}}$$

The last limb is degenerate.

$$V_{(4,3)} = \gamma_{(4,3)}\Big[\beta_{0(4,3)} + \beta_{1(4,3)}f(X_{1(4,3)}) + \beta_{2(4,3)}f(X_{2(4,3)}) + \ldots + \beta_{K(4,3)}f(X_{K(4,3)}) + \frac{1}{\lambda_{(4,3)}} \times IV_{(4,3)}\Big]$$

Assuming that the utility was specified at a lower level:

$$V_{(4,3)} = \gamma_{(4,3)}\left[\frac{1}{\lambda_{(4,3)}} \times IV_{(4,3)}\right]$$

where

$$IV_{(4,3)} = \ln(e^{(\lambda_{(7|4,3)}V_{(7|4,3)})}) = \frac{\gamma_{(4,3)}}{\lambda_{(4,3)}} \times \lambda_{(7|4,3)} \times V_{(7|4,3)} = \gamma_{(4,3)} \times V_{(7|4,3)}$$

The probability of the first limb being selected under RU1 is given as:

$$P(1,1) = e^{V_{(1,1)}}/(e^{V_{(1,1)}} + e^{V_{(2,1)}})$$

Through substitution, this may be rewritten as:

$$P(1,1) = \frac{e^{\gamma_{(1,1)}[\beta_{0(1,1)}+\beta_{1(1,1)}f(X_{1(1,1)})+\beta_{2(1,1)}f(X_{2(1,1)})+\beta_{3(1,1)}f(X_{3(1,1)})+\ldots+\beta_{K(1,1)}f(X_{K(1,1)})+\frac{1}{\lambda_{(1,1)}}\times IV_{(1,1)}]}}{e^{\gamma_{(1,1)}[\beta_{0(1,1)}+\beta_{1(1,1)}f(X_{1(1,1)})+\beta_{2(1,1)}f(X_{2(1,1)})+\beta_{3(1,1)}f(X_{3(1,1)})+\ldots+\beta_{K(1,1)}f(X_{K(1,1)})+\frac{1}{\lambda_{(1,1)}}\times IV_{(1,1)}]} + e^{\gamma_{(1,1)}[\beta_{0(2,1)}+\beta_{1(2,1)}f(X_{1(2,1)})+\beta_{2(2,1)}f(X_{2(2,1)})+\beta_{3(2,1)}f(X_{3(2,1)})+\ldots+\beta_{K(2,1)}f(X_{K(2,1)})+\frac{1}{\lambda_{(2,1)}}\times IV_{(2,1)}]}}$$

The probability of limb 2 being chosen is:

$$P(2,1) = e^{V_{(2,1)}}/(e^{V_{(1,1)}} + e^{V_{(2,1)}})$$

Limbs 3 and 4 reside alone within different trunks of the tree. As such, a similar situation arises as with the degenerate alternatives in that the probability of selecting limb 3 is equal to 1 conditional on trunk 3 being chosen and the probability of selecting limb 4 is also equal to 1 conditional on trunk 4 being chosen. We demonstrate later how to handle such cases when we write out the entire PCS under both RU1 and RU2.

RU2 (normalize $\tau_{(l)} = 1$)

Under RU2 $\tau_{(l)} = 1$ hence the IV parameter, $\frac{\gamma_{(i,l)}}{\lambda_{(i,l)}}$, remains unchanged. The within partition IID assumption, however, suggests

$$\lambda_{(1|1,1)} = \lambda_{(2|1,1)} = \lambda_{(1,1)}, \lambda_{(3|2,1)} = \lambda_{(4|2,1)} = \lambda_{(2,1)} \text{ and } \lambda_{(5|3,2)} = \lambda_{(6|3,2)} = \lambda_{(3,2)}$$

For the first limb, (1,1), we may therefore write the utility expression as:

$$V_{(1,1)} = \gamma_{(1,1)}\Big[\beta_{0(1,1)} + \beta_{1(1,1)}f(X_{1(1,1)}) + \beta_{2(1,1)}f(X_{2(1,1)}) + \ldots + \beta_{K(1,1)}f(X_{K(1,1)}) + \frac{1}{\lambda_{(1,1)}} \times IV_{(1,1)}\Big]$$

Where

$$IV_{(1,1)} = \ln(e^{(\lambda_{(1|1,1)}V_{(1|1,1)})} + e^{(\lambda_{(2|1,1)}V_{(2|1,1)})})$$

The remaining equation for each limb may be written as:

$$V_{(2,1)} = \gamma_{(2,1)}\Big[\beta_{0(2,1)} + \beta_{1(2,1)}f(X_{1(2,1)}) + \beta_{2(2,1)}f(X_{2(2,1)}) + \ldots + \beta_{K(2,1)}f(X_{K(2,1)}) + \frac{1}{\lambda_{(1,1)}} \times IV_{(2,1)}\Big]$$

where

$$IV_{(2,1)} = \ln(e^{(\lambda_{(3|2,1)}V_{(3|2,1)})} + e^{(\lambda_{(4|2,1)}V_{(4|2,1)})})$$

$$V_{(3,2)} = \gamma_{(3,2)}\Big[\beta_{0(3,2)} + \beta_{1(3,2)}f(X_{1(3,2)}) + \beta_{2(3,2)}f(X_{2(3,2)}) + \ldots + \beta_{K(3,2)}f(X_{K(3,2)}) + \frac{1}{\lambda_{(1,1)}} \times IV_{(3,2)}\Big]$$

where

$$IV_{(3,2)} = \ln(e^{(\lambda_{(5|3,2)}V_{(5|3,2)})} + e^{(\lambda_{(6|3,2)}V_{(6|3,2)})})$$

Once again, the last limb is degenerate.

$$V_{(4,3)} = \gamma_{(4,3)}\left[\beta_{0(4,3)} + \beta_{1(4,3)}f(X_{1(4,3)}) + \beta_{2(4,3)}f(X_{2(4,3)}) + \ldots + \beta_{K(4,3)}f(X_{K(4,3)}) + \frac{1}{\lambda_{(4,3)}} \times IV_{(4,3)}\right]$$

Assuming that the utility was specified at a lower level:

$$V_{(4,3)} = \gamma_{(4,3)}\left[\frac{1}{\lambda_{(4,3)}} \times IV_{(4,3)}\right]$$

where

$$IV_{(4,3)} = \ln(e^{(\lambda_{(7|4,3)}V_{(7|4,3)})}) = \frac{\gamma_{(4,3)}}{\lambda_{(4,3)}} \times \lambda_{(4|3)} \times V_{(7|4,3)} = \gamma_{(4,3)} \times V_{(7|4,3)}$$

which is the same as under RU1.

The probability of the first limb being selected under RU1 is given as:

$$P(1,1) = e^{V_{(1,1)}}/(e^{V_{(1,1)}} + e^{V_{(2,1)}})$$

Through substitution, this may be rewritten as:

$$P(1,1) = \frac{e^{\gamma_{(1,1)}[\beta_{0(1,1)}+\beta_{1(1,1)}f(X_{1(1,1)})+\beta_{2(1,1)}f(X_{2(1,1)})+\beta_{3(1,1)}f(X_{3(1,1)})+\ldots+\beta_{K(1,1)}f(X_{K(1,1)})+IV_{(1,1)}]}}{e^{\gamma_{(1,1)}[\beta_{0(1,1)}+\beta_{1(1,1)}f(X_{1(1,1)})+\beta_{2(1,1)}f(X_{2(1,1)})+\beta_{3(1,1)}f(X_{3(1,1)})+\ldots+\beta_{K(1,1)}f(X_{K(1,1)})+IV_{(1,1)}]} + e^{\gamma_{(1,1)}[\beta_{0(2,1)}+\beta_{1(2,1)}f(X_{1(2,1)})+\beta_{2(2,1)}f(X_{2(2,1)})+\beta_{3(2,1)}f(X_{3(2,1)})+\ldots+\beta_{K(2,1)}f(X_{K(2,1)})+IV_{(2,1)}]}}$$

The probability of limb 2 being chosen is given by:

$$P(2,1) = e^{V_{(2,1)}}/(e^{V_{(1,1)}} + e^{V_{(2,1)}})$$

As with RU1, we show how limbs 1 and 4 are treated within the PCS when we formally show the entire PCS system under both RU1 and RU2.

Level 4 (Trunk)

Figure 13A.4 reveals the relationship between levels 3 and 4 of the NL tree structure.

For the first trunk, $\tau_{(1)}$, we may write the utility expression as follows.

$$V_{(1)} = \tau_{(1)}\left[\beta_{0(1)} + \beta_{1(1)}f(X_{1(1)}) + \beta_{2(1)}f(X_{2(1)}) + \ldots + \beta_{K(1)}f(X_{K(1)}) + \frac{1}{\gamma_{(l)}} \times IV_{(1)}\right]$$

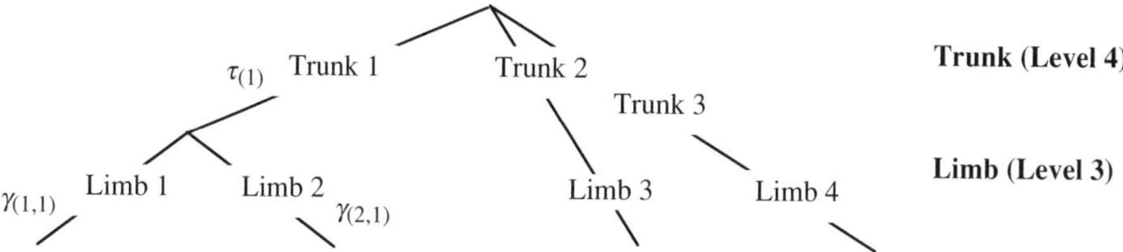

Figure 13A.4 Relationship between the scale parameters at levels 3 and 4 of an NL tree structure

Where

$$\mathrm{IV}_{(1,1)} = \ln(e^{(\gamma_{(1)} V_{(1|1)})} + e^{(\gamma_{(1)} V_{(2|1)})}) \text{ and the IV parameter is } \frac{\tau_{(1)}}{\gamma_{(1)}}.$$

As the IID assumption is maintained within each partition of the tree, the scale parameters for each connected limb are constrained to equal. Hence,

$$\gamma_{(1,1)} = \gamma_{(2,1)} = \gamma_{(1)}, \gamma_{(3,2)} = \gamma_{(2)} \text{ and } \gamma_{(4,3)} = \gamma_{(1)}$$

RU1 (normalize $\mu_{(j|i,l)} = 1$)

For Trunk 1, $\tau_{(1)}$

$$\mathrm{V}_{(1)} = \tau_{(1)}\left[\beta_{0(1)} + \beta_{1(1)} f(\mathrm{X}_{1(1)}) + \beta_{2(1)} f(\mathrm{X}_{2(1)}) + \ldots + \beta_{\mathrm{K}(1)} f(\mathrm{X}_{\mathrm{K}(1)}) + \frac{1}{\gamma_{(1)}} \times \mathrm{IV}_{(1)}\right]$$

Where

$$\mathrm{IV}_{(1)} = \ln(e^{(\gamma_{(1,1)} V_{(1,1)})} + e^{(\gamma_{(2,1)} V_{(2,1)})}) \text{ and the IV parameter is } \frac{\tau_{(1)}}{\gamma_{(1)}}$$

Utility for trunks 2 and 3 reside at lower levels of the tree structure given that the trunks are degenerate at this level of the tree.

$$\mathrm{V}_{(2)} = \tau_{(2)}\left[\beta_{0(2)} + \beta_{1(2)} f(\mathrm{X}_{1(2)}) + \beta_{2(2)} f(\mathrm{X}_{2(2)}) + \ldots + \beta_{\mathrm{K}(2)} f(\mathrm{X}_{\mathrm{K}(2)}) + \frac{1}{\gamma_{(2)}} \times \mathrm{IV}_{(2)}\right]$$

If the utility function was assigned at a lower level:

$$\mathrm{V}_{(2)} = \tau_{(2)}\left[\frac{1}{\gamma_{(2)}} \times \mathrm{IV}_{(2)}\right]$$

where

$$IV_{(2)} = \ln(e^{(\gamma_{(3,2)} V_{(3,2)})}) = \gamma_{(3,2)} \times V_{(3,2)}$$

If the utility function for limb 3 is specified at the trunk level, we have:

$$V_{(2)} = \tau_{(2)}\Big[\beta_{0(2)} + \beta_{1(2)} f(X_{1(2)}) + \beta_{2(2)} f(X_{2(2)}) + \ldots + \beta_{K(2)} f(X_{K(2)}) + \tfrac{1}{\gamma_{(2)}} \times IV_{(2)}\Big]$$

$$V_{(3,2)} = 0$$

$$IV_{(2)} = 0$$

Hence:

$$\begin{aligned} V_{(2)} &= \tau_{(2)}\Big[\beta_{0(2)} + \beta_{1(2)} f(X_{1(2)}) + \beta_{2(2)} f(X_{2(2)}) + \ldots + \beta_{K(2)} f(X_{K(2)}) + \frac{1}{\gamma_{(2)}} \times 0\Big] \\ &= \tau_{(2)}[\beta_{0(2)} + \beta_{1(2)} f(X_{1(2)}) + \beta_{2(2)} f(X_{2(2)}) + \ldots + \beta_{K(2)} f(X_{K(2)})] \end{aligned}$$

The last trunk, associated with degenerative elemental alternative M may be formally represented as:

$$V_{(3)} = \tau_{(3)}\Big[\beta_{0(3)} + \beta_{1(3)} f(X_{1(3)}) + \beta_{2(3)} f(X_{2(3)}) + \ldots + \beta_{K(3)} f(X_{K(3)}) + \frac{1}{\gamma_{(3)}} \times IV_{(3)}\Big]$$

If the utility was assigned at a lower level,

$$V_{(3)} = \tau_{(3)}\left[\frac{1}{\gamma_{(3)}} \times IV_{(3)}\right]$$

where

$$IV_{(3)} = \ln(e^{(\gamma_{(4,3)} V_{(4,3)})}) = \gamma_{(3)} \times V_{(4,3)}$$

The trunk level utility is therefore,

$$V_{(3)} = \tau_{(3)} \times \frac{1}{\gamma_{(3)}} \times \gamma_{(3)} \times V_{(4,3)} = \tau_{(3)} \times V_{(4,3)}$$

We may now write out the probabilities for trunk 1, limb 3 and elemental alternative M. We do so below.

The probability of trunk 1 being selected is:

$$\mathrm{P}(1) = e^{V_{(1)}} / (e^{V_{(1)}} + e^{V_{(3,2)}} + e^{V_{(7|4,2)}})$$

Where

$$e^{V_{(1)}} = e^{(\tau_{(1)}[\beta_{0(1)}+\beta_{(1)}f(x_{1(1)})+\beta_{2(1)}f(X_{2(1)})+\ldots+\beta_{K(1)}f(X_{K(1)})+\frac{1}{\gamma_{(1)}}\times IV_{(1)}])}$$

$$e^{V_{(1)}} + e^{V_{(3,2)}} + e^{V_{(7|4,2)}} = e^{(\tau_{(1)}[\beta_{0(1)}+\beta_{(1)}f(x_{1(1)})+\beta_{2(1)}f(X_{2(1)})+\ldots+\beta_{K(1)}f(X_{K(1)})+\frac{1}{\gamma_{(1)}}\times IV_{(1)}])} + e^{(\gamma_{(3,2)}[\beta_{0(3,2)}+\beta_{1(3,2)}f(x_{1(3,2)})+\beta_{2(3,2)}f(X_{2(3,2)})+\ldots+\beta_{K(3,2)}f(X_{K(3,2)})+IV_{(3,2)}])}$$

We calculate the probability that limb 3 will be selected as:

$$\mathrm{P}(3,2) = e^{V_{(3,2)}} / (e^{V_{(1)}} + e^{V_{(3,2)}} + e^{V_{(7|4,2)}})$$

Finally, the probability that alternative M will be chosen is:

$$\mathrm{P}(M) = e^{V_{(M)}} / (e^{V_{(1)}} + e^{V_{(3,2)}} + e^{V_{(7|4,2)}})$$

RU2 (normalize $\tau_{(l)} = 1$)

Under RU2 $\tau_{(l)} = 1$ hence the IV parameter $\frac{\tau_{(1)}}{\gamma_{(1)}}$ becomes $\frac{1}{\gamma_{(1)}}$

For Trunk 1, $\tau_{(1)}$

$$\mathrm{V}_{(1)} = \beta_{0(1)} + \beta_{1(1)}f(\mathrm{X}_{1(1)}) + \beta_{2(1)}f(\mathrm{X}_{2(1)}) + \ldots + \beta_{\mathrm{K}(1)}f(\mathrm{X}_{\mathrm{K}(1)}) + \frac{1}{\gamma_{(1)}} \times \mathrm{IV}_{(1)}$$

Where

$$\mathrm{IV}_{(1)} = \ln(e^{(\lambda_{(1,1)}\mathrm{V}_{(1,1)})} + e^{(\lambda_{(2,1)}\mathrm{V}_{(2,1)})})$$

The utility for trunk 2 may be expressed as follows:

$$\mathrm{V}_{(2)} = \tau_{(2)}\left[\beta_{0(2)} + \beta_{1(2)}f(\mathrm{X}_{1(2)}) + \beta_{2(2)}f(\mathrm{X}_{2(2)}) + \ldots + \beta_{\mathrm{K}(2)}f(\mathrm{X}_{\mathrm{K}(2)}) + \frac{1}{\gamma_{(2)}} \times \mathrm{IV}_{(2)}\right]$$

Noting that $\tau_{(l)} = 1$

$$\mathrm{V}_{(2)} = \beta_{0(2)} + \beta_{1(2)}f(\mathrm{X}_{1(2)}) + \beta_{2(2)}f(\mathrm{X}_{2(2)}) + \ldots + \beta_{\mathrm{K}(2)}f(\mathrm{X}_{\mathrm{K}(2)}) + \frac{1}{\gamma_{(2)}} \times \mathrm{IV}_{(2)}$$

If the utility was assigned at a lower level:

$$V_{(2)} = \frac{1}{\gamma_{(2)}} \times IV_{(2)}$$

where

$$IV_{(2)} = \ln(e^{(\gamma_{(3,2)} V_{(3,2)})}) = \gamma_{(2)} \times V_{(3,2)}$$

Hence:

$$V_{(2)} = \frac{1}{\gamma_{(2)}} \times \gamma_{(2)} \times V_{(3,2)} = V_{(3,2)}$$

Notice that for the above, there is no IV parameter. The scale parameters in a degenerative partition under RU2 cancel each other out. We show this again for the last trunk associated with the degenerative elemental alternative M.

$$V_{(3)} = \tau_{(3)}\left[\beta_{0(3)} + \beta_{1(3)} f(X_{1(3)}) + \beta_{2(3)} f(X_{2(3)}) + \ldots + \beta_{K(3)} f(X_{K(3)}) + \frac{1}{\gamma_{(3)}} \times IV_{(3)}\right]$$

Noting that $\tau_{(l)} = 1$

$$V_{(3)} = \left[\beta_{0(3)} + \beta_{1(3)} f(X_{1(3)}) + \beta_{2(3)} f(X_{2(3)}) + \ldots + \beta_{K(3)} f(X_{K(3)}) + \frac{1}{\gamma_{(3)}} \times IV_{(3)}\right]$$

If the utility was assigned at a lower level:

$$V_{(3)} = \frac{1}{\gamma_{(3)}} \times IV_{(3)}$$

where

$$IV_{(3)} = \ln(e^{(\gamma_{(4,3)} V_{(4,3)})}) = \gamma_{(3)} \times V_{(4,3)}$$

Hence:

$$V_{(3)} = \frac{1}{\gamma_{(3)}} \times \gamma_{(3)} \times V_{(4,3)} = V_{(4,3)}$$

This finding, first reported by Hunt (2000), suggests that under RU2, the IV parameters of degenerative partitions will not be identifiable at the upper most level of NL models (i.e., they cancel out). NLOGIT automatically recognizes this fact and reverts to RU1 in the case of degenerate partitions. Nevertheless, debate still exists as to the application of degenerative partitions, even under RU1 normalization. Under RU1, the scale parameters at levels 2 to 4 are identifiable only under the assumption that $\mu_{(j|i,l)} = 1$. Intuitively, the variance (scale parameters) for a degenerative partition should be equal at all levels of the NL model (i.e., the variance should not depend on what level the analyst specifies the utility function at), hence we would expect $\tau_{(l)} = \gamma_{(i,l)} = \lambda_{(j|i,l)} = \mu_{(j|i,l,k)}$. Given that $\mu_{(j|i,l,k)} = 1$, $\tau_{(l)}$, $\gamma_{(i,l)}$ and $\lambda_{(j|i,l)}$ must also equal one. If an NL model has two degenerative alternatives, scale parameters for both must be normalized to one, which is equivalent to treating these alternatives as a single nest (with MNL properties).

The probability of trunk 1 being selected is:

$$\mathrm{P}(1) = e^{V_{(1)}} / (e^{V_{(1)}} + e^{V_{(3,2)}} + e^{V_{(7|4,2)}})$$

Where

$$\begin{aligned} e^{V_{(1)}} &= e^{(\beta_{0(1)}+\beta_{(1)} f(x_{1(1)})+\beta_{2(1)} f(X_{2(1)})+\ldots+\beta_{K(1)} f(X_{K(1)})+\frac{1}{\gamma_{(1)}} \times IV_{(1)})} \\ e^{V_{(1)}} + e^{V_{(3,2)}} + e^{V_{(7|4,2)}} &= e^{(\beta_{0(1)}+\beta_{(1)} f(x_{1(1)})+\beta_{2(1)} f(X_{2(1)})+\ldots+\beta_{K(1)} f(X_{K(1)})+\frac{1}{\gamma_{(1)}} \times IV_{(1)})} \\ &\quad + e^{(\gamma_{(3,2)}[\beta_{0(3,2)}+\beta_{1(3,2)} f(x_{1(3,2)})+\beta_{2(3,2)} f(X_{2(3,2)})+\ldots+\beta_{K(3,2)} f(X_{K(3,2)})+IV_{(3,2)}])} \\ &\quad + e^{(\mu_{13}\beta_{0M}+\mu_{13}\beta_{1M} f(x_{1M})+\mu_{13}\beta_{2M} f(X_{2M})+\ldots+\mu_{13}\beta_{KM} f(X_{KM}))} \end{aligned}$$

The PCS

We are now in a position to formally define the entire PCS for the NL model shown in Figure 13A.1. We start by writing out the conditional probabilities for each elemental alternative, branch, limb and trunk, before showing the complete probability calculations as performed at each level of the NL model.

The conditional probabilities are:

$$\begin{aligned} \mathrm{P}(A) &= e^{V_A} / (e^{V_A} + e^{V_B}) \\ \mathrm{P}(B) &= e^{V_B} / (e^{V_A} + e^{V_B}) \\ \mathrm{P}(C) &= e^{V_C} / (e^{V_C} + e^{V_D}) \\ \mathrm{P}(D) &= e^{V_D} / (e^{V_C} + e^{V_D}) \\ \mathrm{P}(E) &= e^{V_E} / (e^{V_E} + e^{V_F}) \\ \mathrm{P}(F) &= e^{V_F} / (e^{V_E} + e^{V_F}) \\ \mathrm{P}(G) &= e^{V_G} / (e^{V_G} + e^{V_H}) \\ \mathrm{P}(H) &= e^{V_H} / (e^{V_G} + e^{V_H}) \\ \mathrm{P}(I) &= e^{V_I} / (e^{V_I} + e^{V_J}) \\ \mathrm{P}(J) &= e^{V_J} / (e^{V_I} + e^{V_J}) \\ \mathrm{P}(K) &= e^{V_K} / (e^{V_K} + e^{V_L}) \\ \mathrm{P}(L) &= e^{V_L} / (e^{V_K} + e^{V_L}) \\ \mathrm{P(M)} &= e^{V_{(M)}} / (e^{V_{(1)}} + e^{V_{(3,2)}} + e^{V_{(7|4,2)}}) \\ \mathrm{P}(1|1,1) &= e^{V_{(1|1,1)}} / (e^{V_{(1|1,1)}} + e^{V_{(2|1,1)}}) \end{aligned}$$

$$P(2|1,1) = e^{V_{(2|1,1)}}/(e^{V_{(1|1,1)}} + e^{V_{(2|1,1)}})$$
$$P(3|2,1) = e^{V_{(3|2,1)}}/(e^{V_{(3|2,1)}} + e^{V_{(4|2,1)}})$$
$$P(4|2,1) = e^{V_{(4|2,1)}}/(e^{V_{(3|2,1)}} + e^{V_{(4|2,1)}})$$
$$P(5|3,1) = e^{V_{(5|3,1)}}/(e^{V_{(5|3,1)}} + e^{V_{(5|3,1)}})$$
$$P(6|3,1) = e^{V_{(6|3,1)}}/(e^{V_{(5|3,1)}} + e^{V_{(5|3,1)}})$$
$$P(1,1) = e^{V_{(1,1)}}/(e^{V_{(1,1)}} + e^{V_{(2,1)}})$$
$$P(2,1) = e^{V_{(2,1)}}/(e^{V_{(1,1)}} + e^{V_{(2,1)}})$$
$$P(3,2) = e^{V_{(3,2)}}/(e^{V_{(1)}} + e^{V_{(3,2)}} + e^{V_{(7|4,2)}})$$
$$P(1) = e^{V_{(1)}}/(e^{V_{(1)}} + e^{V_{(3,2)}} + e^{V_{(7|4,2)}})$$

The probabilities for the elemental alternatives may be calculated as:

$$P(A) = e^{V_A}/(e^{V_A} + e^{V_B}) \times e^{V_{(1|1,1)}}/(e^{V_{(1|1,1)}} + e^{V_{(2|1,1)}}) \times e^{V_{(1,1)}}/(e^{V_{(1,1)}} + e^{V_{(2,1)}}) \times e^{V_{(1)}}/(e^{V_{(1)}} + e^{V_{(3,2)}} + e^{V_{(7|4,2)}})$$
$$P(B) = e^{V_B}/(e^{V_A} + e^{V_B}) \times e^{V_{(1|1,1)}}/(e^{V_{(1|1,1)}} + e^{V_{(2|1,1)}}) \times e^{V_{(1,1)}}/(e^{V_{(1,1)}} + e^{V_{(2,1)}}) \times e^{V_{(1)}}/(e^{V_{(1)}} + e^{V_{(3,2)}} + e^{V_{(7|4,2)}})$$
$$P(C) = e^{V_C}/(e^{V_C} + e^{V_D}) \times e^{V_{(2|1,1)}}/(e^{V_{(1|1,1)}} + e^{V_{(2|1,1)}}) \times e^{V_{(1,1)}}/(e^{V_{(1,1)}} + e^{V_{(2,1)}}) \times e^{V_{(1)}}/(e^{V_{(1)}} + e^{V_{(3,2)}} + e^{V_{(7|4,2)}})$$
$$P(D) = e^{V_D}/(e^{V_C} + e^{V_D}) \times e^{V_{(2|1,1)}}/(e^{V_{(1|1,1)}} + e^{V_{(2|1,1)}}) \times e^{V_{(1,1)}}/(e^{V_{(1,1)}} + e^{V_{(2,1)}}) \times e^{V_{(1)}}/(e^{V_{(1)}} + e^{V_{(3,2)}} + e^{V_{(7|4,2)}})$$
$$P(E) = e^{V_E}/(e^{V_E} + e^{V_F}) \times e^{V_{(3|2,1)}}/(e^{V_{(3|2,1)}} + e^{V_{(4|2,1)}}) \times e^{V_{(2,1)}}/(e^{V_{(1,1)}} + e^{V_{(2,1)}}) \times e^{V_{(1)}}/(e^{V_{(1)}} + e^{V_{(3,2)}} + e^{V_{(7|4,2)}})$$
$$P(F) = e^{V_F}/(e^{V_E} + e^{V_F}) \times e^{V_{(3|2,1)}}/(e^{V_{(3|2,1)}} + e^{V_{(4|2,1)}}) \times e^{V_{(2,1)}}/(e^{V_{(1,1)}} + e^{V_{(2,1)}}) \times e^{V_{(1)}}/(e^{V_{(1)}} + e^{V_{(3,2)}} + e^{V_{(7|4,2)}})$$
$$P(G) = e^{V_G}/(e^{V_G} + e^{V_H}) \times e^{V_{(4|2,1)}}/(e^{V_{(3|2,1)}} + e^{V_{(4|2,1)}}) \times e^{V_{(2,1)}}/(e^{V_{(1,1)}} + e^{V_{(2,1)}}) \times e^{V_{(1)}}/(e^{V_{(1)}} + e^{V_{(3,2)}} + e^{V_{(7|4,2)}})$$
$$P(H) = e^{V_H}/(e^{V_G} + e^{V_H}) \times e^{V_{(4|2,1)}}/(e^{V_{(3|2,1)}} + e^{V_{(4|2,1)}}) \times e^{V_{(2,1)}}/(e^{V_{(1,1)}} + e^{V_{(2,1)}}) \times e^{V_{(1)}}/(e^{V_{(1)}} + e^{V_{(3,2)}} + e^{V_{(7|4,2)}})$$
$$P(I) = e^{V_I}/(e^{V_I} + e^{V_J}) \times e^{V_{(5|3,1)}}/(e^{V_{(5|3,1)}} + e^{V_{(5|3,1)}}) \times e^{V_{(3,2)}}/(e^{V_{(1)}} + e^{V_{(3,2)}} + e^{V_{(7|4,2)}})$$
$$P(J) = e^{V_J}/(e^{V_I} + e^{V_J}) \times e^{V_{(5|3,1)}}/(e^{V_{(5|3,1)}} + e^{V_{(5|3,1)}}) \times e^{V_{(3,2)}}/(e^{V_{(1)}} + e^{V_{(3,2)}} + e^{V_{(7|4,2)}})$$
$$P(K) = e^{V_K}/(e^{V_K} + e^{V_L}) \times e^{V_{(6|3,1)}}/(e^{V_{(5|3,1)}} + e^{V_{(5|3,1)}}) \times e^{V_{(3,2)}}/(e^{V_{(1)}} + e^{V_{(3,2)}} + e^{V_{(7|4,2)}})$$
$$P(L) = e^{V_L}/(e^{V_K} + e^{V_L}) \times e^{V_{(6|3,1)}}/(e^{V_{(5|3,1)}} + e^{V_{(5|3,1)}}) \times e^{V_{(3,2)}}/(e^{V_{(1)}} + e^{V_{(3,2)}} + e^{V_{(7|4,2)}})$$

$$P(M) = e^{V_{(M)}} / (e^{V_{(1)}} + e^{V_{(3,2)}} + e^{V_{(7|4,2)}})$$

The probabilities at the level 2 of the tree are:

$$\begin{aligned}
P(1|1,1) &= e^{V_{(1|1,1)}} / (e^{V_{(1|1,1)}} + e^{V_{(2|1,1)}}) \times e^{V_{(1,1)}} / (e^{V_{(1,1)}} + e^{V_{(2,1)}}) \\
&\quad \times e^{V_{(1)}} / (e^{V_{(1)}} + e^{V_{(3,2)}} + e^{V_{(7|4,2)}}) \\
P(2|1,1) &= e^{V_{(2|1,1)}} / (e^{V_{(1|1,1)}} + e^{V_{(2|1,1)}}) \times e^{V_{(1,1)}} / (e^{V_{(1,1)}} + e^{V_{(2,1)}}) \\
&\quad \times e^{V_{(1)}} / (e^{V_{(1)}} + e^{V_{(3,2)}} + e^{V_{(7|4,2)}}) \\
P(3|2,1) &= e^{V_{(3|2,1)}} / (e^{V_{(3|2,1)}} + e^{V_{(4|2,1)}}) \times e^{V_{(2,1)}} / (e^{V_{(1,1)}} + e^{V_{(2,1)}}) \\
&\quad \times e^{V_{(1)}} / (e^{V_{(1)}} + e^{V_{(3,2)}} + e^{V_{(7|4,2)}}) \\
P(4|2,1) &= e^{V_{(4|2,1)}} / (e^{V_{(3|2,1)}} + e^{V_{(4|2,1)}}) \times e^{V_{(2,1)}} / (e^{V_{(1,1)}} + e^{V_{(2,1)}}) \\
&\quad \times e^{V_{(1)}} / (e^{V_{(1)}} + e^{V_{(3,2)}} + e^{V_{(7|4,2)}}) \\
P(5|3,1) &= e^{V_{(5|3,1)}} / (e^{V_{(5|3,1)}} + e^{V_{(5|3,1)}}) \times e^{V_{(3,2)}} / (e^{V_{(1)}} + e^{V_{(3,2)}} + e^{V_{(7|4,2)}}) \\
P(6|3,1) &= e^{V_{(6|3,1)}} / (e^{V_{(5|3,1)}} + e^{V_{(5|3,1)}}) \times e^{V_{(3,2)}} / (e^{V_{(1)}} + e^{V_{(3,2)}} + e^{V_{(7|4,2)}})
\end{aligned}$$

The probabilities at the level 3 of the tree are calculated as:

$$\begin{aligned}
P(1,1) &= e^{V_{(1,1)}} / (e^{V_{(1,1)}} + e^{V_{(2,1)}}) \times e^{V_{(1)}} / (e^{V_{(1)}} + e^{V_{(3,2)}} + e^{V_{(7|4,2)}}) \\
P(2,1) &= e^{V_{(2,1)}} / (e^{V_{(1,1)}} + e^{V_{(2,1)}}) \times e^{V_{(1)}} / (e^{V_{(1)}} + e^{V_{(3,2)}} + e^{V_{(7|4,2)}}) \\
P(3,2) &= e^{V_{(3,2)}} / (e^{V_{(1)}} + e^{V_{(3,2)}} + e^{V_{(7|4,2)}})
\end{aligned}$$

Finally, the probability at level 4 of the NL tree structure shown in Figure 10A.1 is:

$$P(1) = e^{V_{(1)}} / (e^{V_{(1)}} + e^{V_{(3,2)}} + e^{V_{(7|4,2)}})$$

14 Nested logit estimation

In mathematics you don't understand things. You just get used to them. (Johann von Neumann, 1903–57)

14.1 Introduction

The majority of choice study applications do not progress beyond using the simple MNL model discussed in chapter 10. The ease of computation and the wide availability of software packages capable of estimating the MNL model suggest that this trend will continue well into the future. The ease with which the MNL model may be estimated, however, comes at a price in the form of the assumption of Independence of Identically Distributed (IID) error components. While the IID assumption and the behaviorally comparable assumption of Independence of Irrelevant Alternatives (IIA) allow for ease of computation (as well as providing a closed-form solution[1]), as with any assumption, violations both can and do occur. When violations do occur, the cross-substitution effects observed between pairs of alternatives are no longer equal given the presence or absence of other alternatives within the complete list of available alternatives within the model (Louviere, Hensher, and Swait 2000).

The nested logit (NL) model represents a partial relaxation of the IID and IIA assumptions of the MNL model. As discussed in chapter 13, this relaxation occurs in the variance components of the model together with some correlation within sub-sets of alternatives, and while more advanced models relax the IID assumption more fully (via the covariances), the NL model represents an excellent advance for the analyst in terms of studies of choice. As with the MNL model, the NL model is relatively straightforward to estimate and offers the added benefit of being of a closed-form solution. More advanced models such as multinomial probit (MNP), heteroskedastic extreme value models (HEV), and the random parameter logit (RP), also referred to as the mixed logit (ML) model, relax the

[1] An equation is said to be a "closed-form solution" if it may be solved using mathematical operations and does not require complex, analytical calculations such as integration each time a change occurs somewhere within the system.

IID assumption in terms of the covariances; however, all are of open-form solution and as such require complex analytical calculations to identify changes in the choice probabilities through varying levels of attributes and SDC (see Louviere, Hensher, and Swait 2000 and Train 2003). In this chapter, we demonstrate through the use of the mode-choice data set how to estimate NL models using NLOGIT. As with chapter 10, in this chapter we have been very specific in terms of our explanation of the command syntax as well as the output generated. We begin our discussion-not with the NL model, but with the Hausman-test of the IIA assumption. We do so acknowledging that only once one is confident that the MNL model is deficient should one progress to more advanced models such as the NL model.

14.2 The Hausman-test of the IIA assumption

Underlying the logit model is the assumption of IID error terms which, as discussed in chapter 13, has as an equivalent behavioral assumption, the assumption of IIA. The IIA assumption states that the ratio of the probabilities of any two alternatives should be preserved despite the presence or absence of any other alternative within the set of alternatives included within the model (i.e. P_i/P_j will remain unaffected by the presence or absence of any other alternative within the set of alternatives modeled).

Hausman and McFadden (1984) proposed a specification test for the MNL model to test the IIA assumption. The test, known as the Hausman-test of the IIA assumption, is conducted in two stages; first the analyst estimates an unrestricted model complete with all alternatives before estimating a model synonymous with the alternative hypothesis using a restricted number of alternatives. In specifying the second "restricted" model the same specification (in terms of the attributes and SDC variables) should be used. The test-statistic is shown below:

$$q = [b_u - b_r]' \, [V_r - V_u]^{-1} \, [b_u - b_r] \tag{14.1}$$

where

b_u is a column vector of parameter estimates for the unrestricted model and b_r is a column vector of parameter estimates for the restricted model; and

V_r is the variance–covariance matrix for the restricted model and V_u is the variance–covariance matrix for the unrestricted model.

In NLOGIT, the Hausman-test of the IIA assumption is performed when the following command is added to the MNL command syntax discussed in chapter 10:

```
;ias = <alternative_i>
```

Given the preservation of the ratio of the probabilities for any two alternatives independent of the removal (or addition) of any or all of the remaining alternatives as assumed under the IIA assumption, the Hausman-test of the IIA assumption allows for the simultaneous removal of more than one alternative as part of the restricted model. In NLOGIT, the removal of more than one alternative for the restricted model is conducted as shown below:

```
;ias = <alternative_i>, ..., <alternative_j>
```

The test as performed using the **;ias** specification in NLOGIT may be applied to only a limited number of model specifications. In particular, the restricted model will not be estimable if the absence of one or more alternatives within the restricted model results in an attribute or SDC characteristic becoming constant (i.e. no variability) for the remaining alternatives. This will always be the case when alternatives not present in the restricted model have alternative specific parameter estimates (including constants). To explain, consider a model with four alternatives designated A, B, C, and D. Utility specifications for these alternatives are shown below:

```
U(A) = constant + costa×cost + time×time + income*income
U(B) = constantb + cost×cost + timeb×time
U(C) = constant + cost×cost + time×time
U(D) =            cost×cost + time×time
```

If in the **;ias** specification, the first alternative is removed for the test, the income variable, which is not present within the utility expressions of the three remaining alternatives, is now constant for the restricted model specification (i.e. income is a constant zero for alternatives B, C, and D; which is equivalent to fixing the parameter estimates for income to zero for these remaining alternatives). Similarly, the *costa* parameter associated with alternative A will be zero for alternatives B, C, and D. Removal of alternative B for the restricted model will also not work as the *timeb* parameter will be zero for alternatives A, C, and D. Further, the constant term is specific to this alternative and as such will also be zero for the three remaining alternatives.

The **;ias** specification should work (there is no guarantee as the test is data-specific) if the analyst removes alternative C for the restricted model. For the above example, the constant parameter will be non-zero for alternative A. The *time* attribute will be non-zero for alternatives A and D, and the *cost* attribute will similarly be non-zero for alternatives B and D. All variables associated with this alternative are non-zero in at least one other utility expression. The removal of alternative D from the restricted model raises a special problem in the estimation of the restricted model. If alternative D is not present, the three remaining alternatives each require the estimation of a constant term. As the MNL model is homogeneous of degree zero in the attributes, it is only possible to estimate $J-1$ constant terms. For the restricted model, absent of alternative D, a constant term is now to be estimated for all J remaining alternatives. No such model can be estimated, and the test will fail.

To conduct the Hausman-test of the IIA assumption, the analyst is first required to estimate an unrestricted model inclusive of all alternatives. We do this below using the NLOGIT **;ias** specification. As per chapter 10, this model is estimated for the 30 minutes or less commuting sample only:

```
NLOGIT
;lhs= choice, cset, altij
;Choices = cart, carnt, bus, train, busway, LR
?;ias=carnt
?;Show
;Model:
```

U(cart) = constant + cst*fuel /
U(carnt) =constant+ cst*fuel /
U(bus) = bus + cst*fare /
U(train) = train + cst*fare/
U(busway) = busway + cst*fare /
U(LR) = cst*fare $

For the mode choice case study data, the following model results are produced:

```
+-----------------------------------------------+
| Discrete choice (multinomial logit) model      |
| Maximum Likelihood Estimates                   |
| Model estimated: Feb 30, 2003 at 11:15:00PM.   |
| Dependent variable              Choice         |
| Weighting variable                None         |
| Number of observations            2369         |
| Iterations completed                 4         |
| Log likelihood function        -3246.637       |
| R2=1-LogL/LogL*  Log-L fncn   R-sqrd   RsqAdj  |
| No coefficients  -4244.6782   .23513   .23459  |
| Constants only.   Must be computed directly.   |
|                   Use NLOGIT ;...; RHS=ONE  $  |
| Response data are given as ind. choice.        |
| Number of obs.=   2369,  skipped   0 bad obs.  |
+-----------------------------------------------+
```

Variable	Coefficient	Standard Error	b/St.Er.	P[|Z|>z]
CONSTANT	.14708920	.06733861	2.184	.0289
CST	-.12480466	.01576755	-7.915	.0000
BUS	.02412792	.09853729	.245	.8066
TRAIN	-.04258099	.09318706	-.457	.6477
BUSWAY	.09584390	.08523910	1.124	.2608

The second stage of the test requires the analyst to estimate the restricted model. We show this removing the *carnt* alternative from the model estimation process. We have also included the **;show** specification in this command:

NLOGIT
;lhs= choice, cset, altij
;Choices = cart, carnt, bus, train, busway, LR
;ias=carnt
;Show
;Model:

U(cart) = constant + cst*fuel /
U(carnt) =constant + cst*fuel /
U(bus) = bus + cst*fare /
U(train) = train + cst*fare/
U(busway) = busway + cst*fare /
U(LR) = cst*fare $

The results of the restricted model are shown below:

```
        Tree Structure Specified for the Nested Logit Model
        Sample proportions are marginal, not conditional.
        Choices marked with * are excluded for the IIA test.
+--------------+--------------+----------------+-------------+------+----
Trunk   (prop.) |Limb    (prop.)|Branch   (prop.) |Choice (prop.)|Weight|IIA|
+---------  -----+--------------+----------------+-------------+------+----
Trunk{1} 1.00000|Lmb[1:1]1.00000|B(1:1,1) 1.00000 |CART     .35067| 1.000|
                |               |                 |CARNT    .00000| 1.000|*
                |               |                 |BUS      .14261| 1.000|
                |               |                 |TRAIN    .14202| 1.000|
                |               |                 |BUSWAY   .18644| 1.000|
                |               |                 |LR       .17826| 1.000|
+--------------+--------------+----------------+-------------+------+---+
Model Specification: Utility Functions for Alternatives
Table entry is the attribute that multiplies the indicated parameter.

              Parameter
       Row  1 CONSTANT CST      BUS         TRAIN        BUSWAY
Choice
CART        1 Constant FUEL
CARNT       1 Constant FUEL
BUS         1          FARE     Constant
TRAIN       1          FARE                 Constant
BUSWAY      1          FARE                              Constant
LR          1          FARE


+----------------------------------------------+
| Discrete choice (multinomial logit) model    |
| Maximum Likelihood Estimates                 |
| Model estimated: Feb 30, 2003 at 11:30:00AM. |
| Dependent variable                 Choice    |
| Weighting variable                   None    |
| Number of observations               1711    |
| Iterations completed                    4    |
| Log likelihood function         -1814.646    |
| R2=1-LogL/LogL*  Log-L fncn  R-sqrd  RsqAdj  |
| No coefficients  -3065.7005 .40808  .40721   |
| Constants only.  Must be computed directly.  |
|                  Use NLOGIT ;...; RHS=ONE $  |
| Response data are given as ind. choice.      |
```

```
| Number of obs.= 2369, skipped 658 bad obs.   |
| Hausman-test for IIA. Excluded choices are   |
| CARNT                                        |
| ChiSqrd[5] = 65.8730, Pr(C>c) =     .000000  |
+----------------------------------------------+
```

```
+----------+------------+----------------+----------+----------+
| Variable | Coefficient | Standard Error | b/St.Er. | P[|Z|>z] |
+----------+------------+----------------+----------+----------+
 CONSTANT    -.10490620       .07790176      -1.347      .1781
 CST         -.24264169       .02214527     -10.957      .0000
 BUS          .06343501       .10681205        .594      .5526
 TRAIN        .00698631       .09830069        .071      .9433
 BUSWAY       .08664195       .08971040        .966      .3341
```

The **;Show** command output demonstrates the new choice shares under the restricted set of alternatives. The asterisk in this output (*) is used to indicate which alternatives were removed for the test. As expected, the choice shares for alternatives not present within the restricted model will be zero. For the above example, this is demonstrated for the *carnt* alternative.

We have highlighted the test results in the output. For the restricted model, all observations where a non-present alternative was chosen are removed from the sample. In NLOGIT, these observations are reported as "bad observations." For the above example, 658 of the 2369 choices made in the sample were for the *carnt* alternative, all of which are ignored in the estimation of the restricted model. The test-statistic, q, is given as a Chi-square statistic in the model output. The degrees of freedom for this statistic (five in the above example) are equal to the number of parameters estimated in either model (the number of parameters will be equal for both the unrestricted and restricted models). The p-value for the test is given as Prob($C > c$). For the above example, comparing the p-value for the test to alpha equal to 0.05, we reject the IIA assumption for the model. For the above model, the analyst would have to consider a less restrictive model specification (e.g. NL or mixed logit) in order to proceed.

To demonstrate the test, we chose the model specification so that it would be consistent with the requirements of the test. In practice, one should not use as a determinant of the final model specification constraints imposed by statistical tests such as the Hausman-test of the IIA assumption. Fortunately, it is possible to extend the test to a wider number of model specifications, although not through the **;ias** command. We demonstrate this using the following example for which, we have ASCs but generic fuel and fare parameters. We extend this example further in appendix 14A with a model specified only with alternative-specific parameter estimates. Similar to using the **;ias** specification, to undertake the test, the analyst must to first estimate the unrestricted model. We do so below.

NLOGIT
;lhs= choice, cset, altij
;Choices = cart, carnt, bus, train, busway, LR
;Model:

U(cart) = asccart + fuel*fuel /
U(carnt) = asccarnt + fuel*fuel /
U(bus) = ascbus + fare*fare /
U(train) = asctn + fare*fare /
U(busway) = ascbusw + fare*fare /
U(LR) = fare*fare $

The unrestricted model output for the above model is as follows:

```
+-----------------------------------------------+
| Discrete choice (multinomial logit) model     |
| Maximum Likelihood Estimates                  |
| Model estimated: Feb 30, 2003 at 11:45:00AM.  |
| Dependent variable              Choice        |
| Weighting variable                None        |
| Number of observations            2369        |
| Iterations completed                 5        |
| Log likelihood function      -3215.496        |
| R2=1-LogL/LogL*   Log-L fncn  R-sqrd  RsqAdj  |
| No coefficients   -4244.6782  .24246  .24172  |
| Constants only.   Must be computed directly.  |
|                   Use NLOGIT ;...; RHS=ONE $  |
| Chi-squared[ 2]          =   1648.38887       |
| Prob [chi squared > value ] =     .00000      |
| Response data are given as ind. choice.       |
| Number of obs.= 2369, skipped 0 bad obs.      |
+-----------------------------------------------+
```

```
+----------+-------------+----------------+----------+----------+
|Variable  | Coefficient | Standard Error | b/St.Er. | P[|Z|>z] |
+----------+-------------+----------------+----------+----------+
 ASCCART      -.37341059      .12201823      -3.060     .0022
 FUEL         -.09384597      .04017823      -2.336     .0195
 ASCCARNT     -.09343872      .18348682       -.509     .6106
 ASCBUS        .02274998      .09951495        .229     .8192
 FARE         -.23225084      .02175219     -10.677     .0000
 ASCTN        -.03946351      .09391384       -.420     .6743
 ASCBUSW       .09228428      .08620342       1.071     .2844
```

For each model estimated, NLOGIT saves the parameters in a column vector named B (this matrix is overwritten each time a new model is estimated). The B column vector may be accessed via the project dialog box titled "**Untitled Project 1***" under the *Matrices* folder. The Hausman-test of the IIA assumption is performed using only those parameters that are not constant terms (this is also true when using the **;ias** specification). As such, not all of the parameters of the B column vector are required (i.e. b_u and b_r of (14.1) do not include any parameters that are constant terms). For the above example, b_u will have only two parameters, those being for the *fuel* and *fare* attributes.

To construct b_u, we must first create a permutation matrix, J1, which is used to extract the relevant parameters from the B column vector. The number of rows of the J1 matrix will be equal to the number of parameters required for the b_u column vector, and the number of columns will equal the number of parameters present within the B column vector. This is because each column of the J1 matrix is associated with each row of the B matrix (e.g. column one of the J1 matrix is related to the *asccart* parameter, column two to the *fuel* parameter etc.).

In the construction of the J1 matrix, a zero is placed in each column associated with a row in the B column vector for which the parameter in B is to be discarded. A "1" signifies that the related parameter located in the B column vector is to be retained. For the above example, the J1 matrix is shown below. The command **MATRIX;** is used to either create or manipulate matrices in NLOGIT. The elements of the matrix are enclosed in square brackets (**[ ]**; other brackets such as **( )** and **{}** are also used in the **MATRIX;** commands of NLOGIT but are not required here) and separated by a comma (**,**). A slash (**/**) is used to indicate a new row of the matrix:

```
MATRIX; J1 = [0,1,0,0,0,0,0 /
              0,0,0,0,1,0,0 ] $
```

As an aside, we could simply create b_u as we did for J1 using the relevant parameters from the model output. We did not do this, however, as the parameters shown in the output are displayed only to a number of decimal places which are fewer than the number of decimal places stored in the B matrix and, as such, doing so would produce a less accurate test.

Once J1 is created, b_u and V_u (as with b_u, the elements of the variance–covariance matrix for the test, V_u, are not inclusive of elements related to constant terms) are created using the **MATRIX;** command. We show this below:

```
MATRIX; Bu = J1*B ;Vu = J1*VARB*J1' $
```

By multiplying the column vector of parameter estimates (i.e. B) by the J1 matrix, the resulting matrix, named B_u, is a column vector of the parameter estimates without those parameters associated with the constant terms as obtained from the unrestricted model. The calculation of the B_u matrix is shown below:

$$\begin{bmatrix} 0 & 1 & 0 & 0 & 0 & 0 & 0 \\ 0 & 0 & 0 & 0 & 1 & 0 & 0 \end{bmatrix} \begin{bmatrix} -0.373411 \\ -0.093846 \\ -0.0934387 \\ 0.02275 \\ -0.232251 \\ -0.0394635 \\ 0.0922843 \end{bmatrix} = \begin{bmatrix} -0.093846 \\ -0.232251 \end{bmatrix}$$

As with the b_u column vector, the variance–covariance matrix, V_u, is also not inclusive of elements related to constant terms. To obtain the smaller variance–covariance matrix, the J1 matrix is multiplied by the V_u matrix (saved as *varb* in the *Project* dialog box titled "**Untitled Project 1***" under the *Matrices* folder) which is in turn multiplied by the transpose (when we transpose a matrix, the columns of the matrix become the rows and the rows become the columns; a matrix is transposed using the ' character in NLOGIT) of the J1 matrix. For this example, we show this calculation below:

$$\begin{bmatrix} 0 & 1 & 0 & 0 & 0 & 0 & 0 \\ 0 & 0 & 0 & 0 & 1 & 0 & 0 \end{bmatrix}$$

$$\times \begin{bmatrix} 0.0148884 & -0.00311061 & 0.0194479 & 0.00431227 & 0.00124247 & 0.00380217 & 0.00378675 \\ -0.00311061 & 0.00161429 & -0.00634197 & 0.000056552 & 0.000015019 & 0.000024229 & 0.00000749 \\ 0.0194479 & -0.00634197 & 0.0336674 & 0.00419971 & 0.00121298 & 0.00375465 & 0.00377181 \\ 0.00431227 & 0.000056552 & 0.00419971 & 0.00990322 & 0.00002048 & 0.00453800 & 0.00421324 \\ 0.00124247 & 0.000015019 & 0.00121298 & 0.00002048 & 0.000473158 & -0.00000951 & 0.00002007 \\ 0.00380217 & 0.000024229 & 0.00375465 & 0.004538 & -0.00000951 & 0.00881981 & 0.003252 \\ 0.00378675 & 0.00000749 & .00377181 & 0.00421324 & 0.00002007 & 0.003252 & 0.00743103 \end{bmatrix}$$

$$\times \begin{bmatrix} 0 & 0 \\ 1 & 0 \\ 0 & 0 \\ 0 & 0 \\ 0 & 1 \\ 0 & 0 \\ 0 & 0 \end{bmatrix} = \begin{bmatrix} 0.00161429 & 0.000015020 \\ 0.00001502 & 0.000473158 \end{bmatrix}$$

We now have the b_u and V_u components of (14.1). We now require b_r and V_r in order to calculate the test-statistic, q. This requires estimation of the restricted model. To estimate the restricted model, the analyst must first expunge all observations (i.e. choices) from the sample for which the alternatives which are to be removed were chosen. Fortunately, we have created a series of dummy variables within the data set which are equal to one for choice sets in which specific alternatives where chosen (or zero otherwise). For the *bus* alternative, this variable is called *spbus*. As well as removing choice sets in which the alternatives to be removed were chosen, we are also required to remove any rows of data related to alternatives to be removed from choice sets in which those alternatives were not chosen. Assuming that we are to remove the *bus* alternative (*altij* equal to three), the following **REJECT;** commands will remove all reference to the bus alternative from the sample to be used:

```
REJECT; spbus=1 $
REJECT; altij=3 $
```

The rejection of an alternative such as the *bus* alternative means that for observations where that alternative was once present, the choice set size will be smaller by the number of alternatives removed (e.g. if *bus* was one of four alternatives, removing this alternative will leave three remaining alternatives and hence the choice set size decreases from four to three). This has implications for both *altij* and *cset* in the model commands, neither of which can be used without modification. For data sets with fixed-choice sets, this may be easily fixed by creating a new index variable (say *altijn*) from 1 to J where J is the new number of alternatives within each choice set. Similarly, a new *cset* variable (say *csetn*) may be created such that it is always equal to the new total number of alternatives within each choice set (i.e. *J*).

For data sets that do not have fixed-choice sets (such as the mode-choice data set), a more complex approach is required to obtain *altijn* and *csetn*. For the mode-choice case study, there are six alternatives and hence *altij* takes values from one to six. The removal of the bus alternative (*altij* equal to three) means that there are now five possible remaining alternatives. For alternatives one and two (i.e. *cart* and *carnt*) *altijn* will be the same as *altij*. The removal of the third alternative however means that alternative four (i.e. *train*) should now be designated as alternative three in *altijn*, alternative five (i.e. *busway*) as alternative four and alternative six (i.e. *LR*) as alternative five. As each remaining alternative is not always present within a choice set, the creation of a new index variable for each choice set from one to five will not be consistent with the data.

Further, given the absence of *bus* from some choice sets, the removal of the *bus* alternative will now mean that some choice sets will have three alternatives (those for which *bus* was previously present as an alternative) while others will have four (those for which *bus* was not previously present as an alternative). To create the new *altij* and *cset* variables, we use the following command:

```
CREATE
;if(altij<3)altijn=altij
;if(altij>3)altijn=altij-1
;if(cn<3)csetn=3
;if(cn>2)csetn=cset $
```

The first segment of the above create command creates the new *altijn* variable such that it is equal to *altij* for alternatives one or two but decreases the number assigned to alternatives greater than three by one. Thus alternative four becomes alternative three, alternative five becomes four, etc. The last two lines of the command are used to create the new choice set size variable *csetn*. To do this, we have had to use the *cn* variable from the data set which is used to indicate which alternatives are present within each choice set. Choice sets in which the *bus* alternative is present are represented by *cn* equal to one and two. The command therefore sets *cset* to equal three if the bus alternative is present and four if the *bus* alternative is not present.

With the data setup complete, we now may proceed by estimating the restricted model. We do this below using the newly created *csetn* and *altijn* variables within the specification. Note also that no utility function for the *bus* alternative is estimated:

```
NLOGIT
;lhs= choice, csetn, altijn
;Choices = cart, carnt, train, busway, LR
;Model:
U(cart) = asccart + fuel*fuel /
U(carnt) = asccarnt + fuel*fuel /
?U(bus) = ascbus + fare*fare /
```

U(train) = asctn + fare*fare /
U(busway) = ascbusw + fare*fare /
U(LR) = fare*fare $

For the sample, the restricted model outlined above produces the following model output:

```
+-----------------------------------------------+
| Discrete choice (multinomial logit) model      |
| Maximum Likelihood Estimates                   |
| Model estimated: Feb 30, 2003 at 12:00:00PM.   |
| Dependent variable                 Choice      |
| Weighting variable                   None      |
| Number of observations               2125      |
| Iterations completed                    5      |
| Log likelihood function         -2659.630      |
| R2=1-LogL/LogL*    Log-L fncn  R-sqrd  RsqAdj  |
| No coefficients   -3420.0556  .22234  .22151   |
| Constants only.   Must be computed directly.   |
|                   Use NLOGIT ;...; RHS=ONE $   |
| Chi-squared[ 2]              = 1188.91073      |
| Prob [ chi squared > value] =      .00000      |
| Response data are given as ind. choice.        |
| Number of obs.= 2125, skipped 0 bad obs.       |
+-----------------------------------------------+

+----------+-------------+----------------+----------+----------+
|Variable  | Coefficient | Standard Error | b/St.Er. | P[|Z|>z] |
+----------+-------------+----------------+----------+----------+
 ASCCART     -.35310047      .12755449       -2.768     .0056
 FUEL        -.12019225      .04128175       -2.912     .0036
 ASCCARNT    -.01962300      .18973632        -.103     .9176
 ASCTN       -.04572901      .09486265        -.482     .6298
 FARE        -.24401516      .02542403       -9.598     .0000
 ASCBUSW      .09206082      .08681481        1.060     .2890
```

The parameter estimates for the restricted model will be saved in the B matrix located in the project dialog box titled "**Untitled Project 1***" under the *Matrices* folder (the parameter estimates for the unrestricted model will have been overwritten). Similarly the new variance–covariance matrix will be saved as *VARB* (overwriting that from the previous model). Therefore, to obtain the required b_r and V_r matrices we may use the same method we employed to obtain b_u and V_u. The number of parameters for the restricted model is smaller by the number of alternative specific parameters related to alternatives included in the unrestricted model. As such, the number of columns in the permutation matrix will also be fewer by this number. For the above example, the *bus* alternative had only one alternative-specific parameter (i.e. the constant, the *fare* parameter, is generic with the other public transport fare parameters) and, hence, the permutation matrix will have six columns instead of the previous seven. We show this below:

```
MATRIX; J2 = [0,1,0,0,0,0 /
              0,0,0,0,1,0 ] $
```

Using the new permutation matrix, J2, the relevant parameter estimates and variance–covariance matrix elements can be extracted as shown below:

```
MATRIX; Br = J2*B ;Vr = J2*VARB*J2' $
```

We omit the matrix algebra for this given the similarity to the previous example. What remains is to calculate the test-statistic, q. We show the commands for this below:

```
MATRIX; bd = Bu-Br ;Vd = Vr-Vu $
MATRIX; vdinv=[vd] $
MATRIX; list; q = bd'*vninv*bd $
CALC; list; p = 1-chi(q,2) $
```

The first matrix command creates two matrices. The first matrix created is the difference between the parameter estimates of the unrestricted and restricted models (i.e. $b_u - b_r$). The second matrix created is the difference between the restricted and unrestricted variance–covariance matrices (i.e. $V_r - V_u$). When using the matrix command in NLOGIT, placing a single matrix such as Vd within square brackets ([ ]) creates the inverse of the matrix enclosed. As such, the second matrix command creates the inverse of the difference of the variance–covariances of the two models (i.e. $[V_r - V_u]^{-1}$). The third matrix command computes q. By adding the **list** specification to the command, NLOGIT will display the result in the output file. The command in the above series is a **CALC** command designed to calculate the p-value for the test. The number "2" in this command represents the number of parameters contained within the b_u and b_r matrices.

For the above example, the following NLOGIT output is observed:

```
Matrix Q            has 1 rows and 1 columns.
1
+--------------
1| 8.08460
```

And,

```
P     = .17557046421332600D-01
Calculator: Computed  2 scalar results
```

The test-statistic, q, is equal to 8.0846 and with two degrees of freedom, the p-value for the test is 0.018 (the number after D indicates that the decimal place should be moved that many places. Negative values mean move the decimal place to the left; positive values mean move to the right. Therefore D-01 indicates that the decimal place should be moved one place to the left). Comparing the p-value to 0.05, we reject the null hypothesis of the IIA assumption. This suggests that a more complex model which relaxes the IIA assumption should be considered.

14.3 The nested logit model commands

The simplicity in estimation as well as the empirical appeal of the MNL model arises as a direct result of the IID assumption imposed upon the random component of the utility functions of each alternative. Yet, it has long been recognized that while the IID assumption provides ease of model estimation, it is also represents a potential limitation to the model, in that it is easily violated. The NL model allows for a partial relaxation in the IID assumption of the MNL model by allowing for differential variation in the unobserved effects across partitions of alternatives (but not within those same partitions) with only a marginal increase in difficulty of estimation. While more advanced models relax the IID assumption further and hence may be considered more appealing empirically, they do so at the expense of simplicity and ease of estimation. It is for this reason that the MNL and NL models (and variants with the closed-form set) will remain the primary forms of modeling choice behavior for many years to come.

In this section, we discuss how to estimate NL models using NLOGIT. We use several examples to demonstrate various aspects of NL models and pertinent issues surrounding the specification of such models. As with chapter 10, we use the mode-choice case study as our point of reference in estimating these models. We begin by examining how NL tree structures are specified in NLOGIT.

The majority of NL models estimated as part of choice studies have only two levels. Very few NL models are estimated with three levels, and even fewer with four levels. NLOGIT has the capability to estimate NL models with up to four levels. Within the literature, the three highest levels of NL trees are named, from the highest level (level 4) to the lowest level (level 2), as trunks, limbs, and branches. At the lowest level of NL trees (level one) reside the elemental alternatives (hereafter referred to simply as alternatives) which are sometimes referred to in the literature as "twigs."

NL models estimated by NLOGIT may have up to a maximum of five trunks, 10 limbs, 25 branches, and 100 alternatives. Any tree structure, provided that it does not exceed the maximum number of trunks, limbs, branches, or alternatives allowed, may be estimated. Thus, provided that the total number of alternatives within the tree does not exceed 100, some branches may have only one alternative (known as a *degenerate branch* and discussed in more detail later) while other branches may have two or more alternatives. Similarly, provided that the total number of limbs does not exceed 25, some trunks may have only a single branch, while others may have two or more branches. Trunks may also have any number of limbs, provided that the total number of limbs does not exceed 10 within the overall tree structure. Tree structures in which there is only a single trunk, but two or more limbs, are known as three-level NL models (we often omit the trunk level when we draw such trees; however, the level is still there). Models with only one trunk and one limb but multiple branches are, by implication, called two-level NL models (once more, it is customary when drawing such tree structures to do so without showing the single trunk and limb). Single-level models, where there is only a single trunk, limb and branch, but multiple alternatives, are also possible.

The command syntax structure for the NL model is similar to the command syntax for the MNL model discussed in chapter 10. The addition of the following command to the

MNL command syntax will estimate an NL model using NLOGIT:

;Tree =<tree structure>

Placing the tree specification command within the MNL command syntax, the base NL model command will look as follows:

NLOGIT
;lhs = choice, cset, altij
;Choices =<names of alternatives>
;Tree = <tree structure>
;Model:
U(alternative 1 name) = <utility function 1> /
U(alternative 2 name) = <utility function 2> /
...
U(alternative i name) = <utility function i> $

In defining the tree structure, the following NLOGIT conventions apply:

{} specifies a trunk (level 4)
[] specifies a limb within a trunk (level 3)
() specifies a branch within a limb within a trunk (level 2).

Entries at the same level of a tree are separated by a comma (,). The analyst may name each of the trunks, limbs, and branches; however, if no name is provided, NLOGIT will provide generic names such as Trunk{*l*}, Lmb[*i*|*l*] and B(*j*|*i*,*l*), where *l* is the *l*th trunk, *i* is the *i*th limb, and *j* is the *j*th branch (e.g. B(1|1,1) represents the first branch in limb one within the first trunk; B(1|2,1) represents the second branch in the limb one within trunk one; B(2|2,1) represents the second branch in the limb two within trunk one; Lmb[1:1] represents limb one, trunk one; and Trunk[2] represents trunk two). The naming of a trunk, limb, or branch is done by providing a name (eight characters or fewer) outside the relevant brackets. The alternatives are specified at the lowest level of the tree structure (i.e. at level one) and are entered within the appropriate brackets as they exist within the tree structure. Alternatives within the same trunk, limb, or branch are separated by a comma (,).

To demonstrate the above, consider the following example:

;Tree = car(cart,carnt), PT(bus,train,busway,LR)

The above tree specification will estimate an NL model with the tree structure shown in figure 14.1.

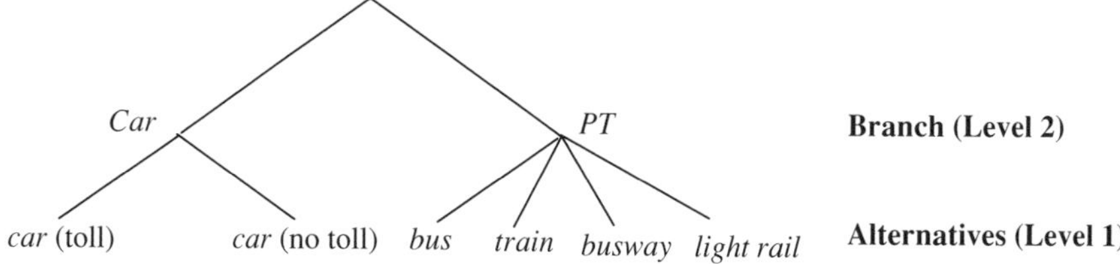

Figure 14.1 Example NL tree structure one

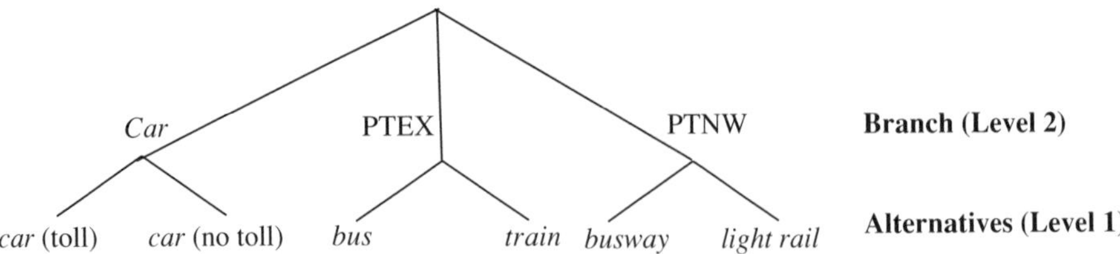

Figure 14.2 Example tree structure two

The tree structure shown in figure 14.1 is the same as that shown in figure 13.1. This structure has two branches and six alternatives, two belonging to the *car* branch, and four to the *PT* branch and hence is a two-level NL model. This tree structure represents one of many possible tree structures that may be explored by the analyst. For example, the analyst may also specify the NL tree structure (using the same alternatives) as follows:

;Tree = car(cart,carnt), PTEX(bus,train), PTNW(busway,LR)

Graphically, the above NL tree structure would look as shown in figure 14.2.

The tree structure in figure 14.2 differs to that in figure 14.1 in that there now exists three branches, each with two alternatives. For the NL model represented by figure 14.2, we have placed the *bus* and *train* alternatives within the same branch named PTEX (for existing modes) and the *busway* and *light rail* modes in a branch named PTNW (for new modes).

As an aside, although, as we have shown, it is possible to omit higher levels from NL models if the higher levels have a single limb or trunk (which we have omitted from our tree diagrams), it is also possible to acknowledge that a higher level exists by providing a name for it. For example:

;Tree = Limb[car(cart,carnt), PTEX(bus,train), PTNW(busway,LR)]

will produce exactly the same NL model as that shown in figure 14.2. In such cases, the IV parameter of the highest level (called *Limb* above) is fixed at 1.0 (see below).

Once again, the tree structure of figure 14.2 represents but one of many possible tree structures that may be of interest. In the following tree specification, we demonstrate a third possible tree structure that may be worth exploring. In this particular structure, we have added an additional level (i.e. a limb) to the tree, thus making this a three-level NL model.

;Tree= CAR[cart,carnt], PT[PTRail(bus,train), PTRoad(busway,LR)]

Graphically, the above tree specification is shown in figure 14.3.

In specifying the tree structure to be adopted, many confuse NL trees with *decision trees* (perhaps this is the fault of authors who tend to use, as examples, NL tree structures that have behaviorally intuitive undertones; the tree structures of figures 14.1, 14.2, and 14.3

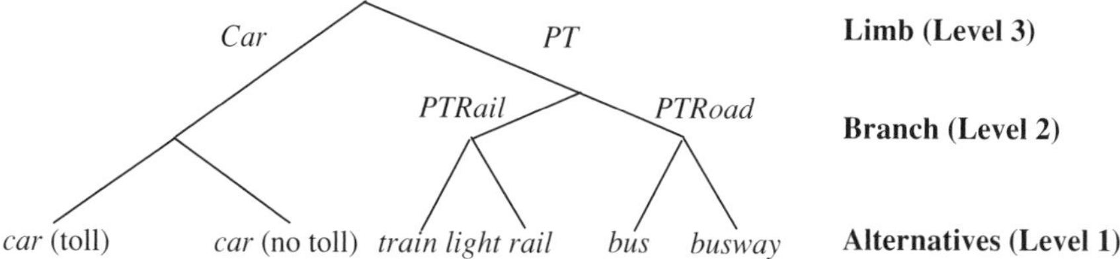

Figure 14.3 Example tree structure three

are examples of this). Nevertheless, any similarity of NL tree structures to decision trees is largely misleading. As discussed in chapter 13, NL tree structures are determined so as to accommodate *differences in variance or scale* that exist in the unobserved components of the utility expressions (i.e. on econometric and not behavioral grounds).

As we learnt from chapter 13, the variance of alternatives that reside together in any partition of an NL tree is constrained so as to equal one another. In the tree structure shown in figure 14.3 this suggests:

$$\sigma^2_{cart|Car} = \sigma^2_{carnt|Car} = \sigma^2_{..|Car};$$
$$\sigma^2_{Train|PTRail} = \sigma^2_{LR|PTRail} = \sigma^2_{..|PTRail};$$
$$\sigma^2_{Bus|PTRoad} = \sigma^2_{Busw|PTRoad} = \sigma^2_{..|PTRoad}; \quad \text{and}$$
$$\sigma^2_{PTRail|PT}\sigma^2_{PTRoad|PT} = \sigma^2_{..|PT}$$

Statistically, the variance of the unobserved effects for a given alternative may be expressed as a function of pertinent information (i.e. variables) omitted from the utility function belonging to that alternative. If the utility functions of two or more alternatives share a common set of missing attributes, all of which would have a similar influence upon the utilities of the various alternatives, then the variance of the unobserved effects for each of those alternatives is more than likely to be similarly influenced, suggesting that such alternatives be situated within the same partition of the NL tree. Given that it is much more likely that (behaviorally) similar alternatives will share a common set of missing attributes, behaviorally intuitive NL tree structures represent an excellent starting point in exploring NL model tree structures. Note, however, that the variance of the unobserved effects for two alternatives may be statistically similar despite the influence of different omitted attributes. It is because of this reason that the tree structures explored should not be confined to behaviorally intuitive partitionings. Thus, for example, without further information, it is possible that the following NL model may represent the best NL tree structure:

```
;Tree= A(cart, busway), B(bus,LR), C(carnt,train)
```

In figure 14.4, we show graphically the above tree specification.

It is therefore extremely important, unless information is known *a priori* about the unobserved effects and their relationships, that the analyst keeps an open mind as to what

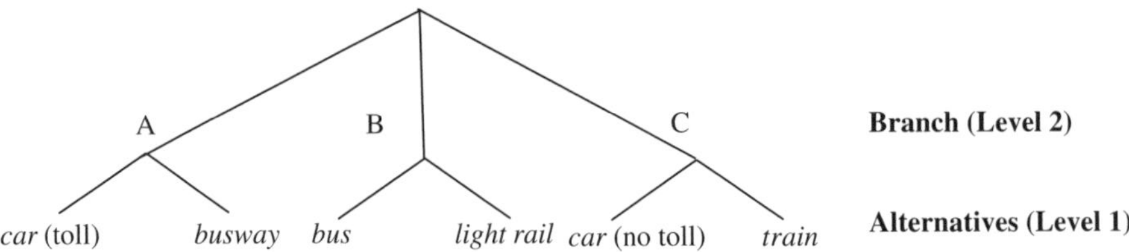

Figure 14.4 Example tree structure four

tree specifications are explored. Assuming the second tree structure as our starting point and using the same utility specifications as the MNL model of chapter 10, the basic NLOGIT NL command would look as follows:

```
NLOGIT
;lhs = choice, cset, altij
;Choices = cart, carnt, bus, train, busway, LR
;Tree= car(cart, carnt), PTEX(bus, train), PTNW(busway, LR)
;Model:
U(cart) = asccart + cst*fuel /
U(carnt) = asccarnt + cst*fuel /
U(bus) = ascbus + cst*fare /
U(train) = asctn + cst*fare /
U(busway) = ascbusw + cst*fare /
U(LR) = cst*fare $
```

14.3.1 Normalizing and constraining IV parameters

For all NL models, there will exist a unique Inclusive Value (IV) parameter for each trunk, limb, and branch specified as part of the tree structure. As with other parameters, the analyst may constrain several of these IV parameters or normalize[2] them (i.e. fix them) to equal some particular value (usually, but not always 1.0). Whether one intends to constrain or normalize an IV parameter, the following command syntax is used:

```
;ivset: (<specification>)
```

For the **;ivset** command specification, we use a colon (**:**) after the **;ivset** command. Whatever the specific specification adopted (discussed below), the specification is placed within round brackets (**( )**). That is, the convention related to the use of brackets for the tree specification command does not apply to the **;ivset** command, no matter at what level of the tree the IV parameter is to be normalized or constrained.

[2] All scale parameters at one level of NL models are normalized to 1.0 due to a problem of identification. This is not the same as normalizing an IV parameter which is the ratio of two scale parameters from two distinct levels of the NL model. NLOGIT will automatically normalize the scale parameters from one level of the model as designated by the analyst according to RU1 or RU2 (discussed later). The normalization of IV parameters is advised but optional.

To constrain two or more scale parameters, the **;ivset** specification takes the following form. In this specification, each IV parameter that is to be constrained is placed within the brackets, separated by a comma (,):

;ivset: (<IV parameter name$_1$>, <IV parameter name$_2$>, . . . , <IV parameter name$_n$>)

For example, assuming the tree structure from figure 14.3, the following command will constrain the IV parameter of the two public transport branches to be equal:

;ivset: (PTrail, PTroad)

It is possible to constrain several IV parameters simultaneously such that various combinations of IV parameters will be equal to one another. Each new simultaneous constraint imposed is separated by a slash, as shown below:

;ivset: (<IV parameter name$_1$>, <IV parameter name$_2$>, . . . , <IV parameter name$_i$>) / (<IV parameter name$_j$>, <IV parameter name$_k$>, . . . , <IV parameter name$_n$>) / . . . / (<IV parameter name$_m$>, <IV parameter name$_n$>, . . . , <IV parameter name$_p$>)

For example, assuming a new branch existed (called D) for the tree structure shown in figure 14.4, with two new alternatives, pushbike and motorbike, the following command would constrain the IV parameters for branches A and C and B, and D:

;ivset: (A, C) / (B, D)

As well as constraining the IV parameters of NL models, it is also possible for the analyst to treat them as *fixed parameters*. Using the terminology associated with the NL literature, when treating an IV parameter as fixed we say that we normalize the IV parameters to (equal) some specific value. The command syntax for this is similar to that shown above for the constraining of the IV parameters, with the parameters to be normalized placed once more within the round brackets of the **;ivset** command. The value that the IV parameter is to be normalized to is specified as follows:

;ivset: (<specification>) = [<value>]

As with the constraining of several IV parameters, it is possible to normalize several IV parameters to some fixed value, simultaneously. Generically, the command syntax to do so is shown below:

;ivset: (<IV parameter name$_1$>, <IV parameter name$_2$>, . . . , <IV parameter name$_n$>) = [<value>]

For example, assuming the tree structure shown in figure 14.3, the following **;ivset** command would normalize the two public transport IV parameters to equal 0.75:

;ivset: (PTRail, PTRoad) = [0.75]

It is also possible to normalize several sets of IV parameters to equal different fixed values simultaneously. We show this below with each set of IV parameters to be normalized separated by a slash (/) in the command syntax:

;ivset: (<IV parameter name$_1$>, <IV parameter name$_2$>, . . . , <IV parameter name$_i$>) = [<value$_1$>] / (<IV parameter name$_j$>, <IV parameter name$_k$>, . . . , <IV parameter name$_n$>) = [<value$_2$>] / . . . / / (<IV parameter name$_m$>, <IV parameter name$_n$>, . . . , <IV parameter name$_p$>) = [<value$_w$>]

For example, the following will normalize the PTRail branch of figure 14.3 to 0.75 while simultaneously normalizing the PTRoad IV parameter to 0.5:

;ivset: (PTRail) = [0.75] / ;ivset: (PTRoad) = [0.5]

Nevertheless, it is customary when normalizing IV parameters that, unless the analyst desires to test some hypothesis with regard to the variance structure of the model, a single IV parameter be normalized to 1.0. The remaining IV parameters which are free to be estimated will therefore be relative to that which was normalized. This approach aids the analyst in determining whether the remaining IV parameters are within the 0–1 bound necessary for global utility maximization.

An interesting question is at which level should one normalize the IV parameter (assuming one is going to normalize an IV parameter at all)? That is, for three- or four-level NL models, does one normalize the IV parameter at the branch, limb, or trunk level (for two-level NL models, the analyst must, if they are going to normalize an IV parameter, normalize the IV parameter at the branch level).

To date, this remains an open question. What is known is that higher levels of NL models exhibit greater levels of variance. This is because higher levels of NL models also incorporate variance at lower connected levels of the model as well as at the level itself. It follows therefore that the scale parameters at higher levels (the ratios of which form the IV parameters) must be smaller in magnitude than those for partitions lower in the tree structure (i.e. the scale parameters are the inverse of the variance; higher variance suggests smaller scale parameters). It is this property which (statistically) imposes the 0–1 bound on the IV parameters.

Given that an IV parameter from any level of the model is defined as the ratio of the scale parameter at that level to the (probability weighted average of the) scale parameter(s) of the level directly below (see appendix 13A or the discussion below), IV parameters observed to be closer to 1.0 suggest that the scale parameters obtained from both levels are close to parity (e.g. $0.4 \div 0.5 = 0.8$; $0.4 \div 0.6 = 0.66$). Given the relationship between the scale parameters and variances, the smaller the difference in variance between two levels of the NL tree, the closer the IV parameter will be to 1.0.

Normalizing an IV parameter, therefore, affects the treatment of at least two scale parameters and hence the variances of at least two levels of the NL model. As such, normalizing different IV parameters, even across the same level of an NL model, will impact upon the model estimation process through the imposition of restrictions upon the variance structure of the model, the outcome of which cannot be predicted *a priori*. As such, the determination of which IV parameter to normalize is a process of trial and error, suggesting that there is strictly no rule to determine at which level one should normalize an IV parameter.

Below, we demonstrate the command to normalize the Car IV parameter to equal 1.0:

```
;ivset: (car)=[1.0]
```

Note that while we have entered the value as 1.0, we need only have entered the value as 1. We have used the decimal place only as a matter of historical convention.

The exception to the above occurs when there exists a single limb or branch which the analyst has named. When a single limb or trunk is named in the command syntax, the IV parameter for that limb or trunk is by default normalized to 1.0. In such cases, the analyst may not normalize this IV parameter (even though it is for the highest level of the tree). For example:

```
;tree = Limb[car(cart,carnt), PTEX(bus,train), PTNW(busway,LR)]
;ivset: (limb)=[0.75]
```

will produce the following NLOGIT error:

```
Error: 1093: You have given a spec for an IV parm that is
  fixed at 1
```

Even the command

```
;Tree = Limb[car(cart,carnt), PTEX(bus,train), PTNW(busway,LR)]
;ivset: (limb)=[1.0]
```

will produce the above error.

For the NL model described by figure 14.2, the command specification normalizing the IV parameter of the Car branch to 1.0 is shown below:

```
NLOGIT
;lhs = choice, cset, altij
;Choices = cart, carnt, bus, train, busway, LR
;Tree= car(cart, carnt), PTEX(bus, train), PTNW(busway, LR)
;ivset: (car)=[1.0]
;Model:
U(cart) = asccart + cst*fuel /
U(carnt) = asccarnt + cst*fuel /
U(bus) = ascbus + cst*fare /
U(train) = asctn + cst*fare /
U(busway) = ascbusw + cst*fare /
U(LR) = cst*fare $
```

As an aside, it is possible to estimate an NL model without normalizing or constraining any of the IV parameters. Such models allow all IV parameters to be estimated freely. We advise against the use of these models for the beginner as the IV parameters will not necessarily be constrained within the (1, 0) bound and as such may be difficult to interpret with regards to model consistency with global utility maximization.

14.3.2 RU1 and RU2

Each trunk, limb, branch, and alternative of an NL model has an associated *scale parameter*. It is from these unique scale parameters that the IV parameters discussed in sub-section 14.3.1 are derived. As we saw in chapter 13 and in sub-section 14.3.1, the IV parameters of NL models are the ratios of the scale parameters from adjoining levels of the NL tree.

An unfortunate property of the NL model is that the model attempts to estimate more parameters than it is possible to estimate with the amount of information available. This is a problem known as *identification*. Rather than not estimate a model at all, the NL model normalizes all scale parameters at one level of the model to 1.0, while estimating all others relative to those normalized. Whereas it is possible to normalize the scale parameters at any level of an NL model, it is customary to normalize either all of the scale parameters at the lowest level (called RU1) or all the scale parameters at the highest level (called RU2) of the tree.

The command syntax to normalize the NL model at the lowest level (i.e. RU1) is:

```
;RU1
```

The addition of

```
;RU2
```

will estimate the model normalizing the scale parameters at the top level of the model. The analyst cannot specify both RU1 and RU2 at the same time, and failure to specify either will have NLOGIT revert to its default setting of RU1.

While the parameter estimates reported from NL models estimated under RU1 will be different to those estimated under RU2, under certain circumstances, the two results will be directly comparable up to a scale factor. As discussed in Louviere, Hensher, and Swait (2000), the estimates of models obtained under RU1 and RU2 will be empirically the same if all attribute parameters within a partition of a nest are alternative specific.

As an aside, the vast majority of studies do not report whether the models estimated were estimated using RU1 or RU2. This makes it difficult, if not impossible, to compare the results of one study to the next. As pointed out by Louviere, Hensher, and Swait (2000), reporting at what level the scale parameters were normalized (as opposed to the IV parameters) would greatly aid in the comparison of research efforts.

14.3.3 Specifying start values for the NL model

In the section on normalizing and constraining IV parameters, we demonstrated how one may either constrain or normalize the IV parameter for any branch, limb, or trunk within the nested tree structure of an NL model. As with the parameter estimates of the MNL model, it is also possible for the analyst to specify the values for the IV parameters within the NL model at which NLOGIT will commence its estimation search. This is accomplished by the following command format whereby the start value is not placed within any brackets:

```
;ivset: (<IV parameter name_1>)= value_1
```

It is possible to specify start values for several IV parameters simultaneously. For example, the following command would instruct NLOGIT to start its search for the IV parameter estimates such that for the CAR branch the start value is 0.8 and for the PTEX and PTNW branches the start values are 0.75:

;ivset: (Car) = 0.8 / (PTEX,PTNW) = 0.75

As an aside, by default, the NLOGIT starting value for all IV parameter estimates is 1.0. The specification of starting values is not limited to the IV parameters of NL models. The analyst may also specify starting values for the remaining parameter estimates contained within the model. While this may be done in a similar manner to the MNL model where the analyst places the requested start value in round brackets (**( )**) after the parameter name, it is also possible to specify as the starting values of the NL model the parameter estimates obtained from a non-nested NL (NNNL) of similar specification to that of the NL model to be estimated. We do so using the following command syntax:

;Start=logit

As an aside, when utility functions are not specified at levels two–four of the NL model (discussed later), the NNNL model first estimated will be equivalent to the equivalently specified MNL model.

The NNNL model provides initial estimates of the parameters at each level of the model, however, does not estimate the IV parameters and as such, will (1) for parameters estimated at level one of the NL model, produce consistent but inefficient parameter estimates and (2) for parameters estimated at higher levels of the NL model, produce inconsistent and inefficient parameter estimates. Nevertheless, the parameter estimates from an initial fitted NNNL model may provide start values for the estimation of the NL model parameters which are possibly different to the default value of zero (assuming statistical significance; start values of zero are also inconsistent; Greene 2002). Given that the log likelihood function of the NL model is complex, the use of start values other than zero for each of the parameters to be estimated is often of benefit to the analyst and may help avoid sub-optimal ML solutions. We therefore advise the beginner to use the NNNL model to uncover the initial start values as a matter of practice in all instances.

We are now ready to estimate our first NL model. Before we do so, however, it is worthwhile reviewing the most significant aspects of the model. In the next section we summarize the most noteworthy sections of the NL model (taken from appendix 13A).

14.3.4 A quick review of the NL model

Adopting the notation used in appendix 13A (as recommended by Louviere, Hensher, and Swait 2000) we represent the scale parameters at each level of the NL model as follows:

Trunk: $\tau_{(l)}$
Limb: $\gamma_{(i,l)}$
Branch: $\lambda_{(j|i,l)}$
Elemental Alternative: $\mu_{(j|i,l)}$

where

$\tau_{(l)}$ (pronounced "tau") is the scale parameter for the lth trunk, $\gamma_{(i,l)}$ (pronounced gamma) is the scale parameter for the ith limb of trunk l, $\lambda_{(j|i,l)}$ (pronounced lambda) is the scale parameter for the jth branch of limb i of trunk l, and $\mu_{(j|i,l)}$ (pronounced mu) is the scale parameter for the elemental alternatives present within branch j of limb i of trunk l.

Using the above notation, the utility functions at each level (one–four) may be expressed as follows (ignoring RU1 and RU2 for the present).

Level 1

$$\begin{aligned} V_J = {} & \mu_{(j|i,l)}\beta_{0J} + \mu_{(j|i,l)}\beta_{1J} f(X_{1J}) + \mu_{(j|i,l)}\beta_{2J} f(X_{2J}) \\ & + \mu_{(j|i,l)}\beta_{3J} f(X_{3J}) + \cdots + \mu_{(j|i,l)}\beta_{KJ} f(X_{KJ}) \end{aligned} \tag{14.2}$$

Due to the IID assumption, $\mu_{(j|i,l)}$will be equal for all elemental alternatives within the same branch.

Level 2

$$\begin{aligned} V_{(j|i,l)} = \lambda_{(j|i,l)}\Big[& \beta_{0(1|1,1)} + \beta_{1(1|1,1)} f(X_{1(1|1,1)}) + \beta_{2(1|1,1)} f(X_{2(1|1,1)}) \\ & + \cdots + \beta_{K(1|1,1)} f(X_{K(1|1,1)}) + \frac{1}{\mu_{(j|i,l)}} \times IV_{(j|i,l)}\Big] \end{aligned} \tag{14.3}$$

where

$IV_{(j|i,l)} = \ln(\sum e^{(\mu(j|i,l)V_j)})$ and $\frac{\lambda_{(j|i,l)}}{\mu_{(j|i,l)}}$ is the IV parameter for the jth branch, of limb i of trunk l.

Level 3

$$\begin{aligned} V_{(i,l)} = \gamma_{(i,l)}\Big[& \beta_{0(1,1)} + \beta_{1(1,1)} f(X_{1(1,1)}) + \beta_{2(1,1)} f(X_{2(1,1)}) \\ & + \cdots + \beta_{K(1,1)} f(X_{K(1,1)}) + \frac{1}{\lambda_{(i,l)}} \times IV_{(i,l)}\Big] \end{aligned} \tag{14.4}$$

where

$IV_{(i,l)} = \ln(\sum e^{(\lambda(i,l)V(j|i,j))})$ and $\frac{\gamma_{(i,l)}}{\lambda_{(i,l)}}$ is the IV parameter for the limb ith of trunk l.

The NL model maintains the IID assumption within each partition, and as such the variances (and hence scale parameters) for branches within the same limb will be equal. Thus, while $\lambda_{(j|i,l)}$ are free to vary at level two of the NL model, at level three of the NL model, branch-level scale parameters *within* the same limb are equal (essentially the IID condition within a partition). The branch-level scale parameters used to estimate the branch-level scale parameter at level three of the NL model are estimated as the probability weighted average of the branch-level scale parameters present within the same limb partition: hence the use of $\lambda_{(i,l)}$ and not $\lambda_{(j|i,l)}$ in (14.4).

Level 4

$$V_{(l)} = \tau_{(l)}[\beta_{0(1)} + \beta_{1(1)}f(X_{1(1)}) + \beta_{2(1)}f(X_{2(1)}) + \cdots \\ + \beta_{K(1)}f(X_{K(1)}) + \frac{1}{\gamma_{(l)}} \times IV_{(l)}] \quad (14.5)$$

where

$$IV_{(l)} = \ln\left(\sum e^{(\gamma_{(l)} V_{i,j})}\right) \text{ and } \frac{\tau_{(l)}}{\gamma_{(l)}} \text{is the IV parameter for the } l\text{th trunk.}$$

Once more, the IID assumption is maintained across each partition at level four of the NL model. Hence, while the limb-level scale parameters were free to vary at level three of the model (i.e. $\gamma_{(i,l)}$), at level four of the model they are constrained to be equal so that the IID assumption may be maintained. Notation-wise, we represent at level four of the NL model, $\gamma_{(i,l)}$ as $\gamma_{(l)}$, which is equal to the probability weighted average of all $\gamma_{(i,l)}$ present within the same trunk of the model.

14.4 Estimating an NL model and interpreting the output

We are now in a position to estimate our first NL model. The model we use here for demonstration purposes is estimated using the 30 minutes or less commuting segment from the mode choice case study described in chapter 9. The model we will explore is shown in figure 14.2. In setting up the command syntax, we normalize the IV parameter for the CAR branch of the model and use the NNNL model to provide the initial start values for the maximum likelihood (ML) search procedure. We also have limited NLOGIT to a maximum of 100 iterations in this search. The omission of either the **RU1** or **RU2** command reverts NLOGIT to its default setting of RU1 (i.e. normalizing the scale parameters at level one of the model):

```
NLOGIT
;lhs = choice, cset, altij
;Choices = cart, carnt, bus, train, busway, LR
;Tree = car(cart, carnt), ptex(bus, train), ptnw(busway, LR)
;Start = logit
;ivset: (car)=[1.0]
;Maxit = 100
;Model:
U(cart) = asccart + cst*fuel /
U(carnt) = asccarnt + cst*fuel /
U(bus) = ascbus + cst*fare /
U(train) = asctn + cst*fare/
U(busway) = ascbusw + cst*fare /
U(LR) = cst*fare $
```

Estimating the above model using the 30 minutes or less commuting segment, we observe the following NLOGIT output. NLOGIT first provides the MNL output used to locate the start values for the NL ML estimation search. Note that this is the same model as shown on p. 316:

```
+---------------------------------------------+
| Discrete choice (multinomial logit) model   |
| Maximum Likelihood Estimates                |
| Model estimated: Feb 30, 2003 at 12:15:00PM. |
| Dependent variable               Choice     |
| Weighting variable                 None     |
| Number of observations             2369     |
| Iterations completed                  5     |
| Log likelihood function       -3220.150     |
| R2=1-LogL/LogL*   Log-L fncn  R-sqrd  RsqAdj |
| No coefficients   -4244.6782  .24137  .24051 |
| Constants only.   Must be computed directly. |
|                   Use NLOGIT ;...; RHS=ONE $ |
| Chi-squared[ 1]          =   1639.08085     |
| Prob [ chi squared > value ] =   .00000     |
| Response data are given as ind. choice.     |
| Number of obs.= 2369, skipped 0 bad obs.    |
+---------------------------------------------+
```

Variable	Coefficient	Standard Error	b/St.Er.	P[|Z|>z]
ASCCART	-.08252881	.07552527	-1.093	.2745
CST	-.20180890	.01916932	-10.528	.0000
ASCCARNT	.41384399	.07640648	5.416	.0000
ASCBUS	.01966141	.09923321	.198	.8429
ASCTN	-.04174518	.09373128	-.445	.6561
ASCBUSW	.09250653	.08587656	1.077	.2814

The above model is multinomial logit model, estimated to obtain the start values for the NL model. We present the NL model output produced by NLOGIT below:

```
+----------------------------------------------+
| FIML: Nested Multinomial Logit Model         |
| Maximum Likelihood Estimates                 |
| Model estimated: Feb 30, 2003 at 12:17:03PM.  |
| Dependent variable               CHOICE      |
| Weighting variable                 None      |
| Number of observations             9476      |
| Iterations completed                 13      |
| Log likelihood function       -3219.011      |
```

```
| Restricted log likelihood      -4244.678               |
| Chi squared                     2051.335               |
| Degrees of freedom                     8               |
| Prob[ChiSqd > value] =          .0000000               |
| R2=1-LogL/LogL*     Log-L fncn   R-sqrd   RsqAdj       |
| No coefficients     -4244.6782   .24164   .24078       |
| Constants only. Must be computed directly.             |
|                     Use NLOGIT ;...; RHS=ONE  $        |
| At start values   -3220.1497    .00035  -.00077        |
| Response data are given as ind. choice.                |
+--------------------------------------------------------+

+----------------------------------------------------+
| FIML: Nested Multinomial Logit Model               |
| The model has 2 levels.                            |
| Nested Logit form:IV parms = tauji,l,sil           |
| and fl. No normalizations imposed a priori.        |
| p(alt=k|b=j,l=i,t=l)=exp[bX_k|jil]/Sum             |
| p(b=j|l=i,t=l)=exp[aY_j|il+tauj|ilIVj|il)]/        |
| Sum. p(l=i|t=l)=exp[cZ_i|l+si|lIVi|l)]/Sum         |
| p(t=l)=exp[exp[qW_l+flIVl]/Sum...                  |
| Number of obs.= 2369, skipped 0 bad obs.           |
+----------------------------------------------------+

+----------+-------------+----------------+----------+----------+
|Variable  | Coefficient | Standard Error | b/St.Er. | P[|Z|>z] |
+----------+-------------+----------------+----------+----------+
          Attributes in the Utility Functions (beta)
 ASCCART     -.09937636       .07881488      -1.261    .2074
 CST         -.21576542       .02333323      -9.247    .0000
 ASCCARNT     .42502208       .08582425       4.952    .0000
 ASCBUS      -.05784125       .14341067       -.403    .6867
 ASCTN       -.14225115       .14741225       -.965    .3346
 ASCBUSW      .09386517       .08671559       1.082    .2791
          IV parameters, tau(j|i,l), sigma(i|l),phi(l)
 CAR         1.00000000       ......(Fixed Parameter).......
 PTEX         .78869033       .13740095       5.740    .0000
 PTNW         .98684458       .12725606       7.755    .0000
```

The first output box of the NL model is similar to that produced for the MNL model discussed in chapter 10. The interpretation of the majority of this output box is the same as that provided for the MNL model. We therefore limit our discussion to new output either not presented with the MNL model output or where the interpretation between that provided for the MNL and that provided for the NL model differs. The first difference of note is in the first line of the output box, which we reproduce below:

```
FIML: Nested Multinomial Logit Model
```

The first line of output informs the analyst that an NL model was obtained using an estimation technique known as *full information maximum likelihood* (FIML). NL models may be estimated either sequentially or simultaneously. Sequential estimation (known as *limited information maximum likelihood* estimators or LIML) involves the estimation of separate levels of the NL tree in sequential order from the lowest level of the tree to the highest level. Beginning at the branch level, LIML will estimate the utility specifications of the alternatives present within each branch, including the scale parameters, as well as the scale parameters for each branch of the tree. Once the scale parameters are estimated, the IV parameters at the branch level may be calculated. These IV parameters are then used as explanatory variables for the next level of the tree. This process is repeated until the entire tree structure of the NL Model is estimated. Hensher (1986) has shown that using LIML to estimate NL models is statistically inefficient as the parameter estimates of levels three and higher are not minimum variance parameter estimates resulting from the use of estimates to estimate yet more estimates. For NL models with between two and four levels, it is therefore more common to use simultaneous estimation procedures which provide statistically efficient parameter estimates. The simultaneous estimation of the branches, limbs, and trunks of an NL model is achieved using FIML. The sequential estimation of each partition of the NL tree offers no advantages over the simultaneous estimation of the entire NL model, other than the possibility to estimate models with greater than four levels (which will rarely be required); hence, we advise against this for the beginner. Those interested in learning more about the differences between sequential and simultaneous estimation of NL models are referred to Louviere, Hensher, and Swait (2000, 149–152) while those interested in estimating such models are referred to the reference manuals that accompany the NLOGIT software.

NLOGIT next provides information on the choice variable used, whether a weighting variable was employed, the number of observations, and the number of iterations completed before no further improvement was observed in the ML function. The number of observations reported above is 9476, four times greater than the 2369 observations reported for the NNNL (MNL) model:

```
Number of observations                9476
```

The number of observations reported in the NL model is not the number of choices made as reported by the MNL model, but rather the total number of alternatives, chosen or not chosen, across the entire sampled data set. For this example, each choice set consisted of four alternatives. Thus across all 2369 choice sets (observations) there were a total of 9476 alternatives considered by the sampled respondents.

NLOGIT next reports the restricted and unrestricted LL functions for the model. The LL functions of the NL model may be interpreted in exactly the same manner as the LL functions of the MNL model. Indeed, if the two models are estimated on the same sample, the LL functions for both are directly comparable. The LL function reported is that for the model fitted as specified through the utility functions, while the unrestricted LL function is the LL function for a model estimated with constant terms only (assuming equal choice shares). As with the MNL model, the test of model significance for the NL model is the LL ratio test using the reported LL values discussed above. The analyst may use spreadsheet programs such as Excel to perform this test (as shown in chapter 10); however, NL performs this test automatically and hence there is no need for the analyst to perform this test manually (the analyst will have to perform the test manually if they wish to test the model against the sample data choice shares, however).

The LL ratio test is Chi-square distributed with degrees of freedom equal to the number of parameters estimated within the model. The number of parameters is inclusive of the IV parameters estimated but not those which were normalized (and hence not estimated). As with the MNL model, the Chi-square test-statistic for this test is

$$-2(ll_{Restricted} - ll_{Unrestricted}) \sim \chi^2_{(\text{difference in the number of parameters estimated between the two models})} \tag{14.6}$$

For the model output above, the test is shown below. The test has eight degrees of freedom (i.e. six parameter estimates and two IV parameters):

$$-2(-4244.678 - (-3219.011)) = 2051.334 \sim \chi^2_{(8)}$$

2051.334 is equal to the value we observe in the NLOGIT output. To determine the overall model fit, the analyst may compare the test-statistic to the critical Chi-square with eight degrees of freedom (see sub-section 2.8.3) or use the p-value provided by NLOGIT, which for this example is given as zero. As the p-value is less than alpha equal to 0.05 (i.e. the 95 percent confidence level) we conclude that the NL model estimated represents an improvement in the LL function of a model estimated with constants only (assuming equal market shares). As such, we conclude that the parameters estimated for the attributes and SDC included in the utility functions improve the overall model fit.

NLOGIT next estimates the pseudo-R^2 and adjusted pseudo-R^2. As with the MNL model, the pseudo-R^2 for the NL model is estimated using the ratio of the LL function of the model estimated here over the LL function of a base model estimated assuming equal choice shares across the alternatives. The resulting pseudo-R^2 is therefore informative as to how much variation in choice is explained from this model in comparison to a model estimated assuming only equal choice shares. It is often worthwhile estimating an NL model assuming the choice shares observed in the sample data and compare the LL function of this model to that of the fitted model. Doing so for this example, we observe an LL function of -3276.833 for the base model assuming the sample data choice shares. From (10.14) the pseudo-R^2 becomes 0.018 and not 0.242, as reported above:

$$R^2 = 1 - \frac{ll_{Estimated\ model}}{ll_{Base\ model}} = 1 - \frac{-3219}{-3276} = 0.018$$

This suggests that the fitted NL model explains far more of the variation in choice compared to a model fitted with equal choice shares than to one fitted using the sample data choice shares. In either case, however, whatever pseudo-R^2 one reports, the conversion suggested in figure 10.6 is required if a comparison is to be made with the R^2 obtained from linear models.

If the MNL model was first estimated to provide the start values for the maximum likelihood estimation procedure of the NL model, NLOGIT also provides the pseudo-R^2 and adjusted pseudo-R^2 values comparing the NL model to that of the initial MNL model. We show this below where the first value provided is the LL function of the MNL model, the second value the pseudo-R^2 value and the last number is the adjusted pseudo-R^2:

```
start values -3220.1497 .00035 -.00077
```

To get the pseudo-R^2 reported here, we once more rely on (10.14). This calculation is shown below. The value we calculate is the same as that estimated by NLOGIT:

$$R^2 = 1 - \frac{ll_{Estimated\ model}}{ll_{Base\ model}} = 1 - \frac{-3219}{-3220} = 0.00035$$

Even taking into account the transformation required (see figure 10.6), a pseudo-R^2 value of 0.00035 suggests that the NL model performs (statistically) no better than the MNL model for this example.

The next output box provided by NLOGIT provides technical details as to the normalization process used. This box is of no interest to the beginning choice modeler and we will not discuss its contents here. The final series of output contains the parameter estimates and associated statistics. For ease, we present this output once more below. The parameter estimates, standard errors, Wald-statistics, and p-values specified within the utility functions of the NL model are provided first, after which the IV parameters and associated statistics are given:

```
+----------+-------------+---------------+----------+---------+
|Variable  | Coefficient |  Standard Error|  b/St.Er.|P[|Z|>z]  |
+----------+-------------+---------------+----------+---------+
      Attributes in the Utility Functions (beta)
 ASCCART      -.09937636        .07881488       -1.261    .2074
 CST          -.21576542        .02333323       -9.247    .0000
 ASCCARNT      .42502208        .08582425        4.952    .0000
 ASCBUS       -.05784125        .14341067        -.403    .6867
 ASCTN        -.14225115        .14741225        -.965    .3346
 ASCBUSW       .09386517        .08671559        1.082    .2791
      IV parameters, tau(j|i,l), sigma(i|l),phi(l)
 CAR          1.00000000      ......(Fixed Parameter)........
 PTEX          .78869033       .13740095        5.740    .0000
 PTNW          .98684458        .12725606       7.755    .0000
```

For the above example, the cost parameter is statistically significant and of the correct sign (i.e. negative). The general form for the utility functions of NL models is given as (14.2)–(14.5). The inclusion of the scale parameters in the utility functions of NL models has important ramifications on how we present the utility functions, and how we interpret them. For the above model, we have normalized the model using the RU1 assumption. Under RU1, the scale parameters at level one of the model are normalized to 1.0 for all alternatives independent of what branch the alternative is assigned. As such, for the above example, we do not have to worry about the scale parameters in writing out the utility functions at level one of the model for each of the alternatives as they are all assumed to equal one (in a following section, we will specify two models, one using the RU1 and the other using the RU2 normalization procedure and compare the results). For the present, we may write out the utility functions for each of the alternatives directly from the output without having to be concerned with the scale parameters of the model (they all equal one). We do this in (14.7a)–(14.7f):

$$V_{cart} = -0.09937636480 - 0.2157654209 \times \text{Fuel} \tag{14.7a}$$

$$V_{carnt} = 0.4250220772 - 0.2157654209 \times \text{Fuel} \tag{14.7b}$$

$$V_{bus} = -0.05784125441 - 0.2157654209 \times \text{Fare} \tag{14.7c}$$

$$V_{train} = -0.1422511493 - 0.2157654209 \times \text{Fare} \tag{14.7d}$$

$$V_{busway} = -0.09386516774 - 0.2157654209 \times \text{Fare} \tag{14.7e}$$

$$V_{LR} = -0.2157654209 \times \text{Fare} \tag{14.7f}$$

As an aside, as with all other choice models, the utilities derived from the above utility specifications are relative. Hence, to determine the utility for any one alternative, the analyst must take the difference between the utility for that alternative and that of a second alternative.

The final results produced are the estimates of the IV parameters for each of the trunks, limbs, and branches of the model. As with the parameter estimates for the attributes and SDCs specified within the utility functions, NLOGIT reports for each IV parameter a standard error, a Wald-statistic, and a p-value. An interesting question arises as to what an "insignificant IV parameter" means. The test-statistic, the Wald-statistic, is calculated by dividing the IV parameter estimate by its associated standard error and comparing the resulting value to some critical value (usually ± 1.96, representing a 95 percent confidence level). This test is exactly the same as the one-sample t-test and is used in this case to determine whether the IV parameter is statistically equal to zero. If the parameter is found to be statistically equal to zero (i.e. the parameter is not significant), the parameter remains within the 0–1 bound (it equals zero). This is important; as mentioned in chapter 10, we have two totally independent choice models for the upper and lower levels and hence there exists evidence for a partition of the tree structure at this section of the model.

As an aside, an insignificant IV parameter (i.e. one that is statistically equal to zero) suggests that the two scale parameters taken from the different levels to form the IV parameter are statistically very different (e.g. 0.1 divided by 0.8 equals 0.125, which is closer to zero than 0.1 divided by 0.2 which equals 0.5; of course, the standard errors must also be accounted for). This does not mean that the variance is not statistically significant.

The alternative finding of a significant IV parameter estimate suggests that the parameter is not equal to zero, but does not indicate whether the parameter lies outside the upper bound of the 0–1 range (recall that an IV parameter cannot be less than zero). Thus, for significant IV parameters, a second test is required to determine whether the upper bound has been exceeded. This test may be undertaken with a simple modification to the test conducted to determine whether the parameter is statistically equal to zero. We show this modification below:

$$\text{Wald-test} = \frac{IV_{parameter} - 1}{\text{std error}} \tag{14.8}$$

For the above example, the IV parameter for the PTEX branch is statistically different to zero. As such, it is necessary to undertake the test described in (14.8) to determine whether the variable is statistically different to one. We perform this test below:

$$\text{Wald-test} = \frac{0.7886903275 - 1}{0.13740095} = -1.53791$$

Comparing the test-statistic of -1.54 to the critical value of ± 1.96 (i.e. at alpha equal to 0.05), we cannot reject the hypothesis that the PTEX parameter is statistically equal to one. This is an interesting finding. Having normalized the IV parameter for the CAR branch to 1.0, we now find that the IV parameter for the PTEX branch is also (statistically) equal to 1.0, meaning that the two branches should collapse into a single branch. But what of the PTNW IV parameter? This parameter is also statistically different to zero. Undertaking the same test we used for the PTEX IV parameter, we find that we cannot reject the null hypothesis that this parameter is also statistically equal to one. We show this test below:

$$\text{Wald-test} = \frac{0.9868445842 - 1}{0.12725606} = -0.10338$$

All three IV parameters in our model are statistically equal to 1.0, and as such should collapse into a single branch, which is equivalent to a MNL model. Thus for the above example, our preference would be to use the simpler MNL model rather than an NL model.

This result is not surprising. Had we bothered to estimate the same model specification as an MNL model and undertake the Hausman-test of the IIA assumption we would have observed a test-statistic, q, equal to 0.78 and a p-value equal to 0.38 (we leave it to the reader to show this). The model specification we employed conforms to the IID assumption and, hence, the NL model should collapse to the MNL model form.

The discussion above highlights only two of the four possible outcomes that may arise with regard to the significance or otherwise of IV parameter estimates. The first possibility is that an IV parameter is statistically equal to zero. The second possibility is that an IV parameter may be found to be statistically equal to one. A third possible outcome is that the IV parameter is not statistically equal to either zero or one but is observed to remain within the 1, 0 bound (e.g. an IV parameter equal to 0.6825920296 with a standard error of 0.15359718). In such cases, the partitioning of the branch, limb, or trunk from that for which the IV parameter was normalized to 1.0 is warranted (but the IV parameter may be equal to other IV parameters also not equal to either zero or one, suggesting further possible collapses of the tree structure). The fourth and final possible outcome occurs when an IV parameter is not statistically equal to either zero or one but is statistically greater than one (e.g. an IV parameter equal to 1.464979425 with a standard error of 0.23162559). In such cases, the global utility maximization assumption is no longer valid and cross-elasticities with the wrong sign will be observed. The analyst will be required to (1) explore new tree structures, (2) normalize a different IV parameter using the same tree structure and re-estimate the model, or (3) move to more advanced models (see chapter 13) in order to proceed.

As an aside, Ben-Akiva and Lerman (1985) show that

$$\frac{\lambda_{(i|j,l)}}{\mu_{(i|j,l)}} = \sqrt{(1 - \text{corr}(V_j, V_i))} \tag{14.9a}$$

where

$$\frac{\lambda_{(i|j,l)}}{\mu_{(i|j,l)}}$$

is an IV parameter (for convenience we have used the notation for a branch-level IV parameter; however, the formula holds at all levels of the NL model), 'corr' indicates correlation and V_j and V_i are the utility functions of two alternatives within the same nest or partition.

Rearranging, we observe

$$\left(\frac{\lambda_{(i|j,l)}}{\mu_{(i|j,l)}}\right)^2 = 1 - \text{corr}(V_j, V_i)$$

$$\text{corr}(V_j, V_i) = 1 - \left(\frac{\lambda_{(i|j,l)}}{\mu_{(i|j,l)}}\right)^2 \tag{14.9b}$$

Thus,

$$1 - \left(\frac{\lambda_{(i|j,l)}}{\mu_{(i|j,l)}}\right)^2$$

equals the correlation of the utility functions for any pair of alternatives present within the same nest or partition of an NL model. For the above example, ignoring the insignificance of the IV parameters, the correlations between the *bus* and *train* and *busway* and *LR* alternatives may be calculated as follows:

$$\text{corr}\,(\textit{bus, train}) = 1 - (0.78869033)^2 = 0.37797$$
$$\text{corr}\,(\textit{busway, LR}\,) = 1 - (0.98684458)^2 = 0.02614$$

Thus, IV parameters closer to 1.0 not only indicate a smaller difference in the variance between adjoining levels, but also smaller correlation structures between the utility functions of alternatives present within the lower level of the nest.

14.4.1 Estimating the probabilities of a two-level NL model

The estimation of the probabilities for each alternative of an NL model is far more complex than the calculations for a MNL model. This is because the probability of choosing an alternative (at level one) is conditional upon the branch to which that alternative belongs. For models with more than two levels, the probability of the branch being chosen is in turn conditional upon the limb to which the branch belongs which, for four-level NL models, is also conditional upon the trunk to which the limb belongs. Thus, the probability that a lower level of an NL model is chosen is said to be conditional upon all higher levels connected with that lower level first being chosen. For example, for the model estimated above, the probability of the *bus* mode being selected is conditional upon the PTEX branch first being chosen. Similarly, the probability of the car with toll alternative being chosen is conditional on the CAR branch being selected first.

Equations (14.7a)–(14.7f) represent the utility functions at level one of the NL model. Higher levels of NL models also have utility, the functions for which we may write out in a form of (14.3). Utility functions at higher levels of the NL model are connected to the lower levels of the model via two means. First, the utility function of higher levels of NL models are connected to the level directly below via the inclusion of the lower level's scale parameter within the upper level's utility function (i.e. $\mu_{(j|i,l)}$ in (14.3) is the scale parameter for the elemental alternatives in branch one). The second connection occurs through the inclusion of the IV variable (i.e. the index of expected maximum utility or EMU) which relates the utility expressions of the level directly below to that of the upper level (i.e. $IV_{(j|i,l)}$ in (14.3)).

As we have not specified any variables in the utility functions at the branch level (we will do so in a later section), (14.3) collapses to:

$$V_{(j|i,l)} = \lambda_{(j|i,l)} \times \frac{1}{\mu_{(j|i,l)}} \times IV_{(j|i,l)} = \frac{\lambda_{(j|i,l)}}{\mu_{(j|i,l)}} \times IV_{(j|i,l)}$$

In words, the utility for the jth branch belonging to limb i of trunk l is equal to the IV parameter multiplied by the IV variable (or EMU).

The utility function for the CAR branch in our example may be written as follows:

$$V_{Car} = \frac{\lambda_{Car}}{\mu_{(Car|1,1)}} \times IV_{Car}$$

Normalization using the RU1 specification (as we have done) suggests that the scale parameters at level 1 are all normalized to 1.0 and hence, $\mu_{(Car|1,1)}$will be equal to 1.0. The utility for the CAR branch therefore becomes:

$$V_{Car} = \frac{\lambda_{Car}}{1} \times IV_{Car} = \lambda_{Car} \times IV_{Car}$$

where

λ_{Car} is the scale factor for branch 1 (CAR) and $IV_{car}$is the index of EMU for the CAR branch of the tree. From chapter 10, the EMU for the CAR branch may be calculated as:

$$IV_{Car} = \ln(e^{(\mu_{(car|1,1)} \times V_{cart})} + e^{(\mu_{(car|1,1)} \times V_{carnt})})$$

Given that the scale parameters at level 1 were normalized to 1.0 ($\mu_{(car|1,1)}$equals 1.0 given RU1), we may substitute the utility functions presented in (14.7a) and (14.7b) into the index of EMU for each branch without modification. Hence:

$$IV_{Car} = \ln\left(e^{(-0.09937636480-0.2157654209\times\text{Fuel})} + e^{(0.4250220772-0.2157654209\times\text{Fuel})}\right)$$

For the two remaining branches we observe (given that the scale parameters at level 1 have also been normalized to 1.0; i.e. $\mu_{(PTEX|1,1)} = \mu_{(PTNW|1,1)} = 1.0$):

$$V_{PTEX} = \frac{\lambda_{PTEX}}{\mu_{(PTEX|1,1)}} \times IV_{PTEX} = \lambda_{PTEX} \times IV_{PTEX} \text{ and}$$
$$V_{PTNW} = \frac{\lambda_{PTNW}}{\mu_{(PTNW|1,1)}} \times IV_{PTNW} = \lambda_{PTNW} \times IV_{PTNW}$$

where

$$IV_{PTEX} = \ln\left(e^{(\lambda_{(PTEX|2,1)} \times V_{bus})} + e^{(\lambda_{(PTEX|2,1)} \times V_{train})}\right) \text{ and}$$
$$IV_{PTNW} = \ln\left(e^{(\lambda_{(PTNW|3,1)} \times V_{busw})} + e^{(\lambda_{(PTNW|3,1)} \times V_{LR})}\right)$$

The IV variables or EMUs for the PTEX and PTNW (i.e. IV_{PTEX} and IV_{PTNW}) branches may be expressed in a fashion similar to that for the EMU for the CAR branch. Thus:

$$IV_{PTEX} = \ln\left(e^{(-0.05784125441-0.2157654209\times\text{Fare})} + e^{(-0.1422511493-0.2157654209\times\text{Fare})}\right)$$
$$IV_{PTNW} = \ln\left(e^{(-0.09386516774-0.2157654209\times\text{Fare})} + e^{(VLR=-0.2157654209\times\text{Fare})}\right)$$

We are now able to formally write out the full utility functions at the branch level.

From the model output, we know the IV parameters for each of the branches. By a simple process of substitution, the utility functions for each of the branches become:

$$V_{Car} = \lambda_{Car} \times IV_{Car} = 1 \times \ln\left(e^{(-0.09937636480-0.2157654209\times\text{Fuel})} + e^{(0.4250220772-0.2157654209\times\text{Fuel})}\right)$$

and

$$\begin{aligned} V_{PTEX} &= \lambda_{PTEX} \times IV_{PTEX} \\ &= 0.7886903275 \times \ln\left(e^{(-0.05784125441-0.2157654209\times\text{Fare})} + e^{(-0.1422511493-0.2157654209\times\text{Fare})}\right) \\ V_{PTNW} &= \lambda_{PTNW} \times IV_{PTNW} \\ &= 0.9868445842 \times \ln\left(e^{(-0.09386516774-0.2157654209\times\text{Fare})} + e^{(VLR=-0.2157654209\times\text{Fare})}\right) \end{aligned}$$

Now that we have formally derived all of the utility functions of the NL model, it is possible to derive the calculations necessary to estimate the probabilities for each alternative. Before we do so, however, recall that the probability of an alternative being chosen is conditional upon the branch to which the alternative belongs being chosen. The conditional probabilities are, at the lower level of the model:

$$\mathrm{P}(cart\,|Car) = \frac{e^{(0.09937636480-0.2157654209\times \text{Fuel})}}{e^{(0.09937636480-0.2157654209\times \text{Fuel})} + e^{(0.4250220772-0.2157654209\times \text{Fuel})}}$$

$$\mathrm{P}(carnt\,|Car) = \frac{e^{(0.4250220772-0.2157654209\times \text{Fuel})}}{e^{(0.09937636480-0.2157654209\times \text{Fuel})} + e^{(0.4250220772-0.2157654209\times \text{Fuel})}}$$

$$\mathrm{P}(bus\,|\mathrm{PTEX}) = \frac{e^{(-0.05784125441-0.2157654209\times \text{Fare})}}{e^{(-0.05784125441-0.2157654209\times \text{Fare})} + e^{(-0.1422511493-0.2157654209\times \text{Fare})}}$$

$$\mathrm{P}(train\,|\mathrm{PTEX}) = \frac{e^{(-0.1422511493-0.2157654209\times \text{Fare})}}{e^{(-0.05784125441-0.2157654209\times \text{Fare})} + e^{(-0.1422511493-0.2157654209\times \text{Fare})}}$$

$$\mathrm{P}(busway\,|\mathrm{PTNE}) = \frac{e^{(-0.09386516774-0.2157654209\times \text{Fare})}}{e^{(-0.09386516774-0.2157654209\times \text{Fare})} + e^{(-0.2157654209\times \text{Fare})}}$$

$$\mathrm{P}(LR|\mathrm{PTNE}) = \frac{e^{(-0.2157654209\times \text{Fare})}}{e^{(-0.09386516774-0.2157654209\times \text{Fare})} + e^{(-0.2157654209\times \text{Fare})}}$$

For the upper level of the model, the (marginal) probabilities become:

$$\mathrm{P}(car) = \frac{\left[\ln(e^{(-0.09937636480-0.2157654209\times \text{Fuel})} + e^{(0.4250220772-0.2157654209\times \text{Fuel})})\right]}{\begin{array}{l}\ln(e^{(-0.09937636480-0.2157654209\times \text{Fuel})} + e^{(0.4250220772-0.2157654209\times \text{Fuel})}) \\ +0.7886903275 \times \ln\left(e^{(-0.05784125441-0.2157654209\times \text{Fare})}\right. \\ \left.+e^{(-0.1422511493-0.2157654209\times \text{Fare})}\right) \\ +0.9868445842 \times \ln\left(e^{(-0.09386516774-0.2157654209\times \text{Fare})} + e^{(-0.2157654209\times \text{Fare})}\right)\end{array}}$$

$$\mathrm{P}(\mathrm{PTEX}) = \frac{[0.7886903275 \times \ln(e^{(-0.05784125441-0.2157654209\times \text{Fare})} + e^{(-0.1422511493-0.2157654209\times \text{Fare})})]}{\begin{array}{l}\ln(e^{(-0.09937636480-0.2157654209\times \text{Fuel})} + e^{(0.4250220772-0.2157654209\times\text{Fuel})}) + 0.7886903275 \\ \times \ln(e^{(-0.05784125441-0.2157654209\times \text{Fare})} + e^{(-0.1422511493-0.2157654209\times \text{Fare})}) \\ +0.9868445842 \times \ln(e^{(-0.09386516774-0.2157654209\times \text{Fare})} + e^{(-0.2157654209\times \text{Fare})})\end{array}}$$

$$\mathrm{P}(\mathrm{PTNE}) = \frac{[0.9868445842 \times \ln(e^{(-0.09386516774-0.2157654209\times \text{Fare})} + e^{(-0.2157654209\times \text{Fare})})]}{\begin{array}{l}\ln(e^{(-0.09937636480-0.2157654209\times \text{Fuel})} + e^{(0.4250220772-0.2157654209\times \text{Fuel})}) + 0.7886903275 \\ \times \ln(e^{(-0.05784125441-0.2157654209\times \text{Fare})} + e^{(-0.1422511493-0.2157654209\times \text{Fare})}) + 0.9868445842 \\ \times \ln(e^{(-0.09386516774-0.2157654209\times \text{Fare})} + e^{(-0.2157654209\times \text{Fare})})\end{array}}$$

The unconditional probabilities for each alternative are calculated for the above example as:

$$\begin{aligned}
\mathrm{P}(cart) &= (cart\,|car) \times \mathrm{P}(Car) \\
\mathrm{P}(carnt) &= (carnt\,|\mathrm{Car}) \times \mathrm{P}(Car) \\
\mathrm{P}(bus) &= P(bus|\mathrm{PTEX}) \times \mathrm{P}(\mathrm{PTEX}) \\
\mathrm{P}(train) &= P(train|\mathrm{PTEX}) \times \mathrm{P}(\mathrm{PTEX}) \\
\mathrm{P}(busway) &= P(busway|\mathrm{PTNE}) \times \mathrm{P}(\mathrm{PTNE}) \\
\mathrm{P}(LR) &= P(LR|\mathrm{PTNE}) \times \mathrm{P}(\mathrm{PTNE})
\end{aligned}$$

Formally:

$$P(cart) = \frac{e^{(0.09937636480-0.2157654209\times\mathrm{Fuel})}}{e^{(0.09937636480-0.2157654209\times\mathrm{Fuel})}+e^{(0.4250220772-0.2157654209\times\mathrm{Fuel})}}$$

$$\times \frac{\left[\ln(e^{(-0.09937636480-0.2157654209\times\mathrm{Fuel})}+e^{(0.4250220772-0.2157654209\times\mathrm{Fuel})})\right]}{\ln\left(e^{(-0.09937636480-0.2157654209\times\mathrm{Fuel})}+e^{(0.4250220772-0.2157654209\times\mathrm{Fuel})}\right)+0.7886903275}$$

$$\times \ln\left(e^{(-0.05784125441-0.2157654209\times\mathrm{Fare})}+e^{(-0.1422511493-0.2157654209\times\mathrm{Fare})}\right)$$

$$+0.9868445842\times\ln\left(e^{(-0.09386516774-0.2157654209\times\mathrm{Fare})}+e^{(-0.2157654209\times\mathrm{Fare})}\right)$$

$$P(carnt) = \frac{e^{(0.4250220772-0.2157654209\times\mathrm{Fuel})}}{e^{(0.09937636480-0.2157654209\times\mathrm{Fuel})}+e^{(0.4250220772-0.2157654209\times\mathrm{Fuel})}}$$

$$\times \frac{\left[\ln(e^{(-0.09937636480-0.2157654209\times\mathrm{Fuel})}+e^{(0.4250220772-0.2157654209\times\mathrm{Fuel})})\right]}{\ln\left(e^{(-0.09937636480-0.2157654209\times\mathrm{Fuel})}+e^{(0.4250220772-0.2157654209\times\mathrm{Fuel})}\right)+0.7886903275}$$

$$\times \ln\left(e^{(-0.05784125441-0.2157654209\times\mathrm{Fare})}+e^{(-0.1422511493-0.2157654209\times\mathrm{Fare})}\right)$$

$$+0.9868445842\times\ln\left(e^{(-0.09386516774-0.2157654209\times\mathrm{Fare})}+e^{(-0.2157654209\times\mathrm{Fare})}\right)$$

$$P(bus) = \frac{e^{(-0.05784125441-0.2157654209\times\mathrm{Fare})}}{e^{(-0.05784125441-0.2157654209\times\mathrm{Fare})}+e^{(-0.1422511493-0.2157654209\times\mathrm{Fare})}}$$

$$\times \frac{\left[0.7886903275\times\ln(e^{(-0.05784125441-0.2157654209\times\mathrm{Fare})}+e^{(-0.1422511493-0.2157654209\times\mathrm{Fare})})\right]}{\ln(e^{(-0.09937636480-0.2157654209\times\mathrm{Fuel})}+e^{(0.4250220772-0.2157654209\times\mathrm{Fuel})})+0.7886903275}$$

$$\times \ln(e^{(-0.05784125441-0.2157654209\times\mathrm{Fare})}+e^{(-0.1422511493-0.2157654209\times\mathrm{Fare})})$$

$$+0.9868445842\times\ln(e^{(-0.09386516774-0.2157654209\times\mathrm{Fare})}+e^{(-0.2157654209\times\mathrm{Fare})})$$

$$P(train) = \frac{e^{(-0.1422511493-0.2157654209\times\mathrm{Fare})}}{e^{(-0.05784125441-0.2157654209\times\mathrm{Fare})}+e^{(-0.1422511493-0.2157654209\times\mathrm{Fare})}}$$

$$\times \frac{\left[0.7886903275\times\ln(e^{(-0.05784125441-0.2157654209\times\mathrm{Fare})}+e^{(-0.1422511493-0.2157654209\times\mathrm{Fare})})\right]}{\ln(e^{(-0.09937636480-0.2157654209\times\mathrm{Fuel})}+e^{(0.4250220772-0.2157654209\times\mathrm{Fuel})})+0.7886903275}$$

$$\times \ln(e^{(-0.05784125441-0.2157654209\times\mathrm{Fare})}+e^{(-0.1422511493-0.2157654209\times\mathrm{Fare})})$$

$$+0.9868445842\times\ln(e^{(-0.09386516774-0.2157654209\times\mathrm{Fare})}+e^{(-0.2157654209\times\mathrm{Fare})})$$

$$P(busway) = \frac{e^{(-0.09386516774-0.2157654209\times\mathrm{Fare})}}{e^{(-0.09386516774-0.2157654209\times\mathrm{Fare})}+e^{(-0.2157654209\times\mathrm{Fare})}}$$

$$\times \frac{\left[0.9868445842\times\ln(e^{(-0.09386516774-0.2157654209\times\mathrm{Fare})}+e^{(-0.2157654209\times\mathrm{Fare})})\right]}{\ln\left(e^{(-0.09937636480-0.2157654209\times\mathrm{Fuel})}+e^{(0.4250220772-0.2157654209\times\mathrm{Fuel})}\right)+0.7886903275}$$

$$\times \ln\left(e^{(-0.05784125441-0.2157654209\times\mathrm{Fare})}+e^{(-0.1422511493-0.2157654209\times\mathrm{Fare})}\right)$$

$$+0.9868445842\times\ln\left(e^{(-0.09386516774-0.2157654209\times\mathrm{Fare})}+e^{(VLR=-0.2157654209\times\mathrm{Fare})}\right)$$

	A	B	C	D	E	F	G
1		Utility (Nlogit)	Prob (Nlogit)	P(my calcs)			
2	CART	-3.15E-01	0.288221	=G15*G9			
3	CARNT	-6.54E-01	0.205422	=G15*G10			
4	TRAIN	-3.58E-01	0.297825	=G16*G11			
5	LR	-6.47E-01	0.208531	=G17*G12			
6							
7	Level 1						
8		Constant	Cost Parameter	Cost	Utility	exp(U)	P(alts)
9	CART	-9.94E-02	-0.215765421	1	=B9+C9*D9	=EXP(E9)	=F9/C$33
10	CARNT	0.425022077	-0.215765421	5	=B10+C10*D10	=EXP(E10)	=F10/C$33
11	TRAIN	-0.142251149	-0.215765421	1	=B11+C11*D11	=EXP(E11)	=F11/C16
12	LR		-0.215765421	3	=B12+C12*D12	=EXP(E12)	=F12/C17
13	Level 2						
14		IV parameter	sum exp	EMU	Vbranches	exp(Ubranches)	P(branches)
15	CAR	1	=F9+F10	=LN(C15)	=D15*B15	=EXP(E15)	=F15/F$36
16	PTEX	0.788690328	=F11	=LN(C16)	=D16*B16	=EXP(E16)	=F16/F$36
17	PTNW	0.986844584	=F12	=LN(C17)	=D17*B17	=EXP(E17)	=F17/F$36
18						**=SUM(F15:F17)**	

Figure 14.5 Calculating probability and utilities of an NL model using NLOGIT

$$P(LR) = \frac{e^{(-0.2157654209 \times \text{Fare})}}{e^{(-0.09386516774 - 0.2157654209 \times \text{Fare})} + e^{(-0.2157654209 \times \text{Fare})}}$$

$$\times \frac{[0.9868445842 \times \ln(e^{(-0.09386516774 - 0.2157654209 \times \text{Fare})} + e^{(-0.2157654209 \times \text{Fare})})]}{\ln\left(e^{(-0.09937636480 - 0.2157654209 \times \text{Fuel})} + e^{(0.4250220772 - 0.2157654209 \times \text{Fuel})}\right) + 0.7886903275 \times \ln\left(e^{(-0.05784125441 - 0.2157654209 \times \text{Fare})} + e^{(-0.1422511493 - 0.2157654209 \times \text{Fare})}\right) + 0.9868445842 \times \ln\left(e^{(-0.09386516774 - 0.2157654209 \times \text{Fare})} + e^{(VLR = -0.2157654209 \times \text{Fare})}\right)}$$

For the beginner, the above may seem overly complicated. We therefore show these same calculations using Microsoft Excel in figure 14.5 for the first-choice set of the first respondent within the mode-choice data set. The first respondent observed four alternatives in the first choice set, *cart*, *carnt*, *train*, and *LR*. Cells B2–B5 of figure 14.5 show the utility estimates obtained for the above model using the NLOGIT **;Utility** command (the analyst may use the utility and **;Prob** command to obtain the **;Utility** and probability estimates for the sample as with the MNL model) and cells C2–C5 the probabilities. Cells B9–B11 show the ASC terms obtained from the model, and cells C9–C12 the cost parameter (which was treated as generic and hence is the same in each cell). The respondent observed fuel attribute levels of \$1 and \$5 for the *cart* and *carnt* alternatives, respectively, within the first-choice set and fare attribute levels of \$1 and \$3 for the *train* and *LR* alternatives, respectively. These attribute levels are represented in cells D9–D12. The utility functions for the elemental alternatives ((14.4a)–(14.4f)) are calculated in cells E9 and E10 of figure 14.5. The exponentials of the utility functions at level one of the model (required to estimate the conditional probabilities at level one) are calculated in cells F9–F12.

The conditional probability that an elemental alternative will be chosen is the exponential of the utility function of that alternative, divided by the sum of the exponentials of the utility functions of all alternatives contained within the same branch of the NL model.

For the *cart* alternative, the denominator of the conditional probability will be the sum of the exponentials of the utility function of the *cart* alternative and the utility function of the *carnt* alternative. The *train* and *LR* alternatives belong to different branches and therefore do not figure into the conditional probability for the *cart* alternative. In cell C15, we calculate the denominator for the elemental alternatives within the CAR branch of the tree. The *train* alternative resides with the *bus* alternative in the PTEX branch of the model; however, the *bus* alternative was not present in the first choice set for respondent one. Thus, the conditional probability of choosing the *train* alternative is equal to one. That is, if the PTEX branch is chosen, the decision maker must chose the *train* alternative as the *bus* alternative is not available. In terms of the probability calculation, the numerator for the *train* alternative will be the same as the denominator given the absence of other alternatives within this partition of the tree. Similarly, the conditional probability of choosing the *LR* alternative will also be one given the absence of the *busway* alternative from the choice set. Cells C16 and 17 are equal to cells F11 and F12, respectively, suggesting that the numerators and denominators for *train* and *LR* are equal and hence the conditional probabilities calculated in cells G11–G12 will be equal to one for these two alternatives. The conditional probabilities for the *cart* and *carnt* alternatives are provided in cells G9 and G11, which together must sum to one.

The IV parameters for the model are provided in cells B15–B17. The EMU values are calculated in cells D15–D17, which are the natural logarithms (i.e. ln( ) in Excel) of the denominators of each of the branches within the model. Given that we have used RU1 in this example, there is no need to account for the scale parameters at level one of the model which have all been normalized to 1.0. The utility function for each branch is calculated as the IV parameter multiplied by the associated EMU (or IV) variable. The calculations for the utility functions for each branch of the NL model are undertaken in cells E15–E17 in figure 14.5. The conditional probabilities at level two of the model rely on the same calculation as the conditional probabilities at level one of the model. That is, the conditional probability that any branch will be chosen may be calculated as the exponential of the utility function of that branch, divided by the sum of the exponentials of the utility functions of all available branches. The exponentials of the utilities of the branches are calculated in cells F15–F17. The denominator, the sum of the exponentials of the branch level utility functions, is calculated in cell F18 of figure 14.5. The conditional probabilities at level two of the NL model are calculated in cells G15–G17, which divide the exponential of the branch level utilities by the sum of the exponential of the branch level utilities calculated in cell F18.

Cells G9–G12 represent the conditional probabilities of each of the elemental alternatives. The unconditional probabilities for the elemental alternatives are equal to the conditional probabilities multiplied by the probability that the branch to which the elemental alternative belongs is first chosen. In figure 14.5, we show these calculations in cells D2–D5.

Figure 14.6 shows the values observed in the calculations shown in figure 14.5. Comparing cells D2–D5 with the probabilities calculated by NLOGIT, shown in cells C2–C5, it is clear that the calculations we have performed are exactly those undertaken by NLOGIT. By varying the fuel and fare costs in cells D9–D12, the analyst may perform a "*what-if*"

	A	B	C	D	E	F	G
1		Utility (Nlogit)	Prob (Nlogit)	P(my calcs)			
2	CART	-3.15E-01	0.288221	0.288221			
3	CARNT	-6.54E-01	0.205422	0.205422			
4	TRAIN	-3.58E-01	0.297825	0.297825			
5	LR	-6.47E-01	0.208531	0.208531			
6							
7	Level 1						
8		Constant	Cost Parameter	Cost	Utility	exp(U)	P(alts)
9	CART	-9.94E-02	-0.215765421	1	-3.15E-01	0.729685408	0.583865772
10	CARNT	0.425022077	-0.215765421	5	-6.54E-01	0.520063153	0.416134228
11	TRAIN	-0.142251149	-0.215765421	1	-3.58E-01	0.699061491	1
12	LR		-0.215765421	3	-6.47E-01	0.523459161	1
13	Level 2						
14		IV parameter	sum exp	EMU	Vbranches	exp(Ubranches)	P(branches)
15	CAR	1	1.249748561	0.22294238	0.22294238	1.249748561	0.49364333
16	PTEX	0.788690328	0.699061491	-0.35801657	-0.282364206	0.753999024	0.297825179
17	PTNW	0.986844584	0.523459161	-0.647296263	-0.638780811	0.527935685	0.20853149
18						**2.531683269**	

Figure 14.6 Example calculations of the probabilities and utilities of an NL model using NLOGIT

analysis to determine changes in the probabilities for this respondent (note that the analyst would be best to use spreadsheet calculations for the entire sample rather than for sampled individuals; we have done so only so as to compare the probabilities of our calculations with those obtained from NLOGIT).

For two-level NL models, establishing the system of equations of NL models in a spreadsheet similar to that shown in figures 14.5 and 14.6 may prove anything but relatively straightforward for the beginner. For three- or four-level NL models, the task is likely to prove impossible. Rather than use spreadsheet programs, the simulation capability of NLOGIT discussed in chapter 11 may also be applied to the NL model using exactly the same syntax commands. This represents a far better method for the beginner (and the expert) than having to revert to programs such as Excel. Indeed, we advise using spreadsheet programs in the manner discussed above only for pedagogical reasons.

14.4.2 Comparing RU1 to RU2

The model we specified in sub-section 14.4.1 had the cost parameter as generic both within and across branches of the NL model. As such, there is no direct parallel between that model (estimated using RU1) and exactly the same model specification estimated using RU2. In this section, we estimate NL models specified with ASCs and alternative-specific cost parameters using both RU1 and RU2 normalizations and compare the two. For this we will use the following model:

```
NLOGIT
;lhs = choice, cset, altij
;Choices = cart, carnt, bus, train, busway, LR
;Tree = car(cart,carnt), ptex(bus,train), ptnw(busway,LR)
```

```
;Start=logit
;ivset: (car)=[1.0]
;Maxit=100
;RU1
;Model:
U(cart) = asccart + cartc*fuel /
U(carnt) = asccarnt + carntc*fuel /
U(bus) = ascbus + bsc*fare /
U(train) = asctn + tnc*fare /
U(busway) = ascbusw + bswc*fare /
U(LR) = lrc*fare $
```

The above model specification will produce the following NLOGIT when estimated on the 30 minutes or less commuter segment of the mode choice case study. We omit the results from the MNL model used to obtain the start values for the NL model shown, as well as the second output box detailing the technical formations of the model:

```
+----------------------------------------------+
| FIML: Nested Multinomial Logit Model          |
| Maximum Likelihood Estimates                  |
| Model estimated: Feb 30, 2003 at 12:30:00PM.  |
| Dependent variable              CHOICE        |
| Weighting variable                None        |
| Number of observations            9476        |
| Iterations completed                21        |
| Log likelihood function      -3211.791        |
| Restricted log likelihood    -4244.678        |
| Chi squared                   2065.775        |
| Degrees of freedom                  13        |
| Prob[ChiSqd > value] =        .0000000        |
| R2=1-LogL/LogL*   Log-L fncn  R-sqrd  RsqAdj  |
| No coefficients   -4244.6782  .24334  .24195  |
| Constants only.   Must be computed directly.  |
|                   Use NLOGIT ;...; RHS=ONE $  |
| At start values   -3214.2405  .00076 -.00107  |
| Response data are given as ind. choice.       |
+----------------------------------------------+

+----------+-------------+----------------+----------+----------+
|Variable  | Coefficient | Standard Error | b/St.Er. | P[|Z|>z] |
+----------+-------------+----------------+----------+----------+
         Attributes in the Utility Functions (beta)
 ASCCART      -.46416295       .16826598      -2.759     .0058
 CARTC        -.09731776       .05796054      -1.679     .0931
```

```
ASCCARNT      -.19407367       .25630350       -.757      .4489
CARNTC        -.09306988       .05646578      -1.648      .0993
ASCBUS        -.22555722       .26182795       -.861      .3890
BSC           -.24049125       .06802551      -3.535      .0004
ASCTN         -.19753411       .25304489       -.781      .4350
TNC           -.28647161       .07038598      -4.070      .0000
ASCBUSW        .13709007       .20168914        .680      .4967
BSWC          -.30532063       .05506268      -5.545      .0000
LRC           -.29426902       .05450482      -5.399      .0000
         IV parameters, lambda(j|i),gamma(i)
CAR           1.00000000       ......(Fixed Parameter).......
PUB            .68259203       .15359718        4.444     .0000
NEWPUB         .81176131       .12868405        6.308     .0000
         Underlying standard deviation = pi/(IVparm*sqr(6))
CAR           1.28254980      ......(Fixed Parameter).......
PTEX          1.87894049      .42280007         4.444     .0000
PTNW          1.57995926      .25046225         6.308     .0000
```

An examination of the first output provided suggests that the model is superior to that of a model estimated with constants only assuming equal market shares, but is perhaps no better than the MNL model used to obtain the start values used in estimating the NL model. Of significance, all cost parameters are of the correct sign; however, at alpha equal to 0.05, the cost parameters for either *car* alternative are not statistically significant. Examining the IV parameters for the above model, both non-normalized IV parameters are statistically different to zero; however, only the PTEX IV parameter is statistically different to one. We show the calculation to test the upper bounds of the two IV parameters below:

$$\text{Wald-test PTEX} = \frac{0.6825920296 - 1}{0.15359718} = -2.07$$

$$\text{Wald-test PTNW} = \frac{0.8117613111 - 1}{0.12868405} = -1.46$$

As we have estimated the model under the RU1 condition, the scale parameters at level one of the model are normalized to 1.0. As such, we are able to write the utility functions for each alternative directly from output. We do so below, ignoring significance of the parameters:

$$\begin{aligned}
V_{cart} &= -0.4641629491 - 0.09731776419 \times \text{Fuel}\\
V_{carnt} &= -0.1940736722 - 0.09306987773 \times \text{Fuel}\\
V_{bus} &= -0.2255572188 - 0.2404912452 \times \text{Fare}\\
V_{train} &= -0.1975341054 - 0.2864716093 \times \text{Fare}\\
V_{busway} &= 0.1370900704 - 0.3053206278 \times \text{Fare}\\
V_{LR} &= -0.29426902 \times \text{Fare}
\end{aligned}$$

Unlike previous output, NLOGIT now reports the underlying standard deviations of the IV parameters which are calculated using (14.10):

$$\sigma = \frac{\pi}{\sqrt{6}\lambda} \tag{14.10}$$

In previous examples, we failed to specify whether NLOGIT should normalize using RU1 or RU2. When the analyst fails to specify which normalization assumption should be used, NLOGIT defaults to RU1 but does not calculate the underlying standard deviations of the IV parameters. When the analyst explicitly specifies that either RU1 or RU2 is to be used, NLOGIT will report the underlying standard deviations of the IV parameters, as seen here.

As an aside, extreme care must be taken in interpreting reported values of the underlying standard deviations of the IV parameters. Consider a three-level NL model estimated using RU1 (we will discuss the case of RU2 in section 14.4). The IV parameter at level three is the ratio of two scale parameters such that $IV_{(1|1)}$ equals

$$\frac{\gamma_{(i,l)}}{\lambda_{(i,l)}}$$

As such, substitution of the IV parameter into (14.10) produces

$$\sigma = \frac{\pi}{\sqrt{6}\frac{\gamma_{(i,l)}}{\lambda_{(i,l)}}}$$

The exact interpretation of the above is not clear as the standard deviation (variance) is no longer related to a single scale parameter but rather the ratio of two scale parameters. Nevertheless, for models estimated using RU1, reported values of the underlying standard deviations of the IV parameters at level two of the model are interpretatively valid as all $\mu_{(j|i,l)}$ are normalized to 1.0 and hence the IV parameter,

$$\frac{\lambda_{(j|i,l)}}{\mu_{(j|i,l)}},$$

becomes $\lambda_{(j|i,l)}$. Thus, (14.10) equals

$$\sigma = \frac{\pi}{\sqrt{6}\lambda_{(j|i,l)}}$$

The corollary of this is that for models estimated using RU1, the reported values of the underlying standard deviations of the IV parameters have substantive interpretational meaning only when examined at level two of the NL model.

The same model specification may be estimated under the RU2 condition using the following command:

```
NLOGIT
;lhs = choice, cset, altij
;Choices = cart, carnt, bus, train, busway, LR
```

```
;Tree = car(cart,carnt), ptex(bus,train), ptnw(busway,LR)
;Start=logit
;ivset: (car)=[1.0]
;Maxit=100
;RU2
;Model:
U(cart) = asccart + cartc*fuel /
U(carnt) = asccarnt + carntc*fuel /
U(bus) = ascbus + bsc*fare /
U(train) = asctn + tnc*fare /
U(busway) = ascbusw + bswc*fare /
U(LR) = lrc*fare $
```

The RU2 model results produced by NLOGIT are presented below. As with the RU1 model, we omit the MNL model estimated to obtain the start values for the NL model:

```
+--------------------------------------------+
| FIML: Nested Multinomial Logit Model       |
| Maximum Likelihood Estimates               |
| Model estimated: Feb 30, 2003 at 12:45:00PM.|
| Dependent variable              CHOICE     |
| Weighting variable                None     |
| Number of observations            9476     |
| Iterations completed                19     |
| Log likelihood function      -3211.791     |
| Restricted log likelihood    -4244.678     |
| Chi squared                   2065.775     |
| Degrees of freedom                  13     |
| Prob[ChiSqd > value] =        .0000000     |
| R2=1-LogL/LogL*  Log-L fncn  R-sqrd  RsqAdj |
| No coefficients  -4244.6782  .24334  .24195 |
| Constants only.  Must be computed directly. |
|                  Use NLOGIT ;...; RHS=ON  $ |
| At start values  -3214.2405 .00076  -.00107 |
| Response data are given as ind. choice.     |
+--------------------------------------------+

+----------+------------+---------------+----------+----------+
|Variable  | Coefficient | Standard Error | b/St.Er. | P[|Z|>z] |
+----------+------------+---------------+----------+----------+
          Attributes in the Utility Functions (beta)
 ASCCART     -.46416298      .16777156      -2.767      .0057
 CARTC       -.09731776      .05761844      -1.689      .0912
 ASCCARNT    -.19407365      .25650729       -.757      .4493
 CARNTC      -.09306989      .05696147      -1.634      .1023
```

```
ASCBUS        -.15396358     .17952724      -.858      .3911
BSC           -.16415740     .04447547     -3.691      .0002
ASCTN         -.13483523     .16902495      -.798      .4250
TNC           -.19554323     .04296818     -4.551      .0000
ASCBUSW        .11128438     .16186000       .688      .4917
BSWC          -.24784746     .04174862     -5.937      .0000
LRC           -.23887622     .04267174     -5.598      .0000
            IV parameters, RU2 form = mu(ji),gamma(i)
CAR           1.00000000     ......(Fixed Parameter)........
PUB            .68259203     .15359718      4.444      .0000
NEWPUB         .81176131     .12868405      6.308      .0000
            Underlying standard deviation = pi/(IVparm*sqr(6))
CAR          1.28254980     ......(Fixed Parameter).........
PTEX         1.87894049     .42280007       4.444      .0000
PTNW          1.57995926     .25046225       6.308     .0000
```

Examining the first NLOGIT output box, the results are exactly the same as when the model was estimated normalizing the scale parameters under RU1. This suggests that there are no differences in terms of the model fits when estimated under RU1 and RU2. All cost parameters are also of the correct sign and, as with the RU1 model, neither *car* cost parameter is statistically significant. Examination of the model results reveals that the parameter estimates are the same for both *car* modes; however, the parameter estimates for the remaining modes are different to those obtained when estimating the same model using RU1:

$$
\begin{aligned}
V_{cart} &= -0.4641629778 - 0.09731775957 \times \text{Fuel} \\
V_{carnt} &= -0.1940736546 - 0.9306988683 \times \text{Fuel} \\
V_{bus} &= -0.1539635774 - 0.1641574047 \times \text{Fare} \\
V_{train} &= -0.1348352254 - 0.1955432321 \times \text{Fare} \\
V_{busway} &= 0.1112843789 - 0.2478474647 \times \text{Fare} \\
V_{LR} &= -0.2388762189 \times \text{Fare}
\end{aligned}
$$

This finding should be of no surprise to the reader, as (14.2) suggests that each parameter be multiplied by a scale parameter, $\mu_{(j|i,l)}$. Previously we normalized the model using RU1 which normalizes each of the scale parameters at the elemental alternative level to 1.0. The RU1 normalization in effect allowed us to ignore the scale parameters at this level of the model. Under the RU2 normalization process, however, the scale parameters are normalized at the top level of the NL model, meaning that the scale parameters at level one of the NL tree are free to be estimated. As the IID property is maintained within each partition at each level of the NL model, the scale parameters for alternatives resident within the same branch are forced to be equal (i.e. the IID assumption is valid for each partition hence the variances and scale parameters for alternatives within each branch, must be equal). The scale parameter for the *cart* alternative will thus be equal to that of the *carnt* alternative at this level of the model. Similarly, the scale parameters for the *bus* and *train* will be equal as will the scale parameters of the *busway* and *LR* alternatives. For the above example, the Car branch IV parameter was normalized to 1.0. Under RU2, the scale parameter at the branch level (level two) of the tree is also normalized to 1.0. This suggests that in order to reconcile the Car IV parameter to equal 1.0, the scale parameters for each of the elemental alternatives at level one must also be equal to 1.0 (i.e. $1 \div 1 = 1$) within this branch. It is for this reason that the utility functions for the *car* modes are the same under RU2 as they were under RU1 as for both models the scale parameters at level one for this partition are equal to 1.0.

For the public transport modes, the IV parameters were allowed to vary. Examining the IV parameters reported by NLOGIT reveals that the IV parameters are exactly the same as those reported for the same model estimated under the RU1 assumption. Thus, the only observable difference between these two models is in the parameters of the *utility functions* estimated. However, we know that the IV parameters at level two of the NL model are given as

$$\frac{\lambda_{(j|i,l)}}{\mu_{(j|i,l)}}$$

and that under the RU2 normalization assumption, $\lambda_{(j|i,l)}$ is normalized to 1.0 (RU2 normalizes the scale parameters at the top level of the model; as this is a two-level NL model, the scale parameters normalized are at the branch level). Thus, we can easily establish the scale parameter values at level one of the model. For the PTEX branch, the scale parameters (i.e. $\mu_{(2|1,1)}$) may be calculated as:

$$\begin{aligned} IV_{PTEX} &= 0.68259200 = \frac{\lambda_{(2|1,1)}}{\mu_{(2|1,1)}} \\ &= \mu_{(2|2,1)} = \frac{1}{0.68259200} = 1.465003989 \end{aligned}$$

Similarly, the scale parameters for the PTNW branch (i.e. $\mu_{(3|1,1)}$) is given by

$$\begin{aligned} IV_{PTNW} &= 0.81176131 = \frac{\lambda_{(3|1,1)}}{\mu_{(3|1,1)}} \\ &= \mu_{(3|1,1)} = \frac{1}{0.81176131} = 1.231889276 \end{aligned}$$

Multiplying each utility function by the relevant scale parameter, as suggested by (14.2), the utility functions at level one of the RU2 model become:

$$\begin{aligned} V_{cart} &= 1 \times -0.46416297781 \times -0.09731775957 \times \text{Fuel} \\ V_{carnt} &= 1 \times -0.1940736546 + 1 \times -0.9306988683 \times \text{Fuel} \\ V_{bus} &= 1.465003989 \times -0.1539635774 + 1.465003989 \times -0.1641574047 \times \text{Fare} \\ V_{train} &= 1.465003989 \times -0.1348352254 + 1.465003989 \times -0.1955432321 \times \text{Fare} \\ V_{busway} &= 1.231889276 \times 0.1112843789 + 1.231889276 \times -0.2478474647 \times \text{Fare} \\ V_{LR} &= 1.231889276 \times -0.2388762189 \times \text{Fare} \end{aligned}$$

which equal:

$$V_{cart} = -0.4641629491 - 0.09731776419 \times \text{Fuel}$$
$$V_{carnt} = -0.1940736722 - 0.09306987773 \times \text{Fuel}$$
$$V_{bus} = -0.2255572188 - 0.2404912452 \times \text{Fare}$$
$$V_{train} = -0.1975341054 - 0.2864716093 \times \text{Fare}$$
$$V_{busway} = 0.1370900704 - 0.3053206278 \times \text{Fare}$$
$$V_{LR} = -0.294226902 \times \text{Fare}$$

Comparing the above utility functions to those of the same model estimated using RU1 reveals that the two sets of utility functions are identical. This finding confirms that, provided all parameters are specified alternative-specific, models estimated using RU1 are identical to those estimated using RU2.

As an aside, analysts using pre-August 2003 versions of NLOGIT will not observe the results we report above, as pre-August 2003 versions of NLOGIT have a minor reporting error for NL models estimated using RU2. For such versions, NLOGIT reports the level one scale parameters rather than the IV parameters. We show this below:

```
+----------+------------+---------------+----------+----------+
|Variable  | Coefficient | Standard Error | b/St.Er. | P[|Z|>z] |
+----------+------------+---------------+----------+----------+
        Attributes in the Utility Functions (beta)
 ASCCART     -.4641629778       .16777156      -2.767     .0057
 CARTC       -.0973177596       .05761844      -1.689     .0912
 ASCCARNT    -.1940736546       .25650729       -.757     .4493
 CARNTC     -0.9306988683       .05696147      -1.634     .1023
 ASCBUS      -.1539635774       .17952724       -.858     .3911
 BSC         -.1641574047       .04447548      -3.691     .0002
 ASCTN       -.1348352254       .16902495       -.798     .4250
 TNC         -.1955432321       .04296818      -4.551     .0000
 ASCBUSW      .1112843789       .16186000        .688     .4917
 BSWC        -.2478474647       .04174862      -5.937     .0000
 LRC         -.2388762189       .04267174      -5.598     .0000
      IV parameters, RU2 form = mu(ji),gamma(i)
 CAR         1.000000000     ........(Fixed Parameter)........
 PTEX        1.465003989       .28579048       5.126     .0000
 PTNW        1.231889276       .19630467       6.275     .0000
 Underlying standard deviation = pi/(IVparm*sqr(6))
 CAR         1.282549800     ........(Fixed Parameter)........
 PTEX        .8754582304       .17078290       5.126     .0000
 PTNW        1.041124251       .16590578       6.275     .0000
```

Analysts using pre-August 2003 releases of NLOGIT will be required to take the reciprocal of the reported IV value (which is, in fact, the scale parameter) to obtain the correct IV parameter value for two-level NL models estimated using the RU2 normalization. We show this below:

$$IV_{PTEX} = \frac{\lambda_{(2|1,1)}}{\mu_{(2|1,1)}} = \frac{1}{1.465} = 0.683$$

$$IV_{PTEX} = \frac{\lambda_{(3|1,1)}}{\mu_{(3|1,1)}} = \frac{1}{1.232} = 0.812$$

which is the IV parameter obtained when estimating the same model using RU1. The important point to note is that IV parameters lie within the 0–1 bound required for global utility maximization, a point that would escape most analysts (indeed, this went unnoticed even by the authors for some time).

This minor reporting problem also extends to the underlying standard deviations of the IV parameters. In order to calculate the true standard deviations, the analyst will be required to once more take the reciprocal of the reported IV value and use this as the scale parameter in (14.9) in order to calculate the true standard deviations. Thus, for the PTEX branch, substitution of the reciprocal of the reported PTEX IV parameter (really the scale parameter) produces the following results:

$$\sigma_{PTEX} = \frac{\pi}{\sqrt{6}\lambda_{PTEX}} = \frac{3.141593}{\sqrt{6} \times \dfrac{1}{1.465003989}} = 1.87894049$$

This is exactly the same value reported by post-August 2003 release versions of NLOGIT. Again, this is a reporting problem that arises only for pre-August 2003 versions of NLOGIT and only when the NL model is estimated using the RU2 normalization procedure.

14.5 Specifying utility functions at higher levels of the NL tree

Equations (14.3)–(14.5) imply that the analyst may include attributes and/or observation-specific SDC or contextual variables in utility expressions at levels greater than level one of an NL model. This is accomplished with the following command syntax where the name provided for the utility expression is a name provided in the **;Tree** specification:

U(<branch, limb or trunk name>) = <utility function 1> /

While the *attributes of elemental alternatives* may be assigned to utility expressions of higher levels of NL models, a great level of care is required in doing so. Attribute levels distinguish between alternatives which by design are placed at level one of the model. Unless it can be shown that a common set of attributes is used by respondents to distinguish between higher choices (i.e. higher-level partitions of the model), attributes should be assigned only at level one of the model. Thus, while we do not rule out the possibility that attribute levels be used in the utility expressions at higher levels of an NL model, we advise the beginner to limit themselves to the use of SDC or contextual variables within the utility functions at levels two–four of NL models.

In the following NL model specification, we assign the number of drivers within each sampled household and the number of household vehicles to the Car branch utility function and ASCs to the utility functions of the PTEX and PTNW branches. As with level one, each level of the NL model is treated as a separate MNL (i.e. this is equivalent to stating that the IID assumption is maintained within each partition of the model), hence the analyst will only ever be able to estimate constants for *J*–1 utility functions at each level and *J*–1 SDC or contextual characteristic parameters:

```
NLOGIT
;lhs=choice, cset, altij
;Choices=cart,carnt,bus,train,busway,LR
;Tree= Car(cart,carnt),PTEX(bus,train),PTNW(busway,LR)
;Start=logit
;ivset: (Car)=[1.0]
;Maxit=100
;Model:
U(car)= ndrivlic*ndrivlic + numbvehs*numbvehs /
u(ptex) = ptex /
u(ptnw) = ptnw /
U(cart) = asccart + cst*fuel /
U(carnt) = asccarnt + cst*fuel /
U(bus) = ascbus + cst*fare /
U(train) = asctn + cst*fare /
U(busway) = ascbusw + cst*fare /
U(LR) = cst*fare $
```

The first results presented are those of the MNL model used to obtain the starting values for the ML search used for the NL model. Note that the NNNL model is no longer equivalent to a simple MNL model which is indicated in the first output line, which previously stated:

```
FIML: Nested Multinomial Logit Model
```

For the 30 minutes or less commuter segment, the following model results are obtained:

```
+-----------------------------------------------+
| Start values obtained using nonnested model   |
| Maximum Likelihood Estimates                  |
| Model estimated: Feb 30, 2003 at 01:00:00PM.  |
| Dependent variable              Choice        |
| Weighting variable                None        |
| Number of observations            2369        |
| Iterations completed                 5        |
| Log likelihood function      -5184.638        |
| Log-L for Choice model =    -3220.1497        |
| R2=1-LogL/LogL*   Log-L fncn  R-sqrd  RsqAdj  |
| No coefficients   -4244.6782  .24137  .24008  |
```

```
| Constants only.   Must be computed directly. |
|                   Use NLOGIT ;...; RHS=ONE $ |
| Chi-squared[ 1]                = 1639.08085 |
| Prob [ chi squared > value ] =       .00000 |
| Log-L for Branch model =         -1964.4887 |
| Response data are given as ind. choice.     |
| Number of obs.= 2369,  skipped  0 bad obs.  |
+---------------------------------------------+

+----------+------------+---------------+----------+----------+
|Variable  | Coefficient | Standard Error | b/St.Er. | P[|Z|>z] |
+----------+------------+---------------+----------+----------+
          Model for Choice Among Alternatives
 ASCCART    -.08252881      .07552527     -1.093    .2745
 CST        -.20180890      .01916932    -10.528    .0000
 ASCCARNT    .41384399      .07640648      5.416    .0000
 ASCBUS      .01966141      .09923321       .198    .8429
 ASCTN      -.04174518      .09373128      -.445    .6561
 ASCBUSW     .09250653      .08587656      1.077    .2814
          Model for Choice Among Branches
 NDRIVLIC   -.11254276      .06334253     -1.777    .0756
 NUMBVEHS    .48617942      .06546039      7.427    .0000
 PTEX        .29826865      .09318183      3.201    .0014
 PTNW        .38982532      .08792904      4.433    .0000
```

For the NNNL model results, the parameter estimates at the lowest level of the model will be exactly the same as those obtained for the same model when utility functions were not specified at higher levels of the model (to see this, compare the results above with those presented on p. 542).

It is worthwhile reiterating at this point that the NNNL model used to derive start values for the estimation of the NL model is *not* equivalent to an NNNL model estimated with all IV parameters normalized to 1.0 (i.e. a MNL model) when utility functions are specified at levels greater than level one of the NL model. If no utility functions are specified at levels two–four (or any sub-set thereof) of the NL model, the non-nested MNL model will be equivalent to the basic MNL model and the LL ratio test reported by NLOGIT is, in reality, a comparison of the NL model to the equivalent MNL model. However, when utility functions are specified at levels two–four (or sub-sets thereof), the NNNL model estimated to provide the start values is not equivalent to the basic MNL model. Thus, if the analyst desires a test of the NL model to the equivalent MNL model (with utility functions specified at higher levels of the model), the analyst will be required to estimate the NL model normalizing all IV parameters to 1.0 (e.g. **;ivset: (Car, PTEX, PTNW) = [1.0]**) and set up the LL ratio-test themselves. Alternatively a stand alone MNL model can be estimated. The test-statistic will be twice the difference in the log likelihoods producing a Chi-squared test-statistic with degrees of freedom equal to the number of free IV parameters.

The NL model results are presented below:

```
+-----------------------------------------------+
| FIML: Nested Multinomial Logit Model           |
| Maximum Likelihood Estimates                   |
| Model estimated: Feb 30, 2003 at 01:02:04PM.   |
| Dependent variable                 CHOICE      |
| Weighting variable                   None      |
| Number of observations               9476      |
| Iterations completed                   20      |
| Log likelihood function         -3187.142      |
| Restricted log likelihood       -4244.678      |
| Chi squared                      2115.073      |
| Degrees of freedom                     12      |
| Prob[ChiSqd > value] =           .0000000      |
| R2=1-LogL/LogL*    Log-L fncn  R-sqrd  RsqAdj  |
| No coefficients   -4244.6782  .24914  .24787   |
| Constants only.   Must be computed directly.   |
|                  Use NLOGIT ;...; RHS=ONE  $   |
| At start values  -3239.6898   .01622  .01456   |
| Response data are given as ind. choice.        |
+-----------------------------------------------+
```

```
+----------+-----------+--------------+---------+---------+
|Variable  | Coefficient | Standard Error | b/St.Er. | P[|Z|>z] |
+----------+-----------+--------------+---------+---------+
          Attributes in the Utility Functions (beta)
ASCCART     -.57012562      .16685520     -3.417    .0006
CST         -.21466427      .02431829     -8.827    .0000
ASCCARNT    -.04811598      .17912908      -.269    .7882
ASCBUS      -.16668514      .28378017      -.587    .5570
ASCTN       -.23571739      .24563386      -.960    .3372
ASCBUSW      .12632204      .10140284      1.246    .2129
          Attributes of Branch Choice Equations (alpha)
NDRIVLIC    -.19772035      .06814564     -2.901    .0037
NUMBVEHS     .45441022      .06557843      6.929    .0000
PTEX         .04343987      .16875118       .257    .7969
PTNW        -.07485068      .17609317      -.425    .6708
          IV parameters, tau(ji,l),sigma(il),phi(l)
CAR         1.00000000      ......(Fixed Parameter).......
PTEX         .77774892      .16056894      4.844    .0000
PTNW        1.01792857      .16155904      6.301    .0000
```

The interpretation of the above output is no different to that for other models discussed to date. The overall model is statistically significant when compared to a model assuming equal choice shares only. Given that the model was estimated using RU1, the utility functions at the lowest level of the model may be written directly from the output (i.e. $\mu_{cart} = \mu_{carnt} = \mu_{bus} = \mu_{train} = \mu_{busway} = 1.0$ and the scale parameters at level two of the model are free to vary, hence λ_{car}, λ_{PTEX}, and λ_{PTNW} do not have to be equal (though they may be, in which case the model will collapse to the MNL form)). We write these out below:

$$\begin{aligned}
V_{cart} &= -0.5701256207 - 0.2146642674 \times \text{Fuel} \\
V_{carnt} &= -0.04811598158 - 0.2146642674 \times \text{Fuel} \\
V_{bus} &= -0.1666851413 - 0.2146642674 \times \text{Fare} \\
V_{train} &= -0.2357173916 - 0.2146642674 \times \text{Fare} \\
V_{busway} &= 0.1263220416 - 0.2146642674 \times \text{Fare} \\
V_{LR} &= -0.2146642674 \times \text{Fare}
\end{aligned}$$

For the above model, at the upper level of the model, the number of drivers in a household holding drivers' licenses and the number of vehicles are statistically significant (i.e. p-values less than 0.05); however, the ASCs for the public transport branches are not statistically significant. Given that the Car branch IV parameter has been normalized (i.e. $\lambda_{Car} = 1.0$), and given that the scale parameter at level one was also normalized to 1.0 (given RU1), the scale parameter at level 2 of the Car branch must, by logical deduction, also be normalized to 1.0 in order for the IV parameter to equal 1.0 (i.e. $1 = 1 \div 1$). From (14.3) we therefore obtain:

$$V_{(Car)} = 1 \times \left[-0.1125427605 \times ndrivlic + 0.4544102206 \times numbvehs + \frac{1}{1} \times IV_{Car}\right]$$

where

$$\begin{aligned}
IV_{Car} &= \ln(e^{\mu_{Car} V_{cart}} + e^{\mu_{Car} V_{carnt}}) \\
&= \ln\left(e^{1\times(-0.5701256207 - 0.2146642674 \times \text{Fuel})} + e^{1\times(-0.04811598158 - 0.2146642674 \times \text{Fuel})}\right) \\
&= \ln\left(e^{(-0.5701256207 - 0.2146642674 \times \text{Fuel})} + e^{(-0.04811598158 - 0.2146642674 \times \text{Fuel})}\right)
\end{aligned}$$

In full, the utility function for the Car branch is:

$$\begin{aligned}
V_{(Car)} = &-0.1125427605 \times ndrivlic + 0.4544102206 \times numbvehs \\
&+ \ln(e^{(-0.5701256207 - 0.2146642674 \times \text{Fuel})} + e^{(-0.0481159818 - 0.2146642674 \times \text{Fuel})})
\end{aligned}$$

The utility functions for the remaining two branches are:

$$V_{(PTEX)} = 0.7777489234 \times \left[0.4343987104 + \frac{1}{1} \times IV_{PTEX}\right]$$

where

$$\begin{aligned}
IV_{PTEX} &= \ln(e^{\mu_{PTEX} V_{bus}} + e^{\mu_{PTEX} V_{train}}) \\
&= \ln(e^{(-0.1666851413 - 0.2146642674 \times \text{Fare})} + e^{(-0.2357173916 - 0.2146642674 \times \text{Fare})})
\end{aligned}$$

Hence:

$$V_{(PTEX)} = 0.7777489234 \times \big[0.4343987104 + \ln\big(e^{(-0.1666851413-0.2146642674\times \text{Fare})} + e^{(-0.2357173916-0.2146642674\times \text{Fare})}\big)\big]$$

and

$$V_{(PTNW)} = 1.017928571 \times \left[-0.7485067881 + \frac{1}{1} \times IV_{PTNW}\right]$$

where

$$IV_{PTNW} = \ln(e^{\mu_{PTNW}V_{Busway}} + e^{\mu_{PTNW}V_{LR}}) = \ln(e^{(0.1263220416-0.2146642674\times \text{Fare})} + e^{(-0.2146642674\times \text{Fare})})$$

Leading to:

$$V_{(PTNW)} = 1.017928571 \times [-0.7485067881 + \ln(e^{(0.1263220416-0.2146642674\times \text{Fare})} + e^{(-0.2146642674\times \text{Fare})})]$$

The conditional probabilities are, at lower level of the model:

$$\text{P}(cart|Car) = \frac{e^{(-0.5701256207-0.2146642674\times \text{Fuel})}}{e^{(-0.5701256207-0.2146642674\times \text{Fuel})} + e^{(-0.04811598158-0.2146642674\times \text{Fuel})}}$$

$$\text{P}(carnt|Car) = \frac{e^{(-0.04811598158-0.2146642674\times \text{Fuel})}}{e^{(-0.5701256207-0.2146642674\times \text{Fuel})} + e^{(-0.04811598158-0.2146642674\times \text{Fuel})}}$$

$$\text{P}(bus|PTEX) = \frac{e^{(-0.1666851413-0.2146642674\times \text{Fare})}}{e^{(-0.1666851413-0.2146642674\times \text{Fare})} + e^{(-0.2357173916-0.2146642674\times \text{Fare})}}$$

$$\text{P}(train|PTEX) = \frac{e^{(-0.2357173916-0.2146642674\times \text{Fare})}}{e^{(-0.1666851413-0.2146642674\times \text{Fare})} + e^{(-0.2357173916-0.2146642674\times \text{Fare})}}$$

$$\text{P}(busway|PTNE) = \frac{e^{(0.1263220416-0.2146642674\times \text{Fare})}}{e^{(0.1263220416-0.2146642674\times \text{Fare})} + e^{(-0.2146642674\times \text{Fare})}}$$

$$P(LR|PTNE) = \frac{e^{(-0.2146642674\times \text{Fare})}}{e^{(0.1263220416-0.2146642674\times \text{Fare})} + e^{(-0.2146642674\times \text{Fare})}}$$

For the upper level of the model, the probabilities are:

$$\text{P}(Car) = \frac{[-0.1125427605 \times ndrivlic + 0.4544102206 \times numbvehs + \ln(e^{(-0.5701256207-0.2146642674\times \text{Fuel})} + e^{(-0.0481159818-0.2146642674\times \text{Fuel})})]}{\begin{array}{l}[-0.1125427605 \times ndrivlic + 0.4544102206 \times numbvehs + \ln(e^{(-0.5701256207-0.2146642674\times \text{Fuel})} + e^{(-0.0481159818-0.2146642674\times \text{Fuel})})] \\ + [0.7777489234 \times [0.4343987104 + \ln(e^{(-0.1666851413-0.2146642674\times \text{Fare})} + e^{(-0.2357173916-0.2146642674\times \text{Fare})})] \\ + [1.017928571 \times [-0.7485067881 + \ln(e^{(0.1263220416-0.2146642674\times \text{Fare})} + e^{(-0.2146642674\times \text{Fare})})]\end{array}}$$

$$\mathrm{P}(PTEX) = \frac{0.7777489234 \times [0.4343987104 + \ln(e^{(-0.1666851413-0.2146642674\times \text{Fare})} + e^{(-0.2357173916-0.2146642674\times \text{Fare})})]}{\begin{array}{l}[-0.1125427605 \times ndrivlic + 0.4544102206 \times numbvehs \\ + \ln(e^{(-0.5701256207-0.2146642674\times \text{Fuel})} + e^{(-0.0481159818-0.2146642674\times \text{Fuel})})] \\ + [0.7777489234 \times [0.4343987104 \\ + \ln(e^{(-0.1666851413-0.2146642674\times \text{Fare})} + e^{(-0.2357173916-0.2146642674\times \text{Fare})})] \\ + [1.017928571 \times [-0.7485067881 \\ + \ln(e^{(0.1263220416-0.2146642674\times \text{Fare})} + e^{(-0.2146642674\times \text{Fare})})]\end{array}}$$

$$\mathrm{P}(PTNE) = \frac{1.017928571 \times [-0.7485067881 + \ln(e^{(0.1263220416=-0.2146642674\times \text{Fare})} + e^{(-0.2146642674\times \text{Fare})})]}{\begin{array}{l}[-0.1125427605 \times ndrivlic + 0.4544102206 \times numbvehs \\ + \ln(e^{(-0.5701256207-0.2146642674\times \text{Fuel})} + e^{(-0.0481159818-0.2146642674\times \text{Fuel})})] \\ + [0.7777489234 \times [0.4343987104 \\ + \ln(e^{(-0.1666851413-0.2146642674\times \text{Fare})} + e^{(-0.2357173916-0.2146642674\times \text{Fare})})] \\ + [1.017928571 \times [-0.7485067881 \\ + \ln(e^{(0.1263220416-0.2146642674\times \text{Fare})} + e^{(-0.2146642674\times \text{Fare})})]\end{array}}$$

As before, the unconditional probabilities for each alternative are calculated for the above example as:

$$\begin{aligned}
\mathrm{P}(cart) &= (cart\,|Car) \times \mathrm{P}(Car) \\
\mathrm{P}(carnt) &= (carnt\,|Car) \times \mathrm{P}(Car) \\
\mathrm{P}(bus) &= \mathrm{P}(bus\,|PTEX) \times \mathrm{P}(PTEX) \\
\mathrm{P}(train) &= \mathrm{P}(train\,|PTEX) \times \mathrm{P}(PTEX) \\
\mathrm{P}(busway) &= \mathrm{P}(busway\,|PTNE) \times \mathrm{P}(PTNE) \\
\mathrm{P}(LR) &= \mathrm{P}(LR\,|PTNE\,) \times \mathrm{P}(PTNE)
\end{aligned}$$

We leave it to the reader to write these out in full.

14.6 Handling degenerate branches in NL models

It is common in many applications to have partitions with only one alternative present. Such partitions are called "degenerate partitions." For example, consider the NL tree structure shown in figure 14.7 in which the *LR* alternative resides within a branch by itself.

Degenerate partitions in NL models require careful consideration on how they are to be operationalized by the analyst. Under RU1, the scale parameter at level one is normalized to 1.0, hence the utility may be written directly as follows:

$$V_{lr} = \beta_{1lr} f(X_{1lr}) + \beta_{2lr} f(X_{2lr}) + \beta_{3lr} f(X_{3lr}) + \cdots + \beta_{Klr} f(X_{Klr})$$

Given that the *LR* alternative is the sole-alternative within branch C, it follows that the conditional choice probability at level one for the *LR* must be equal to one. We show this

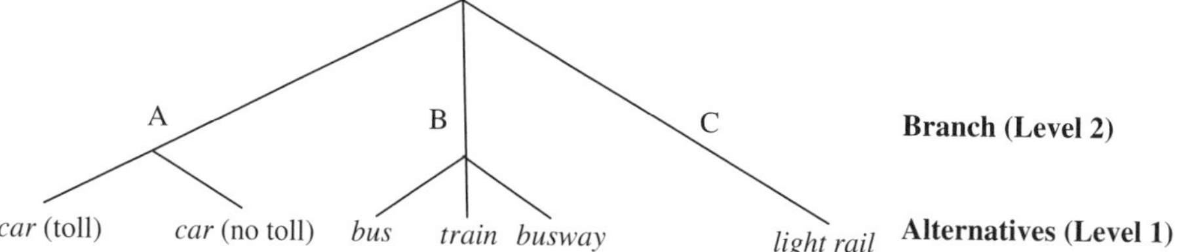

Figure 14.7 An NL tree structure with a degenerate alternative

below:

$$\mathrm{P}(LR) = \frac{e^{V_{LR}}}{e^{V_{LR}}} = 1$$

The utility function at level two for branch C is given as:

$$V_C = \lambda_C \left[\frac{1}{\mu_c} \times IV_{(LR)} \right] = \lambda_C \left[\frac{1}{1} \times \ln(e^{V_{LR}}) \right] = \lambda_C \times V_{LR}$$

As the utility for a degenerate alternative can reside at only one level of the NL model (it does not matter whether we specify it at level one or two), the variance must be the same at each level of a degenerate nest. That is, V_{LR} may be specified at levels one or two in the above example; however, if specified at level one, the scale parameter, μ_C, is normalized to 1.0 while if specified at level two, the scale parameter, λ_C, is free to vary. This is counterintuitive since the variance (and hence the scale parameters) for a degenerate alternative should be equal no matter at what level one specifies the utility function. That is, the variance structure of the NL model is such that higher-level partitions incorporate the variance of lower adjoining partitions as well as that partition's own variance. With a degenerate alternative, higher-level partitions should theoretically not have their own variance, as nothing is being explained at that level. As such, the only level at which variance should be explained is at the level at which the utility function for that alternative is placed. Under RU1, μ_C is normalized to 1.0, hence it follows that λ_C must also be equal to 1.0 (see appendix 13A).

Normalization of the NL model using RU2 yields the following *LR* utility function:

$$\mu_C \times V_{lr} = \mu_C \times \beta_{1lr} f(X_{1lr}) + \mu_C \times \beta_{2lr} f(X_{2lr}) + \cdots + \mu_C \times \beta_{Klr} f(X_{Klr})$$

The utility function at level two of the model may be represented as follows:

$$V_C = 1 \left[\frac{1}{\mu_C} \times IV_{(LR)} \right] = \frac{1}{\mu_C} \times \ln(e^{\mu_C V_{LR}}) = \frac{1}{\mu_C} \times \mu_C V_{LR} = V_{LR}$$

Under RU2, the scale parameters cancel each other. That is, the IV parameter is no longer identifiable! NLOGIT recognises this and automatically reverts to RU1, Nevertheless, at least one scale parameter is identifiable under RU1; however, for reasons discussed, this should be normalized to 1.0 (NLOGIT will not automatically do this).

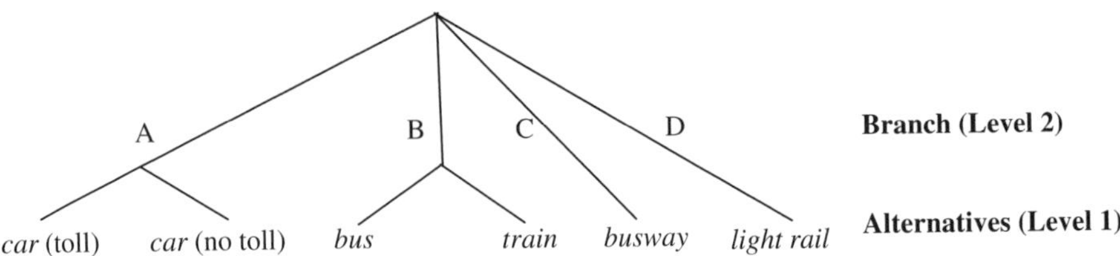

Figure 14.8 An NL tree structure with two degenerate alternatives

An important aspect of the above discussion, not recognized in the literature (at least that we know of), is that if an NL model has two degenerate alternatives, scale parameters for both must be normalized to one, which is equivalent to treating these alternatives as a single nest (with MNL properties). To demonstrate, consider the NL tree structure in figure 14.8.

Under RU1 (RU2 is not estimatable), both μ_C and μ_D are normalized to 1.0. Given the above reasoning, both λ_C and λ_D must also be normalized to 1.0. The scale parameters, and hence variances, of the two degenerate branches are the same and figure 14.8 will collapse to figure 14.2.

Taking the above into account, the following NLOGIT command syntax will estimate an NL model of the form suggested by figure 14.7. We have normalized the branch C IV parameter to 1.0:

```
NLOGIT
;lhs = choice, cset, altij
;Choices = cart, carnt, bus, train, busway, LR
;Tree = A(cart,carnt), B(bus,train,busway),C(LR)
;Start=logit
;ivset: (C)=[1.0]
;Maxit=100
;Model:
U(cart) = asccart+cst*fuel /
U(carnt) = asccarnt + cst*fuel /
U(bus) = ascbus + cst*fare /
U(train) = asctn + cst*fare /
U(busway) = ascbusw + cst*fare /
U(D) = cst*fare $
```

For the 30 minutes or less commuting segment, the above command syntax will generate the following NLOGIT results. We have omitted the non-nested MNL model results used to obtain the NL model start values:

```
+--------------------------------------------+
| FIML: Nested Multinomial Logit Model        |
| Maximum Likelihood Estimates                |
| Model estimated: Feb 30, 2003 at 01:15:00PM. |
| Dependent variable              CHOICE      |
```

```
| Weighting variable                    None        |
| Number of observations                9476        |
| Iterations completed                    22        |
| Log likelihood function          -3218.149        |
| Restricted log likelihood        -4360.073        |
| Chi squared                       2283.849        |
| Degrees of freedom                       8        |
| Prob[ChiSqd > value] =            .0000000        |
| R2=1-LogL/LogL*  Log-L fncn  R-sqrd  RsqAdj       |
| No coefficients  -4360.0732  .26190  .26107       |
| Constants only.  Must be computed directly.       |
|                  Use NLOGIT ;...; RHS=ONE $       |
| At start values  -3465.1102  .07127  .07022       |
| Response data are given as ind. choice.           |
+---------------------------------------------------+

+----------+-------------+----------------+----------+----------+
|Variable  | Coefficient | Standard Error | b/St.Er. | P[|Z|>z] |
+----------+-------------+----------------+----------+----------+
           Attributes in the Utility Functions (beta)
 ASCCART       .02655801       .23377128        .114      .9095
 CST          -.22516186       .02335807      -9.640      .0000
 ASCCARNT      .56991570       .22844399       2.495      .0126
 ASCBUS       -.01155319       .12273402       -.094      .9250
 ASCTN        -.13796595       .13573518      -1.016      .3094
 ASCBUSW       .00255961       .12674207        .020      .9839
           Attributes of Branch Choice Equations (alpha)
 CST          -.22516186       .02335807      -9.640      .0000
           IV parameters, tau(j| i,l),sigma(i| l),phi(l)
 A             .55701107       .32603759       1.708      .0876
 B             .80076806       .11250244       7.118      .0000
 C            1.00000000        ......(Fixed Parameter)......
```

The cost parameter is statistically significant, and of the correct sign. The utility functions for the above model may be written out directly (the model was estimated using RU1). We do so below:

$$
\begin{aligned}
V_{cart} &= 0.02655801050 - 0.2251618652 \times \text{Fuel}\\
V_{carnt} &= -0.5699156988 - 0.2251618652 \times \text{Fuel}\\
V_{bus} &= -0.1155319932 - 0.2251618652 \times \text{Fare}\\
V_{train} &= -0.1379659510 - 0.2251618652 \times \text{Fare}\\
V_{busway} &= 0.002559610651 - 0.2251618652 \times \text{Fare}\\
V_{LR} &= -0.2251618652 \times \text{Fare}
\end{aligned}
$$

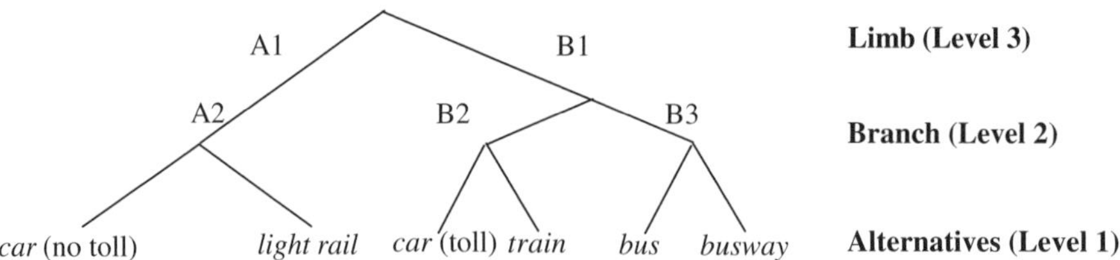

Figure 14.9 A three-level NL tree structure with degenerate branches

The utility function for branch C is given as:

$$V_C = \lambda_C \left[\frac{1}{\mu_C} \times IV_{(LR)} \right] = 1 \left[\frac{1}{1} \times \ln(e^{V_{LR}}) \right] = V_{LR}$$

The remaining branch-level utilities, level one conditional and level two marginal probabilities may be expressed as in previous examples. We leave it to the reader to write these out in full.

The above example demonstrates the case whereby the degenerate nest is at the elemental alternative level of the model. It is possible that, for three-level or four-level NL models, a degenerate partition occurs at higher levels of the model. This represents a partial degeneration. Consider the three-level NL model in figure 14.9.

The NL model shown in figure 14.9 places the *carnt* and *LR* in branch A2; however, the upper nest of this partition, A1, is degenerate in the sense that A1 is the sole limb in the partition. Following the same reasoning before, the scale parameters (and hence the variances) for A1 and A2 must be equal. Given that the model is econometrically operational only under RU1, the scale A1 and A2 scale parameters must be the same as the scale parameters at level one of the model, and as such, must be normalized to 1.0. We show how to handle such cases in section 14.7.

14.7 Three-level NL models

All the NL models we have estimated to date have been two-level NL models. Using the tree structure shown in figure 14.9, we now estimate a three-level NL model. As previously discussed, the A1 and A2 scale parameters must be normalized to equal one another, and given that the level one scale parameter must be normalized to 1.0 (under RU1; the IV parameters are not identifiable under RU2), the A1 and A2 IV parameters should be normalized to 1.0 also. The NLOGIT command to estimate this NL model is given below:

```
NLOGIT
;lhs=choice,cset,altij
;Choices=cart,carnt,bus,train,busway,LR
;Tree= A1[A2(carnt,LR)], B1[B2(cart,train), B3(busway,bus)]
;Start=logit
```

```
;ivset: (A1,A2)=[1.0]
;Maxit=100
;Model:
U(cart) = asccart + cartc*fuel /
U(carnt) = asccarnt + carntc*fuel /
U(bus) = ascbus + bsc*fare /
U(train) = asctn + tnc*fare/
U(busway) = ascbusw + bswc*fare /
U(LR) = lrc*fare $
```

The above model specification produces the following NL model results:

```
+-----------------------------------------------+
| FIML: Nested Multinomial Logit Model          |
| Maximum Likelihood Estimates                  |
| Model estimated: Feb 30, 2003 at 01:30:00PM.  |
| Dependent variable              CHOICE        |
| Weighting variable                None        |
| Number of observations            9476        |
| Iterations completed                19        |
| Log likelihood function      -3212.906        |
| Restricted log likelihood    -4258.696        |
| Chi squared                   2091.581        |
| Degrees of freedom                  14        |
| Prob[ChiSqd > value] =        .0000000        |
| R2=1-LogL/LogL*  Log-L fncn  R-sqrd  RsqAdj   |
| No coefficients  -4258.6963  .24557  .24408   |
| Constants only.  Must be computed directly.   |
|                  Use NLOGIT ;...; RHS=ONE    $|
| At start values  -3214.2405  .00042 -.00156   |
| Response data are given as ind. choice.       |
+-----------------------------------------------+
```

Variable	Coefficient	Standard Error	b/St.Er.	P[|Z|>z]
	Attributes in the Utility Functions (beta)			
ASCCART	-.44492353	.21530430	-2.066	.0388
CARTC	-.12848325	.06801255	-1.889	.0589
ASCCARNT	-.17322340	.26241457	-.660	.5092
CARNTC	-.09234387	.05696107	-1.621	.1050
ASCBUS	-.17779550	.23978597	-.741	.4584
BSC	-.20780102	.05611155	-3.703	.0002
ASCTN	-.11992895	.21989965	-.545	.5855
TNC	-.23506445	.04944917	-4.754	.0000

```
ASCBUSW          .15534048        .22195906          .700      .4840
BSWC            -.30045488        .06177535        -4.864      .0000
LRC             -.25615717        .04207730        -6.088      .0000
           IV parameters, tau(j|i,l),sigma(i|l),phi(l)
A2              1.00000000       ......(Fixed Parameter).........
B2               .82283333        .14755086         5.577      .0000
B3               .85333569        .14738959         5.790      .0000
A1              1.00000000       ......(Fixed Parameter).........
B1               .97211621        .19492260         4.987      .0000
```

For the above model, comparing the LL function at model convergence to the base model assuming equal choice shares, the model produces a Chi-square value of 2091.581 with 14 degrees of freedom. The related p-value reported is 0.0000, which is statistically significant at the 95 percent confidence level. Thus, the model is statistically superior to a model assuming equal choice shares only. Estimation of a constants-only model with constants estimated from the data choice shares provides an LL function at convergence of −3276.796. Comparison of the above model to a model assuming the choice shares obtained from the sample data yields the following test. Note that for the constants-only model, there are five parameters estimated (all ASCs), while the model above estimates 14 parameters (not including the two fixed IV parameters). Thus the test is performed against a Chi-square with nine degrees of freedom:

$$-2(-3276.796 - (-3212.906)) = 127.78 \sim \chi^2_{(9)}$$

From sub-section 2.8.3 or NLOGIT, $\chi^2_{(9)}$ is equal to 16.919. Comparing the test-statistic of 127.78 to the Chi-square critical value of 16.919, we reject the null hypothesis that the above model fit is statistically the same as that of the constants-only model assuming data-specific choice shares.

Comparing the three-level NL model in the above example to the two-level NL model shown on p. 542, we may undertake a test similar to that above to determine which of the two models has the better overall model fit. The model shown on p. 542 has an LL function of −3219.011 and eight estimated parameters. The test therefore is:

$$-2(-3219.011 - (-3212.906)) = 12.12 \sim \chi^2_{(4)}$$

Critical $\chi^2_{(4)}$ (see sub-section 2.8.3) from the statistical tables is equal to 9.488, which is less than the test-statistic of 12.12. Thus we reject the null hypothesis that the LL function of the three-level NL model is statistically equal to that of the two-level model, and conclude that the three-level NL model of the above example has a better model fit to that shown on p. 542. Similar tests may be performed in comparison to other models shown in earlier examples.

All cost parameters are in the expected direction (i.e. negative); however, the cost parameters for both *car* alternatives are not statistically significant. While the analyst may consider removing these and re-running the model, we do not do so here. Nevertheless, if there is sufficient theoretical justification for including a specific attribute, then removing it is not recommended; rather, it hints at the appropriateness of a particular specification.

All IV parameters are observed to be within the necessary 1–0 range. Examination of the IV parameters suggests that all IV parameters are statistically different to zero. Wald-tests for each IV parameter to test-statistical difference from 1.0 are therefore necessary and are shown below:

$$B1 = \frac{0.97211621 - 1}{0.19492260} = -0.14305$$
$$B2 = \frac{0.82283333 - 1}{0.14755086} = -1.20072$$
$$B3 = \frac{0.85333569 - 1}{0.14738959} = -0.99508$$

In each case, we are unable to reject the null hypothesis that each IV parameter is statistically different to 1.0. This finding suggests that all IV parameters in the above specified model should be normalized to 1.0, which will collapse the model to the simple MNL form.

Although we have done so on several occasions already, it is worthwhile exploring the system of equations generated by three-level NL models such as the model in the above example. For those interested, we provide the full set of utility functions generated for the above model as well as the PCS in appendix 14B.

14.8 Searching for the best NL tree structure: the degenerate nested logit

It should be fairly obvious at this point that NL models may adopt many different tree structures (even for a fixed number of alternatives), some of which may be considered better than others on such criteria as overall model fit, revealed behavioral responses (e.g. attribute or SDC elasticities or marginal effects), and/or predictive ability. Further, the best NL tree structure will be *data-specific*, meaning that it is possible that two NL models estimated on different data sets but collected on the same subject matter may require different tree structures. Thus, while previous experience may help identify certain tree structures to explore, limiting the search to a sub-set of all possible tree structures may result in a sub-optimal model (on whatever criteria used). To demonstrate, consider the NL model, the results of which are shown on p. 575. This model may be considered no better or worse than most other models we have explored within this chapter, despite the nesting of alternatives that intuitively do not belong together.

Hensher (1999) proposed the use of the HEV model as a search strategy for the most likely preferred NL model tree structure. Unfortunately, HEV models are notorious for failing to converge (although many do). These models usually require a significant time lapse to decide that they are not going to converge. Thus, depending on the computer processing speed available to the analyst, there is a reasonable chance that the analyst estimating a HEV model will not obtain guidance on an appropriate NL tree structure to employ.

Given the above, the authors have explored the use of a fully degenerate tree structure in NL using the resulting scale parameters to guide the final NL model tree adopted. Through personal correspondence, we have advised a number of colleagues of this approach and it would appear, from feedback given, that the strategy does indeed direct one to the preferred NL tree structure on all the usual selection criteria.

From a theoretical standpoint, as the NL-DG model is to be used expressly as a search mechanism for assigning alternatives to branches, the problem associated with the handling of degenerate branches can be ignored. Even so, however, the fact that each branch represents a separate alternative may mean that this is not a problem at all with these models (further research is required before anything definitive can be confirmed). Further, in specifying the model, one need not normalize an IV parameter as the 0–1 range is not applicable; we are simply using the model to look for IV parameters which are of similar values. Nevertheless, doing so may aid in deciding which alternatives should be partitioned with other alternatives in the NL model.

To demonstrate the NL-DG, consider the following command syntax in which we have assigned each alternative to a separate branch. In this model we have normalized branch B partitioning the *carnt* alternative, although any branch could have been chosen for this. Also for this model, we have specified more complex utility functions. We have done this as models using the simpler utility functions we have used previously have all collapsed to an MNL model:

```
NLOGIT
;lhs = choice, cset, altij
;Choices =cart, carnt, bus, train, busway, LR
;Tree = A(cart), B(carnt), C(bus), D(train), E(busway), F(LR)
;Start = logit
;ivset: (b) = [1.0]
;Maxit = 100
;Model:
U(cart) = asccart + cst*fuel + cartt*time + toll*toll /
U(carnt) = asccarnt + cst*fuel + carntt*time /
U(bus) = ascbus + cst*fare + bust*time /
U(train) = asctn + cst*fare + tnt*time /
U(busway) = ascbusw + cst*fare + bswt*time /
U(LR) = cst*fare + lrt*time $
```

For the 30 minutes commuter segment, the following NLOGIT NL-DG results are produced:

```
+-----------------------------------------------+
| FIML: Nested Multinomial Logit Model          |
| Maximum Likelihood Estimates                  |
| Model estimated: Feb 30, 2003 at 01:45:00PM.  |
| Dependent variable               CHOICE       |
| Weighting variable                 None       |
| Number of observations             9476       |
| Iterations completed                 76       |
| Log likelihood function       -3186.997       |
```

```
| Restricted log likelihood      -4244.678         |
| Chi squared                     2115.362         |
| Degrees of freedom                    18         |
| Prob[ChiSqd > value] =          .0000000         |
| R2=1-LogL/LogL*    Log-L fncn  R-sqrd  RsqAdj    |
| No coefficients    -4244.6782  .24918  .24727    |
| Constants only.    Must be computed directly.    |
|                    Use NLOGIT ;...; RHS=ONE $    |
| At start values    -3191.9824  .00156 -.00097    |
| Response data are given as ind. choice.          |
+-------------------------------------------------+
```

Variable	Coefficient	Standard Error	b/St.Er.	P[|Z|>z]
	Attributes in the Utility Functions (beta)			
ASCCART	-.85622320	.83212125	-1.029	.3035
CST	-.10211592	.05734830	-1.781	.0750
CARTT	.01150402	.02388894	.482	.6301
TOLL	-.16961326	.14742179	-1.151	.2499
ASCCARNT	.05490723	.44827047	.122	.9025
CARNTT	-.03521031	.01161163	-3.032	.0024
ASCBUS	-.27266469	.30499775	-.894	.3713
BUST	-.00872512	.01189834	-.733	.4634
ASCTN	.23513908	.23974542	.981	.3267
TNT	-.03889516	.02629297	-1.479	.1391
ASCBUSW	.16387714	.16740552	.979	.3276
BSWT	-.02176574	.01365419	-1.594	.1109
LRT	-.01448372	.01073229	-1.350	.1772
	IV parameters, tau(j|i,l),sigma(i|l),phi(l)			
A	1.04391822	.82855301	1.260	.2077
B	1.00000000	......(Fixed Parameter).........		
C	1.75204681	1.08176477	1.620	.1053
D	2.02891653	1.23124452	1.648	.0994
E	2.59815886	1.50673977	1.724	.0846
F	2.46367373	1.44164270	1.709	.0875

As with the HEV model, the NL-DG model is helpful primarily in determining two-level NL model tree structures. Ignoring the parameter estimates, examining the IV parameters suggests similarity between branches A and B (*cart* and *carnt*), C and D (*bus* and *train*), and E and F (*busway* and *LR*). Judgment of similarity between IV parameters is largely subjective in nature, as some may view branches A and B as being more similar, branches D, E, and F as being similar, and branch C (*bus*) as being unlike all other branches and hence being retained in the NL model as a degenerate branch. Significantly, all IV parameters in the above model are statistically insignificant, suggesting that the model should collapse to a single branch and be re-estimated as an MNL model, a fact that we have conveniently ignored in our determination of what belongs where. Thus, NL-DG models should be used carefully in determining the final model form to be adopted and should only ever be used as an aid. We leave it to the reader to decide what the best NL model tree structure is; however, it may take a few iterations before the best model structure is defined.

As an aside, for those interested in estimating HEV models, the addition of the following command syntax to the base MNL model command is used:

;Hetero

The **hetero** command is added to the base MNL command syntax and not the NL command syntax. In estimating HEV models, one does not specify the tree structure. Nor should the **ivset** command be used. For example, the following command will estimate an HEV model. Using non-random draws such as Halton or Shuffled Sequences will improve convergence:

```
NLOGIT
;lhs = choice, cset, altij
;Choices =cart, carnt, bus, train, busway, LR
;Maxit=100
;Hetero
;Model:
U(cart) = asccart + cst*fuel + cartt*time + toll*toll /
U(carnt) = asccarnt + cst*fuel + carntt*time /
U(bus) = ascbus + cst*fare + bust*time /
U(train) = asctn + cst*fare + tnt*time /
U(busway) = ascbusw + cst*fare + bswt*time /
U(LR) = cst*fare + lrt*time $
```

For the 30 minutes or less commuter segment, the above command will produce the following NLOGIT output:

```
Line search does not improve fn. Exit iterations. Status=3
  Error 806: Line search does not improve fn. Exit
iterations. Status=3
Function= .52869519171D+04, at entry, .32717072241D+04 at
exit
  Error 1025: Failed to fit model. See earlier diagnostic.
```

The above demonstrates one of the problems with the HEV model. While extrememly good at identifying differences in scale across alternatives, the model will often fail to converge.

14.9 Combining sources of data: SP-RP

Given that the attributes and variables contained within the RP data sets are likely to be ill conditioned (i.e. be largely invariant, suffer from multicollinearity, etc.), parameter estimates (other than the constant terms) obtained from models estimated from RP data are likely to be biased (this is one reason that some prefer stated preference (SP) data). While the level of ill-conditioning can be determined by the analyst (e.g. see chapters 8 and 9 on testing for multicollinearity), the analyst may be limited in available actions to correct any deficiencies once detected. Thus, the extent of the problem may not be known prior to the collection of the data. The attributes of SP data sets, on the other hand, are likely to be of good condition and hence the associated parameter estimates from models estimated from such data are likely to be unbiased.

Nevertheless, the ASCs estimated from SP data are likely to be behaviorally meaningless while those obtained from RP data sources are likely to be of substantive behavioral value. As discussed previously, the ASCs obtained from discrete choice models represent not only the average unobserved effect for each alternative but also reflect the choice shares within the data set from which it was estimated (if we excluded all attributes and SDCs). For SP data, the choice shares will be obtained over a number of hypothetical choice sets derived from some underlying experimental design, each of which is given to multiple individuals. Beyond representing the average unobserved effects, the ASCs obtained from SP data will be meaningless (particularly so for studies involving demand forecasting). On the other hand, ASCs acquired from RP data (assuming that the sample was randomly drawn and the data itself correctly collected) with or without other attributes and SDCs should reflect the true choice shares observed over the population.

It is not uncommon for practitioners to combine a number of data sets (more so SP and RP, although SP and SP, and RP and RP combinations are not unheard of) when estimating models of discrete choice. Doing so, it is argued (see Louviere, Hensher, and Swait 2000, chapter 8 for a review of the current thinking in this area), allows the analyst to exploit the strengths of both data sources while discarding the weakness displayed by each (see chapter 4 for a review of these). Certainly, pooling SP and RP data provides many benefits.

The choice sets need not be the same across the two data sources (i.e. the alternatives, attributes and/or attribute levels may differ). The combination of two data sources will allow the analyst to estimate models using information that, if they had only one of the data sources available, they might not otherwise have been able to estimate due to missing data on attributes or attribute levels. The ability to include non-existent alternatives and manipulate currently non-experienced attributes and attribute levels via an SP choice experiment is appealing. In cases where an alternative is present in the RP data set but not the SP data set (e.g. bike is an alternative within the RP data set but not in the SP data set of the mode-choice case study), the analyst will have no other option but to use the RP data (ill conditioned or not) to estimate the preference function for that alternative. Similarly, where an alternative is present within the SP component of a data set but not within the RP component, the analyst will have to use the SP data to obtain the preference function for that alternative, including the SP ASCs.

As an aside, the respondents sampled for each data source need not be the same. The pooling of data sets represents one possible method of reducing the cognitive burden through reducing the size of surveys deemed too long for any one individual to complete.

As we have noted, the attribute levels obtained from RP preference data are likely to be such that models estimated from RP data will be so poor, as judged on any criteria, as to be of limited value to the analyst (this will not always be the case but is, at least in the experience of the authors, the most likely outcome). The question therefore is: why collect and model choices based on RP data? While many argue that SP data may be used to enrich RP data, why use RP data at all if SP data are judged to be superior (again, this should be determined on a case-by-case basis)? If RP data are collected solely for the purpose of providing SP data with constants, then why not simply collect information on choices (and forget about information on attributes and attribute levels) and use the choice share information to *calibrate the constants* of models estimated from SP data, as discussed in chapter 12? Further, if SP experiments are constructed and designed by the analyst, then why would there be missing alternatives or attributes? A study conducted by Hensher and Rose (2003) demonstrates that larger, more complex, designs are easily handled by respondents despite what many would have you believe. Respondents were shown 10 choice sets with between three and seven alternatives and up to a total of 46 attributes each at four levels. For each alternative in the choice set, respondents were asked to select an embedded sub-alternative as well as the single most preferred overall alternative. A total of 453 respondents completed the study without incentive. An additional question that must be answered by the researcher is whether the SP and RP data should be weighted to give each equal representation. RP data generally consist of one observation per respondent while SP data generally have multiple observations per respondent (we prefer that no such weighting occurs as it restricts the main benefit of using SP data in the first place).

As an aside, the mode-choice case study, the data of which we use here, was completed in a more "innocent" age and if conducted today would probably not have different alternatives across the SP and RP components of the data.

We are not convinced of the merits of combining SP and RP preference data in most cases (as mentioned, RP data may be useful for modeling but this will need to be shown on a case-by-case basis). We do, however, strongly support the collection and use of RP data to provide information on the likely attribute levels experienced within markets from which SP experimental design attribute levels can be pivoted (see chapter 6). Even when used in this manner, RP data must be carefully checked for outliers, which will translate through to the pivoted SP experiment. The study mentioned above was conducted using this approach, in which respondents were asked for the attribute levels for both chosen (actual attribute levels) and non-chosen alternatives (perceived attribute levels). While increasing the time required to complete the survey, respondents were willing to complete the study without incentive (this is one of the best data sets that we have collected – unfortunately it is proprietary, otherwise we would have used it as our case study.)

Nevertheless, many practitioners do combine SP and RP data sets. It is therefore worthwhile demonstrating how this is accomplished. In order to pool the two data sets, the following command syntax is required to reinstate the sample. The **Reject;** command in the second line is used to reject respondents for whom we have either missing SP or RP observations. This is not a necessary command and is done here only for convenience (the reader may attempt to estimate models using the entire sample). The second **Reject;** command removes RP observations in which one or both of the alternatives were either

Table 14.1. *SPRP alti2 values*

alti2	Data set	Alternative	Name
1	RP	Drive alone	RPDA
2	RP	Ride share	RPRS
3	RP	Bus	RPBS
4	RP	Train	RPTN
5	SP	Car (with toll)	Cart
6	SP	Car (no toll)	Carnt
7	SP	Bus	Bus
8	SP	Train	Train
9	SP	Busway	Busway
10	SP	Light rail	LR

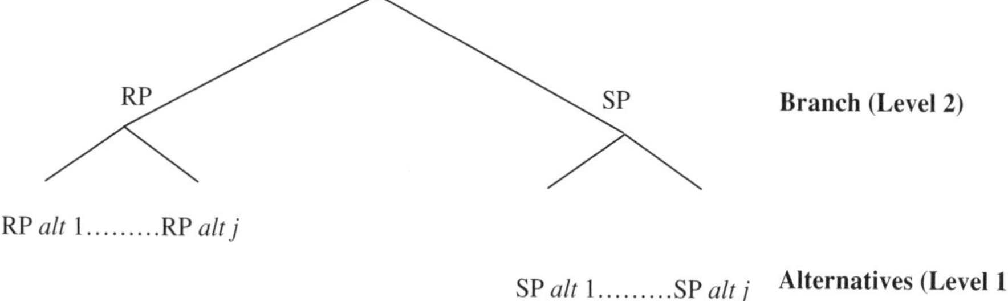

Figure 14.10 Pooling RP and SP data sources

bicycle or *walk*. Again, we have done this for convenience and leave it to the reader to estimate models with these observations present:

```
Sample;all $
Reject;RPSPWKBK=1 $
Reject;sprpmiss=1 $
Dstats;rhs=* $
```

Had the *bike* and *walk* alternatives been retained in the sample, the *alti sprp* variable could have been used to identify each of the alternatives in the model. The removal of these alternatives necessitates the creation of a new alternative identification variable. We create this new variable using the following command syntax:

```
CREATE
;if(sprp=2)alti2=altij+4
;if(sprp=1)alti2=altij $
```

Table 14.1 shows the values for each of the alternatives using the new identification variable.

In pooling RP and SP data sources, the most common practice is to use a two-level NL model with one branch including all the RP alternatives and a second branch for the SP alternatives. We show this in figure 14.10.

The following NLOGIT command demonstrates the pooling of RP and SP data sources for use in a single model. In specifying this model, at least one constant from each data set must be omitted from the utility expressions. For this example, we have elected to omit the constant terms of the *train* alternatives for both data sources (note that the omitted constant term does not necessarily have to belong to an alternative common across both data sets: it does make the process easier, however). Also, in the following model we have specified the constant, cost, and time parameters for the RP car modes as generic. Although we previously advised against this practice, for the following model, specifying a generic *car* constant will produce a single constant parameter for the RP *car* modes that will relate to the choice shares of both *car* alternatives. For the SP *car* utility functions, we have specified the cost, travel time, and parking cost parameters as generic also. We show why we have done this later.

As an aside, in the following model we have allowed both IV parameters to be free (i.e. we have not normalized either of the IV parameters). When combining data sets, the restriction that the IV parameters be between the 0 and 1 bound no longer holds. The combining of data sets in the manner we describe here is designed to uncover differences in scale (i.e. variance) between the data sets and there is no theoretical restriction that the variance of either data set be confined within any limit. While we have not normalized either IV parameter in this example, the analyst may chose to normalize at least one for estimation purposes. If the analyst does decide to normalize either the SP or RP IV parameter, the above discussion suggests that the free parameter when estimated does not have to be less than one:

```
NLOGIT
;lhs= choice, cset, alti2
;Choices= RPDA, RPRS, RPBS, RPTN, cart, carnt, bus, train, busway, LR
;Tree=RP(RPDA, RPRS, RPBS, RPTN),SP(cart, carnt, bus, train, busway, LR)
;Maxit=100
;Start=logit
;Model:
U(RPDA) = rpcar + rpcarc*fcost + rpcartt*autotime /
U(RPRS) = rpcar + rpcarc*fcost + rpcartt*autotime +
rppass*autopass /
U(RPBS) = rpbsasc + rpbsc*mptrfare + rpbstt*mptrtime /
U(RPTN) =                rptnc*mptrfare + rptntt*mptrtime /
U(cart) = asccart + carc*fuel + cartt*time + parking*parking + toll*toll /
U(carnt) = asccarnt + carc*fuel + cartt*time +
parking*parking /
U(bus) = ascbs + bsc*fare + bustt*time /
U(train) =          tnc*fare + trntt*time /
U(busway) = ascbusw + bswc*fare + bswtt*time /
U(LR) = asclr + lrc*fare + lrtt*time $
```

For the mode-choice case study, the above syntax command produces the following results for the NL model:

```
NOTE: Convergence in initial iterations is rarely
at a true function optimum. This may not be a
solution (especially if initial iterations stopped).
Exit from iterative procedure. 1 iterations completed.
Check convergence values shown below.
Gradient value: Tolerance= .1000D-05, current value= .1569D-10
Function chg. : Tolerance= .0000D+00, current value= .2705D+04
Parameters chg: Tolerance= .0000D+00, current value= .1850D-08
Smallest abs. param. change from start value = .0000D+00
At least one parameter did not leave start value.
Normal exit from iterations. Exit status=0.
+-----------------------------------------------+
| FIML Nested Multinomial Logit Model           |
| Maximum Likelihood Estimates                  |
| Model estimated: Feb 30, 2003 at 02:00:00PM.  |
| Dependent variable  CHOICE                    |
| Weighting variable    None                    |
| Number of observations9512                    |
| Iterations completed     1                    |
| Log likelihood function -2704.883             |
| Restricted log likelihood      -6476.586      |
| Chi squared7543.405                           |
| Degrees of freedom       28                   |
| Prob[ChiSqd > value] =    .0000000            |
| R2=1-LogL/LogL*   Log-L fncn  R-sqrd  RsqAdj  |
| No coefficients   -6476.5860  .58236  .58063  |
| Constants only.   Must be computed directly.  |
|                   Use NLOGIT ;...; RHS=ONE $  |
| At start values   -2704.8835  .00000 -.00414  |
| Response data are given as ind. choice.       |
+-----------------------------------------------+

+----------+-------------+----------------+----------+----------+
|Variable  | Coefficient | Standard Error | b/St.Er. | P[|Z|>z] |
+----------+-------------+----------------+----------+----------+
           Attributes in the Utility Functions (beta)
 RPCAR        -.42161371       .45130332       -.934      .3502
 RPCARC       -.00406663       .13357746       -.030      .9757
 RPCARTT      -.03268331       .01130176      -2.892      .0038
 RPPASS       -.42934685       .04305872      -9.971      .0000
```

```
RPBSASC     -2.40746743      .56590188     -4.254     .0000
RPBSC        -.23063822      .10743785     -2.147     .0318
RPBSTT       -.00205542      .01073623      -.191     .8482
RPTNC       -1.30281504      .24178326     -5.388     .0000
RPTNTT       -.02087861      .01275791     -1.637     .1017
ASCCART      1.09008811      .23415115      4.655     .0000
CARC         -.09529843      .02726540     -3.495     .0005
CARTT        -.05521421      .00642193     -8.598     .0000
PARKING      -.10491901      .00544875    -19.256     .0000
TOLL         -.14351787      .04373249     -3.282     .0010
ASCCARNT     1.79230152      .23843948      7.517     .0000
ASCBS         .47135707      .29509493      1.597     .1102
BSC          -.19377136      .04751606     -4.078     .0000
BUSTT        -.04592512      .01102256     -4.166     .0000
TNC          -.28501171      .04722733     -6.035     .0000
TRNTT        -.00658713      .01119429      -.588     .5562
ASCBUSW      -.04344600      .28327470      -.153     .8781
BSWC         -.16310598      .04104829     -3.974     .0001
BSWTT        -.01879697      .00944695     -1.990     .0466
ASCLR         .43147513      .26895985      1.604     .1087
LRC          -.23263067      .04238621     -5.488     .0000
LRTT         -.03869647      .00956595     -4.045     .0001
           IV parameters, tau(j|i,l), sigma(i|l), phi(l)
RP           1.00000000     .151010D+16       .000    1.0000
SP           1.00000000     .839389D+15       .000    1.0000
```

The error message observed prior to the NL model output suggests that the parameter estimates for the combined SP-RP NL model did not move from the initial MNL model estimated to provide start values for the SP-RP NL model. As the error states: "Convergence in initial iterations is rarely at a true function optimum. This may not be a solution (especially if initial iterations stopped)." Because the parameter estimates for the NL model did not move from those of the MNL model, the IV parameters for the branches both equal 1.0 (suggesting an MNL model) and produced extremely large standard errors. While this occurrence is specific to this data set, it does highlight a situation that the authors have observed within many SP-RP data sets. As we show later, it is not uncommon for the variance structure of SP-RP data not to be such that the variance differs between data sets, but rather across different sets of alternatives independent of the data source.

Despite the model not moving beyond the parameters observed for the initial MNL model, we will progress with the steps necessary to combine SP and RP data sources. The first step, the estimation of a joint SP-RP NL model with each data source in a separate branch, has already been executed. The second step of the process we describe below.

The utility functions for each of the alternatives for the joint SP-RP model are shown below (we have used RU1; the equivalent RU2 model would not converge):

$$V_{RPDA} = -0.42161371 - 0.00406663 \times RPCARC - 0.03268331 \times \text{RPCARTT}$$

$$V_{RPRS} = -0.42161371 - 0.00406663 \times \text{RPCARC} - 0.03268331 \times \text{RPCARTT} - 0.42934685 \times \text{RPPASS}$$

$$V_{RPBS} = -2.40746743 - 0.023063822 \times \text{RPBSC} - 0.00205542 \times \text{RPBSTT}$$

$$V_{RPTN} = \qquad - 1.30281504 \times \text{RPTNC} - 0.02087861 \times \text{RPTNTT}$$

$$V_{cart} = 1.09008811 - 0.09529843 \times \text{CARNTC} - 0.05521421 \times \text{CARTT} - 0.10491901 \times \text{PARKING} - 0.14351787 \times \text{TOLL}$$

$$V_{carnt} = 1.79230152 - 0.09529843 \times \text{CARNTC} - 0.05521421 \times \text{CARTT} - 0.10491901 \times \text{PARKING}$$

$$V_{bus} = 0.47135707 - 0.19377136 \times \text{BSC} - 0.04592512 \times \text{BUSTT}$$

$$V_{train} = \qquad - 0.28501171 \times \text{TNC} - 0.00658713 \times \text{TRNTT}$$

$$V_{busway} = -0.04344600 - 0.16310598 \times \text{BSWC} - 0.01879697 \times \text{BSWTT}$$

$$V_{LR} = 0.43147513 - 0.23263067 \times \text{LRC} - 0.03869647 \times \text{LRTT}$$

Common practice associated with the pooling of SP and RP data sources is to discard the RP parameter estimates and the SP constant terms and use the remaining parameters to form composite utility functions. For SP alternatives with no corresponding RP alternative (e.g. *busway* and *LR*), we have no choice but to use the SP constant terms. Also, as the RP data set had two *car* alternatives, neither of which directly corresponds to either of the SP *car* alternatives, in setting up the model we specified the RP utility constant terms as generic so that we could use the single RP resulting constant as the constant term for both SP *car* alternatives (in combining data sets in this manner, the analyst will always need to think carefully ahead).

In discarding the parameter estimates from the RP data set and retaining the constant terms, it is necessary in creating the composite utility functions to recalibrate the RP constant terms. To demonstrate why, consider (14.11) which is the equation used to calculate constant terms in discrete choice models.[3]

$$\beta_{0i}^{RP} = \bar{V}_i^{RP} - \sum_{k=1}^{k} \beta_k^{RP} \bar{x}_k^{RP} \tag{14.11}$$

The latter part of (14.11) accounts for the RP parameter estimates which are to be discarded in constructing the composite utility functions while failing to account for the SP parameter

[3] This is the same formula used to calculate constant terms in linear regression models.

estimates that are to be used. So why use the RP attributes in the first place? In estimating the initial SP-RP NL model, the inclusion or exclusion of an attribute in either data set will affect all other the parameter estimates within the model. Hence, failure to include the RP attributes in the RP component of the NL model (i.e. simply estimate the RP model with constants only) will impact upon the SP parameter estimates obtained from the model. Thus it is necessary, despite potential problems with RP parameter estimates (given data issues), to include the RP attributes in the model, otherwise all information for these components will be accounted for solely by the unobserved effects of the RP utility functions which enter the utility functions through the $\bar{V}_i^{RP}$ (nevertheless, at the same time, the constant terms will preserve information on the choice shares within the data set).

The calibration of the RP constant terms occurs through (14.12).

$$\beta_{0i}^{RP} = \bar{V}_i^{RP} - \sum_{k=1}^{k} \lambda^{SP} \beta_k^{SP} \bar{x}_k^{RP} \tag{14.12}$$

In (14.12), the RP parameter estimates are replaced by the SP parameter estimates obtained from the initial SP-RP model (taking into account scale differences that may exist between the two data sets) while the remaining components of (14.11) are left as are. To operationalize (14.12) requires the analyst to re-estimate the constant terms of alternatives common across the data sets, fixing the RP parameter estimates to the values observed for the SP parameters. Parameters unique to the RP data set should be allowed to be estimated freely.

To calibrate the RP constants, the analyst is first required to reject the SP data set. For the mode choice case study, this is done through the following **Reject;** command:

```
REJECT;sprp=2 $
```

Next, the analyst must estimate an MNL model on the RP data set fixing the common SP-RP parameters to the SP parameter estimates obtained in the initial SP-RP model. We do this below. Where possible, we have fixed the parameter estimates to be the same as the SP parameters multiplied by the SP scale parameter (which in this case was equal to 1.0). The number of passengers in the RP *ride share* utility function did not have an equivalent SP parameter and is therefore left free to vary. Also, the SP *parking cost* parameter and *toll* parameter do not share a common attribute with the RP data set and are therefore out of necessity left out of the estimation process:

```
NLOGIT
;lhs= choice, cset, alti2
;Choices= RPDA, RPRS, RPBS, RPTN
;Maxit=100
;Model:
U(RPDA) = rpcar + rpcarc[-0.09529843]*fcost + rpcartt[-0.05521421]*autotime /
U(RPRS) = rpcar + rpcarc[-0.09529843]*fcost + rpcartt[-0.05521421]*autotime +
rppass*autopass /
```

U(RPBS) = rpbsasc + rpbsc[-0.19377136]*mptrfare + rpbstt[-0.04592512]*mptrtime /
U(RPTN) = rptnc[-0.28501171]*mptrfare + rptntt[-0.00658713]*mptrtime $

For the mode-choice case study estimated on the RP data component, the above model syntax produces the following:

```
+---------------------------------------------+
| Discrete choice (multinomial logit) model   |
| Maximum Likelihood Estimates                |
| Model estimated: Feb 30, 2003 at 02:15:00PM.|
| Dependent variable               Choice     |
| Weighting variable                 None     |
| Number of observations              678     |
| Iterations completed                  6     |
| Log likelihood function      -294.6934      |
| R2=1-LogL/LogL*  Log-L fncn   R-sqrd  RsqAdj |
| No coefficients  -939.9076    .68647  .68507 |
| Constants only.   Must be computed directly. |
|                   Use NLOGIT ;...; RHS=ONE $ |
| Response data are given as ind. choice.      |
| Number of obs.=   678,  skipped  0  bad obs. |
+---------------------------------------------+
```

```
+----------+------------+---------------+---------+---------+
|Variable  | Coefficient | Standard Error | b/St.Er. | P[|Z|>z] |
+----------+------------+---------------+---------+---------+
 RPCAR       2.82788939      .18802255       15.040    .0000
 RPCARC      -.09529843   ......(Fixed Parameter)     .......
 RPCARTT     -.05521421   ......(Fixed Parameter)     .......
 RPPASS      -.44312049      .04066331      -10.897    .0000
 RPBSASC     1.28924832      .19988480        6.450    .0000
 RPBSC       -.19377136   ......(Fixed Parameter)     .......
 RPBSTT      -.04592512   ......(Fixed Parameter)     .......
 RPTNC       -.28501171   ......(Fixed Parameter)     .......
 RPTNTT      -.00658713   ......(Fixed Parameter)     .......
```

The calibrated constant terms may be taken from the above model and inserted in the composite utility functions. The utility functions for the two unique SP alternatives (i.e. *busway* and *LR*) are taken directly from the joint SP-RP model. As such, the composite utilities become:

$$V_{cart} = 2.82788939 - 0.09529843 \times \text{CARNTC} - 0.05521421 \times \text{CARTT} - 0.10491901 \times \text{PARKING} - 0.14351787 \times \text{TOLL}$$

$V_{carnt} = 2.82788939 - 0.09529843 \times \text{CARNTC} - 0.05521421 \times \text{CARTT} -$
$0.10491901 \times \text{PARKING}$

$$V_{bus} = -0.19377136 - 0.19377136 \times \text{BSC} - 0.04592512 \times \text{BUSTT}$$

$$V_{train} = -0.28501171 \times \text{TNC} - 0.00658713 \times \text{TRNTT}$$

$$V_{busway} = -0.04344600 - 0.16310598 \times \text{BSWC} - 0.01879697 \times \text{BSWTT}$$

$$V_{LR} = 0.43147513 - 0.23263067 \times \text{LRC} - 0.03869647 \times \text{LRTT}$$

We argue that given the necessity of having to recalibrate the RP constants to account for the use of the SP parameter estimates and the common practice of discarding the RP parameter estimates, researchers would be best to invest their time and energy in either collecting either better RP data or SP data rather than both (unless one is using RP data to pivot the attribute levels of SP data). If SP data are the preferred method, the analyst may obtain constant terms consistent with the population choice shares by a recalibration process that does not require the use of RP data, thus rendering the option of combining both preference data sources even more undesirable (see chapter 11).

As we mentioned previously, it is not an uncommon experience of the authors that when combining preference data sources, the variance structure is such that common alternatives display similar variances, despite what data set they belong to. In the following model, we place all *car* alternatives in one branch and all *public transport* alternatives in a second branch. Before estimating the model, we re-set the sample:

```
Sample;all $
Reject;RPSPWKBK=1 $
Reject;sprpmiss=1 $
Dstats;rhs=* $
```

Using the same utility specifications (in this instance, there is no need to treat the RP *car* constants as generic; we do so for consistency purposes only):

```
NLOGIT
;lhs= choice, cset, alti2
;Choices= RPDA, RPRS, RPBS, RPTN, cart, carnt, bus, train, busway, LR
;Tree=Car(RPDA,RPRS,cart,carnt),PT(RPBS,RPTN,bus,train,
busway,LR)
;ivset:(car)=[1.0]
;Maxit=100
;Start=logit
;Model:
U(RPDA) = rpcar + rpcarc*fcost + rpcartt*autotime /
U(RPRS) = rpcar + rpcarc*fcost + rpcartt*autotime + rppass*autopass /
U(RPBS) = rpbsasc + rpbsc*mptrfare + rpbstt*mptrtime /
```

U(RPTN) = rptnc*mptrfare + rptntt*mptrtime /
U(cart) = asccart + carc*fuel + cartt*time + parking*parking + toll*toll /
U(carnt) = asccarnt + carc*fuel + cartt*time + parking*parking/
U(bus) = ascbs + bsc*fare + bustt*time /
U(train) = tnc*fare + trntt*time /
U(busway) = ascbusw + bswc*fare + bswtt*time /
U(LR) = asclr + lrc*fare + lrtt*time $

We show the model output below:

```
+-----------------------------------------------+
| FIML Nested Multinomial Logit Model            |
| Maximum Likelihood Estimates                   |
| Model estimated: Feb 30, 2003 at 02:30:00PM.   |
| Dependent variable              CHOICE         |
| Weighting variable                None         |
| Number of observations            9512         |
| Iterations completed                48         |
| Log likelihood function      -2692.399         |
| Restricted log likelihood    -6175.325         |
| Chi squared                   6965.853         |
| Degrees of freedom                  27         |
| Prob[ChiSqd > value] =        .0000000         |
| R2=1-LogL/LogL*   Log-L fncn  R-sqrd  RsqAdj   |
| No coefficients   -6175.3254  .56401  .56227   |
| Constants only.   Must be computed directly.   |
|                   Use NLOGIT ;...; RHS=ONE $   |
| At start values   -2704.8835  .00462  .00064   |
| Response data are given as ind. choice.        |
+-----------------------------------------------+
```

Variable	Coefficient	Standard Error	b/St.Er.	P[|Z|>z]
	Attributes in the Utility Functions (beta)			
RPCAR	.30488102	.46217679	.660	.5095
RPCARC	-.01289064	.14041763	-.092	.9269
RPCARTT	-.03200011	.01206720	-2.652	.0080
RPPASS	-.41922723	.03990688	-10.505	.0000
RPBSASC	-4.07591107	1.12083322	-3.637	.0003
RPBSC	-.83956700	.39637884	-2.118	.0342
RPBSTT	.00186551	.02547105	.073	.9416
RPTNC	-2.53267988	.57181051	-4.429	.0000
RPTNTT	-.03577312	.02506188	-1.427	.1535

```
ASCCART        .85798621      .15007824      5.717      .0000
CARC         -.08412596      .02675659     -3.144      .0017
CARTT        -.04672664      .00666274     -7.013      .0000
PARKING      -.10387916      .00559281    -18.574      .0000
TOLL         -.12036487      .04389649     -2.742      .0061
ASCCARNT     1.48041401      .16766094      8.830      .0000
ASCBS         .62539226      .34789007      1.798      .0722
BSC          -.27567935      .05698394     -4.838      .0000
BUSTT        -.06668700      .01242921     -5.365      .0000
TNC          -.34386855      .05685969     -6.048      .0000
TRNTT        -.02348347      .01350355     -1.739      .0820
ASCBUSW      -.08180111      .34650050      -.236      .8134
BSWC         -.23509763      .05098302     -4.611      .0000
BSWTT        -.03388265      .01171012     -2.893      .0038
ASCLR         .39127581      .30649955      1.277      .2017
LRC          -.31696351      .05059252     -6.265      .0000
LRTT         -.05311882      .01148405     -4.625      .0000
          IV parameters, tau(j|i,l),sigma(i|l),phi(l)
CAR          1.00000000      ......(Fixed Parameter)......
PT            .37804907      .09048388      4.178      .0000
```

In setting up the NL tree structure in the manner that we have, the combined SP-RP NL model now differs from the initial MNL model estimated to obtain start values for the NL model. Examination of the IV parameters suggests common variance structures within the *Car* and PT branches of the model, independent of the data source of the alternatives resident in each branch. Combining the data sources using the above tree structure, however, does not negate the necessity of having to recalibrate the RP constants in defining the composite utility functions as described above.

14.10 Additional commands

The NL model in NLOGIT supports all of the additional commands described for the MNL model in chapter 11. Thus, the **;Show**, **;Descriptives**, **;Crosstab**, **;Effects** (both elasticities and marginal effects; although there are some differences in their calculation, see Louviere, Hensher, and Swait 2000), and **;Weight** (both exogenous and endogenous) commands may be equally applied to the NL model as to the MNL model. Similarly, the **;Simulation** and **;Scenario** capability may also be used for NL model applications. Given the similarity between the output generated using these commands for NL models and MNL models, we do not demonstrate any of these commands here.

Some additional commands do produce different results when applied to an NL model application than when applied to a simple MNL model. In particular, the saving of probabilities is handled differently, particularly as each alternative will have multiple probabilities in an NL model (i.e. one for each associated partition).

The predicted probabilities (the multiplication of all relevant conditional probabilities) in NL models may be retained as a new variable in the data set with the addition of the following command:

```
;Prob = <name>
```

This is the same command used for the MNL model to save the probabilities. Conditional probabilities for elemental alternatives (level 1 probabilities) are retained using the following command syntax:

```
;Cprob = <name>
```

The IV variables (not parameters), otherwise known as EMUs, may also be saved as new variables in the data set. The commands to save the IV parameters at each level are:

Branch level: **ivb = <name>**
Limb level: **ivl = <name>**
Trunk level: **ivt = <name>**

For example, the following command syntax will save the predicted probabilities, the level 1 conditional probabilities, and the IV parameters at the branch level of the model:

```
;Prob = margprob
;Cprob = altprob
;ivb = ivbranch
```

Specifically, for the model shown on p. 542, the above command syntax will look as follows:

```
NLOGIT
;lhs = choice, cset, altij
;Choices = cart, carnt, bus, train, busway, LR
;Tree = car(cart,carnt), ptex(bus,train), ptnw(busway,LR)
;Start=logit
;ivset: (car)=[1.0]
;Prob = predprob
;Cprob = altprob
;ivb = ivbranch
;Maxit=100
;Model:
U(cart) = asccart+cst*fuel /
U(carnt) = asccarnt + cst*fuel /
U(bus) = ascbus + cst*fare /
U(train) = asctn + cst*fare /
U(busway) = ascbusw + cst*fare /
U(LR) = cst*fare $
```

For the 30 minutes or less commuter segment, the predicted probabilities, conditional probabilities, and branch-level IV parameters will appear at the end of the data set as shown in figure 14.11.

ALTI2	IVBRANCH	PREDPROB	ALTPROB
1			
4			
5	0.222942	0.288221	0.583866
6	0.222942	0.205422	0.416134
8	-0.358017	0.297825	1
10	-0.647296	0.208531	1
5	0.328416	0.229215	0.423448
6	0.328416	0.312091	0.576552
9	0.164987	0.145247	0.316653
10	0.164987	0.313447	0.683347
5	0.112651	0.244668	0.423448
6	0.112651	0.333131	0.576552
7	-0.254974	0.174825	0.414081
8	-0.254974	0.247375	0.585919
1			
2			
5	0.222942	0.288221	0.583866
6	0.222942	0.205422	0.416134
8	-0.358017	0.297825	1
10	-0.647296	0.208531	1
5	0.112651	0.244668	0.423448

Figure 14.11 Saving predicted probabilities, conditional probabilities, and IV parameters

The first two rows in figure 14.11 do not show values for the predicted probabilities, conditional probabilities or the branch-level IV parameters, since these two rows of data relate to the RP component and hence were not included in the analysis. The level 1 conditional probabilities are shown in the last column of the data set and are called *altprob*. These probabilities are calculated for each observation (i.e. choice set) within the data. Rows 3–6 therefore represent the first choice set for respondent one, in which the respondent observed the *cart*, *carnt*, *train*, and *LR* alternatives. Given the nesting structure for the model used to obtain these values, the *cart* and *carnt* alternatives belong within the same partition while the *train* and *LR* alternatives belong to distinct partitions. Thus, the conditional probabilities for the *cart* and *carnt* alternatives must sum to one, while the conditional probabilities for the *train* and *LR* alternatives must be both equal to one. For the first choice set, this is precisely what we observe.

The predicted probabilities for each alternative are saved in the second last column of the data set in a new variable titled *predprob*. These are the unconditional probabilities for each of the alternatives which are estimated by multiplying the conditional probabilities with the relevant marginal probabilities (which are not saved by NLOGIT). Within each choice set, the predicted probabilities must sum to one.

IVBRANCH	PREDPROB	ALTPROB	U1
0.222942	0.288221	0.583866	-0.315142
0.222942	0.205422	0.416134	-0.653805
-0.358017	0.297825	1	-0.358017
-0.647296	0.208531	1	-0.647296

Figure 14.12 Saving the utility estimates in NL models

The branch-level EMUs are saved as the third last column in the data set, as shown in figure 14.11. For the first choice set shown in figure 14.11, the equations necessary to estimate the EMU for each alternative are as follows:

$$IV_{(cart)} = \ln(e^{\mu_{car} V_{Cart}} + e^{\mu_{Car} V_{carnt}})$$
$$IV_{(carnt)} = \ln(e^{\mu_{car} V_{Cart}} + e^{\mu_{Car} V_{carnt}})$$
$$IV_{(train)} = \ln(e^{\mu_{PTEX} V_{train}}) = \mu_{PTEX} V_{train}$$
$$IV_{(LR)} = \ln(e^{\mu_{PTNW} V_{LR}}) = \mu_{PTNW} V_{LR}$$

Given that the model has been estimated using the RU1 normalization procedure, μ_{Car}, μ_{PTEX}, and μ_{PTNW} are all equal to 1.0, and hence drop out of the above equations. The utilities for each of the elemental alternatives required for the calculation may be acquired from the **;Utility = <name>** command which, as with the MNL model, will save in memory the utility values for each choice set for each respondent. For the above model, the utilities saved using the **;Utility = <name>** command are shown in the last column of figure 14.12.

The EMU or IV variable calculations are shown below, using the utility values shown in figure 14.12:

$$IV_{(cart)} = IV_{(carnt)} = \ln(e^{V_{cart}} + e^{V_{carnt}}) = \ln(e^{-0.315142} + e^{-0.653805})$$
$$= 0.222942$$
$$IV_{(train)} = V_{train} = -0.358017$$
$$IV_{(LR)} = V_{LR} = -0.647296$$

Comparision of our results to those shown in figures 14.11 and 14.12 reveals that these match precisly the EMU values estimated by NLOGIT.

Appendix 14A: The Hausman-test of the IIA assumption for models with alternative-specific parameter estimates

In this section, we demonstrate how one may use the Hausman-test of the IIA assumption for models in which alternative specific parameters are estimated for alternatives removed from the restricted model. For this example, we will remove the first alternative, that being *cart* for the restricted model. Before doing so, we must first re-set the sample. We do this as follows:

```
Sample;all $
Reject;sprp=1 $
Reject;splength#1 $
```

Once the sample has been re-set, the unrestricted model is estimated. For this example, we chosen to estimate a model specified only with alternative-specific parameter estimates:

```
NLOGIT
;lhs= choice, cset, altij
;Choices = cart, carnt, bus, train, busway, LR
;Model:
U(cart) = asccart + tmcart*time /
U(carnt) = asccarnt + tmcarnt*time /
U(bus) = ascbus + tmbus*time /
U(train) = asctn + tmtn*time /
U(busway) = ascbusw + tmbusw*time /
U(LR) = tmlr*time $
```

The results of this model are shown below:

```
+------------------------------------------------+
| Discrete choice (multinomial logit) model      |
| Maximum Likelihood Estimates                   |
| Model estimated: Feb 30, 2003 at 02:45:00PM.   |
| Dependent variable               Choice        |
| Weighting variable                 None        |
| Number of observations             2369        |
| Iterations completed                  5        |
| Log likelihood function       -3251.456        |
| R2=1-LogL/LogL*  Log-L fncn  R-sqrd  RsqAdj    |
| No coefficients  -4244.6782  .23399  .23280    |
| Constants only.  Must be computed directly.    |
|                  Use NLOGIT ;...; RHS=ONE $    |
| Chi-squared[ 6]  =          1576.46825         |
| Prob [ chi squared > value ] =  .00000         |
| Response data are given as ind. choice.        |
| Number of obs.=  2369,  skipped 0 bad obs.     |
+------------------------------------------------+

+----------+-------------+----------------+----------+----------+
|Variable  | Coefficient | Standard Error | b/St.Er. | P[|Z|>z] |
+----------+-------------+----------------+----------+----------+
 ASCCART      -.58357510      .38140846      -1.530     .1260
 TMCART        .00683567      .02304262        .297     .7667
 ASCCARNT      .33894834      .36031092        .941     .3469
 TMCARNT      -.03759584      .01154720      -3.256     .0011
```

ASCBUS	-.32919959	.37673999	-.874	.3822
TMBUS	-.01643034	.01807821	-.909	.3634
ASCTN	.49876175	.35763106	1.395	.1631
TMTN	-.07740700	.01848344	-4.188	.0000
ASCBUSW	.37377990	.34680033	1.078	.2811
TMBUSW	-.05960742	.01602948	-3.719	.0002
TMLR	-.04020070	.01635244	-2.458	.0140

Once the unrestricted model is estimated and the matrix of parameters and variance–covariance matrix saved, the analyst must next create the permutation matrix used to extract the relevant elements from B and VARB required for the test (that is, discard all information related to the ASCs). The construction of the permutation matrix, J1, is as described within the main text. For the above example, we require the second, fourth, sixth, eighth, tenth, and eleventh parameter estimates (a total of six parameters requiring six columns within the J1 matrix; the remaining parameters are ASCs and are not required for the test). As such, the **MATRIX;** command for J1 would appear as follows:

```
MATRIX; J1 = [0, 1, 0, 0, 0, 0, 0, 0, 0, 0, 0/
              0, 0, 0, 1, 0, 0, 0, 0, 0, 0, 0/
              0, 0, 0, 0, 0, 1, 0, 0, 0, 0, 0/
              0, 0, 0, 0, 0, 0, 0, 1, 0, 0, 0/
              0, 0, 0, 0, 0, 0, 0, 0, 0, 1, 0/
              0, 0, 0, 0, 0, 0, 0, 0, 0, 0, 1]$
```

The B_u and V_u matrices are created using J1, as shown below:

```
MATRIX; Bu = J1*B ;Vu = J1*VARB*J1' $
```

To estimate the restricted model, the appropriate alternatives must be expunged from the sample. For this example, we restrict the first alternative, that being the *cart* alternative. The **Reject;** commands for this are shown below. The first **Reject;** command removes any choice sets in which the *cart* alternative was chosen. The second removes the *cart* alternative from all choice sets in which that alternative was present but not chosen:

```
Reject;spcart=1 $
Reject;altij=1 $
```

Before the restricted model can be estimated, the *altij* and *cset* variables must be modified to reflect the absence of the *cart* alternative. For the mode-choice case study, the *cart* alternative is present within each choice set. As such, the new *cset* variable should equal three (it was previously four) for each and every choice set for the restricted model. As it was the first alternative that was removed, each remaining alternative will be represented as one less than *altij* for the new index variable, *altijn*. We show this below:

```
CREATE
;if(altij>1)altijn=altij-1
;csetn=3 $
```

The restricted model is estimated using the new *altijn* and *csetn* variables. No utility function is estimated for alternatives that are removed:

```
NLOGIT
;lhs = choice, csetn, altijn
;Choices = carnt, bus, train, busway, LR
;Model:
?U(cart) = asccart + tmcart*time /
U(carnt) = asccarnt + tmcarnt*time /
U(bus) = ascbus + tmbus*time /
U(train) = asctn + tmtn*time /
U(busway) = ascbusw + tmbusw*time /
U(LR) = tmlr*time $
```

The results of the restricted model are as now shown:

```
+-----------------------------------------------+
| Discrete choice (multinomial logit) model      |
| Maximum Likelihood Estimates                   |
| Model estimated: Feb 30, 2003 at 03:00:00PM.   |
| Dependent variable                 Choice      |
| Weighting variable                   None      |
| Number of observations               1769      |
| Iterations completed                    5      |
| Log likelihood function         -1914.645      |
| R2=1-LogL/LogL*  Log-L fncn  R-sqrd  RsqAdj    |
| No coefficients  -2847.0957  .32751  .32579    |
| Constants only.  Must be computed directly.    |
|                  Use NLOGIT ;...; RHS=ONE    $ |
| Chi-squared[ 5]          = 1568.85306          |
| Prob [ chi squared > value ] = .00000          |
| Response data are given as ind. choice.        |
| Number of obs.= 1769, skipped 0 bad obs.       |
+-----------------------------------------------+
+----------+-------------+----------------+----------+----------+
|Variable  | Coefficient | Standard Error | b/St.Er. | P[|Z|>z] |
+----------+-------------+----------------+----------+----------+
 ASCCARNT      .37660012       .40372896        .933     .3509
 TMCARNT      -.03690005       .01272788      -2.899     .0037
 ASCBUS       -.20480982       .41221300       -.497     .6193
 TMBUS        -.02106549       .01956805      -1.077     .2817
 ASCTN         .51296455       .37272321       1.376     .1687
 TMTN         -.07537897       .01949406      -3.867     .0001
 ASCBUSW       .41035541       .37438960       1.096     .2731
```

TMBUSW	-.05826122	.01721488	-3.384	.0007
TMLR	-.03697153	.01752762	-2.109	.0349

The test does not require that the parameters associated with the constants be retained. To discard these unneeded parameter estimates, a second permutation matrix, J2, is required. However, in creating J2, it should be noted that b_r and b_u must be of the same dimension (i.e. have the same number of rows and the same number of columns) in order for the test to work. The b_u column vector has six rows, one of which is for the time parameter for the *cart* alternative. For the restricted model, we will retain only five parameters from the restricted model as the *time* parameter for the *cart* alternative was not estimated. As such, the b_r column vector will have only five rows. A similar problem exists for V_r which must be of the same dimensionality as V_u.

Thus, in b_r(and similarly in V_r), all elements corresponding to a parameter estimated in the unrestricted model but not in the restricted model must be set to zero. Thus, for the example, as the *time* parameter in b_u was the first element in the column vector, the corresponding first element in the b_r column vector must be set equal to zero. In creating the permutation matrix, J2, all elements of the first row will therefore be equal to zero. We show this below:

```
MATRIX; J2 = [0,0,0,0,0,0,0,0,0 /
               0,1,0,0,0,0,0,0,0 /
               0,0,0,1,0,0,0,0,0 /
               0,0,0,0,0,1,0,0,0 /
               0,0,0,0,0,0,0,1,0 /
               0,0,0,0,0,0,0,0,1 ] $
```

Once J2 has been created, b_r and V_r may be created. This is shown in the following matrix command:

```
MATRIX; Br = J2*B ;Vr = J2*VARB*J2' $
```

We show the matrix multiplication for the above command as it applies to the creation of the b_r column vector. Note that the first element of b_r, corresponding to the *time* parameter for the *cart* alternative, is zero:

$$\begin{bmatrix} 0 & 0 & 0 & 0 & 0 & 0 & 0 & 0 & 0 \\ 0 & 1 & 0 & 0 & 0 & 0 & 0 & 0 & 0 \\ 0 & 0 & 0 & 1 & 0 & 0 & 0 & 0 & 0 \\ 0 & 0 & 0 & 0 & 0 & 1 & 0 & 0 & 0 \\ 0 & 0 & 0 & 0 & 0 & 0 & 0 & 1 & 0 \\ 0 & 0 & 0 & 0 & 0 & 0 & 0 & 0 & 1 \end{bmatrix} \begin{bmatrix} 0.3766000 \\ -0.0369001 \\ -0.2048100 \\ -0.0210655 \\ 0.5129650 \\ -0.0753790 \\ 0.4103550 \\ -0.0582612 \\ -0.0369715 \end{bmatrix} = \begin{bmatrix} 0.0000000 \\ -0.0369001 \\ -0.0210655 \\ -0.075379 \\ -0.0582612 \\ -0.03697157 \end{bmatrix}$$

The matrix multiplication resulting in the creation of the V_r matrix is shown below:

$$
\begin{bmatrix}
0 & 0 & 0 & 0 & 0 & 0 & 0 & 0 & 0 \\
0 & 1 & 0 & 0 & 0 & 0 & 0 & 0 & 0 \\
0 & 0 & 0 & 1 & 0 & 0 & 0 & 0 & 0 \\
0 & 0 & 0 & 0 & 0 & 1 & 0 & 0 & 0 \\
0 & 0 & 0 & 0 & 0 & 0 & 0 & 1 & 0 \\
0 & 0 & 0 & 0 & 0 & 0 & 0 & 0 & 1
\end{bmatrix}
$$

$$
\times \begin{bmatrix}
0.162997 & -0.003871 & 0.106101 & -0.001382 & 0.068792 & 0.001036 & 0.090165 & -0.000376 & 0.005436 \\
-0.003871 & 0.000162 & -0.001499 & 0.000056 & -0.000315 & -0.000023 & -0.000870 & 0.000013 & -0.000044 \\
0.106101 & -0.001499 & 0.169920 & -0.005931 & 0.060046 & 0.001036 & 0.073436 & 0.000159 & 0.004805 \\
-0.001382 & 0.000056 & -0.005931 & 0.000383 & 0.000225 & -0.000030 & -0.000015 & -0.000017 & -0.000017 \\
0.068792 & -0.000315 & 0.060046 & 0.000225 & 0.138923 & -0.004933 & 0.062828 & -0.000092 & 0.003962 \\
0.001036 & -0.000023 & 0.001036 & -0.000030 & -0.004933 & 0.000380 & 0.000597 & -0.000001 & 0.000038 \\
0.090165 & -0.000870 & 0.073436 & -0.000015 & 0.062828 & 0.000597 & 0.140168 & -0.004397 & 0.004652 \\
-0.000376 & 0.000013 & 0.000159 & -0.000017 & -0.000092 & -0.000001 & -0.004397 & 0.000296 & -0.000007 \\
0.005436 & -0.000044 & 0.004805 & -0.000017 & 0.003962 & 0.000038 & 0.004652 & -0.000007 & 0.000307
\end{bmatrix}
$$

$$
\times \begin{bmatrix}
0 & 0 & 0 & 0 & 0 & 0 \\
0 & 1 & 0 & 0 & 0 & 0 \\
0 & 0 & 0 & 0 & 0 & 0 \\
0 & 0 & 1 & 0 & 0 & 0 \\
0 & 0 & 0 & 0 & 0 & 0 \\
0 & 0 & 0 & 1 & 0 & 0 \\
0 & 0 & 0 & 0 & 0 & 0 \\
0 & 0 & 0 & 0 & 1 & 0 \\
0 & 0 & 0 & 0 & 0 & 1
\end{bmatrix}
=
\begin{bmatrix}
0.000000 & 0.000000 & 0.000000 & 0.000000 & 0.000000 & 0.000000 \\
0.000000 & 0.000162 & 0.000056 & -0.000023 & 0.000013 & -0.000044 \\
0.000000 & 0.000056 & 0.000383 & -0.000030 & -0.000017 & -0.000017 \\
0.000000 & -0.000023 & -0.000030 & 0.000380 & -0.000001 & 0.000038 \\
0.000000 & 0.000013 & -0.000017 & -0.000001 & 0.000296 & -0.000007 \\
0.000000 & -0.000044 & -0.000017 & 0.000038 & -0.000007 & 0.000307
\end{bmatrix}
$$

Once b_r and V_r have been obtained, the test-statistic q may be calculated. The commands to calculate q and obtain the p-value for this test are shown below. In calculating the p-value, the degrees of freedom used are six, as both the unrestricted and restricted models have six parameters (albeit one of the parameter estimates for the restricted model was constrained to equal one):

```
MATRIX; bn = Bu-Br;vn=Vr-Vu $
MATRIX; vninv=[vn] $
MATRIX; list;q = bn'*vninv*bn $
Calc; list;p=1-chi(q,6) $
```

For this example, NLOGIT produces the following output:

```
Matrix Q          has   1 rows and  1  columns.
                      1
          +--------------
1|                  1.82170
```

and,

```
P = .93534439249754890D+00
```

For this example, q equals 1.8217 and p equals 0.935. Comparing the p-value for the test to alpha equal to 0.05, we cannot reject the IIA assumption. The constant variance assumption holds, and hence the MNL model is sufficient.

Appendix 14B: Three-level NL model system of equations

In the chapter, we estimated a three-level NL model. In this section, we write out the full system of equations associated with that model. The utility functions for the elemental alternatives of the three-level NL model discussed on p. 575 may be directly taken from the model output without reference to the scale parameter (RU1). These are shown below:

$$V_{cart} = -0.4449235338 - 0.1284832480 \times \text{Fuel}$$

$$V_{carnt} = -0.1732233955 - 0.09234387421 \times \text{Fuel}$$

$$V_{bus} = -0.1777955033 - 0.2078010234 \times \text{Fare}$$

$$V_{train} = -0.1199289538 - 0.2350644458 \times \text{Fare}$$

$$V_{busway} = 0.1553404831 - 0.3004548811 \times \text{Fare}$$

$$V_{LR} = -0.2561571696 \times \text{Fare}$$

The utility functions for the second and third levels are shown below.

Level 2

In general notation, the A2 branch utility function is:

$$V_{A2} = \lambda_{(1|1,1)}[\alpha_{(1|1,1)} + \beta_{1(1|1,1)} f(X_{1(1|1,1)}) + \beta_{2(1|1,1)} f(X_{2(1|1,1)}) + \cdots + \beta_{K(1|1,1)} f(X_{K(1|1,1)}) + \frac{1}{\mu_{(1|1,1)}} \times IV_{(1|1,1)}]$$

Under RU1, $\mu_{(1|1,1)} = 1.0$. Normalization of the A2 IV parameter means that $\lambda_{(1|1,1)}$ also $= 1.0$. No parameters other than the IV parameter are estimated at this level of the partition, therefore:

$$V_{A2} = 1 \times \left[\frac{1}{1} \times IV_{A2}\right]$$

where

$$IV_{A2} = \ln(e^{\mu_{A2} V_{carnt}} + e^{\mu_{A2} V_{LR}}) = \ln(e^{V_{carnt}} + e^{V_{LR}}) = \ln(e^{(-0.4449235338 - 0.1284832480 \times \text{Fuel})} + e^{(-0.2561571696 \times \text{Fare})})$$

The second branch utility function is:

$$V_{B2} = 0.8228333254 \times \left[\frac{1}{1} \times IV_{B2}\right]$$

where

$$IV_{B2} = \ln(e^{\mu_{B2}V_{cart}} + e^{\mu_{B2}V_{train}}) = \ln(e^{V_{cart}} + e^{V_{train}})$$
$$= \ln(e^{(-0.4449235338 - 0.1284832480 \times \text{Fuel})} + e^{(-0.1199289538 - 0.2350644458 \times \text{Fare})})$$

Therefore,

$$V_{B2} = 0.8228333254$$
$$\times \ln(e^{(-0.4449235338 - 0.1284832480 \times \text{Fuel})} + e^{(-0.1199289538 - 0.2350644458 \times \text{Fare})})$$

The final branch utility function is shown below:

$$V_{B3} = 0.8533356936 \times \left[\frac{1}{1} \times IV_{B3}\right]$$

where

$$IV_{B3} = \ln(e^{\mu_{B3}V_{busway}} + e^{\mu_{B3}V_{Bus}}) = \ln(e^{V_{busway}} + e^{V_{Bus}})$$
$$= \ln(e^{(0.1553404831 - 0.3004548811 \times \text{Fare})} + e^{(-0.1777955033 - 0.2078010234 \times \text{Fare})})$$

Hence,

$$V_{B3} = 0.8533356936 \times \left[\frac{1}{1} \times IV_{B3}\right]$$
$$\times \ln(e^{(-0.4449235338 - 0.1284832480 \times \text{Fuel})} + e^{(-0.1199289538 - 0.2350644458 \times \text{Fare})})$$

Level 3

For the first limb, A1, we may write the utility expression as follows:

$$V_{(A1)} = \gamma_{(A1)}\Big[\alpha_{(A1)} + \beta_{1(A1)}f(X_{1(A1)}) + \beta_{2(A1)}f(X_{2(A1)})$$
$$+ \cdots + \beta_{K(A1)}f(X_{K(A1)}) + \frac{1}{\lambda_{(A1)}} \times IV_{(A1)}\Big]$$

As no utility function was specified at this level:

$$V_{A1} = \frac{\gamma_{(A1)}}{\lambda_{(A1)}} \times IV_{(A1)}$$

where $\frac{\gamma_{(A1)}}{\lambda_{(A1)}}$ is the IV parameter for limb A1 and $\text{IV}_{(A1)}$ is the IV variable for the same limb. We therefore have:

$$IV_{(A1)} = \ln(e^{\lambda_{A2}V_{A2}}) = \lambda_{A2}V_{A2}$$
$$= \lambda_{A2} \times \ln(e^{(-0.4449235338 - 0.1284832480 \times \text{Fuel})} + e^{(-0.2561571696 \times \text{Fare})})$$

λ_{A2} is the probability weighted average of λ_{cart} and λ_{LR}, both of which are equal to one. Hence, λ_{A_2} must also be equal to one, giving:

$$\begin{aligned} IV_{(A1)} &= 1 \times \ln(e^{(-0.4449235338-0.1284832480\times \text{Fuel})} + e^{(-0.2561571696\times \text{Fare})}) \\ &= \ln(e^{-0.4449235338-0.1284832480\times \text{Fuel})} + e^{(-0.2561571696\times \text{Fare})}) \end{aligned}$$

For the second limb, B1, we may write the utility expression as follows:

$$\begin{aligned} V_{(B1)} = \gamma_{(B1)}\Big[&\alpha_{(B1)} + \beta_{1(B1)}f(X_{1(B1)}) + \beta_{2(B1)}f(X_{2(B1)}) \\ &+ \cdots + \beta_{K(B1)}f(X_{K(B1)}) + \frac{1}{\lambda_{(B1)}} \times IV_{(V1)}\Big] \end{aligned}$$

As no utility function was specified at this level:

$$V_{B1} = \frac{\gamma_{(B1)}}{\lambda_{(B1)}} \times IV_{(B1)}$$

where $\frac{\gamma_{(B1)}}{\lambda_{(B1)}}$ is the IV parameter for limb B1 and $\text{IV}_{(B1)}$ is the IV variable for the same limb.

$$IV_{(B1)} = \ln(e^{\lambda_{B2}V_{B2}} + e^{\lambda_{B3}V_{B3}})$$

From the output:

$$\begin{aligned} &IV_{(B1)} \\ &\quad = \ln\left\{e^{[0.82283333\times \ln(e^{(-0.4449235338\ -0.1284832480\times \text{Fuel})})]} + e^{[0.85333569\times \ln(e^{(-0.1199289538\ -0.2350644458\times \text{Fare})})]}\right\} \end{aligned}$$

The utility for B1 becomes:

$$\begin{aligned} &V_{B1} = 0.97211621 \\ &\quad \times \ln\left\{e^{[0.82283333\times \ln(e^{(-0.4449235338\ -0.1284832480\times \text{Fuel})})]} + e^{[0.85333569\times \ln(e^{(-0.1199289538\ -0.2350644458\times \text{Fare})})]}\right\} \end{aligned}$$

As an aside, if a utility specification was estimated for B1, we would be unable to write out the utility specification. This is because the utility equation at this level must be multiplied by $\gamma_{(B1)}$. Unfortunately, NLOGIT reports the values of the IV parameters and not the scale parameters. Thus $\gamma_{(B1)}$ is not identifiable in the following equation. This is an important point to note, given that, in many applications, discrete choice models such as this are often transferred to larger network models. As $\gamma_{(B1)}$ will not be identifiable, the analyst will not be able to use this model outside of NLOGIT's simulation capability:

$$\begin{aligned} V_{(B1)} = \gamma_{(B1)}\Big[&\alpha_{(B1)} + \beta_{1(B1)}f(X_{1(B1)}) + \beta_{2(B1)}f(X_{2(B1)}) \\ &+ \cdots + \beta_{K(B1)}f(X_{K(B1)}) + \frac{1}{\lambda_{(B1)}} \times IV_{(B1)}\Big] \end{aligned}$$

We are now in a position to write out the probability equations for the model. We begin with the level 1 conditional probabilities.

Level 1 conditional probabilities

$$P(carnt) = e^{V_{carnt}}/(e^{V_{carnt}} + e^{V_{LR}})$$
$$P(LR) = e^{V_{LR}}/(e^{V_{carnt}} + e^{V_{LR}})$$
$$P(cart) = e^{V_{cart}}/(e^{V_{cart}} + e^{V_{train}})$$
$$P(train) = e^{V_{train}}/(e^{V_{cart}} + e^{V_{train}})$$
$$P(bus) = e^{V_{bus}}/(e^{V_{busway}} + e^{V_{bus}})$$
$$P(busway) = e^{V_{busway}}/(e^{V_{busway}} + e^{V_{bus}})$$

Level 2 conditional probabilities

$$P(A2) = e^{V_{A2}}/(e^{V_{A2}}) = 1$$
$$P(B2) = e^{V_{B2}}/(e^{V_{B2}} + e^{V_{B3}})$$
$$P(B3) = e^{V_{B3}}/(e^{V_{B2}} + e^{V_{B3}})$$

Level 3 conditional probabilities

$$P(A1) = e^{V_{A1}}/(e^{V_{A1}} + e^{V_{B1}})$$
$$P(B1) = e^{V_{B1}}/(e^{V_{A1}} + e^{V_{B1}})$$

The marginal probabilities for each of the elemental alternatives are calculated as now shown.

Marginal probabilities

$$P(carnt\,|A2|A1) = e^{V_{carnt}}/(e^{V_{carnt}} + e^{V_{LR}}) \times 1 \times e^{V_{A1}}/(e^{V_{A1}} + e^{V_{B1}})$$
$$P(LR\,|A2|A1) = e^{V_{LR}}/(e^{V_{carnt}} + e^{V_{LR}}) \times 1 \times e^{V_{A1}}/(e^{V_{A1}} + e^{V_{B1}})$$
$$P(cart\,|B2|B1) = e^{V_{cart}}/(e^{V_{cart}} + e^{V_{train}}) \times e^{V_{B2}}/(e^{V_{B2}} + e^{V_{B3}}) \times e^{V_{B1}}/(e^{V_{A1}} + e^{V_{B1}})$$
$$P(train\,|B2|B1) = e^{V_{train}}/(e^{V_{cart}} + e^{V_{train}}) \times e^{V_{B2}}/(e^{V_{B2}} + e^{V_{B3}}) \times e^{V_{B1}}/(e^{V_{A1}} + e^{V_{B1}})$$
$$P(bus\,|B3|B1) = e^{V_{bus}}/(e^{V_{busway}} + e^{V_{bus}}) \times e^{V_{B2}}/(e^{V_{B2}} + e^{V_{B3}}) \times e^{V_{B1}}/(e^{V_{A1}} + e^{V_{B1}})$$
$$p(busway\,|B3|B1) = e^{V_{busway}}/(e^{V_{busway}} + e^{V_{bus}}) \times e^{V_{B2}}/(e^{V_{B2}} + e^{V_{B3}}) \times e^{V_{B1}}/(e^{V_{A1}} + e^{V_{B1}})$$

15 The mixed logit model

We used to think that if we knew one, we knew two, because one and one are two. We are finding that we must learn a great deal more about "and." (Sir Arthur Eddington, 1882–1944, quoted in *The Harvest of a Quiet Eye*, London, Institute of Physics, 1977).

15.1 Introduction

The most popular choice models in use are the multinomial logit (MNL) and nested logit (NL). This is likely to remain true for a long time for the majority of practitioners. These models provide closed-form choice probability calculations and offer a framework within which many interesting behaviorally based questions can be investigated and answered. Given that the challenges to input high-quality data on the relevant set of attributes of alternatives and characteristics of individuals extends to all choice models, no matter how simple or complex the model structure might be, there is a large amount of credibility invested in the estimation and application of the familiar, tried and true MNL and NL models. But there is room for alternative choice models, provided that they add value to the established workhorses. Some of the large number of new choice models proposed in the literature have turned out to be tools that have aided the research community in its search for truly improved behavioral specifications. One such choice model is the mixed logit model. (It is also referred to as the "random parameter logit," "mixed multinomial logit," or "hybrid logit" model.[1] We shall use the most popular parlance of "mixed logit" (ML).

Writing a chapter on ML choice models in a primer for beginners might seem somewhat ambitious. We are now entering advanced territory. However, we felt that, sooner or later, beginners would want to venture into this space simply because the software to estimate such models is readily available in NLOGIT and the implementation involves few changes to the input code already used to estimate MNL and NL models. Having recently devoted

[1] Discussions with Ken Train on mixed logit models over the last four years have been invaluable.

a large amount of effort to reviewing this literature and writing a paper on the state of practice of ML modeling (Hensher and Greene 2003) we were persuaded to include this chapter. Ken Train has recently published an excellent book on discrete choice methods which also devotes a large amount of space to mixed logit models (Train 2003). We warn the beginner, however, that this is challenging material.

15.2 Mixed logit choice models

We continue to assume that a sampled individual ($q = 1, \ldots, Q$) faces a choice among J alternatives in each of T choice situations.[2] Individual q is assumed to consider the full set of offered alternatives in choice situation t and to choose the alternative with the highest utility. The utility associated with each alternative j, as evaluated by each individual q in choice situation t, is represented in a discrete choice model by a utility expression of the general form in (15.1). (It will be convenient to use matrix notation in this chapter (unemboldened) to represent the components of a utility expression and other model components.)

$$\begin{aligned} U_{jtq} &= \sum_{k=1}^{K} \beta_{qk} x_{jtqk} + \varepsilon_{jtq} \\ &= \beta'_q \mathbf{x}_{jtq} + \varepsilon_{jtq} \end{aligned}, \tag{15.1}$$

where $\mathbf{x}_{jtq}$ is the full vector of explanatory variables that are observed by the analyst, including attributes of the alternatives, socio-economic characteristics of the individual and descriptors of the decision context and choice task itself in choice situation t. The complexity of the choice task in stated-choice experiments as defined by number of choice situations, number of alternatives, attribute ranges, data collection method, etc., can be included to condition specific parameters associated with attributes of alternatives. The components β_q and ε_{jtq} are not observed by the analyst and are treated as stochastic influences. Note that the first of these, unlike its counterpart in the other models we have examined thus far, is assumed to vary across individuals.

Within the logit context, we impose the familiar condition that ε_{jtq} is independent and identically distributed (IID) extreme value type 1 across individuals, alternatives, and choice situations. The IID assumption is most restrictive in that it does not allow for the error components of different alternatives to be correlated (see chapter 3). We would want to be able to take this into account in some way. One way to do this is to introduce into the utility function through β_q additional stochastic elements that may be heteroskedastic and

[2] A single-choice situation refers to a set of alternatives (or choice set) from which an individual chooses one alternative. An individual who faces a choice situation on more than one occasion (e.g. in a longitudinal panel) or a number of choice sets, one after the other as in stated-choice experiments, is described as facing a number of choice situations (see chapter 5).

correlated across alternatives. Thus:

$$\boldsymbol{\beta}_q = \boldsymbol{\beta} + \boldsymbol{\Delta}\mathbf{z}_q + \boldsymbol{\Gamma}\mathbf{v}_q = \boldsymbol{\beta} + \boldsymbol{\Delta}\mathbf{z}_q + \boldsymbol{\eta}_q \tag{15.2}$$

or $\boldsymbol{\beta}_{qk} = \boldsymbol{\beta}_k + \boldsymbol{\delta}_k'\mathbf{z}_q + \boldsymbol{\eta}_{qk}$, where $\boldsymbol{\eta}_{qk}$ is a random term whose distribution over individuals depends in general on underlying parameters, and $\mathbf{z}_q$ is observed data, $\mathbf{v}_\varepsilon$ is a vector of uncorrelated random variables with known variances on the diagonal of a variance–covariance matrix, ε, and $\boldsymbol{\Gamma}$ is a lower triangular matrix which, because $\text{var}[\boldsymbol{\beta}_q] = \boldsymbol{\Gamma}\varepsilon\boldsymbol{\Gamma}'$, allows free variances and correlations of the parameters. Note that since $\boldsymbol{\beta}_q$ may contain alternative-specific constants, $\boldsymbol{\eta}_{qk}$ may also vary across choices, and, in addition, may thus induce correlation across choices.

The ML class of models assumes a general distribution for $\boldsymbol{\eta}_{qk}$ and an IID extreme value type 1 distribution for $\boldsymbol{\varepsilon}_{jtq}$. That is, $\boldsymbol{\eta}_{qk}$ can take on different distributional forms such as normal, lognormal, uniform, or triangular. Denote the joint density of $[\boldsymbol{\eta}_{q1}, \boldsymbol{\eta}_{q2}, \ldots, \boldsymbol{\eta}_{qK}]$ by $f(\boldsymbol{\eta}_q|\boldsymbol{\Omega}\mathbf{z}_q)$, where the elements of $\boldsymbol{\Omega}$ are the underlying parameters of the distribution of $\boldsymbol{\beta}_q(\boldsymbol{\beta}, \boldsymbol{\Delta}, \boldsymbol{\Gamma})$, $\mathbf{z}_q$ is observed data specific to the individual, such as socio-demographic characteristics, and $\boldsymbol{\eta}_q$ denotes a vector of K random components in the set of utility functions in addition to the J random elements in $\boldsymbol{\varepsilon}_{jtq}$.

For a given value of $\boldsymbol{\eta}_q$, the *conditional* probability for choice j is logit, since the remaining error term is IID extreme value:

$$\mathrm{L}_{jq}(\boldsymbol{\beta}_q|\mathbf{X}_q, \boldsymbol{\eta}_q) = \exp(\boldsymbol{\beta}_q'\mathbf{x}_{jq}) \Big/ \sum_j \exp(\boldsymbol{\beta}_q'\mathbf{x}_{jq}) \tag{15.3}$$

Equation (15.3) is the simple MNL model, but with the proviso that, for each sampled individual, we have additional information defined by $\boldsymbol{\eta}_q$. This is where the use of the word "*conditional*" applies – the probability is conditional on $\boldsymbol{\eta}_q$, that is $\mathbf{v}_q$ (and $\mathbf{z}_q$). This additional information influences the choice outcome.

The *unconditional* choice probability is the expected value of the logit probability over all the possible values of $\boldsymbol{\beta}_q$, that is, integrated over these values, weighted by the density of $\boldsymbol{\beta}_q$. From (15.2), we see that this probability density is induced by the random component in the model for $\boldsymbol{\beta}_q$ (Hensher and Greene 2003, Train 2003): Thus, the unconditional probability is

$$\mathrm{P}_{jq}(\mathbf{X}_q, \mathbf{z}_q, \boldsymbol{\Omega}) = \int_{\boldsymbol{\beta}_q} \mathrm{L}_{jq}(\boldsymbol{\beta}_q|\mathbf{X}_q, \boldsymbol{\eta}_q) f(\boldsymbol{\eta}_q|\mathbf{z}_q, \boldsymbol{\Omega}) d\boldsymbol{\eta}_q \tag{15.4}$$

where, once again, $\boldsymbol{\beta}_q = \boldsymbol{\beta} + \boldsymbol{\Delta}\mathbf{z}_q + \boldsymbol{\eta}_q$. Thus, the *unconditional* probability that individual q will choose alternative j given the specific characteristics of their choice set and the underlying model parameters is equal to the expected value of the conditional probability as it ranges over the possible values of $\boldsymbol{\beta}_q$. The random variation in $\boldsymbol{\beta}_q$ is induced by the random vector $\boldsymbol{\eta}_q$, hence that is the variable of integration in (15.4).

Models of this form are called *mixed logit* because the choice probability P_{jq} is a mixture of logits with f as the mixing distribution. The probabilities will not exhibit the questionable IIA property, and different substitution patterns may be obtained by appropriate specifications of f. This is handled through the random parameters, specifying each element of $\boldsymbol{\beta}_q$ associated with an attribute of an alternative as having both a mean and a standard deviation (i.e. it is treated as a random parameter instead of a fixed parameter).[3]

The standard deviation of an element of the $\boldsymbol{\beta}_q$ parameter vector, which we denote σ_k, accommodates the presence of unobservable preference heterogeneity in the sampled population (i.e. allows for individuals within the sampled population to have different $\boldsymbol{\beta}_q$ as opposed to a single $\boldsymbol{\beta}$ representing the entire sample population). One might handle this heterogeneity in the context of a fixed β_{qk} parameter through data segmentation (e.g. a different model for each socio-economic stratum such as age, gender, and income of each individual in the sample) and/or attribute segmentation (e.g. separate β_{qk}s for different trip length ranges for the travel time attribute in a travel choice study), in contrast to treating it all as random. The challenge of these (deterministic) segmentation strategies is in picking the right segmentation criteria and range cut-offs that account for statistically significant sources of preference heterogeneity. The random parameters representation of preference heterogeneity is more general; albeit with an unknown distribution of parameters, selecting such a distribution presents a challenge.

One can construct estimates of 'individual-specific preferences' by deriving the individual's conditional distribution based (within-sample) on their known choices (i.e. prior knowledge). These conditional parameter estimates are strictly 'same-choice-specific' parameters, or the mean of the parameters of the sub-population of individuals who, when faced with the same choice situation would hence made the same choices. This is an important distinction since we are not able to establish, for each individuals, their unique set of estimates, but rather identify a mean (and standard deviation) estimate for the sub-population who make the same choice. For convenience, let $\mathbf{Y}_q$ denote the observed information on choices by individual q, and let $\mathbf{X}_q$ denote all elements of $\mathbf{x}_{jtq}$ for all j and t. Using Bayes Rule, we find the conditional density for the random parameters:

$$\mathbf{H}(\boldsymbol{\beta}_q|\mathbf{Y}_q, \mathbf{X}_q, \mathbf{z}_q, \boldsymbol{\Omega}) = \frac{f(\mathbf{Y}_q|\boldsymbol{\beta}_q, \mathbf{X}_q, \mathbf{z}_q, \boldsymbol{\Omega})P(\boldsymbol{\beta}_q|\mathbf{z}_q, \boldsymbol{\Omega})}{f(\mathbf{Y}_q|\mathbf{X}_q, \mathbf{z}_q, \boldsymbol{\Omega})} \tag{15.5}$$

The left-hand side gives the density of the random parameter vector given the underlying parameters and the data on individual q. In the numerator of the right-hand side, the first term gives the probability in the conditional likelihood – this is in (15.3). The second term gives the probability density for the random $\boldsymbol{\beta}_q$ given in (15.2) with the assumed distribution of $\boldsymbol{\eta}_q$. The denominator is the unconditional choice probability – this is given by (15.4). Note that the denominator in (15.5) is the integral of the numerator, as given in (15.4). This result will be used to estimate the common choice-specific parameters, utilities, or choice probabilities as a function of the underlying parameters of the distribution of the random parameters. We return to this type of computation in section 15.3.

[3] A fixed parameter essentially treats the standard deviation as zero such that all the behavioral information is captured by the mean.

The choice probability in the denominator of (15.5) generally cannot be calculated exactly because the integral in (15.4) will not have a closed form. The integral is approximated through simulation. For a given value of the parameters, $\mathbf{\Omega}$, and the observed data, $\mathbf{z}_q$, a value of $\boldsymbol{\beta}_q$ is drawn from its distribution based on (15.2). Using this draw, the logit formula (15.3) for $L_{iq}(\boldsymbol{\beta}_q)$ is calculated. This process is repeated for many draws, and the mean of the resulting $L_{jq}(\boldsymbol{\beta}_q)$s is taken as the approximate choice probability giving the simulated probability in (15.6):

$$\hat{f}(\mathbf{Y}_q|\mathbf{X}_q, \mathbf{z}_q, \mathbf{\Omega}) = \mathrm{SP}_{jq}(\mathbf{X}_q, \mathbf{z}_q, \mathbf{\Omega}) = \frac{1}{R}\sum_{r=1}^{R} L_{jq}(\boldsymbol{\beta}_{qr}|\mathbf{X}_q, \boldsymbol{\eta}_{qr}) \tag{15.6}$$

R is the number of replications (i.e. draws of $\boldsymbol{\beta}_{qr}$), $\boldsymbol{\beta}_{qr}$ is the rth draw, and SP_{jq} is the simulated probability that an individual chooses alternative i.[4] It remains to specify the structure of the random vector $\boldsymbol{\beta}_q$. In our application of this model, we will use the structure in (15.2), $\boldsymbol{\beta}_q = \boldsymbol{\beta} + \boldsymbol{\Delta}\mathbf{z}_q + \boldsymbol{\Gamma}\mathbf{v}_q$, where the fixed underlying parameters are $\mathbf{\Omega} = (\boldsymbol{\beta}, \boldsymbol{\Delta}, \boldsymbol{\Gamma})$, $\boldsymbol{\beta}$ is the fixed *mean* of the distribution, $\mathbf{z}_q$ is a set of person-specific influences (also referred to a heterogeneity around the mean), $\boldsymbol{\Delta}$ is a matrix of parameters, $\mathbf{v}_q$ is a vector of uncorrelated random variables with known variances on the diagonal of a variance–covariance matrix, $\boldsymbol{\Sigma}$, and $\boldsymbol{\Gamma}$ is a lower triangular matrix which, because $\mathrm{var}[\boldsymbol{\beta}_q] = \boldsymbol{\Gamma}\boldsymbol{\Sigma}\boldsymbol{\Gamma}'$, allows free variances and correlations of the parameters. Thus, a "draw" from the distribution of $\boldsymbol{\beta}_q$ consists of a "draw" from the distribution of $\mathbf{v}_q$ which is then used to compute $\boldsymbol{\beta}_q$, as shown above.

The simulation method was initially proposed by Geweke (and improved by Keane, McFadden, Börsch-Supan, and Hajivassiliou, see Geweke, Keane, and Runkle 1994; McFadden and Ruud, 1994) to compute random variates from a multivariate truncated normal distribution. The method produces consistent estimators of the choice probabilities. The cumulative distribution function in their research is assumed to be multivariate normal and characterized by the covariance matrix $\mathbf{M}$. The approach is quick and generated draws and simulated probabilities depend smoothly on the parameters $\boldsymbol{\beta}$ and $\mathbf{M}$. This latter dependence enables one to use conventional numerical methods such as quadratic hill climbing or gradient methods to solve the first-order conditions for maximising the simulated likelihood function (15.6) across a sample of $q = 1, \ldots, Q$ individuals; hence the term maximum *simulated* likelihood (MSL) (Stern 1997).

After model estimation, there are many results for interpretation. An early warning – parameter estimates typically obtained from a random parameter specification can be interpreted as stand-alone parameters but the greatest behavioral value occurs in using each parameter with other linked parameter estimates. For example, the mean parameter estimate for travel time, its associated heterogeneity in mean parameter (e.g. for trip length), and

[4] By construction, SP_j is a consistent estimator of P_j for any R; its variance decreases as R increases. It is strictly positive for any R, so that $\ln(\mathrm{SP}_j)$ is always defined in a log likelihood function. It is smooth (i.e. twice differentiable) in parameters and variables, which helps in the numerical search for the maximum of the likelihood function. The simulated probabilities sum to one over alternatives. Train (1998) provides further commentary on this.

the standard deviation parameter estimate for travel time represent the marginal utility of travel time associated with a specific alternative *and* individual. The most general formula will be written out with due allowance for the distributional assumption on the random parameter. Four common specifications of the marginal utility of travel time associated with a set of parameter distributions using the population moments (and unconditional distributions in the sense of those that do not condition on the chosen outcome) are those defined in (15.7a)–(15.7d), using a travel time function in which we have re-parameterized the mean estimate of the travel time random parameter by trip length to establish heterogeneity associated with observable influences:

$$\textit{Lognormal: } \mathrm{Exp}(\beta_{mean\ travel\ time} + \beta_{trip\ length}\mathbf{X}_{trip\ length} + \sigma_{travel\ time\ standard\ deviation}\mathbf{X}\,N) \tag{15.7a}$$

$$\textit{Normal: } \beta_{mean\ travel\ time} + \beta_{trip\ length}\mathbf{X}_{trip\ length} + \sigma_{travel\ time\ standard\ deviation}\mathbf{X}\,N \tag{15.7b}$$

$$\textit{Uniform: } \beta_{mean\ travel\ time} + \beta_{trip\ length}\mathbf{X}_{trip\ length} + \sigma_{travel\ time\ spread}\mathbf{X}\,u \tag{15.7c}$$

$$\textit{Triangular: } \beta_{mean\ travel\ time} + \beta_{trip\ length}\mathbf{X}_{trip\ length} + \sigma_{travel\ time\ spread}\mathbf{X}\,t \tag{15.7d}$$

where ε has a standard normal distribution, u has a uniform distribution, and t has a triangular distribution.

15.3 Conditional distribution for sub-populations with common choices

The most recent advance in the application of mixed logit models is a recognition that the analyst can use the additional information on which alternative is chosen, as a way of establishing a more behaviorally useful location on the distribution curve for a random parameter to position each individual (in contrast to a fully random assignment within the entire sampled population). We might refer to these parameter estimates as 'common- or same-choice-specific' parameters. The conditional 'common-choice-specific' parameter estimates, however, are strictly not individual-specific but represent the mean and standard deviation of the parameters of the sub-population of individuals who, when faced with the same choice situation, would have made the same choices. Random assignment still applies, but is now specialized to the sub-set of the sample with common choices. The Bayesian literature has always advocated the view that the inclusion of this additional information (a subjective prior) adds power to the performance of a model. While this position is correct, it is by no means the unique preserve of the Bayesian method *per se*, and indeed is also applicable to classical inference methods that are presented in this book.

The following sections of this chapter set out some important issues that analysts consider when specifying and estimating mixed logit models. The material draws on the contributions in Hensher and Greene (2003) and Hensher, Greene, and Rose (2003).

15.4 Model specification issues

15.4.1 Selecting the random parameters

The random parameters provide a rich array of preference information. They define the degree of preference heterogeneity through the standard deviation of the parameters and through interactions between the mean parameter estimate and deterministic segmentation criteria (the latter including other attributes of alternatives, socio-economic and contextual descriptors, and even descriptors of the data collection method and instrument). They are also the basis for accommodating correlation across alternatives and across choice situations.

It is important to allocate a good proportion of time to estimating models in which many of the attributes of alternatives are considered as having random parameters. The possibility of different distributional assumptions for each attribute should also be investigated, especially where the sign is important (e.g. we expect a negative sign on the *travel time* parameter). The findings will not necessarily be independent of the number of random draws in the simulation (see (15.7)). Establishing the appropriate set of random parameters requires consideration of the number (and type) of draws, the distributional assumptions, and, in the case of multiple choice situations per individual, whether correlated choice situations are accounted for (see below). These interdependencies may make for a lengthy estimation process.

Estimation of an MNL model is an essential starting point for establishing candidate attributes and their (deterministic) functional form,[5] however, it is of limited value in the *a priori* selection of random parameterized attributes unless extensive segmentation on each attribute occurs.

To assist in the establishment of candidate random parameters, the Lagrange Multiplier tests proposed in McFadden and Train (2000) provide one statistical basis for accepting/rejecting the preservation of fixed parameters in the model. Brownstone (2001) provides a succinct summary of the test. These tests work by constructing artificial variables, as in (15.8):

$$z_{in} = (x_{in} - \overline{x}_i)^2, \text{ with } \overline{x}_i = \sum\nolimits_j x_{jn} \mathrm{P}_{jn} \tag{15.8}$$

where P_{jn} is the MNL choice probability. The MNL model is then re-estimated including these artificial variables and the null hypothesis of no random coefficients on attributes x is rejected if the coefficients of the artificial variables are significantly different from zero. The actual test for the joint significance of the z-variables can be carried out using either a Wald or Likelihood Ratio test-statistic (as shown in earlier chapters). These Lagrange Multiplier tests can be easily carried out in any software package that estimates the MNL model. Brownstone (2001) suggests that these tests are easy to calculate and appear to be

[5] Regardless of what is said about advanced discrete choice models, the MNL model should always be the starting point for empirical investigation. It remains a major input into the modeling process, helping to ensure that the data are clean, and that sensible results (e.g. parameter signs and significance) can be obtained from models that are not "cluttered" with complex relationships (see Louviere, Hensher, and Swait 2000).

quite powerful omnibus tests; however, they are not as good for identifying which random factors to include in a more general ML specification. An alternative test is to assume that all parameters are random and then examine their estimated standard deviations, using a zero-based (asymptotic) t-test for individual parameters or the likelihood-ratio test to establish the overall contribution of the additional information. While appealing, this is very demanding for a large number of explanatory variables and might be problematic in establishing the model with a full set of random parameters.

15.4.2 Selecting the distribution of the random parameters

If there is one single issue that can cause much concern it is the influence of the distributional assumptions of random parameters.[6] The layering of selected random parameters can take a number of predefined functional forms, the most popular being normal, triangular, uniform, and lognormal. The lognormal form is often used if the response parameter needs to be a specific (non-negative) sign. A uniform distribution with a (0, 1) bound is sensible when we have dummy variables.

Distributions are essentially arbitrary approximations to the real behavioral profile. We select specific distributions because we have a sense that the "empirical truth" is somewhere in their domain. Many distributions in common practice unfortunately have at least one major deficiency – typically with respect to sign and length of the tail(s). Truncated or constrained distributions appear to be the most promising direction in the future, given recent concerns. For example, we might propose a constrained triangular in which the spread of the distribution is allowed to vary within 10 percent of the mean. The truncated normal is another candidate. The uniform, triangular and lognormal are less well known and are documented below. In chapter 16, we show how the analyst can constrain distributions in NLOGIT to satisfy certain *a priori* requirements.

Uniform distribution

The standard deviation of a random variable that is uniformly distributed between mean $- s$ and mean $+ s$ is $\sigma = (\text{Upper Limit} - \text{Lower Limit})/(2\sqrt{3}) = s/\sqrt{3}$. The strategy

[6] One can use different distributions on each attribute. The reason you can do this is that you are not using the distributional information in constructing the estimator. The variance estimator is based on the method of moments. Essentially, one is estimating the variance parameters just by computing sums of squares and cross-products. In more detail (in response to a student inquiry) Ken Train comments that it is possible to have underlying parameters jointly normal with full covariance and then transform these underlying parameters to get the parameters that enter the utility function. For example, suppose $V = \alpha_1 x_1 + \alpha_2 x_2$. We can say that β_1 and β_2 are jointly normal with correlation and that $\alpha_2 = \exp(\beta_2)$ and $\alpha_1 = \beta_1$. That gives a lognormal and a normal with correlation between them. The correlation between α_1 and α_2 can be calculated from the estimated correlation between β_1 and β_2 if you know the formula. Alternatively, one can calculate it by simulating many α_1s and α_2s from many draws of β_1s and β_2s from their estimated distribution and then calculate the correlation between the α_1s and α_2s. This can be applied for any distributions. Let α_2 have density $g(\alpha_2)$ with cumulative distribution $G(\alpha_2)$, and let α_1 be normal. $F(\beta_2|\beta_1)$ is the normal CDF for β_2 given β_1. Then α_2 is calculated as $\alpha_2 = G^{-1}(F(\beta_2|\beta_1))$. For some Gs, there must be limits on the correlation that can be attained between α_1 and α_2 using this procedure.

for simulating a draw on the parameter with this distribution is (mean parameter estimate $+s(2u-1)$), where u is the standard uniformly distributed random variable. Since the distribution of u is uniform from 0 to 1, $2u-1$ is uniform from -1 to $+1$; then multiplying by s gives a uniform $\pm s$ from the mean. The spread can be derived from the standard deviation by multiplying the standard deviation by $\sqrt{3}$.

Triangular distribution

For the triangular distribution, the density function looks like a tent: a peak in the center and dropping off linearly on both sides of the center. Let c be the center and s the spread. The density starts at $c-s$, rises linearly to its upper value at c, and then drops linearly to zero again at $c+s$. It is zero below $c-s$ and above $c+s$. The mean and mode are c. The standard deviation is the spread divided by $\sqrt{6}$; hence the spread is the standard deviation times $\sqrt{6}$. The height of the tent at c is $1/s$ (such that each side of the tent has area $s \times (1/s) \times (1/2) = 1/2$, and both sides have area $1/2 + 1/2 = 1$, as required for a density). The slope is $1/s^2$. See Evans, Hastings and Peacock (1993) for formal proofs.

Normal distribution

The normal distribution is symmetrical around a mean. Since chapter 2 uses the normal distribution, we need not set out its properties, other than to note that the distribution permits standard deviations that can result in a change in sign throughout the full range.

Lognormal distribution

The lognormal distribution is very popular for the following reasons. The central limit theorems explain the genesis of a normal random variable. If a large number of random shocks, some positive, some negative, change the size of a particular attribute, x, in an additive fashion, the distribution of that attribute will tend to become normal as the number of shocks increases. But if these shocks act multiplicatively, changing the value of x by randomly distributed proportions instead of absolute amounts, the central limit theorems applied to $Y = \ln(x)$ tend to produce a normal distribution. Hence x has a lognormal distribution. The substitution of multiplicative for additive random shocks generates a positively skewed, leptokurtic, lognormal distribution instead of a symmetric, mesokurtic, normal distribution. Lognormals are appealing in that they are limited to the non-negative domain; however, they typically have a very long right-hand tail which is a disadvantage (especially for WTP calculations). It is this large proportion of "unreasonable" values that often casts doubt of the appropriateness of the lognormal.

In parameter estimation, experience has demonstrated that entering an attribute in a utility expression specified with a random parameter that is lognormally distributed, and which is expected *a priori* to produce a negative mean estimate, typically causes the model either not to converge or to converge with unacceptably large mean estimates. The trick to overcome this is to reverse the sign of the attribute prior to model estimation (i.e. define the negative of the attribute instead of imposing a sign change on the estimated parameter). The logic is as follows. The lognormal has a non-zero density only for positive numbers. So to ensure that an attribute has a negative parameter for all sampled individuals, one has to enter the negative of the attribute. A positive lognormal parameter for the negative of the attribute is the same as a negative lognormal parameter on the attribute itself.

15.4.3 Imposing constraints on a distribution

In practice, we may find that a particular distribution has strengths and weaknesses. The weakness is usually associated with the *spread* or *standard deviation* of the distribution at its extremes including behaviorally unacceptable sign changes for the symmetrical distributions. The lognormal has a long upper tail. The normal, uniform, and triangular may give the "wrong" sign for some parameters depending on the standard deviation. One appealing "solution" is to make the spread or standard deviation of each random parameter a function of the mean. For example, the usual specification in terms of a normal distribution is to define $\beta_{q,k} = \beta_k + \sigma v_{q,k}$, where $v_{q,k}$ is the random variable. A constrained specification might be $\beta_{q,k} = \beta_k + \beta v_{q,k}$, where the standard deviation equals the mean or $\beta_{q,k} = \beta_k + z\beta v_{q,k}$, where z is the coefficient of variation taking any positive value. We would generally expect z to lie in the 0–1 range since a standard deviation greater than the mean estimate *typically* results in behaviorally unacceptable parameter estimates.

This constraint specification can be applied to any distribution. For example, for a triangular with mean equal to spread, the density starts at zero, rises linearly to the mean, and then declines to zero again at twice the mean. It is peaked, as one would expect. It is bounded below at zero, bounded above at a reasonable value that is estimated, and is symmetric such that the mean is easy to interpret. It is appealing for handling WTP parameters. Also with $\beta_{q,k} = \beta_k + \beta v_{q,k}$, where v_{qk} has support from -1 to $+1$, it does not matter if β is negative or positive. A negative coefficient on $v_{q,k}$ simply reverses all the signs of the draws, but does not change the interpretation.[7]

15.4.4 Selecting the number of points for the simulations

Computation of ML choice probabilities by simulation typically requires Monte Carlo integration, as in (15.7). The computation involves the generation of "pseudo-random sequences" that are intended to mimic independent draws from a uniform distribution on the unit interval. Although these pseudo-random sequences cannot be distinguished from draws from a uniform distribution, they are not spread uniformly over the unit interval. Bhat (2000a) proposed replacing these pseudo-random sequences with sequences constructed from number theory to be more uniformly spread over the unit interval. These sequences yield much more accurate approximations in Monte Carlo integration relative to standard pseudo-random sequences. The reason for the superior performance of these sequences is shown in figure 15.1. Even with 1000 draws, the pseudo-random sequences leave noticeable holes in the unit square, while the Halton sequence suggested by Bhat (see the discussion below) gives very uniform coverage.

[7] One could specify the relationship as $\beta(i) = \beta + |\beta| v(i)$, but that would create numerical problems in the optimization routine.

The number of draws required to secure a stable set of parameter estimates varies enormously. In general, it appears that as the model specification becomes more complex in terms of the number of random parameters and the treatment of preference heterogeneity around the mean, correlation of attributes and alternatives, the number of required draws increases for a given type of draw. There is no agreed-upon prescription, but experience suggests that a choice model with three alternatives and one or two random parameters (with no correlation between the attributes and no decomposition of heterogeneity around the mean) can produce stability with as low as 25 *intelligent* draws (e.g. Halton sequences,

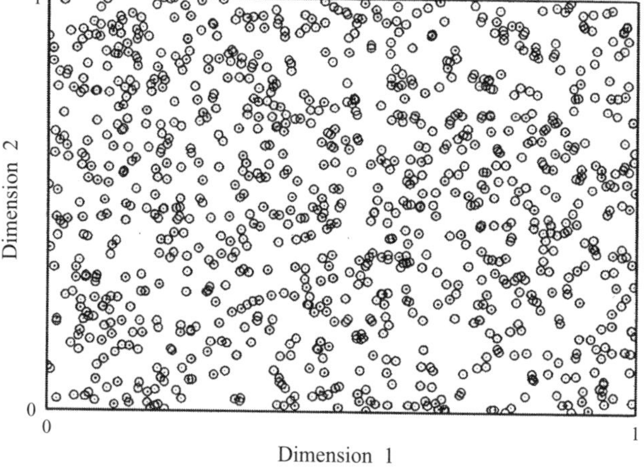

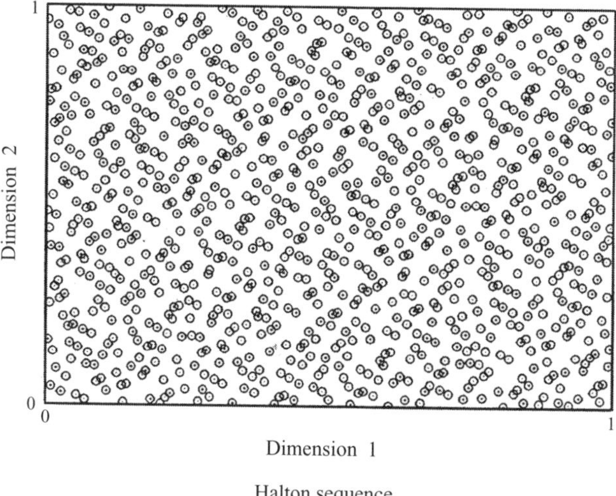

Figure 15.1 1000 draws on the unit square
Source: Bhat (2002).

see Bhat 2001 and Train 2003 for a discussion), although 100 appears to be a "good" number. The best test, however, is always to estimate models over a range of draws (e.g. 25, 50, 100, 250, 500, 1000, and 2000 draws). Confirmation of stability/precision for *each and every model* is very important.

One might ask why the analyst does not simply select a larger number of draws in recognition of the greater likelihood of arriving at the appropriate set of stable parameter estimates. The reason why a smaller number of draws is a relevant consideration is essentially practical – the ability to explore alternative model specifications relatively quickly before estimating the preferred model on a large number of draws. Even with fast computers, it can take hours of run time with many random parameters, large sample sizes, and thousands of draws. To know when parameter stability cuts in is of immense practical virtue, enabling the analyst to search for improved models in a draw domain that is less likely to mislead the inferential process.

Bhat (2001) and Train (1999) found that the simulation variance in the estimated parameters was lower using 100 Halton numbers than with 1000 random numbers. With 125 Halton draws, they both found the simulation error to be half as large as with 1000 random draws and smaller than with 2000 random draws. The estimation procedure is much faster (often 10 times faster). Hensher (2001) investigated Halton sequences involving draws of 10, 25, 50, 100, 150, and 200 (with three random generic parameters) and compared the findings in the context of valuation of travel time savings (VTTS) with random draws. In all models investigated, Hensher concluded that a small number of draws (as low as 25) produced model fits and mean VTTS that were almost indistinguishable.

As an aside, research by Bhat (2003) on the type of draws *vis-à-vis* the dimensionality of integration suggests that the uniformity of the standard Halton sequence breaks down in high dimensions because of the correlation in sequences of high dimension. Bhat proposes a scrambled version to break these correlations, and a randomized version to compute variance estimates. Hess, Train, and Polack (2003) propose the use of randomly shifted and shuffled uniform vectors that avoid the undesirable correlation patterns that arise in standard Halton sequences. These vectors provide more uniform coverage. They show that randomly shifted and shuffled uniform vectors significantly outperform standard, scrambled, and shuffled versions of Halton draws. All of these examples of recent research demonstrate the need for ongoing inquiry into simulated draws, especially as the number of attributes with imposed distributions increases.

15.4.5 Preference heterogeneity around the mean of a random parameter

Introducing an interaction between the mean estimate of the random parameter and a covariate is equivalent to revealing the presence or absence of preference heterogeneity around the mean parameter estimate. This is the role of the term $\boldsymbol{\delta}'_k \mathbf{z}_q$ in (15.2), as the utility function now involves terms

$$\beta_q x_{jtqk} = \beta_k x_{jtqk} + (\boldsymbol{\delta}'_k \mathbf{z}_q) x_{jtqk} + (\boldsymbol{\gamma}'_k \mathbf{v}_q) x_{jtqk}$$

If the interaction is not statistically significant then we can conclude that there is an absence of preference heterogeneity around the mean on the basis of the observed covariates, z_q. This does not imply that there is no preference heterogeneity around the mean, however, but simply that we have failed to reveal its presence in the second term above. This then means that the analyst relies fully on the fixed mean and standard deviation of the parameter estimate, with the latter representing all sources of preference heterogeneity (around the mean).

15.4.6 Accounting for observations drawn from the same individual correlated choice situations

Observations drawn from the same individual, as in SP choice experiments, are a common source of data for ML estimation. In part, this is the result of a recognition that SP data are usually much richer than RP data and hence that SP data open up real opportunities to enhance the behavioral capability of the ML model.

The presence of multiple observations on stated-choice responses for each sampled individual means that the potential for correlated responses across observations is a violation of the independence of observations assumption in classical choice-model estimation. This correlation can be the product of many sources including the commonality of socio-economic descriptors that do not vary across the choice situations for a given sampled individual and the sequencing of offered choice situations that results in mixtures of learning and inertia effects, among other possible influences on choice response.

ML models, through the relaxation of the IIA property, allow the model to be specified in such a way that the error components in different choice situations from a given individual are correlated. To motivate this point and show in particular that correlation and preference heterogeneity are related and hence a key as to how mixed logits handle correlation across choice situations, think of the unobserved sources of utility and how they might be treated. Consider a simple random utility model, in which there are heterogeneous preferences for observed and unobserved attributes of offered alternatives:

$$U_{jtq} = \beta_{0jq} + \gamma_q P_{jtq} + \beta_q x_{jtq} + \varepsilon_{jtq} \tag{15.9}$$

where most terms are defined earlier except for P_{jtq} which denotes price, x_{jtq} denotes some other observed attribute of choice j (which for complete generality varies across individuals and choice situations). The constant, β_{0jq}, denotes the individual, choice-specific intercept for alternative j, arising from q's preferences for unobserved attributes of j. γ_q and β_q are individual-specific utility parameters that are intrinsic to the individual and hence invariant over choice situations. The ε_{jtq} can be interpreted as task-specific variation in q's tastes, which as usual are assumed to be independent over choice situations, alternatives, and individuals. Suppose we estimate an MNL model, incorrectly assuming that the intercept and slope parameters are homogeneous in the population. The random component in this model will be

$$W_{itq} = \Delta\beta_{0iq} + \Delta\gamma_q P_{itq} + \Delta\beta_q x_{itq} + \varepsilon_{itq}$$

where Δ denotes the deviation of the individual-specific parameter from the population mean; for example, $\Delta\beta_{0iq} = (\beta_{0iq} - \mathrm{E}[\beta_{0iq}])$. Observe that (from the analyst's perspective) the variance of this random component for individual q in choice situation t is

$$\mathrm{var}(W_{itq}) = \sigma^2_{\beta_0} + \sigma^2_\gamma P^2_{itq} + \sigma^{2^2}_{\beta_x\, itq} + \sigma^2_\varepsilon \tag{15.10}$$

and the covariance between choice situations t and $t-1$ is

$$\mathrm{cov}(W_{itq}, W_{i.t-1.q}) = \sigma^2_{\beta_0} + \sigma^2_\gamma P^2_{i.t-1.q} + \sigma^{2^2}_{\beta x i.t-1.q} \tag{15.11}$$

Equations (15.10) and (15.11) (which both assume independence between the various random effects) reveal two interesting consequences of ignoring preference heterogeneity. First, the error variance will differ across choice situations as the price p and attribute x are varied. If one estimates an MNL model with a constant error variance, this will show up as variation in the intercept and slope parameters across choice situations. Second, (15.11) shows how preference heterogeneity leads to correlated errors across choice situations. This is revealed through the parameterization of the interactions between the prices and between other attributes in two choice situations. *That heterogeneity is a special type of choice situation correlation is not well understood.* To obtain efficient estimates of choice model parameters one should include a specification of the heterogeneity structure in the model. Daniels and Hensher (2000) and Bhat and Castelar (2003) indicate that the inter-alternative error correlation could be confounded with unobserved preference heterogeneity if the latter is not explicitly taken into account. One such way is to specify the parameters associated with each attribute (including price) as random,[8] exactly what mixed logit permits.[9] As long as one recognizes that preference heterogeneity for all alternatives must be treated as a source of variance across all choice situations defining an individual's choice responses, then correlation is automatically accommodated through the explicit modeling of preference heterogeneity present across all choice situations, as defined by the underlying covariance matrix for the random parameters. This correlation is not likely to be autoregressive for "instantaneous" stated choices since it is not the product of a long period of accumulated experience commonly attributed to state dependence. Rather, it is

[8] Some empirical evidence (e.g. Daniels and Hensher 2000) suggests that once unobserved heterogeneity is taken into account via a random parameters specification such as ML or RPL, serial correlation may be negligible or absent. That is, serial correlation may be spurious due to the failure to account for unobserved heterogeneity.

[9] But, more importantly, if preference heterogeneity is present it is not merely a statistical nuisance requiring correction. Rather, one should model the heterogeneity in order to obtain accurate choice-model predictions, because the presence of heterogeneity will impact on the marginal rates of substitution between attributes, and lead to IIA violations.

recognition in a very short time span of the sharing of preference heterogeneity between choice situations that is evaluated by the same individual. The discussion herein assumes that each attribute specified with a random parameter is independent of other such specified attributes in a given choice situation (within and between alternatives). This restriction, discussed in sub-section 15.4.7, can be relaxed and tested.

15.4.7 Accounting for correlation between parameters

All data sets, regardless of the number of choice situations per sampled individual, may have unobserved effects that are correlated among alternatives in a given choice situation. One way to recognize this is to permit correlation of random parameters of attributes that are common across alternatives. This engenders a covariance matrix with off-diagonal estimates identifying the dependency of one attribute on another within and between alternatives (depending on whether the attribute parameters are generic or alternative-specific). It also has interesting ramifications for the correlated choice situation issue in sub-section 15.4.6.

Let us define the utility expression for each alternative as before (see (15.1)): $U_{itq} = \boldsymbol{\beta}'_q \mathbf{x}_{itq} + \varepsilon_{itq}$. Since $\boldsymbol{\beta}_q$ is random, it can be rewritten as $\boldsymbol{\beta}_q = \boldsymbol{\beta} + \mathbf{u}_q$ where $\boldsymbol{\beta}$ is fixed (i.e. the mean) and $\mathbf{u}_q$ is the deviation from the mean. Then $U_{itq} = \boldsymbol{\beta}'\mathbf{x}_{itq} + (\mathbf{u}'_q \mathbf{x}_{itq} + \varepsilon_{itq})$. There is correlation over alternatives because $\mathbf{u}_q$ is the same for all alternatives. That is, each individual's preferences are used in the evaluation of the alternatives. For a single random coefficient, for example, it would follow that $\text{cov}[(u_q x_{itq} + \varepsilon_{itq}), (u_q x_{isq} + \varepsilon_{isq})]$ equals $\sigma_u^2 \times x_{itq} \times x_{isq}$, where σ_u^2 is the variance of u_q. In addition, however, there is also correlation over choice situations for each alternative, because u_q is the same in each choice situation as well. Again another way of stating this is that each individual uses the same preferences to evaluate (relative) utilities in each choice situation (or time period). The behavioral implication is that random preferences induce correlation over alternatives *and* choice situations.

Thus, both correlated alternatives and choice situations usually go hand in hand (assuming that one identifies the set of choice situations associated with each individual).[10] Correlation over alternatives and not over choice situations could, however, be established by specifying utility as $U_{itq} = \beta_{tq} X_{itq} + \varepsilon_{itq}$, where β_{tq} represents preferences instead of β_q. Thus preferences vary over individuals *and* over choice situations, with β_{tq} independent over choice situations for each individual. This is likely to be an unreasonable assumption for most situations. In particular, although for an individual, preferences might vary over choice situations, it is doubtful that they are independent across these choice situations. In general, the ML model can accommodate (i) correlation over alternatives and not over choice situations by assuming that β_{tq} is IID over choice situations, or (ii) correlation across choice situations but not over alternatives by fixing all of the parameters except

[10] The only circumstance in which you can distinguish correlated-choice situations from correlated alternatives is by ignoring the dependency between choice situations or assuming that it does not exist.

those representing the alternative-specific constants (ASCs), and assuming that ASC parameters are IID over alternatives but the same for each individual across the choice situations.

15.5 Willingness-to-pay challenges

Although selecting distributions for individual parameters is challenge enough, it is compounded when interest focuses on ratios of random parameters, as in the derivation of estimates of willingness to pay (WTP). For example, the ratio of two triangular parameters has a discontinuous distribution with a singularity unless the range of the denominator variable is forced to exclude zero. This otherwise produces an infinite mean and variance. The ratio of two normals has the same problem with the singularity at zero for the denominator. In deriving WTP estimates based on random parameters, one can use all the information in the distribution or just the mean and standard deviation. The former is preferred, but is more complicated. Simulation is generally used in the former case. Suppose we have a model with a fixed cost parameter β_1, and an attribute whose parameter is normally distributed with mean β_2 and standard deviation σ_2. Then the WTP for the attribute is distributed normally with mean β_2/β_1 and standard deviation σ_2/β_1. We can use the point estimates of β_1, β_2, and σ_2 to calculate these ratios. This approach takes the point estimates as given and ignores the sampling variance in these point estimates. To incorporate the sampling variance let β be the vector with elements β_1, β_2, and σ_2. The estimation process yields a covariance matrix for all the estimated parameters. One extracts the part for β (call it $\mathbf{W}$), which is a three by three symmetric matrix. We now wish to draw random observations from the normal distribution which has mean, β, and covariance matrix $\mathbf{W}$. The Cholesky decomposition provides a convenient way to do so.

The matrix $\mathbf{W}$ is decomposed into the product $\mathbf{LL}'$ where $\mathbf{L}$ is a lower triangular matrix. Then, the sample we seek can be drawn by first obtaining a set of three independent standard normal draws in a vector $\mathbf{u}$, which is simple since the three draws can be drawn independently. Then, the desired vector is computed as $\boldsymbol{\beta} + \mathbf{Lu}$. Thus, we generate draws of β_1, β_2, and σ_2 as $\hat{\boldsymbol{\beta}} + \mathbf{Lu}$, where $\mathbf{u}$ is a three by one vector of IID standard normal deviates drawn from a random number generator and $\hat{\boldsymbol{\beta}}$ is the point estimate of β. For each draw, calculate β_2/β_1 and σ_2/β_1, which are the mean WTP and the standard deviation in WTP implied by those draws. Do this for many draws. Then calculate the mean and standard deviation of β_2/β_1 over these draws. That gives you the estimated mean WTP and the standard error in this estimated mean. Also calculate the mean and standard deviation of σ_2/β_1 over these draws to get the estimated standard deviation of WTP and the standard error of this estimate.

To accommodate the entire distribution of WTP (rather than just the mean and standard deviation), take a draw of β_1, β_2, and σ_2 as described above (as $\hat{\boldsymbol{\beta}} + \mathbf{Lu}$). For this draw, one takes numerous draws of WTP, with each draw constructed as $(\beta_2 + \sigma_2 u)/\beta_1$, where u is a standard normal deviate from a random number generator. Repeat for many draws of β_1, β_2, and β_3, to get many sets of draws of WTP. Then, you can calculate whatever you want to know about WTP from the combined set of WTP draws; e.g. you can calculate the probability that WTP exceeds some amount. When the random parameters are assumed to be correlated the Cholesky decomposition is used to identify the standard deviations (or spread).

The discussion above on WTP focuses on using the population moments to derive a distribution. Each sampled individual is randomly assigned along the continuous distribution, since there is no information imported that might assist in a more accurate allocation along the distribution. This is referred to as an *unconditional* distribution. Another way of establishing a WTP distribution is to recognize (within-sample) the additional information available on the alternative chosen. Utilizing this information means that the allocation is *conditional* on the knowledge of which alternative is chosen. The classical inference setting within which ML models are estimated and from which we derive WTP distributions is capable of developing such conditional outputs. Such an approach (popular in Bayesian paradigms) enables the analyst to identify common-choice-specific parameters based on subjective priors (in our case, knowledge of the chosen alternative) and to derive more behaviorally accurate distributions of WTP and associated mean and standard deviation indicators of WTP. We remind the reader that these conditional means relate to the sub-population of individuals who, when faced with the same choice situation, would have made the same choices.

Of particular interest is the derivation of the conditional individual-specific parameter estimates and the associated WTP for a specific attribute for each individual, as described above. Hensher, Greene, and Rose (2003) obtain both population-derived WTP measures and individual-specific values based on the classical "mixed logit" model using a constrained triangular distribution for all random parameters. They illustrate the benefits of calculating WTP measures from ratios of individual parameters that are behaviorally a more appealing approximation to the true values of each individual, in contrast to draws from population distributions. The latter run the risk of allocating two parameters that are poorly juxtaposed in a relative sense, resulting in extreme value estimates.

15.6 Conclusions

The continuing challenges we face with ML models are derived in the main from the *quality of the data*. ML certainly demands better-quality data than MNL and NL, since it offers an extended framework within which to capture a greater amount of true behavioral variability in choice making. Broadly speaking the ML model aligns itself much more with reality where every individual has their own inter-related systematic and random components for each alternative in their perceptual choice set(s).

As discrete choice models become less restrictive in their behavioral assumptions, the possibility of identifying sources of preference heterogeneity associated with the mean and variance of systematic and random components increases. Ultimately we want to improve on our modeling capability to improve the predictability of a model when individuals are faced with changes in the decision environment as represented by a set of attributes of alternatives, characteristics of decision makers, and other contextual effects (which can include task complexity for data collection, especially stated-choice experiments). The sources of explanatory power reside within the systematic and random components in potentially complex ways, and can be captured by both the mean and the variance of parameters representing observed and unobserved effects. The ML model certainly opens up new opportunities to research these behavioral phenomena. In chapter 16, we use the case study data set to estimate a range of ML models to illustrate the capabilities of NLOGIT.

16 Mixed logit estimation

The secret of greatness is simple: do better work than any other man in your field – and keep on doing it. (Wilfred A. Peterson)

16.1 Introduction

The choice modeler has available a number of econometric models. Traditionally, the more common models applied to choice data are the multinomial logit (MNL) and nested logit (NL) models. The mixed logit (ML) model represents the latest development in the econometric toolkit available to the choice modeler.[1] In chapter 15, we outlined the theory behind this class of models. In this chapter, we estimate a range of ML models using NLOGIT. As with chapter 10 (MNL model) and chapter 14 (NL model), we explain in detail the commands necessary to estimate ML models as well as the interpretation of the output generated by NLOGIT. While a complete understanding of the theory behind the ML model is beneficial, it is hoped that in reading this chapter you will have a better understanding of the model, at least from an empirical standpoint.

16.2 The mixed logit model basic commands

The ML model syntax commands build on the commands of the MNL model discussed in chapter 10. We begin with the *basic* ML syntax command, building upon this in later sections as we add to the complexity of the ML model.

[1] Other models exist such as the multinomial probit model (which assumes a normally distributed error structure), ordered logit and probit models (used when the order of the dependent choice variable has some meaning), latent class models (used to uncover possible different preference patterns among assumed respondent segments), and generalized nested logit (GNL). We have deferred discussion of these models in preference to the mixed logit (ML) model, but all models can be estimated using NLOGIT.

The minimum set of commands necessary for the estimation of ML models in NLOGIT are as follows:

```
NLOGIT
;lhs = choice, cset, altij
;Choices =<names of alternatives>
;rpl
;fcn = <parameter name>(<distribution label>)
;Model:
U(alternative 1 name) = <utility function 1> /
U(alternative 2 name) = <utility function 2> /
...
U(alternative i name) = <utility function i> $
```

The **;rpl** command, which stands for "random parameter logit" (an alternative name for the ML model), is the base command responsible for the estimation of the most general ML model form. It is this command in conjunction with the **;fcn** ("fcn" stands for "function") command which distinguishes the ML command syntax from the basic MNL syntax. The **;fcn** command is used to specify which parameters are to be treated as random parameters within the ML model framework. The utility specifications are written in the exact same format as the MNL and NL model command syntax. Within the ML model framework, parameters named in at least one utility specification as well as in the **;fcn** command will be estimated as random parameter estimates. Parameters that are named solely within the utility specifications will be estimated as non-random or fixed parameters.

As an aside, the term "fixed parameter" with reference to a non-random parameter within the ML literature can be at times confusing. In the MNL and NL model frameworks, fixed parameters are parameter estimates which are fixed at some specific value by the analyst (such as zero). That is, they are not estimates at all but rather some *analyst-specified value* (although in some cases we may think of these as an analyst-inspired estimate of the true parameter value). It is also possible to fix parameter estimates within the ML model framework in a similar manner. Thus, in the ML model framework, fixed parameters may refer to either a parameter set to some predetermined value by an analyst or a non-random parameter. For this reason, we use the phrase, "non-random" parameter rather than fixed parameter.

Within the **;fcn** command, the command **(<distribution label>)** is used to specify the distribution that the analyst wishes to impose upon each of random parameters. The popular distributions (available in NLOGIT) are:

N the parameter will be normally distributed
L the parameter will be lognormally distributed
U the parameter will be uniformly distributed
T the parameter will have a triangular distribution
C the parameter will is non-stochastic (i.e. the variance equals zero).

Any of the above distributions may be assigned to any random parameter named in the **;fcn** command syntax. For example, the command:

;fcn = cartc(n)

will specify that a parameter named *cartc* will be a random parameter drawn from a normal distribution. Note that this command refers to the *parameter name* and not the attribute name for an attribute entering utility expression (15.1).

In estimating ML models, more than one parameter may be treated as a random parameter. Indeed, it is possible that all parameter estimates be treated as random. When more than one parameter is estimated as random, there is no requirement that the distributions be the same. Multiple random parameters are separated in the **;fcn** command by commas (,). In the following example, the *cartt* parameter will be estimated as a random parameter estimated from a normal distribution while the *bst* parameter will be treated as a random parameter distributed with a triangular distribution:

;fcn=cartt(n),bst(t)

Recall from chapter 15 that the random parameters assigned over the sampled population are obtained from repeated simulated draws. The number of replications of simulated draws, *R*, from which the random parameters are derived, may be specified by the analyst using the following command:

;pts= <number of replications>

The default number of replications and method of simulation in NLOGIT is 100 *random* draws. Train (1999) recommends that several hundred random draws be employed in estimation while Bhat (2001) recommends 1000 random draws. Whatever number is selected, ML models are time-intensive in estimation. Depending on the speed of the computer used in the estimation as well as the number of alternatives, number of random parameters, etc. of the model, an ML model with 100 random draws may take several hours before converging (authors' note: like any model, it is possible that an ML model may fail to converge even after several hours of estimation). For this reason, Greene (2002) recommends that *R* be set to as low as 10 or 20 for exploratory purposes, but set at much higher values once a final model specification is identified.

Historically, the approach used in the estimation of random parameter models has been to use *R random* draws from some derived empirical distribution (imposed upon each of the random parameters by the analyst). Random draws require a large number of replications if one is to be satisfied with the accuracy of the model results obtained. When combined with a sizeable sample size and a significant number of parameters to estimate, a large number of random draws is computationally time-consuming. A number of intelligent draw methods are available which have been shown to provide dramatic gains in limiting the time taken for model convergence while producing no discernible degradation in model results. Bhat (2001) reports that when using Halton intelligent draws, comparable model results to models estimated using random draws may be obtained with only one-tenth the total number of draws.

Unlike random draws which may over-sample (in assigning parameters over the sampled population) from areas of a distribution while leaving other areas of the distribution under-sampled, intelligent draw methods are designed to sample the entire parameter space in accordance with the empirical distribution imposed. For example, with a random draw, it is possible, although statistically unlikely, that one may draw observations solely from one tail of the distribution; it is for this very reason that we rely on multiple replications in estimating random parameters as opposed to using just a single draw. Nevertheless, as suggested within the literature, less numerous intelligent draws appear to give empirically similar results to numerically larger numbers of random draws. Hence, intelligent draw methods are designed to reduce the possibility of drawing parameters from limited sections of a distribution and thus creating what would be considered anomalous results.

NLOGIT offers two intelligent draw methods; standard Halton sequence (SHS) and shuffled uniform vectors (see Hess, Train, and Polack 2003). The former method has become very popular; however, recognition that SHS may induce correlation across the space of the draws has motivated shuffling in order to reduce this correlation. The most common form of intelligent draw used in model estimation to date has been SHS.

In NLOGIT, the default method of drawing from a distribution is random draws. If no command is provided by the analyst within the ML command syntax (other than the **;rpl** and **;fcn** commands), NLOGIT will automatically employ random draws to draw off of the distribution provided in the **;fcn** command for each random parameter (note that non-random parameters are estimated in the same manner as in the MNL and NL models). To make use of SHS intelligent draws, the analyst is required to add the following command syntax to the base ML command:

;Halton

Rather than use random or SHS draws, shuffled uniform vectors may be used instead. The necessary command used to request shuffled uniform vectors is as follows (note that it is possible to use only one draw method in the estimation process; i.e. random or SHS or shuffled uniform vectors):

;Shuffle

The very nature of using simulated methods to draw parameters from a distribution means that even with the exact same model specification, each estimation task should produce a different set of model results. To avoid this possibility, it is necessary to re-set the seed of the random number generator to the same value each time an ML model is estimated. The re-setting of the random seed generator is by no means compulsory; the ML model will run without re-setting the random seed generator; however, the results may differ with each estimation. The command to re-set the seed of the random number generator is:

Calc; ran(<seed value>) $

The analyst can specify any number in the above command as the actual value adopted is of no consequence. For consistency, it is suggested that the analyst select one value and always use this (much as one would use the same PIN number for one's bank account). Whatever value is used, the **;Calc** command must be given before the ML model syntax because the re-setting of the random number generator is a separate command to that of the ML command (hence the $ at the end).

Throughout this chapter, we will use the following **;Calc** command to re-set the random number generator; but, as suggested above, any number could be used (noting that there is no replicability problem if Halton draws are used):

```
Calc;ran (12345)$
```

In section 16.3, we will estimate an ML model using the above commands and discuss the output generated by NLOGIT for this model. In later sections, we will add to the above set of commands to estimate more complex forms of the ML model capable of detecting a wider range of effects than those discussed immediately below. We finish the chapter by discussing how to derive individual specific parameter estimates and issues surrounding willingness to pay (WTP) measures derived from random parameter estimates.

16.3 NLOGIT output: interpreting the mixed logit model

In this section, we interpret the output from an ML model fitted using the data accompanying this text. As with chapters 10 and 14, we will concentrate on interpreting the output from this model and not concern ourselves with how to improve the model's overall performance (this we leave to the reader). Subsequent sections will add to the output generated through the estimation of more complex ML models.

The ML model shown in the following example is estimated using the mode-choice case study on the 30 minutes or less commuting segments. In the following model, we first re-set the random number generator as suggested in section 16.2. Through the command **;Halton**, we have requested that standard Halton sequences draws be used to estimate each of the random parameters. The **;fcn** command specification is used to stipulate that the *toll* (drawn from a uniform distribution) and *cartc* (drawn from a normal distribution) attributes be treated as random parameters. Other attributes in the utility functions will be treated as non-random parameters. To reduce the amount of time necessary for model convergence, (which will be useful in the classroom to reproduce the results), we have restricted the number of replications to 10:

```
Calc;ran (12345)$
NLOGIT
;lhs = choice, cset, altij
;Choices = cart, carnt, bus, train, busway, LR
;Halton
;rpl
;fcn=toll(t),cartc(n)
;pts=10
;Model:
U(cart) = asccart + cartc*fuel + cartt*time + toll*toll /
U(carnt) = asccarnt + carntc*fuel + carntt*time /
U(bus) = ascbus + bsc*fare + bst*time /
```

U(train) = asctn + tnc*fare + tnt*time /
U(busway) = ascbusw + bswc*fare + bswt*time /
U(LR) = lrc*fare + lrt*time $

For the 30 minutes or less commuting segment, the above command will produce the following NLOGIT output. As with the NL models, NLOGIT will first estimate an MNL model to derive the initial start values for each of the parameters in the ML model. In the case of the ML model, the estimation of the MNL model to obtain starting values for the parameter estimates is not optional and as such does not require the addition of commands such as **;Start=logit** (see chapter 14):

```
+----------------------------------------------+
| Start values obtained using nonnested model  |
| Maximum Likelihood Estimates                 |
| Model estimated: Feb 30, 2003 at 03:15:00PM. |
| Dependent variable               Choice      |
| Weighting variable                 None      |
| Number of observations             2369      |
| Iterations completed                  5      |
| Log likelihood function       -3186.997      |
| R2=1-LogL/LogL*  Log-L fncn  R-sqrd  RsqAdj  |
| No coefficients  -4244.6782  .24918  .24706  |
| Constants only.  Must be computed directly.  |
|                  Use NLOGIT ;...; RHS=ONE $  |
| Chi-squared[13]           =   1705.38596     |
| Prob [ chi squared > value ] =    .00000     |
| Response data are given as ind. choice.      |
| Number of obs.= 2369, skipped    0 bad obs.  |
+----------------------------------------------+

+----------+-------------+----------------+----------+----------+
| Variable | Coefficient | Standard Error | b/St.Er. | P[|Z|>z] |
+----------+-------------+----------------+----------+----------+
TOLL         -.17706237      .06196088       -2.858     .0043
CARTC        -.10660068      .05848307       -1.823     .0683
ASCCART      -.89382699      .41313430       -2.164     .0305
CARTT         .01200925      .02321262         .517     .6049
ASCCARNT      .05490720      .44827049         .122     .9025
CARNTC       -.10211593      .05734831       -1.781     .0750
CARNTT       -.03521031      .01161163       -3.032     .0024
ASCBUS       -.47772133      .41926806       -1.139     .2545
BSC          -.17891188      .04597048       -3.892     .0001
BST          -.01528681      .01836580        -.832     .4052
ASCTN         .47707755      .39471618        1.209     .2268
```

```
TNC          -.20718469     .04626656    -4.478      .0000
TNT          -.07891504     .01874538    -4.210      .0000
ASCBUSW       .42577877     .38421968     1.108      .2678
BSWC         -.26531339     .04188879    -6.334      .0000
BSWT         -.05655085     .01636715    -3.455      .0005
LRC          -.25158031     .04204295    -5.984      .0000
LRT          -.03568315     .01669707    -2.137      .0326
```

The preceding output is interpreted in exactly the same manner as described in chapters 10 and 14. The only discernible difference between this model and those of earlier chapters is the order in which the parameter estimates are given. Those parameter estimates that are specified as random parameters are shown first, irrespective of their order within the utility specification. The initial MNL model is statistically significant (Chi-square value equal to 1705.385 with 13 degrees of freedom) and all parameters (except *cartt* which is statistically insignificant; p-value equal to 0.6049) have the correct sign.

Next we show the ML model output generated by NLOGIT. The first series of output provides information similar to that provided within the first output box of both the MNL and NL models. Provided in this series of output is information on any weighting variable used, number of observations (as with the NL model, the value given is the number of alternatives considered over the sample and not the number of choice sets viewed), the number of iterations to convergence, the log likelihood function at convergence and the log likelihood function assuming equal choice shares only. Also provided is a Chi-squared statistic for the log likelihood ratio-test (using as the base comparison model, a model with equal choice shares only) and information on the pseudo-R^2. In the above example, the model is statistically significant (Chi-square equal to 2119.618 with 20 degrees of freedom and a p-value equal to zero) and has a pseudo-R^2 of 0.25. The overall model fit of this model is adequate (see figure 10.7); however, in comparison to the MNL model estimated to provide the start values for the parameter estimates, we are unable to conclude on the evidence provided that the fitted ML model is any better (the log likelihood ratio-test produces a Chi-square value equal to 4.256 (i.e. $-2 \times (-3186.997 - (-3184.869))$); compare this to a Chi-square critical value with two degrees of freedom (the ML model estimated here has two additional standard deviation parameter estimates) of 5.991:

```
+-----------------------------------------------+
| Random Parameters Logit Model                 |
| Maximum Likelihood Estimates                  |
| Model estimated: Feb 30, 2003 at 03:30:00PM   |
| Dependent variable                 CHOICE     |
| Weighting variable                   None     |
| Number of observations               9476     |
| Iterations completed                   26     |
| Log likelihood function         -3184.869     |
| Restricted log likelihood       -4244.678     |
| Chi squared                      2119.618     |
```

```
| Degrees of freedom                          20       |
| Prob[ChiSqd > value] =               .0000000       |
| R2=1-LogL/LogL*    Log-L fncn  R-sqrd  RsqAdj |
| No coefficients    -4244.6782  .24968  .24756 |
| Constants only.    Must be computed directly. |
|                    Use NLOGIT ;...; RHS=ONE $ |
| At start values    -3186.9971  .00067 -.00215 |
| Response data are given as ind. choice.       |
+-----------------------------------------------+
+-----------------------------------------------+
| Random Parameters Logit Model                 |
| Replications for simulated probs. = 10        |
| Halton sequences used for simulations         |
| Number of obs.= 2369,  skipped  0 bad obs.        |
+-----------------------------------------------+
+---------+-------------+---------------+--------+---------+
|Variable | Coefficient | Standard Error |b/St.Er.|P[|Z|>z] |
+---------+-------------+---------------+--------+---------+
          Random parameters in utility functions
TOLL          -.19079857       .06787110     -2.811    .0049
CARTC         -.18100899       .08977465     -2.016    .0438
          Nonrandom parameters in utility functions
ASCCART       -.82184199       .43244614     -1.900    .0574
CARTT          .01141943       .02466412       .463    .6434
ASCCARNT       .03723827       .45308018       .082    .9345
CARNTC        -.09953307       .05793010     -1.718    .0858
CARNTT        -.03543708       .01173352     -3.020    .0025
ASCBUS        -.46421089       .42354593     -1.096    .2731
BSC           -.18106600       .04635673     -3.906    .0001
BST           -.01650135       .01855446      -.889    .3738
ASCTN          .46699495       .39697364      1.176    .2394
TNC           -.20741394       .04654342     -4.456    .0000
TNT           -.07917195       .01889057     -4.191    .0000
ASCBUSW        .41508128       .38664996      1.074    .2830
BSWC          -.26828461       .04221157     -6.356    .0000
BSWT          -.05583525       .01647527     -3.389    .0007
LRC           -.25371839       .04235201     -5.991    .0000
LRT           -.03606504       .01681554     -2.145    .0320
          Derived standard deviations of parameter distributions
TsTOLL         .17958067       .45765350       .392    .6948
NsCARTC        .27981371       .13790757      2.029    .0425
```

The second output box provides the analyst with information on the number of replications used in the simulated draws as well as the type of draw used. In this example, the output indicates that SHS draws were used in the estimation process with 10 replications. The **;ias** specification (see chapter 14) was not applied to this model, hence no *bad* observations were removed during model estimation.

The last section of the output provides information on the parameter estimates of the ML model. The first and last output generated in this section relates to the random parameters estimated as part of the ML model. The first series of parameter estimate output relates to the random parameters and is used to determine whether the mean of the sample population random parameters obtained from the 10 SHS draws is statistically different to zero. We show this output below:

```
+----------+------------+--------------+---------+---------+
| Variable | Coefficient | Standard Error | b/St.Er. | P[|Z|>z] |
+----------+------------+--------------+---------+---------+
         Random parameters in utility functions
TOLL            -.19079857       .06787110     -2.811      .0049
CARTC           -.18100899       .08977465     -2.016      .0438
```

Random parameters estimated within the most basic ML framework are estimated over the sampled population from a number of draws (either random draws or intelligent draws; SHS or shuffled uniform vectors). The parameter estimates thus obtained are derived at the sample-population level only. This is not the same as estimating individual-specific parameter estimates. Parameter estimates estimated at the sample-population level are called *unconditional* parameter estimates, as the parameters are not conditioned on any particular individual's choice pattern but rather on the sample population as a whole. The process of estimating *unconditional* random parameters is similar to the estimation process of non-random parameters in the MNL and ML models; that is, maximization of the LL function over the data for the sample population. In section 16.4 and 16.8, we demonstrate how to estimate individual-specific or *conditional* parameter estimates. We leave it until then to discuss the differences between the two types of estimates but note that the two often produce widely varying results.

Each draw taken from some specified distribution will produce a unique sample population parameter estimate for each random parameter estimated. To avoid spurious results (for example, drawing a single observation from the tail of the distribution), R replications of draws are used. It is from these R replicated draws that the mean random parameter is derived. Simply put, the mean of each random parameter is the average of the parameters drawn over the R replications from the appropriate distribution. It is this value that is given in the above output. For the toll attribute, the parameter estimate of -0.191 represents the mean of the R draws over the 10 SHS draws requested within the command syntax.

The interpretation of the output associated with the mean of a random parameter estimate is much the same as with non-random parameters discussed in previous chapters. The p-value for the toll attribute random parameter is 0.0049, which is less than alpha equal to 0.05 (i.e. 95 percent confidence interval). As the p-value is less than the analyst-determined critical value, we reject the null hypothesis at the 95 percent level of confidence and conclude that the mean of the random parameter is statistically different to zero. We show this test

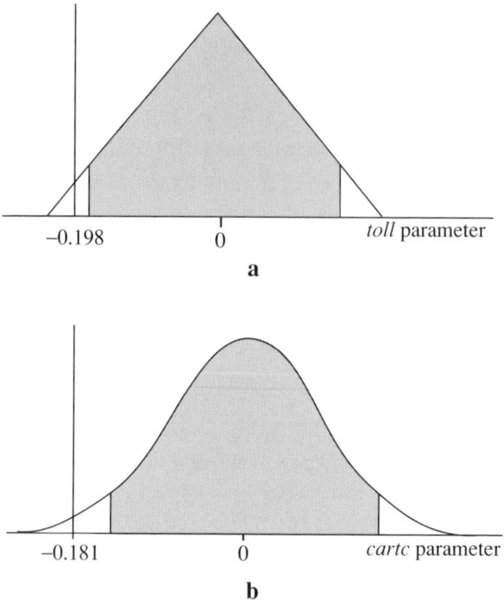

Figure 16.1 Testing for statistical differences in means of triangular and normal distributions

graphically in figure 16.1a (where the imposed distribution is triangular; for the present, we show the triangular distribution with an undetermined amount of spread; in the next series of output that we discuss we are able to determine first whether there exists any spread around the mean, and if there does, how much spread exists). The p-value for the *car with toll cost* parameter is similarly less than alpha equal to 0.05, suggesting that the mean parameter estimate of -0.181 for this random parameter is also statistically different to zero. Graphically, this test is shown in figure 16.1b (where *cartc* is normally distributed; once more, we show the distribution with an as-yet unknown level of variance). Both random parameters have means that are, at the sample population level, statistically different to zero.

The second set of output pertaining to each of the random parameters is reproduced below:

Variable	Coefficient	Standard Error	b/St.Er.	P[|Z|>z]
	Derived standard deviations of parameter distributions			
TsTOLL	.17958067	.45765350	.392	.6948
NsCARTC	.27981371	.13790757	2.029	.0425

while the first set of output relates to the means of each of the random parameters, the second series of output relates to the amount of *spread or dispersion* that exists around the sample population. The parameter estimates given in the output are the derived standard

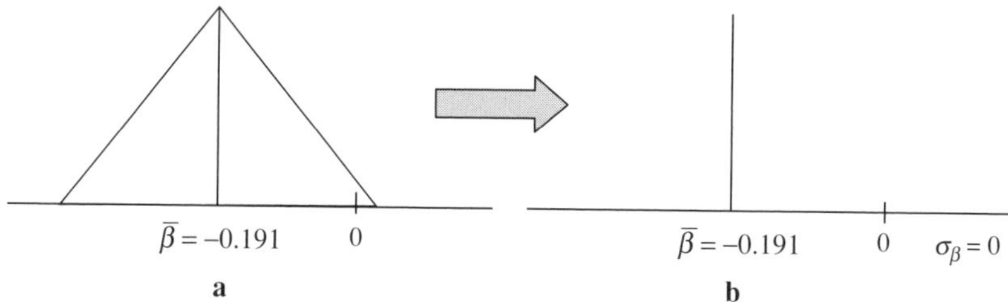

Figure 16.2 Testing dispersion of the *toll* random parameter

deviations calculated over each of the R draws. Insignificant parameter estimates for derived standard deviations indicate that the dispersion around the mean is statistically equal to zero, suggesting that all information in the distribution is captured within the mean. Statistically significant parameter estimates for derived standard deviations for a random parameter suggest the existence of heterogeneity in the parameter estimates over the sampled population around the mean parameter estimate (i.e. different individuals possess individual-specific parameter estimates that may be different from the sample population mean parameter estimate).

As an aside, the reader will note that the names of the parameters in the above output are preceded by two letters. These letters are used to identify the analytical distribution imposed on the random parameter estimate. Random parameters drawn from normal distributions will have the letters Ns, lognormal Ls, uniform Us, triangular distributions Ts, and non-stochastic distributions Cs (we discuss the special case of using a non-stochastic distribution in sub-section 16.6.1).

For the above example, the dispersion of the *toll* random parameter represented by a derived standard deviation of 0.180 is not statistically significant, given a Wald-statistic of 0.392 (within the ± 1.96 range) and a p-value of 0.6948 (which is greater than our critical value of alpha equal to 0.05). We show this test graphically in figures 16.2a and 16.2b where the triangular distribution imposed upon the toll attribute (figure 16.2a) collapses to a single point represented by its mean (figure 16.2b). In this case, all individuals within the sample may be (statistically) represented by a *toll* parameter of -0.191. This is equivalent to treating the *toll* parameter as a non-random or fixed parameter in which the single parameter value represents the entire sampled population.

Dispersion of the *car with toll* cost parameter is statistically significant, as suggested by a Wald-statistic of 2.029 (outside the ± 1.96 critical value range) and a p-value of 0.0425. Unlike the *toll* parameter, the model does not suggest that the *cartc* parameter should collapse to a single-point representative of the entire sampled population. For the analyst, this suggests the presence of heterogeneity over the sampled population with regard to individual-level *cartc* parameter estimates. As such, a single parameter estimate of -0.181 is insufficient to represent all sampled individuals. We show this in figure 16.3.

At this point, the analyst may wish to re-specify the *toll* parameter as a non-random parameter or re-estimate the model maintaining the *toll* parameter as a random parameter but assign to it some other distribution from which it may be derived. Despite supporting evidence that the *cartc* parameter should be treated as a normally distributed random

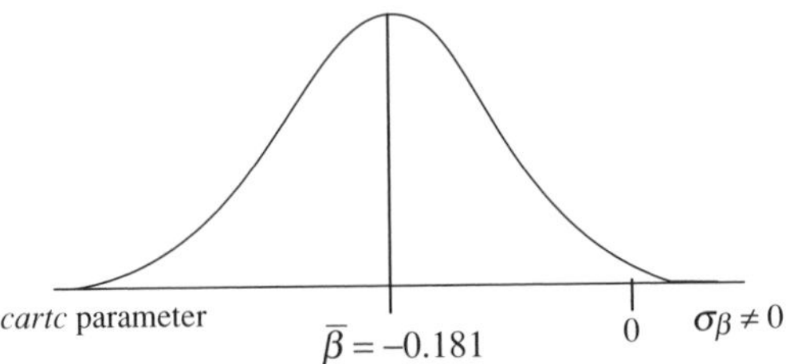

Figure 16.3 Testing dispersion of the *cartc* random parameter

parameter, the analyst may also wish to assign different distributional forms to test for better model fits. Also, other parameters formerly treated as non-random may be estimated as random parameters in further exploratory work. Once the analyst is content with the model results, the model should be re-estimated with a greater number of draws to confirm stability in the results.

As an aside, the statistical significance of attributes does vary as the number of draws changes, so one must exercise some judgment in the initial determination of statistically significant effects. Practical experience suggests that an attribute with a *z*-value (see chapter 15) over 1.5 for a small number of draws may indeed become statistically significant (i.e. over 1.96) with a larger number of draws. This has been observed more for the standard deviation parameters (i.e. those derived from normal and lognormal distributions).

In order to write out the utility functions for the above model, we need to consider (15.7a)–(15.7d) which account for the distributional assumptions placed upon the random parameters of the model. In the above example, we have no associated heterogeneity in the mean parameter estimate (we explore this option in a later section). As such, we may rewrite equations (15.8a)–(15.8d) as (16.1a)–(16.1d), as shown below:

$$\textit{Lognormal: } \mathrm{Exp}(\beta_{\textit{attribute mean}} + \sigma_{\textit{attribute standard deviation}} \times N) \tag{16.1a}$$

$$\textit{Normal: } \beta_{\textit{attribute mean}} + \sigma_{\textit{attribute standard deviation}} \times N \tag{16.1b}$$

$$\textit{Uniform: } \beta_{\textit{attribute mean}} + \sigma_{\textit{attribute time spread}} \times u \tag{16.1c}$$

$$\textit{Triangular: } \beta_{\textit{attribute mean}} + \sigma_{\textit{attribute time spread}} \times t \tag{16.1d}$$

where N has a standard normal distribution, u has a uniform distribution, and t has a triangular distribution.

For the *toll* random parameter, the distribution from which the random parameter was derived was triangularly distributed. From the model results, we observe a mean of −0.191 and a standard deviation of 0.180 (ignoring statistical insignificance) for this parameter. By way of (16.1d), we may write this as such:

$$\text{Toll} = -0.19079857 + 0.17958067 \times \text{t}$$

The car with toll cost random parameter was derived from a normal distribution and had a mean of −0.181 and a standard deviation of 0.279. From (16.1b), we may write out the marginal utility for the attribute as follows:

$$\text{Cartc} = -0.18100899 + 0.27981371 \times \varepsilon$$

The remaining output relates to those attributes estimated as *non-random parameters*. Non-random parameters are interpreted in the exact same manner as parameters estimated with the MNL or NL model forms. This is equivalent to figure 16.2b, in which all information is captured in the mean parameter estimate, the single value of which is used to represent the marginal utility for that attribute (or SDC) for all sampled individuals. In the above example, we observe that the *cartt* non-random parameter has the wrong sign. Nevertheless, this fact is somewhat offset by the fact that the parameter is not statistically significant (and hence is statistically equal to zero). All other parameter estimates are of the correct sign although the *carntc* and *busc* parameters are also observed to be statistically insignificant. Ignoring this, we may write out the utility functions for this model as below:

$$\begin{aligned}
V_{cart} &= -0.82184199 + (-0.18100899 + 0.27981371 \times N) \times \text{CARTC} \\
&\quad + 0.01141943 \times \text{CARTT} + (-0.19079857 + 0.17958067 \times t) \\
&\quad \times \text{TOLL} \\
V_{carnt} &= 0.03723827 - 0.09953307 \times \text{CARNTC} - 0.03543708 \\
&\quad \times \text{CARNTT} \\
V_{bus} &= -0.46421089 - 0.18106600 \times \text{BSC} - 0.01650135 \times \text{BST} \\
V_{train} &= -0.07917195 - 0.20741394 \times \text{TNC} - 0.07917195 \times \text{TNT} \\
V_{busway} &= 0.41508128 - 0.26828461 \times \text{BSWC} - 0.05583525 \times \text{BSWT} \\
V_{\text{LR}} &= -0.25371839 \times \text{LRC} - 0.03606504 \times \text{LRT}
\end{aligned}$$

Given that no random parameter estimates were assigned to the *public transport* and *car with no toll* (*carnt*) alternatives, we may interpret the public transport utility functions in the exact same manner that we would interpret similar utility functions obtained from MNL or NL models (i.e. all the parameters are non-random).

16.4 How can we use random parameter estimates?

The inclusion of the distributional form (i.e. N, t, u) within the utility formula for each random parameter estimate requires special treatment in establishing the marginal utility possessed by any individual towards the alternative for which the random parameter estimate belongs. In a later section, we demonstrate how to estimate the conditional mean parameter estimates (i.e. common-choice-specific parameter estimates conditioned on the choices observed within the data) which may be used to decide where on the distribution (of marginal utility) an individual resides. These parameter estimates may then be used to derive outputs, such as WTP measures, elasticities, etc., or be exported to other systems such as a larger network model.

The ML output generated by NLOGIT (as demonstrated to date), however, is that of the unconditional parameter estimates. The output shown is representative of the entire sampled population. The output provides the mean and standard deviation of each of the random parameter distributions. As such, in using the unconditional parameter estimates, the specific location on the distribution for any given individual is unknown. If one is interested in the population profile, this does not represent a problem.

As an aside, the conditional 'common-choice-specific' mean parameter estimates (see chapter 15) are for each sampled individual (or each choice set, in the case of SP data). The use of these individual parameter estimates, while scientifically rigorous (they are obtained Bayesian-like, conditioned on the choice data), means that any output generated is limited to within the sample drawn as part of the study. Prediction outside of the sample is not possible unless one has a very robust set of mapping variables to assign a hold out sample observation to an observation used in model estimation. Thus, without a robust mapping capability if the analyst wishes to predict outside of the sample, the unconditional parameter estimates are preferred (see Hensher and Jones 2004).

The NLOGIT commands **;Utilities** and **;Prob** work within the ML model framework in the same manner as for the MNL and NL models. The **;Simulation** command (see chapter 11) may be used to test policy implications resulting from changes in attribute levels; however, the results cannot be easily transferred to other domains without a robust mapping capability at the individual-observation level. That is, the analyst requires some method to map the probabilities and/or utilities obtained for sampled individuals and to a domain outside of the sample, a difficult task given the presence of the random parameter estimates. In the absence of such mapping capability, it remains possible to use the information captured in the unconditional parameter estimates to construct hypothetical samples with the same distributional information (i.e. mean, spread) which in turn may be easily exported to other systems.

The unconditional parameter estimates capture information on (1) the distributional form of the marginal utilities of each random parameter (specified by the analyst), (2) the means of the distributions, and (3) the dispersion of the distributions provided in the output as the standard deviation or spread parameters. With this knowledge, it is possible to reconstruct the random parameter distribution out of sample such that the same distribution is randomly assigned over a hypothetical sample of individuals. The process to do this will depend on the distributional form of the random parameter.

Lognormal

The following commands may be used to create a hypothetical sample of individual-specific parameter estimates for a random parameter with a lognormal distribution. In using these commands (as well as for those of other distributional forms), the individual-specific parameter estimates for a hypothetical sample of individuals will be simulated with a sample size equal to the number of rows contained within the active data set. For small data sets, this will mean that only a small hypothetical sample of individuals will be simulated. For this reason, it may be worthwhile creating a dummy data set with a large number of rows of data (at least 10,000; this can be easily done in Microsoft Excel by

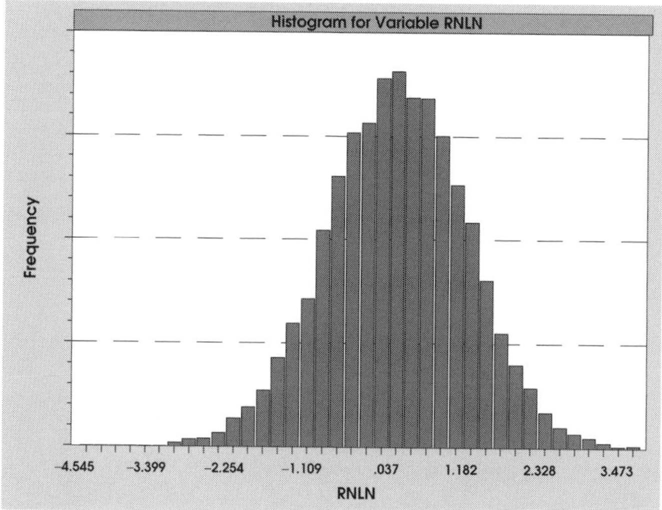

Figure 16.4 Histogram of a randomly drawn normal distribution with mean zero and standard deviation one

dragging a value in the first cell down to the required number of rows and exporting this sheet into NLOGIT):

```
Calc;ran(12345) $
CREATE
;rnln=rnn(0,1) $
Histogram;rhs=rnln $
```

The **Calc;ran(12345)$** command is given first to re-set the random number generator used to randomly assign hypothetical individuals to points on the distribution. The next command (i.e. **CREATE;rnln=rnn(0,1) $**) will draw a sample with a normal distribution with a mean of zero and a standard deviation of one. The final command will produce a histogram plot of the sample drawn to confirm that the distribution is indeed normal (see figure 16.4).

The marginal utility for a lognormal distribution is given in (16.1a). Assuming a mean parameter estimate of −2.79956445 and a standard deviation parameter of 2.30738512, we can now use the newly created *rnln* variable to locate each hypothetical individual on the distribution. This is achieved via the following command syntax:

```
CREATE
;logbet=(exp(-2.79956445 + 2.30738512*rnln)) $
Histogram;rhs=logbet $
```

The calculation undertaken in the **CREATE** command is equivalent to (16.1a) and will create a variable in the data set called *logbet* which will consist of each hypothetical

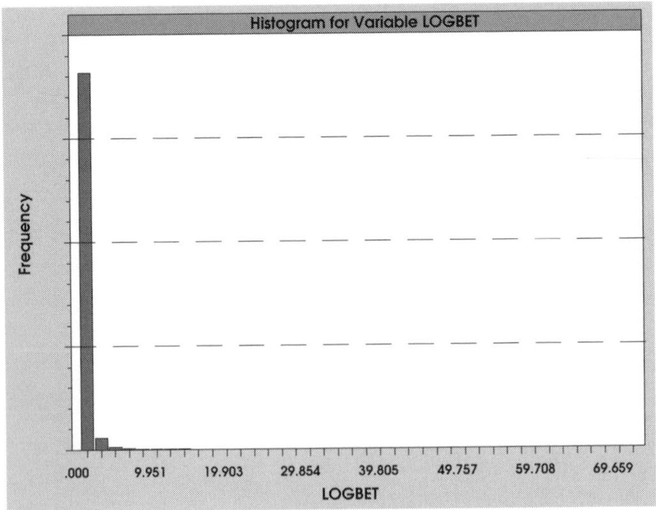

Figure 16.5 Histogram of a hypothetical sample for a lognormal distributed random parameter

	NUM	RNLN	LOGBET
1 »	1	0.53487	0.209002
2 »	2	0.789158	0.37581
3 »	3	-0.921178	0.00726217
4 »	4	-0.301615	0.0303334
5 »	5	0.0406775	0.0668232
6 »	6	1.00284	0.615306
7 »	7	0.514318	0.199322
8 »	8	1.03924	0.669222
9 »	9	-0.502558	0.0190792
10 »	10	-0.443441	0.0218675
11 »	11	-1.25443	0.00336604
12 »	12	-0.527586	0.0180086

Figure 16.6 Hypothetical individual-specific parameter estimates derived from a lognormal distribution

individual's location on the lognormal distribution. To confirm that the shape of the distribution is lognormal, we produce a histogram of the *logbet* variable. We show this as figure 16.5.

As shown in Figure 16.6, each hypothetical individual up to the number of rows of data will be assigned a position on the distribution in terms of a hypothetical parameter estimate. While the parameter estimate for each specific hypothetical individual will be largely meaningless (it was randomly assigned), the overall distribution will match that

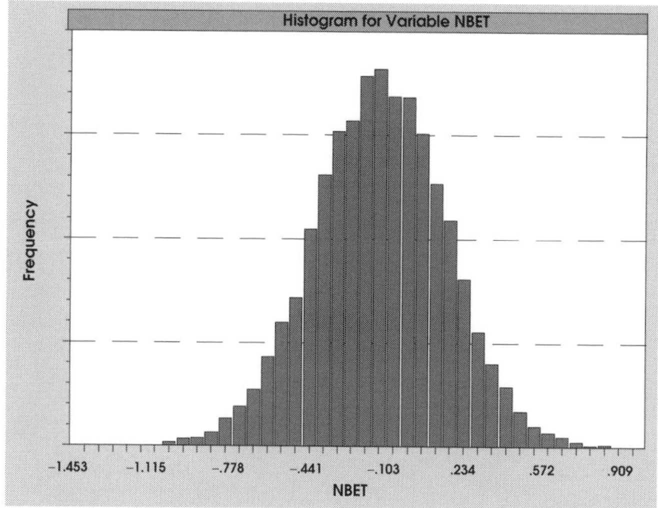

Figure 16.7 Hypothetical parameter distribution for a standard normal distribution

from which the sample was drawn. Provided a large enough sample is drawn, these may then be exported to other external systems.

Normal

The procedure of drawing a hypothetical sample of individual-level parameter estimates which follow a normal distribution is similar to that of drawing a sample following a lognormal distribution. In the previous example, we have already drawn a sample with a standard normal distribution (i.e. a normal distribution with a mean of zero and a standard deviation of one). We can use this same distribution in (16.1b) to derive a hypothetical sample of individual specific parameter estimates over a normally distributed random parameter. The command to do this is shown below:

```
CREATE
;nbet=(-0.18100899 +0.27981371*rnln)$
Histogram;rhs=nbet$
```

The **CREATE** command shown above is equivalent to (16.1b) using the parameter estimates from the previously estimated model. The parameter distribution is plotted using a histogram requested in the last line of syntax. The histogram is shown as figure 16.7.

As with the lognormal example, the hypothetical individual specific parameter estimates may be found in the data set.

Uniform

The final distribution discussed is that of the uniform distribution. In the commands that follow, we demonstrate how to draw a continuous uniform distribution. Once more, we

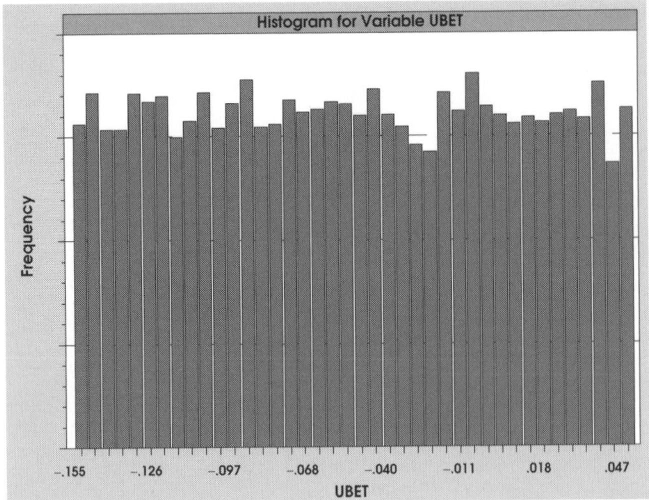

Figure 16.8 Histogram of hypothetical parameter estimates for a uniform distribution

must first re-set the random number generator:

```
Calc;ran(12345) $
CREATE
;U=rnu(0,1)
Histogram;rhs=U $
```

The **rnu( )** command is used to draw a sample from a continuous uniform distribution in the indicated range. In the above example, the range is between zero and one and the values will be stored in a variable named U.

Assuming a mean of −0.20535800 and a standard deviation parameter of 0.54850582, the following command syntax may be used to assign each of our hypothetical individuals to a location on the parameter distribution:

```
CREATE
;Ubet=(-.20535800 + 0.54850582*U)$
Histogram;rhs=Ubet$
```

The above syntax will assign each individual to a location on the uniform distribution based on the random variable U. This is equivalent to (16.1c). The final command will generate a histogram of the parameter distribution to confirm that it is indeed uniform (figure 16.8).

As before, the hypothetical individual specific parameter estimates may be found in the data set (under a variable called *Ubet*).

Triangular

Deriving a hypothetical sample for a random parameter estimate with a triangular distribution is a little more involved. The commands are shown below:

```
Calc;ran(12345)$
CREATE
;V=rnu(0,1)
;if(v<=0.5)T=sqr(2*V)-1;(ELSE) T=1-sqr(2*(1-V))$
Histogram;rhs=V,T $
```

The first command re-sets the random number generator so as to provide consistency over simulations. Any odd number may be used in re-setting the generator. The next **CREATE** command will draw observations from a uniform distribution with a range between 0 and 1. This distribution will be saved as a variable called V. Next, a **CREATE** command is used to create a variable called T which will be the square of two times V minus one if V is less than or equal to 0.5 or one minus the square of two times one minus V if V is greater than 0.5. It is this last command which transforms the continuous uniform distribution into a triangular distribution. The final command which requests the production of a histogram for V and T, confirms this (see figure 16.9).

Once the triangular distribution has been drawn, the individual-specific parameter estimates may be simulated using the following command:

```
CREATE
;Tbet=(-0.18870403 + 0.71645749*T)$
Histogram;rhs=Tbet$
```

The above command follows (16.1d) in assigning an individual to a specific location on a triangular-distributed random parameter. Note we have assumed a mean parameter estimate of −0.18870403 and a standard deviation parameter of 0.71645749 in simulating our hypothetical sample. The last command will produce a histogram of the individual parameter estimates for the hypothetical sample (figure 16.10).

As with the other distributions, the hypothetical individual specific parameter estimates may be found in the data set. These parameter estimates may then be exported and used in wider network models or to create a DSS aggregating over the entire simulated sample.

16.4.1 A note on using the lognormal distribution

In taking the log of a normal distribution, the result must be positive. The lognormal distribution must therefore produce positive parameter values which may be contrary to *a priori* expectations for certain attributes. We demonstrated this earlier without making comment. The observant reader may have noticed that the individual-level parameter estimates for *logbet* in figure 16.6 are all positive, despite the expectation that the parameter estimates for cost should be negative. When using the lognormal distribution for a random parameter for which we have an expectation that the individual-specific parameter estimates should be negative, the analyst must re-code the attribute such that the values it takes are multiplied by minus one. We show this in the following **CREATE** command where we create a new variable called F which is the negative of the fuel attribute. In the same **CREATE** command we also create a new variable named *park* which is the negative of the *parking*

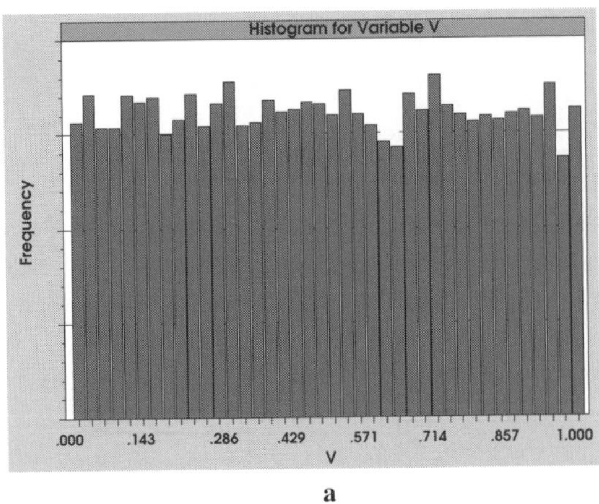

a

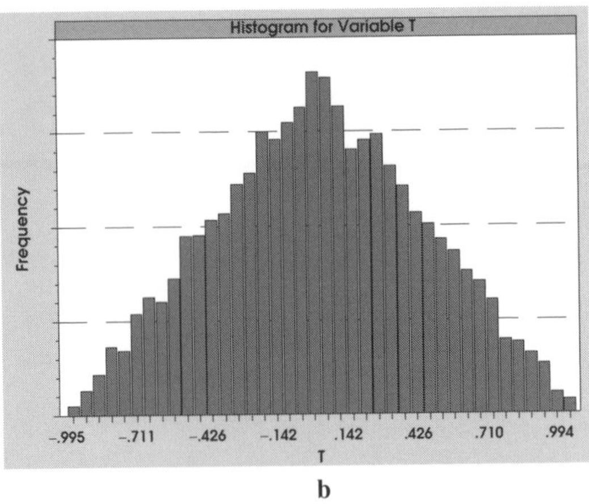

b

Figure 16.9 Transforming a uniform distribution into a triangular distribution
a. Continuous uniform distribution
b. Resulting triangular distribution

attribute:

```
CREATE
;f=-fuel
;park=-parking$
```

In estimating the ML model with a lognormal distribution assigned to an attribute for which we suspect that the sign should be negative, we use the newly created negative of the attribute variable. In the following example, we estimate an ML model with a lognormal distribution assigned to the random parameter estimate for the *fuel* and *parking* attributes for the both *car* alternatives. In specifying the model, we have specified generic parameters for the *car* alternatives and *public transport* alternatives. The exceptions to this are the *toll* and the constants which are specified as alternative-specific parameter estimates. The

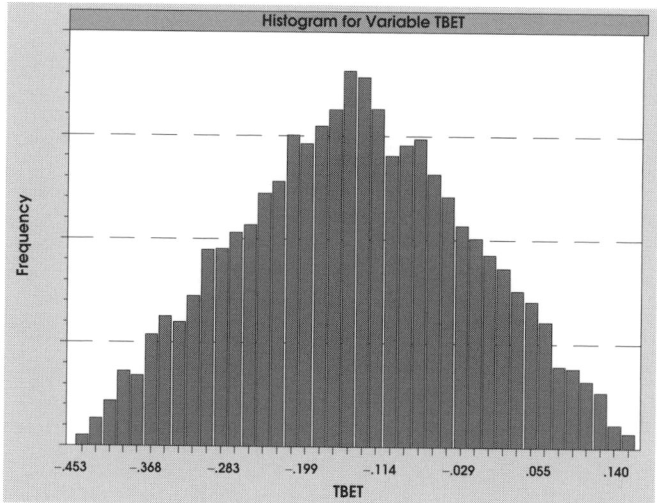

Figure 16.10 Histogram of hypothetical parameter estimates for a triangular distribution

model is estimated on the 30 minutes or less commuter segment with 100 SHS draws:

```
Calc;ran(12345)$
NLOGIT
;lhs = choice, cset, altij
;Choices = cart, carnt, bus, train, busway, LR
;Halton
;rpl
;fcn=cartc(l), park(l)
;pts=100
;Model:
U(cart) = asccart + cartc*F + cartt*time + toll*toll + park*park /
U(carnt) = asccarnt + cartc*F + cartt*time + park*park /
U(bus) = ascbus + ptf*fare + pttt*time /
U(train) = asctn + ptf*fare + pttt*time /
U(busway) = ascbusw +ptf*fare + pttt*time /
U(LR) = ptf*fare + pttt*time $
```

The above model specification produces the following results:

```
+----------------------------------------------+
| Random Parameters Logit Model                |
| Maximum Likelihood Estimates                 |
| Model estimated: Feb 30, 2003 at 03:45:00PM  |
| Dependent variable              CHOICE       |
| Weighting variable                None       |
```

```
| Number of observations                   9476      |
| Iterations completed                      101      |
| Log likelihood function             -2893.386      |
| Restricted log likelihood           -4244.678      |
| Chi squared                          2702.584      |
| Degrees of freedom                         13      |
| Prob[ChiSqd > value] =               .0000000      |
| R2=1-LogL/LogL*  Log-L fncn  R-sqrd  RsqAdj |
| No coefficients  -4244.6782  .31835  .31710 |
| Constants only.  Must be computed directly. |
|                  Use NLOGIT ;...; RHS=ONE $ |
| At start values  -2937.7224  .01509  .01329 |
| Response data are given as ind. choice.     |
+---------------------------------------------+

+---------------------------------------------+
| Random Parameters Logit Model               |
| Replications for simulated probs. = 100     |
| Halton sequences used for simulations       |
| Hessian was not PD. Using BHHH estimator.   |
| Number of obs.= 2369, skipped 0 bad obs.    |
+---------------------------------------------+
+----------+-------------+----------------+----------+----------+
| Variable | Coefficient | Standard Error | b/St.Er. | P[|Z|>z] |
+----------+-------------+----------------+----------+----------+
          Random parameters in utility functions
 CARTC     -4.17496133     2.25644644       -1.850     .0643
 PARK      -1.58329179      .19786924       -8.002     .0000
          Nonrandom parameters in utility functions
 ASCCART    4.05280340     1.16291814        3.485     .0005
 CARTT      -.05962105      .01723131       -3.460     .0005
 TOLL       -.40179755      .10378572       -3.871     .0001
 ASCCARNT   4.35637421     1.23024998        3.541     .0004
 ASCBUS      .20889679      .13321105        1.568     .1168
 PTF        -.34934581      .02931726      -11.916     .0000
 PTTT       -.05435348      .01223328       -4.443     .0000
 ASCTN       .04296112      .11657268         .369     .7125
 ASCBUSW     .13044046      .10148081        1.285     .1987
          Derived standard deviations of parameter distributions
 LsCARTC   11.6648879      5.22245165        2.234     .0255
 LsPARK     1.80582801      .38729966        4.663     .0000
```

The above model is statistically significant overall ($\chi^2 = 2702.584$ with 13 degrees of freedom) with a pseudo-R^2 of 0.31835. The mean of the *cartc* random parameter is not

	NUM	RNLN	CARTCP	PARKP	COSTPN	PARKPN
1 »	1	0.53487	7.87929	0.53934	-7.87929	-0.53934
2 »	2	0.789158	153.006	0.853672	-153.006	-0.853672
3 »	3	-0.921178	3.31249e-007	0.0388992	-3.31249e-007	-0.0388992
4 »	4	-0.301615	0.000455885	0.11908	-0.000455885	-0.11908
5 »	5	0.0406775	0.0247121	0.220946	-0.0247121	-0.220946
6 »	6	1.00284	1850.13	1.25566	-1850.13	-1.25566
7 »	7	0.514318	6.19971	0.519691	-6.19971	-0.519691
8 »	8	1.03924	2828.9	1.34097	-2828.9	-1.34097
9 »	9	-0.502558	4.37404e-005	0.0828417	-4.37404e-005	-0.0828417
10 »	10	-0.443441	8.71696e-005	0.0921746	-8.71696e-005	-0.0921746
11 »	11	-1.25443	6.79039e-009	0.02131	-6.79039e-009	-0.02131
12 »	12	-0.527586	3.26656e-005	0.0791809	-3.26656e-005	-0.0791809

Figure 16.11 Individual-specific parameter estimates derived from an unconditional lognormal random parameter

significantly different to zero, however the standard deviation parameter is (at alpha equal to 0.05). Both the mean and standard deviation parameters for the *park* random parameter are statistically significant at alpha equal to 0.05.

In simulating the individual-specific parameter estimates from the unconditional parameters given above, we use the previously described process, after taking the negative of each parameter. For the above example, the following commands may be used to do this:

```
Calc;ran(12345) $
CREATE ;rnln=rnn(0,1) $
CREATE
;cartcp=EXP(-4.17496133  + 11.6648879  *rnln)
;parkp=EXP(-1.58329179  + 1.80582801  *rnln) $
CREATE
;costpn=-1*cartcp
;parkpn=-1*parkp $
```

The newly created *costpn* and *parkpn* variables are those that should be used in wider application settings. Figure 16.11 shows how the new variables are stored in the data set.

16.5 Imposing constraints on a distribution

The ML models we have estimated above have been estimated with no restrictions placed upon the distributions from which the random parameter estimates are drawn. For several reasons it may be desirable (even necessary) to place restrictions on the random parameter distributions. Each random parameter has at least two population moments representing the mean and spread of the distribution from which it was drawn. The spread of the distribution, represented in the output as a standard deviation parameter, is unrestricted in the sense that it is left free to be estimated at whatever value the log likelihood function of the

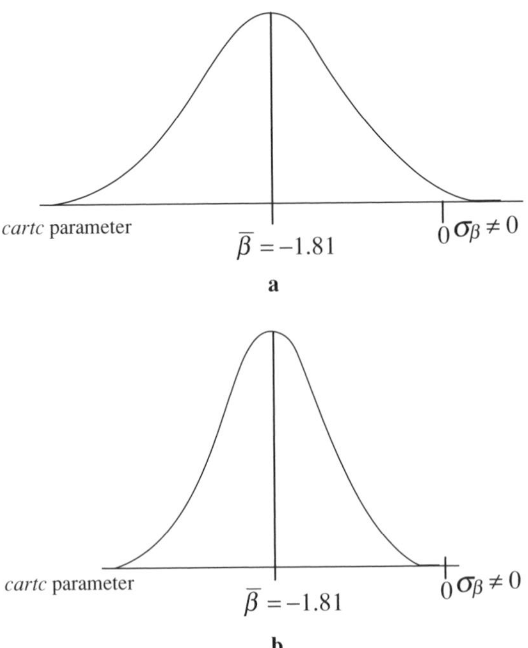

Figure 16.12 Placing a constraint upon the dispersion of the *cartc* random parameter estimate

model is maximized (or the negative log likelihood is minimized; see chapter 10). It is not unforeseeable that, in some instances, the spread of a distribution will be much smaller or much larger than that at which the negative log likelihood function is minimized. For instance, the distribution may be leptokurtic with the individual parameter estimates very close to the mean parameter estimate. That is, there are a greater number of observations immediately around the mean and less in the tails. Figure 16.12 contrasts a normal distribution (which is mesokurtic) with a leptokurtic distribution. The opposite, or platykurtic, distribution, where the individual parameter estimates are spread a great distance around the mean parameter estimate, is also possible (however, as we discuss shortly, this is not desirable).

To impose a constraint on the distribution from which individual-specific parameter estimates are drawn, the following command syntax is used (note that this option is available only to users of post-August 2003 release versions of NLOGIT):

;fcn = <parameter name>(<distribution label>, <constraint>)

When this command is used, the variance (or spread) of the distributions from which the random parameters are drawn takes on a value of $z \times \bar{\beta}$ (making the variance of the imposed distribution a function of the mean; see chapter 15). z may take any positive value; however, values greater than 1.0 may result in behaviorally meaningless parameter estimates (a particular problem observed more with normal distributions). It is therefore suggested that the value entered within the above command syntax be between 0 and 1 (if 1, the variance of the distribution is made equal to the mean). To demonstrate, the following command specifies that the value of z be 0.5 and hence, the variance of the toll attribute (triangularly distributed) will be exactly half that of the mean:

```
;fcn=toll(t,0.5)
```

As an aside, the analyst may use the asterisk as a special case to specify z as two for triangular distributions only. That is, **;fcn=toll(t,*)** the same as **;fcn=toll(t,2)** for triangular distributions.

We use the above constraint to estimate the following ML model:

```
Calc;ran(12345)$
NLOGIT
;lhs = choice, cset, altij
;Choices = cart, carnt, bus, train, busway, LR
;Halton
;rpl
;fcn=toll(t,0.5),cartc(n)
;pts=10
;Model:
U(cart) = asccart + cartc*fuel + cartt*time + toll*toll/
U(carnt) = asccarnt + carntc*fuel + carntt*time /
U(bus) = ascbus + bsc*fare + bst*time /
U(train) = asctn + tnc*fare + tnt*time /
U(busway) = ascbusw + bswc*fare + bswt*time /
U(LR) = lrc*fare + lrt*time $
```

Ignoring the initial MNL model, the following ML model results are produced using the 30 minutes or less commuter segment of the mode-choice case study:

```
+----------------------------------------------+
| Random Parameters Logit Model                |
| Maximum Likelihood Estimates                 |
| Model estimated: Feb 30, 2003 at 04:00:00PM. |
| Dependent variable                CHOICE     |
| Weighting variable                  None     |
| Number of observations              9476     |
| Iterations completed                  26     |
| Log likelihood function        -3185.047     |
| Restricted log likelihood      -4244.678     |
| Chi squared                     2119.262     |
| Degrees of freedom                    19     |
| Prob[ChiSqd > value] =          .0000000     |
| R2=1-LogL/LogL*   Log-L fncn  R-sqrd  RsqAdj |
| No coefficients   -4244 .6782 .24964  .24763 |
```

```
| Constants only.    Must be computed directly.  |
|                    Use NLOGIT ;...; RHS=ONE $  |
| At start values -3187.0518    .00063 -.00205   |
| Response data are given as ind. choice.        |
+------------------------------------------------+
+------------------------------------------------+
| Random Parameters Logit Model                  |
| Replications for simulated probs. = 10         |
| Halton sequences used for simulations          |
| Number of obs.= 2369, skipped 0 bad obs.       |
+------------------------------------------------+

+----------+-------------+----------------+----------+----------+
| Variable | Coefficient | Standard Error | b/St.Er. | P[|Z|>z] |
+----------+-------------+----------------+----------+----------+
         Random parameters in utility functions
 TOLL      -.18589573      .06655981       -2.793     .0052
 CARTC     -.17764099      .08847430       -2.008     .0447
         Nonrandom parameters in utility functions
 ASCCART   -.82672842      .43109769       -1.918     .0551
 CARTT      .01133991      .02456541         .462     .6444
 ASCCARNT   .03714388      .45273764         .082     .9346
 CARNTC    -.09962415      .05789144       -1.721     .0853
 CARNTT    -.03538734      .01172597       -3.018     .0025
 ASCBUS    -.46420751      .42332734       -1.097     .2728
 BSC       -.18085377      .04633328       -3.903     .0001
 BST       -.01647995      .01854661        -.889     .3742
 ASCTN      .46591993      .39682394        1.174     .2403
 TNC       -.20714163      .04652294       -4.452     .0000
 TNT       -.07911114      .01888257       -4.190     .0000
 ASCBUSW    .41580545      .38647888        1.076     .2820
 BSWC      -.26800506      .04218543       -6.353     .0000
 BSWT      -.05591574      .01646810       -3.395     .0007
 LRC       -.25351362      .04232836       -5.989     .0000
 LRT       -.03609439      .01680700       -2.148     .0317
         Derived standard deviations of parameter distributions
 TsTOLL     .09294787      .03327991        2.793     .0052
 NsCARTC    .27263847      .13604768        2.004     .0451
```

As with the first ML model example, the overall model is statistically significant (Chi-square value of 2119.262 with 19 degrees of freedom) and has an acceptable model fit (pseudo-R^2 value of 0.24964). Comparison of the adjusted pseudo-R^2 and log likelihood function at model convergence of this model with that of the first model estimated suggests a slight worsening in the overall model fit.

Examining the results for the random parameters, the parameters representing the sample means for both are statistically significant and of the expected sign. This represents no change from the previous model, in which no constraint was imposed on the distribution from which the *toll* random parameter was drawn. Examination of the spread of the random parameters, however, suggests that where once all information about the *toll* parameter was explained solely by the mean of the *toll* sample population parameter, there now exist observable levels of heterogeneity at the individual level. Whereas before we were unable to observe any statistically significant heterogeneity within the sample population for this parameter, by imposing a different empirical distribution (via a constraint as opposed to a different distributional form) we are now able to detect preference heterogeneity within the sampled population for the *toll* attribute.

As an aside, note that the parameter estimate for the standard deviation of the *toll* parameter is exactly half that of the absolute value of the mean *toll* parameter estimate (i.e. 0.09294787 is exactly half of $|-0.18589573|$). The significance level (i.e. the t- and p-value) statistics for the mean and standard deviation parameters of the random *toll* parameter are exactly the same. It is worth noting that imposing a spread equal to the mean in the triangular distribution guarantees the same sign for the parameter estimate across the entire distribution. This is useful where a change of sign does not make sense.

As before, the marginal utilities for the random parameters may be written out in the form of (16.1b) and (16.1d):

$$\text{Toll} = -0.18589573 + 0.09294787 \times \text{t}$$
$$\text{Cartc} = -0.17764099 + 0.27263847 \times \text{N}$$

The full system of utility functions becomes:

$$V_{cart} = -0.82672842 + (-0.17764099 + 0.27263847 \times N) \times \text{CARTC} + 0.01133991 \times \text{CARTT} + (-0.18589573 + 0.09294787 \times \text{t}) \times \text{TOLL}$$

$$V_{carnt} = 0.03714388 - 0.09962415 \times \text{CARNTC} - 0.03538734 \times \text{CARNTT}$$

$$V_{bus} = -0.46420751 - 0.18085377 \times \text{BSC} - 0.01647995 \times \text{BST}$$

$$V_{train} = 0.46591993 - 0.20714163 \times \text{TNC} - 0.07911114 \times \text{TNT}$$

$$V_{busway} = 0.41580545 - 0.26800506 \times \text{BSWC} - 0.05591574 \times \text{BSWT}$$

$$V_{LR} = -0.25351362 \times \text{LRC} - 0.03609439 \times \text{LRT}$$

The ability to place restrictions upon the distributions from which random parameter estimates are drawn means that even for random parameter estimates without a significant standard deviation parameter, that preference heterogeneity may exist but is not detectable without the placing of a constraint. This means that the analyst may have to estimate a number of models, changing not only the distributional forms of the random parameter estimates, but also testing various restrictions before being satisfied that no preference heterogeneity is present over the sampled population.

16.6 Revealing preference heterogeneity around the mean of a random parameter

In previous sections, we demonstrated how the ML model may be used to determine whether there exists heterogeneity around the mean population parameter through the estimation of a standard deviation parameter associated with each random parameter estimate. One of the appeals of the ML model is its ability to determine the possible *sources* of any heterogeneity that may exist. This is accomplished through the interaction of each random parameter with other attributes or variables that one suspects may be possible sources of preference heterogeneity (for example, if one suspects that observed heterogeneity in a price parameter may be the result of gender differences, one may interact the price random parameter with a variable indicating each respondent's gender to determine if this indeed the case). Rather than create the interactions through the data (as per chapter 10), the heterogeneity around the mean interaction effects are estimated using the following command syntax:

;rpl = <variable name>

In the previous sections, the **rpl** command was given without = **<variable name>**. If this segment of the command is omitted, the ML model will be estimated without attempting to reveal any possible causes of heterogeneity that may be observed.

The variable (attribute or SDC) named in the above command need not be a variable that appears in the utility specifications, nor in the **;fcn** command specification. Any variable in the data set can be used. For example, in the previously estimated models, the following **;rpl** could have been used despite the *pincome* variable not being present anywhere within the model specification:

;rpl = pincome

It is also possible to name multiple variables within the above command. Each additional variable is separated by a comma (,) as shown below:

;rpl=<variable name 1>, <variable name 2>, . . . , <variable name i>

For example (note that *fuel* was included as an attribute in the previous model specification):

;rpl = fuel, pincome

As mentioned above, variables named in the **;rpl** command are interacted with the random parameters specified in the **;fcn** function to determine the presence of preference heterogeneity around the mean of the random parameters. For example, the commands:

;rpl = fuel, pincome
;fcn=toll(t),cartc(n)

will produce the following interaction effects:

toll(t) × *fuel,*
toll(t) × *pincome*
cartc(n) × *fuel*
cartc(n) × *pincome*

Rather than estimate interaction effects for all random parameters, the analyst may restrict the interaction effects which are estimated through the **fcn** command. For example, it is possible that the analyst may not wish to test for preference heterogeneity around the mean of the random parameter of the fuel attribute. To restrict the set of interaction effects estimated, the analyst places the distribution label inside square brackets (**[ ]**) instead of the customary round brackets. For example:

```
;rpl = fuel, pincome
;fcn=toll(t),cartc[n]
```

will produce the following interaction effects only:

toll(t) × *fuel,*
toll(t) × *pincome*

while still estimating the *cartc* parameter as a random parameter estimate drawn from a normal distribution.

As an aside, an equivalent way to handle the above is to use round brackets but indicate with a hash symbol (**#**) separated by a straight line (**|**) which interaction effects are not to be estimated. That is

```
;rpl = fuel, pincome
;fcn=toll(t),cartc(n | #)
```

will produce the same interaction effects as mentioned above.

To demonstrate the above, we estimate the following model using all SP observations (i.e. all commuting segments) of the mode case choice study. To re-set the sample, the following syntax is required:

```
Sample;all$
Reject;sprp=1$
Dstats;rhs=*$
```

As an aside, it is often useful to include the **Dstats** command when using the **Reject** or **Sample;all** commands in order to check that the data are being correctly read by NLOGIT.

In the model that follows, we test for two possible sources of heterogeneity in the *cartt* and *carntt* random parameters (but not the *tnt* random parameter) around the mean using the covariates trip length (*splength*) and personal income levels (*pincome*):

```
Calc;ran(12345)$
NLOGIT
;lhs = choice, cset, altij
```

```
;Choices = cart, carnt, bus, train, busway, LR
;Halton
;rpl=splength,pincome
;fcn=cartt(t),carntt(n),tnt[u]
;pts=10
;Model:
U(cart) = asccart + cartc*fuel + cartt*time + toll*toll /
U(carnt) = asccarnt + carntc*fuel + carntt*time /
U(bus) = ascbus + bsc*fare + bst*time /
U(train) = asctn + tnc*fare + tnt*time /
U(busway) = ascbusw + bswc*fare + bswt*time /
U(LR) = lrc*fare + lrt*time $
```

For the complete SP data set, the following model results are produced (omitting the initial MNL model results):

```
+-----------------------------------------------+
| Random Parameters Logit Model                  |
| Maximum Likelihood Estimates                   |
| Model estimated: Feb 30, 2003 at 04:15:00PM.  |
| Dependent variable                  CHOICE     |
| Weighting variable                    None     |
| Number of observations               14456     |
| Iterations completed                    49     |
| Log likelihood function          -4762.570     |
| Restricted log likelihood        -6475.419     |
| Chi squared                       3425.697     |
| Degrees of freedom                      25     |
| Prob[ChiSqd > value] =            .0000000     |
| R2=1-LogL/LogL*  Log-L fncn  R-sqrd  RsqAdj    |
| No coefficients  -6475 .4187 .26452  .26282    |
| Constants only.  Must be computed directly.    |
|                  Use NLOGIT ;...; RHS=ONE $    |
| At start values  -4771.6360  .00190 -.00041    |
| Response data are given as ind. choice.        |
+-----------------------------------------------+

+-----------------------------------------------+
| Random Parameters Logit Model                  |
| Replications for simulated probs. = 10         |
| Halton sequences used for simulations          |
| Hessian was not PD. Using BHHH estimator.      |
| Number of obs.= 3614,  skipped   0 bad obs.    |
+-----------------------------------------------+
```

```
+----------+------------+---------------+---------+---------+
| Variable | Coefficient | Standard Error | b/St.Er. | P[|Z|>z] |
+----------+------------+---------------+---------+---------+
          Random parameters in utility functions
CARTT        -.08865192      .02203655     -4.023     .0001
CARNTT       -.04589967      .00791793     -5.797     .0000
TNT          -.02806206      .00864399     -3.246     .0012
          Nonrandom parameters in utility functions
ASCCART      -.10448942      .24573099      -.425     .6707
CARTC        -.13981358      .04446617     -3.144     .0017
TOLL         -.11348288      .04966514     -2.285     .0223
ASCCARNT      .12419677      .19819848       .627     .5309
CARNTC       -.12743794      .02702014     -4.716     .0000
ASCBUS       -.17396980      .22206779      -.783     .4334
BSC          -.18295311      .03554486     -5.147     .0000
BST          -.04976854      .00883185     -5.635     .0000
ASCTN        -.39830338      .20152316     -1.976     .0481
TNC          -.22543298      .03537086     -6.373     .0000
ASCBUSW      -.28212809      .18618442     -1.515     .1297
BSWC         -.22703642      .03204485     -7.085     .0000
BSWT         -.02816057      .00770748     -3.654     .0003
LRC          -.28266136      .03270256     -8.643     .0000
LRT          -.04275156      .00783880     -5.454     .0000
          Heterogeneity in mean, Parameter:Variable
CART:SPL     -.01496405      .00476248     -3.142     .0017
CART:PIN      .00059994      .00021231      2.826     .0047
CARN:SPL     -.00140865      .00215290      -.654     .5129
CARN:PIN      .00012859      .00010958      1.173     .2406
TNT:SPL       .000000      ......(Fixed Parameter)...........
TNT:PIN       .000000      ......(Fixed Parameter)...........
          Derived standard deviations of parameter distributions
TsCARTT       .18346155      .05002020      3.668     .0002
NsCARNTT      .01269689      .00806823      1.574     .1156
UsTNT         .00650307      .03448356       .189     .8504

Parameter Matrix for Heterogeneity in Means.

Matrix Delta    has  3 rows and  2 columns.
                 SPLENGTH          PINCOME
              +--------------------------
CARTT         |   -.01496         .00060
CARNTT        |   -.00141         .00013
TNT           | .0000000D+00   .0000000D+00
```

The overall model is statistically significant (Chi-square value of 3425.697 with 25 degrees of freedom). The dependent variable for this model includes all SP observations, hence the adjusted pseudo-R^2 of this model is not directly comparable to that of the previous estimated models (the adjusted pseudo-R^2 is directly comparable only if the model has been estimated using the same dependent variable, which in this instance, despite being estimated using the same data set, is not the case). The overall model fit for this model obtained from the pseudo-R^2 is 0.26452, which is statistically acceptable for this class of model (see figure 10.7).

Examining the output pertaining to the random parameters, the mean sample population parameter estimates are all statistically significant and of the correct sign. Nevertheless, only the spread or dispersion of the *cartt* attribute is statistically significant, suggesting that all information for the *carntt* and *tnt* attributes is captured within their respective means (the distributions of sample population random parameter estimates (statistically) collapse to their respective means). Also provided in the output are interaction effects between the random parameter estimates and covariates named in the **rpl** command. We reproduce these results below:

Heterogeneity in mean, Parameter:Variable

Variable	Coefficient	Standard Error	b/St.Er.	P[|Z|>z]
CART:SPL	-.01496405	.00476248	-3.142	.0017
CART:PIN	.00059994	.00021231	2.826	.0047
CARN:SPL	-.00140865	.00215290	-.654	.5129
CARN:PIN	.00012859	.00010958	1.173	.2406
TNT:SPL	.000000	......(Fixed Parameter)...........		
TNT:PIN	.000000	......(Fixed Parameter)...........		

The interaction terms obtained by interacting random parameters with other covariates in effect decompose any heterogeneity observed within the random parameter, offering an explanation as to why that heterogeneity may exist. For example, if the *toll(t)* × *pincome* interaction term is found to be statistically significant, then the model suggests that differences in the marginal utilities held for the *toll* attribute may be, in part, explained by differences in personal income levels. The interaction terms between the covariates named and the *tnt* random parameter were not estimated (i.e. we used square brackets in specifying the *tnt* distribution within the **;fcn** specification). NLOGIT reports the parameter estimate for these interactions as being fixed (at zero). The *carntt* random parameter was observed to have an insignificant spread (it collapsed to its mean) indicating no heterogeneity (at least that we could observe, given the distribution from which the parameter was derived). Given this result, it is not surprising to observe that interacting the *carntt* random parameter with the trip length and personal income-level covariates produces a statistically insignificant result (although, as we show later, instances where the standard deviation parameter is not statistically significant but heterogeneity around the mean is still observed are possible).

Neither trip length nor personal income explain preference heterogeneity in the *carntt* random parameter; however, both the *cartt* × trip length and *cartt* × person income-level interactions are statistically significant (Wald-statistic values of −3.142 and 2.826, respectively). The heterogeneity in the mean parameter estimate for the *cartt*×trip length of −0.015 suggests that across the sampled population, the sensitivity to travel times with regard to traveling in a car along a toll road increases as the length of trip increases, *ceteris paribus*. That is, individuals with larger trip times are more sensitive to travel times. The statistically significant and positive *cartt* × person income-level parameter suggests that as personal income increases, sampled individuals tend to have individual specific travel time parameter estimates that are closer to zero. This suggests that higher-income individuals tend to be less time-sensitive as those with smaller incomes tend to have marginal utilities further from zero.

The last output provided by NLOGIT (under the heading **Parameter Matrix for Heterogeneity in Means**) is a reproduction of the heterogeneity in the mean parameter estimates observed in the main output.

The inclusion of the heterogeneity around the mean parameter estimates requires that they be included within the marginal utilities for each attribute estimated as a random parameter, as per (15.7a)–(15.7d). The marginal utilities for the above model are:

$$\begin{aligned}
\text{CARTT} &= -0.08865192 - 0.01496405 \times SPL + 0.00059994 \times PINC \\
&\quad + 0.18346155 \times t \\
\text{CARNTT} &= -0.04589967 - 0.00140865 \times SPL + 0.00012859 \times PINC \\
&\quad + 0.01269689 \times N \\
\text{TNT} &= -0.02806206 + 0.00650307 \times u
\end{aligned}$$

These may then be used to write out the utility functions as a whole.

As an aside, NLOGIT makes use of the first four characters of parameters named within the **;fcn** specification only. This may cause problems if the first four characters of two or more random parameters are exactly the same. For example, assuming that the two *car travel* parameters were named cartt1 and cartt2 instead of *cartt* and *carntt*, respectively, the **fcn** specification would look as follows:

```
;fcn=cartt1(t),cartt2(n),tnt[u]
```

As NLOGIT examines the first four characters only, the program will be unable to distinguish between the two car travel time random parameters. In the estimation process, NLOGIT will assume that the parameter that appears first in the utility specification (in this case it would be *cartt1*) is the parameter for which the test of heterogeneity around the mean is to be applied. While it is possible that the analyst may wish this to be the case, NLOGIT will also assume that the *cartt2* random parameter is the *cartt1* parameter and estimate the test of heterogeneity around the mean for the *cartt1* random parameter a second time. As such, the test will be applied twice to the *cartt1* random parameter and not at all to the *cartt2* random parameter. In estimating the test for the *carrtt1* twice, the model results will be meaningless (recall that the estimation of one parameter impacts upon the estimation of all other parameters estimated as part of the model; this applies even for heterogeneity in the mean parameter estimates).

Using the same model specification above but renaming the car travel time parameters to *cartt1* and *cartt2*, the following heterogeneity around the mean parameter estimates are produced, demonstrating our discussion above:

	Heterogeneity in mean, Parameter:Variable			
CART:SPL	−.1037808495E-02	.19907584E-02	−.521	.6021
CART:PIN	.9346630381E-04	.10493456E-03	.891	.3731
CART:SPL	−.1037808495E-02	.19907584E-02	−.521	.6021
CART:PIN	.9346630381E-04	.10493456E-03	.891	.3731
TNT:SPL	.0000000000	........(Fixed Parameter).......		
TNT:PIN	.0000000000	........(Fixed Parameter).......		

The analyst may also ask that a random parameter estimate not be interacted with a given covariate while at the same time imposing a restriction on that same random parameter's distribution. For example, either of the following commands will restrict NLOGIT from interacting the *tnt* random parameter with named covariates while at the same time imposing the restriction that the variance of the distribution be a quarter of the mean:

```
;fcn=cartt(t),carntt(n),tnt(u } #,0.25)
```

or

```
;fcn=cartt(t),carntt(n),tnt[u,0.25]
```

As an aside, when the sign of a parameter needs to be preserved over the entire distribution, we can impose a constraint on the standard deviation or spread (in the case of a triangular distribution we set the **mean-spread**). Unfortunately, when we add in heterogeneity around the mean as shown above, the preservation of the sign is not guaranteed.

16.6.1 Using the non-stochastic distribution

Consider the following model estimated on the 30 minutes or less commuter travel data. The model is estimated with the *toll* and *cartc* coefficients being treated as random parameter estimates (drawn from triangular and normal distributions respectively). Both random coefficients are interacted with a single level of an effects coded city specific variable representing Canberra. The interacted variable takes the value one if the sampled individual is from Canberra, minus one if from Perth, and zero if from another major Australian city. Ten SHS intelligent draws are used and the maximum number of iterations allowed is 50:

```
Calc;ran(12345)$
NLOGIT
;lhs = choice, cset, altij
;Choices = cart, carnt, bus, train, busway, LR
;Halton
;rpl=can
;fcn=toll(t),cartc(n)
;Maxit=50
;pts=10
;Model:
```

U(cart) = asccart + cartc*fuel + cartt*time + toll*toll /
U(carnt) = asccarnt + carntc*fuel + carntt*time /
U(bus) = ascbus + bsc*fare + bst*time /
U(train) = asctn + tnc*fare + tnt*time /
U(busway) = ascbusw + bswc*fare + bswt*time /
U(LR) = lrc*fare + lrt*time $

The above model produces the following parameter estimates:

```
+----------------------------------------------+
| Random Parameters Logit Model                |
| Maximum Likelihood Estimates                 |
| Model estimated: Feb 30, 2003 at 04:30:00PM. |
| Dependent variable              CHOICE       |
| Weighting variable                None       |
| Number of observations            9476       |
| Iterations completed                29       |
| Log likelihood function      -3182.422       |
| Restricted log likelihood    -4244.678       |
| Chi squared                   2124.512       |
| Degrees of freedom                  22       |
| Prob[ChiSqd > value] =        .0000000       |
| R2=1-LogL/LogL* Log-L fncn R-sqrd    RsqAdj  |
| No coefficients -4244.6782 .25026    .24793  |
| Constants only. Must be computed  directly.  |
|                Use NLOGIT ;...; RHS=ONE  $   |
| At start values -3186.9971 .00144   -.00167  |
| Response data are given as ind. choice.      |
+----------------------------------------------+
+----------------------------------------------+
| Random Parameters Logit Model                |
| Replications for simulated probs. = 10       |
| Halton sequences used for simulations        |
| Hessian was not PD. Using BHHH estimator.    |
| Number of obs.=  2369, skipped   0 bad obs.  |
+----------------------------------------------+
+---------+-------------+---------------+--------+---------+
|Variable | Coefficient | Standard Error |b/St.Er.|P[|Z|>z] |
+---------+-------------+---------------+--------+---------+
         Random parameters in utility functions
TOLL      -.20028619       .07244104      -2.765    .0057
CARTC     -.18376792       .10325811      -1.780    .0751
         Nonrandom parameters in utility functions
ASCCART   -.80101205       .43173914      -1.855    .0636
```

```
CARTT         .01112197        .02492568          .446     .6554
ASCCARNT      .03797069        .45514430          .083     .9335
CARNTC       -.09804454        .05823141        -1.684     .0922
CARNTT       -.03561894        .01167120        -3.052     .0023
ASCBUS       -.45796211        .42352748        -1.081     .2796
BSC          -.18116905        .04802885        -3.772     .0002
BST          -.01662225        .01888081         -.880     .3787
ASCTN         .46573188        .39733852         1.172     .2411
TNC          -.20735600        .04536067        -4.571     .0000
TNT          -.07890522        .01890510        -4.174     .0000
ASCBUSW       .41442376        .39091391         1.060     .2891
BSWC         -.26912231        .04247220        -6.336     .0000
BSWT         -.05542031        .01648419        -3.362     .0008
LRC          -.25403903        .04236176        -5.997     .0000
LRT          -.03585608        .01708013        -2.099     .0358
             Heterogeneity in mean, Parameter:Variable
TOLL:CAN     -.24531250        .15154530        -1.619     .1055
CART:CAN      .20334407        .09247040         2.199     .0279
             Derived standard deviations of parameter distributions
TsTOLL       .14509583        .98287789           .148     .8826
NsCARTC      .28949471        .17395809          1.664     .0961

Parameter Matrix for Heterogeneity in Means.

Matrix Delta     has   2  rows and      1 columns.
             CAN
            +-------------
TOLL        |     -.24531
CARTC       |      .20334
```

The overall model is statistically significant with a Chi-square statistic of 2124.512 against a Chi-square critical value of 33.924 (with 22 degrees of freedom at alpha equal to 0.05). Examination of the mean of the random parameter estimates suggests that the sample population mean estimate for the *toll* parameter is statistically different to zero while the mean of the *cartc* random parameter is not. At alpha equal to 0.05, neither standard deviation parameter is statistically significantly different to zero. Ignoring the heterogeneity around the mean parameter estimates, the above model would suggest that, over the population, the marginal utility for the *toll* attribute should collapse to a single non-zero value (and hence the coefficient should be treated as if a non-random parameter; increasing the number of draws or respecifying the distributional form adopted may result in a different finding) while the marginal utility for the *cartc* attribute is zero over the entire sample population.

Examination of the heterogeneity around the mean parameter estimates, however, suggests that despite a lack of evidence for the existence of heterogeneity in the marginal utilities held for the *cartc* attribute over the sampled population (the standard deviation parameter estimate is statistically equal to zero), there does exist some heterogeneity around the mean parameter estimate. This intuitively unappealing result suggests the presence of heterogeneity that is not captured by the distributional form used to estimate the random parameter. In such cases, the analyst may: (1) test other mixing distributions, (2) increase the number of draws used, (3) test for the existence of correlation between the random parameters (see sub-section 16.6.2), (4) combine some or all of the aforementioned strategies, and/or (5) impose a non-stochastic distribution upon the afflicted random coefficient.

A *non-stochastic* (stochastic meaning random, hence non-stochastic meaning non-random) *distribution* is a distribution that does not conform in terms of shape or form to one of the more common distributions used (i.e. normal, lognormal, triangular, or uniform). The advantage of using a non-stochastic distribution to estimate a random parameter is that no distribution is imposed upon the random coefficient *a priori*. This allows for tests of heterogeneity around the mean of a random parameter estimate without having to worry about the distribution from which it was drawn. The disadvantage in using a non-stochastic distribution to estimate a random parameter is that with no known distribution form from which the random parameters are drawn, the spread around the mean value cannot be estimated (i.e. the standard deviation parameter is fixed at zero).

To demonstrate the non-stochastic distribution, consider the following model, equivalent to the previously estimated model, with the exception that the *cartc* random parameter is drawn from a non-stochastic distribution:

```
Calc;ran(12345)$
NLOGIT
;lhs = choice, cset, altij
;Choices = cart, carnt, bus, train, busway, LR
;Halton
;rpl=can
;fcn=toll(t),cartc(c)
;pts=10
;Model:
U(cart) = asccart + cartc*fuel + cartt*time + toll*toll /
U(carnt) = asccarnt + carntc*fuel + carntt*time /
U(bus) = ascbus + bsc*fare + bst*time /
U(train) = asctn + tnc*fare + tnt*time /
U(busway) = ascbusw + bswc*fare + bswt*time /
U(LR) = lrc*fare + lrt*time $
```

```
+----------------------------------------------+
| Random Parameters Logit Model                |
| Maximum Likelihood Estimates                 |
| Model estimated: Feb 30, 2003 at 04:45:00PM. |
| Dependent variable                CHOICE     |
| Weighting variable                  None     |
| Number of observations              9476     |
| Iterations completed                  25     |
```

```
| Log likelihood function          -3184.669         |
| Restricted log likelihood        -4244.678         |
| Chi squared                       2120.018         |
| Degrees of freedom                      21         |
| Prob[ChiSqd > value] =            .0000000         |
| R2=1-LogL/LogL*    Log-L fncn  R-sqrd  RsqAdj      |
| No coefficients    -4244.6782  .24973  .24750      |
| Constants only.    Must be computed directly.      |
|                    Use NLOGIT ;...; RHS=ONE $      |
| At start values   -3186.9971   .00073 -.00223      |
| Response data are given as ind. choice.            |
+----------------------------------------------------+

+----------------------------------------------------+
| Random Parameters Logit Model                      |
| Replications for simulated probs. = 10             |
| Halton sequences used for simulations              |
| Hessian was not PD. Using BHHH estimator.          |
| Number of obs.= 2369,    skipped  0 bad obs.       |
+----------------------------------------------------+

+---------+-------------+----------------+---------+----------+
|Variable | Coefficient | Standard Error | b/St.Er.| P[|Z|>z] |
+---------+-------------+----------------+---------+----------+
          Random parameters in utility functions
TOLL      -.18566994      .06533914      -2.842     .0045
CARTC     -.10531656      .05858765      -1.798     .0722
          Nonrandom parameters in utility functions
ASCCART   -.87747643      .41277741      -2.126     .0335
CARTT      .01172873      .02344891        .500     .6169
ASCCARNT   .05659805      .45107112        .125     .9001
CARNTC    -.10066074      .05769445      -1.745     .0810
CARNTT    -.03539173      .01154649      -3.065     .0022
ASCBUS    -.47185498      .41964840      -1.124     .2608
BSC       -.17894152      .04770815      -3.751     .0002
BST       -.01534620      .01869325       -.821     .4117
ASCTN      .47731400      .39562432       1.206     .2276
TNC       -.20729552      .04507074      -4.599     .0000
TNT       -.07865361      .01872860      -4.200     .0000
ASCBUSW    .42602818      .38884127       1.096     .2732
BSWC      -.26622652      .04212233      -6.320     .0000
BSWT      -.05613036      .01636004      -3.431     .0006
LRC       -.25191966      .04198087      -6.001     .0000
LRT       -.03541045      .01695181      -2.089     .0367
```

```
              Heterogeneity in mean, Parameter:Variable
TOLL:CAN      -.21679543        .14136321        -1.534    .1251
CART:CAN       .18102804        .08334663         2.172    .0299
              Derived standard deviations of parameter distributions
TsTOLL         .07116718       1.22946563          .058    .9538
CsCARTC          .000000    ......(Fixed Parameter)..........

Parameter Matrix for Heterogeneity in Means.

Matrix  Delta   has   2 rows and  1 columns.
          CAN
         +--------------
TOLL     |     -.21680
CARTC    |      .18103
```

The overall model is statistically significant (Chi-square value of 2120.018 compared against a critical Chi-square value of 32.671 with 21 degrees of freedom taken at alpha equal to 0.05). As with the previous model, the mean of the *toll* random parameter is statistically significant as is the standard deviation parameter representing preference heterogeneity over the sampled population. Similar also to the previously estimated model, the mean of the *cartc* random parameter is not statistically significant; however, in this model, the standard deviation of the parameter is fixed at zero. The heterogeneity around the mean parameter estimate for the *toll* parameter remains statistically insignificant; however, the heterogeneity around the mean parameter estimate for the *cartc* random parameter is statistically significant. The model suggests that heterogeneity in the marginal utilities held for this attribute across the sampled population does exist; however, the distributional form taken by such heterogeneity is indeterminate.

As an aside, the use of the non-stochastic or constant distribution is useful when the analyst wishes to include statistically significant parameters for heterogeneity around the mean in the presence of a statistically insignificant standard deviation parameter. The only way to include the heterogeneity around the mean in NLOGIT is to use the **;rpl** command.

16.6.2 Handling insignificant heterogeneity around the mean parameter estimates

When used in the manner described above, the **;rpl=<variable name n>** specification is used to interact each of the named variables in the specification with each of the random parameter estimates, except when square brackets are used in defining the random parameter distributions. For the model specified, the interaction terms that are estimated are either estimated for all random parameters (if the random parameter distribution is specified in round (i.e. **( )**) brackets) or for a sub-set of random parameter estimates (if the random parameter mixing distribution is specified in square (i.e. **[ ]**) brackets).

Consider the following model estimated on the entire SP sample. In the model, the *tnt* and *carntc* parameters are estimated as random parameter estimates drawn from normal and triangular distributions, respectively. Three covariates are tested as possible sources of heterogeneity around the means of each of the random parameter estimates. The three covariates, *can*, *mel*, and *syd* represent city-specific effects coded variables such that if a sampled individual is from Perth, all three equal minus one, if the sampled individual is from Canberra, *can* equals one, if from Melbourne, *mel* equals one, and if from Sydney, *syd* equals one. If the sampled respondent is from another Australian city, *can*, *mel*, and *syd* simultaneously take the value of zero. Twenty SHS draws are used in the estimation process:

```
NLOGIT
;lhs = choice, cset, altij
;Choices = cart, carnt, bus, train, busway, LR
;Halton
;rpl=can,mel,syd
;fcn=tnt(n),carntc(t)
;pts=20
;Model:
U(cart) = asccart + cartc*fuel + cartt*time + toll*toll/
U(carnt) = asccarnt + carntc*fuel + carntt*time /
U(bus) = ascbus + bsc*fare + bst*time /
U(train) = asctn + tnc*fare + tnt*time /
U(busway) = ascbusw + bswc*fare + bswt*time /
U(LR) = lrc*fare + lrt*time $
```

The following output is generated for the above command syntax:

```
+---------------------------------------------+
| Random Parameters Logit Model               |
| Maximum Likelihood Estimates                |
| Model estimated: Feb 30, 2003 at 05:00:00PM.|
| Dependent variable               CHOICE     |
| Weighting variable                 None     |
| Number of observations             9476     |
| Iterations completed                 43     |
| Log likelihood function       -3172.205     |
| Restricted log likelihood     -4244.678     |
| Chi squared                    2144.946     |
| Degrees of freedom                   26     |
| Prob[ChiSqd > value] =         .0000000     |
| R2=1-LogL/LogL*   Log-L  fncn R-sqrd RsqAdj |
| No coefficients   -4244.6782  .25266 .24992 |
| Constants only.   Must be computed directly.|
|                   Use NLOGIT ;...; RHS=ONE $|
| At start values   -3186.9971  .00464 .00099 |
| Response data are given as ind. choice.     |
+---------------------------------------------+
```

```
+------------------------------------------+
| Random Parameters Logit Model            |
| Replications for simulated probs. = 20   |
| Halton sequences used for simulations    |
| Hessian was not PD. Using BHHH estimator.|
| Number of obs.= 2369, skipped 0 bad obs. |
+------------------------------------------+
```

Variable	Coefficient	Standard Error	b/St.Er.	P[|Z|>z]
	Random parameters in utility functions			
TNT	-.08161559	.02429821	-3.359	.0008
CARNTC	-.42272240	.23093769	-1.830	.0672
	Nonrandom parameters in utility functions			
ASCCART	-1.05824550	.43414398	-2.438	.0148
CARTC	-.12641431	.06168226	-2.049	.0404
CARTT	.01548883	.02457798	.630	.5286
TOLL	-.15441105	.06613089	-2.335	.0195
ASCCARNT	.97566026	.90631693	1.077	.2817
CARNTT	-.06396814	.02760849	-2.317	.0205
ASCBUS	-.53854068	.44138139	-1.220	.2224
BSC	-.20213990	.04971615	-4.066	.0000
BST	-.01523577	.01946483	-.783	.4338
ASCTN	.52429288	.43334432	1.210	.2263
TNC	-.25878156	.05045499	-5.129	.0000
ASCBUSW	.41903191	.40889411	1.025	.3055
BSWC	-.27253143	.04450408	-6.124	.0000
BSWT	-.06375271	.01716878	-3.713	.0002
LRC	-.27219198	.04403684	-6.181	.0000
LRT	-.04054272	.01783240	-2.274	.0230
	Heterogeneity in mean, Parameter:Variable			
TNT:CAN	.03482934	.01638155	2.126	.0335
TNT:MEL	.01805784	.01568064	1.152	.2495
TNT:SYD	-.05209090	.02018043	-2.581	.0098
CARN:CAN	-.09845389	.07481997	-1.316	.1882
CARN:MEL	.21862895	.08419796	2.597	.0094
CARN:SYD	-.11604563	.06603993	-1.757	.0789
	Derived standard deviations of parameter distributions			
NsTNT	.01117636	.07743143	.144	.8852
TsCARNTC	1.38162826	.62432224	2.213	.0269

Parameter Matrix for Heterogeneity in Means.

```
Matrix Delta    has 2 rows and     3 columns.
                  CAN              MEL             SYD
              +--------------------------------------------
TNT           |  .03483          .01806         -.05209
CARNTC        | -.09845          .21863         -.11605
```

Ignoring all but the heterogeneity around the mean parameter estimates, we note that the interactions for those residing in Canberra are statistically significant for the *tnt* random parameter but not for the *carntc* random parameter. This suggests that those residing in Canberra have different marginal utilities for traveling times on trains than those who reside in other cities (it is positive, suggesting values closer to zero; that is, those living in Canberra are less sensitive to time spent traveling on trains than other Australian citizens) but are no different to other city residents in terms of preference heterogeneity for fuel costs when traveling on non-toll roads. The opposite pattern is observed for those residing in Melbourne, with a significant heterogeneity around the mean parameter estimate being observed for the *carntc* attribute but not for the *tnt* attribute. The model suggests that Melbournians are no different to other Australians (except possibly Canberrians) in terms of the marginal utilities they hold for train travel, but are different in terms of the marginal utilities held for non-toll road car fuel costs. Sydneysiders appear to be more sensitive to train travel times than other Australian residents but no different in terms of preferences for fuel costs when traveling along non-toll roads (at alpha equal to 0.05). The above discussion can clearly be seen in writing out the marginal utility expressions for each of the random parameters:

$$\begin{aligned}\text{TNT} = &-0.08161559 + 0.03482934 \times \text{can} + 0.01805784 \times \text{mel} - 0.05209090 \times \text{syd}\\ &+ 0.01117636 \times N\end{aligned}$$

$$\begin{aligned}\text{CARNTC} = &-0.42272240 - 0.09845389 \times \text{can} + 0.21862895 \times \text{mel}\\ &- 0.11604563 \times \text{syd} + 1.38162826 \times N\end{aligned}$$

The inclusion or exclusion of an attribute in the system of utility functions of a choice model are likely to impact upon the parameter estimates of all other parameter estimates. This is also true of insignificant parameter estimates, suggesting that the insignificant heterogeneity in the mean parameter estimates will have an effect upon all other parameter estimates within the model. It is therefore suggested that the insignificant heterogeneity around the mean parameter estimates be removed and the model re-estimated.

In removing the insignificant heterogeneity around the mean parameter estimates, we are unable to use the process described earlier (i.e. using square brackets), as this process will have NLOGIT not estimate any heterogeneity around the mean interactions for the entire random parameter estimate, including those we know to be significant. In post-June 2003 release versions of NLOGIT, it is possible to specify which specific interactions between random parameter estimates and covariates defining heterogeneity around the mean should be included. This is achieved by placing a series of ones and zeros following both a straight line (i.e. |) and a hash (i.e. #) when specifying the distribution from which a random parameter is to be drawn.

To demonstrate, consider the above example in which three covariates were used to estimate heterogeneity around the mean parameter estimates. In determining which interaction is to be estimated, each covariate will be represented, in the same order given in the **;rpl** command, by a series of ones and zeros, where a one indicates that the interaction for that covariate should be estimated and a zero indicates that the interaction should not be estimated. Based on the above model results, for the *tnt* random parameter we may wish to estimate heterogeneity around the mean random parameter estimates for the *can* and *syd* covariates but not for the *mel* covariate. The command syntax will be:

```
;fcn=tnt(n|#101)
```

where the first "1" is associated with the *can* covariate, the zero is related to the *mel* covariate, and the last "1" is related to the *syd* covariate.

Similarly,

```
carntc(t|#011)
```

will have NLOGIT estimate heterogeneity around the mean parameter estimates for the *mel* and *syd* covariates but not for the *can* covariate.

Using the above, the model is re-estimated using the following commands:

```
NLOGIT
;lhs = choice, cset, altij
;Choices = cart, carnt, bus, train, busway, LR
;Halton
;rpl=can,mel,syd
;fcn=tnt(n|#101),carntc(t|#011)
;pts=20
;Model:
U(cart) = asccart + cartc*fuel + cartt*time + toll*toll /
U(carnt) = asccarnt + carntc*fuel + carntt*time /
U(bus) = ascbus + bsc*fare + bst*time /
U(train) = asctn + tnc*fare + tnt*time /
U(busway) = ascbusw + bswc*fare + bswt*time /
U(LR) = lrc*fare + lrt*time $
```

For the 30 minutes or less commuting segment, the following model results are produced:

```
+----------------------------------------------+
| Random Parameters Logit Model                |
| Maximum Likelihood Estimates                 |
| Model estimated: Feb 30, 2003 at 05:15:00PM. |
| Dependent variable               CHOICE      |
| Weighting variable                 None      |
| Number of observations             9476      |
| Iterations completed                 39      |
| Log likelihood function       -3173.916      |
```

```
| Restricted log likelihood      -4244.678      |
| Chi squared                     2141.524      |
| Degrees of freedom                    24      |
| Prob[ChiSqd > value] =          .0000000      |
| R2=1-LogL/LogL*   Log-L  fncn R-sqrd  RsqAdj |
| No coefficients   -4244.6782  .25226  .24973 |
| Constants only.   Must be computed directly. |
|                   Use NLOGIT ;...; RHS=ONE $ |
| At start values   -3186.9971  .00410  .00073 |
| Response data are given as ind. choice.      |
+----------------------------------------------+

+----------------------------------------------+
| Random Parameters Logit Model                |
| Replications for simulated probs. = 20       |
| Halton sequences used for simulations        |
| Hessian was not PD. Using BHHH estimator.    |
| Number of obs.= 2369,  skipped   0 bad obs.  |
+----------------------------------------------+
+----------+-------------+----------------+----------+----------+
| Variable | Coefficient | Standard Error | b/St.Er. | P[|Z|>z] |
+----------+-------------+----------------+----------+----------+
          Random parameters in utility functions
 TNT        -.08213187      .02501636        -3.283      .0010
 CARNTC     -.34653083      .19282131        -1.797      .0723
          Nonrandom parameters in utility functions
 ASCCART   -1.04182956      .43118955        -2.416      .0157
 CARTC      -.12461006      .06121724        -2.036      .0418
 CARTT       .01535370      .02440517          .629      .5293
 TOLL       -.15776420      .06577536        -2.399      .0165
 ASCCARNT    .75716103      .79497647          .952      .3409
 CARNTT     -.05689398      .02336956        -2.435      .0149
 ASCBUS     -.53669897      .43811953        -1.225      .2206
 BSC        -.19820584      .04943001        -4.010      .0001
 BST        -.01513808      .01935749         -.782      .4342
 ASCTN       .52204775      .43400074         1.203      .2290
 TNC        -.24897053      .05004600        -4.975      .0000
 ASCBUSW     .41979873      .40560874         1.035      .3007
 BSWC       -.27263687      .04418907        -6.170      .0000
 BSWT       -.06280485      .01705195        -3.683      .0002
 LRC        -.27079162      .04377539        -6.186      .0000
 LRT        -.03991806      .01770621        -2.254      .0242
          Heterogeneity in mean, Parameter:Variable
 TNT:CAN     .04248643      .01583293         2.683      .0073
```

```
TNT:MEL       .000000      ......(Fixed Parameter).......
TNT:SYD     -.04473899      .01840582         -2.431      .0151
CARN:CAN      .000000      ......(Fixed Parameter).......
CARN:MEL      .16228339     .06049550          2.683      .0073
CARN:SYD    -.13274475      .05807256         -2.286      .0223
            Derived standard deviations of parameter distributions
NsTNT        .01152567      .08077762           .143      .8865
TsCARNTC    1.13662857      .51886229          2.191      .0285

Parameter Matrix for Heterogeneity in Means.
Matrix Delta    has 2 rows and    3 columns.
          CAN                     MEL            SYD
         +-----------------------------------------
TNT      |        .04249    .0000000D+00   -.04474
CARNTC   |    .0000000D+00     .16228      -.13274
```

Examining the heterogeneity around the mean parameter estimates, all are now statistically significant at alpha equal to 0.05. Comparing the mean and standard deviation parameter estimates for the *carntc* random parameter suggests significant changes in the parameter estimates from when the insignificant heterogeneity parameters were present. In our discussion we have ignored the insignificant *tnt* standard deviation parameter estimate.

16.7 Correlated parameters

The above model assumes that the random parameters are uncorrelated. As discussed in chapter 15, all data sets, regardless of the number of choice situations per sampled individual (i.e. choice sets), may have *unobserved effects* that are correlated among alternatives in a given choice situation. ML models enable the model to be specified in such a way that the error components in different choice situations from a given individual are correlated. In NLOGIT, this is achieved with the following command syntax:

;Correlation (shortened to **;cor**)

As an aside, for current versions of NLOGIT, the **;Correlation** command syntax will not work in conjunction with constraints imposed on any random parameter distributions.

The following ML model is estimated allowing for correlation among the random parameters of the model:

```
Calc;ran(12345) $
NLOGIT
;lhs = choice, cset, altij
;Choices = cart, carnt, bus, train, busway, LR
;Halton
;rpl
;fcn=ctc(u),cntc(n),ctp(t),cntp(t)
```

```
;pts=10
;Correlation
;Model:
U(cart) = asccart + ctc*fuel + ctt*time + toll*toll + ctp*parking /
U(carnt) = asccarnt + cntc*fuel + cntt*time + cntp*parking /
U(bus) = ascbus + bsc*fare + bst*time + bsf*freq /
U(train) = asctn + tnc*fare + tnt*time + tnf*freq /
U(busway) = ascbusw + bswc*fare + bswt*time + bswf*freq /
U(LR) = lrc*fare + lrt*time + lrf*freq $
```

As an aside, the naming of random parameters is also an issue for ML models using the correlation option. Indeed for ML models using this option, random parameter names must differ in at least the first three (not four) characters, as the output provides only the first three characters (see below), making interpretation difficult.

Estimated on the 30 minutes or less commuter segment of the mode-case study, the following ML model results are produced:

```
+----------------------------------------------+
| Random Parameters Logit Model                 |
| Maximum Likelihood Estimates                  |
| Model estimated: Feb 30, 2003 at 05:30:00PM.  |
| Dependent variable               CHOICE       |
| Weighting variable                 None       |
| Number of observations             9476       |
| Iterations completed                 59       |
| Log likelihood function       -2887.461       |
| Restricted log likelihood     -4244.678       |
| Chi squared                    2714.435       |
| Degrees of freedom                   34       |
| Prob[ChiSqd > value] =         .0000000       |
| R2=1-LogL/LogL*   Log-L  fncn  R-sqrd RsqAdj  |
| No coefficients   -4244.6782   .31975 .31648  |
| Constants only.   Must be computed directly.  |
|                   Use NLOGIT ;...; RHS=ONE $  |
| At start values   -2914.0214   .00911  .00435 |
| Response data are given as ind. choice.       |
+----------------------------------------------+
+----------------------------------------------+
| Random Parameters Logit Model                 |
| Replications for simulated probs. = 10        |
| Halton sequences used for simulations         |
| RPL model has correlated parameters           |
| Hessian was not PD. Using BHHH estimator.     |
| Number of obs.= 2369, skipped 0 bad obs.      |
+----------------------------------------------+
```

Variable	Coefficient	Standard Error	b/St.Er.	P[|Z|>z]
Random parameters in utility functions				
CTC	-.21266271	.10710586	-1.986	.0471
CNTC	-.17003912	.09758271	-1.743	.0814
CTP	-.17018797	.01947385	-8.739	.0000
CNTP	-.17963862	.02867177	-6.265	.0000
Nonrandom parameters in utility functions				
ASCCART	.39234026	.57680457	.680	.4964
CTT	-.02221060	.03211095	-.692	.4891
TOLL	-.20696526	.08615618	-2.402	.0163
ASCCARNT	1.30237710	.65475533	1.989	.0467
CNTT	-.06021319	.01799337	-3.346	.0008
ASCBUS	.12500894	.54216150	.231	.8176
BSC	-.26398469	.05478859	-4.818	.0000
BST	-.02115159	.02177631	-.971	.3314
BSF	-.05648598	.01063530	-5.311	.0000
ASCTN	.52222086	.49571177	1.053	.2921
TNC	-.32666743	.05332250	-6.126	.0000
TNT	-.07506255	.02243601	-3.346	.0008
TNF	-.02154335	.01099883	-1.959	.0501
ASCBUSW	.02335739	.48896909	.048	.9619
BSWC	-.27798190	.04988251	-5.573	.0000
BSWT	-.04565222	.01924386	-2.372	.0177
BSWF	-.01846118	.00949048	-1.945	.0517
LRC	-.31539990	.05013937	-6.290	.0000
LRT	-.04708827	.01963803	-2.398	.0165
LRF	-.01461773	.00966106	-1.513	.1303
Diagonal values in Cholesky matrix, L.				
UsCTC	1.36129698	.24253523	5.613	.0000
NsCNTC	.09445525	.09704604	.973	.3304
TsCTP	.21889601	.05465811	4.005	.0001
TsCNTP	.03900974	.04860811	.803	.4222
Below diagonal values in L matrix. V = L*Lt				
CNTC:CTC	.61341814	.14690672	4.176	.0000
CTP:CTC	-.07231832	.03660327	-1.976	.0482
CTP:CNT	-.03735979	.02238622	-1.669	.0951
CNTP:CTC	.10553796	.05330632	1.980	.0477
CNTP:CNT	.10923760	.03300261	3.310	.0009
CNTP:CTP	-.09499480	.05148272	-1.845	.0650
Standard deviations of parameter distributions				
sdCTC	1.36129698	.24253523	5.613	.0000
sdCNTC	.62064773	.14680653	4.228	.0000

```
sdCTP        .23354048      .05098340      4.581      .0000
sdCNTP       .18334908      .04530980      4.047      .0001

Correlation Matrix for Random Parameters

Matrix COR.MAT. has    4 rows and    4 columns.

            CTC         CNTC        CTP         CNTP
         +--------------------------------------------
CTC      | 1.00000     .98835    -.30966      .57561
CNTC     |  .98835    1.00000    -.33040      .65958
CTP      | -.30966    -.33040    1.00000     -.75917
CNTP     |  .57561     .65958    -.75917     1.00000

Covariance Matrix for Random Parameters

Matrix COV.MAT. has 4 rows and 4 columns.
            CTC         CNTC        CTP         CNTP
         +--------------------------------------------------------
CTC      |  1.85313     .83504    -.09845      .14367
CNTC     |   .83504     .38520    -.04789      .07506
CTP      |  -.09845    -.04789     .05454     -.03251
CNTP     |   .14367     .07506    -.03251      .03362

Cholesky Matrix for Random Parameters

Matrix Cholesky has    4 rows and    4 columns.
            CTC            CNTC            CTP             CNTP
         +--------------------------------------------------------
CTC      |  1.36130    .0000000D+00    .0000000D+00    .0000000D+00
CNTC     |   .61342      .09446       .0000000D+00    .0000000D+00
CTP      |  -.07232     -.03736         .21890        .0000000D+00
CNTP     |   .10554      .10924        -.09499           .03901
```

The above model is statistically significant with a Chi-square value of 2114.435 with 34 degrees of freedom and a pseudo-R^2 value of 0.31975. The mean of the *car with toll fuel cost* parameter is statistically significant (p-value $= 0.0471$ at the 95 percent confidence level). At the 95 percent confidence level, the mean of *car traveling on a non-tolled road fuel cost* parameter is not statistically significant in the above model (p-value $= 0.0814$). The means of the *parking cost* random parameters for both car modes are statistically different to zero (p-values $= 0.0000$). Examination of the spreads of each of the random parameters around their respective means reveals that all attributes exhibit preference heterogeneity. The shapes of each of the random parameter distributions are represented graphically in figures 16.13a–16.13d.

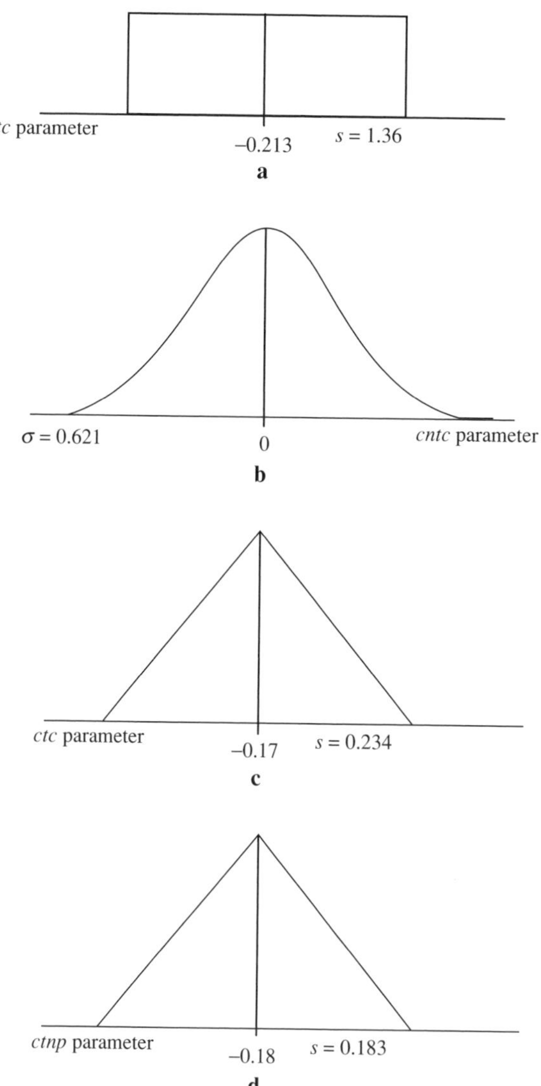

Figure 16.13 Means and spreads of *ctc*, *ctnc*, *ctp*, and *cntp* random parameters

All of the non-random or fixed parameter estimates are of the expected sign, though several are not statistically significant.

The addition of the correlation command in NLOGIT produces a great deal of new output. It is first worth examining the last series of output generated which is represented as several matrices. The first matrix is the correlation matrix. The correlation matrix (shown once more below) suggests several numerically large correlations. The *ctc* random parameter has correlations of −0.98835, −0.30966, and 0.57561 with the *cntc*, *ctp*, and *cntp* random parameters. The *ctnc* random parameter has correlations of −0.3304 and 0.65958 with the *ctp* and *cntp* random parameters and the *ctp* random parameter has a correlation of −0.75917 with the *cntp* random parameter:

```
Correlation Matrix for Random Parameters

Matrix COR.MAT. has 4 rows and 4 columns.

              CTC          CNTC          CTP          CNTP
          +----------------------------------------------------
CTC       |   1.00000      .98835     -.30966       .57561
CNTC      |    .98835     1.00000     -.33040       .65958
CTP       |   -.30966     -.33040     1.00000      -.75917
CNTP      |    .57561      .65958     -.75917      1.00000
```

The variance and covariance of each random parameter are given as the diagonal and off-diagonal elements, respectively, in the next matrix reported:

```
Matrix COV.MAT. has 4 rows and 4 columns.

              CTC          CNTC          CTP          CNTP
          +----------------------------------------------------
CTC       |   1.85313      .83504     -.09845       .14367
CNTC      |    .83504      .38520     -.04789       .07506
CTP       |   -.09845     -.04789      .05454      -.03251
CNTP      |    .14367      .07506     -.03251       .03362
```

The variance (values on the diagonal of the variance–covariance matrix) of each random parameter is calculated as the square of the reported standard deviations given in the main series of output. The calculations for this are as shown below:

$$\mathrm{var}(CTC) = 1.36129698^2 = 1.85313$$
$$\mathrm{var}(CNTC) = 0.62064773^2 = 0.38520$$
$$\mathrm{var}(CTP) = 0.23354048^2 = 0.05454$$
$$\mathrm{var}(CNTP) = 0.18334908^2 = 0.03362$$

The covariances, reported as the off-diagonal elements of the above matrix, are calculated directly from the data (each covariance is the average of the products of deviations for each data point pair). It is therefore impossible to show this calculation, although equation (16.2) shows the formula used in the calculation process; this is the same equation as (2.13):

$$\mathrm{cov}(x, y) = \frac{1}{n}\sum_{i=1}^{N}(X_i - U_i)(Y_i - U_i) \tag{16.2}$$

Positive covariances suggest that larger parameter estimates for individuals along the distribution on one attribute are generally associated with larger parameter estimates for that same individual in the parameter space for the second attribute. For example, the covariance of 0.83504 between the *ctc* and *ctnc* random parameters suggests that individuals with larger (i.e. more negative – the marginal utilities for this attribute are expected to be negative) sensitivities to fuel costs traveling along toll roads are likely to have higher (negative) marginal utilities to fuel costs. The larger the covariance, the greater the relationship between the two random parameters. Hence, 0.83504 suggests a stronger (positive) relationship between the *ctc* and *ctnc* random parameters than between the *ctc* and *ctp* random parameters, with a covariance statistic of −0.09845 (a negative relationship; larger values of *ctc* result in smaller values of *ctp*).

There exists a direct relationship between the variances and covariances and the correlations observed. The correlation coefficient used to produce the correlations previously reported was given as (2.17):

$$\rho = \frac{\text{cov}(X_1, X_2)}{\sigma_{x_1} \times \sigma_{x_2}}$$

To demonstrate this relationship, consider the correlation exhibited between the *cartt* and *carntt* random parameters:

$$\rho = \frac{\text{cov}(ctc, cntc)}{\sigma_{ctc} \times \sigma_{cntc}} = \frac{0.83504}{\sqrt{1.85313} \times \sqrt{0.38520}} = 0.988346$$

which is the correlation reported between the *ctc* and *cntc* random parameters by NLOGIT (note that it is the *standard deviations* and not variances that make up the denominator of the correlation coefficient).

The last matrix is the Cholesky decomposition matrix. The Cholesky decomposition matrix is a lower triangular matrix (meaning that the upper off-diagonal elements of the matrix are all zero). The above output illustrates the presence of correlated alternatives due to correlated random parameters, one uniformly distributed, one normally distributed, and two triangularly distributed. When we have more than one random parameter and we permit correlated random parameters then the standard deviations are no longer independent. To assess this, we have to decompose the standard deviation parameters into their attribute-specific (e.g. *ctc* and *cntc*) and attribute-interaction (e.g. *ctc* × *cntc*) standard deviations. Cholesky decomposition is the method used to do this. The ML model is extended to accommodate this case by allowing the set of random parameters to have an unrestricted covariance matrix. The non-zero off-diagonal element of this matrix carries the cross-parameter correlations:

```
Matrix Cholesky has 4 rows and 4 columns.

           CTC          CNTC            CTP               CNTP
        +--------------------------------------------------------
CTC     |   1.36130   .0000000D+00    .0000000D+00    .0000000D+00
CNTC    |    .61342     .09446        .0000000D+00    .0000000D+00
CTP     |  -.07232     -.03736          .21890        .0000000D+00
CNTP    |    .10554     .10924         -.09499           .03901
```

The Cholesky matrix is obtained from the variance–covariance matrix. To demonstrate how this matrix is constructed, consider the following variance–covariance matrix in which the variances are represented as the diagonal elements a_{ij} where $i = j$ and the covariances are represented as the off-diagonal a_{ij} elements where $i \neq j$:

$$\begin{bmatrix} a_{11} & a_{12} & a_{13} & \cdots & a_{1i} \\ a_{21} & a_{22} & a_{23} & \cdots & a_{2i} \\ a_{31} & a_{32} & a_{33} & \cdots & a_{3i} \\ & & & \cdots & \\ & & & \cdots & \\ & & & \cdots & \\ a_{j1} & a_{j2} & a_{j3} & \cdots & a_{ji} \end{bmatrix} = \begin{bmatrix} b_{11} & 0 & 0 & \cdots & 0 \\ b_{21} & b_{22} & 0 & \cdots & 0 \\ b_{31} & b_{32} & b_{33} & \cdots & 0 \\ . & . & . & . & 0 \\ . & . & . & . & 0 \\ . & . & . & . & 0 \\ b_{j1} & b_{j2} & b_{j3} & \cdots & b_{ji} \end{bmatrix} \begin{bmatrix} b_{11} & b_{12} & b_{13} & \cdots & b_{1i} \\ 0 & b_{22} & b_{23} & \cdots & b_{2i} \\ 0 & 0 & b_{33} & \cdots & b_{3i} \\ 0 & 0 & 0 & . & . \\ . & . & . & . & . \\ . & . & . & . & . \\ 0 & 0 & 0 & \cdots & b_{ji} \end{bmatrix} \tag{16.3}$$

The Cholesky decomposition matrix is that matrix given immediately to the right of the equal sign in (16.3), in which the upper off-diagonal elements are all equal to zero. To calculate the elements of this matrix, the following equations are required:

$$b_{ij} = \sqrt{a_{ij}} \text{ for } i = j = 1 \text{ (the first diagonal element) else} \tag{16.4a}$$

$$b_{ij} = \sqrt{a_{ij} - \sum_{i}^{i-1} b_{ij}^2} \text{ if } i = j \neq 1 \text{ (all other diagonal elements) else} \tag{16.4b}$$

$$b_{ij} = (a_{ij})/b_{ii} \text{ for } j = 1 \text{ and } i \neq j$$
$$\text{(lower off-diagonal elements in the first column) else} \tag{16.4c}$$

$$b_{ij} = (a_{ij} - \sum_{i}^{i-1} b_{jk}b_{ki})/b_{ii} \text{ for } j \neq 1 \text{ and } i \neq j$$
$$\text{(lower off-diagonal elements not in the first column)} \tag{16.4d}$$

The Cholesky decomposition matrix for the above example may be calculated as follows:

$$\begin{bmatrix} 1.85313 & 0.83504 & -0.09845 & 0.14367 \\ 0.83504 & 0.3852 & -0.04789 & 0.07506 \\ -0.09845 & -0.04789 & 0.05454 & -0.03251 \\ 0.14367 & 0.07506 & -0.03251 & 0.03362 \end{bmatrix}$$
$$= \begin{bmatrix} b_{11} & 0 & 0 & 0 \\ b_{21} & b_{22} & 0 & 0 \\ b_{31} & b_{32} & b_{33} & 0 \\ b_{41} & b_{42} & b_{43} & b_{44} \end{bmatrix} \begin{bmatrix} b_{11} & b_{21} & b_{31} & b_{41} \\ 0 & b_{22} & b_{23} & b_{24} \\ 0 & 0 & b_{33} & b_{34} \\ 0 & 0 & 0 & b_{44} \end{bmatrix}$$

where

$$b_{11} = \sqrt{a_{11}} = \sqrt{1.85313} = 1.361297 \qquad \text{from (16.4a)}$$

$$b_{21} = (a_{21})/b_{11} = (0.83504)/(1.361297) = 0.613415 \qquad \text{from (16.4c)}$$

$$b_{22} = \sqrt{a_{22} - b_{21}^2} = \sqrt{0.3852} - (0.613415)^2 = 0.094457 \qquad \text{from (16.4b)}$$

$$b_{31} = (a_{31})/b_{11} = (-0.09845)/(1.361297) = -0.07232 \qquad \text{from (16.4c)}$$

$$\begin{aligned} b_{32} &= \left\lfloor \sqrt{a_{32} - b_{31} \times b_{21}} \right\rfloor / b_{22} \\ &= \left\lfloor \sqrt{-0.04789 - (-0.07232 \times 0.613415)} \right\rfloor \Big/ 0.094457 \\ &= -0.03734 \qquad \text{from (16.4d)} \end{aligned}$$

$$\begin{aligned} b_{33} &= \sqrt{a_{33} - b_{32}^2 \times b_{31}^2} = \sqrt{-0.09845 - \left\lfloor(-0.03734)^2 \times (-0.07232)^2\right\rfloor} \\ &= \sqrt{0.218895} \qquad \text{from (16.4b)} \end{aligned}$$

$$b_{41} = (a_{41})/b_{11} = (0.14367)/(1.361297) = 0.105539 \qquad \text{from (16.4c)}$$

$$\begin{aligned} b_{42} &= \left\lfloor \sqrt{a_{42} - b_{41} \times b_{21}} \right\rfloor / b_{22} \\ &= \left\lfloor \sqrt{0.07506 - (0.105539 \times 0.613415)} \right\rfloor \Big/ 0.094457 = 0.109264 \\ & \qquad \text{from (16.4d)} \end{aligned}$$

$$\begin{aligned} b_{43} &= \left\lfloor \sqrt{a_{43} - b_{42} \times b_{32} - b_{41} \times b_{31}} \right\rfloor \Big/ b_{33} \\ &= \left\lfloor \sqrt{0.07506 - (0.105539 \times 0.613415)} \right\rfloor \Big/ -0.09501 \\ &= -0.09501 \qquad \text{from (16.4d)} \end{aligned}$$

$$\begin{aligned} b_{44} &= \sqrt{a_{44} - b_{43}^2 \times b_{42}^2 \times b_{41}^2} \\ &= \sqrt{0.03362 - \left[(-0.09501)^2 \times (0.109264)^2 \times (0.105539)^2\right]} \\ &= 0.038938 \qquad \text{from (16.4b)} \end{aligned}$$

The Cholesky decomposition matrix is therefore:

$$\begin{bmatrix} 1.361297 & 0 & 0 & 0 \\ 0.613415 & 0.094457 & 0 & 0 \\ -0.07232 & -0.03734 & 0.218895 & 0 \\ 0.105539 & 0.109264 & -0.09501 & 0.038938 \end{bmatrix}$$

which is equivalent (within rounding) to that provided in the ML output given by NLOGIT.

As noted, the standard deviations of random parameter estimates under conditions of correlated parameters may not be independent. To establish the independent contribution of each random parameter estimate, the Cholesky decomposition matrix separates the contribution to each standard deviation parameter made through correlation with other random parameter estimates and the actual contribution made solely through heterogeneity around the mean of each random parameter estimate; thus unconfounding the correlation structure over random parameter estimates with their associated standard deviation parameters. This allows the parameters to be freely correlated and have an unrestricted scale, as well, while ensuring that the covariance matrix that we estimate is positive definite at all times (see chapter 2 for a definition of a positive definite matrix).

The first element of the Cholesky decomposition matrix will always be equal to the standard deviation parameter of the first specified random coefficient.[2] Subsequent diagonal elements of the Cholesky decomposition matrix represent the amount of variance attributable to that random parameter when the covariances (correlations) with subsequently named random parameters have been removed. In the above example, the amount of variance directly attributable for the CNTC random parameter is 0.09 and not 0.62. Off-diagonal elements of the matrix represent the amount of cross-parameter correlations previously confounded with the standard deviation parameters of the model. For the standard deviation parameter associated with the CNTC random parameter, 0.61 is attributable to a cross-product correlation with the CTC random parameter estimate.

Returning to the parameter estimates of the model output, the Cholesky decomposition matrix estimates are reported once more. We reproduce these results below:

```
          Diagonal values in Cholesky matrix, L.
UsCTC           1.36129698        .24253523      5.613     .0000
NsCNTC           .09445525        .09704604       .973     .3304
TsCTP            .21889601        .05465811      4.005     .0001
TsCNTP           .03900974        .04860811       .803     .4222
          Below diagonal values in L matrix. V = L*Lt
CNTC:CTC         .61341814        .14690672      4.176     .0000
CTP:CTC         -.07231832        .03660327     -1.976     .0482
```

[2] Random parameters in NLOGIT are created independent of the generation of other random parameter estimates. Correlation between two random parameters is created by running the random parameter estimates through a Cholesky matrix. The distribution of the resulting vector will differ depending on the order that was specified for the coefficients in the **;fcn** command. This means that different orderings of random parameters can result in different parameterizations when non-normal distributions are used. Using an example offered by Ken Train (in private correspondence with the authors), assume two random parameters X_1 and X_2 specified with normal and uniform distributions with correlation. NLOGIT creates a standard normal and a standard uniform distribution that are uncorrelated, N_1 and U_2, and multiplies these by use of a Cholesky matrix. For matrix $C = a\ 0\ b\ c$ the resulting coefficients are $X_1 = a \times N_1$, which is normal, and $X_2 = b \times e_1 + c \times U_2$, which is the sum of a uniform and a normal. X_2 is not uniform but has the distribution defined by the sum of a uniform and normal. If the order is reversed, such that N_1 is uniform and U_2 is normal, X_1 will be uniform and X_2 will be the sum of a uniform and normal. By ordering the random parameters differently, the user is implicitly changing the *distribution* of the resulting coefficients.

```
CTP:CNT        -.03735979        .02238622      -1.669      .0951
CNTP:CTC        .10553796        .05330632       1.980      .0477
CNTP:CNT        .10923760        .03300261       3.310      .0009
CNTP:CTP       -.09499480        .05148272      -1.845      .0650
```

Examination of the results for the diagonal values in the matrix reveals significant effects for the CTC and CNTP diagonal elements of the matrix. As suggested above, the first element of this output representing the CTC random parameter estimate is exactly the same as that for the first reported standard deviation parameter. The diagonal values reported in the Cholesky matrix represent the true level variance of variance for each random parameter once the cross-correlated parameter terms have been unconfounded. In the above example, it can be seen that despite all standard deviation parameter estimates being statistically significant at alpha equal to 0.05, only the CTC and CTP diagonal elements in the Cholesky decomposition matrix are statistically significant. This suggests that the significant result observed for the standard deviation parameter estimates for the CNTC, and CNTP random parameter estimates are due to cross-product correlations with the other random parameter estimates. Significant below-diagonal elements in the Cholesky decomposition matrix suggest significant cross-correlations among the random parameter estimates that otherwise would be confounded within the standard deviation parameter estimates. In the above model, significant cross-product correlations are observed to exist between the CTC and CNTC, CTC and CTP, CTC and CNTP, CNT and CNTP, and CTP and CNTP random parameter estimates (at alpha equal to 0.05). Without the Cholesky decomposition method, these significant cross-product correlations would be confounded within the standard deviation parameter estimates of each of the random parameters.

In writing out the marginal utility estimates of the random parameters, the analyst may either use the standard deviation parameter estimates or utilize the decomposed values obtained from the model output. The use of the standard deviation parameter estimates ignores the additional information obtained in decomposing the sources of variation through the Cholesky decomposition method. Using the elements of the Cholesky decomposition matrix, on the other hand, requires that the analyst must first locate the position of all simulated individuals on the each of the elements of the matrix (i.e. on the diagonals and off-diagonals of the matrix) in order to reconstruct the empirical distribution of the standard deviation parameter estimates. To demonstrate this concept more clearly, consider (16.5), which shows the formula for the decomposed standard deviation parameter:

$$\text{Standard deviation parameter} = \beta_{\textit{diagonal element}} \times f(X_0) + \beta_{\textit{off-diagonal element } 1} \times f(X_1) + \cdots + \beta_{\textit{off-diagonal element } k} \times f(X_k) \tag{16.5}$$

where $f(X_k)$ is a location parameter used to locate individual i on some distribution for each element of the matrix.

The location parameter, $f(X_k)$, may take on any distribution; however, it is most common to use the normal distribution.

The marginal utilities may therefore be written as (16.6):

$$\begin{aligned} \textit{Marginal Utility}(\textit{attribute}) = {} & \beta_{\textit{attribute mean}} + \beta_{\textit{covariate}} \times x_{\textit{covariate}} \\ & + (\beta_{\textit{diagonal element}} + \beta_{\textit{off-diagonal element 1}} \\ & \times \varepsilon + \cdots + \beta_{\textit{off-diagonal element k}} \times N) \times f(N, T \text{ or } U) \end{aligned} \tag{16.6}$$

where $f(N, T \text{ or } U)$ is the mixing distribution.

Assuming each $f(X_k)$ are normally distributed, for the above example, the standard deviation parameters may be reconstructed as follows. Note that the first standard deviation parameter was not deconstructed and hence does not appear in this series of calculations:

$$\text{CNTC}_{\text{stdev}} = 0.61341814 \times N + 0.09445525 \times N$$
$$\text{CTP}_{\text{stdev}} = -0.07232 \times N - 0.03736 \times N + 0.21890 \times N$$
$$\text{CTP}_{\text{stdev}} = 0.10554 \times N + 0.10924 \times N - 0.09499 \times N + 0.03901 \times N$$

In NLOGIT, these calculations may be performed using the following syntax commands:

```
Calc;ran(12345)$
CREATE
;rna=rnn(0,1)
;rnb=rnn(0,1)
;rnc=rnn(0,1)
;rnd=rnn(0,1)
;rne=rnn(0,1)
;rnf=rnn(0,1)
;rng=rnn(0,1)
;rnh=rnn(0,1)
;rni=rnn(0,1)$

CREATE
;cntcsd = 0.61342*rna + 0.09446*rnb
;ctpsd = -0.07232*rnc -0.03736*rnd +0.21890*rne
;cntpsd = 0.10554*rnf +  0.10924*rng -0.094998*rnh + 0.03901*rni$
```

The marginal utilities therefore may be written as follows:

$$\text{CTC} = -0.21266271 + 1.36129698 \times u$$
$$\text{CNTC} = -0.17003912 + (0.61341814 \times N + 0.09445525 \times N) \times t$$
$$\text{CTP} = -0.17018797 + (-0.07232 \times N - 0.03736 \times N + 0.21890 \times N) \times N$$
$$\begin{aligned} \text{CTP} = {} & -0.17963862 + (0.10554 \times N + 0.10924 \times N - 0.09499 \times N \\ & + 0.03901 \times N) \times t \end{aligned}$$

The NLOGIT commands used to construct the unconditional parameter estimates are therefore as shown below:

```
Calc;ran(12345)$
CREATE
;U=rnu(0,1)$
Calc;ran(12345)$
CREATE
;rnt1=rnu(0,1)
;if(rnt1<=0.5)T1=sqr(2*rnt1)-1;(ELSE) T1=1-sqr(2*(1-rnt1))
;rnt2=rnu(0,1)
;if(rnt2<=0.5)T2=sqr(2*rnt2)-1;(ELSE) T2=1-sqr(2*(1-rnt2)) $

Calc;ran(12345)$
CREATE
;rnn=rnn(0,1)$

CREATE
;ctc=-0.21266271 + 1.36129698*U
;cntc=-0.17003912 + cntcsd*T1
;ctp= -.17018797 + ctpsd*rnn
;cntp= -.17963862 + cntpsd * T2 $
```

Figures 16.14a–16.14d plot the marginal utility (unconditional) distributions for the four random parameter estimates derived above (see section 16.9 on how these graphs are obtained). The uniform distribution imposed upon the marginal utilities for the *cart* fuel cost attribute can be seen in figure 16.14a. The triangular distributions are also identifiable in for the *carnt* fuel cost and parking cost parameters (figures 16.14b and 16.14d). Less obvious is the normal distribution imposed upon the marginal utilities for *cart* parking cost attribute (figure 16.4c).

As an aside, NLOGIT presents output in a hierarchical fashion, starting with MNL and building up to more advanced models. The standard deviation parameters in mixed logit are meaningful under the condition of uncorrelated attributes and alternatives. However, when correlation is accounted for, the standard deviation parameters in the output should be ignored and the Cholesky decomposition matrix parameters used instead (as shown above).

16.8 Common-choice-specific parameter estimates: conditional parameters

The output provided by NLOGIT details the population moments of the random parameter estimates for ML models. As we have shown, these population moments may be used to simulate out-of-sample populations and construct what are known as *unconditional parameter estimates*. Rather than rely on randomly allocating each sampled individual within a full distribution as a way of allocating preference information, it is possible to utilize the additional information about the common choices each sub-set of individuals

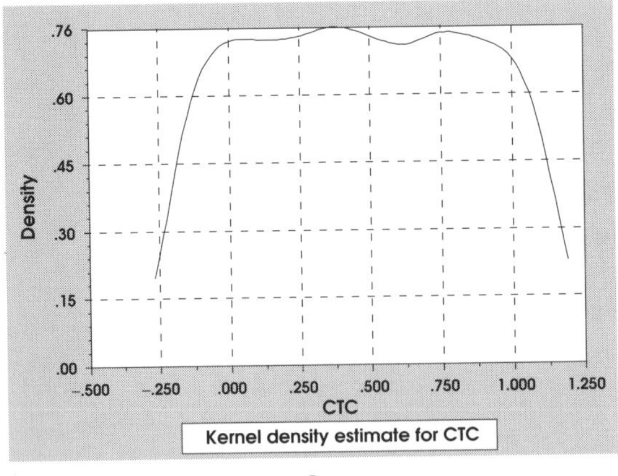

a

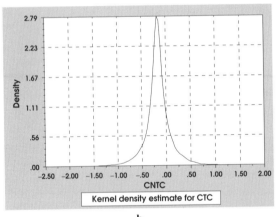

b

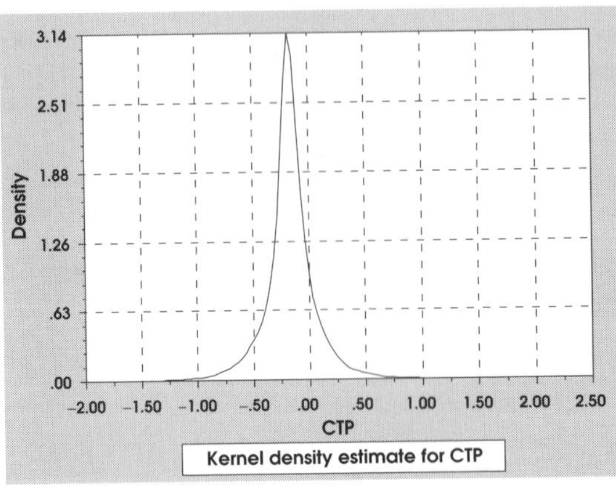

c

Figure 16.14 Plotting the marginal utilities from unconditional parameter estimates

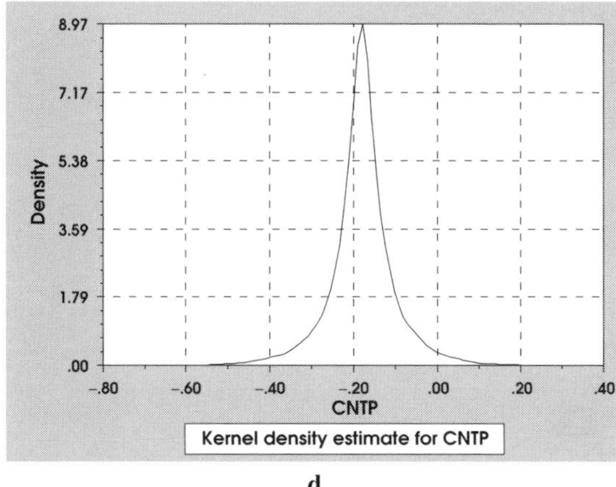

d

Figure 16.14 *(Cont.)*

was observed to have made as a way of increasing the accuracy of the preference allocation. In this way, it is possible to derive common-choice-specific parameter estimates which are *conditioned* on the choices observed to have been made.

NLOGIT will estimate the conditional mean parameter estimates with the following command syntax:

;Parameters (or **;Par** for short)

To demonstrate the estimation of the conditional parameter estimates, we will estimate an ML model on the 30 minutes or less commuter trip segment within the data set. The commands necessary to re-set the correct segment are shown below:

```
Sample;all $
Reject;sprp=1 $
Reject;splength#1 $
Dstats;rhs=* $
```

The model we estimate, including the parameters command syntax, is given below:

```
Calc;ran(12345)$
NLOGIT
;lhs = choice, cset, altij
;Choices = cart, carnt, bus, train, busway, LR
;Halton
;rpl
;fcn=toll(t,0.5),cartc(n)
;parameters
;pts=10
;Model:
```

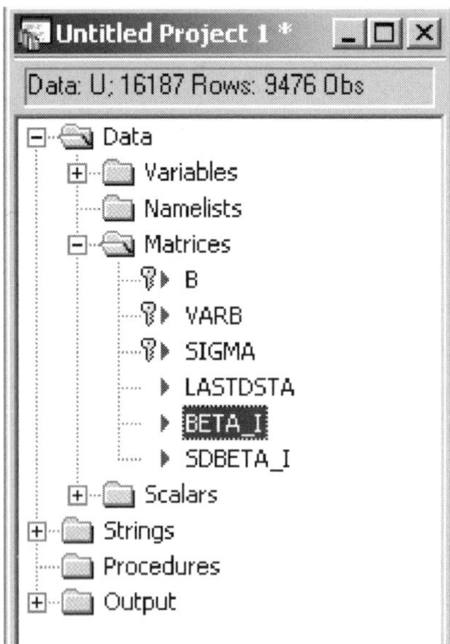

Figure 16.15 Locating the conditional parameter estimates

U(cart) = asccart + cartc*fuel + cartt*time + toll*toll /
U(carnt) = asccarnt + carntc*fuel + carntt*time /
U(bus) = ascbus + bsc*fare + bst*time /
U(train) = asctn + tnc*fare + tnt*time /
U(busway) = ascbusw + bswc*fare + bswt*time /
U(LR) = lrc*fare + lrt*time $

We omit the NLOGIT output for the above model, instead choosing to concentrate on the conditional parameter estimates. The conditional parameter estimates may be found under the *Matrices* folder in the "**Untitled Project 1**" box, shown as figure 16.15.

The conditional parameter estimates will be made available to the analyst by double clicking on the BETA_I option in the *Matrices* folder of the "**Untitled Project 1**" box. Double clicking on this option will open up a new matrix data sheet with the saved conditional parameter estimates. Figure 16.16 shows the stored conditional parameters for the above model. The column headings of the matrix are numbered with the parameters appearing in the same order provided in the NLOGIT output for the model. This means that the random parameter estimates will appear in the first few columns of the matrix, with the remaining columns devoted to the non-random parameter estimates of the model. For the above example, two random parameters were estimated, with the *toll* random parameter appearing first and the *cartc* random parameter appearing second in the model output. Hence, the first column of the BETA_I matrix will correspond to the conditional parameter

Matrix - BETA_I

[2369, 18] Cell -0.183723

	1	2	3	4	5	6	7	8	9
1	-0.183723	-0.201582	-0.826728	0.0113399	0.0371439	-0.0996241	-0.0353873	-0.464208	-0.180854
2	-0.188702	-0.173239	-0.826728	0.0113399	0.0371439	-0.0996241	-0.0353873	-0.464208	-0.180854
3	-0.181539	-0.188864	-0.826728	0.0113399	0.0371439	-0.0996241	-0.0353873	-0.464208	-0.180854
4	-0.185899	-0.236289	-0.826728	0.0113399	0.0371439	-0.0996241	-0.0353873	-0.464208	-0.180854
5	-0.186139	0.00220074	-0.826728	0.0113399	0.0371439	-0.0996241	-0.0353873	-0.464208	-0.180854
6	-0.183854	-0.201969	-0.826728	0.0113399	0.0371439	-0.0996241	-0.0353873	-0.464208	-0.180854
7	-0.185882	-0.298002	-0.826728	0.0113399	0.0371439	-0.0996241	-0.0353873	-0.464208	-0.180854
8	-0.181376	0.0884195	-0.826728	0.0113399	0.0371439	-0.0996241	-0.0353873	-0.464208	-0.180854
9	-0.185856	-0.198544	-0.826728	0.0113399	0.0371439	-0.0996241	-0.0353873	-0.464208	-0.180854
10	-0.189466	-0.242302	-0.826728	0.0113399	0.0371439	-0.0996241	-0.0353873	-0.464208	-0.180854
11	-0.188082	-0.0549653	-0.826728	0.0113399	0.0371439	-0.0996241	-0.0353873	-0.464208	-0.180854
12	-0.188564	-0.16052	-0.826728	0.0113399	0.0371439	-0.0996241	-0.0353873	-0.464208	-0.180854
13	-0.182018	-0.230811	-0.826728	0.0113399	0.0371439	-0.0996241	-0.0353873	-0.464208	-0.180854
14	-0.178897	-0.0812538	-0.826728	0.0113399	0.0371439	-0.0996241	-0.0353873	-0.464208	-0.180854
15	-0.191036	-0.110517	-0.826728	0.0113399	0.0371439	-0.0996241	-0.0353873	-0.464208	-0.180854
16	-0.17853	-0.0911752	-0.826728	0.0113399	0.0371439	-0.0996241	-0.0353873	-0.464208	-0.180854
17	-0.186654	-0.184037	-0.826728	0.0113399	0.0371439	-0.0996241	-0.0353873	-0.464208	-0.180854
18	-0.190431	-0.212839	-0.826728	0.0113399	0.0371439	-0.0996241	-0.0353873	-0.464208	-0.180854
19	-0.182251	-0.197028	-0.826728	0.0113399	0.0371439	-0.0996241	-0.0353873	-0.464208	-0.180854
20	-0.185352	-0.18505	-0.826728	0.0113399	0.0371439	-0.0996241	-0.0353873	-0.464208	-0.180854
21	-0.189471	-0.240175	-0.826728	0.0113399	0.0371439	-0.0996241	-0.0353873	-0.464208	-0.180854

Figure 16.16 A matrix with the stored conditional random parameter estimates

estimates for the *toll* parameter and the second column of the matrix to the conditional parameter estimates for the *cartc* attribute.

Each row of the matrix will correspond to a choice set within the data. For the example data set from which these conditional parameter estimates were derived, each respondent was shown three choice sets each. As such, the first three rows of the matrix correspond to the three choice sets shown to the first respondent, the next three rows to the three choice sets shown to the second respondent, and so forth. The total number of rows will therefore equal the total number of choice sets in the data.

As mentioned previously, the conditional parameter estimates are estimated within the sample. While the conditional parameter estimates may be exported to other application settings and randomly assigned to observations in a hold out or application sample, unless the sample of respondents was drawn so as to be representative of the population from which it was derived, the conditional parameter estimates may be poor predictors of population behavioral reactions to policy changes in the scenarios tested (this may be particularly true if a non-random sample such as choice-based sampling (CBS) was employed). Nevertheless, while certainly true of the conditional parameter estimates, the same problem will likely be witnessed in using unconditional parameter estimates obtained from models estimated using non-representative samples.

As an aside, the reason for this concern is that the choice distribution can be quite different in the application sample, and imposing the choice distribution from the estimation sample is a source of information that is a burden if the known sample choice distribution is so different. Additional information is useful only if it is *portable* across data settings. The use of the population moments associated with the unconditional estimates of parameters seems to be more appealing when applying a model using another sample of individuals.

Despite our earlier warning of using the conditional mean parameter estimates to predict out-of-sample, the conditional parameter estimates often prove particularly useful. Given the non-random assignment of each individual to a specific location on the random parameter distribution, the conditional parameter estimates may be used to derive individual-specific behavioral outputs. Placement is now conditional on the common choices made and hence there remains random assignment, given mean and standard deviation of the estimated parameter, within the common-choice sub-set of individuals. For example, it is possible to derive individual-specific elasticities and marginal effects (see chapter 11 for clues as to how you might do this). It is also possible to begin to build consumer segments based on the utilities held by individuals for given attributes (often called *benefit segments* in marketing) rather than on the traditional marketing segmentation methods of grouping consumers based on socio-demographic or psychographic information. Further, having individual-specific marginal utilities allows for the mapping between the utilities held for product bundles and other (consumer) characteristics (such as socio-demographic or psychographic information) using other statistical modeling techniques such as multiple linear regression.

16.9 Presenting the distributional outputs graphically using a kernel density estimator

The kernel density estimator is a useful device for graphically presenting many of the outputs of ML models, especially the distributions of parameter estimates and WTP values derived from parameter distributions. It is for this reason that we introduce it in this chapter (although it is useful in the presentation of results for all model forms).The *kernel density* is a modification of the familiar histogram used to describe the distribution of a sample of observations graphically. The disadvantages of the histogram that are overcome with kernel estimators are, first, that histograms are discontinuous whereas (our models assume) the underlying distributions are continuous and, second, the shape of the histogram is crucially dependent on the assumed widths and placements of the bins. Intuition suggests that the first of these problems is mitigated by taking narrower bins, but the cost of doing so is that the number of observations that land in each bin falls so that the larger picture painted by the histogram becomes increasingly variable and imprecise. The kernel density estimator is a "smoothed" plot that shows, for each selected point, the proportion of the sample that is "near" it (hence, the name "density"). "Nearness" is defined by a weighting function called the *kernel function*, which will have the characteristic that the farther a sample observation is from the selected point, the smaller will be the weight that it receives.

The kernel density function for a single attribute is computed using (16.7):

$$f(z_j) = \frac{1}{n}\sum\nolimits_{i=1}^{n} \frac{K\left[\left(z_j - x_i\right)/h\right]}{h}, \; j = 1, \ldots, M. \tag{16.7}$$

The function is computed for a specified set of values of interest, z_j, $j = 1, \ldots, M$, where z_j is a partition of the range of the attribute. Each value requires a sum over the full sample of n-values, x_i, $i = 1 \ldots n$. The primary component of the computation is the kernel, or weighting function, $K[.]$, which takes a number of forms. For example, the normal kernel is $K[z] = \phi(z)$ (normal density). Thus, for the normal kernel, the weights range from $\phi(0) = 0.399$ when $x_i = z_j$ to values approaching zero when x_i is far from z_j. Thus, again, what the kernel density function is measuring is the proportion of the sample of values that is close to the chosen z_j.

The other essential part of the computation is the smoothing (bandwidth) parameter, h, to ensure a good plot resolution. The bandwidth parameter is exactly analogous to the bin width in a common histogram. Thus, as noted earlier, narrower bins (smaller bandwidths) produce unstable histograms (kernel density estimators) because not many points are "in the neighborhood" of the value of interest. Large values of h stabilize the function, but tend to flatten it and reduce the resolution – imagine a histogram with only two or three bins, for example. Small values of h produce greater detail, but also cause the estimator to become less stable. An example of a bandwidth is given in (16.8), which is a standard form used in several contemporary computer programs:

$$h = 0.9Q/n^{0.2} \tag{16.8}$$

where Q = min(standard deviation, range/1.5)

A number of points have to be specified. The set of points z_j is (for any number of points) defined by (16.9):

$$z_j = z_{LOWER} + j^*[(z_{UPPER} - z_{LOWER})/M], j = 1, \ldots, Mz_{LOWER}$$
$$= \min(x) - h \text{ to } z_{UPPER} = \max(x) + h \tag{16.9}$$

The procedure produces an $M \times 2$ matrix in which the first column contains z_j and the second column contains the values of $f(z_j)$ and plot of the second column against the first – this is the estimated density function. The NLOGIT command used to obtain plots of the kernel densities is shown generically below. Note that it is the *attribute name* and not the parameter name that is used within the command syntax:

Kernel;rhs= <attribute> $

Using the kernel density to graphically describe the empirical distributions for two parameters, fuel and toll cost (figure 16.17), we can establish the empirical shape of each distribution. The specific NLOGIT commands for this are as shown below:

Kernel;rhs=fuel $
Kernel;rhs=toll $

A close inspection of the properties of each distribution (i.e. kurtosis and skewness) suggests approximate analytical distributions. Both parameters, for example, appear lognormal.

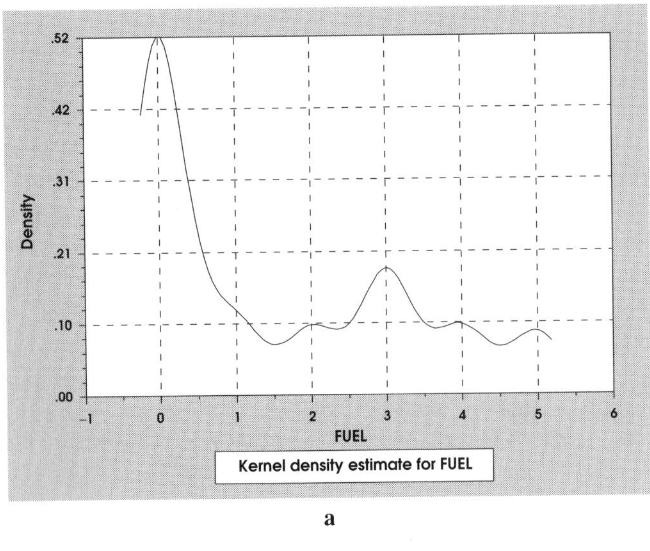

a

Density
2.38
1.90
1.43
.95
.48
.00
–.50
.00
.50
1.00
1.50
2.00
2.50
TOLL
Kernel density estimate for TOLL

b

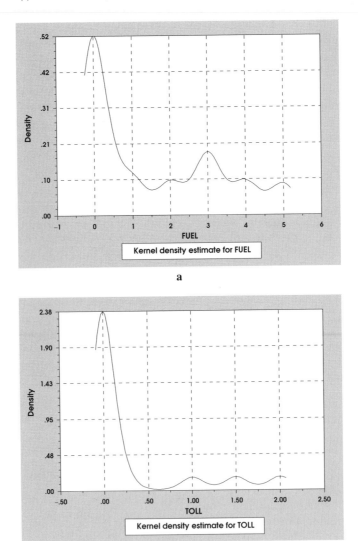

Figure 16.17 Kernel density function for *fuel* and *toll cost* parameters

16.10 Willingness-to-pay issues and the mixed logit model

We discussed in chapter 10 how to derive measures of WTP from the MNL model. If in the ML model, the two parameters used in deriving measures of WTP are estimated as non-random parameters, the methodology of calculating WTP remains unchanged. If, however, one or the other of the parameters is estimated as a random parameter, then the WTP calculations must take this into account. To demonstrate the derivation of WTP measures using random parameter estimates, consider the following two choice models.

In estimating the first model, we estimate a generic car cost parameter, *c*, as a random parameter estimate with a triangular distribution and a generic public transport travel time parameter drawn from a normal distribution. In the estimation process, we have not constrained the distributions, 20 SHS draws are used and the model is estimated on the 30 minutes or less commuter segment:

```
Calc;ran(12345)$
NLOGIT
;lhs = choice, cset, altij
;Choices = cart, carnt, bus, train, busway, LR
;rpl
;fcn=c(t),pt(n)
;Halton
;pts=20
;Parameters
;wtp=tt/c
;Model:
U(cart)  = asccart + c*fuel + tt*time + tl*toll + pk*parking /
U(carnt) = asccarnt + c*fuel + tt*time + pk*parking /
U(bus)   = ascbus + pc*fare + pt*time + fq*freq /
U(train) =          pc*fare + pt*time + fq*freq /
U(busway)= ascbusw + pc*fare + pt*time + fq*freq /
U(LR)    = asclr + pc*fare + pt*time + fq*freq $
```

The following NLOGIT output is produced for this model:

```
+-----------------------------------------------+
| Random Parameters Logit Model                  |
| Maximum Likelihood Estimates                   |
| Model estimated: Feb 30, 2003 at 05:45:00PM.   |
| Dependent variable              CHOICE         |
| Weighting variable                None         |
| Number of observations            9476         |
| Iterations completed                28         |
| Log likelihood function      -2909.884         |
| Restricted log likelihood    -4244.678         |
| Chi squared                   2669.588         |
| Degrees of freedom                  14         |
| Prob[ChiSqd > value] =        .0000000         |
| R2=1-LogL/LogL*    Log-L fncn  R-sqrd  RsqAdj  |
| No coefficients    -4244.6782  .31446  .31311  |
| Constants only.    Must be computed directly.  |
|                    Use NLOGIT ;...; RHS=ONE $  |
| At start values    -2924.9284  .00514  .00318  |
| Response data are given as ind. choice.        |
+-----------------------------------------------+
```

```
+------------------------------------------------+
| Random Parameters Logit Model                  |
| Replications for simulated probs. = 20         |
| Halton sequences used for simulations          |
| Number of obs.=  2369, skipped   0 bad obs.    |
+------------------------------------------------+

+----------+-------------+----------------+----------+----------+
| Variable | Coefficient | Standard Error | b/St.Er. | P[|Z|>z] |
+----------+-------------+----------------+----------+----------+
          Random parameters in utility functions
C             -.21242053       .07301025      -2.909      .0036
PT            -.08754103       .03039003      -2.881      .0040
          Nonrandom parameters in utility functions
ASCCART        .17020687       .51021809        .334      .7387
TT            -.05322133       .01528195      -3.483      .0005
TL            -.23162567       .08587784      -2.697      .0070
PK            -.12830201       .00912735     -14.057      .0000
ASCCARNT       .55598847       .56422966        .985      .3244
ASCBUS         .08019698       .11225723        .714      .4750
PC            -.29657234       .03052860      -9.715      .0000
FQ            -.02791986       .00556176      -5.020      .0000
ASCBUSW        .11653191       .11871065        .982      .3263
ASCLR          .04150513       .10680010        .389      .6976
          Derived standard deviations of parameter distributions
TsC           1.15213773       .26977389       4.271      .0000
NsPT           .10152930       .04005109       2.535      .0112
```

The model is statistically significant overall with a Chi-square statistic of 2669.588 with 14 degrees of freedom and a pseudo-R^2 of 0.31446. The mean and standard deviation parameters of the two random parameters are statistically significant at the 95 percent confidence level and in the expected directions. The non-random parameter estimates for each of the attributes are statistically significant at the 95 percent confidence level and of the expected signs.

The WTP for an attribute is calculated in exactly the same manner as described in chapter 10. That is, the WTP for an attribute is the ratio of that attribute's parameter estimate to the parameter estimate of the cost parameter. For values of travel time savings (VTTS), we multiply the resulting WTP measure by 60 if the time attribute was measured in minutes. This converts the VTTS to a measure of WTP for time per hour.

VTTS and WTP measures may be constructed using either the unconditional parameter estimates (population moments) or the common-choice-specific conditional parameter estimates. In order to obtain a WTP or VTTS measure using the unconditional parameter estimates, the population must be simulated. The following command syntax may be used to simulate a population for the above example. VTTS will be saved in the data set under

E2 ▾ fx =B2/A2*60

	A	B	C	D	E	F
1	C	TT	PTC	PT	VTTSCar	VTTSPT
2	0.12068	-0.05322	-0.29657	-0.10954	-$26.46	$22.16
3	-0.35716	-0.05322	-0.29657	-0.02777	$8.94	$5.62
4	-0.47625	-0.05322	-0.29657	-0.00846	$6.71	$1.71
5	0.153415	-0.05322	-0.29657	-0.11245	-$20.81	$22.75
6	-0.10372	-0.05322	-0.29657	-0.12772	$30.79	$25.84

Figure 16.18

the names *VTTSCAR* and *VTTSPT*. We have multiplied the VTTS by 60 to convert from $/min to $/hour. The results for the following commands are shown in table 16.1 (p. 692).

```
Calc;ran(12345)$
CREATE
;rna=rnn(0,1)
;V=rnu(0,1)
;if(v<=0.5)T=sqr(2*V)-1;(ELSE) T=1-sqr(2*(1-V))$

CREATE
;vttscar=60*(-0.05322133)/(-0.21242053 + 1.15213773*T)
;vttspt=60*(-0.08754103+ 0.10152930*rna)/(-0.29657234)$
```

	A	B	C	D	E	F
1	C	TT/C car	PC	PT	VTTSCar	VTTSPT
2	0.12068	-0.3193	-0.29657	-0.10954	$19.16	$22.16
3	-0.35716	0.491382	-0.29657	-0.02777	-$29.48	$5.62
4	-0.47625	-0.1313	-0.29657	-0.00846	$7.88	$1.71
5	0.153415	0.307044	-0.29657	-0.11245	-$18.42	$22.75
6	-0.10372	-0.85012	-0.29657	-0.12772	$51.01	$25.84

Figure 16.19

Figure 16.19 highlights the possibility of obtaining negative VTTS when using unconstrained distributions to calculate VTTS from the conditional parameter estimates. As negative values of VTTS suggest that individuals require payment to save an hour of travel time as opposed to their being willing to pay to save time traveling, such values represent a behaviorally implausible position (especially in the current application). In using random parameter estimates to obtain WTP measures, Hensher and Greene (2003) suggest that to derive behaviorally meaningful values, the distributions from which random parameters are drawn be constrained.[3] Although little is reported in the literature as to the best constraint to use, constraining the standard deviation parameter estimate to that of the mean of the random parameter for a triangular distribution guarantees non-negative WTP measures.

[3] The constraining of a random parameter distribution is an econometric consideration based upon the underlying empirical distribution of that parameter. The reader is cautioned against confusing such a constraint on the empirical distribution with a constraint upon the *behavioral distributions* in the population.

A second-choice model is estimated in which the standard deviation parameters are constrained to equal the means of each random parameter estimate respectively. The NLOGIT command syntax for this model is as shown below:

```
Calc;ran(12345)$
NLOGIT
;lhs = choice, cset, altij
;Choices = cart, carnt, bus, train, busway, LR
;rpl
;fcn=c(t,1),pt(n,1)
;Halton
;pts=20
;parameters
;wtp=tt/c
;Model:
U(cart)   = asccart + c*fuel + tt*time + tl*toll + pk*parking /
U(carnt)  = asccarnt + c*fuel + tt*time + pk*parking /
U(bus)    = ascbus + pc*fare + pt*time + fq*freq /
U(train)  =          pc*fare + pt*time + fq*freq /
U(busway) = ascbusw + pc*fare + pt*time + fq*freq /
U(LR)     = asclr + pc*fare + pt*time + fq*freq $
```

Estimated on the 30 minutes or less commuter segment, the above syntax produces the following model output:

```
+----------------------------------------------+
| Random Parameters Logit Model                |
| Maximum Likelihood Estimates                 |
| Model estimated: Feb 30, 2003 at 06:00:00PM. |
| Dependent variable               CHOICE      |
| Weighting variable                 None      |
| Number of observations             9476      |
| Iterations completed                 19      |
| Log likelihood function       -2917.469      |
| Restricted log likelihood     -4244.678      |
| Chi squared                    2654.418      |
| Degrees of freedom                   12      |
| Prob[ChiSqd > value] =         .0000000      |
| R2=1-LogL/LogL*  Log-L  fncn R-sqrd RsqAdj   |
| No coefficients  -4244.6782  .31268  .31151  |
| Constants only.  Must be computed directly.  |
|                  Use NLOGIT ;...; RHS=ONE $  |
| At start values  -2922.8994  .00186  .00017  |
| Response data are given as ind. choice.      |
+----------------------------------------------+
```

```
+------------------------------------------------+
| Random Parameters Logit Model                  |
| Replications for simulated probs. = 20         |
| Halton sequences used for simulations          |
| Number of obs.= 2369, skipped 0 bad obs.       |
+------------------------------------------------+
```

Variable	Coefficient	Standard Error	b/St.Er.	P[|Z|>z]
Random parameters in utility functions				
C	-.09674326	.05293829	-1.827	.0676
PT	-.11077398	.02747050	-4.032	.0001
Nonrandom parameters in utility functions				
ASCCART	-.64779213	.39541059	-1.638	.1014
TT	-.04006352	.01273571	-3.146	.0017
TL	-.22868428	.07878422	-2.903	.0037
PK	-.11207428	.00655237	-17.104	.0000
ASCCARNT	-.27881266	.46099393	-.605	.5453
ASCBUS	.08237295	.10884923	.757	.4492
PC	-.27300900	.02812753	-9.706	.0000
FQ	-.02669383	.00514895	-5.184	.0000
ASCBUSW	.10545547	.11440470	.922	.3566
ASCLR	.02825173	.10376308	.272	.7854
Derived standard deviations of parameter distributions				
TsC	.09674326	.05293829	1.827	.0676
NsPT	.11077398	.02747050	4.032	.0001

The overall model is statistically significant, $\chi^2_{12} = 2654.418$, and has a pseudo-R^2 of 0.31268. The mean and standard deviation parameters for the *public transport travel time* random parameter are statistically significant at the 95 percent level of confidence and are of the expected sign. The mean and standard deviation parameters for the *car fuel cost* random parameter are statistically significant at the 90 percent level of confidence and are also of the expected sign. All non-random parameters estimated for the remaining design attributes are also statistically significant and of the expected signs. Once more, the WTP ratios for each observation are saved in the WTP_I Matrix and the choice-specific-conditional parameter estimates within the BETA_I Matrix.

In table 16.1 we compare the VTTS derived from using (i) the unconditional parameter estimates, (ii) the conditional but unconstrained parameter estimates, and (iii) the conditional and constrained parameter estimates. The VTTS derived from the unconditional parameter estimates produced behaviorally implausible results. For travel by car, a negative VTTS value of −\$5.05 was observed and maximum and minimum VTTS of \$ 44,657.56 and −\$37, 357.09 were produced. A mean of \$17.67 was observed for the public transport

Table 16.1. *Comparison of the VTTS derived from unconditional parameter estimates, conditional (unconstrained), and conditional (constrained) parameter estimates*

	Unconditional parameters		Conditional (unconstrained) distribution		Conditional (constrained) distribution	
	car ($)	*public transport* ($)	*car* ($)	*public transport* ($)	*car* ($)	*public transport* ($)
Mean	−5.05	3.77	49.12	17.81	34.48	24.26
St. dev.	880.35	253.13	2,414.01	9.56	12.38	13.37
Maximum	46,657.56	6,071.40	114,434.72	41.16	421.60	50.67
Minimum	−37,357.09	−6,297.60	−18,438.22	−11.80	24.68	−12.52

E2 fx =B2/A2*60

	A	B	C	D	E	F
1	C	TT	PT	PTC	VTTSCar	VTTSPT
2	-0.09361	-0.04006	-0.27301	-0.15638	$25.68	$34.37
3	-0.09375	-0.04006	-0.27301	-0.03121	$25.64	$6.86
4	-0.10659	-0.04006	-0.27301	-0.01648	$22.55	$3.62
5	-0.09388	-0.04006	-0.27301	-0.17289	$25.60	$38.00
6	-0.09829	-0.04006	-0.27301	-0.1578	$24.46	$34.68

Figure 16.20

VTTS with a standard deviation of $20.31. The VTTS produced using the conditional but unconstrained parameter estimates had a mean of $3.71 and $17.81 for the *car* and *public transport* modes, respectively. For the *car* alternatives, a standard deviation of $253.13 is observed, a result of a number of very large positive and very small negative VTTS produced in the random draw process. Using the conditional but unconstrained parameter estimates for the public transport alternatives produces a mean and standard deviation for the VTTS measure of $17.81 and $9.56, respectively. The VTTS derived when using the conditional but constrained parameter estimates are closer to the values suggested within the literature (although the public transport values are high and have a negative range due to the use of a normal distribution). The mean of the car VTTS is $34.48 with a standard deviation of $12.38 and therefore no negative values are observed due to the use of a triangular distribution. The public transport VTTS from the same model has a mean of $24.26 and a standard deviation of $13.37.

For WTP measures estimated using the conditional random parameter estimates, it is possible to generate distributions of WTP. Figures 16.21 and 16.22 plot the VTTS values obtained for the above example. It is worth noting that what is being plotted are strictly not "individual-specific values" but rather the distribution of conditional means. In plotting WTP or VTTS distributions, the observed values should first be ordered. Figure 16.22 shows the VTTS distributions for the *car* alternatives (we have restricted the Y-axis of the graph to be between minus $150 and $150). Clearly demonstrated in figure 16.21 is the

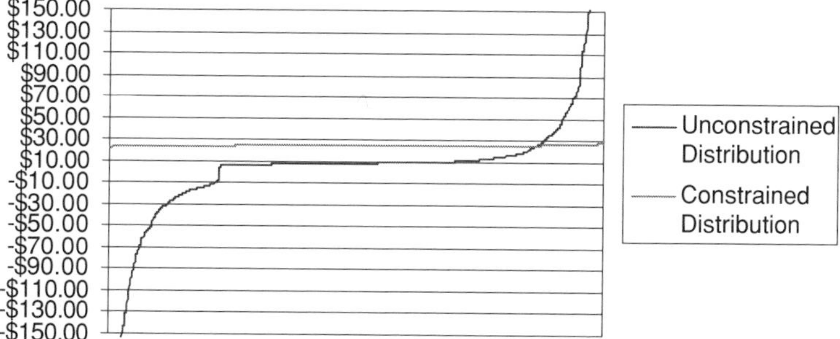

Figure 16.21 The *car* VTTS distribution

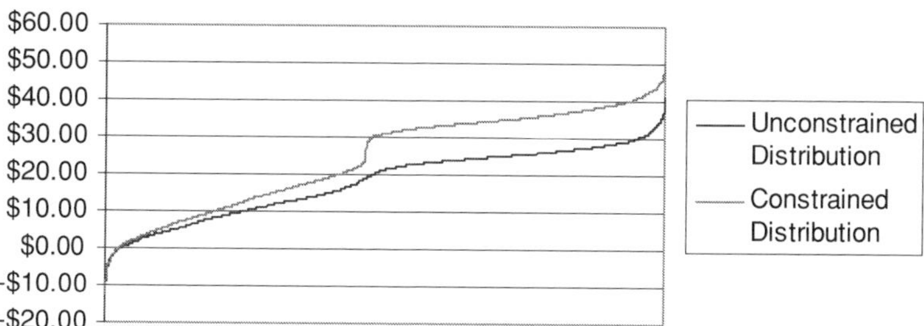

Figure 16.22 The *public transport* VTTS distribution

influence of drawing observations from the tails of unconstrained distributions in deriving behavioral outputs.

Figure 16.22 shows the VTTS distributions for the *public transport* modes. Figure 16.22 suggests that the left-hand tail of the two VTTS distributions are almost identical, however, as one moves along the distribution, the VTTS are larger when using the constrained distributions than the unconstrained distributions. In both cases, negative VTTS are observed.

What the above discussion highlights are some of the challenges in estimating ML models when the objective of the estimation process is to produce behaviorally meaningful individual-level outputs. In the above example, we have estimated constrained and unconstrained models using a triangular and normal distribution from which we draw the random parameters. Accrued experience, however, suggests that the triangular distribution is the best distribution to derive such individual-level outputs.

Figure 16.23 plots the VTTS for the *car* and *public transport* modes derived from the above model. The distributions for both modes show similar patterns with little deviation in the tails. The VTTS for the public transport mode has a neater distribution than when a normal distribution was applied with behaviorally acceptable properties (see table 16.1).

There is much work still required in deriving WTP measures using the ML model. In this, section, we have highlighted some of the challenges as well as the accumulated experiences (often unreported) of researchers in this field. In providing the reader with the mode-choice data, we hope that you will use the data to estimate statistically and behaviorally superior

Table 16.2. *Statistical outputs for VTTS estimated using triangular distributions*

	car ($)	*public transport* ($)
Mean	24.74	11.06
St. Dev.	0.75	0.68
Maximum	27.96	12.71
Minimum	22.65	8.69

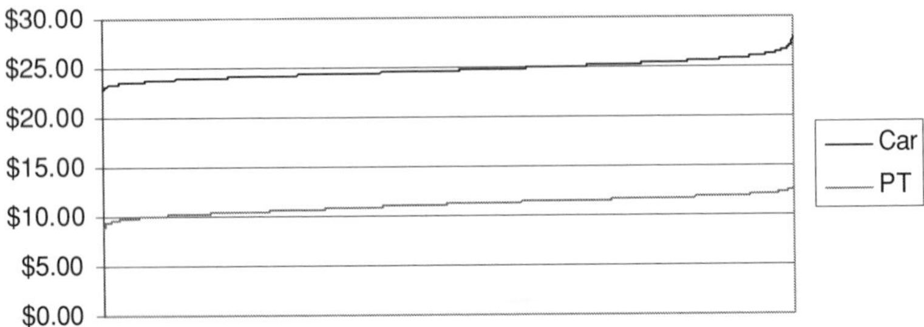

Figure 16.23 Plotting the VTTS derived from triangular distributions

models to those we have used as examples in this, and other, chapters. In doing so, we hope that you too, will add to the collective experience of the international community of choice modelers.

Glossary

General statistical terms

a priori	Latin for "before the fact"
Alternative hypothesis	the outcome of the hypothesis test for which one wishes to find supporting evidence
Alternative-specific constant (ASC)	a parameter for a particular alternative that is used to represent the role of unobserved sources of utility
Alternatives	options containing specified levels of attributes
Arc elasticity	an elasticity calculated over a range of values for the reference variable
Attribute invariance	limited variation in the levels of attributes observed in the market
Attribute-level label	the narrative description corresponding to an attribute
Attribute levels	a specific value taken by an attribute; experimental designs require that each attribute takes on two or more levels, which may be quantitative or qualitative
Attributes	characteristics of an alternative
Balanced design	a design in which the levels of any given attribute appear the same number of times as all other levels for that particular attribute
Bayesian determination	the assignment of weights to RP and SP data according to the behavioral strengths each data source has
Bias	a force that leads to incorrect inferences regarding behavior

Blocking	the use of an additional design column to assign sub-sets of treatment combinations to decision makers
Bounded rationality	acting consistently with rational behavior, with the constraint that only a sub-set of all available information is considered
Branch	the third division of alternatives in a nested model
Calibrate	to adjust the constant terms in a model in order to replicate actual market shares through model estimation
Calibration constant	constants used to allow the model to correspond to actual choice shares
Cardinal	a numerical value that is directly comparable to all other such values (i.e. a value of ten is twice as good as a value of five)
Ceteris paribus	Latin for "all other things held constant"
Choice-based sampling (CBS)	a sampling method involving the deliberate over- and under-sampling of groups that make particular choices
Choice outcome	the observed choice behavior of an individual
Choice set	the set of alternatives over which an agent makes a choice
Choice set generation	the process of identifying the choices that are relevant to a particular problem
Choice setting	the scenario in which an agent's choice takes place
Choice shares	the proportion of the population that chooses a particular alternative
Cholesky matrix	a lower off-diagonal matrix **L** which is used in the factorization of a matrix **A**, such that $\mathbf{A} = \mathbf{L}\mathbf{L}'$
Closed-form	mathematically tractable, involving only mathematical operations
Code book	a blueprint of the form that the data will take when entered into a computer for analysis
Coding	the use of numbers to designate a particular state of an attribute (e.g. zero denotes male and one denotes female)
Coefficient	a scalar value by which a particular element in a model is multiplied in the estimation process
Cognitive burden	the level of difficulty faced by a respondent in considering a set of choice menus
Column vector	a matrix containing only one column

Composite alternatives alternatives incorporating more than one component alternative (e.g. choosing to drive a car and choosing to drive that car during rush hour)

Computer-aided personal interview (CAPI) the use of a computer in face-to-face data collection

Conditional choice a choice that is predicated on a prior condition (e.g. the choice of commuting mode is conditional on the decision whether to work)

Conditional probability density function (CPDF) a function yielding the probability of observing a particular value for a variable given the observation of a particular value for another variable

Confoundment the state of being unable to break apart the effects of multiple forces

Conjoint analysis the analysis of experiments in which individuals rank or rate each treatment combination

Constraints obstacles to selecting an alternative that would yield the highest possible level of utility or satisfaction (e.g. income, time, scarcity, technology)

Contingency table a cross-tabulation of actual versus predicted choices

Continuous a variable that can take an infinite level of values

Correlation a measure of the strength of magnitude of the relationship that may exist between two random variables

Covariance a statistical measure representative of the degree to which two random variables vary together

Cross-section data relating to multiple members of a population

Cumulative distribution function (CDF) a function yielding a value equal to the probability that a random variable is observed to take on a value less than or equal to some known value

Data cleaning the inspection of the data for inaccuracies

Decision support system (DSS) a program used to embed the resulting utility expressions from a model so that analysts can predict the impact of changes in the levels of attributes on choice shares and absolute numbers choosing each alternative

Degenerate outcome	occurs when there is no dependence between choice models at the upper and lower levels
Degrees of freedom	the number of observations in a sample minus the number of independent (linear) constraints imposed during the modeling process; these constraints are the estimated parameters
Delay choice alternative	the alternative to delay a choice of alternatives
Design degrees of freedom	the number of treatment combinations required to obtain the necessary degrees of freedom
Discrete	a variable that can take only a finite level of values
Discrete choice	the selection of one alternative among a set of mutually exclusive alternatives
Distribution	the range over which the value of a variable may be, and the frequency with which each of those values is observed to occur
Dummy coding	denoting the existence of a particular attribute with a one and its absence with a zero
Effect	the impact of a particular treatment upon a response variable
Effects coding	*see* orthogonal coding
Elasticity	the percentage change in one variable with respect to a percentage change in another
Elemental alternatives	alternatives that are not composites of other alternatives (e.g. choosing to drive a car, choosing to take a train)
Endogenous	within the control of the decision maker (e.g. which alternative to choose)
Endogenous weighting	the weighting of choice-data based on information regarding true market shares
Exogenous	outside of the control of the decision maker (e.g. gender or age)
Exogenous weighting	the weighting of any data besides choice
Expected value	the average value of a set of values observed for a particular variable
Experiment	the manipulation of one variable with the purpose of observing the effect of that manipulation upon a second variable
Experimental design	the specification of attributes and attribute levels for use in an experiment

Factor levels a specific value taken by a factor; experimental designs require that each factor takes on two or more levels, which may be quantitative or qualitative

Fixed parameter a parameter with a constant value; also refers to a non-random parameter

Foldover the reproduction of a design in which the factor levels of the design are reversed (e.g. replace 0 with 1 and replace 1 with 0)

Full factorial design a design in which all possible treatment combinations are enumerated

Functional form of the attributes the manner in which the relevant attributes in a model are assumed to influence choice (e.g. linearly, non-linearly, logarithmic)

Functional form of the parameters the manner in which the importance weights enter the model (e.g. fixed or random)

Generalized cost a measure of cost that allows for the direct comparison of the costs of all alternatives; this involves the conversion of attribute levels into a common measure, generally a monetary value (e.g. converting travel time into a value of travel time)

Hausman-test a test for the existence of the independence of irrelevant alternatives

Heterogeneity variation in behavior that can be attributed to differences in the tastes and decision making processes of individuals in the population

Hypothesis testing the process by which one determines the worth of an estimate of a population parameter or a sample parameter

IID condition the assumption that the unobserved components of utility of all alternatives are uncorrelated with the unobserved components of utility for all other alternatives, combined with the assumption that each of these error terms has the exact same distribution

Importance weight the relative contribution of an attribute to utility

Inclusive value (IV) a parameter estimate used to establish the extent of dependence or independence between linked choices

Income effect — the change in quantity demanded that can be attributed to a change in an individual's income

Independence of irrelevant alternatives (IIA) — a restrictive assumption, which is part of the multinomial logit model; the IIA property states that the ratio of the choice probabilities is independent of the presence or absence of any other alternative in a choice set

Indifference curves — all combinations of two attributes that yield the same level of utility

Indirect utility function — the function used to estimate the utility derived from a particular set of observed attributes

Insignificant — having no systematic influence

Interaction effect — an effect upon the response variable obtained by combining two or more attributes which would not have been observed had each of the attributes been estimated separately

Inter-attribute correlation — the subjective interrelation between two attributes (e.g. a higher price may signal higher quality)

Internet-aided survey (IAS) — the collection of survey data via the internet

Interval scaled data — data in which the levels of an object under study are assigned values which are unique, provide an indication of order, and have an equal distance between scale points (e.g. temperature measured in Centigrade or Fahrenheit)

Joint probability density function (JPDF) — a function yielding the probabilities of observing sets of individual values for multiple variables

Kernel density — a smoothed plot used to describe the distribution of a sample of observations

Labeled experiment — containing a description of the alternative (e.g. naming a particular item model)

Leptokurtic — having a small spread around the mean

Limb — the second division of alternatives in a nested model

Linear restriction — a constraint that a parameter takes on a particular value

Lower off-diagonal matrix — a matrix in which all values above and to the right of the diagonal are equal to zero

Main effect the direct independent effect of each factor upon a response variable; for experimental designs, the main effect is the difference in the means of each level of an attribute and the overall or grand mean

Maintained assumption an assumption that cannot be tested

Marginal effects the change in the probability of selecting an alternative with respect to a one-unit change in an attribute

Marginal probability density function (MPDF) a function yielding the probabilities of observing a particular value for a variable in a multivariate environment independent of what value is observed for the other variable(s)

Marginal rate of substitution The amount of a particular item that must be given to an agent in order to exactly compensate that agent for the loss of one unit of another item

Marginal utility the increase in utility due to an incremental increase of an attribute

Maximum likelihood estimation (MLE) a method used to find parameter estimates that best explain the data

Mesokurtic having a moderate spread around the mean

Mixing distribution a distribution mixing the multiple logit (ML) models used in a mixed (or random parameters) logit model

Moment a property of a distribution, such as its mean (first population moment of a distribution) or variance (second population moment of a distribution)

Multicollinearity the state of two variables being so closely correlated that the effects of one cannot be isolated from the effects of the other

Multivariate involving more than one variable

Naive pooling the calculation of marginal effects for each decision maker without weighting by the decision maker's associated choice probability

Nested hierarchical, or belonging to a mutually exclusive sub-set of a group of outcomes

No-choice alternative the alternative not to choose any of the alternatives in the choice set

Nominal qualitative attribute a labeled attribute for which no natural order exists

Nominal scaled data data in which the levels observed are assigned unique values which provide classification, but which do not provide any indication of order

Non-random draws error components obtained using systematic elements, designed to cover the range of the error term more efficiently than random draws

Non-random parameter a parameter that takes on only one value

Non-stochastic not random, a constant

Normalize to fix to a particular value in order to enable comparison

Null hypothesis a statement that outlines the possible outcome of the hypothesis test that one does not want to observe

Observation a choice made by an individual in a choice setting

One-tailed test a hypothesis test in which the analyst is investigating whether a test-statistic is outside one particular critical value (e.g. whether a *t*-statistic is greater than 1.812, to test at the 5 percent significance level with 10 degrees of freedom)

Ordinal a numerical value that is indirectly comparable to all other such values (i.e. a value of ten is better than a value of five, but it is unknown how much better it is)

Ordinal qualitative attribute a labeled attribute for which some natural order exists

Ordinal scaled data data in which the values assigned to levels observed for an object are both unique and provide an indication of order (i.e. a ranking)

Orthogonal independent of all other factors

Orthogonal coding coding in which all values for a given attribute sum to zero; in the case of even numbers of code levels, each positive code level is matched by its negative value, in the case of odd numbers of code levels, the median level is assigned the value zero – for example, in the two-level case, the levels assigned are -1 and 1; in the three-level case, the levels assigned are -1, 0, and 1

Orthogonal main effects only design	an orthogonal design in which only the main effects are estimated; all other interactions are assumed to be insignificant
Over-identified	having too many variables to be estimated by the available information
Over-sampling	sampling a proportion of a particular group that is greater than that group's proportion in the population
Panel data	data incorporating multiple observations per sampled individual
Parameter	a unique weight used to describe the systematic contribution of a particular element in a model
Partial degeneration	occurs when degenerate partitions occur before the final level of the model
Part-worth	the proportion of utility that can be attributed to a specific attribute
Platykurtic	having a large spread around the mean
Point elasticity	an elasticity calculated at a particular point
Preference heterogeneity	differing preferences across the population
Preferences	the forces leading an individual to select one alternative over another
Probability density function (PDF)	the probability distribution over the various values that a variable might take (bounded by zero and one, inclusively)
Probability-weighted sample enumeration	the calculation of marginal effects for each decision maker, weighted by the decision maker's associated choice probability
Profiles	combinations of attributes, each with unique levels
Pseudo-R^2	a measure of model fit for discrete choice models, giving the proportion of variation in the data that is explained by the model
***p*-value**	represents the probability of an erroneous finding in terms of accepting the conclusion drawn from a test conducted on a sample as being valid, or representative of the population
Qualitative	involving description
Quantitative	involving numbers
Random parameter	a parameter with a mean value and an associated standard deviation, yielding a distribution of estimated values

Random utility maximization the analysis of the maximization of utility, taking into account the unobserved sources of utility for all alternatives

Random variable a variable that can take on more than one value

Randomization changing the order of elements

Ratio scale the level of satisfaction or utility of an alternative relative to that of another alternative

Ratio scaled data data in which the values assigned to levels of an object are unique, provide an indication of order, have an equal distance between scale points, and the zero point on the scale of measure used represents an absence of the object being observed (e.g. expenditure, or temperature measured in Kelvin or Rankin)

Rationality taking into account all matters that are relevant, regardless of the amount of information at one's disposal to assist one's deliberations

Rejection level a value representing the probability that the analyst is willing to reject the null hypothesis when in fact the null hypothesis is correct; alternatively, a value representing the probability that the analyst has not rejected the null hypothesis when it is correct

Relative frequency the proportion of occurrence of an outcome observed in relation to all outcomes observed

Reliability the concept that results similar to those from a given sample would be obtained through repeated samples

Research question the chief question the research is intended to address

Response rate out of the total number of individuals requested to participate in an experiment, the proportion of those who take part

Response stimulus an element used to invoke a desired response (e.g. a choice)

Responses the observed outcomes in a choice setting

Restricted involving parameters that are constrained to a particular value

Revealed preference (RP) responses observed in a market setting

Row vector a matrix containing only one row

Sampling distribution	the distribution of a sample statistic over repeated sampling from a fixed population: a measure of sample-to-sample variability
Sampling distribution mean	the distribution of the means over repeated samples from the (fixed) population from which multiple samples are drawn
Sampling error	random variability resulting from the particular sample that is drawn; that is, if different samples are drawn, different means, variances, correlations and covariances are likely to be observed
Sampling frame	the sub-set of the population to whom the experiment may be administered
Satisfaction	the amount or level of happiness that an alternative yields to an individual *see* utility
Scale parameter	a parameter used to normalize utility expressions across alternatives; a reference measure used to allow for the comparison of utility for different alternatives
Significance	the probability that a given parameter estimate is equal to a particular value, generally given in reference to zero
Significance level	a value representing the probability that the analyst is willing to reject the null hypothesis when in fact the null hypothesis is correct; alternatively, a value representing the probability that the analyst has not rejected the null hypothesis when it is correct
Socio-demographic characteristic (SDC)	information regarding respondents, such as age, income, and gender
Socio-economic characteristics	information regarding individuals that serves as a proxy for their tastes; examples include income, age, gender, and occupation
Standard deviation	the square root of the variance
Standard error	the standard deviation of the sample distribution, representing the standard deviation of the sampling distribution
Stated-preference (SP)	responses observed in an experimental setting
Stated-preference experiment	an experiment involving hypothetical choice scenarios and researcher-specified attributes and attribute levels
Statistical independence	the state in which the value of one variable is not influenced by the value of another

Step function a function involving a discrete variable (a variable that can take on only particular values), in which there is no increase in the value of the function until it jumps at a particular point; for example, the cumulative distribution function for a discrete variable is a step function, because the probability of observing an outcome in between two consecutive values x and y for the variable is zero – the function will maintain the same value from x up to y and then jump to a new value at y

Stimulus refinement brainstorming and then narrowing the range of alternatives to consider in the experiment

Stochastic random

Substitution effect the change in quantity demanded that can be attributed to a change in the relative prices of two goods

Substitution patterns the manner in which it is inferred that people move away from one alternative toward another in response to changes in attribute levels

Survey instrument the survey to be used in the experiment

Synthetic household a representative hypothetical group, used in analysis to represent the proportion of agents of a particular type

Tastes the component of an individual's personal preferences which are specific to that individual, rather than being tied to the relevant attributes in the choice set

Test statistic the result of a statistical test that relates some sample statistic to that of a population statistic

Testable assumption an assumption that can be refuted or confirmed

Transpose a transformation of a matrix in which the rows and columns of a matrix are interchanged

Treatment the specific factor level for a particular attribute

Treatment combination combinations of attributes, each with unique levels

Trunk the first division of alternatives in a nested model

***t*-test** A test-statistic relating to the sample standard deviation through a normal distribution

Two-tailed test a hypothesis test in which the analyst is investigating whether a test-statistic is outside one of two critical values (e.g. whether a t-statistic is greater than 2.228 or less than −2.228, to test at the 5 percent significance level (2.5 percent significance level at each tail) with 10 degrees of freedom)

Type I error the act of rejecting the null hypothesis when it is, in fact, correct

Type II error the act of accepting the null hypothesis when it is, in fact, false

Unbalanced design a design in which the levels of any given attribute do not appear the same number of times as all other levels for that particular attribute

Unconditional choice a choice that is independent of all previous choices

Under-sampling sampling a proportion of a particular group that is less than that group's proportion in the population

Univariate involving one variable

Unlabeled experiment containing no description of the alternative (e.g. listed as "Product A")

Utility the level of happiness that an alternative yields to an individual

Utility maximization the act of seeking the alternative that yields the highest level of utility

Validity a significant relationship between the results inferred through estimation and real world behavior

Variance the second population moment of a distribution; it provides the analyst with an understanding of how dispersed or spread observations are around the mean of a distribution

Vector a matrix containing either only one row or one column

Wald-statistic the ratio of an importance weight to its standard error

Wald-test a test of whether a Wald-statistic is significantly different to zero

***Z*-test** a test-statistic relating to the population standard deviation through a normal distribution

NLOGIT terms and commands

#	used to specify which observations should remain in the data to be analysed
$	denotes the end of a command sequence
*	denotes all alternatives
/	used to separate utility functions
;Choices	used in the process of endogenous weighting
;Correlation	enables a mixed logit model to be specified in such a way that the error components in different choice situations from a given individual are correlated
;Cprob	yields conditional probabilities
;Crosstab	generates contingency tables
;Descriptives	gives descriptive statistics for each alternative
;Effects	used to calculate marginal effects or elasticities
;Halton	specifies the form of random draws as intelligent (pseudo-random) draws
;Hetero	used in the estimation of HEV models
;Histogram	used to plot a histogram for a variable
;ias	used to conduct the Hausman-test
;if	used in the generation of values for new variables
;ivset:	used to constrain or normalize an inclusive value parameter
;lhs	refers to the left-hand side variables
;Maxit=n	specifies the maximum number of iterations in the search for the global maximum of the likelihood function
;Means	allows for the calculation of point elasticities at the sample means
;Model:	used to begin the specification of a utility function
;Prob	used to produce choice probabilities
;pts	specifies the number of replications for simulated draws
;pwt	allows for the use of probability-weighted sample enumeration
;rpl	specifies the model as a mixed (random parameter) logit model
;Scenario	used to simulate a change in an attribute
;Show	generates output informative of both the market shares and utility structures
;Shuffle	specifies the form of random draws as a shuffled sequence of intelligent (pseudo-random) draws
;Simulation	used to restrict the set of alternatives
;Start	specifies staring values of the nested logit model parameter estimates
;Start=logit	establishes multinomial logit values of parameters as the starting point in the search for the global maximum of the likelihood function
;tlg	denotes the desired tolerance level in the search for the global maximum of the likelihood function
;Tree	used in the specification of the tree structure

;Utility	used to generate utility estimates
;wts	used in the process of exogenous weighting
alti	an accounting index that informs NLOGIT which alternative is assigned a line of data
Calc;	used for performing a range of mathematical functions
;Choices	indicates which alternative within a choice set was chosen
;Create	used to construct new variables
;Cset	informs NLOGIT of the number of alternatives within a particular choice set
Dstats;	generates descriptive statistics
;Format	used to specify the format of the data file
;IVB	used to specify the inclusive value at the branch level
;IVL	used to specify the inclusive value at the limb level
;IVT	used to specify the inclusive value at the trunk level
;List	displays results in the output file
;Kernel	used to plot a kernel density for a variable
;Load	used to open data sets which have already been written or read into NLOGIT and saved during previous work sessions
;Matrix	creates and manipulates matrices
;Names	used to specify the names of the variables
NLOGIT	informs the program that the analyst intends to perform a discrete choice model
;Nobs	denotes the number of observations
;Nvar	denotes the number of variables
;One	denotes the constant in a model
;Output	used to generate covariance matrices (output=1$), correlation matrices (output=2$), or both (output=3$)
;READ	used to read data into NLOGIT
;Regress	used to perform a regression analysis
Reject;	removes specified observations from the sub-set of data to be analysed
;rhs	refers to all right-hand side variables
;rnln	used to include a lognormal random variable
;rnu	used to include a uniform random variable
;RU1	used in estimation where the model is normalized at the lowest level of the tree
;RU2	used in estimation where the model is normalized at the top level of the tree
Sample;	used to finalize the sub-set of the data to be analyzed
;Wald	used to test linear restrictions
;WRITE	allows the user to create a new data set from an existing data set

References

Aaker, D.A., Kumar, V., and Day, G.S. (2001). *Marketing Research*, New York: Wiley

Ben-Akiva, M. and Lerman, S.R. (1985). *Discrete Choice Analysis: Theory and Application to Travel Demand*, Cambridge, MA: MIT Press

Bhat C.R. (2000a). Flexible model structures for discrete choice analysis, in D.A. Hensher and K.J. Button (eds.), *Handbook of Transport Modelling*, vol. 1, *Handbooks in Transport*, Oxford: Pergamon Press, 71–90

(2000b). Incorporating observed and unobserved heterogeneity in urban work mode choice modeling, *Transportation Science*, 34(2), 228–238

(2001). Quasi-random maximum simulated likelihood estimation of the mixed multinomial logit model, *Transportation Research B*, 35(7), 677–695

(2003). Simulation estimation of mixed discrete choice models using randomised and scrambled Halton sequences, *Transportation Research B*, 37(9), 837–855

Bhat, C.R. and Castelar, S. (2003). A unified mixed logit framework for modeling revealed and stated preferences: formulation and application to congestion pricing analysis in the San Francisco Bay Area, *Transportation Research B*, 36(7), 593–616

Bhat, C.R. and Zhao, H. (2002). The spatial analysis of activity stop generation, *Transportation Research B*, 36(6), 557–575

Brownstone, D. (2001). Discrete choice modelling for transportation, in D.A. Hensher (ed.), *Travel Behaviour Research: The Leading Edge*, Oxford: Pergamon Press, 97–124

Brownstone, D. and Train, K. (1999). Forecasting new product penetration with flexible substitution patterns, *Journal of Econometrics*, 89(1–2), 109–129

Bunch, D.S., Louviere, J.J., and Anderson, D. (1996). A comparison of experimental design strategies for choice-based conjoint analysis with generic-attribute multinomial logit models, Working Paper, Graduate School of Management, University of California, Davis

Churchill, G.A. (1999). *Marketing Research: Methodological Foundations* 7th edn., Fort Worth, TX: Dryden Press

Cochran, W.G. and Cox, G.M. (1957). *Experimental Designs*, New York: Wiley

Cox, D.R. (1958). *Planning of Experiments*, New York: Wiley

Daly, A.J. (1982). Policy analysis using sample enumeration: an application to car ownership forecasting, in *Proceedings of the 10th PTRC Summer Annual Meeting*, Transport Planning Methods Seminar, 1–13

Daniels, R. and Hensher, D.A. (2000). Valuation of environmental impacts of transportation projects: the challenge of self-interest proximity, *Journal of Transport Economics and Policy*, 34(2), 189–214

Dawes, R. and Corrigan, B. (1974). Linear models in decision making, *Psychological Bulletin*, 81, 95–106

Dillman, D.A. (2000). *Mail and Internet Surveys: The Tailored Design Method*, 2nd edn., New York and Chichester: Wiley

Domencich, T. and McFadden, D. (1975). *Urban Travel Demand A Behavioural Analysis*, New York and Oxford: Elsevier

Esar, E. (1943). *Esar's Comic Dictionary*, New York: Harvest House

Evans, M., Hastings, N., and Peacock, B. (1993). *Statistical Distribution*, New York: Wiley

Foddy, W.H. (1994). *Constructing Questions for Interviews and Questionnaires: Theory and Practice in Social Research*, Melbourne: Cambridge University Press

Frazer, L. and Lawley, M. (2000). *Questionnaire Design and Administration: A Practical Guide*, Brisbane: Wiley

Geweke J., Keane, M., and Runkle, D. (1994). Alternative computational approaches to inference in the multinomial probit model, *Review of Economics and Statistics*, 76(4), 609–632

Greene W.H. (2002). *NLOGIT Version 3.0 Reference Guide*, New York: Econometric Software Inc.

(2003). *Econometric Analysis*, 6th edn. Englewood Cliffs, NJ: Prentice Hall

Greene, W.H., Hensher, D.A. and Rose, J. (2004). Accounting for heterogeneity in the variance of unobserved effects in mixed logit models, Institute of Transport Studies, The University of Sydney, August

Gujarati, D. (1995). *Basic Econometrics*, 3rd edn., New York: McGraw-Hill

(1999). *Essentials of Econometrics*, 2nd edn., New York: McGraw-Hill

Hausman, J. and McFadden, D. (1984). Specification tests for the multinomial logit model, *Econometrica*, 52, 1219–1240

Hensher, D.A. (1986). Sequential and full information maximum likelihood estimation of a nested logit model, *Review of Economics and Statistics*, 68(4), 657–667

(1999). HEV choice models as a search engine for specification of nested logit tree structures, *Marketing Letters*, 10(4), 333–343

(2001). The valuation of commuter travel time savings for car drivers in New Zealand: evaluating alternative model specifications, *Transportation*, 28(2), 101–118

(2002). A systematic assessment of the environmental impacts of transport policy: an end use perspective, prepared for an invitational Special Issue of *Environmental and Resource Economics*, 22, on "Tools of the Trade for Environmental Economists," guest edited by Richard Carson, 185–217

Hensher, D.A. and Brewer, A.M. (2001). *Transport: An Economics and Management Perspective*, Oxford: Oxford Universtiy Press

Hensher, D.A. and Greene, W.G. (2001). Choosing between conventional, electric and LPG/CNG vehicles in single-vehicle households, in D.A. Hensher (ed.), *The Leading Edge of Travel Behaviour Research*, Oxford: Pergamon Press, 725–750

(2002). Specification and estimation of nested logit models, *Transportation Research*, *B* 36(1), 1–18

(2003). The mixed logit model: the state of practice, *Transportation*, 30(2), 133–176

Hensher, D.A., Greene, W.H., and Rose, J.M. (2003). Using classical inference methods to reveal individual-specific parameter estimates and avoid the potential complexities of WTP derived from population moments, The University of Sydney, September

Hensher, D.A. and Jones, S. (2004). Predicting the financial distress of firms: an assessment of the performance of conditional and unconditional distributions within a mixed logit framework, Working Paper, Institute of Transport Studies, The University of Sydney, January

Hensher, D.A. and Rose, J.M. (2003). The North-West Transport Study Patronage Survey: stated choice model estimation for work and non-work travel, Report prepared for the North-West Sydney Transportation Study, Institute of Transport Studies, The University of Sydney, July

Hensher, D.A. and Smith, N.A. (1984). Automobile classification and demand modelling, *Transport Reviews*, 4(3), 245–271

Hensher, D.A., Smith, N., Milthorpe, F., and Barnard, P. (1992). *Dimensions of Automobile Demand: A Longitudinal Study of Household Automobile Ownership and Use*, Amsterdam: North-Holland

Hensher, D.A. and Sullivan, C. (2003). Willingness to pay for road curviness and road type, *Transportation Research D*, 8(2), 139–155

Hess, S., Train, K., and Polack, J. (2003). On the use of randomly shifted and shuffled uniform vectors in the estimation of a Mixed Logit model for vehicle choice, Paper submitted for Transportation Research Board 2004 Annual Meeting

Holmes, O.W. (1858). *The Autocrat of the Breakfast Table*, Cambridge: H.O. Houghton & Co.

Howell, D.C. (1999). *Fundamental Statistics for the Behavioral Sciences*, 4th edn., Pacific Grove, CA: Duxbury Press

Huber, J. and Zwerina, K. (1996). The importance of utility balance and efficient choice designs, *Journal of Marketing Research*, 33, 307–317

Hunt, G.L. (2000). Alternative nested logit model structures and the special case of partial degeneracy, *Journal of Regional Science*, 40(1), 89–113

Kanninen, B.J. (2002). Optimal design for multinomial choice experiments, *Journal of Marketing Research*, 39, 214–217

Klein, L.R. (1962). *An Introduction to Econometrics*, Englewood Cliffs, NJ: Prentice-Hall

Kuehl, R.O. (2000). *Statistical Principles of Research Design and Analysis*, 2nd edn., Pacific Grove, CA: Duxbury Press

Kuhfeld, W.F., Tobias, R.D., and Garratt, M. (1994). Efficient experimental design with marketing research applications, *Journal of Marketing Research*, 21, 545–557

Lazari, A.G. and Anderson, D.A. (1994). Design of discrete choice set experiments for estimating both attribute and availability cross effects, *Journal of Marketing Research*, 21, 375–383

Lehman, D.R., Gupta, S., and Steckel, J.H. (1998). *Marketing Research*, Englewood Cliffs, NJ: Prentice-Hall

Louviere, J.J., Hensher, D.A., and Swait, J. (2000). *Stated Choice Methods: Analysis and Applications in Marketing, Transportation and Environmental Valuation*, Cambridge: Cambridge University Press

Mackay, D. (ed.) (1977). *The Harvest of a Quiet Eye*, Bristol and London: Institute of Physics

Maddala, G.S. (1992). *Introduction to Econometrics*, 2nd edn., New York: Macmillan

McFadden, D. (1974). Conditional logit analysis of qualitative choice behavior, in P. Zarembka (ed.), *Frontiers of Econometrics*, New York: Academic Press, 105–142

McFadden, D. and Ruud, P.A. (1994). Estimation by simulation, *Review of Economics and Statistics*, 76(4), 591–608

McFadden, D. and Train, K. (2000). Mixed MNL models for discrete response, *Applied Econometrics*, 15(5), 447–470

Powers, D.A. and Xie, Y. (2000). *Statistical Methods for Categorical Data Analysis*, New York: Academic Press

Rose, J.M. and Bliemer, M.C.J. (2004). The design of stated choice experiments: the state of practice, Working Paper, Institute of Transport Studies, The University of Sydney

Rowntree, D. (1991). *Statistics Without Tears: A Primer for Non-Mathematicians*, London: Penguin Books

Sandor, Z. and Train, K. (2004). Quasi-random simulation of discrete choice models, *Transport Research B*, 38(4), 313–327

Sandor, Z. and Wedel, M. (2001). Designing conjoint choice experiments using managers' prior beliefs, *Journal of Marketing Research*, 38, 430–444

Siegel S. and Castellan, J.N., Jr. (1988). *Nonparametric Statistics for the Behavioral Sciences International*, 2nd edn., Singapore: McGraw-Hill

Stern, S. (1997). Simulation-based estimation, *Journal of Economic Literature*, 35, 2006–2039

Stevens, S.S. (1951). Mathematics, measurement, and psychophysics, in S.S. Stevens (ed.), *Handbook of Experimental Psychology*, New York: Wiley

Train, K. (1998). Unobserved taste variation in recreation demand models, *Land Economics*, 74(2), 230–239

(1999). Halton sequences for mixed logits, Department of Economics, University of California at Berkeley, August 2

(2003). *Discrete Choice Methods with Simulation*, Cambridge: Cambridge University Press

Twain, M. (1894). Pudd'nhead Wilson, *The Century*, 48(1), 16–24

Wittink, D.R. and Nutter, J.B. (1982). Comparing derived importance weights across attributes, *Journal of Consumer Research*, 8, 471–474

Wittink, D.R., Krishnamurthi, L., and Reibstein, D.J. (1990). The effect of differences in the number of attribute levels on conjoint results, *Marketing Letters*, 1(2), 113–129

Zappo's Shoe store, retrieved on December 13, 2002, from http://shop.zappos.com/

Index